£28

PUBLICATIONS OF
THE ISRAEL ACADEMY OF SCIENCES
AND HUMANITIES

SECTION OF HUMANITIES

———

FONTES AD RES JUDAICAS SPECTANTES

Greek and Latin Authors
on Jews and Judaism

Volume Two
FROM TACITUS TO SIMPLICIUS

GREEK AND LATIN AUTHORS
ON JEWS AND JUDAISM

Edited with Introductions, Translations

and Commentary

by

MENAHEM STERN

Volume Two

FROM TACITUS TO SIMPLICIUS

Jerusalem 1980

The Israel Academy of Sciences and Humanities

Preparation and publication of this volume
was made possible by a grant from the
Memorial Foundation for Jewish Culture

ISBN 965–208–035–7
ISBN 965–208–037–3

Printed in Israel
at the Jerusalem Academic Press

Memoriae Alexandri Fuks

PREFACE

THIS VOLUME CONTAINS TEXTS on Jews and Judaism found in works of Greek and Latin authors from Tacitus to the late pagan thinkers of the sixth century, continuing Volume I. In the second volume I have endeavoured to take into consideration scholarly contributions published to 1978.

The third volume will include an Appendix comprising texts ranging from a fragment of a poem of Alcaeus to the scholia to Aristophanes and Plato where some of the references to Jews or Judaism are less obvious or certain than those given in the first two volumes (e.g., the Neo-Pythagorean texts from Stobaeus). I also propose to discuss some problematical passages (e.g., the references to Moses attributed by Pseudo-Justin to ancient Greek historians, like Hellanicus and Philochorus), and to add geographical texts, which according to the strict criteria established in the Preface to Volume I were not brought in the first two volumes. Volume III will also include the indexes to the whole work.

I wish to express my thanks to the staff of the Israel Academy of Sciences and Humanities, above all to Mrs Yvonne Glikson who spared no effort in preparing the volume for and seeing it through the press. I also wish to acknowledge my debt to Mr J. Elron for his proofreading of the English and the Latin texts, and to the Academic Press, especially to Miss Elyse Schapira and Mr Avraham Gino. Miss Norma Schneider helped with the preparation of both volumes.

I am grateful to Harvard University Press for permission to reprint translations published in the Loeb Classical Library Series, to Dr H. Chadwick and the Cambridge University Press for allowing me to use the translation of Origen's *Contra Celsum*, and for permission to use translations of passages from Galen's works given by Oxford University Press and from Jerome's Commentary to Daniel given by Baker Book House.

My colleague Dr D. Rokeah helped me read the proofs.

This volume is dedicated to the memory of my friend Alexander Fuks (1917–1978), Professor of Ancient History in the Hebrew University of Jerusalem, who from the very start followed the progress of this work with keen interest and sympathy and whose death is felt as a grave loss to scholarship.

Menahem Stern

The Hebrew University of Jerusalem, 1980

TABLE OF CONTENTS

ix

Table of Contents

Table of Contents

LIST OF ABBREVIATIONS

AASOR	*Annual of the American Schools of Oriental Research*
Abel	F. M. Abel, *Géographie de la Palestine*, I–II, Paris 1933–1938
AJA	*American Journal of Archeology*
AJP	*American Journal of Philology*
Alt	A. Alt, *Kleine Schriften zur Geschichte des Volkes Israel*, I–III, Munich 1953–1959
Avi-Yonah	M. Avi-Yonah, *The Holy Land from the Persian to the Arab Conquests (536 B. C. to A. D. 640), Historical Geography*, Grand Rapids, Michigan 1966
BASOR	*Bulletin of the American Schools of Oriental Research*
Bengtson	H. Bengtson, *Die Strategie in der hellenistischen Zeit*, I–III, Munich 1937–1952
Bernays	J. Bernays, *Gesammelte Abhandlungen*, I–II, Berlin 1885
BGU	*Aegyptische Urkunden aus den Königlichen Museen zu Berlin. Griechische Urkunden*, Berlin 1895 →
Bidez & Cumont	J. Bidez & F. Cumont, *Les mages hellénisés*, I–II, Paris 1938
BIFAO	*Bulletin de l'institut français d'archéologie orientale*
Böhl	F. M. T. de Liagre Böhl, *Opera Minora*, Groningen–Djakarta 1953
CAH	*The Cambridge Ancient History*, I–XII, Cambridge 1923–1939
CCSL	*Corpus Christianorum, Series Latina*
Cichorius	C. Cichorius, *Römische Studien*, Leipzig–Berlin 1922
CII	J. B. Frey, *Corpus Inscriptionum Iudaicarum*, I–II, Rome–Paris 1936–1952
CIL	*Corpus Inscriptionum Latinarum*
CPJ	V. A. Tcherikover, A. Fuks & M. Stern, *Corpus Papyrorum Judaicarum*, I–III, Cambridge (Mass.) 1957–1964
CQ	*The Classical Quarterly*
CRAI	*Comptes rendus de l'Académie des Inscriptions et Belles Lettres*
Cramer	F. H. Cramer, *Astrology in Roman Law and Politics*, Philadelphia 1954
CSEL	*Corpus Scriptorum Ecclesiasticorum Latinorum*
Derenbourg	J. Derenbourg, *Essai sur l'histoire et la géographie de la Palestine*, Paris 1867

List of Abbreviations

F. Gr. Hist.	F. Jacoby, *Die Fragmente der griechischen Historiker,* Berlin–Leiden 1923 →
FHG	C. & T. Müller, *Fragmenta Historicorum Graecorum,* I–V
Fraser	P. M. Fraser, *Ptolemaic Alexandria,* I–III, Oxford 1972
Freudenthal	J. Freudenthal, *Hellenistische Studien,* I–II, *Alexander Polyhistor und die von ihm erhaltenen Reste jüdischer und samaritanischer Geschichtswerke,* Breslau 1874–1875
Friedländer	L. Friedländer, *Darstellungen aus der Sittengeschichte Roms in der Zeit von Augustus bis zum Ausgang der Antonine,* Leipzig I–II, 1922; III, 1923; IV, 1921
Gabba	E. Gabba, *Iscrizioni greche e latine per lo studio della Bibbia,* Turin 1958
Gager	J. G. Gager, *Moses in Greco-Roman Paganism,* Nashville 1972
Geyer	P. Geyer, *Itinera Hierosolymitana Saeculi IIII–VIII,* Prague–Vienna–Leipzig 1898
Ginzberg	L. Ginzberg, *The Legends of the Jews,* I–VII, Philadelphia 1925–1938
Goodenough	E. R. Goodenough, *Jewish Symbols in the Greco-Roman Period,* I–XII, New York 1953–1965
Gutschmid	A. v. Gutschmid, *Kleine Schriften,* I–V, Leipzig 1889–1894
Harnack	A. v. Harnack, *Die Mission und Ausbreitung des Christentums,* I–II⁴, Leipzig 1924
Hengel	M. Hengel, *Judentum und Hellenismus — Studien zu ihrer Begegnung unter besonderer Berücksichtigung Palästinas bis zur Mitte des 2 Jh. v. Chr.,* Tübingen 1969
HTR	*The Harvard Theological Review*
HUCA	*Hebrew Union College Annual*
IEJ	*Israel Exploration Journal*
IG	*Inscriptiones Graecae*
IGLS	*Inscriptions grecques et latines de la Syrie,* I–VII, ed. L. Jalabert, R. Mouterde, C. Mondésert, & J. P. Rey-Coquais, Paris 1929–1970
IGRR	*Inscriptiones Graecae ad Res Romanas Pertinentes,* I, Paris 1911; III, 1906; IV, 1927
ILS	H. Dessau, *Inscriptiones Latinae Selectae,* I–III, Berlin 1892–1916
JAOS	*Journal of the American Oriental Society*
JBL	*Journal of Biblical Literature*
JEA	*The Journal of Egyptian Archeology*
Jeremias	J. Jeremias, *Jerusalem zur Zeit Jesu³,* Göttingen 1962
JHS	*The Journal of Hellenic Studies*

xiv

List of Abbreviations

JNES	*Journal of Near Eastern Studies*
JQR	*The Jewish Quarterly Review*
JR	*Journal of Religion*
JRS	*The Journal of Roman Studies*
JTS	*The Journal of Theological Studies*
Juster	J. Juster, *Les Juifs dans l'empire Romain*, I–II, Paris 1914
Kahrstedt	U. Kahrstedt, *Syrische Territorien in hellenistischer Zeit*, Berlin 1926
LCL	The Loeb Classical Library, Cambridge (Mass.)–London
Leon	H. J. Leon, *The Jews of Ancient Rome*, Philadelphia 1960
Lifshitz	B. Lifshitz, *Donateurs et fondateurs dans les synagogues juives*, Paris 1967
Linsenmayer	A. Linsenmayer, *Die Bekämpfung des Christentums durch den römischen Staat bis zum Tode des Kaisers Julian (363)*, Munich 1905
Ed. Meyer	E. Meyer, *Ursprung und Anfänge des Christentums*, I–III, Stuttgart-Berlin 1921–1923
MGWJ	*Monatsschrift für Geschichte und Wissenschaft des Judentums*
Momigliano	A. Momigliano, *Ricerche sull' organizzazione della Giudea sotto il dominio romano (Annali della R. Scuola Normale Superiore de Pisa)*, Series II, Vol. III (1934)
Moore	G. F. Moore, *Judaism in the First Centuries of the Christian Era*, I–II, Cambridge (Mass.) 1927–1930
Müller	J. G. Müller, *Des Flavius Josephus Schrift gegen den Apion*, Basel 1877
Nicols	J. Nicols, *Vespasian and the* Partes Flavianae, Wiesbaden 1978
Niese	B. Niese, *Geschichte der griechischen und makedonischen Staaten seit der Schlacht bei Chaeronea*, I–III, Gotha 1893–1903
NNM	*Numismatic Notes and Monographs*
Nock	A. D. Nock, *Essays on Religion and the Ancient World*, I–II, Oxford 1972
Norden	E. Norden, *Kleine Schriften zum klassischen Altertum*, Berlin 1966
NTS	*New Testament Studies*
OGIS	W. Dittenberger, *Orientis Graeci Inscriptiones Selectae*, I–II, Leipzig 1903–1905
Otto	W. Otto, *Herodes — Beiträge zur Geschichte des letzten jüdischen Königshauses*, Stuttgart 1913
PAAJR	*Proceedings of the American Academy for Jewish Research*

P. Columbia Zenon	W. L. Westermann et al., *Zenon Papyri — Business Papers in the Third Century B. C. dealing with Palestine and Egypt* (*Columbia Papyri, Greek Series*, Nos. 3–4), I–II, New York 1934–1940
PCZ	C. C. Edgar, *Zenon Papyri*, I–IV, Cairo 1925–1931
PEQ	*Palestine Exploration Fund Quarterly Statement*
PG	*Patrologia Graeca*
PIR²	*Prosopographia Imperii Romani Saeculi I. II. III,* editio altera, Berlin–Leipzig 1933 →
PJB	*Palästinajahrbuch*
PL	*Patrologia Latina* →
P. Lond.	*Greek Papyri in the British Museum*, London 1893 →
PLRE	A. H. M. Jones, J. R. Martindale & J. Morris, *The Prosopography of the Later Roman Empire*, I, Cambridge 1971
P. Oslo	*Papyri Osloenses*, I–III, Oslo 1925–1936
P. Oxy.	*The Oxyrhynchus Papyri*, London 1898 →
P. Rylands	*Catalogue of the Greek (and Latin) Papyri in the John Rylands Library*, I–IV, Manchester 1911–1952
PSI	Papiri greci e latini — *Pubblicazioni della Società italiana per la ricerca dei Papiri greci e latini in Egitto*, Florence 1912 →
P. Tebtunis	*The Tebtunis Papyri*, I–III, London–New York–California 1902 →
PW	Pauly-Wissowa, *Real-Encyclopädie der classischen Altertumswissenschaft*, Stuttgart 1893 →
QDAP	*The Quarterly of the Department of Antiquities in Palestine*
R	T. Reinach, *Textes d'auteurs grecs et romains relatifs au Judaïsme*, Paris 1895
Radin	M. Radin, *The Jews among the Greeks and Romans*, Philadelphia 1915
RB	*Revue biblique*
REA	*Revue des études anciennes*
REG	*Revue des études grecques*
Reinach (Budé)	Flavius Josèphe, Contre Apion, texte établi et annoté par T. Reinach, Collection de l'Association Guillaume Budé, Paris 1930
REJ	*Revue des études juives*
REL	*Revue des études latines*
RFIC	*Rivista di Filologia e di Istruzione Classica*
Rhein. Museum	Rheinisches Museum für Philologie
RHR	*Revue de l'histoire des religions*
RIDA	*Revue internationale des droits de l'antiquité*
Saxer	R. Saxer, *Untersuchungen zu den Vexillationen des römischen Kaiserheeres* (= *Epigraphische Studien*, I), Köln–Graz 1967

Schanz & Hosius	M. Schanz & C. Hosius, *Geschichte der römischen Literatur*, I–II⁴, Munich 1927–1935
Schmid & Stählin, II	*Wilhelm von Christs Geschichte der griechischen Litteratur,* sechste Auflage unter Mitwirkung von O. Stählin bearbeitet von Wilhelm Schmid, Part II, Munich 1920–1924
Schürer	E. Schürer, *Geschichte des jüdischen Volkes im Zeitalter Jesu Christi*, I–III, Leipzig 1901–1909
Schürer, ed. Vermes & Millar	*The History of the Jewish People in the Age of Jesus Christ (175 B. C.–A. D. 135) by Emil Schürer,* new English version revised and edited by Geza Vermes & Fergus Millar, I, Edinburgh 1973
SEG	*Supplementum Epigraphicum Graecum,* Leiden 1923 →
SEHHW	M. Rostovtzeff, *Social and Economic History of the Hellenistic World*, I–III, Oxford 1953
Sevenster	J. N. Sevenster, *The Roots of Pagan Anti-Semitism in the Ancient World*, Leiden 1975
Simon	M. Simon, *Verus Israel — Étude sur les relations entre Chrétiens et Juifs sous l'empire romain (135–425),* Paris 1964
Smallwood	E. M. Smallwood, *The Jews under Roman Rule,* Leiden 1976
Stähelin	F. Stähelin, *Der Antisemitismus des Altertums,* Basel 1905
Strack & Billerbeck	H. L. Strack, P. Billerbeck & J. Jeremias, *Kommentar zum Neuen Testament aus Talmud und Midrasch,* I–VI, Munich 1922–1961
Susemihl	F. Susemihl, *Geschichte der griechischen Litteratur in der Alexandrinerzeit*, I–II, Leipzig 1891–1892
SVF	J. [H.] de Arnim, *Stoicorum Veterum Fragmenta,* I–IV, Leipzig 1903–1924
Sylloge	W. Dittenberger, *Sylloge Inscriptionum Graecarum,* I–IV, Leipzig 1915–1924
Syme	R. Syme, *Tacitus*, I–II, Oxford 1958
TAPA	*Transactions and Proceedings of the American Philological Association*
Tcherikover	V. Tcherikover, *Hellenistic Civilization and the Jews,* Philadelphia 1959
Weber	W. Weber, *Josephus und Vespasian*, Berlin–Stuttgart–Leipzig 1921
YCS	*Yale Classical Studies*
ZAW	*Zeitschrift für die alttestamentliche Wissenschaft*
ZDMG	*Zeitschrift der Deutschen morgenländischen Gesellschaft*
ZDPV	*Zeitschrift des Deutschen Palästinavereins*
ZNTW	*Zeitschrift für die neutestamentliche Wissenschaft*
ZPE	*Zeitschrift für Papyrologie und Epigraphik*

XCII. TACITUS

c. 56 C.E. — 120 C.E.

Tacitus refers to Jews and Judaea in several places in the Histories and Annals. His main treatment of the subject, however, is to be found in the excursus at the beginning of Historiae, *Book V, Sections 2–13 (No. 281). This is the most detailed account of the history and religion of the Jewish people extant in classical Latin literature; the only exposition even comparable is that of Pompeius Trogus found in the epitome of Justin (No. 137). Tacitus' account, written in the first decade of the second century C.E., reflects the feelings of influential circles of Roman society in the age following the destruction of the Temple, when Judaism nevertheless still constituted an important and militant factor in the Mediterranean world. Since this description is found in the work of the greatest historian of Rome, its subsequent influence, especially after the revival of interest in Tacitus in the sixteenth century, may be considered out of all proportion to its inherent merits.*

The form of the excursus follows the tradition of ancient historiography, of which Sallust, Tacitus' model, was one of the most conspicuous exponents. As the formal justification for its inclusion, Tacitus states that he is about to describe the last days of Jerusalem (Historiae, V, 2:1). The account falls into the following parts: the origin of the Jewish people, their religion and customs, a geographical description of Judaea, and a cursory historical survey.

Tacitus offers six explanations for the origin of the Jews. The first of these, namely, their Cretan origin, is mentioned only by him. Another, which points to the Assyrian antecedents of the Jewish people, their subsequent emigration to Egypt, and then again to their settlement of the Hebrew territories, is in noteworthy accord with the biblical tradition. A third explanation mentioned by Tacitus indeed adds to the lustre of the Jewish people by associating them with the Solymi celebrated in the Homeric poems. The sixth and last version of the genesis of the Jewish nation connects them with Egypt and presents the ancestors of the Jews as people who had been disfigured by a plague, and were in consequence expelled from Egypt. Their misfortune is said to account for many of the religious practices introduced by their leader Moses. This consistently hostile explanation of Jewish ancestry reflects

1

the old Graeco-Egyptian version which found its way into Latin literature at least as early as the age of Augustus, as testified by its inclusion in the History of Pompeius Trogus. The details given by Tacitus resemble most closely those related by Lysimachus (No. 158).

Formally, Tacitus abstains from deciding in favour of any one of the six versions, as customary with the ethnographic genre.[1] Similarly, the sentence of transition, leading to Tacitus' own exposition of the character of the contemporary Jewish religion, expresses doubt as to the veracity of the accounts transmitted by him (Historiae, V, 5:1): "hi ritus quoquo modo inducti". Yet the large amount of space allotted by Tacitus to the last version, which exceeds that given to the other five put together, the impressive episodes it covers, and the fact that it is the only one that supplies aetiological interpretations of actual features of the Jewish religion, together with its general tone, which conforms to that of Tacitus' own mode of exposition, are all features that lend special weight to the sixth version and tend to identify it with the views of the historian himself. That impression is accentuated by the transition in the middle of the account from oratio obliqua to oratio recta. It should be noted that, in contrast to Pompeius Trogus, Tacitus does not resort to contamination of his various sources.

However, Tacitus does not conceal his true opinion of Judaism, the customs of which he declares to be sinister and abominable. Hate and enmity towards other people are the counterpart to the strong solidarity which the Jews display towards one another. Their proselytes follow the same course and are imbued with contempt for the gods and indifference to their country and families. Tacitus refers to Jewish monotheism and to Jewish objections to material representations of God, but he does not state here his own views. He disapproves of the comparison sometimes made between Jewish customs and the Dionysiac cult in strong terms (ibid., 5:5): "quippe Liber festos laetosque ritus posuit, Iudaeorum mos absurdus sordidusque".

The geographical survey of Judaea by Tacitus contains little that is specific. Like many writers before him, he concentrates on the region of the Dead Sea and its products, on the balsam and bitumen.[2]

---

1 See R.M. Ogilvie & I. Richmond, *Cornelii Taciti de Vita Agricolae*, Oxford 1967, p. 174.

2 The influence of Posidonius has been postulated by some scholars, e.g., Theissen and Morr, but was denied by Reinhardt and Hahn. (References for scholars on Tacitus are given in the bibliography below, p. 6.)

2

The historical summary ignores the biblical period of Jewish independence and depicts the Jews as a nation generally subject to great foreign powers. Accordingly, King Antiochus was precluded from abolishing their superstition by the outbreak of the Parthian War, and a favourable political constellation offered the Jews an opportunity to establish a kingdom of their own. This had a priestly character and fostered superstition, acquired the bad traits of an oriental monarchy, and was finally subdued by Pompey (ibid., 8:2–9:1).

In his account of Roman rule in Judaea, Tacitus nowhere blames the Jews for their mutinous conduct, nor does he impute to them the responsibility for the Jewish war against Rome. He implies rather that the Roman procurators were to blame. Although the Jews had resorted to arms in the time of Caligula, Tacitus states that they did so only after the emperor had ordered them to set up his statue in the Temple, and the death of Gaius put an end to the uproar this had caused. Among the procurators, the freedman Felix practised cruelty and lust, while Gessius Florus finally broke the patience of the Jews.

What remains of Tacitus' story of the revolt (ibid., 10–13) invites comparison with the Jewish War *of Josephus. Some resemblances occur, the most conspicuous relating to the portents preceding the great events, the sight of contending hosts in the skies, the opening of the doors of the Temple and the divine departure from it, and above all the prophecy that the world would be ruled by men hailing from Judaea. However, striking discrepancies between the two accounts may also be detected. Thus the number of the besieged given by Tacitus (ibid., 13:3) contradicts that of Josephus. Moreover, the Roman historian confuses John of Gischala with Simon bar Giora, and dwells on the end of Cestius Gallus (ibid., 10:1), which is ignored by Josephus. Direct use by Tacitus of the Jewish historian's work seems out of the question, but indirect influence cannot be excluded on principle, though its assumption is by no means necessary.[3] Other sources have been suggested, especially Pliny the Elder, Antonius Julianus and the* Commentarii *of Vespasian and Titus, which were used by Josephus also. For the archaeology, Apion has been pointed to as a possible*

---

3 That Tacitus made use of Josephus has been maintained by some scholars, e.g., Lehmann and Schürer, and above all by Dornseiff. Against any direct dependence of this kind, cf. the studies of Clason, Hild, Thiaucourt and Groag. The last-mentioned scholar suggests the use by the Roman historian of a source dependent on Josephus besides Pliny the Elder.

source.[4] *Certainty is impossible in view of the very fragmentary nature of the sources and the existence of many works bearing upon the Jewish war by authors now unknown (see No. 200).*

The following observations may elucidate this question:

a. Tacitus' source or sources for the archaeology need by no means be identical with those for the siege of Jerusalem.

b. Even if the identity of the ignotus *common to Plutarch's Galba and Otho and to Tacitus' account was certain, no conclusion could be drawn as to his source for the narrative of the siege, and still less concerning that for the archaeology.[5]*

c. There is no reason to assume that the various views adduced by Tacitus about the origin of the Jewish people derive from a single source.[6] He probably consulted more than one work, as he also did for his excursus on the founding of the cult of Serapis (Historiae, IV, 83 f.). But we must not go to the other extreme and maintain that every view expressed by the Roman historian may be traced to a specific source.

d. Tacitus did not have to consult Graeco-Alexandrian writers directly, since presumably the main material was available in Latin works.[7]

The Annales *were composed later than the* Historiae, *and at least the later books belong to the years subsequent to the violent Jewish revolts at*

---

4 The influence of Pliny the Elder was stressed by Fabia, that of Antonius Julianus by Hild, Wolff-Beckh, Norden and Paratore. Tacitus' indebtedness to Vespasian's *Commentarii* for his information on the Dead Sea was suggested by K. Peter; cf. also H. Peter, *Historicorum Romanorum Reliquiae*, II, Leipzig 1906, p. CXXXXIV. Weber maintains that Tacitus did not use all these sources directly, their influence being felt only through Pliny. For the view that Apion was the source for Tacitus' archaeology, see Gutschmid, IV, p. 367. Nissen suggested Pliny, yet was refuted with strong arguments by Detlefsen. Some scholars suggest Mucianus as a source of facts concerning the geography of Palestine and the topography of Jerusalem; see, e.g., W. A. Spooner, *The Histories of Tacitus*, London 1891, p. 21.

5 Thus Groag, although he inclines to identify the *ignotus* with Fabius Rusticus, still would not identify him as the source of Tacitus' archaeology.

6 See also Syme, I, p. 190.

7 It seems otherwise with the excursus on the establishment of the cult of Serapis, where Tacitus expressly states in *Historiae*, IV, 83: "Origo dei nondum nostris auctoribus celebrata."

the end of Trajan's reign.[8] *However, these events make little impact in the few chapters dealing with Jews in the extant portions of the* Annales. *Loss of Jewish life is considered "vile damnum" in* Annales, *II, 85 (No. 284), whether we take this as the view of the historian himself or of the instigators of the "senatus consultum", as surmised by Tacitus. The villains of the piece are mainly the Roman procurators and not the Jews in* Annales, *XII, 54 (No. 288), and the burden of taxation in the province of Judaea is barely mentioned in* Annales, *II, 42 (No. 283). In the famous passage in* Annales, *XV, 44 (No. 294), Judaea is stated to be the "origo eius mali" (scil. Christianity), but the historian adds no comment concerning Judaism.*

The antipathy displayed by Tacitus towards the Jewish religion is in line with that shown by some of the other great representatives of Latin literature, from Seneca onwards, and particularly by Quintilian and Juvenal. The indignation of Tacitus, like that of Juvenal, is not confined to faults found in Judaism, but includes intrusions of other foreign cults. The Egyptian is no less superstitious in Tacitus' estimation,[9] *and he shows a remarkably cold attitude to Hellenism as well.*[10] *Significant for Tacitus, as well as for Seneca and Juvenal, is the success of the Jewish proselytizing movement, which he considers a menace to the structure of Roman society.*[11] *It is the danger inherent in Judaism to this society that colours his attitude rather than any political or military consequences for the Roman empire that might be caused by other forms of Jewish activity.*[12]

8 For the date of the *Annales*, see Syme, II, p. 473; J. Beaujeu, *REL*, XXXVIII (1960), pp. 200 ff.; see also S. Borzsák, PW, Suppl. XI, pp. 467 ff.; K. Meister, *Eranos*, XLVI (1948), pp. 94 ff. Meister distinguishes between the first books written between 105 and 115 C.E. and the later books which might have been published under Hadrian.

9 See Tacitus, *Historiae*, IV, 81:1: "dedita superstitionibus gens".

10 See B. Hardinghaus, "Tacitus und das Griechentum", Ph.D. Thesis, Münster 1932; Syme, II, pp. 504 ff.

11 We do not have to accept the view that the antipathy felt towards the Jews by Roman authors of the type of Tacitus was due to the Jewish support of the principate; cf. W.L. Knox, *JRS*, XXXIX (1949), p. 30.

12 I have not included *Annales*, XVI, 6, among the excerpts; this passage, in recording the death and burial of Poppaea Sabina, states that "corpus non igni abolitum, ut Romanus mos, sed regum externorum consuetudine differtum odoribus conditur tumuloque Iuliorum infertur". That Poppaea was buried and not cremated should not be explained by her alleged leanings towards Judaism. Though the empress sometimes displayed sympathy towards the Jewish cause and is described by

Bibliography

C. Worm, *De Corruptis Antiquitatum Hebraearum apud Tacitum et Martialem Vestigiis*, Copenhagen 1694; F. Jacob, *Über eine Stelle des Tacitus Geschichtsbüchern*, 5, 2–5, Lübeck 1840; J.G. Müller, *Theologische Studien und Kritiken* (1843), pp. 893 ff.; Leonhard, *Über den Bericht des Tacitus über die Juden, Hist.*, 5, 2–6, Ellwangen 1852; H. Lehmann, *Claudius und Nero und ihre Zeit*, I, Gotha 1858, pp. 33 ff.; O. Clason, *Tacitus und Sueton*, Breslau 1870, pp. 90 ff.; K. Peter, *Flavius Josephus und der jüdische Krieg*, Programm, Perleberg 1871, pp. 5 ff.; H. Nissen, *Rhein. Museum*, XXVI (1871), pp. 541 ff.; L. Geiger, *Quid de Iudaeorum Moribus atque Institutis Scriptoribus Romanis Persuasum Fuerit*, Berlin 1872, pp. 31 ff.; D. Detlefsen, *Philologus*, XXXIV (1876), pp. 43 f.; J.A. Hild, *REJ*, XI (1885), pp. 174 ff.; C. Thiaucourt, *REJ*, XIX (1889), pp. 57 ff.; XX (1890), pp. 312 ff.; W.A. Spooner, *The Histories of Tacitus*, London 1891, pp. 22 f.; P. Fabia, *Les sources de Tacite dans les Histoires et les Annales*, Paris 1893, pp. 247 ff.; E. Groag, "Zur Kritik von Tacitus' Quellen in den Historien", *Jahrbücher für classische Philologie*, Suppl. XXIII (1897), pp. 783 f.; G. Boissier, *Mélanges Cabrières*, I, Paris 1899, pp. 81 ff.; B. Wolff-Beckh, *Neue Jahrbücher für das klassische Altertum*, XI (1903), pp. 469 f.; Schürer, II, p. 604, n. 27; V. Ussani, *RFIC*, XXXIX (1911), pp. 390 ff.; (W.)G. Theissen, "De Sallustii, Livii, Taciti Digressionibus", Ph.D. Thesis, Berlin 1912, pp. 76 ff.; E. Norden, *Neue Jahrbücher für das klassische Altertum*, XXXI (1913), pp. 637 ff. = Norden, pp. 241 ff.; K. Trüdinger, *Studien zur Geschichte der griechisch-römischen Ethnographie*, Basel 1918, pp. 156 ff.; Weber, pp. 147 ff., 179; C. Marchesi, *Tacito*, Messina–Rome 1924, pp. 172 ff.; J. Morr, *Philologus*, LXXXI (1926), pp. 271 ff.; K. Reinhardt, *Poseidonios über Ursprung und Entartung*, Heidelberg 1928, pp. 64 ff.; W. Capelle, *Philologus*, LXXXIV (1929), pp. 491 f.; E. Hahn, "Die Exkurse in den Annalen des Tacitus", Ph.D. Thesis, Munich 1933, pp. 84 f.; F. Dornseiff, *ZNTW*, XXXV (1936), pp. 143 ff.; (H.)J. Lewy, *Zion*, VIII (1942/3), pp. 1 ff. = *Studies in Jewish Hellenism*, Jerusalem 1960, pp. 115 ff. (in Hebrew); I. Lévy, *Latomus*, V (1946), pp. 331 ff.; A.M.A. Hospers-Jansen, *Tacitus over de Joden*, Groningen 1949; L. Herrmann, *Latomus*, IX (1950), pp. 472 f.; B. Blumenkranz, *REJ*, NS, XI (1951–1952), pp. 187 ff.; Syme, I, pp. 310 f.; E. Paratore, *Tacito*², Rome 1962, pp. 653 ff.; G. Townend, *Rhein. Museum*, CV (1962), p. 363; A. Toaff, *La Rassegna mensile di Israel*, XXIX (1963), pp. 394 ff.; Gager, pp. 127 f.; Sevenster, pp. 10 f.

Josephus as ϑεοσεβής (*Ant.*, XX, 195), we cannot interpret this to imply exclusive sympathy. Against the view that ϑεοσεβής here constitutes a technical term, see E.M. Smallwood, *JTS*, NS, X (1959), pp. 329 ff.; W.H.C. Frend, *Martyrdom and Persecution in the Early Church*, Oxford 1965, p. 175 (n. 70 still supports the view that Poppaea was a "semi-proselyte"). It seems worthwhile to recall the example of Julia Severa in Phrygian Acmonia; she built a synagogue (*CII*, No. 766 = Lifshitz, No. 33) and yet acted as priestess of a pagan cult. On her, see Groag, PW, X, pp. 946 ff.; C.S. Walton, *JRS*, XIX (1929), pp. 44 f.

Historiae, I, 10:3; 11:1 — Koestermann

(10:3) Bellum Iudaicum Flavius Vespasianus (ducem eum Nero delegerat) tribus legionibus administrabat. Nec Vespasiano adversus Galbam votum aut animus: quippe Titum filium ad venerationem cultumque eius miserat, ut suo loco memorabimus. Occulta fati et
5 ostentis ac responsis destinatum Vespasiano liberisque eius imperium post fortunam credidimus. (11:1) Aegyptum copiasque, quibus coerceretur, iam inde a divo Augusto equites Romani obtinent loco regum: ita visum expedire, provinciam aditu difficilem, annonae fecundam, superstitione ac lascivia discordem et mobilem,
10 insciam legum, ignaram magistratuum, dom⟨u⟩i retinere. Regebat tum Tiberius Alexander, eiusdem nationis.

1 *Iudei cum* M   4 *occultis fatis* L   *occulta* ⟨*patefacta*⟩ *fati* Koestermann
10 *dom*⟨*u*⟩*i* Ricklefs   *domi* ML

(10:3) The war against the Jews was being directed with three legions by Flavius Vespasianus, whom Nero had selected as general. Neither Vespasian's desires nor sentiments were opposed to Galba, for he sent his son, Titus, to pay his respects and to show his allegiance to him, as we shall tell at the proper time. The secrets of Fate, and the signs and oracles which predestined Vespasian and his sons for power, we believed only after his success was secured. (11:1) Egypt with the troops to keep it in order, has been managed from the time of the deified Augustus by Roman knights in place of their former kings. It had seemed wise to keep thus under the direct control of the imperial house a province which is difficult of access, productive of great harvests, but given to civil strife and sudden disturbances because of the fanaticism and superstition of its inhabitants, ignorant as they are of laws and unacquainted with civil magistrates. At this time the governor was Tiberius Alexander, himself an Egyptian.

(trans. C.H. Moore, *LCL*)

10:3 *ducem eum Nero delegerat*: Cf. *BJ*, III, 3 ff.
tribus legionibus administrabat: These legions were the Fifth, the Tenth and the Fifteenth; cf. *BJ*, III, 65, and Tacitus, *Historiae*, V, 1 (No. 281).
11:1 *Regebat tum Tiberius Alexander*: For the previous career of Tiberius Alexander, see Tacitus, *Annales*, XV, 28 (No. 292), and the commentary *ad loc*. The prefecture of Egypt was the next stage in his career known to us. He was appointed prefect in 66 C.E.; see A. Stein, *Die Präfekten von Ägypten in*

der römischen Kaiserzeit, Bern 1950, p. 37; O. W. Reinmuth, PW, Suppl. VIII (1956), p. 528; idem, *Bulletin of the American Society of Papyrologists*, IV (1967), p. 83; P. A. Brunt, *JRS*, LXV (1975), p. 143; G. Bastianini, *Zeitschrift für Papyrologie und Epigraphik*, XVII (1975), p. 274. As prefect of Egypt he ruthlessly quelled the Jewish disturbances at Alexandria in 66 C.E.; see *BJ*, II, 490 ff. For the edict promulgated by him in 68 C.E. after the accession of Galba, see G. Chalon, *L'édit de Tiberius Julius Alexander*, Olten–Lausanne 1964. In the summer of 69 C.E. he was instrumental in raising Vespasian to the throne.

eiusdem nationis: Scil. *Aegyptiae*. Tacitus consistently ignores the Jewish antecedents of Tiberius Alexander. See also Iuvenalis, *Saturae*, I, 130 (No. 295). The expression "eiusdem nationis" implies no more than that Tiberius Alexander came from Egypt; see J. Schwartz, *Annuaire de l'Institut de Philologie et d'Histoire orientales et slaves*, XIII (1953), p. 602, n. 3.

274

Historiae, I, 76:2 — Koestermann

Longiquae provinciae et quidquid armorum mari dirimitur penes Othonem manebat, non partium studio, sed erat grande momentum in nomine urbis ac praetexto senatus, et occupaverat animos prior auditus. Iudaicum exercitum Vespasianus, Syriae legiones Mucianus
5 sacramento Othonis adegere.

   3 *praetextu* L   4 *Iudeicum* M   *iudaeorum* L / *exercitus* L

The distant provinces and all the armed forces across the sea remained on Otho's side, not from any enthusiasm for his party, but because the name of the city and the splendour of the senate had great weight; moreover the emperor of whom they first heard pre-empted their regard. The oath of allegiance to Otho was administered to the army in Judaea by Vespasian, to the legions in Syria by Mucianus.   (trans. C. H. Moore, *LCL*)

Iudaicum exercitum: See Tacitus, *Historiae*, II, 79 (No. 279)

275

Historiae, II, 1:1; 2:1 — Koestermann

(1:1) Titus Vespasianus, e Iudaea incolumi adhuc Galba missus a patre, causam profectionis officium erga principem et maturam petendis honoribus iuventam ferebat, sed volgus fingendi avidum

8

disperserat accitum in adoptionem ... (2:1) His ac talibus inter spem
5 metumque iactatum spes vicit. Fuere qui accensum desiderio
Berenices reginae vertisse iter crederent; neque abhorrebat a
Berenice iuvenilis animus, sed gerendis rebus nullum ex eo
impedimentum: laetam voluptatibus adulescentiam egit, suo quam
patris imperio moderatior.

5 *fuerunt* ab

(1:1) Titus Vespasianus had been dispatched by his father from
Judaea while Galba was still alive. The reason given out for his
journey was a desire to pay his respects to the emperor, and the fact
that Titus was now old enough to begin his political career. But the
common people, who are always ready to invent, had spread the
report that he had been summoned to Rome to be adopted...(2:1)
These considerations and others like them made him waver between
hope and fear; but hope finally won. Some believed that he turned
back because of his passionate longing to see again Queen Berenice;
and the young man's heart was not insensible to Berenice, but his
feelings towards her proved no obstacle to action. He spent his youth
in the delights of self-indulgence, but he showed more self-restraint in
his own reign than in that of his father.   (trans. C.H. Moore, *LCL*)

1:1 *e Iudaea incolumi adhuc Galba missus*: I.e. in any case before January
69 C.E.; cf. *BJ*, IV, 497 ff. See also M. Fortina, *L'imperatore Tito*, Turin 1955,
pp. 32 f.
2:1 *desiderio Berenices reginae vertisse iter*: For Berenice and her
relationship with Titus, see Quintilianus, IV, 1:19 (No. 231), and the
commentary *ad loc.*; Suetonius, *Divus Titus*, 7 (No. 318); Iuvenalis, *Saturae*,
VI, 156 (No. 298); Cassius Dio, LXVI, 15 (No. 433).

276

Historiae, II, 4:3–4; 5:2; 6:1–2 — Koestermann = F178R

(4:3) Profligaverat bellum Iudaicum Vespasianus, obpugnatione
Hierosolymorum reliqua, duro magis et arduo opere ob ingenium
montis et pervicaciam superstitionis quam quo satis virium obsessis
ad tolerandas necessitates superesset. (4:4) Tres, ut supra
5 memoravimus, ipsi Vespasiano legiones erant, exercitae bello ...

1 *Iudei cum* M   *cum iudaeis* L

(5:2) Ceterum hic ⟨scil. Mucianus⟩ Syriae, ille ⟨scil. Vespasianus⟩ Iudaeae praepositus, vicinis provinciarum administrationibus invidia discordes, exitu demum Neronis positis odiis in medium consuluere, ... (6:1) Auditique saepius in Syria Iudaeaque Caesares quam
10 inspecti. Nulla seditio legionum, tantum adversus Parthos minae, vario eventu; et proximo civili bello turbatis aliis inconcussa ibi pax, dein fides erga Galbam. (6:2) Mox, ut Othonem ac Vitellium scelestis armis res Romanas raptum ire volgatum est, ne penes ceteros imperii praemia, penes ipsos tantum servitii necessitas esset, fremere miles et
15 vires suas circumspicere: septem legiones statim et cum ingentibus auxiliis Syria Iudaeaque.

(4:3) Vespasian had almost put an end to the war with the Jews. The siege of Jerusalem, however, remained, a task rendered difficult and arduous by the character of the mountain-citadel and the obstinate superstition of the Jews rather than by any adequate resources which the besieged possessed to withstand the inevitable hardships of a siege. (4:4) As we have stated above, Vespasian himself had three legions experienced in war... (5:2) But Mucianus was governor of Syria, Vespasian of Judaea. They had quarrelled through jealousy because they governed neighbouring provinces. Finally at Nero's death they had laid aside their hostilities and consulted together... (6:1) And in Syria and Judaea the Caesars had been oftener heard of than seen. There was no mutiny on the part of the legions, only some threatening demonstrations against the Parthians which met with varied success. In the last civil struggle, while other provinces had been shaken, in the East peace was undisturbed, and then adhesion to Galba followed. (6:2) Presently, when the news spread abroad that Otho and Vitellius were proceeding with their impious arms to make spoil of the imperial power, the soldiers began to murmur and examine their own resources, that the rewards of empire might not fall to the rest, to them only the necessity of servitude. They could count at once on seven legions, and they had besides Syria and Judaea with the great auxiliary forces that they could furnish.

(trans. C. H. Moore, *LCL*)

4:3 *Profligaverat bellum Iudaicum Vespasianus, obpugnatione Hierosolymorum reliqua*: Cf. Tacitus, *Historiae*, V, 10 (No. 281), and the commentary *ad loc.*
arduo opere ob ingenium montis: Cf. *ibid.*, 11 (No. 281).
et pervicaciam superstitionis: Cf. *ibid.*, 12:2 (No. 281): "nam pervicacissimus

quisque illuc perfugerat". "Superstitio" is the common designation for
Judaism by Tacitus; see *ibid.*, 13:1 (No. 281), and the commentary *ad loc.*
quam quo satis virium obsessis ad tolerandas necessitates superesset: Cf. *ibid.*,
13:3: "et plures quam pro numero audebant".
5:2 *Ceterum hic Syriae, ille Iudaeae praepositus*: The official position of
Vespasian seems to have been that of a *legatus pro praetore*; see Weynand,
PW, VI, p. 2630.
6:2 *septem legiones statim et cum ingentibus auxiliis Syria Iudaeaque*: Four
legions belonged to the province of Syria, and three were attached to
Vespasian for his campaign against the Jews.

277

Historiae, II, 73; 74:1; 76:1, 5 — Koestermann

(73) Vix credibile memoratu est, quantum superbiae socordiaeque
Vitellio adoleverit, postquam speculatores e Syria Iudaeaque
adactum in verba eius Orientem nuntiavere ... (74:1) At
Vespasianus bellum armaque et procul vel iuxta sitas vires
5 circumspectabat. Miles ipsi adeo paratus, ut praeeuntem sacramen-
tum et fausta Vitellio omnia precantem per silentium audierint;
Muciani animus nec Vespasiano alienus et in Titum pronior;
praefectus Aegypti ⟨Ti.⟩ Alexander consilia sociaverat ... (76:1) His
pavoribus nutantem et alii legati amicique firmabant et Mucianus
10 post multos secretosque sermones iam et coram ita locutus ... (76:5)
"Tibi e Iudaea et Syria et Aegypto novem legiones integrae, nulla
acie exhaustae..."

8 ⟨*Ti.*⟩ Ursinus

(73) The degree to which the insolent pride of Vitellius increased
after couriers arrived from Syria and Judaea and reported that the
East had sworn allegiance to him is almost past belief ... (74:1) As for
Vespasian, he now began to reflect on the possibilities of war and
armed combat and to review the strength of the forces near and far.
His own soldiers were so ready that when he administered the oath
and made vows for the success of Vitellius, they listened in complete
silence. The sentiments of Mucianus were not hostile to him and
indeed were favourable to Titus; Tiberius Alexander, the prefect of
Egypt, had already cast his lot with his side ... (76:1) While he was
hesitating, moved by such fears as these, his mind was confirmed by
his officers and friends and especially by Mucianus, who first had long

11

private conversations with him and then spoke openly before the rest
...(76:5) "You have in Syria, Judaea and Egypt nine legions at their
full strength not worn out by fighting..."   (trans. C. H. Moore, *LCL*)

73 *postquam speculatores e Syria Iudaeaque adactum in verba eius Orientem
nuntiavere*: As it was then summer, it took only a short time for the
"speculatores" to pass the news to Vitellius; cf. "celeri navigatione", below,
Tacitus, *Historiae*, II, 81 (No. 279), and the commentary *ad loc.*
76:5 *Tibi e Iudaea et Syria et Aegypto novem legiones integrae*: From the
speech of Mucianus; see A. Briessmann, *Tacitus und das flavische
Geschichtsbild*, Wiesbaden 1955, p. 13.

278

Historiae, II, 78:2–4 — Koestermann = F179R

(2) Recursabant animo vetera omina: cupressus arbor in agris eius
conspicua altitudine repente prociderat ac postera die eodem vestigio
resurgens procera et latior virebat. Grande id prosperumque
consensu haruspicum et summa claritudo iuveni admodum Vespasiano promissa, sed primo triumphalia et consulatus et Iudaicae
victoriae decus implesse fidem ominis videbatur: ut haec adeptus est,
portendi sibi imperium credebat. (3) Est Iudaeam inter Syriamque
Carmelus: ita vocant montem deumque. Nec simulacrum deo aut
templum — sic tradidere maiores — ara tantum et reverentia. Illic
sacrificanti Vespasiano, cum spes occultas versaret animo, Basilides
sacerdos inspectis identidem extis "quidquid est," inquit, "Vespasiane, quod paras, seu domum exstruere seu prolatare agros sive
ampliare servitia, datur tibi magna sedes, ingentes termini, multum
hominum." (4) Has ambages et statim exceperat fama et tunc
aperiebat: nec quidquam magis in ore volgi. Crebriores apud ipsum
sermones, quanto sperantibus plura dicuntur. Haud dubia de-
stinatione discessere Mucianus Antiochiam, Vespasianus
Caesaream: illa Suriae, hoc Iudaeae caput est.

| 3 *laetior* Triller | 5 *Iudaeicae* M | 6 *hominis* M | 7 *et* M |
| 9 *aram...reverentiam* M | 12 *prolatare* M | *plantare* L | 18 *hoc*] *haec* L |

(2) Old omens came back to his mind: once on his country estate a
cypress of conspicuous height suddenly fell, but the next day it rose
again on the selfsame spot, fresh, tall, and with wider expanse than
before. This occurrence was a favourable omen of great significance,

as the haruspices all agreed, and promised the highest distinctions for Vespasian, who was then still a young man. At first, however, the insignia of a triumph, his consulship, and his victory over Judaea appeared to have fulfilled the promise given by the omen; yet after he had gained these honours, he began to think that it was the imperial throne that was foretold. (3) Between Judaea and Syria lies Carmel: this is the name given to both the mountain and the divinity. The god has no image or temple — such is the rule handed down by the fathers; there is only an altar and the worship of the god. When Vespasian was sacrificing there and thinking over his secret hopes in his heart, the priest Basilides, after repeated inspection of the victim's vitals, said to him: "Whatever you are planning, Vespasian, whether to build a house, or to enlarge your holdings, or to increase the number of your slaves, the god grants you a mighty home, limitless bounds, and a multitude of men". (4) This obscure oracle rumour had caught up at the time, and now was trying to interpret; nothing indeed was more often on men's lips. It was discussed even more in Vespasian's presence — for men have the more to say to those who are filled with hope. The two leaders now separated with clear purposes before them, Mucianus going to Antioch, Vespasian to Caesarea. Antioch is the capital of Syria, Caesarea of Judaea.

(trans. C.H. Moore, *LCL*)

2 *Recursabant animo vetera omina*: Cf. Suetonius, *Divus Vespasianus*, 5 (No. 313).
ut haec adeptus est, portendi sibi imperium: In contrast to Suetonius (*loc. cit.*), where the prophecy on the Carmelus is followed by that of Josephus, Tacitus wholly ignores the latter's prediction of Vespasian's future glory.
3 *Est Iudaeam inter Syriamque Carmelus*: The boundary between the provinces of Judaea and Syria passed south of the Carmel, as Judaea certainly did not include Dora.
ita vocant montem deumque: Cf. also "Carmelus deus" in Suetonius (*loc. cit.*) and the late second- or early third-century C.E. inscription which reads: Διὶ Ἡλιοπολείτῃ Καρμήλῳ; see M. Avi-Yonah, *IEJ*, II (1952), pp. 118 ff. The assertion that Carmelus is the name of the god derives from a mistaken translation of בעל כרמל, the Baal of the Carmel; see Alt, II, p. 139, n. 1. The cult on the Carmel is implied also in the ὄρος ἱερὸν Διός mentioned in Pseudo-Scylax, 66; cf. C. Müller, *Geographi Graeci Minores*, I, p. 79 (No. 558); see K. Galling, *Studien zur Geschichte Israels im persischen Zeitalter*, Tübingen 1964, p. 197. See also Iamblichus, *Vita Pythagorae*, III, 15; cf. the commentary to Porphyrius, *Vita Pythagorae*, 11 (No. 456a). The deer of the Carmel, but not their cult, are referred to in Aelianus, *De Natura Animalium*, V, 56. Pliny mentions only "promunturium Carmelum et in

monte oppidum eodem nomine"; cf. Plinius, *Naturalis Historia*, V, 75. See also Strabo, *Geographica*, XVI, 2:27, p. 758 (No. 114); cf. also H.J. Katzenstein, *The History of Tyre*, Jerusalem 1973, p. 151, n. 113.

ara tantum et reverentia: For the style of the whole passage, see B.R. Voss, *Der pointierte Stil des Tacitus*, Münster 1963, pp. 17 f.

Basilides sacerdos: On this personage, see K. Scott, *JRS*, XXIV (1934), pp. 138 ff.; idem, *The Imperial Cult under the Flavians*, Stuttgart–Berlin 1936, pp. 11 ff. Scott maintains that he is identical with the Basilides who appeared to Vespasian in his vision at the temple of Sarapis; cf. Tacitus, *Historiae*, IV, 82. See also P. Derchain & J. Hubaux, *Latomus*, XII (1953), pp. 51 f.; L. Herrmann, *ibid.*, pp. 312 ff. Scott suggests that Basilides acted as a representative of Tiberius Alexander at the conference held by Vespasian with Mucianus at the Carmel. See also E. Schäfer, *Hermes*, CV (1977), pp. 455 ff.

4 *hoc Iudaeae caput est*: For Caesarea as the provincial capital of Judaea, cf. *BJ*, II, 171, 230, 332, 407; *Ant.*, XVIII, 57; XX, 116; Acts, xxiii: 23; xxv. There is no foundation for Juster's claim that Caesarea became the capital of the province only after the destruction of the Temple and that consequently Tacitus' statement is anachronistic; see Juster, II, p. 4, n. 3. For the history of Caesarea, see now L.I. Levine, *Caesarea under Roman Rule*, Leiden 1975 (on the period preceding the Jewish war against Rome, pp. 18 ff., on the second century C.E., pp. 34 ff.). In the time of Tacitus it was a Roman colony, a status obtained under Vespasian; cf. Plinius, *Naturalis Historia*, V, 69 (No. 204).

279

Historiae, II, 79, 81–82 — Koestermann

(79) Initium ferendi ad Vespasianum imperii Alexandriae coeptum, festinante Tiberio Alexandro, qui kalendis Iuliis sacramento eius legiones adegit. Isque primus principatus dies in posterum celebratus, quamvis Iudaicus exercitus V nonas Iulias apud ipsum
5 iurasset, eo ardore, ut ne Titus quidem filius exspectaretur, Syria remeans et consiliorum inter Mucianum ac patrem nuntius... (81:1) Ante idus Iulias Syria omnis in eodem sacramento fuit. Accessere cum regno Sohaemus haud spernendis viribus, Antiochus vetustis opibus ingens et servientium regum ditissimus, mox per occultos
10 suorum nuntios excitus ab urbe Agrippa: ignaro adhuc Vitellio celeri navigatione properaverat. (81:2) Nec minore animo regina Berenice partes iuvabat, florens aetate formaque et seni quoque Vespasiano magnificentia munerum grata. Quidquid provinciarum adluitur mari Asia atque Achaia tenus quantumque introrsus in Pontum et

4 *apud eum* L   9 *inservientium* M   10 *exercitus* M

14

15 Armenios patescit, iuravere; sed inermes legati regebant, nondum
additis Cappadociae legionibus. (81 : 3) Consilium de summa rerum
Beryti habitum. Illuc Mucianus cum legatis tribunisque et splendidis-
simo quoque centurionum ac militum venit, et e Iudaico exercitu
lecta decora: tantum simul peditum equitumque et aemulantium
20 inter se regum paratus speciem fortunae principalis effecerant...
(82:3) Titum instare Iudaeae, Vespasianum obtinere claustra
Aegypti placuit.

(79) The transfer of the imperial power to Vespasian began at
Alexandria, where Tiberius Alexander acted quickly, administering
to his troops the oath of allegiance on the first of July. This day has
been celebrated in later times as the first of Vespasian's reign,
although it was on the third of July that the army in Judaea took the
oath before Vespasian himself, and did it with such enthusiasm that
they did not wait even for his son Titus, who was on his way back from
Syria and was the medium of communication between Mucianus and
his father ... (81 : 1) Before the fifteenth of July all Syria had sworn the
same allegiance. Vespasian's cause was now joined also by Sohaemus
with his entire kingdom, whose strength was not to be despised, and
by Antiochus who had enormous ancestral wealth, and was in fact the
richest of the subject princes. Presently Agrippa, summoned from
Rome by private messages from his friends, while Vitellius was still
unaware of his action, quickly crossed the sea and joined the cause.
(81:2) Queen Berenice showed equal spirit in helping Vespasian's
party: she had great youthful-beauty, and commended herself to
Vespasian for all his years by the splendid gifts she made him. All the
provinces on the coast to the frontiers of Achaia and Asia, as well as
all the inland provinces as far as Pontus and Armenia, took the oath
of allegiance; but their governors had no armed forces, since
Cappadocia had as yet no legions. (81 : 3) A grand council was held at
Berytus. Mucianus came there with all his lieutenants and tribunes, as
well as his most distinguished centurions and soldiers; the army in
Judaea also sent its best representatives. This great concourse of foot
and horse, with princes who rivalled one another in splendid display,
made a gathering that befitted the high fortune of an emperor ...
(82:3) It was decided that Titus should follow up the war in Judaea,
Vespasian hold the keys to Egypt.   (trans. C. H. Moore, *LCL*)

79 *festinante Tiberio Alexandro, qui kalendis Iuliis sacramento eius legiones
adegit*: This event seems to be the subject of *CPJ*, No. 418a; see Fuks's

introduction to the papyrus; Stein, *op. cit.* (supra, p. 7 f.), p. 38; V. Burr, *Tiberius Iulius Alexander*, Bonn 1955, pp. 60 ff. It is not easy to determine the exact date for the end of the Egyptian prefecture of Tiberius Alexander. In any case, in the spring of 70 C.E. he took a prominent part in the siege of Jerusalem. It seems that his direct successor was one L. Peducaeus Colonus; cf. R. Syme, *JRS*, XLIV (1954), p. 116; Turner, *ibid.*, p. 61, n. 44a. That Colonus was prefect before 27 July 70 C.E. emerges from *P. Oxy.*, XXII, No. 2349, l. 26. See J.D. Thomas, *ZEP*, XXI (1976), pp. 153 ff.

81:1 *Sohaemus haud spernendis viribus*: Sohaemus, king of Emesa, took part in the expedition of Cestius Gallus; see *BJ*, II, 501. He was later in the army of Titus at the siege of Jerusalem; cf. Tacitus, *Historiae*, V, 1 (No. 281); *BJ*, III, 68. See Stein, PW, Ser. 2, III, pp. 796 ff.; A. A. Barrett, *AJP*, XCVIII (1977), pp. 153 ff.

celeri navigatione properaverat: For record speeds, cf. Plinius, *Naturalis Historia*, XIX, 3 (seven and six days for voyages from Sicily to Alexandria and nine from Puteoli to Alexandria). Such speeds, however, were unusual. In general, see M.P. Charlesworth, *Trade-Routes and Commerce of the Roman Empire*, Cambridge 1924, pp. 22 f., 44; W. Riepl, *Das Nachrichtenwesen des Altertums*, Leipzig–Berlin 1913, p. 167; Nicols, pp. 41 f.

280

Historiae, IV, 3:3; 51:2 — Koestermann

(3:3) At Romae senatus cuncta principibus solita Vespasiano decernit, laetus et spei certus: quippe sumpta per Gallias Hispaniasque civilia arma, motis ad bellum Germaniis, mox Illyrico, postquam Aegyptum Iudaeam Syriamque et omnis provincias
5 exercitusque lustraverant, velut expiato terrarum orbe cepisse finem videbantur ... (51:2) Vespasianus in Italiam resque urbis intentus adversam de Domitiano famam accipit, tamquam terminos aetatis et concessa filio egrederetur: igitur validissimam exercitus partem Tito tradit ad reliqua Iudaici belli perpetranda.

(3:3) But at Rome the senators voted to Vespasian all the honours and privileges usually given the emperors. They were filled with joy and confident hope, for it seemed to them that civil warfare, which, breaking out in the Gallic and Spanish provinces, had moved to arms first the Germanies, then Illyricum, and which had traversed Egypt, Judaea, Syria, and all provinces and armies, was now at an end, as if the expiation of the whole world had been completed ... (51:2) While Vespasian was absorbed with thoughts of Italy and conditions in Rome, he heard an unfavourable report concerning Domitian to the effect that he was transgressing the bounds set by his youth and what might be permissible in a son: accordingly he turned over to Titus the main force of his army to complete the war with the Jews.

(trans. C.H. Moore, *LCL*)

51:2 *igitur validissimam exercitus partem Tito tradit ad reliqua Iudaici belli perpetranda*: Cf. *BJ*, IV, 658: τὸν δὲ υἱὸν Τίτον μετὰ τῆς ἐκκρίτου δυνάμεως ἀπέστειλεν ἐξαιρήσοντα τὰ Ἱεροσόλυμα.

281

Historiae, V, 1–13 — Koestermann = F 180 R

(1:1) Eiusdem anni principio Caesar Titus, perdomandae Iudaeae delectus a patre et privatis utriusque rebus militia clarus, maiore tum vi famaque agebat, certantibus provinciarum et exercituum studiis. Atque ipse, ut super fortunam crederetur, decorum se promptumque
5 in armis ostendebat, comitate et adloquiis officia provocans ac plerumque in opere, in agmine gregario militi mixtus, incorrupto ducis honore. (2) Tres eum in Iudaea legiones, quinta et decima ac quinta decima, vetus Vespasiani miles, excepere. Addidit e Syria duodecumam et adductos Alexandria duoetvicensimanos tertianos-
10 que; comitabantur viginti sociae cohortes, octo equitum alae, simul Agrippa Sohaemusque reges et auxilia regis Antiochi validaque et solito inter accolas odio infensa Iudaeis Arabum manus multi⟨que⟩, quos urbe atque Italia sua quemque spes adciverat occupandi principem adhuc vacuum. His cum copiis fines hostium ingressus
15 composito agmine, cuncta explorans paratusque decernere, haud procul Hierosolymis castra facit.
(2:1) Sed quoniam famosae urbis supremum diem tradituri sumus, congruens videtur primordia eius aperire. Iudaeos Creta insula profugos novissima Libyae insedisse memorant, qua tempestate
20 Saturnus vi Iovis pulsus cesserit regnis. Argumentum e nomine petitur: inclutum in Creta Idam montem, accolas Idaeos aucto in barbarum cognomento Iudaeos vocitari. (2) Quidam regnante Iside exundantem per Aegyptum multitudinem ducibus Hierosolymo ac

2 *privatis* Rhenanus *p̄latis* M *prelatis* L   4 *super fortunam* Lipsius   *superiori*
unam M   *superior omnibus* L   6 *et in agmine* L   12 *infensaque* L   /
           multique Halm   *multi* ML   13 ⟨*ex*⟩ *urbe* Nipperday
           16 *hierusolimis* M   22 *Iudeos* M

Iuda proximas in terras exoneratam; plerique Aethiopum prolem,
25 quos rege Cepheo metus atque odium mutare sedes perpulerit. (3)
Sunt qui tradant Assyrios convenas, indigum agrorum populum,
parte Aegypti potitos, mox proprias urbes Hebraeasque terras et
propiora Syriae coluisse. Clara alii Iudaeorum initia: Solymos,
carminibus Homeri celebratam gentem, conditae urbi Hierosolyma
30 nomen e suo fecisse.

(3:1) Plurimi auctores consentiunt orta per Aegyptum tabe, quae
corpora foedaret, regem Bocchorim adito Hammonis oraculo
remedium petentem purgare regnum et id genus hominum ut invisum
deis alias in terras avehere iussum. Sic conquisitum collectumque
35 volgus postquam vastis locis relictum sit, ceteris per lacrimas
torpentibus, Moysen, unum exulum, monuisse, ne quam deorum
hominumve opem exspectarent utrisque deserti, et sibimet duce
caelesti crederent, primo cuius auxilio praesentes miserias pepulis-
sent. Adsensere atque omnium ignari fortuitum iter incipiunt. (2) Sed
40 nihil aeque quam inopia aquae fatigabat, iamque haud procul exitio
totis campis procubuerant, cum grex asinorum agrestium e pastu in
rupem nemore opacam concessit. Secutus Moyses coniectura herbidi
soli largas aquarum venas aperit. Id levamen, et continuum sex
dierum iter emensi septimo pulsis cultoribus obtinuere terras, in quis
45 urbs et templum dicata.

(4:1) Moyses quo sibi in posterum gentem firmaret, novos ritus
contrariosque ceteris mortalibus indidit. Profana illic omnia quae
apud nos sacra, rursum concessa apud illos quae nobis incesta. (2)
Effigiem animalis, quo monstrante errorem sitimque depulerant,
50 penetrali sacravere, caeso ariete velut in contumeliam Hammonis;
bos quoque immolatur, quia Aegyptii Apin colunt. Sue abstinent
memoria cladis, quod ipsos scabies quondam turpaverat, cui id
animal obnoxium. (3) Longam olim famem crebris adhuc ieiuniis
fatentur, et raptarum frugum argumentum panis Iudaicus nullo
55 fermento detinetur. Septimo die otium placuisse ferunt, quia is finem
laborum tulerit; dein blandiente inertia septimum quoque annum
ignaviae datum. (4) Alii honorem eum Saturno haberi, seu principia

---

24 *pleriqui auctores consentiunt prolem* *Aethiopum* L   30 *nomen e* Rhenanus
nomine ML   36 *mosen* M y superscr. m. post. / *exulem* L   37 *et* ex *ex*
corr. M¹ / *duci* L   38 *praesentes* Orosius   *credentes praesentes* ML
41 *pastum* Damsté, *Mnemosyne*, LV, p. 117   42 *conscendit* L
47 *illis* Acidalius   51 *quia* Bipontini *q̄* M   *quem* L / *sue* ex *sues* corr. M¹
52 *meria* M   *memoria* superscr. m. vetus   55 *diei* M

religionis tradentibus Idaeis, quos cum Saturno pulsos et conditores gentis accepimus, seu quod e septem sideribus, quis mortales
60 reguntur, altissimo orbe et praecipua potentia stella Saturni feratur; ac pleraque caelestium vi⟨a⟩m suam et cursus septenos per numeros commeare.

(5:1) Hi ritus quoquo modo inducti antiquitate defenduntur: cetera instituta, sinistra foeda, pravitate valuere. Nam pessimus quisque
65 spretis religionibus patriis tributa et stipes illuc ⟨con⟩gerebant, unde auctae Iudaeorum res, et quia apud ipsos fides obstinata, misericordia in promptu, sed adversus omnes alios hostile odium. (2) Separati epulis, discreti cubilibus, proiectissima ad libidinem gens, alienarum concubitu abstinent; inter se nihil inlicitum. Circumcidere
70 genitalia instituerunt, ut diversitate noscantur. Transgressi in morem eorum idem usurpant, nec quidquam prius imbuuntur quam contemnere deos, exuere patriam, parentes liberos fratres vilia habere. (3) Augendae tamen multitudini consulitur; nam et necare quemquam ex agnatis nefas, animosque proelio aut suppliciis
75 peremptorum aeternos putant: hinc generandi amor et moriendi contemptus. Corpora condere quam cremare e more Aegyptio, eademque cura et de infernis persuasio, caelestium contra. (4) Aegyptii pleraque animalia effigiesque compositas venerantur, Iudaei mente sola unumque numen intellegunt: profanos, qui deum
80 imagines mortalibus materiis in species hominum effingant; summum illud et aeternum neque imitabile neque interiturum. Igitur nulla simulacra urbibus suis, nedum templis s⟨ist⟩unt; non regibus haec adulatio, non Caesaribus honor. (5) Sed quia sacerdotes eorum tibia tympanisque concinebant, hedera vinciebantur vitisque aurea ⟨in⟩
85 templo reperta, Liberum patrem coli, domitorem Orientis, quidam arbitrati sunt, nequaquam congruentibus institutis: quippe Liber festos laetosque ritus posuit, Iudaeorum mos absurdus sordidusque.

(6:1) Terra finesque, qua ad Orientem vergunt, Arabia terminantur; a meridie Aegyptus obiacet, ab occasu Phoenices et mare;

58 *Idaeis* Lipsius   *Iudeis* M   *iudaeis* L   59 *e* Novák *de* ML /   *mortales* ⟨*res*⟩ Wurm   ⟨*res*⟩ *mortales* Halm   61 *viam* Bezzenberger   *vim* ML /   *septenos* Halm   *septimos* ML   62 *commearent* M sed *nt* del M[1]   *coniiciant* L   *vim...conficiant* Lipsius   63 *Hi* L, ed. Spirensis   *Is* M   65 *congerebant* Puteolanus   *gerebant* ML   70 *transgressique* L   74 *ex gnatis* Lipsius   76 *condire* Triller   76–77 *Aegyptio cura, eademque et* C. Heraeus   79 *unum tantum* L   82 *s*⟨*ist*⟩*unt* Doederlein   *sunt* ML   *statuunt* Gudeman   *sinunt* J. F. Gronovius   84 *concinebant*] *continebantur* M   86 *neque* L

19

90 septemtrionem e latere Syriae longe prospectant. Corpora hominum salubria et ferentia laborum. Rari imbres, uber solum, fruges nostrum ad morem praeterque eas balsamum et palmae. Palmetis proceritas et decor, balsamum modica arbor; ut quisque ramus intumuit, si vim ferri adhibeas, pavent venae; fragmine lapidis aut
95 testa aperiuntur; umor in usu medentium est. (2) Praecipuum montium Libanum erigit, mirum dictu tantos inter ardores opacum fidumque nivibus; idem amnem Iordanen alit funditque. Nec Iordanes pelago accipitur, sed unum atque alterum lacum integer perfluit, tertio retinetur. Lacus immenso ambitu, specie maris, sapore
100 corruptior, gravitate odoris accolis pestifer, neque vento impellitur neque pisces aut suetas aquis volucres patitur. Inertes undae superiacta ut solido ferunt; periti imperitique nandi perinde attoluntur. (3) Certo anni tempore bitumen egerit, cuius legendi usum, ut ceteras artes, experientia docuit. Ater suapte natura liquor
105 et sparso aceto concretus innatat; hunc manu captum, quibus ea cura in summa navis trahunt; inde nullo iuvante influit oneratque, donec abscindas. Nec abscindere aere ferrove possis: fugit cruorem vestemque infectam sanguine, quo feminae per menses exsolvuntur. (4) Sic veteres auctores, sed gnari locorum tradunt undantes bitumine
110 moles pelli manuque trahi ad litus, mox, ubi vapore terrae, vi solis inaruerint, securibus cuneisque ut trabes aut saxa discindi.
(7:1) Haud procul inde campi, quos ferunt olim uberes magnisque urbibus habitatos fulminum iactu arsisse; et manere vestigia terramque ipsam specie torridam vim frugiferam perdidisse. Nam
115 cuncta sponte edita aut manu sata, sive herba tenus aut flore seu solidam in speciem adolevere, atra et inania velut in cinerem vanescunt. (2) Ego sicut inclutas quondam urbes igne caelesti flagrasse concesserim, ita halitu lacus infici terram, conrumpi superfusum spiritum, eoque fetus segetum et autumni putrescere
120 reor solo caeloque iuxta gravi. Et Belus amnis Iudaico mari inlabitur, circa cuius os lectae harenae admixto nitro in vitrum excocuntur. Modicum id litus et egerentibus inexhaustum.

91 *fruges* Lipsius   *exuberant fruges* ML   96 *inter tantos* L   101 *inertes*
undae Heinsius   *incertes* (erasa *s*) *undae* M   *incerteum unde* L   104 *acer* L
            109 *bituminis* L   110 *trahique manu* L   /   *vique* L
        113 *ictu* Orosius cod. B   /   *et*] *sed* Orosius   114 *torrida* M
    115 *herba tenus aut flore* Rhenanus   *herbas* (*herbae* L) *tenues aut flores* ML
116 *solidam* Salmasius   *solitam* ML / *qatra* M, sed *q* erasum   *putria* Thomas
taetra Meiser   117 *inclitas* L Orosius   *Indicas* M   120 *Belus* Rhenanus
        bel Ius M   *bellus* superscr. m. vetus. L

(8:1) Magna pars Iudaeae vicis dispergitur; habent et oppida; Hierosolyma genti caput. Illic immensae opulentiae templum, et
125 primis munimentis urbs, dein ⟨re⟩gia, templum intimis clausum. Ad fores tantum Iudaeo aditus, limine praeter sacerdotes arcebantur. (2) Dum Assyrios penes Medosque et Persas Oriens fuit, despectissima pars servientium: postquam Macedones praepolluere, rex Antiochus demere superstitionem et mores Graecorum dare adnisus, quo minus
130 taeterrimam gentem in melius mutaret, Parthorum bello prohibitus est; nam ea tempestate Arsaces desciverat. (3) Tum Iudaei Macedonibus invalidis, Parthis nondum adultis (et Romani procul erant), si⟨bi⟩ ipsi reges imposuere; qui mobilitate volgi expulsi, resumpta per arma dominatione fugas civium, urbium eversiones,
135 fratrum coniugum parentum neces aliaque solita regibus ausi superstitionem fovebant, quia honor sacerdotii firmamentum potentiae adsumebatur.

(9:1) Romanorum primus Cn. Pompeius Iudaeos domuit templum-que iure victoriae ingressus est: inde volgatum nulla intus deum
140 effigie vacuam sedem et inania arcana. Muri Hierosolymorum diruti, delubrum mansit. Mox civili inter nos bello, postquam in dicionem M. Antonii provinciae cesserant, rex Parthorum Pacorus Iudaea potitus interfectusque a P. Ventidio, et Parthi trans Euphraten redacti: Iudaeos C. Sosius subegit. (2) Regnum ab Antonio Herodi
145 datum victor Augustus auxit. Post mortem Herodis nihil exspectato Caesare Simo quidam regium nomen invaserat. Is a Quintilio Varo obtinente Syriam punitus, et gentem coercitam liberi Herodis tripertito rexere. Sub Tiberio quies; dein iussi a C. Caesare effigiem eius in templo locare arma potius sumpsere, quem motum Caesaris
150 mors diremit. (3) Claudius defunctis regibus aut ad modicum redactis Iudaeam provinciam equitibus Romanis aut libertis permisit, e quibus Antonius Felix per omnem saevitiam ac libidinem ius regium servili ingenio exercuit, Drusilla Cleopatrae et Antonii nepte in matrimonium accepta, ut eiusdem Antonii Felix progener, Claudius
155 nepos esset.

124 *caput genti* L   125 *dein regia* Mercerus   *de Ingia* M
124–125 *ex primis munimentis urbis alienigenis templum interius clausum* L
126 ⟨*omnes*⟩ *arcebantur* Koestermann   127 *persaxas* M   128 *praepolluere*
      Halm   *praepotuere* ML   133 *si* M, *bi* superscr. m. post   *sed* L   /
volgis epulsi M   141 *inter nos*] *Interno* M   142 ⟨*Orientis*⟩ *provinciae* Ritter
provinciae ⟨*Orientis*⟩ C. Heraeus   143 *eusphraten* M, sed *s* erasum   *eufratem* L
144 *sestius* L   146 *Simo* Ernesti   *simon* M   *symon* L   152 *omnia* M, sed *a*
in *em* corr. M[1] et in marg. add. *peromnem*   154 *matrimonia* M   *matrimonio* L

21

(10:1) Duravit tamen patientia Iudaeis usque ad Gessium Florum procuratorem: sub eo bellum ortum. Et comprimere coeptantem Cestium Gallum Syriae legatum varia proelia ac saepius adversa excepere. Qui ubi fato aut taedio occidit, missu Neronis Vespasianus
160 fortuna famaque et egregiis ministris intra duas aestates cuncta camporum omnesque praeter Hierosolyma urbes victore exercitu tenebat. (2) Proximus annus civili bello intentus quantum ad Iudaeos per otium transiit. Pace per Italiam parta et externae curae rediere: augebat iras, quod soli Iudaei non cessissent; simul manere apud
165 exercitus Titum ad omnes principatus novi eventus casusve utile videbatur.

(11:1) Igitur castris, uti diximus, ante moenia Hierosolymorum positis instructas legiones ostentavit: Iudaei sub ipsos muros struxere aciem, rebus secundis longius ausuri et, si pellerentur, parato
170 perfugio. Missus in eos eques cum expeditis cohortibus ambigue certavit; mox cessere hostes et sequentibus diebus crebra pro portis proelia serebant, donec assiduis damnis intra moenia pellerentur. (2) Romani ad obpugnandum versi; neque enim dignum videbatur famem hostium opperiri, poscebantque pericula, pars virtute, multi
175 ferocia et cupidine praemiorum. Ipsi Tito Roma et opes voluptatesque ante oculos, ac ni statim Hierosolyma conciderent, morari videbantur. (3) Sed urbem arduam situ opera molesque firmaverant, quis vel plana satis munirentur. Nam duos colles in immensum editos claudebant muri per artem obliqui aut introrsus sinuati, ut latera
180 obpugnantium ad ictus patescerent; extrema rupis abrupta, et turres, ubi mons iuvisset, in sexagenos pedes, inter devexa in centenos vicenosque attollebantur mira specie ac procul intuentibus pares. Alia intus moenia regiae circumiecta, conspicuoque fastigio turris Antonia, in honorem M. Antonii ab Herode appellata.

185 (12:1) Templum in modum arcis propriique muri, labore et opere ante alios; ipsae porticus, quis templum ambibatur, egregium propugnaculum. Fons perennis aquae, cavati sub terra montes et piscinae cisternaeque servandis imbribus. (2) Providerant conditores ex diversitate morum crebra bella: inde cuncta quamvis adversus
190 longum obsidium; et a Pompeio expugnatis metus atque usus

158 *sestium* L   159 *excipere* M
accepere L   /   *missus neroni* (corr. ex *neronis*) L   160 *intra*] *inter* M
160–161 *cuncta camporum*] *cuncta composuit* L   163 *parata* ML   /
redire M   165 *utilis* M   *utilius* Pichena   181 *sexagenos* Bekker   *sexaginta* ML
182 *vicenos* Haase   185 *opera* ML   189 *adversus quamvis* C. Heraeus

22

pleraque monstravere. Atque per avaritiam Claudianorum temporum empto iure muniendi struxere muros in pace tamquam ad bellum, magna conluvie et ceterarum urbium clade aucti; nam pervicacissimus quisque illuc perfugerat, eoque seditiosius agebant.

195 (3) Tres duces, totidem exercitus: extrema et latissima moenium Simo, mediam urbem Ioannes quem et Bargioram vocabant, templum Eleazarus firmaverat. Multitudine et armis Ioannes ac Simo, Eleazarus loco pollebat; sed proelia dolus incendia inter ipsos, et magna vis frumenti ambusta. (4) Mox Ioannes, missis per speciem

200 sacrificandi qui Eleazarum manumque eius obtruncarent, templo potitur. Ita in duas factiones civitas discessit, donec propinquantibus Romanis bellum externum concordiam pareret.

(13:1) Evenerant prodigia, quae neque hostiis neque votis piare fas habet gens superstitioni obnoxia, religionibus adversa. Visae per

205 caelum concurrere acies, rutilantia arma et subito nubium igne conlucere templum. Apertae repente delubri fores et audita maior humana vox, excedere deos; simul ingens motus excedentium. (2) Quae pauci in metum trahebant: pluribus persuasio inerat antiquis sacerdotum litteris contineri, eo ipso tempore fore ut valesceret

210 Oriens profectique Iudaea rerum potirentur. Quae ambages Vespasianum ac Titum praedixerat, sed volgus more humanae cupidinis sibi tantam fatorum altitudinem interpretati ne adversis quidem ad vera mutabantur. (3) Multitudinem obsessorum omnis aetatis, virile ac muliebre secus, sexcenta milia fuisse accepimus:

215 arma cunctis, qui ferre possent, et plures quam pro numero audebant. Obstinatio viris feminisque par ac si transferre sedes cogerentur, maior vitae metus quam mortis. (4) Hanc adversus urbem gentemque Caesar Titus, quando impetus et subita belli locus abnueret, aggeribus vineisque certare statuit: dividuntur legionibus munia, et

220 quies proeliorum fuit, donec cuncta expugnandis urbibus reperta apud veteres aut novis ingeniis ⟨inventa⟩ struerentur.

193 *conluvies* Nipperdey / *exterarum urbium* L   196 *symon* L /
iohs (*h* lineola perfosa) M / *Bargioram* Rhenanus *barbagioram* ML
quem et Bargioram vocabant secl. Bipontini post *Simo* Salinerius posuit
197 *alazarus* M   198 *alazarus* M   200 *lazarum* M   206 *apertae*]
expertae M, sed *ex* in ras. m. post   212 *altitudinem*] *magnitudinem* M
213 *hominis* M   214 *virilis ac muliebris sexus* L
221 ⟨*inventa*⟩ Koestermann

(1:1) At the beginning of this same year Titus Caesar, who had been selected by his father to complete the subjugation of Judaea, and who had already won distinction as a soldier while both were still private citizens, began to enjoy greater power and reputation, for provinces and armies now vied with one another in enthusiasm for him. Moreover, in his own conduct, wishing to be thought greater than his fortune, he always showed himself dignified and energetic in the field; by his affable address he called forth devotion, and he often mingled with the common soldiers both at work or on the march without impairing his position as general. (2) He found awaiting him in Judaea three legions, Vespasian's old troops, the Fifth, the Tenth and the Fifteenth. He reinforced these with the Twelfth from Syria and with some soldiers from the Twenty-second and the Third which he brought from Alexandria; these troops were accompanied by twenty cohorts of allied infantry, eight squadrons of cavalry, as well as by the princes Agrippa and Sohaemus, the auxiliaries sent by King Antiochus and by a strong contingent of Arabs, who hated the Jews with all that hatred that is common among neighbours; there were besides many Romans who had been prompted to leave the capital and Italy by the hope that each entertained of securing the prince's favour while he was yet free from engagements. With these forces Titus entered the enemy's land: his troops advanced in strict order, he reconnoitred at every step and was always ready for battle; not far from Jerusalem he pitched camp.

(2:1) However, as I am about to describe the last days of a famous city, it seems proper for me to give some account of its origin. It is said that the Jews were originally exiles from the island of Crete who settled in the farthest parts of Libya at the time when Saturn had been deposed and expelled by Jove. An argument in favour of this is derived from the name: there is a famous mountain in Crete called Ida, and hence the inhabitants were called the Idaei, which was later lengthened into the barbarous form Iudaei. (2) Some hold that in the reign of Isis the superfluous population of Egypt, under the leadership of Hierosolymus and Iuda, discharged itself on the neighbouring lands; many others think that they were an Ethiopian stock, which in the reign of Cepheus was forced to migrate by fear and hatred. (3) Still others report that they were Assyrian refugees, a landless people, who first got control of a part of Egypt, then later they had their own cities and lived in the Hebrew territory and the nearer parts of Syria. Still others say that the Jews are of illustrious origin, being the Solymi, a people celebrated in Homer's poems, who founded a city and gave it the name Hierosolyma, formed from their own.

(3:1) Most authors agree that once during a plague in Egypt, which caused bodily disfigurement, King Bocchoris approached the oracle of Ammon and asked for a remedy whereupon he was told to purge his kingdom and to transport this race into other lands, since it was hateful to the gods. So the crowd was searched out and gathered together, then, being abandoned in the desert, while all others lay idle and weeping, one only of the exiles, Moses by name, warned them not to hope for help from gods or men; for they were deserted by both; but to trust to themselves, regarding as a guide sent from heaven the one whose assistance should first give them escape from their present distress. They agreed, and then set out on their journey in utter ignorance, but trusting to chance. (2) Nothing caused them so much distress as scarcity of water, and in fact they had already fallen exhausted over the plain nigh unto death, when a herd of wild asses moved from their pasturage to a rock that was shaded by a grove of trees. Moses followed them, and, conjecturing the truth from the grassy ground, discovered abundant streams of water. This relieved them, and they then marched six days continuously, and on the seventh seized a country, expelling the former inhabitants; there they founded a city and dedicated a temple.

(4:1) To establish his influence over this people for all time, Moses introduced new religious practices, quite opposed to those of all other religions. The Jews regard as profane all that we hold sacred; on the other hand, they permit all that we abhor. (2) They dedicated, in a shrine, a statue of that creature whose guidance enabled them to put an end to their wandering and thirst, sacrificing a ram, apparently in derision of Ammon. They likewise offer the ox, because the Egyptians worship Apis. They abstain from pork, in recollection of a plague, for the scab to which this animal is subject once afflicted them. (3) By frequent fasts even now they bear witness to the long hunger with which they were once distressed, and the unleavened Jewish bread is still employed in memory of the haste with which they seized the grain. They say that they first chose to rest on the seventh day because that day ended their toils; but after a time they were led by the charms of indolence to give over the seventh year as well to inactivity. (4) Others say that this is done in honour of Saturn, whether it be that the primitive elements of their religion were given

25

by the Idaeans, who, according to tradition, were expelled with Saturn and became the founders of the Jewish race, or is due to the fact that, of the seven planets that rule the fortunes of mankind, Saturn moves in the highest orbit and has the greatest potency; and that many of the heavenly bodies traverse their paths and courses in multiples of seven.

(5:1) Whatever their origin, these rites are maintained by their antiquity: the other customs of the Jews are base and abominable, and owe their persistence to their depravity: for the worst rascals among other peoples, renouncing their ancestral religions, always kept sending tribute and contributing to Jerusalem, thereby increasing the wealth of the Jews; again, the Jews are extremely loyal toward one another, and always ready to show compassion, but toward every other people they feel only hate and enmity. (2) They sit apart at meals and they sleep apart, and although as a race, they are prone to lust, they abstain from intercourse with foreign women; yet among themselves nothing is unlawful. They adopted circumcision to distinguish themselves from other peoples by this difference. Those who are converted to their ways follow the same practice, and the earliest lesson they receive is to despise the gods, to disown their country, and to regard their parents, children, and brothers as of little account. (3) However, they take thought to increase their numbers; for they regard it as a crime to kill any late-born child, and they believe that the souls of those who are killed in battle or by the executioner are immortal: hence comes their passion for begetting children, and their scorn of death. They bury the body rather than burn it, thus following the Egyptians' custom; they likewise bestow the same care on the dead, and hold the same belief about the world below; but their ideas of heavenly things are quite the opposite. (4) The Egyptians worship many animals and monstrous images; the Jews conceive of one god only, and that with the mind only: they regard as impious those who make from perishable materials representations of gods in man's image; that supreme and eternal being is to them incapable of representation and without end. Therefore they set up no statues in their cities, still less in their temples; this flattery is not paid their kings, nor this honour given to the Caesars. (5) But since their priests used to chant to the accompaniment of pipes and drums and to wear garlands of ivy, and because a golden vine was found in their temple, some have thought that they were devotees of Father Liber, the conqueror of the East, in spite of the incongruity of their customs. For Liber established festive rites of a joyous nature, while the ways of the Jews are preposterous and mean.

(6:1) Their land is bounded by Arabia on the east, Egypt lies on the south, on the west are Phoenicia and the sea, and toward the north the people enjoy a wide prospect over Syria. The inhabitants are healthy and hardy. Rains are rare; the soil is fertile: its products are like ours, save that the balsam and the palm also grow there. The palm is a tall and handsome tree; the balsam a mere shrub: if a branch, when swollen with sap, is pierced with steel, the veins shrivel up; so a piece of stone or a potsherd is used to open them; the juice is employed by physicians. (2) Of the mountains, Lebanon rises to the greatest height, and is in fact a marvel, for in the midst of the excessive heat its summit is shaded by trees and covered by snow; it likewise is the source and supply of the river Jordan. This river does not empty into the sea, but after flowing with volume undiminished through two lakes is lost in the third. The last is a lake of great size: it is like the sea, but its water has a nauseous taste, and its offensive odour is injurious to those who live near it. Its waters are not moved by the wind, and neither fish nor water-fowl can live there. Its lifeless waves bear up whatever is thrown upon them as on a solid surface; all swimmers, whether skilled or not, are buoyed up by them. (3) At a certain season of the year the sea throws up bitumen, and experience has taught the natives how to collect this, as she teaches all arts. Bitumen is by nature a dark fluid which coagulates when sprinkled with vinegar, and swims on the surface. Those whose business it is, catch hold of it with their hands and haul it on shipboard: then with no artificial aid the bitumen flows in and loads the ship until the stream is cut off. Yet you cannot use bronze or iron to cut the bituminous stream; it shrinks from blood or from a cloth stained with a woman's menses. (4) Such is the story told by ancient writers, but those who are acquainted with the country aver that the floating masses of bitumen are driven by the winds or drawn by hand to shore, where later, after they have been dried by vapours from the earth or by the heat of the sun, they are split like timber or stone with axes and wedges.

(7:1) Not far from this lake is a plain which, according to report, was once fertile and the site of great cities, but which was later devastated by lightning; and it is said that traces of this disaster still exist there, and that the very ground looks burnt and has lost its fertility. In fact, all the plants there, whether wild or cultivated, turn black, become sterile and seem to wither into dust, either in leaf or in flower or after they have reached their usual mature form. (2) Now for my part, although I should grant that famous cities were once destroyed by fire from heaven, I still think that it is the exhalations from the lake that infect the ground and poison the atmosphere about this district and that this is the reason that crops and fruits decay, since both soil and climate are deleterious. The river Belus also empties into the Jewish Sea; around its mouth a kind of sand is gathered, which when mixed with soda is fused into glass. The beach is of moderate size, but it furnishes an inexhaustible supply.

(8:1) A great part of Judaea is covered with scattered villages, but there are some towns also; Jerusalem is the capital of the Jews. In it was a temple possessing enormous riches. The first line of fortifications protected the city, the next the palace, and the innermost wall the temple. Only a Jew might approach its doors, and all save the priests were forbidden to cross the threshold. (2) While the East was under the dominion of the Assyrians, Medes and Persians, the Jews were regarded as the meanest of their subjects: but after the Macedonians gained supremacy, King Antiochus endeavoured to abolish Jewish superstition and to introduce Greek civilization; the war with the Parthians, however, prevented his improving this basest of peoples; for it was exactly at that time that Arsaces had revolted. (3) Later on, since the power of Macedon had waned, the Parthians were not yet come to their strength, and the Romans were far away, the Jews selected their own kings. These in turn were expelled by the fickle mob; but recovering their throne by force of arms, they banished citizens, destroyed towns, killed brothers, wives, and parents, and dared essay every other kind of royal crime without hesitation; but they fostered the national superstition, for they had assumed the priesthood to support their civil authority.

(9:1) The first Roman to subdue the Jews and set foot in their temple by right of conquest was Gnaeus Pompey: thereafter it was a matter of common knowledge that there were no representations of the gods within, but that the place was empty and the secret shrine contained nothing. The walls of Jerusalem were razed, but the temple remained standing. Later, in the time of our civil wars, when these eastern provinces had fallen into the hands of Mark Antony, the Parthian prince, Pacorus, seized Judaea, but he was slain by Publius Ventidius, and the Parthians were thrown back across the Euphrates: the Jews

28

were subdued by Gaius Sosius. (2) Antony gave the throne to Herod, and Augustus, after his victory, increased his territory. After Herod's death, a certain Simon assumed the name of king without waiting for Caesar's decision. He, however, was put to death by Quintillius Varus, governor of Syria; the Jews were repressed; and the kingdom was divided into three parts and given to Herod's sons. Under Tiberius all was quiet. Then, when Caligula ordered the Jews to set up his statue in their temple, they chose rather to resort to arms, but the emperor's death put an end to their uprising. (3) The princes now being dead or reduced to insignificance, Claudius made Judaea a province and entrusted it to Roman knights or to freedmen; one of the latter, Antonius Felix, practised every kind of cruelty and lust, wielding the power of king with all the instincts of a slave; he had married Drusilla, the granddaughter of Cleopatra and Antony, and so was Antony's grandson-in-law, while Claudius was Antony's grandson.

(10:1) Still the Jews' patience lasted until Gessius Florus became procurator: in his time war began. When Cestius Gallus, governor of Syria, tried to stop it, he suffered varied fortunes and met defeat more often than he gained victory. On his death, whether in the course of nature or from vexation, Nero sent out Vespasian, who, aided by his good fortune and reputation as well as by his excellent subordinates, within two summers occupied with his victorious army, the whole of the level country and all the cities except Jerusalem. (2) The next year was taken up with civil war, and thus was passed in inactivity, so far as the Jews were concerned. When peace had been secured throughout Italy, foreign troubles began again; and the fact that the Jews alone had failed to surrender increased our resentment; at the same time, having regard to all the possibilities and hazards of a new reign, it seemed expedient for Titus to remain with the army.

(11:1) Therefore, as I have said above, Titus pitched his camp before the walls of Jerusalem and displayed his legions in battle array: the Jews formed their line close beneath their walls, being thus ready to advance if successful, and having a refuge at hand in case they were driven back. Some horse and light-armed foot were sent against them, but fought indecisively; later the enemy retired, and during the following days they engaged in many skirmishes before their gates until at last their continual defeats drove them within their walls. (2) The Romans now turned to preparations for an assault; for the soldiers thought it beneath their dignity to wait for the enemy to be starved out, and so they began to clamour for danger, part being prompted by bravery, but many were moved by their savage natures and their desire for booty. Titus himself had before his eyes a vision of Rome, its wealth and its pleasures, and he felt that if Jerusalem did not fall at once his enjoyment of them was delayed. (3) But the city stands on an eminence, and the Jews had defended it with works and fortifications sufficient to protect even level ground; for the two hills that rise to a great height had been included within walls that had been skilfully built, projecting out or bending in so as to put the flanks of an assailing body under fire. The rocks terminated in sheer cliffs, and towers rose to a height of sixty feet where the hill assisted the fortifications, and in the valleys they reached one hundred and twenty; they presented a wonderful sight, and appeared of equal height when viewed from a distance. An inner line of walls had been built around the palace, and on a conspicuous height stands Antony's tower, so named by Herod in honour of Mark Antony.

(12:1) The temple was built like a citadel, with walls of its own, which were constructed with more care and effort than any of the rest; the very colonnades about the temple made a splendid defence. Within the enclosure is an ever-flowing spring; in the hills are subterraneous excavations, with pools and cisterns for holding rain-water. (2) The founders of the city had foreseen that there would be many wars because the ways of their people differed so from those of the neighbours: therefore they had built at every point as if they expected a long siege; and after the city had been stormed by Pompey, their fears and experience taught them much. Moreover, profiting by the greed displayed during the reign of Claudius, they had bought the privilege of fortifying their city, and in time of peace had built walls as if for war. The population at this time had been increased by streams of rabble that flowed in from the other captured cities, for the most desperate rebels had taken refuge here, and consequently sedition was the more rife. (3) There were three generals, three armies: the outermost and largest circuit of the walls was held by Simon, the middle of the city by John, and the temple was guarded by Eleazar. John and Simon were strong in numbers and equipment, Eleazar had the advantage of position: between these three there was constant fighting, treachery, and arson, and a great store of grain was consumed. (4) Then John got possession of the temple by sending a party under pretence of offering sacrifice, to slay Eleazar and his troops. So the citizens were divided into two factions until, at the approach of the Romans, foreign war produced concord.

(13:1) Prodigies had indeed occurred, but to avert them either by victims or by vows is held unlawful by a people which, though prone to superstition, is opposed to all propitiatory rites. Contending hosts were seen meeting in the skies, arms flashed and suddenly the temple was illuminated with fire from the clouds. Of a sudden the doors of the shrine opened and a superhuman voice cried: "The gods are departing": at the same moment the mighty stir of their going was heard. (2) Few interpreted these omens as fearful; the majority firmly believed that their ancient priestly writings contained the prophecy that this was the very time when the East should grow strong and that men starting from Judaea should possess the world. This mysterious prophecy had in reality pointed to Vespasian and Titus, but the common people, as is the way of human ambition, interpreted these great destinies in their own favour, and could not be turned to the truth even by adversity. (3) We have heard that the total number of the besieged of every age and both sexes was six hundred thousand: there were arms for all who could use them, and the number ready to fight was larger than could have been anticipated from the total population. Both men and women showed the same determination; and if they were to be forced to change their home, they feared life more than death. (4) Such was the city and people against which Titus Caesar proceeded; since the nature of the ground did not allow him to assault or employ any sudden operations, he decided to use earthworks and mantlets: the legions were assigned to their several tasks, and there was a respite of fighting until they made ready every device for storming a town that the ancients had ever employed or modern ingenuity invented.   (trans. C. H. Moore, *LCL*)

1:1 *Eiusdem anni principio*: The beginning of 70 C.E.
perdomandae Iudaeae delectus a patre: Cf. Tacitus, *Historiae*, IV, 51 (No. 280).
privatis utriusque rebus militia clarus: The former military achievements of Titus were connected with his service in Germany and Britain (Suetonius, *Divus Titus*, 4), and with the conquest of Galilaea; see M. Fortina, *L'imperatore Tito*, Turin 1955, pp. 16 ff.; Weynand, PW, pp. 2697 ff.
Atque ipse ... decorum se promptumque in armis ostendebat ... incorrupto ducis honore: On Titus as a soldier and leader, see Weber, pp. 226 ff.
1:2 *quinta*: For the part played by the Fifth Legion (the Macedonian) in the siege, cf. *BJ*, V, 68, 467; VI, 68. Its commander was Sextus Cerialis; cf. *ibid.*, 237.

decima: Cf. *BJ*, V, 69, 135, 269, 468; its commander was Larcius Lepidus; cf. *BJ*, VI, 237.

quinta decima: Cf. *BJ*, V, 468; its commander was Tittius Frugi; cf. *BJ*, VI, 237; see Ritterling, PW, XII, p. 1751.

Addidit e Syria duodecumam: The Twelfth Legion (the Fulminata) bore the brunt of the battle during the expedition of Cestius Gallus and suffered an ignominious repulse; see below, the commentary to Tacitus, *Historiae*, V, 10:1.

adductos Alexandria duoetvicensimanos tertianosque: These legions were represented at the siege only by *vexillationes* of a thousand men from each legion; cf. *BJ*, V, 44: δισχίλιοι μὲν γὰρ αὐτῷ τῶν ἀπ' Ἀλεξανδρείας στρατευμάτων ἐπίλεκτοι, τρισχίλιοι δὲ συνείποντο τῶν ἀπ' Εὐφράτου φυλάκων; ibid., 287: τῶν ἀπ' Ἀλεξανδρείας ἐπιλέκτων. They were commanded by Fronto Liternius (or Aeternius); cf. *BJ*, VI, 238: στρατοπεδάρχης τῶν ἀπὸ Ἀλεξανδρείας δύο ταγμάτων; see Saxer, p. 21. *Sohaemusque*: Cf. Tacitus, *Historiae*, II, 81 (No. 279).

auxilia regis Antiochi: On the part played by Antiochus in the siege, cf. *BJ*, V, 460 ff.

infensa Iudaeis Arabum manus: Malchus the Arab is linked with Antiochus, Agrippa and Sohaemus in *BJ*, III, 68: συχνὸν δὲ καὶ παρὰ τῶν βασιλέων συνήχθη συμμαχικόν, Ἀντιόχου μὲν καὶ Ἀγρίππα καὶ Σοαίμου παρασχομένων ἀνὰ δισχιλίους πεζοὺς τοξότας καὶ χιλίους ἱππεῖς, τοῦ δὲ Ἄραβος Μάλχου χιλίους πέμψαντος ἱππεῖς ἐπὶ πεζοῖς πεντακισχιλίοις. For the reign of Malchus, see P.C. Hammond, *The Nabataeans — Their History, Culture and Archaeology*, Gothenburg 1973, pp. 27 ff.; Y. Meshorer, *Nabataean Coins*, Jerusalem 1975, pp. 63 ff. For the enmity of the Arabs towards the Jews at the time of the expedition of Varus in 4 B.C.E., cf. *BJ*, II, 68 ff.; *Ant.*, XVII, 290. On the forces of Titus at the siege in general, see Weynand, PW, VI, p. 2700.

2:1 *Sed quoniam*: For other examples of "sed quoniam" at the start of a digression, cf. Tacitus, *Historiae*, IV, 5; Sallustius, *Bellum Iugurthinum*, 79; 95:2; see Theissen, *op. cit.* (supra, p. 6), p. 91.

famosae urbis: "Famosa" may have a neutral meaning in Tacitus, i.e. just famous; cf. Tacitus, *Historiae*, I, 10. It has such a meaning in Horatius, *Ars Poetica*, 469, as Heubner remarks in his commentary *ad loc*. The adjective is in any case less explicit than the "Hierosolyma, longe clarissima urbium Orientis" of Plinius, *Naturalis Historia*, V, 70 (No. 204).

primordia eius aperire: Cf. Livius, *Periochae*, XVI: "origo Carthaginiensium et primordia urbis eorum" (in connection with the outbreak of the First Punic War); see B.R. Voss, *Der pointierte Stil des Tacitus*, Münster 1963, p. 29; R. Häussler, *Tacitus und das historische Bewusstsein*, Heidelberg 1965, p. 274.

Iudaeos Creta insula profugos: Reinach suggests that this view should be related to the Cretan origins of the Philistines, but we can hardly look for historical reality behind the learned mythological combination based on the supposed connection between the Jews and Saturn. Nor is there any need to explain the Cretan origins of the Jews by the existence of Jewish communities there under the Roman empire; for these, see Josephus, *Ant.*, XVII, 327; *BJ*, II, 103 (help given by Cretan Jews to Pseudo-Alexander); *Vita*, 427 (Josephus marries a Cretan Jewess). Cf. also the inscriptions: A.C. Bandy, *Hesperia*, XXXII (1963), p. 227 (a Gortynian Jewess Sophia plays an important part in the life of the Jewish community of Kisamos); *Inscriptiones Creticae*, ed. M. Guarducci, I, Rome 1935, p. 12, No. 17 (third or fourth century); *ibid.*, IV, 1950, p. 414, No. 509 (which, however, may be Christian); *Inscriptiones Creticae*, II, Rome 1939, p. 179, n. 8. However, Cretan Jews were by no means conspicuous in the Diaspora. It has been suggested that the fantastic etymology may have been invented by Hellenistic Jews who wanted to connect the origins of their people with Greek civilization; see G. La Piana, *HTR*, XX (1927), p. 382. For the frequent mention of "profugi" in foundation-sagas of colonies, see F. Kuntz, "Die Sprache des Tacitus und die Tradition der lateinischen Historikersprache", Ph.D. Thesis, Heidelberg 1962, p. 131,

novissima Libyae: Cf. Herodotus, III, 115: ἐσχατιαί εἰσι καὶ ἐν τῇ Λιβύῃ (i.e. the dwelling-place of the Ethiopians). This connects the first explanation of Jewish origins brought by Tacitus with the third, which regards the Jews as descendants of the Ethiopians; see H. Lewy, *MGWJ*, LXXXI (1937), pp. 65 ff.; see also our commentary below.

qua tempestate Saturnus vi Iovis pulsus cesserit regnis: On the connection between Saturnus and the Jews, cf. also below, Tacitus, *Historiae*, V, 4. On Saturn as a fugitive from Crete, cf., e.g., Minucius Felix, *Octavius*, 23:10 (21:5): "Saturnus Creta profugus Italiam metu filii saevientis accesserat"; Servius, *In Aeneidem*, VIII, 319.

inclutum in Creta: For the use of "inclutus", see O. Prinz, *Glotta*, XXIX (1942), pp. 138 ff.

accolas Idaeos aucto in barbarum cognomento Iudaeos vocitari: The classic example of changes in the names of nations is found in Strabo, *Geographica*, VII, 2:2, p. 293: Κιμμερίους τοὺς Κίμβρους ὀνομασάντων τῶν Ἑλλήνων. Cf. also Posidonius, apud: Strabo, *Geographica*, I, 2:34, p. 42 = *F. Gr. Hist.*, II, A 87, F 105; Claudius Iolaus (No. 249): Οὐδαῖος = Ἰουδαῖος, and in Vergilius, *Aeneis*, I, 267 f. In favour of a Latin source for the identification of Idaei with Iudaei, see Hospers-Jansen, *op. cit.* (supra, p. 6), p. 112. For the use of "barbarus" by Tacitus, see G. Walser, *Rom, das Reich und die fremden Völker in der Geschichtsschreibung der frühen Kaiserzeit*, Baden-Baden 1951, pp. 70 f.

2:2 *exundantem per Aegyptum multitudinem*: On the over-population of Egypt and its establishment of colonies in many parts of the world, cf. the remark of Diodorus, I, 29:5 (presumably from Hecataeus). Cf. also *ibid.*, I, 31:6; Aristoteles, *De Animalium Generatione*, 770a, 34 f.; Strabo, *Geographica*, XV, 1:22, p. 695; Philo, *De Specialibus Legibus*, I, 2; Plinius, *Naturalis Historia*, VII, 33.

ducibus Hierosolymo ac Iuda: The same version is reflected in Plutarchus, *De Iside et Osiride*, 31 (No. 259), where Hierosolymus and Iudaeus appear as sons of Typhon.

proximas in terras exoneratam: Cf. Livius, X, 6:2; Seneca, *Consolatio ad*

Helviam, 7:4: "Nec omnibus eadem causa relinquendi...alios domestica seditio summovit; alios nimia superfluentis populi frequentia ad exonerandas vires emisit."

rege Cepheo: For the connection between the father of Andromeda and Aethiopia, cf. Euripides, *Andromeda*, in: Nauck, *Tragicorum Graecorum Fragmenta*, No. 113; Agatharchides, *De Mari Erythraeo*, I, 4 (Müller, *Geographi Graeci Minores*, I, p. 112); Ovidius, *Metamorphoses*, IV, 669; Lucianus, *Dialogi Marini*, XIV.

The question whether the location of the myth of Andromeda at Jaffa originated independently or derived from the Ethiopian location is difficult to answer; see the commentary to Pausanias, *Graeciae Descriptio*, IV, 35:9 (No. 354). The first possibility seems preferable since, even by the fifth century B.C.E., a fragment from a comedy by Cratinus connects Perseus with Syria; see C. Dugas, *REG*, LXIX (1956), p. 9. In any case the connection between Jaffa and Cepheus is clearly seen in Conon, apud: Photius, *Bibliotheca*, Cod. 186 (ed. Bekker, pp. 138b–139a = No. 145), and in Plinius, *Naturalis Historia*, VI, 182: "et Syriae imperitasse eam [scil. Aethiopiam] nostroque litori aetate regis Cephei patet Andromedae fabulis"; Stephanus Byzantius, s.v. Ἰόπη (ed. Meineke, p. 333). This identification drew much of its probability from the similarity of the name Jope–Jaffa to that of Cassiepeia (Cassiope), Cepheus' wife, as well as to that of Aethiopia.

2:3 *Sunt qui tradant Assyrios convenas...parte Aegypti potitos*: Here we are given in outline the biblical account, namely, the Mesopotamian origin of the people, a sojourn in a part of Egypt, and a return to the "Hebrew lands". In recording this version, which includes these three stages, Tacitus is rather exceptional among the pagan writers. The Mesopotamian ancestry of the Jewish people is also stated by Nicolaus of Damascus, who, more in accord with the Bible, speaks of τῆς γῆς τῆς ὑπὲρ Βαβυλῶνος Χαλδαίων λεγομένης; see *Ant.*, I, 159 (No. 83). Pompeius Trogus, who also notes some national traditions, attributes Damascene ancestry to the Jewish people (Pompeius Trogus, apud: Iustinus, XXXVI, 2 = No. 137; see commentary *ad loc.*). That Tacitus calls the ancient Jews "Assyrii convenae" and not "Babylonii" merely reflects the broad use of the name Assyria. It is noteworthy that the province of Assyria created by Trajan may have been identical with ancient Babylonia; see A. Maricq, *Syria*, XXXVI (1959), pp. 254 ff.; cf., however, the reservations of L. Dillemann, *Haute Mésopotamie orientale et pays adjacents*, Paris 1962, pp. 287 ff. Also in the period of the later empire, Babylon itself is considered one of the cities of Assyria; cf. Ammianus Marcellinus, XXIII, 6:23.

Hebraeasque terras: Used proleptically. It is the only place where Tacitus calls the Jews by the name "Hebrews". His use of the term is not surprising in a writer of the early second century C.E., since it is also attested by such authors as Statius, Appian, Antonius Diogenes, Pausanias and Charax of Pergamum; see the commentary to Charax (No. 335).

Solymos, carminibus Homeri celebratam gentem...nomen e suo fecisse: Cf. *Ilias*, VI, 184; *Odyssea*, V, 283. For the first use of Solymi, or rather Σολυμῖται, for the inhabitants of Jerusalem, cf. Manetho, apud: Josephus,

Contra Apionem, I, 248 (No. 21). It became widespread among Hellenistic Jewry; cf. *Oracula Sibyllina*, IV, 126; *Ant.*, I, 180; VII, 67; *BJ*, VI, 438. For the interpretation put on the Solymi in a passage of the poet Choirilus of Samos, see No. 557. See also, T. Labhardt, *Quae de Iudaeorum Origine Iudicaverint Veteres*, Augsburg 1881, pp. 28 ff.; Lévy, *op. cit.* (supra, p. 6), pp. 334 ff.; E. J. Bickerman, *Classical Philology*, XLVII (1952), p. 79, n. 32. Bickerman doubts whether the identification of the Jews with the Solymi derives from a Jewish source.

In the time of Tacitus the name Solyma was often used in poetry and prose for Jerusalem; cf. Valerius Flaccus, *Argonautica*, I, 13 (No. 226); Statius, *Silvae*, V, 2 : 138 (No. 237); Martialis, *Epigrammata*, VII, 55 (No. 242); XI, 94 (No. 245); Pausanias, *Graeciae Descriptio*, VIII, 16 : 5 (No. 358); Philostratus, *Vita Apollonii*, VI, 29 (No. 404). For a different, hostile, explanation of the name Hierosolyma, cf. Lysimachus, apud: Josephus, *Contra Apionem*, I, 311 (No. 158); cf. also Choirilus of Samos (No. 557) and the commentary *ad loc.*

3 : 1 *orta per Aegyptum tabe, quae corpora foedaret*: It is in line with Tacitus' well-known avoidance of vulgar and common *voces* that he does not specify the nature of the "tabes", in contrast to Pompeius Trogus, who defines it as "scabies" and "vitiligo" (Pompeius Trogus, apud: Iustinus, XXXVI, 2 : 12 = No. 137), though in a later passage Tacitus refers to scabies (4 : 2). The explanation that a plague was the reason for the expulsion of the Jews from Egypt goes back as far as the beginning of the Hellenistic age. According to Hecataeus, it was a general λοιμικὴ περίστασις in Egypt, which the natives attributed to the sojourn of foreigners in their country (Hecataeus, apud: Diodorus, XL, 3 : 1 = No. 11). Manetho states that it was the king's wish to see the gods, and the fulfilment depended on the expulsion of the lepers and other polluted persons (Manetho, apud: Josephus, *Contra Apionem*, I, 232 f. = No. 21). The ancestors of the Jews were ἀλφοὶ ἢ λέπρας ἔχοντες and therefore expelled, according to Diodorus, XXXIV, 1 : 2 (No. 63); Chaeremon records that Egypt was purged of its contaminated people in order to appease Isis (Chaeremon, apud: Josephus, *Contra Apionem*, I, 289 f. = No. 178), while Lysimachus says that the Jewish people, being afflicted with leprosy, scurvy and other maladies, took refuge in the temples, and that consequently the crops failed throughout Egypt: the country was purged of these people at the command of the god Ammon (Lysimachus, apud: Josephus, *Contra Apionem*, I, 305 f. = No. 158). The version of Tacitus differs from that of Lysimachus, who states at the outset that it was the Jewish people who fell sick and took refuge in the temples, while Tacitus' version regards the emergence of the Jewish people as resulting from the expulsion of the contaminated rabble. However, as the writings of Lysimachus are known only through Josephus, his exact language cannot be determined; possibly his use of the "Jewish people" is proleptical. Moreover, Tacitus speaks only of the "tabes" but Lysimachus dwells also on the resulting ἀκαρπία. See Morr, *op. cit.* (supra, p. 6), p. 277, n. 54.

regem Bocchorim: The expulsion of the Jews is also dated to the reign of this king by Lysimachus, apud: Josephus, *Contra Apionem*, I, 305 (No. 158), and see the commentary *ad loc.*; it seems that Apion too assigned approximately the same date to the Exodus. Incidentally, the only other Egyptian king mentioned by Tacitus is Sesostris (Sesosis) in *Annales*, VI, 28.

adìto Hammonis oraculo: Cf. Lysimachus, apud: Josephus, *Contra Apionem*, I, 306: Βόκχοριν δὲ τὸν τῶν Αἰγυπτίων βασιλέα εἰς Ἄμμωνος πέμψαι.

vastis locis relictum sit: Cf. ibid., 308: συναθροισθέντας εἰς τόπους ἐρήμους ἐκτεθῆναι ἐπ᾽ ἀπωλείᾳ. However, the condensed summary of Tacitus lacks details found in Lysimachus.

Moysen, unum exulum: For the form "Moyses", cf. I. Heinemann, PW, XVI, p. 360. See also E. Nestle, *ZAW*, XXVII (1907), pp. 111 ff.

Adsensere: Cf. Lysimachus, apud: Josephus, *Contra Apionem*, I, 310: συναινεσάντων δὲ τῶν ἄλλων.

3:2 *haud procul exitio totis campis procubuerant*: For a similar description, cf. Curtius Rufus, IV, 7:10 ff.

cum grex asinorum...: This provides the aetiology for what Tacitus has to say later; see below, *Historiae*, V, 4. Cf. Ampelius, *Liber Memorialis*, II, 1; Hermippus, apud: Hyginus, *Astronomica*, II, 20; Servius, *In Aeneidem*, IV, 196; Lactantius Placidus, *In Thebaidem*, III, 476, where not an ass, but a ram is the animal. See also E. Bickermann, *MGWJ*, LXXI (1927), p. 257; Nock, I, p. 142. It is worthwhile here pointing out the view that before the conquest of Canaan the ancient Hebrews were ass-nomads or "donkey caravaners"; see W.F. Albright, *Yahweh and the Gods of Canaan*, London 1968, p. 135.

et continuum sex dierum iter emensi septimo pulsis cultoribus obtinuere terras: That the march of the Jewish people from Egypt to Judaea took a week emerges also from Pompeius Trogus, apud: Iustinus, XXXVI, 2:14 (No. 137); cf. also Apion, apud: Josephus, *Contra Apionem*, II, 21 (No. 165); Plutarchus, *De Iside et Osiride*, 31 (No. 259). Thus it served as an aetiological explanation for the Sabbath. It seems, however, that the recurring statement about the seven days' march can also be connected with the simple fact that the minimum time needed for crossing by land from Egypt to Palestine was a week; cf. Arrianus, *Anabasis*, III, 1:1; Curtius Rufus, IV, 7:2. Normally the same journey took more time; see V. Tscherikower, *Miẓraim*, IV–V (1937), pp. 27 f.

4:1 *novos ritus contrariosque ceteris mortalibus indidit*: Cf. Herodotus, II, 35:2: Αἰγύπτιοι...τὰ πολλὰ πάντα ἔμπαλιν τοῖσι ἄλλοισι ἀνθρώποισι ἐστήσαντο ἤθεά τε καὶ νόμους. However, the reasons given by Herodotus for the difference between the Egyptians and other people are the physical nature of their country and climate. The Jewish "diversitas morum" is stressed also below by Tacitus, *Historiae*, V, 12; Diodorus, XXXIV, 1:2 (No. 63): καὶ νόμιμα παντελῶς ἐξηλλαγμένα καταδεῖξαι. Hecataeus explains the differences between the Jews and other people in regard to their mode of sacrificing and way of life as follows (Hecataeus, apud: Diodorus, XL, 3:4 = No. 11): διὰ γὰρ τὴν ἰδίαν ξενηλασίαν ἀπάνθρωπόν τινα καὶ μισόξενον βίον εἰσηγήσατο. Like pagan writers concerning the Jews from Hecataeus onwards, and in keeping with his assertion that the journey from Egypt to Judaea took a week, Tacitus dates the legislation of Moses subsequent to the conquest of the land, the foundation of Jerusalem and the construction of the Temple.

4:2 *Effigiem animalis...penetrali sacravere*: Since the time of Tertullian Tacitus has been blamed for a grave inconsistency here; cf. Tertullianus, *Apologeticus*, 16:1–4. For Tacitus later states that the Jews, in contrast to Egyptians, "mente sola unumque numen intellegunt", etc. (see below, *Historiae*, V, 5:4), and, in connection with Pompey's intrusion into the Temple of Jerusalem, he adds (below, *ibid.*, 9:1): "inde volgatum nulla intus deum effigie vacuam sedem et inania arcana". Yet Tacitus' consistency can be maintained at least formally when one considers that what he says here about the "effigies animalis" (i.e. of an ass) is imputed to the opinion of "plurimi auctores", so that, notwithstanding the consideration he gives them, he is not absolutely committed. Moreover, we may suppose that the "effigies" here implies only an ἀνάθημα and not an object of worship. Thus, e.g., Spooner, *op. cit.* (supra, p. 6), p. 461; E. Bickermann, *Der Gott der Makkabäer*, Berlin 1937, p. 104, n. 1; (H.)J. Lewy, *Zion*, VIII (1942/3), p. 5, n. 26. An excellent example is afforded by Pausanias, *Graeciae Descriptio*, X, 18:4: ἀνέθεσαν δὲ καὶ 'Αμβρακιῶται χαλκοῦν ὄνον (after they had been saved by an ass from the danger of the Molossians). Other authors who connect an ass with Jewish worship are Mnaseas, apud: Josephus, *Contra Apionem*, II, 114 (No. 28); Diodorus, XXXIV, 1:3 (No. 63); Damocritus (No. 247), and Plutarchus, *De Iside et Osiride*, 31 (No. 259). In general, see the introduction to Mnaseas (No. 28).

caeso ariete: Cf. Lev. xvi:3.

velut in contumeliam Hammonis: Cf. Manetho, apud: Josephus, *Contra Apionem*, I, 249 (No. 21).

Sue abstinent memoria cladis: Cf. Petronius (No. 195); Plutarchus, *Quaestiones Convivales*, IV, 5 (No. 258); Sextus Empiricus, *Hypotyposes*, III, 222 f. (No. 334), where the Jews are coupled with Egyptian priests as having an abhorrence for pork; Macrobius, *Saturnalia*, II, 4:11 (No. 543). Petronius (*loc. cit.*) accounts for the abstention of Jews from pork by their worship of the pig; cf. Plutarch (*loc. cit.*), where the question is raised whether this abstention arises from worship or aversion.

4:3 *crebris adhuc ieiuniis*: For the belief that the Sabbath was a fast-day, cf., e.g., Suetonius, *Divus Augustus*, 76 (No. 303); Strabo, *Historica Hypomnemata*, apud: Josephus, *Ant.*, XIV, 66 (No. 104); *Geographica*, XVI, 2:40, p. 763 (No. 115); Pompeius Trogus, apud: Iustinus, XXXVI, 2:14 (No. 137); see also Sevenster, pp. 130 ff. For the attraction that Jewish fasts had for gentiles, see Tertullianus, *De Ieiuniis*, 16: "Iudaicum certe ieiunium ubique celebratur."

raptarum frugum argumentum panis Iudaicus nullo fermento detinetur: Tacitus is the only pagan writer to refer to this. On the passage, see also J J. Hartman, *Mnemosyne*, NS, XXXII (1904), pp. 148 f. Segal finds it noteworthy that both in the explanation for the eating of unleavened bread, and in the figure 600,000 (see below, Tacitus, *Historiae*, V, 13), Tacitus appears to echo a single passage of the Bible (Exod. xii:37–39); see J. B. Segal, *The Hebrew Passover*, London 1963, p. 39, n. 8.

quia is finem laborum tulerit: Cf. Pompeius Trogus, apud: Iustinus, XXXVI, 2:14 (No. 137); Apion, apud: Josephus, *Contra Apionem*, II, 21 (No. 165).

blandiente inertia septimum quoque annum ignaviae datum: Cf. Seneca, apud: Augustinus, *De Civitate Dei*, VI : 11 (No. 186): "septimam fere partem aetatis suae perdant vacando"; for an answer to similar accusations, see Philo, *Hypothetica*, apud: Eusebius, *Praeparatio Evangelica*, VIII, 7 : 14: ἀρά σοι δοκεῖ ταῦτα ἀργούντων εἶναι καὶ οὐ παντὸς σπουδάσματος μᾶλλον ἀναγκαῖα αὐτοῖς;

Tacitus is the only pagan writer to refer to the Jewish sabbatical year (the *Shemiṭṭa*) apart from some allusion by Suetonius, *Tiberius*, 32:2 (No. 305). However Tacitus gives the false impression that it involves rest from all work, and not merely agricultural labour, an assumption arising from the preponderance of agriculture in Jewish economic life. A similar formulation is found also in *Ant.*, XIII, 234: ἐνίσταται τὸ ἔτος ἐκεῖνο, καθ' ὃ συμβαίνει τοὺς Ἰουδαίους ἀργεῖν· κατὰ δὲ ἑπτὰ ἔτη τοῦτο παρατηροῦσιν, ὡς ἐν ταῖς ἑβδομάσιν ἡμέραις· Cf. *BJ*, I, 60. The gentile mocking at the Jewish Seventh Year is reflected also in *Midrasch Echa Rabbati*, Petiḥta, 17 (ed. Buber, p. 14).

For the Seventh Year in the Second Temple period and after, see B. Zuckermann, *Über Sabbatjahrcyklus und Jobelperiode*, Breslau 1857; C. E. Caspari, *Theologische Studien und Kritiken* (1877), pp. 181 ff.; J. Jeremias, *ZNTW*, XXVII, (1928), pp. 98 ff.; R. North, *Biblica*, XXXIV (1953), pp. 501 ff.; S. Safrai, *Tarbiẓ*, XXXV (1966), pp. 304 ff.; B. Wacholder, *HUCA*, XLIV (1973), pp. 153 ff.

4:4 *seu principia religionis tradentibus Idaeis*: See above, Tacitus, *Historiae*, V, 2.

altissimo orbe et praecipua potentia stella Saturni feratur: For the names of the planets, see F. Cumont, *L'Antiquité classique*, IV (1935), pp. 5 ff. Saturn is identical with Kronos, who in his turn was identified with the Babylonian Ninib as the most powerful planet; cf. Diodorus, II, 30:3; Chrysippus, in: *SVF*, II, F527, p. 169: τῶν δὲ πλανωμένων ὑψηλοτάτην εἶναι μετὰ τὴν ⟨τῶν⟩ ἀπλανῶν τὴν τοῦ Κρόνου; Epigenes, apud: Seneca, *Naturales Quaestiones*, VII, 4; Diodorus of Tarsus, apud: Photius (ed. Bekker), Cod. 223, p. 211b, 1. 29: Ὁ Κρόνος, μείζων (ὥς φασι) τῶν ἄλλων ὑπάρχων πλανήτων, ὅτι τούτων ἀνώτερον διατρέχει κύκλον (= ed. Henry, IV, p. 17). See also A. Bouché-Leclercq, *L'astrologie grecque*, Paris 1899, pp. 94 f.; F. H. Cramer, *Astrology in Roman Law and Politics*, Philadelphia 1954, p. 68.

For the Sabbath as "dies Saturni", see Tibullus, I, 3 : 18 (No. 126); Cassius Dio, XXXVII, 17 : 3 (No. 406). For the relation of the Jewish to the planetary week, see F. H. Colson, *The Week*, Cambridge 1926, pp. 39 ff.

septenos per numeros commeare: For the importance of the number seven in celestial motions, see Aulus Gellius, *Noctes Atticae*, III, 10: "M. Varro in primo librorum, qui inscribuntur hebdomades vel de imaginibus, septenarii numeri, quem Graece ἑβδομάδα appellant, virtutes potestatesque multas variasque dicit. 'Is namque numerus,' inquit, 'septentriones maiores minoresque in caelo facit, item vergilias, quas πλειάδας Graeci vocant, facit etiam stellas, quas alii "erraticas", P. Nigidius "errones" appellat'... Praeterea scribit lunae curriculum confici integris quater septenis diebus..., id est octo et viginti diebus conficeret luna iter suum...".

5:1 *Hi ritus... antiquitate defenduntur*: I.e. abstention from pork, the use of Jewish bread, the observance of the Sabbath and the sabbatical year, all of which are customs rooted in the remote past of the Jews and given an aetiological explanation by Tacitus. That the antiquity of laws and customs entitle them to a place of honour is a fairly common view. The importance to be attached to the antiquity of laws is basic to Josephus' argument in *Contra Apionem*; cf. also *Ant.*, XVI, 44. The same sentiment is echoed in patristic literature; cf., e.g., Arnobius, *Adversus Gentes*, II, 71; Minucius Felix, *Octavius*, 6:3. This also anticipates the contentions of Celsus and Porphyry.

pessimus quisque... tributa et stipes illuc congerebant: For an example of financial aid offered to Jerusalem by proselytes, see, e.g., on the gifts of Fulvia, *Ant.*, XVIII, 82.

unde auctae Iudaeorum res: Cf. also below, Tacitus, *Historiae*, V, 8: "immensae opulentiae templum"; see also the speech of Titus, *BJ*, VI, 335: τὸ δὲ μέγιστον, δασμολογεῖν τε ὑμῖν ἐπὶ τῷ θεῷ καὶ ἀναθήματα συλλέγειν ἐπετρέψαμεν... ἵν' ἡμῖν γένησθε πλουσιώτεροι.

apud ipsos fides obstinata: Cf. Tertullianus, *Apologeticus*, 27:7: "pro fideli obstinatione", though Tacitus does not imply so much the religious obstinacy of the believers as the trust the Jews have in each other; cf. the "fidei obstinatio" of Tacitus, *Historiae*, III, 39.

misericordia in promptu... adversus omnes alios hostile odium: For a similar sentiment, see Iuvenalis, XIV, 103 f. (No. 301). This emphasizes Jewish fellow feelings of compassion and probably derives from knowledge of the organization of charity among the Jews. Regarding people who wanted to imitate Jewish concord and charity, see Josephus, *Contra Apionem*, II, 283: μιμεῖσθαι δὲ πειρῶνται καὶ τὴν πρὸς ἀλλήλους ἡμῶν ὁμόνοιαν καὶ τὴν τῶν ὄντων ἀνάδοσιν. See M. Weinberg, *MGWJ*, XLI (1897), pp. 678 ff.; S. Krauss, *Talmudische Archäologie*, III, Leipzig 1912, pp. 63 ff.; Moore, II, pp. 162 ff.; cf. Iulianus, *Epistula ad Arsacium*, 84a (ed. Bidez & Cumont) (No. 482) and the commentary *ad loc.*

5:2 *Separati epulis, discreti cubilibus*: Jewish separateness is stressed from the time of Hecataeus onwards; cf. Hecataeus, apud: Diodorus, XL, 3:4 (No. 11); Apollonius Molon, apud: *Contra Apionem*, II, 258 (No. 50); Diodorus, XXXIV, 1:2 (No. 63): τὸ μηδενὶ ἄλλῳ ἔθνει τραπέζης κοινωνεῖν μηδ' εὐνοεῖν τὸ παράπαν; Strabo, *Geographica*, XVI, 2:37, p. 761 (No. 115): ἐκ μὲν τῆς δεισιδαιμονίας αἱ τῶν βρωμάτων ἀποσχέσεις, where it is imputed merely to superstition and not to hate; Cassius Dio, XXXVII, 17:2 (No. 406): κεχωρίδαται δὲ ἀπὸ τῶν λοιπῶν ἀνθρώπων ἔς τε τἆλλα τὰ περὶ τὴν δίαιταν πάνθ' ὡς εἰπεῖν. Cf. also the formulation of Paul in I Thess. ii:14–15: Ἰουδαίων... πᾶσιν ἀνθρώποις ἐναντίων. In general, cf. Dan. i:8 ff.; Judith xii:1 f.; Tobit i:10 f.; III Macc. iii:4; Jubilees xxii:16; Josephus, *Vita*, 74 ff.; *BJ*, II, 591 f.

During the first century C.E., the separation of Jews from gentiles in dietary matters became more marked; cf. *TP Shabbat*, i, 3c; H. Graetz, *Geschichte der Juden*, Vol. III, Part 2⁵, Leipzig 1906, pp. 805 ff.; M. Hengel, *Die Zeloten²*, Leiden–Cologne 1976, pp. 204 ff. Cf. also the later rabbinic sources, as, e.g., *Agadat Esther*, iii:14 f. (ed. Buber, p. 37); *Midrasch Aba Gorion*, 3 (ed.

Buber, p. 31); *Tosefta 'Avoda Zara*, 4:6. For the reflection of gentile accusations against Jews in midrashic literature in general, see M. D. Herr, *Benjamin de Vries Memorial Volume*, Jerusalem 1968, pp. 149 ff.; idem, *Scripta Hierosolymitana*, XXIII (1972), pp. 85 ff.; I. Heinemann, *Zion*, IV (1939), pp. 269 ff.

proiectissima ad libidinem gens: This statement is probably connected with the alleged prolific nature of the Jews; cf. below: "augendae tamen multitudini consulitur"; for the Jews as "obscena gens", cf. also Rutilius Namatianus, *De Reditu Suo*, I, 387 (No. 542). However, the notion is mostly based on the common typology of the strong sexual passions credited to barbarians, especially to those of the East; see Tacitus, *Annales*, XI, 16: "vinolentiam ac libidines, grata barbaris, usurpans". Thus Justin states that the Parthians are "in libidinem proiecti" and "uxores dulcedine variae libidinis singuli plures habent" (Iustinus, XLI, 3:1). On the other hand, Tacitus stresses the chastity prevailing among the Germani (Tacitus, *Germania*, 19). See E. Wolff, *Hermes*, LXIX (1934), p. 132. For the motif of Jewish profligacy continued in patristic literature, see Juster, I, p. 47; Simon, p. 251, n. 1.

alienarum concubitu abstinent: Abstention from marriage and cohabitation with gentile women became common practice from the time of Ezra and Nehemiah and is well reflected in the literature of the Second Temple; cf., e.g., Jubilees xxx:14 ff.; Philo, *De Specialibus Legibus*, III, 29; *Ant.*, VIII, 191; *TB 'Avoda Zara*, 36b; *TP Megilla*, iv, 75c; *TP Sanhedrin*, ix, 27b; *Midrasch Tannaim on Deuteronomium*, ed. D. Hoffmann, Berlin 1909, pp. 23, 109; *Midrasch Aba Gorion*, 3 (ed. Buber, p. 31); *Midrasch Panim Acherim*, Version A (ed. Buber, p. 50); *Agadat Esther*, iii:14 (ed. Buber, p. 37); *Das Targum Scheni*, ed. M. David, Berlin 1898, p. 23; *Joseph et Aseneth* (ed. Philonenko), VII, 6 f.

A good example of Jewish sexual ἀμιξία is afforded by *Aboth de Rabbi Nathan*, ed. Schechter (First Version, chap. XVI), p. 63 = English translation by J. Goldin, *Yale Iudaica*, X (1955), p. 84: "When he [scil. R. Aqiva] went to Rome, he was slandered before a certain hegemon. He sent two beautiful women to him. They were bathed and anointed and outfitted like brides...But he sat there in disgust and would not turn to them...The hegemon sent for him and asked: Now why didst thou not do with these women as men generally do with women? Are they not beautiful? Are they not human beings like thyself? Did not he who created thee create them?" In general, see A. Bertholet, *Die Stellung der Israeliten und der Juden zu den Fremden*, Freiburg im Breisgau–Leipzig 1896, pp. 308 ff.; W. Bousset & H. Gressmann, *Die Religion des Judentums im späthellenistischen Zeitalter*, Tübingen 1926, p. 93; Hengel, *op. cit.* (supra, p. 39), pp. 192 ff.; G. Alon, *Tarbiz*, VI (1935), pp. 32 f. In reality there were exceptions, such as those humorously alluded to by poets like Meleager, *Anthologia Graeca*, V, 160 (No. 43); Martialis, VII, 30 (No. 240); idem, XI, 94 (No. 245).

inter se nihil inlicitum: That strange remark is the logical inference from the allegation of Jewish lustfulness and seems also to rest on the affinity between Judaism and Christianity, the latter religion having been accused of extreme licentiousness (so also Reinach, following J. A. Hild, *REJ*, XI (1885), pp. 178 f.).

Circumcidere genitalia instituerunt, ut diversitate noscantur: Tacitus ignores, as does, e.g., Strabo, the Egyptian origins of circumcision; cf. Herodotus, II, 104:1–3 (No. 1); Diodorus, I, 28:3 (No. 55). For circumcision as a "nota Iudaica", cf. Petronius, *Satyricon*, 102:13–14 (No. 194); *Codex Theodosianus*, XVI, 8:22. Cf. *Midrash Bamidbar Rabba*, 10:1: כל מעשיהם של ישראל מבדלים מן אומות העולם "All the deeds of Israel are separate from those of the nations".

Transgressi in morem eorum idem usurpant: The first century C. E. and the beginning of the second saw the heyday of Jewish proselytism; in general, see M. Guttmann, *Das Judentum und seine Umwelt*, Berlin 1927, pp. 66 ff.; B. J. Bamberger, *Proselytism in the Talmudic Period*, Cincinnati 1939; W. G. Braude, *Jewish Proselyting in the First Five Centuries of the Common Era*, Providence 1940, K. G. Kuhn & H. Stegemann, PW, Suppl. IX, pp. 1248 ff.; for the diffusion of Judaism even in senatorial circles, see the commentary to Cassius Dio, LXVII, 14:1–3 (No. 435).

nec quidquam prius imbuuntur quam contemnere deos, exuere patriam... vilia habere: Cf. Philo, *De Specialibus Legibus*, I, 52: ἀπολελειπότες, φησί, πατρίδα καὶ φίλους καὶ συγγενεῖς δι᾽ ἀρετὴν καὶ ὁσιότητα, and ibid., IV, 178: ὅτι τοὺς συγγενεῖς, οὓς μόνους εἰκὸς ἔχειν συναγωνιστάς, ἐχθροὺς ἀσυμβάτους εἰργάσατο ἑαυτῷ μεταναστὰς εἰς ἀλήθειαν καὶ τὴν τοῦ ἑνὸς τιμίου τιμὴν ἀπὸ μυθικῶν πλασμάτων... (the same argument is also found in Philo's *De Virtutibus*, 102). For "contemnere deos", cf. Plinius, *Naturalis Historia*, XIII, 46 (No. 214), characterizing the Jews as "gens contumelia numinum insignis".

5:3 *necare quemquam ex agnatis nefas*: This feature of Jewish life, so sharply contrasting with the usage of the Greeks and Romans, was conspicuous enough to draw the attention of Hecataeus, apud: Diodorus, XL, 3:8 (No. 11); cf. the commentary *ad loc*. See also Iuvenalis, VI, 592 ff. ("abortio partus" had not yet been considered a crime in Roman law), and Tertullianus, *Apologeticus*, 9:6 ff., where pagan infanticide is contrasted with the Christian opposition to the exposure of children and abortion. See also Minucius Felix, *Octavius*, 30:2. Especially instructive is Musonius Rufus (ed. Hense, p. 80): ὃ δέ μοι δοκεῖ δεινότατον, οὐδὲ πενίαν ἔνιοι προφασίζεσθαι ἔχοντες, ἀλλ᾽ εὔποροι χρημάτων ὄντες, τινὲς δὲ καὶ πλούσιοι, τολμῶσιν ὅμως τὰ ἐπιγινόμενα τέκνα μὴ τρέφειν. Only the exposure of defective children is referred to by Seneca, *De Ira*, I, 15:2. See also P. A. Brunt, *Italian Manpower 225 B. C.–A. D. 14*, Oxford 1971, pp. 147 ff. For the Germans' aversion to infanticide, see Tacitus, *Germania*, 19.

animosque proelio aut suppliciis peremptorum aeternos putant: Belief in the immortality of the soul became universal among Jews in both Judaea and the Diaspora during the period of the Second Temple; cf. R. H. Charles, *A Critical History of the Doctrine of a Future Life in Israel, in Judaism, and in Christianity*², London 1913; Moore, II, pp. 279 ff. Tacitus has in view here not the general notion of immortality, but its specific connection with death in battle and martyrdom. For martyrdom as a bridge to immortality, cf., e.g.,

II Macc. vii:9. Josephus sees death on the battlefield as the easiest form of death, but that accompanied by torture as the hardest; see *Contra Apionem*, II, 232; see also W.H.C. Frend, *Martyrdom and Persecution in the Early Church*, Oxford 1965, pp. 31 ff. On immortality reserved for those who fall in battle, cf. a speech of Titus in *BJ*, VI, 46f. It is worthwhile pointing out here a passage in *Midrash Tanhuma*, Ki Tavo, 2, as translated by Lieberman: "The [Gentile] people who witness [the execution of the martyrs] say: They [i.e. the martyrs] are full of decay, crimes are on their hands, and for this they are executed, and die because of their corruption, but they do not know that the lot of the martyrs is in the eternal life" (trans. from the *editio princeps*); see S. Lieberman, *Annuaire de l'institut de philologie et d'histoire orientales et slaves*, VII (1939–1944), p. 433.

hinc generandi amor: Cf. Hieronymus, *In Esaiam*, xlviii:17 (*PL*, XXIV, Col. 462 = ed. Adriaen, *CCSL*, LXXIII A, p. 531): "usque in praesentem diem instar vermiculorum pullulant filios et nepotes".

et moriendi contemptus: Cf., e.g., the fortitude of the Essenes in face of torture (*BJ*, II, 151): τὸν δὲ θάνατον, εἰ μετ᾽ εὐκλείας προσίοι, νομίζοντες ἀθανασίας ἀμείνονα: or that of the Sicarii, who suffered death in Egypt (*BJ*, VII, 417 ff.). See also the celebrated speech of Eleazar ben Yair at Massada with its philosophical tenor (*BJ*, VII, 341 ff.). See W. Morel, *Rhein. Museum*, LXXV (1926), pp. 106 ff.; O. Bauernfeind & O. Michel, *ZNTW*, LVIII (1967), pp. 267 ff.; A. Wolff, "De Flavii Iosephi Belli Iudaici Scriptoris Studiis Rhetoricis", Ph.D. Thesis, Halle 1908, pp. 17 ff.; V. Nikiprowetzky, *Hommages à André Dupont-Sommer*, Paris 1971, pp. 461 ff. A connection between belief in immortality and courage in battle constituted an ethnographical motif; see A. Schröder, "De Ethnographiae Antiquae Locis Quibusdam Communibus Observationes", Ph.D. Thesis, Halle 1921, pp. 10 ff.; cf. also Ammianus Marcellinus, XXIII, 6:44 (from the description of the Parthians): "ut iudicetur inter alios omnes beatus, qui in proelio profuderit animam."

Corpora condere quam cremare e more Aegyptio: Though the custom of burial probably preceded that of cremation at Rome (see K. Latte, *Römische Religionsgeschichte*, Munich 1960, pp. 100 f.), and in the last century of the Republic both burial and cremation were familiar, the common practice at Rome during the early Empire was cremation. A change occurred in the second century C.E., see A.D. Nock, *HTR*, XXV (1932), pp. 321 ff.; see especially, p. 323: "At Pompeii there appears to be only one burial known between the time of Sulla and the eruption"; F. Cumont, *Lux perpetua*, Paris 1949, pp. 387 ff. For the reemergence of inhumation in the second century C.E., see R. Turcan, *REA*, LX (1958), pp. 323 ff.

On Jewish burial customs, see recently, E.M. Myers, *Jewish Ossuaries — Reburial and Rebirth*, Rome 1971; on Jewish tombs of Palestine, see Goodenough, I, pp. 61 ff. Jewish burial customs were in no way similar to Egyptian embalming (for some influence of Egyptian embalming among Jews, see Juster, I, p. 480, n. 3). Tacitus equates the two because they both contrasted with cremation. There seems no justification here for substituting "condire" for "condere", as by, e.g., W. Ridgeway, *Journal of Philology*, XII

(1883), p. 31. On the death of Poppaea Sabina, see also Tacitus, *Annales*, XVI, 6: "corpus non igni abolitum ut Romanis mos, sed regum externorum consuetudine differtum odoribus conditur."

5:4 *summum illud et aeternum neque imitabile neque interiturum*: On the abstract character of Jewish monotheism in that period, see Bousset & Gressmann, *op. cit.* (supra, p. 40), pp. 308 ff. A philosophical statement of the abstract nature of God is given by Josephus, *Contra Apionem*, II, 190 ff.

nulla simulacra urbibus suis, nedum templis sistunt: Cf. Tacitus, *Germania*, 9: "ceterum nec cohibere parietibus deos neque in ullam humani oris speciem adsimulare ex magnitudine caelestium arbitrantur". See also R.T. Scott, *Religion and Philosophy in the Histories of Tacitus*, Rome 1968, p. 82, n. 79. We miss in Tacitus' remarks about the Jews the explanation "ex magnitudine caelestium". On the difference in tone between Tacitus' treatment of the same phenomenon among Jews and Germani, see E. Wolff, *Hermes*, LXIX (1934), p. 135. By "templa" Tacitus can only mean the synagogues; cf. Agatharchides, apud: Josephus, *Contra Apionem*, I, 209 (No. 30a): ἀλλ' ἐν τοῖς ἱεροῖς ἐκτετακότες τὰς χεῖρας.

non regibus haec adulatio, non Caesaribus honor: On the exemption of Jews from participating in the imperial cult, see Juster, I, pp. 339 ff.; A. D. Nock, *Classical Review*, LVII (1943), p. 80 = Nock, II, p. 564.

5:5 *hedera vinciebantur*: For comparison of this description with Jubilees, xvi:30, see A. Büchler, *REJ*, XXXVII (1898), p. 196. In Jubilees wreaths are mentioned in connection with the Feast of the Tabernacles, though not specifically those of ivy.

vitisque aurea in templo reperta: Cf. *Ant.*, XV, 395; *BJ*, V, 210; Florus, I, 40:30 (No. 321); *M. Middot*, iii:8; see also J. Scheftelowitz, *MGWJ*, LXV (1921), pp. 115 f.

Liberum patrem coli ... quidam arbitrati sunt: Cf. also Plutarchus, *Quaestiones Convivales*, IV, 6 (No. 258); Lydus, *De Mensibus*, IV, 53 (ed. Wünsch, p. 109). See also A. Alföldi, *Chiron*, III (1973), pp. 131 ff. The identification of Liber with Dionysus was an old one. For the etymology of Liber, cf. E. Benveniste, *REL*, XIV (1936), p. 52.

Iudaeorum mos absurdus sordidusque: By describing the Jewish "mos" as "sordidus", Tacitus certainly makes much of the contrast between the rites of Liber and the adjective "sordidus"; see I. Heinemann, PW, Suppl. V (1931), p. 20. On "absurdus sordidusque", see also C. Brakman, *Mnemosyne*, NS, LIII (1925), p. 178.

6:1 *Terra finesque ... Arabia terminantur*: I.e. by the Nabataean kingdom (until the times of Trajan) and by the province of Arabia (after its incorporation into the Roman empire). On the limits of the Nabataean kingdom, see Hammond, *op. cit.* (supra, p. 32), pp. 29 ff. Cf., in general, Tacitus' remark in *Annales*, IV, 33: "nam situs gentium ... redintegrant legentium animum."

ab occasu Phoenices et mare: Here Tacitus is remarkably accurate, for the north-western border of the province of Judaea (north of the Carmel) did not extend to the sea; all the Phoenician cities from Dora and Ptolemais northwards were included in the province of Syria.

Corpora hominum salubria et ferentia laborum: Cf. Philo, *Legatio*, 215, where the inhabitants of Judaea are described as τὰ σώματα γενναιότατοι. An evaluation of the health and physique of nations was a *topos* in ethnographical literature; see Trüdinger, *op. cit.* (supra, p. 6), p. 155.

Sallust expresses himself in language similar to that of Tacitus in his description of the people of Africa; cf. Sallustius, *Bellum Iugurthinum*, 17:6: "genus hominum salubri corpore ... patiens laborum". See also, on the Ligurians, Diodorus, V, 39:2; on Spain, Pompeius Trogus, apud: Iustinus, XLIV, 2:1. Concerning the Germani, on the other hand, Tacitus states (*Germania*, 4): "magna corpora et tantum ad impetum valida; laboris atque operum non eadem patientia." See also Capelle, *op. cit.* (supra, p. 6), pp. 351 f.; Ammianus Marcellinus (XXVII, 4:14) on the people of Thrace: "omnes paene agrestes ... salubritate virium ... nos anteire."

si vim ferri adhibeas, pavent venae: Cf. Plinius, *Naturalis Historia*, XII, 115 (No. 213): "ferro laedi vitalia odit, emoritur protinus."

fragmine lapidis aut testa aperiuntur: Cf. *ibid.*: "Inciditur vitro, lapide, osseisve cultellis." On "fragmen", see Kuntz, *op. cit.* (supra, p. 33), pp. 110 f.

umor in usu medentium est: Diodorus expresses himself in the same general way; see Diodorus, II, 48:9 (No. 59) = XIX, 98 (No. 62): τῆς δ' ἐξ αὐτοῦ χρείας εἰς φάρμακα τοῖς ἰατροῖς καθ' ὑπερβολὴν εὐθετούσης. Pliny states only (*Naturalis Historia*, XII, 118 = No. 213): "Corticis etiam ad medicamenta pretium"; Strabo, who is more specific, refers to its use for curing headaches and dimness of sight; see Strabo, *Geographica*, XVI, 2:41, p. 763 (No. 115).

6:2 *Libanum erigit, mirum dictu ... opacum fidumque nivibus*: This description is more suited to the Hermon; see Abel, I, pp. 347 ff. For "fidum nivibus", cf., e.g., Claudianus, *De Raptu Proserpinae*, I, 167: "scit nivibus servare fidem".

Iordanes ... unum atque alterum lacum integer perfluit, tertio retinetur: Cf. Strabo, *Geographica*, XVI, 2:16, p. 755 (No. 112); Plinius, *Naturalis Historia*, V, 71 (No. 204). See also *BJ*, III, 509 ff. The river is called Ἰάρδανος in Pausanias, V, 7:4 (No. 356); cf. the commentary *ad loc.*; cf. also Galenus, *De Simplicium Medicamentorum Temperamentis ac Facultatibus*, IV, 20 (No. 381); Polybius, V, 70:4.

Lacus immenso ambitu, specie maris: Tacitus does not normally give measurements; contrast Diodorus, II, 48:7 (No. 59) = XIX, 98 (No. 62); Strabo, *Geographica*, XVI, 2:42, p. 763 (No. 115), where, however, the Dead Sea is confused with Lake Sirbonis; Plinius, *Naturalis Historia*, V, 72 (No. 204); Josephus, *BJ*, IV, 482. Pompeius Trogus (apud: Iustinus, XXXVI, 3:6 = No. 137) states that the lake "propter magnitudinem aquae et inmobilitatem Mortuum Mare dicitur". Cf. also Pausanias, *loc. cit.* (No. 356); Galenus, *loc. cit.* (No. 381).

periti imperitique nandi perinde attoluntur: Cf. *BJ*, IV, 476 f., and the commentary to Diodorus, XIX, 99 (No. 62).

6:3 *Certo anni tempore bitumen egerit*: In contrast to this, Strabo states in *Geographica*, XVI, 2:42, p. 763 (No. 115): αὕτη δὲ ἀναφυσᾶται κατὰ καιροὺς ἀτάκτους, while Diodorus alludes only in general terms to an annual emission of asphalt from the lake.

Ater suapte natura liquor et sparso aceto concretus innatat: There is no close parallel to this statement by any other writer.

fugit cruorem ... quo feminae per menses exsolvuntur: Cf. Plinius, *Naturalis Historia*, VII, 65 (No. 207); *BJ*, IV, 480 (see also *ibid.*, VII, 181): πληρώσασι δὲ ἀποκόπτειν οὐ ῥᾴδιον ... ἕως ἂν ἐμμηνίῳ γυναικῶν αἵματι καὶ οὔρῳ διαλύσωσιν αὐτήν, οἷς μόνοις εἴκει. Cf. also Posidonius, apud: Strabo, *Geographica*, XVI, 2:43, p. 764 (No. 45).

6:4 *Sic veteres auctores*: Among these Tacitus probably has Pliny in view; against this supposition, see Groag, *op. cit.* (supra, p. 6), p. 784, n. 2. Whether Tacitus alludes also to Josephus is more doubtful, since his knowledge of Josephus' works remains to be proved; see the introduction to Tacitus, supra, p. 3.

sed gnari locorum tradunt ... securibus cuneisque ut trabes aut saxa discindi: Tacitus' source may be oral information, but it is equally possible that he here uses some recent author. Cf. also Fabia, *op. cit.* (supra, p. 6), pp. 254 f.; Weber, p. 147; Capelle, *op. cit.* (supra, p. 6), p. 492, n. 166; Hospers-Jansen, *op. cit.* (supra, p. 6), pp. 148 f. We may also refer to the factual, though different, description of Diodorus, XIX, 99:2 (No. 62): Ὅταν δὲ πλησίον γένωνται τῆς ἀσφάλτου, πελέκεις ἔχοντες ἐπιπηδῶσι, καὶ καθάπερ μαλακῆς πέτρας ἀποκόπτοντες γεμίζουσι τὴν δέσμην. See also Reinhardt, *op. cit.* (supra, p. 6), pp. 65 f.

7:1 *Haud procul inde campi, quos ferunt ... fulminum iactu arsisse*: Cf. Strabo, *Geographica*, XVI, 2:44, p. 764 (No. 115): ὥστε πιστεύειν τοῖς θρυλουμένοις ὑπὸ τῶν ἐγχωρίων, ὡς ἄρα ᾠκοῦντό ποτε τρισκαίδεκα πόλεις ἐνταῦθα ... Strabo ascribes the cause of the destruction to the lake's bursting its shores because of the earthquakes and eruptions of fire and hot water brimming with asphalt, so that the cities were engulfed. On the other hand, an explanation closer to that of Tacitus for the destruction of the neighbouring land is given in *BJ*, IV, 483 f.; cf. Josephus' γειτνιᾷ with Tacitus' "haud procul".

et manere vestigia: Cf. the expression in Tacitus, *Annales*, IV, 43; XV, 42, interpreted by E. Norden, *Die germanische Urgeschichte*, Leipzig–Berlin 1920, p. 273, n. 1.

sive herba tenus aut flore seu solidam in speciem adolevere: Cf. Tacitus, *Dialogus de Oratoribus*, 9, 4: "velut in herba vel flore praecerpta, ad nullam certam et solidam pervenit frugem."

atra et inania velut in cinerem vanescunt: Cf. *BJ*, IV, 484: δρεψαμένων δὲ χερσὶν εἰς καπνὸν διαλύονται καὶ τέφραν.

7:2 *Et Belus amnis Iudaico mari inlabitur*: The transition from the description of the vicinity of the Dead Sea to that of the river Belus is very abrupt. The Belus is to be located far from the Dead Sea in the north-west of Palestine, near Acre–Ptolemais, i.e. outside the province of Judaea. Tacitus made the Belus follow upon the Dead Sea because both constitute "mirabilia". For the Belus, cf. also Plinius, *Naturalis Historia*, V, 75; XXXVI, 190; *BJ*, II, 189 ff.; Stephanus Byzantius, s.v. Ἄκη. The Belus is to be identified with the Naaman; see A. Schlatter, *Zur Topographie und Geschichte Palästinas*, Stuttgart 1893, pp. 352 f.; Abel, I, pp. 465 ff. It is assumed that the Jordan does not flow into the Dead Sea but to another river, which the context implies to be the Belus, in the *Letter of Aristeas*, 116 f. Tacitus' expression "Iudaico mari" is rather loose. It means the part of the Mediterranean adjoining Judaea, and Tacitus ignores the fact that the Belus is outside the boundaries of the province. The explanation suggested by Juster that the Jewish preponderance in the glass industry misled Tacitus does not seem plausible; cf. Juster, II, p. 307, n. 6.

circa cuius os lectae harenae ... in vitrum excocuntur: Cf. Plinius, *Naturalis Historia*, XXXVI, 190 ff.

et egerentibus inexhaustum: The expression is paralleled by Tacitus, *Germania*, 20: "inexhausta pubertas". It goes back to Vergilius, *Aeneis*, X, 174: "insula inexhaustis Chalybum generosa metallis".

8:1 *habent et oppida*: As Tacitus does not restrict his use of the name Judaea to Judaea proper, the "oppida" may include even such places as Tiberias and Sepphoris. In Judaea proper they may include the administrative centres of the ten or eleven toparchies; cf. Plinius, *Naturalis Historia*, V, 70 (No. 204). Among them Jericho was conspicuous as a large and populous town; cf. *BJ*, IV, 432; *TP Ta'anit*, iv, 67d; *TB Ta'anit*, 27a; see A. Büchler, *Die Priester und der Cultus im letzten Jahrzehnt des jerusalemischen Tempels*, Vienna 1895, pp. 161 f. Of Lydda, Josephus states that it was a village not inferior in size to a city (*Ant.*, XX, 130): εἰς κώμην τινὰ παραγενόμενος Λύδδαν πόλεως τὸ μέγεθος οὐκ ἀποδέουσαν. Engedi is designated by him as a πολίχνη (*BJ*, IV, 402), and so is Hebron (*ibid.*, 529). On Jamnia, there is the evidence of Philo that it was ἐν τοῖς μάλιστα πολυάνθρωπος (*Legatio*, 200).

Hierosolyma genti caput: Cf. "hoc [scil. Caesarea] Iudaeae caput" in Tacitus, *Historiae*, II, 78 (No. 278). Tacitus clearly distinguishes between the national capital of the Jews, and the capital of the Roman province. On Jerusalem, cf. *BJ*, III, 54: μερίζεται δ᾽ εἰς ἕνδεκα κληρουχίας, ὧν ἄρχει μὲν βασίλειον τὰ Ἱεροσόλυμα προανίσχουσα τῆς περιοίκου πάσης ὥσπερ ἡ κεφαλὴ σώματος.

Illic immensae opulentiae templum: For the wealth of the Temple of Jerusalem, where the Temple treasury contained enormous quantities of money, raiment and other valuables, cf. *BJ*, VI, 282: συνελόντι δ᾽ εἰπεῖν, πᾶς ὁ Ἰουδαίων σεσώρευτο πλοῦτος.

et primis munimentis urbs, dein regia, templum intimis clausum: Tacitus does not distinguish, as do Josephus and the modern archaeologists who follow him, between the three walls surrounding Jerusalem. He implies that there was one line of fortifications surrounding the whole town and emphasizes the specific fortifications of the royal palace and the Temple. On the Temple, see also below, Tacitus, *Historiae*, V, 12; for the main description of the walls of Jerusalem, see *BJ*, V, 142 ff. The "regia", the palace of Herod, is singled out by Tacitus for its strength due to the three adjoining towers built by that king, namely, Hippicus, Phasael and Mariamme. Josephus goes out of his way to extol their construction (*BJ*, V, 161): μέγεθος δὲ καὶ κάλλος ἦσαν καὶ

Tacitus

ὀχυρότητα τῶν κατὰ τὴν οἰκουμένην διάφοροι. This palace and the three towers constituted the main bulwark of the Upper City of Jerusalem. On the "regia" and the towers, see J. Simons, *Jerusalem in the Old Testament*, Leiden 1952, pp. 265 ff.

Ad fores tantum Iudaeo aditus: Gentiles were allowed entrance only to the outer court, which was surrounded by splendid porticos; cf. *BJ*, V, 190 ff. Entrance to the inner court was debarred to them and tablets were erected warning foreigners not to enter the place; cf. Josephus, *BJ*, V, 194; VI, 125; *Ant.*, XV, 417; *Contra Apionem*, II, 103 f.; Philo, *Legatio*, 212. Such an inscription was found by Clermont-Ganneau in 1871; see *OGIS*, No. 598. Another copy has been published by J. H. Iliffe, *QDAP*, VI (1938), pp. 1 ff. = *SEG*, VIII, No. 169. See now also *CII*, No. 1400, and Gabba, No. XXIV, with Gabba's commentary. The inscription reads as follows: Μηθένα ἀλλογενῆ εἰσπορεύεσθαι ἐντὸς τοῦ περὶ τὸ ἱερὸν τρυφάκτου καὶ περιβόλου. ὃς δ' ἂν ληφθῇ ἑαυτῷ αἴτιος ἔσται διὰ τὸ ἐξακολουθεῖν θάνατον. Cf. also Acts xxi: 27 ff. For interpretations of the inscription, see E. J. Bickerman, *JQR*, XXXVII (1946/7), pp. 387 ff.; A. M. Rabello, *Miscellanea Disegni*, Turin 1969, pp. 199 ff.

limine praeter sacerdotes arcebantur: Cf. *Ant.*, XV, 419: ἐκείνου δ' ἐνδοτέρω τρίτον, ὅπου τοῖς ἱερεῦσιν εἰσελθεῖν ἐξὸν ἦν μόνοις. See also M. *Kelim*, i: 8. On the various precincts of the Herodian Temple of Jerusalem, see F. J. Hollis, *The Archaeology of Herod's Temple*, London 1934, pp. 103 ff.

8:2 *Dum Assyrios penes Medosque et Persas Oriens fuit*: The succession of empires may be traced back to Ctesias. In Latin literature the enumeration first appears in Velleius Paterculus, I, 6:6 (deriving from Aemilius Sura): "Assyrii principes omnium gentium rerum potiti sunt, deinde Medi, postea Persae, deinde Macedones." See also O. Seel, *Die Praefatio des Pompeius Trogus*, Erlangen 1955, pp. 74 f. Cf. Appianus, *Praefatio*, 9; Claudianus, *De Consulatu Stilichonis*, III, 159 ff. See the discussion by J. W. Swain, *Classical Philology*, XXXV (1940), pp. 1 ff.

despectissima pars servientium: Cf. Cicero, *De Provinciis Consularibus*, 5:10 (No. 70): "Iudaeis et Syris, nationibus natis servituti."

rex Antiochus demere superstitionem et mores Graecorum dare adnisus... in melius mutaret: It has been suggested that this passage echoes traces of the anti-Semitic version of Antiochus' policy, a version also found in Diodorus, XXXIV–XXXV, 1:1–5 (No. 63); see E. Bickermann, *Der Gott der Makkabäer*, Berlin 1937, p. 24. This point of view presumably regarded Antiochus as a champion of civilization and classed the Jews among the low barbarians whom the king was trying to civilize by force. Tacitus' designation of the Jewish faith as "superstitio" recurs below, in *Historiae*, V, 8:3: "superstitionem fovebant"; *ibid.*, 13: "gens superstitioni obnoxia"; see also *Annales*, II, 85 (No. 284). Tacitus evaluates Antiochus' religious policy as the enforcement of Hellenization, a view that accords well with the official documents contemporary with the persecution; cf. *Ant.*, XII, 263, where the authenticity of the whole document (*Ant.*, XII, 258 ff.) has been upheld by E. Bikerman, *Revue de l'histoire des religions*, CXV (1937), pp. 188 ff. Cf. also II Macc. xi: 24: ἐπὶ τὰ Ἑλληνικὰ μεταθέσει.

Parthorum bello prohibitus: Some scholars assume that Tacitus confuses the events of the reign of Antiochus Epiphanes with those of Antiochus VII Sidetes because there is no express record of military activities against Parthia during the reign of the former. The latter was deeply involved in a war against the Parthians in which he met his death (129 B.C.E.), thereby leaving the way clear for attaining Jewish independence. Meyer assumes that the Antiochus of Tacitus should be identified with Sidetes; see Ed. Meyer, II, p. 153, n. 2. Otto thinks that Tacitus combined activities pertaining to two Antiochi in the same sentence; see W. Otto, *Zur Geschichte der Zeit des 6. Ptolemäers*, Munich 1934, p. 85, n. 3; Jacoby states (*F. Gr. Hist.*, II, C, p. 208, commentary to Posidonius): "Tacitus V.8 wo Antiochos Epiphanes und Antiochos Grypos flüchtig zusammengeworfen sind" (the substitution of Grypos for Sidetes seems to be a slip on the part of Jacoby). Cf. also the recent work of O. Mørkholm, *Antiochus IV of Syria*, Copenhagen 1966, pp. 176 f.; Mørkholm inclines to accept the interpretation of Otto. Yet, it does not seem necessary to suppose that Tacitus had Antiochus Sidetes in view. Although the Parthians are not specifically mentioned in connection with the last activities of Antiochus Epiphanes, the sources relate much about his eastern expedition during which he met his death; see I Macc. vi: 1 ff.; II Macc. i: 13 ff.; *Ant.*, XII, 354 f.; Appianus, *Syriacus Liber*, 66:352. This may imply a clash with the Parthians; see W. W. Tarn, *The Greeks in Bactria and India*², Cambridge 1951, pp. 183 ff. Even if we minimize the importance of the part played by the Parthians in the policy of Antiochus in his last years (cf. Mørkholm, *op. cit.*, pp. 172 ff.), Tacitus could still interpret any Seleucid expedition to the East in terms of a Parthian war. See also W. Kolbe, *Beiträge zur syrischen und jüdischen Geschichte*, Stuttgart 1926, pp. 156 f.; F. Altheim, *Weltgeschichte Asiens im griechischen Zeitalter*, II, Halle 1948, p. 36.

ea tempestate Arsaces desciverat: Arsaces, the name of the founder of the dynasty, became a dynastic designation for all Parthian kings and was used alongside their personal names; cf. Strabo, *Geographica*, XV, 1:36, p. 702: Ἀρσάκαι γὰρ καλοῦνται πάντες, ἰδίᾳ δὲ ὁ μὲν Ὀρώδης, ὁ δὲ Φραάτης, ὁ δ᾽ ἄλλο τι; Iustinus, XLI, 5:6. See P. Treves, *Il mito di Alessandro e la Roma d'Augusto*, Milan–Naples 1953, pp. 173 f. The Arsaces contemporary with Antiochus Epiphanes was Arsaces VI, better known as Mithridates I, the ruler who made Parthia a great power; cf. Diodorus, XXXIII, 18; see E. Breccia, *Klio*, V (1905), pp. 39 ff.; G. Le Rider, *Suse sous les Séleucides et les Parthes*, Paris 1965, pp. 78 f., pp. 316 ff. He is called simply Arsaces also in I Macc. xiv:2; xv:22. Thus there is no ground for the view — the latest exponent of which is Hospers-Jansen, *op. cit.* (supra, p. 6), p. 155 — that Tacitus committed an anachronism by connecting Arsaces, the founder of the dynasty in the third century B.C.E., with the reign of Antiochus. Some of the older editors were even inclined to athetize the words "ea tempestate Arsaces desciverat"; see, e.g., Heraeus.

8:3 *Macedonibus invalidis*: The use of "Macedones" for the rulers of the Seleucid empire is quite natural and common; cf. Pompeius Trogus, apud: Iustinus, XXXVI, 1:10 (No. 137), and the commentary *ad loc.*

Parthis nondum adultis ... sibi ipsi reges imposuere: Although this remark is prejudiced, and consonant with Tacitus' previous animadversion against the Jews as a "despectissima pars servientium", it still shows the insight of a political historian. Tacitus felt that the political significance of the Hasmonaean state was dependent on political constellations, and these prevented the great powers in whose orbit Palestine was included from effectively interfering in its affairs.

qui mobilitate volgi expulsi ...: Tacitus presents us here with a typology of monarchical rule that partly accorded with the traditional Roman view of *reges* but was mainly influenced by the example of the oriental monarchies. The last one in line was the contemporary Parthian monarchy, but perhaps Tacitus had no less in mind the Hellenistic kingdoms of Seleucid Syria and Ptolemaic Egypt (cf., e.g., Iustinus, XXXVIII, 8:4), or for that matter the kingdom of Pontus under Mithridates Eupator (cf. Memnon, apud: Photius, *Bibliotheca*, cod. 224 = *F. Gr. Hist.*, III, B 434, F 22). Most of the statements by Tacitus here about internal strife during the Hasmonaean monarchy may be illustrated by actual events in the reigns of Aristobulus I and Alexander Jannaeus, as related mainly by Josephus. Aristobulus had imprisoned his mother and most of his brothers and had starved his mother to death (*Ant.*, XIII, 302). He also brought about, though reluctantly, the death of his beloved brother Antigonus (*ibid.*, 303 ff.). However, Josephus' statements are strongly coloured by the hostile version of Nicolaus of Damascus; see the introduction to this author, supra, Vol. I, pp. 229 ff. Of Alexander Jannaeus Josephus states that he murdered one of his brothers (*Ant.*, XIII, 323). The rebellion of his Jewish subjects brought him to the brink of ruin. For an example of the murder of a *coniunx* we have to wait until the reign of Herod. A good parallel to this passage of Tacitus is furnished by Syncellus, whose summary of this period has been supposed to draw, at least partially, on older sources independent of Josephus; cf. Syncellus, I, p. 558 (ed. Dindorf) (see H. Gelzer, *Sextus Julius Africanus*, I, Leipzig 1880, pp. 256 ff.): Ἰανναῖος τοὺς λοιποὺς ἀδελφοὺς καὶ συγγενεῖς ἀνεῖλε, μηδένα τοῦ γένους ὑπολειψάμενος. διὰ τοῦτο καὶ πᾶσαι αἱ πόλεις Ἰουδαίων ἀπέστησαν αὐτοῦ ... καὶ τῶν ἀποστατησάντων Ἰουδαίων τὰς πόλεις ἀφανίζων καὶ τοὺς ὁμογενεῖς ἀφειδῶς ἀποσφάττων μέχρι γυναικῶν καὶ παίδων. The tyranny of Alexander Jannaeus is reflected also in the Dead Sea Scrolls; see the commentary on Nahum, in: J. M. Allegro, *Discoveries in the Judaean Desert of Jordan*, V (Qumran Cave 4), Oxford 1968, p. 38. Here the king is called כפיר החרון ("Lion of Wrath").

honor sacerdotii firmamentum potentiae adsumebatur: Cf. Pompeius Trogus, as summarized in Iustinus, XXXVI, 2:16 (No. 137): "semperque exinde hic mos apud Iudaeos fuit, ut eosdem reges et sacerdotes haberent, quorum iustitia religione permixta incredibile quantum coaluere."

9:1 *templumque iure victoriae ingressus est*: Cf. *Ant.*, XIV, 71 f.: παρηνομήθη δὲ οὐ σμικρὰ περὶ τὸν ναὸν ἄβατόν τε ὄντα ἐν τῷ πρὶν χρόνῳ καὶ ἀόρατον· παρῆλθεν γὰρ εἰς τὸ ἐντὸς ὁ Πομπήιος καὶ τῶν περὶ αὐτὸν οὐκ ὀλίγοι καὶ εἶδον ὅσα μὴ θεμιτὸν ἦν τοῖς ἄλλοις ἀνθρώποις ἢ μόνοις τοῖς ἀρχιερεῦσιν. In *BJ*, I, 152, Josephus stresses that none of the calamities of that time so deeply affected the nation as the fact that the holy place, hitherto unseen, was exposed to alien eyes; cf. also Livius, *Periochae*, CII (No. 131); Florus, I, 40:30 (No. 321); Cassius Dio, XXXVII, 16 (No. 406).

nulla intus deum effigie vacuam sedem: Presumably a similar connection between the statement that no statue was to be found in the Temple and the capture of the Temple by Pompey was suggested by Livy; that connection is implicitly assumed by Cassius Dio.

Muri Hierosolymorum diruti: Cf. *Ant.*, XIV, 82; *BJ*, I, 160. Josephus does not expressly refer to the demolition of the walls in connection with the capture of Jerusalem by Pompey, but this seems to be implied both by the subsequent attempt of Alexander the Hasmonaean to rebuild the walls and by the actual restoration of the city walls in the time of Caesar; see *Ant.*, XIV, 144; Momigliano, p. 198.

rex Parthorum Pacorus Iudaea potitus: Cf. the commentary to Strabo, *Historica Hypomnemata*, apud: *Ant.*, XV, 8–10 (No. 108).

Iudaeos C. Sosius subegit: Cf. also Seneca Rhetor, *Suosoriae*, II, 21 (No. 149).

9:2 *Regnum ... victor Augustus auxit*: Cf. Cassius Dio, LIV, 9:3 (No. 416) and the commentary *ad loc.*

nihil exspectato Caesare Simo quidam regium nomen invaserat: This Simon was one of the three leaders (the other two were Athrongaeus and Judas the Galilaean) who stirred the Jewish nation to revolt after Herod's death (4 B.C.E.). He is the only one mentioned by Tacitus. According to Josephus, Simon was handsome, of fine build and great bodily vigour. The unsettled conditions of Judaea tempted him to assume the crown and he was proclaimed king by his followers. He set on fire the royal palace in Jericho and gave a free hand to his men to plunder the country; cf. *Ant.*, XVII, 273 ff.; *BJ*, II, 57 ff. For the disturbances after Herod's death, cf. Nicolaus of Damascus, *De Vita Sua*, apud: Constantinus Porphyrogenitus, *Excerpta de Insidiis*, p. 2 (No. 97) and the commentary *ad loc.* Tacitus asserts that Simon did not wait for Caesar (i.e. for confirmation by Augustus) before assuming the royal title. But what hope could there be for a slave, without any rights to the throne, to have his accession approved by Augustus? Tacitus' puzzling statement is probably due to his compression of the narrative. An accusation was in fact made by the opponents of Archelaus, Herod's primary heir, that he had not waited for Augustus' ratification of his father's will but had assumed all the prerogatives of royalty; cf. the speech of Antipater, Archelaus' cousin and enemy, before Augustus, in *Ant.*, XVII, 230: Ἀρχελάῳ παιδιὰν τὸν περὶ τῆς ἀρχῆς εἶναι λόγον, ἔργῳ τὴν δύναμιν αὐτῆς πρότερον ἢ Καίσαρα συγχωρῆσαι παραλειφότι ... Cf. *BJ*, II, 26: κατηγόρει φάσκων τοῖς μὲν λόγοις ἀμφισβητεῖν ἄρτι βασιλείας Ἀρχέλαον, τοῖς δ' ἔργοις πάλαι γεγονέναι βασιλέα, κατειρωνεύεσθαι δὲ νῦν τῶν Καίσαρος ἀκοῶν, ὃν δικαστὴν τῆς διαδοχῆς οὐ περιέμεινεν.

Is a Quintilio Varo obtinente Syriam punitus: The major part played by Varus, governor of Syria, in the suppression of the revolt clearly emerges from Josephus' account. Yet the death of Simon is specifically ascribed by the latter to Gratus, one of the late king's officers; cf. *Ant.*, XVII, 275 f.; *BJ*, II, 58 f.

liberi Herodis tripertito rexere: Archelaus received Judaea, Idumaea and

Samaria, Herod Antipas was given Galilaea and the Peraea as his share, and Philip obtained some of the northern and north-eastern parts of his father's kingdom.

Sub Tiberio quies: The description "quies" should be taken only as meaning that there were no open rebellions under Tiberius. For the tension that prevailed in Judaea in the last years of Tiberius, when Pontius Pilatus was *praefectus* (26–36 C. E.), see C. H. Kraeling, *HTR*, XXXV (1942), pp. 263 ff.; E. Stauffer, *La nouvelle Clio*, I–II (1949–1950), pp. 495 ff.; J. Blinzler, *Novum Testamentum*, II (1957–1958), p. 24 ff.

iussi a C. Caesare effigiem eius in templo locare: According to Philo, Gaius ordered a colossal statue named after Zeus to be erected (*Legatio*, 188): ἀνδριάντα ... Διὸς ἐπίκλησιν αὐτοῦ. We learn that this order envisaged a gilded statue of gigantic proportions, to be set up in the Temple (*ibid.*, 203), but Philo does not specify there whose statue was intended. However, in connection with Gaius' proposed treatment of the Jews, Philo mentions that the emperor intended to turn the Temple into a shrine of his own, namely, that of Gaius Zeus Epiphanes Neos (*ibid.*, 346). This passage probably implies that the statue was of the emperor himself, though presumably in the style of a Zeus; cf. also E. M. Smallwood, *Philonis Alexandrini Legatio ad Gaium*, Leiden 1961, pp. 256 f.; P. J. Sijpesteijn, *Journal of Jewish Studies*, XV (1964), p. 91, n. 17. Josephus, like Tacitus, merely relates that a statue of Gaius was to be erected in the Temple; see *Ant.*, XVIII, 261; *BJ*, II, 185.

arma potius sumpsere: In contrast to the Jewish sources (Philo and Josephus), Tacitus stresses, probably with much justification, that armed resistance was offered by the Jews. Yet some allusions to the threat of rebellion may also be traced in Philo; cf., e.g., *Legatio ad Gaium*, 208, 215. The possibility of active resistance was inherent in the logic of the situation and would have played a large part in the considerations of Petronius, the governor of Syria, who had to execute Gaius' plan.

quem motum Caesaris mors diremit: Although Gaius apparently cancelled the order to set up the statue in the Temple on Agrippa's request, there is much to be said for Tacitus' statement. As we learn from Philo, the cancellation of the order to erect the statue did not preclude the establishment of altars, the offering of sacrifices and the erection of images or statues outside Jerusalem; cf. *Legatio ad Gaium*, 334 f. According to the apt remark of Philo, this was no less than στάσεων καὶ ἐμφυλίων πολέμων ἀρχή. It is noteworthy that Josephus, who in *BJ* does not mention the intervention of Agrippa and ignores the cancellation of the order to set up the statue in the Temple, attributes the end of the crisis only to the death of Gaius; cf. *BJ*, II, 199 ff. Cf. also Tacitus, *Annales*, XII, 54 (No. 288).

9:3 *Claudius defunctis regibus aut ad modicum redactis Iudaeam provinciam equitibus Romanis aut libertis permisit*: This statement may give the false impression that Claudius inaugurated the provincial system and that the Jews had previously been ruled by the sons of Herod. What Tacitus refers to here is the restoration of the provincial system in Judaea after the death in 44 C. E. of Agrippa I, who had ruled over the whole country for the last three years of his life; cf. also Tacitus, *Annales*, XII, 23 (No. 287). The only Roman governor of Judaea known to have been a "libertus" is Felix. According to the prevalent view he was promoted to the equestrian order; see H. Smilda, *C. Suetonii Tranquilli Vita Divi Claudii*, Groningen 1896, p. 141; O. Hirschfeld, *Die kaiserlichen Verwaltungsbeamten*[2], Berlin 1905, p. 380; A. Stein, *Der römische Ritterstand*, Munich 1927, p. 114; P. R. C. Weaver, *Historia*, XIV (1965), p. 466. For the view that this assumption is not warranted by the sources, see F. Millar, *Historia*, XIII (1964), p. 182, n. 13.

Antonius Felix: On the basis of this passage, and on the assumption that the *gentilicium* of his brother Pallas was "Antonius" (though he is never so referred to by Tacitus), it has been almost uhiversally agreed that the *gentilicium* of Felix too was "Antonius" and that consequently we should deny the validity of the readings found in the manuscripts of Josephus that give his *gentilicium* as "Claudius"; cf. *Ant.*, XX, 137: πέμπει [scil. Claudius] δὲ καὶ Κλαύδιον Φήλικα Πάλλαντος ἀδελφόν. The epitome alone has Κλαύδιος instead, leaving Felix without a *gentilicium*; the conservative Niese left Κλαύδιον in his text, but most scholars read differently. The evidence of the Suda (s. v. Κλαύδιος) is rightly thought unimportant because it is dependent on Josephus; see Schürer, I, p. 571, n. 18; A. Stein, *PIR*[2], I, pp. 157 f. Since Pallas had been a slave of Antonia (cf. *Ant.*, XVIII, 182, referring to events of 31 C.E.) and presumably freed by her under Tiberius — see S. I. Oost, *AJP*, LXXIX (1958), p. 116 — it has been suggested (e.g. by von Rohden, PW, I, p. 2617; Smilda, *loc. cit.*) that Felix was a freedman of Antonia, and like his brother received the *gentilicium* of her father. However, this view has recently been called into question by the implications of a new inscription published by M. Avi-Yonah, *IEJ*, XVI (1966), pp. 258 ff. Avi-Yonah reads (p. 259, ll. 7 f.): Τιβερίου Κλαυδίο[υ Φήλικος] ἐπιτρόπου Σε[βάστου Ἰουδαίας]. If we accept Avi-Yonah's restoration, this would settle the question in favour of the manuscripts of Josephus, i.e. that the name of the procurator of Judaea was Claudius Felix. However, it seems that Avi-Yonah's restoration was wrong; cf. *L'Année épigraphique*, 1967, No. 525. Cf. also *P. Oxy.*, XLI, No. 2957 (91 C.E.), ll. 11 f., with G. M. Browne's comments. This mentions one Marcus Antonius Pallas. For Felix, cf. also Tacitus, *Annales*, XII, 54 (No. 288); Suetonius, *Divus Claudius*, 28 (No. 308); *Epitome de Caesaribus*, 4:7 (No. 530); Schürer, I, pp. 571 ff.; B. W. Henderson, *The Life and Principate of the Emperor Nero*, London 1903, pp. 363 ff.; Ed. Meyer, III, pp. 46 ff.; J. Dobiáš, *Dějiny římské provincie syrské*, I, Prague 1924, pp. 454 ff.; Schürer, ed. Vermes & Millar, I, pp. 460 ff. Felix succeeded Cumanus in 52 C.E. and continued to govern Judaea until *c.* 60 C.E. The view that Felix ended his term in 55 C.E. (see, e.g., E. Schwartz, *Gesammelte Schriften*, V, Berlin 1963, pp. 151 ff.; Lambertz, PW, XXII, pp. 220 ff.; C. Saumagne, *Mélanges Piganiol*, Paris 1966, pp. 1373 ff.) carries less conviction; see M. Stern, in: S. Safrai & M. Stern (eds), *The Jewish People in the First Century*, I, Assen 1974, pp. 74 ff.

per omnem saevitiam ac libidinem ius regium servili ingenio exercuit: Cf. Tacitus, *Annales*, XII, 54 (No. 288). The image of Felix hardly improves in Josephus' account; cf. *Ant.*, XX, 137 ff.; 160 ff.; *BJ*, II, 252 ff. An attempt to rehabilitate Felix somewhat (see Henderson, *loc. cit.*) has little foundation.

Drusilla Cleopatrae et Antonii nepte in matrimonium accepta: Felix married three queens according to Suetonius, *Divus Claudius*, 28 (No. 308). One was a grand-daughter of Antony. Antony had three children by Cleopatra; cf. Cassius Dio, XLIX, 32; see W. W. Tarn, *JRS*, XXII (1932), pp. 144 f.; H. Volkmann, *Cleopatra*, Munich 1953, p. 143. These were two sons and a daughter. The daughter Cleopatra Selene became the wife of King Juba of Mauretania, and possibly her daughter was one of the three wives of Felix. (So, e.g., Stein, in: *PIR²*, I, p. 158.) In any case, it seems likely that her name was not Drusilla; since that was the name of another of Felix's wives, the daughter of Agrippa I. Tacitus therefore may have confused the two. Drusilla was the youngest of the three daughters of Agrippa I (*Ant.*, XVIII, 132; XIX, 354; *BJ*, II, 220) and was born *c.* 38 C. E. Her first husband was Azizus, the ruler of Emesa, who underwent circumcision in order to marry her; cf. *Ant.*, XX, 139. She was so beautiful that Felix was overcome by passion for her and persuaded her to leave her husband and marry him A son named Agrippa was born to them; cf. *ibid.*, 142 ff.; cf. also Acts xxiv : 24; see H. Willrich, *Das Haus des Herodes*, Heidelberg 1929, pp. 159 f.; A. H. M. Jones, *The Herods of Judaea*, Oxford 1938, p. 219.

10 : 1 *Duravit tamen patientia Iudaeis usque ad Gessium Florum*: The single sentence devoted by Tacitus to Florus implies that the years of his procuratorship were hard times for the Jews. This is more than borne out by the narrative of Josephus, who thinks him the worst procurator of them all; see *Ant.*, XX, 253 ff.: οὕτω δὲ περὶ τὴν ἐξουσίαν ἐγένετο κακὸς καὶ βίαιος, ὥστε διὰ τὴν ὑπερβολὴν τῶν κακῶν Ἀλβῖνον ἐπῄνουν ὡς εὐεργέτην Ἰουδαῖοι ... ἦν γὰρ ἄτεγκτος μὲν πρὸς ἔλεον, παντὸς δὲ κέρδους ἄπληστος ... τὸν γὰρ πρὸς Ῥωμαίους πόλεμον ὁ καταναγκάσας ἡμᾶς ἄρασθαι Φλῶρος ἦν κρεῖττον ἡγουμένους ἀθρόως ἢ κατ' ὀλίγον ἀπολέσθαι; *Ant.*, XVIII, 25: Φλώρου ... ἀπονοήσαντος αὐτοὺς ἀποστῆναι Ῥωμαίων; cf. also *BJ*, II, 277 f. On the procuratorship of Florus, see also Dobiáš, *op. cit.* (supra, p. 52), pp. 460 ff.; H. Dessau, *Geschichte der römischen Kaiserzeit*, Vol. II, Part 2, Berlin 1930, pp. 800, 803 f. Florus was a Greek from Clazomenae, who owed his appointment as procurator of Judaea (64 C. E.) to the friendship of his wife Cleopatra with the Empress Poppaea Sabina; cf. *Ant.*, XX, 252. Florus, like Felix, who was also a Greek, naturally felt sympathy for the Greek cities in the rivalry of their members with the Jewish population of the province. His appointment, like that of Felix, was in line with the rise of the Graeco-Oriental elements in the administration of the Roman eastern provinces; cf. G. Schumann, "Hellenistische und griechische Elemente in der Regierung Neros", Ph.D. Thesis, Leipzig 1930, pp. 34 ff.; A. N. Sherwin-White, *Papers of the British School at Rome*, XV, NS II (1939), p. 25; H. G. Pflaum, *Les procurateurs équestres sous le Haut-Empire romain*, Paris 1950, pp. 172 ff. Tacitus does not attribute the revolt directly to the rebellious nature of the Jews, and his remarks about such governors as Felix and Florus imply that these had a large share of the responsibility for causing the war. *Cestium Gallum Syriae legatum varia proelia ... excepere*: On Cestium Gallus' attempt to crush the revolt and defeat at the hands of the rebels, see Suetonius, *Divus Vespasianus*, 4 : 5 (No. 312). The main source is *BJ*, II, 499 ff.

The course of military operations was as follows: Cestius concentrated a strong force, consisting of the entire Twelfth Legion, *vexillationes* detached from other legions stationed in Syria, and contingents furnished by the allied kings; with this force Cestius left Antiochia for Ptolemais and advanced into the province of Judaea. He captured Chabulon in western Galilaea, sent a detachment to Jaffa and after reducing Galilaea marched on Jerusalem by way of Antipatris and Lydda without meeting with much serious opposition; he pitched camp at Gibeon, north-west of Jerusalem. Agrippa II made an attempt to mediate between Cestius and the insurgents, but failed. Cestius resumed the offensive. He pitched camp in the vicinity of Jerusalem, and even penetrated into the suburbs. He set fire to the New City (Bezetha), encamping opposite the royal palace; see above, the commentary to *Historiae*, V, 8. Yet the Roman attacks on the fortifications of the Temple seem to have failed, despite the contrary assertion of Josephus, and Cestius' retreat was probably dictated more by military needs than Josephus allows. The retreat, however, ended in the complete rout of the Roman army, which was continuously harassed by the pursuing Jews. Above all fatal to Cestius' army was the pass of Bet Ḥoron, the traditional battleground for Jewish victories; see F. M. Abel, *RB*, XXXII (1923), pp. 503 f.; B. Bar-Kochva, *PEQ*, CVIII (1976), pp. 13 ff. Josephus records numerous infantry casualties, apart from 480 losses sustained by the cavalry. The defeat of Cestius Gallus was a turning-point in the history of the revolt. One legion (presumably the Twelfth) lost its *aquila*, cf. Suetonius, *loc. cit.* See also Dessau, *op. cit.* (súpra, p. 53), pp. 805 ff.; Dobiáš, *op. cit.* (supra, p. 52), pp. 470 ff.; F. M. Abel, *Histoire de la Palestine*, I, Paris 1952, pp. 487 ff.

fato aut taedio occidit: Cestius Gallus' fate is not recorded in other sources.

et egregiis ministris: Some of Vespasian's adjutants are known from Josephus' more circumstantial account. Thus, we hear of Placidus and the decurion Aebutius who invested Jotapata (*BJ*, III, 144); Traianus, commander of the Tenth Legion (*ibid.*, 289); Cerialis, commander of the Fifth Legion (*ibid.*, 310); tribunes such as Domitius Sabinus (*ibid.*, 324), Sextus Calvarius (*ibid.*, 325), Paulinus and Gallicanus (*ibid.*, 344), Nicanor (*ibid.*, 346), the decurion Valerianus (*ibid.*, 448), the commander of the archers Antonius Silo (*ibid.*, 486), and Lucius Annius (*ibid.*, IV, 487 ff.).

intra duas aestates cuncta camporum omnesque praeter Hierosolyma urbes victore exercitu tenebat: Vespasian was appointed commander-in-chief of the Judaean campaign on the defeat of Cestius Gallus. He started his military operations in the spring of 67 C. E. On the 21st of the month of Artemisius, Josephus entered Jotapata to defend it against Vespasian (*BJ*, III, 142). The township of Japhia in its vicinity was captured by the Romans on the 25th of Daisius (*ibid.*, 306); Jotapata itself was taken on the new moon of Panemus — cf. *ibid.*, 339; for the slight chronological inconsistency connected with the last date, see B. Niese, *Hermes*, XXVIII (1893), pp. 202 f. — while the storming of Taricheae took place on the 8th of Gorpiaeus (*BJ*, III, 542), and that of Gamala in the Gaulanitis on the 23rd of Hyperberetaeus (*BJ*, IV, 69, 83). The latter date, falling in November of 67 C.E., is the last given by Josephus in connection with Vespasian's Galilaean campaign, excepting the reference to the fall of the Jewish stronghold of Gischala a short time afterwards. See also Nicols, pp. 40 ff.

Military operations were resumed in the following spring (68 C.E.). Gadara (not the famous Hellenistic city, but es-Salt, the capital of the Jewish Peraea) was captured by the Romans on the 4th of Dystrus (*ibid.*, 413), and this was followed by the subjugation of the whole of Peraea, apart from the southern fortress of Machaerus (*ibid.*, 439). In Josephus' narrative these events precede the arrival of the tidings of the revolt of Vindex. Later Josephus records Vespasian's conquest of the various toparchies of Judaea (Thamna, Lydda, Jamnia and Emmaus), and of some villages in central Idumaea (*ibid.*, 447 f.). Vespasian next turned northwards, again via Emmaus, to Samaria and the Jordan. He reached Jericho on the 3rd of Daisius (*ibid.*, 449 f.). Thereafter he began the investment of Jerusalem, establishing garrison camps at Jericho and Adida in the toparchy of Lydda (*ibid.*, 486). Almost the whole country, apart from Jerusalem and some of the strongholds, was thus subdued between the spring of 67 C.E. and the summer of 68 C.E. Josephus' description of these events excellently illustrates Tacitus' remarks; see Schürer, I, pp. 610 ff.; Schürer, ed. Vermes & Millar, I, pp. 497 ff.; Weber, pp. 136 ff.

It has been suggested that the coins of Vitellius on which *Victoria* is associated with a palm tree were meant to celebrate the previous defeats of the Jews and anticipate the final victory; see H. St J. Hart, *JTS*, NS, III (1952), pp. 191 f.

10:2 *Proximus annus ... quantum ad Iudaeos per otium transiit*: Josephus also emphasizes that Vespasian suspended his operations against Jerusalem in view of the civil war; cf. *BJ*, IV, 497: Οὐεσπασιανὸς τοίνυν τὸ μὲν πρῶτον ἀνεβάλλετο τὴν τῶν Ἱεροσολύμων στρατείαν. Cf. also *ibid.*, 502: διὰ τὸν περὶ τῆς πατρίδος φόβον τὴν ἐπὶ τοὺς ἀλλοφύλους ὁρμὴν ἄωρον ἐνόμιζον [scil. Vespasian and Titus].

Pace per Italiam parta et externae curae rediere: Cf. *BJ*, IV, 656 ff. Titus with his army appeared before the walls of Jerusalem in the spring of 70 C.E., shortly before the festival of Passover.

11:1 *Igitur castris, uti diximus, ante moenia Hierosolymorum positis*: Cf. above, *Historiae*, V, 1. The main source for the siege of Jerusalem is *BJ*, V, 47 ff. But the brief summary included in Cassius Dio, LXVI, 4–7 (No. 430), is of great importance. Some details are also supplied by Suetonius, *Divus Titus*, 5:2 (No. 317); *OGIS*, No. 586 = *IGLS*, VII, No. 4011; cf. also H. C. Newton, "The Epigraphical Evidence for the Reigns of Vespasian and Titus", *Cornell Studies in Classical Philology*, XVI (1901), pp. 9 ff. For the relevant talmudic literature, cf. Derenbourg, pp. 255 ff. See also F. de Saulcy, *Les derniers jours de Jérusalem*, Paris 1866; Schürer, I, pp. 624 ff.; B. Wolff-Beckh, *Neue Jahrbücher für das klass. Altertum*, XI (1903), pp. 449 ff.; Weber, pp. 185 ff.; A. Momigliano, *CAH*, X (1934), pp. 861 ff.; F. M. Abel, *RB*, LVI (1949), pp. 238 ff.; Fortina, *op. cit.* (supra, p. 31), pp. 49 ff.; Schürer, ed. Vermes & Millar, I, pp. 484 ff.; R. Furneaux, *The Roman Siege of Jerusalem*, London 1973, pp. 87 ff.; Smallwood, pp. 293 ff.

instructas legiones ostentavit: Tacitus certainly alludes here to what we read in

BJ, V, 349 ff.: ἐνστάσης γὰρ τῆς προθεσμίας, καθ' ἣν ἔδει διαδοῦναι τοῖς στρατιώταις τροφάς, ἐν ἀπόπτῳ τοῖς πολεμίοις ἐκέλευσε τοὺς ἡγεμόνας ἐκτάξαντας τὴν δύναμιν ἀπαριθμεῖν ἑκάστῳ τἀργύριον. οἱ δ᾽, ὥσπερ ἔθος, ἀποκαλύψαντες τὰ ὅπλα θήκαις ἐσκεπασμένα τέως, κατάφρακτοι προῇεσαν καὶ τοὺς ἵππους ἄγοντες ... καὶ τῆς ὄψεως ἐκείνης οὐδὲν οὔτε τοῖς σφετέροις ἐπιτερπέστερον οὔτε τοῖς πολεμίοις παρέστη φοβερώτερον
...See also Fortina, *op. cit.* (supra, p. 31), p. 66, n. 32. Yet Josephus relates this display of the Roman forces not to the first stages of the siege, but to the period following the storming of the first and second walls of Jerusalem by the Romans. Tacitus, on the other hand, suggests the false notion that it occurred at the initial stage.

Missus in eos eques ... ambigue certavit: Also according to Josephus the first skirmish between the besieged and Titus' army involved the Roman cavalry; cf. *BJ*, V, 54 ff. The engagement is described as an attack by the Jews on a reconnoitring troop of horse led by Titus, whose life was endangered by the daring of the Jews.

crebra pro portis proelia serebant: Notable among these were the Jewish assault on the Tenth Legion, which had pitched its camp on the Mount of Olives (*BJ*, V, 75 ff.); a ruse which involved the death of many Romans (*ibid.*, 109 ff.); and the attempts to hinder the erection of the Roman earthworks (*ibid.*, 284 ff.).

11:2 *Romani ad obpugnandum versi; neque enim dignum videbatur famem hostium opperiri*: It seems that at first Titus expected to capture Jerusalem by a swift attack. His army succeeded in storming the third wall (i.e. the first from the point of view of the besiegers) on the 7th of Artemisius, and five days later the second wall was taken (*BJ*, V, 302, 331). Yet he failed at that stage to force an entry into the city, as the defenders demolished the Roman earthworks (*ibid.*, 466 ff.). Hence there was a change in the siege-plan and the decision was taken to raise a wall of encirclement. This implied that the Romans expected to force the Jews to surrender by famine, in spite of Josephus' representation of the project as combining speed with security. See also Weber, pp. 241 ff.

11:3 *Nam duos colles in immensum editos*: Cf. *BJ*, V, 136, where it is stated that Jerusalem was built on two hills separated by a valley. On the western hill lay the upper city, while the lower one was situated on the eastern hill. Josephus emphasizes that the two hills were surrounded by deep ravines, while the precipitous cliffs hindered access; cf. *ibid.*, 141. See G. Dalman, *Jerusalem und sein Gelände*, Gütersloh 1930, pp. 65 ff.; article of M. Avi-Yonah (ed.), *The Herodian Period* (*The World History of the Jewish People*, First Series, VII), Tel Aviv 1975, p. 211.

et turres ... in sexagenos pedes: Josephus dwells at length on the towers; cf. *BJ*, V, 156 ff. The third wall had ninety towers, the second fourteen and the first sixty. Specifically he mentions the Tower of Psephinus at the north-west angle of the third wall, and the three towers connected with Herod's palace and the first wall (Hippicus, Phasael, Mariamme). Measurements of the towers are supplied also by *BJ*, V, 156, 160, 163, 166 f., 170.

mira specie: Josephus too expresses his admiration of the towers, mainly in

BJ, V, 156, 159, 161, 172 ff.; yet "procul intuentibus pares" is peculiar to Tacitus.

turris Antonia, in honorem M. Antonii ab Herode appellata: Cf. *Ant.*, XV, 409: τότε δ' οὖν ὁ τῶν Ἰουδαίων βασιλεὺς Ἡρώδης ... χαριζόμενος Ἀντωνίῳ φίλῳ μὲν αὑτοῦ Ῥωμαίων δὲ ἄρχοντι προσηγόρευσεν Ἀντωνίαν. The fortress Antonia, situated to the north-west of the Temple, was a key position in the whole defence system of Jerusalem. Its storming by the Romans, who razed it to its foundations (*BJ*, VI, 23 ff.), decided the fate of the Temple and of the other parts of the city. Its description is found in *BJ*, V, 238 ff. In view of its designation by Tacitus as "turris" it is worthwhile quoting Josephus on its appearance (*ibid.*, 242): πυργοειδὴς δὲ οὖσα τὸ πᾶν σχῆμα κατὰ γωνίαν τέσσαρσιν ἑτέροις διείληπτο πύργοις. Because of the strategical value of Antonia, the Romans used it before the revolt to quarter the cohort that kept order in Jerusalem; on the topography, see H. Vincent, *RB*, LXI (1954), pp. 87 ff.; St Marie Aline de Sion, *La Forteresse Antonia à Jérusalem et la question du prétoire*, Jerusalem 1955; C. Maurer, *ZDPV*, LXXX (1964), pp. 137 ff.; P. Benoit, *HTR*, LXIV (1971), pp. 135 ff.; Avi-Yonah, *op. cit.* (supra, p. 56), pp. 228 ff.

12:1 *Templum in modum arcis propriique muri, labore et opere ante alios*: Cf. also above, *Historiae*, V, 8: "templum intimis clausum". As a citadel in itself, the Temple played a prominent military role in the times of Judas Maccabaeus and had already withstood a siege of three months in 63 B.C.E. The Temple again showed its strength in the siege of 70 C.E. and the defenders continued resistance even after the fall of the adjacent Antonia, which dominated it.

Fons perennis aquae ... cisternaeque servandis imbribus: Cf. *Letter of Aristeas*, 89: Ὕδατος δὲ ἀνέκλειπτός ἐστι σύστασις, ὡς ἂν καὶ πηγῆς ἔσωθεν πολυρρύτου φυσικῶς ἐπιρρεούσης, ἔτι δὲ θαυμασίων καὶ ἀδιηγήτων ὑποδοχείων ὑπαρχόντων ὑπὸ γῆν. Cf. also, Siracides 1:3; Philo the Elder, apud: Eusebius, *Praeparatio Evangelica*, IX, 37 = *F. Gr. Hist.*, III, C 729, F 2; *Itinerarium Burdigalense*, in: Geyer, p. 21: "Sunt in Hierusalem piscinae magnae duae ad latus templi ..."; Timochares merely says of Jerusalem generally that it abounded in water; cf. Timochares, apud: Eusebius, *Praeparatio Evangelica*, IX, 35:1 (No. 41); a similar observation is made by Strabo, *Geographica*, XVI, 2:36, p. 761 (No. 115); a specific fountain is mentioned in the anonymous Schoinometresis Syriae, apud: Eusebius, *Praeparatio Evangelica*, IX, 36:1 (No. 42). For the water supply in ancient Jerusalem in general, see Dalman, *op. cit.* (supra, p. 56), pp. 266 ff.; Abel, I, pp. 450 f.; M. Hecker, *Sefer Yerushalayim*, I, Jerusalem 1956, pp. 191 ff.; J. Wilkinson, *PEQ*, CVI (1974), pp. 33 ff.

12:2 *Providerant conditores ex diversitate morum crebra bella*: For a similar idea, cf. Anaxandrides, apud: Athenaeus, *Deipnosophistae*, VII, 55, p. 299 F (addressing the Egyptians): οὐκ ἂν δυναίμην συμμαχεῖν ὑμῖν ἐγώ·/ οὔθ' οἱ τρόποι γὰρ ὁμονοοῦσ' οὔθ' οἱ νόμοι/ ἡμῶν, ἀπ' ἀλλήλων δὲ διέχουσιν πολύ./ βοῦν προσκυνεῖς, ἐγὼ δὲ θύω τοῖς θεοῖς·/ τὴν ἔγχελυν μέγιστον ἡγεῖ δαίμονα,/ ἡμεῖς δὲ τῶν ὄψων μέγιστον παρὰ πολύ... See H. C. Baldry, *The Unity of Mankind in Greek Thought*, Cambridge 1965, p. 62.

per avaritiam Claudianorum temporum empto iure muniendi struxere muros: This can refer only to the plan of Agrippa I, who intended to raise a third wall to include the northern suburbs. Tacitus' statement is coloured by his antipathy to the Claudian administration. His wording could imply that the plan was fully executed in the time of Claudius. In any case he makes no mention of the so-called three walls of Jerusalem known from Josephus, and it may even be assumed that Tacitus thought that the city had remained without walls since its capture by Pompey; cf. above, *Historiae*, V, 9; Simons, *op. cit.* (supra, p. 47), p. 475, n. 2. Josephus states that Agrippa started to fortify the walls of the "New City" and that he would have made them too strong to be captured by any human force, but for the intervention of Marsus, the governor of Syria. Instigated by Marsus, Claudius asked Agrippa to desist from the plan, and the latter obeyed; cf. *Ant.*, XIX, 326 f. In the parallel narrative Josephus also records that Agrippa started building a wall that, had it been completed, would have made ineffectual the later Roman siege of Jerusalem; cf. *BJ*, II, 218 f. Yet, contrary to what is stated in *Antiquities*, the reason given here for the interruption of the work is the death of Agrippa. The plan to build the wall is explicitly ascribed to Agrippa I in the general description of Jerusalem found in *BJ*, V, 152 ff. This passage repeats that Jerusalem would have become impregnable had the plan been executed according to the intention of the king, and agrees with the statement in *Antiquities* that the wall was left incomplete by Agrippa through fear of the emperor. It adds that subsequently the Jews, presumably at the time of the revolt, completed the work in a hurry.

The problem of the third wall and its remains has aroused heated archaeological debate. From the time of E. Robinson (1838) it has been customary to identify a line of masonry north of the Old City of Jerusalem with the third wall of the Second Temple, a view apparently corroborated by the excavations of Sukenik and Mayer in 1925–1927; cf. E. L. Sukenik & L. A. Mayer, *The Third Wall of Jerusalem*, Jerusalem 1930, pp. 52 ff. However, dissenting voices have been raised (L. H. Vincent, J. Simons, K. M. Kenyon); see Simons, *op. cit.* (supra, p. 47), pp. 475 ff.; E. W. Hamrick, *BASOR*, 183 (1966), pp. 19 ff. There is nothing in the remains under discussion that reflects in any way the splendour and massiveness that are supposed to have characterized the wall started by Agrippa. The best explanation seems that put forward by W. F. Albright in a postscript to Hamrick's article, *ibid.*, p. 26, n. 21. Albright considers that the so-called "Sukenik's wall" is indeed the third wall mentioned by Josephus, but "that every new discovery has reduced the relative significance of the share of Agrippa in the construction of this wall, which must have been almost entirely the work of the Jews in A. D. 66–70". Wholly mistaken seems to be the argument of Manfrin, who, in an attempt to harmonize the accounts of Josephus and Tacitus, goes to the length of maintaining that there were two stages in the building of the walls, one prior to the death of Agrippa and the second subsequently, but still in the reign of Claudius; see P. Manfrin, *Gli Ebrei sotto la dominazione romana*, III, Rome 1892, pp. 247 ff. In general on the problem, see M. Avi-Yonah, *IEJ*, XVIII (1968), pp. 98 ff.; E. W. Hamrick,

Biblical Archeologist, XL (1977), pp. 18 ff. On the consecration of the third wall, cf. also A. Schwarz, *MGWJ*, LXI (1917), pp. 392 ff.

magna conluvie et ceterarum urbium clade aucti; nam pervicacissimus quisque illuc perfugerat: As often, Tacitus leaves some doubt as to his exact meaning. Does this imply a permanent process that had already started under Claudius, or the events of the Jewish war? The first interpretation is favoured by the connection with the building of the walls in the time of Claudius, the second by the reference to the "clades urbium". Historically both are possible, but the second is more probable. Thus only a minority of the rebel leaders and their followers came from Jerusalem. Menahem, the leader of the Sicarii, hailed from Galilaea, and Niger, who played a conspicuous part in the first stages of the Revolt, from the Peraea; the main heroes of the siege, John and Simon Bar Giora, were from Gischala and Gerasa, respectively. How great was the number of people streaming to Jerusalem as a result of "clades urbium" is demonstrated by the fact that the refugees from Tiberias furnished the defence of Jerusalem with some two thousand fighters; cf. Josephus, *Vita*, 354.

12:3 *Tres duces, totidem exercitus*: The division given here is identical with that of Josephus, *BJ*, V, 248 ff.; however, the Jewish historian depicts the Idumaeans as a separate fighting force, though also under Simon's orders; cf. ibid., 249: Ἰδουμαῖοι δ' αὐτῷ συντελοῦντες.

extrema et latissima moenium Simo ... firmaverat: Simo is given priority here and in the above-mentioned passage in Josephus, as justified by his position as commander of the largest Jewish force (10,000 men of his own and 5,000 Idumaeans) and by the part he played in the defence of Jerusalem. This Simo is undoubtedly Simon Bar Giora. By inadvertence Tacitus, or perhaps his source, attaches the name of Bar Giora to his rival John, but there is no reason to impute the mistake to the manuscript tradition and to transpose Bar Giora, as Salinerus did (cf. apparatus criticus). Against this, cf. also Hospers-Jansen, *op. cit.* (supra, p. 6), p. 158. Presumably of a proselyte family from Gerasa, Simon Bar Giora was preeminently the leader of the revolutionary lower classes and liberated slaves (*BJ*, IV, 508). He was adored by his followers, who were ready to do everything at his behest (*BJ*, V, 309). He was singled out by the Flavian victors to die as commander-in-chief of the Jews at the triumph commemorating their defeat; cf. *BJ*, VII, 154. Concerning him, cf. also Cassius Dio, LXVI, 7 (No. 430); M. Hengel, *Die Zeloten*[2], Leiden–Cologne 1976, pp. 303 f.; M. Stern, *JRS*, LII (1962), pp. 258 f.; idem, *Encyclopaedia Judaica, Year-Book 1973*, Jerusalem, pp. 145 ff.; O. Michel, *NTS*, XIV (1967–1968), pp. 402 ff.

Ioannes: Yohanan ben Levi was the rival of Josephus during the latter's Galilaean activities. At first a moderate, and closely connected with the upper and middle classes, he gradually adopted a more extremist policy. However he never became a prophet of social revolution, nor was he considered by his followers a king and Messiah.

Eleazarus: Of a priestly family (*BJ*, IV, 225), he may be regarded as the leader of the Jerusalem group of Zealots. His fighting force consisted of 2,400 men (*BJ*, V, 250).

magna vis frumenti ambusta: Cf. *BJ*, V, 25: κατακαῆναι δὲ πλὴν ὀλίγου πάντα τὸν σῖτον, ὃς ἂν αὐτοῖς οὐκ ἐπ᾽ ὀλίγα διήρκεσεν ἔτη πολιορκουμένοις; *Aboth de R. Nathan*, Chapter xiii, Second Version, ed. Schechter, p. 31; *Qohelet Rabba*, vii : 11; *TB Giṭṭin*, 56a. See also A. Büchler, in: M. Brann & F. Rosenthal (eds), *Gedenkbuch zur Erinnerung an David Kaufmann*, Breslau 1900, pp. 16 ff.

12 : 4 *Ioannes ... templo potitur*: John exploited the occasion of Passover (cf. Tacitus' "per speciem sacrificandi"), when Eleazar admitted outsiders to the Temple, to capture the place; cf. *BJ*, V, 100 ff. Yet Eleazar was not killed, and he is mentioned later in command of his men (*ibid.*, 250), though presumably in a subordinate position to John.

propinquantibus Romanis bellum externum concordiam pareret: Cf. *ibid.*, 71 (after the appearance of Titus and the encampment of the Tenth Legion on the Mount of Olives): Τῶν δ᾽ ἀνὰ τὸ ἄστυ συρρηγνυμένων ἀδιαλείπτως τότε πρῶτον ἀνέπαυσεν τὴν ἐπ᾽ ἀλλήλοις ἔριν ὁ ἔξωθεν πόλεμος ἐξαίφνης πολὺς ἐπελθὼν ...

13 : 1 *Evenerant prodigia ... gens superstitioni obnoxia, religionibus adversa*: For the "prodigia" witnessed in Jerusalem, cf. *BJ*, VI, 288 ff. On the handling of "prodigia" in Rome, see K. Latte, *Römische Religionsgeschichte*, Munich 1960, p. 204. For "superstitioni obnoxia", cf. Livius, I, 31 : 6.

Regarding the contrast between "religio" and "superstitio", cf., e.g., Cicero, *De Natura Deorum*, II, 71: "Maiores nostri superstitionem a religione separaverunt". Tacitus uses here for the third time in his excursus on the Jews the term "superstitio" to designate Judaism; cf. above, *Historiae*, V, 8. Cf. also Cicero, *Pro Flacco*, 28 : 67 (No. 68). Tacitus uses "superstitio" to designate barbarian religions in general (*Germania*, 39, 43; *Agricola*, 11); in his eyes Christianity is "superstitio" (*Annales*, XV, 44 = No. 294); on "superstitio", see also D. Grodzynski, *REA*, LXXVI (1974), pp. 36 ff.

Visae per caelum concurrere acies ... igne conlucere templum: Cf. *BJ*, VI, 298 f.: πρὸ γὰρ ἡλίου δύσεως ὤφθη μετέωρα περὶ πᾶσαν τὴν χώραν ἅρματα καὶ φάλαγγες ἔνοπλοι διᾴττουσαι τῶν νεφῶν καὶ κυκλούμεναι τὰς πόλεις. See also Tacitus, *Historiae*, I, 86; II Macc. v : 2 ff.; Tibullus, II, 5 : 71 ff.; Plinius, *Naturalis Historia*, II, 148; Cassius Dio, XLVII, 40 : 2; LXV, 8 : 2.

rutilantia arma: For *rutilare*, see Kuntz, *op. cit.* (supra, p. 33), p. 18.

Apertae repente delubri fores: Cf. *BJ*, VI, 293 f.; *TB Yoma*, 39b = *TP Yoma*, vi, 43c. On the motif of the opening of doors in general, see O. Weinreich, *Genethliakon Wilhelm Schmid*, Stuttgart 1929, pp. 200 ff., and especially, pp. 271 ff. (a comparison between Tacitus and Josephus concerning the prodigies bearing upon the destruction of the Temple); see also K. J. McKay, *CQ*, NS, XVII (1967), pp. 184 ff.

audita maior humana vox, excedere deos: Cf. *BJ*, VI, 299: πρῶτον μὲν κινήσεως ἔφασαν ἀντιλαβέσθαι καὶ κτύπου, μετὰ δὲ ταῦτα φωνῆς ἀθρόας «μεταβαίνομεν ἐντεῦθεν». There are many examples of the abandonment of people by their gods as a prelude to complete ruin; cf., e.g., Chares of Mytilene, in: Plutarchus, *Alexander*, 24 = *F. Gr. Hist.*, II, B 125, F7; Vergilius, *Aeneis*, II, 351 f.; Livius, V, 15; Silius Italicus, *Punica*, II, 365. See also, on the departure of Dionysus, Plutarchus, *Antonius*, 75; cf. H. J. Rose,

Annals of Archaeology and Anthropology, XI (1924), pp. 25 ff. See also *Scriptores Historiae Augustae, Commodus Antoninus*, 16:1–2: "Crinita stella apparuit. Vestigia deorum in foro visa sunt exeuntia. Et ante bellum desertorum caelum arsit."

13:2 *Quae pauci in metum trahebant*: Cf. *BJ*, VI, 291, 295: πάλιν τοῦτο τοῖς μὲν ἰδιώταις κάλλιστον ἐδόκει τέρας ...

antiquis sacerdotum litteris contineri ... fore ut valesceret Oriens profectique Iudaea rerum potirentur: Almost identical is Suetonius, *Divus Vespasianus*, 4:5 (No. 312). Cf. also the "regnum Hierosolymorum" of idem, *Nero*, 40:2 (No. 309). Josephus relates in *BJ*, VI, 312: τὸ δ' ἐπᾶραν αὐτοὺς μάλιστα πρὸς τὸν πόλεμον ἦν χρησμὸς ἀμφίβολος ὁμοίως ἐν τοῖς ἱεροῖς εὑρημένος γράμμασιν ὡς κατὰ τὸν καιρὸν ἐκεῖνον ἀπὸ τῆς χώρας αὐτῶν τις ἄρξει τῆς οἰκουμένης. See A. Schalit, in: H. Temporini & W. Haase (eds), *Aufstieg und Niedergang der römischen Welt*, Vol. II, Part 2, Berlin–New York 1975, pp. 208 ff.

Tacitus uses the traditional language of the oracles and prophecies which, from the first half of the second century B.C.E., embodied the aspirations of the peoples of the Orient who were hostile to Roman hegemony; cf. E. Norden, *Neue Jahrbücher für das klassische Altertum*, XXXI (1913), pp. 656 ff. = Norden, pp. 263 ff.; H. Fuchs, *Der geistige Widerstand gegen Rom*, Berlin 1938; F. Altheim, *Gnomon*, XXIII (1951), p. 433; see also Schalit, *op. cit.*, pp. 218 ff. Noteworthy in this connection is the prophecy transmitted by Lactantius, *Divinae Institutiones*, VII, 15:11: "et imperium in Asiam revertetur, ac rursus Oriens dominabitur"; for a discussion of this passage, see H. Windisch, *Die Orakel des Hystaspes*, Amsterdam 1929, pp. 50 ff. The same language could be adapted to other situations as well. As Bickermann puts it: "Ein Aufstand setzt in der Regel die Siegeshoffnung voraus; der Sieg über das Weltreich bedeutet aber die Weltherrschaft"; see E. Bickermann, *Gnomon*, VII (1931), p. 279. Thus, according to Tacitus (*Historiae*, IV, 54), the Druids maintained that the burning of the Capitol signified the transference of world rule ("possessio rerum humanarum") to the Transalpine nations. Cf. also Suetonius, *Galba*, 9: "orituram quandoque ex Hispania principem dominumque rerum"; Athenaeus, *Deipnosophistae*, V, 50, p. 213 B = F. Gr. Hist., II, A 87, F 36 (p. 246), relating to Mithridates VI of Pontus.

Undoubtedly the substance of the prophecy, as formulated by Josephus, Tacitus and Suetonius in connection with the Jewish revolt, was the Messianic expectation of the Jewish nation, which constituted one of the mainsprings of the Jewish War against Rome. Jewish Messianic belief envisaged a King Messiah, the future ruler of the world; cf. P. Volz, *Die Eschatologie der jüdischen Gemeinde im neutestamentlichen Zeitalter*, Tübingen 1934, pp. 173 ff.; W. Bousset & H. Gressmann, *Die Religion des Judentums im späthellenistischen Zeitalter*, Tübingen 1926, pp. 222 ff. It is consonant with this belief that Josephus has τις, the singular, instead of the "profecti Iudaea" of Tacitus and Suetonius. Presumably these Jewish expectations had become a matter of common knowledge by the initial stages of the rebellion, and did not sound strange to a world already familiar with eschatological terminology. Nourished by prophecy, these beliefs were held to the end by the defenders of Jerusalem and the Temple and were not without some influence even on the besieging army; cf. Cassius Dio, LXVI, 5:4 (No. 430).

Reports of the Jewish Messianic expectations probably belonged to the common stock of historical data incorporated in the accounts of the Jewish War and the siege of Jerusalem to be found in the many works dealing with those subjects. However the identity of the first author to give it literary formulation, or whether it is really necessary to assume a single first literary source, is a matter for conjecture only.

Friedländer's opinion that by "antiquis sacerdotum litteris" Tacitus alludes to the Sibylline oracles is not very likely; see M. Friedländer, *REJ*, XXX (1895), pp. 122 ff. Tacitus expresses in Latin terminology the ἐν τοῖς ἱεροῖς γράμμασιν of Josephus, who could only have had in mind the sacred books of the Bible. Even more doubt attaches to the view of J. G. Griffiths, *Rhein. Museum*, CXIII (1970), pp. 363 ff., who sees an allusion to the Dead Sea Scrolls.

Quae ambages: Cf. the χρησμὸς ἀμφίβολος of *BJ*, VI, 312.

Vespasianum ac Titum praedixerat, sed volgus ... sibi ... interpretati: For other passages reflecting the same official Flavian propaganda, cf. *BJ*, VI, 313; Suetonius, *Divus Vespasianus*, 4:5 (No. 312). See also E. M. Sanford, *AJP*, LVIII (1937), pp. 447 f.

13:3 *Multitudinem obsessorum ... sexcenta milia fuisse accepimus*: The number given here seems very exaggerated, although there was a multitude of refugees and fighters from all parts of Jewish Palestine concentrated in Jerusalem in addition to the permanent population. Josephus gives even higher figures. The casualties incurred by the Jews during the siege amounted to 1,100,000, while 97,000 were taken prisoners by the Romans according to *BJ*, VI, 420. The number that emerges from the census described by Josephus on the basis of the Passover sacrifices is still higher: *ibid.*, 422 f.; cf. *BJ*, II, 280; *TB Pesaḥim*, 64b; see H. Graetz, *Geschichte der Juden*, Vol. III, Part 2, Leipzig 1906, pp. 815 ff. This accords with other figures that may be extracted from Josephus. Thus, e.g., Josephus states that Galilaea numbered 204 towns and villages (*Vita*, 235), the least of which had 15,000 inhabitants (*BJ*, III, 43). Hence the total for Galilaea only was at least three million. Philo expresses himself in general terms on the populousness of Judaea, in *Legatio ad Gaium*, 215: τοὺς τὴν Ἰουδαίαν κατοικοῦντας ἀπείρους τε εἶναι τὸ πλῆθος. Cf. also idem, *In Flaccum*, 45 f.

Modern scholars have arrived at differing conclusions concerning the ancient population of the country. Most of these are sheer hypotheses deriving from the authors' preconceptions, as the reliable data are too scanty to build upon. A minimalist view is that the whole Jewish population of Judaea and the Galilee numbered only 300,000; see C. C. McCown, *JBL*, LXVI (1947), pp. 425 ff.; cf. the summary, p. 436. For the view that the population of Palestine numbered some two million and that of Jerusalem itself 100,000, see J. Beloch, *Bevölkerung der griechisch-römischen Welt*, Leipzig 1886, pp. 242 ff.; cf. p. 248. The last figure is accepted also by McCown, *loc. cit.* Baron assumes 2,500,000 people for the whole Palestinian population (2,000,000 Jews and some 500,000 Samaritans, "Greeks" and Nabataeans); see S. W. Baron, *A Social and Religious History of the Jews*, I, New York 1952, p. 168. A maximalist view seems to have been taken by Cumont, who thinks that the figures of Beloch concerning Syria and Palestine (some five to six millions for the first century C.E.) fall far short of the truth; see F. Cumont, *JRS*, XXIV (1934), pp. 187 ff. Concerning the population of Jerusalem, its permanent population is assessed as 55,000 or 95,000 inhabitants by Jeremias, p. 96; for an estimate of the population of Jerusalem and its environs at 220,000, see A. Byatt, *PEQ*, CV (1973), pp. 51 ff.; the latter is held to be too high by Wilkinson, *op. cit.* (supra, p. 57), pp. 46 ff.; for the conclusion that the population of Jerusalem at that time surpassed 80,000, a figure higher than at any other period in the history of ancient Jerusalem, see M. Broshi, *RB*, LXXXII (1975), pp. 5 ff. (cf. the Table, p. 13). It seems that we must reject the exaggerated figures of Josephus, and to a lesser degree those of Tacitus, and make use instead of the few data that have a ring of reality. Such are, above all, those relating to the respective fighting groups that defended Jerusalem during the siege. Thus, according to Josephus, the force commanded by Simon Bar Giora amounted to 10,000 men, to whom were also attached 5,000 Idumaeans; there were 6,000 fighters at the disposal of John, and 2,400 were led by Eleazar; cf. *BJ*, V, 248 ff. We arrive, therefore, at a total of 23,400 fighting men, who were besieged by some 60,000 Roman and allied soldiers.

ac si transferre sedes cogerentur, maior vitae metus quam mortis: There is no record of any Roman plan or proposal to remove the defenders of Jerusalem elsewhere. On the contrary, at one stage of the siege, after the burning of the Temple, the Jewish leaders suggested abandoning Jerusalem for the desert; cf. *BJ*, VI, 351. Is this remark of Tacitus a *topos* to exemplify the obstinacy of the defence? At the siege of Carthage, for instance, when in 149 B.C.E. the Romans ordered the Carthaginians to leave their ancestral city and to settle elsewhere, at a place at least 80 stadia from the coast, the Carthaginians refused to accede to this demand; cf. Appianus, *Libycus Liber*, 81 : 378 ff.; see U. Kahrstedt, *Geschichte der Karthager von 218–146*, Berlin 1913, pp. 643 ff.; G. de Sanctis, *Storia dei Romani*, Vol. IV, Part 3, Florence 1964, pp. 36 f.

13:4 *quando impetus et subita belli locus abnueret*: Cf. above, Tacitus, *Historiae*, V, 11, and the commentary *ad loc.*

dividuntur legionibus munia: For the distribution of the work of circumvallation among the legions, cf. *BJ*, V, 502 ff.

donec cuncta expugnandis urbibus reperta apud veteres aut novis ingeniis ⟨inventa⟩ struerentur: Cf. Tacitus, *Annales*, III, 5 : 1: "cuncta a maioribus reperta aut quae posteri invenerint".

282

apud: Sulpicius Severus, *Chronica*, II, 30:3, 6, 7 — Halm = F181R

(3) Interea Iudaei obsidione clausi, quia nulla neque pacis neque deditionis copia dabatur, ad extremum fame interibant, passimque viae oppleri cadaveribus coepere, victo iam officio humandi ... (6) Fertur Titus adhibito consilio prius deliberasse, an templum tanti
5 operis everteret. Etenim nonnullis videbatur, aedem sacratam ultra omnia mortalia illustrem non oportere deleri, quae servata modestiae Romanae testimonium, diruta perennem crudelitatis notam praeberet. (7) At contra alii et Titus ipse evertendum in primis templum censebant, quo plenius Iudaeorum et Christianorum religio
10 tolleretur: quippe has religiones, licet contrarias sibi, isdem tamen ⟨ab⟩ auctoribus profectas; Christianos ex Iudaeis extitisse: radice sublata stirpem facile perituram.

2 *interiebant* P	6 *oportere*] *deberi* b	7 *perenne* P
8–9 *templum in primis* b	/ 9 *plenius*] *penitius* Bernays	11 ⟨*ab*⟩ de Prato

(3) Meanwhile the Jews, hemmed in by the siege, since no opportunity for peace or surrender had been given, at last perished of hunger, and everywhere the roads began to be filled with corpses, so that the duty of burying them could not be performed ... (6) It is said that Titus summoned his council, and before taking action consulted it whether he should overthrow a sanctuary of such workmanship, since it seemed to many that a sacred building, one more remarkable than any other human work, should not be destroyed. For if preserved it would testify to the moderation of the Romans, while if demolished it would be a perpetual sign of cruelty. (7) On the other hand, others, and Titus himself, expressed their opinion that the Temple should be destroyed without delay, in order that the religion of the Jews and Christians should be more completely exterminated. For those religions, though opposed to one another, derive from the same founders; the Christians stemmed from the Jews and the extirpation of the root would easily cause the offspring to perish.

On this passage, see J. Bernays, *Ueber die Chronik des Sulpicius Severus*, Breslau 1861, pp. 48 ff. = Bernays, II, p. 159 ff.; K. Peter, *Flavius Josephus und der jüdische Krieg*, Programm, Perleberg 1871, pp. 10 ff.; C. Thiaucourt, *REJ*, XIX (1889), pp. 64 ff.; Gutschmid, IV, p. 345; V, pp. 282 f.; P. Fabia, *Les sources de Tacite*, Paris 1893, p. 256; B. Niese, *Historische Zeitschrift*, NS, XL (1896), p. 203; I. M. J. Valeton, *Mnemosyne*, NS, XXVII (1899), pp. 78 ff.;

Schürer, I, p. 631, n. 115; B. Wolff-Beckh, *Neue Jahrbücher für das klassische Altertum*, XI (1903), pp. 467 ff.; H. Graetz, *Geschichte der Juden*, Vol. III⁵, Part 2, Leipzig 1906, p. 540, n. 1; Weynand, PW, VI, p. 2703; E. Norden, *Neue Jahrbücher für das klassische Altertum*, XXXI (1913), p. 653 = Norden, pp. 259 f.; Juster, I, p. 225, n. 3; Weber, pp. 72 f.; H. St J. Thackeray, *Josephus the Man and the Historian*, New York 1929, p. 48; H. Dessau, *Geschichte der römischen Kaiserzeit*, Vol. II, Part 2, Berlin 1930, pp. 825 f.; A. Momigliano, *CAH*, X (1934), p. 862, n. 1; G. Ricciotti, *Flavio Giuseppe — Introduzione*, Turin 1937, pp. 83 ff.; (H.)J. Lewy, *Zion*, VIII (1942/3), pp. 81 ff. = *Studies in Jewish Hellenism*, 1960, pp. 190 ff. (in Hebrew); M. Fortina, *L'imperatore Tito*, Turin 1955, pp. 66 ff.; G. Alon, *Studies in Jewish History*, I, Tel Aviv 1957, pp. 206 ff. (in Hebrew); S. Prete, *Paideia*, VIII (1953), pp. 350 ff.; H. Montefiore, *Historia*, XI (1962), pp. 156 ff.; I. Weiler, *Klio*, L (1968), pp. 139 ff.; H. Lindner, *Die Geschichtsauffassung des Flavius Josephus im Bellum Judaicum*, Leiden 1972, pp. 122 f.; A. Momigliano, *Quinto contributo alla storia degli studi classici e del mondo antico*, Rome 1975, pp. 146 f.; A. Schalit, in: H. Temporini & W. Haase (eds), *Aufstieg und Niedergang der römischen Welt*, Vol. II, Part 2, Berlin–New York 1975, p. 261, n. 108; T. D. Barnes, *Classical Philology*, LXXII (1977), pp. 226 ff.

The chronicle of the Christian writer Sulpicius Severus contains details concerning the siege and capture of Jerusalem by Titus that are not found in the account of Josephus, or the tradition dependent on him. Thus Sulpicius stresses that the Jews were given no opportunity to make peace or surrender, while Josephus insists on emphasizing Titus' clemency and his proposals to arrive at a peaceful settlement.

More important is the other disagreement with Josephus. Both Josephus and Sulpicius report the council of war convoked by Titus to decide the fate of the Temple. According to Josephus, the three respective commanders of the Fifth, Tenth and Fifteenth legions, as well as Tiberius Julius Alexander, who acted as "praefectus exercitus Iudaici" (cf. *OGIS*, No. 586 = *IGLS*, VII, No. 4011), and Fronto Liternius, who commanded the *vexillationes* of the two Alexandrian legions, took part in the deliberations; cf. *BJ*, VI, 237 ff.; see H. G. Pflaum, *Les procurateurs équestres sous le Haut-Empire romain*, Paris 1950, pp. 144 ff. Cf. Saxer, p. 21. Some of the commanders suggested that the Temple should be destroyed, since the Jews would never cease to rebel while it remained the focus for concourse from every quarter: μὴ γὰρ ἄν ποτε Ἰουδαίους παύσασθαι νεωτερίζοντας τοῦ ναοῦ μένοντος, ἐφ' ὃν οἱ πανταχόθεν συλλέγονται. Others expressed the view that the Temple should be saved only if the Jews abandoned it, but that it should be burnt down if they continued to defend it. Yet Titus himself, with whom three of the officers concurred, asserted that in no circumstances would he burn down the Temple: Ῥωμαίων γὰρ ἔσεσθαι τὴν βλάβην, ὥσπερ καὶ κόσμον τῆς ἡγεμονίας αὐτοῦ μένοντος. On the other hand, Sulpicius declares that it was Titus, among others, who urged the destruction of the Temple, and that he did so in order to extirpate the religion of both the Jews and the Christians which, though mutually hostile, sprang from the same source. Thus as the Christians derived from the Jews, the extermination of the root would involve that of the stock. The view that Sulpicius' statement in this passage derives from Tacitus was already expressed by Bernays in 1861. Many scholars agreed with him, e.g., K. Peter, Thiaucourt, A.v. Gutschmid, Fabia, Niese, Wolff-Beckh, Weber, Dessau, Momigliano, Alon, Prete, though not a few objected, e.g., Schürer, Graetz, Weynand, Juster, Fortina, and more recently, with specific arguments, Montefiore; see the bibliography for this passage, above, pp. 64 f.

It seems certain that Sulpicius used a historical source independent of Josephus and his tradition for the description of Jerusalem and the burning of the Temple. As he had certainly used Tacitus elsewhere (*Annales*, XV, 37 = Sulpicius Severus, II, 28:2; *Annales*, XV, 44 = Sulpicius Severus, II, 29:1–3), the hypothesis that Sulpicius here also draws on Tacitus appears very plausible. This conjecture cannot be strictly proven, and some of the stylistic arguments of Bernays have been refuted by Montefiore, but it seems more likely that Tacitus was the direct source used by the Christian chronicler rather than another historian, such as Antonius Julianus whom Montefiore suggests. However, the Christian colouring of Titus' argumentation seems to be an addition. It accords with the statement of Origenes (Rufinus), *Homiliae*, on Josh. ix:10 (*PG*, XII, Col. 879): "Convenerunt enim reges terrae, senatus, populusque et principes Romani, ut expugnarent nomen Jesu et Israel simul." It is also paralleled by the account of a Christian motivation for the anti-Jewish policy of Hadrian given by Sulpicius, II, 31:3 f.; on this passage, see especially Lewy, *op. cit.* (supra, p. 65).

The number of Jews killed during the siege given by Sulpicius is 1,100,000. This agrees with the figure of Josephus (*BJ*, VI, 420), but conflicts with that of Tacitus (*Historiae*, V, 13 = No. 281), who gives 600,000 as the number of Jewish casualties. However, this discrepancy could be explained by assuming that Sulpicius had access to the tradition of Josephus as well as that used by Tacitus.

Another account of the deliberations of the council of Titus before the burning of the Temple, similar to that of Sulpicius but lacking its Christian colouring, is found in Orosius, VII, 9:5 f.: "quod tamen postquam in potestatem redactum ... diu deliberavit utrum tamquam incitamentum hostium incenderet an in testimonium victoriae reservaret."

To decide whether the version of events given by Josephus or the source presumed to be Tacitus is correct, it must be borne in mind that the Jewish historian published his work under the auspices of the Flavian dynasty (75–79 C.E.); cf. H. Vincent, *RB*, NS, VIII (1911), pp. 370 f. Thus he was obliged to draw a sympathetic picture of his benefactors and to try to make them acceptable to his Jewish readers, possibly even at the expense of the truth. In several places in his *Jewish War* Josephus consciously points out that Titus continually displayed clemency towards the Jewish people during both the Galilaean campaign and the siege of Jerusalem; cf. *BJ*, III, 501 (on the capture of Taricheae); IV, 92, 96 (on that of Gischala); V, 334: περὶ πλείστου γὰρ ἐποιεῖτο σῶσαι τὴν μὲν πόλιν αὐτῷ, τὸν δὲ ναὸν τῇ πόλει; V, 450: Τίτῳ μὲν οὖν οἰκτρὸν τὸ πάθος κατεφαίνετο; V, 519: ἐστέναξέ τε καὶ τὰς χεῖρας ἀνατείνας κατεμαρτύρατο τὸν θεόν, ὡς οὐκ εἴη τὸ ἔργον αὐτοῦ; VI, 324: ὁ

δὲ καὶ διὰ τὸ φιλάνθρωπον φύσει τὸ γοῦν ἄστυ περισῶσαι προαιρούμενος;
VI, 383; see also VII, 107 ff. (on Titus' attitude to the Jews of Antioch); VII,
112: ᾤκτειρε τῆς πόλεως τὸν ὄλεθρον. A writer like Tacitus, on the other
hand, was free from such considerations.

However, Josephus evidently felt no need to conceal the truth concerning the
schismatic Jewish temple of Onias at Leontopolis in Egypt and a parallel act
in which Titus was not involved. In this case Josephus himself relates that the
Jewish temple in Egypt was demolished on the express order of Vespasian,
and the reason suggested was the interminable Jewish tendency to revolution
(*BJ*, VII, 421): ὁ δὲ τῶν Ἰουδαίων τὴν ἀκατάπαυστον ὑφορώμενος
νεωτεροποιίαν καὶ δείσας, μὴ πάλιν εἰς ἓν ἀθρόοι συλλεγῶσι καί τινας
αὐτοῖς συνεπισπάσωνται, προσέταξε τῷ Λούπῳ τὸν ἐν τῇ Ὀνίου
καλουμένῃ νεὼν καθελεῖν τῶν Ἰουδαίων. Presumably the same policy
dictated the burning of the Temple of Jerusalem by the Flavians.

In his account of the burning of the Temple of Jerusalem Josephus alludes
also to the σκυθρωπὰ παραγγέλματα of Vespasian (*BJ*, VI, 344). Later he
expressly states that, apart from the three towers, Phasael, Hippicus and
Mariamme, Titus found it convenient to destroy whatever remained of the
sanctuary (*BJ*, VII, 1): κελεύει Καῖσαρ ἤδη τήν τε πόλιν ἅπασαν καὶ τὸν
νεὼν κατασκάπτειν.

For Titus' responsibility for the burning of the Temple, see now especially
Alon, *op. cit.* (supra, p. 65); Weiler, *op. cit.* (supra, p. 65). That Titus was
responsible seems much more likely than what Josephus states in his efforts
to whitewash his friend and protector, or the qualifications adopted by some
modern scholars that Josephus gives an accurate account of Titus' formal
orders, while Sulpicius' source represents Titus' true intentions; cf. Valeton,
op. cit. (supra, p. 64); Montefiore, *op. cit.* (supra, p. 65).

An interesting parallel to the discussion that took place in the council of Titus
prior to the burning of the Temple is to be found in midrashic literature. This
relates that R. Yohanan b. Zakkai, when inside the Roman camp, tried to
prevent the destruction of the Temple in a disputation with the enemy
commanders; cf. *Midrasch Echa Rabbati* (ed. Buber, p. 68): התחילו הדוכוסין
מושלין לפניו משלות, מגדל שקינן בו נחש מה עושים לו, א״ל מביאין חרב והורגין
הנחש, אמר אמגר אדרבא נותצים את המגדל והורגין הנחש. חבית שקינן בה נחש מה
עושין לה, א״ל מביאין חרב והורגין את הנחש ומצילין את החבית, אמר אמגר הורגין
הנחש ושוברין החבית.

283

Annales, II, 42:5 — Koestermann = F174R

Per idem tempus Antiocho Commagenorum, Philopatore Cilicum
regibus defunctis turbabantur nationes, plerisque Romanum, aliis
regium imperium cupientibus; et provinciae Syria atque Iudaea
fessae oneribus deminutionem tributi orabant.

About the same time, the death of the two kings, Antiochus of Commagene and Philopator of Cilicia, disturbed the peace of their countries, where the majority of men desired a Roman governor, and the minority a monarch. The provinces, too, of Syria and Judaea, exhausted by their burdens, were pressing for a diminution of the tribute. (trans. J. Jackson, *LCL*)

et provinciae Syria atque Iudaea: Tacitus clearly treats Syria and Judaea as separate provinces in contrast to *Annales*, XII, 23 (No. 287), where he alludes to Judaea as annexed to Syria; cf. the commentary *ad loc*. That they were separate provinces, however, is in agreement with his own account in *Historiae*, V, 9 (No. 281); Suetonius, *Divus Claudius*, 28 (No. 308); Josephus, *BJ*, II, 117: τῆς δὲ 'Αρχελάου χώρας εἰς ἐπαρχίαν περιγραφείσης (6 C. E.). *fessae oneribus deminutionem tributi orabant*: For the system of taxation in Syria and Judaea under Roman rule, see F. M. Heichelheim, "Roman Syria", in: T. Frank (ed.), *An Economic Survey of Ancient Rome*, IV, Baltimore 1938, pp. 231 ff. For the stress of taxation in the provinces under Tiberius, see G. Alföldy, *Latomus*, XXIV (1965), pp. 834 f. After the death of Herod (4 B.C.E.), Augustus reduced the tribute payable by Samaria by one-fourth as a reward for keeping the peace when the Jewish sectors of the country revolted; cf. *BJ*, II, 96 = *Ant.* XVII, 319. Among the events of 17 C.E., during the consulate of Caelius and Pomponius, Tacitus relates that the provinces demanded a reduction of tribute. At that time Judaea was governed by Valerius Gratus (15–26 C.E.). Josephus does not refer to taxation during the governorship of Gratus, though Graetz has attempted, without much success, to find a talmudic allusion to the event here related by Tacitus; see H. Graetz, *Geschichte der Juden*, Vol. III, Part 2[5], Leipzig 1906, pp. 741 f. However the problem of taxation in Judaea under Roman rule was always acute. The edicts of Julius Caesar evidence that in his time the tribute from Judaea amounted to 12.5 per cent of the annual crop; cf. *Ant.*, XIV, 203. There is no similar information for the period of direct Roman rule in the first century C.E., though demands for reductions in taxes are mentioned; cf. *Ant.*, XVII, 205; *BJ*, II, 4: οἱ μὲν γὰρ ἐβόων ἐπικουφίζειν τὰς εἰσφοράς (after the death of Herod); *Ant.*, XVIII, 90 (Vitellius abolishes τὰ τέλη τῶν ὠνουμένων καρπῶν, in 36 C.E.); *Ant.*, XIX, 299: ἀνῆκε γοῦν αὐτοῖς τὰ ὑπὲρ ἑκάστης οἰκίας. For a remedy proposed by Tiberius to alleviate the burden of the provinces of Achaia and Macedonia in 15 C.E., cf. *Annales*, I, 76:2.

284

Annales, II, 85:4 — Koestermann = F175R

Actum et de sacris Aegyptiis Iudaicisque pellendis, factumque patrum consultum, ut quattuor milia libertini generis ea superstitione

infecta, quis idonea aetas, in insulam Sardiniam veherentur, coercendis illic latrociniis et, si ob gravitatem caeli interissent, vile
5 damnum; ceteri cederent Italia, nisi certam ante diem profanos ritus exuissent.

Another debate dealt with the proscription of the Egyptian and Jewish rites, and a senatorial edict directed that four thousand descendants of enfranchised slaves, tainted with that superstition and suitable in point of age, were to be shipped to Sardinia and there employed in suppressing brigandage: "if they succumbed to the pestilential climate, it was a cheap loss". The rest had orders to leave Italy, unless they had renounced their impious ceremonial by a given date. (trans. J. Jackson, *LCL*)

On this passage, see G. Volkmar, *Jahrbücher für protestantische Theologie* (1885), pp. 136 ff.; F. A. C. Schemann, "Die Quellen des Flavius Josephus in der jüdischen Archäologie", Ph.D. Thesis, Marburg 1887, pp. 55 f.; T. Mommsen, *Historische Zeitschrift*, LXIV (1890), pp. 407 f.; H. Vogelstein & P. Rieger, *Geschichte der Juden in Rom*, I, Berlin 1896, pp. 14 ff.; Schürer, III, pp. 60 f., 679; Juster, II, pp. 170 f.; E. Norden, *Neue Jahrbücher für das klassische Altertum*, XXXI (1913), p. 641, n. 2 = Norden, p. 246, n. 8; Radin, pp. 304 ff.; C. A. Holtzhausser, *An Epigraphic Commentary on Suetonius's Life of Tiberius*, Philadelphia 1918, pp. 31 f.; E. T. Merrill, *Classical Philology*, XIV (1919), pp. 365 ff.; W. A. Heidel, *AJP*, XLI (1920), pp. 38 ff.; Harnack, I, p. 10; G. La Piana, *HTR*, XX (1927), p. 375, n. 6; J. R. Rietra, *C. Suetoni Tranquilli Vita Tiberi*, Amsterdam 1928, pp. 39 ff.; R. S. Rogers, *AJP*, LIII (1932), pp. 252 ff.; A. Momigliano, *Claudius the Emperor and His Achievement*, Oxford 1934, p. 30; p. 95, n. 24; H. Last, *JRS*, XXVII (1937), p. 88; H. Janne, *Latomus*, I (1937), p. 47 ff.; G. May, *Revue historique de droit français et étranger*, Ser. IV, XVII (1938), pp. 19 ff.; M. Brücklmeier, "Beiträge zur rechtlichen Stellung der Juden im römischen Reich", Ph.D. Thesis, Munich 1939, p. 61; A. M. A. Hospers-Jansen, *Tacitus over de Joden*, Groningen 1949, pp. 105 f.; L. Herrmann, *Revue Belge de philologie et d'histoire*, XXVII (1949), p. 644, n. 3; E. M. Smallwood, *Latomus*, XV (1956), pp. 314 ff.; H. R. Moehring, *Novum Testamentum*, III (1959), pp. 293 ff.; Leon, pp. 16 ff.; C. Questa, *Studi sulle fonti degli Annales di Tacito*, Rome 1960, p. 82, n. 11; E. M. Smallwood, *Philonis Alexandrini Legatio ad Gaium*, Leiden 1961, pp. 243 f.; E. Koestermann, *Cornelius Tacitus, Annalen*, commentary, I, Heidelberg 1963, p. 411; W. H. C. Frend, *Martyrdom and Persecution in the Early Church*, Oxford 1965, pp. 141 f.; E. L. Abel, *REJ*, CXXVII (1968), pp. 383 ff.; W. Orth, *Die Provinzialpolitik des Tiberius*, Munich 1970, p. 18; M. Malaise, *Les conditions de pénétration et de diffusion des cultes égyptiens en Italie*, Leiden 1972, pp. 389 ff.; R. F. Newbold, *Athenaeum*, LII (1974), pp. 123 ff.; Sevenster, p. 56; D. Hennig, *L. Aelius Seianus*, Munich 1975, pp. 161 ff.; B. Levick, *Tiberius the Politician*, London 1976, p. 106.

Tacitus mentions the expulsion of the Jews from Rome by Tiberius among the events of 19 C.E. This action of Tiberius is also described by Suetonius, *Tiberius*, 36 (No. 306). Like Tacitus, Suetonius connects it with the measures taken against Egyptian worship, but he does not mention a date. It is clear from the short but perceptive fragment of Cassius Dio, LVII, 18:5a (No. 419), preserved by John of Antioch, that Tiberius expelled most of the Roman Jews and that the main reason for this step was their proselytizing activity. The place of this passage in Cassius Dio tallies with the date given by Tacitus. The most circumstantial evidence of the clash between the Roman authorities and the Jews is found in Josephus, *Ant.*, XVIII, 81 ff. Before relating this event, Josephus dwells at length on an act of sexual outrage committed on a Roman lady with the help of priests of Isis; see O. Weinreich, *Der Trug des Nektanebos*, Leipzig–Berlin 1911, pp. 17 ff. For this they were severely punished by the Roman authorities; the priests were crucified and the statue of the goddess was thrown into the Tiber. Josephus then proceeds to tell of a persecution of the Jews that took place following an act of embezzlement committed by four Jewish impostors, who appropriated some purple cloth and gold given to them by a Roman lady Fulvia, a proselyte to Judaism (καὶ νομίμοις προσεληλυθυῖαν τοῖς Ἰουδαϊκοῖς) to be sent as a donation to the Temple of Jerusalem. It has been suggested that the same lady who was involved with the priests of Isis is implied and that her name was Fulvia Paulina; see Rogers, *op. cit.* (supra, p. 69). (An attempt has been made to connect the story with the institution of Temple prostitution; see Heidel's speculations, *loc. cit.*, endorsed by Rogers, *op. cit.*, p. 252. But such practices were so remote from Jewish life in the period of the Second Temple that they hardly require refutation.) When this embezzlement was reported to Tiberius by the husband of the lady, the emperor, according to Josephus, ordered all the Jews to leave Rome, while the consuls enrolled from among them four thousand men for fighting in Sardinia. Josephus dates the whole story towards the end of the procuratorship of Pontius Pilate (26–36 C.E.), but the date given by Tacitus is supported by Cassius Dio; cf. already Volkmar, *op. cit.* (supra, p. 69), p. 141. Volkmar tries to solve the contradiction by interpreting καὶ ὑπὸ τοὺς αὐτοὺς χρόνους of *Ant.*, XVIII, 65, as referring to the time of Tiberius in general. The chronological sequence of events given by Josephus elsewhere in *Antiquities*, XVIII, is also unsatisfactory. For example, the Jewish historian mentions first the founding of the city of Tiberias, i.e. 17–22 C.E. or 23 C.E.; on the date, see H.W. Hoehner, *Herod Antipas*, Cambridge 1972, pp. 93 ff.; Y. Meshorer, *Jewish Coins of the Second Temple*, Tel Aviv 1967, p. 74; T. Rajak, *CQ*, NS, XXIII (1973), p. 349, n. 7. He then mentions the death of the Parthian king Phraates (IV), who died many years earlier (in 2 B.C.E.), connecting both events by the phrase κατὰ τοῦτον τὸν χρόνον; cf. *Ant.*, XVIII, 39; see G. Hölscher, *Die Quellen des Josephus*, Leipzig 1904, p. 62.

It seems also that Seneca had the events of 19 C.E. in mind in his *Epistulae Morales*, CVIII, 22 (No. 189). Philo does not expressly record the expulsion of the Jews in 19 C.E. but mentions in general terms that there were disturbances in Italy, when Sejanus was planning his attack; cf. *Legatio ad*

Gaium, 159 ff. However, Philo adds that after the death of that minister (31 C.E.) the emperor realized that the charges brought against the Jews of Rome were only slanders fabricated by Sejanus. He therefore issued instructions to the governors throughout the empire to protect the Jews and thus reassure them: ὡς οὐκ εἰς πάντας προβάσης τῆς ἐπεξελεύσεως, ἀλλ' ἐπὶ μόνους τοὺς αἰτίους. Sejanus, who had already been *praefectus praetorio* in 13–14 C.E., could have had a hand in framing policy towards the Jews of Rome in 19 C.E. On the other hand, as Philo states that Tiberius' reference to guilty Jews (*ibid.*, 161: ἐπὶ μόνους τοὺς αἰτίους) was made in 31 C.E., and that slanders were fabricated by Sejanus against Roman Jews at that time, it seems that some new anti-Jewish attack planned by Sejanus is meant. This was different in character and later in time from that of 19 C.E., and involved the provinces as well; see Merrill, *op. cit.* (supra, p. 69), p. 372; Smallwood, *Latomus, op. cit.* (supra, p. 69), pp. 325 ff. The anti-Jewish policy of Sejanus may be reflected in the actions of Pontius Pilatus; see E. Stauffer, *La Nouvelle Clio*, I–II (1949–1950), pp. 495 ff.; E. Bammel, *Journal of Jewish Studies*, II (1950/51), pp. 108 ff.; idem, *Theologische Literaturzeitung*, LXXVII (1952), p. 207; Smallwood, *Latomus*, pp. 327 f.; H. W. Bird, *Latomus*, XXIX (1970), pp. 1046 ff. One should be sceptical of the suggestion that Josephus' narrative implies a different set of events from those related by Tacitus and Suetonius; cf. Malaise, *op. cit.* (supra, p. 69), pp. 391 f. Malaise prefers to connect the account of Josephus with what Philo has to say about Sejanus. On the other hand, for arguments against any supposed connection between Pilate and Sejanus, and that Sejanus did not play any part in the events of 19 C.E., see Hennig, *op. cit.* (supra, p. 69), pp. 160 ff. Cf. also Levick, *op. cit.* (supra, p. 69), pp. 136 f.

The *senatus consultum* of 19 C.E. was the first enactment of the Roman authorities, so far as is known, to check the spread of Judaism among the population of the capital, excepting the measure taken in 139 B.C.E.; cf. the statement of Valerius Maximus (No. 147). Josephus states that its immediate cause was an act of embezzlement connected with a Roman lady proselyte. Cassius Dio suggests a connection with Jewish proselytizing activity. Tacitus and Suetonius give no reason for the *senatus consultum*, but the latter mentions that proselytes as well as born Jews were affected by the terms of the *senatus consultum* ("reliquos gentis eiusdem vel similia sectantes urbe summovit"). Possibly Tacitus, too, alluding to the people envisaged by the order, implied that proselytes were also among them ("quattuor milia ... ea superstitione infecta"). See also Rietra, *op. cit.* (supra, p. 69), p. 42; Smallwood, *Latomus, op. cit.* (supra, p. 69), pp. 319 ff.; Newbold, *op. cit.* (supra. p. 69), pp. 124 ff.; M. Aberbach, *The Roman-Jewish War (66–70 A.D.)*, London 1966, p. 43.

On the whole the *senatus consultum* of 19 C.E. is important evidence for the wide diffusion of Judaism among the various strata of the Roman population at the beginning of the first century C.E., ranging from freedmen (as testified by Tacitus) to the upper classes (the case of Fulvia). Josephus emphasizes that the order to leave Rome included all the Jews in the capital; cf. *Ant.*, XVIII, 83: Κελεύει πᾶν τὸ Ἰουδαϊκὸν τῆς Ῥώμης ἀπελθεῖν. There is no record of when the edict of expulsion was revoked, but it seems that at the end of Tiberius' reign many Jews lived at Rome and that at the beginning of the rule of Claudius (41 C.E.) the Jews in Rome were again numerous; cf. Cassius Dio, LX, 6:6 (No. 422): τούς τε Ἰουδαίους πλεονάσαντας αὖθις ...

de sacris Aegyptiis Iudaicisque pellendis: Tiberius' action against foreign cults was in line with the general religious policy of the Roman government after Actium. Although the last step taken against the cult of Isis known before 19 C.E. dates to 21 B.C.E., the senate consistently tried to check the diffusion of oriental cults, especially that of Isis; see F. Cumont, *Les religions orientales dans le paganisme romain*[4], Paris 1929, p. 77; K. Latte, *Römische Religionsgeschichte*, Munich 1960, p. 283; Malaise, *op. cit.*, pp. 386 f.

factumque patrum consultum: Tacitus is the only source to mention the *senatus consultum*. Josephus and Suetonius attribute the initiative to Tiberius, who is not referred to by Tacitus. Josephus also relates the part played by the consuls in sending the Jewish recruits to Sardinia.

quattuor milia libertini generis ea superstitione infecta: By his use of the singular "ea superstitione" Tacitus must mean the Jewish religion only, and not the Egyptian faith as well. That four thousand Jews were sent to Sardinia is borne out by *Ant.*, XVIII, 84. Suetonius, *Tiberius*, 36 (No. 306), states: "Iudaeorum iuventutem per speciem sacramenti in provincias gravioris caeli distribuit". Enrolment into the army was the only way to remove Roman citizens from Rome, and the other Jews expelled were not citizens; see Hennig, *op. cit.* (supra, p. 69), p. 163. Neither Josephus nor Suetonius mentions the sending of devotees of Isis to Sardinia. The phrase "ea superstitione" has been explained as a compression by Tacitus, who was so preoccupied with the Jews that "although he begins with both religions, he reduces them abruptly to one, the votaries of which were deported"; see Syme, II, p. 468, n. 3; cf. the commentary to Suetonius, *loc. cit.* The number four thousand is one of the two figures extant concerning the Jews of Rome in the Julio-Claudian period. The other relates to the time of Augustus (4 B.C.E.), when, according to Josephus, over eight thousand Roman Jews supported the remonstrance of the opponents of Archelaus against this prince; cf. *Ant.*, XVII, 300 = *BJ*, II, 80.

libertini generis: Philo asserts that most of the Roman Jews were enfranchized slaves; cf. *Legatio ad Gaium*, 155. Tacitus probably has in mind here not only actual freedmen but their descendants as well; see Merrill, *op. cit.* (supra, p. 69), pp. 366 f., 371; for a different opinion, see Radin, pp. 307 f. In the strict legal terminology of the imperial period these, however, were not considered "libertini"; see A.M. Duff, *Freedmen in the Early Roman Empire*, Oxford 1928, p. 50. For the expression "libertinum genus" by Tacitus, see *Annales*, IV, 62: "Atilius quidam libertini generis".

coercendis illic latrociniis: For the situation in Sardinia, see P. Meloni, *L'amministrazione della Sardegna da Augusto all'invasione vandalica*, Rome 1958, pp. 16 f. See also E. Pais, *Storia della Sardegna e della Corsica durante il dominio romano*, I, Rome 1923, pp. 282 f.

ob gravitatem caeli: Cf. Suetonius, *loc. cit.*: "in provincias gravioris caeli distribuit". Suetonius does not expressly mention Sardinia, which is designated by Josephus, in addition to Tacitus, as the place of the deportation of the Jews in *Ant.*, XVIII, 84. For the "gravitas caeli" of Sardinia, cf. Livius, XXIII, 34:11; Strabo, *Geographica*, V, 2:7, p. 225: νοσηρὰ γὰρ ἡ νῆσος τοῦ θέρους. See also Mela, II, 7:123; Martialis, IV, 60:6.

vile damnum: This sentiment is aptly compared with that expressed on the fate of the gladiators in Tacitus, *Annales*, I, 76:3; see Furneaux, in his commentary *ad loc.*

cederent Italia: Tacitus alone mentions an expulsion from the whole of Italy. Suetonius and Josephus refer only to an expulsion from Rome, perhaps supported by the Scholia to Juvenal (No. 538), if they refer to the events of 19 C.E. and not to 41 C.E. Nevertheless, although Josephus and Suetonius must be correct concerning the general scope and purpose of the *senatus consultum*, it may have included something that had a bearing on Italy as a whole.

nisi certam ante diem profanos ritus exuissent: Cf. Suetonius, *loc. cit.*: "expulit et mathematicos, sed deprecantibus ac se artem desituros promittentibus veniam dedit". Tacitus may allude here to proselytes who were left with a choice of giving up Judaism or leaving Italy.

285

Annales, VI, 40:2 — Koestermann

Ne Tigranes quidem, Armenia quondam potitus ac tunc reus, nomine regio supplicia civium effugit.

Not even Tigranes, once monarch of Armenia and now a defendant, was preserved by his royal title from the doom of Roman citizens.

(trans. J. Jackson, *LCL*)

Tigranes quidem: Tigranes, king of Armenia, was convicted under the charge of *maiestas*. On him, see Geyer, PW, Ser. 2, VI, p. 980; A. H. M. Jones, *The Herods of Judaea*, Oxford 1938, p. 260; M. Pani, *Roma e i re d'Oriente da Augusto a Tiberio*, Bari 1972, pp. 58 ff. He was the second son of Alexander, the son of Herod, by Glaphyra the Cappadocian; cf. *Ant.*, XVIII, 139; *BJ*, II, 222: ἡ δὲ Ἀλεξάνδρου γενεὰ τῆς μεγάλης Ἀρμενίας ἐβασίλευσεν. Raised by Augustus to the throne of Greater Armenia, he was soon expelled and he died childless.

286

Annales, XII, 13:1; 14:1 — Koestermann

(13:1) Exim nivibus et montibus fessi, postquam campos propinquabant, copiis Carenis adiunguntur, transmissoque amne Tigri

permeant Adiabenos, quorum rex Izates societatem Meherdatis
palam induerat, in Gotarzen per occulta et magis fida inclinabat ...
5 (14:1) Ex quis Izates Adiabenus, mox Acbarus Arabum rex cum
exercitu abscedunt, levitate gentili, et quia experimentis cognitum est
barbaros malle Roma petere reges quam habere.

3 *Izates* Freinsheim   *iuliates* ML   5 *Adiabeno* J.F. Gronovius

(13:1) At last, when, outworn by snows and mountains, they were
nearing the plains, they effected a junction with the forces of Carenes,
and, crossing the Tigris, struck through the country of the Adiabeni,
whose king, Izates, had in public leagued himself with Meherdates,
whilst in private, and with more sincerity, he inclined to Gotarzes ...
(14:1) ... First Izates and the contingents of Adiabene then Acbarus
and those of the Arabs, took their departure, in accordance with the
levity of their race and with the fact, proved by experience, that
barbarians are more inclined to seek their kings from Rome than to
keep them.

(trans. J. Jackson, LCL)

13:1 *transmissoque amne Tigri permeant Adiabenos*: Tacitus relates these
events among those of 49 C.E. The Parthian enemies of King Gotarzes
arrived at Rome to ask Claudius to send them Meherdates, the grandson of
Phraates, to be king over them. Claudius agreed, and Meherdates was
accompanied to the Euphrates by Cassius the legate of Syria. At the
suggestion of Abgar (Acbar) the Arab, Meherdates chose to advance to the
Parthian kingdom through Armenia; cf. V.M. Scramuzza, *The Emperor
Claudius*, Cambridge (Mass.) 1940, pp. 188 f.
quorum rex Izates: Josephus relates that this king of Adiabene, influenced by
Jewish missionaries, had become a proselyte in the reign of the Parthian king
Artabanus. His mother Helena, his brother Monobazus, and other relatives
followed his example (*Ant.*, XX, 17 ff.). See H. Graetz, *Geschichte der Juden*,
Vol. III, Part 2⁵, Leipzig 1906, pp. 789 f.; Schürer, III, pp. 169 f.;
N.C. Debevoise, *A Political History of Parthia*, Chicago 1938, pp. 165 f.;
J. Neusner, *JBL*, LXXXIII (1964), pp. 60 ff. Josephus makes no mention of
the events related here by Tacitus. Regarding the relations between Izates
and the Parthian kings, Josephus alludes only to the support lent by Izates to
Artabanus and his opposition to Vardanes regarding the declaration of war
on the Romans. Josephus also refers briefly to the reign of Gotarzes but
without dwelling on his relations with Izates (*Ant.*, XX, 74). Tacitus,
however, makes no allusion to the Jewish affinities of the rulers of Adiabene.
On the boundaries of Adiabene, see L. Dillemann, *Haute Mésopotamie
orientale et pays adjacents*, Paris 1962, p. 112.

287

Annales, XII, 23:1 — Koestermann = F176R

Ituraeique et Iudaei defunctis regibus Sohaema atque Agrippa provinciae Suriae additi.

1 *ituraei* L / *sohaemo* L

Ituraea and Judaea, on the death of their sovereigns, Sohaemus and Agrippa, were attached to the province of Syria.

(trans. J. Jackson, *LCL*)

defunctis regibus Sohaema atque Agrippa: Tacitus records the death of Agrippa I among the events of 49 C.E. (the consulate of Gaius Pompeius and Quintus Veranius), but Agrippa died earlier, in 44 C.E. Tacitus may have here confused the date of the death of Agrippa with that of his brother Herod of Chalcis, which occurred in 48 C.E. (*Ant.*, XX, 104); see Ed. Meyer, III, p. 43; the same view is accepted by M.P. Charlesworth, *CAH*, X (1934), p. 681, n. 2, and by Syme, II, p. 747.

provinciae Suriae additi: For the view that Tacitus' statement could be taken at its face value, and that after Agrippa I's death Judaea proper, in contrast to Samaria and Galilaea, did not constitute part of a separate province but was incorporated for a short time into the province of Syria, see E. Schwartz, *Zur Chronologie des Paulus* (*Nachrichten von der Königlichen Gesellschaft der Wissenschaften zu Göttingen, Philologisch-historische Klasse*, Fasc. 3, 1907), pp. 286 f. = *Gesammelte Schriften*, V, Berlin 1963, pp. 152 f. In favour of this interpretation Schwartz adduces Tacitus, *Annales*, XII, 54 (No. 288), where Tacitus mentions only Galilaea and Samaria as the regions ruled by two Roman procurators, wholly ignoring Judaea proper. But at most this may prove that Tacitus was consistent in his mistake and not that Judaea proper formed a part of Syria at that time. That Judaea proper was then ruled by a procurator and did not constitute a part of Syria is fully proved by Josephus, who circumstantially relates the events in Judaea proper under the procurators Fadus (44–46 C.E.), Tiberius Alexander (46–48 C.E.) and Cumanus (48–52 C.E.). Nevertheless, there remains the question whether Tacitus really meant that Judaea proper had been incorporated into the province of Syria. Momigliano considers that Tacitus meant this, and makes light of the argument of Ed. Meyer that Tacitus cannot be so interpreted since he would be contradicting himself in *Historiae*, V, 9 (No. 281); see Momigliano, pp. 389 f.; Ed. Meyer, *loc. cit.*; P. Horovitz, *Revue Belge de Philologie et d'Histoire*, XVII (1938), p. 786. However, against Momigliano's argument is the possibility that Tacitus is expressing himself loosely. Since the procurator of Judaea was dependent on the legate of Syria, above all in questions of security (see H.G. Pflaum, *Les procurateurs équestres sous le Haut-Empire romain*, Paris 1950, pp. 146 ff.), Tacitus might have regarded the restoration of the provincial regime after the death of Agrippa I as tantamount to incorporation into Syria. Tacitus was not the only writer to do this. Josephus himself, when speaking of the Roman reorganization after the banishment of Archelaus (6 C.E.), says that Judaea was incorporated into Syria; cf. *Ant.*, XVII, 355: τῆς δ᾽ Ἀρχελάου χώρας ὑποτελοῦς προσνεμηθείσης τῇ Σύρων, though in his parallel account he emphasizes the creation of the separate province of Judaea; cf. *BJ*, II, 117: τῆς δὲ Ἀρχελάου χώρας εἰς ἐπαρχίαν περιγραφείσης. Indeed, Josephus' famous description of Judaea as a προσθήκη of Syria (*Ant.*, XVIII, 2) means in the language of this writer nothing less than incorporation; cf. *Ant.*, XVIII, 252: τὴν τετραρχίαν ἀφελόμενος αὐτὸν προσθήκην τῇ Ἀγρίππου βασιλείᾳ ποιεῖται. Cf. also *ibid.*, XIX, 274: προσθήκην τε αὐτῷ ποιεῖται πᾶσαν τὴν ὑπὸ Ἡρώδου βασιλευθεῖσαν, ὃς ἦν πάππος αὐτοῦ, Ἰουδαίαν καὶ Σαμάρειαν (against the view of Schürer, I, p. 456, n. 29).

Sohaemus was only a tetrarch; see Stein, PW, Ser. 2, III, p. 796. He is coupled here with Agrippa under the common designation of "king".

288

Annales, XII, 54 — Koestermann

(1) At non frater eius, cognomento Felix, pari moderatione agebat, iam pridem Iudaeae impositus et cuncta malefacta sibi impune ratus tanta potentia subnixo. Sane praebuerant Iudaei speciem motus orta seditione, postquam *** cognita caede eius haud obtemperatum
5   esset, manebat metus, ne quis principum eadem imperitaret. (2) Atque interim Felix intempestivis remediis delicta accendebat, aemulo ad deterrima Ventidio ⟨ Cumano⟩, cui pars provinciae habebatur, ita divisis, ut huic Galilaeorum natio, Felici Samaritae parerent, discordes olim et tum contemptu regentium minus coercitis
10   odiis. (3) Igitur raptare inter se, immittere latronum globos, componere insidias et aliquando proeliis congredi, spoliaque et praedas ad procuratores referre. Hique primo laetari, mox gliscente pernicie cum arma [militum] interiecissent, caesi milites; arsissetque bello provincia, ni Quadratus Syriae rector subvenisset. (4) Nec diu
15   adversus Iudaeos, qui in necem militum proruperant, dubitatum quin capite poenas luerent: Cumanus et Felix cunctationem adferebant, quia Claudius causis rebellionis auditis ius statuendi etiam de procuratoribus dederat. Sed Quadratus Felicem inter iudices

2 *iam pridem*] *tum primum* L   3 *patientia* M
4 lacunam Haase ex Hist. V, 9 sic supplevit *postquam* ⟨ *a C. Caesare iussi erant effigiem eius in templo locare; et quamquam*⟩ *cognita caede*
7 ⟨*Cumano*⟩ suppl. in marg. M. m. post.   13 *militum* secl. Hartman

ostentavit, receptum in tribunal, quo studia accusantium
20 deterrerentur; damnatusque flagitiorum, quae duo deliquerant,
Cumanus, et quies provinciae reddita.

20 damnatosque M

(1) The like moderation, however, was not shown by his brother,
surnamed Felix; who for a while past had held the governorship of
Judaea, and considered that with such influences behind him all
malefactions would be venial. The Jews, it is true, had given signs of
disaffection in the rioting prompted [by the demand of Gaius Caesar
for an effigy of himself in the Temple; and though] the news of his
murder had made compliance needless, the fear remained that some
emperor might issue an identical mandate. (2) In the interval, Felix
was fostering crime by misconceived remedies, his worst efforts being
emulated by Ventidius Cumanus, his colleague in the other half of the
province — which was so divided that the natives of Galilee were
subject to Ventidius, Samaria to Felix. The districts had long been at
variance, and their animosities were now under the less restraint, as
they could despise their regents. (3) Accordingly, they harried each
other, unleashed their troops of bandits, fought an occasional field,
and carried their trophies and their thefts to the procurators. At first,
the pair rejoiced; then, when the growth of the mischief forced them
to interpose the army of their troops, the troops were beaten, and the
province would have been ablaze with war but for the intervention of
Quadratus, the governor of Syria. (4) With regard to the Jews, who
had gone so far as to shed the blood of regular soldiers, there were no
protracted doubts as to the infliction of the death penalty: Cumanus
and Felix were answerable for more embarrassment, as Claudius, on
learning the motives of the revolt, had authorized Quadratus to deal
with the case of the procurators themselves. Quadratus, however,
displayed Felix among the judges, his admission to the tribunal being
intended to cool the zeal of his accusers: Cumanus was sentenced for
the delinquencies of two, and quietude returned to the province.

(trans. J. Jackson, LCL)

On this passage, see H. Smilda, *C. Suetonii Tranquilli Vita Divi Claudii*,
Groningen 1896, p. 141; P. v. Rohden, PW, I, p. 2617; Schürer, I, p. 570, n. 14;
H. Graetz, *Geschichte der Juden*, Vol. III, Part 2[5], Leipzig 1906, pp. 728 ff.;
E. Schwartz, *Zur Chronologie des Paulus (Nachrichten von der Königlichen
Gesellschaft der Wissenschaften zu Göttingen, Philologisch-historische*

From Tacitus to Simplicius

Klasse, Fasc. 3, 1907), pp. 285 ff. = *Gesammelte Schriften*, V, Berlin 1963, pp. 152 ff.; A. v. Domaszewski, *Philologus*, LXVII (1908), pp. 10 f.; Ed. Meyer, III, pp. 44 ff.; J. Dobíaš, *Dějiny římské provincie syrské*, Prague 1924, pp. 430 ff.; H. Dessau, *Geschichte der römischen Kaiserzeit*, Vol. II, Part 2, Berlin 1930, pp. 798 f.; Momigliano, pp. 388 ff.; V. M. Scramuzza, *The Emperor Claudius*, Cambridge (Mass.) 1940, p. 87; M. Aberbach, *JQR*, XL (1949/50), pp. 1 ff.; R. Hanslik, PW, Ser. 2, VIII, p. 817; Syme, II, p. 747; E. M. Smallwood, *Latomus*, XVIII (1959), pp. 560 ff.; P. A. Brunt, *Historia*, X (1961), p. 214, n. 78; E. Haenchen, *Die Apostelgeschichte*[13], Göttingen 1961, pp. 60 ff.; Fergus Millar, *JRS*, LVI (1966), p. 159, n. 35; E. Koestermann, *Cornelius Tacitus — Annalen*, III, commentary, Heidelberg 1967, pp. 200 ff.; G. Boulvert, *Esclaves et affranchis impériaux sous le Haut-Empire romain*, Naples 1970, pp. 347 f.; M. T. Griffin, *Seneca — a Philosopher in Politics*, Oxford 1976, p. 451.

Josephus gives a fuller account of the same events; cf. *BJ*, II, 232 ff. = *Ant.*, XX, 118 ff. The outbreak of fighting between the Jews and Samaritans was caused by the murder of a Galilaean pilgrim (so *BJ*; according to *Ant.* many people were killed). This occurred near the village of Ginea on the border of Samaria and the Great Plain. The leaders of the Galilaeans asked Cumanus to punish the murderers, but did not obtain satisfaction since he had been bribed by their opponents. They therefore sought the help of their brethren in Judaea, calling for their armed intervention. Despite efforts by the Jewish leaders to calm their compatriots, a number of Jews under the command of the brigand leader Eleazar the son of Dinai, and of Alexander, burnt and pillaged some Samaritan villages. Cumanus took auxiliary forces, one *ala* of cavalry and four cohorts of infantry, supplied the Samaritans also with arms, and opposed the Jews by force, killing and taking many of them prisoner. The riots were brought to the attention of Ummidius Quadratus, governor of Syria, who was then at Tyre. He postponed making a decision until he had arrived in the province of Judaea, where he put to death both the Samaritan and the Jewish prisoners whom he found guilty of rioting. Then, holding trials in Lydda, he pronounced the death sentence on certain Jews who had been found guilty of revolutionary propaganda. He also sent the high priest Ananias and the ex-high priest Jonathan to Rome to be judged by Claudius (*BJ*, II, 243). Likewise the procurator Cumanus, the military tribune Celer and the leaders of the Samaritans were ordered to proceed to Rome, where a struggle ensued between Cumanus and the Samaritans on one side and the Jews on the other to gain the favour of the emperor. The freedmen and "friends" of Claudius sided with Cumanus and the Samaritans, but the Jews had on their side the influence of Agrippa II, who obtained the support of the empress Agrippina — it is a plausible suggestion that not all the freedmen were behind the opponents of the Jews, and that Felix' brother Pallas at least had a hand in enlisting Agrippina's support; on Pallas, see S. I. Oost, *AJP*, LXXIX (1958), pp. 113 ff. Claudius decided against Cumanus and the Samaritans; Cumanus was sentenced to banishment, the representatives of the Samaritans were executed at Rome, while the tribune Celer was sent to Jerusalem to meet his death there (*BJ*, II, 246). Felix, whose candidature had been supported by Jonathan the son of Hanan, an ex-high priest and an influential Jewish politician (*Ant.*, XX, 162), was appointed procurator of Judaea.

Apart from the fact that Tacitus' narrative is much less detailed than that of Josephus, the main difference between the two accounts is that, according to the Jewish historian, Cumanus was governor of Judaea at the time of the disturbances while Felix is not mentioned in any connection with Palestine before his appointment subsequently to the governorship of Judaea. However, Tacitus at first refers to Felix as if he were already governor of Judaea ("iam pridem Iudaeae impositus"), and then explains that while Cumanus ruled over the Galilaeans, the Samaritans had to obey Felix ("ita divisis, ut huic [scil. Cumano] Galilaeorum natio, Felici Samaritae parerent"). Some scholars prefer the version of Josephus to Tacitus without much discussion; so, e.g., Schürer, Ed. Meyer, Millar, P. Garnsey, *Social Status and Legal Privilege in the Roman Empire*, Oxford 1970, p. 73, n. 3. Others accept Tacitus, e.g., Scramuzza, Hanslik, Syme; H. Mattingly, *The Imperial Civil Service of Rome*, Cambridge 1910, p. 144.

But Josephus cannot be wrong in stating that Cumanus, and not Felix, was procurator at least of Judaea proper during the time of the riots and the years preceding them. On the other hand, it is unlikely that Tacitus had no foundation for introducing the activities of Felix in Palestine at the time of Cumanus' governorship. Different solutions have been suggested to account for the discrepancy between the two historians. One of the most convincing seems to be that of Graetz, who maintains that Felix was procurator of part of the province in the time of Cumanus' procuratorship over the rest, but that Tacitus was mistaken in identifying the area under Felix' control with Samaria; Cumanus' jurisdiction must have extended over both Judaea proper and Samaria, which constituted a contiguous territory, while Felix was governor of Galilaea. This change is required by the logic of the situation, since it is hard to assume a partition by which Cumanus' area would be cut in two by that of Felix. Graetz also offers a better explanation of the alliance between Cumanus and the Samaritans. The theory that the country was divided between Cumanus and Felix gains some slight support from *BJ*, II, 247: Μετὰ ταῦτα Ἰουδαίας μὲν ἐπίτροπον Φήλικα τὸν Πάλλαντος ἀδελφὸν ἐκπέμπει τῆς τε Σαμαρείας καὶ Γαλιλαίας καὶ Περαίας. There Josephus mentions the appointment of Felix to the governorship of the whole province, but since he finds it necessary to list all its constituent parts — a procedure that he follows in respect of no other appointment — this might imply that the situation was different at the time of Cumanus. It may also be emphasized that Galilaea had not originally been included in the Roman province of Judaea because it led a separate existence until 39 C. E. Another explanation is that Felix had already been appointed temporarily to the governorship of Samaria during the judicial proceedings against Cumanus and that this had caused the confusion in Tacitus; see Momigliano, *loc. cit.* (supra, p. 78). It is also possible that during Cumanus' governorship Felix filled some procuratorial post that was not strictly the governorship of a part of the province; see Brunt, *loc. cit.* (supra, p. 78). An example is the procuratorship of the imperial estate of Jamneia, mentioned in *Ant.*, XVIII, 158: καὶ γνοὺς Ἐρέννιος Καπίτων ὁ τῆς Ἰαμνείας ἐπίτροπος πέμπει στρατιώτας, οἳ εἰσπράξονται αὐτὸν ἀργυρίου τριάκοντα μυριάδας θησαυρῷ τῷ Καίσαρος ὀφειλομένας ἐπὶ Ῥώμης ... Cf. Philo, *Legatio ad Gaium*, 199, where Capito is described as φόρων ἐκλογεὺς ὁ Καπίτων ἐστὶ τῶν τῆς Ἰουδαίας. Capito was instrumental in instigating the anti-Jewish policy of Gaius Caligula; for his career, see P. Fraccaro, *Athenaeum*, XVIII (1940), pp. 136 ff.; H.G. Pflaum, *Les carrières procuratoriennes équestres sous le Haut-Empire romain*, I, Paris 1960, pp. 23 ff.; cf. also the inscription found in the vicinity of Jabneh, where we read the name of Mellon, a procurator and *libertus* of Tiberius; see M. Avi-Yonah, *QDAP*, XII (1946), p. 84. Cf. also Orth, *op. cit.* (supra, p. 69), pp. 54 f.; P.R.C. Weaver, *Familia Caesaris*, Cambridge 1972, p. 275.

1 *Felix*: For his career, see the commentary to Tacitus, *Historiae*, V (No. 281).

pari moderatione: Ironical. For Felix' brother, Pallas, see above, the introduction to this text.

iam pridem Iudaeae impositus: In view of the subsequent statements that Felix was governor of Samaria while Cumanus had jurisdiction over the Galilaeans, Tacitus' designation of Felix as "Iudaeae impositus" seems a slovenly expression. Usually Tacitus uses the term Judaea for the whole province and not just for Judaea proper. Here he probably means to indicate loosely the general sphere of Felix' appointment, without necessarily implying that he had jurisdiction over Judaea proper. Any suggestion that Felix was governor of Judaea proper in these years is excluded by the detailed references to Cumanus' activities there in the works of Josephus; cf. *Ant.*, XX, 105 ff. = *BJ*, II, 223 ff.

cognita caede eius: This sentence obviously refers to Gaius Caligula; cf. *Historiae*, V, 9 (No. 281): "dein iussi a C. Caesare effigiem eius in templo locare arma potius sumpsere, quem motum Caesaris mors diremit."

2 *intempestivis remediis delicta accendebat*: This characterization accords well with the information given by Josephus about the methods adopted by Felix as procurator of Judaea in 52–60 C.E. His policy ranged from the harshest suppression of any disturbance to an opportunist alliance with the extremist Sicarii; cf. *Ant.*, XX, 160 ff.; *BJ*, II, 253 ff., and the commentary to Tacitus, *loc. cit.*

Ventidio Cumano: In the works of Josephus he is known solely by his cognomen. Only Tacitus gives the *gentilicium*.

ut huic Galilaeorum natio, Felici Samaritae parerent: Missing here is Judaea proper. The omission cannot be accounted for by the interpretation that Judaea proper, in marked contrast to Samaria and Galilaea, had at that time (from 49 C.E. onward) been included in the province of Syria; on this see Schwartz, *op. cit.* (supra, pp. 77 f.), p. 286 = *Gesammelte Schriften*, V, p. 153.

discordes olim: The old-standing enmity between the Jewish and Samaritan communities went back to the formative years of the Second Jewish Commonwealth; cf. the commentaries to Curtius Rufus, IV, 8:9–11 (No. 197), and Hecataeus of Abdera, apud: *Contra Apionem*, II, 43 (No. 13). The policy of the Hasmonaeans, who had destroyed the Samaritan centre of worship, intensified this hostility. At the beginning of the provincial regime in Judaea the Samaritans defiled the Temple of Jerusalem; cf. *Ant.*, XVIII, 30 — the time of Coponius; see J. Carcopino, *Revue historique*, CLXVI (1931), pp. 88 ff. This animosity is taken for granted in various passages of the New Testament.

There were occasions when the Jews and Samaritans were in the same camp struggling against common oppressors. Thus both communities complained to the Roman imperial government about Archelaus (*Ant.*, XVII, 342; *BJ*, II, 111), though the Samaritans had no part in the revolt ten years before. The Samaritans were also active in securing the dismissal by Vitellius of Pilate, the common enemy of both the Samaritans and the Jews (*Ant.*, XVIII, 88 f.); there was also some commotion among the Samaritans at the time of the Jewish war (*BJ*, III, 307 ff.). However in neither case can it be assumed with any degree of certainty that the Samaritans consciously made common cause with the Jews.

3 *Quadratus Syriae rector*: Ummidius Quadratus acted as legate of Syria in the years 50–60 C.E.; see Schürer, I, p. 335; Schürer, ed. Vermes & Millar, I, p. 264; Syme, II, pp. 478 f.; on the Ummidi, see also R. Syme, *Historia*, XVII (1968), pp. 72 ff. This was one of the many interventions by the legates of Syria in the affairs of the province of Judaea. At the time of the creation of the new province (6 C.E.) Quirinius, the legate of Syria, had been sent there to supervise the census (*Ant.*, XVII, 355). Later (36 C.E.), following complaint by the Samaritans, Vitellius intervened, replaced Pilate by Marcellus and regulated the internal affairs of Judaea (*Ant.*, XVIII, 89 ff.). When Gaius Caligula planned the erection of the statue at the Temple of Jerusalem, he ordered Petronius, the legate of Syria, to enter Judaea at the head of an army (*Ant.*, XVIII, 261). Petronius' successor Marsus prevented Agrippa I from completing the fortifications of Jerusalem (*Ant.*, XIX, 326 f.) and dispersed the conference of the vassal kings of the Roman East at Tiberias (*Ant.*, XIX, 340 f.). When there was danger of serious riots at Jerusalem during the procuratorship of Fadus, the legate Cassius Longinus appeared in the city (*Ant.*, XX, 7). On the presence of Cestius Gallus at Jerusalem, cf. *BJ*, II, 280.

4 *Nec diu adversus Iudaeos ... dubitatum*: The "Iudaeos" presumably included the Samaritans; cf. *Ant.*, XX, 129 (= *BJ*, II, 241): Σαμαρέων δὲ καὶ Ἰουδαίων οὕστινας νεωτερίσαντας ἔμαθεν ἀνεσταύρωσεν οὓς Κουμανὸς ἔλαβεν αἰχμαλώτους.

ius statuendi etiam de procuratoribus dederat: This rather implies that generally the legates of Syria had not this right, though Vitellius followed a similar procedure in dismissing Pilate from his post and commanding him to leave for Rome. Pilate obeyed the order; cf. *Ant.*, XVIII, 89: οὐκ ὂν ἀντειπεῖν. See S.J. de Laet, *L'Antiquité Classique*, VIII (1939), p. 417. As Tacitus states, however, Vitellius was not an ordinary governor, since he had received a special commission from Tiberius; cf. *Annales*, VI, 32: "et cunctis, quae apud Orientem parabantur, L. Vitellium praefecit".

Sed Quadratus Felicem inter iudices ostentavit, receptum in tribunal: Josephus also refers to Quadratus sitting in judgement; cf. *Ant.*, XX, 130: καθίσας ἐπὶ βήματος. For the expression itself, cf. Tacitus, *Annales*, XIII, 23: "Burrus quamvis reus inter iudices sententiam dixit".

damnatusque ... Cumanus: Cumanus was only implicitly condemned by Quadratus, being suspended from his post and sent to Rome to be judged by the emperor, who sentenced him to exile.

289

Annales, XIII, 7:1 — Koestermann

Haec atque talia vulgantibus, Nero et iuventutem proximas per provincias quaesitam supplendis Orientis legionibus admovere legionesque ipsas pro⟨p⟩ius Armeniam collocari iubet, duosque veteres reges Agrippam et ⟨Ant⟩iochum expedire copias, quis
5 Parthorum fines ultro intrarent, simul pontes per amnem Euphraten iungi; et minorem Armeniam Aristobulo, regionem Sophenen Sohaemo cum insignibus regiis mandat.

2 *regionibus* M / *admoveri* Pichena 3 *proius* M *per* L
4 ⟨*Ant*⟩*iochum* Lipsius *Iochum* M *Iochium* L 6 *iungi*] *Iun Iu* M

In the midst of these popular discussions, Nero gave orders that both the recruits levied in the adjacent provinces to keep the eastern legions at strength were to be moved up, and the legions themselves stationed closer to Armenia; while the two veteran kings, Agrippa and Antiochus, prepared their forces, so as to take the initiative by crossing the Parthian frontier: at the same time bridges were to be thrown over the Euphrates, and Lesser Armenia was assigned to Aristobulus, the district of Sophene to Sohaemus, each receiving royal insignia. (trans. J. Jackson, *LCL*)

These events, at the beginning of Nero's reign, are included by Tacitus among those of 54 C.E. The Parthian success in Armenia at the end of Claudius' reign roused the Roman government to a military effort to meet the new situation. The direction of operations was given to Domitius Corbulo, and the allied kings were asked to prepare their forces for the new emergency; see J. G. C. Anderson, *CAH*, X, p. 758; M. A. Levi, *Nerone e i suoi tempi*, Milan–Varese 1949, pp. 167 f.

supplendis Orientis legionibus: The legions of the east at that time were the III Gallica, VI Ferrata, X Fretensis and XII Fulminata. This passage of Tacitus is one of the main sources showing that the legions of the east were then recruited from the eastern provinces; cf. Tacitus, *Annales*, XIII, 35: "et habiti per Galatiam Cappadociamque dilectus" (58 C.E.). In general, see G. Forni, *Il reclutamento delle legioni da Augusto a Diocleziano*,

Milan–Rome 1953, pp. 54, 57; G. E. F. Chilver, *JRS*, XLVII (1957), p. 31.

Agrippam: Agrippa II, the son of Agrippa I, had been king of Chalcis in place of his dead uncle, Herod of Chalcis, but in 53 C. E. (the thirteenth year of Claudius; cf. *BJ*, II, 247; *Ant.*, XX, 138) he received instead the Trachonitis, Batanaea and Gaulanitis, together with some adjacent territories. For his early career, see Schürer, I, pp. 585 ff.; Rosenberg, PW, X, p. 146; T. Frankfort, *Hommages à Albert Grenier*, II, Brussels-Berchem 1962, pp. 659 ff.; Schürer, ed. Vermes & Millar, I, pp. 471 ff.

Antiochum: Antiochus IV, king of Commagene, had already been king in 38 C. E., but his kingdom was taken from him by Gaius Caligula and restored to him only by Claudius. He took part in the conference of vassal kings at Tiberias under the chairmanship of Agrippa I and proved an energetic auxiliary of Rome in the war against the Jews; cf. *BJ*, II, 500; III, 68; V, 460 ff.

et minorem Armeniam Aristobulo … mandat: This Aristobulus was a son of Herod king of Chalcis and a cousin of Agrippa II. With his father and Agrippa he had interceded with Claudius on behalf of the Jews regarding the robes of the High Priest; see *Ant.*, XX, 13. For the bestowal upon him of Lesser Armenia, cf. also *BJ*, II, 252 = *Ant.*, XX, 158. On him, see also Wilcken, PW, II, p. 910; A. Stein, in: *PIR*², I, p. 206, No. 1052.

290

Annales, XIV, 26 — Koestermann

(1) Quin et Tiridaten per Medos extrema Armeniae intrantem praemisso cum auxiliis Verulano legato atque ipse ⟨scil. Corbulo⟩ legionibus citis abire procul ac spem belli omittere subegit; quosque nobis alienos animis cognoverat, caedibus et incendiis perpopulatus
5 possessionem Armeniae usurpabat, cum advenit Tigranes a Nerone ad capessendum imperium delectus, Cappadocum e nobilitate, regis Archelai nepos, sed quod diu obses apud urbem fuerat, usque ad servilem patientiam demissus. (2) Ne⟨c⟩ consensu acceptus, durante apud quosdam favore Arsacidarum: at plerique superbiam Partho-
10 rum perosi datum a Romanis regem malebant. Additum et praesidium, mille legionarii, tres sociorum cohortes duaeque equitum alae; et quo facilius novum regnum tueretur, pars Armeniae, ut cuique finitima, Pharasmani Pole⟨moni⟩que et Aristobulo atque Antiocho parere iussae sunt.

1 *tiridatem* ML   4 *ab re animis* M   6 *e] et* LM, sed *t* del. M¹   8 *ne⟨c⟩* Puteolanus
ne ML   9 *plerisque superbia* M   9–10 *parthorum perobsi datum* M
parthorumque obsidatum L   13 *Armeniae ut* Puteolanus   *armenia(-niam* L)
        eunt ML   /   *Pharasmani Pole⟨moni⟩que* J. F. Gronovius
            pars manipulique L   *pars nipulique* M

(1) Moreover, as Tiridates was attempting to penetrate the extreme Armenian frontier by way of Media, he [scil. Corbulo] sent the legate Verulanus in advance with the auxiliaries, and by his own appearance with the legions after a forced march compelled the prince to retire to a distance and abandon the thought of war. After devastating with fire and sword the districts he had found hostile to ourselves, he remained master of Armenia, when Tigranes, who had been chosen by Nero to assume the crown, arrived on the scene — a member of the Cappadocian royal house and a great-grandson of King Archelaus, but by his long residence as a hostage in the capital reduced to a slave-like docility. (2) Nor was his reception unanimous, since in some quarters the popularity of the Arsacidae still persisted: the majority, however, revolted by Parthian arrogance, preferred a king assigned by Rome. He was allowed, further, a garrison of one thousand legionaries, three allied cohorts, and two squadrons of cavalry; while, to make his new kingdom more easily tenable, any district of Armenia adjoining the frontier of Pharasmanes or Polemo, or Aristobulus, or Antiochus was ordered to obey that prince.

(trans. J. Jackson, *LCL*)

1 *cum advenit Tigranes a Nerone ad capessendum imperium delectus ...* *regis Archelai nepos*: For Tigranes' genealogy, see *Ant.*, XVIII, 139 f. In fact this Tigranes was the great-grandson of Archelaus of Cappadocia; see Geyer, PW, Ser. 2, VI, p. 980. His uncle, also named Tigranes, had been king of Armenia; see the commentary to Tacitus, *Annales*, VI, 40 (No. 285). Neither he nor his uncle can be thought to have been practising Jews. Josephus himself testifies that the descendants of Alexander, the son of Herod, did not remain loyal to Judaism; cf. *Ant.*, XVIII, 141: καὶ τὸ μὲν Ἀλεξάνδρου γένος εὐθὺς ἅμα τῷ φυῆναι τὴν θεραπείαν ἐξέλιπεν τῶν Ἰουδαίοις ἐπιχωρίων μεταταξάμενοι πρὸς τὰ Ἕλλησι πάτρια.
2 *pars Armeniae ... Aristobulo atque Antiocho parere iussae sunt*: This passage deals with the events of 60 C.E. Corbulo had succeeded in ousting the Parthian candidate to the Armenian throne, replacing him by Tigranes. Aristobulus, who as king of Armenia Minor was one of the neighbours of Tigranes, gained some territorial advantages from Corbulo's reorganization.

291

Annales, XV, 1:2–3; 2:4; 4:1, 3; 14:3 — Koestermann

(1:2) Atque illum ⟨scil. Vologaesen⟩ ambiguum novus insuper nuntius contumeliae exstimulat: quippe egressus Armenia Tigranes

1 *novus etiam* L

Adiabenos, conterminam nationem, latius ac diutius quam per latrocinia vastaverat, idque primores gentium aegre tolerabant: eo
5 contemptionis descensum, ut ne duce quidem Romano incursarentur, sed temeritate obsidis tot per annos inter mancipia habiti. (1:3) Accendebat dolorem eorum Monabazus, quem penes Adiabenum regimen, quod praesidium aut unde peteret rogitans: iam de Armenia concessum, proxima trahi; et nisi defendant Parthi, levius
10 servitium apud Romanos deditis quam captis esse ... (2:4) Simul diademate caput Tiridatis evinxit ⟨scil. Vologaeses⟩, promptam equitum manum, quae regem ex more sectatur, Monaesi nobili viro tradidit, adiectis Adiabenorum auxiliis, mandavitque Tigranen Armenia exturbandum, dum ipse positis adversus Hyrcanos
15 discordiis vires intimas molemque belli ciet, provinciis Romanis minitans ... (4:1) Ea dum a Corbulone tuendae Syriae parantur, acto raptim agmine Mon⟨a⟩eses, ut famam sui praeiret, non ideo nescium aut incautum Tigranen offendit ... (4:3) Adiabeni cum promovere scalas et machinamenta inciperent ⟨scil. ad Tigranocertam⟩, facile
20 detrusi, mox erumpentibus nostris caeduntur ... (14:3) Et multum in vicem disceptato, Monobazus Adiabenus in diem posterum testis iis quae pepigissent adhibetur.

8 *aut*] *haud* M   21 *his* ML

(1:2) He was still in doubt, when news of a fresh indignity stung him into action, for Tigranes emerging from Armenia, had ravaged the bordering country of Adiabene too widely and too long for a plundering foray, and the grandees of the nations were becoming restive; complaining that they had sunk to a point of humiliation where they could be harried, not even by a Roman general, but by the temerity of a hostage whom for years the enemy had counted among his chattels. (1:3) Their resentment was inflamed by Monobazus, the ruling prince of Adiabene: "What protection," he kept demanding, "was he to seek? or from what quarter?" Armenia had already been ceded; the adjacent country was following; and, if Parthia refused protection, then the Roman yoke pressed more lightly upon a surrendered than upon a conquered nation! ... (2:4) Therewith he bound the diadem on the brows of Tiridates. A body of cavalry, regularly in attendance on the king, was at hand: he transferred it to a noble named Monaeses, adding a number of Adiabenian auxiliaries, and commissioned him to eject Tigranes from Armenia; while he himself laid aside his quarrel with Hyrcania and called up his internal forces, with the full machinery of war, as a threat to the Roman provinces ... (4:1) While Corbulo was thus preparing for the defence of Syria Monaeses, who had marched at full speed in order to outstrip the rumour of his coming, failed nonetheless to catch Tigranes unawares off his guard ... (4:3) The Adiabeni, on beginning to push forward their ladders and machines, were easily thrown back, then cut to pieces by a sally of our men ... (14:3) After much parleying on both sides, Monobazus of Adiabene was called in for the following day as witness to the arrangement concluded.   (trans. J. Jackson, *LCL*)

1:2 *egressus Armenia Tigranes*: These events are dated by Tacitus to 62 C.E., but he combines here the events of 61 and 62; see J.G.C. Anderson, *CAH*, X, p. 765, n. 5.
14:3 *Monobazus ... testis ... adhibetur*: Like Izates, his brother (cf. Tacitus, *Annales*, XII, 14:1 = No. 285), he was a proselyte (*Ant.*, XX, 75), and he succeeded his brother to the throne of Adiabene (*ibid.*, 93); cf. also Cassius Dio, LXII, 20:2–3; 23:4 (No. 424). Here Monobazus acts as a witness to the agreement signed by Paetus, the besieged Roman commander, and Vasaces, the representative of Vologaeses, the Parthian king.

292

Annales, XV, 28:3 — Koestermann

Die pacta Tiberius Alexander, inlustris eques Romanus, minister bello datus, et Vini⟨ci⟩anus Annius, gener Corbulonis, nondum senatoria aetate et pro legato quintae legioni impositus, in castra Tiridatis venere, honore eius ac ne metueret insidias tali pignore;
5 viceni dehinc equites adsumpti.

2 *Vini⟨ci⟩anus* Ryckius   *vinianus* M   *vimanus* L   4 *honor* M
honori Lipsius

On the day fixed upon, Tiberius Alexander, a Roman knight of the first rank, who had been appointed a commissioner for the campaign, and Annius Vinicianus, a son-in-law of Corbulo, still under senatorial age, and acting legate of the fifth legion, entered the camp of Tiridates, partly out of compliment to him, but also, by such a pledge, to remove all fear of treachery. On each side twenty mounted men were then taken into attendance.   (trans. J. Jackson, *LCL*)

Die pacta: This event belongs to the reconciliation between Tiridates, the Parthian king of Armenia, and Domitius Corbulo.

Tiberius Alexander: Tiberius Julius Alexander, son of Alexander the Jewish alabarch of Alexandria and a nephew of the philosopher Philo, may be considered a representative of the Jewish upper class of Alexandria; see A. Fuks, *Zion*, XIII–XIV (1948/9), pp. 10 ff. (in Hebrew); J. Schwartz, *Annuaire de l'institut de philologie et d'histoire orientales et slaves*, XIII, 1953 (1955), pp. 591 ff. He did not remain loyal to his ancestral religion (cf. *Ant.*, XX, 100: τοῖς γὰρ πατρίοις οὐκ ἐνέμεινεν οὗτος ἔθεσιν), but chose the administrative career of a Roman knight. He is first mentioned as the *epistrategos* of the Thebais in 42 C.E. (*OGIS*, No. 663), and later as procurator of Judaea (*Ant.*, XX, 100 ff. = *BJ*, II, 220) in 46–48 C.E., between the procuratorships of Fadus and Cumanus. As governor of Judaea he showed no marked sympathy for the Jewish population. Though his advancement to this post may have partly been due to his patrician Jewish connections, and above all those with the Herodian family, the general trend in Roman administration from Claudius onwards was to promote officials from the Hellenistic population of the East; see the commentary to Tacitus, *Historiae*, V, 10 (No. 281). As procurator of Judaea, Tiberius Alexander sentenced to death two extremist leaders, Jacob and Simon, the sons of Judas the Galilaean; cf. *Ant.*, XX, 102.

inlustris eques Romanus: Tacitus nowhere refers to the Jewish antecedents of Tiberius Alexander. Here he is only "inlustris eques Romanus", while Tacitus describes him as belonging to the Egyptian nation in *Historiae*, I, 11 (No. 273). Since Tiberius Alexander had abandoned the Jewish religion, he ceased to be regarded as a Jew by Tacitus as well as by Juvenal; cf. Iuvenalis, I, 130 (No. 295).

minister bello datus: Possibly in Corbulo's army he fulfilled the same task that he later had in the army of Titus; cf. *BJ*, V, 46; VI, 237; cf. also *OGIS*, No. 586 = *IGLS*, VII, No. 4011. On the beginning of his career, see W. Schur, *Die Orientpolitik des Kaisers Nero*, Leipzig 1923, p. 95; V. Burr, *Tiberius Iulius Alexander*, Bonn 1955, pp. 25 ff.; E. G. Turner, *JRS*, XLIV (1954), pp. 58 f.; H. G. Pflaum, *Les carrières procuratoriennes équestres sous le Haut-Empire romain*, I, Paris 1960, pp. 46 ff.; J. Geudens, *De Epistrategie in romeins Egypte*, Louvain 1967–1968, pp. 47 f.; cf. also Tacitus, *Historiae*, I, 11 (No. 273) and the commentary *ad loc.*

293

Annales, XIII, 32 : 2 — Koestermann

Et Pomponia Graecina insignis femina, Plautio, quem ovasse de Britannis rettuli, nupta ac superstitionis externae rea, mariti iudicio permissa. Isque prisco instituto propinquis coram de capite famaque coniugis cognovit et insontem nuntiavit.

1 *platio* M ⟨*A.*⟩ *Plautio* Nipperdey 1–2 *quem ovasse de Britanniis*
rettuli Acidalius *qui ovans se de britanniis rettulit* M *qui ovasset de*
Britanniis L

Pomponia Graecina, a woman of high family, married to Aulus Plautius — whose ovation after the British campaign I recorded earlier — and now arraigned for alien superstition, was left to the jurisdiction of her husband. Following the ancient custom he held the inquiry, which was to determine the fate and the fame of his wife, before a family council, and announced her innocent.

(trans. J. Jackson, *LCL*)

Pomponia Graecina ... Plautio ... nupta: For the family connections of the Plautii, see the commentary to Cassius Dio, LXVII, 14:1–2 (No. 435); see also E. Koestermann, *Cornelius Tacitus, Annalen*, III, commentary, Heidelberg 1967, p. 297.

superstitionis externae rea: Tacitus does not specify the character of the "superstitio externa". There is much to be said for the view that it was either Judaism or Christianity; see T. Mommsen, *Römisches Strafrecht*, Leipzig 1899, p. 574, n. 3; E. G. Hardy, *Studies in Roman History*, London 1906, p. 43; H. Janne, *Latomus*, I (1937), p. 50. In 57 C.E. they were not yet differentiated by the Roman government. The influence of Druidism has been suggested; see Hofmann, PW, XXI, p. 29. However, the Gallic cults had little attraction outside their ethnic boundaries; see F. Cumont, *Les religions orientales dans le paganisme romain*[4], Paris 1929, pp. 21 f.

294

Annales, XV, 44:2–5 — Koestermann = F177R = W. den Boer, *Scriptorum Paganorum* I–IV *Saec. de Christianis Testimonia*, Leiden 1948, No. II

(2) Sed non ope humana, non largitionibus principis aut deum placamentis decedebat infamia, quin iussum incendium crederetur. Ergo abolendo rumori Nero subdidit reos et quaesitissimis poenis affecit, quos per flagitia invisos vulgus Chrestianos appellabat. (3) Auctor nominis eius Christus Tiberio imperitante per procuratorem Pontium Pilatum supplicio adfectus erat; repressaque in praesens exitiabilis superstitio rursum erumpebat, non modo per Iudaeam, originem eius mali, sed per urbem etiam, quo cuncta undique atrocia aut pudenda confluunt celebranturque. (4) Igitur primum correpti qui fatebantur, deinde indicio eorum multitudo ingens haud proinde in crimine incendii quam odio humani generis convicti sunt. Et pereuntibus addita ludibria, ut ferarum tergis contecti laniatu canum

4 *Christianos* L   corr. ex *chrestianos* M m. post.   *appellat* L
5 *imperante* L   6 *erat* L sup. lin.   10–11 *proinde crimine* L
11 *convicti* L   *con Iuncti* M

interirent aut crucibus adfixi atque flammati, ubi defecisset dies in
usu⟨m⟩ nocturni luminis urerentur. (5) Hortos suos ei spectaculo
15 Nero obtulerat et circense ludicrum edebat, habitu aurigae permixtus
plebi vel curriculo insistens. Unde quamquam adversus sontes et
novissima exempla meritos miseratio oriebatur, tamquam non
utilitate publica, sed in saevitiam unius absumerentur.

> 13 *etque* Hartke   *aut* ML   /   *flammandi* M
> *aut ... flammati* secl. Nipperdey   14 *usu* ML   16 *circulo* M

(2) But neither human help, nor imperial munificence, nor all the
modes of placating Heaven, could stifle scandal or dispel the belief
that the fire had taken place by order. Therefore to scotch the
rumour, Nero substituted as culprits, and punished with the utmost
refinements of cruelty a class of men, loathed for their vices, whom
the crowd styled Christians. (3) Christus, the founder of the name,
had undergone the death penalty in the reign of Tiberius, by sentence
of the procurator Pontius Pilatus, and the pernicious superstition was
checked for a moment, only to break out once more, not merely in
Judaea, the home of the disease, but in the capital itself, where all
things horrible or shameful in the world collect and find a vogue. (4)
First, then, the confessed members of the sect were arrested; next, on
their disclosures vast numbers were convicted, not so much on the
count of arson as for hatred of the human race. And derision
accompanied their end: they were covered with wild beasts' skins and
torn to death by dogs; or they were fastened on crosses, and, when
daylight failed were burned to serve as lamps by night. (5) Nero had
offered his gardens for the spectacle, and gave an exhibition in his
Circus, mixing with the crowd in the habit of a charioteer, or mounted
on his car. Hence, in spite of a guilt, which had earned the most
exemplary punishment, there arose a sentiment of pity, due to the
impression that they were being sacrificed not for the welfare of the
state but to the ferocity of a single man.   (trans. J. Jackson, *LCL*)

On this passage, see C. F. Arnold, *Die neronische Christenverfolgung*, Leipzig
1888; P. Batiffol, *RB*, III (1894), pp. 510 ff.; A. Gercke, *Seneca-Studien*,
Leipzig 1895, pp. 216 ff.; K. Hofbauer, *Die "erste" Christenverfolgung —
Beiträge zur Kritik der Tacitusstelle* (*Dreiunddreissigster Jahres-Bericht des
Staats-Gymnasiums in Oberhollabrunn*), 1903; B. W. Henderson, *The Life
and Principate of the Emperor Nero*, London 1903, pp. 249 ff., 434 ff., 484 f.;
P. Allard, *Histoire des persécutions pendant les deux premiers siècles*[3], Paris
1903, pp. 35 ff.; Linsenmayer, pp. 54 ff.; A. Profumo, *Le fonti ed i tempi dello*

incendio Neroniano, Rome 1905; E.G. Hardy, *Studies in Roman History*, London 1906, pp. 41 ff.; E.T. Klette, *Die Christenkatastrophe unter Nero*, Tübingen 1907; K. Linck, *De Antiquissimis Veterum Quae ad Jesum Nazarenum Spectant Testimoniis*, Giessen 1913, pp. 61 ff.; O. Hirschfeld, *Kleine Schriften*, Berlin 1913, pp. 407 ff.; Radin, pp. 317 ff.; Ed. Meyer, III, pp. 500 ff.; Harnack, I, pp. 66 f., 501 f.; E.T. Merrill, *Essays in Early Christian History*, London 1924, pp. 82 ff.; R. Reitzenstein, *Die hellenistischen Mysterienreligionen*[3], Leipzig–Berlin 1927, pp. 110 ff.; H. Janne, *L'Antiquité Classique*, II (1933), pp. 331 f.; idem, *Latomus*, I (1937), pp. 50 f.; A. Momigliano, *CAH*, X (1934), pp. 725 f., 887 f.; F.R.M. Hitchcock, *Hermathena*, XLIX (1935), pp. 184 ff.; A. Bourgery, *Latomus*, II (1938), pp. 106 ff.; A. Kurfess, *Mnemosyne*, Ser. 3, VI (1938), pp. 261 ff.; M. Dibelius, *Rom und die Christen im ersten Jahrhundert (Sitzungsberichte der Heidelberger Akademie der Wissenschaften, 1941/2*, 1942, No. 2), pp. 31 ff.; M. Goguel, *La naissance du Christianisme*, Paris 1946, pp. 545 ff.; A.G. Roos, in: *Symbolae van Oven*, Leiden 1946, pp. 297 ff.; F.W. Clayton, *CQ*, XLI (1947), pp. 81 ff.; M.A. Levi, *Nerone e i suoi tempi*, Milan–Varese 1949, pp. 203 f.; A.M.A. Hospers-Jansen, *Tacitus over de Joden*, Groningen 1949, pp. 106 ff.; L. Herrmann, *Revue Belge de philologie et d'histoire*, XXVII (1949), pp. 633 ff.; H. Fuchs, *Vigiliae Christianae*, IV (1950), pp. 65 ff.; H. Hommel, *Theologia Viatorum*, III (1951), pp. 10 ff.; A.N. Sherwin-White, *JTS*, NS, III (1952), pp. 207 f.; K. Büchner, *Aegyptus*, XXXIII (1953), pp. 181 ff.; J. Zeiller, *Revue d'histoire ecclésiastique*, L (1955), pp. 393 ff.; B. Doer, *Das Altertum*, II (1956), pp. 15 ff.; A. Ronconi, *Studi in onore di Ugo Enrico Paoli*, Florence 1956, pp. 615 ff.; J.B. Bauer, *Gymnasium*, LXIV (1957), pp. 497 ff.; Syme, II, p. 533, n. 5; H. Heubner, *Hermes*, LXXXVII (1959), pp. 223 ff.; A. Wlosok, *Gymnasium*, LXVI (1959), pp. 20 ff.; J. Beaujeu, *Latomus*, XIX (1960), pp. 65 ff., 291 ff.; Leon, p. 28; C. Questa, *Studi sulle fonti degli Annales di Tacito*, Rome 1960, pp. 163 ff.; L. Herrmann, *Latomus*, XX (1961), pp. 817 ff.; C. Saumagne, *Revue historique*, CCXXVII (1962), pp. 337 ff.; V. Capocci, *Studia et Documenta Historiae et Iuris*, XXVIII (1962), pp. 65 ff.; H. Fuchs, *Museum Helveticum*, XX (1963), pp. 221 ff.; G.B.A. Fletcher, *Annotations on Tacitus*, Brussels–Berchem 1964, p. 49; M. Sordi, *Il Cristianesimo e Roma*, Bologna 1965, pp. 79 ff.; J.E.A. Crake, *Phoenix*, XIX (1965), pp. 68 f.; W.H.C. Frend, *Martyrdom and Persecution in the Early Church*, Oxford 1965, pp. 161 ff.; R.J. Getty, in: *The Classical Tradition — Literary and Historical Studies in Honor of Harry Caplan*, Ithaca (New York) 1966, pp. 285 ff.; E. Koestermann, *Historia*, XVI (1967), pp. 456 ff.; R. Freudenberger, *Das Verhalten der römischen Behörden gegen die Christen im 2. Jahrhundert*, Munich 1967, pp. 180 ff.; P. Winter, *Journal of Historical Studies*, I (1967), pp. 31 ff.; idem, *Klio*, LII (1970), pp. 497 ff.; R. Renehan, *La Parola del Passato*, XXIII (1968), pp. 368 ff.; T.D. Barnes, *JRS*, LVIII (1968), pp. 34 f.; idem, *Tertullian*, Oxford 1971, pp. 151 f.; L. Herrmann, *Chrestos*, Brussels 1970, pp. 8, 161 f.; J. Molthagen, *Der römische Staat und die Christen im zweiten und dritten Jahrhundert*, Göttingen 1970, pp. 21 ff.; J. Rougé, in: *Mélanges Seston*, Paris 1974, pp. 433 ff.; A. Hamman, in: *Studi Pellegrino*, Turin 1975, pp. 96 ff.; Z. Yavetz, in: *Essays in Honour of C.E. Stevens*,

Westmead 1975, pp. 181 ff.; H. Fuchs, *Museum Helveticum*, XXXII (1975), pp. 61 f.

This passage supplies the earliest evidence of the treatment of the Christians as a group to be differentiated by the Roman government from the main body of the Jewish nation, thus requiring measures that would not include the Jews who remained outside the sphere of Christianity.

The spread of Christianity in Rome began at least some twenty-three years before the fire of 64 C. E.; cf. the commentary to Suetonius, *Divus Claudius*, 25:4 (No. 307). At the time it caused disturbances among the Jewish population of the capital and was followed by the drastic intervention of Claudius. Christianity made further progress in the forties and fifties. Probably the appearance of Paul at Rome caused agitation among both Jews and Christians and accelerated the diffusion of the new belief among non-Jewish circles. Thus by 64 C. E. the existence of the new religion could be a matter of common knowledge at the imperial court of Rome, which availed itself of the fact to put the blame on the Christians. It is almost certain that the Jews as such were not involved in Nero's persecution and there is no evidence that the idea of persecuting them had ever entered his mind. The reference to the inclusion of the Jews in the persecution found in the spurious correspondence between Seneca and Paul stands unsupported by older evidence; cf. *Epistolae Senecae ad Paulum et Pauli ad Senecam ⟨quae vocantur⟩*, ed. C. W. Barlow (*Papers and Monographs of the American Academy in Rome*, 1938), § XI, p. 134: "Christiani et Iudaei quasi machinatores incendii — pro! — supplicio adfecti, quod fieri solet." On the other hand, there is nothing in the ancient sources to suggest that the Jews instigated Nero to persecute the Christians, a view held by, e.g., Klette, Harnack and Frend. It is strongly contradicted by, e.g., Linsenmayer, Hirschfeld, Ed. Meyer, Leon, and Herrmann. For agreement with the latter view, see F. Millar, *JRS*, LVI (1966), p. 233. The principal source held to prove it is Clemens Romanus, *Epistula I ad Corinthios*, 6: τούτοις τοῖς ἀνδράσιν ὁσίως πολιτευσαμένοις συνηθροίσθη πολὺ πλῆθος ἐκλεκτῶν, οἵτινες πολλαῖς αἰκίαις καὶ βασάνοις διὰ ζῆλος παθόντες, ὑπόδειγμα κάλλιστον ἐγένοντο ἐν ἡμῖν. διὰ ζῆλος διωχθεῖσαι γυναῖκες ... This does not confirm it at all, however, and at most may allude to some internal dissension among the Christians themselves, though such an interpretation is more than doubtful. Certainly, none of the Christian sources prior to the late and quite unreliable Commodianus implies a Jewish initiative in Nero's persecution; cf. Commodianus, *Carmen Apologeticum*, 840 ff. (perhaps third century C. E.).

2 *quin iussum incendium crederetur*: Tacitus does not commit himself to the view that it was Nero who personally issued the order to set Rome on fire; cf. Tacitus, *Annales*, XV, 38:1: "sequitur clades, forte an dolo principis incertum (nam utrumque auctores prodidere)"; *ibid.*, 38:7: "nec quisquam defendere audebat, crebris multorum minis restinguere prohibentium, et quia alii palam faces iaciebant atque esse sibi auctorem vociferabantur, sive ut raptus licentius exercerent seu iussu". It seems certain that among the "auctores" who blamed Nero for the fire was Pliny the Elder, one of the authorities used by Tacitus in his *Annales* (I, 69; XIII, 20; XV, 53). Pliny expressly speaks of "Neronis principis incendia" in his *Naturalis Historia*, XVII, 5. This view was also shared by Suetonius (*Nero*, 38:1): "incendit urbem tam palam ..." Cf. also Cassius Dio, LXII, 16:1–18:5.

Ergo abolendo rumori Nero subdidit reos: Tacitus clearly intends his readers to understand that Nero charged the Christians with the burning of Rome. Suetonius does not connect the fire with the condemnation of the Christians. The persecution of the Christians is listed by him among the laudable activities of Nero (*Nero*, 16), while the burning of Rome attributed to the emperor finds its place in a later chapter (*ibid.*, 38), among the misdeeds of Nero. This is to be explained by Suetonius' method of arranging his material. Thus the separation of the two facts by him does not in itself constitute any evidence that they had no connection. Tacitus is the only detailed source for this information, and by his manner of expression ("subdidit reos") he does not leave much room for doubt that he intended to stress the legal interrelation between the fire and the persecution; see the argumentation of Roos against the scepticism on this point of scholars like Dibelius; see the bibliography for this passage.

per flagitia invisos: An allusion to the "Thyestean banquets" and "Oedipean connections"; see H. Janne, *L'Antiquité Classique*, II (1933), pp. 331 ff.; D. Berwig, "Mark Aurel und die Christen", Ph.D. Thesis, Munich 1970, p. 72; A. Henrichs, *Festschrift Johannes Quasten*, I, Münster 1970, pp. 18 ff. See already Plinius, *Epistulae*, X, 96:2: "nomen ipsum, si flagitiis careat, an flagitia cohaerentia nomini puniantur".

Chrestianos: This is the original reading of the Mediceus, and we should probably prefer it to "Christianos"; so, e.g., Fuchs, *locc. cit.* (supra, p. 90); Renehan, *loc. cit.* (supra, p. 90); for Chrestus = Christus, cf. Tertullianus, *Apologeticus*, 3:5; Suetonius, *Divus Claudius*, 25:4 (No. 307). The difficulty of this reading of Tacitus lies in his following mention of "Christus". But it is quite possible that in this form Christus reflects a correction in one of the stages of the transmission by copyists who were more at home with Christus than with Chrestus. For the name Christiani, see E. J. Bickerman, *HTR*, XLII (1949), pp. 109 ff.; H. B. Mattingly, *JTS*, NS, IX (1958), pp. 26 ff.; B. Lifshitz, *Vigiliae Christianae*, XVI (1962), pp. 65 ff.

3 *per procuratorem Pontium Pilatum*: Pilate, like all the other governors of Judaea before the time of Claudius, was officially called "praefectus Iudaeae" and not procurator, as may be seen from the inscription discovered at Caesarea; see A. Frova, *Istituto Lombardo, Rendiconti*, XCV (1961), p. 424 = *Scavi di Caesarea maritima*, Rome 1966, p. 217. For the inscription, see also H. Volkmann, *Gymnasium*, LXXV (1968), pp. 124 ff.; A. Degrassi, *Atti della Accademia Nazionale dei Lincei, Rendiconti*, XIX (1964), pp. 59 ff.; E. Weber, *Bonner Jahrbücher*, CLXXI (1971), pp. 194 ff. This was the proper form of his title, as correctly maintained even before the last discovery by such scholars as O. Hirschfeld, *Die kaiserlichen Verwaltungsbeamten bis auf Diocletian*[2], Berlin 1905, pp. 384 f.; A. H. M. Jones, *Studies in Roman Government and Law*, Oxford 1960, pp. 115 ff. The consistent use of "procurator" or its Greek equivalent ($\dot{\epsilon}\pi i\tau\rho o\pi o\varsigma$) is found only from the time of Claudius onwards; cf., e.g., the official document included in *Ant.*, XX, 14. Thus Tacitus transfers the later terminology to the time of Pilate, and the same is sometimes done by Josephus, e.g., *BJ*, II, 117, 169. See also P. A. Brunt, *Latomus*, XXV (1966), p. 463, n. 3.

4 *correpti*: This implies arrest; see Fuchs, *Vigiliae Christianae, op. cit.* (supra, p. 90); Wlosok, *op. cit.* (supra, p. 90).

qui fatebantur: Did they confess to Christianity or to incendiarism? As Tacitus did not believe that the Christians were responsible for the burning of Rome, it would be natural to assume with the majority of scholars that only the first interpretation should be accepted. Scholars such as Gercke and Momigliano maintain that the historian's ambiguity here reflects the use of contradictory sources, while Clayton supposes that Tacitus' vagueness here is intentional; see the bibliography for this passage. In any case such tantalizing brevity is quite characteristic of Tacitus and cannot always be explained by the diversity of his sources.

haud proinde in crimine incendii quam odio humani generis convicti sunt: I prefer to follow the majority of interpreters (recently, e.g., Fuchs, Heubner and Koestermann against Büchner and Bauer) in accepting "convicti" in spite of the "coniuncti" of the Mediceus.

The meaning of the sentence seems to be that though Christians had originally been brought to the trial as incendiaries, their ultimate conviction was due even more to the general nature of their creed, characterized as it was by hatred of humanity. Tacitus does not give the juridical grounds for the condemnation of the Christians, which could hardly have been based on a hatred of humanity. Until the end of Nero's persecution, incendiarism might have served as the main accusation, but to merit a conviction it would have been enough to be one of the Christians whose alleged misanthropy made them suspect of any crime.

odio humani generis: "Odium humani generis" ($\mu\iota\sigma\alpha\nu\vartheta\rho\omega\pi\iota\alpha$) is the old charge raised against the Jews; cf. Diodorus, XXXIV–XXXV, 1:2 (No. 63); Apion, apud: Josephus, *Contra Apionem*, II, 121 (No. 173); Tacitus, *Historiae*, V, 5 (No. 281). Cf. also Seneca, *De Tranquillitate Animi*, 15:1: "occupat enim nonnumquam odium generis humani"; Plinius, *Naturalis Historia*, VII, 80: "Timonem, hunc quidem etiam in totius odium generis humani evectum." Cf. also W. Nestle, *Klio*, XXI (1927), pp. 91 ff. This is the common interpretation and most natural way of understanding the passage. However a different interpretation is that Tacitus implies here the hatred felt by the human race for Christians (so, e.g., Ed. Meyer, Hitchcock, Getty).

Et pereuntibus addita ludibria: Cf. Clemens Romanus, *loc. cit.*: διὰ ζῆλος διωχθεῖσαι γυναῖκες Δαναΐδες καὶ Δίρκαι, αἰκίσματα δεινὰ καὶ ἀνόσια παθοῦσαι.

XCIII. JUVENAL

c. 60–130 C.E.

*Criticism of the intrusion of foreign elements into the capital of imperial
Rome is frequently expressed by its greatest satirist; for Juvenal, Rome
was fast deteriorating into a Greek city, and, even worse, an oriental
Greek city. The Tiber, as he ironically remarks, was in danger of being
engulfed by the Orontes (Saturae, III, 60 ff.):*

> *non possum ferre, Quirites,*
> *Graecam urbem; quamvis quota portio faecis Achaei?*
> *iam pridem Syrus in Tiberim defluxit Orontes.*

*Juvenal could not tolerate either the pliability of the Greeks or the part
played by the Egyptian or Syrian parvenus in the life of Rome.[1]
Particularly abhorrent were the Egyptians, whose barbarian behaviour
appeared in such glaring contrast to the cultured society of the West
(XV, 110 ff.).[2]*

*It was only to be expected that such a writer would include the Jews
among the targets of his satire. Two main aspects of the contemporary
position of Jews and Judaism emerge from Juvenal's allusions to the
Jews of Rome. One was the spread of Judaism there, which gradually
won over whole families. From among the specifically Jewish customs
Juvenal singles out observance of the Sabbath, which was the first to
gain ground among non-Jews. He also refers to the abstention of Jews
from pork, and finally to their practice of circumcision. Juvenal saw
conversion to Judaism mainly as the flouting of the laws of Rome
aimed at the complete subjugation of its followers to the Jewish law, as*

---

1 Cf. *Saturae*, I, 26 ff.: "cum pars Niliacae plebis, cum verna Canopi/
Crispinus Tyrias umero revocante lacernas/ ventilet aestivum digitis
sudantibus aurum". Cf. also *ibid.*, IV, 23 f.: "hoc tu succinctus patria
quondam, Crispine, papyro?" *ibid.*, I, 103 ff.: "natus ad Euphraten,
molles quod in aure fenestrae/ arguerint, licet ipse negem? sed quinque
tabernae/ quadringenta parant".
See, in general, T. Reekmans, *Ancient Society*, II (1971), pp. 127 ff.;
J. Gérard, *Juvénal et la réalité contemporaine*, Paris 1976, pp. 387 ff.;
W. J. Watts, *Acta Classica*, XIX (1976), pp. 83 ff.

2 On Juvenal's religious views, see J. Beaujeu, *Mélanges d'archéologie,
d'épigraphie et d'histoire offerts à Jérôme Carcopino*, Vendôme 1966, pp.
71 ff.

handed down in the secret volume of Moses. Like Tacitus, Juvenal emphasizes Jewish misanthropy (No. 301).

The second feature relating to the Jews that Juvenal brings into prominence is his picture of them as indigents. They are to be seen begging near the Porta Capena, and he relates that a Jew will interpret dreams for the minutest of coins (No. 299). In his allusion to Agrippa and Berenice (No. 298) Juvenal does not refer to them as Jews, while for him the "Arabarches", the Jew Tiberius Alexander, was an Egyptian (No. 295), as also for Tacitus, Historiae, I, 11 (No. 273).[3]

---

3 I have not found sufficient reason to include in this collection *Saturae*, V, 141: "sed tua nunc Mycale pariat licet", etc., on the assumption that "Migale" (the reading in some of the MSS) might be a Jewish name; cf. R. L. Dunbabin, *Classical Review*, XXXIX (1925), p. 112.

Saturae, I, 127–131 — Clausen

Ipse dies pulchro distinguitur ordine rerum:
sportula, deinde forum iurisque peritus Apollo
atque triumphales, inter quas ausus habere
130 nescio quis titulos Aegyptius atque Arabarches,
cuius ad effigiem non tantum meiiere fas est.

The day itself is marked out by a fine round of business. First comes the dole; then the courts, and Apollo learned in the law, and those triumphal statues among which some Egyptian Arabarch or other has dared to set up his titles; against whose statue more than one kind of nuisance may be committed! (trans. G. G. Ramsay, *LCL*)

127 *Ipse dies…*: The day of the client is divided up by various engagements, including the duty of accompanying the patron to the Forum.
128 *forum iurisque peritus Apollo*: I.e. the Forum built by Augustus, in which there was a famous statue of Apollo; cf. Plinius, *Naturalis Historia*, VII, 183.
129 *atque triumphales*: Scil. *statuas*.
129–130 *inter quas ausus habere nescio quis titulos Aegyptius*: It is commonly assumed that this is Tiberius Julius Alexander. That a personality long dead should serve as a target for satire accords with Juvenal's deliberate practice. Cf. also the commentary to Tacitus, *Historiae*, I, 11 (No. 273); and to *Annales*, XV, 28 (No. 292). After Tiberius Julius Alexander had played his part in the siege of Jerusalem, he continued to enjoy the favour of the Flavian dynasty. The wording of a papyrus from Hibeh may even suggest that he was promoted to the rank of *praefectus praetorio*; cf. *The Hibeh Papyri*, II, 1955 (ed. E. G. Turner), No. 215 (b) ll. 6 ff.: Τιβερίου Ἰουλίου Ἀλεξάνδρου τοῦ ἡγεμο[νεύσαντ]ος, γενομένου καὶ ἐπάρχου πραι[τωρίου] with the interpretation of E. G. Turner, *JRS*, XLIV (1954), pp. 61 ff.; H. G. Pflaum, *Les carrières procuratoriennes équestres sous le Haut-empire romain*, I, Paris 1960, pp. 48 f. See, however, the doubts cast on this interpretation by Syme, II, p. 509, n. 6; cf. also *CPJ*, No. 418b, Fuks's introduction. That a person of Tiberius Alexander's standing received a "triumphalis statua" is not surprising. On Juvenal's attitude to Tiberius Alexander, see also M. Coffey, *Roman Satire*, London 1976, p. 138.
Arabarches: The term is mostly taken to denote an inspector of customs on the eastern side of the Nile; cf. Schürer, III, p. 132, n. 42; *OGIS*, No. 570, n. 3; U. Wilcken, *Griechische Ostraka aus Aegypten und Nubien*, I, Leipzig 1899, pp. 350 f., 597 (another explanation which connects "arabarches" with the Hebrew word ערבון seems less convincing; see V. Burr, *Tiberius Iulius Alexander*, Bonn 1955, p. 87, n. 4). The "arabarches" is identical with the "alabarches", in accordance with the well-known interchange through

dissimilation between ρ and λ; cf. E. Mayser, *Grammatik der griechischen Papyri*, I, Berlin–Leipzig 1923, p. 188; S. G. Kapsomenakis, *Voruntersuchungen zu einer Grammatik der nachchristlichen Zeit*, Munich 1938, p. 45. Although it is not stated in other sources that Alexander himself was arabarch or alabarch, Josephus relates that Alexander's father held this position, cf. *Ant.*, XVIII, 159, 259; XIX, 276; XX, 100. Another Jew of the first century C. E., named Demetrius, also fulfilled that function (*Ant.*, XX, 147). As Tcherikover sums up (Prolegomena to *CPJ*, I, p. 49, n. 4): "At any rate it appears that the alabarchs were high officials dealing with finance and that in the early Roman period such an office was sometimes bestowed on wealthy Alexandrian Jews". The institution of the alabarchy is still mentioned by the fourth-century poet Palladas; see *Anthologia Graeca*, XI, 383: ἐξότε γὰρ καὶ τοῦτον ὄνον χαλεπὸς χρόνος ἔσχεν, ἐξ ἀλαβαρχείης γραμματικοῦ γέγονεν.

296

Saturae, III, 10–18 — Clausen = F170aR

Sed dum tota domus raeda componitur una,
substitit ad veteres arcus madidamque Capenam.
Hic, ubi nocturnae Numa constituebat amicae
(nunc sacri fontis nemus et delubra locantur
Iudaeis, quorum cophinus fenumque supellex;
15 omnis enim populo mercedem pendere iussa est
arbor et eiectis mendicat silva Camenis),
in vallem Egeriae descendimus et speluncas
dissimiles veris.

But while all his goods and chattels were being packed upon a single wagon, my friend halted at the dripping archway of the old Porta Capena. Here Numa held his nightly assignations with his mistress; but now the holy fount and grove and shrine are let out to Jews, who possess a basket and a truss of hay for all their furnishings. For as every tree nowadays has to pay toll to the people, the Muses have been ejected, and the wood has to go a-begging. We go down to the Valley of Egeria, and into the caves so unlike to nature.

(trans. G. G. Ramsay, *LCL*)

10 *Sed dum tota domus raeda componitur una*: From the farewell monologue of Umbricius who was leaving Rome in disgust; see G. Highet, *Juvenal the Satirist*, Oxford 1954, pp. 65 ff.; A. Serafini, *Studio sulla satira di Giovenale*, Bari 1957, pp. 32 ff. See also F. Jacoby, *Hermes*, LXXXVII (1959), pp. 449 ff.

11 *madidamque Capenam*: Porta Capena was one of the gates in the Servian wall. It was the starting point of the Via Appia, which led to Capua; cf. S. B. Platner & T. Ashby, *A Topographical Dictionary of Ancient Rome*, Oxford 1929, p. 405. The portal is described here as "madida", since a branch of the Aqua Marcia terminated above it; cf. Frontinus, *De Aquaeductu Urbis Romae*, I, 19.

13 f. *nunc sacri fontis nemus et delubra locantur Iudaeis ...*: Cf. the scholia: "templa Camenarum Iudaeis locabantur". Some scholars even explain the existence of a Jewish settlement there by the proximity to running water, since it was the Jewish practice to construct synagogues at such sites. For this practice, cf. *Ant.*, XIV, 258 (at Halicarnassus); Acts xvi : 13; see also E. L. Sukenik, *Ancient Synagogues in Palestine and Greece*, London 1934, pp. 49 f.; for the supply of water to synagogues, cf. also *CPJ*, No. 432; L. Robert, *Revue de Philologie*, XXXII (1958), pp. 43 ff. (at Side in Pamphylia). Mommsen interpreted the letting of the grove of Egeria to Jews as implying the building of a synagogue; see Mommsen, *Gesammelte Schriften*, III, Berlin 1907, p. 419, n. 3. Cf. also G. La Piana, *HTR*, XX (1927), p. 221, referring to the Jewish settlement outside Porta Capena as the largest of the Jewish quarters. However the words of Juvenal do not seem to imply a permanent Jewish quarter but only a settlement of vagrant beggars; see Leon, p. 137. Juvenal's remarks concerning the letting of sanctuaries to Jews accord with the general tone of the satire, which bewails the fact that Rome was becoming a city of foreigners; see also W. S. Anderson, *YCS*, XV (1957), pp. 62 ff.

14 *quorum cophinus fenumque supellex*: Cf. also *Saturae*, VI (No. 299). The scholiast on Satire VI explains the basket and the hay as a reference to the Jewish custom of keeping food warm on Sabbath in this way, and his explanation sounds very plausible; see Friedländer's commentary *ad loc.*; J. A. Hild, *REJ*, XI (1885), p. 187, n. 1; G. Hirst, *Classical Review*, XXXVIII (1924), p. 171; R. L. Dunbabin, *Classical Review*, XXXIX (1925), p. 112; A. Cameron, *Classical Review*, XL (1926), pp. 62 f. The *cophinus* is also used as a symbol of the Jews in Sidonius Apollinaris, *Epistulae*, VII, 6: " ... Pharao incedat cum diademate, Israelita cum cophino." See also B. L. Ullman, in: *The Classical Tradition — Literary and Historical Studies in Honor of Harry Caplan*, ed. L. Wallach, Ithaca (New York) 1966, p. 276. Ullman, referring to Iuvenalis, XI, 70 f., and Martialis, III, 47 : 14, suggests that the Jews were peddling eggs at the Porta Capena.

16 *et eiectis mendicat silva Camenis*: The grove itself, after the expulsion of the Camenae, has become a beggar.

297

Saturae, III, 290–296 — Clausen = F 170b R

> Stat contra starique iubet. Parere necesse est;
> nam quid agas, cum te furiosus cogat et idem
> fortior? "Unde venis," exclamat, "cuius aceto,

cuius conche tumes? Quis tecum sectile porrum
sutor et elixi vervecis labra comedit?
295 Nil mihi respondes? aut dic aut accipe calcem.
Ede ubi consistas: in qua te quaero proseucha?"

293 *concha* Φ

The fellow stands up against me, and bids me halt; obey I must. What
else can you do when attacked by a madman stronger than yourself?
"Where are you from?" shouts he; "whose vinegar, whose beans
have blown you out? With what cobbler have you been munching cut
leeks and boiled wether's chaps? — What sirrah, no answer? Speak
out, or take that upon your shins! Say, where is your stand? In what
prayer-house shall I find you?" (trans. G. G. Ramsay, *LCL*)

291 *nam quid agas*: This is another episode illustrating the troubles met
with in Rome, an unprovoked fray in which Umbricius had become involved.
296 *Ede ubi consistas: in qua te quaero proseucha?*: I.e. where is your stand
for begging? For the connection between beggars and the synagogue, cf.
Cleomedes, *De Motu Circulari*, II, 1:91 (No. 333). For *proseucha* (προσευχή)
designating the Jewish prayer-house, cf. the commentary to Apion, apud:
Josephus, *Contra Apionem*, II, 10 (No. 164). Cf. also Artemidorus,
Onirocritica, III, 53 (No. 395). For a prayer-house in Rome itself, cf. *CII*, No.
531: "de aggere a proseucha".

298

Saturae, VI, 153–160 — Clausen = F171aR

Mense quidem brumae, cum iam mercator Iason
clausus et armatis obstat casa candida nautis,
155 grandia tolluntur crystallina, maxima rursus
murrina, deinde adamas notissimus et Beronices
in digito factus pretiosior. Hunc dedit olim
barbarus incestae, dedit hunc Agrippa sorori,
observant ubi festa mero pede sabbata reges
160 et vetus indulget senibus clementia porcis.

153 *cum*] *quo* PRA Arou   156 *beronices*] *beronicis* Φ   *bernices* PA Arou
bernicis F   158 *dedit hunc*] *gestare* Housman   159 *mero*] *nudo* PRO Arou

Then in the winter time, when the merchant Jason is shut out from
view, and his armed sailors are blocked out by the white booths, she
will carry off huge crystal vases, vases bigger still of agate, and finally
a diamond of great renown, made precious by the finger of Berenice.

It was given as a present long ago by the barbarian Agrippa to his incestuous sister, in that country where kings celebrate festal sabbaths with bare feet, and where a long-established clemency suffers pigs to attain old age.   (trans. G. G. Ramsay, *LCL*)

The extract is taken from Juvenal's great satire on marriage.

156 f.   *et Beronices in digito factus pretiosior* ...: For Berenice, the sister of Agrippa II, cf. Quintilianus, IV, 1 : 19 (No. 231); Tacitus, *Historiae*, II, 2 (No. 275).

157 f.   *dedit olim barbarus incestae*: On the rumoured sexual relations between Agrippa and Berenice, cf. *Ant.*, XX, 145: φήμης ἐπισχούσης, ὅτι τἀδελφῷ συνείη. For a different interpretation of this passage, see H. J. Rose, *Harvard Studies in Classical Philology*, XLVII (1936), p. 14. Rose shares Housman's feeling that the repetition here of "hunc" is not compatible with the art of Juvenal, but is not ready to accept the emendation *gestare*. He suggests that "barbarus" and "incesta" refer not to Agrippa and Berenice, but to the last of the Ptolemies and Cleopatra VII. In that case Juvenal would here list two stages of the diamond's pedigree: it first belonged to Cleopatra and then passed to Berenice. This solution, though ingenious, is hard to accept in view of the gossip about the incestuous relations between Agrippa and Berenice, as attested by Josephus. A reference to the connection between Cleopatra and her brother seems far-fetched. See also E. Mireaux, *La reine Bérénice*, Paris 1951, pp. 88 ff.; G. H. Macurdy, *AJP*, LVI (1935), pp. 249 f.

159   *observant ubi festa mero pede sabbata reges*: This should be connected with the Jewish custom of ascending the Temple Mount barefoot, cf. *M. Berakhot*, ix : 5. For a suggestion that Juvenal here confuses the Sabbath with the Day of Atonement, on which it was forbidden to Jews to wear shoes, see Heinrich Lewy, *Philologus*, LXXXIV (1929), pp. 390 f.

160   *et vetus indulget senibus clementia porcis*: For the interpretation put on the Jewish abstention from pork, cf. Petronius (No. 195). See also Sextus Empiricus, *Hypotyposes*, III, 222–223 (No. 334); Macrobius, *Saturnalia*, II, 4 : 11 (No. 543). For pork as common food in Rome at that time, see Highet, *op. cit.* (supra, p. 97), pp. 77 f.; p. 258, n. 6. "Senibus" should be taken proleptically (Friedländer), i.e. because of the Jewish "clementia" the pigs will become old.

299

Saturae, VI, 542–547 — Clausen = F171bR

Cum dedit ille locum, cophino fenoque relicto
arcanam Iudaea tremens mendicat in aurem,
interpres legum Solymarum et magna sacerdos
545 arboris ac summi fida internuntia caeli.

Implet et illa manum, sed parcius; aere minuto
qualiacumque voles Iudaei somnia vendunt.

No sooner has that fellow departed than a palsied Jewess, leaving her
basket and her truss of hay, comes begging to her secret ear; she is an
interpreter of the laws of Jerusalem, a high priestess of the tree, a
trusty go-between of highest heaven. She, too, fills her palm, but
more sparingly, for a Jew will tell you dreams of any kind you please
for the minutest of coins. (trans. G. G. Ramsay, *LCL*)

542 *Cum dedit ille locum*: In his indictment of the superstition of Roman
women the poet makes a Jewish interpretress of dreams appear after
representatives of the Egyptian cults.
cophino fenoque relicto: Cf. Iuvenalis, *Saturae*, III, 14 (No. 296). The scholia
state: "ideo dixit 'faenumque supellex', quod his pulmentaria sua et calidam
aquam die sabbati servare consuerunt".
543 *mendicat in aurem*: Cf. Iuvenalis, *Saturae*, III, 16 (No. 296): "eiectis
mendicat silva Camenis". See also below, l. 546: "aere minuto", etc. Again
the Jews are represented by Juvenal as beggars. Cf. also Martialis, XII, 57: 13
(No. 246): "a matre doctus nec rogare Iudaeus". For the economic conditions
of Roman Jews, see Juster, II, p. 320; Leon, pp. 233 ff.
arcanam ... in aurem: "So viel als heimlich ins Ohr" (Friedländer).
544 *interpres legum Solymarum*: To strengthen the effect of the parody the
Jewess is designated by three high-sounding titles. For the view that there is
perhaps an allusion in "interpres legum" to interpreters of Jewish law, and in
"magna sacerdos arboris" to the High Priest, see J. (H.) Lewy, *Studies in
Jewish Hellenism* (1960), pp. 202 f. (in Hebrew). However, "sacerdos
arboris" should rather be interpreted by reference to Iuvenalis, *Saturae*, III,
16 (No. 296). See also L. Herrmann, *REA*, XLII (1940 = *Mélanges Radet*),
pp. 448 f.; Ullman, *op. cit.* (supra, p. 98), p. 276. The comments of
Reitzenstein suggesting a connection with Jewish-Phrygian syncretistic cults
do not carry conviction; see R. Reitzenstein, *Die hellenistischen
Mysterienreligionen*[3], Leipzig–Berlin 1927, pp. 145 f.
545 *ac summi fida internuntia caeli*: For the worship of the "caelum" by
Jews, cf. Iuvenalis, *Saturae*, XIV, 97 (No. 301). See Bernays, II, p. 79.

300

Saturae, VIII, 158–162 — Clausen

Sed cum pervigiles placet instaurare popinas,
obvius adsiduo Syrophoenix udus amomo

159–160 syrophoenix–idymaeae om. F   159 udus] unctus A Vat. Reg. 2029 et

160 currit, Idymaeae Syrophoenix incola portae
    hospitis adfectu dominum regemque salutat,
    et cum venali Cyane succincta lagona.

(*unc* in ras.) P   160 om. AL, del. Jahn   162 *lagona*] *lagoena* Φ

And when it pleases him to go back to the all-night tavern, a
Syro-Phoenician runs forth to meet him — a denizen of the Idumaean
gate perpetually drenched in perfumes — and salutes him as lord and
prince with all the airs of a host; and with him comes Cyane, her dress
tucked up, carrying a flagon of wine for sale.

(trans. G. G. Ramsay, *LCL*)

159 *Syrophoenix*: Cf. Plinius, *Naturalis Historia*, VII, 201.
160 *Idymaeae ... incola portae*: The emigration of Idumaeans — at least to
Egypt — had already begun in the Hellenistic age; cf. the introduction to
Mnaseas of Patara, Vol. I, p. 98. However, after their conversion in the time
of John Hyrcanus, in the twenties of the second century B.C.E., the
Idumaeans should be regarded as full Jews. The Latin poets frequently
confused Judaea with Idumaea in their writings; cf. Vergilius, *Georgica*, III,
12 (No. 125) and the introduction to the text. Yet it is doubtful whether the
Idumaean gate should be identified with the Porta Capena, as suggested by
Ullman, *op. cit.* (supra, p. 98), p. 277, and also by L. Herrmann, *Chrestos*,
Brussels 1970, p. 153.

301

Saturae, XIV, 96–106 — Clausen = F172R

Quidam sortiti metuentem sabbata patrem
nil praeter nubes et caeli numen adorant,
nec distare putant humana carne suillam,
qua pater abstinuit, mox et praeputia ponunt;
100 Romanas autem soliti contemnere leges
Iudaicum ediscunt et servant ac metuunt ius,
tradidit arcano quodcumque volumine Moyses:
non monstrare vias eadem nisi sacra colenti,
quaesitum ad fontem solos deducere verpos.
105 Sed pater in causa, cui septima quaeque fuit lux
ignava et partem vitae non attigit ullam.

Some who have had a father who reveres the Sabbath, worship
nothing but the clouds, and the divinity of the heavens, and see no

difference between eating swine's flesh, from which their father abstained, and that of man; and in time they take to circumcision. Having been wont to flout the laws of Rome, they learn and practice and revere the Jewish law, and all that Moses handed down in his secret tome, forbidding to point out the way to any not worshipping the same rites, and conducting none but the circumcised to the desired fountain. For all which the father was to blame, who gave up every seventh day to idleness, keeping it apart from all the concerns of life. (trans. G. G. Ramsay, *LCL*)

The passage occurs in a satire whose main theme is the bad influence that the vices of parents have on their children. See now J. P. Stein, *Classical Philology*, LXV (1970), pp. 34 ff.

96 *metuentem sabbata patrem*: Cf. 1. 101: "Iudaicum ... metuunt ius". Apparently it is not by chance that *metuere* occurs twice in this passage. Bernays already suggested a connection between the "metuentes" of Juvenal and the expression found in Jewish sources: the "Fearers of God" in the Bible (ירֵאי אדני), the "Fearers of Heaven" (ירֵאי שמים) in the midrashic and talmudic literature, the σεβόμενοι or φοβούμενοι τὸν θεόν in the New Testament, and in one place in the *Antiquities* of Josephus, as well as the "metuentes" in some Latin inscriptions; see Bernays, II, pp. 71 ff. Bernays considers that all these designations refer to the same category of persons, i.e. gentiles attracted by Judaism. Subsequent scholars have defined these Jewish "sympathizers" more specifically. They are considered to be gentiles drawn to Jewish monotheism who kept some of the observances of Judaism, mainly celebration of the Sabbath and the abstention from prohibited food, but who did not go to the length of becoming full proselytes and did not undergo the rite of circumcision. It is above all to this category of persons that Josephus refers in *Contra Apionem*, II, 282, and Tertullian in *Ad Nationes*, I, 13. Circumcision was only the last phase in the conversion of Izates of Adiabene. He was originally persuaded by the Jewish merchant Ananias to forgo the rite, which might anger his subjects, since it would be possible for him to worship God without being circumcised; cf. *Ant.*, XX, 41: δυνάμενον δ' αὐτὸν ἔφη καὶ χωρὶς τῆς περιτομῆς τὸ θεῖον σέβειν, εἴγε πάντως κέκρικε ζηλοῦν τὰ πάτρια τῶν Ἰουδαίων.

See also [H.] Graetz, *Die jüdischen Proselyten im Römerreiche unter den Kaisern Domitian, Nerva, Trajan und Hadrian*, Breslau 1884, p. 13; Schürer, III, pp. 172 ff.; Juster, I, pp. 274 ff.; A. Deissmann, *Licht vom Osten*[4], Tübingen 1923, p. 391; Moore, I, pp. 232 f., 325; W. Fink, *Der Einfluss der jüdischen Religion auf die griechisch-römische*, Bonn 1932, pp. 11 f.; B. J. Bamberger, *Proselytism in the Talmudic Period*, Cincinnati 1939, pp. 135 f.; E. Lerle, *Proselytenwerbung und Urchristentum*, Berlin 1960, p. 28; I. Heinemann, *Zion*, IV (1939), p. 269, n. 1 (in Hebrew). Heinemann accepts in general this view, though he is aware that ירֵאי שמים is not an exclusive designation for sympathizers and may sometimes denote full proselytes and observant Jews as well.

Dissenting voices have been raised also. Thus, it is maintained that the φοβούμενοι and the σεβόμενοι are just προσήλυτοι; see A. Bertholet, *Die Stellung der Israeliten und der Juden zu den Fremden*, Freiburg–Leipzig 1896, pp. 328 ff. On the other hand, it is argued that there is insufficient evidence that the words have any technical sense; see Lake, in: F. J. Foakes Jackson & K. Lake, *The Beginnings of Christianity*, Part I, Vol. V, London 1933, pp. 84 ff.; see also L. H. Feldman, *TAPA*, LXXXI (1950), pp. 200 ff.; E. M. Smallwood, *JTS*, NS, X (1959), pp. 330 f.; N. J. McEleney, *NTS*, XX (1974), pp. 325 ff. Lake, however, admits that the question affects the use of words rather than the facts of history (Foakes Jackson & Lake, *op. cit.*, p. 87). He agrees that φοβούμενος τὸν θεόν and σεβόμενος τὸν θεόν are technical terms applied to this category of persons in the Acts of the Apostles, yet qualifies this by remarking that there are well-known Old Testament phrases which do not bear any technical meaning. However, Lake ignores the midrashic and talmudic evidence, which seems to be decisive on this point. These sources clearly distinguish not only between Jews and "God-fearers" (יראי שמים), but expressly set the last-mentioned in a category apart from the full-fledged proselytes (גרי צדק); cf., e.g., *Mechilta d'Rabbi Ismael*, Tractate Neziqin, xviii (ed. Horovitz–Rabin, p. 312). Here three different categories are mentioned successively: the religious proselytes, the repentant sinners and the God-fearers: וזה יקרא בשם יעקב, אלו גרי צדק וזה יכתוב ידו לד', אלו בעלי תשובה ובשם ישראל יכנה, אלו יראי־שמים. See also *Midrash Tehillim*, xxii:29 (ed. Buber, p. 195): יראי ד' הללוהו, ר' יהושע בן לוי אמר אלו יראי שמים, ר' שמואל בר נחמני אמר אלו גרי הצדק; *Midrash Devarim Rabba*, ii, concerning a Roman noble, martyred for the sake of Judaism, who is designated ירא שמים before he underwent circumcision; *TP Megilla*, iii, 74a; *Bereshit Rabba*, 28 (ed. Theodor, p. 264); *Pesiqta Rabbati*, p. 180a (ed. Friedman): וכל גרים המתגיירים בעולם וכל ירא שמים שיש בעולם. For the study of the relevant midrashic and talmudic material, see I. Lévi, *REJ*, L (1905), pp. 1 ff.; LI (1906), pp. 29 ff.; Strack & Billerbeck, II, pp. 715 ff.; M. Guttmann, *Das Judentum und seine Umwelt*, I, Berlin 1927, pp. 70 f.; Bamberger, *op. cit.* (supra, p. 103), pp. 135 ff.; S. Lieberman, *Greek in Jewish Palestine*, New York 1942, pp. 68 ff. Feldman also admits that in talmudic literature as early as the *Mekhilta* there exists a definite term for "sympathizers", i.e. יראי שמים; cf. Feldman, *op. cit.*, pp. 207 f. However Feldman qualifies his view when he denies the existence of such a term in sources outside of the Midrash and Talmud.

The second most important evidence, that of the New Testament, is confined to the text of Acts, where the expressions φοβούμενοι τὸν θεόν and σεβόμενοι τὸν θεόν occur a number of times. For a recent discussion, see K. Romaniuk, *Aegyptus*, XLIV (1964), pp. 66 ff.; G. Theissen, *ZNTW*, LXV (1974), pp. 264 ff.

The main passages are the following: Acts x:1 f., 22, where the centurion Cornelius, clearly not a full proselyte, is denoted as φοβούμενος τὸν θεόν; Acts xiii:16: ἄνδρες Ἰσραηλῖται καὶ οἱ φοβούμενοι τὸν θεόν; Acts xiii:26: Ἄνδρες ἀδελφοί, υἱοὶ γένους Ἀβραὰμ καὶ οἱ ἐν ὑμῖν φοβούμενοι τὸν θεόν;

Juvenal

Acts x:35: ἀλλ᾽ ἐν παντὶ ἔθνει ὁ φοβούμενος αὐτὸν καὶ ἐργαζόμενος δικαιοσύνην δεκτὸς αὐτῷ ἐστιν.

While these passages have φοβούμενοι τὸν θεόν, others have σεβόμενοι τὸν θεόν, as in Acts xvi:14: καί τις γυνὴ ὀνόματι Λυδία, πορφυρόπωλις πόλεως Θυατίρων, σεβομένη τὸν θεόν; Acts xviii:7: καὶ μεταβὰς ἐκεῖθεν ἦλθεν εἰς οἰκίαν τινὸς ὀνόματι Τιτίου Ἰούστου σεβομένου τὸν θεόν.

Even more important for the quasi-technical character of the designation is that other passages in Acts denote such persons without qualification as σεβόμενοι (or φοβούμενοι), omitting τὸν θεόν; cf. Acts xiii:50: οἱ δὲ Ἰουδαῖοι παρώτρυναν τὰς σεβομένας γυναῖκας τὰς εὐσχήμονας καὶ τοὺς πρώτους τῆς πόλεως; Acts xvii:4: τῶν τε σεβομένων Ἑλλήνων πλῆθος πολύ; Acts xvii:17: διελέγετο μὲν οὖν ἐν τῇ συναγωγῇ τοῖς Ἰουδαίοις καὶ τοῖς σεβομένοις. Though Acts does not distinguish expressly between proselytes and "sympathizers" as do the Midrash and the Talmud, the expressions φοβούμενοι or σεβόμενοι τὸν θεόν seem to denote the latter category, while προσήλυτοι designates the first group (Acts ii:11; vi:5). The one place where the expression τῶν σεβομένων προσηλύτων occurs (Acts xiii:43) may be accounted for by the insertion of a gloss; cf. E. Haenchen, *Die Apostelgeschichte*[13], Göttingen 1961, p. 355, n. 5.

The occurrence in Iustinus, *Dialogus cum Tryphone*, of φοβούμενοι τὸν θεόν is to be explained by a dependence on Acts; cf. *Dialogus cum Tryphone*, 10: καὶ πείθειν ἡμᾶς ἐπιχειρεῖτε ὡς εἰδότες τὸν θεόν, μηδὲν πράσσοντες ὧν οἱ φοβούμενοι τὸν θεόν.

The σεβόμενοι τὸν θεόν are mentioned also by Josephus, *Ant.*, XIV, 110: Θαυμάσῃ δὲ μηδείς, εἰ τοσοῦτος ἦν πλοῦτος ἐν τῷ ἡμετέρῳ ἱερῷ, πάντων τῶν κατὰ τὴν οἰκουμένην Ἰουδαίων καὶ σεβομένων τὸν θεόν, ἔτι δὲ καὶ τῶν ἀπὸ τῆς Ἀσίας καὶ τῆς Εὐρώπης εἰς αὐτὸ συμφερόντων ἐκ πολλῶν πάνυ χρόνων. Marcus renders this into English in the Loeb edition as: "But no one need wonder that there was so much wealth in our temple for all the Jews throughout the habitable world and those who worshipped God, even those from Asia and Europe, had been contributing to it for a very long time". For a justification of the translation from the aspects of both Greek usage and subject matter, see R. Marcus, *Jewish Social Studies*, XIV (1952), pp. 247 ff.; H. Bellen, *Jahrbuch für Antike und Christentum*, VIII–IX (1965–1966), p. 173, n. 19.

Less clear is the evidence from Greek inscriptions, which so far yield no evidence concerning the φοβούμενοι or σεβόμενοι τὸν θεόν. Yet it has been surmised that inscriptions using the designation θεοσεβεῖς point in the same direction; cf., e.g., *Corpus Inscriptionum Graecarum*, No. 2924 = L. Robert, *Études Anatoliennes*, Paris 1937, p. 409 (from Tralles in Asia Minor, third century C.E.) = Lifshitz, No. 30; *SEG*, IV, No. 441 = A. Deissmann, *Licht vom Osten*⁴, Tübingen 1923, pp. 391 f. = *CII*, No. 748 — on this inscription, cf. also B. Schwank, *Biblische Zeitschrift*, XIII (1969), pp. 262 f.; L. Robert, *Nouvelles inscriptions de Sardes*, Paris 1964, p. 39, Nos. 4–5 = Lifshitz, Nos. 17–18; *IG*, Vol. XII, Part 1, No. 593 (from Rhodes). For the possibility that the θεοσεβεῖς are to be identified with the "sympathizers", cf. Schürer, III, p. 174, n. 70; B. Lifshitz, *Journal for the Study of Judaism*, I (1970), pp. 77 ff.;

Bellen, *op. cit.* (supra, p. 105), pp. 171 ff. Bellen also interprets in this way inscriptional material from the kingdom of the Bosporus. On the other hand, Robert is now of the opinion that the ϑεοσεβεῖς are Jews; cf. L. Robert, *Nouvelles inscriptions de Sardes, op. cit.*, pp. 39 ff. See, however, the argumentation of Lifshitz, *loc. cit.*, and H. Hommel, *Istanbuler Mitteilungen*, XXV (1975), pp. 167 ff.

There are references to "metuentes" in Latin epitaphs, which, like the σεβόμενοι in Acts, omit to mention the object of worship; cf. *CII*, Nos. 5, 285, 529. These inscriptions have on sufficient ground been connected with the Jewish "sympathizers"; cf. Schürer, III, p. 174, n. 70; G. La Piana, *HTR*, XX (1927), pp. 391 f.; *CII*, I, p. LXIV; Simon, p. 331; K. G. Kuhn & H. Stegemann, PW, Suppl. IX (1962), p. 1266. This connection is denied by Leon, p. 253. Against the attribution of "metuentes" in these inscriptions to Jewish "sympathizers", Feldman adduces *CIL*, VI, No. 390: "domini metuens I(ovi) O(ptimo) M(aximo) l(ibens) m(erito) sacr(um)"; cf. Feldman, *op. cit.* (supra, p. 104), p. 203. This, as well as the phrase in *Sylloge*, No. 557, 1.7: σε[β]ομένοις Ἀπ[όλλωνα], are certainly of a different kind, since they both mention the object of worship. On the other hand, plain "metuentes" or σεβόμενοι seems to be an abridgement of the fuller Jewish formula, and it is hard to conceive that either *metuens* or σεβόμενος is used in the general sense of "religious".

The Iranian name for Christians (*tarsākān* in Pehlewi), which derives from "Fear [of God]", has been connected with the circles of Jewish God-fearers, who supplied many recruits for nascent Christianity and were largely the Christians with whom the Iranian people came into contact; see S. Pines, "The Iranian Name for Christians and the 'God-Fearers'", *Proceedings of the Israel Academy of Sciences and Humanities*, Vol. II, No. 7 (1968), pp. 143 ff. For the view that there is a direct allusion to the God-fearers also in Commodianus, *Instructiones*, I, 24:11 ff.: "Quid in synagoga decurris saepe bifarius? ... Exis inde foris, iterum tu fana requiris", and that "qui timent" in I, 25, translates the φοβούμενοι, see K. Thraede, *Jahrbuch für Antike und Christentum*, II (1959), pp. 96 ff.; cf. also J. Martin, *Traditio*, XIII (1957), p. 17. On the term φοβούμενοι used by the astrological writer Rhetorius, see also W. Kroll, *Klio*, XVIII (1923), p. 224. Thus it seems that Juvenal uses the verb *metuere* in connection with people who had leanings towards Judaism because of their very common designation as "God-fearers".

On the God-fearers in general, see F. Siegert, *Journal for the Study of Judaism*, IV (1973), pp. 109 ff.

sabbata: The Sabbath seems to have had a special attraction for gentiles. Josephus adduces the widespread observance of the Sabbath as the first instance of the enthusiasm felt by many people for Jewish religious practices; see *Contra Apionem*, II, 282: οὐδ' ἔστιν οὐ πόλις Ἑλλήνων οὐδητισοῦν οὐδὲ βάρβαρον οὐδὲ ἓν ἔθνος, ἔνθα μὴ τὸ τῆς ἑβδομάδος, ἣν ἀργοῦμεν ἡμεῖς, τὸ ἔθος διαπεφοίτηκεν. Philo also takes pride in the universal respect shown for the sacred day (*Vita Mosis*, II, 21). The frequency with which the Sabbath was observed by the gentile population is illustrated by documents from Egypt testifying to the tremendous diffusion of the name Sambathion, deriving from Sabbath (*CPJ*, Section XIII). The existence of a syncretistic community of "Sabbatistae" at Elaeusa in Cilicia points in the same direction (*OGIS*, No. 573). The central position that the Sabbath held in Jewish religious life is shown also by the name "Sabbatheion" for synagogue; cf. *Ant.*, XVI, 164. For the adoption of Sabbath observance by gentiles, cf. also Tertullianus, *Ad Nationes*, I, 13. See also Fink, *op. cit.* (supra, p. 103), pp. 14 ff.

97 *nil praeter nubes*: It has been aptly remarked that "nubes" here has a satiric nuance, "to throw into relief the nebulous nature of such a God of heaven as opposed to the sharply defined outlines of the gods of Greece and Rome"; see J. E. B. Mayor, *Thirteen Satires of Juvenal with a Commentary*, II², London–Cambridge 1878, p. 305 (the commentary *ad loc.*).

100 *Romanas autem soliti contemnere leges*: Cf. Tacitus, *Historiae*, V, 5 : 2 (No. 281): "nec quidquam prius imbuuntur quam contemnere deos".

102 *tradidit arcano quodcumque volumine Moyses*: Use of the indefinite relative pronoun implies that there are many versions of what is written in the Book of Moses, but that its general purport is to inculcate hatred towards all who do not adhere to Judaism. In labelling the Book of Moses, a "secret" work Juvenal is casting on Judaism the disrepute that attached to esoteric religious societies, while pointing out the danger inherent in its exercise; see Lewy, *op. cit.* (supra, p. 101).

103 f. *non monstrare vias ... quaesitum ad fontem solos deducere verpos*: It is customary to refer in this connection to Seneca, *De Beneficiis*, IV, 29 : 1; idem, *Epistulae Morales*, XCV, 51; and to Cicero, *De Officiis*, III, 54. Juvenal could also have had in mind the ceremony of baptism, which, in conjunction with circumcision, were the main acts undertaken on becoming a Jew; see Lewy, *op. cit.* (supra, p. 101), pp. 194 f.; cf. Epictetus, apud: Arrianus, *Dissertationes*, II, 19 : 19–21 (No. 254). The same idea is already suggested by the scholiast who explains "quaesitum ad fontem" by "ubi baptizantur". Rose's comments on the passage and his attempt to find Old Testament references in Juvenal are rather far-fetched; see H. J. Rose, *The Classical Review*, XLV (1931), p. 127.

104 The word "verpos" for circumcised is much favoured by Martial; cf. Martialis, XI, 94 (No. 245). Cf. also the "verpus Priapus" in Catullus, XLVII, 4, where, however, not a Jew but Piso the father-in-law of Caesar is implied; see W. Kroll, *C. Valerius Catullus*², Leipzig–Berlin 1929, p. 87; C. J. Fordyce, *Catullus — A Commentary*, Oxford 1961, pp. 210 ff.

XCIV. SUETONIUS

c. 69 C.E. to the first half of the second century C.E.

In his Lives of the Caesars Suetonius gives some valuable information about Jews in the early imperial period, and for part of the data is the only source. This applies to his statements concerning the mourning among the Jews at the death of Julius Caesar (No. 302); the attitude of Augustus to Judaism (No. 304); the anecdote about Tiberius and the Jewish grammaticus at Rhodes (No. 305); the promise given to Nero about the kingdom of Jerusalem (No. 309); and finally the investigation of the nonagenarian regarding payment of the "Jewish tax" in the reign of Domitian (No. 320). Other incidents recorded by Suetonius are paralleled elsewhere, mainly in the accounts of Tacitus and Cassius Dio.

Suetonius does not explicitly state his views about Jews or Judaism, as he does concerning Christianity (Nero, 16: "afflicti suppliciis Christiani, genus hominum superstitionis novae et maleficae").[1] Nor does he censure anywhere the diffusion of oriental cults in Rome. It is only possible to say that Suetonius was much attached to Roman religious traditions. Thus, while he writes of the aversion of his model emperor, Augustus, to both the Jewish and the Egyptian cults (No. 304), he recounts the connection of a bad emperor like Nero with both the "Dea Syria" (Nero, 56) and the Magi (ibid., 34); likewise he informs us that Otho was attached to the cult of Isis (Otho, 12).[2] Hence foreign cults seem associated in the mind of Suetonius with the so-called bad emperors, while Suetonius himself implicitly endorses the view of the great Augustus.[3] Nevertheless, Vespasian, also a "good" emperor, did not abstain from visiting the temple of Serapis (Divus Vespasianus, 7).

---

1 Describing the expulsion of the Jews from Rome under Claudius (No. 307), Suetonius does not yet distinguish between Jews and Christians. On the other hand, when narrating the steps taken by Nero against the Christians (*Nero*, 16:2), he no longer confuses them with Jews.

2 Cf. also Suetonius, *Vitellius*, 14: "vaticinante Chatta muliere".

3 On the religion of the Caesars as reflected in the work of Suetonius, see F. Della Corte, *Suetonio eques Romanus*², Florence 1967, pp. 55 ff.

Divus Iulius, 84:5 — Ihm = F183R

In summo publico luctu exterarum gentium multitudo circulatim suo
quaeque more lamentata est praecipueque Iudaei, qui etiam noctibus
continuis bustum frequentarunt.

At the height of the public grief a throng of foreigners went about
lamenting each after the fashion of his country, above all the Jews,
who even flocked to the funeral-pyre for several successive nights.

(trans. J.C. Rolfe, *LCL*)

praecipueque Iudaei: There were a number of reasons for the sorrow evinced
by the Jews of Rome at the assassination of Julius Caesar. He had been the
enemy of Pompey, who had put an end to Jewish independence,
sacrilegiously entered the Holy of Holies in the Temple and curtailed the
territory of Judaea. Hence from the outbreak of the civil war Caesar
considered the Jews his natural allies. He even intended to put the former
Jewish king, Aristobulus II, in command of Roman forces against Pompey in
Judaea. The plan was not implemented because Aristobulus died by poison;
cf. *Ant.*, XIV, 123 f.; *BJ*, I, 183 f.; see also Cassius Dio, XLI, 18:1 (No. 409).
After his victory in the civil war, Caesar promulgated a series of edicts on
behalf of the Jews in Palestine, improving their political situation. These
abolished the enactments of Gabinius unfavourable to the interests of
Judaea, returned to it the port of Jaffa, and increased the prestige of the high
priest Hyrcanus; cf. *Ant.*, XIV, 190 ff. On the Judaean policy of Caesar, see
W. Judeich, *Caesar im Orient*, Leipzig 1885, pp. 119 ff.; A. Büchler,
Festschrift Steinschneider, Leipzig 1896, pp. 91 ff.; O. Roth, *Rom und die
Hasmonäer*, Leipzig 1914, pp. 47 ff.; M.S. Ginsburg, *Rome et la Judée*, Paris
1928, pp. 85 ff.; Momigliano, pp. 192 ff.; A. Schalit, *König Herodes*, Berlin
1969, pp. 36 ff.; Smallwood, pp. 38 ff.
The Jews living in Rome itself were also favourably treated by the dictator.
Thus, while Caesar enacted legislation aimed at the abolition of the various
collegia (cf. *Divus Iulius*, 42:3: "cuncta collegia praeter antiquitus constituta
distraxit"), the Jews were included by him among the *collegia* that had their
rights of association confirmed; cf. *Ant.*, XIV, 215: καὶ γὰρ Γάιος Καῖσαρ ὁ
ἡμέτερος στρατηγὸς ὕπατος ἐν τῷ διατάγματι κωλύων θιάσους
συνάγεσθαι κατὰ πόλιν, μόνους τούτους [scil. Ἰουδαίους] οὐκ ἐκώλυσεν
οὔτε χρήματα συνεισφέρειν οὔτε σύνδειπνα ποιεῖν; cf. A.D. Nock,
Gnomon, XXIX (1957), p. 525 (= Nock, II, pp. 896 f.). For Caesar's policy
towards the Jews, see also J.A. Hild, *REJ*, VIII (1884), pp. 26 ff.;
T. Mommsen, *Römische Geschichte*[9], Berlin 1909, pp. 549 ff.; Juster, I, pp.
409 f.; Ed. Meyer, III, p. 461.
The Jews on their side gave proof of their friendship to Caesar by the aid they
offered him when he was in straits in Alexandria in 47 B.C.E. Soldiers sent by

the government of Judaea took part in the expeditionary force led by Mithridates of Pergamum to help Caesar, and the Egyptian Jews who guarded the entrances of the country opened them to the army of Mithridates, having been persuaded to do so by the letters of Hyrcanus, the Jewish high priest and ethnarch; cf. *Ant.*, XIV, 127 ff.; *BJ*, I, 187 ff. See also F. M. Heichelheim, *Zeitschrift für Religions- und Geistesgeschichte*, X (1958), p. 159. For the place of the whole passage in Suetonius' biography of Julius Caesar, see C. Brutscher, *Analysen zu Suetons Divus Julius und der Parallelüberlieferung*, Bern–Stuttgart 1958, p. 136.

303

Divus Augustus, 76:2 — Ihm = F 130 R = Malcovati, *Imperatoris Augusti Operum Fragmenta*[5], Epistulae, XI

Et rursus: "Ne Iudaeus quidem, mi Tiberi, tam diligenter sabbatis ieiunium servat quam ego hodie servavi, qui in balineo demum post horam primam noctis duas buccas manducavi prius quam ungui inciperem."

   2 *balneo* M²HGXΠ   3 *buceas* Π¹   *bucceas* Π²R   *buccatas* H

Once more: "Not even a Jew, my dear Tiberius, fasts so scrupulously on his sabbaths as I have to-day; for it was not until after the first hour of the night that I ate two mouthfuls of bread in the bath before I began to be anointed."   (trans. J. C. Rolfe, *LCL*)

The sentence is a direct quotation from a letter of Augustus to Tiberius. For Augustus' epistolary style, see H. Bardon, *Les empereurs et les lettres latines d'Auguste à Hadrien*, Paris 1940, pp. 39 ff.
sabbatis: The use of the Jewish name for the day, and not of a periphrasis, may be considered typical of the epistolary style of Augustus.
ieiunium servat: Augustus holds the Sabbath to be a fast-day, a view also found in works by his contemporaries; cf. Pompeius Trogus, apud: Iustinus, XXXVI, 2:14 (No. 137); Strabo, *Geographica*, XVI, 2:40, p. 763 (No. 115). The assumption that Augustus was thinking here of the Day of Atonement does not seem tenable; cf. Radin, p. 254. For references to the Jewish Sabbath by Latin classical writers, see J. H. Michael, *The American Journal of Semitic Languages and Literatures*, XL (1923–1924), pp. 117 ff.
manducavi: This is an example of the use of colloquialism by Augustus.

304

Divus Augustus, 93 — Ihm = F 184 R = Malcovati, *op. cit.*, XXIV

At contra non modo in peragranda Aegypto paulo deflectere ad

visendum Apin supersedit, sed et Gaium nepotem, quod Iudaeam
praetervehens apud Hierosolyma[m] non supplicasset, conlaudavit.

3 *Hierosolyma* Burmann   *Hierosolymam* codd.

But on the other hand he not only omitted to make a slight detour to
visit Apis, when he was travelling through Egypt, but highly
commended his grandson Gaius for not offering prayers at Jerusalem
as he passed by Judaea.   (trans. J. C. Rolfe, *LCL*)

Gaium nepotem, quod Iudaeam praetervehens apud Hierosolyma non
supplicasset: Gaius Caesar passed through Judaea in 1 B.C.E., that is, when
Judaea was ruled by Archelaus. Gaius' behaviour on this occasion differed
from that of his father M. Agrippa, the friend of Herod, who visited
Jerusalem in 15 B.C.E. and offered many sacrifices in the Temple of
Jerusalem; cf. *Ant.*, XVI, 12 ff., especially *ibid.*, 14: Ἀγρίππας δὲ τῷ θεῷ
μὲν ἑκατόμβην κατέθυσεν; see also *Ant.*, XVI, 55; Philo, *Legatio ad*
Gaium, 294 ff.
conlaudavit: This is not to be interpreted as the expression of a specific
anti-Jewish attitude on the part of Augustus. It was his general religious
policy to infuse new life into the old Roman tradition and fortify it against the
penetration of foreign cults (cf. the ideal picture of ancient Rome in
Propertius, IV, 1:17: "nulli cura fuit externos quaerere divos"). The Jewish
cult is here coupled with that of the Egyptians as a religion that should have
no interest for a Roman.
In general, Augustus was remembered by the Jews as a great benefactor. In
Asia he continued the policy of Julius Caesar, and the Jews of Egypt and
Cyrenaica enjoyed his protection. For an appreciation of Augustus' attitude
to the Jews, cf. Philo, *Legatio ad Gaium*, 143 ff., 309 ff.; see also Leon, p. 142,
and the inscriptions, *loc. cit.* (Nos. 284, 301, 338, 368, 416, 496). These refer to
the synagogue of the Augustesians, but cf. also the commentary to
Macrobius, *Saturnalia*, II, 4:11 (No. 543).

305

Tiberius, 32:2 — Ihm

Diogenes grammaticus, disputare sabbatis Rhodi solitus, venientem
eum, ut se extra ordinem audiret, non admiserat ac per servolum
suum in septimum diem distulerat; hunc Romae salutandi sui causa
pro foribus adstantem nihil amplius quam ut post septimum annum
rediret admonuit.

4 *ut* del. Bentley

The grammarian Diogenes, who used to lecture every Sabbath at
Rhodes, would not admit Tiberius when he came to hear him on a

different day, but sent a message by a common slave of his, putting him off to the seventh day. When this man waited before the Emperor's door at Rome to pay his respects, Tiberius took no further revenge than to bid him return seven years later.

(trans. J.C. Rolfe, *LCL*)

Diogenes grammaticus: This seems to be the sole source to mention him.
disputare sabbatis Rhodi solitus: Probably this Diogenes was a Jew who used to lecture every Saturday. If so, it is by no means certain that "grammaticus" here is to be understood in the usual meaning of the word; cf. J. Hubaux, *Latomus*, V (1946), pp. 99 ff. See also F.H. Colson, *The Week*, Cambridge (1926), p. 16. Colson thinks that there were so many people at leisure on Sabbath that Diogenes found it a suitable day to collect an audience.
Rhodi: Tiberius sojourned at the island between 6 B.C.E. and 2 C.E. The anecdote seems to indicate the presence of a considerable Jewish community there. Perhaps some slight evidence of this is the mention of Rhodes in I Macc. xv:23 (at the time of Simon the Hasmonaean). See also *IG*, Vol. XII, Part 1, No. 593 (Εὐφρο[σ]ύνα ϑεοσεβὴς χρηστὰ χαῖρε), and the comments of L. Robert, *Études anatoliennes*, Paris 1937, p. 411, n. 5; idem, *Nouvelles inscriptions de Sardes*, Paris 1964, p. 44; *IG*, Vol. XII, Part 1, No. 11: Μένιππος Ἱερ..υμίτα[ς], where the restoration required seems to be Ἱεροσολυμίτας.
pro foribus adstantem: Cf. Friedländer, I, p. 92.
quam ut: For a defence of the "ut" of the MSS, see J.R. Rietra, *C. Suetoni Tranquilli Vita Tiberi, c. 24–c.40*, Amsterdam 1928, p. 30.
post septimum annum: For the suggestion that this is an allusion to the Jewish sabbatical year, see the article of Hubaux, *op. cit.*, p. 101. The servant of Diogenes deferred Tiberius' visit to the following Sabbath, while Tiberius put off that of Diogenes to the next sabbatical year. Tacitus in any case had heard about this institution; cf. Tacitus, *Historiae*, V, 4 (No. 281): "dein blandiente inertia septimum quoque annum ignaviae datum".

306

Tiberius, 36 — Ihm = F185R

Externas caerimonias, Aegyptios Iudaicosque ritus compescuit, coactis qui superstitione ea tenebantur religiosas vestes cum instrumento omni comburere. Iudaeorum iuventutem per speciem sacramenti in provincias gravioris caeli distribuit, reliquos gentis
5   eiusdem vel similia sectantes urbe summovit, sub poena perpetuae servitutis nisi obtemperassent.

He abolished foreign cults, especially the Egyptian and the Jewish rites, compelling all who were addicted to such superstitions to burn their religious vestments and all their paraphernalia. Those of the Jews who were of military age he assigned to provinces of less healthy climate, ostensibly to serve in the army; the others of the same race or of similar beliefs he banished from the city, on pain of slavery for life if they did not obey. (trans. J. C. Rolfe, *LCL*)

Externas caerimonias: For "caerimonia", see K. H. Roloff, *Glotta*, XXXII (1953), pp. 101 ff.

superstitione ea: Cf. "ea superstitione" in Tacitus, *Annales*, II, 85 (No. 284). Tacitus, though initially referring to both the Jewish and Egyptian religions, applies "ea superstitione" only to the Jewish. Suetonius, on the other hand, depicting the action as directed against both the Egyptian and the Jewish rites, reverses the process. This is evidenced by the context, "coactis … religiosas vestes cum instrumento omni comburere", which applies to the votaries of Isis; cf. J. R. Rietra, *op. cit.* (supra, p. 112), p. 44. Both Tacitus and Suetonius apparently derived the expression "superstitione ea" from some common source, either the *senatus consultum* itself or some intermediate work. Suetonius' "in provincias gravioris caeli" may also be compared with Tacitus' "ob gravitatem caeli", a resemblance that also suggests a common ultimate source. To consider that Tacitus and Suetonius saw the Egyptian and Jewish religions as an identical superstition goes too far; cf. G. May, *Revue historique de droit français et étranger*, Ser. IV, XVII (1938), p. 21, n. 1.

religiosas vestes cum instrumento omni comburere: See M. Malaise, *Les conditions de pénétration et de diffusion des cultes égyptiens en Italie*, Leiden 1972, p. 393.

per speciem sacramenti: Since the Jewish freedmen were Roman citizens, they could be enlisted in the Roman army. This seems to show that there was no general exemption from military service for Jews who were Roman citizens, though examples of local and temporary exemptions are known. These include a decree of the consul Lentulus in 49 B.C.E. concerning the Jews of Ephesus; cf. *Ant.*, XIV, 228; for the decree of the Delians, cf. *Ant.*, XIV, 231 f. See also *Ant.*, XIV, 236 f.

in provincias gravioris caeli: It can be learned that Sardinia is meant from Tacitus, *Annales*, II, 85 (No. 284), and see the commentary *ad loc.* This has been cited as an example of a practice characterizing Suetonius' work from his Life of Tiberius on, i.e. omission of names and increasing reference to individuals by vague plurals; see G. Townend, *CQ*, LIII (1959), p. 289.

307

Divus Claudius, 25:4 — Ihm = F 186 R = W. den Boer, *Scriptorum Paganorum — I–IV Saec. de Christianis Testimonia*, Leiden 1968, No. III

Iudaeos impulsore Chresto assidue tumultuantis Roma expulit.

Christo Orosius VII, 6:15

Since the Jews constantly made disturbances at the instigation of Chrestus, he expelled them from Rome. (trans. J. C. Rolfe, *LCL*)

On this passage, see L. Geiger, *Quid de Iudaeorum Moribus atque Institutis Scriptoribus Romanis Persuasum Fuerit*, Berlin 1872, p. 11; J.A. Hild, *REJ*, XI (1885), p. 58, n. 3; T. Mommsen, *Historische Zeitschrift*, LXIV (1890), p. 408; H. Smilda, *C. Suetonii Tranquilli Vita Divi Claudii*, Groningen 1896, pp. 123 ff.; H. Vogelstein & P. Rieger, *Geschichte der Juden in Rom*, I, Berlin 1896, pp. 19 f.; E.G. Hardy, *Studies in Roman History*, London 1906, p. 43; Schürer, III, pp. 61 ff.; K. Linck, *De Antiquissimis Veterum quae ad Jesum Nazarenum Spectant Testimoniis*, Giessen 1913, pp. 104 ff.; Juster, II, p. 171; E. Preuschen, *ZNTW*, XV (1914), p. 96; Radin, pp. 313 ff.; Ed. Meyer, III, pp. 37 f., 462 f.; Harnack, I, p. 10; A. Deissmann, *Paulus*[2], Tübingen 1925, pp. 222 f.; T. Zielinski, *Revue de l'Université de Bruxelles*, XXXII (1926–1927), pp. 143 ff.; G. La Piana, *HTR*, XX (1927), p. 376, n. 7; W. Seston, *Revue d'histoire et de philosophie religieuses*, XI (1931), pp. 299 ff.; M. Goguel, *Vie de Jésus*, Paris 1932, pp. 75 f.; Lake, in: F.J. Foakes Jackson & K. Lake, *The Beginnings of Christianity*, Part I, Vol. V, London 1933, pp. 459 f.; A. Momigliano, *Claudius, the Emperor and his Achievement*, Oxford 1934, pp. 31 f., 98 f.; P. Labriolle, *La Réaction païenne*, Paris 1934, pp. 42 f.; H. Janne, *Annuaire de l'institut de philologie et d'histoire orientales*, II (1934 = *Mélanges Bidez*), pp. 531 ff.; H. Last, *JRS*, XXVII (1937), p. 88; G. May, *Revue historique de droit français et étranger*, Ser. IV, XVII (1938), pp. 37 ff.; V.M. Scramuzza, *The Emperor Claudius*, Cambridge (Mass.) 1940, p. 151, p. 286, n. 20; S.L. Guterman, *Religious Toleration and Persecution in Ancient Rome*, London 1951, pp. 149 f.; H.J. Cadbury, *The Book of Acts in History*, London 1955, pp. 115 f.; E. Bammel, *Zeitschrift für Theologie und Kirche*, LVI (1959), pp. 294 ff.; Leon, pp. 23 ff.; E. Haenchen, *Die Apostelgeschichte*[13], Göttingen 1961, p. 58; F.F. Bruce, *Bulletin of the John Rylands Library*, XLIV (1961–1962), pp. 313 ff.; W.H.C. Frend, *Martyrdom and Persecution in the Early Church*, Oxford 1965, p. 160; M. Sordi, *Il Cristianesimo e Roma*, Bologna 1965, pp. 62 ff.; T.D. Barnes, *JRS*, LVIII (1968), pp. 43 f.; G. Ogg, *The Chronology of the Life of Paul*, London 1968, pp. 99 ff.; S. Benko, *Theologische Zeitschrift*, XXV (1969), pp. 406 ff.; L. Herrmann, *Chrestos*, Brussels 1970, p. 165; A. Hamman, in: *Studi Pellegrino*, Turin 1975, pp. 92 ff.

The disturbances referred to here by Suetonius reflect the earliest stage of the diffusion of Christianity within the city of Rome. They occurred only a few years after the death of Jesus, when the Christians were still considered by the Roman government a part of the Jewish people. It was the express policy of Claudius to revive the Roman religious tradition; see Scramuzza, *op. cit.*, pp. 145 ff.; Momigliano, *op. cit.*, pp. 20 ff. In this respect Claudius followed in the footsteps of Augustus and Tiberius, and therefore did not view favourably the undermining of this tradition by cults from the East. In contrast to Gaius Caligula, however, Claudius enabled the Jews to regain their former religious rights, reversing the policy of his predecessor. On several occasions he acted on their behalf; cf. *Ant.*, XIX, 280 ff.; *ibid.*, 287 ff. Claudius was also the friend of Agrippa I, who had aided him in his dealings with the senate at the time of his accession. Claudius rewarded Agrippa by bestowing upon him, in addition to the territories in northern and eastern

Palestine over which he had already been ruler in the time of Caligula, the former province of Judaea; cf. *Ant.*, XIX, 274; *BJ*, II, 215. Even after the death of Agrippa I, Claudius sometimes expressly met the wishes of the Jews. Thus he acceded to their request on the custody of the robes of the high priest (*Ant.*, XX, 10 ff.), and decided the quarrel between the Jews and the Samaritans in favour of the Jews (Tacitus, *Annales*, XII, 54 = No. 288). The Alexandrian anti-Semites alleged that Claudius was a cast-off son of the Jewess Salome; cf. *CPJ*, No. 156d, ll. 11 f.; see H. A. Musurillo, *The Acts of the Pagan Martyrs*, Oxford 1954, pp. 128 ff.

Nevertheless, Claudius vigorously opposed any Jewish attempt to upset the existing order that might cause harm to other sections of the population of the empire, as may clearly be seen even from his pro-Jewish edict; cf. *Ant.*, XIX, 290: καλῶς οὖν ἔχειν καὶ Ἰουδαίους τοὺς ἐν παντὶ τῷ ὑφ' ἡμᾶς κόσμῳ τὰ πάτρια ἔθη ἀνεπικωλύτως φυλάσσειν, οἷς καὶ αὐτοῖς ἤδη νῦν παραγγέλλω μου ταύτῃ τῇ φιλανθρωπίᾳ ἐπιεικέστερον χρῆσθαι καὶ μὴ τὰς τῶν ἄλλων ἐθνῶν δεισιδαιμονίας ἐξουθενίζειν, τοὺς ἰδίους δὲ νόμους φυλάσσειν.

This attitude especially emerges from his famous letter to the city of Alexandria; see H. I. Bell, *Jews and Christians*, London 1924, p. 25, ll. 88 ff. = *CPJ*, No. 153: καὶ Ἰουδέοις δὲ ἄντικρυς κελεύωι μηδὲν πλήωι ὧν πρότερον ἔσχον περιεργάζεσθαι ... μηδὲ ἐπάγεσθαι ἢ προσείεσθαι ἀπὸ Συρίας ἢ Αἰγύπ⟨τ⟩ου καταπλέοντας Ἰουδαίους.

Even Agrippa I was not allowed full freedom to attain his political aims, and Claudius partially at least approved of the opposition of Marsus, the governor of Syria, to Agrippa's policy.

The riots that broke out in Rome following the Christian propaganda induced Claudius to adopt police measures against the Jewish community of the capital. Suetonius, who simply states that these measures involved the expulsion of the Jews from Rome, is clearly supported by at least two other sources; cf. Acts xviii:2: προσφάτως ἐληλυθότα ἀπὸ τῆς Ἰταλίας ... διὰ τὸ διατεταχέναι Κλαύδιον χωρίζεσθαι πάντας τοὺς Ἰουδαίους ἀπὸ τῆς Ῥώμης; Orosius, *Adversus Paganos*, VII, 6:15: "Anno eiusdem [scil. Claudii] nono expulsos per Claudium urbe Iudaeos Iosephus refert, sed me magis Suetonius movet, qui ait hoc modo"; here follows the passage from Suetonius. There is no record of the expulsion in the works of Josephus. Orosius depends here wholly on Suetonius, except for the date. On the other hand, Claudius' order is alluded to by Cassius Dio, who expressly asserts that it denied the Jews the right of assembly only but did not expel them; cf. Cassius Dio, LX, 6:6 (No. 422): οὐκ ἐξήλασε μέν, τῷ δὲ δὴ πατρίῳ βίῳ χρωμένους ἐκέλευσε μὴ συναθροίζεσθαι. This contradicts Suetonius, and perhaps also the scholiast to Juvenal (No. 538; cf. the commentary *ad loc.*), who refers to a settlement of Roman Jews at Aricia. Cassius Dio also differs from Orosius in regard to the date of Claudius' edict. While Orosius dates it to the ninth year of Claudius, i.e. 49 C.E., Cassius Dio refers to it in connection with Claudius' accession, i.e. 41 C.E. Suetonius does not suggest a date, but the narrative of the New Testament Acts may implicitly lend some support to Orosius. The expression προσφάτως of Acts, in relation to

Aquila's arrival at Corinth, seems to imply that he had only recently arrived from Italy when Paul met him at that city; and Orosius' date of 49 C.E., and not 41 C.E., would be in keeping with the chronology of Paul's travels.

It is suggested by some scholars that there were two different edicts: 1) The prohibition of assembly, by an edict promulgated in 41 C.E., to which Cassius Dio refers. 2) A general order of expulsion, on which there is agreement between Suetonius, Acts and Orosius, dated by the last-mentioned writer to 49 C.E. See, e.g., Smilda, Ed. Meyer, Momigliano, Nock, in: *CAH*, X, p. 500, Bammel, Bruce, and Frend (see the bibliography for this passage).

It seems much more likely, however, that all the authorities allude here to the same event. Possibly Claudius first intended to expel all the Jews from Rome, and even published an edict to that effect. But under pressure from the Jews, and perhaps especially from Agrippa I, to whom Claudius owed so much that year (41 C.E.), he reversed the order of expulsion and changed it into a restriction of the Jewish right of assembly. Not a few of the Jews left Rome, perhaps before the reversal of the first order. These would include, e.g., Aquila or the Jews who went to Africa; cf. Harnack, *op. cit.* (supra, p. 114). The passage in Acts should not cause undue difficulty, since Aquila could have already left Rome in 41 C.E., stayed elsewhere in Italy, and arrived at Corinth only after the lapse of a number of years. It may even be that the first order was not cancelled in respect to people especially involved in the disturbances; cf. also Leon, p. 26.

Regarding the date, the authority of Orosius by itself is not necessarily greater than that of Cassius Dio. Tacitus' account of the year 49 C.E. in *Annales*, XI, makes no mention of an edict of expulsion of the Jews, which he would have undoubtedly mentioned had it been promulgated that year (the part of the *Annales* covering 41 C.E. is lost). These considerations outweigh the view of Schürer, who, though accepting Cassius Dio's version of the nature of the edict, still adheres to the date offered by Orosius; the latter date is also accepted by H. Stuart Jones, *JRS*, XVI (1926), p. 31. Last, Scramuzza, and Benko (see the bibliography for this passage).

The view of Zielinski, *op. cit.* (supra, p. 114), who adheres to Cassius Dio's chronology of 41 C.E. while rejecting that historian's account of the nature of the edict, seems to be implausible; it is approved by Janne, *op. cit.* (supra, p. 114), pp. 534 f.

impulsore Chresto: There exists hardly any serious doubt that here Chrestus = Christus, i.e. Jesus, though Chrestus was common as a proper name; see, e.g., Linck, *op. cit.* (supra, p. 114), p. 106, n. 2; cf. also *CII*, No. 683, an inscription from Panticapaeum mentioning a Jewess called Chreste. If Suetonius had in mind here some other Jew called Chrestus, he would at least have added *quodam* after Chresto; cf. also Janne, *op. cit.* (supra, p. 114), p. 540, and, already, D.C.G. Baumgarten-Crusius, *C. Suetonii Tranquilli Opera*, II, Leipzig 1816, p. 55. However, the words of Suetonius could convey the impression that Christus himself was present at Rome at that time, and that the disturbances were instigated by him personally, while Tacitus, indeed, was better informed on the whereabouts of Christus; cf. *Annales*,

116

XV, 44 (No. 294). It may be that here "impulsore" need not imply physical presence but only an act of instigation, and that Suetonius did not bother to reconcile the chronology with Christ's death; see also the explanation given by May, *op. cit.* (supra, p. 114), p. 40, and Labriolle, *op. cit.* (supra, p. 114), p. 43. Wholly based on fantasy is the interpretation of the passage as an allusion to Simon Magus, given by R. Eisler, Ἰησοῦς βασιλεὺς οὐ βασιλεύσας, I, Heidelberg 1929, p. 133, n. 1; cf. his discussion, pp. 132 ff.

308

Divus Claudius, 28 — Ihm = F 187 R

Libertorum praecipue suspexit Posiden spadonem, quem etiam Britannico triumpho inter militares viros hasta pura donavit; nec minus Felicem, quem cohortibus et alis provinciaeque Iudaeae praeposuit, trium reginarum maritum.

4 ⟨*illus*⟩*trium reginarum maritum* L. Herrmann, *Latomus*, XXVII (1968), p. 437

Of his freedmen he had special regard for the eunuch Posides, whom he even presented with the headless spear at his British triumph, along with those who had served as soldiers. He was equally fond of Felix, giving him the command of cohorts and of troops of horse, as well as of the province of Judaea; and he became the husband of three queens.   (trans. J. C. Rolfe, *LCL*)

Posiden spadonem: On Posides, see Lambertz, PW, XXII, p. 829.
nec minus Felicem: Suetonius does not mention the connection between Felix and Pallas, the "a rationibus" of the emperor; see the commentary to Tacitus, *Annales*, XII, 54 (No. 288).
cohortibus et alis provinciaeque Iudaeae praeposuit: This means simply that Felix was appointed to the procuratorship of Judaea. Since Judaea was one of the procuratorial provinces, its military forces consisted only of *auxilia*, to the exclusion of legionary forces; the command over the auxiliary infantry cohorts and the *alae* of cavalry seemed to Suetonius the main function of the procurator of Judaea, and there is no reason to conclude from this statement that Felix was given a purely military command in Judaea, preceding his procuratorship; see, e.g., M. Aberbach, *JQR*, XL (1949/50), p. 5. For the auxiliary forces stationed in Judaea, see Broughton, in: Foakes Jackson & Lake, *op. cit.* (supra, p. 114), pp. 439 ff.; Momigliano, pp. 376 ff. See also Schürer, I, pp. 458 ff.; Schürer, ed. Vermes & Millar, I, pp. 362 ff. Five cohorts and one *ala* of the Sebastenes and Caesareans constituted the backbone of the army of Judaea; see *Ant.*, XIX, 365; cf. *BJ*, III, 66.

trium reginarum maritum: On the wives of Felix, see the commentary to Tacitus, *Historiae*, V, 9 (No. 281). One was a grand-daughter of Antony and Cleopatra, the second was Drusilla, a daughter of Agrippa I. The name of the third is not known. In any case Suetonius uses the designation "regina" loosely here.

309

Nero, 40:2 — Ihm

Spoponderant tamen quidam ⟨scil. mathematicorum⟩ destituto Orientis dominationem, nonnulli nominatim regnum Hierosolymorum, plures omnis pristinae fortunae restitutionem.

1 *quidem* M

Some of them [of the astrologers], however, had promised him the rule of the East, when he was cast off, a few expressly naming the sovereignty of Jerusalem, and several the restitution of all his former fortunes. (trans. J. C. Rolfe, *LCL*)

regnum Hierosolymorum: This promise should be connected with the prophecies circulating at that time about the transfer of the rule of the ancient world to the East; cf. Tacitus, *Historiae*, V, 13 (No. 281), and the commentary *ad loc*. For the Jewish tradition that Nero became a proselyte and that Rabbi Meir was descended from him, see *TB Giṭṭin*, 56a; W. Bacher, *REJ*, V (1882), pp. 181 ff.; idem, *Die Agada der Tannaiten*, II, Strasbourg 1890, p. 5, n. 6; B. J. Bamberger, *Proselytism in the Talmudic Period*, Cincinnati 1939, pp. 231 f.; N. G. Cohen, *Journal of Jewish Studies*, XXIII (1972), pp. 54 ff.; see also S. J. Bastomsky, *JQR*, NS, LIX (1968/9), pp. 321 ff.

310

Galba, 23 — Ihm

Senatus, ut primum licitum est, statuam ei decreverat rostratae columnae superstantem in parte fori, qua trucidatus est; sed decretum Vespasianus abolevit, percussores sibi ex Hispania in Iudaeam submisisse opinatus.

The senate, as soon as it was allowed to do so, voted him a statue standing upon a column adorned with the beaks of ships, in the part of the Forum where he was slain; but Vespasian annulled this decree, believing that Galba had sent assassins from Spain to Judaea, to take his life. (trans. J. C. Rolfe, *LCL*)

Vespasianus abolevit, percussores ... in Iudaeam submisisse opinatus:
However, according to Suetonius, *Divus Titus*, 5: "Galba mox tenente rem
publicam missus [scil. Titus] ad gratulandum, quaqua iret convertit homines,
quasi adoptionis gratia arcesseretur." The supporters of Otho, the murderer
of Galba, were one of the mainstays of the Flavian party, a factor that may
have played its part in the invention of this apocryphal story.

311

Vitellius, 15:1 — Ihm

Octavo imperii mense desciverunt ab eo exercitus Moesiarum atque
Pannoniae, item ex transmarinis Iudaicus et Syriaticus, ac pars in
absentis pars in praesentis Vespasiani verba iurarunt.

In the eighth month of his reign the armies of the Moesian provinces
and Pannonia revolted from him, and also in the provinces beyond
the seas those of Judaea and Syria, the former swearing allegiance to
Vespasian in his absence and the latter in his presence.

(trans. J.C. Rolfe, *LCL*)

desciverunt ab eo exercitus Moesiarum atque Pannoniae: For the secession of
these legions from Vitellius, cf. Tacitus, *Historiae*, II, 85–86.

312

Divus Vespasianus, 4:5–6 — Ihm = F188R

(5) Percrebruerat Oriente toto vetus et constans opinio esse in fatis ut
eo tempore Iudaea profecti rerum potirentur. Id de imperatore
Romano, quantum postea eventu paruit, praedictum Iudaei ad se
trahentes rebellarunt caesoque praeposito legatum insuper Syriae
consularem suppetias ferentem rapta aquila fugaverunt. Ad hunc
motum comprimendum cum exercitu ampliore et non instrenuo
duce, cui tamen tuto tanta res committeretur, opus esset, ipse
potissimum delectus est ut et industriae expertae nec metuendus ullo
modo ob humilitatem generis ac nominis. (6) Additis igitur ad copias
duabus legionibus, octo alis, cohortibus decem, atque inter legatos
maiore filio assumpto, ut primum provinciam attigit, proximas

4 *debellarunt* Y   *rebellerant* Bentley   8 *industriae expertae* ΠQ
     industria experti MR   *industria expertus* cett.
     11 *provinciam ⟨suam⟩* Becker

quoque convertit in se, correcta statim castrorum disciplina, unoque et altero proelio tam constanter inito, ut in oppugnatione castelli lapidis ictum genu scutoque sagittas aliquot exceperit.

14 *ictu* M   /   *scuto sagittasque* M
scutoque sagittasque G   *scuto sagittas* Y   *scuto sagittas* ⟨*quo*⟩ *que* Bücheler

(5) There had spread over all the Orient an old and established belief, that it was fated at that time for men coming from Judaea to rule the world. This prediction, referring to the emperor of Rome, as afterwards appeared from the event, the people of Judaea took to themselves; accordingly they revolted and after killing their governor they routed the consular ruler of Syria as well, when he came to the rescue, and took one of his eagles. Since to put down the rebellion required a considerable army with a leader of no little enterprise, yet one to whom so great power could be entrusted without risk, Vespasian was chosen for the task, both as a man of tried energy and as one in no wise to be feared because of the obscurity of his family and name. (6) Therefore there were added to the forces in Judaea two legions with eight divisions of cavalry and ten cohorts. He took his elder son as one of his lieutenants and as soon as he reached his province he attracted the attention of the neighbouring provinces also: for he at once reformed the discipline of the army, and fought one or two battles with such daring, that in the storming of a fortress he was wounded in the knee with a stone and received several arrows in his shield.

(trans. J. C. Rolfe, *LCL*)

5   *Percrebruerat Oriente ... ut eo tempore Iudaea profecti rerum potirentur*: Cf. Tacitus, *Historiae*, V, 13 (No. 281): "antiquis sacerdotum litteris contineri, eo ipso tempore fore ut valesceret Oriens profectique Iudaea rerum potirentur. Quae ambages Vespasianum ac Titum praedixerat"; see H. R. Graf, "Kaiser Vespasian", *Untersuchungen zu Suetons Vita Divi Vespasiani*, Stuttgart 1937, pp. 21 ff., and the commentary to Tacitus, *ad loc.*
Id ... praedictum Iudaei ad se trahentes rebellarunt: Cf. *BJ*, VI, 312; see also Tacitus, *Historiae*, V, 13 (No. 281), the commentary *ad loc.*
caesoque praeposito: This statement does not accord with the facts. The procurator of Judaea at that time was Gessius Florus, and Josephus is silent about his death at the hands of the rebels, a fact which he could hardly have suppressed in his detailed narrative. Suetonius' statement is taken at its face value by W. A. Spooner, *The Histories of Tacitus*, London 1891, p. 468. Josephus writes that, having lost control of the situation, Florus left for Caesarea (*BJ*, II, 332). Subsequently he is found in the camp of Cestius Gallus, bribing some of the Roman officers so as to prevent a speedy

conquest of Jerusalem (*BJ*, II, 531; cf. also *ibid.*, 558, according to which Cestius Gallus blamed Florus for the outbreak of the Jewish war against Rome). It may be that Suetonius confused the fate of Florus with that of the Roman garrison of Antonia, where the troops were slaughtered by the rebels while the commander, Metilius, was forced to become a Jew and his life was spared (*BJ*, II, 450 ff.); see Weber, p. 35; Graf, *op. cit.* (supra, p. 120), p. 24. There is also something to be said for the emendation "praesidio" for "praeposito".

legatum insuper Syriae consularem ... fugaverunt: Suetonius refers here to the attempt of Cestius Gallus to capture Jerusalem and put down the rebellion; cf. *BJ*, II, 499 ff.; Tacitus, *Historiae*, V, 10 (No. 281): "comprimere coeptantem Cestium Gallum Syriae legatum varia proelia ac saepius adversa excepere", and cf. the commentary *ad loc.*

rapta aquila: The captured eagle from the army of Cestius Gallus must have belonged to the Legio XII Fulminata, the main striking force of Cestius Gallus' expedition against Jerusalem. This was the only legion of the army of Syria in which all the soldiers took part in the campaign; cf. *BJ*, II, 500: ἀναλαβὼν δὲ ἀπὸ τῆς ᾿Αντιοχείας τὸ μὲν δωδέκατον τάγμα πλῆρες. For this legion, cf. Broughton, *op. cit.* (supra, p. 117), p. 435; Ritterling, PW, XII, pp. 1705 ff. The Twelfth Legion participated in the siege of Jerusalem under Titus; cf. *BJ*, V, 41; Tacitus, *Historiae*, V, 1 (No. 281). Nevertheless the memory of its disgrace was not easily obliterated, and its later transfer from Syria was thought to have been some sort of punishment; cf. *BJ*, VII, 18: μεμνημένος δὲ τοῦ δωδεκάτου τάγματος, ὅτι Κεστίου στρατηγοῦντος ἐνέδωκαν τοῖς ᾿Ιουδαίοις, τῆς μὲν Συρίας αὐτὸ παντάπασιν ἐξήλασεν. Since Josephus nowhere refers to the loss of the eagle by the Twelfth Legion, some doubt on the truth of Suetonius' statement is cast by Ritterling, *op. cit.*, p. 1706. This view is supported by H. Dessau, *Geschichte der römischen Kaiserzeit*, Vol. II, Part 2, Berlin 1930, p. 807, n. 1; A. W. Braithwaite, *C. Suetoni Tranquilli Divus Vespasianus*, Oxford 1927, p. 31. However, the silence of Josephus does not in itself invalidate the statement of Suetonius here, especially since it emerges from Josephus' narrative that a deep disgrace was felt to attach to this legion that may well be explained by the loss of the eagle. Perhaps Suetonius even gains support from numismatic evidence; see H. Mattingly & E. A. Sydenham, *The Roman Imperial Coinage*, II, London 1926, p. 71: "signis receptis"; see also Graf, *op. cit.* (supra, p. 120), p. 118, n. 131.

ipse potissimum delectus: Cf. *BJ*, III, 3 ff.

6 *Additis igitur ad copias duabus legionibus*: Suetonius is not too clear about the "copiae" to which the two legions were added. Reference to Josephus shows that Titus, on arriving at Ptolemais, added the Fifteenth Legion, which he had brought with him from Alexandria, to the two legions of Vespasian, i.e. the Fifth and the Tenth; cf. *BJ*, III, 64 f.; see Schürer, I, p. 610, n. 31. This was then the whole legionary force under the command of Vespasian. It seems that Suetonius confused the forces accompanying Titus with those already serving in Judaea before his arrival. See also Braithwaite, *op. cit.*, pp. 31 f.; Weber, pp. 117 ff.

octo alis, cohortibus decem: Josephus mentions only six *alae* at the disposal of the whole army (*BJ*, III, 66). Weber has suggested combining both sources, Suetonius and Josephus, supposing that Vespasian brought with him eight *alae*, while Titus had six; see Weber, pp. 118 f. The total number of auxiliary cohorts was twenty-three; cf. *BJ*, *loc. cit.*: τούτοις εἴποντο ὀκτωκαίδεκα σπεῖραι. προσεγένοντο δὲ καὶ ἀπὸ Καισαρείας πέντε. If both sources are combined (as by Weber, p. 119) it follows also that while Vespasian had ten cohorts, as stated by Suetonius, Titus had thirteen under his command. Elsewhere Josephus clearly distinguishes between ten and thirteen cohorts, according to their strength as *miliariae* (*BJ*, III, 67).

proximas [scil. *provincias*] *quoque convertit in se*: Especially Syria and Egypt. "Proximas" cannot be taken to describe localities or towns in Vespasian's own province, such as Sepphoris, as proposed by Weber, p. 117.

in oppugnatione castelli lapidis ictum genu scutoque sagittas aliquot exceperit: This is the same episode about which Josephus writes, in connection with the siege of Jotapata, in *BJ*, III, 236: ἔνθα τις τῶν ἀμυνομένων ἀπ' αὐτοῦ βάλλει τὸν Οὐεσπασιανὸν βέλει κατὰ τὸν ταρσὸν τοῦ ποδὸς καὶ τιτρώσκει μὲν ἐπιπολαίως, προεκλύσαντος τὸ βληθὲν τοῦ διαστήματος. The "castellum" referred to by Suetonius should therefore be identified with Jotapata.

313

Divus Vespasianus, 5:6 — Ihm = F188R

Apud Iudaeam Carmeli dei oraculum consulentem ita confirmavere sortes, ut quidquid cogitaret volveretque animo quamlibet magnum, id esse proventurum pollicerentur; et unus ex nobilibus captivis Iosephus, cum coiceretur in vincula, constantissime asseveravit fore
5   ut ab eodem brevi solveretur, verum iam imperatore.

4 *iosepus* M

When he consulted the oracle of the god of Carmel in Judaea, the lots were highly encouraging, promising that whatever he planned or wished, however great it might be, would come to pass; and one of his high-born prisoners, Josephus by name, as he was being put in chains, declared most confidently that he would soon be released by the same man, who would then, however, be emperor.   (trans. J.C. Rolfe, *LCL*)

Apud Iudaeam: Suetonius here uses the official name of the province. Mount Carmel was situated on the border between the provinces of Judaea and Syria; cf. Tacitus, *Historiae*, II, 78 (No. 278): "Est Iudaeam inter Syriamque Carmelus", and the commentary *ad loc.* See also Graf, *op. cit.* (supra, p. 120), p. 39.

ut quidquid cogitaret volveretque animo: Cf. Tacitus, *loc. cit.*: "quidquid est," inquit, "Vespasiane, quod paras, seu domum exstruere seu prolatare agros sive ampliare servitia, datur tibi magna sedes, ingentes termini, multum hominum."

unus ex nobilibus captivis Iosephus: Suetonius does not appear to have known that Josephus was commander of the rebels in Galilee.

cum coiceretur in vincula: Josephus himself relates this episode in *BJ*, III, 400 f.: σὺ μέν, ἔφη, Οὐεσπασιανέ, νομίζεις αἰχμάλωτον αὐτὸ μόνον εἰληφέναι Ἰώσηπον, ἐγὼ δὲ ἄγγελος ἥκω σοι μειζόνων... σὺ Καῖσαρ, Οὐεσπασιανέ, καὶ αὐτοκράτωρ, σὺ καὶ παῖς ὁ σὸς οὗτος. Cf. also Cassius Dio, LXVI, 1 : 2–4 (No. 429); Appianus, apud: Zonaras, XI, 16 (No. 347). The Flavian house obtained similar *oracula* from pagan sources; cf. Suetonius, *Divus Titus*, 5; Tacitus, *Historiae*, II, 4; F. Beckurts, *Zur Quellenkritik des Tacitus, Sueton und Cassius Dio*, Brunswick 1880, pp. 26 f.; A. Schalit, in: H. Temporini & W. Haase, *Aufstieg und Niedergang der römischen Welt*, Vol. II, Part 2, Berlin–New York 1975, pp. 259 ff. The prophecy of another Jew is transmitted by midrashic and talmudic sources in the traditions about R. Yoḥanan ben Zakkai; see *Aboth de-Rabbi Nathan*, Version A, iv, pp. 22 f.; Version B, vi, p. 19 (ed. Schechter); *TB Giṭṭin*, 56ab.

314

Divus Vespasianus, 6:3 — Ihm

Ceterum divulgato facto Tiberius Alexander praefectus Aegypti primus in verba Vespasiani legiones adegit Kal. Iul., qui principatus dies in posterum observatus est; Iudaicus deinde exercitus V. Idus Iul. apud ipsum iuravit.

2 *allegit* Y

But when their action became known, Tiberius Alexander, prefect of Egypt, was the first to compel the legions to take the oath for Vespasian, on the Kalends of July, the day which was afterwards celebrated as that of his accession; then the army in Judaea swore allegiance to him personally on the fifth day before the Ides of July.

(trans. J. C. Rolfe, *LCL*)

Iudaicus deinde exercitus: Suetonius is slightly inaccurate about the date on which the army of Judaea took its oath of fealty to Vespasian. It was 3 July, not 11 July; cf. M. Fortina, *L'imperatore Tito*, Turin 1955, p. 46, n. 84; M. Hammond, *Memoirs of the American Academy in Rome*, XXIV (1956), p. 74; L. Lesiusse, *Revue belge de philologie et d'histoire*, XL (1962), p. 73, n. 1.

315
Divus Vespasianus, 8:1 — Ihm = F188R

Talis tantaque cum fama in urbem reversus acto de Iudaeis triumpho consulatus octo veteri addidit.

Returning to Rome under such auspices and attended by so great renown, after celebrating a triumph over the Jews, he added eight consulships to his former one. (trans. J. C. Rolfe, *LCL*)

acto de Iudaeis triumpho: The description of the triumph is to be found in *BJ*, VII, 121 ff.

316
Divus Titus, 4:3 — Ihm = F189R

Ex quaesturae deinde honore legioni praepositus Tarichaeas et Gamalam urbes Iudaeae validissimas in potestatem redegit, equo quadam acie sub feminibus amisso alteroque inscenso, cuius rector circa se dimicans occubuerat.

1 *Taricheas* Ursinus   *thracias* codd. (*trachias* ΠR)

Then, after holding the office of quaestor, as commander of a legion he subjugated the two strong cities of Taricheae and Gamala in Judaea, having his horse killed under him in one battle and mounting another, whose rider had fallen fighting by his side.

(trans. J. C. Rolfe, *LCL*)

legioni praepositus: Josephus does not connect Titus during the conquest of Galilee with the command of one given legion. In the capture of Gamala three legions took part; cf. *BJ*, III, 65. Before the beginning of hostilities in Galilee, Titus brought with him the Fifteenth Legion (Apollinaris), and incorporated it in his father's army. It may be conjectured that the legion to which Suetonius refers was this legion; cf. G. W. Mooney, *C. Suetoni Tranquilli De Vita Caesarum*, London 1930, p. 475. It is expressly mentioned as taking part in the capture of Gamala, and soldiers of this legion accompanied Titus in scaling the walls of Jotapata; cf. *BJ*, III, 324.
Tarichaeas: Cf. the commentary to Strabo, *Geographica*, XVI, 2:45, p. 764 (No. 115). Its capture is described in *BJ*, III, 462 ff. At first Vespasian sent Titus there at the head of six hundred chosen cavalry (*ibid.*, 470). Subsequently Trajan appeared with four hundred cavalry (*ibid.*, 485) and two thousand archers under the command of Antonius Silo in order to take the mountain facing the town (*ibid.*, 486).

Gamalam: A fortress in the Gaulanitis captured by Alexander Jannaeus; cf. *Ant.*, XIII, 394; *BJ*, I, 105. It was thought to have been one of the strongest in Palestine. For the locale, see Abel, II, p. 325; B. Bar-Kochva, *ZDPV*, XCII (1976), pp. 54 ff.; Avi-Yonah, p. 167. Its capture by the Romans is described by Josephus in *BJ*, IV, 11 ff. The Fifth, Tenth and Fifteenth legions participated in the siege of Gamala. Josephus refers to the presence of Vespasian at the siege; Titus had at first been absent (*ibid.*, 32), and only arrived there later (*ibid.*, 70). Then, according to Josephus, Titus played a decisive role in the final capture of the fortress. The capture of Gamala is to be dated to the 23rd of Hyperberetaeus in 67 C.E.

urbes Iudaeae: Suetonius uses the term Iudaea here in the broadest meaning, which it assumed as a result of the Hasmonaean conquests; cf. Strabo, *Geographica*, XVI, 2:21, p. 756 (No. 113). Taricheae and Gamala were not even included in the procuratorial province of Judaea, since they belonged to the kingdom of Agrippa II.

validissimas: In respect of Taricheae, Josephus states, in *BJ*, III, 464: ἡ μὲν γὰρ πόλις, ὥσπερ ἡ Τιβεριὰς ὑπόρειος οὖσα, καθὰ μὴ τῇ λίμνῃ προσεκλύζετο πάντοθεν ὑπὸ τοῦ Ἰωσήπου τετείχιστο καρτερῶς. The strength of Gamala is described in *BJ*, IV, 4 ff.: Γάμαλα δ' οὐ προσεχώρει πεποιθυῖα τῇ δυσχωρίᾳ πλέον τῶν Ἰωταπάτων ... οὕτως οὖσαν φύσει δυσμήχανον τὴν πόλιν τειχίζων ὁ Ἰώσηπος ἐποίησεν ὀχυρωτέραν ὑπονόμοις τε καὶ διώρυξιν. In addition to the role that Josephus ascribes to Titus in the capture of Taricheae and the storming of Gamala, Josephus makes him conspicuous in the taking of Jotapata (*BJ*, III, 324) and the Galilaean townships of Jafia (*BJ*, III, 298 ff.) and Gischala (*BJ*, IV, 87 ff.).

equo quadam acie ... amisso: The personal valour shown by Titus in the conquest of Galilee is much emphasized by Josephus. Titus was the first to scale the walls of Jotapata; cf. *BJ*, III, 324: καὶ πρῶτος ἐπιβαίνει Τίτος σὺν ἑνὶ τῶν χιλιάρχων Δομετίῳ Σαβίνῳ; he led the conquest of Taricheae; cf. *BJ*, III, 487: ὁ δὲ Τίτος πρῶτος τὸν ἵππον ἤλαυνεν εἰς τοὺς πολεμίους; cf. also *ibid.*, 497: πρῶτος εἰς τὴν πόλιν εἰσέρχεται. On the capture of Gamala, cf. *BJ*, IV, 70 f.: Τίτος δέ, ἤδη γὰρ παρῆν, ὀργῇ τῆς πληγῆς ἣν παρ' αὐτὸν ἐπλήγησαν ἀπόντα Ῥωμαῖοι ... εἰσέρχεται τὴν πόλιν ἡσυχῇ ... οἱ δὲ τὸν Τίτον ὑπαντιάζοντες ἀδιαλείπτως ἔπιπτον. See Weber, pp. 133 f.

317

Divus Titus, 5:2 — Ihm = F189R

Cuius ⟨scil. spei⟩ brevi compos et ad perdomandam Iudaeam relictus, novissima Hierosolymorum oppugnatione duodecim propugnatores totidem sagittarum confecit ictibus, cepitque ea natali filiae suae tanto militum gaudio ac favore, ut in gratulatione imperatorem eum
5 consalutaverint et subinde decedentem provincia detinuerint,

3 *ea* M   *eam* cett.

suppliciter nec non et minaciter efflagitantes, aut remaneret aut secum omnis pariter abduceret.

6 *et flagitantes* MG

Soon realising his hope and left behind to complete the conquest of Judaea, in the final attack on Jerusalem he slew twelve of the defenders with as many arrows; and he took the city on his daughter's birthday, so delighting the soldiers and winning their devotion that they hailed him as imperator and detained him from time to time, when he would leave the province, urging him with prayers and even with threats either to stay or to take them all with him.

(trans. J.C. Rolfe, *LCL*)

et ad perdomandam Iudaeam relictus: Cf. *BJ*, IV, 658, and Tacitus, *Historiae*, V, 1 (No. 281). See also Weber, p. 185.

novissima Hierosolymorum oppugnatione duodecim propugnatores totidem sagittarum confecit ictibus: Cf. *BJ*, V, 288: καὶ δώδεκα μὲν αὐτὸς τῶν προμάχων ἀναιρεῖ, πρὸς δὲ τὸ τούτων πάθος ἐγκλίνοντος τοῦ λοιποῦ πλήθους ἑπόμενος συνελαύνει πάντας εἰς τὴν πόλιν κἀκ τοῦ πυρὸς διασώζει τὰ ἔργα. For Titus' ability as an archer, cf. also *BJ*, V, 340 f.; Eutropius, VII, 21:2 (No. 491), which is dependent on Suetonius.

cepitque ea natali filiae suae: Julia, the daughter of Titus, is meant. Suetonius does not specify which phase of the capture of Jerusalem is implied here, whether the taking of the Temple in the month of Av or of the Upper Town in the month of Elul. However, the first possibility seems to be indicated in view of the information given by Josephus, quoted below in the commentary.

imperatorem eum consalutaverint: Cf. *BJ*, VI, 316: Ῥωμαῖοι δὲ τῶν μὲν στασιαστῶν καταπεφευγότων εἰς τὴν πόλιν, καιομένου δὲ αὐτοῦ τε τοῦ ναοῦ καὶ τῶν πέριξ ἁπάντων, κομίσαντες τὰς σημαίας εἰς τὸ ἱερὸν ... ἔθυσάν τε αὐταῖς αὐτόθι καὶ τὸν Τίτον μετὰ μεγίστων εὐφημιῶν ἀπέφηναν αὐτοκράτορα. Cf. also H. Price, *C. Suetonii Tranquilli de Vita Caesarum Liber VIII, Divus Titus*, Menasha (Wisconsin) 1919, p. 29.

et subinde decedentem provincia detinuerint: There is no allusion to this behaviour of the legions by Josephus; cf. *BJ*, VII, 5 ff.

318

Divus Titus, 7:1-2 — Ihm

(1) Praeter saevitiam suspecta in eo etiam luxuria erat, quod ad mediam noctem comisationes cum profusissimo quoque familiarium extenderet; nec minus libido propter exoletorum et spadonum greges propterque insignem reginae Berenices amorem, cui etiam nuptias

4 *berenicis* MX   *beronicis* G   *beronices* Y

5 pollicitus ferebatur; suspecta rapacitas, quod constabat in
co⟨g⟩n⟨i⟩tionibus patris nundinari praemiarique solitum; denique
propalam alium Neronem et opinabantur et praedicabant. At illi ea
fama pro bono cessit conversaque est in maximas laudes neque vitio
ullo reperto et contra virtutibus summis. (2) Convivia instituit
10 iucunda magis quam profusa. Amicos elegit, quibus etiam post eum
principes ut et sibi et rei publicae necessariis adquieverunt
praecipueque sunt usi. Berenicen statim ab urbe dimisit invitus
invitam.

6 *cognitionibus* Torrentius   *contionibus* codd.   *negotiationibus* Ursinus
12 *beronicem* GY

(1) Besides cruelty, he was also suspected of riotous living, since he
protracted his revels until the middle of the night with the most
prodigal of his friends; likewise of unchastity because of his troops of
catamites and eunuchs, and his notorious passion for queen Berenice,
to whom it was even said that he promised marriage. He was
suspected of greed as well; for it was well known that in cases which
came before his father he put a price on his influence and accepted
bribes. In short, people not only thought, but openly declared, that he
would be a second Nero. But this reputation turned out to his
advantage, and gave place to the highest praise, when no fault was
discovered in him, but on the contrary the highest virtues. (2) His
banquets were pleasant rather than extravagant. He chose as his
friends men whom succeeding emperors also retained as indispensa-
ble alike to themselves and to the State, and of whose services they
made special use. Berenice he sent from Rome at once, against her
will and his own.   (trans. J. C. Rolfe, *LCL*)

1 *propterque insignem reginae Berenices amorem*: For the relations between
Titus and Berenice, cf. the commentaries to Quintilianus, IV, 1 : 19 (No. 231);
Tacitus, *Historiae*, II, 2 (No. 275); Cassius Dio, LXVI, 15 : 3–4 (No. 433).
2 *Berenicen statim ab urbe dimisit*: Suetonius may give the impression that
Berenice had stayed continuously in Rome during the reign of Vespasian and
was dismissed from the capital only after his death. However, it appears from
the account of Cassius Dio that there were two phases. Her first sojourn was
from 75 C. E. to some time shortly before the death of Vespasian; cf. Cassius
Dio, *loc. cit.* (No. 433), where his language (προσεδόκα δὲ γαμηθήσεσθαι)
recalls that of Suetonius' "cui etiam nuptias pollicitus ferebatur". Her second
followed her return to Rome subsequent to the death of Vespasian; cf.
Cassius Dio, LXVI, 18 (No. 434): καίτοι καὶ τῆς Βερενίκης εἰς Ῥώμην
αὖθις ἐλθούσης. Cf. also *Epitome de Caesaribus*, 10 : 6–7 (No. 532): "Sed

haec in melius conversa ... Berenicen nuptias suas sperantem regredi domum ... praecepit". See Wilcken, PW, III, p. 288; G. H. Macurdy, *AJP*, LVI (1935), p. 252; J. A. Crook, *AJP*, LXXII (1951), pp. 162 ff.; M. Fortina, *L'imperatore Tito*, Turin 1955, p. 95, n. 81; G. Luck, *Rhein. Museum*, CVII (1964), p. 67; H. Gugel, *Studien zur biographischen Technik Suetons*, Vienna 1977, pp. 80 f.

319

Domitianus, 2:1 — Ihm = F 190 R

Ob haec correptus, quo magis et aetatis et condicionis admoneretur, habitabat cum patre una sellamque eius ac fratris, quotiens prodirent, lectica sequebatur ac triumphum utriusque Iudaicum equo albo comitatus est.

For this he was reprimanded, and to give him a better realisation of his youth and position, he had to live with his father, and when they appeared in public he followed the emperor's chair and that of his brother in a litter, while he also attended their triumph over Judaea riding on a white horse.   (trans. J. C. Rolfe, *LCL*)

320

Domitianus, 12:2 — Ihm = F 190 R

Praeter ceteros Iudaicus fiscus acerbissime actus est; ad quem deferebantur, qui vel[ut] inprofessi Iudaicam viverent vitam vel dissimulata origine imposita genti tributa non pependissent. Interfuisse me adulescentulum memini, cum a procuratore frequen-
5 tissimoque consilio inspiceretur nonagenarius senex, an circumsectus esset.

> 1 *exactus* G   2 *vel inprofessi* I. F. Gronovius
> *velut inprofessi* MGYδ   *veluti professi* X

Besides other taxes, that on the Jews was levied with the utmost vigour, and those were prosecuted who without publicly acknowledging that faith yet lived as Jews, as well as those who concealed their origin and did not pay the tribute levied upon their people. I recall being present in my youth when the person of a man ninety years old was examined before the procurator and a very crowded court, to see whether he was circumcised.   (trans. J. C. Rolfe, *LCL*)

Iudaicus fiscus: This "fiscus" seems to have been the aggregate of the revenue from the special Jewish tax imposed on all Jews after the destruction of the Second Temple. Officially, the tax had to be paid to Jupiter Capitolinus and superseded the former dues paid by the Jews to the Temple of Jerusalem; cf. Cassius Dio, LXVI, 7:2 (No. 430): καὶ ἀπ᾽ ἐκείνου δίδραχμον ἐτάχθη τοὺς τὰ πάτρια αὐτῶν ἔθη περιστέλλοντας τῷ Καπιτωλίῳ Διὶ κατ᾽ ἔτος ἀποφέρειν. Cf. also *BJ*, VII, 218: ἀνὰ πᾶν ἔτος εἰς τὸ Καπετώλιον φέρειν, ὥσπερ πρότερον εἰς τὸν ἐν Ἱεροσολύμοις νεὼν συνετέλουν. (For the δίδραχμον paid to the Temple, cf. Philo, *Quis Rerum Divinarum Heres Sit.*, 186; *Ant.*, XVIII, 312; Matt. xvii:24.) The documentary evidence from Egypt provides much information about the levy there of the "Jewish tax" in the first and second centuries C.E. The greater part of that evidence is supplied by the *ostraca* from Apollinopolis Magna (Edfu) in Upper Egypt, and dates from 71/2–116 C.E. (*CPJ*, Nos. 160–229). These *ostraca* show that at first the tax had been designated τιμὴ δηναρίων δύο Ἰουδαίων, as is testified by *ostraca* from 71/2 C.E. – 89 C.E. (*CPJ*, Nos. 160–168, 170–182, 183a–188). To this tax there had usually been added, at least from 73 C.E. on, another tax, referred to as ἀπαρχαί, of one drachma a year. The annual rate of the τιμή itself, as emerges from these *ostraca*, was eight Egyptian drachmae. It may be surmised that both taxes together became known as Ἰουδαϊκὸν τέλεσμα. That name already occurs in a papyrus from Arsinoë, dated 73 C.E.; see *CPJ*, No. 421, ll. 154, 172. A πράκτωρ Ἰουδαϊκοῦ τελέσματος at Edfu, who issued a receipt for both the τιμὴ δηναρίων δύο Ἰουδαίων and the ἀπαρχαί, is mentioned in *CPJ*, No. 181 (80 C.E.). It seems that at the first stage of levying the Jewish tax a distinction was made, at least at Edfu, between the τιμὴ τῶν δύο δηναρίων and the ἀπαρχαί, both being collected by the πράκτωρ Ἰουδαϊκοῦ τελέσματος.

The last *ostraca* to show the two items existing separately date from July and August 89 C.E.; see *CPJ*, Nos. 186 and 187. However an earlier record refers only to Ἰουδαϊκὸν τέλεσμα, testifying to a new system; cf. *CPJ*, No. 183 (18 May 85 C.E.). The dated *ostraca* from 92/3 C.E. on merge both taxes into one. It is clear that the Ἰουδαϊκὸν τέλεσμα was more comprehensive than the τιμή, since it was commonly levied at the annual rate of nine drachmae, i.e. consisting of the eight drachmae of the τιμή and the one drachma of the ἀπαρχαί. The last document from Egypt to attest the payment of Ἰουδαϊκὸν τέλεσμα is from Karanis in the Faiyûm dated 145/6 or 167/8 C.E.; cf. *CPJ*, No. 460, l. 7. This tax still existed in the first half of the third century; cf. Origenes, *Ad Africanum*, 14: καὶ νῦν γοῦν Ῥωμαίων βασιλευόντων, καὶ Ἰουδαίων τὸ δίδραχμον αὐτοῖς τελούντων. However, we do not know when it was finally abolished. Some scholars connect its abolition with Julian the Apostate; see Juster, II, p. 286; M.S. Ginsburg, *JQR*, XXI (1930/1), p. 290. For the view that it probably lapsed during the third-century inflation, see A.H.M. Jones, *The Later Roman Empire*, II, Oxford 1964, p. 947.

Apart from the humiliation attached to the Jewish tax it was also a financial burden on the Jewish population of the empire. The *ostraca* of Edfu indicate that the annual rate of the Jewish tax was more than half of that of the poll tax (*laographia*) levied in the same place and period, which seems to have been fixed at sixteen drachmae (cf., e.g., *CPJ*, Nos. 239, 246, 248, 253, 257, 262, 263, 264, 266, 274, 280, 358, 360, 369; although many of the *ostraca* record the sums of four, eight or sometimes twelve drachmae, these amounts were probably only part of the annual rate).

For the problems connected with the Jewish tax, see S. Gsell, *Essai sur le règne de l'empereur Domitien*, Paris 1894, p. 289; O. Hirschfeld, *Die kaiserlichen Verwaltungsbeamten*, Berlin 1905, p. 73; Rostowzew, PW, VI, pp. 2403ff.; Juster, II, pp. 282 ff.; Ginsburg, *op. cit.* (supra, p. 129), pp. 281 ff.; M. Brücklmeier, "Beiträge zur rechtlichen Stellung der Juden im römischen Reich", Ph.D. Thesis, Munich 1939, pp. 54 ff.; E. M. Smallwood, *Classical Philology*, LI (1956), pp. 2 ff.; I. A. F. Bruce, *PEQ*, XCVI (1964), pp. 34 ff.; P. Keresztes, *Vigiliae Christianae*, XXVII (1973), pp. 2 ff.; Smallwood, pp. 371 ff. For the term *fiscus Iudaicus*, cf. similar designations, e.g., *fiscus Alexandrinus, fiscus Asiaticus*. For an interpretation of talmudic passages bearing upon the Jewish tax, see also A. Carlebach, *JQR*, LXVI (1975), pp. 57 ff.

qui vel inprofessi Iudaicam viverent vitam vel dissimulata origine imposita genti tributa non pependissent: Domitian made the levy of the tax more rigorous by exacting it both from those who were not Jews by origin but adhered to the Jewish way of life and from those who were Jews by birth but tried to evade the tax by concealing their origin. Apparently Domitian did not introduce new principles for the application of the tax, but imposed the levy much more harshly. The old suggestion has been revived that by "inprofessi Iudaicam viverent vitam" the Christians are meant; see J. Janssen, *C. Suetonii Tranquilli Vita Domitiani*, Groningen 1919, pp. 59 f.; so also, e.g., P. E. Arias, *Domiziano*, Catania 1945, p. 142. However this interpretation is not easy to accept, since the Roman government was well aware of the difference between Christians and Jews from the time of Nero on, though the tax might sometimes have been exacted from Christians as well on the pretext that they lived a "Jewish life". See also M. Sordi, *Rivista di storia della chiesa in Italia*, XIV (1960), p. 21; J. Speigl, *Der römische Staat und die Christen*, Amsterdam 1970, pp. 20 ff. For "Iudaicam viverent vitam", cf. Ἰουδαϊκὸς βίος in Cassius Dio, LXVIII, 1:2 (No. 436).

me adulescentulum memini: This is one of the few passages in which Suetonius refers to his own experience; cf. Suetonius, *Nero*, 57:2: "denique cum post viginti annos adulescente me extitisset condicionis incertae qui se Neronem esse iactaret", where "adulescente me" refers to 88 C. E.; cf. also his *De Grammaticis*, 4: "me quidem adolescentulo". However the date of the episode in the *Vita Domitiani* cannot be established. The years 82–86 C. E. are suggested by A. Macé, *Essai sur Suétone*, Paris 1900, pp. 45 f.; for the possibility of dating it to the nineties, see Smallwood, *Classical Philology, op. cit.*, p. 12, n. 23, connecting the episode with Martialis, *Epigrammata*, VII, 55:7 f.; *ibid.*, 82 (Nos. 242 and 243), and cf. the commentary to these passages. For the problem of the year of Suetonius' birth, see Funaioli, PW, Ser. 2, IV, pp. 593 f.

cum a procuratore: For the procurator "ad capitularia Iudaeorum", cf. *ILS*, No. 1519. Cf. also *CPJ*, No. 181: πράκτωρ Ἰουδαϊκοῦ τελέσματος; see

Suetonius

G. Boulvert, *Esclaves et affranchis impériaux sous le Haut-Empire romain,* Naples 1970, pp. 230 f. For an alternative explanation of "capitularia", cf. Bruce, *op. cit.* (supra, p. 130), p. 37.

nonagenarius senex: Suetonius' story about the investigation of the nonagenarian apparently contradicts the general view, based on the documentary evidence from Egypt, that the obligation to pay the tax terminated at the age of sixty-two; see S. L. Wallace, *Taxation in Egypt from Augustus to Diocletian*, Princeton 1938, p. 111. It seems unlikely that there was a difference in the taxation systems for Italy and Egypt, to the disadvantage of Italy, or for that matter of Numidian Hippo (on which, see below). The exaction of the tax from a nonagenarian (a ὑπερετής, according to Graeco-Egyptian terminology) may only exemplify the "acerbitas" attaching to its levy under Domitian, who did not show a strict regard for the original regulations. The view that exemption from the Jewish tax was obtained at the age of sixty-two is mainly based on general considerations, in particular, the analogy with the *laographia.*

Suetonius does not state where he witnessed the scrutiny of the nonagenarian. The incident may have taken place in Rome, but it is equally possible that it occurred in Hippo Regius in Numidia, generally considered the native town of Suetonius because of an inscription found there honouring him (*CRAI*, 1952, pp. 76 ff.). See H. G. Pflaum, *Les carrières procuratoriennes équestres sous le Haut-Empire romain*, I, Paris 1960, p. 221; G. B. Townend, *Historia*, X (1961), pp. 105 ff. See also F. Millar, *Historia*, XIV (1965), p. 363. Some scholars prefer the view that Suetonius was a native of Italy. For a suggestion that he was born at Ostia, and that the inscription honouring him at Hippo reflects the importance of Suetonius during his years of administrative influence at the imperial court, see F. Grosso, *Atti della Accademia Nazionale dei Lincei* (Serie Ottava, *Rendiconti, Classe di Scienze Morali, Storiche e Filologiche*), XIV (1959), pp. 263 ff.; cf. C. Baurain, *Les Études Classiques*, XLIV (1976), pp. 124 ff.

XCV. FLORUS

First half of the second century C.E.

For his epitome of the history of the Roman Republic Florus seems to have been dependent on Livy, but to what extent is still an open question. He mentions the Jews once only, in his account of the conquests of Pompey. The epithet "inpia gens", which Florus applies to the Jews, is fairly typical of the attitude of a Roman living at the time of the Jewish revolt under Trajan (see commentary).[1]

---

1 For Florus and his sources, see O. Rossbach, PW, VI, pp. 2761 ff.; Schanz & Hosius, III, 1922, pp. 67 ff.; R. Zimmermann, *Rhein. Museum*, LXXIX (1930), pp. 93 ff.; P. Zancan, *Floro e Livio*, Padua 1942; A. Garzetti, *Athenaeum*, NS, XLII (1964), pp. 136 ff.; P. Jal, *REL*, XLIII (1965), pp. 358 ff.; W. den Boer, *Mnemosyne*, XVIII (1965), pp. 366 ff.; idem, *Some Minor Roman Historians*, Leiden 1972, pp. 1 ff.

321

Epitoma, I, 40:29–30 — Jal = F191R

(29) Nec non et in meridiem verso agmine Libanum Syriae Damascumque transgressus per nemora illa odorata, per turis et balsami silvas Romana circumtulit signa. Arabes, si quid imperaret, praesto fuere. (30) Hierosolyma defendere temptavere Iudaei;
5 verum haec quoque et intravit et vidit illud grande inpiae gentis arcanum patens, sub aurea vite Caelum. Dissidentibusque de regno fratribus arbiter factus regnare iussit Hyrcanum; Aristobolum, quia renovabat imperium, in catenas dedit.

1 *et* om. B	3 *circumtulit signa* e	*signa circumtulit* cett.
4 *Hierosolyma* Rossbach	*(h)ierosoli(y)mam* codd.	6 *aurea vite caelum* B
aureo uti sçelo N	*aureo uti (utis* P) *celo* cett.	7 *aristobolo* C

(29) Furthermore, turning his army southwards, he passed through the Lebanon in Syria and through Damascus, and bore the Roman standards through the famous scented groves and woods of frankincense and balm. He found the Arabs ready to carry out orders which he might give. (30) The Jews attempted to defend Jerusalem; but this also he entered and saw the great secret of that impious nation laid open to view, the heavens beneath a golden vine. Being appointed arbitrator between the two brothers, who were disputing the throne, he decided in favour of Hyrcanus and threw Aristobulus into prison, because he was seeking to restore his power.

(trans. E.S. Forster, *LCL*)

29 *per nemora illa odorata*: These are the groves in the vicinity of Jericho. Pompey passed through them on his march to Jerusalem; cf. *Ant.*, XIV, 54.

30 *et vidit illud ... arcanum patens*: Cf. Tacitus, *Historiae*, V, 9 (No. 281).

inpiae gentis: The designation of the Jews as "inpii", or in Greek ἀνόσιοι, became common especially as a result of their revolt under Trajan; cf. *CPJ*, Nos. 157, ll. 43, 49 f.; 158a, Col. VI, l. 14; 438, l. 4; 443, Col. II, l. 4 f. See also the discussion by A. Fuks, *Aegyptus*, XXXIII (1953), pp. 157 f.

sub aurea vite: Cf. *BJ*, V, 210.

Caelum: This reading of B should stand. For the depiction of the heavenly panorama on the tapestry hanging in the Temple, cf. *BJ*, V, 214. The emendation "cillus" does not commend itself. See also E. Bickermann, *MGWJ*, LXXI (1927), p. 257, n. 2. Florus' emphasis on the picture of the heavens should be accounted for by the view prevalent at Rome of the Jews as sky-worshippers; cf. Iuvenalis, XIV, 97 (No. 301). See also Hecataeus, apud: Diodorus, XL, 3:4 (No. 11).

XCVI. APOLLODORUS OF DAMASCUS

Died in the thirties of the second century C.E.

Apollodorus of Damascus, the celebrated architect of the age of Trajan and Hadrian, wrote his treatise on siege engines in response to a request from Hadrian. This Roman emperor was then encountering the stiff Jewish resistance in the Bar-Kokhba revolt in Judaea.

Although the name of the emperor is not given by Apollodorus in his introductory letter (No. 322), the work is stated by the Anonymous Byzantinus to have been addressed to Hadrian, and was known as τὰ Ἀπολλοδώρου πρὸς Ἀδριανὸν αὐτοκράτορα συνταχθέντα πολιορκητικά.[1] The only war that might have necessitated a handbook of this kind during the reign of Hadrian was the Bar-Kokhba revolt (see the commentary to Cassius Dio, LXIX = No. 440).[2] The suggestion that the letter may allude to events in Thrace at the beginning of Hadrian's reign[3] is precluded by the statement here of the author himself. Apollodorus writes that he had no personal knowledge of the places concerned (ἐπεὶ οὖν ἀγνοῶ τοὺς τόπους), while he was well acquainted with Thrace from his experience in the campaigns of Trajan. Apollodorus was executed by Hadrian after the architect's criticism of the plan for the temple of Venus and Roma, according to Cassius Dio, LXIX, 4. It is now assumed that this temple, which had been inaugurated in 121 C.E., was dedicated only in 136/7.[4] Thus the statement of Cassius Dio contains nothing to invalidate a date in the earlier thirties of the second century for the writing of the Poliorcetica. *That Hadrian himself joined the Roman army at the battle-field in Judaea is implied not only by the letter of Apollodorus, but also by*

---

1 See Schneider's introduction to the *Poliorcetica*, ed. R. Schneider, in: *Abhandlungen der königlichen Gesellschaft der Wissenschaften zu Göttingen, Philologisch-historische Klasse*, NF, Vol. X, Part 1, 1908, p. 6, n. 1.

2 See J. Plew, *Quellenuntersuchungen zur Geschichte des Kaisers Hadrian*, Strasbourg 1890, pp. 89 ff.; Juster, II, p. 194, n. 2; F.M. Abel, *Histoire de la Palestine*, II, Paris 1952, p. 93; F. Millar, *A Study of Cassius Dio*, Oxford 1964, pp. 65 f.; S. Follet, *Revue de Philologie*, XLII (1968), p. 67.

3 So Fabricius, PW, I, p. 2896.

4 See Millar, *loc. cit.*

Cassius Dio, LXIX, 14:3 (No. 440). Compare also Hieronymus, In Joel, i:4 (CCSL, *LXXVI, ed. Adriaen, p. 163*); Chronicon Paschale, *I (ed. Dindorf), p. 474:* ἦλθεν ᾿Αδριανὸς εἰς ῾Ιεροσόλυμα, καὶ ἔλαβε τοὺς ᾿Ιουδαίους αἰχμαλώτους.

Inscriptional evidence may also be adduced for the presence of Hadrian in Judaea during the war. The name of Q. Lollius Urbicus is mentioned as Hadrian's personal adjutant in the Judaean expedition; see ILS, *No. 1065: "Q. Lollio ... legato imp. Hadriani in expeditione Iudaica". Hadrian himself is referred to as "lab] oribus max[imis rempublicam ab ho]ste liberavit"; see* CIL, VI, *No. 974, to be dated to 134 or 135 C.E.*[5]

---

5 It has been suggested that the correspondence between the emperor and Apollodorus might allude to Hadrian's Mauretanian campaign of 122 C.E., and not necessarily to the war in Judaea; see Smallwood, p. 452, n. 93. Still the case for Judaea seems somewhat stronger.

Poliorcetica, ed. R. Schneider, *Abhandlungen der Königlichen Gesellschaft der Wissenschaften zu Göttingen, Philologisch-historische Klasse*, NF, Vol. X, Part I, 1908, pp. 8, 10

Ἀνέγνων σου, δέσποτα, τὴν περὶ τῶν μηχανημάτων ἐπιστολὴν καὶ μακάριος ἐγενόμην, ὅτι με κοινωνῆσαι ταύτης σου τῆς φροντίδος ἄξιον ἔκρινας. ποιήσας οὖν ὑποδείγματά τινα πρὸς πολιορκίαν εὔχρηστα ἔπεμψα διαγράψας, καὶ πᾶσιν ὑπελάλησα καὶ ὑπουργὸν ἀπέλυσα
5 πάντα δείξας καὶ ἐπ' αὐτοῦ ἐργασάμενος, ἵνα πρὸς τὰ ὑποδείγματα ὁμοίως, εἴ τις χρεία γένοιτο, ἐργάσηται. ἐπεὶ οὖν ἀγνοῶ τοὺς τόπους, σχήματα πολλὰ καὶ ποικίλα διέγραψα καὶ τὰς αἰτίας ἐπήνεγκα, ἑκάστῳ βοήθειαν καὶ φυλακὴν καὶ ἀσφάλειαν προσαρμόσας, καὶ ὡς ἐπὶ τὸ πλεῖστον εὐπόριστα, ἐλαφρά, εὐεργῆ, ταχέως ὑπὸ τῶν τυχόντων
10 συντελούμενα. ταῦτά σοι ἐφωδίασα, δέσποτα, ὡς οὐ μόνον ἐπινοεῖν ὑμᾶς τὰ ἔργα ἀλλὰ καὶ χρῆσθαι αὐτοῖς δύνασθαι διδάξας· ἄλλως γὰρ πολιορκεῖται πολίσματα πάσῃ παρασκευῇ καὶ ἀφθονίᾳ καὶ ὕλης καὶ χρόνου, καὶ ἄλλως ἔθνη καὶ κλίματα ὑπὸ τῆς τυχούσης περιτροπῆς εὐτροπούμενα. ὅθεν σκεψάμενος καὶ ἐπινοηθεὶς ταῦτα, βράδιον
15 ἀντέγραψά σοι, οὐδὲν διὰ τὴν καινότητα καὶ τὸ τῆς χρήσεως τάχος ὑπὸ τῶν προγεγενημένων ὠφεληθῆναι δυνηθείς. ἔπεμψα δὲ καὶ τέκτονας ἐγχωρίους καὶ τοὺς ἄλλως ἐργάσασθαι καὶ ποιῆσαι δυναμένους. οἶδα γὰρ μετά σου ἐν ταῖς παρατάξεσι γενόμενος, ὅτε εὐτύχουν στρατιωτῶν εὐπορήσας πρὸς τὸ καλῶς ἐργάσασθαι ἢ συνηθείᾳ ἢ εὐχερείᾳ, οἷον αἱ
20 ἐν τοῖς πολέμοις ἐκ τοῦ παραδόξου χρεῖαι ὡς εὐστρόφων καὶ ἀνθρώπων καὶ μηχανημάτων δέονται. ἐὰν δέ τι ἐν τοῖς ἐπὶ ἑκάστου συστήματος ἐπιλογισμοῖς ἀσαφῶς εἴπω, σύγγνωθι, δέσποτα. καὶ γὰρ τὰ ὀνόματα τῆς ἐπιστήμης ἀσυνήθη ἔσται τοῖς κοινοῖς λόγοις καὶ ποικίλην θεωρίαν ἔχει τὸ ἔργον, καὶ αὐτὸς ἐγὼ εἰπεῖν τάχα ἀσθενέστερος· τάχα
25 δὲ ἡ μεγαλοφυΐα σου διορθοῦται, καὶ συγγινώσκει ἡ εὐμένεια.

9 ταχέα PaV   17 ἐγχωρίους] ἐγχειρητικοὺς Schneider

I have read, my lord, your letter about engines of war, and I felt happy that you found me worthy to participate in your anxiety. Having thus made some models that are serviceable for a siege I have sent you the drawings. I have discussed them with everybody and have sent an assistant, after showing him everything and executing the plan in his presence, so that if the need arises he may work likewise according to the drawings. Since I do not know the places, I have drawn many and variegated designs, and explained their purpose, fitting to each of them means of defence, protection and safety. They were to be constructed with maximum ease, as light, serviceable and capable of quick execution even by untrained people. I have furnished you, my lord, with these things, instructing you to be able not only to construct the engines, but also to use them. For it is one thing to lay siege to towns with all the equipment, and with a plentiful supply of material and time, and yet another when people and regions are easily dealt a reversal by chance. Hence, in examining and conceiving these things, I have been rather slow in answering your letter, since because of the novelty and urgency of the requirement I could profit nothing from the works of my predecessors. I have also sent you native [?][1] carpenters and other fellows who are able to work and manufacture in other ways. For I know, having taken part with you in battles, when I have had the good fortune to have a plentiful supply of soldiers able to work well, either through habit or skill, to what extent unforeseen changes require both well-adapted men and engines. However, if I fail to express myself clearly in the descriptions of each machine, please forgive me, my lord. For the technical terms differ from the common language, the subject requires a complicated exposition, and I am perhaps rather poor in powers of expression. Yet your magnanimity may set matters right, and your goodwill grant forgiveness.

1 Or enterprising (according to the emendation of Schneider).

XCVII. HERENNIUS PHILO OF BYBLUS

Second half of the first century to first half of the second century C.E.

Herennius Philo of Byblus in Phoenicia was born at the time of the accession of Nero as emperor of Rome (c. 54 C.E.). He wrote many works in Greek, including a Phoenician history, a work on famous towns and personalities, and a history of Hadrian (117–138 C.E.).

According to Philo, the contents of his Phoenician history derived from the ancient writer Sanchuniathon of Berytus, whose work Philo claimed to have translated into Greek. Although it has been the fashion to treat Philo's statement with scepticism, the recent discoveries, especially those of Ugarit, have made it more credible that Philo's work included some authentic material that may go back to Sanchuniathon.

Philo was proud of the Phoenician past in general, and above all that of his native Berytus. His history of Phoenicia recalls the works of the Babylonian Berossus, the Egyptians Manetho and Chaeremon, and the Jew Josephus, on the history of their respective countries.

Philo held euhemeristic views, and, living at the time of the Jewish revolt under Hadrian, was not too sympathetic towards the Jews. This is attested both by the remark quoted by Origen (No. 325), and by Helladius' reference to him, quoted by Photius (No. 329).

Bibliography

A. Gudeman, PW, VIII, pp. 650 f.; C. Clemen, *Die phönikische Religion nach Philo von Byblos*, Leipzig 1939; O. Eissfeldt, *Ras Schamra und Sanchunjaton*, Halle 1939; idem, *Taautos und Sanchunjaton*, Berlin 1952; idem, *Sanchunjaton von Berut und Ilumilku von Ugarit*, Halle 1952; idem, *Kleine Schriften*, II, Tübingen 1963, pp. 127 ff., 130 ff.; III, 1966, pp. 398 ff., 407 ff.; T. S. Brown, *HTR*, XXXIX (1946), pp. 271 ff.; P. Nautin, *RB*, LVI (1949), pp. 259 ff., 573 ff.; LVII (1950), pp. 409 ff.; R. Follet, *Biblica*, XXXIV (1953), pp. 81 ff.; F. Løkkegaard, *Studia Theologica*, VIII (1954), pp. 51 ff.; J. Pépin, *Mythe et allégorie, les origines grecques et les contestations judéo-chrétiennes*, Paris 1958, pp. 217 ff.; Hesiod, *Theogony*, ed. M. L. West, with Prolegomena and Commentary, Oxford 1966, pp. 24 ff.; W. F. Albright, *Yahweh and the Gods of Canaan*, London 1968, pp. 194 ff.; S. E. Loewenstamm, *P'raqim*, II, Jerusalem 1974, pp. 315 ff. (in Hebrew); idem, PW, Suppl. XIV (1974), pp. 593 ff., s. v. Sanchuniat(h)on; J. Barr, *Bulletin of the John Rylands University Library of Manchester*, LVII (1974–1975), pp. 17 ff.; L. Troiani, *L'opera storiografica di Filone da Byblos*, Pisa 1974; R. A. Oden, *PEQ*, CX (1978), pp. 115 ff.

apud: Eusebius, *Praeparatio Evangelica*, I, 9: 20–21 — Mras = F79 R = *F. Gr. Hist.*, III, C790, F1

(20) Ἱστορεῖ δὲ ταῦτα Σαγχουνιάθων, ἀνὴρ παλαιότατος καὶ τῶν Τρωϊκῶν χρόνων, ὥς φασι, πρεσβύτερος, ὃν καὶ ἐπ᾽ ἀκριβείᾳ καὶ ἀληθείᾳ τῆς Φοινικικῆς ἱστορίας ἀποδεχθῆναι μαρτυροῦσιν· Φίλων δὲ τούτου πᾶσαν τὴν γραφὴν ὁ Βύβλιος, οὐχ ὁ Ἑβραῖος, μεταβαλὼν ἀπὸ τῆς Φοινίκων
5 γλώττης ἐπὶ τὴν Ἑλλάδα φωνὴν ἐξέδωκε. μέμνηται τούτων ὁ καθ᾽ ἡμᾶς τὴν καθ᾽ ἡμῶν πεποιημένος συσκευὴν ἐν τετάρτῳ τῆς πρὸς ἡμᾶς ὑποθέσεως, ὧδε τῷ ἀνδρὶ μαρτυρῶν πρὸς λέξιν.
(21) « Ἱστορεῖ δὲ τὰ περὶ Ἰουδαίων ἀληθέστατα, ὅτι καὶ τοῖς τόποις καὶ τοῖς ὀνόμασιν αὐτῶν τὰ συμφωνότατα, Σαγχουνιάθων ὁ Βηρύτιος, εἰληφὼς τὰ
10 ὑπομνήματα παρὰ Ἱερομβάλου τοῦ ἱερέως θεοῦ Ἰευώ· ὃς Ἀβιβάλῳ τῷ βασιλεῖ Βηρυτίων τὴν ἱστορίαν ἀναθεὶς ὑπ᾽ ἐκείνου καὶ τῶν κατ᾽ αὐτὸν ἐξεταστῶν τῆς ἀληθείας παρεδέχθη ... τὰ δὲ τοῦ Σαγχουνιάθωνος εἰς Ἑλλάδα γλῶσσαν ἡρμήνευσεν Φίλων ὁ Βύβλιος.»

1 δὴ A / παλαίτατος BONV	2 πρεσβύτατος A	
3 ἀποδειχθῆναι V ἀποδειχθησα B¹	ἀποδειχθείση B²	
4 συγγραφὴν BONV 10 ἱερομβαλίου B / ἀβελβάλῳ BONV		
13 βίβλιος A		

(20) Now the historian of this subject is Sanchuniathon, an author of great antiquity and older, as they say, than the Trojan times, whom they testify to have been approved for the accuracy and truth of his Phoenician History. Philo of Byblos, not the Hebrew, translated his whole work from the Phoenician language into the Greek, and published it. The author in our own day of the compilation against us mentions these things in the fourth book of his treatise "Against the Christians", where he bears the following testimony to Sanchuniathon, word for word:
(21) "Of the affairs of the Jews the truest history, because the most in accordance with their places and names, is that of Sanchuniathon of Berytus who received the records from Hierombalus the priest of the god Jeuo; he dedicated his history to Abibalus king of Berytus, and was approved by him and by the investigators of truth in his time." And the works of Sanchuniathon were translated into the Greek tongue by Philo of Byblos.   (trans. E. H. Gifford, Oxford 1903)

20 μέμνηται τούτων ...: I.e. the writing of the history by Sanchuniathon and its translation by Philo of Byblus.

ὁ καθ' ἡμᾶς τὴν καθ' ἡμῶν πεποιημένος συσκευὴν ...: A reference to Porphyry and his work against the Christians.

21 Ἱστορεῖ δὲ τὰ περὶ Ἰουδαίων ἀληθέστατα...: The preceding sentences of Eusebius do not refer to Jews, but only to Phoenicians; cf. *Praeparatio Evangelica*, I, 9 : 19 f.: ἡ γοῦν τῶν ἐθνῶν ἀπάντων πολύθεος πλάνη μακροῖς ὕστερον αἰῶσι πέφανται, ἀρξαμένη μὲν ἀπὸ Φοινίκων καὶ Αἰγυπτίων ... ἣν καὶ αὐτὴν ἐπισκέψασθαι καιρὸς ἀπὸ τῶν Φοινικικῶν ἀρξαμένους ... ἱστορεῖ δὲ ταῦτα Σαγχουνιάθων ... ὃν καὶ ἐπ' ἀκριβείᾳ καὶ ἀληθείᾳ τῆς Φοινικικῆς ἱστορίας ἀποδεχθῆναι μαρτυροῦσιν. Thus the quotation from Porphyry by Eusebius, which expressly mentions the Jews, comes as a surprise. Moreover, the continuation of the passage contains nothing concerning the Jews. The emendation ἱεουδαίων, i.e. single sons, is proposed by O. Eissfeldt, *Sanchunjaton von Berut, op. cit.* (supra, p. 138), pp. 28 ff.; cf. also idem, *Taautos und Sanchunjaton, op. cit.* (supra, p. 138), p. 28, n. 1; idem, *Wiener Studien*, LXX (1957), pp. 96 f. = *Festschrift Karl Mras*, Vienna 1957. This emendation would imply that Porphyry had in view sacrifices of single sons, of which Philo of Byblus presumably wrote in his Phoenician history. The same emendation was already proposed for Eusebius, *Praeparatio Evangelica*, I, 10 : 42 (No. 326); see Müller, *FHG*, III, p. 571. However, Eissfeldt himself does not wholly exclude the possibility that the text quoted from Porphyry might have had Ἰουδαίων; see *Sanchunjaton von Berut, op. cit.*, pp. 25 f.: "Da uns der Zusammenhang, in dem der von Eusebius aus der Schrift des Porphyrius zitierte Abschnitt in dieser gestanden hat, leider unbekannt ist und auch wohl bleiben wird, lässt sich nicht sagen, ob die ihm da vorangegangenen Ausführungen die Nennung der Juden an seinem Anfang verständlich gemacht haben, etwa in dem Sinne, dass sie 'Juden' im weiteren Sinn, mit Einschluss der Phönizier, gebraucht und damit auch zu solchem Verständnis des am Anfang des Zitates stehenden Wortes 'Juden' angeleitet hätten. Dann könnte man das Ἰουδαίων am Ende dem Porphyrius zutrauen, brauchte also nicht an einen Textfehler zu denken." See now Barr, *op. cit.* (supra, p. 138), p. 32, n. 1. Barr seems right in rejecting the attempt to eliminate Ἰουδαίων and read ἱευδαίων instead; for it is unlikely that a Greek would have understood this to mean "concerning the first-born".

παρὰ Ἱερομβάλου: On the supposition that Sanchuniathon is referring to the Jews, it is natural to search in this passage of Philo for an allusion to the biblical past, so Hierombalos has been identified with Jerubaal (= Gideon); see, e.g., Gudeman, *op. cit.* (supra, p. 138), p. 661. However, this is rather far-fetched and a Phoenician proper name seems more likely. The form Hierembalos is read by W. F. Albright, *JBL*, LX (1941), p. 210. See also Clemen, *op. cit.* (supra, p. 138), pp. 8 f.

Ἰευώ: This name occurs only here. For the reading Ἰαώ, see Theodoretus, *Graecarum Affectionum Curatio*, II, 44; cf. Ganschinietz, PW, IX, p. 702. See also W. W. Baudissin, *Kyrios*, II, Giessen 1929, pp. 205 ff. For an explanation of the occurrence of Ἰευώ (= Ἰάω) as a result of the diffusion of the cult of the biblical Iao among the Phoenicians, see Clemen, *op. cit.* (supra, p. 138),

p. 9. A different view is that Ἰευώ stands for some Phoenician deity and since the inhabitants of Berytus were especially attached to the cult of Poseidon, we should read here "Yam" (ם׳), who appears in the pantheon of Ugarit; see Eissfeldt, *Sanchunjaton von Berut, op. cit.* (supra, p. 138), pp. 32 ff. This interpretation is accepted by G. Capovilla, *Aegyptus*, XXXIX (1959), p. 339. However, Albright points out that the reading Ieu of the codex A reflects the "typical North-Israelite and Phoenician dissimilation of Yahu"; see Albright, *Yahweh, op. cit.* (supra, p. 138), p. 228, n. 155.

Ἀβιβάλῳ τῷ βασιλεῖ Βηρυτίων: This is the name of the father of Hiram, Solomon's contemporary, according to Dius, apud: Josephus, *Contra Apionem*, I, 113 (No. 36).

τὰ δὲ τοῦ Σαγχουνιάθωνος: For the various views held by scholars on Sanchuniathon, see O. Eissfeldt, *Taautos und Sanchunjaton, op. cit.* (supra, p. 138), pp. 50 ff.; Albright, *Yahweh, op. cit.* (supra, p. 138), pp. 195 f. Albright suggests that Sanchuniathon was a refugee from Tyre who settled in Berytus, living in the sixth century B.C.E.

324

apud: Lydus, *De Mensibus*, IV, 53, pp. 110 f. — Wünsch = *F. Gr. Hist.*, III, C790, F7

Ὁ δὲ Ῥωμαῖος Βάρρων περὶ αὐτοῦ ⟨scil. τοῦ παρὰ Ἰουδαίων τιμωμένου θεοῦ⟩ διαλαβών φησι ⟨No. 75⟩ παρὰ Χαλδαίοις ἐν τοῖς μυστικοῖς αὐτὸν λέγεσθαι Ἰάω ἀντὶ τοῦ φῶς νοητὸν τῇ Φοινίκων γλώσσῃ, ὥς φησιν Ἐρέννιος.

The Roman Varro defining him [scil. the Jewish God] says that he is called Iao in the Chaldaean mysteries. That means in the Phoenician language the "intelligible light" according to Herennius.

Ἰάω: For the diffusion of the name Ἰάω in the Graeco-Roman world, see the commentary to Diodorus, I, 94:1–2 (No. 58); Cornelius Labeo, apud: Macrobius, *Saturnalia*, I, 18:18–21 (No. 445). Did Philo give a Phoenician interpretation to this famous name merely from a desire to link it with Phoenicia, or had the name real roots in the Phoenician past? The latter alternative seemed to gain probability following the discoveries at Ugarit, when some scholars thought that they had found a god Iao; see R. Dussaud, *RHR*, CV (1932), p. 247; H. Bauer, *ZAW*, LI (1933), pp. 92 ff.; Clemen, *op. cit.* (supra, p. 138), p. 9. Against these, however, see the doubts of Eissfeldt, *Sanchunjaton von Berut, op. cit.* (supra, p. 138), pp. 32 f.

φῶς νοητόν: It has been suggested that the identification of Ἰάω with φῶς νοητόν is based on that of Iao with Aion, whose name is also found in the magical papyri; see H. Lewy, *Chaldaean Oracles and Theurgy*, Cairo 1956, p. 409, n. 32.

325

apud: Origenes, *Contra Celsum*, I, 15 — Borret = F81R = *F. Gr. Hist.*, III, C790, F9

Καὶ Ἑκαταίου δὲ τοῦ ἱστορικοῦ φέρεται περὶ Ἰουδαίων βιβλίον, ἐν ᾧ
προστίθεται μᾶλλόν πως ὡς σοφῷ τῷ ἔθνει ἐπὶ τοσοῦτον, ὡς καὶ Ἑρέννιον
Φίλωνα ἐν τῷ περὶ Ἰουδαίων συγγράμματι πρῶτον μὲν ἀμφιβάλλειν, εἰ
τοῦ ἱστορικοῦ ἐστι τὸ σύγγραμμα, δεύτερον δὲ λέγειν ὅτι, εἴπερ ἐστὶν
5 αὐτοῦ, εἰκὸς αὐτὸν συνηρπάσθαι ἀπὸ τῆς παρὰ Ἰουδαίοις πιθανότητος
καὶ συγκατατεθεῖσθαι αὐτῶν τῷ λόγῳ.

6 αὐτῶν Bouhéreau   αὐτῷ A

Moreover, a book about the Jews is attributed to Hecataeus the
historian, in which the wisdom of the nation is emphasized even more
strongly — so much so that Herennius Philo in his treatise about the
Jews even doubts in the first place whether it is a genuine work of the
historian, and says in the second place that if it is authentic, he had
probably been carried away by the Jews' powers of persuasion and
accepted their doctrine.   (trans. H. Chadwick, Cambridge 1953)

Καὶ Ἑκαταίου δὲ τοῦ ἱστορικοῦ φέρεται περὶ Ἰουδαίων βιβλίον: It is
commonly assumed that Philo has here in mind the work of Hecataeus of
Abdera on the Jews, on which Josephus draws in *Contra Apionem*, I, 183–204
(No. 12). That Philo intends some other work attributed to Hecataeus, of the
kind referred to in the *Letter of Aristeas*, 31, is suggested by M. Engers,
Mnemosyne, NS, LI (1923), pp. 233 f. But this conjecture is hardly necessary.
See also Troiani, *op. cit.* (supra, p. 138), p. 23, n. 48.

326

apud: Eusebius, *Praeparatio Evangelica*, I, 10:42–44 — Mras = *F. Gr. Hist.*, III, C790,
F10 + 3b

(42) Ὁ δ' αὐτὸς ⟨scil. Philo⟩ ἐν τῷ περὶ Ἰουδαίων συγγράμματι ἔτι καὶ
ταῦτα περὶ τοῦ Κρόνου γράφει· *(43)* «Τάαυτος, ὃν Αἰγύπτιοι
προσαγορεύουσιν Θωύθ, σοφίᾳ διενεγκὼν παρὰ τοῖς Φοίνιξιν, πρῶτος
τὰ κατὰ τὴν θεοσέβειαν ἐκ τῆς τῶν χυδαίων ἀπειρίας εἰς
5 ἐπιστημονικὴν ἐμπειρίαν διέταξεν ... *(44)* Κρόνος τοίνυν, ὃν οἱ
Φοίνικες Ἤλ προσαγορεύουσιν, βασιλεύων τῆς χώρας, καὶ ὕστερον
μετὰ τὴν τοῦ βίου τελευτὴν ἐπὶ τὸν τοῦ Κρόνου ἀστέρα καθιερωθείς,

2 Ταυθός A   4 τῶν om. B   6 Ἤλ] Ἰσραὴλ BGNV
7 ἐπὶ] εἰς BONV

ἐξ ἐπιχωρίας νύμφης Ἀνωβρὲτ λεγομένης υἱὸν ἔχων μονογενῆ (ὂν διὰ
τοῦτο Ἰεοὺδ ἐκάλουν, τοῦ μονογενοῦς οὕτως ἔτι καὶ νῦν καλουμένου
10 παρὰ τοῖς Φοίνιξι) κινδύνων ἐκ πολέμου μεγίστων κατειληφότων τὴν
χώραν βασιλικῷ κοσμήσας σχήματι τὸν υἱὸν βωμόν τε
κατασκευασάμενος κατέθυσεν.»

8 ἄνωβριν Α	9 Ἰεοὺδ Eissfeldt	ἰεδοὺδ Α	ἱεροὺδ Ν
ἱροὺδ BODV	11 χώραν] πόλιν BONV	12 κατασκευάσας ἄσμενος Η	

(42) The same author [scil. Philo], in his history of the Jews, further
writes thus concerning Kronos (43): "Taautos, whom the Egyptians
call Thoyth, excelled in wisdom among the Phoenicians, and was the
first to rescue the worship of the gods from the ignorance of the
vulgar, and arrange it in the order of intelligent experience ... (44)
Kronos then, whom the Phoenicians call El, who was king of the
country and subsequently, after his decease, was deified as the star
Saturn, had by a nymph of the country named Anobret an only
begotten son, whom they on this account called Ieud, the only
begotten being still so called among the Phoenicians; and when very
great dangers from war beset the country, he arrayed his son in royal
apparel, and prepared an altar, and sacrificed him."

(trans. E.H. Gifford, Oxford 1903)

42 Ὁ δ' αὐτὸς ἐν τῷ περὶ Ἰουδαίων συγγράμματι: Here also, as in No. 323,
some doubts arise concerning the reading Ἰουδαίων, though theoretically it
could be possible that Philo referred in some way to Kronos and also to
Taautos in his work on the Jews. The reading Ἰεουδαίων is suggested by
Müller, *op. cit.* (supra, p. 140); see the commentary to No. 323. Another view
is that ὁ δ' αὐτός does not refer to Philo but to Porphyry, with reference to his
work against the Christians; see P. Nautin, *RB*, LVII (1950), pp. 409 ff.
Though Nautin's interpretation is grammatically correct, the assumption
that, by περὶ Ἰουδαίων, Eusebius refers to the work of Porphyry against the
Christians, or even to a part of it, is improbable; see Eissfeldt, *Sanchunjaton
von Berut, op. cit.* (supra, p. 138), p. 29, n. 4 (end).

327

Stephanus Byzantius, s.v. Ἰόπη — Meineke = *F. Gr. Hist.*, III, C790, F38

Ἰόπη πόλις Φοινίκης πλησίον Ἰαμνίας ὡς Φίλων, ὡς δὲ Διονύσιος
Παλαιστίνης.

Jope, according to Philo, is situated in Phoenicia in the vicinity of
Jamnia. According to Dionysus it is situated in Palaestina.

Ἰόπη ... ὡς Φίλων: The extract is from the work of Philo περὶ πόλεων καὶ οὕς ἑκάστη αὐτῶν ἐνδόξους ἤνεγκεν. On the use of Philo of Byblus as a source by Stephanus Byzantius, see Gudeman, *op. cit.* (supra, p. 138), pp. 654 ff. The Phoenician patriotism of Philo finds expression in the inclusion of Jaffa in Phoenicia. This was in accord with the situation in the Persian period, when Jaffa was incorporated in the territory of the Phoenician king Eshmunezer; see the commentary to Diodorus, I, 31:2 (No. 56). It was presumably also within the administrative division of Phoenicia in the Seleucid period, but from the time of Simon the Hasmonaean Jaffa was a Jewish city and the main port of Judaea. Nevertheless even writers like Strabo occasionally continued to regard it as a Phoenician city; cf. *Geographica*, I, 2:35 (No. 109). Philo here defines the situation of Jaffa in relation to Jamnia. The importance of Jamnia is also emphasized in Strabo, *Geographica*, XVI, 2:28, p. 759 (No. 114); see the commentary *ad loc.* For the history of Jamnia at the end of the period of the Second Temple, see Schürer, II, pp. 126 ff. Following the destruction of the Temple it became the chief centre of Judaism.

328

apud: Lydus, *De Magistratibus*, I, 12, p. 17 — Wünsch; cf. *ibid.*, I, 23, p. 27 = F 80 R = F. Gr. Hist., III, C790, F55

Τὸ δὲ Βάρρωνος ἐπώνυμον τὸν ἀνδρεῖον, κατὰ τὴν Κελτῶν φωνήν, κατὰ δὲ Φοίνικας τὸν Ἰουδαῖον σημαίνει, ὡς Ἑρέννιός φησιν·

2 Ἑρέννιος Fussius   ερέννιοι O

According to Herennius the surname Varro denotes in the Celtic language "the brave one", while among the Phoenicians it signifies "the Jew".

Τὸ δὲ Βάρρωνος ... κατὰ δὲ Φοίνικας τὸν Ἰουδαῖον σημαίνει: This explanation of Philo seemingly derives from the similarity of sound between Βάρρων (Varro) and Ἑβραῖος (עברי). Müller connects Philo's explanation with בר־אֹזן (i.e. *filius mendacii*) and detects in it an anti-Semitic vein; see Müller, *op. cit.* (supra, p. 140), p. 562; but this view is rather far-fetched. On the use of Philo by Lydus, see Gudeman, *op. cit.* (supra, p. 138), p. 652.

329

apud: Helladius, *Chrestomathia*, apud: Photius, *Bibliotheca*, Cod. 279, p. 529b; cf. No. 472 = F. Gr. Hist., III, C790, F11

Ὅτι φλυαρεῖ καὶ οὗτος τὸν Μωσῆν Ἄλφα καλεῖσθαι, διότι ἀλφοῖς τὸ σῶμα κατάστικτος ἦν, καὶ καλεῖ τοῦ ψεύδους τὸν Φίλωνα μάρτυρα.

Also Helladius talks nonsense that Moses is called Alpha because his body was spotted with leprosy. To this lie he calls upon Philo to testify.

XCVIII. PHLEGON OF TRALLES

First half of the second century C.E.

The lexicon of Suda shows Phlegon of Tralles (s.v. Φλέγων Τραλλιανός) to have been a prolific and versatile writer. Ranking foremost among his works is "On the Olympiads" in sixteen books,[1] *of which only some fragments remain. This work apparently also covered events of the reign of Hadrian from what is stated about it in Suda: ἔστι δὲ μέχρι τῆς σκϑ΄ ὀλυμπιάδος τὰ πραχϑέντα πανταχοῦ, and in Photius, Bibliotheca, Cod. 97: κάτεισι δέ, ὡς αὐτός φησι, μέχρι τῶν Ἀδριανοῦ χρόνων. Both the general statement of Suda and the fragments of the work quoted in Photius show that Phlegon did not confine himself to details concerning the Olympiads, but related there the main events of political history, such as the expeditions of Murena and Lucullus, the conquest of Crete by Metellus, or changes in the Parthian monarchy.*

Phlegon is referred to as a historian who had briefly mentioned the Jews in a passage also quoted by Suda from the Church historian Philostorgius, who puts him on the same level as Dio (i.e. Cassius Dio). It seems that Philostorgius adduces Phlegon in a passage explaining why the history of the rise of Christianity is omitted in works of historians writing of the Jews.[2]

The letter attributed to Phlegon referring to Jews, in: Scriptores Historiae Augustae, Quadrigae Tyrannorum, 8 (*No. 527*), *is undoubtedly a forgery.*

---

1 See C. Wachsmuth, *Einleitung in das Studium der alten Geschichte*, Leipzig 1895, pp. 147 f. (Wachsmuth refers only to fifteen books); W. Weber, *Untersuchungen zur Geschichte des Kaisers Hadrianus*, Leipzig 1907, pp. 94 ff.; E. Frank, PW, XX, pp. 262 f.
2 See Gutschmid, IV, p. 349.

146

Phlegon of Tralles

330

Suda, s. v. φλέγων — Adler = F. Gr. Hist., II, B257, F34 = Philostorgius, Historia Ecclesiastica, I, 1a, ed. Bidez & Winkelmann, p. 5

Τούτου τοῦ Φλέγοντος, ὥς φησι Φιλοστόργιος, ὅσον τὰ κατὰ τοὺς Ἰουδαίους συμπεσόντα διὰ πλείονος ἐπεξελθεῖν τοῦ πλάτους, Φλέγοντος καὶ Δίωνος βραχέως ἐπιμνησθέντων καὶ παρενθήκην αὐτὰ τοῦ οἰκείου λόγου ποιησαμένων· ἐπεὶ τῶν γε εἰς εὐσέβειαν καὶ τὴν ἄλλην ἀρετὴν
5 ἑλκόντων οὐδ' ὁτιοῦν οὐδ' οὗτος δείκνυται πεφροντικώς, ὅνπερ οὐδ' ἐκεῖνοι τρόπον. τοὐναντίον μὲν οὖν ὁ Ἰώσηπος καὶ δεδοικότι ἔοικε καὶ εὐλαβουμένῳ ὡς μὴ προσκρούσειεν Ἕλλησι.

1 ὅσον] Ἰοῦστον vel potius Ἰώσηπον Valesius   2 ἐξελθεῖν G

As Philostorgius says, Justus [or Josephus?] related the history of the Jews more circumstantially than Phlegon, since both Phlegon and Dio referred to them only briefly, treating them as a parenthesis in their main narrative. However, he [scil. Justus] is shown not to be interested in matters conducing to piety and virtue in general, and in this he is like the two others [scil. Phlegon and Dio]. On the other hand, Josephus seems to be God-fearing and scrupulous to give no offence to the Greeks [?].

ὅσον: The reading ὅσον makes hardly any sense here, and one would expect the name of a writer who related Jewish history more circumstantially than Phlegon. Valesius, therefore, suggested the reading Ἰοῦστον, or more preferably Ἰώσηπον, feeling that the name of a Jewish historian has to be supplied. Later scholars followed his suggestion, though usually preferring the emendation Ἰοῦστον; see, e.g., Wachsmuth, op. cit. (supra, p. 146, n. 1), p. 438, n. 2; Gutschmid, loc. cit. (supra, p. 146, n. 2), and for the view that Philostorgius took Justus for a pagan; Schürer, I, p. 62; H. Luther, Josephus und Justus von Tiberias, Halle 1910, p. 50, n. 1.
On the other hand, the emendation Ἰώσηπον is upheld by Schürer, ed. Vermes & Millar, I, p. 37; T. Rajak, CQ, NS, XXIII (1973), pp. 365 f.

XCIX. PTOLEMY CHENNUS

First half of the second century C.E.

Ptolemy Chennus, son of Hephaestion, was an Alexandrian grammaticus. *It seems that he stayed for some time at Rome.*[1] *His* Καινὴ ἱστορία, *a collection of mainly mythological material, is cited by Photius,* Bibliotheca, *Cod. 190. Ptolemy mentioned famous persons whose nickname derived from one of the letters of the alphabet; the only celebrity among them who was neither Greek nor Roman is Moses.*

---

1 See A. Dihle, PW, XXIII, p. 1862. On Ptolemy Chennus and the extant fragments of his work, see A. Chatzis, *Der Philosoph und Grammatiker Ptolemaios Chennos*, Paderborn 1914; K. H. Tomberg, *Die Kaine Historia des Ptolemaios Chennos*, Bonn 1968.

Ptolemy Chennus

331

Nova Historia, apud: Photius, *Bibliotheca*, Cod. 190, p. 151b, ed. Henry, Vol. III, p. 66 = F74R

(additions et corrections, p. 361) = Chatzis, *Der Philosoph und Grammatiker*

Ptolemaios Chennos, 1914, p. 37

'Ὡς 'Αλφειῷ τῷ ποταμῷ γέρας δωρούμενος 'Ηρακλῆς, νικήσας ἐν
'Ολυμπίᾳ, ἀπ' αὐτοῦ ἐκάλεσε τὸ ἄλφα καὶ προέταξε τῶν στοιχείων. ὅτι
φλυαρῶν οὗτος ὁ μυθογράφος, Μωσῆς, φησίν, ὁ τῶν 'Εβραίων νομοθέτης
ἄλφα ἐκαλεῖτο διὰ τὸ ἀλφοὺς ἔχειν ἐπὶ τοῦ σώματος.

    2 ἀπ' αὐτοῦ Casaubonus   ἄπαν A   ἄπαν M   3 φασίν A

After a victory at Olympia Heracles, presenting the river Alpheus
with a gift, called the "Alpha" after it and put it at the head of the
alphabet. This mythographer is talking nonsense when he says that
Moses the legislator of the Jews was called Alpha because he had
much dull-white leprosy on his body.

ὁ τῶν 'Εβραίων νομοθέτης: The use of the term "Hebrews" instead of
"Jews" by Ptolemy, who probably lived at the end of the first century C.E.
and the beginning of the second, is in accord with the usage of other writers of
that period; see the commentary to Charax of Pergamum (No. 335).
ἄλφα ἐκαλεῖτο ...: This explanation probably derives from Alexandrian
circles, since Ptolemy lived in this city, with which the tradition that the Jews
had originally been lepers was connected. Philo of Byblus, quoted by
Helladius with reference to this explanation (No. 329), apparently suggested
it in his discussion of the Phoenician alphabet. Ptolemy Chennus, however,
need not have derived this from Philo. The name ἄλφα for Moses, with the
same explanation, also occurs in a passage on the Jews by Nicarchus (No.
248). See also Heinemann, PW, XVI, p. 361; Böhl, *Opera Minora*, p. 112;
J.G. Gager, *JTS*, XX (1969), pp. 245 ff.

C. ARRIAN
c. 95–175 C.E.

The historian Arrian makes no reference to Jews in his extant works, apart from the allusions recorded in his Discourses of Epictetus (Nos. 252–254). Even his narrative of the conquest of Palestine by Alexander the Great does not mention the Jews. However he evidently had occasion to do so in his lost work Parthica, *and surviving fragments show that it contained information about the confrontation between the Romans and the Jewish population of the East at the time of Trajan. Arrian's* Parthica *was a major work, in seventeen books, from which only meagre fragments have been preserved in the* Bibliotheca of Photius, *the lexicons of Suda and Stephanus Byzantius, and the works of Lydus.[1] The main part of Arrian's Parthian history concentrated on the campaigns of Trajan in the East, events which were contemporaneous with Arrian although he did not participate in them. This section was preceded by an account of the rise of the Parthian state, its history until the time of Trajan, and the events leading up to the war.*

The nature of the fragments makes it hardly possible to construct a connected narrative of Trajan's campaigns in the East. The chief source for this expedition is Book LXVIII of the history of Cassius Dio, which is dependent on Arrian's Parthica.[2] *However, that part of Cassius Dio's history survives only in the epitome of Xiphilinus.*

Since the Jews played a part in the events of the Parthian War under Trajan and suffered much at the latter's hands, as known from both Cassius Dio (through Xiphilinus) and the Christian tradition (through Eusebius and other Christian writers dependent on him), it may be assumed with certainty that Arrian's Parthica *referred in some way to the relations between the Romans and the Jews. This is fully borne out by the fragment in Suda, relating Trajan's determination to destroy the nation (i.e. the Jews) in view of its presumptuous wickedness (No. 332a). The fragment given by Stephanus Byzantius from Book XI of the* Parthica, *presumably deriving from the story of Trajan's advance*

---

1 On Arrian's *Parthica*, see Gutschmid, III, pp. 125 ff.; A. G. Roos, *Studia Arrianea*, Leipzig 1912; *F. Gr. Hist.*, II, D, pp. 566 ff.; F. A. Lepper, *Trajan's Parthian War*, Oxford 1948, pp. 1 ff.
2 See K. Hartmann, *Philologus*, LXXIV (1917), pp. 73 ff.

150

southwards into Babylonia, mentions a Syrian city in the vicinity of the Euphrates named Naarda (No. 332b). This was inhabited mainly by Jews and was the chief centre of Babylonian Jewry up to the middle of the third century C.E. Less certainly, the mention in the Parthica *of some other places, above all* Χώχη *in the vicinity of Seleucia on the Tigris (see Stephanus Byzantius, s. v.), may imply a direct contact, or even clash, between Jews in these localities and the Roman army.*[3]

3 See Y. Gutman, *Assaf Festschrift*, Jerusalem 1953, pp. 152 f. (in Hebrew).

332a

Parthica, apud: Suda, s.v. ἀτάσθαλα et παρείκοι — Adler = *Parthica*, F79 Roos

Ὁ δὲ Τραϊανὸς ἔγνω μάλιστα μέν, εἰ παρείκοι, ἐξελεῖν τὸ ἔθνος εἰ δὲ μή, ἀλλὰ συντρίψας γε παῦσαι τῆς ἄγαν ἀτασθαλίας.

1 μὲν Suda s. v. ἀτάσθαλα   μάλιστα Suda s. v. παρείκοι, utrumque iunxit Bernhardy

Trajan was determined above all, if it were possible, to destroy the nation utterly, but if not, at least to crush it and stop its presumptuous wickedness.

Although assuming that Suda derives this notice from the lost *Parthica* of Arrian, Roos suggested at first that the nation referred to might be that of the Parthians themselves; see Roos, *op. cit.* (supra, p. 150, n. 1), p. 31; this seems unlikely. First, the description ἀτασθαλία would be more suited to Jewish rebels than to the Parthians; see Hartmann, *op. cit.* (supra, p. 150, n. 2), p. 86; L. Motta, *Aegyptus*, XXXII (1952), pp. 484 ff.; Groag, PW, XIII, p. 1881. Secondly, the plan ascribed here to Trajan accords well with the actions of his general Lusius Quietus, as described in other sources dealing with the same events; see Eusebius, *Historia Ecclesiastica*, IV, 2:5: ὁ δὲ αὐτοκράτωρ ὑποπτεύσας καὶ τοὺς ἐν Μεσοποταμίᾳ Ἰουδαίους ἐπιθήσεσθαι τοῖς αὐτόθι, Λουσίῳ Κυήτῳ προσέταξεν ἐκκαθᾶραι τῆς ἐπαρχίας αὐτούς· ὃς καὶ παραταξάμενος, πάμπολυ πλῆθος τῶν αὐτόθι φονεύει, ἐφ’ ᾧ κατορθώματι Ἰουδαίας ἡγεμὼν ὑπὸ τοῦ αὐτοκράτορος ἀνεδείχθη; Hieronymus, *Chronica* (ed. Helm), p. 196: "Iudaeis Mesopotamiae rebellantibus praecepit imperator Traianus Lysiae Quieto, ut eos provincia exterminaret. Adversum quos Quietus aciem instruens infinita milia eorum interficit et ob hoc procurator Iudaeae ab imperatore decernitur." See also Eusebius, *Die Chronik aus dem armenischen übersetzt* (ed. J. Karst), p. 219; Rufinus, *Historia Ecclesiastica*, IV, 2:5; Syncellus, I (ed. Dindorf), p. 657; Prosper Tiro, *Epitoma Chronicon*, 578, in: *Chronica Minora*, I (ed. Mommsen), p. 421; Nicephorus Callistus, *Ecclesiastica Historia*, III, 22, in: *PG*, CXLV, p. 941: Λουκίῳ Κυέτῳ προσέταττε τῆς ὑπ’ αὐτὸν ἐπαρχίας ὅσον τάχος ἐκκαθαίρειν αὐτούς. On the sources for Nicephorus Callistus, see G. Gentz, *Die Kirchengeschichte des Nicephorus Callistus Xanthopulus und ihre Quellen*, Berlin 1966.

It is difficult to assess the part played by the Jews in the general revolt of the inhabitants of the Roman-occupied lands of the Parthian kingdom. This must be considered in relation to the sequence of events, and its relevance to the uprisings in the Jewish settlements of the Hellenistic Diaspora at Cyrenaica, Egypt and Cyprus.

The general outline of Trajan's campaigns in the East is fairly clear though some doubts still attach to details and chronology. For discussions and summaries, see R.P. Longden, *JRS*, XXI (1931), pp. 1 ff.; idem, *CAH*, XI

(1936), pp. 239 ff., 858 f.; N.C. Debevoise, *A Political History of Parthia*, Chicago 1938, pp. 218 ff.; J. Guey, *Essai sur la guerre parthique de Trajan (114–117)*, Bucharest 1937; Lepper, *op. cit.* (supra, p. 150, n. 1); L. Dillemann, *Haute Mésopotamie orientale et pays adjacents*, Paris 1962, pp. 273 ff.

The chief source for Trajan's Parthian War is Cassius Dio, through the epitome of Xiphilinus. This account may be supplemented by the fragments of Arrian's *Parthica* given by Suda and Stephanus Byzantius, some references in Fronto, *De Bello Parthico* (ed. Van den Hout), 2, p. 206; *Principia Historiae*, 3g, 17, pp. 193, 199, and some late sources like Malalas, XI (ed. Dindorf), pp. 269 ff. = A.S.v. Stauffenberg, *Die römische Kaisergeschichte bei Malalas*, Stuttgart 1931, pp. 42 ff.

The main course of the war may be stated as follows: The invasion of Armenia by the Romans and its annexation were followed by the conquest of Mesopotamia (including Nisibis) and an attack on Adiabene. Trajan left part of his army to accomplish the subjugation of Adiabene, while he himself advanced rapidly down the Euphrates into Babylonia. He brought over his ships into the Tigris, and captured Ctesiphon and Seleucia, thus striking at the heart of the Parthian kingdom. He then sailed down the Tigris to the Persian Gulf. However, when he returned to Babylon alarming news reached him of a general revolt which had broken out in the subjugated Parthian territories, and of the expulsion or annihilation of the garrisons that he had placed there. Trajan dispatched armed forces against the rebels. One of the Roman commanders, Maximus, was defeated and fell in battle. However, Lusius Quietus recaptured Nisibis and sacked Edessa, and two other commanders, Erucius Clarus and Julius Alexander (perhaps a grandson of Tiberius Julius Alexander, the Jewish renegade; cf. Syme, II, p. 511), retook Seleucia and burned down the city. In face of the fierce opposition of the Parthians Trajan decided to attempt some compromise with them and appointed Parthamaspates king of Parthia in the presence of Romans and Parthians at Ctesiphon.

The last events of Trajan's Parthian campaign related by Xiphilinus bear upon the Roman operations against Hatra. Trajan did not succeed in taking the place, and his health began to fail him.

The chronology of the war may be reconstructed as follows: The conquest of Armenia may be placed in 114 C.E., and that of Mesopotamia not later than 115. The campaign that started in the spring of 116 comprised the conquest of Babylonia and Ctesiphon, and the sailing down the Tigris to the Persian Gulf. According to one view, the Parthian revolt took place between midsummer 116 and midsummer 117; see Lepper, *op. cit.*, p. 96. It may be dated roughly to the autumn 116; see Guey, *op. cit.*, p. 142. For a somewhat different chronological scheme of the history of the war, see Longden, *CAH, op. cit.* (supra, pp. 152 f.), pp. 858 f.

There is no reference to a general revolt by the Parthians in the account of Eusebius, *Historia Ecclesiastica*, IV, 2:5, and the Christian sources dependent on it. Eusebius concentrates upon what happened to the Jews in Mesopotamia and connects the events there with those in Cyrene and Egypt.

According to this historian, the emperor suspected that the Jews living in Mesopotamia would attack the inhabitants of the country, as the Jews of Cyrene and Egypt had done, and he therefore ordered Lusius Quietus to put to death all the Jews of the province. Quietus attacked them and killed a great multitude. Eusebius asserts that his account agrees with those of Greek historians.

In his epitome of Cassius Dio Xiphilinus does not explicitly refer to the military actions of Quietus against the Mesopotamian Jews, although he stresses the part played by this general in quelling the eastern rebellion by capturing Edessa and Nisibis; see Cassius Dio, LXVIII, 30. Xiphilinus relates the Jewish disturbances under Trajan to a later date, after the emperor retired from Hatra, i.e. probably in the spring of 117 C.E.; see Cassius Dio, LXVIII, 32 (No. 437). It is only then that Xiphilinus expressly refers to the Jewish revolt in Cyrene, Egypt and Cyprus, when his final sentence implies that the full narrative of Cassius Dio also dealt with a campaign directed against the Jews of Mesopotamia: ἀλλ᾽ Ἰουδαίους μὲν ἄλλοι τε καὶ Λούσιος, ὑπὸ Τραϊανοῦ πεμφθεὶς κατεστρέψατο. Quietus, who took no part in crushing the revolt of the Jews of Egypt, Cyrene or Cyprus, is known from Eusebius and other sources to have played a leading part in the military activities against the Jews of Mesopotamia.

It has been suggested that the suppression of the general eastern, pro-Parthian, revolt should be completely dissociated from the subsequent action against the Jews of Mesopotamia in 117 C.E., i.e. after the Roman failure at Hatra; see Groag, *loc. cit.* However this explanation seems to make too much of the rather meagre narrative and vague chronology of Xiphilinus and to attribute too great an importance to the reason given by Eusebius for the anti-Jewish measures taken by Quietus. The departure of Trajan from Hatra, and his failing health following this departure, is connected by Xiphilinus with the Jewish revolt in Cyrene, Egypt and Cyprus by the words καὶ ἐν τούτῳ. This by no means necessitates Groag's interpretation that a Jewish revolt occurred subsequent to the general revolt. The Greek documents from Egypt make it clear that the Jewish revolt in Egypt started in 115 C.E., and certainly not in 117; see A. Fuks, *JRS*, LI (1961), pp. 100 f.; J. Schwartz, *Chronique d'Égypte*, XXXVII (1962), p. 353. It follows that the ἐν τούτῳ of Xiphilinus should be interpreted not as tantamount to μετὰ ταῦτα, but as meaning that Jewish revolts in the various countries occurred approximately at the same time as the Parthian campaign of Trajan in general, from the annexation of Armenia in 114 C.E. on. Eusebius also lends no support for Groag's case. The church historian wholly ignores the background of the Parthian War for the revolt, stating that the anti-Jewish policy of Trajan in Mesopotamia was prompted by the suspicion that the Jews would attack their neighbours. This seems hardly compatible with the contemporary situation in the conquered parts of the Parthian empire, where the Greek city of Seleucia also took part in the revolt against Rome; see G. Alon, *History of the Jews in the Age of the Mishna and the Talmud*, I³, Tel Aviv 1958, p. 253 (in Hebrew). The reason given by Eusebius seems to be an inference drawn by the author himself from a comparison with the atmosphere characteristic of Greek-Jewish relations in Cyrene and Egypt. Since the advance of the Roman legions took in most of the important centres of eastern Jewry, and cities such as Nisibis and Edessa and the country of Adiabene were expressly connected with the Parthian revolt, the Jews living there must have taken part in it from the beginning. They would not have waited until the others were crushed before raising the standard of revolt themselves. See Guey, *op. cit.* (supra, p. 153), pp. 126 ff.; Debevoise, *op. cit.* (supra, p. 153), pp. 235 f.; Lepper, *op. cit.* (supra, p. 150, n. 1), p. 154; L. Motta, *Aegyptus,* XXXII (1952), p. 480; Fuks, *op. cit.* (supra, p. 154), p. 99. On the importance of Nisibis as a Jewish centre, see *Ant.*, XVIII, 312. On the Jews at Edessa, see J. B. Segal, *Edessa, "The Blessed City"*, Oxford 1970, pp. 41 ff.; see also H. J. W. Drijvers, *Vigiliae Christianae*, XXIV (1970), pp. 4 ff. On Adiabene, see the commentary to Tacitus, *Annales*, XII, 13:1 (No. 286). On Jews in fourth-century Arbela, situated in Adiabene, see E. Sachau, *Die Chronik von Arbela*, Berlin 1915, pp. 73, 75 f.

It may be suggested that because of the fierceness of the Jewish opposition to the Romans, and the concurrent events in the Roman provinces of Cyrenaica, Egypt and Cyprus, Trajan was determined to treat the Jews with more than usual harshness, and even went to the length of ordering that large numbers should be put to death. On the other hand, there is no proof that Adiabene was the mainspring of the Jewish rebellion in the Roman provinces as proposed by F. M. Heichelheim, *JEA*, XXXII (1946), p. 106. For a different view, denying the existence of a concerted plan to stir up a Jewish revolt throughout the East, see Schwartz, *op. cit.* (supra, p. 154), p. 356. Viewed objectively, however, the Jewish revolt in Cyrene, Egypt and Cyprus must have had some effect on the potentialities of the Roman effort against Parthia; see A. Schalit, *Tarbiz*, VII (1936), pp. 178 ff. (in Hebrew).

παρείκοι: For the use of παρείκοι by Arrian, cf., e.g., Arrianus, *Anabasis*, VI, 9:2.

τῆς ἄγαν: Cf. *ibid.*, IV, 7:4; VI, 12:3.

ἀτασθαλίας: Cf. *ibid.*, VII, 14:5; idem, *Indica*, 13:13.

332b

Parthica, apud: Stephanus Byzantius, s.v. Νάαρδα — Meineke = *Parthica*, F10 Roos = *F.Gr.Hist.*, II, B156, F42

Νάαρδα· πόλις Συρίας πρὸς τῷ Εὐφράτῃ, ὡς ᾿Αρριανὸς Παρθικῶν ἐνδεκάτῳ.

1 ἀριανὸς RV   ῥιανὸς A

Naarda. A city of Syria near the Euphrates, as Arrian tells us in the eleventh book of his Parthian history.

Jewish tradition traces the origins and greatness of the Jewish community of Naarda to the exile of King Jehoiachin; see the *Epistle of Rav-Sherira Gaon*, ed. B. M. Lewin, Haifa 1921, pp. 72 f. From Josephus we know that the city of Naarda (or Nearda or Neharde'a) constituted the chief bastion of Babylonian Jewry at least as early as the first century C. E.; see *Ant.*, XVIII, 311: Νέαρδα τῆς Βαβυλωνίας ἐστὶ πόλις ἄλλως τε πολυανδροῦσα καὶ χώραν ἀγαθὴν καὶ πολλὴν ἔχουσα καὶ σὺν ἄλλοις ἀγαθοῖς καὶ ἀνθρώπων ἀνάπλεων. The Jews made use of its strong position to concentrate there the money to be sent to the Temple in Jerusalem (*ibid.*, 312). Naarda was also the home of Asinaeus and Anilaeus, the rebel Jewish brothers who founded a semi-independent state in Babylonia (*ibid.*, 314 ff.). The Babylonians, who ordered the Jews of Naarda to deliver up Anilaeus, met with a blunt refusal (*ibid.*, 369). The Jews of Seleucia on the Tigris fled to Naarda and Nisibis after the disaster that befell them; cf. *ibid.*, 379: ὀχυρότητι τῶν πόλεων κτώμενοι τὴν ἀσφάλειαν, καὶ ἄλλως πληθὺς ἅπασα μαχίμων ἀνδρῶν κατοικεῖται. R. Aqiva visited the place and intercalated the month there; see *M. Yevamot*, xvi: 7; J. Neusner, *A History of the Jews in Babylonia*, I, Leiden 1965, pp. 49 f. Naarda also became the seat of the famous *Amora* Samuel and his academy, which shed the lustre of its scholars on the city.

On Naarda, its location and history, see S. Funk, *Festschrift zum siebzigsten Geburtstage David Hoffmann's*, Berlin 1914, pp. 97 ff.; J. Obermeyer, *Die Landschaft Babylonien*, Frankfurt 1929, pp. 244 ff.; F. H. Weissbach, PW, XVI, pp. 1439 f.

Νάαρδα is mentioned by Ptolemy among the Mesopotamian cities situated along the Euphrates; cf. Ptolemaeus, *Geographia*, V, 18:7 (ed. Nobbe = V, 17:5, ed. Müller).

CI. CLEOMEDES

First or second century C.E.

Cleomedes was the author of an astronomical work inspired by Stoicism. While attacking the vulgar language of Epicurus there, Cleomedes refers incidentally to the Jews. He adduces several examples of the idiom used by the philosopher, a phraseology that seems partly to derive from brothels, partly to resemble that spoken at the Thesmophoria, and partly to have been borrowed from the synagogue.[1]

333

De Motu Circulari, II, 1:91 — Ziegler = F121R

Ἐπεί γε πρὸς τοῖς ἄλλοις καὶ τὰ κατὰ τὴν ἑρμηνείαν αὐτῷ ποικίλως
διεφθορότα ἐστί, σαρκὸς εὐσταθῆ καταστήματα λέγοντι καὶ τὰ περὶ
ταύτης πιστὰ ἐλπίσματα καὶ λίπασμα ὀφθαλμῶν τὸ δάκρυον
ὀνομάζοντι καὶ ἱερὰ ἀνακραυγάσματα καὶ γαργαλισμοὺς σώματος καὶ
5 ληκήματα καὶ ἄλλας τοιαύτας κακὰς ἄτας· ὧν τὰ μὲν ἐκ
χαμαιτυπείων ἄν τις εἶναι φήσειε, τὰ δὲ ὅμοια τοῖς λεγομένοις ἐν τοῖς
Δημητρίοις ὑπὸ τῶν Θεσμοφοριαζουσῶν γυναικῶν, τὰ δὲ ἀπὸ μέσης
τῆς προσευχῆς καὶ τῶν ἐπ᾽ αὐλαῖς προσαιτούντων, Ἰουδαϊκά τινα καὶ
παρακεχαραγμένα καὶ κατὰ πολὺ τῶν ἑρπετῶν ταπεινότερα.

6 χαμαιτυπίων, φήσειεν εἶναι M

1 On Cleomedes, see H.R. Ziegler, "De vita et scriptis Cleomedis", Ph.D. Thesis, Leipzig 1878, pp. 44ff.; H. Lewy, *Philologus*, LXXXIV (1929), pp. 395f.; S. Lieberman, *Greek in Jewish Palestine*, New York 1942, pp. 29f.; F. Büchsel, *ZAW*, LX (1944), pp. 144f.; H.J. Lewy, *Studies in Jewish Hellenism*, Jerusalem 1960, pp. 197ff. (in Hebrew).
On the sources of Cleomedes, see A. Boericke, "Quaestiones Cleomedeae", Ph.D. Thesis, Leipzig 1905; for the view that Cleomedes derives his information from Posidonius, see A.D. Nock, *Gnomon*, XXIII (1951), p. 49, n. 4. See also G. Rudberg, *Forschungen zu Poseidonios*, Uppsala–Leipzig 1918, pp. 32ff. For a different view, which denies any dependence of Cleomedes on Posidonius for the passages bearing on Epicurus, see K. Reinhardt, *Poseidonios*, Munich 1921, p. 186.

Since, in addition to other things, his style [scil. Epicurus'] is also a corrupt motley, making use of expressions like "stable states of the flesh" and "hopeful hopes" concerning it, and calling tears "glistenings of the eyes" and having recourse to phrases like "holy screechings" and "ticklings of the body" and "wenchings" and other bad mischiefs of this kind. One may say that these expressions derive in part from brothels, in part they are similar to those spoken by women celebrating the Thesmophoria at the festivals of Demeter, and in part they issue from the midst of the synagogue and the beggars in its courtyards. These are Jewish and debased and much lower than reptiles.

Ἐπεί γε ... καὶ ἄλλας τοιαύτας κακὰς ἄτας: The frequent use of words with the ending –μα was felt to be a grave stylistic fault; see E. Norden, *Antike Kunstprosa*, I, Leipzig 1898, p. 124, n. 1.

ὅμοια τοῖς λεγομένοις ἐν τοῖς Δημητρίοις ὑπὸ τῶν Θεσμοφοριαζουσῶν γυναικῶν: On the loose speech used by women at the Thesmophoria, see L. Deubner, *Attische Feste*, Berlin 1932, pp. 57 f.

τὰ δὲ ἀπὸ μέσης τῆς προσευχῆς ... προσαιτούντων: From the various words adduced by Cleomedes as typical of Epicurus, ἐλπίσματα may specifically allude to Jewish vain beliefs. On a connection between the synagogue and beggars, cf. Artemidorus, III, 53 (No. 395): Προσευχὴ καὶ μεταῖται.

Ἰουδαϊκά τινα καὶ παρακεχαραγμένα: The passage does not attest that there existed some special Graeco-Jewish language similar to the later development of Yiddish. Cleomedes only refers to the bad Greek spoken by Jews, which he considered to be of the same standard as the Greek of the brothels and the Thesmophoria. The literal translations of Hebrew, especially in connection with religious matters, were made with little regard to Greek grammar and style. They left their mark on the Greek language used by Jews and made it an easy object of contempt for the Greek educated classes. Perhaps also the expression παρακεχαραγμένα implies that in the mouth of a Jew the Greek words had lost their proper meaning.

ταπεινότερα: The term is commonly used by Greek rhetors with reference to vulgar speech.

CII. SEXTUS EMPIRICUS

Second century C.E.

The philosopher Sextus Empiricus[1] adduces the Jews among examples of nations who cleave to dietary observances. They are cited, before the Egyptian priests, as people who prefer to die rather than partake of pork. Other peoples mentioned by Sextus in this connection are the Libyans, Syrians and Thracians.

334

Hypotyposes, III, 222-223 — Mutschmann–Mau = F89 R

(222) Παραπλήσια δὲ τούτοις ἔστιν εὑρεῖν καὶ τὰ ἐν τῇ κατὰ τὴν δίαιταν τῶν ἀνθρώπων θρησκείᾳ περὶ τοὺς θεούς. (223) Ἰουδαῖος μὲν γὰρ ἢ ἱερεὺς Αἰγύπτιος θᾶττον ἂν ἀποθάνοι ἢ χοίρειον φάγοι, Λίβυς δὲ προβατείου γεύσασθαι κρέως τῶν ἀθεσμοτάτων εἶναι δοκεῖ, Σύρων
5 δέ τινες περιστερᾶς, ἄλλοι δὲ ἱερείων.

(222) A similar behaviour may be found in respect of food in people's worship of their gods. (223) A Jew or an Egyptian priest would prefer to die instantly rather than eat pork, while to taste mutton is reckoned an abomination in the eyes of a Libyan, and Syrians think the same about pigeons, and others about cattle.

223 Ἰουδαῖος μὲν γὰρ ἢ ἱερεὺς Αἰγύπτιος θᾶττον ἂν ἀποθάνοι ἢ χοίρειον φάγοι: On the readiness of the Jews to die rather than eat pork, see II Macc. vi : 18 ff.; cf. also Philo, *Legatio ad Gaium*, 361. See also the commentaries to Petronius, *Fragmenta*, No. 37 (No. 195), and Plutarchus, *Quaestiones Convivales*, IV, 5 (No. 258). For abstention by Egyptians from pork, cf. Plutarchus, *De Iside*, 8, pp. 353 F: ὁμοίως δὲ καὶ τὴν ὗν ἀνίερον ζῷον ἡγοῦνται [scil. Αἰγύπτιοι]; Aelianus, *De Natura Animalium*, X, 16: ταύτῃ τοι καὶ ἐμίσησαν Αἰγύπτιοι τὸ ζῷον ὡς μυσαρὸν καὶ πάμβορον. See further M. Wellmann, *Hermes*, XXXI (1896), p. 240; H. Kees, *Ägypten*, Munich 1933, pp. 20 f. Concerning the abstention of Egyptian priests from pork, see also the remark of Josephus, *Contra Apionem*, II, 141.

1 For the date of Sextus Empiricus, see now F. Kudlien, *Rhein. Museum*, CVI (1963), pp. 251 ff. It is suggested that he be placed *c.* 100 C.E.

CIII. CLAUDIUS CHARAX OF PERGAMUM

Second century C.E.

An explanation of the name Ἑβραῖοι by the historian Claudius Charax of Pergamum, Roman consul in 147 C.E.,[1] has been preserved by Stephanus Byzantius. It is not possible to tell in what connection Charax was referring to the Jews here.[2] He was not the only writer from Asia Minor to take an interest in them; see the introduction to Teucer of Cyzicus, above, Vol. I, p. 165.

1 Cf. the inscriptional evidence on Charax published by C. Habicht, *Istanbuler Mitteilungen*, IX–X (1959–1960), pp. 109 ff.
2 In Stephanus Byzantius, s.v. Ἰόπη (= *F. Gr. Hist.*, II, A 103, F 56) we read also: Ἰόπη ... Ἰοπὶς θηλυκὸν παρὰ Χάρακι.

335

Stephanus Byzantius, s.v. Ἑβραῖοι — Meineke = F 82 R = *F. Gr. Hist.*, II, A 103, F 52

Ἑβραῖοι. οὕτως Ἰουδαῖοι ἀπὸ Ἀβράμωνος, ὥς φησι Χάραξ.

Ἀβράμωνος Holstenius   Ἀβραμῶνος Bochartus   ἀβράβωνος codd.

Hebrews. Thus are called Jews after Abramon, as Charax says.

Ἑβραῖοι: The appellation Ἑβραῖοι for Jews was in common use among the Jews themselves in this period, as illustrated in Jewish-Hellenistic literature; cf., e.g., II Macc. vii:31; xi:13; xv:37. The first non-Jewish writer known to use this designation is Alexander Polyhistor (cf. No. 51a). From the end of the first century C.E. its usage spread among Latin and Greek writers; cf. Statius, *Silvae*, V, 1:213 (No. 236); Tacitus, *Historiae*, V, 2 (No. 281); Antonius Diogenes (No. 250); Plutarchus, *Vita Antonii*, 27:4 (No. 265); *Quaestiones Convivales*, IV, 6:1 (No. 258); Ptolemy Chennus, apud: Photius, 190 (No. 331); Appianus, *Bella Civilia*, II, 71:294 (No. 349); Pausanias, I, 5:5; IV, 35:9; V, 5:2; V, 7:4; VI, 24:8; VIII, 16:4–5; X, 12:9 (Nos. 353 ff.); Lucianus, *Alexander*, 13 (No. 373); see Juster, I, p. 174.

ἀπὸ Ἀβράμωνος: The name Abraham was not unknown to Greek writers; cf. Apollonius Molon, apud: Eusebius, *Praeparatio Evangelica*, IX, 19:2 (No. 46); Nicolaus of Damascus, apud: *Ant.*, I, 159 (No. 83). A public document from Pergamum, the city of Charax, of *c.* 112 B.C.E., refers to ancient relations between the Jews and the city in the time of Abraham, who is called πάντων Ἑβραίων πατήρ (*Ant.*, XIV, 255); for the date of the document, see M. Stern, *Zion*, XXVI (1961), pp. 12 ff. The description "Abraham the Hebrew" is already given in the Bible (Gen. xiv:13), but the biblical tradition does not attempt to link the names Abraham and Hebrews. Josephus states that the Jews derived the name "Hebrew" from Eber, grandson of Shem (*Ant.*, I, 146). On the other hand, the explanation given by Charax is to be found in fragments from the work of the Jewish-Hellenistic writer Artapanus, apud: Eusebius, *Praeparatio Evangelica*, IX, 18:1 = *F. Gr. Hist.*, III, C726, F1 = A.M. Denis, *Fragmenta Pseudepigraphorum Quae Supersunt Graeca*, Leiden 1970, p. 186: καλεῖσθαι δὲ αὐτοὺς Ἑβραίους ἀπὸ Ἀβραάμου.

The form Ἀβράμων is not known elsewhere. He is called Ἀβραάμ by Apollonius Molon, and Nicolaus of Damascus gives the Graecized form Ἀβράμης. Inscriptions from Leontopolis have "Abramos"; see L. Robert, *Hellenica*, I, Limoges 1940, p. 18. For papyrological evidence, cf. *CPJ*, Nos. 365, 412; for Ἀβράμις, cf. *ibid.*, No. 374.

CIV. PTOLEMY (CLAUDIUS PTOLEMAEUS)

Second century C. E.

Two of the works of the Alexandrian astronomer contain references to Judaea. These are Ptolemy's Apotelesmatica (= Tetrabiblos) *and his* Geographia.

The Apotelesmatica, *a systematic treatment of astrology, was composed before the* Geographia. *It divides the inhabited world into four quarters and their respective triangles. Judaea, being in the second quarter, is associated with Idumaea, Coele-Syria, Phoenicia, Chaldaea, Orchinia and Arabia Felix among the countries situated towards the north-west of the whole quarter. These countries have affinity to the north-western triangle, and to Aries, Leo and Sagittarius, and have as co-rulers Zeus, Ares and Hermes.*

The list of countries grouped with Judaea may cause some surprise, especially the hardly identifiable Orchinia and Chaldaea; so, too, does the mention of Idumaea as a country apart from Judaea. Syria proper is conspicuous by its absence. Although Orchinia and Chaldaea are listed in this division, Mesopotamia and Babylonia are located in a different part of the second quarter. Little can be inferred from this confused presentation. It presumably reflects the use by Ptolemy of old sources that he did not succeed in rationalizing.[1]

It was the view of Ptolemy that national characteristics are conditioned by the geographical and astrological situation. Accordingly he defines the peoples listed with those of Judaea as especially gifted in trade and exchange, and also as unscrupulous cowards, treacherous, and servile.

---

1 Against Posidonius as the source for the astrological geography in the *Tetrabiblos*, see H. Trüdinger, *Studien zur Geschichte der griechisch-römischen Ethnographie*, Basel 1918, pp. 81 ff.; for the substitution of Serapion (also first century B. C. E.) as a probable source of both Manilius and Ptolemaeus, see E. Honigmann, *Die sieben Klimata*, Heidelberg 1929, p. 48, though Honigmann wisely modifies his suggestion by stating that Serapion should not be considered their sole source. For the astrological geography of Ptolemy, see also F. Boll, "Studien über Claudius Ptolemäus", *Jahrbücher für Classische Philologie*, XXI, Suppl. (1894), pp. 181 ff.

However, the inhabitants of Coele-Syria, Idumaea and Judaea are also labelled bold, godless and scheming.
There can hardly be room for doubt that in referring to the inhabitants of these countries Ptolemy actually had in mind the Jews alone. It was only natural for an Egyptian Greek, a youthful contemporary of the Jewish revolts under Trajan and Hadrian, to stress the boldness (ϑρασύτης) of the Jews besides the godlessness (ἀϑεότης) with which they had been traditionally charged. On the other hand, it may easily be assumed that Ptolemy's general remark concerning these peoples on their excellence in trade and exchange, as well as their cowardice and servility, applies mainly to the Syrians who were famous as merchants in the Roman empire, although Syria proper is not mentioned in that context.[2]
The description of Judaea in the Geographia *(No. 337a) takes much account of contemporary conditions. Many of the names included in it by Ptolemy reflect a situation at least not anterior to the rule of Herod or his sons. Thus he mentions Caesarea, Antipatris, Sebaste and Phasaelis, as well as Julias (Bet Saida), Tiberias, Archelais and Livias. Moreover, he also lists Neapolis, founded by Vespasian, and expressly states that Jerusalem is now, i.e. since the time of Hadrian, called Aelia Capitolina.*
Judaea in the Geographia *is roughly identical with the Roman province of Judaea, but Ptolemy was conscious that the name of the province had been officially changed (V, 15:1). He is correct in not including Dora within the borders of the province. On the other hand, like Pliny, he includes within it both Ascalon and Gaza, although both were excluded from the province of Judaea on its creation by Augustus in 6 C.E.[3] Apart from this broad use of the term Judaea, Ptolemy also has recourse to its narrower meaning of Judaea proper: thus Judaea is classed also with Galilaea, Samaria, the east side of the Jordan (= Peraea) and Idumaea, a usage also met elsewhere, mainly in works by Jewish writers like Josephus, but found also in Plinius,* Naturalis Historia, *V, 70 (No. 204).*
Some inaccuracies have crept into the list of places supplied by Ptolemy.

2 For Syrians in commerce, see V. Pârvan, "Die Nationalität der Kaufleute im römischen Kaiserreiche", Ph.D. Thesis, Breslau 1909, pp. 92 ff., 110 ff.
3 There is no need, in any case, to assume that Ptolemy had recourse here to an official list; see also A. H. M. Jones, *The Cities of the Eastern Roman Provinces*, Oxford 1971, p. 512.

These concern chiefly the location of certain towns. Ptolemy locates Sebaste in Judaea proper instead of in Samaria. Some places, in both Judaea proper and the Peraea, are hard to identify. However, the list of Idumaean towns is a real puzzle. Idumaea is listed separately, though at the end of the Second Temple period it was an integral part of Judaea proper (see the commentary to Pliny, No. 204). There is also a contradiction between the area emerging as Idumaea in the Geographia *of Ptolemy and those territories commonly thought to have constituted Idumaea in the Second Temple period. Thus Beitogabri (Βαιτογαβρεῖ = Bet Gubrin, which superseded Marisa), and Engadda (= 'En Gedi) take their place among the townships of Judaea proper, while Idumaea, as surveyed by Ptolemy, covers places situated further south, although some localities that belonged to the Second Temple Idumaea are also included within it.*[4]

---

4 On the sources of Ptolemy, see E. Polaschek, PW, Suppl., X (1965), pp. 753 ff. On Syria and Palestine in the map of Ptolemy, see also M. Linke, *Wissenschaftliche Zeitschrift der Martin Luther Universität (Mathematisch-naturwissenschaftliche Reihe,* XIV), Halle–Wittenberg 1965, pp. 473 ff.

336a

Apotelesmatica, II, 3:65–66 (29–31) — Boll & Boer

(29) Τὰ δὲ λοιπὰ τοῦ τεταρτημορίου μέρη περὶ τὸ μέσον ἐσχηματισμένα
τῆς ὅλης οἰκουμένης, Ἰδουμαία, Κοίλη Συρία Ἰουδαία Φοινίκη Χαλδαϊκὴ
Ὀρχηνία Ἀραβία εὐδαίμων καὶ τὴν θέσιν ἔχοντα πρὸς βορρόλιβα τοῦ
ὅλου τεταρτημορίου προσλαμβάνει πάλιν τὴν συνοικείωσιν τοῦ βορρο-
5 *λιβικοῦ τριγώνου, Κριοῦ Λέοντος Τοξότου, ἔχει δὲ συνοικοδεσπότας*
τόν τε τοῦ Διὸς καὶ τὸν τοῦ Ἄρεως καὶ ἔτι τὸν τοῦ Ἑρμοῦ. (30) διὸ μᾶλλον
οὗτοι τῶν ἄλλων ἐμπορικώτεροι καὶ συναλλακτικώτεροι, πανουργότεροι
δὲ καὶ δειλοκαταφρόνητοι καὶ ἐπιβουλευτικοὶ καὶ δουλόψυχοι καὶ ὅλως
ἀλλοπρόσαλλοι διὰ τὸν τῶν προκειμένων ἀστέρων συσχηματισμόν. (31)
10 *καὶ τούτων δὲ πάλιν οἱ μὲν περὶ τὴν Κοίλην Συρίαν καὶ Ἰδουμαίαν καὶ*
Ἰουδαίαν τῷ τε Κριῷ καὶ τῷ τοῦ Ἄρεως μᾶλλον συνοικειοῦνται, διόπερ ὡς
ἐπίπαν θρασεῖς τέ εἰσι καὶ ἄθεοι καὶ ἐπιβουλευτικοί· Φοίνικες δὲ καὶ
Χαλδαῖοι καὶ Ὀρχήνιοι τῷ Λέοντι καὶ τῷ ἡλίῳ διόπερ ἁπλούστεροι καὶ
φιλάνθρωποι καὶ φιλαστρόλογοι καὶ μάλιστα πάντων σέβοντες τὸν ἥλιον·

3 ὀρχινία α / ἀρραβία β 5 ἔχει δὲ] ἔτι δὲ V ἔχη Υ
ἔχοντος Σ 7 συναλλακτικοί αβγ / πανοῦργοι τε βγ om. V
πανουργότεροί τε Co (Le) 8 δειλοκαταφρόνηται α
14 φιλανθρωπότεροι αβγ / φιλοστοργότεροι β C om. A

(29) The remaining parts of the quarter, situated about the centre of
the inhabited world, Idumaea, Coele-Syria, Judaea, Phoenicia,
Chaldaea, Orchinia, and Arabia Felix, which are situated toward the
north-west of the whole quarter, have additional familiarity with the
north-western triangle, Aries, Leo, and Sagittarius, and, furthermore, have as co-rulers Jupiter, Mars and Mercury. (30) Therefore
these peoples are, in comparison with the others, more gifted in trade
and exchange; they are more unscrupulous, despicable cowards,
treacherous, servile, and in general fickle, on account of the stars
mentioned. (31) Of these, again the inhabitants of Coele-Syria,
Idumaea, and Judaea are more closely familiar to Aries and Mars,
and therefore these peoples are in general bold, godless, and
scheming. The Phoenicians, Chaldaeans, and Orchinians have
familiarity with Leo and the sun, so that they are simpler, kindly,
addicted to astrology, and beyond all men worshippers of the sun.

(trans. F. E. Robbins, *LCL*)

31 ἄθεοι: For the charge of ἀθεότης lodged against the Jews, cf.
Apollonius Molon, apud: Josephus, *Contra Apionem*, II, 148 (No. 49).

336b

Apotelesmatica, II, 4:73 (1–2) — Boll & Boer

(1) Ἐκθησόμεθα δὲ καὶ διὰ τὸ τῆς χρήσεως εὐεπίβολον ἐφ᾽ ἑκάστου τῶν δωδεκατημορίων κατὰ ψιλὴν παράθεσιν ἕκαστα τῶν συνῳκειωμένων ἐθνῶν ἀκολούθως τοῖς προκατειλεγμένοις περὶ αὐτῶν τὸν τρόπον τοῦτον. (2) Κριῷ· Βρεττανία, Γαλατία, Γερμανία, Βασταρνία· περὶ τὸ μέσον
5 *Κοίλη Συρία, Ἰδουμαία, Ἰουδαία.*

(1) We shall also set forth, for ready use, a list of the several nations which are in familiarity, merely notes against each of the signs, in accordance with what has just been said about them, thus: (2) Aries: Britain, Gaul, Germania, Bastarnia; in the centre, Coele-Syria, Idumaea, Judaea. (trans. F. E. Robbins, *LCL*)

Ptolemy's astrological geography is repeated in the work of Hephaestion of Thebes (second half of the fourth century C.E.); cf. Hephaestio Thebanus, *Apotelesmatica*, I, 1 (ed. Pingree, I, pp. 3 f.): Περὶ τῆς τῶν δωδεκατημορίων ὀνομασίας τε καὶ δυνάμεως ... τούτῳ [scil. κριῷ] δὲ ὑπόκεινται ἀρχαίη Βαβυλών, Τυρίου Βήλοιο πόλισμα ... κατὰ δὲ Πτολεμαῖον Βρετανία, Γαλατία, Γερμανία, Παλαιστίνη, Ἰδουμαία, Ἰουδαία.

337a

Geographia, V, 15:1–7 — Müller = Nobbe, V, 16:1–10

Παλαιστίνης ⟨ἢ⟩ Ἰουδαίας θέσις
(1) Ἡ Παλαιστίνη ἢ Ἰουδαία [Συρία] περιορίζεται ἀπὸ μὲν ἄρκτων καὶ ἀνατολῶν Συρίᾳ κατὰ τὰς ἐκτεθειμένας γραμμάς· ἀπὸ δὲ μεσημβρίας Ἀραβίᾳ Πετραίᾳ κατὰ γραμμὴν τὴν ἀπὸ τοῦ πρὸς τῇ Συρίᾳ ἑωθινοῦ ὁρίου
5 *μέχρι τοῦ πρὸς τῇ Αἰγύπτῳ πέρατος, οὗ πέρατος ἡ θέσις, ὡς εἴρηται, ξδ´δ″ λ´γο″ ἀπὸ δὲ δύσεως τῷ τε ἐντεῦθεν μέχρι θαλάσσης ἐκτεθειμένῳ τῆς Αἰγύπτου μέρει καὶ τῷ ἐφεξῆς πελάγει μέχρι τοῦ ὁρίου τῆς Συρίας κατὰ περιγραφὴν τοιαύτην· (2) Μετὰ τὰς τοῦ Χορσέου ποταμοῦ ἐκβολὰς*

Καισάρεια Στράτωνος	ξϛ´	δ″	λβ´	L″
Ἀπολλωνία	ξϛ´		λβ´	δ″
Ἰόπη	ξε´	γο″	λβ´	ιβ″
Ἰαμνιτῶν λιμήν	ξε´	L″	λβ´	
Ἄζωτος	ξε´	δ″	λα´	L″γ″ιβ″

1 ⟨ἢ⟩ Müller   4 ἑωθινοῦ om. SΩ   8 χορσαίου SXϒ

166

Ptolemy

<table>
<tr><td>Ἀσκαλών</td><td>ξε΄</td><td></td><td>λα΄</td><td>γο΄΄</td></tr>
<tr><td>15 Ἀνθηδών</td><td>ξδ΄</td><td>L΄΄γ΄΄</td><td>λα΄</td><td>γο΄΄</td></tr>
<tr><td>Γαζαίων λιμήν</td><td>ξε΄</td><td>L΄΄δ΄΄</td><td>λα΄</td><td>L΄΄</td></tr>
</table>

(= 3 Nobbe) Διαιρεῖ δὲ τὴν Ἰουδαίαν τὸ πρὸς τῇ Ἀσφαλτίτιδι λίμνῃ τοῦ Ἰορδάνου ποταμοῦ μέρος, ἧς τὸ μέσον ἐπέχει μοίρας ξς΄ L΄΄γ΄΄ λα΄ ς΄΄

(3 = 4 Nobbe) Καὶ πόλεις εἰσὶν ἐν αὐτῇ μεσόγειοι αἵδε Γαλιλαίας

<table>
<tr><td>20 Σαπφουρεί</td><td>ξς΄</td><td>γο΄΄</td><td>λβ΄</td><td>γ΄΄ιβ΄΄</td></tr>
<tr><td>Καπαρκοτνεί</td><td>ξς΄</td><td>L΄΄γ΄΄</td><td>λβ΄</td><td>L΄΄ιβ΄΄</td></tr>
<tr><td>Ἰουλιάς</td><td>ξζ΄</td><td>ιβ΄΄</td><td>λβ΄</td><td>δ΄΄</td></tr>
<tr><td>Τιβεριάς</td><td>ξζ΄</td><td>δ΄΄</td><td>λβ΄</td><td>ιβ΄΄</td></tr>
</table>

(4 = 5 Nobbe) Σαμαρίας δὲ

<table>
<tr><td>25 Νεάπολις</td><td>ξς΄</td><td>L΄΄γ΄΄</td><td>λα΄</td><td>L΄΄γ΄΄</td></tr>
<tr><td>Θήνα</td><td>ξζ΄</td><td>ιβ΄΄</td><td>λα΄</td><td>L΄΄δ΄΄</td></tr>
</table>

(5 = 6 Nobbe) Τῆς δὲ Ἰουδαίας ἀπὸ μὲν δύσεως τοῦ ποταμοῦ τοῦ Ἰορδάνου

<table>
<tr><td>Ῥαφία</td><td>ξε΄</td><td></td><td>λα΄</td><td>ς΄΄</td></tr>
<tr><td>Γάζα</td><td>ξε΄</td><td>γ΄΄ιβ΄΄</td><td>λα΄</td><td>L΄΄δ΄΄</td></tr>
<tr><td>30 Ἰάμνια</td><td>ξε΄</td><td>γο΄΄</td><td>λβ΄</td><td></td></tr>
<tr><td>Λύδδα</td><td>ξς΄</td><td></td><td>λβ΄</td><td></td></tr>
<tr><td>Ἀντιπατρίς</td><td>ξς΄</td><td>γ΄΄</td><td>λβ΄</td><td></td></tr>
<tr><td>Δρουσιάς</td><td>ξς΄</td><td>L΄΄</td><td>λα΄</td><td>L΄΄γ΄΄ιβ΄΄</td></tr>
<tr><td>Σεβαστή</td><td>ξς΄</td><td>γο΄΄</td><td>λβ΄</td><td>ς΄΄</td></tr>
<tr><td>35 Βαιτογαβρεί</td><td>ξε΄</td><td>L΄΄</td><td>λα΄</td><td>L΄΄</td></tr>
<tr><td>Σεβοῦς</td><td>ξε΄</td><td>γο΄΄</td><td>λα΄</td><td>γ΄΄ιβ΄΄</td></tr>
<tr><td>(= 7 Nobbe) Ἐμμαοῦς</td><td>ξε΄</td><td>L΄΄δ΄΄</td><td>λα΄</td><td>L΄΄γ΄΄</td></tr>
<tr><td>Γούφνα</td><td>ξς΄</td><td>ς΄΄</td><td>λα΄</td><td>L΄΄δ΄΄</td></tr>
<tr><td>Ἀρχελαΐς</td><td>ξς΄</td><td>L΄΄</td><td>λα΄</td><td>L΄΄δ΄΄</td></tr>
<tr><td>40 Φασαηλίς</td><td>ξς΄</td><td>L΄΄γ΄΄ιβ΄΄</td><td>λα΄</td><td>L΄΄ιβ΄΄</td></tr>
<tr><td>Ἰερικοῦς</td><td>ξς΄</td><td>L΄΄δ΄΄</td><td>λα΄</td><td>γ΄΄ιβ΄΄</td></tr>
</table>

(= 8 Nobbe) Ἱεροσόλυμα, ἥτις νῦν καλεῖται

<table>
<tr><td>Αἰλία Καπιτωλία</td><td>ξς΄</td><td></td><td>λα΄</td><td>γο΄΄</td></tr>
<tr><td>Θάμνα</td><td>ξς΄</td><td>δ΄΄</td><td>λα΄</td><td>L΄΄</td></tr>
<tr><td>45 Ἐνγάδδα</td><td>ξς΄</td><td>L΄΄</td><td>λα΄</td><td>δ΄΄</td></tr>
<tr><td>Βηδωρώ</td><td>ξς΄</td><td>L΄΄</td><td>λα΄</td><td></td></tr>
<tr><td>Θαμαρώ</td><td>ξς΄</td><td>γ΄΄</td><td>λ΄</td><td>L΄΄γ΄΄</td></tr>
</table>

17 ἀσφαλτίδι FLMΦ   20 σαπφουρί X   σαπφουρίς ACPRVW
σαπφουρά Zm²   26 θήνα BESVZΔΩℲ   θίνα FN   κώμη θηνα x
    30 ἰαμνία ADFℲ   ἰάμνεια PRY   38 γούφνα SΩ
γνούφα AMOΔ   40 Φασαηλίς ed. pr.   φασιλίς A   φασηλίς cett.
   41 Ἰερικοῦς Wilberg   Ἰερεικοῦς ed. pr.   ἐρικοῦς X   ἱερικός Φ
ἐρικός et ἔρικος cett.   45 Ἐνγάδδα Müller   Ἐνγάδα ed. pr.
       ἔργαδδα LSΩℲ   ἔργαδα ADMOΔ

(6 = 9 Nobbe*) ἀπ' ἀνατολῶν δὲ τοῦ ποταμοῦ 'Ιορδάνου*

Κόσμος	ξζ'	δ"	λα'	L"ιβ"
Λιβιάς	ξζ'	ϛ"	λα'	γ"ιβ"
Καλλιρρόη	ξζ'	ιβ"	λα'	ϛ"
Γάζωρος	ξζ'	L"	λα'	δ"
'Επίκαιρος	ξζ'		λα'	

50 (line marker)

(7 = 10 Nobbe*) 'Ιδουμαίας, ἥτις ἐστὶ πᾶσα ἀπὸ δύσεως τοῦ 'Ιορδάνου*
55 *ποταμοῦ*

Βέρζαμα	ξδ'	L"γ"	λα'	δ"
Καπαρόρσα	ξε'	L"	λα'	δ"
Γεμμαρουρίς	ξε'	L"γ"	λα'	ϛ"
'Ελοῦσα	ξε'	ϛ"	λ'	L"γ"
Μάψ	ξε'	γο"	λ'	L"γ"

60 (line marker)

49 *Κόσμος*] ἢ κόρμος add. A   50 λιβυάς BEZ   λιβίας ΟΦ
56 *Βέρζαμα* PSVWXΩ et pr. m. Ͻ   βέρζαμμα et βερζάμμα cett.
60 μαψίς X   μάψα A   μαψή Arg.   μάψ cett.

The Situation of Palaestina or Judaea

(1) The border of Palaestina or Judaea to the North and East is Syria, along the lines stated above; to the South it is bordered by Arabia Petraea along a line drawn from the eastern terminal near Syria to the boundary near Egypt, the location of which boundary is 64° 15′ 30° 40′, as stated; to the West, by that part of Egypt which starts there and extends to the sea, as has been stated above; and by the adjacent sea to the confines of Syria, which coast is described as follows: (2) After the mouth of the Chorseos river

Caesarea Stratonis	66°	15′	32°	30′
Apollonia	66°		32°	15′
Iope	65°	40′	32°	5′
The port of the Jamnites	65°	30′	32°	
Azotus	65°	15′	31°	55′
Ascalon	65°		31°	40′
Anthedon	64°	50′	31°	40′
The port of the Gazaeans	65°	45′	31°	30′

A part of the Jordan river flows through Judaea near the Asphaltite Lake, the middle position of which extends over the degrees 66° 50′ 31° 10′

(3) The interior towns of Judaea are, in Galilaea

168

Sapphuri	66°	40'	32°	25'
Caparcotni	66°	50'	32°	35'
Iulias	67°	5'	32°	15'
Tiberias	67°	15'	32°	5'

(4) in Samaria

Neapolis	66°	50'	31°	50'
Thena	67°	5'	31°	45'

(5) in Judaea to the west of the River Jordan

Raphia	65°		31°	10'
Gaza	65°	25'	31°	45'
Jamnia	65°	40'	32°	
Lydda	66°		32°	
Antipatris	66°	20'	32°	
Drusias	66°	30'	31°	55'
Sebaste	66°	40'	32°	10'
Beitogabri	65°	30'	31°	30'
Sebus	65°	40'	31°	25'
Emmaus	65°	45'	31°	50'
Guphna	66°	10'	31°	45'
Archelais	66°	30'	31°	45'
Phasaelis	66°	55'	31°	35'
Hiericus	66°	45'	31°	25'
Hierosolyma, that is now called				
Aelia Capitolina	66°		31°	40'
Thamna	66°	15'	31°	30'
Engadda	66°	30'	31°	15'
Bedoro	66°	30'	31°	
Thamaro	66°	20'	30°	50'

(6) To the east of the River Jordan

Cosmos	67°	15'	31°	35'
Livias	67°	10'	31°	25'
Callirrhoe	67°	5'	31°	10'
Gazorus	67°	30'	31°	15'
Epicairos	67°		31°	

(7) In Idumaea, all of which is west of the Jordan river

Berzama	64°	50'	31°	15'
Kaparorsa	65°	30'	31°	15'
Gemmaruris	65°	50'	31°	10'
Elusa	65°	10'	30°	50'
Maps	65°	40'	30°	50'

1 Παλαιστίνης Ἰουδαίας: A hybrid form; see M. Noth, *ZDPV*, LXII (1939), p. 131.

2 μετὰ τὰς τοῦ Χορσέου ποταμοῦ ἐκβολάς: For the identification of the River Chorseos with Nahr ez-Zerqa, see Abel, I, pp. 469 f. It is identified with Nahr ed-Difle by P. Thomsen, *ZDPV*, XXIX (1906), p. 104; Avi-Yonah, p. 143. It constituted the northern border of the territory of Caesarea. For other identifications of the places named by Ptolemy, see also Thomsen, *op. cit.*, pp. 101 ff.

Καισάρεια Στράτωνος: This dual form, which combines the name of the older town of Phoenician origin with that of the new foundation of Herod, is also found in patristic texts and in inscriptions; see Schürer, II, p. 136; L. Robert, *Villes d'Asie Mineure*², Paris 1962, p. 82. The name was never official and consequently has not been found on coins.

Ἰαμνιτῶν λιμήν: The port of Jamnia lay to the west of the town; see F. M. Abel, *RB*, XXXIII (1924), p. 207.

Ἄζωτος: In the first century C. E. the population of Azotus was evidently to a large extent Jewish as Vespasian found it necessary to reduce the town by force and to secure it by stationing a garrison there; cf. *BJ*, IV, 130.

Γαζαίων λιμήν: It later became known as Μαϊουμᾶς; cf. Sozomenus, *Historia Ecclesiastica*, V, 3:6; Marcus Diaconus, *Vita Porphyrii*, 57; Hieronymus, *Vita Hilarionis*, 3.

πρὸς τῇ Ἀσφαλτίτιδι λίμνῃ: This name for the Dead Sea is shared by many authors; cf. the commentary to Galenus, *De Simplicium Medicamentorum Temperamentis ac Facultatibus*, IV, 20 (No. 381).

3 Σαπφουρεί: This is the first mention of Sepphoris, the foremost town of Galilee, by a pagan writer. Josephus generally calls it by the Graecized name Σέπφωρις.

Καπαρκοτνεί: On the southern boundary of Galilee, the place is known from the Mishna as Kefar Otni; cf. *M. Giṭṭin*, i:5. It was given the new name of Legio, as it was garrisoned by the Sixth Legion; see B. Lifshitz, *Latomus*, XIX (1960), pp. 109 ff. Cf. Eusebius, *Onomasticon* (ed. Klostermann), p. 14, l. 21; p. 110, l. 21.

Ἰουλιάς: To be identified with Bet Saida at the north of the Sea of Galilee. It was given the name of Julias in honour of Julia, the daughter of Augustus; cf. *Ant.*, XVIII, 28; *BJ*, II, 168.

4 Θῆνα: Cf. Eusebius, *Onomasticon* (ed. Klostermann), p. 98, l. 13: καὶ νῦν ἐστι κώμη Θηνὰ ἀπὸ σημείων ἱ Νέας πόλεως ἐπ᾽ ἀνατολάς, κατιόντων ἐπὶ τὸν Ἰορδάνην. See A. Alt, *PJB* (1929), p. 54; K. Elliger, *ZDPV*, LIII (1930), pp. 277 f.

5 Ἀντιπατρίς: Built by Herod at Hellenistic Pegai; see Avi-Yonah, pp. 145 f.

Δρουσιάς: It is identified with el-Mejdel, near et-Taiyibe, by A. Alt, *PJB* (1931), p. 33, n. 2; with et-Tire to the north of Antipatris, by Thomsen, *op. cit.*, p. 107; and with Khirbet Drusia, 7 km north of Bet Gubrin, by Abel, II, p. 309.

Βαιτογαβρεί: Bet Gubrin became later known as Eleutheropolis. Ptolemy is the first Greek writer to mention Bet Gubrin, never referred to by Josephus.

170

Ptolemy

Σεβοῦς: There is no certainty, or even strong probability, concerning its location; cf. Thomsen, *loc. cit.*

Γούφνα, Θάμνα, 'Ενγάδδα: See the commentary to Plinius, *Naturalis Historia*, V, 70 (No. 204).

Βηδωρώ: This name defies exact identification; cf. Thomsen's attempt, *op. cit.* (supra, p. 170), p. 108.

Θαμαρώ: It occurs as Thamaro in the Tabula Peutingeriana; see Y. Aharoni, *Eretz-Israel*, V (1958), pp. 129 ff. (in Hebrew).

6 Κόσμος: It should perhaps be sought beyond the Jordan, but the place is hardly identifiable.

Λιβιάς, Καλλιρρόη: See the commentary to Plinius, *Naturalis Historia*, V, 72 (No. 204).

Γάζωρος: As the place is undoubtedly located in the Peraea, it should be identified with the centre of the Jewish Peraea, which was named Gadara (*BJ*, IV, 413), but is to be distinguished from the celebrated Hellenistic city of Gadara; see G. Dalman, *PJB* (1910), pp. 22 f.; A. H. M. Jones, *JRS*, XXI (1931), p. 79; Avi-Yonah, p. 179. It should be sought in the vicinity of es-Salt (at 'Ain Jâdûr).

'Επίκαιρος: Does the name stand for that of the fortress Μαχαιροῦς?

7 Βέρζαμα: It appears as Birsama in the *Notitia Dignitatum*, Oriens, XXXIV (ed. Seeck), pp. 72 f. It may be identified with Khirbet el-Far; see A. Alt, *ZDPV*, LVIII (1935), p. 27.

Καπαρόρσα: Perhaps it is to be identified with Khirbet Hreise, south of Marisa; see A. Alt, *PJB* (1931), p. 18, n. 3.

Γεμμαρουρίς: Perhaps identical with Khirbet Gambrure in the territory of Eleutheropolis (= Bet Gubrin). Thus, while Bet Gubrin itself is included by Ptolemy in Judaea, both Καπαρόρσα and Γαμμαρουρίς are included within Idumaea.

Μάψ: This is probably identical with Μάμψις of Eusebius, *Onomasticon* (ed. Klostermann), p. 8, l. 8: λέγεται δέ τις Θαμαρὰ κώμη διεστῶσα Μάψις ἡμέρας ὁδόν, ἀπιόντων ἀπὸ Χεβρὼν εἰς Αἰλάμ, ἥτις νῦν φρούριόν ἐστι τῶν στρατιωτῶν; it is now commonly identified with Qurnub; cf. A. Alt, *ZDPV*, LVIII (1935), p. 26; A. Negev, *IEJ*, XVII (1967), pp. 48 ff.

337b

Geographia, V, 16 — Müller = Nobbe, 17

(16:1 = 17:1 Nobbe) 'Αραβίας Πετραίας θέσις.

'Η Πετραία 'Αραβία περιορίζεται ἀπὸ μὲν δύσεως τῷ ἐκτειθειμένῳ τῆς Αἰγύπτου μέρει· ἀπὸ δὲ ἄρκτων τῇ τε Παλαιστίνῃ ἢ 'Ιουδαίᾳ καὶ τῷ μέρει τῆς Συρίας κατὰ τὰς διωρισμένας αὐτῶν γραμμὰς ...

5 (16:2 = 17:3 Nobbe) Διατείνει δὲ ἐν τῇ χώρᾳ τὰ καλούμενα Μέλανα ὄρη ἀπὸ τοῦ κατὰ Φαρὰν μυχοῦ τοῦ κόλπου ὡς ἐπὶ τὴν 'Ιουδαίαν ...

171

(16:1) The situation of Arabia Petraea.

Arabia Petraea is bounded to the west by the part of Egypt stated above, to the north by Palaestina or Judaea and the part of Syria along their indicated lines ...

(16:2) In the land the so-called Black Mountains extend from the recess of the bay near Pharan in the direction of Judaea ...

CV. VETTIUS VALENS

Second century C.E.

The astrological work of Vettius Valens[1] *contains references to the* σαββατικὴ ἡμέρα *and to Abraham as an astrological authority. Abraham is called* θαυμασιώτατος *and there is an express allusion to his astrological works.*

Abraham's reputation as an astrologer may be traced to the Jewish Hellenistic writer Artapanus, who stated that it was Abraham who taught the Egyptian king Pharethotes the science of astrology; see Eusebius, Praeparatio Evangelica, *IX, 18:1 =* F. Gr. Hist., *III, C 726, F 1.*[2] *A similar tradition is found in the work of the anonymous writer generally known as pseudo-Eupolemus;*[3] *see Eusebius,* Praeparatio Evangelica, *IX, 17:8 =* F. Gr. Hist., *III, C 724, F 1 = A. M. Denis,* Fragmenta Pseudepigraphorum Quae Supersunt Graeca, *Leiden 1970, p. 198:* συζήσαντα δὲ τὸν Ἀβραὰμ ἐν Ἡλιουπόλει τοῖς Αἰγυπτίων ἱερεῦσι πολλὰ μεταδιδάξαι αὐτούς, καὶ τὴν ἀστρολογίαν καὶ τὰ λοιπὰ τοῦτον αὐτοῖς εἰσηγήσασθαι. *The same source (Eusebius,* Praeparatio Evangelica, *IX, 18:2 =* F. Gr. Hist., *III, C 724, F 2) maintains that Abraham also introduced the Phoenicians to astrology.*[4]

The prominence of Abraham as an astrologer is also reflected in the later work of Firmicus Maternus, Mathesis, *IV, Prooemium, 5; IV, 17:2, 17:5, 18:1 (Nos. 473–476).*

---

1 For the chronology, see O. Neugebauer, *HTR*, XLVII (1954), pp. 65 ff. Neugebauer concludes that Vettius Valens wrote the bulk of his work in the decade 152 to 162 C.E.

2 For Abraham and astrology, see also E. Fascher, *Jahrbuch für Antike und Christentum*, Suppl. I, 1964 = Mullus, *Festschrift Theodor Klauser*, p. 122; W. & H. G. Gundel, *Astrologumena*, Wiesbaden 1966, pp. 52 ff.

3 On pseudo-Eupolemus, see B. Wacholder, *HUCA*, XXXIV (1963), pp. 83 ff.; N. Walter, *Klio*, XLIII–XLV (1965), pp. 282 ff.

4 The tradition that God commanded Abraham not to rely on astrology often occurs in rabbinic sources; see Ginzberg, V, p. 227, n. 108.

338

Anthologiae, I, 10 — Kroll

Περὶ ἑπταζώνου ἤτοι σαββατικῆς ἡμέρας ...
Περὶ δὲ τῆς ἑβδομάδος καὶ σαββατικῆς ἡμέρας οὕτως...

On the seven-zoned system or the sabbatical day ...
On the week day and the sabbatical day as follows...

Περὶ δὲ τῆς ἑβδομάδος καὶ σαββατικῆς ἡμέρας: The astrological writers, Vettius Valens among them, customarily equated the Sabbath with Saturn's day, and thought of the Jewish week as a variation of their own planetary week. Thus Valens uses both ἑβδομάς and σαββατικὴ ἡμέρα to denote week day. See also F. H. Colson, *The Week*, Cambridge 1926, p. 60. ἑβδομάς is already sometimes equated with the day of Sabbath in Jewish-Hellenistic literature; see Josephus, *BJ*, II, 147, 392; IV, 99; *Contra Apionem*, II, 175.

339

Anthologiae, II, 28 — Kroll

Περὶ ἀποδημίας ἐκ τῶν Ἑρμίππου ...
ὁ δὲ θαυμασιώτατος Ἄβραμος ἐν τοῖς βιβλίοις αὐτοῦ τούτου τοῦ τόπου δέδειχεν ἡμῖν * ἀλληλόσοά τε καὶ αὐτὸς ἰδίᾳ ἄλλα ἐξευρών τε καὶ δοκιμάσας ἐπὶ τῶν ἀποδηματικῶν μάλιστα γενέσεων.

On travelling, from the works of Hermippus ...
The most wonderful Abramos has shown us about this position in his books ... and he himself on his part invented other things and tested them, especially on genitures inclined to travelling.

ἐκ τῶν Ἑρμίππου: On Hermippus and Jews, see above, Vol. I, pp. 93 ff. Hermippus catalogued and commented upon the verses of Zoroaster, according to Plinius, *Naturalis Historia*, XXX, 4. See also Arnobius, *Adversus Nationes*, I, 52. Cf. Bidez & Cumont, I, pp. 21 f., 85 ff.; F. Wehrli, *Die Schule des Aristoteles* (Suppl. I, *Hermippos der Kallimacheer*), Basel–Stuttgart 1974, pp. 45 ff. On Hermippus as a compiler of a work on the Magi, see Diogenes Laertius, *Prooemium*, 8.

Vettius Valens

340

Anthologiae, II, 29 — Kroll

Περὶ ἀποδημίας ...
τίσι δὲ καὶ καιροῖς καὶ χρόνοις ἔσονται ⟨αἱ⟩ ἀποδημίαι ταῖς τοιαύταις
γενέσεσι, τὰ σχήματα δηλώσει τὰ ὑπὸ ᾽Αβράμου λεγόμενα ...
᾽Επὶ γὰρ τῆς διαιρέσεως τῶν χρόνων τῶν πρακτικῶν κατὰ ῎Αβραμον ...

On travelling ...
At which seasons and times the travels of such genitures will take
place is made clear by the configurations said to be drawn by
Abramos ...
Following the division of times of action according to Abramos ...

CVI. FRONTO

c. 90–170 C.E.

Born in Cirta, Numidia, Fronto became the leading orator of his day,[1] and was tutor and close friend of Marcus Aurelius. Two surviving fragments of his writings contain allusions to Jews. In the first, a letter to the emperor (No. 341), Fronto is probably referring to Jews in his description of the "superstitiosi" who look for a star in order to stop their fasting. In the other fragment he recalls the losses sustained by the Roman forces in the war against the Jews under Hadrian (No. 342).

341

Epistulae ad M. Caesarem et Invicem, II, 9 — Van den Hout

Caesari suo consul

Meum fratrem beatum, qui vos in isto biduo viderit! At ego Romae haereo conpedibus aureis vinctus; nec aliter kal. Sept. expecto quam superstitiosi stellam, qua visa ieiunium polluant. Vale, Caesar, decus
5 patriae et Romani nominis. Vale, domine.

4 *polluant*] *solvant* Schopen

The consul to his own Caesar

Lucky brother of mine to have seen you those two days! But I stick fast in Rome bound with golden fetters, looking forward to the first of September as the superstitious to the star, at sight of which to break their fast. Farewell, Caesar, glory of your country and the Roman name. My lord, farewell. (trans. C. R. Haines, *LCL*)

quam superstitiosi stellam, qua visa ieiunium polluant: As every Jewish fast lasts from sunset to sunset, the appearance of stars signals its termination.

---

1 For the date of Fronto's death, see G. W. Bowersock, *Greek Sophists in the Roman Empire*, Oxford 1969, pp. 124 ff.; A. R. Birley, *Chiron*, II (1972), pp. 463 ff.; E. Champlin, *JRS*, LXIV (1974), pp. 137 ff. Bowersock maintains that Fronto was still alive in 176 C.E., or even *c.* 183. On the other hand, Champlin concludes that Fronto did not survive the year 167.

342

De Bello Parthico, 2 — Van den Hout = F 192 R

Sed ne nimis vetera alte petam, vestrae familiae exemplis utar. Traiani proavi vestri ductu auspicioque nonne in Dacia captus vir consularis? Nonne a Parthis consularis aeque vir in Mesopotamia trucidatus? Quid? Avo vestro Hadriano imperium optinente
5 quantum militum a Iudaeis, quantum ab Britannis caesum? Patre etiam vestro imperante, qui omnium principum ...

      6 *principum ⟨felicissimus fuit⟩* Niebuhr   ⟨*pacatissimus*⟩ Haines

But not to hark back too far into ancient times, I will take instances from your own family. Was not a consular taken prisoner in Dacia under the leadership and auspices of your great grandfather Trajan; Was not a consular likewise slain by the Parthians in Mesopotamia? Again under the rule of your grandfather Hadrian what a number of soldiers were killed by the Jews, what a number by the Britons! Even in the principate of your Father, who was the most fortunate of princes...   (trans. C. R. Haines, *LCL*)

quantum militum a Iudaeis, quantum ab Britannis caesum: This was written in 162 C.E., after the Roman army had suffered a defeat at the hands of the Parthians in Armenia, resulting in the annihilation of a Roman legion and the death of the governor of Cappadocia. Fronto consoles Marcus Aurelius by reminding him of the many reverses that occurred in Roman history in olden times, from the Battle of the Allia to that of Carrhae, as well as other failures that took place more recently, in the reigns of Trajan, Hadrian and Antoninus Pius. In the defeats inflicted by the Jews at the time of Hadrian many Roman soldiers were killed. The losses sustained by Hadrian's forces at the hands of the Jews were connected with the revolt of Bar-Kokhba; cf. Cassius Dio, LXIX, 14:3 (No. 440).

CVII. APPIAN OF ALEXANDRIA

Second century C.E.

Information concerning the Jews appears in various books of Appian's Roman history: in the Syriaca, Mithridatica, *and those comprising the* Bella Civilia. *Book XXII, which treated the history of the empire until the times of Trajan, may have included more material about the Jews and their contact with the Romans, to judge from a surviving fragment (No. 347).*[1]

The Alexandrian historian was conspicuously loyal to imperial Rome and valued the order it imposed throughout the civilized world. He was opposed to Greek circles that harboured anti-Roman feelings. However, as a native of Egypt, Appian also took pride in the past glory of the Ptolemaic monarchy (Prooemium, 10:39 ff.). The tensions and terrors of the Jewish revolt in the time of Trajan were known to Appian from personal experience (No. 348). Nevertheless, the remnants of his work contain little trace of hatred or contempt for the Jews.

1 On the work of Appian, see E. Schwartz, PW, II, pp. 216 ff. = *Griechische Geschichtschreiber*, Leipzig 1959, pp. 361 ff.; A. Rosenberg, *Einleitung und Quellenkunde zur römischen Geschichte*, Berlin 1921, pp. 203 ff.; E. Gabba, *Appiano e la storia delle guerre civili*, Florence 1956.

178

343

Syriacus Liber, 50:251–253 — Viereck, Roos & Gabba = F75R

(251) Οὕτω μὲν δὴ Κιλικίας τε καὶ Συρίας τῆς τε μεσογαίου καὶ Κοίλης καὶ Φοινίκης καὶ Παλαιστίνης, καὶ ὅσα ἄλλα Συρίας ἀπὸ Εὐφράτου μέχρις Αἰγύπτου καὶ μέχρι θαλάσσης ὀνόματα, ἀμαχεὶ Ῥωμαῖοι κατέσχον. (252) ἓν δὲ γένος ἔτι, τὸ Ἰουδαίων, ἐνιστάμενον ὁ
5 Πομπήιος ἐξεῖλε κατὰ κράτος καὶ τὸν βασιλέα Ἀριστόβουλον ἔπεμψεν ἐς Ῥώμην καὶ τὴν μεγίστην πόλιν Ἱεροσόλυμα καὶ ἁγιωτάτην αὐτοῖς κατέσκαψεν, ἣν δὴ καὶ Πτολεμαῖος, ὁ πρῶτος Αἰγύπτου βασιλεύς, καθῃρήκει καὶ Οὐεσπασιανὸς αὖθις οἰκισθεῖσαν κατέσκαψε καὶ Ἀδριανὸς αὖθις ἐπ' ἐμοῦ. (253) καὶ διὰ ταῦτ' ἐστὶν Ἰουδαίοις ἅπασιν ὁ
10 φόρος τῶν σωμάτων βαρύτερος τῆς ἄλλης περιουσίας. ἔστι δὲ καὶ Σύροις καὶ Κίλιξιν ἐτήσιος, ἑκατοστὴ τοῦ τιμήματος ἑκάστῳ.

1 τε² om. i   6 τὴν μεγίστην καὶ ἁγιωτάτην αὐτοῖς πόλιν Ἱεροσόλυμα
Mendelssohn   10 περιουσίας] περιοικίας Musgrave
⟨τοῦ⟩ τῆς ἄλλης περιουσίας Viereck & Roos

(251) In this way the Romans, without fighting, came into possession of Cilicia, inland Syria and Coele-Syria, Phoenicia, Palestine, and all the other countries bearing the Syrian name from the Euphrates to Egypt and the sea. (252) The Jewish nation alone still resisted and Pompey conquered them, sent their king, Aristobulus, to Rome, and destroyed their greatest, and to them holiest, city, Jerusalem, as Ptolemy, the first king of Egypt had formerly done. It was afterward rebuilt and Vespasian destroyed it again, and Hadrian did the same in our time. (253) On account of those rebellions the poll tax imposed upon all Jews is heavier than that imposed upon the surrounding peoples.[1] The Syrians and Cilicians also are subject to an annual tax of one hundredth of the assessed value of the property of each man.

(trans. H. White, LCL)

1 According to the emendation of Musgrave.

252 ἓν δὲ γένος ἔτι, τὸ Ἰουδαίων: Appian summarizes here the conquests of Pompey in the East after his victory over Mithridates. The Romans hardly encountered any resistance in Syria itself, but only in Judaea.
ἐξεῖλε κατὰ κράτος ... κατέσκαψεν: Pompey did not destroy Jerusalem and was satisfied with demolishing its walls; cf. Strabo, Geographica, XVI, 2:40, p. 763 (No. 115); Orosius, VI, 6:4. The expression ἡ ἁγιωτάτη αὐτοῖς πόλις recurs also in Appianus, Mithridaticus Liber, 106:498 (No. 344), but that passage refers only to the capture of Jerusalem (εἷλε) and not to its destruction.

179

ἦν δὴ καὶ Πτολεμαῖος ... καθηρήκει: Agatharchides, apud: Josephus, *Contra Apionem*, I, 205–211 (No. 30), alludes to the same event; for the date, cf. the commentary, *ad loc*. Appian's reference to the destruction of Jerusalem seems too sweeping here also.

καὶ Οὐεσπασιανός: The destruction of Jerusalem by Titus, under Vespasian, is meant.

καὶ Ἀδριανὸς αὖθις ἐπ' ἐμοῦ: I.e. at the time of Bar-Kokhba's revolt. Appian lends support to the view that Jerusalem had for some time fallen into the hands of the rebels, as may also be concluded from the evidence of contemporary coins, which bear on the reverse side the legend, לחרות ירושלים, and on the obverse, שמעון; see F. W. Madden, *Coins of the Jews*, London 1881, pp. 233 ff. Cf. also, Eusebius, *Demonstratio Evangelica*, VI, 18:10. A siege of Jerusalem in the time of Hadrian is implied also by Eusebius, *Historia Ecclesiastica*, IV, 5:2; V, 12:1. The silence of Cassius Dio regarding this event does not prove much, especially as his history of this period is known only from the abridgement of Xiphilinus; cf. No. 440; see Schürer, I, pp. 685 f., 691; Alon, *History of the Jews in Palestine in the Period of the Mishna and Talmud*, II, Tel Aviv 1955, pp. 31 f. (in Hebrew).

253 καὶ διὰ ταῦτ'... βαρύτερος τῆς ἄλλης περιουσίας: The interpretation of this passage has given rise to much discussion; see U. Wilcken, *Griechische Ostraka*, I, Leipzig 1899, p. 247, n. 1; U. v. Wilamowitz-Moellendorff, *Hermes*, XXXV (1900), pp. 546 f.; Schürer, I, p. 512, n. 10; O. Hirschfeld, *Die kaiserlichen Verwaltungsbeamten*, Berlin 1905, p. 73, n. 1; Juster, II, p. 280, n. 1; H. Willrich, *Urkundenfälschung in der hellenistisch-jüdischen Literatur*, Göttingen 1924, p. 81; Momigliano, pp. 210 ff.; F. M. Heichelheim, "Roman Syria", in: T. Frank (ed.), *Economic Survey of Ancient Rome*, IV, Baltimore 1938, p. 231; E. Gabba, Addenda to the Teubner edition of Appianus, I, 1962, pp. 543 f.; cf. also M. Brücklmeier, "Beiträge zur rechtlichen Stellung der Juden im römischen Reich", Ph.D. Thesis, Munich 1939, p. 53, n. 101. In referring here to the heavy taxation weighing on the Jews Appian obviously has in mind contemporary conditions, as attested by his use of the present tense. He certainly considered that these conditions were the direct result (διὰ ταῦτα) of the mutinous temper of the Jews from the time of Pompey onwards, but his words should not be understood to imply that Pompey had actually imposed these conditions, as assumed by Wilamowitz; against this view, cf. already Juster. As Momigliano states: "Di fatto — se ben si considera — egli non collega già il tributo con un avvenimento determinato ma, per mezzo del διὰ ταῦτα, lo mette in relazione con tutto il fenomeno della resistenza presa nel suo complesso."

φόρος τῶν σωμάτων: This phrase should be translated, it seems, by "tributum capitis" and does not imply a special poll-tax for Jews, as suggested by Wilcken. However, Wilcken does not equate it with the Jewish tax; cf. Suetonius, *Domitianus*, 12:2 (No. 320). Some corruption lurks in the words τῆς ἄλλης περιουσίας. Musgrave, who felt that the contrast here is between the φόρος τῶν σωμάτων imposed on Jews and that imposed on the neighbouring peoples, emended περιουσίας to περιοικίας; see the *apparatus criticus* of Viereck, Roos & Gabba. The passage should then mean that as a consequence of the recurring Jewish revolts, the "tributum capitis" levied in Judaea, apart from the special Jewish tax, was higher than that levied in the neighbouring provinces, i.e. Syria and Cilicia, where it was fixed at one-hundredth of the assessed value of a man's property.

Other scholars look for the contrast in the difference between φόρος τῶν σωμάτων and other taxes. Thus περιουσία is taken by Wilcken as equivalent to οὐσία = property. This interpretation is approved in the *apparatus criticus* of Viereck & Roos: "scribe vel intellege ⟨τοῦ⟩ τῆς ἄλλης περιουσίας." However, this late use of περιουσία by a classical author is unattested, as pointed out by Wilamowitz.

Musgrave's emendation, though linguistically not wholly satisfactory, seems more suited to the general meaning of the passage, in which Appian intends to compare the Jews with their neighbours in respect of taxation and to explain the relatively worse condition of the former in consequence of their recurrent rebellions. There would be less point in Appian's comparing one tax paid by Jews with other taxes paid by them also.

A somewhat different explanation, that φόρος τῶν σωμάτων means the "Jewish tax", which for psychological reasons, as well as moral, was strongly resented by the Jews, is accepted by Juster and Momigliano; see also Brücklmeier's considerations.

344

Mithridaticus Liber, 106:498–499 — Viereck, Roos & Gabba

(498) · Ἐπολέμησε δὲ καὶ ῎Αραψι τοῖς Ναβαταίοις, Ἀρέτα βασιλεύοντος αὐτῶν, καὶ Ἰουδαίοις, Ἀριστοβούλου τοῦ βασιλέως ἀποστάντος, ·ἕως εἷλεν Ἱεροσόλυμα, τὴν ἁγιωτάτην αὐτοῖς πόλιν. (499) καὶ Κιλικίας δέ, ὅσα οὔπω Ῥωμαίοις ὑπήκουε, καὶ τὴν ἄλλην Συρίαν,
5 ὅση τε περὶ Εὐφράτην ἐστὶ καὶ Κοίλη καὶ Φοινίκη καὶ Παλαιστίνη λέγεται, καὶ τὴν Ἰδουμαίων καὶ Ἰτουραίων καὶ ὅσα ἄλλα ὀνόματα Συρίας, ἐπιὼν ἀμαχεὶ Ῥωμαίοις καθίστατο ...

3 καθεῖλεν iC

(498) He made war against the Nabataean Arabs, whose king was Aretas, and against the Jews (whose king, Aristobulus, had revolted), until he had captured their holiest city, Jerusalem. (499) He advanced against, and brought under Roman rule without fighting, those parts of Cilicia that were not yet subject to it, and the remainder of Syria which lies along the Euphrates, and the countries called Coele-Syria, Phoenicia, and Palestine, also Idumaea and Ituraea, and the other parts of Syria by whatever name called.   (trans. H. White, *LCL*)

498 Ἀρέτα βασιλεύοντος αὐτῶν: On Aretas III (87–62 B.C.E.), cf.

Schürer, I, pp. 732 ff.; R. Dussaud, *La pénétration des Arabes en Syrie avant l'Islam*, Paris 1955, p. 149; Schürer, ed. Vermes & Millar, I, p. 580; P. C. Hammond, *The Nabataeans — Their History, Culture and Archaeology*, Gothenburg 1973, pp. 17 ff.

'Αριστοβούλου ... ἀποστάντος: The expedition of Pompey to Petra, the capital of Aretas, was in fact stopped because of Aristobulus' change of policy; cf. *Ant.*, XIV, 46 ff.

345

Mithridaticus Liber, 114:556; 115:562 — Viereck, Roos & Gabba

(114:556) Αὐτὸς δέ, ἐνὶ τῷδε πολέμῳ τά τε ληστήρια καθήρας καὶ βασιλέα καθελὼν μέγιστον καὶ συνενεχθεὶς ἐς μάχας, ἄνευ τοῦ Ποντικοῦ πολέμου, Κόλχοις τε καὶ 'Αλβανοῖς καὶ 'Ίβηρσι καὶ 'Αρμενίοις καὶ Μήδοις καὶ "Αραψι καὶ 'Ιουδαίοις καὶ ἑτέροις ἔθνεσιν
5 ἑῴοις, τὴν ἀρχὴν ὡρίσατο 'Ρωμαίοις μέχρις Αἰγύπτου ... *(115:562)* καὶ ἑτέρας πολλαχοῦ κατενεχθείσας ἢ βεβλαμμένας διωρθοῦτο περί τε τὸν Πόντον καὶ Παλαιστίνην καὶ Κοίλην Συρίαν καὶ Κιλικίαν, ἐν ᾗ δὴ καὶ μάλιστα τοὺς ληστὰς συνῴκιζε, καὶ ἡ πόλις ἡ πάλαι Σόλοι νῦν Πομπηιούπολίς ἐστι.

7–8 δὴ μάλιστα i   9 πομπηιόπολις i

(114:556) Pompey, having cleared out the robber dens, and prostrated the greatest king then living in one and the same war, and having fought successful battles, besides those of the Pontic war, with Colchians, Albanians, Iberians, Armenians, Medes, Arabs, Jews and other Eastern nations, extended the Roman sway as far as Egypt ... (115:562) He restored other towns in many places, that had been destroyed or damaged, in Pontus, Palestine, Coele-Syria, and also in Cilicia, where he had settled the greater part of the pirates, and where the city formerly called Soli is now known as Pompeiopolis.

(trans. H. White, *LCL*)

556 καὶ 'Ιουδαίοις: The Jews are mentioned among the other nations who were defeated by Pompey.

346

Mithridaticus Liber, 117:571–573; 576–578 — Viereck, Roos & Gabba

(571) Αὐτοῦ δὲ τοῦ Πομπηίου προῆγον, ὅσοι τῶν πεπολεμημένων βασιλέων ἡγεμόνες ἢ παῖδες ἢ στρατηγοὶ ἦσαν, οἳ μὲν αἰχμάλωτοι

ὄντες, οἳ δὲ ἐς ὁμηρείαν δεδομένοι, τριακόσιοι μάλιστα καὶ εἴκοσι καὶ τέσσαρες. *(572)* ἔνθα δὴ καὶ ὁ Τιγράνους ἦν παῖς Τιγράνης καὶ πέντε
5 Μιθριδάτου, Ἀρταφέρνης τε καὶ Κῦρος καὶ Ὀξάθρης καὶ Δαρεῖος καὶ Ξέρξης, καὶ θυγατέρες Ὀρσάβαρίς τε καὶ Εὐπάτρα. *(573)* παρήγετο δὲ καὶ ὁ Κόλχων σκηπτοῦχος Ὀλθάκης καὶ Ἰουδαίων βασιλεὺς Ἀριστόβουλος καὶ οἱ Κιλίκων τύραννοι καὶ Σκυθῶν βασίλειοι γυναῖκες καὶ ἡγεμόνες τρεῖς Ἰβήρων καὶ Ἀλβανῶν δύο καὶ Μένανδρος ὁ
10 Λαοδικεύς, ἱππάρχης τοῦ Μιθριδάτου γενόμενος ... *(576)* παρεφέρετο δὲ καὶ πίναξ ἐγγεγραμμένων τῶνδε· «νῆες ἑάλωσαν χαλκέμβολοι ὀκτακόσιαι. πόλεις ἐκτίσθησαν Καππαδοκῶν ὀκτώ, Κιλίκων δὲ καὶ Κοίλης Συρίας εἴκοσι, Παλαιστίνης δὲ ἡ νῦν Σελευκίς. βασιλεῖς ἐνικήθησαν Τιγράνης Ἀρμένιος, Ἀρτώκης Ἴβηρ, Ὀροίζης Ἀλβανός,
15 Δαρεῖος Μῆδος, Ἀρέτας Ναβαταῖος, Ἀντίοχος Κομμαγηνός.» *(577)* τοσαῦτα μὲν ἐδήλου τὸ διάγραμμα, αὐτὸς δὲ ὁ Πομπήιος ἐπὶ ἅρματος ἦν, καὶ τοῦδε λιθοκολλήτου, χλαμύδα ἔχων, ὥς φασιν, Ἀλεξάνδρου τοῦ Μακεδόνος, εἴ τῳ πιστόν ἐστιν· ἔοικε δ' αὐτὴν εὑρεῖν ἐν Μιθριδάτου, Κῴων παρὰ Κλεοπάτρας λαβόντων. *(578)* εἵποντο δὲ αὐτῷ μετὰ τὸ
20 ἅρμα οἱ συστρατευσάμενοι τῶν ἡγεμόνων, οἳ μὲν ἐπὶ ἵππων, οἳ δὲ πεζοί. παρελθὼν δ' ἐς τὸ Καπιτώλιον οὐδένα τῶν αἰχμαλώτων ἔκτεινεν ὡς ἕτεροι τῶν θριάμβους παραγαγόντων, ἀλλ' εἰς τὰς πατρίδας ἔπεμψε δημοσίοις δαπανήμασι, χωρὶς τῶν βασιλικῶν· καὶ τούτων μόνος Ἀριστόβουλος εὐθὺς ἀνῃρέθη καὶ Τιγράνης ὕστερον. ὁ μὲν δὴ
25 θρίαμβος ἦν τοιόσδε.

10 ἵππαρχος Mendelssohn ex a   13 ἡ νῦν Σελευκίς corrupta
24 ἀριστόβολος B

(571) Before Pompey himself, at the head of the procession, went the satraps, sons and generals of the kings against whom he had fought, who were present (some having been captured and others given as hostages) to the number of 324. (572) Among them were Tigranes, the son of Tigranes, and five sons of Mithridates, namely, Artaphernes, Cyrus, Oxathres, Darius and Xerxes, and his daughters, Orsabaris and Eupatra. (573) Olthaces, chief of the Colchians, was also led in the procession, and Aristobulus king of the Jews, the tyrants of the Cilicians, and female rulers of the Scythians, three chiefs of the Iberians, two of the Albanians, and Menander the Laodicean who had been chief of cavalry to Mithridates ... (576) Moreover, a tablet was carried along with the inscription: "Ships with brazen beaks captured, 800; cities founded in Cappadocia, 8; in Cilicia and Coele Syria, 20; in Palestine, the one which is now Seleucis.

Kings conquered: Tigranes the Armenian, Artoces the Iberian, Oroezes the Albanian, Darius the Mede, Aretas the Nabataean, Antiochus of Commagene." (577) These were the facts recorded on the inscription. Pompey himself was borne in a chariot studded with gems, wearing, it is said, a cloak of Alexander the Great, if anyone can believe that. It seems to have been found among the possessions of Mithridates that the inhabitants of Cos had received from Cleopatra. (578) His chariot was followed by the officers who shared the campaigns with him, some on horseback and others on foot. When he arrived at the Capitol he did not put any of the prisoners to death, as had been the custom of other triumphs, but sent them all home at the public expense, except the kings. Of these Aristobulus alone was at once put to death and Tigranes somewhat later. Such was the character of Pompey's triumph.   (trans. H. White, *LCL*)

---

571 Αὐτοῦ δὲ τοῦ Πομπηίου προῆγον: For the triumph celebrated by Pompey at the end of September 61 B.C.E., see J. van Ooteghem, *Pompée le Grand*, Brussels 1954, pp. 281 ff.; M. Gelzer, *Pompeius*, Munich 1949, pp. 132 f. For the description of the triumph, cf. Plutarchus, *Pompeius*, 45 (No. 262).

573 καὶ Ἰουδαίων βασιλεὺς Ἀριστόβουλος: The Jews were expressly mentioned on the official placard carried at the triumphal procession after the appearance of the magistrates and senators; cf. Plinius, *Naturalis Historia*, VII, 98 (No. 208). See also Diodorus, XL, 4 (No. 66); Plutarchus, *loc. cit.*

578 Ἀριστόβουλος εὐθὺς ἀνῃρέθη: Aristobulus was not put to death immediately, but played a further part in Jewish history for many years. In 56 B.C.E. he was again active in Judaea and was for a second time taken prisoner to Rome, where he continued to reside. When war broke out between Pompey and Caesar, the latter decided to use him against the supporters of Pompey (49 B.C.E.), but those at Rome succeeded in poisoning Aristobulus before he could start his activities on behalf of Caesar; cf. *Ant.*, XIV, 123 ff.; *BJ*, I, 183 f. See also Cassius Dio, XLI, 18:1 (No. 409). For the whole passage, see F. Arnold, *Quaestionum de Fontibus Appiani Specimen*, Königsberg 1882, pp. 14 f. The death of Aristobulus occurred some twelve years after the triumph of Pompey described here by Appian. For this kind of mistake in Appian, see also E. Gabba, *Appiano e la storia delle guerre civili*, Florence 1956, p. 120, n. 5.

καὶ Τιγράνης ὕστερον: This statement also seems doubtful. The reference is to Tigranes the Younger, who was set free by the tribune Publius Clodius in 58 B.C.E., according to Cassius Dio, XXXVIII, 30:1.

Appian of Alexandria

347

apud: Zonaras, *Epitome Historiarum*, XI, 16 — Dindorf = Viereck, Roos & Gabba, F17

Ὁ γὰρ Ἰώσηπος, ὡς αὐτὸς ἐκεῖνος ἱστόρησε, χρησμόν τινα ἐν γράμμασιν ἱεροῖς εὑρηκὼς δηλοῦντα ὡς ἄρξει τις ἀπὸ τῆς χώρας αὐτῶν τῆς οἰκουμένης ... τούτου δὲ τοῦ χρησμοῦ μέμνηται καὶ Ἀππιανὸς ἐν τῷ εἰκοστῷ δευτέρῳ λόγῳ τῆς Ῥωμαϊκῆς ἱστορίας αὐτοῦ.

For Josephus, as he related himself, found in the sacred writings some oracle which revealed that one from their own country would become the ruler of the world ... This oracle Appian also mentions in the twenty-second book of his Roman history.

For the prophecy, see *BJ*, VI, 312: τὸ δ᾽ ἐπᾶραν αὐτοὺς μάλιστα πρὸς τὸν πόλεμον ἦν χρησμὸς ἀμφίβολος ὁμοίως ἐν τοῖς ἱεροῖς εὑρημένος γράμμασιν, ὡς κατὰ τὸν καιρὸν ἐκεῖνον ἀπὸ τῆς χώρας αὐτῶν τις ἄρξει τῆς οἰκουμένης.

348

Arabicus Liber, F19 — Viereck, Roos & Gabba = F77R

(1) Περὶ Ἀράβων μαντείας. Ἀππιανός φησι τῷ τέλει τοῦ κδ´ βιβλίου. φεύγοντί μοί ποτε τοὺς Ἰουδαίους ἀνὰ τὸν πόλεμον τὸν ἐν Αἰγύπτῳ γενόμενον καὶ ἰόντι διὰ τῆς Πετραίας Ἀραβίας ἐπὶ ποταμόν, ἔνθα με σκάφος περιμένον ἔμελλε διοίσειν ἐς Πηλούσιον, Ἄραψ ἀνὴρ δ᾽
5 ἡγεῖτό μοι τῆς ὁδοῦ νυκτός, οἰομένῳ πλησίον εἶναι τοῦ σκάφους κρωζούσης ἄρτι πρὸς ἕω κορώνης ἔφη συνταραχθείς· «πεπλανήμεθα.» καὶ κρωζούσης αὖθις εἶπεν· «ἄγαν πεπλανήμεθα.» *(2)* θορυβουμένῳ δέ μοι καὶ σκοποῦντι, εἴ τις ὁδοιπόρος ὀφθήσεται, καὶ οὐδένα ὁρῶντι ὡς ἐν ὄρθρῳ ἔτι πολλῷ καὶ γῇ πολεμουμένῃ, τὸ τρίτον ὁ Ἄραψ τοῦ
10 ὀρνέου πυθόμενος εἶπεν ἡσθείς· «ἐπὶ συμφέροντι πεπλανήμεθα καὶ ἐχόμεθα τῆς ὁδοῦ.» *(3)* ἐγὼ δὲ ἐγέλων μέν, εἰ καὶ νῦν ἐξόμεθα τῆς πλανώσης, καὶ ἀπεγίνωσκον ἐμαυτοῦ, πάντων πολεμίων ὄντων, οὐκ ὄν μοι δυνατὸν οὐδ᾽ ἀναστρέψαι διὰ τοὺς ὄπισθεν, οὓς δὴ καὶ φεύγων ἠρχόμην, ὑπὸ δ᾽ ἀπορίας εἰπόμην ἐκδοὺς ἐμαυτὸν τῷ μαντεύματι. *(4)*
15 οὕτω δὲ ἔχοντί μοι παρὰ δόξαν ἕτερος ποταμὸς ἐκφαίνεται, ὁ ἀγχοτάτω

4–5 δ᾽ ἡγεῖτο Mendelssohn   διηγεῖτο codd.   11 ἐξόμεθα Nauck
ἐγὼ δὲ διετέλουν μὲν ⟨δεδοικώς, μὴ⟩ ἐξόμεθα vel ἐγὼ δὲ ἐγέλων μέν, εἰ καὶ ⟨δε-
δοικώς, μὴ⟩ ἐξόμεθα Müller / νῦν om. Miller   12 πλανωμένης cod.
Milleri / πάντῃ Mendelssohn   15 ἐπιφαίνεται Mendelssohn

μάλιστα τοῦ Πηλουσίου, καὶ τριήρης ἐς τὸ Πηλούσιον παραπλέουσα,
ἧς ἐπιβὰς διεσωζόμην· τὸ σκάφος δέ, ὅ με ἐν τῷ ἑτέρῳ ποταμῷ
ὑπέμεινεν, ὑπὸ Ἰουδαίων ἐλήφθη. τοσοῦτον ὠνάμην τῆς τύχης καὶ
τοσοῦτον ἐθαύμασα τοῦ μαντεύματος.

17 με Mendelssohn   μὲν codd.
18 τοσούτου ὠνάμην (omisso τῆς τύχης) cod. Treuii

(1) About the Arabian power of divination. At the end of the
twenty-fourth book Appian says as follows: When I was fleeing from
the Jews during the war which was being waged in Egypt and I was
passing through Arabia Petraea in the direction of the river, where a
boat had been waiting in order to carry me over to Pelusium, an Arab
served me as guide at night. When I believed us to be near the boat a
crow croaked, just about day-break, and the troubled man said: "We
have gone astray." And when the crow croaked again, he said: "We
have gone much astray." (2) Then I became disturbed and looked for
some wayfarer. I saw none, since it was early morning and the country
was in a state of war. When the Arab heard the crow a third time, he
said rejoicing: "We have gone astray to our advantage and we have
gained the road." (3) I only laughed, thinking we would gain the
wrong path again, and despaired of myself as we were surrounded
everywhere by enemies, and it was not possible for me to turn back
because of those behind from whom I was fleeing. However, being at
a loss, I followed and gave myself up to the augury. (4) Being in such a
state, unexpectedly I perceived another river very near to Pelusium
and a trireme sailing to Pelusium. I embarked and was saved, while
the boat which awaited me at the other river was captured by the
Jews. So much I had good luck and marvelled at the augury.

This fragment affords a lively picture of the atmosphere in Egypt during the
Jewish revolt under Trajan and illustrates the wide diffusion of the hostilities;
cf. the general statement of Orosius, VII, 12:7: "Aegyptum vero totam ...
cruentis seditionibus turbaverunt"; see A. Fuks, *JRS*, LI (1961), p. 99.
Although there is no other documentary evidence for the activities of the
Jewish rebels in the vicinity of Pelusium, the presence of the ancient and
strong Jewish element in north-eastern Egypt would well account for such
operations; for the Jewry of Pelusium, cf. *Ant.*, XIV, 99; *BJ*, I, 175.
For the fear that the Jewish revolt inspired, cf. a letter from the χώρα (*CPJ*,
No. 437); Cassius Dio, LXVIII, 32 (No. 437), and the commentary *ad loc.*
1 ἀνὰ τὸν πόλεμον: The Jewish revolt is also called πόλεμος in
Artemidorus, *Onirocritica*, IV, 24 (No. 396).

349

Bella Civilia, II, 71:294 — Mendelssohn & Viereck

Ἐπὶ δὲ τοῖς Ἕλλησιν ὀλίγου πάντες, ὅσοι περιιόντι τὴν ἐν κύκλῳ
θάλασσαν ἐπὶ τὴν ἔω, Θρᾷκές τε καὶ Ἑλλησπόντιοι καὶ Βιθυνοὶ καὶ
Φρύγες καὶ Ἴωνες, Λυδοί τε καὶ Παμφύλιοι καὶ Πισίδαι καὶ
Παφλαγόνες, καὶ Κιλικία καὶ Συρία καὶ Φοινίκη καὶ τὸ Ἑβραίων γένος
5 καὶ Ἄραβες οἱ τούτων ἐχόμενοι Κύπριοί τε καὶ Ῥόδιοι καὶ Κρῆτες
σφενδονῆται καὶ ὅσοι ἄλλοι νησιῶται.

Besides the Greeks almost all the nations of the Levant sent aid to
Pompey: Thracians, Hellespontines, Bithynians, Phrygians, Ionians,
Lydians, Pamphylians, Pisidians, Paphlagonians; Cilicia, Syria,
Phoenicia, the Hebrews and their neighbours the Arabs; Cyprians,
Rhodians, Cretan slingers, and all the other islanders.

(trans. H. White, LCL)

Ἐπὶ δὲ τοῖς Ἕλλησιν ὀλίγου πάντες: Appian enumerates here the various
national contingents that assisted Pompey in his struggle against Caesar; cf.
Lucanus, Pharsalia, III, 214–217 (No. 192). The verb of this sentence
(συνεμάχουν or ἐστρατεύοντο) has to be supplied from the former passage.
καὶ τὸ Ἑβραίων γένος: For the appellation Ἑβραῖοι, cf. the commentary to
Charax of Pergamum (No. 335). It is common also in non-Jewish literature
from the end of the first century C.E. The Jewish soldiers at Pharsalus were
sent by Hyrcanus and Antipater, then loyal supporters of Pompey. They
presumably constituted part of the forces led from Syria by its governor
Scipio, the father-in-law of Pompey, who commanded the centre in the battle
of Pharsalus.

350

Bella Civilia, II, 90:380 — Mendelssohn & Viereck = F76R

Τὴν δὲ κεφαλὴν τοῦ Πομπηίου προσφερομένην οὐκ ὑπέστη, ἀλλὰ
προσέταξε ταφῆναι, καί τι αὐτῇ τέμενος βραχὺ πρὸ τῆς πόλεως
περιτεθὲν Νεμέσεως τέμενος ἐκαλεῖτο· ὅπερ ἐπ' ἐμοῦ κατὰ Ῥωμαίων
αὐτοκράτορα Τραϊανόν, ἐξολλύντα τὸ ἐν Αἰγύπτῳ Ἰουδαίων γένος, ὑπὸ
5 τῶν Ἰουδαίων ἐς τὰς τοῦ πολέμου χρείας κατηρείφθη.

5 τῶν om. b

Caesar could not bear to look at the head of Pompey when it was
brought to him but ordered that it be buried, and he set apart for it a
small plot of ground near the city which was dedicated to Nemesis,

but in my time, while the Roman emperor Trajan was exterminating the Jewish race in Egypt, it was devastated by them in the exigencies of the war. (trans. H. White, *LCL*)

ἐς τὰς τοῦ πολέμου χρείας κατηρείφθη: For the policy of the Jewish rebels in destroying pagan temples, see S. Applebaum, *Zion*, XIX (1954), pp. 33 ff.; A. Fuks, *JRS*, LI (1961), p. 104. On the other hand, it is argued that the Jewish rebels during the revolt under Trajan had no such specific policy; see Alon, *op. cit.* (supra, p. 180), I, p. 239. No definite conclusions can be reached from the wording of Appian, since the historian expressly states that the temple of Nemesis was destroyed ἐς τὰς τοῦ πολέμου χρείας, but the view about a general destructive policy of the Jews is supported by archaeological evidence from Cyrenaica. For the location of the temple of Nemesis, see E. Bernand, *Recueil des inscriptions grecques du Fayoum*, I, Leiden 1975, pp. 202 ff.

351

Bella Civilia, V, 7:31 — Mendelssohn & Viereck

Ἐπιπαριὼν ⟨scil. ᾿Αντώνιος⟩ δὲ Φρυγίαν τε καὶ Μυσίαν καὶ Γαλάτας τοὺς ἐν ᾿Ασίᾳ Καππαδοκίαν τε καὶ Κιλικίαν καὶ Συρίαν τὴν κοίλην καὶ Παλαιστίνην καὶ τὴν ᾿Ιτουραίαν καὶ ὅσα ἄλλη γένη Σύρων, ἅπασιν ἐσφορὰς ἐπέβαλλε βαρείας καὶ διῆτα πόλεσι καὶ βασιλεῦσιν, ἐν μὲν
5 Καππαδοκίᾳ ᾿Αριαράθῃ τε καὶ Σισίνῃ ...

3 τουραίωνα i C   4 ἐς φορὰς B

Proceeding onward to Phrygia, Mysia, Galatia, Cappadocia, Cilicia, Coele-Syria, Palestine, Iturea, and the other provinces of Syria, he [scil. Antony] imposed heavy contributions on all, and acted as arbiter between kings and cities, — in Cappadocia, for example, between Ariarathes and Sisina, ... (trans. H. White, *LCL*)

On the activities of Antony in the East after the victory of Philippi, see H. Buchheim, *Die Orientpolitik des Triumvirn M. Antonius*, Heidelberg 1960; E. Gabba, *Appiani Bellorum Civilium Liber Quintus*, Florence 1970, pp. 22 f. καὶ Παλαιστίνην: Appian does not explicitly mention Judaea, but the country is here certainly included in Palestine. On the relations then existing between Antony and the Jews, cf. *Ant.*, XIV, 301 ff.; *BJ*, I, 242 ff.

352

Bella Civilia, V, 75:318–319 — Mendelssohn & Viereck

(318) Ἐπὶ δὲ τούτοις ὁ μὲν Καῖσαρ ἐς τὴν Κελτικὴν ἐξώρμα

Appian of Alexandria

ταρασσομένην, ὁ δὲ Ἀντώνιος ἐπὶ τὸν πόλεμον τῶν Παρθυαίων. καὶ αὐτῷ τῆς βουλῆς ψηφισαμένης εἶναι κύρια, ὅσα ἔπραξέ τε καὶ πράξει, αὖθις στρατηγοὺς πανταχῇ περιέπεμπε καὶ τἆλλα ὡς ἐπενόει πάντα
5 διεκόσμει. (319) ἵστη δέ πῃ καὶ βασιλέας, οὓς δοκιμάσειεν, ἐπὶ φόροις ἄρα τεταγμένοις, Πόντου μὲν Δαρεῖον τὸν Φαρνάκους τοῦ Μιθριδάτου, Ἰδουμαίων δὲ καὶ Σαμαρέων Ἡρῴδην, Ἀμύνταν δὲ Πισιδῶν καὶ Πολέμωνα μέρους Κιλικίας καὶ ἑτέρους ἐς ἕτερα ἔθνη.

5 ποι i   7 Ἰδουμαίων] Ἰουδαίων Musgrave   /   Ἡρῴδην Viereck
Ἡρῴδην codd.

(318) After these events Octavian set forth on an expedition to Gaul, which was in a disturbed state, and Antony started for the war against the Parthians. The Senate having voted to ratify all that he had done or should do Antony again despatched his lieutenants in all directions and arranged everything else as he wished. (319) He set up kings here and there as he pleased, on condition of their paying a prescribed tribute: in Pontus, Darius, the son of Pharnaces and grandson of Mithridates; in Idumaea and Samaria, Herod; in Pisidia, Amyntas; in a part of Cilicia, Polemon, and others in other countries.

(trans. H. White, *LCL*)

319 ἵστη δὲ πῇ καὶ βασιλέας ... Ἰδουμαίων δὲ καὶ Σαμαρέων Ἡρῴδην: The text of Appian, as it stands, refers only to the appointment of Herod as the king of the Idumaeans and the Samaritans, while the Jews are not mentioned at all. Herod became king of Judaea by the grace of Rome in 40 B.C.E., after he had escaped from the Parthians and Antigonus, Antony being his main supporter; cf. *Ant.*, XIV, 381 ff.; *BJ*, I, 282. The opinion that Appian here had the same event in mind is held by Schürer, I, p. 355, n. 3; Otto, pp. 28 f. However, the passage occurs within the framework of the events in the East dated to 39 B.C.E., and while Josephus recounts the original appointment of Herod by the Senate, Appian relates its somewhat later confirmation by the triumvir among many similar acts. On the other hand, it seems artificial to explain the omission of Judaea proper by Herod's supposed exemption from payment of taxes for Judaea while he had to pay for Samaria and Idumaea; see T. Mommsen, *Römische Geschichte*, V, Berlin 1909, p. 501, n.1. The most important fact in this passage is not the obligation to pay taxes but the confirmation of the monarchies of the clients. Also there is no sufficient reason to assume that Herod did not pay taxes for Judaea proper; see Momigliano, p. 349. It would be preferable to suppose that Appian implies an addition of territory to the kingdom of Herod not included in the original grant of 40 B.C.E.; see Buchheim, *op. cit.* (supra, p. 188), pp. 66 f. This interpretation gains some support from the fact that Samaria, and perhaps parts of Idumaea, e.g., Marisa, had not been included in the ethnarchy of Hyrcanus, Herod's predecessor as ruler of Judaea. Even so, the omission of Judaea proper in the confirmatory act of M. Antonius may be noted. Musgrave, who felt the difficulty, emended Ἰδουμαίων into Ἰουδαίων, as noted in the *apparatus criticus*, but it is better to assume that Ἰουδαίων was dropped here by haplography, following Ἰδουμαίων; see also A. H. M. Jones, *JRS*, XXV (1935), p. 229; Gabba, *Appiani Bellorum, op. cit.* (supra, p. 188), p. 129.

CVIII. PAUSANIAS

Second century C.E.

Since Pausanias is thought to have been a native of Asia Minor,[1] it has been suggested, with some plausibility, that his Description of Greece was intended mainly for the Greek inhabitants of his native region.[2] Pausanias travelled widely, not only in Greece, but also in the lands of the East. From his own assertion it is clear that he visited Palestine (cf. No. 356: καὶ αὐτὸς οἶδα), but his description of it contains nothing to corroborate the view that he was a native of Syria and is to be identified with Pausanias of Damascus.[3]

As Pausanias' theme is the description of Greece, his work naturally does not contain much information on either the Jews or their land. References occur only by way of comparison or in excurses. Pausanias never uses the names "Judaea" or "Jews", but consistently employs the terms "the land of the Hebrews" and "Hebrews" respectively. This accords well with the common usage of the second century C.E. "The Land of the Hebrews" in Pausanias' terminology includes Jaffa, the Lake of Tiberias, and the Jordan, and covers an area undoubtedly identical with Judaea in the meaning acquired by that name as a result of the Hasmonaean conquests.

The present collection of passages does not include that found in Chapter 12:4 of Book V of Pausanias' work, although some scholars have suggested that it alludes to the activities of Antiochus Epiphanes in connection with the Temple of Jerusalem.[4]

1 See W. Gurlitt, *Über Pausanias*, Graz 1890, pp. 56 f.; J. G. Frazer, *Pausanias's Description of Greece*, I, London 1913, p. XIX; O. Strid, *Über Sprache und Stil des Periegeten Pausanias*, Uppsala 1976, p. 11.

2 See O. Regenbogen, PW, Suppl, VIII, p. 1093.

3 See C. Robert, *Pausanias als Schriftsteller*, Berlin 1909, pp. 271 ff.; G. Pasquali, *Hermes*, XLVIII (1913), pp. 222 f. Against this supposition, cf. O. Seel, PW, XVIII, p. 2404; H. Diller, *TAPA*, LXXXVI (1955), pp. 268 ff. (on the authors named Pausanias; Pausanias of Damascus is excluded from the company of second-century writers of that name).

4 Against this view, cf. A. Pelletier, *Syria*, XXXII (1955), pp. 289 ff.; see also idem, *REG*, LXIX (1956), p. XII; O. Mørkholm, *Antiochus IV of Syria*, Copenhagen 1966, p. 62, n. 43. The text of Pausanias reads: ἐν δὲ Ὀλυμπίᾳ παραπέτασμα ἐρεοῦν κεκοσμημένον ὑφάσμασιν Ἀσσυρίοις καὶ βαφῇ πορφύρας τῆς Φοινίκων ἀνέθηκεν Ἀντίοχος.

353

Graeciae Descriptio, I, 5:5 — Spiro

Οἵδε μὲν εἰσιν Ἀθηναίοις ἐπώνυμοι τῶν ἀρχαίων· ὕστερον δὲ καὶ ἀπὸ
τῶνδε φυλὰς ἔχουσιν, Ἀττάλου τοῦ Μυσοῦ καὶ Πτολεμαίου τοῦ
Αἰγυπτίου καὶ κατ' ἐμὲ ἤδη βασιλέως Ἀδριανοῦ τῆς τε ἐς τὸ θεῖον
τιμῆς ἐπὶ πλεῖστον ἐλθόντος καὶ τῶν ἀρχομένων ἐς εὐδαιμονίαν τὰ
5 μέγιστα ἑκάστοις παρασχομένου. καὶ ἐς μὲν πόλεμον οὐδένα ἑκούσιος
κατέστη, Ἑβραίους δὲ τοὺς ὑπὲρ Σύρων ἐχειρώσατο ἀποστάντας ...

6 κατέστη] κατέβη L¹y

These are the Athenian eponymoi who belong to the ancients. And of
a later date than these they have tribes named after the following,
Attalus the Mysian and Ptolemy the Egyptian, and within my own
time the emperor Hadrian, who was extremely religious in the
respect he paid to the deity and contributed very much to the
happiness of his various subjects. He never voluntarily entered upon
a war, but he reduced the Hebrews beyond Syria, who had
rebelled.   (trans. W. H. S. Jones, *LCL*)

Ἑβραίους δὲ τοὺς ὑπὲρ Σύρων ἐχειρώσατο ἀποστάντας: Pausanias refers
here to Hadrian in connection with the Athenian φυλαί. That Pausanias finds
it appropriate to mention the Jewish revolt as the only event that disturbed
the peace under the rule of this emperor is the measure of the impression left
by the revolt in subsequent years. The first book of Pausanias was written not
long after the crushing of the rebellion and the death of Hadrian; for the date
of composition, see Diller, *op. cit.* (supra, p. 191, n. 3), p. 268.

354

Graeciae Descriptio, IV, 35:9 — Spiro

Γλαυκότατον μὲν οἶδα ὕδωρ θεασάμενος τὸ ἐν Θερμοπύλαις, οὔτι που
πᾶν, ἀλλ' ὅσον κάτεισιν ἐς τὴν κολυμβήθραν ἥντινα ὀνομάζουσιν οἱ
ἐπιχώριοι Χύτρους γυναικείους· ξανθὸν δὲ ὕδωρ, οὐδέν τι ἀποδέον τὴν
χρόαν αἵματος, Ἑβραίων ἡ γῆ παρέχεται πρὸς Ἰόππῃ πόλει·
5 θαλάσσης μὲν ἐγγυτάτω τὸ ὕδωρ ἐστί, λόγον δὲ ἐς τὴν πηγὴν
λέγουσιν οἱ ταύτῃ, Περσέα ἀνελόντα τὸ κῆτος, ᾧ τὴν παῖδα
προκεῖσθαι τοῦ Κηφέως, ἐνταῦθα τὸ αἷμα ἀπονίψασθαι.

1 γλαυκότερον P   7 τὴν Κηφέως Schubart

The bluest water that I know from personal experience is that at Thermopylae, not all of it, but that which flows into the swimming-baths, called locally the Women's Pots. Red water, in colour like blood, is found in the land of the Hebrews near the city of Joppa. The water is close to the sea, and the account which the natives give of the spring is that Perseus, after destroying the sea-monster, to which the daughter of Cepheus was exposed, washed off the blood in the spring.

(trans. H. A. Ormerod, *LCL*)

ξανθὸν δὲ ὕδωρ ...: The story of Pausanias that the water near Jaffa used to become red with blood stands almost alone in Greek literature. The nearest parallel to it is the tale that the river Adonis changed its colour because of the blood flowing into it when Adonis was wounded on Mount Libanus; see Lucianus, *De Dea Syria*, 8; cf. examples collected from places throughout the world by Frazer, *op. cit.* (supra, p. 191, n. 1), III, p. 454.

Περσέα ἀνελόντα τὸ κῆτος ...: The main Greek tradition placed the legend of Perseus and Andromeda in Ethiopia; cf. Apollodorus, *Bibliotheca*, II, 4:3; see also Ovidius, *Metamorphoses*, IV, 668 ff. However by the fourth century B.C.E. another version was current which connected the legend with the shore of Jaffa; cf. Pseudo-Scylax, in: C. Müller, *Geographi Graeci Minores*, I, p. 79 = K. Galling, *ZDPV*, LXI (1938), p. 90 (No. 558). It even seems, to judge from a fragment of a comedy by Cratinus, that some tradition in the fifth century already connected Perseus with Syria; see J. M. Edmonds, *The Fragments of Attic Comedy*, I, Leiden 1957, F 207, p. 94: ἐς Συρίαν δ'ἔνθενδ' ἀφικνῆ μετέωρος ὑπ'αὔρας. Cf. also C. Dugas, *REG*, LXIX (1956), p. 9. The location of the story of Andromeda at Jaffa is mentioned by many writers; cf. Strabo, *Geographica*, I, 2:35, p. 43 (No. 109); XVI, 2:28 (No. 114); Pomponius Mela, I, 11:64 (No. 152); Plinius, *Naturalis Historia*, V, 69 (No. 204); IX, 11 (No. 209); *BJ*, III, 420. See also Conon, *Narrationes*, apud: Photius, *Bibliotheca*, Cod. 186 (ed. Bekker, pp. 138b–139a = No. 145); Stephanus Byzantius, s.v. 'Ιόπη; Tzetzes, in his scholia to Lycophron, *Alexandra*, l. 836; see *Lycophronis Alexandra*, ed. E. Scheer, Berlin 1908, II, p. 268; cf. H. Schmidt, *Jona*, Göttingen 1907, p. 17, n. 3. Jerome asserts that in his day the rocks to which Andromeda was bound still used to be shown; cf. Hieronymus, *Commentarii in Ionam* (*PL*, XXV, Col. 1123); idem, *Epistulae*, 108 (*PL*, XXII, Col. 883). Apparently a local tradition in Jaffa about a sea monster early merged into the story of Perseus and Andromeda. The similarity in the names Jope–Jaffa and Aethiopia certainly played its part in this amalgamation of traditions. It is also noteworthy that the mother of Andromeda was called Cassiepeia and that in poetry the name sometimes assumed the form Cassiope. See also K. B. Stark, *Gaza und die philistäische Küste*, Jena 1852, pp. 255 ff., p. 593; Schürer, II, pp. 32 f.; Schmidt, *op. cit.*, p. 12 ff.; W. W. Baudissin, *Studien zur semitischen Religionsgeschichte*, II, Leipzig 1911, p. 178; H. Lewy, *MGWJ*, LXXXI (1937), pp. 65 ff.; Dugas, *op. cit.*, p. 4, n. 3; K. Schauenburg, *Perseus in der Kunst des Altertums*, Bonn 1960, pp. 55 ff. See also the commentary to Tacitus, *Historiae*, V, 2 (No. 281), and the Appendix, Pseudo-Scylax (No. 558).

355

Graeciae Descriptio, V, 5:2 — Spiro = F90R

Ἡ δὲ βύσσος ἡ ἐν τῇ Ἠλείᾳ λεπτότητος μὲν ἕνεκα οὐκ ἀποδεῖ τῆς Ἑβραίων, ἔστι δὲ οὐχ ὁμοίως ξανθή.

The fine flax of Elis is as fine as that of the Hebrews, but it is not so yellow.   (trans. W.H.S. Jones, *LCL*)

ἡ δὲ βύσσος ἡ ἐν τῇ Ἠλείᾳ: For the byssus of Elis, cf. J.A.O. Larsen, "Roman Greece", in: T. Frank (ed.), *Economic Survey of the Roman Empire*, IV, Baltimore 1938, pp. 471, 484 ff.
οὐκ ἀποδεῖ τῆς Ἑβραίων: See also the comparison made by Pausanias between the dates of Boeotia and those of Palestine (No. 359). The byssus was probably a species of flax; see Larsen, *op. cit.*, p. 485, n. 3; S. Krauss, *Talmudische Archäologie*, I, Leipzig 1910, p. 536, n. 119. It served as material for the dress of the priests in Jerusalem (*BJ*, V, 229), and in general, like purple, was considered suitable for the rich; cf. *TB Bava Meẓi'a*, 29b.
On the skill of Jews in the production of byssus, cf. also Cosmas Indicopleustes, *Topographia Christiana*, ed. E.O. Winstedt, Cambridge 1909, p. 121 = ed. W. Wolska-Conus, III, 70, Vol. I, p. 511.

356

Graeciae Descriptio, V, 7:4–5 — Spiro = F91R

(4) Ἐν δὲ τῇ γῇ ποταμὸν τῇ Ἑβραίων Ἰάρδανον καὶ αὐτὸς οἶδα λίμνην Τιβεριάδα ὀνομαζομένην διοδεύοντα, ἐς δὲ λίμνην ἑτέραν καλουμένην θάλασσαν Νεκράν, ἐς ταύτην ἐσιόντα καὶ ὑπὸ τῆς λίμνης αὐτὸν ἀναλούμενον. (5) ἡ δὲ θάλασσα ἡ Νεκρὰ πάσχει παντὶ ὕδατι ἄλλῳ τὰ
5 ἐναντία· ἐν ᾗ γε τὰ μὲν ζῶντα πέφυκεν οὐ νηχόμενα ἐποχεῖσθαι, τὰ δὲ θνήσκοντα ἐς βυθὸν χωρεῖν. ταύτῃ ἄκαρπος καὶ ἰχθύων ἡ λίμνη· ἅτε ἀπὸ τοῦ φανερωτάτου κινδύνου ἐπὶ τὸ ὕδωρ ἀναφεύγουσιν ὀπίσω τὸ οἰκεῖον.

2 Τιβεριάδα Sylburg   τιβερίδα codd.

(4) And in the land of the Hebrews, as I can myself bear witness, the river Jordan passes through a lake called Tiberias, and then entering another lake called the Dead Sea, it disappears in it. (5) The Dead Sea has the opposite qualities to those of any other water. Living

Pausanias

creatures float in it naturally without swimming; dying creatures sink to the bottom. Hence the lake is barren of fish; their danger stares them in the face, and they flee back to the water which is their native element.   (trans. W.H.S.Jones, *LCL*)

4 ποταμὸν ... Ἰάρδανον: The common name for the river in Greek is Ἰορδάνης. The peculiar form Ἰάρδανος used by Pausanias is phonetically nearer to the original Hebrew name (יַרְדֵּן), while sounding more familiar to the Greek ear. Albright thinks that the original form of the name of the river was probably Yurdan, while Yordan is the form retained in "Amorite"; in Canaanite proper the form in the thirteenth century B.C.E. was spelled Yardon, and the biblical Yarden is an Aramaicizing development from Canaanite Hebrew; see W.F. Albright, *Yahweh and the Gods of Canaan*, London 1968, p. 97, n. 5. Cf. also L. Köhler, *ZDPV*, LXII (1939), pp. 115 ff.; W. von Soden, *ZAW*, LVII (1939), pp. 153 f. A description of the Jordan is given in both Plinius, *Naturalis Historia*, V, 71 (No. 204), and Tacitus, *Historiae*, V, 6 (No. 281). Cf. *BJ*, III, 509 ff. The following explanation of the name of the river Ἰορδάνης has been falsely attributed to Plutarch; see the fragment of Iohannes Antiochensis, *Archaeologia*, in: J.A.Cramer, *Anecdota Graeca e Codd. Manuscriptis Bibliothecae Regiae Parisiensis*, II, Oxford 1839, p. 388 = Plutarchus, *Moralia*, VII, Leipzig 1967, F187: Ἰορδάνης λέγεται ὁ ποταμὸς διότι δύο ἅμα μίγνυνται ποταμοί, Ἰόρ τε καὶ Δάνης, καὶ ἀποτελοῦσιν αὐτόν, ὥς φησι Πλούταρχος.
5 θάλασσα ἡ Νεκρά: The same name in its Latin translation "Mortuum Mare" occurs in Pompeius Trogus, apud: Iustinus, XXXVI, 3:6 (No. 137); see the commentary *ad loc*.
ἐν ᾗ γε τὰ μὲν ζῶντα: In describing the nature of the Dead Sea Pausanias takes a position similar to that of Pompeius Trogus, *loc. cit*. Pausanias expressly distinguishes between living bodies and dead ones, only the latter sinking to the bottom of the sea.
ἄκαρπος καὶ ἰχθύων ἡ λίμνη: On fish being unable to live there, cf. already Aristoteles, *Meteorologica*, II, p. 359a (No. 3).

357
Graeciae Descriptio, VI, 24:8 — Spiro = F92R

Θνητὸν δὲ εἶναι τὸ γένος τῶν Σιληνῶν εἰκάσαι τις ἂν μάλιστα ἐπὶ τοῖς τάφοις αὐτῶν· ἐν γὰρ τῇ Ἑβραίων χώρᾳ Σιληνοῦ μνῆμα καὶ ἄλλου Σιληνοῦ Περγαμηνοῖς ἐστιν.

That the Silenuses are a mortal race you may infer especially from their graves, for there is a tomb of a Silenus in the land of the Hebrews, and of another at Pergamum.   (trans. W.H.S.Jones, *LCL*)

Σιληνοῦ μνῆμα: It is hard to tell what topographical feature in "the land of the Hebrews" Pausanias had in mind here. One of the sacred hills of the Canaanite and early Israelite period is implied. The statement could reflect the common view on the connection between the Jewish cult and that of Dionysus since the Sileni were the companions of Dionysus; see Frazer, *op. cit.* (supra, p. 191, n. 1), IV, p. 104. See also T. Labhardt, *Quae de Iudaeorum Origine Iudicaverint Veteres*, Augsburg 1881, p. 27, n. 2.

358

Graeciae Descriptio, VIII, 16:4–5 — Spiro = F93 R

(4) Τάφους δὲ ἀξίους θαύματος ἐπιστάμενος πολλοὺς δυοῖν ἐξ αὐτῶν
ἐπιμνησθήσομαι, τοῦ τε ἐν Ἀλικαρνασσῷ καὶ ἐν τῇ Ἑβραίων. ὁ μὲν δὴ ἐν
Ἀλικαρνασσῷ Μαυσώλῳ βασιλεύσαντι Ἀλικαρνασσέων πεποίηται,
μέγεθος δὲ οὕτω δή τί ἐστι μέγας καὶ ἐς κατασκευὴν περίβλεπτος τὴν
5 πᾶσαν, ὥστε καὶ Ῥωμαῖοι μεγάλως δή τι αὐτὸν θαυμάζοντες τὰ παρὰ
σφίσιν ἐπιφανῆ μνήματα Μαυσώλεια ὀνομάζουσιν· *(5)* Ἑβραίοις δὲ
Ἑλένης γυναικὸς ἐπιχωρίας τάφος ἐστὶν ἐν πόλει Σολύμοις, ἣν ἐς ἔδαφος
κατέβαλεν ὁ Ῥωμαίων βασιλεύς. μεμηχάνηται δὲ ἐν τῷ τάφῳ τὴν θύραν,
ὁμοίως παντὶ οὖσαν τῷ τάφῳ λιθίνην, μὴ πρότερον ἀνοίγεσθαι, πρὶν ἂν
10 ἡμέραν τε ἀεὶ καὶ ὥραν τὸ ἔτος ἐπαγάγῃ τὴν αὐτήν· τότε δὲ ὑπὸ μόνου τοῦ
μηχανήματος ἀνοιχθεῖσα καὶ οὐ πολὺ ἐπισχοῦσα συνεκλείσθη δι᾽ ἑαυτῆς.
τοῦτον μὲν δὴ οὕτω, τὸν δὲ ἄλλον χρόνον ἀνοῖξαι πειρώμενος ἀνοίξαις μὲν
οὐκ ἄν, κατάξεις δὲ αὐτὴν πρότερον βιαζόμενος.

2 τε om. y   9 παντὶ Bekker   πάντα codd. /   ἀνοίγεσθαι P
    ἐσανοίγεσθαι cett.   10 ἐπαγάγῃ L²   ἀπαγάγῃ cett.
    11 δι᾽ ἑαυτῆς Mayor   δι᾽ ὀλίγης codd.

(4) I know many wonderful graves, and will mention two of them, the one at Halicarnassus and one in the land of the Hebrews. The one of Halicarnassus was made for Mausolus, king of the city, and it is of such vast size and so notable for all its ornament, that the Romans in their great admiration of it call remarkable tombs in their country Mausolea. (5) The Hebrews have a grave, that of Helen, a native woman, in the city of Jerusalem, which the Roman Emperor razed to the ground. There is a contrivance in the grave whereby the door, which like all the grave is of stone, does not open until the year brings back the same day and the same hour. Then the mechanism, unaided, opens the door, which, after a short interval, shuts itself. This happens at that time, but should you at any other try to open the door you cannot do so; force will not open it, but only break it down.

(trans. W.H.S. Jones, *LCL*)

4 Τάφους δὲ ἀξίους θαύματος: The Mausoleum at Halicarnassus was considered one of the seven wonders of the world; cf. Strabo, *Geographica*, XIV, 2:16, p. 656; Plinius, *Naturalis Historia*, XXXVI, 30. That Pausanias puts the tomb of Queen Helene at Jerusalem on the same level indicates the tremendous impression it made on him.

5 γυναικὸς ἐπιχωρίας: Helene can hardly be considered ἐπιχώρια in Judaea, since she was the wife of the king of Adiabene, and became a proselyte with her two sons, Izates and Monobazus (*Ant.*, XX, 17 ff.), successive kings of Adiabene. Helene had stayed for some time at Jerusalem and helped the inhabitants of Judaea during the famine at the time of Claudius (*Ant.*, XX, 51). After Helene died in Adiabene her bones and those of Izates were sent by King Monobazus to be buried in the pyramids built by her at a distance of three stadia from Jerusalem; cf. *Ant.*, XX, 95: ἃς ἡ μήτηρ κατεσκευάκει τρεῖς τὸν ἀριθμὸν τρία στάδια τῆς Ἱεροσολυμιτῶν πόλεως ἀπεχούσας. On the Adiabene tombs, see also *BJ*, V, 55, 119, 147. Cf. also Eusebius, *Historia Ecclesiastica*, II, 12:3; Hieronymus, *Epistulae*, 108 (*PL*, XXII, Col. 883). The monument should be identified with the "Royal Tombs" in the northern part of Jerusalem; see M. Kon, *The Royal Tombs*, Tel Aviv 1947, p. 27 (in Hebrew). See also C. Schick, *PEQ* (1897), pp. 182 ff.; E. Pfennigsdorf, *ZDPV*, XXVII (1904), pp. 173 ff.; H. Graetz, *Geschichte der Juden*, Vol. III, Part 2⁵, Leipzig 1906, pp. 786 ff.; Schürer, III, pp. 169 ff.; S. Klein, *Jüdisch-palästinisches Corpus Inscriptionum*, Vienna–Berlin 1920, p. 26; Jeremias, pp. 77 f.; J. Pirenne, *Syria*, XL (1963), pp. 102 ff. For talmudic sources bearing on Queen Helene, cf. Derenbourg, pp. 223 ff. See also Tacitus, *Annales*, XV, 14 (No. 291), and the commentary *ad loc.*

κατέβαλεν ὁ Ῥωμαίων βασιλεύς: Pausanias does not mention the name of the Roman emperor who destroyed Jerusalem.

μεμηχάνηται δὲ ἐν τῷ τάφῳ τὴν θύραν: The description of the mechanism here may be compared with that of similar machines found in the works of the Greek mathematician Hiero of Alexandria; cf. *Hieronis Alexandrini Opera Quae Supersunt* (ed. Schmidt), I, pp. 175 ff.; see Vincent, *Comptes rendus de l'Académie des Inscriptions et Belles-Lettres*, II (1866), pp. 120 ff.; see also Kon, *op. cit.*, pp. 56 ff. The archaeological remains, as described and interpreted by Kon, seem to confirm Pausanias' description.

359

Graeciae Descriptio, IX, 19:8 — Spiro

Φοίνικες δὲ πρὸ τοῦ ἱεροῦ πεφύκασιν, οὐκ ἐς ἅπαν ἐδώδιμον παρεχόμενοι καρπὸν ὥσπερ ἐν τῇ Παλαιστίνῃ, τοῦ δὲ ἐν Ἰωνίᾳ τῶν φοινίκων καρποῦ πεπανώτερον.

1 ἐδώδιμοι P¹y²

In front of the sanctuary grow palm-trees, the fruit of which, though not wholly edible like the dates of Palestine, yet are riper than those of Ionia.   (trans. W. H. S. Jones, *LCL*)

Φοίνικες ... ἐν τῇ Παλαιστίνῃ: This is the first time that Pausanias uses in place of the "land of the Hebrews" the name Palestine, which became the official name of the former province of Judaea in the time of Hadrian; cf. the commentary to Ovidius, *Ars Amatoria*, I, 413–416 (No. 142). Pausanias mentions the date-palms of Palestine in comparison with those growing in front of the sanctuary of Artemis at Aulis in Boeotia. Pausanias probably had in mind the date-palms of Jericho.

360

Graeciae Descriptio, X, 12:9 — Spiro = F94R

Ἐπετράφη δὲ καὶ ὕστερον τῆς Δημοῦς παρ' Ἑβραίοις τοῖς ὑπὲρ τῆς Παλαιστίνης γυνὴ χρησμολόγος, ὄνομα δὲ αὐτῇ Σάββη· Βηρόσου δὲ εἶναι πατρὸς καὶ Ἐρυμάνθης μητρός φασι Σάββην· οἱ δὲ αὐτὴν Βαβυλωνίαν, ἕτεροι δὲ Σίβυλλαν καλοῦσιν Αἰγυπτίαν.

1 ἐπετράφη Schubart-Walz   ἐπεγράφη codd.   /   καὶ om. L¹
2 σαββηκη ροσου Py²

Later than Demo there grew up among the Hebrews above Palestine a woman who gave oracles and was named Sabbe. They say that the father of Sabbe was Berosus, and her mother Erymanthe. But some call her a Babylonian Sibyl, others an Egyptian.

(trans. W. H. S. Jones, *LCL*)

ἐπετράφη ... παρ' Ἑβραίοις: The Hebrew Sibyl is referred to by Pausanias in his general discussion of the Sibyls. While describing Delphi, he digresses to tell of the Libyan Sibyl, and deals in a more detailed manner with Hierophyle, the Sibyl of Asia Minor, claimed as their own by both the people of Marpessus and those of Erythrae. As the third, he mentions Demo, the Sibyl of Cumae in Italy, and the fourth is the eastern Sibyl. Pausanias calls her "Sabbe", and first stresses her Hebrew origin. On the other hand, he states that Sabbe is thought to be the daughter of Berossus and Erymanthe and that she was known to some as an Egyptian.
Some scholars have expressed the opinion that the catalogue of Sibyls of Pausanias derives from a work by Alexander Polyhistor; see E. Maass, "De Sibyllarum Indicibus", Ph.D. Thesis, Greifswald, 1879, pp. 4 ff.; Tümpel, PW, VI, pp. 565 f.; P. Schnabel, *Berossos und die babylonisch-hellenistische Literatur*, Leipzig 1923, p. 85; A. Peretti, *La Sibilla babilonese nella*

Pausanias

propaganda ellenistica, Florence 1943, p. 51, n. 51, and p. 72. No cogent argument has been adduced to prove this; see Regenbogen, *op. cit.* (supra, p. 191, n. 2), p. 1053.

τοῖς ὑπὲρ τῆς Παλαιστίνης: Pausanias locates the Hebrews ὑπὲρ Παλαιστίνης and not ἐν Παλαιστίνῃ. Thus he follows here the old and limited meaning of Palestine; cf. also Pausanias, *Graeciae Descriptio*, I, 14:7: καὶ Φοινίκων τοῖς Ἀσκάλωνα ἔχουσιν ἐν τῇ Παλαιστίνῃ.

Σάββη: The name given here to the Hebrew Sibyl derives from the fuller name Σαμβήθη, borne by the Jewish Sibyl in other sources; see Rzach, PW, Ser. 2, II, p. 2098. The full name Σαμβήθη for the Jewish Sibyl appears, e.g., in the following sources: "Theosophy of Tübingen", in: K. Buresch (ed.), *Klaros*, Leipzig 1889, p. 121; *Scholia Platonica ad Phaedrum*, 244B (No. 571); the Prologue to *Oracula Sibyllina*, 33: ἡ κυρίῳ ὀνόματι καλουμένη Σαμβήθη; Suda (ed. Adler), IV, p. 354; Photius, *PG*, CI, Col. 811. In the *Oracula Sibyllina* there is no mention of a proper name for the Jewish Sibyl, except in the prologue, and its existence there was only surmised by J. Geffcken, *Komposition und Entstehungszeit der Oracula Sibyllina*, Leipzig 1902, p. 4.

A plausible explanation of the name Sambethe maintains that it was originally the name of the Babylonian Sibyl, later adopted by the Jews. This explanation is supported by the argument that the Jewish Sibyl herself asserts her Babylonian origin in *Oracula Sibyllina*, III, 809 f.: Ἀσσυρίης Βαβυλώνια τείχεα μακρὰ οἰστρομανὴς προλιποῦσα. A Babylonian origin would also account for the connection of Sambethe–Sabbe with Berossus. The impression that the name Sambethe was first attached to the Chaldaean Sibyl is also given by the *Scholia Platonica ad Phaedrum, loc. cit.*: Σίβυλλαι μὲν γεγόνασι δέκα, ὧν πρώτη ὄνομα Σαμβήθη. Χαλδαίαν δέ φασιν αὐτὴν οἱ παλαιοὶ λόγοι, οἱ δὲ μᾶλλον Ἑβραίαν. Cf. Photius, *loc. cit.* See also W. Bousset, *ZNTW*, III (1902), pp. 24 f.; Peretti, *op. cit.* (supra, pp. 198 f.), pp. 71 ff.; H.C. Youtie, *HTR*, XXXVII (1944), pp. 214 f. = *Scriptiunculae*, I, Amsterdam 1973, pp. 472 f.

Another explanation is afforded by connecting Σάββη = Σαμβήθη with the Sabbath, the observance of which was widely diffused throughout the Mediterranean world; see V. Tcherikover, *Scripta Hierosolymitana*, I (1954), pp. 86 ff. (A somewhat far-fetched theory is that the origin of the name is to be found in the story of the river related in Plinius, *Naturalis Historia*, XXXI, 24 = No. 222: "In Iudaea rivus sabbatis omnibus siccatur"; cf. *BJ*, VII, 96 ff. See Beer, PW, Ser. 2, I, p. 2121.)

It may also be suggested that a similarly sounding Babylonian name was somewhat changed to give it a Sabbatical ring in order to connect the Sibyl with the Sabbath.

Βηρόσου: The true form of this Babylonian-Hellenistic name in Greek was Βηρωσσός. Erymanthe, here the mother of the Sibyl, is unknown from other sources, but Berossus is thought to have been the father of the Sibyl elsewhere; cf. [Iustinus], *Cohortatio ad Graecos*, 37 = *F. Gr. Hist.*, III, C680, T7c: τῆς παλαιᾶς Σιβύλλης ... ταύτην δὲ ἐκ μὲν Βαβυλῶνος ὁρμῆσαί φασι, Βηρωσσοῦ τοῦ τὴν Χαλδαικὴν ἱστορίαν γράψαντος θυγατέρα οὖσαν;

199

and also Suda, *op. cit.*, p. 353. See also the discussion by V. Nikiprowetzky, *La troisième Sibylle*, Paris 1970, pp. 15 f.

It is somewhat hard to grasp how the historian Berossus became a mythical figure and the father of the Sibyl, although it stands to reason that Berossus referred to the Babylonian Sibyl in his work; see Youtie, *op. cit.* (supra, p. 199), p. 214. He may have been cited in some connection with the Sibyl. Similarly, some misunderstood expression may have given rise to the idea that the Sibyl was really his daughter; see Bousset, *op. cit.* (supra, p. 199), p. 25.

οἱ δὲ αὐτὴν Βαβυλωνίαν ...: The dual Jewish and Babylonian tradition about the Sibyl Sambethe is found also in the *Scholia Platonica ad Phaedrum*, *loc. cit.* (No. 571), and Suda, *loc. cit.* Neither a Hebrew nor a Babylonian Sibyl is included in the catalogue of the Sibyls by Varro, apud: Lactantius, *Institutiones*, I, 6:7 ff. His eastern Sibyl, the first enumerated by him, is designated a Persian; cf. *Oracula Sibyllina*, 32 f., Prologue. The Persian Sibyl occupies the place after the Hebrew Sibyl in *Chronicon Paschale* (ed. Dindorf), I, p. 201. See, in general, Nikiprowetzky, *op. cit.*, pp. 37 ff.

Αἰγυπτίαν: An Egyptian Sibyl is also mentioned in Aelianus, *Varia Historia*, XII, 35 (No. 444); see Rzach, *op. cit.* (supra, p. 199), p. 2102.

CIX. APULEIUS

Second century C.E.

Popularly known as the author of "The Golden Ass", Apuleius was born in Madauros, Numidia. He refers at least twice to Jews in his works. In his Apologia, *probably delivered in 158/9 C.E.,[1] Apuleius lists Moses and the Jewish magician Iohannes among prominent sorcerers who were active after Zoroaster and Ostanes (No. 361). In the* Florida, *he characterizes the Egyptians as "eruditi" in a declamation in honour of the Indian Gymnosophists, and describes other nations — Nabataeans, Parthians, Ituraeans and Arabs — according to their activities, dress or the natural products of their country, the Jews alone being stigmatized as "superstitiosi" (No. 362).*

Much more problematic in its Jewish content is a passage in Apuleius' Metamorphoses, IX. *In it he recounts that the miller's wife despised and trampled upon the divine powers, and instead of believing in a sure religion she made a sacrilegious declaration of faith in a god whom she affirmed to be the only one.[2] The woman feigned empty rites, deceived everyone, including her husband, and gave up her body to drinking wine from the morning on, and to continued lewdness.[3] The description implies her attachment to a monotheistic creed, either to Judaism or to the sect of God-fearers, i.e. Jewish sympathizers (cf. Iuvenalis, Saturae, XIV, 96–106 = No. 301, and the commentary ad loc.), or the woman could have been a Christian.[4] Certainly Judaism continued to be a living force, and retained some power of attraction, not only in the*

---

1 For the date of the *Apologia*, see R. Syme, *REA*, LXI (1959), pp. 316 f.

2 On the episode of the miller, see H. van Thiel, *Der Eselroman*, I (*Untersuchungen*), Munich 1971, pp. 133 ff.

3 See Apuleius, *Metamorphoses*, IX, 14: "Tunc spretis atque calcatis divinis numinibus in vicem certae religionis mentita sacrilega praesumptione dei, quem praedicaret unicum, confictis observationibus vacuis, fallens omnis homines et miserum maritum decipiens matutino mero et continuo stupro corpus manciparat."

4 See A. D. Nock, *Conversion*, Oxford 1933, p. 283.

second century⁵ but even later.⁶ However it seems more probable that Apuleius has Christianity in mind rather than Judaism.⁷

5 For the date of Apuleius' *Metamorphoses*, see T. D. Barnes, *Tertullian — A Historical and Literary Study*, Oxford 1971, p. 272.

6 On "sympathizers", see Commodianus, *Instructiones*, I, 24:11 ff. (probably third century), or the late (*c.* 500 C.E.) astrological writer Rhetorius, in: *Catalogus Codicum Astrologorum Graecorum*, ed. P. Boudreaux, Vol. VIII, Part 4, Brussels 1921, p. 159, l. 8: ϑεοσεβῆ γυναῖκα; p. 164, l. 16. Cf. the interpretation by W. Kroll, *Klio*, XVIII (1923), p. 224.

7 For the likelihood that Apuleius considered the woman to be a convert to Judaism, see P. de Labriolle, *La réaction païenne*, Paris 1934, p. 70. Most scholars prefer the interpretation that she was a Christian; see Barnes, *loc. cit.*; L. Herrmann, *Latomus*, XII (1953), pp. 189 f. Herrmann founds much of his view on the connotation of the *stuprum* attributed to the miller's wife, which recalls the *flagitia* popularly associated with the Christians; cf. Tacitus, *Historiae*, XV, 44:2 (No. 294), and the correspondence of Pliny the Younger with Trajan (*Epistulae*, X, 96:2). See also M. Simon, in: *Mélanges H. C. Puech*, Paris 1974, pp. 299 ff.

361

Apologia, 90 — Vallette = F193R = Bidez & Cumont, II, F B3

Reputate vobiscum quanta fiducia innocentiae meae quantoque despectu vestri agam: si una causa vel minima fuerit inventa, cur ego debuerim Pudentillae nuptias ob aliquod meum commodum appetere, si quamlibet modicum emolumentum probaveritis, ego ille

5 sim Carmendas vel Damigeron vel ⋆ his ⋆ Moses vel Iohannes vel Apollobex vel ipse Dardanus vel quicumque alius post Zoroastren et Hostanen inter magos celebratus est.

5 *his moses* F   *hismesos* φ   *iste Moses* Brakman   /   *Iannes* Colvius
    6 *Apollobex* Helm   *apollo haec* F φ   *Apollobeches* Krueger /
        alius] *alias* F φ

Consider what confidence in my innocence and what contempt of you is implied by my conduct. If you can discover one trivial reason that might have led me to woo Pudentilla for the sake of some personal advantage, if you can prove that I have made the very slightest profit of my marriage, I am ready to be any magician you please — the great Carmendas himself or Damigeron or Moses of whom you have heard, or Iohannes[1] or Apollobex or Dardanus himself or any sorcerer of note from the time of Zoroaster and Ostanes till now.

(trans. H.E. Butler, Oxford 1909)

1 Jannes in Butler's translation.

On this passage, see A. Abt, *Die Apologie des Apuleius von Madaura und die antike Zauberei* (*Religionsgeschichtliche Versuche und Vorarbeiten*, Vol. IV, Part 2), Giessen 1908, pp. 318 (244) ff.; H.E. Butler & A.S. Owen, *Apulei Apologia, with Introduction and Commentary*, Oxford 1914, pp. 161 ff.; C. Marchesi, *Apuleio, della Magia*, Bologna 1957, pp. 220 f.

Carmendas: The name is not mentioned elsewhere though it would not be an unnatural one for a magician "qui carmen dat"; see Butler & Owen, *op. cit.* Pliny's list of the great magicians includes a certain Tarmoendas the Assyrian; cf. Plinius, *Naturalis Historia*, XXX, 5. It has therefore been suggested that Carmendas should be emended to Tarmoendas; see Bidez & Cumont, II, p. 15, n. 1; see also W. Kroll, PW, Ser. 2, IV, p. 2326. However, as mention of this Tarmoendas is confined to Pliny, and almost nothing about him is known, little is to be gained by the emendation, even if both writers had the same person in mind.

Damigeron: He wrote a well-known book on stones; his name appears in Tertullianus, *De Anima*, 57: "Ostanes et Typhon et Dardanus et Damigeron et Nectabis et Berenice"; Arnobius, *Adversus Nationes*, I, 52. Cf. V. Rose,

Hermes, IX (1875), pp. 471 ff.; Abt, *op. cit.* (supra, p. 203), p. 319 (245). For a suggested likeness between the name Damigeron and a literal translation of the Old Testament term "Elders of the People", see A. A. Barb, in: A. Momigliano (ed.), *The Conflict between Paganism and Christianity*, Oxford 1963, p. 118.

his: Various emendations of this corrupt passage have been suggested. *Iste* is proposed by C. Brakman, *Mnemosyne*, XXXVII (1909), p. 75 (for the use of *iste* in Apuleius, see M. Bernhard, *Der Stil des Apuleius*, Stuttgart 1927, p. 115). Against this, see Butler & Owen, *op. cit.* (supra, p. 203). These authors do not see much reason for particularizing Moses with a pronoun, but prefer to regard *his* as a corruption of JHS, the sacred name, which presumably stands in the MSS of Apuleius for Jesus, who too was famed as a magician. In that case it is assumed that *vel* has been omitted by the copyist between the words "Jesus" and "Moses".

Moses: That Moses is named among the prominent magicians is not surprising; see Abt, *op. cit.* (supra, p. 203), pp. 321 (247) f.; cf. Plinius, *Naturalis Historia*, XXX, 11 (No. 221), and the commentary *ad loc.*

Iohannes: Iohannes stands in the MSS for the well known magician Iannes, one of the Egyptian rivals of Moses; cf. Numenius, apud: Eusebius, *Praeparatio Evangelica*, IX, 8:1-2 (No. 365), and the commentary *ad loc.* The name appears as Iannes in the Greek sources, in the *Targum Yerushalmi*, and in most midrashic sources, but as יוחנא in *TB Menahot*, 85a; יוחני in *Yalqut Shim'oni*, §235; and יחנה in *The Zadokite Fragments*[2], ed. C. Rabin, Oxford 1958, V, 17 ff. (p. 21). This, of course, conforms to the manuscript tradition of Apuleius and renders emendation here unnecessary.

Apollobex: The emendation Apollobex is very plausible indeed; cf. Plinius, *Naturalis Historia*, XXX, 9.

Dardanus: Josephus thus transcribes into Greek the name Darda in I Kings v:11; cf. *Ant.*, VIII, 43, which relates that King Solomon surpassed even Dardanus in wisdom. See R. Reitzenstein, *Poimandres*, Leipzig 1904, pp. 163 f.; K. Preisendanz (ed.), *Papyri Graecae Magicae*[2], I, Stuttgart 1973, No. IV, l. 1716.

et Hostanen: Pliny also considered that Ostanes was foremost among magicians; cf. Plinius, *Naturalis Historia*, XXX, 8; see Bidez & Cumont, I, pp. 167 ff. He is mentioned previously by Apuleius in conjunction with Epimenides, Orpheus and Pythagoras in *Apologia*, 27. The casual enumeration of the relatively long list of the great magicians is meant to exhibit the vast erudition of Apuleius and is characteristic of the style of other parts of his *Apologia*; see R. Helm, *Das Altertum*, I (1955), p. 101.

362

Florida, 6 — Vallette = F 194 R

Indi, gens populosa cultoribus et finibus maxima, procul a nobis ad orientem siti, prope oceani reflexus et solis exortus, primis sideribus,

ultimis terris, super Aegyptios eruditos et Iudaeos superstitiosos et
Nabathaeos mercatores et fluxos vestium Arsacidas et frugum
5 pauperes Ityraeos et odorum divites Arabas ...

India is a populous country of enormous extent. It lies far to the east
of us, close to the point where ocean turns back upon himself and the
sun rises, on that verge where meet the last of lands and the first stars
of heaven. Far away it lies, beyond the learned Egyptians, beyond the
superstitious Jews and the merchants of Nabataea, beyond the
children of Arsaces in their long flowing robes, the Ituraeans to whom
earth gives but scanty harvest, and the Arabs, whose perfumes are
their wealth.   (trans. H. E. Butler, Oxford 1909)

super Aegyptios eruditos: A deep respect for the Egyptians pervades the
writings of Apuleius; cf. the enthusiasm for the cult of Isis manifest in Book
XI of his *Metamorphoses*; his tribute to the "sanctissimi Aegyptiorum
sacerdotes" (*Apologia*, 56) and his account of the respect shown to Egypt and
to Zoroaster by Pythagoras (*Florida*, 15).
et Iudaeos superstitiosos: The designation of the Jews as "superstitiosi" gains
in significance by comparison with the praises that Apuleius bestows upon
the Egyptians and Persians; cf. also *Apologia*, 25–26. Apart from the Jews,
the only representatives of the oriental religions of which Apuleius
disapproves are the priests of the "Syrian Goddess"; cf. *Metamorphoses*,
VIII, 24 ff. (The same disparagement of the priests of the Syrian goddess is
also expressed in Lucianus, *Asinus*, 35: κίναιδος γὰρ καὶ γέρων ἦν τούτων
εἷς τῶν τὴν θεὸν τὴν Συρίαν εἰς τὰς κώμας καὶ τοὺς ἀγροὺς περιφερόντων
καὶ τὴν θεὸν ἐπαιτεῖν ἀναγκαζόντων. Presumably Apuleius received his
picture of the priests of the "Syrian Goddess" from his Greek model.)

CX. NUMENIUS OF APAMEA

Second half of the second century C.E.

Numenius of Apamea, an avowed disciple of Plato, is characterized "the Pythagorean" in ancient sources and is generally thought of as the main precursor of the Neoplatonists.[1] He greatly admired oriental religious beliefs, irrespective of the amount he actually owed them in forming his philosophy.[2] Numenius found parallels in the teachings of Pythagoras and Plato to the rituals and doctrines of the Brahmans, Jews, Magi and Egyptians. He included the Jews among the representatives of oriental civilizations he most revered, thereby resembling the early writers of the Hellenistic era, such as Theophrastus, apud: Porphyrius, De Abstinentia, II, 26 (No. 4); Megasthenes, apud: Clemens Alexandrinus, Stromata, I, 15:72:5 (No. 14); and Clearchus, apud: Contra Apionem, I, 176–183 (No. 15). *He thus stands in glaring contrast to some of the writers nearer to his time, who, though fervent admirers of oriental wisdom, despised Judaism. A case in point is Apuleius.*
The enthusiasm of Numenius for Moses, called in one of the fragments by the name Musaios (No. 365), is unequalled in the whole range of Greek literature, apart from the praise of the lawgiver found in the famous passage of De Sublimitate, IX, 9 (No. 148). Numenius even goes to the length of defining Plato as an Atticizing Moses (No. 363a).

1 For the date of Numenius, see E.A.Leemans, *Studie over den wijsgeer Numenius van Apamea met uitgave der fragmenten*, Brussels 1937, p. 13; G.Martano, *Numenio d'Apamea*, Naples 1960, pp. 9 f.; *Numénius, Fragments*, ed. E.des Places, Paris 1973, pp. 7 f.; for a date in the first half of the second century C.E., see R.Beutler, PW, Suppl. VII, p. 665.
2 This debt is assessed very highly by H.C.Puech, in: *Mélanges Bidez = Annuaire de l'institut de philologie et d'histoire orientales* (1934), II, pp. 745 ff. It is rated much lower by Le P.R. (A.J.) Festugière, *La révélation d'Hermes Trismégiste*, III, Paris 1953, p. 42, n. 1; E.R.Dodds, in: *Les Sources de Plotin (Fondation Hardt pour l'étude de l'antiquité classique, Entretiens, V, 1957)*, pp. 4 ff.; and P. Merlan, in: *The Cambridge History of Later Greek and Early Medieval Philosophy*, Cambridge 1967, pp. 99, 103. In general, see also A.Momigliano, *Alien Wisdom*, Cambridge 1975, p. 147.

206

Moses seems to have been considered by Numenius "the Prophet" par excellence. A direct quotation by Numenius from Genesis is given by Porphyry (No. 368), and Numenius' frequent use of both the Pentateuch and the Prophets, which he interpreted allegorically, is attested by Origen (No. 366). According to the same authority this had been Numenius' procedure not only in one of his works, but in at least three. In addition to the biblical traditions, Numenius had recourse to the apocryphal tale of the struggle between Moses and the Egyptian magicians, which occurs in various types of literature, and evidently enjoyed much popularity.

According to Lydus (No. 367), Numenius described the Jewish God as the "father of all the gods" and stressed his intolerance of other gods. Probably Numenius had learned much about Judaism in his native Apamea, which had a considerable Jewish population.[3] Apamea was one of the three cities of Syria that in 66 C.E. had shown a sympathetic attitude to their Jewish inhabitants during the war against Rome (BJ, II, 479). Its citizens did the Jews no harm, while in other cities of Syria Jews were massacred.

There is not much plausibility in the view that Numenius himself was a Jew.[4] His teaching contains hardly anything specifically Jewish, and all the characteristics of his philosophy may be accounted for by the Graeco-Oriental environment of that period. The esteem in which Numenius held Moses and the Jewish religious traditions may be sufficiently explained by the continuing trend of sympathy for Judaism (represented also by the sentiments expressed in De Sublimitate) which existed simultaneously with the much better attested opposite stream of anti-Semitism. It may also be suggested that the conditions then prevailing at Apamea could go far to explain Numenius' outlook.[5]

---

3 It seems unnecessary to explain the influence of Judaism on Numenius by presuming a sojourn at Alexandria as suggested by Martano, *op. cit.* (supra, p. 206, n. 1), p. 11.

4 This was suggested by C. Bigg, *The Christian Platonists of Alexandria*, Oxford 1913, p. 300, n. 1. Against this view, cf. Dodds, *op. cit.* (supra, p. 206, n. 2), p. 6. See also J. Whittaker, *Phoenix*, XXI (1967), p. 197; Gager, pp. 68 f.

5 For the presumable influence of Philo on Numenius, see K. S. Guthrie, *Numenius of Apamea*, London 1917, pp. 145 ff.; E. R. Dodds, *CQ*, XXII (1928), p. 140, n. 1; W. Theiler, *Museum Helveticum*, I (1944), p. 216; and especially J. H. Waszink, *Porphyre (Fondation Hardt, Entretiens*, XII, 1965), pp. 50 f. On the other hand, it is maintained that Numenius' debt to

The influence of Numenius on Porphyry was considerable.[6] *Numenius is probably also implied by the reference to the "philosophus" in Augustinus,* De Consensu Evangelistarum, *I, 29:45.*[7] *There is also some plausibility in the argument that the references to "Hebraica philosophia" by Calcidius go back, through Porphyry, to Numenius.*[8]

Philo is no more demonstrable than that owed Philo by Plotinus; see H. Lewy, *Chaldaean Oracles and Theurgy*, Cairo 1956, p. 314, n. 7. See also H. Chadwick, *Early Christian Thought and the Classical Tradition*, Oxford 1966, p. 129, n. 31.

6 See Waszink, *op. cit.* (supra, p. 207, n. 5), pp. 35 ff.

7 The text of Augustine reads as follows: "Audivi quendam eorum dicere se legisse aput nescio quem philosophum, quod ex his quae Iudaei in suis sacramentis agerent intellexisset, quem deum colerent: praepositum, inquit, istorum elementorum, quibus iste visibilis et corporeus mundus extructus est."

8 See Waszink, *op. cit.* (supra, p. 207, n. 5), pp. 58 ff. The relevant passages are to be found in *Timaeus a Calcidio Translatus Commentarioque Instructus*, ed. J. H. Waszink, London–Leiden 1962. Thus, cf. *ibid.*, CCC: "Quibus Hebraei concinunt, cum dicunt homini quidem a deo datam esse animam ex inspiratione caelesti, quam rationem et animam rationabilem appellant, mutis vero et agrestibus ex silva rationis expertem iussu dei vivis et animantibus bestiis terrae gremio profusis; quorum in numero fuerit etiam ille serpens, qui primitias generis humani malis suasionibus illaqueaverit"; *ibid.*, CCXIX: "Hebraei quoque videntur secundum hunc opinari de animae principali, cum dicunt: Clamat apud me sanguis fratris tui et item alio loco: Non edetis carnem cum sanguine, quia omnium animalium sanguis anima est. Quae si ita intelleguntur ut debent, animam esse animalium sanguinem, quia sit vehiculum inrationabilis animae, cuius partes sunt importuni appetitus, habet plane rationem talis assertio. Si autem confitentur animam hominis rationabilem fore, credant sibi, quod deus a se hominibus factis inspiraverit divinum spiritum, quo ratiocinamur quoque intellegimus et quo veneramur pie deum estque nobis cum divinitate cognatio diique esse dicimur et filii summi dei. Quam cognationem cum deo et omnino rationem qua ratiocinamur sanguinem putare esse non recte opinantis est"; *ibid.*, LV: "Quod quidem verum esse testatur eminens quaedam doctrina sectae sanctioris et in comprehensione divinae rei prudentioris, quae perhibet deum absoluto illustratoque sensili mundo genus hominum instituentem corpus quidem eius parte humi sumpta iuxta hanc effigiem aedificasse formasseque, vitam vero eidem ex convexis accersisse caelestibus postque intimis eius inspirationem proprio flatu intimasse, inspirationem hanc dei consilium animae rationemque significans."

Numenius of Apamea

363a

apud: Clemens Alexandrinus, *Stromata*, I, 22:150:4 — Stählin & Früchtel = Leemans, F10

Νουμήνιος δὲ ὁ Πυθαγόρειος φιλόσοφος ἄντικρυς γράφει· «Τί γὰρ ἐστι Πλάτων ἢ Μωυσῆς ἀττικίζων;»

1 πυθαγόριος L   Πυθαγορικὸς Eus.   2 Μωσῆς Eus.

Numenius the Pythagorean philosopher writes expressly: "For what is Plato, but Moses speaking in Attic?"

Τί γὰρ ἐστι Πλάτων ἢ Μωυσῆς ἀττικίζων: This quotation from Numenius is preceded in Clemens' work by one from the Alexandrian Jewish philosopher Aristobulus concerning the ancient translations of the Bible into Greek prior to the Septuagint. The similarity between the teachings of Moses and of Greek philosophy is also implied in Philo's thought, and Numenius may have been influenced by him in that direction; see F. Thedinga, *De Numenio Philosopho Platonico*, Bonn 1875, p. 3.
Clemens explicitly states that he uses the very words of Numenius (Νουμήνιος ἄντικρυς γράφει). Therefore one cannot endorse the doubts of Schürer, who bases himself on the parallel passage in Eusebius, *Praeparatio Evangelica*, XI, 10:14 (No. 363c): εἰκότως δῆτα εἰς αὐτὸν ἐκεῖνο τὸ λόγιον περιφέρεται; see Schürer, III, p. 627; against him, cf. Puech, *op. cit.* (supra, p. 206, n. 2), p. 753. See also A. B. Hulen, *Porphyry's Work Against the Christians*, New Haven 1933, p. 26.
In referrring to Plato as an "Atticizing Moses", Numenius implied only a similarity in their teachings. From this the later Christian tradition derived a notion foreign to Numenius, that Plato stole Moses' doctrine; cf. the passage from Suda, s.v. Νουμήνιος (No. 363e).
It is impossible to tell in which context Numenius drew the comparison between Moses and Plato. It has been suggested that Numenius had in mind the way in which Plato, introducing the Artificer, used the term τὸ ὂν ἀεί which Numenius combines with the ὁ ὤν of the Septuagint; see Merlan, *op. cit.* (supra, p. 206, n. 2), p. 100.

363b

apud: Eusebius, *Praeparatio Evangelica*, IX, 6:9 — Mras

Νουμήνιος δὲ ὁ Πυθαγορικὸς φιλόσοφος ἄντικρυς γράφει· «Τί γὰρ ἐστι Πλάτων ἢ Μωσῆς ἀττικίζων;» ταῦτα ὁ Κλήμης.

1 Πυθαγόρειος Clemens / φιλόσοφος om. B / ἄντικρὺ B
2 Μωυσῆς Clemens Theodoretus / ταῦτα ὁ Κλήμης om. B

209

And Numenius, the Pythagorean philosopher, writes expressly: "For what is Plato, but Moses speaking in Attic Greek?" Thus Clemens.

(trans. E. H. Gifford, Oxford 1903)

363c

apud: Eusebius, *Praeparatio Evangelica*, XI, 10:14 — Mras

Ταῦτα μὲν οὖν ὁ Νουμήνιος, ὁμοῦ τὰ Πλάτωνος καὶ πολὺ πρότερον τὰ Μωσέως ἐπὶ τὸ σαφὲς διερμηνεύων. εἰκότως δῆτα εἰς αὐτὸν ἐκεῖνο τὸ λόγιον περιφέρεται, δι' οὗ μνημονεύεται· «Τί γάρ ἐστι Πλάτων ἢ Μωσῆς ἀττικίζων;»

1 οὖν om. I   2 σαφέστερον ON / διερμηνεύων] ἄγων ND
        3 δι ... μνημονεύεται om. ND / τὸ τί ND

Thus then speaks Numenius, explaining clearly both Plato's doctrines and the much earlier doctrines of Moses. With reason therefore is that saying attributed to him, in which it is recorded that he said, "For what else is Plato than Moses speaking Attic Greek?"

(trans. E. H. Gifford, Oxford 1903)

363d

apud: Theodoretus, *Graecarum Affectionum Curatio*, II, 114 — Raeder

Τῷ Πυθαγορικῷ Νουμηνίῳ πιστεύσει λέγοντι· «Τί γάρ ἐστι Πλάτων ἢ Μωϋσῆς ἀττικίζων;»

2 μωσῆς C

Will he believe Numenius the Pythagorean philosopher when he says: "For what is Plato, but Moses speaking in Attic?"

363e

Suda, s.v. Νουμήνιος — Adler = Leemans, T1

Νουμήνιος, Ἀπαμεύς, ἀπὸ Συρίας φιλόσοφος Πυθαγόρειος. οὗτός ἐστιν ὁ τὴν τοῦ Πλάτωνος ἐξελέγξας δίανοιαν, ὡς ἐκ τῶν Μωσαϊκῶν τὰ περὶ θεοῦ καὶ κόσμου γενέσεως ἀποσυλήσασαν. καὶ διὰ τοῦτό φησι· «τί γάρ ἐστι Πλάτων ἢ Μωσῆς ἀττικίζων;»

3 φασι V

210

Numenius of Apamea

Numenius of Apamea, a Pythagorean philosopher from Syria. It was he who convicted the mind of Plato of stealing from the works of Moses his views about God and the creation of the world, and because of this he says: "For what is Plato, but Moses speaking in Attic?"

364a

De Bono, apud: Eusebius, *Praeparatio Evangelica*, IX, 7:1 — Mras = Leemans, F9a = Des Places, *Numenius, Fragments*, Paris 1973, F1a

Καὶ αὐτοῦ δὲ τοῦ Πυθαγορικοῦ φιλοσόφου, τοῦ Νουμηνίου λέγω, ἀπὸ τοῦ πρώτου Περὶ τἀγαθοῦ τάδε παραθήσομαι·
«Εἰς δὲ τοῦτο δεήσει εἰπόντα καὶ σημηνάμενον ταῖς μαρτυρίαις ταῖς Πλάτωνος ἀναχωρήσασθαι καὶ ξυνδήσασθαι τοῖς λόγοις τοῦ Πυθαγόρου,
5 ἐπικαλέσασθαι δὲ τὰ ἔθνη τὰ εὐδοκιμοῦντα, προσφερόμενον αὐτῶν τὰς τελετὰς καὶ τὰ δόγματα τάς τε ἱδρύσεις συντελουμένας Πλάτωνι ὁμολογουμένως, ὁπόσας Βραχμᾶνες καὶ Ἰουδαῖοι καὶ Μάγοι καὶ Αἰγύπτιοι διέθεντο.»

1 Καὶ ... λέγω] οὖ B   3 εἰ B   /   ταῖς²] τοῦ ON
5 τὰ εὐδοκιμοῦντα ἔθνη B   6 ἱδρύσεις] ἰδέας B

Also from the Pythagorean philosopher himself, I mean Numenius, I will quote as follows from his first book "On the Good":
"But when one has spoken upon this point, and sealed it by the testimonies of Plato, it will be necessary to go back and connect it with the precepts of Pythagoras, and to appeal to the nations of good repute, bringing forward their rites and doctrines, and their institutions which are formed in agreement with those of Plato, all that the Brahmans, and Jews, and Magi and Egyptians arranged."

(trans. E. H. Gifford, Oxford 1903)

ἀπὸ τοῦ πρώτου Περὶ τἀγαθοῦ: On this work, see Thedinga, *op. cit.* (supra, p. 209), pp. 6 ff.; Beutler, *op. cit.* (supra, p. 206, n. 1), p. 669; H.J. Krämer, *Der Ursprung der Geistmetaphysik*, Amsterdam 1964, p. 69. The work had, it seems, the form of a dialogue; see H. Lewy, *loc. cit.* (supra, p. 208, n. 5). See also des Places, *op. cit.* (supra, p. 206, n. 1), pp. 8 f.; Festugière, *op. cit.* (supra, p. 206, n. 2), IV, 1954, pp. 124 ff.
ἀναχωρήσασθαι: This expression implies that the ancients were in possession of truth; see des Places, *op. cit.* (supra, p. 206, n. 1), pp. 22 f., 103.
Βραχμᾶνες καὶ Ἰουδαῖοι καὶ Μάγοι καὶ Αἰγύπτιοι διέθεντο: See, in general, the survey of the subject by Festugière, *op. cit.* (supra, p. 206, n. 2), I², 1950, pp. 19 ff.

On Jews and Brahmins, cf. Megasthenes, apud: Clemens Alexandrinus, *Stromata*, I, 15:72:5 (No. 14). On Jews and Magi, cf. Diogenes Laertius, I, 9 (No. 397).

364b

De Bono, apud: Origenes, *Contra Celsum*, I, 15 — Borrett = Leemans, F9b = Des Places, *op. cit.*,
F1b

Πόσῳ δὲ βελτίων Κέλσου καὶ διὰ πολλῶν δείξας ἐλλογιμώτατος καὶ
πλείονα βασανίσας δόγματα καὶ ἀπὸ πλειόνων συναγαγὼν ἃ ἐφαντάσθη
εἶναι ἀληθῆ ὁ Πυθαγόρειος Νουμήνιος, ὅστις ἐν τῷ πρώτῳ Περὶ τἀγαθοῦ
λέγων περὶ τῶν ἐθνῶν, ὅσα περὶ τοῦ θεοῦ ὡς ἀσωμάτου διείληφεν,
5 ἐγκατέταξεν αὐτοῖς καὶ Ἰουδαίους, οὐκ ὀκνήσας ἐν τῇ συγγραφῇ αὐτοῦ
χρήσασθαι καὶ λόγοις προφητικοῖς καὶ τροπολογῆσαι αὐτούς.

How much better than Celsus is Numenius the Pythagorean, a man who showed himself in many works to be very learned and who by studying several doctrines made from many sources a synthesis of those which seemed to him to be true. In the first book on "The Good" where he speaks of the nations that believe God to be incorporeal, he also included the Jews among them, and did not hesitate to quote the sayings of the prophets in his book and to give them an allegorical interpretation.

(trans. H. Chadwick, Cambridge 1953)

365

De Bono, apud: Eusebius, *Praeparatio Evangelica*, IX, 8:1–2 — Mras = F95R = Leemans, F18 =
Des Places, *op. cit.*, F9

*(1) Καὶ ἐν τῇ τρίτῃ δὲ βίβλῳ Μωσέως ὁ αὐτὸς ⟨scil. Νουμήνιος⟩ τάδε λέγων
μνημονεύει· «Τὰ δ᾽ ἑξῆς Ἰαννῆς καὶ Ἰαμβρῆς Αἰγύπτιοι ἱερο-
γραμματεῖς, ἄνδρες οὐδενὸς ἥττους μαγεῦσαι κριθέντες εἶναι, ἐπὶ
Ἰουδαίων ἐξελαυνομένων ἐξ Αἰγύπτου. (2) Μουσαίῳ γοῦν τῷ Ἰουδαίων
5 ἐξηγησαμένῳ, ἀνδρὶ γενομένῳ θεῷ εὔξασθαι δυνατωτάτῳ, οἱ παραστῆναι
ἀξιωθέντες ὑπὸ τοῦ πλήθους τοῦ τῶν Αἰγυπτίων οὗτοι ἦσαν τῶν τε
συμφορῶν, ἃς ὁ Μουσαῖος ἐπῆγε τῇ Αἰγύπτῳ, τὰς νεανικωτάτας αὐτῶν ἐπιλύεσθαι ὤφθησαν δυνατοί.»*

6 τοῦ² om. B

(1) Also in his third book the same author makes mention of Moses speaking as follows: "And next in order came Jannes and Jambres,

Egyptian sacred scribes, men judged to have no superiors in the practice of magic at the time when the Jews were being driven out of Egypt. (2) So then these were the men chosen by the people of Egypt as fit to stand beside Musaeus, who led forth the Jews, a man who was most powerful in prayer to God; and of the plagues which Musaeus brought upon Egypt, these men showed themselves able to disperse the most violent." (trans. E. H. Gifford, Oxford 1903)

1 Ἰαννῆς καὶ Ἰαμβρῆς: Cf. also Plinius, *Naturalis Historia*, XXX, 11 (No. 221); Apuleius, *Apologia*, 90 (No. 361). These two Egyptian magicians appear as Moses' opponents in various sources; cf. the Second Pauline Epistle to Timothy (II Tim. iii:8): ὃν τρόπον δὲ Ἰαννῆς καὶ Ἰαμβρῆς ἀντέστησαν Μωϋσεῖ, οὕτως καὶ οὗτοι ἀνθίστανται τῇ ἀληθείᾳ; *TB Menaḥot*, 85a; *Targum Yerushalmi* to Exod. vii:11. According to a Jewish tradition the two were sons of Balaam; cf. *Targum Yerushalmi* to Num. xxii:22. See also *Tanḥuma*, Ki-Tisa, 19; Jellinek, *Bet ha-Midrasch*, II², Jerusalem 1938, Chronik des Moses, p. 5. The Book of the Covenant of Damascus states (5, 18 f.): "And Belial raised Jannes and his brother by his evil device, when Israel was delivered for the first time"; see *The Zadokite Documents²*, ed. C. Rabin, Oxford 1958. The existence of an apocryphal work on Jannes and Jambres is mentioned in Origenes, *Ad Mattheum*, XXVII:9 (ed. Klostermann, 1933, p. 250). For other patristic evidence, see A. M. Denis, *Introduction aux pseudépigraphes grecs de l'ancien Testament*, Leiden 1970, pp. 146 ff.; P. Maraval, *ZPE*, XXIV (1977), pp. 199 ff.
Probably Numenius drew on some Jewish source, but the complicated literary tradition about Jannes and Jambres makes it idle to speculate on the nature of that source — thus it is identified with Artapanus, the Jewish-Hellenistic writer, by Freudenthal, p. 173; with either II Tim. iii:8, or pseudo-Jonathan (*Targum Yerushalmi*) by Bigg, *loc. cit.* For Jannes and Jambres, see also Schürer, III, pp. 402 ff.; Strack & Billerbeck, III, pp. 660 ff.; Bidez & Cumont, II, p. 14, n. 23; Ginzberg, II, pp. 334 f.; III, pp. 28 f.; V, p. 407, n. 80; p. 425, n. 161; V. Aptowitzer, *Parteipolitik der Hasmonäerzeit im rabbinischen und pseudoepigraphischen Schrifttum*, Vienna–New York 1927, pp. XI ff.; S. Weinstock, *CQ*, XLII (1948), pp. 41 ff.; Festugière, *op. cit.* (supra, p. 206, n. 2), I², pp. 280, 435 f.; V. Nikiprowetzky, *REJ*, CXXX (1971), pp. 370 f.; Gager, pp. 137 f.
2 Μουσαίῳ: For this name, see Artapanus, apud: Eusebius, *Praeparatio Evangelica*, IX, 27:3 = *F. Gr. Hist.*, III, C726, F3, p. 682 = *Fragmenta Pseudepigraphorum Quae Supersunt Graeca*, ed. A. M. Denis, Leiden 1970, p. 188: ὑπὸ δὲ τῶν Ἑλλήνων αὐτὸν ἀνδρωθέντα Μουσαῖον προσαγορευθῆναι.
τὰς νεανικωτάτας αὐτῶν ἐπιλύεσθαι ὤφθησαν δυνατοί: Against the translation of Reinach and his remarks on the passage, cf. the just criticism of Puech, *loc. cit.* (supra, p. 206, n. 2). That Jannes and Jambres were capable of resisting Moses is implied also by II Timothy and the Jewish tradition; see the commentary above on § 1.

366

De Bono, apud: Origenes, *Contra Celsum*, IV, 51 —Borret = Leemans, F32 + 19 = Des Places, *op. cit.* F1c + 10a

Ἐγὼ δ' οἶδα καὶ Νουμήνιον τὸν Πυθαγόρειον, ἄνδρα πολλῷ κρεῖττον διηγησάμενον Πλάτωνα καὶ ⟨περὶ⟩ τῶν Πυθαγορείων δογμάτων πρεσβεύσαντα, πολλαχοῦ τῶν συγγραμμάτων αὐτοῦ ἐκτιθέμενον τὰ Μωϋσέως καὶ τῶν προφητῶν καὶ οὐκ ἀπιθάνως αὐτὰ τροπολογοῦντα, ὥσπερ ἐν τῷ καλουμένῳ Ἔποπι καὶ ἐν τοῖς περὶ ἀριθμῶν καὶ ἐν τοῖς περὶ τόπου. ἐν δὲ τῷ τρίτῳ περὶ τἀγαθοῦ ἐκτίθεται καὶ περὶ τοῦ Ἰησοῦ ἱστορίαν τινά, τὸ ὄνομα αὐτοῦ οὐ λέγων, καὶ τροπολογεῖ αὐτήν· πότερον δ' ἐπιτετευγμένως ἢ ἀποτετευγμένως, ἄλλου καιροῦ ἐστιν εἰπεῖν. ἐκτίθεται καὶ τὴν περὶ Μωϋσέως καὶ Ἰαννοῦ καὶ Ἰαμβροῦ ἱστορίαν.

I am also aware that Numenius the Pythagorean, a man who expounded Plato with great skill and maintained the Pythagorean doctrines, quotes Moses and the prophets in many passages in his writings, and gives them no improbable allegorical interpretation, as in the book entitled "Hoopoe" (Epops) and in that "Concerning Numbers" and in that "Concerning Place". In the third book "Concerning the Good" he even quotes a story about Jesus, though without mentioning his name, and interprets it allegorically; whether his interpretation is successful or not we discuss at another time. He also quotes the story about Moses and Jannes and Jambres.

(trans. H. Chadwick, Cambridge 1953)

ἐκτιθέμενον τὰ Μωϋσέως καὶ τῶν προφητῶν: Among the Hellenistic writers Numenius is quite conspicuous in his use of biblical references to the prophets, his knowledge not being confined to the first chapters of Genesis. Ἔποπι: For the Ἔποψ, see Thedinga, *op. cit.* (supra, p. 209), p. 18; Leemans, *op. cit.* (supra, p. 206, n. 1), pp. 159 f.; des Places, *op. cit.* (supra, p. 206, n. 1), p. 104, P. Thillet's note.

367

apud: Lydus, *De Mensibus*, IV, 53, pp. 109— Wünsch = Leemans, F34 = Des Places, *op. cit.*, F56

Τούτῳ ⟨scil. Λιβίῳ⟩ δὲ ἀκολούθως ὁ Λούκανος ἀδήλου θεοῦ τὸν ἐν Ἱεροσολύμοις ναὸν εἶναι λέγει, ὁ δὲ Νουμήνιος ἀκοινώνητον αὐτὸν καὶ πατέρα πάντων τῶν θεῶν εἶναι λέγει, ἀπαξιοῦντα κοινωνεῖν αὐτῷ τῆς τιμῆς τινα.

In conformity with Livy Lucan says that the temple of Jerusalem belongs to an uncertain god, while Numenius says that the power of this god is not to be shared by any other, and that he is the father of all the gods, and that he deems any other god unworthy of having a share in his cult.

ἀκοινώνητον: See *Sapientia Salomonis*, xiv:21: τὸ ἀκοινώνητον ὄνομα λίθοις καὶ ξύλοις περιέθεσαν; cf. the discussion by E. des Places, *Journal des Savants* (1973), pp. 292 f.; idem, in: *Hommages à Claire Préaux*, Brussels 1975, pp. 340 ff.

ἀπαξιοῦντα κοινωνεῖν αὐτῷ τῆς τιμῆς τινα: See Exod. xx:3; xxxiv:14; Deut. iv:24. Cf. Iulianus, *Contra Galilaeos* (No. 481).

368

apud: Porphyrius, *De Antro Nympharum*, 10 — Nauck = Leemans, T46 = Des Places, *op. cit.*, F30

Ἡγοῦντο γὰρ προσιζάνειν τῷ ὕδατι τὰς ψυχὰς θεοπνόῳ ὄντι, ὡς φησὶν ὁ Νουμήνιος, διὰ τοῦτο λέγων καὶ τὸν προφήτην εἰρηκέναι ἐμφέρεσθαι ἐπάνω τοῦ ὕδατος θεοῦ πνεῦμα.

1 συνιζάνειν M

They [scil. the Jews] believed that the souls rest on the water which is divinely animated, so Numenius asserts, saying that because of this the prophet said that the spirit of God is carried above the water.

θεοπνόῳ: This adjective combines the words θεοῦ πνεῦμα of the quotation from Gen. i:2; see Gager, p. 66.

369

apud: Eusebius, *Praeparatio Evangelica*, XI, 18:14 — Mras = Leemans, F22 = W. Scott, *Hermetica*, II, 1925, p. 79 = Des Places, *op. cit.*, F13

Ὥσπερ δὲ πάλιν λόγος ἐστὶ γεωργῷ πρὸς τὸν φυτεύοντα ἀναφερόμενος, τὸν αὐτὸν λόγον μάλιστά ἐστιν ὁ πρῶτος θεὸς πρὸς τὸν δημιουργόν. ὁ μέν γε ὢν σπέρμα πάσης ψυχῆς σπείρει εἰς τὰ μεταλαγχάνοντα αὐτοῦ χρήματα ξύμπαντα· ὁ νομοθέτης δὲ φυτεύει καὶ διανέμει καὶ μετα-
5 φυτεύει εἰς ἡμᾶς ἑκάστους τὰ ἐκεῖθεν προκαταβεβλημένα.

3 γε ὢν secl. W. Scott   ὁ μέν γε α´ ὢν (= πρῶτος ὢν) E. R. Dodds, *Les Sources de Plotin (Fondation Hardt pour l'étude de l'antiquité classique*, V, *Entretiens*, 1957), p. 15   γεννῶν Thillet, apud: Des Places

And as again there is a relation between the husbandman and him that planteth, exactly in the same way is the First God related to the Demiurge. The former being the seed of all soul sows it in all things that partake of Himself. But the Lawgiver plants, and distributes and transplants into each of us the germs which have been previously deposited from the higher source.   (trans. E. H. Gifford, Oxford 1903)

ὁ μέν γε ὥν: The most natural interpretation of this designation for the First God here is that Numenius was influenced by the Septuagint translation of Exod. iii:14: ἐγώ εἰμι ὁ ὥν; see already Festugière, *op. cit.* (supra, p. 206, n. 2), III, p. 44, nn. 2 and 3; for a more detailed discussion, see Whittaker, *op. cit.* (supra, p. 207, n. 4), pp. 196 ff. The expression was used not infrequently by Philo and other Jewish Hellenistic and Christian writers. It could easily serve as a link between the Judaic and Platonic conceptions of God. Thus its appearance in the writings of Numenius should cause no surprise, though whether he was directly indebted here to Philo cannot be stated with certainty. Against the emendation of the text by Dodds, *op. cit.* (supra, p. 206, n. 2), p. 15, see Waszink, *op. cit.* (supra, p. 207, n. 5), p. 50, n. 4. See also J. Whittaker, *Phoenix*, XXXII (1978), pp. 144 ff.

216

CXI. AELIUS ARISTIDES

Second century C.E.

The orator Aelius Aristides[1] found an opportunity to attack contemporary philosophers in his vindication of the four great Athenians — Pericles, Cymon, Miltiades and Themistocles — against the accusation supposedly levelled at them by Plato. The character and behaviour of the philosophers are compared by Aristides to those of the "impious in Palestine" (No. 371). It may now be accepted that his invective is aimed only at the philosophers.[2] There is a strong presumption that the people in Palestine to whom Aristides refers here are Jews and not Christians, since he employs the expression "in Palestine", and not "from Palestine", i.e. originating from Palestine.[3] In the second century C.E. Palestine still had a large Jewish population, while the Christians constituted only a negligible minority.[4] Aristides, who in his childhood or youth witnessed the fierce revolt of Palestinian Jews under Bar-Kokhba, might well have chosen the Jews as suitable for comparison with the philosophers, the tertium comparationis *being the fact that both fail to acknowledge their betters.*

1 On the dates of the birth and death of Aelius Aristides (118 C.E.–c. 180 C.E.), see C.A. Behr, *Aelius Aristides and the Sacred Tales*, Amsterdam 1968, p. 1, n. 2; 114, n. 80; cf. C.A. de Leeuw, *Aelius Aristides*, Amsterdam–Paris 1939, p. 1, n. 3.
2 See A. Boulanger, *Aelius Aristide*, Paris 1923, pp. 249 ff.; U.v. Wilamowitz-Moellendorff, *"Der Rhetor Aristeides"*, Sitzungsberichte der preussischen Akademie der Wissenschaften, Philosophisch-historische Klasse (1925), p. 350.
3 See Boulanger, *op. cit.* (supra, n. 2), p. 259, n. 3. For the suggestion that both Jews and Christians are implied, see J. Bernays, *Lucian und die Kyniker*, Berlin 1879, p. 39. Cf. also the remarks of E. Norden, *Jahrbücher für classische Philologie*, Suppl. XIX, Part 2 (1893), pp. 407 ff. The opinion that this refers to Christians is expressed, e.g., by Friedlaender, III, p. 237; P. de Labriolle, *La Réaction païenne*, Paris 1934, p. 83. Against Labriolle, cf. now C. Andresen, *Logos und Nomos*, Berlin 1955, p. 214, n. 9. This passage was already interpreted as referring to Jews by J. Masson, in the "Collectanea Historica ad Aristidis Vitam", printed in Dindorf's edition of the works of Aelius Aristides, III, Leipzig 1829, pp. XLII f.
4 See Harnack, II, pp. 642 f.

This hypothesis is not entirely certain, however, since, of the features that Aristides believed to be common to philosophers and Palestinians, namely self-abasement (ταπεινότης) and stubbornness (αὐθαδεία), the first perhaps attached more to Christians.

Aristides also refers to Palestine, or more precisely to its official name at that time of "Syria-Palaestina", in connection with a natural phenomenon of which he had heard: that a lake near the place where the famous dates and balsam grew indicated the annual rise of the Nile (No. 370). There is no doubt that Aristides had in mind the Dead Sea. He reverts to the lake, in the same speech, in order to explain why it is called a "sea". In this context, however, he defines it as a sea situated in Syria near Phoenicia: ἐν τῇ κατὰ Φοινίκην Συρίᾳ θάλατταν, or as a lake in Syria: καὶ ἧς ἀρτίως ἐμνήσθην λίμνης, τῆς ἐν τῇ Συρίᾳ.

370

Oratio, XXXVI, Aegyptiacus, 82, 88–89 — Keil = Dindorf, XLVIII

(82) Ἤκουσα δὲ ἔγωγε καὶ τῆς Παλαιστίνης Συρίας ἐν Σκυθῶν πόλει περὶ τὸν τόπον, ὃς τάς τε δὴ βαλάνους τῶν φοινίκων τὰς ὀνομαστὰς καὶ τὸν ὀπὸν φέρει, λίμνην εἶναι, ἥν, ἐπειδὰν ὁ Νεῖλος ἀνέλθῃ σημαίνειν· καὶ γὰρ τὸ ῥῆμα τοῦτ' ἦν τῶν ξένων, ἔλεγον δὲ ὡς αὐξανομένης ... (88) ἦν γὰρ ἐν τῇ
5 κατὰ Φοινίκην Συρίᾳ θάλατταν καλοῦσί τινες νῦν, τὴν ἄγονον ταύτην, αὐτίκα ἐροῦμεν πόθεν εἴληφεν τοὔνομα. (89) ἔπειτα ταύτας πάσας, οἶμαι, συμβέβηκεν τὴν αὐτὴν ταύτην ἔχειν φύσιν ἀλλήλαις τε καὶ τῇ πηγῇ, καὶ οὐδείς ἐστιν ὅστις ὑπεξείλετο εἶναί τιν' αὐτῶν γλυκεῖαν, ἀλλ' ὁμοῦ θάλατταν εἰρήκασι. καὶ δήλη ἐστὶν ἡ τοῦ ὕδατος φύσις ἰδία τε καὶ μόνης
10 τῆς θαλάττης οὖσα, ὥστε καὶ τῶν φρεάτων ὅσα πρὸς τὸ ἁλμυρὸν κέκλικεν θάλατταν καλοῦσιν οἱ πολλοί, καὶ ἧς ἀρτίως ἐμνήσθην λίμνης, τῆς ἐν τῇ Συρίᾳ, τὸ ὕδωρ ἅλμην ἔχον ⋆ τῆς γῆς θαλάττης ἐπωνυμίαν παρὰ τοῖς πολλοῖς πεποίηκεν.

4 ξένων] λέξεων D   5 συρίαν D /   θάλασσαν SU   8 ὁμοῦ
⟨πάσας⟩ Reiske   ὁμοῦ ⟨αὐτὰς⟩ Keil   12 ἔχον ⟨ἐκ⟩ vel ⟨ἀπὸ⟩ Reiske
τῆς γῆς del. Wilamowitz

(82) I heard it myself at Scythopolis, the city of Palaestina-Syria, that in the place which brings forth the famous dates and the juice [i.e. of balsam], there is a lake which indicates whenever the Nile rises. That was said by my hosts, who maintained that it happened during the increase of the lake ... (88) As for the lake in Syria near Phoenicia

which some now call a sea, I mean that sterile one, we shall presently state whence it took its name. (89) Since all these [scil. seas] have the same nature, as well as their source, no one has ever made an exception for one of them as being sweet but called them alike "sea". As the nature of their water is manifestly distinct and specific only to the sea, many people also call those wells "sea" which have a tendency to saltiness. And as for the lake, the one in Syria which I have just mentioned, its briny water * procured it the cognomen "sea" among the multitude.

82 Ἤκουσα δὲ ἔγωγε ... ἐν Σκυθῶν πόλει: From what Aelius Aristides says here it is clear that he had visited Scythopolis. It was surmised long ago that this visit should be connected with Aristides' return from his Egyptian journey; see J. Masson, op. cit. (supra, p. 217, n. 3), p. XL. It is now accepted that Aelius was in Egypt in 142 C.E.; on his journey, see Boulanger, op. cit. (supra, p. 217, n. 2), pp. 120 ff., 489 ff.; Behr, op. cit. (supra, p. 217, n. 1), pp. 15 ff. Behr thinks that Aelius arrived in Egypt around May 141 C.E. and left the country in April 142 C.E. (ibid., p. 21). However, Behr does not mention Aelius' sojourn in Scythopolis. The Egyptian Oration of Aristides was written some years after the journey; see Behr, op. cit., p. 19, n. 63, dating it provisionally to c. 147/149 C.E.
Scythopolis was undoubtedly a city of some Greek culture in the second century C.E.; Basilides, a teacher of Marcus Aurelius, came from that city; see Hieronymus, Chronica (ed. Helm), p. 203; Syncellus, I (ed. Dindorf), p. 663. Basilides may have been the man referred to as a Stoic by Sextus Empiricus, Adversus Mathematicos, VIII (= Adversus Logicos, II), 258: οἱ στωικοί, ὡς οἱ περὶ τὸν Βασιλείδην. From the third century Porphyry mentions a physician from Scythopolis who was among the pupils of Plotinus; see Porphyrius, Vita Plotini, 7: ἔσχε [scil. Πλωτῖνος] δὲ καὶ ἰατρικόν τινα Σκυθοπολίτην Παυλῖνον ὃν ὁ Ἀμέλιος Μίκκαλον προσηγόρευε.
βαλάνους τῶν φοινίκων ... καὶ τὸν ὀπόν: In other orations Aristides mentions that he used the juice of both balsam and dates for medicinal purposes; see Orationes (ed. Keil), XLVIII, 10: μετὰ δὲ ταῦτα ἐδίδου τὰ ἰάματα αὐτῷ μοί, ὧν πρῶτον ἦν, ὡς γ' ἐγὼ μέμνημαι, ὁ τοῦ βαλσάμου ὀπός; ibid., XLIX, 24.
88 θάλατταν ... τὴν ἄγονον ταύτην: Cf. BJ, IV, 456: ἡ μὲν γὰρ ἁλμυρώδης καὶ ἄγονος [scil. the Sea of Asphalt].

371

Oratio, XLVI, De Quattuorviris, 309 — Dindorf

Ἤδη δέ τινες καὶ τοῦθ', ὡς ἀκούω, δόγμα πεποίηνται, προσίεσθαι μὲν τὸ διδόμενον, λαμβάνοντες δὲ λοιδορεῖν. μόνους δὲ τούτους οὔτ' ἐν κόλαξιν

οὔτ᾽ ἐν ἐλευθέροις ἄξιον θεῖναι. ἐξαπατῶσι μὲν γὰρ ὡς κόλακες, προπηλακίζουσι δ᾽ ὡς κρείττονες, δύο τοῖς ἐσχάτοις καὶ τοῖς ἐναντιωτάτοις
5 ἔνοχοι κακοῖς ὄντες, ταπεινότητι καὶ αὐθαδείᾳ, τοῖς ἐν τῇ Παλαιστίνῃ δυσσεβέσι παραπλήσιοι τοὺς τρόπους. καὶ γὰρ ἐκείνοις τοῦτ᾽ ἐστὶ σύμβολον τῆς δυσσεβείας, ὅτι τοὺς κρείττους οὐ νομίζουσι, καὶ οὗτοι τρόπον τινὰ ἀφεστᾶσι τῶν Ἑλλήνων, μᾶλλον δὲ καὶ πάντων τῶν κρειττόνων.

3 θεῖναι] κρῖναι N in marg.   8 ἐφεστᾶσι N

There are some persons, so I have heard, who even laid down this principle for themselves: to accept what is given but to abuse it while accepting. Only such as these is it proper to rank neither among flatterers nor among free men. For they beguile like flatterers, but behave disdainfully [i.e. towards those from whom they obtain gifts] like their betters. Thus they are prone to two contradictory vices, self-abasement and stubbornness. In this they are similar in character to the impious who live in Palaestina. For, as to them, the sign of their impiety consists in that they do not recognize their betters [i.e. believe in gods], and these also have in some way seceded from the Greeks or rather from all the better people.

κρείττους ... κρειττόνων: The first κρείττους implies the gods in whom the Jews do not believe. The phrase πάντων τῶν κρειττόνων means the better class of people from whom the philosophers seceded. In his customary manner Aristides here plays upon the double meaning of κρείττονες; see Boulanger, *op. cit.* (supra, p. 217, n. 2), p. 253, n. 2.

CXII. LUCIAN OF SAMOSATA

Second century C.E.

Lucian was an enemy of all belief in the supernatural and had no sympathy for the religious trends of his age.[1] *He does not display much interest in Judaism, and its believers scarcely served even as targets for his wit.*[2]

One of his few allusions to Jews seems to occur in the Philopseudeis[3] *(No. 372), which tells of a Syrian from Palestine*[4] *who practised as an exorcist. A Jewish thaumaturgist also appears in the* Tragodopodagra *(No. 374). In the* Alexander Pseudopropheta *(No. 373), the false prophet is said to have uttered some meaningless words which sounded like the language of the Hebrews or Phoenicians.*[5]

1 For a short summary of Lucian's attitude to religion, see M.P. Nilsson, *Geschichte der griechischen Religion*[2], II, Munich 1961, p. 559 ff.

2 Lucian presumably took more interest in Christianity, as may be inferred from his *De Morte Peregrini*; see M. Caster, *Lucien et la pensée religieuse de son temps*, Paris 1937, pp. 346 ff.; H.D. Betz, *Lukian von Samosata und das Neue Testament*, Berlin 1961, pp. 5 ff.; J. Bernays, *Lucian und die Kyniker*, Berlin 1879, pp. 55 f.

3 For the date of the *Philopseudeis* (between 166 and 170 C.E.), cf. J. Schwartz, *Biographie de Lucien de Samosate*, Brussels–Berchem 1965, p. 108.

4 For this expression indicating a Jew, see Ovidius, *Ars Amatoria*, I, 416 (No. 142). It is not necessary here to assume an allusion to the Gospels; cf. also J. Schwartz (ed.), *Philopseudès et De Morte Peregrini*, Paris 1951, p. 45.

5 Lucian makes some allusion to the "Seventh Day", as an offensive nickname for a man who acted in the assemblies as children do on the Seventh Day, joking and making fun, in *Pseudologista*, 16: καὶ ὁ μὲν κόθορνόν τινα εἶπεν ... ὁ δὲ ἑβδόμην, ὅτι ὥσπερ οἱ παῖδες ἐν ταῖς ἑβδόμαις κἀκεῖνος ἐν ταῖς ἐκκλησίαις ἔπαιζεν καὶ διεγέλα καὶ παιδιὰν ἐποιεῖτο τὴν σπουδὴν τοῦ δήμου. However, there is no reason to assume here an allusion to the Sabbath, the more so as the examples of Lucian presumably belong to the age of classical Athens, and Lucian expressly refers to οἱ πάλαι before citing them. The "buskin" (κόθορνος) adduced first seems to be an allusion to Theramenes.

221

372

Philopseudeis, 16 — Macleod

Ἐγὼ γοῦν ἡδέως ἂν ἐροίμην σε, τί περὶ τούτων φῇς ὅσοι τοὺς δαιμονῶντας
ἀπαλλάττουσι τῶν δειμάτων οὕτως σαφῶς ἐξᾴδοντες τὰ φάσματα. καὶ
ταῦτα οὐκ ἐμὲ χρὴ λέγειν, ἀλλὰ πάντες ἴσασι τὸν Σύρον τὸν ἐκ τῆς
Παλαιστίνης, τὸν ἐπὶ τούτῳ σοφιστήν, ὅσους παραλαβὼν καταπίπτοντας
5 πρὸς τὴν σελήνην καὶ τὼ ὀφθαλμὼ διαστρέφοντας καὶ ἀφροῦ πιμ-
πλαμένους τὸ στόμα ὅμως ἀνίστησιν καὶ ἀποπέμπει ἀρτίους τὴν γνώμην,
ἐπὶ μισθῷ μεγάλῳ ἀπαλλάξας τῶν δεινῶν. ἐπειδὰν γὰρ ἐπιστὰς
κειμένοις ἔρηται ὅθεν εἰσεληλύθασιν εἰς τὸ σῶμα, ὁ μὲν νοσῶν αὐτὸς
σιωπᾷ, ὁ δαίμων δὲ ἀποκρίνεται, ἑλληνίζων ἢ βαρβαρίζων ὁπόθεν ἂν
10 αὐτὸς ᾖ, ὅπως τε καὶ ὁπότε εἰσῆλθεν ἐς τὸν ἄνθρωπον· ὁ δὲ ὅρκους
ἐπάγων, εἰ δὲ μὴ πεισθείη, καὶ ἀπειλῶν ἐξελαύνει τὸν δαίμονα.

2 τὰ β   καὶ τὰ γ   4 καταλαβὼν β   5 καὶ¹ om. β / καὶ² om. β
   6–7 ἀρτίους τὴν γνώμην ἐπὶ Γᵃ β   om. γ   7 γὰρ om. P
8 ἐσεληλύθεισαν N   9 ὁπόθεν β   ἢ ὅθεν γ   11 εἰ δὲ μὴ πεισθείη]
   εἰ δὲ μὴ πειθοίη γ   εἰ δὴ ἀπειθοίη Γᵃ β

For my part, I should like to ask you what you say to those who free
possessed men from their terrors by exorcising the spirits so
manifestly? I need not discuss this; everyone knows about the Syrian
from Palestine, the adept in it how many he takes in hand who fall
down in the light of the moon and roll their eyes and fill their mouths
with foam; nevertheless he restores them to health and sends them
away normal in mind, delivering them from their straits for a large
fee. When he stands beside them as they lie there and asks: "Whence
came you into his body?" the patient himself is silent, but the spirit
answers in Greek or in the language of whatever foreign country he
comes from, telling how and whence he entered into the man;
whereupon, by adjuring the spirit and if he does not obey threatening
him, he drives him out.   (trans. A. M. Harmon, *LCL*)

373

Alexander Pseudopropheta, 13 — Macleod

Οἱ παρόντες δέ — συνδεδραμήκει γὰρ σχεδὸν ἅπασα ἡ πόλις ἅμα γυναιξὶ
καὶ γέρουσι καὶ παιδίοις — ἐτεθήπεσαν καὶ ηὔχοντο καὶ προσεκύνουν. ὁ
δὲ φωνάς τινας ἀσήμους φθεγγόμενος, οἷαι γένοιντο ἂν Ἑβραίων ἢ

Φοινίκων, ἐξέπληττε τοὺς ἀνθρώπους οὐκ εἰδότας ὅ τι καὶ λέγοι, πλὴν
τοῦτο μόνον, ὅτι πᾶσιν ἐγκατεμίγνυ τὸν ᾿Απόλλω καὶ τὸν ᾿Ασκληπιόν.

5

4 ὅτι λέγοι γ   5 ᾿Απόλλωνα γ

The assembly — for almost the whole city, including women, old men
and boys, had come running — marvelled, prayed and made
obeisance. Uttering a few meaningless words like Hebrew or
Phoenician, he dazed the creatures, who did not know what he was
saying save only that he everywhere brought in Apollo and
Asclepius.   (trans. A. M. Harmon, *LCL*)

374

Tragodopodagra, 171–173 (655–657) — Iacobitz = F84R

῎Αλλος δὲ πίνων τὴν ἱερὰν καθαίρεται,
ἄλλος ἐπαοιδαῖς ἐπιθετῶν ἐμπαίζεται,
᾿Ιουδαῖος ἕτερον μωρὸν ἐξᾴδει λαβών.

Some purge themselves with sacred medicine;
Others are mocked by chants impostors sell,
And other fools fall for the spells of Jews.

(trans. M. D. Macleod, *LCL*)

CXIII. CELSUS PHILOSOPHUS

Second century C.E.

The place, the personality, and the connections of Celsus, as well as the external circumstances of his literary activity, remain unknown to us, as they were even to his third-century literary opponent, Origen (see Origenes, Contra Celsum, I, 8). His sole known work, the Ἀληθὴς Λόγος "The True Doctrine", has been preserved only in the quotations included by Origen in his reply to Celsus' arguments (No. 375). It may be stated with certainty that Celsus launched his great attack on Christianity in the reign of Marcus Aurelius, or at the earliest towards the end of the reign of Antoninus Pius.[1] He may have originated from Egypt, or more probably from Syria. However neither Rome nor Asia Minor should be excluded as possible candidates for the place where Celsus composed his work.[2]

1 For dating the work at the end of the reign of Marcus Aurelius (178 C.E.), see T. Keim, *Celsus' Wahres Wort*, Zürich 1873, pp. 261 ff. Not a few scholars accept his view, e.g. R. Bader, *Der Ἀληθὴς Λόγος des Kelsos*, Stuttgart-Berlin 1940; P. Merlan, *Reallexikon für Antike und Christentum*, II (1954), pp. 954 ff.; C. Andresen, *Logos und Nomos*, Berlin 1955, p. 309; H. O. Schröder, *Die Welt als Geschichte*, XVII (1957), p. 190. Chadwick assigns the work to the years 177–180 C.E.; see Chadwick's introduction to his translation, pp. XXVI ff. For dating the Ἀληθὴς Λόγος to the reign of Antoninus Pius, see J. B. Lightfoot, *The Apostolic Fathers*, Vol. II, Part 1², London 1889, pp. 530 f. For a date in the sixties of the second century C.E., and that Celsus was acquainted with the *De Morte Peregrini* by Lucian, see J. Schwartz, *Revue d'histoire et de philosophie religieuses*, XL (1960), pp. 126 ff.; idem, *Biographie de Lucien de Samosate*, Brussels–Berchem 1965, p. 24; H. U. Rosenbaum, *Vigiliae Christianae*, XXVI (1972), pp. 102 ff. Rosenbaum inclines to accept a date approximate to that of Schwartz (some twenty years before the date accepted by most scholars). On the other hand, for a defence of the date 178 C.E., and emphasizing that neither Tatian nor Athenagoras shows any knowledge of the work, see J. M. Vermander, *Revue des études augustiniennes*, XVIII (1972), p. 27, n. 2.

2 For the location in Rome of Celsus' literary activity, see Keim, *op. cit.* (supra, n. 1), pp. 274 f. For arguments in favour of Alexandria, see Chadwick, in the introduction to his translation, pp. XXVIII f. The view that Celsus was writing "somewhere in the broad area between

Origen calls Celsus an "Epicurean" (see, e.g., Contra Celsum, I, 8: εὐρίσκεται ... ἐπικούρειος ὤν). Yet the parts of Celsus' work included in Contra Celsum *furnish no proof that he adhered to this school of thought, and it seems that even Origen himself began to doubt his own assertion (see* ibid.*).*[3] *Celsus may be defined rather as an eclectic philosopher, whose views were tinged mainly by Middle Platonism, the prevalent philosophy of his time, and who also made free use of the arsenal of Stoic argumentation.*

Origen's quotations from the work show that Celsus had a lofty concept of the Supreme God, who is transcendental, unchangeable, abstract and worshipped under different names. In the accepted tradition of Greek philosophy Celsus combines a kind of monotheism on principle with acquiescence in the existing polytheism, as enshrined in popular cults and beliefs, since it was believed that he who worships the different deities ultimately adores the Supreme God. To Celsus Christianity appears as a false and destructive doctrine, by no means a pure monotheism (VIII, 12), but a creed characterized by an irrational belief in Christ, a doctrine originating among the Jews, and appealing mainly to the most foolish and lowest elements of society. He sees in the Christian state of mind a threat to civilization and to the future of the Roman state. Celsus therefore exhorted the Christians to help the Roman emperor by changing their minds and by cooperating with him in what was right (VIII, 73).

On the whole it should be remarked that Celsus' work is more a refutation of the "False Doctrine", i.e. Christianity, than an exposition

Alexandria and Antioch" is taken by Frend, *Martyrdom and Persecution in the Early Church*, p. 297, n. 56. Because of the special knowledge of Egypt and Syria displayed in the work, it has been suggested that Celsus was a Roman official who functioned in Syria and also perhaps lived in Asia Minor; see Schwartz, in his article in *Revue d'histoire et philosophie religieuses*, p. 144. That Celsus was a Roman official acquainted with the eastern countries, and above all with Palestine and Egypt, was also surmised by O. Glöckner, *Philologus*, LXXXII (1927), p. 351.

3 For other allusions by Origen to Epicureanism, see *Contra Celsum*, I, 10, 20; II, 60; III, 80; IV, 4 (here Origen wavers concerning the Epicureanism of Celsus), 54 (again Origen shows awareness that Celsus may not have been an Epicurean), 75; V, 3 (where it is expressly stated by Origen that throughout the treatise Celsus has not admitted that he was an Epicurean).

of the Ἀληϑὴς Λόγος, the *"True Doctrine"*.[4] *His own systematic statement of the "True Doctrine" is reserved by Celsus only for the future (VIII, 76).*

Celsus' attitude to the Jews and their religion was conditioned above all by the inherent connection between Judaism and Christianity. To disprove the intellectual and religious foundations of Christianity he found it necessary to strike at Judaism as the root of the evil. His views on the Jewish religion are deeply influenced by the opinions traditionally held by many Greek and Latin authors, and Celsus does not share the sympathetic approach to Judaism of his contemporary Numenius (Nos. 363a–369). Celsus' criticism is marked by coolness and reluctance to admit that the Jews also share with other nations a common ancient religious tradition. Moreover, in Celsus' view, whatever may be of value in Jewish beliefs and customs — the alleged worship of heaven, circumcision — is neither original nor specific to Judaism.

Celsus nevertheless abstains from recourse to the hostile myths in the Graeco-Egyptian anti-Jewish tradition recounted by writers like Lysimachus, Chaeremon and Apion. Thus Celsus ignores the allegations that the ancestors of the Jewish nation were tainted by physical disabilities during their sojourn in Egypt, causing the pollution of the country and the resulting divine displeasure. In stating that Moses and the Jews were of Egyptian ancestry Celsus accords with the version of Jewish history related not only by Manetho and Chaeremon but also by Strabo, both in his Historica Hypomnemata, *apud: Josephus,* Ant., *XIV, 118 (No. 105), and his* Geographica, *XVI, 2:34 f., p. 760 (No. 115). Strabo, however, displays a sincere admiration for the personality of Moses, approving of the Egyptian followers who accepted his religious teachings and only criticizing the later development of the Jewish religion, while Celsus views Moses with the greatest antipathy. Celsus explains that the goatherds and shepherds who became attached to Moses were deluded by clumsy deceits into thinking that there was only one God. They abandoned polytheistic worship without any rational cause.*

When Celsus alludes to the contribution of the Jews to human civilization as meagre, he has as precursors in this opinion both the Egyptian Apion and Apollonius Molon, as well as a successor in

---

4 For the Platonic antecedents of the expression, see Andresen, *op. cit.* (supra, n. 1), pp. 108 ff.

Julian. Celsus also resorts to an argument against Judaism based on the political failure of the Jews as a nation, an argument used not only by Apion, but also by Cicero in his Pro Flacco, *28:69 (No. 68).*

The other arguments which Celsus uses against Judaism fall mainly under the following headings:

a. The absurdity of Jewish messianic beliefs, concerning which Celsus compares the controversy between the Jews and Christians as to whether the expected Messiah has already come to the proverbial tale of the dispute over the shadow of an ass. He also objects to the belief in resurrection supposedly held by Jews and Christians, and praises those Jews who deny it.

b. The anthropocentricism of Judaism and Christianity.

c. The nature of what is said concerning the Jews by Moses and the prophets which Celsus maintains is biased in favour of their own doctrine.

d. The figurative and allegorical interpretation of Mosaic history.

e. The Mosaic cosmogony and history itself, which Celsus considers extremely silly. The assignment of certain days to the making of the world, even before the days themselves existed, and the story of paradise both serve as targets for his attack. According to Celsus, God emerges from the creation story in Genesis as the bad workman who tires of his work and needs a holiday for rest. Celsus maintains that God could not have created man in His own image, because He does not resemble man, or any other form. In particular Celsus singles out for ridicule the biblical passages attributing human passions to God. Apart from the cosmology of Genesis, Celsus also attacks its later narrative, the story of the Flood and the Tower of Babel. The Flood, according to him, is no more than a debased version of the story of Deucalion, and the iniquities related of Lot are worse than the Thyestian sins. Celsus also deprecates other stories in Genesis, such as the story of Joseph and the relation of the dreams of the chief butler and the chief baker of Pharaoh.

f. The angel-worship that Celsus states is practised by the Jews.

g. The humble origins of Moses' followers, who in the eyes of Celsus belonged to the lowest sectors of the population. He refers to them as "goatherds and shepherds" and views them as people who had raised the standard of rebellion against their country (Egypt) and society, being runaway slaves from Egypt. Celsus states that in thus isolating themselves from their country and society, and in finding recruits from the lowest classes, they foreshadowed the rebels of his own day, i.e. the Christians.

227

Celsus is the first pagan writer known to have drawn abundantly on the Bible, principally on Genesis. However his range of interest is not confined to this book or to the Pentateuch only, and he refers also to the stories of Daniel and Jonah.

In his criticism of Judaism, Celsus is more penetrating than any of his pagan predecessors. He also shows awareness of a fundamental distinction between the religion of the Jews and Christianity. For while displaying hostility towards Judaism, Celsus sees it, in contrast to Christianity, as a national religion, and to him it is therefore only natural that the Jews should adhere to it. In this at least they behave like the rest of mankind, not only because different peoples think differently on matters of religion, and it is always necessary to preserve the established social order, but also because different parts of the earth are apparently assigned to different overseers. In this attitude to Judaism Celsus may be considered the forerunner of Porphyry and Julian, the protagonists of the later Neoplatonic opposition to Christianity. These writers sometimes even use the same arguments as Celsus employs. Yet, while Porphyry, at least in some of his works, allots to Judaism an honourable place among the religions of the East, Celsus makes a detrimental distinction between the Jews and other barbarian nations, the Egyptians, Assyrians, Indians and Persians.

It is a main feature of the ʼΑληϑὴς Λόγος *that the arguments against Christianity are put into the mouth of a Jew. Celsus may have been influenced in his use of a Jew as the disputant against Christianity by the similar device in Justin's* Dialogus cum Tryphone.[5]

The points of attack on Christianity by Celsus' Jew are only partly paralleled in Jewish literature. Thus Jesus is accused by the Jew of having fabricated the story of his virgin birth, whereas in fact he was the child of a poor Jewish village woman, who earned her living by spinning and was driven out by her carpenter husband after she had been convicted of adultery with a soldier named Panthera. She gave birth to his son, Jesus, who later became a hired labourer in Egypt. He learned the arts of magic from the Egyptians and then returned to Judaea. There, trusting in his magical powers, he assumed the title of God.

5 See H. Chadwick, *Early Christian Thought and the Classical Tradition*, Oxford 1966, p. 133. For the view that the ʼΑληϑὴς Λόγος was in some way a reply to Justin's doctrine of Logos, see Andresen, *op. cit.* (supra, n. 1), pp. 308 ff.; A. D. Nock, *JTS*, NS, VII (1956), pp. 316 f.

The subsequent argumentation, based mainly on criticism of material found in the Gospels, is generally rationalistic in nature, sometimes tinged with sarcasm. The Jew asks whether the mother of Jesus was beautiful, and whether it was not for this reason that God had sexual relations with her.

One of the arguments put forward by the Jew is a refutation of Jesus' claims to messiahship. The Jew asks why Jesus in particular should be singled out as the Messiah of the biblical prophecies, among the multitudes of other people who had lived after the prophecies were uttered. Then it is asked why Jesus, if he were the son of God, did not become king when he grew up but instead lived a life of wandering, cowering in fear and destitution. As to the miracles said to have been wrought by Jesus, the Jew maintains that even if these had been performed, they should only be put on the same level as the works of other Egyptian-style sorcerers. Additionally, unlike Jesus, a god would not have had a corruptible body, he would not have been born as he was, and would not have eaten the food he did.

The beginning of Book II of Origen's Contra Celsum *contains an argument specifically addressed by the Jew to the Jewish Christians, his coreligionists, who had joined Jesus, having been deluded into abandoning their ancestral law. Celsus' Jew again emphasizes the fact that many others similar to Jesus had appeared to deceive people who wanted to be deceived. Jews could not regard as God one who in general did not fulfil anything that he had promised to do, who had been condemned by the Jews, caught in hiding and betrayed by his own disciples. If he was a god, it is asked how all this could happen. The Jew argues that the messianic claims of Jesus are refuted by the actual words of the prophets, who tell that the one who comes will be a great prince, ruler of all nations and of the whole earth. The same criticism applies also to the Christian equation of the Son of God with the Logos, for the Christians' Son of God is not a pure and holy Logos but a man who was arrested by the authorities and crucified. In regard to the resurrection of Jesus, this was witnessed only by a hysterical female and possibly by another deluded by the same sorcery. To prove his divine power Jesus ought to have shown himself before those who maltreated and condemned him, and to display his divinity he should have disappeared from the cross. When he was punished he was seen by all, but when he rose again he was observed only by one woman and by his own followers, whereas logically the opposite ought to have happened. It is obvious from the parallels to be found between the arguments of*

229

Celsus' Jew and those occurring in Jewish talmudic and later literature that Celsus had drawn on Jewish sources here, whether written or oral.[6] *Celsus' Jew even addresses part of his discourse specifically to the Jewish Christians, in whom Celsus could hardly have had an actual interest. However, it should by no means be assumed that all the arguments put into the mouth of the Jew are derived by Celsus from Jewish sources.*

The Jew depicted by Celsus undoubtedly belongs to a Hellenistic Jewish cultural milieu, as may be deduced from the knowledge that he displays of Greek literature and mythology.[7] *He also makes use of the Logos concept familiar to Hellenistic Jewry.*[8]

Bibliography

For reconstructions of the text, see O. Glöckner, *Celsi 'Αληθὴς Λόγος* (*Kleine Texte*, No. 151), Bonn 1924; R. Bader, *Der 'Αληθὴς Λόγος des Kelsos*, Stuttgart–Berlin 1940; *Origen — Contra Celsum*, translated by H. Chadwick, with introduction and notes, Cambridge 1953.

On this work in general, see T. Keim, *Celsus' Wahres Wort*, Zürich 1873; L. Rougier, *Celse ou le conflit de la civilisation antique et du christianisme primitif*, Paris 1925; A. Miura-Stange, *Celsus und Origenes — das Gemeinsame ihrer Weltanschauung*, Giessen 1926; O. Glöckner, *Philologus*, LXXXII (1927), pp. 329 ff.; J. S. Whale, *Expository Times*, XLII (1930–1931), pp. 119 ff.; E. Stein, *Eos*, XXXIV (1932–1933), pp. 205 ff.; A. D. Nock, *Conversion*, Oxford 1933, pp. 204 ff.; P. de Labriolle, *La Réaction païenne*, Paris 1934, pp. 111 ff.; A. L. Williams, *Adversus Judaeos*, Cambridge 1935, pp. 79 ff.; A. Wifstrand, "Die wahre Lehre des Kelsos", *Bulletin de la Société Royale des Lettres de Lund* (1941–1942), pp. 391 ff.; P. Merlan, *Reallexikon für Antike und Christentum*, II (1954), pp. 954 ff.; Le R. P. (A. J.) Festugière, *La révélation d'Hermès Trismégiste*, IV, Paris 1954, pp. 115 ff.; C. Andresen, *Logos und Nomos; Die Polemik des Kelsos wider das Christentum*, Berlin

6 See M. Lods, *Revue d'histoire et de philosophie religieuses*, XXI (1941), pp. 1 ff.

7 See, e.g., the reference to famous persons in Greek mythology, Perseus, Amphion, Aeacus and Minos (*Contra Celsum*, I, 67); the quotation from the *Bacchae* and an allusion to Pentheus (II, 34); the references to the deeds of Zalmoxis among the Scythians, Pythagoras in Italy and Rhampsinitus in Egypt, as well as of Orpheus among the Odrysians, Protesilaus in Thessaly, Heracles at Taenarum, and Theseus (II, 55).

8 See Simon, p. 208, n. 5; see also the remarks of M. Freimann, *MGWJ*, LV (1911), pp. 561 f.; LVI (1912), pp. 52 ff.

1955; A.D. Nock, *JTS*, NS, VII (1956), pp. 314 ff.; H.O. Schröder, *Die Welt als Geschichte*, XVII (1957), pp. 190 ff.; W.H.C. Frend, *Martyrdom and Persecution in the Early Church*, Oxford 1965, pp. 276 ff.; H. Chadwick, *Early Christian Thought and the Classical Tradition*, Oxford 1966, pp. 22 ff.; J. Speigl, *Der römische Staat und die Christen*, Amsterdam 1970, pp. 185 ff.; Gager, pp. 92 ff.; J.C.M. van Winden, in: *Festschrift Johannes Quasten*, I, Münster 1970, pp. 209 ff.; D. Rokeah, *Tarbiz*, XL (1970/1), pp. 463 f.; H. Bietenhard, *Caesarea, Origenes und die Juden*, Stuttgart 1974, pp. 42 ff.; N.R.M. de Lange, *Origen and the Jews*, Cambridge 1976, pp. 63 ff.; M. Borret, *Origène, Contre Celse*, V (Introduction générale), Paris 1976, pp. 122 ff.; W. den Boer, *Athenaeum*, NS, LIV (1976), pp. 300 ff.

375

'Αληθὴς Λόγος, apud: Origenes, *Contra Celsum* — Borret = O. Glöckner, *Celsi 'Αληθὴς Λόγος* (*Klein Texte*, No. 151), Bonn 1924 = R. Bader, *Der 'Αληθὴς Λόγος des Kelsos*, Stuttgart–Berlin 1940

(I, 2) Ἑξῆς βάρβαρόν φησιν ἄνωθεν εἶναι τὸ δόγμα, δηλονότι τὸν
ἰουδαϊσμόν, οὗ χριστιανισμὸς ἤρτηται. καὶ εὐγνωμόνως γε οὐκ
ὀνειδίζει ἐπὶ τῇ ἀπὸ βαρβάρων ἀρχῇ τῷ λόγῳ, ἐπαινῶν ὡς ἱκανοὺς
εὑρεῖν δόγματα τοὺς βαρβάρους· προστίθησι δὲ τούτοις ὅτι κρῖναι
5 καὶ βεβαιώσασθαι καὶ ἀσκῆσαι πρὸς ἀρετὴν τὰ ὑπὸ
βαρβάρων εὑρεθέντα ἀμείνονές εἰσιν Ἕλληνες ... *(14)*
Συγγένειαν παρὰ πολλοῖς τῶν ἐθνῶν νομίζων εἶναι ὁ Κέλσος τοῦ
αὐτοῦ λόγου πάντα μὲν ὀνομάζει τὰ ἔθνη ὡς ἀρξάμενα τοῦ τοιοῦδε
δόγματος· οὐκ οἶδα δ' ὅπως μόνους Ἰουδαίους συκοφαντεῖ, οὐ
10 συγκαταλέγων αὐτῶν τὸ ἔθνος τοῖς λοιποῖς, ὡς εἴτε συμφιλοπονῆσαν
ἐκείνοις καὶ ὁμοφρονῆσαν εἴτε παραπλήσια ἐν πολλοῖς δογματίσαν ...
εἰ δὲ κεχαρισμένως Μωϋσῆς καὶ οἱ προφῆται τῷ ἑαυτῶν λόγῳ πολλὰ
ἀνέγραψαν περὶ τῶν παρὰ σφίσιν αὐτοῖς, διὰ τί τὸ παραπλήσιον οὐκ
ἐροῦμεν καὶ περὶ τῶν ἐν τοῖς λοιποῖς ἔθνεσι συγγραφέων; ἢ Αἰγύπτιοι
15 μὲν ἐν ταῖς ἑαυτῶν ἱστορίαις Ἰουδαίους κακολογοῦντες πιστοί εἰσι
περὶ Ἰουδαίων· ταὐτὰ δὲ λέγοντες Ἰουδαῖοι περὶ Αἰγυπτίων, πολλὰ
ἀδίκως πεπονθέναι ἀναγράφοντες ἑαυτοὺς καὶ διὰ τοῦτο λέγοντες
αὐτοὺς κεκολάσθαι ὑπὸ θεοῦ, ψεύδονται; ... ὅρα οὖν εὐθέως τὸ
φίλαυτον τοῦ τοῖσδε μέν τισι πιστεύοντος ὡς σοφοῖς ἔθνεσι τῶνδε δὲ
20 καταγινώσκοντος ὡς πάντῃ ἀνοήτων. ἄκουε γὰρ λέγοντος τοῦ Κέλσου
ὅτι ἔστιν ἀρχαῖος ἄνωθεν λόγος, περὶ ὃν δὴ ἀεὶ καὶ τὰ ἔθνη τὰ
σοφώτατα καὶ πόλεις καὶ ἄνδρες σοφοὶ κατεγένοντο. καὶ οὐκ
ἐβουλήθη ἔθνος σοφώτατον εἰπεῖν κἂν παραπλησίως Αἰγυπτίοις
καὶ Ἀσσυρίοις καὶ Ἰνδοῖς καὶ Πέρσαις καὶ Ὀδρύσαις καὶ
25 Σαμόθραξι καὶ Ἐλευσινίοις τοὺς Ἰουδαίους ... *(16)* Θαυμάζω δέ,
πῶς Ὀδρύσας μὲν καὶ Σαμόθρακας καὶ Ἐλευσινίους καὶ
Ὑπερβορέους ἐν τοῖς ἀρχαιοτάτοις καὶ σοφωτάτοις ἔταξεν
ἔθνεσιν ὁ Κέλσος, τοὺς δὲ Ἰουδαίους οὐκ ἠξίωσεν οὔτε εἰς σοφοὺς
παραδέξασθαι οὔτε εἰς ἀρχαίους· ... ἀλλὰ καὶ τοὺς μὲν Ὁμήρου
30 Γαλακτοφάγους καὶ τοὺς Γαλατῶν Δρυΐδας καὶ τοὺς Γέτας
σοφώτατα λέγει ἔθνη εἶναι καὶ ἀρχαῖα, περὶ τῶν συγγενῶν
τοῖς Ἰουδαϊκοῖς λόγοις διαλαμβάνοντας ... πάλιν τε αὖ
κατάλογον ποιούμενος ἀνδρῶν ἀρχαίων καὶ σοφῶν,
ὠφελησάντων τοὺς κατ' αὐτοὺς καὶ διὰ συγγραμμάτων τοὺς

1 δῆλον ὅτι A   9 οἶδα δ' ὅπως M²   οἶδ' ὅπως A

35 μετ᾽ αὐτούς, Μωϋσέα ἐξέβαλε τοῦ καταλόγου τῶν σοφῶν ... Λίνον
δὲ καὶ Μουσαῖον καὶ Ὀρφέα καὶ τὸν Φερεκύδην καὶ τὸν
Πέρσην Ζωροάστρην καὶ Πυθαγόραν φήσας περὶ τῶνδε
διειληφέναι, καὶ ἐς βίβλους κατατεθεῖσθαι τὰ ἑαυτῶν
δόγματα καὶ πεφυλάχθαι αὐτὰ μέχρι δεῦρο ... (17) Ἐν δὲ τοῖς
40 ἑξῆς κατηγορῶν τῆς Μωϋσέως ἱστορίας αἰτιᾶται τοὺς τροπολογοῦντας
καὶ ἀλληγοροῦντας αὐτήν ... καὶ γὰρ οὗτος κατηγορήσας, ὡς οἴεται,
τῶν παρὰ Μωϋσεῖ ἱστοριῶν καὶ μεμψάμενος τοῖς ἀλληγοροῦσι μετὰ
τοῦ καὶ ἔπαινόν τινα περὶ αὐτῶν λέγειν, ὅτι εἰσὶν οἱ ἐπιεικέστεροι,
οἱονεὶ κωλύει κατηγορήσας, ὡς βούλεται, ἀπολογεῖσθαι τοὺς
45 δυναμένους, ὡς πέφυκεν ἔχειν τὰ πράγματα ... (19) Ἑξῆς τούτοις ὁ
Κέλσος λεληθότως βουλόμενος διαβαλεῖν τὴν κατὰ Μωϋσέα
κοσμοποιΐαν, ἐμφαίνοντα μηδέπω μυρίων ἐτῶν ἀριθμὸν ἔχειν τὸν
κόσμον ἀλλὰ πολλῷ τούτου λειπόμενον, προστίθεται κλέπτων αὐτοῦ τὸ
βούλημα τοῖς λέγουσιν ἀγένητον εἶναι τὸν κόσμον. τὸ γὰρ πολλὰς ἐκ
50 παντὸς αἰῶνος ἐκπυρώσεις γεγονέναι πολλὰς δ᾽ ἐπικλύσεις
καὶ νεώτερον εἶναι τὸν ἐπὶ Δευκαλίωνος κατακλυσμὸν
ἔναγχος γεγενημένον σαφῶς τοῖς ἀκούειν αὐτοῦ δυναμένοις
παρίστησι τὸ κατ᾽ αὐτὸν τοῦ κόσμου ἀγένητον. λεγέτω δὴ ἡμῖν ὁ τῇ
πίστει Χριστιανῶν ἐγκαλῶν, ποίοις ἀποδεικτικοῖς λόγοις ἠναγκάσθη
55 παραδέξασθαι πολλὰς γεγονέναι ἐκπυρώσεις καὶ πολλοὺς
κατακλυσμούς, πάντων δὲ νεώτερον εἶναι κατακλυσμὸν μὲν τὸν ἐπὶ
Δευκαλίωνος ἐκπύρωσιν δὲ τὴν ἐπὶ Φαέθοντος ... (21) Τούτου
οὖν, φησί, τοῦ λόγου τοῦ παρὰ τοῖς σοφοῖς ἔθνεσι καὶ
ἐλλογίμοις ἀνδράσιν ἐπακηκοὼς ὄνομα δαιμόνιον ἔσχε
60 Μωϋσῆς ... εἰ δ᾽, ὡς σὺ φῇς, συγκατέθετο δόγμασι σοφοῖς καὶ
ἀληθέσι καὶ ἐπαίδευσε τοὺς οἰκείους δι᾽ αὐτῶν, τί κατηγορίας ἄξιον
πεποίηκεν; ... (22) Μετὰ ταῦτα τὸ περιτέμνεσθαι τὰ αἰδοῖα μὴ
διαβαλὼν ὁ Κέλσος ὑπὸ Ἰουδαίων γινόμενον, φησὶν ἀπὸ Αἰγυπτίων
αὐτὸ ἐληλυθέναι ... (23) Ἑξῆς τούτοις φησὶν ὁ Κέλσος ὅτι τῷ
65 ἡγησαμένῳ σφῶν ἑπόμενοι Μωϋσεῖ αἰπόλοι καὶ ποιμένες,
ἀγροίκοις ἀπάταις ψυχαγωγηθέντες ἕνα ἐνόμισαν εἶναι
θεόν. δεικνύτω τοίνυν πῶς, αἰπόλων καὶ ποιμένων ἀλόγως, ὡς
οἴεται, ἀποστάντων τοῦ σέβειν θεούς, αὐτὸς δύναται παραστῆσαι
τὸ πλῆθος τῶν καθ᾽ Ἕλληνας θεῶν ἢ τοὺς λοιποὺς βαρβάρους ... (24)
70 Μετὰ ταῦτά φησιν ὅτι οἱ αἰπόλοι καὶ ποιμένες ἕνα ἐνόμισαν
θεόν, εἴτε Ὕψιστον εἴτ᾽ Ἀδωναῒ εἴτ᾽ Οὐράνιον εἴτε Σαβαώθ,

44 κωλύει Guiet   κωλύεται A
50 γεγονέναι post ἐπικλύσεις transp. Pap.   61 τί ποτε M
71 Ἀδωναΐ (ι in ras.) A¹   ἀδωναῖον Φ Borret / οὐράνιον A²   οὐρανὸν A

εἴτε καὶ ὅπῃ καὶ ὅπως χαίρουσιν ὀνομάζοντες τόνδε τὸν
κόσμον· καὶ πλεῖον οὐδὲν ἔγνωσαν. καὶ ἐν τοῖς ἑξῆς δέ φησι
μηδὲν διαφέρειν τῷ παρ' Ἕλλησι φερομένῳ ὀνόματι τὸν ἐπὶ
75 πᾶσι θεὸν καλεῖν Δία ἢ τῷ δεῖνα, φέρ' εἰπεῖν, παρ' Ἰνδοῖς ἢ
τῷ δεῖνα παρ' Αἰγυπτίοις ... (26) Ἴδωμεν δὲ τίνα τρόπον
συκοφαντεῖ Ἰουδαιοὺς ὁ παντ' ἐπαγγελλόμενος εἰδέναι Κέλσος λέγων
αὐτοὺς σέβειν ἀγγέλους καὶ γοητείᾳ προσκεῖσθαι, ἧς ὁ
Μωϋσῆς αὐτοῖς γέγονεν ἐξηγητής ... ἐπαγγέλλεται δὲ διδάξειν
80 ἑξῆς, πῶς καὶ Ἰουδαῖοι ὑπὸ ἀμαθίας ἐσφάλησαν
ἐξαπατώμενοι ... ἐπαγγειλάμενος δ' ὁ Κέλσος ὕστερον διδάξειν
τὰ περὶ Ἰουδαίων, πρῶτον ποιεῖται τὸν λόγον περὶ τοῦ σωτῆρος
ἡμῶν ... (28) μετὰ ταῦτα προσωποποιεῖ Ἰουδαῖον αὐτῷ διαλεγόμενον
τῷ Ἰησοῦ καὶ ἐλέγχοντα αὐτὸν περὶ πολλῶν μέν, ὡς οἴεται, πρῶτον δὲ
85 ὡς πλασαμένου αὐτοῦ τὴν ἐκ παρθένου γένεσιν· ὀνειδίζει δ'
αὐτῷ καὶ ἐπὶ τῷ ἐκ κώμης αὐτὸν γεγονέναι Ἰουδαϊκῆς καὶ
ἀπὸ γυναικὸς ἐγχωρίου καὶ πενιχρᾶς καὶ χερνήτιδος. φησὶ δ'
αὐτὴν καὶ ὑπὸ τοῦ γήμαντος, τέκτονος τὴν τέχνην ὄντος,
ἐξεῶσθαι ἐλεγχθεῖσαν ὡς μεμοιχευμένην. εἶτα λέγει ὡς
90 ἐκβληθεῖσα ὑπὸ τοῦ ἀνδρὸς καὶ πλανωμένη ἀτίμως σκότιον
ἐγέννησε τὸν Ἰησοῦν· καὶ ὅτι οὗτος διὰ πενίαν εἰς Αἴγυπτον
μισθαρνήσας κἀκεῖ δυνάμεών τινων πειραθείς, ἐφ' αἷς
Αἰγύπτιοι σεμνύνονται, ἐπανῆλθεν ἐν ταῖς δυνάμεσι μέγα
φρονῶν, καὶ δι' αὐτὰς θεὸν αὐτὸν ἀνηγόρευσε ... (32) Ἀλλὰ γὰρ
95 ἐπανέλθωμεν εἰς τὴν τοῦ Ἰουδαίου προσωποποιίαν ἐν ᾗ ἀναγέγραπται
ἡ τοῦ Ἰησοῦ μήτηρ ὡς ἐξωσθεῖσα ὑπὸ τοῦ μνηστευσαμένου
αὐτὴν τέκτονος, ἐλεχθεῖσα ἐπὶ μοιχείᾳ καὶ τίκτουσα ἀπό
τινος στρατιώτου Πανθήρα τοὔνομα ... (37) ἐπεὶ δὲ τὸν Ἰουδαῖον
ὁ Κέλσος εἰσήγαγε διαλεγόμενον τῷ Ἰησοῦ καὶ διασύροντα τήν, ὡς
100 οἴεται, προσποίησιν τῆς ἐκ παρθένου γενέσεως αὐτοῦ, φέροντα τοὺς
Ἑλληνικοὺς μύθους περὶ Δανάης καὶ Μελανίππης καὶ Αὔγης καὶ
Ἀντιόπης, λεκτέον ὅτι ταῦτα βωμολόχῳ ἔπρεπε τὰ ῥήματα καὶ οὐ
σπουδάζοντι ἐν τῇ ἀπαγγελίᾳ ... (39) εἰ ἄρα καλὴ ἦν ἡ μήτηρ τοῦ
Ἰησοῦ, καὶ ὡς καλῇ αὐτῇ ἐμίγνυτο ὁ θεός, οὐ πεφυκὼς ἐρᾶν
105 φθαρτοῦ σώματος; ἢ ὅτι οὐδ' εἰκὸς ἦν ἐρασθήσεσθαι αὐτῆς
τὸν θεόν, οὔσης οὔτ' εὐδαίμονος οὔτε βασιλικῆς, ἐπεὶ μηδεὶς
αὐτὴν ᾔδει μηδὲ τῶν γειτόνων· παίζει δὲ λέγων καὶ ὅτι
μισουμένην αὐτὴν ὑπὸ τοῦ τέκτονος καὶ ἐκβαλλομένην οὐκ

73 ἐν τοῖς ἑξῆς Φ Borret   ἑξῆς Α
97 τίκτουσα] κύουσα Pap. mgΑ¹ et Μ¹ Borret   99 εἰσήγαγε Α¹
          ἤγαγε Α

ἔσωσε θεία δύναμις οὐδὲ λόγος πειστικός, οὐδὲν οὖν, φησί,
110 ταῦτα πρὸς τὴν τοῦ θεοῦ βασιλείαν ... (41) ἔστι δ' ὁ Ἰουδαῖος
αὐτῷ ἔτι ταῦτα λέγων, πρὸς ὃν ὁμολογοῦμεν εἶναι κύριον ἡμῶν τὸν
Ἰησοῦν· λουομένῳ, φησί, σοὶ παρὰ τῷ Ἰωάννῃ φάσμα ὄρνιθος
ἐξ ἀέρος λέγεις ἐπιπτῆναι. εἶτα πυνθανόμενος ὁ παρ' αὐτῷ
Ἰουδαῖός φησι· τίς τοῦτο εἶδεν ἀξιόχρεως μάρτυς τὸ φάσμα, ἢ
115 τίς ἤκουσεν ἐξ οὐρανοῦ φωνῆς εἰσποιούσης σε υἱὸν τῷ θεῷ;
πλὴν ὅτι σὺ φῇς καί τινα ἕνα ἐπάγῃ τῶν μετὰ σοῦ
κεκολασμένων ... (49) ἀλλ' εἶπεν ἐμὸς προφήτης ἐν
Ἱεροσολύμοις ποτέ, ὅτι ἥξει θεοῦ υἱός, τῶν ὁσίων κριτὴς καὶ
τῶν ἀδίκων κολαστής ... (50) εἶτα ὡς οὐ μόνου προφητευθέντος
120 τούτου, ὁσίων αὐτὸν εἶναι κριτὴν καὶ τῶν ἀδίκων κολαστήν, ... φησί· τί
μᾶλλον σὺ ἢ ἄλλοι μυρίοι οἱ μετὰ τὴν προφητείαν γενόμενοί
εἰσι, περὶ ὧν ταῦτα ἐπροφητεύετο; καὶ οὐκ οἶδ' ὅπως βουλόμενος
καὶ ἑτέροις περιθεῖναι τὸ δύνασθαι ὑπονοεῖσθαι ὅτι αὐτοὶ ἦσαν οἱ
προφητευθέντες φησὶν ὅτι οἱ μὲν ἐνθουσιῶντες οἱ δὲ ἀγείροντές
125 φασιν ἥκειν ἄνωθεν υἱὸν θεοῦ ... (54) Ἐπεὶ δὲ ὁ ἐπαγγελλόμενος
εἰδέναι τὰ τοῦ λόγου πάντα Κέλσος ὀνειδίζει τῷ σωτῆρι ἐπὶ τῷ πάθει
ὡς μὴ βοηθηθέντι ὑπὸ τοῦ πατρὸς ἢ μὴ δυνηθέντι ἑαυτῷ
βοηθῆσαι, παραθετέον ... (57) Ἔτι δὲ πρὸς τὸν σωτῆρα αὐτῷ ὁ
Ἰουδαῖός φησιν ὅτι, εἰ τοῦτο λέγεις, ὅτι πᾶς ἄνθρωπος κατὰ
130 θείαν πρόνοιαν γεγονὼς υἱός ἐστι θεοῦ, τί ἂν σὺ ἄλλου
διαφέροις; ... τινὲς δὲ καὶ ἐλέγχουσιν, ὥς φησιν ὁ παρὰ Κέλσῳ
Ἰουδαῖος, μυρίοι τὸν Ἰησοῦν φάσκοντες περὶ ἑαυτῶν ταῦτα
εἰρῆσθαι, ἅπερ περὶ ἐκείνου ἐπροφητεύετο ... (40) καὶ μετὰ
ταῦτα ἀνατρέχει ἐπὶ τὸ ἑξῆς τῇ γενέσει τοῦ Ἰησοῦ ἀναγεγραμμένον,
135 τὸ περὶ τοῦ ἀστέρος διήγημα καὶ τῶν ἐληλυθότων ἀπὸ ἀνατολῆς
μάγων προσκυνῆσαι τῷ παιδίῳ ... (34) ὅτι δὲ κακουργῶν ὁ Κέλσος οὐκ
ἐξέθετο τὴν προφητείαν, δῆλόν μοι γίνεται ἐκ τοῦ παραθέμενον αὐτὸν
πολλὰ ἀπὸ τοῦ κατὰ Ματθαῖον εὐαγγελίου, ὥσπερ τὸν ἀνατείλαντα
ἀστέρα ἐπὶ τῇ γενέσει τοῦ Ἰησοῦ καὶ ἄλλα τῶν παραδόξων, μηδὲ
140 τὴν ἀρχὴν τούτου ἐμνημονευκέναι ... (58) Μετὰ ταῦτα ὁ παρὰ τῷ
Κέλσῳ Ἰουδαῖος ἀντὶ τῶν ἐν τῷ εὐαγγελίῳ μάγων Χαλδαίους φησὶν
ὑπὸ τοῦ Ἰησοῦ λελέχθαι κινηθέντας ἐπὶ τῇ γενέσει αὐτοῦ
ἐληλυθέναι, προσκυνήσοντας αὐτὸν ἔτι νήπιον ὡς θεόν· καὶ
Ἡρώδῃ τῷ τετράρχῃ τοῦτο δεδηλωκέναι· τὸν δὲ πέμψαντα
145 ἀποκτεῖναι τοὺς ἐν τῷ αὐτῷ χρόνῳ γεγεννημένους, οἰόμενον

109 πειστικός Ktr Borret   πιστικός Α
125 υἱὸν] υἱοὶ Wifstrand Chadwick   131 διαφέροις Α²P   διαφέρῃς ΑΜ
141 φησὶν] λέγει Pap.

235

καὶ τοῦτον ἀνελεῖν σὺν αὐτοῖς, μή πως τὸν αὐτάρκη
ἐπιβιώσας χρόνον βασιλεύσῃ ... (61) ταῦτα δ' εἰ ἑωράκει ὁ
Κέλσος, οὐκ ἂν ἔλεγεν· εἰ δ' ὅπως μὴ σὺ αὐξηθεὶς ἀντ' ἐκείνου
βασιλεύῃς; τί ἐπειδή γε ηὐξήθης, οὐ βασιλεύεις, ἀλλ' ὁ τοῦ
150 θεοῦ παῖς οὕτως ἀγεννῶς ἀγείρεις κυπτάζων ὑπὸ φόβου καὶ
περιφθειρόμενος ἄνω κάτω; ... (62) Μετὰ ταῦτα δ' ἐπεὶ μηδὲ τὸν
ἀριθμὸν τῶν ἀποστόλων ἐπιστάμενος δέκα εἶπεν ἢ ἕνδεκά τινας
ἐξαρτησάμενον τὸν Ἰησοῦν ἑαυτῷ ἐπιρρήτους ἀνθρώπους,
τελώνας καὶ ναύτας τοὺς πονηροτάτους, μετὰ τούτων τῇδε
155 κἀκεῖσε αὐτὸν ἀποδεδρακέναι, αἰσχρῶς καὶ γλίσχρως τροφὰς
συνάγοντα ... (66) Ἐπὶ δὲ τούτοις ἑξῆς ὁ Ἰουδαῖος πρὸς τὸν
Ἰησοῦν παρὰ τῷ Κέλσῳ λέγει, τί δὲ καί σε νήπιον ἔτι ἐχρῆν
εἰς Αἴγυπτον ἐκκομίζεσθαι, μὴ ἀποσφαγῇς; θεὸν γὰρ οὐκ
εἰκὸς ἦν περὶ θανάτου δεδιέναι. ἀλλ' ἄγγελος μὲν ἧκεν ἐξ
160 οὐρανοῦ, κελεύων σοι καὶ τοῖς σοῖς οἰκείοις φεύγειν, μὴ
ἐγκαταλειφθέντες ἀποθάνητε. φυλάσσειν δέ σε αὐτόθι ὁ δύο
ἤδη διὰ σὲ πεπομφὼς ἀγγέλους, ὁ μέγας θεὸς τὸν ἴδιον υἱόν,
οὐκ ἐδύνατο; ... (67) Μετὰ ταῦτά φησιν ὁ παρὰ τῷ Κέλσῳ Ἰουδαῖος
ὡς φιλομαθής τις Ἕλλην καὶ τὰ Ἑλλήνων πεπαιδευμένος ὅτι οἱ μὲν
165 παλαιοὶ μῦθοι Περσεῖ καὶ Ἀμφίονι καὶ Αἰακῷ καὶ Μίνωϊ
θείαν σπορὰν νείμαντες — οὐδ' αὐτοῖς ἐπιστεύσαμεν —
ὅμως ἐπέδειξαν αὐτῶν ἔργα μεγάλα καὶ θαυμαστὰ ἀληθῶς
τε ὑπὲρ ἄνθρωπον, ἵνα μὴ ἀπίθανοι δοκῶσι· σὺ δὲ δή, τί
καλὸν ἢ θαυμάσιον ἔργῳ ἢ λόγῳ πεποίηκας; ἡμῖν οὐδὲν
170 ἐπεδείξω, καίτοι προκαλουμένων ἐν τῷ ἱερῷ σε παρασχέσθαι
τι ἐναργὲς γνώρισμα, ὡς εἴης ὁ τοῦ θεοῦ παῖς ... (68) Ἑξῆς δὲ
τούτοις ὁ Κέλσος ὑπιδόμενος τὰ ἐπιδειχθησόμενα ὑπὸ τοῦ Ἰησοῦ
γεγενημένα μεγάλα ... προσποιεῖται συγχωρεῖν ἀληθῆ εἶναι ὅσα
περὶ θεραπειῶν ἢ ἀναστάσεως ἢ περὶ ἄρτων ὀλίγων
175 θρεψάντων πολλοὺς ἀναγέγραπται, ἀφ' ὧν λείψανα πολλὰ
καταλέλειπται, ἢ ὅσα ἄλλα οἴεται τερατευσαμένους τοὺς
μαθητὰς ἱστορηκέναι, καὶ ἐπιφέρει αὐτοῖς· φέρε πιστεύσωμεν
εἶναί σοι ταῦτ' εἰργασμένα. καὶ εὐθέως κοινοποιεῖ αὐτὰ πρὸς τὰ
ἔργα τῶν γοήτων, ὡς ὑπισχνουμένων θαυμασιώτερα, καὶ πρὸς
180 τὰ ὑπὸ τῶν μαθόντων ἀπὸ Αἰγυπτίων ἐπιτελούμενα, ἐν
μέσαις ἀγοραῖς ὀλίγων ὀβολῶν ἀποδιδομένων τὰ σεμνὰ
μαθήματα καὶ δαίμονας ἀπὸ ἀνθρώπων ἐξελαυνόντων καὶ

149 βασιλεύσῃς M   158 μὴ] ἵνα μὴ BC   167 αὐτῶν Delarue
      ἑαυτῶν A   176 τερατευομένους V   τερατευσομένους A
      181 ἀποδιδομένων Wendland Borret   ἀποδομένων A

νόσους ἀποφυσώντων καὶ ψυχὰς ἡρώων ἀνακαλούντων
δεῖπνά τε πολυτελῆ καὶ τραπέζας καὶ πέμματα καὶ ὄψα τὰ
185 οὐκ ὄντα δεικνύντων καὶ ὡς ζῷα κινούντων οὐκ ἀληθῶς ὄντα
ζῷα ἀλλὰ μέχρι φαντασίας φαινόμενα τοιαῦτα, καί φησιν· ἆρ᾽
ἐπεὶ ταῦτα ποιοῦσιν ἐκεῖνοι, δεήσει ἡμᾶς αὐτοὺς ἡγεῖσθαι
υἱοὺς εἶναι θεοῦ; ἢ λεκτέον αὐτὰ ἐπιτηδεύματα εἶναι
ἀνθρώπων πονηρῶν καὶ κακοδαιμόνων; ... (69) Μετὰ ταῦτα
190 φύρων τὸν λόγον καὶ τὰ ὑπὸ αἱρέσεώς τινος λεγόμενα ὡς κοινὰ
Χριστιανῶν ἐγκλήματα πᾶσι τοῖς ἀπὸ τοῦ θείου προσάγων λόγου
φησὶν ὅτι θεοῦ οὐκ ἂν εἴη τοιοῦτον σῶμα, οἷον τὸ σόν ... εἶτα ὁ
Κέλσος φησὶν ὅτι οὐκ ἂν εἴη θεοῦ σῶμα τὸ οὕτω σπαρέν, ὡς σύ,
ὦ Ἰησοῦ, ἐσπάρης ... (70) λέγει δ᾽ ὅτι οὐδὲ τοιαῦτα σιτεῖται
195 σῶμα θεοῦ, ὡς ἔχων αὐτὸν παραστῆσαι ἀπὸ τῶν εὐαγγελικῶν
γραμμάτων σιτούμενον, καὶ ποῖα σιτούμενον. ἀλλ᾽ ἔστω, λεγέτω αὐτὸν
βεβρωκέναι μετὰ τῶν μαθητῶν τὸ πάσχα, οὐ μόνον εἰπόντα τὸ
«ἐπιθυμίᾳ ἐπεθύμησα τοῦτο τὸ πάσχα φαγεῖν μεθ᾽ ὑμῶν» ἀλλὰ καὶ
βεβρωκότα, λεγέτω δ᾽ αὐτὸν καὶ διψήσαντα παρὰ τῇ πηγῇ τοῦ Ἰακὼβ
200 πεπωκέναι ... ἀλλ᾽ οὐδὲ σῶμα, φησί, θεοῦ χρῆται τοιαύτῃ φωνῇ
οὐδὲ τοιᾷδε πειθοῖ ... (71) Εἶτά φησι λοιδορούμενος τῷ Ἰησοῦ ὁ διὰ
τὴν ἀσέβειαν καὶ τὰ μοχθηρὰ δόγματα, ἵνα οὕτως εἴπω, θεομισὴς ὅτι
ταῦτα θεομισοῦς ἦν τινος καὶ μοχθηροῦ γόητος ...
(II, 1) ... Φησὶν αὐτοὺς καταλιπόντας τὸν πάτριον νόμον τῷ
205 ἐψυχαγωγῆσθαι ὑπὸ τοῦ Ἰησοῦ ἠπατῆσθαι πάνυ γελοίως καὶ
ἀπηυτομοληκέναι εἰς ἄλλο ὄνομα καὶ εἰς ἄλλον βίον ... ταῦτα δὲ
πάντα εἰ ἠπίστατο ὁ Κέλσος, οὐκ ἂν ἐπροσωποποίησατο τὸν Ἰουδαῖον
λέγοντα πρὸς τοὺς ἀπὸ ἰουδαϊσμοῦ πιστεύοντας τό· τί παθόντες, ὦ
πολῖται, κατελίπετε τὸν πάτριον νόμον καὶ ὑπ᾽ ἐκείνου, πρὸς
210 ὃν ἄρτι διειλέγμεθα, ψυχαγωγηθέντες πάνυ γελοίως
ἐξηπατήθητε καὶ ἀφ᾽ ἡμῶν ἀπηυτομολήσατε εἰς ἄλλο ὄνομα
καὶ εἰς ἄλλον βίον; ... (4) Εἶτα λέγει ὁ παρ᾽ αὐτῷ Ἰουδαῖος πρὸς
τοὺς ἀπὸ τοῦ λαοῦ πιστεύσαντας ὅτι χθὲς καὶ πρώην καὶ ὁπηνίκα
τοῦτον ἐκολάζομεν βουκολοῦντα ὑμᾶς, ἀπέστητε τοῦ πατρίου
215 νόμου ... μετὰ δὲ ταῦτα δοκεῖ μοι δεινότητος ἔχεσθαι τὸ ἢ πῶς
ἄρχεσθε μὲν ἀπὸ τῶν ἡμετέρων ἱερῶν, προϊόντες δὲ αὐτὰ
ἀτιμάζετε, οὐκ ἔχοντες ἄλλην ἀρχὴν εἰπεῖν τοῦ δόγματος ἢ
τὸν ἡμέτερον νόμον; ... τί οὖν καθ᾽ ἡμῶν λέγεται ὑπὸ τοῦ παρὰ τῷ
Κέλσῳ Ἰουδαίου ἐν τῷ· εἴτε γὰρ προηγόρευσέ τις ὑμῖν ὅτι ἄρα ὁ
220 τοῦ θεοῦ παῖς εἰς ἀνθρώπους ἀφίξεται, οὗτος ἡμέτερος ἦν ὁ
προφήτης καὶ τοῦ ἡμετέρου θεοῦ· ... (5) Μετὰ ταῦτα εἰ καὶ

207 ἐπροσωποποίησεν Pap. A¹   209 κατελίπετε] κατελίπατε Pap.

ταυτολογεῖ ὁ Κέλσος περὶ τοῦ Ἰησοῦ, δεύτερον ἤδη λέγων
πλημμελήσαντα αὐτὸν δεδωκέναι παρὰ Ἰουδαίοις δίκην,
ἀλλ᾽ ἡμεῖς οὐκ ἐπαναληψόμεθα τὴν ἀπολογίαν ... ἐπεὶ ὡς ἔωλα τὰ
225 περὶ ἀναστάσεως νεκρῶν καὶ κρίσεως θεοῦ καὶ τιμῆς μὲν ἐπὶ
τοὺς δικαίους πυρὸς δ᾽ ἐπὶ τοὺς ἀδίκους εὐτελίζει ὁ παρ᾽ αὐτῷ
Ἰουδαῖος, μηδὲν δὲ καινὸν ἐν τούτοις διδάσκεσθαι φάσκων
Χριστιανοὺς οἴεται ἀνατρέπειν χριστιανισμόν · λεκτέον ... (6) Ἔστω
δὲ καὶ πάντα τὰ κατὰ Ἰουδαίους ἔθη μέχρι καὶ τῶν παρ᾽
230 αὐτοῖς θυσιῶν πεποιηκέναι τὸν Ἰησοῦν· τί τοῦτο συμβάλλεται
πρὸς τὸ μὴ δεῖν πιστεύειν αὐτῷ ὡς υἱῷ τοῦ θεοῦ; ... (7)
Δεικνύτωσαν δέ, ποῦ κἂν ἔμφασις λέξεως ἀπὸ ἀλαζονείας
προφερομένης παρὰ τῷ Ἰησοῦ εὑρίσκεται ... ἐλεγχέτω δέ τις, τίνα
ἐψεύσατο, καὶ παραστησάτω μεγάλα καὶ μικρὰ ψεύδη, ἵνα δείξῃ τὰ
235 μεγάλα ψευσάμενον τὸν Ἰησοῦν ... τίνα δὲ καὶ τὰ ἀνόσια τοῦ
Ἰησοῦ, ἀπαγγελλέτω καὶ μάλιστα ὁ παρὰ τῷ Κέλσῳ Ἰουδαῖος ... (8)
Φησὶ δὲ πολλοὺς ἂν καὶ ἄλλους φανῆναι τοιούτους τοῖς
ἐξαπατᾶσθαι θέλουσιν, ὁποῖος ἦν ὁ Ἰησοῦς ... φησὶ δὲ τοῦτο
ἔγκλημα ἀπὸ τῶν εἰς τὸν Χριστὸν πιστευόντων προσάγεσθαι
240 Ἰουδαίοις, ἐπεὶ μὴ πεπιστεύκασιν ὡς εἰς θεὸν τὸν Ἰησοῦν ...
πῶς δέ, φησίν, ἡμεῖς οἱ πᾶσιν ἀνθρώποις δηλώσαντες ἥξειν
ἀπὸ θεοῦ τὸν κολάσοντα τοὺς ἀδίκους ἐλθόντα ἠτιμάζομεν;
... διὰ τί ἠτιμάζομεν ὃν προεκηρύσσομεν; ἢ ἵνα πλέον τῶν
ἄλλων κολασθῶμεν; ... (9) Μετὰ ταῦτά φησιν ὁ Ἰουδαῖος· πῶς δ᾽
245 ἐμέλλομεν τοῦτον νομίζειν θεόν, ὃς τά τε ἄλλα, ὥσπερ
ἐπηκούετο, οὐδὲν ὧν ἐπηγγέλλετο ἐπεδείκνυτο, καὶ ἐπειδὴ
ἡμεῖς ἐλέγξαντες αὐτὸν καὶ καταγνόντες ἠξιοῦμεν
κολάζεσθαι, κρυπτόμενος μὲν καὶ διαδιδράσκων
ἐπονειδιστότατα ἑάλω, ὑπ᾽ αὐτῶν δὲ ὧν ὠνόμαζε μαθητῶν
250 προὐδόθη; καίτοι θεόν, φησίν, ὄντα οὔτε φεύγειν ἐνῆν οὔτε
δεθέντα ἀπάγεσθαι, ἥκιστα δὲ ὑπὸ τῶν συνόντων αὐτῷ καὶ
παντὸς ἰδίᾳ κεκοινωνηκότων καὶ διδασκάλῳ χρωμένων
σωτῆρα νομιζόμενον καὶ θεοῦ τοῦ μεγίστου παῖδα καὶ
ἄγγελον ἐγκαταλείπεσθαί τε καὶ ἐκδίδοσθαι ... (12)
255 Παιδαριώδη δέ μοι δοκεῖ καὶ τὰ τοιαῦτα, ὅτι στρατηγὸς μὲν ἀγαθὸς
καὶ πολλῶν μυριάδων ἡγησάμενος οὐδεπώποτε προὐδόθη,
ἀλλ᾽ οὐδὲ λήσταρχος πονηρὸς καὶ παμπονήρων ἄρχων,
ὠφέλιμος τοῖς συνοῦσιν εἶναι δοκῶν· αὐτὸς δὲ προδοθεὶς ὑπὸ
τῶν ὑπ᾽ αὐτῷ οὔτε ὡς στρατηγὸς ἦρξεν ἀγαθός, οὔτ᾽ ἀπατήσας

222 Ἰησοῦ edd.   ἰω̅ (= Ἰωάννου A) codd.   229 ἰουδαίων AV
253 καὶ σωτῆρα M

260 τοὺς μαθητὰς κἂν τὴν ὡς πρὸς λήσταρχον, ἵν' οὕτως ὀνομάσω,
εὔνοιαν ἐνεποίησε τοῖς ἀπατηθεῖσι ... *(13)* Μετὰ ταῦτά φησιν ὁ
παρὰ τῷ Κέλσῳ Ἰουδαῖος ὅτι πολλὰ ἔχων λέγειν περὶ τῶν κατὰ
τὸν Ἰησοῦν γενομένων καὶ ἀληθῆ καὶ οὐ παραπλήσια τοῖς
ὑπὸ τῶν μαθητῶν τοῦ Ἰησοῦ γραφεῖσιν ἑκὼν ἐκεῖνα
265 παραλείπω ... ἐγκαλεῖ δὲ τοῖς μαθηταῖς ὡς πλασαμένοις ὅτι
πάντα τὰ συμβάντα αὐτῷ ἐκεῖνος προῄδει καὶ προειρήκει ...
(15) Φησὶ δὲ ὁ Κέλσος ὅτι καὶ οἱ μαθηταὶ τοῦ Ἰησοῦ ἐπὶ
πράγματι περιφανεῖ μηδὲν ἔχοντες ἐπισκήψασθαι τοῦτο
ἐπενόησαν, τὸ λέγειν αὐτὸν πάντα προεγνωκέναι ... *(16)* Πάνυ
270 δ' εὐήθως φησὶ τοὺς μαθητὰς πρὸς παραίτησιν τῶν κατὰ τὸν
Ἰησοῦν ἀναγεγραφέναι περὶ αὐτοῦ τοιαῦτα· ὥσπερ, φησίν, εἴ
τις λέγων εἶναί τινα δίκαιον δεικνύει αὐτὸν ἀδικοῦντα, καὶ
λέγων ὅσιον δεικνύει φονεύοντα, καὶ λέγων ἀθάνατον
δεικνύει νεκρόν, πᾶσι τούτοις ἐπιφέρων ὅτι προειρηκὼς αὐτὰ
275 ἔτυχεν ... οὐ γὰρ ἐγνωκὼς εἶπε τό· οὐδὲ γὰρ τοῦτο εἴπατε ὅτι
ἐδόκει μὲν τοῖς ἀσεβέσι ἀνθρώποις ταῦτα πάσχειν οὐκ
ἔπασχε δέ, ἀλλ' ἄντικρυς παθεῖν ὁμολογεῖτε ... πόθεν οὖν
πιστὸν τὸ προειρηκέναι ... πόθεν ἀθάνατος ὁ νεκρός; ... *(17)*
τίς ἂν ἢ θεὸς ἢ δαίμων ἢ ἄνθρωπος φρόνιμος προειδὼς αὐτῷ
280 τοιαῦτα συμβησόμενα οὐκ ἄν, εἴ γε ἐδύνατο, ἐξέκλινεν ἀλλὰ
συνέπιπτεν οἷς προηπίστατο; ... *(18)* Ἑξῆς δὲ τούτῳ καὶ ἄλλο
εὔηθές φησιν ὁ παρὰ τῷ Κέλσῳ Ἰουδαῖος, ὅτι πῶς, εἴπερ προεῖπε
καὶ τὸν προδώσοντα καὶ τὸν ἀρνησόμενον, οὐκ ἂν ὡς θεὸν
ἐφοβήθησαν, ὡς τὸν μὲν μὴ προδοῦναι ἔτι τὸν δὲ μὴ
285 ἀρνήσασθαι; ... ἀλλ' αὐτοὶ προέδωκάν τε καὶ ἠρνήσαντο
μηδὲν αὐτοῦ φροντίσαντες ... *(19)* ἤδη γάρ που καὶ ἄνθρωπος
ἐπιβουλευόμενός τε καὶ προαισθόμενος ἐὰν προείπῃ τοῖς
ἐπιβουλεύουσιν, ἀποτρέπονται καὶ φυλάσσονται ... ἑξῆς
ὥσπερεὶ τὸ συμπέρασμα ἐπάγων τῷ λόγῳ φησίν· οὔκουν ἐπειδὴ
290 προείρητο ταῦτα, γέγονεν, ἀδύνατον γάρ· ἀλλ' ἐπειδὴ γέγονε,
ψεῦδος ἐλέγχεται τὸ προειρηκέναι· πάντῃ γὰρ ἀμήχανον
τοὺς προακούσαντας ἔτι προδοῦναι καὶ ἀρνήσασθαι ... *(20)*
ταῦτα θεός, φησίν, ὢν προεῖπε, καὶ πάντως ἐχρῆν γενέσθαι τὸ
προειρημένον. θεὸς οὖν τοὺς αὐτοῦ μαθητὰς καὶ προφήτας,
295 μεθ' ὧν συνεδείπνει καὶ συνέπινεν, εἰς τοῦτο περιήγαγεν,
ὥστε ἀσεβεῖς καὶ ἀνοσίους γενέσθαι, ὃν ἐχρῆν μάλιστα
πάντας ἀνθρώπους εὐεργετεῖν, διαφερόντως δὲ τοὺς ἑαυτοῦ

283 ἀρνησόμενον Pap. A² P   ἀρνησάμενον A   288 ἑξῆς δὲ M²
294 αὐτοῦ Bouhéreau Delarue   αὑτοῦ A

συνεστίους. ἢ ἀνθρώπῳ μὲν ὁ κοινωνήσας τραπέζης οὐκ ἄν
ἔτι ἐπεβούλευσε, θεῷ δὲ ⟨ὁ⟩ συνευωχηθεὶς ἐπίβουλος
300 ἐγίνετο; καὶ ὅπερ ἔτι ἀτοπώτερον, αὐτὸς ὁ θεὸς τοῖς
συντραπέζοις ἐπεβούλευσε, προδότας καὶ δυσσεβεῖς ποιῶν
... (23) Μετὰ ταῦτα λέγει ὅτι, εἰ δέδοκτο αὐτῷ ταῦτα, καὶ τῷ
πατρὶ πειθόμενος ἐκολάζετο, δῆλον ὅτι θεῷ γε ὄντι καὶ
βουλομένῳ οὔτ' ἀλγεινὰ οὔτ' ἀνιαρὰ ἦν τὰ κατὰ γνώμην
305 δρώμενα ... (24) Ἑξῆς δὲ τούτοις θέλων παραστῆσαι ὅτι ἀλγεινὰ καὶ
ἀνιαρὰ ἦν τὰ συμβάντα αὐτῷ καὶ ὅτι οὐχ οἷόν τε ἦν βουληθέντα αὐτὸν
ποιῆσαι εἶναι αὐτὰ μὴ τοιαῦτα λέγει· τί οὖν ποτνιᾶται καὶ
ὀδύρεται καὶ τὸν τοῦ ὀλέθρου φόβον εὔχεται παραδραμεῖν,
λέγων ὧδέ πως· «ὦ πάτερ, εἰ δύναται τὸ ποτήριον τοῦτο
310 παρελθεῖν;» ... (26) Ἔτι δὲ λέγει ὁ παρὰ τῷ Κέλσῳ Ἰουδαῖος πρὸς
τοὺς Ἰησοῦ μαθητὰς ὡς πλασαμένους ταῦτα, ὅτι οὐδὲ ψευδόμενοι
τὰ πλάσματα ὑμῶν πιθανῶς ἐπικαλύψαι ἠδυνήθητε ... (27)
Μετὰ ταῦτά τινας τῶν πιστευόντων φησὶν ὡς ἐκ μέθης ἥκοντας
εἰς τὸ ἐφεστάναι αὑτοῖς μεταχαράττειν ἐκ τῆς πρώτης
315 γραφῆς τὸ εὐαγγέλιον τριχῇ καὶ τετραχῇ καὶ πολλαχῇ καὶ
μεταπλάττειν, ἵν' ἔχοιεν πρὸς τοὺς ἐλέγχους ἀρνεῖσθαι ...
(28) Ἐπεὶ δὲ μετὰ ταῦτα καὶ τὸ προφήταις χρῆσθαι Χριστιανοὺς
προκηρύξασι τὰ περὶ Ἰησοῦ ὀνειδίζει ὁ παρὰ τῷ Κέλσῳ Ἰουδαῖος,
φήσομεν πρὸς τοῖς ἀνωτέρω εἰς τοῦτο λελεγμένοις καὶ ὅτι ἐχρῆν αὐτόν,
320 ὥς φησι, φειδόμενον ἀνθρώπων, αὐτὰς ἐκθέσθαι τὰς προφητείας καὶ
συναγορεύσαντα ταῖς πιθανότησιν αὐτῶν τὴν φαινομένην αὐτῷ
ἀνατροπὴν τῆς χρήσεως τῶν προφητικῶν ἐκθέσθαι. οὕτω γὰρ ἂν ἔδοξε
μὴ συναρπάζειν τηλικοῦτον κεφάλαιον διὰ λεξειδίων ὀλίγων, καὶ
μάλιστα ἐπεί φησι μυρίοις ἄλλοις ἐφαρμοσθῆναι δύνασθαι
325 πολὺ πιθανώτερον τὰ προφητικὰ ἢ τῷ Ἰησοῦ ... (29) διόπερ
οὐκέτι χρεία ἡμᾶς ἀπολογήσασθαι πρὸς τὸ λεγόμενον ὡς ὑπὸ τοῦ
Ἰουδαίου, ὅτι μέγαν καὶ δυνάστην καὶ πάσης τῆς γῆς καὶ
πάντων τῶν ἐθνῶν καὶ στρατοπέδων κύριόν φασιν οἱ
προφῆται εἶναι τὸν ἐπιδημήσοντα. Ἰουδαϊκῶς δ' οἶμαι εἶπε καὶ
330 κατὰ τὴν ἐκείνων χολὴν μετὰ τοῦ χωρὶς ἀποδείξεως κἂν πιθανῆς
λοιδορεῖν τὸν Ἰησοῦν, ὅτι οὐχὶ ⟨δὲ⟩ τοιοῦτον ὄλεθρον
κατήγγειλαν ... (30) Παρέρριψε δ' ὁ Κέλσος καὶ τό· θεὸν δὲ καὶ

298 ἀνθρώπῳ A[1]   ἀνθρώπων A   299 ἐπιβουλεύσειε Ktr / ⟨ὁ⟩ Ktr
305 δρώμενα A[3] Koetschau   χρώμενα Pap. A   γινόμενα Velser
314 αὐτοῖς Bouhéreau Delarue   αὑτοῖς A   321 αὐτῷ A[3] Bouhéreau
αὐτῶν A   328 φασιν A[1]   φησιν A
330 πιθανῆς Bouhéreau   πιθανῶς A   331 ⟨δὲ⟩ Bouhéreau

θεοῦ υἱὸν οὐδεὶς ἐκ τοιούτων συμβόλων καὶ παρακουσμάτων
οὐδ' ἐξ οὕτως ἀγεννῶν τεκμηρίων συνίστησιν ... ὡς γὰρ ὁ
335 ἥλιος, φησί, πάντα τὰ ἄλλα φωτίζων πρῶτον αὐτὸν δεικνύει,
οὕτως ἐχρῆν πεποιηκέναι τὸν υἱὸν τοῦ θεοῦ ... (31) Μετὰ ταῦτα
Χριστιανοῖς ἐγκαλεῖ ὡς σοφιζομένοις ἐν τῷ λέγειν τὸν υἱὸν τοῦ
θεοῦ εἶναι αὐτολόγον, καὶ οἴεταί γε κρατύνειν τὸ ἔγκλημα, ἐπεὶ
λόγον ἐπαγγελλόμενοι υἱὸν εἶναι τοῦ θεοῦ ἀποδείκνυμεν οὐ
340 λόγον καθαρὸν καὶ ἅγιον ἀλλὰ ἄνθρωπον ἀτιμότατα
ἀπαχθέντα καὶ ἀποτυμπανισθέντα ... καὶ τοῦτο περιάπτων τῷ
τοῦ Ἰουδαίου προσώπῳ λέγοντος· ὡς εἴ γε ὁ λόγος ἐστὶν ὑμῖν υἱὸς τοῦ
θεοῦ, καὶ ἡμεῖς ἐπαινοῦμεν ... (32) Προείρηται δ' ἡμῖν ὅτι οὔτ' ἀλαζὼν
οὔτε γόης δύναται εἶναι ὁ Ἰησοῦς· διὸ οὐκ ἀναγκαῖον ἐπανα-
345 λαμβάνειν τὰ εἰρημένα, ἵνα μὴ πρὸς τὰς ταυτολογίας Κέλσου
καὶ ἡμεῖς ταυτολογῶμεν ... Φησὶ δὲ ἀπηυθαδῆσθαι τοὺς
γενεαλογήσαντας ἀπὸ τοῦ πρώτου φύντος καὶ τῶν ἐν
Ἰουδαίοις βασιλέων τὸν Ἰησοῦν. καὶ οἴεταί τι εἰσφέρειν γενναῖον,
ὅτι οὐκ ἂν ἡ τοῦ τέκτονος γυνὴ τηλικούτου γένους
350 τυγχάνουσα ἠγνόει ... (33) Τί δέ, φησί, καὶ γενναῖον ἔδρασεν
οἷον θεός, καταφρονῶν ἀνθρώπων καὶ διαγελῶν καὶ παίζων
τὸ συμβαῖνον ὁ Ἰησοῦς; ... (34) Παίζων δ', ὡς οἴεται, τὸν Ἰησοῦν ὁ
παρὰ τῷ Κέλσῳ Ἰουδαῖος εἰδέναι ἀναγέγραπται τὸν Εὐριπίδου
Βάκχον λέγοντα ⟨Bacchae, 498⟩ «Λύσει μ' ὁ δαίμων αὐτός, ὅταν ἐγὼ
355 θέλω»
... ἀλλ' οὐδ' ὁ καταδικάσας, φησίν, αὐτὸν ἔπαθέ τι, οἷον ὁ
Πενθεὺς μανεὶς ἢ σπαραχθείς ... πάλιν τε αὖ σιωπῶν τὰ
ἐμφαίνοντα τὴν τοῦ Ἰησοῦ θειότητα ὁ Κέλσος ὀνειδίζει ἐκ τῶν
γεγραμμένων ἐν τῷ εὐαγγελίῳ περὶ Ἰησοῦ, παρατιθέμενος τοὺς
360 ἐμπαίξαντας αὐτῷ καὶ φοινικίδα περιθέντας καὶ τὸν ἐξ
ἀκανθῶν στέφανον καὶ τὸν ἐν τῇ χειρὶ κάλαμον ... (35) Πρὸς δὲ
τό· τί οὐκ εἰ μὴ πρόσθεν ἀλλὰ νῦν γοῦν θεῖόν τι ἐπιδείκνυται
καὶ τῆς αἰσχύνης ταύτης ἑαυτὸν ῥύεται καὶ τοὺς ὑβρίζοντας
εἰς ἑαυτόν τε καὶ τὸν πατέρα δικαιοῖ;
365 ... (36) Εἶτά φησιν ὁ Κέλσος· τί φησι καὶ
ἀνασκολοπιζομένου. τοῦ σώματος; ποῖος ⟨Ilias, V, 340⟩
«ἰχώρ, οἷός πέρ τε ῥέει μακάρεσσι θεοῖσιν;» ... (37) Μετὰ
ταῦθ' ὁ ⟨Ἰουδαῖος⟩ ἀπὸ τοῦ εὐαγγελίου ἐκλαβὼν λέξεις, ὧν
κατηγορεῖν νομίζει, τὸ ὄξος καὶ τὴν χολὴν ὀνειδίζει τῷ Ἰησοῦ
370 ὡς χανδὸν ἐπὶ τὸ πιεῖν ὡρμημένῳ καὶ μὴ

333 θεοῦ A²   τὸ θεοῦ A   τοῦ θεοῦ Delarue   334 ὡς A²   om A
335 αὐτὸν edd.   αὐτὸν A   368 ⟨Ἰουδαῖος⟩ Ktr Bader Chadwick

241

διακαρτερήσαντι τὴν δίψαν, ὡς καὶ ὁ τυχὼν ἄνθρωπος
πολλάκις διακαρτερεῖ ... (38) Μετὰ ταῦτά φησιν ἔτι πρὸς
ἡμᾶς ὁ Ἰουδαῖος· ταῦτα οὖν ἡμῖν ἐγκαλεῖτε, ὦ
πιστότατοι, διότι τοῦτον οὐ νομίζομεν θεὸν οὐδὲ
375 συντιθέμεθα ὑμῖν ὅτι ἐπ᾽ ἀνθρώπων ὠφελείᾳ ταῦτα
ὑπέμεινεν, ἵνα καὶ ἡμεῖς κολάσεων καταφρονῶμεν ...
(39) πῶς δ᾽ οὐκ ἄντικρυς ψεῦδος τὸ ὑπὸ παρὰ τῷ Κέλσῳ
Ἰουδαίου λεγόμενον, ὅτι μηδένα πείσας μέχρι ἔζη ὅ γε
μηδὲ τοὺς ἑαυτοῦ μαθητὰς ἐκολάσθη καὶ τοιαῦτα
380 ὑπέμεινε; ... (41) Ἔτι δ᾽ ἐγκαλεῖ τῷ Ἰησοῦ ὁ Κέλσος διὰ τοῦ
ἰουδαϊκοῦ προσώπου, ὡς μὴ δείξαντι ἑαυτὸν πάντων δὴ
κακῶν καθαρεύοντα ... (42) Ἔτι δ᾽ ἐπεὶ βούλεται μηδὲ
ἀνεπίληπτον γεγονέναι τὸν Ἰησοῦν ὁ Κέλσος,
παραστησάτω, τίς τῶν ἀρεσκομένων τῷ λόγῳ αὐτοῦ τὸ ἀληθῶς
385 ἐπίληπτον τοῦ Ἰησοῦ ἀνέγραψεν ... οὐκ οἶδα δ᾽ ἀπὸ ποίων
μειζόνων καὶ ἐναργεστέρων ἐβούλετο αὐτὸν πιστὰ ποιῆσαι τὰ
προειρημένα ὁ Κέλσος· εἰ μὴ ἄρα, ὡς φαίνεται, μὴ
ἐπιστάμενος τὸν λόγον τὸν Ἰησοῦν ἄνθρωπον γενόμενον
ἐβούλετο μηδὲν ἀνθρώπινον παθεῖν μηδὲ γενέσθαι ἀνθρώποις
390 παράδειγμα γενναῖον περὶ τοῦ φέρειν τὰ συμβαίνοντα ... (43)
Μετὰ δὲ ταῦτα λέγει πρὸς ἡμᾶς ὅτι οὐ δή που φήσετε περὶ
αὐτοῦ ὅτι μὴ πείσας τοὺς ὧδε ὄντας ἐστέλλετο εἰς ᾅδου
πείσων τοὺς ἐκεῖ ... (44) Ἑξῆς δὲ τούτοις οὐκ οἶδ᾽ ὅπως
σφόδρα εὔηθες λέγει ὅτι, εἴπερ ἀτόπους ἀπολογίας
395 εὑρίσκοντες, ἐφ᾽ αἷς καταγελάστως ἐξηπατήθητε,
οἴεσθε ἀληθῶς ἀπολογεῖσθαι, τί κωλύει καὶ ἄλλους,
ὅσοι καταγνωσθέντες κακοδαιμονέστερον ἀπήλλαξαν,
μείζονας νομίζειν εἶναι καὶ θειοτέρους τούτου
ἀγγέλους; ... ἐπεὶ δὲ καὶ λῃσταῖς αὐτὸν παραβαλὼν ὁ παρὰ
400 τῷ Κέλσῳ Ἰουδαῖός φησιν ὅτι δύναιτο ἄν τις ὁμοίως
ἀναισχυντῶν καὶ περὶ λῃστοῦ καὶ ἀνδροφόνου
κολασθέντος εἰπεῖν ὅτι οὗτός γε οὐχὶ λῃστὴς ἀλλὰ
θεὸς ἦν· προεῖπε γὰρ τοῖς συλλῃσταις ὅτι πείσεται
τοιαῦτα, οἷα δὴ πέπονθε ... (45) Εἶτα οἱ μὲν τότε ζῶντι
405 αὐτῷ συνόντες καὶ τῆς φωνῆς ἐπακούοντες αὐτοῦ καὶ
διδασκάλῳ χρώμενοι κολαζόμενον καὶ ἀποθνῄσκοντα
ὁρῶντες, οὔτε συναπέθανον οὔτε ὑπεραπέθανον αὐτοῦ
οὐδὲ κολάσεων καταφρονεῖν ἐπείσθησαν, ἀλλὰ καὶ

383 ἀνεπίληπτον A¹   ἀνεπιβούλευτον A   385 δ᾽ ἀπὸ ποίων A¹
     ποῖον A   395 αἷς] οἷς Bouhéreau Borret

242

ἠρνήσαντο εἶναι μαθηταί· νῦν δὲ ὑμεῖς αὐτῷ
410 συναποθνήσκετε ... (46) Πῶς δ' οὐ ψεύδεται ὁ λέγων παρὰ
τῷ Κέλσῳ Ἰουδαῖος ὅτι παρὼν δέκα ναύτας καὶ τελώνας
τοὺς ἐξωλεστάτους μόνους εἷλε καὶ οὐδὲ τούτους
ἅπαντας; ... καὶ ἐν τῷ προκειμένῳ τοίνυν λόγῳ καθ' ἣν
ἔχομεν τάξιν τῆς γραφῆς φησιν· εἰ ζῶν μὲν αὐτὸς μηδένα
415 ἔπεισεν, ἀποθανόντος δ' αὐτοῦ πείθουσιν οἱ
βουλόμενοι τοσούτους, πῶς τοῦτο οὐχ ὑπεράτοπόν ἐστι;
... (47) Ἑαυτῷ δὲ λαμβάνει ὡς ἡμετέραν ἀπόκρισιν πρὸς
πεῦσιν αὐτοῦ λεγομένην φήσαντος· τίνι προσήχθητε
λογισμῷ τοῦτον νομίζειν υἱὸν θεοῦ; πεποίηκε γὰρ ἡμᾶς
420 ἀποκρινομένους ὅτι τούτῳ προσήχθημεν, ἐπεὶ ἴσμεν τὴν
κόλασιν αὐτοῦ ὑπὲρ καθαιρέσεως τοῦ πατρὸς τῆς
κακίας γεγονυῖαν ... καὶ ὡς ἡμῶν γε λεγόντων ὅτι υἱὸν
αὐτὸν νομίζομεν θεοῦ, ἐπεὶ ἐκολάσθη, φησί· τί οὖν;
οὐχὶ καὶ ἄλλοι πολλοὶ ἐκολάσθησαν, καὶ οὐχ ἧττον ἀγεννῶς;
425 ... (48) Πολλάκις δ' ὁ Κέλσος ἤδη μὴ δυνάμενος ἀντιβλέπειν
αἷς ἀναγέγραπται πεποιηκέναι δυνάμεσιν ὁ Ἰησοῦς διαβάλλει
αὐτὰς ὡς γοητείας· καὶ πολλάκις τῷ λόγῳ κατὰ τὸ δυνατὸν ἡμῖν
ἀντείπομεν. καὶ νῦν δέ φησιν οἱονεὶ ἡμᾶς ἀποκρίνασθαι ὅτι
διὰ τοῦτ' ἐνομίσαμεν αὐτὸν εἶναι υἱὸν θεοῦ, ἐπεὶ
430 χωλοὺς καὶ τυφλοὺς ἐθεράπευσε. προστίθησι δὲ καὶ τό·
ὥς ὑμεῖς φατε, ἀνέστη νεκρούς ... (49) Ὁ δὲ Κέλσος
κοινοποιῆσαι βουλόμενος τὰ τεράστια τοῦ Ἰησοῦ πρὸς τὴν ἐν
ἀνθρώποις γοητείαν φησὶν αὐταῖς λέξεσιν· ὦ φῶς καὶ
ἀλήθεια, τῇ αὐτοῦ φωνῇ διαρρήδην ἐξαγορεύει, καθὰ
435 καὶ ὑμεῖς συγγεγράφατε, διότι παρέσονται ὑμῖν καὶ
ἕτεροι δυνάμεσιν ὁμοίαις χρώμενοι, κακοὶ καὶ γόητες,
καὶ Σατανᾶν τινα τοιαῦτα παραμηχανώμενον
ὀνομάζει· ὥστ' οὐδὲ αὐτὸς ἔξαρνός ἐστιν, ὡς ταῦτά γε
οὐδὲν θεῖον ἀλλὰ πονηρῶν ἐστιν ἔργα. βιαζόμενος δὲ
440 ὑπὸ τῆς ἀληθείας ὁμοῦ καὶ τὰ τῶν ἄλλων ἀπεκάλυψε
καὶ τὰ καθ' αὐτὸν ἤλεγξε. πῶς οὖν οὐ σχέτλιον ἀπὸ τῶν
αὐτῶν ἔργων τὸν μὲν θεὸν τοὺς δὲ γόητας ἡγεῖσθαι; τί
γὰρ μᾶλλον ἀπό γε τούτων τοὺς ἄλλους πονηροὺς ἢ
τοῦτον νομιστέον αὐτῷ χρωμένους μάρτυρι; ταῦτα μέν
445 γε καὶ αὐτὸς ὡμολόγησεν οὐχὶ θείας φύσεως ἀλλ'

420 ἐπεὶ Bouhéreau Bader Borret   εἰ καὶ A   ἐπεὶ καὶ Koetschau
431 καὶ νεκρούς Glöckner Bader   437 τινα τοιαῦτα Bouhéreau Koetschau
    τοιαῦτά τινα A

ἀπατεώνων τινῶν καὶ παμπονήρων εἶναι γνωρίσματα
... (54) Μετὰ ταῦτά φησι πρὸς ἡμᾶς δῆθεν — ἵνα τηρήσω τὸ
ἀπ' ἀρχῆς τῷ Ἰουδαίῳ προτεθέν — ὁ τοῦ Κέλσου Ἰουδαῖος ἐν
τῷ πρὸς τοὺς πολίτας ἑαυτοῦ λόγῳ πιστεύσαντας· τίνι οὖν
450 προσήχθητε ἢ διότι προεῖπεν, ὡς ἀποθανὼν
ἀναστήσεται ... (55) Μετὰ ταῦτά φησιν ὁ Ἰουδαῖος πρὸς τοὺς
ἑαυτοῦ πολίτας τῷ Ἰησοῦ πιστεύοντας· Φέρε δὴ καὶ
πιστεύωμεν ὑμῖν τοῦτ' εἰρῆσθαι. πόσοι δ' ἄλλοι
τοιαῦτα τερατεύονται, πειθοῦς ἕνεκα τῶν εὐήθως
455 ἀκουόντων ἐνεργολαβοῦντες τῇ πλάνῃ; ὅπερ οὖν καὶ
Ζάμολξιν ἐν Σκύθαις φασί, τὸν Πυθαγόρου δοῦλον, καὶ
αὐτὸν Πυθαγόραν ἐν Ἰταλίᾳ καὶ Ῥαμψίνιτον ἐν
Αἰγύπτῳ· τοῦτον μὲν καὶ «συγκυβεύειν» ἐν ᾅδου «τῇ
Δήμητρι» καὶ ἀνελεῖν «δῶρον» «παρ' αὐτῆς
460 χειρόμακτρον χρυσοῦν» φέροντα· καὶ μὴν καὶ Ὀρφέα
ἐν Ὀδρύσαις καὶ Πρωτεσίλαον ἐν Θεσσαλίᾳ καὶ
Ἡρακλέα ἐπὶ Ταινάρῳ καὶ Θησέα. ἀλλ' ἐκεῖνο
σκεπτέον εἴ τις ὡς ἀληθῶς ἀποθανὼν ἀνέστη ποτὲ
αὐτῷ σώματι· ἢ οἴεσθε τὰ μὲν τῶν ἄλλων μύθους εἶναί
465 τε καὶ δοκεῖν, ὑμῖν δὲ τὴν καταστροφὴν τοῦ δράματος
εὐσχημόνως ἢ πιθανῶς ἐφευρῆσθαι, τὴν ἐπὶ τοῦ
σκόλοπος αὐτοῦ φωνήν, ὅτ' ἀπέπνει, καὶ «τὸν σεισμὸν»
καὶ τὸν σκότον; ὅτι δὴ ζῶν μὲν οὐκ ἐπήρκεσεν ἑαυτῷ,
νεκρὸς δ' ἀνέστη καὶ τὰ σημεῖα τῆς κολάσεως ἔδειξε
470 καὶ τὰς χεῖρας ὡς ἦσαν πεπερονημέναι, τίς τοῦτο εἶδε;
γυνὴ πάροιστρος, ὥς φατε, καὶ εἴ τις ἄλλος τῶν ἐκ τῆς
αὐτῆς γοητείας, ἤτοι κατά τινα διάθεσιν ὀνειρώξας καὶ
κατὰ τὴν αὐτοῦ βούλησιν δόξῃ πεπλανημένῃ
φαντασιωθείς, ὅπερ ἤδη μυρίοις συμβέβηκεν, ἤ, ὅπερ
475 μᾶλλον, ἐκπλῆξαι τοὺς λοιποὺς τῇ τερατείᾳ ταύτῃ
θελήσας καὶ διὰ τοῦ τοιούτου ψεύσματος ἀφορμὴν
ἄλλοις ἀγύρταις παρασχεῖν ... (61) Ἦν οὖν καὶ ὁ Ἰησοῦς
μετὰ θάνατον, ὡς μὲν ὁ Κέλσος οἴεται, φαντασίαν
ἐξαποστέλλων τῶν ἐπὶ τῷ σταυρῷ τραυμάτων καὶ οὐκ ἀληθῶς
480 τοιοῦτος ὢν τραυματίας ... (63) Μετὰ ταῦτα ὁ Κέλσος οὐκ
εὐκαταφρονήτως τὰ γεγραμμένα κακολογῶν φησιν ὅτι ἐχρῆν,
εἴπερ ὄντως θείαν δύναμιν ἐκφῆναι ἤθελεν ὁ Ἰησοῦς,
αὐτοῖς τοῖς ἐπηρεάσασιν καὶ τῷ καταδικάσαντι καὶ

452 δὴ καὶ P   καὶ δὴ A   453 πιστεύωμεν M^corr   πιστεύομεν A
459 ἀνελεῖν] ἀνελθεῖν P^corr Koetschau   474 ἤδη A²   δὲ A   δὴ M

ὅλως πᾶσιν ὀφθῆναι ... (67) Καὶ μάτην παρελήφθη τῷ
485 Κέλσῳ τὸ οὐ γὰρ δὴ ἐφοβεῖτό τινα ἀνθρώπων ἀποθανὼν
καί, ὥς φατε, θεὸς ὤν, οὐδ' ἐπὶ τοῦτ' ἐπέμφθη τὴν
ἀρχήν, ἵνα λάθῃ ... (68) Ἴδωμεν δὲ τίνα τρόπον φησὶν ὁ
παρὰ τῷ Κέλσῳ Ἰουδαῖος ὅτι εἰ δ' οὖν τό γε τοσοῦτον
ὤφειλεν εἰς ἐπίδειξιν θεότητος ἀπὸ τοῦ σκόλοπος γοῦν
490 εὐθὺς ἀφανὴς γενέσθαι ... (70) Πόθεν δὲ τῷ Κέλσου
Ἰουδαίῳ λέλεκται ὅτι ἐκρύπτετο Ἰησοῦς; λέγει γὰρ περὶ αὐτοῦ·
τίς δὲ πώποτε πεμφθεὶς ἄγγελος, δέον ἀγγέλλειν τὰ
κεκελευσμένα, κρύπτεται ... ἢ ὅτε μὲν ἠπιστεῖτο ⟨ὢν⟩
ἐν σώματι, πᾶσιν ἀνέδην ἐκήρυττεν· ὅτε δὲ πίστιν ἂν
495 ἰσχυρὰν παρεῖχεν ἐκ νεκρῶν ἀναστάς, ἑνὶ μόνῳ γυναίῳ
καὶ τοῖς ἑαυτοῦ θιασώταις κρύβδην παρεφαίνετο; ...
κολαζόμενος μὲν ἄρα πᾶσιν ἑωρᾶτο, ἀναστὰς δὲ ἑνί ...
οὗπερ ἐχρῆν τοὐναντίον; ... (71) Ἐδίδαξε δὲ ἡμᾶς ὁ Ἰησοῦς
καὶ ὅστις ἦν ὁ πέμψας ... καὶ ἐφ' οἷς ἔπεμψεν αὐτὸν ὁ
500 πατὴρ μυρία ἐστίν ... ἀλλὰ καὶ τοὺς μὲν εὐσεβοῦντας οὗτος
φωταγωγεῖ τοὺς δὲ ἁμαρτάνοντας κολάσει, ὅπερ οὐκ ἰδὼν ὁ
Κέλσος πεποίηκε· καὶ τοὺς μὲν εὐσεβοῦντας
φωταγωγήσων τοὺς δὲ ἁμαρτάνοντας ἢ μεταγνόντας ⟨ἢ
μὴ⟩ ἐλεήσων ... (72) Μετὰ ταῦτά φησιν· εἰ μὲν ἐβούλετο
505 λανθάνειν, τί ἠκούετο ἡ ἐξ οὐρανοῦ φωνὴ κηρύττουσα
αὐτὸν υἱὸν θεοῦ; εἰ δ' οὐκ ἐβούλετο λανθάνειν, τί
ἐκολάζετο ἢ τί ἀπέθνῃσκε; ... (73) Ἐκτίθεται δὲ μετὰ
ταῦτα ὁ Κέλσου Ἰουδαῖος ὡς ἀκόλουθον τὸ μὴ ἀκόλουθον. οὐ
γὰρ ἀκολουθεῖ τῷ ἠθέλησεν ἡμᾶς δι' ὧν πέπονθε
510 κολάσεων διδάξαι καὶ θανάτου καταφρονεῖν τὸ
ἀναστάντα αὐτὸν ἐκ νεκρῶν φανερῶς εἰς φῶς καλέσαι
πάντας καὶ διδάξαι, οὗ χάριν κατεληλύθει ... (74) Καὶ
πᾶσί γε τούτοις ἐπιλέγει ὁ Κέλσου Ἰουδαῖος· ταῦτα μὲν οὖν
ὑμῖν ἐκ τῶν ὑμετέρων συγγραμμάτων, ἐφ' οἷς οὐδενὸς
515 ἄλλου μάρτυρος χρῄζομεν· αὐτοὶ γὰρ ἑαυτοῖς
περιπίπτετε ... ἐπεὶ δὲ προστίθησι τούτοις ὁ Ἰουδαῖος αὐτοῦ
ὅτι ὅλως, ὦ Ὕψιστε καὶ Οὐράνιε, τίς θεὸς παρὼν εἰς
ἀνθρώπους ἀπιστεῖται ... (75) ἢ τί δή ποτε τοῖς πάλαι
προσδεχομένοις οὐ γνωρίζεται; ... (76) Μέμφεται γὰρ τὸν
520 Ἰησοῦν τοιαῦτα λέγων περὶ αὐτοῦ· ἀπειλεῖ, καὶ λοιδορεῖ
κούφως ὁπόταν λέγῃ 'οὐαὶ ὑμῖν' καὶ «προλέγω ὑμῖν». ἐν

493 ⟨ὢν⟩ Ktr   503–504 ⟨ἢ μὴ⟩ Mosheim Bader
      514 ὑμετέρων P²   ἡμετέρων A

245

γὰρ τούτοις ἄντικρυς ὁμολογεῖ ὅτι πεῖσαι ἀδυνατεῖ,
ὅπερ οὐκ ἄν θεὸς ἀλλ' οὐδ' ἄνθρωπος φρόνιμος πάθοι
... (77) Μετὰ ταῦτα ὁ Ἰουδαῖος αὐτῷ λέγει, δηλονότι κατὰ τὸ
525 Ἰουδαίοις ἀρέσκον, ὅτι ἐλπίζομεν δή που ἀναστήσεσθαι
ἐν σώματι καὶ βιοτὴν ἕξειν αἰώνιον, καὶ τούτου
παράδειγμα καὶ ἀρχηγέτην τὸν πεμπόμενον ἡμῖν
ἔσεσθαι, δεικνύντα ὅτι οὐκ ἀδύνατόν τινα τῷ θεῷ σὺν
τῷ σώματι ⟨ἀναστῆσαι⟩ ... μετὰ ταῦτά φησι· ποῦ οὖν
530 ἐστιν; ἵνα ἴδωμεν καὶ πιστεύσωμεν ... (78) Μετὰ ταῦτα
λέγει ὁ Ἰουδαῖος· ἢ ἐπὶ τοῦτο κατῆλθεν, ἵν' ἀπιστήσωμεν
... (79) Εἶτ' ἐπίλογος τοῦ Ἰουδαίου ἐπὶ τούτοις πᾶσί φησι περὶ
τοῦ Ἰησοῦ· ἐκεῖνος μὲν οὖν ἄνθρωπος ἦν, καὶ τοιοῦτος,
οἷον αὐτὸ τὸ ἀληθὲς ἐμφανίζει καὶ ὁ λόγος δείκνυσιν.
535 (III, 1) Φησὶ δὴ ὅτι εὐηθέστατα ἐρίζουσι πρὸς ἀλλήλους
Χριστιανοὶ καὶ Ἰουδαῖοι, καὶ λέγει μηδὲν διαφέρειν
ἡμῶν τὸν πρὸς ἀλλήλους διάλογον περὶ Χρίστου τῆς
κατὰ τὴν παροιμίαν καλουμένης ὄνου σκιᾶς μάχης· καὶ
οἴεται μηδὲν σεμνὸν εἶναι ἐν τῇ Ἰουδαίων καὶ
540 Χριστιανῶν πρὸς ἀλλήλους ζητήσει, πιστευόντων μὲν
ἀμφοτέρων ὅτι ἀπὸ θείου πνεύματος ἐπροφητεύθη τις
ἐπιδημήσων σωτὴρ τῷ γένει τῶν ἀνθρώπων οὐκέτι δ'
ὁμολογούντων περὶ τοῦ ἐληλυθέναι τὸν
προφητευόμενον ἢ μή ... (5) Ἑξῆς δὲ τούτοις ὁ Κέλσος
545 οἰόμενος τοὺς Ἰουδαίους, Αἰγυπτίους τῷ γένει
τυγχάνοντας, καταλελοιπέναι τὴν Αἴγυπτον,
στασιάσαντας πρὸς τὸ κοινὸν τῶν Αἰγυπτίων καὶ τὸ
ἐν Αἰγύπτῳ σύνηθες περὶ τὰς θρησκείας
ὑπερφρονήσαντας, φησὶν αὐτοὺς ἅπερ ἐποίησαν
550 Αἰγυπτίοις πεπονθέναι ὑπὸ τῶν προσθεμένων τῷ
Ἰησοῦ καὶ πιστευσάντων αὐτῷ ὡς Χρίστῳ, καὶ
ἀμφοτέροις αἴτιον γεγονέναι τῆς καινοτομίας τὸ
στασιάζειν πρὸς τὸ κοινόν ... (6) Τοῦτο δέ μοι βούλεται ὁ
λόγος συνάγειν ὅτι ψεῦδος τὸ Αἰγυπτίους τὸ γένος ὄντας
555 τινὰς ἐστασιακέναι πρὸς Αἰγυπτίους καὶ τὴν Αἴγυπτον
καταλελοιπέναι καὶ ἐπὶ τὴν Παλαιστίνην ἐληλυθέναι
τήν τε νῦν καλουμένην Ἰουδαίαν ᾠκηκέναι ... (8)
Ὁμοίως δὲ ψεῦδος τὸ Αἰγυπτίους ὄντας ἀπὸ στάσεως τὴν
ἀρχὴν εἰληφέναι τοὺς Ἑβραίους, καὶ τὸ Ἰουδαίους
560 ὄντας ἄλλους κατὰ τοὺς Ἰησοῦ χρόνους ἐστασιακέναι

528 τινα] τι παρὰ P   529 ⟨ἀναστῆσαι⟩ Koetschau Borret

246

πρὸς τὸ κοινὸν τῶν Ἰουδαίων καὶ τῷ Ἰησοῦ κατηκολουθηκέναι ... ταῦτα μὲν πρὸς τὰ ὑπὸ Κέλσου εἰρημένα περὶ τοῦ στάσιν γεγονέναι τὴν ἀρχὴν πάλαι μὲν τοῦ συστῆναι Ἰουδαίους ...

565 (IV, 1) Καὶ μάλιστα χρεία ἡμῖν πρὸς τὰ νῦν ἑξῆς τοῖς προειρημένοις τῷ Κέλσῳ λεγόμενα κατασκευάσαι ὅτι καλῶς τὰ περὶ τοῦ Χρίστου πεπροφήτευται. ἅμα γὰρ πρὸς τοὺς ἀμφοτέρους ἱστάμενος ὁ Κέλσος, Ἰουδαίους μὲν ἀρνουμένους γεγονέναι τὴν Χριστοῦ ἐπιδημίαν ἐλπίζοντας δ' αὐτὴν ἔσεσθαι, Χριστιανοὺς δὲ ὁμολογοῦντας τὸν
570 Ἰησοῦν εἶναι τὸν προφητευθέντα Χριστόν, φησίν· (2) Ὅτι δὲ καὶ Χριστιανῶν τινες καὶ Ἰουδαῖοι οἱ μὲν καταβεβηκέναι ⟨λέγουσιν⟩, οἱ δὲ καταβήσεσθαι εἰς τὴν γῆν τινα θεὸν ἢ θεοῦ υἱὸν τῶν τῇ δε δικαιωτήν, τοῦτ' αἴσχιστον, καὶ οὐδὲ δεῖται μακροῦ λόγου ὁ ἔλεγχος ... (3) τίς ⟨γὰρ⟩ ὁ νοῦς τῆς τοιᾶσδε
575 καθόδου τῷ θεῷ; ... ἢ ἵνα μάθῃ τὰ ἐν ἀνθρώποις ... οὐ γὰρ οἶδε πάντα; ... ἆρ' οὐχ οἷόν τε αὐτῷ δυνάμει θείᾳ ἐπανορθοῦν, ἐὰν μὴ φύσει τινὰ ἐπὶ τοῦτο πέμψῃ; ... (5) Μετὰ ταῦθ' ὁ γενναιότατος Κέλσος οὐκ οἶδ' ὁπόθεν λαβὼν ἐπαπορεῖ πρὸς ἡμᾶς ὡς λέγοντας ὅτι αὐτὸς κάτεισι πρὸς ἀνθρώπους ὁ θεός· καὶ οἴεται
580 ἀκολουθεῖν τούτῳ τὸ τὴν ἑαυτοῦ ἕδραν αὐτὸν καταλιπεῖν ... ὡς ὁ Κέλσος οἴεται, λέγων· εἰ γὰρ ἕν τι τῶν τῇδε τοὐλάχιστον μεταβάλοις, ἀνατραπέντα οἰχήσεταί σοι τὰ πάντα ... (6) Εἰ δὲ καὶ πρὸς τὰ καταγελαστότατα τοῦ Κέλσου θέλεις ἡμᾶς ἀπαντᾶν, ἄκουε αὐτοῦ λέγοντος· ἀλλὰ γὰρ ἀγνοούμενος ὁ θεὸς ἐν
585 ἀνθρώποις καὶ παρὰ τοῦτ' ἔλαττον ἔχειν δοκῶν ἐθέλοι ἂν γνωσθῆναι καὶ τοὺς πιστεύοντάς τε καὶ ἀπιστοῦντας διαπειράσαι, καθάπερ οἱ νεόπλουτοι τῶν ἀνθρώπων ἐπιδεικτιῶντες; πολλὴν ⟨δή⟩ τινα καὶ πάνυ θνητὴν φιλοτιμίαν τοῦ θεοῦ καταμαρτυροῦσι. (11) Μετὰ ταῦτα
590 βουλόμενος ἡμᾶς παραδεῖξαι μηδὲν παράδοξον μηδὲ καινὸν λέγειν περὶ κατακλυσμοῦ ἢ ἐκπυρώσεως, ἀλλὰ καὶ παρακούσαντας τῶν παρ' Ἕλλησιν ἢ βαρβάροις περὶ τούτων λεγομένων ταῖς ἡμετέραις πεπιστευκέναι περὶ αὐτῶν γραφαῖς, φησὶ ταῦτα· ἐπῆλθε δ' αὐτοῖς καὶ ταῦτα ἐκείνων παρακούσασιν, ὅτι δὴ κατὰ χρόνων
595 μάκρων κύκλους καὶ ἄστρων ἐπανόδους τε καὶ συνόδους ἐκπυρώσεις καὶ ἐπικλύσεις συμβαίνουσι, καὶ ὅτι μετὰ τὸν τελευταῖον ἐπὶ Δευκαλίωνος κατακλυσμὸν ἡ περίοδος κατὰ τὴν ὅλων ἀμοιβὴν ἐκπύρωσιν ἀπαιτεῖ· ταῦτ' αὐτοὺς ἐποίησεν

---

572 ⟨λέγουσιν⟩ Koetschau   574 ⟨γὰρ⟩ Bader   588 ⟨δή⟩ Glöckner

ἐσφαλμένῃ δόξῃ λέγειν ὅτι ὁ θεὸς καταβήσεται δίκην
600 βασανιστοῦ πῦρ φέρων ... *(20)* Εἶτ' ἐπεὶ προσωποποιεῖ ἰδίᾳ μὲν
Ἰουδαίους αἰτιολογοῦντας τὴν κατ' αὐτοὺς μέλλουσαν Χριστοῦ
ἐπιδημίαν ἰδίᾳ δὲ Χριστιανοὺς λέγοντας περὶ τῆς ἤδη γεγενημένης
ἐπιδημίας εἰς τὸν βίον τῶν ἀνθρώπων τοῦ υἱοῦ τοῦ θεοῦ· φέρε καὶ
ταῦτα, ὡς οἷόν τε ἐστί, διὰ βραχέων κατανοήσωμεν. Ἰουδαῖοι δὴ
605 παρ' αὐτῷ λέγουσι πληρωθέντα τὸν βίον πάσης κακίας
δεῖσθαι τοῦ καταπεμπομένου ἀπὸ θεοῦ, ἵν' οἱ μὲν ἄδικοι
κολασθῶσι, τὰ δὲ πάντα καθαρθῇ ἀνάλογον τῷ πρώτῳ
συμβάντι κατακλυσμῷ ... *(21)* Οὐκ οἶδα δ' ὅπως παραπλησίως
τῷ κατακλυσμῷ καθήραντι τὴν γῆν ὡς ὁ Ἰουδαίων καὶ
610 Χριστιανῶν βούλεται λόγος, οἴεται καὶ τὴν τοῦ πύργου κατάρριψιν
γεγονέναι. ἵνα γὰρ μηδὲν αἰνίσσηται ἡ κατὰ τὸν πύργον
ἱστορία κειμένη ἐν τῇ Γενέσει ἀλλ' ὡς οἴεται Κέλσος, σαφὴς
τυγχάνῃ, οὐ δ' οὕτως φαίνεται ἐπὶ καθαρσίῳ τῆς γῆς τοῦτο
συμβεβηκέναι· εἰ μὴ ἄρα καθάρσιον τῆς γῆς οἴεται τὴν καλουμένην
615 τῶν γλωσσῶν «σύγχυσιν» ... ἐπεὶ δ' οἴεται Μωϋσέα, τὸν
ἀναγράψαντα τὰ περὶ τοῦ πύργου καὶ τῆς τῶν διαλέκτων
συγχύσεως, παραφθείροντα τὰ περὶ τῶν Ἀλωέως υἱῶν
ἱστορούμενα τοιαῦτα περὶ τοῦ πύργου ἀναγεγραφέναι,
λεκτέον ὅτι ... καὶ τὰ περὶ Σοδόμων δὲ καὶ Γομόρρων ὑπὸ
620 Μωϋσέως ἱστορούμενα ἐν τῇ Γενέσει, ὡς διὰ τὴν ἁμαρτίαν πυρὶ
ἐξαφανισθέντων, παραβάλλει ὁ Κέλσος τῇ κατὰ τὸν Φαέθοντα
ἱστορίᾳ, ἑνὶ σφάλματι, τῷ περὶ τοῦ μὴ τετηρηκέναι τὰ τῆς Μωϋσέως
ἀρχαιότητος, ἀκολούθως πάντα ποιήσας ... *(22)* Καὶ Χριστιανοὶ δὲ
κατὰ τὸν Κέλσον προστιθέντες τινὰς λόγους τοῖς ὑπὸ Ἰουδαίων
625 λεγομένοις φασὶ διὰ τὰς τῶν Ἰουδαίων ἁμαρτίας ἤδη
πεπέμφθαι τὸν υἱὸν τοῦ θεοῦ, καὶ ὅτι Ἰουδαῖοι κολάσαντες
τὸν Ἰησοῦν καὶ χολὴν ποτίσαντες ἐπὶ σφᾶς αὐτοὺς ἐκ θεοῦ
χόλον ἐπεσπάσαντο ... *(23)* Μετὰ ταῦτα συνήθως ἑαυτῷ γελῶν τὸ
Ἰουδαίων καὶ Χριστιανῶν γένος πάντας παραβέβληκε
630 νυκτερίδων ὁρμαθῷ ἢ μύρμηξιν ἐκ καλιᾶς προελθοῦσιν ἢ
βατράχοις περὶ τέλμα συνεδρεύουσιν ἢ σκώληξιν ἐν
βορβόρου γωνίᾳ ἐκκλησιάζουσι καὶ πρὸς ἀλλήλους
διαφερομένοις, τίνες αὐτῶν εἶεν ἁμαρτωλότεροι, καὶ
φάσκουσιν ὅτι πάντα ἡμῖν ὁ θεὸς προδηλοῖ καὶ
635 προκαταγγέλλει, καὶ τὸν πάντα κόσμον καὶ τὴν οὐράνιον

---

607 πρώτῳ PM   πρῶτον A   617 παραφθείραντα M   /
Αλωέως υἱῶν Koetschau   ἁλωιῶν A   624 προστιθέντες Reg
                   προτιθέντες A

φορὰν ἀπολιπὼν καὶ τὴν τοσαύτην γῆν παριδὼν ἡμῖν μόνοις
πολιτεύεται καὶ πρὸς ἡμᾶς μόνους ἐπικηρυκεύεται καὶ
πέμπων οὐ διαλείπει καὶ ζητῶν, ὅπως ἀεὶ συνῶμεν αὐτῷ. καὶ
ἐν τῷ ἀναπλάσματί γε ἑαυτοῦ παραπλησίους ἡμᾶς ποιεῖ
640 σκώληξι, φάσκουσιν ὅτι ὁ θεός ἐστιν, εἶτα μετ᾽ ἐκεῖνον ἡμεῖς
ὑπ᾽ αὐτοῦ γεγονότες πάντῃ ὅμοιοι τῷ θεῷ, καὶ ἡμῖν πάντα
ὑποβέβληται, γῆ καὶ ὕδωρ καὶ ἀὴρ καὶ ἄστρα, καὶ ἡμῶν ἕνεκα
πάντα, καὶ ἡμῖν δουλεύειν τέτακται. λέγουσι δ᾽ ἔτι παρ᾽ αὐτῷ οἱ
σκώληκες, ἡμεῖς δηλαδή, ὅτι νῦν, ἐπειδή τινες ⟨ἐν⟩ ἡμῖν
645 πλημμελοῦσιν, ἀφίξεται θεὸς ἢ πέμψει τὸν υἱόν, ἵνα
καταφλέξῃ τοὺς ἀδίκους, καὶ οἱ λοιποὶ σὺν αὐτῷ ζωὴν αἰώνιον
ἔχωμεν. καὶ ἐπιφέρει γε πᾶσιν ὅτι ταῦτα ⟨μᾶλλον⟩ ἀνεκτά,
σκωλήκων καὶ βατράχων, ἢ Ἰουδαίων καὶ Χριστιανῶν πρὸς
ἀλλήλους διαφερομένων ... (31) Μετὰ ταῦτα βουλόμενος
650 κατασκευάζειν ὅτι μηδὲν τῶν προειρημένων παρ᾽ αὐτῷ ζῴων
διαφέρουσιν Ἰουδαῖοι καὶ Χριστιανοί φησιν Ἰουδαίους ἀπ᾽ Αἰγύπτου
δραπέτας γεγονέναι, μηδὲν πώποτε ἀξιόλογον πράξαντας, οὔτ᾽ ἐν
λόγῳ οὔτ᾽ ἐν ἀριθμῷ αὐτούς ποτε γεγενημένους ... εἰ δὲ τὸ μήτ᾽
ἐν λόγῳ μήτ᾽ ἐν ἀριθμῷ αὐτοὺς γεγονέναι κατασκευάζεσθαι νομίζει
655 ἐκ τοῦ μὴ πάνυ τι τὴν περὶ αὐτῶν ἱστορίαν εὑρίσκεσθαι παρὰ τοῖς
Ἕλλησι, φήσομεν ὅτι ... (33) Ἑξῆς δὲ τούτοις ὁ Κέλσος ἐπιτρέχων τὰ
ἀπὸ τῆς πρώτης βίβλου Μωϋσέως, ἥτις ἐπιγέγραπται Γένεσις, φησίν·
⟨ἀναισχύντ⟩ως ἄρα ἐπεχείρησαν γενεαλογεῖν αὐτοὺς ἀπὸ
πρώτης σπορᾶς γοήτων καὶ πλάνων ἀνθρώπων ἀμυδρὰς καὶ
660 ἀμφιβόλους φωνὰς ἐν σκότῳ που κρυφίους ἐπιμαρτυρόμενοι
καὶ τοῖς ἀμαθέσι καὶ ἀνοήτοις παρεξηγούμενοι, καὶ ταῦτα
μηδὲ πώποτ᾽ ἐν πολλῷ τῷ πρόσθεν χρόνῳ τοῦ τοιοῦδε μηδ᾽
ἀμφισβητηθέντος ... (35) ἀλλὰ νῦν Ἰουδαῖοι πρὸς ἑτέρους
τινάς, οὓς οὐκ ὠνόμασε, περὶ τούτων ἀμφισβητοῦσι ... (36) Μετὰ
665 ταῦτα ὁ Κέλσος ἐκτιθέμενος τὰ ἀπὸ τῆς ἔξω τοῦ θείου λόγου ἱστορίας,
τὰ περὶ τῶν ἐπιδικασαμένων ἀνθρώπων τῆς ἀρχαιότητος, οἷον
Ἀθηναίων καὶ Αἰγυπτίων καὶ Ἀρκάδων καὶ Φρυγῶν, καὶ
γηγενεῖς τινας παρὰ σφίσιν γεγονέναι λεγόντων καὶ
τεκμήρια τούτων παρεχομένων ἑκάστων, φησὶν ὡς ἄρα
670 Ἰουδαῖοι ἐν γωνίᾳ που τῆς Παλαιστίνης συγκύψαντες,
παντελῶς ἀπαίδευτοι καὶ οὐ προακηκόοτες πάλαι ταῦτα

637 ἐμπολιτεύεται M² 640 ὁ om M 643 δ᾽ ἔτι Borret δέ τι A
644 ⟨ἐν⟩ Bouhéreau 647 ⟨μᾶλλον⟩ Bouhéreau
648 καὶ Delarue ἢ A (bis) 658 ⟨ἀναισχύντ⟩ως Koetschau Borret /
αὐτοὺς M αὐτοὺς A 659 σπορᾶς A¹ φορᾶς A

Ἡσιόδῳ καὶ ἄλλοις μυρίοις ἀνδράσιν ἐνθέοις ὑμνημένα,
συνέθεσαν ἀπιθανώτατα καὶ ἀμουσότατα, ἄνθρωπόν τινα
ὑπὸ χειρῶν θεοῦ πλασσόμενόν τε καὶ ἐμφυσώμενον καὶ
675 γύναιον ἐκ τῆς πλευρᾶς καὶ παραγγέλματα τοῦ θεοῦ καὶ ὄφιν
τούτοις ἀντιπράσσοντα καὶ περιγινόμενον τῶν θεοῦ
προσταγμάτων τὸν ὄφιν, μῦθόν τινα ὡς γραυσὶ διηγούμενοι
καὶ ποιοῦντες ἀνοσιώτατα τὸν θεόν, εὐθὺς ἀπ᾽ ἀρχῆς
ἀσθενοῦντα καὶ μηδ᾽ ἕν᾽ ἄνθρωπον, ὃν αὐτὸς ἔπλασε, πεῖσαι
680 δυνάμενον ... (41) Ἑξῆς δὲ τοιαῦτά φησιν· εἶτα κατακλυσμόν
τινα καὶ κιβωτὸν ἀλλόκοτον, ἅπαντα ἔνδον ἔχουσαν, καὶ
περιστεράν τινα καὶ κορώνην ἀγγέλους, παραχαράττοντες
καὶ ῥαδιουργοῦντες τὸν Δευκαλίωνα· οὐ γὰρ οἶμαι
προσεδόκησαν ὅτι ταῦτ᾽ εἰς φῶς πρόεισιν, ἀλλ᾽ ἀτεχνῶς
685 παισὶ νηπίοις ἐμυθολόγησαν ... (43) Ἀτοπωτάτην δὲ λέγει καὶ
ἔξωρον παιδοποιΐαν, εἰ καὶ μὴ ὠνόμασε, δῆλον δ᾽ ὅτι λέγων τὴν
τοῦ Ἀβραὰμ καὶ τῆς Σάρρας. ῥίπτων δὲ καὶ τὰς τῶν ἀδελφῶν
ἐπιβουλὰς ἤτοι τὸν Κάϊν ἐπιβουλεύσαντα τῷ Ἄβελ λέγει ἢ πρὸς
τούτῳ καὶ τὸν Ἡσαῦ τῷ Ἰακώβ· πατρὸς δὲ λύπην, τάχα μὲν καὶ τὴν
690 Ἰσαὰκ ἐπὶ τῇ τοῦ Ἰακὼβ ἀποδημίᾳ τάχα δὲ καὶ τὴν τοῦ Ἰακὼβ διὰ
τὸν Ἰωσὴφ πραθέντα εἰς Αἴγυπτον. μητέρων δ᾽ οἶμαι ἐνέδρας
ἀναγράφοντα αὐτὸν δηλοῦν τὴν Ῥεβέκκαν, οἰκονομήσασαν τὰς τοῦ
Ἰσαὰκ εὐχὰς μὴ ἐπὶ τὸν Ἡσαῦ ἀλλ᾽ ἐπὶ τὸν Ἰακὼβ φθάσαι. ἄγχιστα
δὲ τούτοις πᾶσι συμπολιτευόμενον εἴ φαμεν τὸν θεόν, τί ἄτοπον
695 πράσσομεν ... ; ἐχλεύασε δὲ τὴν παρὰ τῷ Λάβαν κτῆσιν τοῦ Ἰακώβ,
μὴ νοήσας, ἐπὶ τί ἀναφέρεται τὸ «καὶ ἦν τὰ ἄσημα τοῦ Λάβαν, τὰ δὲ
ἐπίσημα τοῦ Ἰακώβ», καί φησι τὸν θεὸν τοῖς υἱοῖς ὀνάρια καὶ
προβάτια καὶ καμήλους δεδωρῆσθαι ... (44) Πόρρω δὲ τυγχάνων
τοῦ βουλήματος τῶν γεγραμμένων φησὶ τὸν θεὸν καὶ φρέατα τοῖς
700 δικαίοις δεδωκέναι ... πολλαχοῦ δὲ ἱστορίαις γενομέναις
συγχρησάμενος ὁ λόγος ἀνέγραψεν αὐτὰς εἰς παράστασιν μειζόνων
καὶ ἐν ὑπονοίᾳ δηλουμένων· ὁποῖά ἐστι καὶ τὰ περὶ φρέατα καὶ τὰ
περὶ τοὺς γάμους καὶ τὰς διαφόρους μίξεις τῶν δικαίων ...
νύμφας τε καὶ θεραπαινίδας ἀνάγεσθαι ἐπὶ τροπολογίαν οὐχ
705 ἡμεῖς διδάσκομεν, ἀλλ᾽ ἄνωθεν ἀπὸ σοφῶν παρειλήφαμεν ... (45)
Δέον δ᾽ αὐτὸν τὸ φιλάληθες τῶν ἀναγραψάντων τὰς θείας γραφὰς
ἀποδεξάμενον, μὴ κρυψάντων καὶ τὰ ἀπεμφαίνοντα, προσαχθῆναι καὶ
περὶ τῶν λοιπῶν καὶ παραδοξοτέρων ὡς οὐ πεπλασμένων, ὁ δὲ

676 ἀντιπράσσοντα] ἀντιπροστάσσοντα Hoeschel Spencer / περιγενόμενον M
    686 δῆλον ὅτι M^{corr}   698 πρόβατα M   700 γενομέναις M
        γενόμενος A   702 τὰ φρέατα M

τοὐναντίον πεποίηκε καὶ τὰ περὶ τὸν Λὼτ καὶ τὰς θυγατέρας, οὔτε
710 κατὰ τὸ ῥητὸν ἐξετάσας οὔτε κατὰ τὴν ἀναγωγὴν ἐρευνήσας, τῶν
Θυεστείων εἶπε κακῶν ἀνομώτερα ... (46) Παραρρίπτει δ' ὁ
Κέλσος τὴν ἀπέχθειαν, οἶμαι τοῦ Ἠσαῦ πρὸς τὸν Ἰακώβ, ἀνδρὸς
κατὰ τὴν γραφὴν ὁμολογουμένου φαύλου· καὶ μὴ σαφῶς ἐκτιθέμενος
τὰ περὶ τὸν Συμεὼν καὶ τὸν Λευῒ ἐπεξελθόντας τῇ ὕβρει
715 τῆς ἀδελφῆς, βιασθείσης ὑπὸ τοῦ υἱοῦ τοῦ βασιλέως Σικίμων,
σφᾶς αἰτιᾶται· ἀδελφοὺς δὲ πωλοῦντας τοὺς υἱοὺς λέγει τοῦ
Ἰακώβ. καὶ ἀδελφὸν πιπρασκόμενον τὸν Ἰωσήφ, καὶ πατέρα
ἐξαπατώμενον τὸν Ἰακώβ ... (47) Μετὰ ταῦτα ὁ Κέλσος ὁσίας
ἕνεκεν μετὰ πάσης ἀσαφείας ὑπομιμνήσκεται τῶν ὀνειράτων τοῦ
720 ἀρχιοινοχόου καὶ ἀρχισιτοποιοῦ καὶ τοῦ Φαραὼ καὶ τῆς λύσεως αὐτῶν
... καὶ τοῖς πωλήσασί γε ἀδελφοῖς λιμώττουσι καὶ σταλεῖσι
κατ' ἐμπορίαν μετὰ τῶν ὄνων φησὶ χαριζόμενον τὸν πραθέντα
πεποιηκέναι ἃ οὐδὲ παρέστησεν ὁ Κέλσος. καὶ τὸν ἀναγνωρισμὸν
δὲ τίθησιν, οὐκ οἶδα τί βουλόμενος καὶ τί ἐμφαίνων ἄτοπον ἐκ τοῦ
725 ἀναγνωρισμοῦ ... τίθησι δὲ καὶ τὸν εἰς δοῦλον πραθέντα Ἰωσὴφ
ἐλευθερούμενον καὶ μετὰ πομπῆς ἐπανιόντα πρὸς τὸν τοῦ
πατρὸς τάφον καὶ νομίζει κατηγορίαν περιέχειν τὸν λόγον εἰπὼν τό·
Ὑφ' οὗ — δῆλον δ' ὅτι τοῦ Ἰωσήφ — τὸ λαμπρὸν καὶ θεσπέσιον
Ἰουδαίων γένος ἐπὶ πλῆθος ἐν Αἰγύπτῳ σπαρέν, ἔξω που
730 παροικεῖν καὶ ποιμαίνειν ἐν τοῖς ἀτίμοις ἐκελεύσθη ... τὴν
δ' ἀπ' Αἰγύπτου ἔξοδον τοῦ λαοῦ φυγὴν ὠνόμασεν, οὐδὲ τὴν ἀρχὴν
ὑπομνησθεὶς τῶν ἐν τῇ Ἐξόδῳ γεγραμμένων περὶ τῆς ἐξόδου τῶν
Ἑβραίων ἐκ γῆς Αἰγύπτου ... (48) Εἶτα ὡς εἰς τὸ μισεῖν μόνον καὶ
ἀπεχθάνεσθαι τῷ κατ' Ἰουδαίους καὶ Χριστιανοὺς λόγῳ ἑαυτὸν
735 ἐπιδεδωκώς, φησὶν ὅτι καὶ Ἰουδαίων καὶ Χριστιανῶν οἱ
ἐπιεικέστεροι ταῦτ' ἀλληγοροῦσι· λέγει δὲ αἰσχυνομένους
ἐπὶ τούτοις καταφεύγειν ἐπὶ τὴν ἀλληγορίαν ... (50) Ἐπὶ
πλεῖον δ' ἐξέτεινα τὸν λόγον βουλόμενος παραστῆσαι μὴ ὑγιῶς
εἰρῆσθαι τῷ Κέλσῳ ὅτι οἱ ἐπιεικέστεροι Ἰουδαίων καὶ
740 Χριστιανῶν πειρῶνταί πως ἀλληγορεῖν αὐτά, ἔστι δ' οὐχ οἷα
ἀλληγορίαν ἐπιδέχεσθαί τινα ἄλλ' ἄντικρυς εὐηθέστατα
μεμυθολόγηται ... (51) Δοκεῖ δέ μοι ἀκηκοέναι ὅτι ἐστὶ
συγγράμματα περιέχοντα τὰς τοῦ νόμου ἀλληγορίας, ἅπερ εἰ
ἀνεγνώκει, οὐκ ἂν ἔλεγεν· αἱ γοῦν δοκοῦσαι περὶ αὐτῶν
745 ἀλληγορίαι γεγράφθαι πολὺ τῶν μύθων αἰσχίους εἰσὶ καὶ
ἀτοπώτεραι, τὰ μηδαμῇ μηδαμῶς ἁρμοσθῆναι δυνάμενα

727 νομίζει edd.   νομίζειν Α   730 ἐκελεύσθη P   κελευσθὲν Α
741 εὐηθέστατα Iol²   ἀληθέστατα Α

251

θαυμαστῇ τινι καὶ παντάπασιν ἀναισθήτῳ μωρίᾳ
συνάπτουσαι ... *(71)* Ἐπεὶ δὲ μετὰ ταῦτα μὴ νοήσας τὰς περὶ θεοῦ
ὡς ἀνθρωποπαθοῦς ἐν ταῖς γράφαις λέξεις διασύρει ὁ Κέλσος ἐν αἷς
750 ὀργῆς λέγονται κατὰ τῶν ἀσεβῶν φωναὶ καὶ ἀπειλαὶ κατὰ τῶν
ἡμαρτηκότων, λεκτέον ὅτι ... *(72)* Οὐκ ἀνθρώπινα οὖν πάθη
προσάπτομεν τῷ θεῷ οὐδὲ δυσσεβεῖς δόξας ἔχομεν περὶ
αὐτοῦ οὐδὲ πλανώμενοι τὰς περὶ τοῦτον διηγήσεις ἀπ' αὐτῶν τῶν
γραμμάτων συνεξεταζομένων ἀλλήλοις παρίσταμεν ... *(73)*
755 Ἀκολούθως δὲ τῷ μὴ νενοηκέναι τὰ περὶ ὀργῆς ἀναγεγραμμένα θεοῦ
φησιν· ἢ γὰρ οὐ καταγέλαστον, εἰ ἄνθρωπος μὲν ὀργισθεὶς,
Ἰουδαίοις πάντας αὐτοὺς ἡβηδὸν ἀπώλεσεν καὶ ἐπυρ-
πόλησεν, οὕτως οὐδὲν ἦσαν, θεὸς δ' ὁ μέγιστος, ὥς φασιν, ὀργιζόμενος καὶ θυμούμενος καὶ ἀπειλῶν πέμπει τὸν υἱὸν αὐτοῦ,
760 καὶ τοιαῦτα πάσχει; ... ἀλλ' ὅπως μὴ περὶ μόνων
Ἰουδαίων — οὐ γὰρ τοῦτο λέγω — ἀλλὰ περὶ τῆς ὅλης φύσεως,
ὅπερ ἐπηγγειλάμην, ὁ λόγος ᾖ, σαφέστερον ἐμφανιῶ τὰ
προειρημένα ... *(74)* Διὰ πολλῶν δ' ἑξῆς ἐγκαλεῖ ἡμῖν ὡς τῷ
ἀνθρώπῳ φάσκουσι πάντα πεποιηκέναι τὸν θεόν. καὶ βούλεται
765 ἐκ τῆς περὶ τῶν ζώων ἱστορίας καὶ τῆς ἐμφαινομένης αὐτοῖς ἀγχινοίας
δεικνύναι ὅτι οὐδὲν μᾶλλον ἀνθρώπων ἢ τῶν ἀλόγων ζώων
ἕνεκεν γέγονε τὰ πάντα ... *(75)* Οἴεται γὰρ πρῶτον μὲν μὴ ἔργα
θεοῦ εἶναι βροντὰς καὶ ἀστραπὰς καὶ ὑετούς, ἤδη σαφέστερον
ἐπικουρίζων· δεύτερον δέ φησιν ὅτι, εἰ καὶ διδῴη τις ταῦτα ἔργα
770 εἶναι θεοῦ, οὐ μᾶλλον ἡμῖν τοῖς ἀνθρώποις ταῦτα γίνεται
πρὸς τροφὴν ἢ τοῖς φυτοῖς δένδροις τε καὶ πόαις καὶ
ἀκάνθαις ... εἶτά φησιν ὅτι κἂν ταῦτα λέγῃς ἀνθρώποις
φύεσθαι ... , τί μᾶλλον αὐτὰ ἀνθρώποις φήσεις φύεσθαι ἢ
τοῖς ἀλόγοις ζῴοις τοῖς ἀγριωτάτοις; ... *(76)* Ἑξῆς τούτοις ὁ
775 Κέλσος ... φησίν· ἡμεῖς μέν γε κάμνοντες καὶ προσ-
ταλαιπωροῦντες μόλις καὶ ἐπιπόνως τρεφόμεθα· τοῖς δ'
⟨*Odyssea*, IX, 109⟩ «ἄσπαρτα καὶ ἀνήροτα πάντα φύονται» ... *(77)*
Ἔχει δ' οὕτως ἡ τοῦ Κέλσου λέξις· εἰ δὲ καὶ τὸ Εὐριπίδειον ἐρεῖς,
ὅτι ⟨*Phoenissae*, 546⟩, «Ἥλιος μὲν νὺξ τε δουλεύει βροτοῖς», τί
780 μᾶλλον ἢ τοῖς μύρμηξι καὶ ταῖς μυίαις; καὶ γὰρ ἐκείνοις ἡ
μὲν νὺξ γίνεται πρὸς ἀνάπαυσιν ἡ δ' ἡμέρα πρὸς τὸ ὁρᾶν τε
καὶ ἐνεργεῖν ... *(78)* Ἑξῆς δὲ τούτοις ἑαυτῷ ἀνθυποφέρει τὰ ὡς ὑπὲρ

753 περὶ τούτων M   754 περιστῶμεν P   763 δ'] δὴ Φ
764 καὶ om. A   765 τῶν om. Φ   αὐτοῖς Pat C   αὐτῷ AB
766 ὅτι Φ   om. AM   768 σαφῶς Φ   769 διδοίη M   (διδόη B¹) B² C
774 ἑξῆς δὲ Φ   776 καὶ μόλις Pat C   777 πάντα om. Pat C   /   φύεται Φ

ἀνθρώπων λεγόμενα, ὅτι δι' αὐτοὺς τὰ ἄλογα ζῷα δεδημιούργηται, καί
φησιν ὅτι, εἴ τις ἡμᾶς λέγοι ἄρχοντας τῶν ἀλόγων, ἐπεὶ ἡμεῖς
785 τὰ ἄλογα ζῷα θηρῶμέν τε καὶ δαινύμεθα, φήσομεν, ὅτι τί δ'
οὐχὶ μᾶλλον ἡμεῖς δι' ἐκεῖνα γεγόναμεν, ἐπεὶ ἐκεῖνα
θηρᾶται ἡμᾶς καὶ ἐσθίει; ἀλλὰ καὶ ἡμῖν μὲν ἀρκύων καὶ
ὅπλων δεῖ καὶ ἀνθρώπων πλειόνων βοηθῶν καὶ κυνῶν κατὰ
τῶν θηρευομένων· ἐκείνοις δ' αὐτίκα καὶ καθ' αὐτὰ ἡ φύσις
790 ὅπλα δέδωκεν εὐχερῶς ἡμᾶς ὑπάγουσα ἐκείνοις ... (99) Ἐπεὶ
οὖν τούτοις πᾶσιν ἐπιφέρει ὁ Κέλσος τό· οὔκουν ἀνθρώπῳ
πεποίηται τὰ πάντα, ὥσπερ οὐδὲ λέοντι οὐδὲ ἀετῷ οὐδὲ
δελφῖνι, ἀλλ' ὅπως ὅδε ὁ κόσμος ὡς ἂν θεοῦ ἔργον ὁλόκληρον
καὶ τέλειον ἐξ ἁπάντων γένηται· τούτου χάριν μεμέτρηται τὰ
795 πάντα, οὐκ ἀλλήλων, ἀλλ' εἰ μὴ πάρεργον, ἀλλὰ τοῦ ὅλου. καὶ
μέλει τῷ θεῷ τοῦ ὅλου, καὶ τοῦτ' οὔ ποτ' ἀπολείπει πρόνοια,
οὐδὲ κάκιον γίνεται, οὐδὲ διὰ χρόνου πρὸς ἑαυτὸν ὁ θεὸς
ἐπιστρέφει, οὐδ' ἀνθρώπων ἕνεκα ὀργίζεται, ὥσπερ οὐδὲ
πιθήκων οὐδὲ μυῶν οὐδὲ τούτοις ἀπειλεῖ, ὧν ἕκαστον ἔν τῷ
800 μέρει τὴν αὐτοῦ μοῖραν εἴληφε ...
(V, 2) Πρόκειται οὖν νῦν τὴν οὕτως ἔχουσαν αὐτοῦ ἀνατρέψαι λέξιν·
θεὸς μέν, ὦ Ἰουδαῖοι καὶ Χριστιανοί, καὶ θεοῦ παῖς οὐδεὶς
οὔτε κατῆλθεν οὔτ' ⟨ἂν⟩ κατέλθοι. εἰ δέ τινας ἀγγέλους φατέ,
τίνας τούτους λέγετε, θεοὺς ἢ ἄλλο τι γένος; ἄλλο τι ὡς εἰκός,
805 τοὺς δαίμονας ... (6) Μετὰ ταῦτα δὲ τοιαύτην ἐκτίθεται περὶ
Ἰουδαίων λέξιν· πρῶτον οὖν τῶν Ἰουδαίων θαυμάζειν ἄξιον, εἰ
τὸν μὲν οὐρανὸν καὶ τοὺς ἐν τῷδε ἀγγέλους σέβουσι, τὰ
σεμνότατα δὲ αὐτοῦ μέρη καὶ δυνατώτατα, ἥλιον καὶ
σελήνην καὶ τοὺς ἄλλους ἀστέρας ἀπλανεῖς τε καὶ πλανήτας,
810 ταῦτα παραπέμπουσιν· ὡς ἐνδεχόμενον τὸ μὲν ὅλον εἶναι
θεόν, τὰ δὲ μέρη αὐτοῦ μὴ θεῖα, ἢ τοὺς μὲν ἐν σκότῳ που ἐκ
γοητείας οὐκ ὀρθῆς τυφλώττουσιν ἢ δι' ἀμυδρῶν φασμάτων
ὀνειρώττουσιν ἐγχρίμπτειν λεγομένους εὖ μάλα θρησκεύειν,
τοὺς δ' ἐναργῶς οὕτως καὶ λαμπρῶς ἅπασι προφητεύοντας, δι'
815 ὧν ὑετούς τε καὶ θάλπη καὶ νέφη καὶ βροντάς, ἃς
προσκυνοῦσι, καὶ ἀστραπὰς καὶ καρποὺς καὶ γονὰς ἁπάσας

782–783 Ἑξῆς ... δεδημιούργηται Φ om. A   784 λέγει Φ / ἀλόγων Φ Borret
785 ἄλογα Φ Borret   ἄλλα A Koetschau / ζῴων A Koetschau
792 τὰ πάντα Φ   ταῦτα A   795 πάρεργον Koetschau Borret
πᾶν ἔργον A Pat C   πάρεστιν B / ἀλλὰ A² Φ   om. A   del. Koetschau
797 ἑαυτὸν Delarue Koetschau Borret   αὐτὸ A Φ   798 ἐπιστρέψει Pat B
800 αὐτοῦ] ἑαυτοῦ Pat C / εἴληφε] εἴληχεν Pat B   803 ⟨ἂν⟩ Ktr Borret

ταμιεύεσθαι, δι' ὧν αὐτοῖς ἀνακαλύπτεσθαι τὸν θεόν, τοὺς
φανερωτάτους τῶν ἄνω κήρυκας, τοὺς ὡς ἀληθῶς οὐρανίους
ἀγγέλους, τούτους ἡγεῖσθαι τὸ μηδέν ... *(14) Λέγει οὖν ταῦτα·*
820 ἠλίθιον δ' αὐτῶν καὶ τὸ νομίζειν, ἐπειδὰν ὁ θεὸς ὥσπερ
μάγειρος ἐπενέγκῃ τὸ πῦρ, τὸ μὲν ἄλλο πᾶν ἐξοπτήσεσθαι
γένος, αὐτοὺς δὲ μόνους διαμενεῖν, οὐ μόνον τοὺς ζῶντας
ἀλλὰ καὶ τοὺς πάλαι ποτὲ ἀποθανόντας αὐταῖς σαρξὶν
ἐκείναις ἀπὸ τῆς γῆς ἀναδύντας, ἀτεχνῶς σκωλήκων ἡ ἐλπίς.
825 ποία γὰρ ἀνθρώπου ψυχὴ ποθήσειεν ⟨ἂν⟩ ἔτι σῶμα σεσηπός;
ὁπότε μηδ' ὑμῶν τὸ δόγμα καὶ τῶν Χριστιανῶν ἐνίοις κοινόν
ἐστι, καὶ τὸ σφόδρα μιαρὸν αὐτοῦ καὶ ἀπόπτυστον ἅμα καὶ
ἀδύνατον ἀποφαίνειν· ποῖον γὰρ σῶμα πάντη διαφθαρὲν οἷόν
τε ἐπανελθεῖν εἰς τὴν ἐξ ἀρχῆς φύσιν καὶ αὐτὴν ἐκείνην, ἐξ
830 ἧς ἐλύθη, τὴν πρώτην σύστασιν; οὐδὲν ἔχοντες
ἀποκρίνασθαι καταφεύγουσιν εἰς ἀτοπωτάτην ἀναχώρησιν
ὅτι πᾶν δυνατὸν τῷ θεῷ. ἀλλ' οὔτι γε τὰ αἰσχρὰ ὁ θεὸς
δύναται οὐδὲ τὰ παρὰ φύσιν βούλεται· οὐδ' ἂν σύ τι
ἐπιθυμήσῃς κατὰ τὴν σαυτοῦ μοχθηρίαν βδελυρόν, ὁ θεὸς
835 τοῦτο δυνήσεται, καὶ χρὴ πιστεύειν εὐθὺς ὅτι ἔσται. οὐ γὰρ
τῆς πλημμελοῦς ὀρέξεως οὐδὲ τῆς πεπλανημένης ἀκοσμίας
ἀλλὰ τῆς ὀρθῆς καὶ δικαίας φύσεως ὁ θεός ἐστιν ἀρχηγέτης.
καὶ ψυχῆς μὲν αἰώνιον βιοτὴν δύναιτ' ἂν παρασχεῖν· «νέκυες
δέ» φησὶν Ἡράκλειτος, «κοπρίων ἐκβλητότεροι». σάρκα δή,
840 μεστὴν ὧν οὐδὲ εἰπεῖν καλόν, αἰώνιον ἀποφῆναι παραλόγως
οὔτε βουλήσεται ὁ θεὸς οὔτε δυνήσεται. αὐτὸς γάρ ἐστιν ὁ
πάντων τῶν ὄντων λόγος· οὐδὲν οὖν οἷός τε παράλογον οὐδὲ
παρ' ἑαυτὸν ἐργάσασθαι ... *(25) Ἴδωμεν δὲ καὶ τὴν ἑξῆς τοῦ*
Κέλσου λέξιν, οὕτως ἔχουσαν· Ἰουδαῖοι μὲν οὖν ἔθνος ἴδιον
845 γενόμενοι καὶ κατὰ τὸ ἐπιχώριον νόμους θέμενοι καὶ τούτους
ἐν σφίσιν ἔτι νῦν περιστέλλοντες καὶ θρησκείαν ὁποίαν δή,
πάτριον δ' οὖν, φυλάσσοντες ὅμοια τοῖς ἄλλοις ἀνθρώποις
δρῶσιν, ὅτι ἕκαστοι τὰ πάτρια, ὁποῖά ποτ' ἂν τύχῃ
καθεστηκότα περιέπουσι. δοκεῖ δ' οὕτως καὶ συμφέρειν, οὐ
850 μόνον καθότι ἐπὶ νοῦν ἦλθεν ἄλλοις ἄλλως νομίσαι καὶ δεῖ
φυλάττειν τὰ ἐς κοινὸν κεκυρωμένα, ἀλλὰ καὶ ὅτι ὡς εἰκὸς τὰ

817 ταμιεύεσθαι δῆλον Bouhéreau   822 διαμενεῖν Μ   διαμένειν Α
824 ἀπὸ Μ   ὑπὸ Α   825 ⟨ἂν⟩ Bader Borret   826 ὑμῶν edd.
ἡμῶν Α   828 ἀποφαίνειν Koetschau Borret   ἀποφαίνει Ρ
ἀποφαίνεις Α   848 ὁποῖά Φ   ὅπῃ Α
849 καθεστηκότα Φ om. Α   851 ἐς] εἰς Φ

μέρη τῆς γῆς ἐξ ἀρχῆς ἄλλα ἄλλοις ἐπόπταις νενεμημένα καὶ
κατά τινας ἐπικρατείας διειλημμένα ταύτῃ καὶ διοικεῖται. καὶ δὴ τὰ
παρ' ἑκάστοις ὀρθῶς ἂν πράττοιτο ταύτῃ δρώμενα, ὅπῃ ἐκείνοις φίλον·
855 παραλύειν δὲ οὐχ ὅσιον εἶναι τὰ ἐξ ἀρχῆς κατὰ τόπους νενομισμένα ...
(34) Ἵνα δὲ μὴ παρέλθωμεν τὰ ἐν τοῖς μεταξὺ λελεγμένα τῷ Κέλσῳ,
φέρ' ἐκθώμεθα καὶ ταῦτα· χρήσαιτο δ' ἄν τις καὶ Ἡροδότῳ πρὸς
τόδε μάρτυρι, λέγοντι ὧδε ⟨*Historiae*, II, 18⟩· «οἱ γὰρ δὴ ἐκ
Μαρέης τε πόλιος καὶ Ἄπιος οἰκέοντες Αἰγύπτου τὰ
860 πρόσουρα Λιβύῃ, αὐτοί τε δοκέοντες εἶναι Λίβυες καὶ οὐκ
Αἰγύπτιοι καὶ ἀχθόμενοι τῇ περὶ τὰ ἱερὰ θρησκείῃ,
βουλόμενοι θηλέων βοῶν μὴ εἴργεσθαι, ἔπεμψαν εἰς
Ἄμμωνα φάμενοι οὐδὲν σφίσι τε καὶ Αἰγυπτίοισι κοινὸν
εἶναι· οἰκέειν γὰρ ἔξω τοῦ Δέλτα καὶ οὐκ ὁμολογέειν αὐτοῖσι,
865 βούλεσθαί τε πάντων σφίσιν ἐξεῖναι γεύεσθαι· ὁ δὲ θεὸς οὐκ
ἔα σφέας ποιέειν ταῦτα, φὰς Αἴγυπτον εἶναι ταύτην, ἣν ὁ
Νεῖλος ἐπιὼν ἄρδει, καὶ Αἰγυπτίους εἶναι τούτους, οἳ
ἔνερθεν Ἐλεφαντίνης πόλιος οἰκέοντες ἀπὸ τοῦ ποταμοῦ
τούτου πίνουσιν.» Ἡροδότῳ μὲν τάδε ἱστόρηται. ὁ δ' Ἄμμων
870 οὐδέν τι κακίων διαπρεσβεῦσαι τὰ δαιμόνια ἢ οἱ Ἰουδαίων
ἄγγελοι· ὥστε οὐδὲν ἄδικον ἑκάστους τὰ σφέτερα νόμιμα
θρησκεύειν. ἀμέλει πλεῖστον αὐτῶν εὑρήσομεν κατὰ ἔθνη τὸ
διαφέρον, καὶ ὅμως ἕκαστοι αὐτοὶ μάλιστα εὖ νομίζειν
δοκοῦσιν· Αἰθιόπων μὲν οἱ Μερόην οἰκοῦντες ⟨*Historiae*, II, 29⟩
875 «Δία καὶ Διόνυσον μόνους» σέβοντες, Ἀράβιοι δὲ τὴν
Οὐρανίαν καὶ Διόνυσον τούτους μόνους, Αἰγύπτιοι δὲ πάντες
μὲν Ὄσιρίν τε καὶ Ἶσιν, Σαῖται δὲ Ἀθηνᾶν, Ναυκρατῖται δέ,
οὐ πάλαι ἀρξάμενοι, ὠνόμασαν Σάραπιν, καὶ οἱ λοιποὶ κατὰ
νόμους ὡς ἕκαστοι. καὶ οἱ μὲν οἴων ἀπέχονται, σέβοντες ὡς
880 ἱερούς, οἱ δὲ αἰγῶν, οἱ δὲ κροκοδείλων, οἱ δὲ βοῶν θηλείων,
συῶν δὲ ἀπέχονται βδελυττόμενοι, Σκύθαις γε μὴν καὶ
ἀνθρώπους δαίνυσθαι καλόν· Ἰνδῶν δέ εἰσιν οἳ καὶ τοὺς
πατέρας ἐσθίοντες ὅσια δρᾶν νομίζουσι. καί που φησὶν ὁ
αὐτὸς Ἡρόδοτος· χρήσομαι δὲ αὖθις αὐταῖς ἐκείνου λέξεσι
885 πίστεως εἵνεκα· ἱστορεῖ δὲ ὧδε· ⟨*Historiae*, III, 38⟩ «εἰ γάρ τις
προσθείη πᾶσιν ἀνθρώποισι ἐκλέξασθαι κελεύων νόμους
τοὺς καλλίστους τοὺς ἐκ ⟨τῶν⟩ πάντων νόμων, διασκεψάμενοι

---

862 ἔργεσθαι Koetschau   863 φάμενοι Herodotus   εἰργόμενοι A
866 ἥν] τὴν Herodotus Koetschau   867 Αἰγυπτίους Herodotus   αἰγύπτου A
   871 ἑκάστους M^corr   ἑκάστου A   879 νομοὺς Koetschau
886 προθείη M^corr Koetschau   887 ⟨τῶν⟩ ex Herodoto add. Koetschau

ἂν ἑλοίατο πολύ τι καλλίστους ἑωτῶν νόμους ἕκαστοι εἶναι.
οὔκων εἰκός ἐστιν ἄλλον γε ἢ μαινόμενον ἄνδρα ⟨γέλωτα⟩ τὰ
890 τοιαῦτα τίθεσθαι. ὡς δ᾽ οὕτως νενομίκασι τὰ περὶ τοὺς
νόμους οἱ πάντες ἄνθρωποι, πολλοῖσι καὶ ἄλλοισι
τεκμηρίοισι πάρεστι σταθμώσασθαι, ἐν δὲ δὴ καὶ ⟨τῷδε⟩.
Δαρεῖος ἐπὶ τῆς ἑωυτοῦ ἀρχῆς καλέσας Ἑλλήνων τοὺς
παρεόντας εἴρετο ἐπὶ κόσῳ ἂν χρήματι βουλοίατο τοὺς
895 πατέρας ἀποθνήσκοντας κατασιτέεσθαι· οἱ δὲ ἔφασαν ἐπ᾽
οὐδενὶ ἔρδειν ἂν ταῦτα. Δαρεῖος δὲ μετὰ ταῦτα καλέσας
Ἰνδῶν τοὺς καλεομένους Καλλατίας, οἳ τοὺς γονέας
κατεσθίουσιν, εἴρετο, παρεόντων τῶν Ἑλλήνων καὶ δι᾽
ἑρμηνέος μανθανόντων τὰ λεγόμενα, ἐπὶ τίνι χρήματι
900 δεξαίατ᾽ ἂν τελευτῶντας τοὺς πατέρας κατακαίειν πυρί· οἱ δὲ
ἀμβώσαντες μέγα εὐφημέειν μιν ἐκέλευον. οὕτω μὲν νῦν
τάδε νενόμισται, καὶ ὀρθῶς μοι δοκέει Πίνδαρος ποιῆσαι,
νόμον πάντων βασιλέα φήσας εἶναι.» ... (41) Ἴδωμεν δὲ καὶ τὰ
ἑξῆς τῷ Κέλσῳ λεγόμενα, ἐν οἷς σφόδρα μὲν ἐλάχιστά ἐστι τὰ περὶ
905 Χριστιανῶν πλεῖστα δὲ ὅσα περὶ Ἰουδαίων. φησὶν οὖν· εἰ μὲν δὴ
κατὰ ταῦτα περιστέλλοιεν Ἰουδαῖοι τὸν ἴδιον νόμον, οὐ
μεμπτὰ αὐτῶν, ἐκείνων δὲ μᾶλλον, τῶν καταλιπόντων τὰ
σφέτερα καὶ τὰ Ἰουδαίων προσποιουμένων. εἰ δ᾽ ὥς τι
σοφώτερον εἰδότες σεμνύνονταί τε καὶ τὴν ἄλλων κοινωνίαν
910 ⟨ὡς⟩ οὐκ ἐξ ἴσου καθαρῶν ἀποστρέφονται, ἤδη ἀκηκόασιν ὅτι
οὐδὲ τὸ περὶ οὐρανοῦ δόγμα ἴδιον λέγουσιν ἀλλ᾽ ἵνα πάντα
ἐάσω, καὶ Πέρσαις, ὥς που δηλοῖ καὶ Ἡρόδοτος, πάλαι
δεδογμένον. «νομίζουσι γάρ», φησί, «Διῒ μὲν ἐπὶ τὰ
ὑψηλότατα τῶν ὀρέων ἀναβαίνοντες θυσίας ἔρδειν, τὸν
915 κύκλον πάντα τοῦ οὐρανοῦ Δία καλέοντες». οὐδὲν οὖν οἶμαι
διαφέρειν Δία Ὕψιστον καλεῖν ἢ Ζῆνα ἢ Ἀδωναῖον ἢ
Σαβαὼθ ἢ Ἀμοῦν, ὡς Αἰγύπτιοι, ἢ Παπαῖον ὡς Σκύθαι. οὐ

---

888 πολύ] πολλὸν ex Herodoto Koetschau   889 οὔκων] οὐκ ὂν A /
γέλωτα ex Herodoto add. Koetschau   892 τεκμηρίοισι Herodotus
τεκμηρίοις A / ⟨τῷδε⟩ ex Herodoto add. Koetschau   894 εἴρετο Herodotus
ἤρετο M^{corr}   ἐρεῖ τὸ A   895 κατασιτέεσθαι M Herodotus
κατασιτεύεσθαι A   896 ταῦτα] τοῦτο Koetschau   899 ἑρμηνέος Herodotus
ἑρμηνέων A / μανθανόντων Herodotus   μανθανόντος A
900 δεξαίατ᾽ Herodotus   δέξαιο A / τελευτέοντας Koetschau
902 τάδε A   ταῦτα Herodotus Koetschau   907 μεμπτὸν Koetschau
μεμπτέον Guiet   910 ὡς οὐκ ... καθαρῶν edd.   οὐκ ... καθαρῶς A
914 ὀρέων Herodotus P   ὁράσεων A   916 ἀδωναῖον M²
ἀδωναῖ A¹   ἀδωνέα A   917 Παπαῖον edd.   παπταῖον A

μὴν οὐδὲ κατὰ ταῦτα ἁγιώτεροι τῶν ἄλλων ἂν εἶεν, ὅτι
περιτέμνονται· τοῦτο γὰρ Αἰγύπτιοι καὶ Κόλχοι πρότεροι·
920 οὐδ' ὅτι συῶν ἀπέχονται· καὶ γὰρ τοῦτ' Αἰγύπτιοι, καὶ
προσέτι αἰγῶν τε καὶ οἰῶν καὶ βοῶν τε καὶ ἰχθύων, καὶ
κυάμων γε Πυθαγόρας τε καὶ οἱ μαθηταὶ καὶ ἐμψύχων
ἁπάντων. οὐ μὴν οὐδ' εὐδοκιμεῖν παρὰ τῷ θεῷ καὶ
στέργεσθαι διαφόρως τι τῶν ἄλλων τούτους εἰκός, καὶ
925 πέμπεσθαι μόνοις αὐτοῖς ἐκεῖθεν ἀγγέλους, οἷον δή τινα
μακάρων χώραν λαχοῦσιν· ὁρῶμεν γὰρ αὐτούς τε καὶ τὴν
χώραν τίνων ἠξίωνται. οὗτος μὲν οὖν ὁ χορὸς ἀπίτω δίκην
ἀλαζονείας ὑποσχών, οὐκ εἰδὼς τὸν μέγαν θεὸν ἀλλ' ὑπὸ τῆς
Μωϋσέως γοητείας ὑπαχθείς τε καὶ ψευσθεὶς κἀκείνης οὐκ
930 ἐπ' ἀγαθῷ τέλει γεγονὼς μαθητής ... (33) ἀλλὰ καὶ μετρίως
προλαμβάνουσι τὰ ὑπὸ τοῦ Κέλσου πρὸς ἡμᾶς λεγόμενα, ἐν οἷς φησιν·
ἴτω δὲ ὁ δεύτερος· ἐρήσομαι δὲ αὐτούς, πόθεν ἥκουσιν ἢ τίνα
ἔχουσιν ἀρχηγέτην πατρίων νόμων. οὐδένα φήσουσιν, οἵ γε
ἐκεῖθεν μὲν ὥρμηνται καὶ αὐτοὶ καὶ τὸν διδάσκαλόν τε καὶ
935 χοροστάτην οὐκ ἄλλοθέν ποθεν φέρουσιν· ὅμως δ'
ἀφεστήκασιν Ἰουδαίων ... (52) Ἢν δὲ βουλόμεθα ἐξετάσαι
νῦν τοῦ Κέλσου λέξιν οὕτως ἔχει· καὶ δὴ παραλείπομεν ὅσα
περὶ τοῦ διδασκάλου διελέγχονται, καὶ δοκείτω τις ὡς
ἀληθῶς ἄγγελος. ἧκε δὲ πότερον οὗτος πρῶτος καὶ μόνος, ἢ καὶ
940 ἄλλοι πρότερον; εἰ μὲν φαῖεν ὅτι μόνος, ἐλέγχοιντο ἂν ἐναντία
σφίσι ψευδόμενοι. ἐλθεῖν γὰρ καὶ ἄλλους λέγουσι πολλάκις,
καὶ ὁμοῦ γε ἑξήκοντα ἢ ἑβδομήκοντα· οὓς δὴ γενέσθαι
κακοὺς καὶ κολάζεσθαι δεσμοῖς ὑποβληθέντας ἐν γῇ, ὅθεν
καὶ τὰς θερμὰς πηγὰς εἶναι τὰ ἐκείνων δάκρυα. καὶ μὴν καὶ
945 πρὸς τὸν αὐτοῦ τοῦδε τάφον ἐλθεῖν ἄγγελον, οἱ μὲν ἕνα, οἱ δὲ
δύο, τοὺς ἀποκρινομένους ταῖς γυναιξὶν ὅτι ἀνέστη. ὁ γὰρ τοῦ
θεοῦ παῖς, ὡς ἔοικεν, οὐκ ἐδύνατο ἀνοῖξαι τὸν τάφον, ἀλλ'
ἐδεήθη ἄλλου ἀποκινήσοντος τὴν πέτραν. ἔτι μὴν καὶ ὑπὲρ
τῆς Μαρίας κυούσης πρὸς τὸν τέκτονα ἧκεν ἄγγελος, καὶ
950 ὑπὲρ τοῦ τὸ βρέφος ἐξαρπάσαντας φυγεῖν ἄλλος ἄγγελος. καὶ
τί δεῖ πάντα ἀκριβολογεῖσθαι καὶ τοὺς Μωϋσεῖ τε καὶ ἄλλοις
αὐτῶν πεμφθῆναι λεγομένους ἀπαριθμεῖν; εἰ τοίνυν
ἐπέμφθησαν καὶ ἄλλοι, δῆλον ὅτι καὶ ὅδε παρὰ τοῦ αὐτοῦ
θεοῦ. πλεῖον δέ τι ἀγγέλλειν δοκείτω, φέρε, ὥσπερ

---

920 τουτ'] ταυτ' M   921 τε² M   om. A   933 πατρίων νόμων Delarue
πάτριον νόμον A   937 παραλείπωμεν Gelenius Delarue
940 ἐλέγχοιτο A   954 δοκείτω M   δοκεῖ τῷ A

955 πλημμελούντων τι Ἰουδαίων ἢ παραχαραττόντων τὴν εὐσέβειαν ἢ οὐχ ὅσια δρώντων· ταῦτα γὰρ αἰνίττονται ... (59)
Εἶθ' ἑξῆς φησιν ὁ Κέλσος· οὐκοῦν ὁ αὐτὸς θεὸς Ἰουδαίοις τε καὶ
τοῖσδε, δῆλον δ' ὅτι τοῖς Χριστιανοῖς· καὶ ὡσπερεὶ τὸ οὐκ ἂν
διδόμενον συνάγων τοῦτό φησι· σαφῶς γε τῶν ἀπὸ μεγάλης
960 ἐκκλησίας τοῦτο ὁμολογούντων καὶ τὰ τῆς παρὰ Ἰουδαίοις
φερομένης κοσμογονίας προσιεμένων ὡς ἀληθῆ περί γε τῶν
ἓξ ἡμερῶν καὶ τῆς ἑβδόμης, ἐν ᾗ, ὡς μὲν ἡ γραφὴ λέγει,
«κατέπαυσεν ἀπὸ τῶν ἔργων ἑαυτοῦ» ὁ θεὸς ἀναχωρῶν εἰς τὴν ἑαυτοῦ
περιωπήν, ὡς δ' ὁ Κέλσος μὴ τηρήσας τὰ γεγραμμένα μηδὲ συνιεὶς
965 αὐτά φησιν, ἀναπαυσάμενος, ὅπερ οὐ γέγραπται ... εἶτα δοκεῖ μοι
τὸ βιβλίον συμπληρῶσαι θέλων καὶ μέγα δοκεῖν εἶναι ποιῶν εἰκῇ
προστιθέναι τινά, ὁποῖά ἐστι καὶ τὰ κατὰ τὸν πρῶτον ἄνθρωπον,
ὡς ἄρα λέγομεν τὸν αὐτὸν εἶναι ὡς καὶ Ἰουδαῖοι καὶ τὴν ἀπ'
ἐκείνου διαδοχὴν ὁμοίως αὐτοῖς γενεαλογοῦμεν. ἀλλὰ καὶ εἰς
970 ἀλλήλους μὲν ἐπιβουλὴν ἀδελφῶν οὐκ ἴσμεν, τὸν δὲ Κάϊν
ἐπιβεβουλευκέναι τῷ Ἄβελ καὶ τὸν Ἡσαῦ τῷ Ἰακώβ · οὐ γὰρ Ἄβελ
τῷ Κάϊν ἐπεβούλευσεν οὐδὲ ὁ Ἰακὼβ τῷ Ἡσαῦ· ὅπερ εἰ ἐγεγόνει,
ἀκολούθως ἂν εἶπεν ὁ Κέλσος τὰς εἰς ἀλλήλους τῶν ἀδελφῶν
ἐπιβουλὰς τὰς αὐτὰς ἡμᾶς Ἰουδαίοις ἱστορεῖν. ἔστω δὲ καὶ τὴν
975 εἰς Αἴγυπτον ἡμᾶς ἀποδημίαν τὴν αὐτὴν λέγειν ἐκείνοις καὶ
τὴν ἐκεῖθεν ἐπάνοδον καὶ οὐ φυγήν, ὡς ὁ Κέλσος νομίζει ... (61)
Ἑξῆς δὲ τούτοις φησί· μή με οἰηθῇ τις ἀγνοεῖν, ὡς οἱ μὲν αὐτῶν
συνθήσονται τὸν αὐτὸν εἶναι σφίσιν ὅνπερ Ἰουδαίοις θεόν,
οἱ δ' ἄλλον, ᾧ τοῦτον ἐναντίον, παρ' ἐκείνου τε ἐλθεῖν τὸν
980 υἱόν ... ἔστωσαν δέ τινες καὶ τὸν Ἰησοῦν ἀποδεχόμενοι ὡς παρὰ
τοῦτο Χριστιανοὶ εἶναι αὐχοῦντες, ἔτι δὲ καὶ κατὰ τὸν Ἰουδαίων
νόμον ὡς τὰ Ἰουδαίων πλήθη βιοῦν ἐθέλοντες ... (65) καὶ
ἐνδιατρίβει γε κατηγορῶν τῆς ἐν ταῖς αἱρέσεσι διαφορᾶς· οὐ πάνυ δέ
μοι δοκεῖ διαρθροῦν ἃ λέγει οὐδ' ἐπιμελῶς αὐτὰ τεθεωρηκέναι οὐδὲ
985 κατανενοηκέναι, πῶς πλεῖον Ἰουδαίων ἐπίστασθαι λέγουσιν
ἑαυτοὺς οἱ ἐν τοῖς λόγοις διαβεβηκότες Χριστιανοί, ...
(VI, 19) Ἑξῆς δὲ τούτοις φησὶν ὁ Κέλσος παρακούσαντάς τινας
Χριστιανοὺς Πλατωνικῶν λέξεων αὐχεῖν τὸν ὑπερουράνιον
θεόν, ὑπεραναβαίνοντας τὸν Ἰουδαίων οὐρανόν ... (22) Ἔδοξε
990 δέ μοι τὸ ἐκθέσθαι τὴν λέξιν ἐν τούτοις τοῦ Κέλσου ἄτοπον εἶναι καὶ
ὅμοιον ᾧ αὐτὸς πεποίηκεν εἰς τὴν περὶ Χριστιανῶν καὶ Ἰουδαίων
κατηγορίαν ἀκαίρως παραλαβὼν οὐ μόνον τὰ Πλάτωνος, ὡς ἐκείνοις
ἀρκεῖσθαι, ἀλλὰ καὶ τά, ὥς φησι, Περσῶν τοῦ Μίθρου μυστήρια

961 κοσμογενείας Μ   975 ἀποδημίαν Α¹   ἐπιδημίαν Α

258

καὶ τὴν διήγησιν αὐτῶν ... (27) Εἶτ᾽ ἐπιλαβόμενος τῆς λέξεως
995 εὐλόγως κατηγορεῖ τῶν τοῦτο τολμώντων λέγειν· τούτου δ᾽ ἕνεκα καὶ
ἡμεῖς συναγανακτοῦμεν τοῖς μεμφομένοις τοὺς τοιούτους, εἰ δή τινες
εἰσὶ λέγοντες θεὸν κατηραμένον τὸν Ἰουδαίων, τὸν ὕοντα καὶ
βροντῶντα καὶ τοῦδε τοῦ κόσμου δημιουργὸν καὶ Μωϋσέως
καὶ τῆς κατ᾽ αὐτὸν κοσμοποιίας θεόν ... (28) φύρων δὲ τὰ
1000 πράγματα καὶ τὴν αἰτίαν ἐκτίθεται τοῦ κατηραμένον λέγεσθαι τὸν τῆς
κατὰ Μωϋσέα κοσμοποιίας θεὸν φάσκων ὅτι τοιοῦτός ἐστιν καὶ
ἀρᾶς ἄξιος κατὰ τοὺς ταῦτα περὶ αὐτοῦ δοξάζοντας, ἐπείπερ
τῷ ὄφει, γνῶσιν καλοῦ καὶ κακοῦ τοῖς πρώτοις ἀνθρώποις
εἰσηγουμένῳ, κατηράσατο ... (29) Εἶθ᾽ ἑξῆς ὡς Χριστιανοῖς
1005 λοιδορούμενος καὶ κατηγορῶν τῶν κατηραμένον εἰπόντων τὸν
Μωϋσέως καὶ τοῦ κατ᾽ αὐτὸν νόμου θεὸν καὶ οἰόμενος Χριστιανοὺς
εἶναι τοὺς ταῦτα λέγοντάς φησι· τί ἂν ἠλιθιώτερον ἢ
μανικώτερον ταύτης τῆς ἀναισθήτου σοφίας γένοιτο; τί γὰρ
ἐσφάλη ὁ Ἰουδαίων νομοθέτης; καὶ πῶς τὴν ἐκείνου
1010 κοσμογένειαν σαυτῷ διά τινος, ὡς φῇς, τυπώδους ἀλληγορίας
λαμβάνεις ἢ τὸν Ἰουδαίων νόμον, ἐπαινεῖς δὲ ἄκων, ὦ
δυσσεβέστατε, τὸν τοῦ κόσμου δημιουργόν, τὸν πάντα
ὑποσχόμενον αὐτοῖς, τὸν τὸ γένος αὐτῶν αὐξήσειν μέχρι
περάτων γῆς ἐπαγγειλάμενον καὶ ἀναστήσειν ἐκ νεκρῶν
1015 αὐτῇ σαρκὶ καὶ αἵματι καὶ τοῖς προφήταις ἐμπνέοντα, καὶ
πάλιν τοῦτον λοιδορεῖς; ἀλλ᾽ ὅταν μὲν ὑπὸ τούτων βιάζῃ, τὸν
αὐτὸν θεὸν σέβειν ὁμολογεῖς; ὅταν δὲ τὰ ἐναντία ὁ σὸς
διδάσκαλος Ἰησοῦς καὶ ὁ Ἰουδαίων Μωϋσῆς νομοθέτῃ, θεὸν
ἄλλον ἀντὶ τούτου καὶ τοῦ πατρὸς ζητεῖς ... (42) Ἑξῆς δὲ τούτοις
1020 ἀπὸ ἄλλης ἀρχῆς ὁ Κέλσος τοιαῦτά φησι καθ᾽ ἡμῶν· σφάλλονται δὲ
ἀσεβέστατα ἄττα καὶ περὶ τήνδε τὴν μεγίστην ἄγνοιαν,
ὁμοίως ἀπὸ θείων αἰνιγμάτων πεπλανημένην, ποιοῦντες τῷ
θεῷ ἐναντίον τινά, διάβολόν τε καὶ γλώττῃ Ἑβραίᾳ Σατανᾶν
ὀνομάζοντες τὸν αὐτόν. ἄλλως μὲν οὖν παντελῶς θνητὰ
1025 ταῦτα καὶ οὐδ᾽ ὅσια λέγειν, ὅτι δὴ ὁ μέγιστος θεός,
βουλόμενός τι ἀνθρώπους ὠφελῆσαι, τὸν ἀντιπράσσοντα
ἔχει καὶ ἀδυνατεῖ. ὁ τοῦ θεοῦ παῖς ἄρα ἡττᾶται ὑπὸ τοῦ
διαβόλου, καὶ κολαζόμενος ὑπ᾽ αὐτοῦ διδάσκει καὶ ἡμᾶς τῶν
ὑπὸ τούτῳ κολάσεων καταφρονεῖν, προαγορεύων ὡς ἄρα ὁ

---

995 ἕνεκα Α¹   ἕνεκεν Α   1009 ἐσφάλη Bader Borret
ἐσφάλετο Α   1010 φῇς Bouhéreau Koetschau Borret   φησι Α
1024 θνητὰ] πτηκτὰ Guiet   ἀνόητα Gundermann   ψεκτὰ Koetschau
1026 ἀνθρώποις Μ   1029 τούτου Ρ

1030 Σατανᾶς καὶ αὐτὸς ὁμοίως φανεὶς ἐπιδείξεται μεγάλα ἔργα
καὶ θαυμαστά, σφετεριζόμενος τὴν τοῦ θεοῦ δόξαν· οἷς οὐ
χρῆναι βουκοληθέντας ἀποτρέπεσθαι πρὸς ἐκεῖνον, ἀλλὰ
μόνῳ πιστεύειν ἑαυτῷ· ταῦτα μέν γε ἐστὶν ἄντικρυς
ἀνθρώπου γόητος, ἐργολαβοῦντος καὶ προφυλαττομένου τοὺς
1035 ἀντιδοξοῦντάς τε καὶ ἀνταγείροντας ... (49) Ἴδωμεν δὲ καὶ τὰ
ἑξῆς, ἐν οἷς μιᾷ λέξει ἀποφηνάμενος καὶ μηδὲ κατὰ τὸ πιθανόν τι
λέγων κατηγορεῖ τῆς κατὰ Μωϋσέα κοσμοποιΐας εἰπών· ἔτι γε μὴν
καὶ ἡ κοσμογένεια μάλα εὐηθική ... ἀπεφήνατο δὲ μάλα
εὐηθικὴν εἶναι καὶ τὴν περὶ ἀνθρώπων γενέσεως γραφήν,
1040 μήτε τιθεὶς τὰς λέξεις μήτ' ἀγωνιζόμενος πρὸς αὐτάς· οὐ γὰρ εἶχεν
οἶμαι λόγους ἀνατρέψαι δυναμένους τὸ «κατ' εἰκόνα θεοῦ»
πεποιῆσθαι τὸν ἄνθρωπον. ἀλλ' οὐδὲ συνίει τὸν ὑπὸ θεοῦ
φυτευθέντα «παράδεισον» καὶ τὴν προηγουμένην ἐν αὐτῷ
τοῦ ἀνθρώπου ζωὴν καὶ τὴν ἐκ περιστάσεως γενομένην,
1045 ἐκβληθέντος διὰ τὴν ἁμαρτίαν καὶ κατοικισθέντος ἐναντίον
«τοῦ παραδείσου τῆς τρυφῆς». ὁ δὲ λέγων μάλα εὐηθικῶς ταῦτ'
εἰρῆσθαι πρῶτον ἐπιστησάτω καὶ ἑκάστῳ μὲν καὶ τῷ δέ· «ἔταξε τὰ
χερουβὶμ καὶ τὴν φλογίνην ῥομφαίαν τὴν στρεφομένην, φυλάσσειν τὴν
ὁδὸν τοῦ ξύλου τῆς ζωῆς» εἰ δ' ἄρα μηδὲν νοήσας Μωϋσῆς
1050 ἀνέγραψε ταῦτα ἀλλὰ παραπλήσιόν τι ποιῶν οἷς παίζοντες οἱ
τῆς ἀρχαίας κωμῳδίας ποιηταὶ ἀνεγράψαντο· Προῖτος ἔγημε
Βελλεροφόντην, ὁ δὲ Πήγασος ἦν ἐξ Ἀρκαδίας· ἀλλ' ἐκεῖνοι
μὲν γελωτοποιεῖν θέλοντες τοιαῦτα συνέταττον ... (50) Ἐξῆς
δὲ τούτοις συμφορήσας ἐν ψιλαῖς ἀποφάσεσι τὰς διαφορὰς τῶν περὶ
1055 κόσμου καὶ ἀνθρώπων γενέσεώς τισι τῶν ἀρχαίων εἰρημένων
φησὶ τοὺς τὰ ἡμέτερα συγγράμματα λιπόντας Μωϋσέα καὶ
τοὺς προφήτας, οὐκ εἰδότας ἥτις ποτέ ἐστιν ἡ τοῦ κόσμου καὶ
τῶν ἀνθρώπων φύσις, συνθεῖναι λῆρον βαθύν ... (60) Μετὰ δὲ
τὴν ἐξετασθεῖσαν λέξιν ὡσπερεὶ σκοπὸν ἔχων τὸ ὅπως ποτὲ πολλῶν
1060 λόγων πληρῶσαι τὸ βιβλίον, ἄλλαις λέξεσι τὰ παραπλήσιά φησι τοῖς
ὀλίγῳ ἀνωτέρω ἐξετασθεῖσιν, ἐν οἷς ἔλεγε· μακρῷ δ' εὐηθέστερον
τὸ καὶ ἡμέρας τινὰς ἐπιδιανεῖμαι τῇ κοσμογονίᾳ, πρὶν εἶναι
ἡμέρας· οὐρανοῦ γὰρ οὔπω γεγονότος οὐδὲ γῆς πω

1032 χρῆναι βουκοληθέντας Wifstrand Chadwick Borret   χρῆναι
βουληθέντας A   χρῆναι προσέχειν βουληθέντας M²   χρὴ πλανηθῆναι
βουληθέντας Koetschau / πρὸς del. M²   1040 λέξεις Wendland Borret
   δείξεις A   1047 τῷ δέ Ktr Chadwick   τῷδε A Koetschau Borret
1051 ἔγημε A   ἔκτεινε in marg. M²   1055 εἰρημένων Wendland
Chadwick Borret   εἰρημένας A Koetschau   1056 καταλιπόντας Koetschau

ἐρηρεισμένης οὐδ' ἡλίου πω τῇδε φερομένου, πῶς ἡμέραι
ἦσαν; τί γὰρ διαφέρει ταῦτα τοῦ ἔτι δ' ἄνωθεν λαβόντες
ἐπισκεψώμεθα, πῶς οὐκ ἂν ἄτοπος εἴη θεὸς ὁ πρῶτος καὶ ὁ
μέγιστος κελεύων· γενέσθω τόδε καὶ ἕτερον τόδε ἢ τόδε, καὶ
μιᾷ μὲν ἡμέρᾳ τοσόνδε τεκταινόμενος τῇ δευτέρᾳ δ' αὖθις
τοσῷδε πλέον καὶ τρίτῃ καὶ τετάρτῃ καὶ πέμπτῃ καὶ ἕκτῃ; ...
1070 (52) Μετὰ δὲ ταῦτα Κέλσος φησίν· ἐγὼ δὲ περὶ μὲν γενέσεως
κόσμου καὶ φθορᾶς, ἢ ὡς ἀγένητος καὶ ἄφθαρτος, ἢ ὡς
γενητὸς μὲν ἄφθαρτος δέ, ἢ ὡς τὸ ἔμπαλιν, οὐδὲν περὶ τοῦδε
νυνὶ λέγω ... ἀλλ' οὐδὲ πνεῦμα τοῦ ἐπὶ πᾶσι θεοῦ φαμεν ὡς ἐν
ἀλλοτρίοις τοῖς τῇδε γεγονέναι κατὰ τὸ «πνεῦμα θεοῦ ἐπεφέρετο
1075 ἐπάνω τοῦ ὕδατος», οὐδὲ κακῶς μηχανώμενά τινα ὡς ὑπὸ ἑτέρου
τοῦ δημιουργοῦ παρὰ τὸν μέγαν θεὸν κατὰ τοῦ πνεύματος
αὐτοῦ φαμεν, ἀνεχομένου τοῦ ἀνωτέρω θεοῦ, δεδεῆσθαι
καθαιρέσεως ... (61) Εἶτα πάλιν ... φησί· μετὰ τοῦτο μὴν ὥσπερ
τις ἀτεχνῶς πονηρὸς χειροτέχνης ἐκκαμὼν καὶ πρὸς
1080 ἀνάπαυσιν ἀργίας δεηθείς ... εἶτα ὡς ἤτοι τῶν γραφῶν οὕτω
λεγουσῶν ἢ καὶ ἡμῶν αὐτῶν οὕτως διηγουμένων περὶ θεοῦ, ὅτι καμὼν
ἀνεπαύσατο, φησὶν ὅτι οὐ θέμις τὸν πρῶτον θεὸν κάμνειν
οὔτε χειρουργεῖν, οὔτε κελεύειν ... (62) Πάλιν τε αὖ ὁ Κέλσος ...
φησίν· οὐδὲ στόμα αὐτῷ ἐστιν οὐδὲ φωνή ... ἀλλ' οὐδ' ἄλλο
1085 φησὶν εἶναι τῷ θεῷ, ὧν ἡμεῖς ἴσμεν ... (63) Εἶτά ... φησι τό· οὐδ'
ἄνθρωπον ἐποίησεν εἰκόνα αὐτοῦ· οὐ γὰρ τοιόσδε ὁ θεὸς οὔτ'
ἄλλῳ εἴδει οὐδενὶ ὅμοιος ... (78) Ἑξῆς δὲ τοιαῦτά τινα λέγει ὁ
Κέλσος· ἔτι μὴν εἴπερ ἐβούλετο ὁ θεὸς ὥσπερ ὁ παρὰ τῷ
κωμῳδῷ Ζεὺς ἐκ τοῦ μακροῦ ὕπνου διϋπνίσας ῥύσασθαι τὸ
1090 τῶν ἀνθρώπων γένος ἐκ κακῶν, τί δή ποτε εἰς μίαν γωνίαν
ἔπεμψε τοῦτο, ὅ φατε, πνεῦμα; δέον πολλὰ ὁμοίως
διαφυσῆσαι σώματα καὶ κατὰ πᾶσαν ἀποστεῖλαι τὴν
οἰκουμένην. ἀλλ' ὁ μὲν κωμῳδὸς ἐν τῷ θεάτρῳ γελωτοποιῶν
συνέγραψεν ὅτι Ζεὺς ἐξυπνισθεὶς Ἀθηναίοις καὶ
1095 Λακεδαιμονίοις τὸν Ἑρμῆν ἔπεμψε· σὺ δὲ οὐκ οἴει
καταγελαστότερον πεποιηκέναι Ἰουδαίοις πεμπόμενον τοῦ
θεοῦ τὸν υἱόν ... (80) Ἑξῆς δὲ τούτοις ἐν θεώτατα ἐξ ἀρχῆς ἔδοξε
Κέλσῳ λέγειν ἔθνη Χαλδαίους, ἀφ' ὧν ἡ ἀπατηλὸς γενεθλιαλογία
νενέμηται τοὺς ἀνθρώπους. ἀλλὰ καὶ Μάγους τοῖς ἐνθεωτάτοις
1100 κατατάττει ἔθνεσιν ὁ Κέλσος, ἀφ' ὧν ἡ παρώνυμος τοῦ ἔθνους αὐτῶν

1072 τοῦδε] τούτου M   1075 μηχανώμενά τινα M^corr   μηχανῶμεν ἄτινα A
       1080 ἀργίας M²   ἀργοῦ A   1090 τῶν M   om. A

From Tacitus to Simplicius

μαγεία καὶ τοῖς λοιποῖς ἔθνεσιν ἐπὶ διαφθορᾷ καὶ ὀλέθρῳ τῶν
χρωμένων αὐτῇ ἐπιδεδήμηκε. καὶ Αἰγύπτιοι μὲν ἐν μὲν τοῖς
ἀνωτέρω καὶ παρὰ τῷ Κέλσῳ ἐπλανῶντο, ὡς σεμνοὺς μὲν ἔχοντες
περιβόλους τῶν νομιζομένων ἱερῶν ἔνδον δὲ οὐδὲν ἀλλ᾽ ἢ πιθήκους ἢ
1105 κροκοδείλους ἢ αἶγας ἢ ἀσπίδας ἤ τι τῶν ζῴων· νῦν δὲ ἔδοξε Κέλσῳ
ἐνθεώτατον εἰπεῖν καὶ τὸ Αἰγυπτίων ἔθνος, καὶ ἐνθεώτατον ἐξ
ἀρχῆς, τάχα ἐπεὶ Ἰουδαίοις προσπεπολεμήκασι. καὶ Πέρσαι δὲ οἱ
τὰς μητέρας γαμοῦντες καὶ θυγατράσι μιγνύμενοι ἔνθεον ἔθνος εἶναι
τῷ Κέλσῳ δοκοῦσιν, ἀλλὰ καὶ Ἰνδοί, ὧν τινας ἐν τοῖς προειρημένοις
1110 ἔλεγε καὶ ἀνθρωπείων γεγεῦσθαι σαρκῶν. μηδὲν δὲ τούτων
Ἰουδαίους μάλιστα τοὺς πάλαι πράττοντας οὐ μόνον οὐκ εἶπεν
ἐνθεωτάτους ἀλλὰ καὶ αὐτίκα ἀπολουμένους ...
(VII, 3) Φησὶν οὖν· τὰ μὲν ὑπὸ τῆς Πυθίας ἢ Δωδωνίδων ἢ
Κλαρίου ἢ ἐν Βραγχίδαις ἢ ἐν Ἄμμωνος ὑπὸ μυρίων τε
1115 ἄλλων θεοπρόπων προειρημένα, ὑφ᾽ ὧν ἐπιεικῶς πᾶσα γῆ
κατῳκίσθη, ταῦτα μὲν ⟨ἐν⟩ οὐδενὶ λόγῳ τίθενται· τὰ δὲ ὑπὸ
τῶν ἐν Ἰουδαίᾳ τῷ ἐκείνων τρόπῳ λεχθέντα ἢ μὴ λεχθέντα,
καὶ ὥσπερ εἰώθασιν ἔτι νῦν οἱ περὶ Φοινίκην τε καὶ
Παλαιστίνην, ταῦτά γε θαυμαστὰ καὶ ἀπαράλλακτα
1120 ἡγοῦνται ... (18) Ἑξῆς δὲ τούτοις τοιαῦτά φησιν ὁ Κέλσος· ἐκεῖνο δ᾽
οὐκ ἐνθυμηθήσονται πάλιν; εἰ προεῖπον οἱ τοῦ Ἰουδαίων
θεοῦ προφῆται τοῦτον ἐκείνου παῖδα ἐσόμενον, πῶς ἐκεῖνος
μὲν διὰ Μωϋσέως νομοθετεῖ πλουτεῖν καὶ δυναστεύειν καὶ
καταπιμπλάναι τὴν γῆν καὶ καταφονεύειν τοὺς πολεμίους
1125 ἡβηδὸν καὶ παγγενεὶ κτείνειν, ὅπερ καὶ αὐτὸς ἐν ὀφθαλμοῖς
τῶν Ἰουδαίων, ὥς φησι Μωϋσῆς, ποιεῖ καὶ πρὸς ταῦτα, ἂν μὴ
πείθωνται, διαρρήδην αὐτοὺς τὰ τῶν πολεμίων δράσειν
ἀπειλεῖ, ὁ δ᾽ υἱὸς ἄρα αὐτοῦ, ὁ «Ναζωραῖος» ἄνθρωπος,
ἀντινομοθετεῖ μηδὲ παριτητὸν εἶναι πρὸς τὸν πατέρα τῷ
1130 πλουτοῦντι ἢ φιλαρχιῶντι ἢ σοφίας ἢ δόξης ἀντιποιουμένῳ,
δεῖν δὲ σίτων μὲν καὶ ταμείου μὴ μᾶλλόν τι φροντίζειν ἢ
«τοὺς κόρακας», ἐσθῆτος δὲ ἧττον ἢ «τὰ κρίνα», τῷ δ᾽ ἅπαξ
τυπτήσαντι παρέχειν καὶ αὖθις τύπτειν; πότερον Μωϋσῆς ἢ
Ἰησοῦς ψεύδεται; ἢ ὁ πατὴρ τοῦτον πέμπων ἐπελάθετο, τίνα
1135 Μωϋσεῖ διετάξατο; ἢ καταγνοὺς τῶν ἰδίων νόμων μετέγνω
καὶ τὸν ἄγγελον ἐπὶ τοῖς ἐναντίοις ἀποστέλλει; ... (53) Μετὰ

1109 Ἰνδοί edd.   ἰνδῶν A   1113 Δωδωνίδων edd.   δωδωνίων A
1114 βραγχίδαις P²   βραχὶ(δ super χ) A   1126 ποιεῖ Mᶜᵒʳʳ   ποιεῖν A
1131 δεῖν Mᶜᵒʳʳ   δεῖ A   1135 διετάξατο edd.   διελέξατο A
1136 ἐπὶ Bouhéreau Bader Borret   καὶ ἐπὶ A Koetschau

262

ταῦτα ... φησὶ πρὸς ἡμᾶς· πόσῳ δ' ἦν ὑμῖν ἄμεινον, ἐπειδή γε
καινοτομῆσαί τι ἐπεθυμήσατε, περὶ ἄλλον τινὰ τῶν
γενναίως ἀποθανόντων καὶ θεῖον μῦθον δέξασθαι
1140 δυναμένων σπουδάσαι; φέρε, εἰ μὴ ἤρεσκεν Ἡρακλῆς καὶ
Ἀσκληπιὸς καὶ οἱ πάλαι δεδοξασμένοι, Ὀρφέα εἴχετε,
ἄνδρα ὁμολογουμένως ὁσίῳ χρησάμενον πνεύματι καὶ αὐτὸν
βιαίως ἀποθανόντα. ἀλλ' ἴσως ὑπ' ἄλλων προείληπτο.
Ἀνάξαρχον γοῦν, ὃς εἰς ὅλμον ἐμβληθεὶς καὶ παρανομώτατα
1145 συντριβόμενος εὖ μάλα κατεφρόνει τῆς κολάσεως λέγων·
«πτίσσε, πτίσσε τὸν Ἀναξάρχου θύλακον, αὐτὸν γὰρ οὐ
πτίσσεις»· θείου τινὸς ὡς ἀληθῶς πνεύματος ἡ φωνή· ἀλλὰ
καὶ τούτῳ φθάσαντές τινες ἠκολούθησαν φυσικοί· οὐκοῦν
Ἐπίκτητον; ὃς τοῦ δεσπότου στρεβλοῦντος αὐτοῦ τὸ σκέλος
1150 ὑπομειδιῶν ἀνεκπλήκτως ἔλεγε· «κατάσσεις», καὶ
κατάξαντος «οὐκ ἔλεγον», εἶπεν, «ὅτι κατάσσεις»; τί τοιοῦτον
ὁ ὑμέτερος θεὸς κολαζόμενος ἐφθέγξατο; ὑμεῖς δὲ κἂν
Σίβυλλαν ᾗ χρῶνταί τινες ὑμῶν, εἰκότως ἂν μᾶλλον
προεστήσασθε ὡς τοῦ θεοῦ παῖδα· νῦν δὲ παρεγγράφειν μὲν
1155 εἰς τὰ ἐκείνης πολλὰ καὶ βλάσφημα εἰκῇ δύνασθε, τὸν δὲ βίῳ
μὲν ἐπιρρητοτάτῳ θανάτῳ δὲ οἰκτίστῳ χρησάμενον θεὸν
τίθεσθε. πόσῳ τοῦδε ἐπιτηδειότερος ἦν ὑμῖν Ἰωνᾶς «ἐπὶ τῇ
κολοκύντῃ» ἢ Δανιὴλ ὁ ἐκ τῶν θηρίων ἢ οἱ τῶνδε ἔτι
τερατωδέστεροι; ...
1160 (VIII, 69) Εἶτα ἑαυτοῦ μὴ ἀκούσας ὁ Κέλσος ... φησίν· οὐ μὲν δὴ
τοῦτο φήσεις, ὡς, ἄν πεισθέντες σοι Ῥωμαῖοι καὶ τῶν
νενομισμένων αὐτοῖς πρὸς θεούς τε καὶ ἀνθρώπους
ἀμελήσαντες τὸν σὸν Ὕψιστον, ἢ ὅντινα βούλει,
προσκαλέσωνται, καταβὰς ὑπερμαχεῖται αὐτῶν, καὶ
1165 οὐδεμιᾶς ἄλλης ἀλκῆς δεήσει. καὶ γὰρ πρότερον ὁ αὐτὸς θεὸς
τοῖς προσέχουσιν αὐτῷ ταῦτά τε καὶ πολὺ μείζω τούτων, ὡς
ὑμεῖς φατε, ὑπισχνούμενος ὁρᾶτε ὅσα ὠφέλησεν ἐκείνους τε
καὶ ὑμᾶς· ὧν τοῖς μὲν ἀντὶ ⟨τοῦ⟩ γῆς ἁπάσης εἶναι δεσπόταις
οὐδ' ὁποία τις βῶλος οὐδ' ἑστία λείπεται, ὑμῶν δὲ κἂν
1170 πλανᾶταί τις ἔτι λανθάνων, ἀλλὰ ζητεῖται πρὸς θανάτου
δίκην.

1137 ὑμῖν Μ^corr   ἡμῖν Α   1155 δύνασθε] δεδύνησθε Bouhéreau
        1164 προσκαλέσωνται Koetschau   προσκαλέσασθαι Α
    1168 ⟨τοῦ⟩ Μ^corr Koetschau   1169 λείπεται] καταλείπεται Μ^corr

(I, 2) Next he says that *the doctrine* (obviously meaning Judaism with which Christianity is connected) *was originally barbarian*. Having an open mind he does not reproach the gospel for its barbarian origin, but praises *the barbarians* for being *capable of discovering doctrines*; but he adds to this that *the Greeks are better able to judge the value of what the barbarians have discovered, and to establish the doctrines and put them into practice by virtue* ... (14) Thinking that *between many of the nations there is an affinity* in that *they hold the same doctrine*, Celsus names all the nations which he supposes to have held this doctrine originally. But for some unknown reason he misrepresents the Jews alone, and does not include their race in the list with the others; nor does he say of them either that they *took part in labours* equal to theirs and *had the same notions* or that they *held similar doctrines in many respects* ... If *Moses and the prophets wrote much about their own people which is biased in favour of their own doctrine*, why may we not say as much of the compositions of the other nations also? Or are the *Egyptians* reliable authorities when in their histories they speak evil of the Jews? And when the Jews say the same about the Egyptians, recording that they suffered much wrongfully and saying that for this reason they were punished by God, are they lying? ... See then the wilfulness of the man who believes some particular nations to be *wise* while he condemns others as *utterly stupid*. Hear Celsus' words: *There is an ancient doctrine which has existed from the beginning, which has always been maintained by the wisest nations and cities and wise men*. And he would not speak of the Jews as being a very wise nation on a par with the *Egyptians, Assyrians, Indians, Persians, Odrysians, Samothracians, and Eleusinians* ... (16) I am surprised that Celsus numbers *the Odrysians, Samothracians, Eleusinians, and Hyperboreans among the most ancient and wise nations*, and yet does not reckon the Jews worth including with the wise or the ancient ... He says, moreover, that *the Galactophagi of Homer, the Druids of the Gauls, and the Getae are very wise and ancient nations, who believe doctrines akin to those of the Jews* ... Again, when he makes a list of *ancient and wise men who were of service to their contemporaries and to posterity by their writings*, he rejects Moses from the list of wise men ... For he says that *Linus, Musaeus, Orpheus, Pherecydes, Zoroaster the Persian, and Pythagoras understood these doctrines, and their opinions were put down in books and are preserved to this day* ... (17) But later when he criticizes the Mosaic history he finds fault with those who interpret it figuratively

264

and allegorically ... So when Celsus attacks, as he thinks, the Mosaic history and finds fault with *those who treat it allegorically*, although at the same time he gives them some credit for being *the more reasonable*, by the form of his criticism as it were he hinders (as he intends to do) those who are able to explain in reply how matters really stand ... (19) After this, secretly wishing to attack the Mosaic cosmography which indicates that the world is not yet ten thousand years old but is much less than this, Celsus agrees with those who say that the world is uncreated, although he hides his real intention. For in saying that *there have been many conflagrations from all eternity and many floods, and that the deluge which lately happened in the time of Deucalion was the most recent*, he clearly suggests to those able to understand him that he thinks the world is uncreated. But let this man who attacks the faith of the Christians tell us by what sort of arguments he was forced to accept the doctrine that *there have been many conflagrations and many floods, and that more recent than all others is the flood in the time of Deucalion and the conflagration in the time of Phaethon* ... (21) *Accordingly*, he says, *Moses heard of this doctrine which was current among the wise nations and distinguished men and acquired a name for divine power* ... But if, as you say, *he accepted wise and true doctrines and educated his own people by them*, what did he do deserving of criticism? ... (22) After this, though he does not attack the circumcision of the private parts which is the custom of the Jews, Celsus says that *it came from the Egyptians* ... (23) Celsus next says: *The goatherds and shepherds who followed Moses as their leader were deluded by clumsy deceits into thinking that there was only one God.* Let him show how, since it was, as he thinks, *without any rational cause* that *these goatherds and shepherds abandoned the worship of many gods*, he is able to commend the large number of gods among the Greeks or the other barbarian deities ... (24) After this he says: *The goatherds and shepherds thought that there was one God called the Most High, or Adonai, or the Heavenly One, or Sabaoth, or however they like to call this world; and they acknowledged nothing more.* Later he says that *it makes no difference whether one calls the supreme God by the name used among the Greeks, or by that, for example, used among the Indians, or by that among the Egyptians* ... (26) Let us see how Celsus, who professes to know everything, misrepresents the Jews when he says that *they worship angels and are addicted to sorcery of which Moses was their teacher* ... He next promises *to teach* us *how the Jews fell into error through ignorance and*

265

were deceived ... After Celsus has promised that *later* he *will teach about the Jewish doctrines,* he first discusses our Saviour ... (28) After this, he represents the Jew as having a conversation with Jesus himself and refuting him on many charges, as he thinks: first, because *he fabricated the story of his birth from a virgin*; and he reproaches him because *he came from a Jewish village and from a poor country woman who earned her living by spinning.* He says that *she was driven out by her husband, who was a carpenter by trade, as she was convicted of adultery.* Then he says that *after she had been driven out by her husband and while she was wandering about in a disgraceful way she secretly gave birth to Jesus.* And he says that *because he was poor he hired himself out as a workman in Egypt, and there tried his hand at certain magical powers on which the Egyptians pride themselves; he returned full of conceit, because of these powers, and on account of them gave himself the title of God* ... (32) Let us return, however, to the words put into the mouth of the Jew, where *the mother of Jesus* is described as having been *turned out by the carpenter who was betrothed to her, as she had been convicted of adultery and had a child by a certain soldier named Panthera* ... (37) But when Celsus has introduced the Jew as disputing with Jesus and pouring ridicule on the presence, as he thinks, of his birth from a virgin, and as quoting the Greek myths about *Danae* and *Melanippe* and *Auge* and *Antiope,* I have to reply that these words would be appropriate to a vulgar buffoon and not to a man who takes his professed task seriously ... (39) *Then was the mother of Jesus beautiful? And because she was beautiful did God have sexual intercourse with her, although by nature He cannot love a corruptible body? It is not likely that God would have fallen in love with her since she was neither wealthy nor of royal birth; for nobody knew her, not even her neighbours.* It is just ridicule also when he says: *When she was hated by the carpenter and turned out, neither divine power nor the gift of persuasion saved her. Therefore,* he says, *these things have nothing to do with the kingdom of God* ... (41) His Jew continues by saying this to him whom we confess to be our Lord Jesus: *When,* he says, *you were bathing near John, you say that you saw what appeared to be a bird fly towards you out of the air.* His Jew then asks: *What trustworthy witness saw this apparition, or who heard a voice from heaven adopting you as son of God? There is no proof except for your word and the evidence which you may produce of one of the men who were punished with you* ... (49) *But my prophet said once in Jerusalem that God's son would come to judge the holy and to punish the unrighteous* ... (50) As if it was not he alone of whom the prophets foretold that he would *judge the holy and punish the unrighteous* ... he says: *Why should you be the subject of these prophecies rather than the thousands of others who lived after the prophecy was uttered?* For some unknown reason he wants to ascribe to others the possibility that they may be supposed to have been referred to by the prophecies, and says: *Some people in ecstasy and others who go about begging say that they are sons of God who have come from above* ... (54) Since Celsus, who professes to know everything about the gospel, reproaches the Saviour for his passion, saying that he *was not helped by his Father, nor was able to help himself*, I have to affirm ... (57) Again, his Jew says to the Saviour: *If you say that every man has become a son of God by divine providence, what is the difference between you and anyone else?* ... *But some thousands*, so Celsus' Jew says, *will refute Jesus by asserting that the prophecies which were applied to him were spoken of them* ... (40) And after that he runs back to what is recorded after the birth of Jesus, the story about the star and the magi who came from the east to worship the child ... (34) That it was out of wickedness that Celsus did not quote the prophecy is made clear to me from the fact that although he has quoted several things from the gospel according to Matthew, such as *the star that arose at the birth of Jesus* and other miracles, yet he has not even mentioned this at all [scil. the prophecy of Isaiah about Emmanuel] ... (58) After this instead of the magi of the gospel, Celsus' Jew speaks of *Chaldaeans*, saying that *according to the account of Jesus they were moved to come to his birth to worship him as God although he was still an infant; and they informed Herod the Tetrarch of this: but he sent men to kill those born just at that time, thinking that he would destroy him also with them, lest somehow, after he had lived for the time sufficient for him to grow up, he should become king* ... (61) If Celsus had seen these things, he would not have said: *If Herod did this in order that when you were grown up you might not reign instead of him, why then when you had grown up did you not become king, but, though son of God, go about begging so disgracefully, cowering from fear, and wandering up and down in destitution?* ... (62) After this, not even knowing the number of the apostles, he says: *Jesus collected round him ten or eleven infamous men, the most wicked tax-collectors and sailors, and with these fled hither and thither, collecting a means of livelihood in a disgraceful and importunate way* ... (66) After these remarks the Jew of Celsus next says to Jesus: *Why also when you were still an infant did you have to be taken to Egypt lest you should be murdered? It is not likely that a god would be afraid of death. But an angel came from heaven, commanding you and your family to escape, lest by being left behind you should die. And could not the great God, who had already sent two angels on your account, guard you, His own son, at that very place?* ... (67) After this Celsus' Jew, as though he were some Greek that loved learning and had been educated to Greek literature, says: *The old myths that attributed a divine birth to Perseus and Amphion and Aeacus and Minos (we do not believe even them) are nevertheless evidence of their great and truly wonderful works for mankind, so that they do not appear lacking in plausibility; but as for you, what have you done in word or deed that is fine or wonderful? You showed nothing to us, although they challenged you in the temple to produce some obvious token that you were the son of God* ... (68) After this, suspecting that the great works done by Jesus would be pointed out, Celsus pretends to grant that the scriptures may be true when they speak of *cures or resurrection or a few loaves feeding many people, from which many fragments were left over, or any other monstrous tales,* as he thinks, *related by the disciples.* And he goes on to say: *Come let us believe that these miracles really were done by you.* Then he at once puts them on a level with *the works of sorcerers who profess to do wonderful miracles, and the accomplishments of those who are taught by the Egyptians, who for a few obols make known their sacred lore in the middle of the market-place and drive daemons out of men and blow away diseases and invoke the souls of heroes, displaying expensive banquets and dining tables and cakes and dishes which are non-existent and who make things move as though they were alive although they are not really so, but only appear as such in the imagination.* And he says: *Since these men do these wonders, ought we think them sons of God? Or ought we to say that they are the practices of wicked men possessed by an evil daemon?* ... (69) After this he muddles Christianity with the view of some sect as though Christians shared their opinions and applies his objections to all people converted by the divine word, saying *a god would not have had a body such as yours* ... Celsus then says: *The body of a god would not have been as you, Jesus, were begotten* ... (70) He says that *the body of a god would also not eat such food,* as though able to show from the gospels both that he ate and what kind of food he ate. However, supposing that he can do this, he might mention that he ate the passover with the disciples, holding that he did not merely say "with desire I have desired to eat this passover with you," but also actually ate it. He might also mention that when he was thirsty he drank at Jacob's well ... Furthermore, he says: *The body of a god does not use a voice of that kind, nor that method of persuasion* ... (71) Then this man who is, so to speak, *hated by God* for his impiety and *wicked* doctrines, hurls abuse at Jesus and says: *These were the actions of one hated by God and of a wicked sorcerer* ...

(II, 1) He says that *deluded by Jesus, they have left the law of their fathers, and have been quite ludicrously deceived, and have deserted to another name and another life* ... If Celsus had known all this, he would not have represented the Jew as saying to converts from Judaism: *What was wrong with you, citizens, that you left the law of our fathers, and being deluded by that man whom we were addressing just now, were quite ludicrously deceived and have deserted us for another name and another life?* ... (4) His Jew then says to believers from the Jewish people: *Quite recently, when we punished this fellow who cheated you, you abandoned the law of your fathers,*.. After this he seems to me to possess shrewdness when he says: *Or why do you take your origin from our religion, and then, as if you are progressing in knowledge, despise these things, although you cannot name any other origin of your doctrine than our law?* ... Why therefore does Celsus' Jew speak against us and say: *For if there was anyone who proclaimed to you that the son of God would come down to men, it was our prophet, the prophet of our God?* ... (5) After this, even though Celsus repeats himself about Jesus, saying now for the second time that *as an offender he was punished by the Jews,* nevertheless I will not repeat the defence ... Then his Jew disparages as stale stuff *the doctrine of the resurrection of the dead and of God's judgment giving reward to the righteous but fire to the unrighteous.* He thinks he can overthrow Christianity by saying that in these matters *Christians teach nothing new.* My answer to him is ... (6) Supposing also that *Jesus kept all the Jewish customs, and even took part in their sacrifices;* Why does this lend support to the view that *we ought not to believe in him as Son of God?* ... (7) I challenge anyone to show where there can be found even a suggestion of a saying uttered by Jesus from *arrogance* ... I challenge anyone to prove what *lies* he told; and let him give an account of great and small lies, that he may prove that *Jesus told great lies* ... And let Celsus' Jew in particular tell us what were the *profane* actions of Jesus ... (8) He says that *many others of the same type as*

269

Jesus have appeared to people who are willing to be deceived ... He remarks that *this charge is brought against the Jews by believers in Christ, that they have not believed in Jesus as God ... But how,* says he, *would we despise him when he came, when we declare plainly to all men that the one who will punish the unrighteous will come from God? ... Why should we have despised the one whom we proclaimed beforehand? Or was it that we might be punished more than others? ...* (9) After this the Jew says: *How could we regard him as God when in other matters, as people perceived, he did not manifest anything which he professed to do, and when we had convicted him, condemned him and decided that he should be punished, was caught hiding himself and escaping most disgracefully, and indeed was betrayed by those whom he called disciples? And yet,* says the Jew, *if he was God he could not run away nor be led away under arrest, and least of all could he, who was regarded as Saviour, and Son of the greatest God and an angel, be deserted and betrayed by his associates who had privately shared everything with him and had been under him as their teacher* ... (12) This objection also seems to me to be puerile: *No good general who led many thousands was ever betrayed, nor was any wicked robber-chieftain, who was captain of very bad men, while he appeared to bring some advantage to his associates. But he, who was betrayed by those under his authority, neither ruled like a good general; nor, when he had deceived his disciples, did he even inspire in the men so deceived that good will, if I may call it that, which robbers feel towards their chieftain* ... (13) After this Celsus' Jew says: *Although I could say much about what happened to Jesus which is true, and nothing like the account which has been written by the disciples of Jesus, I leave that out intentionally* ... He accuses the disciples of having *invented the statement that Jesus foreknew and foretold all that happened to him ...* (15) Celsus says: *As the disciples of Jesus were unable to conceal the self-evident fact, they conceived this idea of saying that he foreknew everything* ... (16) He makes the very silly statement that *the disciples recorded such things about Jesus to excuse the events of his life.* He says: *It is as if someone, while saying that a certain man is righteous, shows him to be doing wrong, and, while saying that he is holy, shows him to be a murderer, and, while saying that he is immortal, shows him to be dead, and to all this adds that he had predicted it* ... If he had known he would not have said this: *For you do not even say that he seemed to the impious men to endure these sufferings although he did not really do so; but on the contrary, you admit that he did suffer ...*

270

*What trustworthy evidence is there that he made these predictions? ...
How can a dead man be immortal? ...* (17) This too is very stupid:
*Who, whether god or daemon, or sensible man, if he foreknew that such
things would happen to him, would not avoid them if at least he could
do so, instead of meeting with just the events which he had foreseen? ...*
(18) After this Celsus' Jew makes yet another silly remark: *If he
foretold both the one who was to betray him and the one who was to
deny him, why did they not fear him as God, so that the one did not
betray him nor the other deny him? ... But they betrayed and denied
him without any respect for him? ...* (19) *Furthermore, if people conspire
against a man and he perceives it, then if he predicts it to the
conspirators they turn back and are on their guard ...* He next as it were
brings his argument to a conclusion by saying: *These things certainly
did not happen because they were foretold, for that is impossible; but
since they did happen, the assertion that he predicted them is proved to
be false. For it should be utterly inconceivable that those who had
already heard that Jesus knew their intentions would still have betrayed
him and denied him ...* (20) *If he foretold these events as being a god,* he
says, *then what he foretold must assuredly have come to pass. A god,
therefore, led his own disciples and prophets with whom he used to eat
and drink so far astray that they became impious and wicked. But a
god above all ought to have done good to all men, in particular to those
who have lived with him. A man who had shared meals with another
would not further plot against him. Would one who had eaten a
banquet with a god have become a conspirator against him? And what
is more outrageous still, God himself conspired against those who ate
with him, by making them traitors and impious men ...* (23) After this
he says *that if these things had been decreed for him and if he was
punished in obedience to his Father, it is obvious that since he was a god
and acted intentionally, what was done of deliberate purpose was
neither painful nor grievous to him ...* (24) After this he wants to argue
that the things that happened to Jesus *were painful and grievous,* and
that it was impossible for him to prevent them being so, even if he
desired, saying: *Why then does he utter loud laments and wailings, and
pray that he may avoid the fear of death, saying something like this: "O
Father, if this cup could pass by me?" ...* (26) Moreover, Celsus' Jew
charges the disciples of Jesus with having invented these stories,
saying: *Although you lied you were not able to conceal plausibly your
fictitious tales ...* (27) After this he says that *some believers, as though
from a drinking bout, go so far as to oppose themselves and alter the*

271

original text of the gospel three or four or several times over, and they change its character to enable them to deny difficulties in face of criticism ... (28) As after this Celsus' Jew also reproaches Christians for *quoting prophets who proclaimed beforehand the facts of Jesus' life*, we will say this in addition to what we have already said earlier on this subject. If, as he says, he *has consideration for men*, he ought to have quoted the prophecies and while admitting their plausible characteristics, to have set forth such a refutation of our use of the prophecies as might seem fitting to him. For then he would not have seemed to jump to such an important conclusion after a Jew's minor remarks. This is particularly true when he says that *the prophecies could be applied to thousands of others far more plausibly than to Jesus* ... (29) For this reason we have no need to reply to this remark attributed to the Jew: *The prophets say that the one who will come will be a great prince, lord of the whole earth and of all nations and armies.* But it is just like a Jew, I think, and consistent with their bitterness, when he reviles Jesus without giving even any plausible argument, saying: *But they did not proclaim a pestilent fellow like him* ... (30) Celsus also threw out this remark: *But no one gives a proof of a god or a son of a god by such signs and false stories, nor by such disreputable evidence* ... *for*, he says, *as the sun which illuminates everything else first shows itself, so ought the Son of God to have done* ... (31) After this he accuses Christians of *sophistry when they say that the Son of God is the very Logos himself*, and actually thinks he can substantiate the accusation by saying that *although we proclaim the Son of God to be Logos we do not bring forward as evidence a pure and holy Logos, but a man who was arrested most disgracefully and crucified* ... as Celsus has said when he attributes this to the Jew, representing him as saying: *Now if the Logos in your view is Son of God, we too approve of that.* (32) We have said earlier that Jesus could not have been either a *boaster* or a *sorcerer* ... But he says that *the men who compiled the genealogy boldly said that Jesus was descended from the first man and from the kings of the Jews.* He thinks he makes a fine point in saying that *the carpenter's wife would not have been ignorant of it had she had such a distinguished ancestry* ... (33) *Moreover*, he says, *what fine action did Jesus do like a god? Did he despise men's opposition and laugh and mock at the disaster that befell him?*
... (34) Celsus' Jew, while mocking Jesus, as he thinks, is described as having some knowledge *of the remark of Bacchus in Euripides* [*Bacchae*, 498]: "*The god himself will set me free whenever I wish it*".

... But the one who condemned him did not even suffer any such fate as that of Pentheus by going mad or being torn in pieces, he says ... And again, Celsus says nothing of the facts which point to the divinity of Jesus and reproaches him on the ground of what is written in the Gospel about Jesus, mentioning *those who mocked him and put a purple robe around him and the crown of thorns and the reed in his hand* ... (35) Then he says: *Why, if not before, does he not at any rate now show forth something divine, and deliver himself from this shame, and take his revenge on those who insult both him and his Father?* ... (36) Then Celsus says: *What does he say while his body is being crucified? Was his blood like [Ilias, V, 340] "Ichor such as flows in the veins of the blessed gods"?*

... (37) After this the Jew, who takes out of the gospel texts which, he thinks, provide opportunity for criticism, reproaches Jesus with *the vinegar and the gall,* saying that *he rushed greedily to drink and did not bear his thirst patiently as even an ordinary man often bears it* ... (38) After this the Jew further says to us: *Do you, who are such great believers, criticize us because we do not regard this man as a god nor agree with you that he endured these sufferings for the benefit of mankind, in order that we also may despise punishments* ... (39) How is it anything but a downright lie when Celsus' Jew asserts that *as long as he lived he convinced nobody, not even his own disciples, and was punished and endured such shame?* ... (41) Celsus further criticizes Jesus by words put into the mouth of the Jew, saying that *he did not show himself to be pure from all evils* ... (42) Moreover, as Celsus wants to make out that *Jesus was also not free from blame,* let him show who among those who assented to his doctrine recorded anything really blameworthy about Jesus ... But I do not know by what greater and clearer facts Celsus wanted Jesus to confirm the truth of the predictions. Perhaps, as it seems, he did not understand the doctrine that Jesus was a man, and did not want him to have any human experience, nor to become a noble example to men to show how to bear calamities ... (43) After this he says to us: *You will not say of him, I presume, that having failed to convince men on earth he travelled to Hades to convince them there* ... (44) After this for some unknown reason he makes a very silly remark: *If you think that you provide a true defence by discovering absurd justifications for those doctrines in which you have been ridiculously deceived, why may we not think that everyone else as well who has been condemned and come to an unfortunate end is an angel greater and more divine than Jesus?*

... Celsus' Jew also compares him with robbers saying that *anyone with similar shamelessness could say even of a robber and murderer who had been punished that he, forsooth, was not a robber but a god; for he foretold to his robber-gang that he would suffer the sort of things that he did in fact suffer* ... (45) *When those who were living with him at the time, who heard him speak and were taught by him, saw that he was being punished and was dying, they did not die with him, or for his sake, nor were they persuaded to despise punishments. But they even denied that they were disciples. Yet now you die with him* ... (46) Is it anything but lying when Celsus' Jew says: *When he was alive he won over only ten sailors and tax-collectors of the most abominable character, and not even all of these?* ... On the point in question, the next thing which he says in his book is this: *Is it not utterly ludicrous that when he was alive himself he convinced nobody; but now that he is dead, those who wish to do so convince multitudes* ... (47) He invents out of his own head what he asserts to be our answer to his question when he says: *What argument led you to regard this man as Son of God?* He has made us reply that *we were led by this argument because we know that his punishment was meant to destroy the father of evil* ... Also, as though we maintained that *we regard him as Son of God because he was punished,* he says: *What then? Have not many others also been punished and that no less disgracefully* ... (48) Many times already when Celsus has been unable to disregard the miracles which Jesus is recorded to have done he has misrepresented them as sorceries; and often we have replied to his arguments to the best of our ability. But here he says that this is the reply, as it were, which we make, that *we regarded him as Son of God for this reason, because he healed the lame and the blind.* And he goes on to say: *He raised the dead also, so you say* ... (49) Celsus wants to put the wonders of Jesus on a level with human sorcery and says in these very words: *O light and truth, with his own voice he explicitly confesses, as even you have recorded, that there will come among you others also who employ similar miracles, wicked men and sorcerers, and he names one Satan as devising this; so that not even he denies that these wonders have nothing divine about them, but are works of wicked men. Nevertheless, being compelled by the truth, he both reveals the deeds of others and proves his own to be wrong. Is it not a miserable argument to infer from the same works that he is a god while they are sorcerers? Why should we conclude from these works that the others were any more wicked than this fellow, taking the witness of Jesus himself? In fact, even he*

274

admitted that these works were not produced by any divine nature, but were the signs of certain cheats and wicked men ... (54) After this Celsus' Jew (to keep the part given to the Jew from the beginning) in the address to his fellow-citizens who believe says to us, forsooth: *What led you to believe, except that he foretold that after his death he would rise again?* ... (55) After this the Jew says to his fellow-citizens who believe in Jesus: *Come now, let us believe your view that he actually said this: How many others produce wonders like this to convince simple hearers whom they exploit by deceit? They say that Zamolxis, the slave of Pythagoras, also did this among the Scythians, and Pythagoras himself in Italy, and Rhampsinitus in Egypt. The last-named played dice with Demeter in Hades and returned bearing a gift from her, a golden napkin. Moreover, they say that Orpheus did this among the Odrysians and Protesilaus in Thessaly, and Heracles at Taenarum, and Theseus. But we must examine this question whether anyone who really died ever rose again with the same body. Or do you think that the stories of these others really are the legends which they appear to be, and yet that the ending of your tragedy is to be regarded as noble and convincing — his cry from the cross when he expired, and the earthquake and the darkness? While he was alive he did not help himself, but after death he rose again and showed the marks of his punishment and how his hands had been pierced. But who saw this? An hysterical female, as you say, and perhaps some other one of those who were deluded by the same sorcery, who either dreamt in a certain state of mind and through wishful thinking had a hallucination due to some mistaken notion (an experience which has happened to thousands), or, which is more likely, wanted to impress the others by telling this fantastic tale, and so by this cock-and-bull story to provide a chance for other beggars* ... (61) *After his death,* Celsus thinks, *Jesus used to produce only a mental impression of the wounds he received on the cross, and did not really appear wounded in this way* ... (63) After this Celsus speaks evil of the biblical story in a way that cannot be lightly passed over, when he says that *if Jesus really wanted to show forth divine power, he ought to have appeared to the very men who treated him despitefully and to the man who condemned him and to everyone elsewhere* ... (67) This was a futile argument of Celsus: *For he no longer feared any man after he died and, as you say, was a god; and he was not sent at all with the intention that he might be hid* ... (68) Let us see the way in which Celsus' Jew continues: *But if he really was so great he ought, in order to display his divinity, to have disappeared suddenly from the cross* ... (70) What source had Celsus' Jew for the assertion that *Jesus hid himself?* For he says of Jesus: *But what messenger that has been sent ever hid himself when he ought to be delivering the message that he had been commanded to proclaim? ... At the time when he was disbelieved while in the body, he preached without restraint to all; but when he would establish a strong faith after rising from the dead, he appeared secretly to just one woman and to those of his own confraternity... When he was punished he was seen by all; but by only one person after he rose again, whereas the opposite ought to have happened...* (71) Jesus taught us *who it was that sent him* ... furthermore, *the reasons why the Father sent him* are innumerable ... Moreover, Jesus enlightens the pious but punishes sinners, which Celsus did not say when he wrote: *And he will enlighten the pious while he will have mercy on sinners whether they repent or not* ... (72) After this he says: *If he wanted to be unnoticed, why was the voice from heaven heard, proclaiming him as Son of God? Yet if he did not want to be unnoticed why was he punished or why did he die? ...* (73) After this Celsus' Jew draws a conclusion which does not follow at all. For it does not follow from the fact that *he wanted to teach us even to despise death by the punishments which he suffered that after his resurrection from the dead he ought to have called all men clearly to the light and taught them why he came down* ... (74) To all this Celsus' Jew adds: *However, these objections come from your own writings, and we need no other witness; for you provide your own refutation* ... His Jew goes on after this: *O most high and heavenly one, what God that comes among men is completely disbelieved? ...* (75) *Or why ever is he not recognized by people who had been long expecting him? ...* (76) For he finds fault with Jesus, saying of him that *he utters threats and empty abuse whenever he says,* Woe unto you, *and,* I declare unto you. *For in these words he openly admits his inability to carry conviction, which no god, nor even a sensible man, would fail to do* ... (77) After this his Jew says, as though his remarks were consistent with the doctrine of the Jews: *We hope, it is true, to be resurrected in the body and to have everlasting life, and that he who is sent to us will be a pattern and leader of this by showing that it is not impossible for God to raise someone up again with his body* ... After this he says: *Where is he then, that we see and believe? ...* (78) After this the Jew says: *Or was his purpose in coming down that we might disbelieve? ...* (79) The Jew then concludes all this by saying about Jesus: *However, he was a mere man,*

*and of such a character as the truth itself makes obvious and as reason
shows* ...

(III, 1) He says now that *Christians and Jews quarrel with one another
very foolishly,* and that *our wrangle with one another about Christ is no
different from that called in the proverb a fight about the shadow of an
ass.* And he thinks *there is nothing worthy of attention in the dispute of
Jews and Christians with one another, since they both believe that by
divine inspiration a certain saviour was prophesied to be coming to
dwell among mankind; but they do not agree as to whether the one
prophesied has come or not* ... (5) In his next remarks Celsus imagines
that *the Jews were Egyptian by race, and left Egypt after revolting
against the Egyptian community and despising the religious customs of
Egypt.* He says that *what they did to the Egyptians they suffered in turn
through those who followed Jesus and believed him to be the Christ; in
both instances a revolt against the community led to the introduction of
new ideas* ... (6) My argument aims at proving the falsehood of the
assertion that *certain people who were Egyptian by race revolted
against the Egyptians and left Egypt, and came to Palestine where they
inhabited the part now called Judaea* ... (7) Just as it is false that the
Hebrews, being Egyptians, originated from a revolt, it is equally false
that others who were Jews revolted at the time of Jesus against the
Jewish community and followed Jesus ... (8) This is my reply to
Celsus' assertion that a revolt was the origin of the establishment of
the Jews in ancient times, and later of the existence of the Christians
...

(IV, 1) Our main task now is to reply to what Celsus says immediately
after the remarks we have quoted, to show that the prophecies about
Christ were true. For Celsus opposes both Jews and Christians at
once: the Jews who deny Christ has come, but hope that he will do so;
and the Christians who affirm that Jesus was the prophesied Christ.
This is what he says: (2) *The assertion made both by some of the
Christians and by the Jews, the former saying that some God or son of
God has come down to earth as judge of mankind, the latter saying that
he will come, is most shameful, and no lengthy argument is required to
refute it* ... (3) *What is the purpose of such a descent on the part of God?
... was it in order to learn what was going on among men? ... does not
he know everything? ... was he then unable to correct men merely by
divine power, without sending someone specially endowed for this
purpose?* ... (5) After this the most estimable Celsus for some

unknown reason brings up the objection against us that we affirm that *God Himself will come down to men.* And he thinks it follows from this that he leaves his throne ... as Celsus thinks when he says: *for if you changed any one quite insignificant thing on earth, you would upset and destroy everything ...* (6) If you want us to meet even the most ludicrous arguments of Celsus, listen to him when he says: *Furthermore, if God was unknown among men and on this account thought Himself to be underrated, would he want to make himself known, and try out both those who believe Him and those who do not, just like men who have just come into wealth and show off? It is, indeed, a strong and very mortal ambition which they attribute to God ...* (11) After this he wants to make out that we have nothing either remarkable or original to say about a *flood or conflagration,* and furthermore that it is because we have *misunderstood what is said by the Greeks or barbarians about these matters* that we have believed the accounts of them in our scriptures. This is what he says: *This idea occurred to them because they misunderstood the doctrine of Greeks and barbarians, namely, that after cycles of long periods and after returns and conjunctions of stars there are conflagrations and floods, and that after the last flood in the time of Deucalion the cycle demands a conflagration in accordance with the alternating succession of the universe. This was responsible for their mistaken opinion that God will come down and bring fire like a torturer ...* (20) He then represents the Jews, on the one hand, as finding reasons for their belief that the advent of the Christ is still in the future, and the Christians, on the other hand, as saying that the advent into human life of the Son of God has already happened. Accordingly, let us give our mind to this briefly, as far as possible: *The Jews say,* thinks Celsus, *that as life is filled with all manner of evil, it is necessary for God to send someone down that the wicked may be punished and everything purified, as it was when the first flood occurred ...* (21) For some unknown reason he thinks that *the overthrow of the tower had a similar purpose to that of the flood which,* according to the doctrine of Jews and Christians, *purified the earth.* Supposing that *the story about the tower* in Genesis contains *no hidden truth but,* as Celsus thinks, *is obvious,* even so its overthrow does not seem to have happened for the purification of the earth ... He thinks, however, that *Moses* who *wrote about the tower* and the confusion of languages *corrupted the story about the sons of Aloeus when he composed the narrative about the tower ...* Celsus also compares with *the story of Phaethon the narrative told* by Moses in

Genesis *about Sodom and Gomorrah, that they were destroyed by fire on account of their sins.* All that he has done in the consequence of one mistake: he failed to notice the evidence of Moses' antiquity ... (22) According to Celsus: *Christians also add certain doctrines to those maintained by the Jews, and assert that the Son of God has already come on account of the sins of the Jews, and that because the Jews punished Jesus and gave him gall to drink they drew down upon themselves the bitter anger of God ...* (23) After this he continues as usual by laughing at *the race of Jews and Christians,* comparing them *all to a cluster of bats or ants coming out of a nest, or frogs holding council round a marsh, or worms assembling in some filthy corner, disagreeing with one another about which of them are the worse sinners. They say: God shows and proclaims everything to us beforehand, and He has even deserted the whole world and the motion of the heavens, and disregarded the vast earth to give attention to us alone; and He sends messengers to us alone and never stops sending them and seeking that we may be with Him forever.* In the words which he invents he asserts that we are *like worms who say: There is God first, and we are next after Him in rank since He has made us entirely like God, and all things have been put under us, earth, water, air, and stars; and all things exist for our benefit, and have been appointed to serve us.* Celsus' worms, that is we Christians, further say: *Since some among us are in error, God will come or will send His Son to consume the unrighteous, and that the rest of us may have eternal life with Him.* And he adds to all this, that *these assertions would be more tolerable coming from worms and frogs than from Jews and Christians disagreeing with one another ...* (31) After this, from a desire to argue that Jews and Christians are no better than the animals which he mentioned above, he says: *The Jews were runaway slaves who escaped from Egypt; they never did anything important, nor have they ever been of any significance or prominence ...* If he thinks that he can argue that they were never of any significance or prominence from the fact that *nothing about their history is to be found among the Greeks,* we will say ... (33) After this Celsus attacks the first book of Moses entitled Genesis, saying that *they shamelessly undertook to trace their genealogy back to the first offspring of sorcerers and deceivers, invoking the witness of vague and ambiguous utterances concealed in some dark obscurity, which they misinterpreted to uneducated and stupid people, in spite of the fact that throughout the length of past history such an idea has never been claimed ...* (35) *yet now the Jews make claims about them in answer to certain others* ... (36) After this Celsus quotes from literature outside the divine Scripture the stories about *the men who claimed antiquity such as the Athenians, Egyptians, Arcadians and Phrygians, who hold that some among them were born of earth, and each of whom produce evidence for these assertions.* He says that *the Jews, being bowed down in some corner of Palestine, were totally uneducated and had not heard of these things which were sung in poetry long before by Hesiod and thousands of other inspired men. They composed a most improbable and crude history that a man was formed by the hands of God and given breath, that a woman was formed out of his side, that God gave commands, and that a serpent opposed them and even proved superior to the ordinances of God — a legend which they expound to old women, most impiously making God into a weakling right from the beginning, and incapable of persuading even one man whom He had formed* ... (41) He next speaks as follows: *They then tell of a flood and a prodigious ark holding everything inside it, and that a dove and a crow were messengers. This is a debased and unscrupulous version of the story of Deucalion, I suppose they did not expect that this would come to light, but simply recounted the myth to small children* ... (43) *Utterly absurd also,* he says, *is the begetting of children when the parents were too old,* and though he does not say so he obviously means the case of Abraham and Sarah. He rejects also *the conspiracies of the brothers,* referring either to Cain's plot against Abel, or both this and that of Esau against Jacob. He mentions *the father's grief,* perhaps referring to that of Isaac at the departure of Jacob, but perhaps also to that of Jacob when Joseph was sold into Egypt. When he writes of *the treacheries of mothers,* I think he means Rebecca when she contrived that the blessings of Isaac should not come to Esau but to Jacob. If we say that *God entered into the closest contact with* these men, why are we doing anything *absurd?* ... He has ridiculed the property which Jacob acquired when he was with Laban, because he did not understand the reference in the words "And the unbranded sheep were Laban's and the branded sheep were Jacob's". He says that *God made a present to the sons of asses, sheep, and camels* ... (44) He had missed the meaning of the Bible when he says that *God also gave wells to the righteous* ... In many passages the Word made use of stories about actual events and recorded them to exhibit deeper truths, which are indicated by means of hints. Of this sort are the stories about *the wells,* and *the marriages,* and *the intercourse* of righteous *men with* different *women* ... It is not we who teach that *brides and maidservants* are to be interpreted allegorically, but we have received this from wise men before us ... (45) Although Celsus ought to have approved the honesty of the authors of the divine scriptures, who did not even conceal discreditable events, and ought to have been won over also to regard even the other more remarkable stories as being not fictitious, yet he did the opposite. Concerning the story of Lot and his *daughters*, where he neither examined its ordinary meaning, nor looked into its mystical interpretation, he says that the story is *more iniquitous than Thyestian sins* ... (46) Celsus objects to the *hatred*, referring, I think, to that of Esau towards Jacob. Esau is a man admitted by the Bible to be bad. And without clearly quoting the story, he attacks that of Simon and Levi who *went forth because of the insult to their sister* after she had been forced by the son of the king of Shechem. He speaks of *brothers trading*, meaning Jacob's sons, and of *a brother sold*, meaning Joseph, and *a father who was deceived*, meaning Jacob ... (47) After this, for form's sake, Celsus makes exceedingly obscure references to the *dreams* of the chief butler and the chief baker of Pharaoh, and to *their explanation* ... And he says that *the one who was sold was kind to his brothers who sold him when they were hungry and had been sent with the asses to do some trading*, though Celsus does not specify what he did for them. He also mentions *the time when Joseph made himself known*, though I have no idea what his intention is in so doing, and what absurdity he produces from the fact that he made himself known ... And he says that Joseph, *the man who was sold to be a slave, was set free and with a solemn procession returned to his father's tomb*. He thinks that the story contains a ground for an objection when he says: *By him* (clearly meaning Joseph) *the distinguished and marvellous race of the Jews, which in Egypt had increased to be a multitude, were commanded to live somewhere outside and to tend their flocks in land that was valueless* ... He has called the departure of the people from Egypt a *flight*, not even mentioning at all what is written in the Exodus about the Hebrews' departure from the land of Egypt ... (48) Then, as though he had devoted himself only to hatred and hostility towards the doctrines of Jews and Christians, he says that *the more reasonable Jews and Christians allegorize these things*. He asserts that *because they are ashamed of them, they take refuge in allegory* ... (50) I have ventured upon an extended discussion from a desire to show that Celsus is incorrect when he says that *the more reasonable Jews and Christians try somehow to allegorize them, but they are incapable*

281

of being explained in this way, and are manifestly very stupid fables ...
(51) He seems to me to have heard also that there are treatises
containing allegories of the law. But if he had read them he would not
have said: *At any rate, the allegories which seem to have been written
about them are far more shameful and preposterous than the myths,
since they connect with some amazing and utterly senseless folly ideas
which cannot by any means be made to fit* ... (71) After this because
Celsus failed to understand them, he ridicules passages in the Bible
which speak of God as though he were subject to human passions, in
which *angry utterances* are spoken against the impious and threats
against people who have sinned. I reply that ... (72) we do not
attribute human passions to God, nor do we hold impious opinions
about Him, nor are we in error when we produce explanations
concerning Him from the scriptures themselves by comparing them
with one another ... (73) As a result of the fact that he has not
understood what is written of God's wrath, he says: *Is it not ridiculous
that when a man was angry with the Jews and destroyed them all from
the youth upwards and burnt down their city, in this case they were
annihilated; yet when the supreme God, as they say, was angry and
wrathful and sent His Son with threats, he suffered such indignities?* ...
After this he says: *However, that the discussion may not be confined to
the Jews alone (for that is not my theme) but may concern the whole of
nature, as I promised, I will show what has just been said with greater
clarity* ... (74) He next embarks on a lengthy discussion, criticizing us
on the ground that *we assert that God made all things for man.* From
the history of animals and from the sagacity which they display he
wants to show that *everything was made just as much for the irrational
animals as for men* ... (75) He thinks, in the first place that *thunders
and lightnings and rainstorms are not made by God*, at last displaying
his Epicurean views more clearly. And in the second place he says
that *even if one were to allow that these things are made by God, they
are not created for the nourishment for us men any more than for plants,
trees, grass and thorns* ... Then he says: *Even if you say that these
things grow for men ... why do you say that they grow for men any more
than for the wildest of irrational animals?* ... (76) After this Celsus ...
says: *Though we struggle and persevere we sustain ourselves only with
difficulty and toil, whereas for them* [*Odyssea*, IX, 109] *"everything
grows without sowing and tillage"*
... (77) Celsus' words are as follows: *But if you were to quote the verse
of Euripides that* [*Phoenissae*, 546] *"sun and night serve mortals" why*

do they exist for us any more than for ants and flies? For in their case too the night is for rest and the day for seeing and doing ... (78) After this he refers to the objections to his view which point to the superiority of men and hold that on their account the irrational animals have been created. He says that *if anyone were to call us rulers of the irrational animals because we hunt them and feast on them, we will reply by asking why rather were we not made on their account since they hunt and eat us? Furthermore, we need nets and weapons and many men and dogs to help us against the hunted prey. Whereas to them nature has given weapons from the start in their natural powers, making it easy for them to subdue us* ... (99) To all this Celsus adds the following remark: *Accordingly, all things have not been made for man any more than for the lion or the eagle or the dolphin, but so that this world, as God's work, may be made complete and perfect in all its parts. For this purpose all things have been proportioned, not for one another except incidentally, but for the universe as a whole. And God takes care of the universe, and providence never abandons it, nor does it become more evil; nor does God turn it back to Himself after a time, nor is He angry because of men any more than He is because of monkeys or mice; nor does He threaten them. For each of them has received his destiny in his turn* ...

(V, 2) It is our object now to refute his words which read as follows: *Jews and Christians, no God or child of God either has come down or would have come down. And if it is certain angels of which you speak, whom do you mean by them, gods or some other kind of being? You presumably mean some other kind — daemons* ... (6) After this he writes the following statement about the Jews: *The first thing about the Jews which may well cause amazement is that although they worship the heaven and the angels in it, yet they reject its most sacred and powerful parts, the sun, moon, and the other stars, both the fixed stars and the planets. They behave as though it were possible that the whole could be God but its parts not divine, or that one might quite rightly worship beings which are alleged to draw near to people blinded in darkness somewhere as a result of black magic, or who have dreams of obscure phantoms. But as for those beings who prophesy so clearly and distinctly to everyone, through whom showers and heat, clouds and thunders, which they worship, and lightnings and fruitfulness and all productivity are controlled, by whom God is revealed to them, the clearest heralds of the powers above, the truly heavenly messengers (angels), these are thought to be of no account* ... (14) This is what he says! *It is foolish of them also to suppose that, when God applies the fire (like a cook!), all the rest of mankind will be thoroughly roasted and that they alone will survive, not merely those who are alive at the time but those also long dead who will rise up from the earth possessing the same bodies as before. This is simply the hope of worms. For what sort of human soul would have any further desire for a body that has rotted? The fact that this doctrine is not shared by some of you (Jews) and by some Christians shows its utter repulsiveness, and that it is both revolting and impossible. For what sort of body, after being entirely corrupted, could return to its original nature and that same condition which it had before it was dissolved? As they have nothing to say in reply, they escape to a most outrageous refuge by saying that "anything is possible to God". But indeed neither can God do what is shameful nor does He desire what is contrary to nature. If you were to desire something abominable in your wickedness, not even God would be able to do this, and you ought not to believe at all that your desire will be fulfilled. For God is not the author of sinful desire or of disorderly confusion, but of what is naturally just and right. For the soul He might be able to provide everlasting life; but as Heraclitus says, "corpses ought to be thrown away as worse than dung". As for the flesh, which is full of things which are not even nice to mention, God would neither desire nor be able to make it everlasting, contrary to reason. For He Himself is the reason of everything that exists; therefore He is not able to do anything contrary to reason or to His own character* ... (25) Let us look at Celsus' next passage which reads as follows: *Now the Jews became an individual nation, and made laws according to the custom of their country; and they maintain these laws among themselves at the present day, and observe a worship which may be very peculiar but is at least traditional. In this respect they behave like the rest of mankind, because each nation follows its traditional customs, whatever kind may happen to be established. This situation seems to have come to pass not only because it came into the head of different people to think differently and because it is necessary to preserve the established social conventions, but also because it is probable that from the beginning the different parts of the earth were allotted to different overseers, and are governed in this way by having been divided between certain authorities. In fact, the practices done by each nation are right when they are done in the way that pleases the overseers; and it is impious to abandon the customs which have existed in each locality from the beginning* ... (34) That we may not pass by the remarks which Celsus has made in between these last two, let us also quote these: *One might also call Herodotus as witness for this, when he speaks as follows* [Historiae, II, 18]: *"Now the people of the cities Marea and Apis who live in the part of Egypt bordering on Libya, thinking that they were Libyans and not Egyptians, objected to the worship of the temples, not wanting to abstain from eating cows; so they sent to Ammon, saying that they had nothing in common with the Egyptians for they lived outside the Delta and did not agree with them; and they wanted Ammon to allow them to taste all meats. But the god did not allow them to do this, saying that land which the Nile passed over and watered was Egypt, and that those who lived below the city of Elephantine and drank from this river were Egyptians." This is the story of Herodotus. Ammon is not any less competent to give an account of these things of God than the angels of the Jews. Thus there is nothing wrong if each nation observes its own laws of worship. Actually we will find that the difference between each nation is very considerable, and nevertheless each one of them appears to think its own by far the best. The Ethiopians who live at Meroe worship only Zeus and Dionysus* [Historiae, II, 29]. *The Arabians worship only Ourania and Dionysus. The Egyptians all worship Osiris and Isis, the people of Sais Athena, the Naucratites, though they did not begin long ago, invoke Sarapis, and the rest act in each case according to their respective laws. Some abstain from sheep, reverencing them as sacred, others from goats, others from crocodiles, others from cows, and they abstain from pigs because they loathe them. Indeed, among the Scythians cannibalism is a good thing; and there are some Indians who think they are acting piously when they eat even their fathers. And the same Herodotus says this somewhere (and I will again quote his actual words to guarantee its genuineness). He tells the following story* [Historiae, III, 38]: *"For if anyone were to propose to call men and to tell them to choose which of all the laws were the best, on consideration each would choose his own. Therefore, it is not likely that anyone but a lunatic would make a mock of these things. But that all men have believed this of their laws can be concluded by this proof among many others. While he was ruler Darius called the Greeks who were with him, and asked for how much money they would be willing to feed on their dead fathers. They said that they would not do this at any price. After this Darius called those Indians called Calatians who feed on their parents, and in the presence of the Greeks, and learning their reply through an interpreter, he asked for what money they would be ready to burn their dead fathers with fire. But they uttered a loud cry and told him to keep silence. These customs have in fact existed, and Pindar seems to me to have been right when he said that custom is king of all"* ... (41) Let us see what Celsus has to say next, where there is very little about the Christians but a great deal about the Jews. He says: *If indeed in accordance with these principles the Jews maintained their own law, we should not find fault with them but rather with those who have abandoned their own traditions and professed those of the Jews. If, as though they had some deeper wisdom, they are proud and turn away from the society of others on the ground that they are not on the same level of piety, they have already heard that not even their doctrine of heaven is their own but, to omit all other instances, was also held long ago by the Persians, as Herodotus shows in one place. "For their custom,"* he says, *"is to go up to the highest peaks of the mountains to offer sacrifice to Zeus, and to call the whole circle of heaven Zeus". I think, therefore, that it makes no difference whether we call Zeus the Most High, or Zen, or Adonai, or Sabaoth, or Ammon like the Egyptians, or Papaeus like the Scythians. Moreover, they would certainly not be holier than other people because they are circumcised; for the Egyptians and Colchians did this before they did. Nor because they abstain from pigs; for the Egyptians also do this, and in addition abstain also from goats, sheep, oxen and fish. And Pythagoras and his disciples abstain from beans and from all living things. Nor is it at all likely that they are in favour with God and are loved any more than other folk, and that angels are sent to them alone, as though indeed they had been assigned some land of the blessed. For we see of what fate both they and their land were thought worthy.*[1] *Let this chorus depart, then, after suffering the penalty of their arrogance. For they do not know the great God, but have been led on and deceived by Moses' sorcery and have learnt about that for no good purpose* ... (33) But to some extent it anticipates what Celsus says to us in these remarks: *Now let us take the second chorus. I will ask them where they have come from, or who is the author of their traditional laws. Nobody, they will say. In fact, they themselves originated from Judaism, and they cannot name any other source for their teacher and chorus-leader. Nevertheless they rebelled against the Jews* ... (52) The passage of Celsus which we now want to examine reads as follows: *We leave on one side the many arguments which refute what they say about their teacher; and let us assume that he really was some angel. Was he the first and only one to have come?*

---

1 The translation printed here differs somewhat from that of Chadwick.

Or were there also others before him? If they were to say that he is the only one, they would be convicted of telling lies and contradicting themselves. For they say that others also have often come, and, in fact, sixty or seventy at once, who became evil and were punished by being cast under the earth in chains. And they say that their tears are the cause of hot springs. Furthermore, they say that an angel came to the tomb of this very man (some say one angel, some two), who replied to the women that he was risen. The Son of God, it seems, was not able to open the tomb, but needed someone else to move the stone. What is more, an angel came to the carpenter to defend Mary when she was pregnant, and another angel that they might rescue the infant and escape. And why should I give a careful list of them all and enumerate those alleged to have been sent to Moses and to others of them? If therefore others also were sent, obviously Jesus too came from the same God. Apparently he had a mission of greater significance because, for example, the Jews were doing something wrong, or were debasing their religion, or were behaving impiously; for these things are hinted at ...
(59) Then Celsus next says: *Therefore both the Jews and these people have the same God,* clearly by the latter meaning the Christians. And as if he were drawing a conclusion which would not be accepted, he says this: *Obviously the members of the great Church confess this, and believe that the story of the making of the world current among the Jews is true even in respect of the six days and the seventh* in which, according to the Bible, God ceased from His work and retired into the contemplation of Himself, though Celsus, because he did not read the scriptures carefully and did not understand them, says that God *rested,* which is not the word used ... Then he seems to me to want to fill up his book and to make it look big. For he irrelevantly adds some words such as these about the first man, to the effect that *we say he was the same man as the Jews do, and we trace the genealogical descent from him like them.* But we know nothing about *a plot of brothers against one another,* although we do know that Cain plotted against Abel and Esau against Jacob. For Abel did not plot against Cain, nor Jacob against Esau. Had this been the case, Celsus would have been right in saying that we *tell the same plots of brothers against one another as the Jews do.* Suppose also that we do talk of *the same departure to Egypt as they do,* and the same return *from there* (it was not a *flight,* as Celsus thinks) ... (61) After this he says: *Let no one imagine I do not know that some of them will agree that they have the same God as the Jews, while some think there is another God to whom*

the former is opposed, and that the Son came from the latter ... Let us admit that *some also accept Jesus* and on that account boast they are Christians *although they still want to live according to the law of the Jews like the multitude of the Jews* ... (65) And he dwells on his criticism of the difference between the sects; but he does not seem to me to have any clear idea at all of what he means, nor to have looked into them carefully, nor to understand how *Christians who have made some progress in education say that they know more than the Jews* ...

(VI, 19) After this Celsus says: *It is because certain Christians have misunderstood sayings of Plato that they boast of a God who is above the heavens and place Him higher than the heaven in which the Jews believe* ... (22) It seemed to me that to quote Celsus' words here would be absurd, for it would be to do what he himself has done when, for the purpose of criticizing Christians and Jews, he inappropriately compared their teaching not merely with the remarks of Plato with which he might have rested content, but also, as he says, with *the mysteries of the Persian Mithras and their interpretation of them* ... (27) He then objects to this expression and with good reason criticizes those who venture to say this. On this ground we too share the annoyance of those who find fault with such people, if any there are, who *maintain that the God of the Jews is accursed, being the God who sends rain and thunder, and who is the Creator of this world and the God of Moses, described in his account of the creation of the world* ... (28) That he is confusing the issue is shown when he gives the reason why the God of the Mosaic cosmogony is said to be accursed. For he says that *such a God even deserves to be cursed in the opinion of those who hold this view of him, because he cursed the serpent which imparted to the first men knowledge of good and evil* ... (29) Then next, as though it were the Christians upon whom he is pouring scorn when he criticizes those who say that the God of Moses and his law is accursed and imagining that those who hold these views are Christians, he says: *What could be sillier or crazier than this blockheaded wisdom? For why did the Jews' lawgiver make a mistake? And if he did, why do you accept his cosmogony, or the law of the Jews, interpreting it as an allegory, as you say, while you only grudgingly praise the Creator of the world, you most impious fellow, though he promised the Jews everything, declaring that he would increase their race to the ends of the earth and would raise them up from the dead with the same flesh and blood, and inspired the prophets; and yet you pour abuse on him? But when you are put in difficulties by the Jews, you*

288

confess that you worship the same God. Yet when your master Jesus and Moses, in whom the Jews believe, lay down contradictory laws, you try to find another God instead of this one who is the Father ... (42) After these remarks Celsus brings the following objections against us from another angle: *That they make some quite blasphemous errors is also shown by his example of their utter ignorance, which has similarly led them to depart from the true meaning of the divine enigmas, when they make a being opposed to God; devil, and in the Hebrews' tongue, Satanas are the names which they give to this same being. At all events these notions are entirely of mortal origin, and it is blasphemy to say that when the greatest God indeed wishes to confer some benefit upon men, he has a power which is opposed to Him, and so is unable to do it. The Son of God, then, is worsted by the devil, and is punished by him so that he may teach us also to despise the punishments which he inflicts on us. He declares that even Satan himself will appear in a similar way to that in which he has done and will manifest great and amazing works, usurping the glory of God. We must not be deceived by these, nor desire to turn away to Satan, but must believe in him alone. This is blatantly the utterance of a man who is a sorcerer, who is out for profit and is taking precautions against possible rivals to his opinions and to his begging* ... (49) Let us also consider the next remarks where he objects to the Mosaic story of the creation of the world with a single bare assertion without even saying anything plausible. Besides, *the cosmogony too is very silly* ... He asserted that *the record of the origin of man is also very silly*, without either quoting the texts or combating with them. For I imagine he had no arguments able to refute the saying that man was made in God's image. Furthermore, he does not understand *the paradise planted by God, and the life which the man lived in it in the first place, and that which came to pass through force of circumstances when the man was banished on account of his sin and made to live opposite the paradise of luxury.* Let the fellow who says that *those statements are very silly* first pay attention to each point, in particular to this: "He places the cherubim and the flaming sword that turned itself to guard the way of the tree of life." But perhaps *Moses wrote these stories because he understood nothing, but did much the same as the poets of the Old Comedy who mockingly wrote "Proetus married Bellerophon, and Pegasus came from Arcadia".* Yet they composed this from a desire to raise a laugh ... (50) After this he piles up mere assertions about the *different views concerning the origin of the world and of mankind held by some of the ancients* whom he has

289

mentioned, and says *that Moses and the prophets who left our books had no idea what the nature of the world and of mankind really is, and put together utter trash* ... (60) After the passage we have examined, as though it were his object to fill his book somehow with lengthy verbosity, he makes a remark which, though in different words, is to the same effect as that which we examined a little above, where he said: *But far more silly is to have allotted certain days to the making of the world before days existed. For when the heaven had not yet been made or the earth yet fixed, or the sun borne round it, how could days exist?* What difference is there between these words and this remark: *Moreover, taking the question from the beginning, let us consider this. Would it not be absurd for the first and greatest God to command, "Let this come into existence", or something else, or that, so that He made so much on one day and again so much more on the second, and so on with the third, fourth, fifth, and sixth?* ... (52) After this Celsus says: *But I say nothing now about the beginning and the destruction of the world, whether it is uncreated and indestructible, or created and indestructible, or vice versa.* For this reason neither do we speak now about these questions ... However, we do not say that *the Spirit of the supreme God came among men on earth as to strangers,* when we say that "the Spirit of God was borne above the water". Nor do we say that *some things were devised by another Creator, different from the great God, against his Spirit while the higher God restrained himself, and that they needed to be destroyed.* (61) Then again ... he says: *After this, indeed, God, exactly like a bad workman, was worn out, and needed a holiday to have a rest* ... Then, as if it were either what the scriptures say or what we ourselves expound them to say about God, that he rested because He was tired, he says: *It is not right for the first God to be tired or to work with his hands or to give orders* ... (62) Again Celsus ... says: *He has neither mouth nor voice ... nor does God have any other of the characteristics of which we know* ... (63) Then ... he says: *Nor did he make man his image: for God is not like that, nor does he resemble any other form at all* ... (78) Celsus next says something to this effect: *Furthermore, if God, like Zeus in the comic poet, woke up out of his long slumber and wanted to deliver the human race from evils, why on earth did he send this spirit that you mention into one corner? He ought to have breathed into many bodies in the same way and sent them all over the world. The comic poet wrote that Zeus woke up and sent Hermes to the Athenians and Spartans because he wanted to raise a*

290

laughter in the theatre. Yet do you not think it is more ludicrous to make the Son of God to be sent to the Jews? ... (80) After this Celsus thought fit to say that *the Chaldaeans have been a race endowed with the highest inspiration from the beginning,* though it was from them that the deceitful art of astrology spread among men. Celsus also reckons *the Magi* among the most inspired races, though from them magic, which takes its name from their race, has come to other nations as well, to the destruction and ruin of those who use it. *The Egyptians,* whom Celsus also mentioned earlier, went astray in having impressive precincts about their supposed temples, but inside nothing but cats or crocodiles or goats or snakes or some other animals. Yet now Celsus thought fit to remark that *the nation of the Egyptians* is also endowed with the highest inspiration, and that from the beginning, probably because from the beginning they fought against the Jews. *The Persians,* who marry their mothers and have sexual intercourse with their daughters, appear to Celsus to be an inspired race; and the *Indians* also of whom in the previous pages he said that some had tasted human flesh. But although the Jews, especially those of early times, did none of these things, not only does he not call them *endowed with the highest inspiration,* but even says that *they will presently perish ...*

(VII, 3) He says: *The predictions of the Pythian priestess or of the priestesses of Dodona or of the Clarian Apollo or at Branchidae or at the shrine of Zeus Ammon, and of countless other prophets, are reckoned of no account, although it is probable that by them the whole earth became inhabited. But the predictions, whether they were actually spoken or not, made by the people of Judaea after their usual manner, as even now is customary with those who live round about Phoenicia and Palestine, are thought to be wonderful and unalterable ...* (18) After this Celsus continues as follows: *Will they not ponder that again? If the prophets of the God of the Jews foretold that Jesus would be his son, why did he give them laws by Moses that they were to become rich and powerful and to fill the earth and to massacre their enemies, children and all, and slaughter their entire race, which he himself did, so Moses says, before the eyes of the Jews? And besides this, if they were not obedient, why does he expressly threaten to do to them what he did to their enemies? Yet his son, the man of Nazareth, gives contradictory laws, saying that a man cannot come forward to the father if he is rich or loves power or lays "claim to any intelligence or reputation", and that he must not pay attention to food or to his storehouse any more than the ravens, or to clothing any more than the lilies, and that to a man who has struck him once he should offer himself to be struck once again. Who is wrong? Moses or Jesus? Or when the Father sent Jesus had he forgotten what commands he gave to Moses? Or did he condemn his own laws and change his mind, and send his messenger for quite the opposite purpose?* ... (53) Then after these remarks ... he says to us: *How much better it would have been for you, since you conceived a desire to introduce some new doctrine, to have addressed your attentions to some other man among those who have died noble deaths and are sufficiently distinguished to have a myth about them like the gods. For example, if Heracles and Asclepius and those who since early times have been held in honour failed to please you, you had Orpheus, a man who, as all agree, possessed a pious spirit and also died a violent death. But perhaps he had been chosen by others before you. At any rate you had Anaxarchus who, when cast into a mortar and while he was being beaten with great violence, nobly showed contempt for the punishment, saying "Beat on, beat the pouch of Anaxarchus for you are not beating him." The utterance is surely one of some divine spirit. But some natural philosophers have preceded you in taking him for their master. What about Epictetus then? When his master was twisting his leg he smiled gently and calmly said "You are breaking it." And when he had broken it he said, "Did I not tell you that you were breaking it?" What comparable saying did your God utter while he was being punished? If you had put forward the Sibyl, whom some of you use, as a child of God, you would have had more to be said in your favour. However, you have had the presumption to interpolate many blasphemous things in her verses, and assert that a man who lived a most infamous life and died a most miserable death was a god. A far more suitable person for you than Jesus would have been Jonah with his gourd, or Daniel who escaped from wild beasts, or those of whom stories yet more incredible than these are told* ...

(VIII, 69) Then as Celsus did not understand himself ... he says: *You will surely not say that if the Romans were convinced by you and were to neglect their customary honours to both gods and men and were to call upon your Most High, or whatever name you prefer, He would come down and fight on their side, and they would have no need for any other defence. In earlier times also the same God made these promises and some far greater than these, so you say, to those who pay regard to him. But see how much help he has been to both them and you. Instead of being masters of the whole world, they have been left no land or home of any kind. While in your case, if anyone does still wander about in secret, yet he is sought out and condemned to death...*

(trans. H. Chadwick, Cambridge 1953)

I, 2 ἐπαινῶν ὡς ἱκανοὺς εὑρεῖν δόγματα τοὺς βαρβάρους: The view tracing the origin of Greek philosophy to the Orient was of long standing and gained strength in the second century C.E.; see Festugière, *op. cit.* (supra, p. 230), I, pp. 19 ff.; cf. also T. Hopfner, *Orient und griechische Philosophie*, Leipzig 1925. Yet Celsus qualifies his view about barbarians by what he says in the succeeding sentence, where he maintains that the Greeks are superior to the barbarians, and that the Greeks are the best judges of the value of the discoveries of the barbarians. For the evaluation of the barbarians by the Greeks, see, in general, H. Dörrie, in: *Festschrift H. E. Stier*, Münster 1972, pp. 146 ff.

κρῖναι ... τὰ ὑπὸ βαρβάρων εὑρεθέντα ἀμείνονές εἰσιν Ἕλληνες: This shows a direct influence of [Plato] *Epinomis*, 987 E: ὅ τί περ ἂν Ἕλληνες βαρβάρων παραλάβωσι, κάλλιον τοῦτο εἰς τέλος ἀπεργάζονται. For the limitations of Celsus' positive evaluation of "barbarism", see Andresen, *op. cit.* (supra, p. 230), p. 210.

14 ἀρχαῖος ἄνωθεν λόγος, περὶ ὃν δὴ ἀεὶ καὶ τὰ ἔθνη τὰ σοφώτατα καὶ πόλεις καὶ ἄνδρες σοφοί κατεγένοντο: See *Contra Celsum*, III, 16: τὰ τοῦ παλαιοῦ λόγου παρακούσματα; cf. also Plato, *Leges*, IV, 715 E: ὥσπερ καὶ ὁ παλαιὸς λόγος, quoted in *Contra Celsum*, VI, 15.

Αἰγυπτίοις: That the Egyptians take their place as the first among the wise nations is in line with the literary tradition of the Greeks from the times of Herodotus and Plato; see Herodotus, II, 58; *ibid.*, 123 (the Egyptians were teachers of the Greeks in matters of religion; concerning the transmigration of souls); Plato, *Phaedrus*, 274 C–D (Egypt is the country where the sciences were invented); Diodorus, I, 69 (on the sojourns of Homer, Orpheus, Pythagoras and Solon in Egypt); Diogenes Laertius, *Prologus*, I, 11 (the Egyptians legislated laws of justice, they invented geometry, astrology and arithmetic). We read again that Celsus held the view that the Egyptians were a nation endowed with the highest inspiration from the beginning; see below, *Contra Celsum*, VI, 80.

καὶ Ἀσσυρίοις: Among the Assyrians the Chaldaeans are certainly included, with all the connotations attaching to them; see Andresen, *op. cit.* (supra, p. 230), p. 201.

Ἰνδοῖς: For the high respect shown to the Indians, see also Philostratus, *Vita Apollonii*.

Πέρσαις: In spite of the Persian objection to temples and images, an objection which they shared with Jews and Christians (cf. *Contra Celsum*, VII, 62), Celsus still counts the Persians among the wise nations, reflecting thereby the traditional respect felt for the Persian religion and way of life by many Greeks.

16 πῶς Ὀδρύσας μὲν καὶ Σαμόθρᾳκας καὶ Ἐλευσινίους: The Odrysians are probably included here because of the connection with Orpheus, and the

Samothracians and Eleusinians because of the mysteries proper to them. The mysteries of the Cabeiri of Samothrace are alluded to again in *Contra Celsum*, VI, 23.

καὶ Ὑπερβορέους: See J.D.P. Bolton, *Aristeas of Proconnesus*, Oxford 1962, pp. 195 ff.; A.J. van Windekens, *Rhein. Museum*, C (1957), pp. 164 ff.

Γαλακτοφάγους: See *Ilias*, XIII, 6.

Δρυΐδας: For descriptions of the Druids in ancient literature, see Diodorus, V, 31:2; Strabo, *Geographica*, IV, 4:4, p. 197; Diogenes Laertius, *Prologus*, I, 6; Caesar, *Bellum Gallicum*, VI, 13 f.

καὶ τοὺς Γέτας: The Getae are thought to be the bravest and most just among the Thracians in Herodotus, IV, 93.

Λίνον ... καὶ Πυθαγόραν: Celsus joins Linus, Musaeus and Orpheus with Pherecydes and Zoroaster. Origen censures Celsus for not having included Moses in the list of the wise men; cf. Gager, p. 96. For the equation of Moses with Musaeus, see Numenius, apud: Eusebius, *Praeparatio Evangelica*, IX, 8:1 (No. 365).

17 αἰτιᾶται τοὺς τροπολογοῦντας καὶ ἀλληγοροῦντας: The allegorical method of interpretation of Scripture is characteristic of Philo and the Alexandrian school, from which it passed to the Christians. In general, see E. Stein, *Die allegorische Exegese des Philo aus Alexandreia*, Giessen 1929; C. Kraus-Reggiani, *RFIC*, CI (1973), pp. 162 ff.; J. Pépin, *Mythe et allégorie — Les origines grecques et les contestations judéo-chrétiennes*, Paris 1958, especially, pp. 215 ff., 448 ff.; I. Christiansen, *Die Technik der allegorischen Auslegungswissenschaft bei Philon von Alexandrien*, Tübingen 1969.

19 προστίθεται ... τοῖς λέγουσιν ἀγένητον εἶναι τὸν κόσμον: Origen's allusion to the supposed views of Celsus on the eternity of the world seems to be aimed at the Epicureanism attributed to him by this Church Father. For the Jewish view on the creation of the world *ex nihilo*, see II Macc. vii:28.

21 συγκατέθετο δόγμασι σοφοῖς ...: Andresen (following Wifstrand) maintains convincingly that this also is a fragment of Celsus' work (to be added to the passages collected by Bader); see Andresen, *op. cit.* (supra, p. 230), p. 11.

22 τὸ περιτέμνεσθαι τὰ αἰδοῖα ... φησὶν ἀπὸ Αἰγυπτίων αὐτὸ ἐληλυθέναι: This is an old view already held in Herodotus, II, 104:3 (No. 1), and repeated in Diodorus, I, 28:3 (No. 55). In any case Celsus does not view circumcision as an expression of the superstition and decline of the Jewish religion, as is undoubtedly indicated by Strabo, *Geographica*, XVI, 2:37, p. 761 (No. 115). Celsus is only interested in proving that Jewish customs and institutions are not original but draw on the traditions of other people.

23 ἑπόμενοι Μωϋσεῖ αἰπόλοι καὶ ποιμένες: This characterization of Moses' followers draws upon Gen. xlvii:3. It is in accord with the general tone of the work of Celsus in which he maintains that the Christians, foreshadowed in this respect by their Jewish predecessors, had an appeal only for the uneducated and baser elements of the population; on this, see J. Vogt, *Gymnasium*, LXXXII (1975), pp. 401 ff.

24 εἴτε Ὕψιστον: Hypsistos (a translation of עליון) became a common designation for the Jewish God among the Jews themselves. For its use in

Jewish-Hellenistic literature, see R. Marcus, *PAAJR*, III (1931–1932), p. 115.
Cf. E. R. Goodenough, *JQR*, XLVII (1956/7), pp. 221 ff., and the
commentary to Damascius, *Vita Isidori*, 141 (No. 548). See now also
P. Boyancé, in: *Mélanges H. C. Puech*, Paris 1974, pp. 139 ff.
Σαβαώϑ: Cf. the commentary to Valerius Maximus, I, 3:3 (No. 147b).
μηδὲν διαφέρειν ... καλεῖν Δία ... ἢ τῷ δεῖνα ... παρ' Αἰγυπτίοις: Cf.
Labeo, apud: Macrobius, *Saturnalia*, I, 18:18–21 (No. 445), and the
commentary *ad loc.*

26 λέγων αὐτοὺς σέβειν ἀγγέλους: Cf. Col. ii:18; on this, see Strack &
Billerbeck, III, p. 629; J. B. Lightfoot, *Saint Paul's Epistles to the Colossians
and to Philemon*, London 1904, p. 194; Clemens Alexandrinus, *Stromata*, VI,
5:41:2; Origenes, *Commentarii in Ioannem*, XIII:17; Aristides, *Apologia*,
14:4 (ed. J. Geffcken, *Zwei griechische Apologeten*, Leipzig–Berlin 1907, p.
22). Celsus returns to this point and couples angel worship with that of
Heaven; see below, *Contra Celsum*, V, 6. For allusions to the existence of
angel worship in popular Judaism, see *Tosefta Ḥullin*, 2:18 (ed.
Zuckermandel, p. 503). Cf. W. Bousset & H. Gressmann, *Die Religion des
Judentums im späthellenistischen Zeitalter*, Tübingen 1926, pp. 330 f.; Simon,
p. 402; idem, *CRAI* (1971), pp. 120 ff.

28 The attack launched by Celsus' Jew on Christianity first impugns the
origin and the way of life of Jesus. The following passages state that he was
born of a woman convicted of adultery and driven out by her husband. Jesus'
real father was a soldier named Panthera, and he himself was very poor and
hired himself out as a labourer in Egypt. There he became an adept in magic.
This information, including the name of the father Panthera, Jesus' sojourn
in Egypt, and his study there of magic arts, has close parallels in Jewish
literature. The emphasis on the low connections of Jesus, the poverty of his
mother, who earned her living by spinning, and the fact that her husband was
a carpenter, is based on the Gospels and is given greater prominence by
Celsus than in the Jewish tradition as expressed in the Talmud and Midrash.
For the talmudic and midrashic parallels to the story of Jesus as recounted by
Celsus, as well as for the later development of the life of Jesus in Jewish
tradition, see R. Sinker, *Essays and Studies*, Cambridge 1900, pp. 58 ff.; S.
Krauss, *Das Leben Jesu nach jüdischen Quellen*, Berlin 1902; R. T. Herford,
Christianity in Talmud and Midrash, London 1903; H. L. Strack, *Jesus — Die
Häretiker und die Christen nach den ältesten jüdischen Angaben*, Leipzig
1910; Strack & Billerbeck, I, pp. 36 ff.; S. Krauss, *MGWJ*, LXXVI (1932), pp.
586 ff.; S. Zeitlin, *Abhandlungen zur Erinnerung an Hirsch Perez Chajes*,
Vienna 1933, pp. 295 ff.; B. Heller, *MGWJ*, LXXVII (1933), pp. 204 ff.; M.
Goldstein, *Jesus in the Jewish Tradition*, New York 1950; J. Z. Lauterbach,
Rabbinic Essays, Cincinnati 1951, pp. 473 ff.; E. Bammel, *NTS*, XIII
(1966–1967), pp. 317 ff.; D. Rokeah, *Tarbiẓ*, XXXIX (1970), pp. 9 ff. For the
parallels to Celsus' life of Jesus in contemporary Christian literature, cf. also
W. Bauer, *Das Leben Jesu im Zeitalter der neutestamentlichen Apokryphen*,
Tübingen 1909.

For Egypt as the centre *par excellence* of magic, see *TB Qiddushin* 49b: עשרה
קבים כשפים ירדו לעולם, תשעה נטלה מצרים. This accords with both the biblical

traditions about Egyptian sorcerers contending with Moses (Exod. vii:11 f.; cf. Numenius, apud: Eusebius, *Praeparatio Evangelica*, IX, 8:1–2 = No. 365) and the fame achieved by Egypt in this sphere throughout the Hellenistic and Roman world.

For Jesus as a magician, see also *Contra Celsum*, I, 6, 38, 46, 68, 71; II, 9, 14, 16; III, 1; V, 51; VI, 42. Cf. also Iustinus, *Apologia*, I, 30; *Dialogus cum Tryphone*, 69: καὶ γὰρ μάγον εἶναι αὐτὸν ἐτόλμων λέγειν καὶ λαοπλάνον; *Acta Pionii*, 10:13:8, in: H. Musurillo, *The Acts of the Christian Martyrs*, Oxford 1972, pp. 152 f.: λέγουσι δὲ καὶ νεκυομαντείαν πεποιηκέναι καὶ ἀνηγειοχέναι τὸν Χριστὸν μετὰ τοῦ σταυροῦ; Tertullianus, *Apologeticum*, 23:12; Lactantius, *Institutiones Divinae*, V, 3:19: "magum putassemus, ut et vos nunc putatis et Iudaei tunc putaverunt". For additional references, see Bauer, *op. cit.* (supra, p. 295), p. 465. Against the supposed equation in Jewish literature of Jesus with Balaam, see E. E. Urbach, *Tarbiẓ*, XXV (1956), pp. 272 ff.

32 κύουσα ἀπό τινος στρατιώτου Πανθήρα τοὔνομα: This name occurs in Jewish sources as the name of the father of Jesus, sometimes even as the name of Jesus himself. We meet also with the variant Pandera; see *Tosefta Ḥullin*, 2, 22 f. (ed. Zuckermandel, p. 503): ישוע בן פנטרא; *TP Shabbat* xiv, 14d; *'Avoda Zara*, ii, 40d; *Tosefta Ḥullin*, 2, 24: ישוע בן פנטירי.

Panthera as a proper name is well attested in Latin inscriptions; see A. Deissmann, *Orientalische Studien Theodor Nöldeke gewidmet*, II, Giessen 1906, pp. 871 ff.; idem, *Licht vom Osten*[4], Tübingen 1923, p. 57. For the suggestion that some controversialist seized on this name because of its similarity to the word παρθένος, see L. Patterson, *JTS*, XIX (1918), pp. 79 f. Allusions to Jesus' mother as an adulteress appear in the so-called *Toledot Yeshu*, deriving from a much later period; for the text, see Krauss, *Das Leben Jesu, op. cit.* (supra, p. 295), from a Strasbourg MS, giving the name of the adulterer as Joseph ben Pandera, see pp. 38 f.; from a Vienna MS, where Joseph Pandria is the lawful husband of Miriam, Jesus' mother, see pp. 64 f. He appears here as a God-fearing man. The wicked adulterer is given the name of John. Cf. also Tertullianus, *De Spectaculis*, 30: "fabri aut quaestuariae filius". Celsus is the only source for the explicit statement that Jesus' father was a Roman soldier; cf. Bammel, *op. cit.* (supra, p. 295), p. 324.

37 τοὺς Ἑλληνικοὺς μύθους περὶ Δανάης καὶ Μελανίππης καὶ Αὔγης καὶ Ἀντιόπης: On Danae, cf. Apollodorus, II, 4:1; on Melanippe, cf. Hyginus, *Fabulae*, 186; R. Wünsch, *Rhein. Museum*, XLIX (1894), pp. 91 ff.; on Auge, cf. Apollodorus, II, 7:4; III, 9:1; Diodorus, IV, 33:7; Strabo, *Geographica*, XIII, 1:69, p. 615; Pausanias, VIII, 4:9; 47:4; 48:7; X, 28:8; Hyginus, 99; on Antiope, cf. Apollodorus, III, 5:5; Pausanias, II, 6:1 ff.; IX, 25:3; Hyginus, *Fabulae*, 7–8.

39 τὴν τοῦ θεοῦ βασιλείαν: The biblical concept of the Kingdom of God is used again by Celsus; cf. *Contra Celsum*, III, 59; VI, 17; VIII, 11.

49 ἥξει θεοῦ υἱός, τῶν ὁσίων κριτὴς καὶ τῶν ἀδίκων κολαστής: For an allusion to future reward and punishment, and to the day of judgement in general, see *Contra Celsum*, II, 5, 8; IV, 7, 20, 23; V, 14; VII, 9.

50 Perhaps this is an allusion to the view that all believers are the sons of

Celsus Philosophus

God, as implied by Matt. v : 9, 45, and Rom. viii : 14: ὅσοι γὰρ πνεύματι θεοῦ ἄγονται, οὗτοι υἱοί εἰσιν θεοῦ.

40 ἐληλυθότων ἀπὸ ἀνατολῆς μάγων: Cf. Matt. ii : 1 ff.

58 Celsus substitutes here the Chaldaeans for the Magi of the Gospel. The confusion between Chaldaean priests and Magi goes back to the early Hellenistic age; see A. Momigliano, *Alien Wisdom*, Cambridge 1975, p. 143; cf. Bidez & Cumont, I, p. 35. Celsus clearly confuses here Herod the Great with Herod Antipas, tetrarch of Galilee (Luke iii : 1).

66 Ἀλλ᾽ ἄγγελος μὲν ἧκεν ἐξ οὐρανοῦ, κελεύων σοι ... φεύγειν: Cf. Matt. ii : 13.

ὁ δύο ... πεπομφὼς ἀγγέλους: For references to Luke i : 26 ff., and ii : 9 ff., see Bader, *op. cit.* (supra, p. 230); see, however, the note of Borret *ad loc.*

67 The argument of the Jew that the old myths attributing divine birth to men like Perseus are evidence of the benefits they bestowed upon mankind, while Jesus can show no such remarkable achievement, is by no means surprising when adduced by a Hellenistic Jew; cf. Philo, *Legatio ad Gaium*, 86: οὗτοι πάντες, ὦ Γάιε, διὰ τὰς ὑπηργμένας εὐεργεσίας ἐθαυμάσθησαν καὶ ἔτι νῦν θαυμάζονται καὶ σεβασμοῦ τε καὶ τῶν ἀνωτάτω τιμῶν ἠξιώθησαν. εἰπὲ δὴ καὶ αὐτὸς ἡμῖν, ἐπὶ τίνι γαυριᾷς καὶ πεφύσησαι τῶν παραπλησίων. Here Gaius, who claimed divine honours, is contrasted with the Dioscuri, Heracles and Dionysus. On the function of the old myths relating to legendary figures of the Greek past within the cultural framework of Celsus' work, see also Andresen, *op. cit.* (supra, p. 230), p. 53.

68 καὶ δαίμονας ἀπὸ ἀνθρώπων ἐξελαυνόντων: For the New Testament demonology in its contemporary setting, see S. Eitrem, *Some Notes on the Demonology in the New Testament*[2], Oslo 1966.

70 See John iv : 5 ff.; according to the Gospel of John, Jacob's Well was situated near Sichar.

II, 1 τί παθόντες, ὦ πολῖται, κατελίπετε τὸν πάτριον νόμον: Clearly Celsus' Jew is addressing here Jewish Christians, though Celsus himself nowhere expressly refers to the difference between Jewish and gentile Christians. The complaint of Celsus' Jew against the Jews who seceded from Judaism is in line with what Celsus himself has to say about gentiles who abandoned their own laws and adopted the Jewish commandments.

From the vast literature on the Judaeo-Christians, see Simon, pp. 277 ff.; H. J. Schoeps, *Theologie und Geschichte des Judenchristentums*, Tübingen 1949; A. F. J. Klijn & G. J. Reinink, *Patristic Evidence for Jewish-Christian Sects*, Leiden 1973 (for the texts from Origen, see pp. 124 ff.).

ψυχαγωγηθέντες ... ἀπηυτομολήσατε: For similar language concerning the followers of Moses, above, cf. *Contra Celsum*, I, 23. In the same manner as these seceded from the Egyptians for Moses, so the Judaeo-Christians deserted Judaism for Jesus.

5 Apparently Celsus' Jew argues not against the idea of resurrection in itself, or that of reward and punishment for good and evil, but against the use put by the Christians to an old-established Jewish concept. Thus in what follows Celsus' Jew argues that Jesus kept all the Jewish customs, even taking part in Jewish sacrifices.

8 Here the Jew answers the accusation of the Christians that although the Jews had foretold the advent of the Saviour they denied him their recognition when he appeared. The core of the Jew's argumentation is that Jesus was only one of the many persons who claimed to be the Messiah. Celsus' Jew does not mention names, some of which are known to us through Josephus.

18 προεῖπε καὶ τὸν προδώσοντα: Celsus alludes here to passages from the Gospels; cf. the list in Bader, *op. cit.* (supra, p. 230), p. 67.

24 See Matt. xxvi:39, 42; Luke xxii:42.

27 μεταχαράττειν ... καὶ μεταπλάττειν: Chadwick thinks that Origen may be right in interpreting it as gnostic alterations (μεταχαράξαντας δὲ τὸ εὐαγγέλιον ἄλλους οὐκ οἶδα ἢ τοὺς ἀπὸ Μαρκίωνος καὶ τοὺς ἀπὸ Οὐαλεντίνου οἶμαι δὲ καὶ τοὺς ἀπὸ Λουκάνου).

29 ὅτι μέγαν καὶ δυνάστην ... εἶναι τὸν ἐπιδημήσοντα: For the figure of the Messiah in Jewish eschatology, see P. Volz, *Die Eschatologie der jüdischen Gemeinde im neutestamentlichen Zeitalter*, Tübingen 1934, pp. 173 ff.; J. Klausner, *The Messianic Idea in Israel from Its Beginning to the Completion of the Mishnah*, London 1956; Strack & Billerbeck, Vol. IV, Part 2, pp. 799 ff.; E. E. Urbach, *The Sages — Their Concepts and Beliefs*, Jerusalem 1975, I, pp. 649 ff.; II, pp. 990 ff.

31 ὡς εἴ γε ὁ λόγος ἐστὶν ὑμῖν υἱὸς τοῦ θεοῦ, καὶ ἡμεῖς ἐπαινοῦμεν: Celsus' Jew, representing the Hellenistic trend in Jewish society, expresses his adhesion to the Jewish-Hellenistic Logos theory. For this, see H. A. Wolfson, *Philo*, I, Cambridge (Mass.) 1947, pp. 226 ff.

32 ἡ τοῦ τέκτονος γυνὴ τηλικούτου γένους τυγχάνουσα ἠγνόει: Origen already perceives that Celsus here missed the opportunity of attacking the genealogical discrepancies in the Gospels concerning the origins of Jesus. Such arguments against Christianity are used indeed by Iulianus, *Contra Galilaeos*, p. 253E.

34 λύσει μ' ὁ δαίμων αὐτὸς ...: The comparison with the story of Pentheus and Dionysus emphasizes the difference between Dionysus, whose persecutor Pentheus was punished, and Jesus, whose persecutor Pilate went unpunished.

36 ἰχώρ, οἷός πέρ τε ῥέει μακάρεσσι θεοῖσι: This Homeric quotation is frequently repeated in the tradition relating the history of Alexander the Great; see Aristobulus, apud: Athenaeus, *Deipnosophistae*, VI, p. 251a = *F. Gr. Hist.*, II, B 139, F 47; cf. *F. Gr. Hist.*, II, D, p. 519; C. A. Robinson, *The History of Alexander the Great*, I, Providence 1953, p. 223.

37 τὸ ὄξος καὶ τὴν χολὴν ὀνειδίζει τῷ Ἰησοῦ: See Matt. xxvii:34, 48; Mark xv:36; Luke xxiii:36; John xix:29 f.

46 δέκα ναύτας καὶ τελώνας: Cf. above, *Contra Celsum*, I, 62.

54 ἐν τῷ πρὸς τοὺς πολίτας ἑαυτοῦ λόγῳ πιστεύσαντας: I.e. the Judaeo-Christians.

55 Ζάμολξιν ... τὸν Πυθαγόρου δοῦλον: Cf. Herodotus, IV, 94 ff.; Lucianus, *Deorum Concilium*, 9.

καὶ αὐτὸν Πυθαγόραν ἐν Ἰταλίᾳ: Cf. Hermippus, apud: Diogenes Laertius, VIII, 41.

καὶ Ῥαμψίνιτον: Cf. Herodotus, II, 122.

Celsus Philosophus

καὶ Ὀρφέα ἐν Ὀδρύσαις: Cf. Apollodorus, *Bibliotheca*, I, 3:2.

καὶ Πρωτεσίλαον ἐν Θεσσαλίᾳ: Cf. Apollodorus, *Epitoma*, III, 30.

τὴν ἐπὶ τοῦ σκόλοπος αὐτοῦ φωνήν: Cf. Matt. xxvii:46; Mark xv:34.

τίς τοῦτο εἶδε; γυνὴ πάροιστρος: Cf. Mark xvi:9; Luke viii:2; John xx:1 ff.

καὶ εἴ τις ἄλλος: Peter is implied.

74 ὦ Ὕψιστε καὶ Οὐράνιε: Cf. above, *Contra Celsum*, I, 24. Celsus puts what seemed to him the most typical appellations of the Jewish God into the mouth of the Jew.

75 τοῖς πάλαι προσδεχομένοις οὐ γνωρίζεται: I.e. the Jews with their messianic expectations.

77 ἵνα ἴδωμεν καὶ πιστεύσωμεν: Cf. Mark xv:32.

III, 1 κατὰ τὴν παροιμίαν καλουμένης ὄνου σκιᾶς μάχης: An old popular proverb to denote a wrangle about trifles, which may be traced from the fourth century B.C.E.; see Plato, *Phaedrus*, 260C; cf. also Dio Chrysostomus, XXXIV, 48; *Corpus Paroemiographorum Graecorum* (ed. E. L. Leutsch & F. G. Schneidewin), Göttingen 1839, I, pp. 169 f., 439 f.; 1851, II, 42 f., 566, 703; Suda, s.v. ὄνου σκιά (ed. Adler, III, p. 543).

οὐκέτι δ᾽ ὁμολογούντων περὶ τοῦ ἐληλυθέναι τὸν προφητευόμενον ἢ μή: This is also correctly singled out as the chief bone of contention between Christianity and Judaism by Tertullianus, *Apologeticum*, 21:15: "Sciebant et Iudaei venturum esse Christum, scilicet quibus prophetae loquebantur. Nam et nunc adventum eius expectant, nec alia magis inter nos et illos compulsatio est quam quod iam venisse non credunt."

5 Αἰγυπτίους τῷ γένει τυγχάνοντας: The view that the Jews were originally Egyptians appears clearly in Strabo, *Geographica*, XVI, 2:34 f., pp. 760 f. (No. 115); idem, apud: Josephus, *Ant.*, XIV, 118 (No. 105). An Egyptian origin is already implied in the second version of Manetho, apud: Josephus, *Contra Apionem*, I, 238 ff. (No. 21). This tells of the lepers and other polluted persons led by Osarsiph, one of the priests of Heliopolis, who is identified with Moses and described as being intent from the first upon defying the Egyptian religion. The idea that the Jewish people were of Egyptian origin also emerges from Chaeremon, apud: Josephus, *Contra Apionem*, I, 288 ff. (No. 178), where the leaders of the Jews, Tisithen (= Moses) and Peteseph (= Joseph), are stated to have been Egyptians. One should also bear in mind Plutarch's remarks on the sons of Typhon called Hierosolymus and Iudaeus in *De Iside et Osiride*, 31 (No. 259); cf. also the kindred version found in Tacitus, *Historiae*, V, 2 (No. 281).

καταλελοιπέναι τὴν Αἴγυπτον, στασιάσαντας: Celsus emphasizes the motif of rebellion in his version of Jewish history, since the revolutionary character of Christianity was one of the main targets of his polemic. According to his view the Christians behaved towards the Jews as the latter had behaved towards the Egyptians; see Andresen, *op. cit.* (supra, p. 230), pp. 215 ff.

IV, 21 παραφθείροντα τὰ περὶ τῶν Ἀλωέως υἱῶν ἱστορούμενα: The myth of Aloeus is found first in *Ilias*, V, 385 ff.; *Odyssea*, XI, 305 ff. Philo noticed the similarity between this myth and the story of the Tower of Babel in Genesis; see his *De Confusione Linguarum*, 4 f. It may be surmised that he was not the first to point this out. The story of the Tower also suggested the myth of Aloeus to Julian; see Iulianus, *Contra Galilaeos*, 135 A (No. 481).

παραβάλλει ὁ Κέλσος τῇ κατὰ τὸν Φαέθοντα ἱστορίᾳ: Cf. Hesiodus, *Theogonia*, 987; Hyginus, *Fabulae*, 154; Ovidius, *Metamorphoses*, I, 751 ff.; Euripides, *Hippolytus*, 735 ff.; idem, *Fragmenta* (ed. Nauck), 771–784; cf. the Prolegomena to J. Diggle (ed.), *Phaethon*, Cambridge 1970, pp. 3 ff.; A. H. Krappe, *Review of Religion*, VIII (1943), pp. 115 ff. Cf. the contemporary Lucianus, *De Astrologia*, 19; A. G. Galanopulos, *Das Altertum*, XIV (1968), pp. 158 ff.

23 The passage connects motifs from Greek literature and uses them to satirize both Jews and Christians; see Andresen, *op. cit.* (supra, p. 230), pp. 226 ff.

παραβέβληκε νυκτερίδων ὁρμαθῷ: The cluster of bats goes back to *Odyssea*, XXIV, 6 ff., quoted by Plato, *Respublica*, 387 A.

ἢ μύρμηξιν ... ἢ βατράχοις περὶ τέλμα συνεδρεύουσιν: Cf. Plato, *Phaedo*, 109 B. The same reference is found also in *Contra Celsum*, VII, 28.

συνεδρεύουσιν ... ἐκκλησιάζουσι: "Es ist die Schilderung von dem Sumpfsynhedrion der Juden und dem Regenwürmerkonzil der Christen"; see Andresen, *op. cit.* (supra, p. 230), p. 226.

πάντῃ ὅμοιοι τῷ θεῷ: Cf. Gen. i : 26.

καὶ ἡμῖν πάντα ὑποβέβληται ... καὶ ἡμῖν δουλεύειν τέτακται: Cf. Gen. i : 28; I Cor. iii : 21 f.

31 Ἰουδαίους ἀπ' Αἰγύπτου δραπέτας γεγονέναι: Again Celsus emphasizes the inferior social status of the Jews.

μηδὲν πώποτε ἀξιόλογον πράξαντας: This is the old argument used by Apollonius Molon, apud: Josephus, *Contra Apionem*, II, 148 (No. 49), and Apion, apud: Josephus, *Contra Apionem*, II, 135 (No. 175). The first writer states that the Jews were the least gifted among the barbarians and the only ones among them who had contributed no useful invention to the civilization of mankind. The second that the Jews had not produced any such outstanding personalities as Socrates, Zeno and Cleanthes. The same line of argument is followed by Julian, who asserts that one cannot find among the Hebrews a single general like Alexander or Caesar, cf. Iulianus, *Contra Galilaeos*, 218 B–C (No. 481). He also adds that in matters concerning the constitution and law-courts, the administration of cities and excellence of laws, or the advancement of learning and cultivation of the liberal arts, the Hebrews were in a miserable and barbarous state (*ibid.*, p. 221 E).

οὔτ' ἐν λόγῳ οὔτ' ἐν ἀριθμῷ αὐτούς ποτε γεγενημένους: A well-known expression in Greek literature originally concerning the Megarians; cf. Callimachus, *Epigrammata*, XXV, 6 (ed. Pfeiffer, II, Oxford 1953, p. 87); Theocritus, XIV, 48 f.; Deinias of Argos (in the scholia to Theocritus); see *F. Gr. Hist.*, III, B 306, F 6; cf. the commentary in *F. Gr. Hist.*, IIIb, p. 31; Philo, *Quod Deus Immutabilis Sit*, 90.

33 ἐπεχείρησαν γενεαλογεῖν αὐτοὺς ἀπὸ πρώτης σπορᾶς γοήτων καὶ πλάνων ἀνθρώπων: This somewhat obscure passage is not wholly clarified by the succeeding quotation from Celsus (IV, 35). Celsus probably had in mind the connection of the Jews with Abraham, Isaac and Jacob, names used for magical purposes, as is well attested by the papyri. Cf. also M. Rist, *JBL*, LVII (1938), pp. 289 ff.; Goodenough, II, pp. 190 ff.

36 ἐπιδικασαμένων ἀνθρώπων τῆς ἀρχαιότητος: The claim to an origin in remote antiquity made by different nations, and even that of being the most ancient among them, is an old one. For the claim of the Phrygians and Egyptians, cf. Herodotus, II, 2; see also the list drawn up by Chadwick, in his note *ad loc.*

ἄνθρωπόν τινα ὑπὸ χειρῶν θεοῦ πλασσόμενόν ... καὶ περιγινόμενον τῶν θεοῦ προσταγμάτων τὸν ὄφιν: An allusion to Gen. ii:7, 16 f., 21 f.; iii:1 ff.; Philo interprets the story of the serpent allegorically; cf. Philo, *De Opificio Mundi*, 157 ff.: ἔστι δὲ ταῦτα οὐ μύθου πλάσματα ... ἑπόμενος δέ τις εἰκότι στοχασμῷ φήσει προσηκόντως τὸν εἰρημένον ὄφιν ἡδονῆς εἶναι σύμβολον.

41 παραχαράττοντες καὶ ῥᾳδιουργοῦντες τὸν Δευκαλίωνα: On Deucalion, see Ovidius, *Metamorphoses*, I, 318 ff.; Apollodorus, *Bibliotheca*, I, 7:2. Deucalion had already been identified with Noah by Philo, *De Praemiis et Poenis*, 23. This identification probably became common among Hellenistic Jewry and is repeated in patristic literature; see Iustinus, *Apologia*, II, 7; Theophilus, *Ad Autolycum*, III, 19.

43 ἔξωρον παιδοποιΐαν ... τὴν τοῦ Ἀβραὰμ καὶ τῆς Σάρρας: See Gen. xvii:17 ff.; xviii:9 ff.; xxi:1 ff.

ἤτοι τὸν Κάϊν ἐπιβουλεύσαντα τῷ Ἄβελ: See Gen. iv:2 ff.

καὶ τὸν Ἠσαῦ τῷ Ἰακώβ: See Gen. xxvii:30 ff.

πατρὸς δὲ λύπην, τάχα μὲν καὶ τὴν Ἰσαὰκ ... καὶ τὴν τοῦ Ἰακώβ: See Gen. xxviii:1 ff.; Gen. xxxvii:34.

τὴν Ῥεβέκκαν ... ἐπὶ τὸν Ἰακὼβ φθάσαι: See Gen. xxvii:1 ff.

καὶ ἥν τὰ ἄσημα τοῦ Λάβαν, τὰ δὲ ἐπίσημα τοῦ Ἰακώβ: See Gen. xxx:42. On this, cf. Philo's interpretation in *De Fuga et Inventione*, 9: ὁ Λάβαν τοῦ γένους ἐστὶ τούτου· τὴν γὰρ ἄσημον αὐτῷ ποίμνην οἱ χρησμοὶ προσνέμουσιν· ἄσημος δὲ ἐν μὲν τοῖς ὅλοις ἡ ἄποιος ὕλη, ἐν ἀνθρώποις δὲ ἡ ἀμαθὴς ψυχὴ καὶ ἀπαιδαγώγητος.

ὀνάρια καὶ προβάτια καὶ καμήλους δεδωρῆσθαι: Probably an allusion to such passages as Gen. xxx:43.

44 καὶ φρέατα τοῖς δικαίοις δεδωκέναι: For the reading διψίοις for δικαίοις, see E. Stein, *Eos*, XXXIV (1932–1933), p. 214, n. 25. The emendation is opposed by Bader, *op. cit.* (supra, p. 230), but accepted by Chadwick in his translation. In any case it seems to be an allusion to passages like Gen. xxi:19; xxvi:19 ff.

νύμφας τε καὶ θεραπαινίδας ἀνάγεσθαι: This is apparently an allusion to Sara and Hagar (Gen. xvi), and it was thus interpreted by Origen.

45 περὶ τὸν Λὼτ καὶ τὰς θυγατέρας: See Gen. xix:30 ff.; see Geffcken, *op. cit.* (supra, p. 295), p. 231. The equation by Celsus of the incest of Lot's daughters with Thyestian sins sounds like a pagan answer to the Jewish-Christian criticism of the immoral sexual behaviour attributed to Greek gods.

τῶν Θυεστείων εἶπε κακῶν ἀνομώτερα: For the accusation of Θυέστεια κακά levelled against Galilaeans, see the commentary to Tacitus, *Annales*, XV, 44 (No. 294).

46 Παραρρίπτει δ᾽ ὁ Κέλσος τὴν ἀπέχθειαν, οἶμαι τοῦ Ἠσαῦ πρὸς τὸν Ἰακώβ: See Gen. xxvii:41 ff.

ἐκτιθέμενος τὰ περὶ τὸν Συμεὼν καὶ τὸν Λευὶ ἐπεξελθόντας τῇ ὕβρει τῆς ἀδελφῆς: See Gen. xxxiv.

ἀδελφοὺς δὲ πωλοῦντας ... ἐξαπατώμενον τὸν Ἰακώβ: See Gen. xxxvii.

47 ὑπομιμνήσκεται τῶν ὀνειράτων τοῦ ἀρχιοινοχόου καὶ ... τῆς λύσεως αὐτῶν: See Gen. xl:1 ff.; xli:1 ff.

καὶ τοῖς πωλήσασί γε ἀδελφοῖς λιμώττουσι καὶ σταλεῖσι κατ᾽ ἐμπορίαν μετὰ τῶν ὄνων ... τὸν ἀναγνωρισμόν: See Gen. xliii–xlv. For μετὰ τῶν ὄνων, see Gen. xliv:13.

Ἰωσὴφ ... ἐπανιόντα πρὸς τὸν τοῦ πατρὸς τάφον: See Gen. l:4 ff.

48 καταφεύγειν ἐπὶ τὴν ἀλληγορίαν: See already above, *Contra Celsum*, I, 17; and cf. IV, 38.

72 That God could be angry was against the view held by philosophers; see H. Usener (ed.), *Epicurea*, Leipzig 1887, F363, p. 242; Philo, *Quod Deus Immutabilis Sit*, 52: τινὲς ... ὑπολαμβάνουσι θυμοῖς καὶ ὀργαῖς χρῆσθαι τὸ ὄν. ἔστι δ᾽ οὐδενὶ ληπτὸν πάθει τὸ παράπαν; cf. also Athenagoras, *Apologia*, 21 (ed. Geffcken, p. 137): οὔτε γὰρ ὀργὴ οὔτε ἐπιθυμία καὶ ὄρεξις οὐδὲ παιδοποιὸν σπέρμα ἐν τῷ θεῷ. For Celsus' views on the transcendence of God, see Miura-Stange, *op. cit.* (supra, p. 230), pp. 38 ff.

73 εἰ ἄνθρωπος: Titus is implied.

74 ἐγκαλεῖ ἡμῖν ὡς τῷ ἀνθρώπῳ φάσκουσι πάντα πεποιηκέναι τὸν θεόν: Celsus attacks the anthropocentric view of Jews and Christians that God made all things for man; cf. Gen. i:26; Aristides, *Apologia*, I, 3 (ed. Geffcken, p. 4). His criticism has its counterpart in the academic argumentation against the Stoics. See also W. Nestle, *Archiv für Religionswissenschaft*, XXXVII (1941–1942), pp. 84 f.

99 καὶ μέλει τῷ θεῷ τοῦ ὅλου ... πρόνοια: Celsus, without committing himself to either the Middle Platonic or the Stoic view of the workings of Divine Providence, is interested only in showing its universalism; see Andresen, *op. cit.* (supra, p. 230), pp. 82 f.

V, 6 τὸν μὲν οὐρανὸν καὶ τοὺς ἐν τῷδε ἀγγέλους σέβουσι: For the supposed Jewish worship of Heaven, see Hecataeus, apud: Diodorus, XL, 3:4 (No. 11): ἀλλὰ τὸν περιέχοντα τὴν γῆν οὐρανὸν μόνον εἶναι θεὸν καὶ τῶν ὅλων κύριον; cf. Strabo, *Geographica*, XVI, 2:35, p. 761 (No. 115); Iuvenalis, *Saturae*, XIV, 97 (No. 301): "nil praeter nubes et caeli numen adorant". For the worship of angels, cf. above, *Contra Celsum*, I, 26, and the commentary *ad loc.*

14 Celsus attacks Jewish-Christian eschatological expectations, and above all the belief in bodily resurrection; see H. Chadwick, *HTR*, XLI (1948), pp. 83 ff. Celsus represents here the Greek philosophical view, known to us also from his contemporary Galen, that not all is possible to God, who cannot do what is contrary to nature; see Galenus, *De Usu Partium*, XI, 14 (No. 376). For Christian replies to the pagan criticism of belief in resurrection, see Geffcken, *op. cit.* (supra, p. 295), pp. 235 ff.

ὁπότε μηδ᾽ ὑμῶν τοῦτο τὸ δόγμα καὶ τῶν Χριστιανῶν ἐνίοις κοινόν ἐστι: By ὑμῶν only the Jews can be meant. Among the Jews the idea of bodily

302

Celsus Philosophus

resurrection was repugnant, at least to the Sadducees; cf. Acts xxiii:8: Σαδδουκαῖοι γὰρ λέγουσιν μὴ εἶναι ἀνάστασιν. See J.Le Moyne, *Les Sadducéens*, Paris 1972, pp. 167 ff.

25 Ἰουδαῖοι μὲν οὖν ἔθνος ἴδιον γενόμενοι καὶ κατὰ τὸ ἐπιχώριον νόμους ... περιστέλλοντες ... ὅμοια τοῖς ἄλλοις ἀνθρώποις δρῶσιν: This justification for adherence to their laws and customs by the Jews was put forward even by their opponents a long time before Celsus; see Seneca, *De Superstitione*, apud: Augustinus, *De Civitate Dei*, VI, 11 (No. 186); Tacitus, *Historiae*, V, 5 (No. 281). Cf. also the general formulation of this view by Porphyrius, *Ad Marcellam*, 18: οὗτος γὰρ μέγιστος καρπὸς εὐσεβείας τιμᾶν τὸ θεῖον κατὰ τὰ πάτρια. See also the argumentation of the pagan disputant in Minucius Felix, *Octavius*, 6:1.

τὰ μέρη τῆς γῆς ἐξ ἀρχῆς ἄλλα ἄλλοις ἐπόπταις νενεμημένα ... διοικεῖται: In keeping its proper laws, each nation acts in accordance with the wish of the specific divine power which supervises it; see Chadwick, *op. cit.* (supra, p. 230), introduction, p. XX.

41 Δία Ὕψιστον καλεῖν: Cf. above, *Contra Celsum*, I, 24, and the commentary *ad loc.*

Παπαῖον, ὡς Σκύθαι: See Herodotus, IV, 59.

τοῦτο γὰρ Αἰγύπτιοι καὶ Κόλχοι πρότεροι: The same argument was used before by Celsus; cf. above, *Contra Celsum*, I, 22.

καὶ κυάμων γε Πυθαγόρας ... καὶ ἐμψύχων ἁπάντων: For the Pythagorean abstention from beans, cf. the explanations in Diogenes Laertius, VIII, 34; see W. K. C. Guthrie, *A History of Greek Philosophy*, I, Cambridge 1962, pp. 184 f. There is a variety of evidence for the Pythagorean abstention from animal flesh; cf., e.g., among the comic poets, Antiphanes, in: J. M. Edmonds, *The Fragments of Attic Comedy*, II, Leiden 1959, F135, p. 226 (*Corycus*); Mnesimachus, *ibid.*, F1, p. 360 (*Alcmaeon*); Alexis, *ibid.*, F220–221, p. 480 (*The Tarentines*); Eudoxus, apud: Porphyrius, *Vita Pythagorae*, 7. The Pythagorean abstention from both animal food and beans is designated an antiquated and erroneous notion, though one of long standing, by Aulus Gellius, *Noctes Atticae*, IV, 11:1. See also Lucianus, *Gallus*, 4; idem, *Dialogi Mortuorum*, 6:3.

ὁρῶμεν γὰρ αὐτούς τε καὶ τὴν χώραν τίνων ἠξίωνται: The argument against the Jews based on the low political status to which they had fallen is adduced by pagan writers from Cicero onwards; see Cicero, *Pro Flacco*, 69 (No. 68); Apion, apud: Josephus, *Contra Apionem*, II, 125 (No. 174); cf. also Minucius Felix, *Octavius*, 10:4. Celsus refers again to the low status of the Jews; see below, *Contra Celsum*, VIII, 69. Thus it seems that the correct translation of the present passage would be: "For we see of what fate both they and their land were thought worthy" rather than "For we see both the sort of people they are and what sort of a land it was of which they were thought worthy". Cf. also Borret's translation: "nous voyons assez quel traitement ils ont mérité eux et leur pays". This translation renders irrelevant the reference to Strabo, pp. 759–761, made by Bader, *op. cit.* (supra, p. 230), p. 134, n. 1. According to Bader this might imply Strabo's explanation that Moses easily took possession of the territory in which Jerusalem was later founded "since it was not a place that would be looked on with envy, nor yet one for which anyone would make a serious fight"; see Strabo, *Geographica*, XVI, 2, 36, p. 761 (No. 115).

ὑπὸ τῆς Μωϋσέως γοητείας ὑπαχθείς: Cf. above, *Contra Celsum*, I, 23. Moses had already been designated γοής by the earlier anti-Jewish writers Apollonius Molon and Lysimachus; see Josephus, *Contra Apionem*, II, 145 (Nos. 49, 161).

33 ἀφεστήκασιν Ἰουδαίων: Cf. already above, *Contra Celsum*, III, 5.

59 κατέπαυσεν ἀπὸ τῶν ἔργων ἑαυτοῦ: See Gen. ii:2.

ἀναχωρῶν εἰς τὴν ἑαυτοῦ περιωπήν: This constitutes a quotation from Plato, *Politicus*, 272 E.

ὁμοίως αὐτοῖς γενεαλογοῦμεν: See Matt. i:1 ff.; Luke iii:23 ff.

61 ὡς τὰ Ἰουδαίων πλήθη βιοῦν ἐθέλοντες: An allusion to the Judaeo-Christians, the Ebionites.

VI, 19 παρακούσαντάς τινας Χριστιανοὺς Πλατωνικῶν λέξεων ... ὑπεραναβαίνοντας τὸν Ἰουδαίων οὐρανόν: The statement that there were sayings of Plato which certain Christians misunderstood seems to be an allusion to *Phaedrus*, 247C. Celsus' conception of this misunderstanding is explained as follows by Andresen, *op. cit.* (supra, p. 230), pp. 157 f.: "Während die Christen in naivem Optimismus wähnen, den 'überhimmlischen Gott' gefunden zu haben, hat Platons Sachkenntnis nur dem abstrakt denkenden Nus den Zugang zu jenem Bereich der Transzendenz vorbehalten. Gott selbst aber steht noch darüber, er ist jenseits allen Seins. Darin besteht also das 'Misverständnis' der Christen, dass sie meinen, weiter als die Juden in der Suche nach dem jenseitigen Gott vorgestossen zu sein, und doch auf halbem Wege stehengeblieben sind."

Chadwick suggests that Celsus' statement that the Christians place God higher than the heaven in which the Jews believe implies the notion that the Jews located God in the seventh celestial sphere, while the Christians, working on a system of eight, located God's dwelling within the eighth region, the sphere of fixed stars above the seven planets.

27 In the preceding passage Celsus relates the views of one of the Gnostic sects. According to them seven angels stand on either side of the soul when the body is dying, one group consisting of angels of light and the other consisting of the so-called archontic angels. The chief of those archontic angels is said to be an accursed God (καὶ λέγει τὸν ἄρχοντα τῶν ὀνομαζομένων ἀρχοντικῶν λέγεσθαι θεὸν κατηραμένον). On a fourth-century sect called Archontici, see Epiphanius, *Panarion Haeresium*, XL (κατὰ Ἀρχοντικῶν).

28 ἐπείπερ τῷ ὄφει ... κατηράσατο: See Gen. iii:14. For the Ophites, see A. Hönig, *Die Ophiten — Ein Beitrag zur Geschichte des jüdischen Gnosticismus*, Berlin 1889.

42 Celsus' anti-dualistic view is also expressed in *Contra Celsum*, VIII, 11.

49 τὸ κατ' εἰκόνα θεοῦ πεποιῆσθαι τὸν ἄνθρωπον: See Gen. i:27; cf. Ecphantus, *De Regno*, apud: Stobaeus, IV, 7:64 (No. 563): ἀρχετύπῳ χρώμενος ἑαυτῷ.

φυτευθέντα παράδεισον: See Gen. ii:8.

καὶ τὴν φλογίνην ῥομφαίαν: See Gen. iii:24.

60 μακρῷ δ᾿ εὐηθέστερον τὸ καὶ ἡμέρας τινὰς ἐπιδιανεῖμαι τῇ κοσμογονίᾳ, πρὶν εἶναι ἡμέρας: This very difficulty had already been felt by Philo, *Legum Allegoria*, I, 2.

52 πνεῦμα θεοῦ ἐπεφέρετο ἐπάνω τοῦ ὕδατος: See Gen. i:2; cf. Numenius, apud: Porphyrius, *De Antro Nympharum*, 10 (No. 368).

ὡς ὑπὸ ἑτέρου τοῦ δημιουργοῦ παρὰ τὸν μέγαν θεόν: Obviously Celsus implies here the doctrines of Marcion.

61 ὥσπερ τις ἀτεχνῶς πονηρὸς χειροτέχνης ἐκκαμών: This became a recurrent argument in pagan polemics; see Iulianus, *Adversus Galilaeos* (No. 481); Rutilius Namatianus, *De Reditu Suo*, I, 392 (No. 542). Origen's reply here is that Celsus' argumentation derived from a fallacious interpretation of Genesis, which equated "He ceased on the seventh day" (κατέπαυσε τῇ ἡμέρᾳ τῇ ἑβδόμῃ) with "He rested on the seventh day" (ἀνεπαύσατο τῇ ἡμέρᾳ τῇ ἑβδόμῃ). However, we see that the text called for a reply on the part of Jewish thinkers from the earliest stages of Jewish-Hellenistic theology. The passage is already mentioned in the fragment of Aristobulus, apud: Eusebius, *Praeparatio Evangelica*, XIII, 12:11; Philo, *Legum Allegoria*, I, 5–6.

80 νῦν δὲ ἔδοξε Κέλσῳ ἐνθεώτατον εἰπεῖν καὶ τὸ Αἰγυπτίων ἔθνος: In his high appreciation of the Egyptians Celsus follows a long line of tradition in the ancient world with contemporary parallels in, e.g., Apuleius or Aelius Aristides. See Andresen, *op. cit.* (supra, p. 230), p. 200.

VII, 3 καὶ ὥσπερ εἰώθασιν ἔτι νῦν οἱ περὶ Φοινίκην τε καὶ Παλαιστίνην: Cf. *Contra Celsum*, VII, 9: ἐπεὶ δὲ καὶ τὸν τρόπον τῶν ἐν Φοινίκῃ καὶ Παλαιστίνῃ μαντείων ἐπαγγέλλεται φράσειν ὁ Κέλσος ὡς ἀκούσας καὶ πάνυ καταμαθών, ... πολλοί, φησί, καὶ ἀνώνυμοι ῥᾷστα ἐκ τῆς προστυχούσης αἰτίας καὶ ἐν ἱεροῖς καὶ ἔξω ἱερῶν, οἱ δὲ καὶ ἀγείροντες καὶ ἐπιφοιτῶντες πόλεσιν ἢ στρατοπέδοις, κινοῦνται δῆθεν ὡς θεσπίζοντες. πρόχειρον δ᾿ ἑκάστῳ καὶ σύνηθες εἰπεῖν· ἐγὼ ὁ θεός εἰμι θεοῦ παῖς ἢ πνεῦμα θεῖον.

18 πλουτεῖν καὶ δυναστεύειν: See Deut. xv:6, and especially xxviii:11 ff.

καὶ καταπιμπλάναι τὴν γῆν: See Gen. viii:17; ix:1, 7.

καὶ καταφονεύειν ... καὶ παγγενεὶ κτείνειν: See Exod. xvii:13 ff.; Num. xxi:34 f.; Deut. xxv:19.

ὅπερ καὶ αὐτὸς ἐν ὀφθαλμοῖς τῶν Ἰουδαίων, ὥς φησι Μωϋσῆς, ποιεῖ: See Exod. xxxiv:10; Deut. xxix:1 f.

τὰ τῶν πολεμίων δράσειν ἀπειλεῖ: See Deut. vii:4; xxviii:15 ff.

53 Ἀνάξαρχον γοῦν: For the story of the death of Anaxarchus of Abdera, the pupil of Democritus, at the hands of Nicocreon in Cyprus, see Cicero, *Tusculanae Disputationes*, II, 52; idem, *De Natura Deorum*, III, 82; Philo, *Quod Omnis Probus Liber Sit*, 109, and the parallel references, many of them in patristic literature. See Chadwick's note to his translation, p. 439, n. 8.

VIII, 69 ὧν τοῖς μὲν ἀντὶ τοῦ γῆς ἁπάσης εἶναι δεσπόταις οὐδ᾿ ὁποία τις βῶλος οὐδ᾿ ἑστία λείπεται: For the same argument deriving from the deplorable political state of the Jews at this time, see above, *Contra Celsum*, V, 41.

CXIV. GALEN

129–c. 200 C.E.

The illustrious physician of the ancient world was born in Pergamum, and stayed in several of the great Jewish centres, including Smyrna, Alexandria and Rome. He also visited Palestine. Galen does not allot any special place to the Jews in his works, but mentions them, like the Christians, mainly to exemplify a certain cast of mind which he considers does not conform to that of the true scientist and philosopher. Five passages in which Judaism is referred to expressly have been traced in the works of Galen. Three are to be found in his extant Greek works: one in De Usu Partium *and two in* De Pulsuum Differentiis. *Two other passages have been recovered from Arabic translations.[1]*

The most elaborate passage is that in De Usu Partium *(No. 376), a work composed between 169 and 176 C.E.,[2] roughly contemporaneous with the* Ἀληθὴς Λόγος *of Celsus (No. 375). The reference constitutes a criticism of the Mosaic cosmogony and is found in the middle of Galen's discussion of the constant length of the eyelashes. The problem posed is whether this constant should be attributed to the hair's fear of its master's command, or to reverence for the god who ordered it so, or to the fact that the hair itself believes this to be best. This problem provides*

---

1 See the texts and the exhaustive discussion in R. Walzer, *Galen on Jews and Christians*, Oxford 1949, and the reviews by A. Momigliano, *Rivista storica italiana*, LXII (1950), pp. 575 ff.; A. D. Nock, *Gnomon*, XXIII (1951), pp. 48 ff.; G. Levi della Vida, *Journal of the American Oriental Society*, LXX (1950), pp. 182 ff.

The two Arabic passages are given with an English translation in Walzer, *op. cit.*, pp. 11 and 15. The first is a quotation from a lost work of Galen on Hippocrates' *Anatomy*. In Walzer's translation it reads as follows: "They compare those who practise medicine without scientific knowledge to Moses, who framed laws for the tribe of the Jews, since it is his method in his books to write without offering proofs, saying 'God commanded, God spake'." The other is a quotation from Galen's work against the theology of Aristotle: "If I had in mind people who taught their pupils in the same way as the followers of Moses and Christ teach theirs — for they order them to accept everything on faith — I should not have given you a definition."

2 See *ibid.*, p. 11.

the context for the statement that while the Mosaic interpretation of nature is preferable to that of Epicurus, the best system is that which does not confine itself, like that of Moses, to the principle of the demiurge as the source of the whole creation but adds to it the material principle. In the specific case of the length of the eyelashes, the demiurge created it thus because he thought it good, and consequent upon his decision he took care that the proper material conditions should exist in which to execute it, since the will alone certainly did not suffice.

In this lies what Galen considers to be the essential difference between the opinion of Moses and that of Plato and the other Greeks who follow the right method in dealing with the questions of Nature. For Moses, it was sufficient to say that God willed the arrangement of matter, while the Greeks think that certain things are physically impossible and that God only chooses the best out of the available possibilities. Thus, even if God should exert His will numberless times, the eyelashes will never come into being out of a soft substance and it is only possible for them to stand erect when fixed to something hard. Hence God planted them firmly in a cartilaginous body. Otherwise the deity would have been inferior not only to Moses, but also to a bad general who places a wall or a camp in marshy ground. In the words of Walzer, by Galen "it is appreciated that Moses retained the causa motrix *by introducing the demiurge as a principle of becoming, but he is censured for having omitted the* causa materialis *and — we may add — for having thus postulated the* creatio ex nihilo *to which later Christians, Muhamme-dans, and Jews explicitly adhered."*[3]

Galen's four other references to the Jews bear mainly on two features that characterize them, common to both Jews and Christians. These are acceptance of everything on faith and obstinate loyalty to their doctrine. Two of the passages derive from De Pulsuum Differentiis. *They occur in connection with Galen's criticism of Archigenes, a famous physician of the former generation, for having associated eight qualities with the pulses without giving any proofs for this statement (No. 377). Galen argues that it would have been much better to add to the statement, if not cogent proof, at least a reassuring and adequate explanation. For one should not from the start, as if one had come into the* διατριβή *(school) of Moses and Christ, hear about laws that have not been demonstrated, particularly in a case where it is least appropriate. The other passage from the same work (No. 378) is an attack on the school dogmatism*

3 See *ibid.*, p. 26.

implied in unqualified adherence to a particular doctrine. This is compared by Galen to the attachment of the Christians and Jews to their respective beliefs, for "one might more easily teach novelties to the followers of Moses and Christ than to the physicians and philosophers, who cling fast to their schools".

An Arabic version of a passage by Galen bearing upon the Jews comes from his lost work on Hippocrates' Anatomy, one of Galen's early compositions, written between 162 and 166 C.E. Thus it precedes in strict chronological order the excerpt from the De Usu Partium. The work itself is dedicated to Flavius Boethus, a native of Acre–Ptolemais and a governor of Syria Palaestina, a position presumably obtained by him before 166 C.E.[4] *The relevant passage compares those who practise medicine without scientific knowledge to Moses, who legislated for the tribe of the Jews, since it is his method to write without offering proofs. Another passage, extant in Arabic translation, couples the followers of Moses with those of Christ in teaching the acceptance of everything on faith. The quotation derives from a work of Galen opposing Aristotelian theology, the date of which is uncertain.*[5]

In the Arabic rendering of a passage from Galen's summary of Plato's Republic Galen makes no mention of the Jews when he states that the people called Christians, though drawing their inspiration from parables and miracles, sometimes act in the same way as philosophers. Galen then lists the features of Christian behaviour that cause him to assert that some of the Christians have attained a degree of intellectual understanding on a par with that of genuine philosophers. They display contempt of death and practise abstention from cohabitation, self-control in matters of food and drink, and a keen pursuit of justice.[6] *As may be seen, Galen's references bearing upon Jews and Judaism concern the fundamental principle of Mosaic philosophy and cosmogony, and the habit of mind prevalent among Jews that undoubtedly results from what Galen considers are the defects of this underlying principle of faith. Yet characteristically Galen nowhere*

4 See Kappelmacher, PW, VI, pp. 2534 f.; Nock, *op. cit.* (supra, p. 306, n. 1), p. 50; Smallwood, p. 552 ff. On Flavius Boethus, cf. Galenus, *De Anatomicis Administrationibus*, I, 1 (ed. Kühn, II, pp. 215 f.); *De Libris Propriis*, 1 (ed. Kühn, XIX, p. 16): ὁ Βοηθὸς ἐξῆλθε τῆς πόλεως ἐμοῦ πρότερος, ἄρξων τότε τῆς Παλαιστίνης Συρίας, ἐν ᾗ καὶ ἀπέθανε.

5 See Walzer, *op. cit.* (supra, p. 306, n. 1), pp. 14 f.

6 See *ibid.*, p. 15.

*makes carping remarks about the Jewish way of life or the misanthropy,
superstitious customs, or other frequently heard anti-Jewish allegations.
This omission may be accounted for in part at least by the period in
which Galen wrote. After 160 C.E. the "Jewish question" had become
less acute both in its effect on Roman imperial policy and in the life of
the Greek cities.*

*The references to the Jews by Galen do not necessitate the assumption of
a solid knowledge of Judaism. In his places of residence, Galen had
certainly met Jews, and presumably not a few of his patients and some
of his colleagues were Jews.[7] While Galen expressly testifies to his
sojourn in Palestine (Nos. 382, 384, 385, 390), he does not mention Jews
in this connection.*

7 On the relations between Rufus of Samaria and Galen, see F. Pfaff,
Hermes, LXVII (1932), pp. 356 ff. Pfaff offers a German rendering of
passages from Galen's commentary on Book VI of Hippocrates'
Epidemica, preserved in Arabic in the translation of Ḥunain ibn Isḥaq.
From these it appears that Rufus of Samaria was among the
commentators on Hippocrates' works, but that he was more of a
compiler than an original thinker. According to Galen, Rufus did not
know Greek before he came to Rome, and should have been ashamed of
the fact that although he had been living among Greeks his knowledge of
the language was so poor that he aroused derision; see *ibid.*, p. 357. Galen
states expressly that Rufus of Samaria was a Jew, and adds a general
remark about his nation, which lacked the ability to interpret books of
antiquity independently; Rufus had collected interpretations from
commentaries written by others, since they were all in his possession; see
ibid., p. 358. The passages bearing upon Rufus are now to be found in
*Galens Kommentare zu dem VI. Buche der Epidemien des Hippokrates
aus dem Arabischen ins Deutsche*, translated by F. Pfaff, Berlin 1956, pp.
413 f., 293; see also pp. 213, 289, 347, 476 f., 503. It may be that Galen did
not distinguish Jews from Samaritans. The absence of information about
Jews living in the city of Samaria (= Sebaste) at that period allows some
presumption that Rufus was a Samaritan. There is also an allusion to an
ἀρχίατρος named Solomon in *De Remediis Parabilibus*, I, 17 (ed. Kühn,
XIV, p. 389): εἰ δέ σοι χρεία γένηται καὶ τοῦ πρὸς Σαλομῶντα τὸν
ἀρχίητρον γεγραμμένου ἡμῖν συντάγματος. However, Solomon may
be a Christian rather than a Jew if the work derives from a later period;
see H. Usener, *Das Weihnachtsfest*[2], Bonn 1911, p. 235, n. 3. In any case,
the work is not authentic; see J. Ilberg, *Rhein. Museum*, LI (1896), p. 191.
For later mediaeval traditions identifying Galen with Gamaliel, see
G. Vajda, *Annuaire de l'institut de philologie et d'histoire orientales et
slaves*, XIII (1953; published 1955), pp. 641 ff.

Galen makes several references in his works to the Dead Sea.[8] *He gives a description of the water of the lake in Syria Palaestina, called by some "the Dead Sea" and by others "the Lake of Asphalt", in his* De Simplicium Medicamentorum Temperamentis ac Facultatibus, *IV, 20 (No. 381). In the same work he stresses the beauty of the asphalt of the Dead Sea and points out its medicinal qualities; see ibid., XI, 2, 10 (No. 386).*

The asphalt of the Dead Sea is also referred to as "Judaean asphalt" in De Symptomatum Causis, *III, 7 (No. 380), in* De Antidotis, *I, 12 (No. 392), in* De Compositione Medicamentorum per Genera, *II, 17:22 (No. 388), and in* Ad Pisonem de Theriaca *(No. 389). The excellence of the Jewish opobalsamum is stressed in* De Antidotis, *I, 2 (No. 390).*

In a chapter dealing with dates in De Alimentorum Facultatibus, *II, 26:2 (No. 379), there is mention of the soft, moist and sweet caryotic dates, the finest of which are said to grow in Jericho "situated in Syria Palaestina". The term for the area used by Galen accords with the official usage that obtained from the time of Hadrian.*

The medical use for what is called the "Judaean stone" is dealt with in De Simplicium Medicamentorum Temperamentis ac Facultatibus, *IX, 2:5 (No. 383). Galen doubts whether it is of much help to the bladder, for which purpose it is commonly used, but he finds it good for the kidneys.*

An especially interesting passage dealing with the year and the intercalary month of the inhabitants of Palestine is Ad Hippocratis Epidemiarum Libros, *I, 1 (No. 394).*

Galen mentions Palestine also in connection with watery wine; see Hippocratis de Acutorum Morborum Victu Liber et Galeni Commentarius, *III, 8 (ed. Kühn, XV, p. 648):* ἐγὼ γοῦν καὶ κατὰ τὴν Κιλικίαν καὶ Φοινικίην καὶ Παλαιστίνην καὶ Σκῦρον καὶ Κρήτην εὗρον οἴνους τοιούτους. *However, there is nothing here to suggest a specific connection with Jews.*

8 On Galen's visit to the Dead Sea, see J. Walsh, *Bulletin of the Geographical Society of Philadelphia*, XXV (1927), pp. 93 ff. For dating the visit in 157 or 161–162 C.E., see V. Nutton, *CQ*, NS, XXIII (1973), pp. 169 f.

De Usu Partium, XI, 14 — Helmreich = Kühn, III, pp. 904 ff.

Ἆρ' οὖν προσέταξε ταύταις μόναις ταῖς θριξὶν ὁ δημιουργὸς ἡμῶν ἴσον ἀεὶ
φυλάττειν τὸ μέγεθος, αἱ δ' ἤτοι δεδοικυῖαι τὴν ἐπίταξιν τοῦ δεσπότου ἢ
αἰδούμεναι τὸν προστάξαντα θεὸν ἢ αὐταὶ πεπεισμέναι βέλτιον εἶναι
δρᾶν τοῦτο διαφυλάττουσιν, ὡς ἐκελεύσθησαν; ἢ Μωσῆς μὲν οὕτως
5 ἐφυσιολόγει, καὶ βέλτιον οὕτως ἢ ὡς Ἐπίκουρος; ἄριστον μέντοι μηδ-
ετέρως, ἀλλὰ τὴν ἐκ τοῦ δημιουργοῦ φυλάττοντας ἀρχὴν γενέσεως ⟨ἐν⟩
ἅπασι τοῖς γεννητοῖς ὁμοίως Μωσεῖ τὴν ἐκ τῆς ὕλης αὐτῇ προστιθέναι.
διὰ τοῦτο μὲν γὰρ ἴσον ἀεὶ φυλάττειν αὐτὰς δεομένας τὸ μέγεθος ὁ
δημιουργὸς ἡμῶν ἀπειργάσατο, διότι τοῦτ' ἦν τὸ βέλτιον· ἐπεὶ δ' ἔγνω
10 τοιαύτας δεῖν ἐργάζεσθαι, διὰ τοῦτο ταῖς μὲν οἷον χόνδρον τιν' ὑπέτεινε
σκληρὸν σῶμα, ταῖς δὲ σκληρὸν δέρμα συμφυὲς τῷ χόνδρῳ διὰ τῶν
ὀφρύων. οὐ γὰρ δὴ τὸ βουληθῆναι τοιαύτας γενέσθαι μόνον ἦν αὔταρκες·
οὐδὲ γάρ, εἰ τὴν πέτραν ἐξαίφνης ἐθελήσειεν ἄνθρωπον ποιῆσαι, δυνατὸν
αὐτῷ. καὶ τοῦτ' ἔστι, καθ' ὃ τῆς Μωσοῦ δόξης ἥδ' ἡμετέρα καὶ ἡ Πλάτωνος
15 καὶ ἡ τῶν ἄλλων τῶν παρ' Ἕλλησιν ὀρθῶς μεταχειρισαμένων τοὺς περὶ
φύσεως λόγους διαφέρει. τῷ μὲν γὰρ ἀρκεῖ τὸ βουληθῆναι τὸν θεὸν
κοσμῆσαι τὴν ὕλην, ἡ δ' εὐθὺς κεκόσμηται· πάντα γὰρ εἶναι νομίζει τῷ
θεῷ δυνατά, κἂν εἰ τὴν τέφραν ἵππον ἢ βοῦν ἐθέλοι ποιεῖν. ἡμεῖς δ' οὐχ
οὕτω γινώσκομεν, ἀλλ' εἶναι γάρ τινα λέγομεν ἀδύνατα φύσει καὶ τούτοις
20 μηδ' ἐπιχειρεῖν ὅλως τὸν θεόν, ἀλλ' ἐκ τῶν δυνατῶν γενέσθαι τὸ
βέλτιστον αἱρεῖσθαι. καὶ τοίνυν καὶ τρίχας ἐπὶ τοῖς βλεφάροις ἐπειδὴ
βέλτιον ἦν ἴσας ἀεὶ καὶ μέγεθος εἶναι καὶ ἀριθμόν, οὐ τὸν μὲν
βουληθῆναι λέγομεν τὰς δ' εὐθὺς γεγονέναι· μὴ γὰρ ἄν, μηδ' εἰ μυριάκις
βουληθείη, γενέσθαι ποτ' ἂν τοιαύτας αὐτὰς ἐκ δέρματος μαλακοῦ
25 πεφυκυίας· τά τε γὰρ ἄλλα καὶ ὀρθὰς ἀνεστηκέναι παντάπασιν ἀδύνατον
ἦν μὴ κατὰ σκληροῦ πεπηγυίας. ἀμφοτέρων οὖν τὸν θεὸν αἴτιον εἶναί
φαμεν, τῆς τε τοῦ βελτίονος ἐν αὐτοῖς δημιουργουμένοις αἱρέσεως καὶ τῆς
περὶ τὴν ὕλην ἐκλέξεως. ἐπεὶ γὰρ ἅμα μὲν ὀρθὰς ἀνεστηκέναι τὰς ἐπὶ τῶν
βλεφάρων τρίχας ἐχρῆν, ἅμα δ' ἴσας ἀεὶ φυλάττεσθαι μέγεθός τε καὶ
30 ἀριθμόν, εἰς χονδρῶδες αὐτὰς κατέπηξε σῶμα. εἰ δ' εἰς μαλακὴν οὐσίαν
καὶ σαρκοειδῆ κατεπήξατο, φαυλότερος ἂν ἦν οὐ Μωσοῦ μόνον, ἀλλὰ καὶ
στρατηγοῦ μοχθηροῦ κατὰ τέλματος τεῖχος ἢ χάρακα πηγνυμένου.

5 οὕτως] οὗτος B   6 ⟨ἐν⟩ Helmreich   7 ἅπασι om. D /
γεννητικοῖς B   γενητοῖς LU / μωσῆ LU   8 ἀεὶ ἴσον D
10 ἐργάσασθαι B   11 χονδρώδει BL   14 μωσῆ U in ras.
μωσέως D   17 νομίζει post δυνατά colloc. D   18 ἐθέλει BD
21 βέλτιον D   22 οὐ om. D   23 μηδὲ γὰρ L   27 τοῦ om. DU
28 ὀρθῶς D   31 μωσῆν B   μωσέως D

Did our demiurge simply enjoin this hair to preserve its length always equal, and does it strictly observe this order either from fear of its master's command, or from reverence for the god who gave this order, or is it because it itself believes it better to do this? Is not this Moses' way of treating Nature and is it not superior to that of Epicurus? The best way, of course, is to follow neither of these but to maintain like Moses the principle of the demiurge as the origin of every created thing, while adding the material principle to it. For our demiurge created it to preserve a constant length, because this was better. When he had determined to make it so, he set under part of it a hard body as a kind of cartilage, and under another part a hard skin attached to the cartilage through the eyebrows. For it was certainly not sufficient merely to will their becoming such: it would not have been possible for him to make a man out of a stone in an instant, by simply wishing so.

It is precisely this point in which our own opinion and that of Plato and of the other Greeks who follow the right method in natural science differs from the position taken by Moses. For the latter it seems enough to say that God simply willed the arrangement of matter and it was presently arranged in due order; for he believes everything to be possible with God, even should He wish to make a bull or a horse out of ashes. We however do not hold this; we say that certain things are impossible by nature and that God does not even attempt such things at all but that He chooses the best out of the possibilities of becoming. We say therefore that since it was better that the eyelashes should always be equal in length and number, it was not that He just willed and they were instantly there; for even if He should just will numberless times, they would never come into being in this manner out of a soft skin; and, in particular, it was altogether impossible for them to stand erect unless fixed on something hard. We say thus that God is the cause both of the choice of the best in the products of creation themselves and of the selection of the matter. For since it was required, first that the eyelashes should stand erect and secondly that they should be kept equal in length and number, He planted them firmly in a cartilaginous body. If He had planted them in a soft and fleshy substance He would have suffered a worse failure not only than Moses but also than a bad general who plants a wall or a camp in marshy ground.

(trans. R. Walzer, Oxford 1949)

Galen

On this passage, see Walzer, *op. cit.* (supra, p. 306, n. 1), pp. 26 ff. The discussion and censure of the view that God, equated here with the demiurge, can do the impossible appears here in connection with Judaism for the first time in Galen's works. It is paralleled in the criticism of the Jewish and Christian belief in resurrection voiced by Galen's contemporary Celsus; cf. Origenes, *Contra Celsum*, V, 14 (No. 375). Both writers had forerunners in the Academic critics of the Stoic tenet of divine omnipotence; see H. Chadwick, *HTR*, XLI (1948), p. 85; cf. Cicero, *De Divinatione*, II, 86; idem, *De Natura Deorum*, III, 92.

The omnipotence of God was generally invoked by Christian writers in justification of the belief in bodily resurrection; see Chadwick, *op. cit.*, p. 84. A reference to Porphyry's views is included in the commentary to Job by Didymus the Blind, in: D. Hagedorn & R. Merkelbach, *Vigiliae Christianae*, XX (1966), p. 86: σοφίζονται γάρ τινες, ὧν ἐστι καὶ Πορφύριος καὶ ὅμοιοι, ὅτι εἰ πάντα δυνατὰ τῷ θεῷ, καὶ τὸ ψεύσασθαι. καὶ εἰ πάντα δυνατὰ τῷ πιστῷ (Matt. xvii : 20), δύναται καὶ κλίνην ποιῆσαι καὶ ἄνθρωπον ποιῆσαι. Christians and Epicureans are coupled in Lucianus, *Alexander*, 38. On Epicureans and Christians in the second century, see also A. D. Simpson, *TAPA*, LXXII (1941), pp. 372 ff.

377

De Pulsuum Differentiis, II, 4 — Kühn, VIII, pp. 578 ff.

Ταῦτα μὲν οὖν εὐθὺς κατ᾽ ἀρχὰς ἡμάρτηται τῷ Ἀρχιγένει περὶ τὴν
ἐξαρίθμησιν τῶν πρώτων ποιοτήτων, ἅς οὐδ᾽ ἀποδεῖξαι, πῶς τοσαῦται τὸν
ἀριθμόν εἰσιν, ἠξίωσεν, ἀλλ᾽ ἁπλῶς ὡδί πως ἔρριψε τὸν λόγον. ὀκτὼ
λέγονται ποιότητες παρέπεσθαι τοῖς σφυγμοῖς, αἱ διηχημέναι παρά γ᾽
5 οὖν τοῖς καθαρείοις. ἐγὼ δὲ τί μέν ἐστι τὸ διηχημέναι, ἀκριβῶς συμβαλεῖν
οὐ δύναμαι. οὐδὲ γὰρ εὗρον τοὔνομα παρά τινι τῶν Ἑλλήνων. ὥστε οὐδὲ
καθ᾽ οὗ τέτακται πράγματος ὑπ᾽ Ἀρχιγένους ἐπίσταμαι, καὶ ταῦτα μηδὲ
γράψαντος αὐτοῦ βιβλίον περὶ τῆς ἰδίας διαλέκτου, καθάπερ Χρύσιππος
ὑπὲρ ὧν ἔθετο κατὰ τὴν διαλεκτικὴν ὀνομάτων· μόνως γὰρ ἂν οὕτως
10 συνίεμεν αὐτοῦ. ἐκ μέντοι τῆς ὅλης λέξεως ὑπονοήσειεν ἄν τις, κατὰ τοῦ
παρὰ πᾶσι λεγομένου τε καὶ πεπιστευμένου τὸ διηχημέναι φέρειν αὐτόν.
καίτοι γε οὐδὲ τοῦτ᾽ ἐστὶν ἁπλῶς ὑπονοῆσαι δυνατόν. οὐ γὰρ ἅπασιν, ἀλλὰ
τοῖς καθαρείοις φησίν, οὕς οὐδ᾽ αὐτοὺς πάλιν ἐπίσταμαι, τίνες ποτέ εἰσι.
καίτοι μαθεῖν γε ἐδεόμην, ἵνα σκέψωμαι πότερον πιστευτέον αὐτοῖς χωρὶς
15 ἀποδείξεως, ἢ μή. παρὰ μὲν γὰρ Ἀριστοτέλους ἔνδοξα λήμματα ἤκουσα,
τὰ πᾶσιν ἀνθρώποις, ἢ τοῖς πλείστοις, ἢ τοῖς σοφοῖς δοκοῦντα. νυνὶ δέ, εἰ
τοὺς καθαρείους ἀντὶ τῶν σοφῶν χρὴ νοεῖν, οὐκ οἶδα. κάλλιον δ᾽ ἂν ἦν
πολλῷ προσθεῖναί τινα, εἰ καὶ μὴ βεβαίαν ἀπόδειξιν, παραμυθίαν γ᾽ οὖν
ἱκανὴν τῷ λόγῳ περὶ τῶν ὀκτὼ ποιοτήτων, ἵνα μή τις εὐθὺς κατ᾽ ἀρχάς, ὡς

20 εἰς Μωϋσοῦ καὶ Χριστοῦ διατριβὴν ἀφιγμένος, νόμων ἀναποδείκτων ἀκούῃ, καὶ ταῦτα ἐν οἷς ἥκιστα χρή. μέλλων γὰρ ἐρεῖν ὑπὲρ ἁπάντων τῶν σφυγμῶν, ὡς ἄν τις ἐξ ὧν προῦγραψεν εἰκάσειεν, ὁπόσοι γ᾽ εἰσίν, οὐδεμιᾷ μεθόδῳ λογικῇ προβιβάζειν ἡμᾶς ἠξίωσεν, ἀλλ᾽ ἐμπειρικὴν ἐποιήσατο διδασκαλίαν ὀκτὼ τοῖς καθαρείων λέγων διηχεῖσθαι ποιότητας.

This mistake Archigenes committed at the very beginning in his enumeration of the first qualities, about which he did not even consider it necessary to demonstrate how their number is so constituted, but simply hurled his statement in some such manner: "Eight qualities, those commonly spoken of among the 'purists', are said to be associated with the pulses." However, I cannot precisely understand what "commonly spoken" (αἱ διηχημέναι) means, since I did not find the word in use among anyone of the Greeks; so that I do not know to what matter Archigenes referred, the more so as he did not write a book about his special language, as did Chrysippus about the words he used in his dialectic, for only in this way are we able to understand him. One indeed may surmise from the whole discourse that by "commonly spoken" he refers to what is said and believed by all; however, it is impossible simply to surmise even this. For he talks about what is spoken of, not among all, but only among the "purists" (καθαρεῖοι),[1] and again I do not know who they are, although I wanted to know this in order to consider whether they may be believed without a proof or not. For I learned from Aristotle that probable statements are those approved by all people, or by the majority, or by the wise. Yet I do not know if we should consider the "purists" as being tantamount to the wise. I should have thought it much more proper to add some adequate reason, if not a cogent demonstration, to the argument about the eight qualities. Thus one would not, at the very start, as if one had come into the school of Moses and Christ, hear about laws that have not been demonstrated, and concerning a matter where it is least appropriate. Since, intending to speak about all the pulses, as one might presume from what he [Archigenes] wrote before, how many they are, he did not consider it necessary to guide us by any logical method but adopted an empirical fashion of teaching, saying that eight qualities are "commonly spoken" of by the "purists".

1 The translation "prominent people" is given by Walzer, *op. cit.* (supra, p. 306, n. 1).

Galen

378

De Pulsuum Differentiis, III, 3 — Kühn, VIII, p. 657

Θᾶττον γὰρ ἄν τις τοὺς ἀπὸ Μωϋσοῦ καὶ Χριστοῦ μεταδιδάξειεν ἢ τοὺς ταῖς αἱρέσεσι προστετηκότας ἰατρούς τε καὶ φιλοσόφους. ὥστ᾿ ἐγὼ τελευτῶν ἔγνων κερδαίνειν μακρὰν ἀδολεσχίαν περὶ μηδενὸς αὐτοῖς ὅλως διαλεγόμενος.

One might more easily teach novelties to the followers of Moses and Christ than to the physicians and philosophers, who cling fast to their schools. So that at the end I determined to spare myself much idle talk by not discussing anything at all with them.

379

De Alimentorum Facultatibus, II, 26:2 — Helmreich, *Corpus Medicorum Graecorum* = Kühn, VI, pp. 606 f.

῎Εστι δ᾿ ἐν αὐτοῖς οὐ σμικρὰ διαφορά. τινὲς μὲν γὰρ ξηροί τέ εἰσι καὶ στύφοντες ὥσπερ οἱ Αἰγύπτιοι, τινὲς δὲ μαλακοὶ καὶ ὑγροὶ καὶ γλυκεῖς ὥσπερ οἱ καλούμενοι καρυωτοί, κάλλιστοι δ᾿ οὗτοι γεννῶνται κατὰ τὴν Παλαιστίνην Συρίαν ἐν Ἱεριχοῦντι.

1 ξηρότεροι AB   4 ἱερακοῦντι B

There is no small difference between them; some of the dates are dry and astringent, as for instance the Egyptian, others are soft, moist and sweet, as for instance those called *caryotoi*. Those are most beautiful and grown in Jericho, in Syria Palaestina.

καρυωτοί, κάλλιστοι δ᾿ οὗτοι γεννῶνται κατὰ τὴν Παλαιστίνην Συρίαν: On the caryotic dates of Judaea, cf. Strabo, *Geographica*, XVI, 2:41, p. 763 (No. 115); Varro, *Res Rusticae*, II, 1:27 (No. 73). Strabo, like Galen, connects them with the vicinity of Jericho.

380

De Symptomatum Causis, III, 7 — Kühn, VII, p. 245

Αἷμα μὲν γὰρ αὐτὸ καθ᾿ ἑαυτὸ μελαινόμενον ἐν τῷ ψύχεσθαι, πρὸς τῷ μηδεμίαν ἐπικτᾶσθαι στιλπνότητα, καὶ ἣν ἐξ ἀρχῆς εἶχεν ἀπόλλυσιν· ἡ μέλαινα δὲ χολὴ στιλπνοτέρα καὶ αὐτοῦ τοῦ αἵματός ἐστιν, ὥσπερ καὶ ἡ ἐκ τῆς νεκρᾶς θαλάττης ἄσφαλτος, ἣν Ἰουδαϊκὴν ὀνομάζουσιν.

The blood itself, which becomes black by being cooled, not only does not acquire any additional glitter thereby but also loses that which it had before. The black bile is more glittering even than the blood itself, like the asphalt from the "Dead Sea" that is called "the Judaean".

ἐκ τῆς νεκρᾶς θαλάττης: Galen gives this as one of two alternative names in the *De Simplicium Medicamentorum Temperamentis ac Facultatibus*, IV, 20 (No. 381). See also *ibid.*, XI, 2:10 (No. 384). The designation Θάλασσα Νεκρά is used by Pausanias, V, 7:4 (No. 356), and *Mortuum Mare* by Pompeius Trogus, apud: Iustinus, XXXVI, 3:6 (No. 137); see also Dio Chrysostomus (No. 251): τὸ νεκρὸν ὕδωρ.
ἄσφαλτος, ἣν Ἰουδαϊκὴν ὀνομάζουσιν: Cf. Galenus, *De Antidotis*, I, 12 (No. 392). The Dead Sea asphalt was known as the "Judaean asphalt", or *bitumen Iudaicum*, cf. Scribonius Largus, 207, 209 (Nos. 155, 156); Pelagonius, *Ars Veterinaria*, 194, 338, 340, 491 (No. 534); *Mulomedicina Chironis*, 193, 870, 872, 874 (No. 533).

381

De Simplicium Medicamentorum Temperamentis ac Facultatibus, IV, 20 — Kühn, XI, pp. 690 ff. =
F85R

Ἀψίνθιον μὲν γὰρ οὐ πικρὸν μόνον, ἀλλὰ καὶ στρυφνόν ἐστιν, ἡ θάλαττα δ' ἁλμυρὰ μᾶλλον ἢ πικρὰ καὶ πλείστου μετέχουσα τοῦ ποτίμου, καθάπερ καὶ Ἀριστοτέλει πάλαι τοῦθ' ἱκανῶς ἐπιδέδεικται. τὸ δὲ τῆς ἐν Παλαιστίνῃ Συρίᾳ λίμνης ὕδωρ, ἣν ὀνομάζουσιν οἱ μὲν θάλασσαν νεκράν,
5 οἱ δὲ λίμνην ἀσφαλτῖτιν, ἔστι μὲν καὶ γευομένοις οὐχ ἁλυκὸν μόνον, ἀλλὰ καὶ πικρόν. ἔχει δὲ καὶ τοὺς ἐξ ἑαυτοῦ γεννωμένους ἅλας ὑποπίκρους ὁμοίως καὶ κατὰ τὴν ὄψιν εὐθὺς ἅμα πάσης θαλάσσης λευκότερόν τε καὶ παχύτερον φαίνεται, ἅλμῃ κατακορεῖ προσεοικός, εἰς ἣν οὐδ' ἂν ἐμβάλῃς ἅλας, ἔτι τακήσονται, πλεῖστον γὰρ τούτων μετέχει. καὶ εἴ τις εἰς αὐτὴν
10 καταδὺς ἀνακύψειεν, ἄχνην ἁλῶν ἂν εὐθέως κύκλῳ περὶ πᾶν ἴσχει τὸ σῶμα, καὶ διὰ τοῦτό τε βαρύτερόν ἐστι τῆς ἄλλης θαλάττης τὸ ὕδωρ ἐκεῖνο τοσοῦτον ὅσον ἡ θάλαττα τῶν ποταμῶν, ὥστ' οὐδ' εἰ βούλοιο κατὰ τοῦ βάθους καθεὶς ἑαυτὸν φέρεσθαι κάτω, δυνηθείης ἄν· οὕτως ἐξαίρει τε καὶ κουφίζει τὸ ὕδωρ, οὐχ ὡς φύσει κοῦφον ὑπάρχον, ὅπερ ἤδη τις εἶπε τῶν
15 παλαιῶν σοφιστῶν, ἀλλ' ὡς Ἀριστοτέλης ἔλεγε, διὰ βαρύτητα δίκην πηλοῦ βαστάζον τὰ κουφότερα. καὶ κατὰ τοῦτό γέ τοι καὶ εἰ συνδήσας ἀνθρώπου τὼ χεῖρε καὶ τὼ πόδε μεθείης εἰς τὸ τῆς λίμνης ἐκείνης ὕδωρ, οὐχ οἰχήσεται κάτω. καὶ μὲν δὴ καὶ ὡς ἐν τῇ θαλάττῃ πλείονα φορτία τῶν ἐν ταῖς λίμναις τε καὶ ποταμοῖς βαστάζει τὰ πλοῖα μὴ βυθιζόμενα, κατὰ
20 τὸν αὐτὸν τρόπον ἐν τῇ νεκρᾷ λίμνῃ πολλαπλάσια τῶν ἐν τῇ θαλάττῃ.

τοσούτῳ γάρ ἐστιν τὸ κατ' αὐτὴν ὕδωρ τοῦ θαλαττίου βαρύτερον ὅσον τὸ
θαλάττιον τοῦ λιμναίου τε καὶ ποταμίου. πρόσεστι γὰρ ἡ τῶν ἁλῶν οὐσία,
γεώδης τε καὶ βαρεῖα. καί σοι καὶ αὐτῷ γεννῆσαι θάλατταν ἔξεστιν, ἅλας
ὕδατι ποτίμῳ διατήξαντι καὶ γνῶναι πόσῳ βαρύτερον ἀποτελεῖται τὸ
25 τοιοῦτο ὕδωρ τοῦ γλυκέος. ἀλλὰ καὶ μέτρον ἤδη τι πεποίηνται τοῦ τὴν
ἅλμην εὔκρατον ὑπάρχειν εἰς τὰς ταριχείας, εἰ φαίνοιτο κατ' αὐτὴν
ἐπιπλέον ᾠόν, ὡς ἔτι γε καταφερομένου καὶ μήπω περὶ τὴν ἐπιφάνειαν
τῆς ἅλμης ἐννηχομένου μᾶλλον ὑδατώδης ἐστὶ καὶ γλυκεῖα. δεινῶς δ'
ἁλμυρὰ γίνεται τοσούτων ἐμβληθέντων ἁλῶν, ὡς μηκέτ' ἐγχωρεῖν
30 ἐπιτήκεσθαι τοὺς ἐπεμβαλλομένους. καὶ τοῦτό σοι στήσαντι τὸ ὕδωρ
ἁπάντων ὑδάτων εὑρεθήσεται βαρύτερον. ὥστ' ἔγωγέ ποτε μάταιον
ἀπέδειξα τοῦ πλουσίου τὴν φιλοτιμίαν, ἐκ τῆς νεκρᾶς θαλάττης τοσοῦτο
ὕδωρ κομίσαντος εἰς Ἰταλίαν, ὡς πληρῶσαι δεξαμένην. ἑτοίμως γὰρ
ἐποίησα ταὐτό, ἅλας παμπόλλους ἐμβαλὼν ὕδατι ποτίμῳ. μᾶλλον δ' ἂν
35 ἔτι βαρύτερον ἐργάσαιο τὸ τοιοῦτο ὕδωρ, εἰ τήξας τοὺς ἅλας ὡς πλείστους
ὑπὸ κυνὸς ἐπιτολήν, ἡνίκα μάλιστα θάλπος ἐστὶ σφοδρότατον, ἐάσαις
ἐξοπτηθῆναι, παραπλησίως τῷ κατὰ τὴν ἀσφαλτῖτιν λίμνην. οὕτω γὰρ
ἔσται καὶ τοῦτο βαρὺ τὸ ὕδωρ ὡς ἐκεῖνο. καὶ εἰ ἐνδήσειας ἢ ἄνθρωπον ἢ
ὁτιοῦν ἄλλο ἐμβάλλοις ζῷον εἰς αὐτό, παραπλησίως τοῖς πλοίοις
40 ἐποχήσεται τῷ ὕδατι. καὶ μὲν δὴ καὶ πικρότερον εὐθὺς ἔσται τὸ ποιοῦτο
ὕδωρ, ὡς εἰ καὶ καθεψεῖν ὑπὸ πυρὸς αὐτὸ βουληθείης· ὅ τι γὰρ ἂν ἁλυκὸν
ἐπὶ πλέον ἐκθερμήνῃς, ἔσται σοι πικρόν. οὕτω γοῦν καὶ αὐτὸ τὸ τῆς
ἀσφαλτίτιδος λίμνης ὕδωρ ἐν κοίλῳ καὶ θερμῷ χωρίῳ περιεχόμενον
ἐξοπτώμενόν θ' ὑπὸ τοῦ ἡλίου γίγνεται πικρόν. διὰ τοῦτό γε τοι καὶ τοῦ
45 θέρους μᾶλλον ἢ χειμῶνός ἐστι πικρόν. καὶ εἰ ἀρυσάμενος αὐτοῦ τι
καταθείης ἐν ἀγγείῳ κοίλῳ καὶ προσηλίῳ χωρίῳ, καθάπερ καὶ ἡμεῖς
ἐποιήσαμεν ὥρᾳ θέρους αὐτίκα μάλα πικρότερον αὐτοῦ φαίνεταί σοι
γεγονός. ἀλλὰ ταῦτα μὲν ἅπαντα τοῖς ὀλίγον ἔμπροσθεν ὑπὲρ τῆς τοῦ
πικροῦ γενέσεως εἰρημένοις ἱκανῶς μαρτυρεῖ. οὗ δ' ἕνεκεν ὁ λόγος ἐπὶ τὴν
50 ἀσφαλτῖτιν ἐξετράπετο λίμνην, οὔπω μοι πᾶν λέλεκται. φαίνεται γὰρ ἐν
ἐκείνῳ τῷ ὕδατι μήτε ζῷον ἐγγινόμενόν τι μήτε φυτόν, ἀλλὰ καὶ τῶν εἰς
αὐτὴν ἐμβαλόντων ποταμῶν ἀμφοτέρων, μεγίστους καὶ πλείστους
ἐχόντων ἰχθύας, καὶ μάλιστα τοῦ πλησίον Ἱεριχοῦντος, ὃν Ἰορδάνην
ὀνομάζουσιν, οὐδ' εἷς τῶν ἰχθύων ὑπερβαίνει τὰ στόματα τῶν ποταμῶν.
55 κἂν εἰ συλλαβὼν δέ τις αὐτοὺς ἐμβάλοι τῇ λίμνῃ, διαφθειρομένους ὄψεται
ταχέως· οὕτως τ' ἀκριβῶς πικρὸν ἅπασίν ἐστι καὶ ζῴοις καὶ φυτοῖς
πολέμιον, αὐχμῶδές τε καὶ ξηρὸν καὶ τὴν φύσιν οἷόν περ αἴθαλος ὑπὸ τῆς
κατοπτήσεως γεγενημένον. καίτοι γε οὐδὲ τὸ τῆς λίμνης ἐκείνης ὕδωρ
ἀκριβῶς ἐστι πικρόν, ὅτι μηδ' οἱ ἅλες αὐτοί. προσαγορεύουσι δ' αὐτοὺς
60 Σοδομηνοὺς ἀπὸ τῶν περιεχόντων τὴν λίμνην ὀρῶν ἃ καλεῖται Σόδομα,

317

καὶ χρῶνται πολλοὶ τῶν περιοίκων εἰς ὅσα περ ἡμεῖς τοῖς ἄλλοις ἁλσί.
δύναμις δ᾽ αὐτῶν οὐ ξηραντικὴ μόνον ἐπὶ μᾶλλόν ἐστι τῶν ἄλλων ἁλῶν,
ἀλλὰ καὶ λεπτυντική, διότι μᾶλλον τῶν ἄλλων ἐξώπτηνται. πᾶσι μὲν γὰρ
τοῖς ἁλσὶν ὑπάρχει τι καὶ στυπτικὸν ἀμυδρόν, ᾧ δὴ καὶ σφίγγουσι καὶ
65 πιλοῦσι τὰ ταριχευόμενα τῶν κρεῶν καὶ μάλισθ᾽ ὅταν ὦσι χόνδροι τε καὶ
δύσθραυστοι. τοιοῦτοι δὲ εἰσὶν ἀκριβέστατοι μὲν οἱ πλεῖστοι τῶν ὀρυκτῶν,
ἧττον δ᾽ αὐτῶν οἵ τ᾽ ἐκ τῆς θαλάττης καὶ πολλαχόθι τῆς γῆς ἐξ ὑδάτων
ἐλαφρῶν ἀναξηρανθέντων γεννώμενοι. τρίτοι δ᾽ ἐπὶ τούτοις ὑπάρχουσιν οἱ
ὀρυκτοί, ῥύπτειν μᾶλλον ἢ στύφειν τε καὶ συνάγειν πεφυκότες. ἐγγὺς δὲ
70 τούτων εἰσὶ κατὰ τὴν δύναμιν οἱ Σοδομηνοὶ χόνδροι μὲν ὄντες ὁμοίως τοῖς
θαλαττίοις, ἀλλὰ διὰ τὴν ἀναμεμιγμένην αὐτοῖς πικρότητα ῥυπτικώτεροί
τε καὶ διαφορητικώτεροι τῶν ἐκ τῆς θαλάττης ὑπάρχοντες. οὕτω δὲ δὴ καὶ
τὸ νίτρον αὐτὸ καὶ ἀφρὸς αὐτοῦ καὶ τὸ συνθέτῳ προσηγορίᾳ καλούμενον
ἀφρόνιτρον ἔτι μᾶλλον τῶν ἄλλων πέφυκε ῥύπτειν, ὡς ἂν ἥκιστα μὲν
75 στύφοντα, πικρὰ δ᾽ ἀκριβῶς ὑπάρχοντα.

Wormwood is not only bitter, but also astringent, while the sea is salty
rather than bitter even when it contains drinking water in a very large
quantity, as has been sufficiently shown long ago by Aristotle. The
water of the lake in Palaestina Syria, which some call the Dead Sea
and others Lake Asphaltitis, is to those who taste of it not only salty,
but also bitter. Likewise the salt from it is somewhat bitter and whiter
and thicker in appearance than that of any sea, resembling saturated
sea-water. Into which lake if you throw salt it does not dissolve, since
the water already has a great deal of salt in it. Moreover, if somebody
plunges into the lake and then emerges from the water, he forthwith
has a salty foam around the whole body; and therefore this water is
heavier than that of other seas in the same way as sea-water is heavier
than that of rivers, so that even if you want to be carried downwards
and plunge into the deep water you will not be able to do so. The
water lifts up and elevates in this way not because it is light by nature,
as was said by some of the ancient sophists, but, as Aristotle said,
because of its heaviness, since like mud it lifts up lighter things.
Accordingly, if you bind the hands and feet of a man and throw him
into the water of that lake he will not go down. And as in the sea the
ships carry bigger cargoes than those in the lakes and rivers, and do
not sink, in the same way in the Dead Sea the ships carry cargoes
many times bigger than those in the sea, for its water is heavier than
sea-water in the same degree as this is heavier than lake or river water
since it has the earthy and heavy salty substance. You yourself can

produce sea-water by melting salt in drinking water, and you may perceive how much heavier such water is rendered than sweet water. And a measure has been fixed for the salt water to be well-tempered for pickling, namely, if you see an egg floating upon it — for when it still sinks and does not swim over the surface of the salt water then the water rather is watery and sweet. It becomes strongly salty when so much salt is thrown into it that it is no longer possible for the salt thrown into it to dissolve. And when you weigh this water it will be found heavier than any of the other water. Consequently I indeed found foolish the zeal of the rich who imported a container full of water from the Dead Sea to Italy while I readily achieved the same by throwing large quantities of salt into drinking water. And you will make such water even heavier if you dissolve the greatest amount of salt at the time of the rise of the dog-star, when the heat is at its height, and allow it to be baked like that in the Asphaltite Lake, for this water will be as heavy as that of Lake Asphaltitis. And if you bind a man or any living creature and throw it in, it will float on the water like ships. And such water will immediately become more bitter if you want to boil it over a fire. For everything salty that you warm for a long time becomes bitter to you. In this manner the water of Lake Asphaltitis itself, being surrounded by a hollow and hot place and thoroughly baked by the sun, becomes bitter, and indeed for this reason it is more bitter in the summer than in the winter. And if you draw from this water and put it in a hollow vessel and a sunny place as we have done, it will immediately be found to have become more bitter. Anyhow all this sufficiently testifies to what has been said a little way above about the production of the bitterness. However the reason for my digression on the Asphaltitis has not yet been stated by me, for it appears that in this water no living being and no plant spring up, and though both the rivers which empty themselves into it contain the biggest fish in the largest number, and especially the river in the vicinity of Jericho which is called Jordan, no fish crosses the mouths of the rivers, and one who catches them and throws them into the lake will see them quickly destroyed. It is so bitter to everything, and hostile to living beings and plants, squalid and dry, and by nature becoming like ash by being burned, though the water of that lake is not strictly bitter apart from the salt itself. They call the salt Sodomene from the name of the mountains surrounding the lake which are called Sodoma, and many of the people living around them use it for the same purposes as other salt is used among us. This salt

319

has not only more drying power than other salt, but also an attenuating one because it is baked more than others. For every kind of salt has some modicum of astringent property by which it binds and compresses meat which is being pickled, especially when the salt is in the form of lumps and hard to break. Of that kind the most potent is most of the salt that is dug up, while that produced from the sea, or, as in many places, from evaporated light water, is less so. After this, in the third place, comes salt that has been dug up but having more a cleansing than an astringent and contracting capacity. Near to this in potency is the Sodomene salt that consists of lumps like that coming from the sea, but owing to the bitterness mixed with it is more cleansing and discutient than that from the sea. In the same way also nitre itself and its foam, as well as that called by a synthetic name "aphronitrium", have an even greater capacity to cleanse than other materials, possessing the least astringency but being exceedingly bitter.

τὸ δὲ τῆς ἐν Παλαιστίνῃ Συρίᾳ λίμνης ὕδωρ: A λίμνη ἐν Παλαιστίνῃ is mentioned in this connection by Aristoteles, *Meteorologica*, II, p. 359a (No. 3). Hieronymus of Cardia, and, following him, Diodorus, locate it in the land of the Nabataeans; see Diodorus, II, 48:6 (No. 59). Later writers, such as Pliny and Tacitus, naturally connect it with Judaea. On the other hand it is said to be situated ἐν τῇ γῇ τῇ Ἑβραίων by Pausanias, V, 7:4 (No. 356), while it is referred to either as a sea in Syria near Phoenicia or as a lake in Syria by Aelius Aristides, *Aegyptiacus*, 88, 89 (No. 370). Galen uses the term Παλαιστίνη Συρία here, as well as in another passage in this work; cf. below, IX, 2:5 (No. 383), as also in *De Antidotis*, I, 2 (No. 390). He refers simply to Παλαιστίνη in this work, below, IX, 1:2 (No. 382), and so too in *Ad Hippocratis Epidemiarum Libros*, I, 1 (No. 394), where Κοίλη Συρία is defined as a part of Παλαιστίνη.

λίμνην ἀσφαλτῖτιν: Cf. Diodorus, XIX, 98:1 (No. 62); Plinius, *Naturalis Historia*, V, 72 (No. 204); *ibid.*, II, 226 (No. 203); this is the common name for the Dead Sea in the works of Josephus; cf., e.g., *Ant.*, I, 174; *BJ*, IV, 476; *Contra Apionem*, I, 174.

ἅμα πάσης θαλάσσης λευκότερον: Scientists have pointed out that in August 1943 the whole of the Dead Sea was observed to have become milky white: apparently one million tons of calcium carbonate had spread over it during the night; see R. Bloch, H. Z. Littman & B. Elazari-Volcani, *Nature*, CLIV (1944), pp. 402 f. This description by Galen of the Dead Sea had already been referred to by D. Flusser; see *ibid.*

ὡς Ἀριστοτέλης ἔλεγε: Cf. Aristoteles, *Meteorologica*, II, 359a (No. 3).
εἰ συνδήσας ἀνθρώπου τὼ χεῖρε ... οὐκ οἰχήσεται κάτω: Cf. *BJ*, IV, 477: ἀφικόμενος γοῦν καθ᾽ ἱστορίαν ἐπ᾽ αὐτὴν Οὐεσπασιανὸς ἐκέλευσέ τινας τῶν νεῖν οὐκ ἐπισταμένων, δεθέντας ὀπίσω τὰς χεῖρας, ῥιφῆναι κατὰ τοῦ

Galen

βυθοῦ, καὶ συνέβη πάντας ἐπινήξασθαι, καθάπερ ὑπὸ πνεύματος ἄνω βιαζομένους.

ὃν Ἰορδάνην ὀνομάζουσιν: A description of the River Jordan is given in Plinius, *Naturalis Historia*, V, 71 (No. 204); Tacitus, *Historiae*, V, 6 (No. 281). The form Ἰάρδανος occurs in Pausanias, V, 7:4 (No. 356).

ἃ καλεῖται Σόδομα: Cf. Dio Chrysostomus (No. 251); Strabo, *Geographica*, XVI, 2:44, p. 764 (No. 115). For Strabo, at least, "Sodoma" was undoubtedly the name of a city (τῆς μητροπόλεως Σοδόμων), and not of mountains. Galen himself refers to our passage later in his work; see *De Simplicium Medicamentorum Temperamentis ac Facultatibus*, XI, 2:4 (ed. Kühn, XII, p. 373): λέλεκται δὲ καὶ περὶ τῶν Σοδομηνῶν [scil. ἁλῶν] τῶν ἐν τῇ νεκρᾷ θαλάσσῃ καλουμένῃ γεννωμένων ἐν τῷ τετάρτῳ γράμματι, καὶ εἴ τις ἐκεῖνο τὸ βιβλίον ἀνέγνωκεν ἐπιμελῶς, ἀναμνήσεως αὐτῷ μόνον δεήσει νῦν, ὥστε ῥηθείσης τῆς γευστῆς ποιότητος αὐτὸν ἐπίστασθαι τὴν δύναμιν τοῦ φαρμάκου.

382

De Simplicium Medicamentorum Temperamentis ac Facultatibus, IX, 1:2 — Kühn, XII, p. 171

Ἀνεγνωκὼς δὲ ἐγὼ παρά τε Διοσκορίδῃ καὶ ἄλλοις τισὶ μίγνυσθαι τράγειον αἷμα τῇ Λημνίᾳ γῇ, κἀκ τοῦ διὰ μίξεως ταύτης γενομένου πηλοῦ τὴν ἱέρειαν ἀναπλάττειν τε καὶ σφραγίζειν ἃς ὀνομάζουσι Λημνίας σφραγῖδας, ὠρέχθην αὐτὸς ἱστορῆσαι τὴν συμμετρίαν τῆς μίξεως. ὥσπερ
5 οὖν εἰς Κύπρον ἕνεκα τῶν ἐν αὐτῇ μετάλλων, εἴς τε τὴν κοίλην Συρίαν, μόριον οὖσαν τῆς Παλαιστίνης, ἕνεκεν ἀσφάλτου καί τινων ἄλλων κατ' αὐτὴν ἀξίων ἱστορίας ἐπορεύθην, οὕτως καὶ εἰς Λῆμνον οὐκ ὤκνησα πλεῦσαι.

Having read in Dioscorides and other writers that the blood of a he-goat is mixed with Lemnian earth, and that the priestess moulds the mud deriving from this mixture and certifies the so-called "Lemnian seals", I myself strove to examine the right proportion of the mixture. As I went to Cyprus because of its mines and to Coele-Syria, which constitutes a part of Palaestina, because of the asphalt and some other things worthy of investigation, so in like manner I did not shrink from sailing to Lemnos.

ὥσπερ οὖν εἰς Κύπρον ἕνεκα τῶν ἐν αὐτῇ μετάλλων: Cf. also Galenus, *De Antidotis*, I, 2 (No. 390). On the mines of Cyprus, see T. R. S. Broughton, in: T. Frank (ed.), *An Economic Survey of Ancient Rome*, IV, Baltimore 1938, p. 655; O. Davies, *The Annual of the British School at Athens*, XXX (1932), pp. 74 ff.

ἕνεκεν ἀσφάλτου ... ἐπορεύθην: Here Galen expressly states that he visited Palestine; cf. also his *De Simplicium Medicamentorum Temperamentis ac Facultatibus*, IX, 2:10 (No. 384); *ibid.*, 3:8 (No. 385).

383

De Simplicium Medicamentorum Temperamentis ac Facultatibus, IX, 2:5 — Kühn, XII, p. 199 = F86R

Περὶ Ἰουδαϊκοῦ. ἔστι δὲ καὶ ἄλλος λίθος ἰσχυρότερος τὴν δύναμιν ἐν τῇ Παλαιστίνῃ Συρίᾳ γινόμενος, λευκὸς μὲν τὴν χρόαν, εὔρυθμος δὲ κατὰ τὸ σχῆμα καὶ γραμμὰς ἔχων ὡς ἀπὸ τόρνου γεγονυίας. ὀνομάζουσι δ᾽ αὐτὸν ἀπὸ τῆς χώρας ἐν ᾗ γεννᾶσθαι πέφυκεν Ἰουδαϊκόν, καὶ χρῶνται πρὸς τοὺς
5   ἐν τῇ κύστει λίθους, ἀνιέντες μὲν ἐπ᾽ ἀκόνης, ποτίζοντες δὲ δι᾽ ὕδατος θερμοῦ κυάθων τριῶν. ἡμεῖς δ᾽ ἐφ᾽ ὧν ἐπειράθημεν οὐδὲν ἤνυσεν ὡς πρὸς τοὺς ἐν κύστει λίθους, ἐπὶ δὲ τῶν ἐν νεφροῖς συνιζομένων ἐστὶ δραστήριος.

7 συνιζομένων vel συνημμένων Wasserstein   συνιμένων Kühn

About the Judaean stone. There is another, more powerful, stone produced in Syria Palaestina, white-coloured, and well-proportioned in form, which has lines as though made by a turning-lathe. It is called "the Judaean" after the land in which it is produced. They use it against stones of the bladder, dissolving it on a whetstone, and moistening it with three cyathi of hot water. However, in the cases in which we tried it it accomplished nothing against the stones in the bladder but it is effective for those adhering to the kidneys.

Cf. Dioscorides, *De Materia Medica*, V, 137 (No. 184).

384

De Simplicium Medicamentorum Temperamentis ac Facultatibus, IX, 2:10 — Kühn, XII, p. 203

Πλακώδεις δὲ λίθους μελαίνας, εἰ κατὰ πυρὸς ἐπιτεθεῖεν, ἀσθενῆ φλόγα γεννῶντας ἐκόμισα πολλὰς ἐκ τῆς κοίλης Συρίας, ἐν τῷ λόφῳ γεννωμένας τῷ περιέχοντι τὴν νεκρὰν ὀνομαζομένην θάλασσαν, ἐν τοῖς ἀνατολικοῖς αὐτῆς μέρεσιν, ἔνθα καὶ ἡ ἄσφαλτος γίνεται. καὶ ἦν ἡ ὀσμὴ τῶν λίθων τῇ
5   ἀσφάλτῳ παραπλησία.

I brought from Coele Syria many black laminated stones, which, if put on a fire, generate a weak fire. They are produced in the hill surrounding the Sea called Dead, in the eastern parts of which the asphalt is also produced. The smell of the stone is similar to that of asphalt.

385

De Simplicium Medicamentorum Temperamentis ac Facultatibus, IX, 3 : 8 — Kühn, XII, pp. 215 f.

Προσθήσω δέ τι τῷ κατ' αὐτὸ λόγῳ χρήσιμον οὐ περὶ διφρυγοῦς μόνον γινώσκειν, ἀλλὰ καὶ περὶ Λημνίας σφραγῖδος καὶ πομφόλυγος καὶ ὀποβαλσάμου καὶ λυκίου τοῦ Ἰνδικοῦ. τούτων γὰρ ἔμαθον ἔτι μειράκιον ὢν σκευασίας, ἀδιάγνωστον τὸ σκευασθὲν ἐργαζόμενος τῶν ἀληθινῶν. ἦν
5 δὲ ὁ διδάξας ἄνθρωπος ἐπὶ μισθῷ μεγάλῳ περιεργότατος οὐκ ἐς ταῦτα μόνον, ἀλλὰ καὶ ἄλλα παραπλήσια. διὰ τοῦτο τοιγαροῦν ἔς τε Λῆμνον καὶ Κύπρον καὶ τὴν Παλαιστίνην Συρίαν ἐσπούδασα πορευθεὶς ἑκάστου τῶν φαρμάκων τούτων πολὺ πλῆθος εἰς ὅλον ἐμαυτοῦ παραθέσθαι τὸν βίον, ἀλλὰ καὶ τὸ λύκιον τὸ Ἰνδικὸν ἀρτίως ἐνηνεγμένον ἐς Φοινίκην ἅμα τῇ
10 Ἰνδικῇ ἀλόῃ κατ' ἐκεῖνον τὸν χρόνον εὐτύχησα λαβεῖν, ἡνίκα τὴν ἀπὸ τῆς Παλαιστίνης ὁδὸν ἐπανῄειν, αὐτῷ τε τῷ κεκομίσθαι διὰ τῶν καμήλων, σὺν τῷ παντὶ φορτίῳ, πεισθεὶς Ἰνδικὸν ὑπάρχειν αὐτὸ καὶ τῷ τὸ νοθευόμενον οὐ δύνασθαι πρὸς τῶν κομιζόντων γινώσκεσθαι, τῆς ὕλης ἐξ ἧς σκευάζεται κατὰ τοὺς τόπους ἐκείνους μὴ γεννωμένης.

I shall add something to the discussion that is useful to learn not only about pyrites, but also about the Lemnian seal and zinc oxide and opobalsamum and the Indian lycium. When still a boy I learned the manner of their fabrication, making the fabricated indiscernible from the authentic. The fellow that taught me it for a high pay was most curious not only concerning these, but about other similar things as well. Therefore I was eager indeed to go to Lemnos and Cyprus and Palaestina Syria and to store up a large quantity of these medicines for my whole life. Moreover I had the good fortune to lay hold of the Indian lycium which had been recently imported to Phoenicia together with the Indian aloe. This happened when I was back on my way from Palaestina, and I was persuaded that the lycium was Indian both by the very fact that it was brought by camels, together with the whole cargo, and because the spurious one could not be known to those who brought the lycium as the material from which it is prepared is not produced in their localities.

386

De Simplicium Medicamentorum Temperamentis ac Facultatibus, XI, 2:10 — Kühn, XII, p. 375

Περὶ ἀσφάλτου γεννωμένου ἐν τῇ νεκρᾷ θαλάσσῃ. καλλίστη δ᾽ ἄσφαλτος
γεννᾶται κατὰ τὴν νεκρὰν ὀνομαζομένην θάλασσαν. ἔστι δ᾽ αὐτὴ λίμνη
τις ἁλμυρὰ κατὰ τὴν κοίλην Συρίαν. ἡ δὲ δύναμις τοῦ φαρμάκου ξηραντική
τ᾽ ἐστὶ καὶ θερμαντικὴ κατὰ τὴν δευτέραν που τάξιν. εἰκότως οὖν αὐτῷ
5 χρῶνται πρός γε τὰς κολλήσεις τῶν ἐναίμων τραυμάτων πρὸς τἄλλα, ὅσα
ξηραίνειν δεόμενα μετὰ τοῦ θερμῆναι μετρίως.

About the asphalt produced in the Dead Sea. The most beautiful
asphalt is produced in the Sea called "Dead". This is a salty lake in
Coele Syria. The potency of this medicine consists in its drying and
next in its heating capabilities. It is indeed appropriate that people
use it for closing bleeding wounds and for other things that need to be
dried and moderately warmed.

387

De Compositione Medicamentorum per Genera, II, 7 — Kühn, XIII, p. 507

Ἄλλη Σαλώμη πρὸς πᾶσαν περιωδυνίαν καὶ συνάγχην μετὰ σικύας καὶ
πρὸς πλευρᾶς πόνον.

Salome with gourd is good for every pain and sore throat as well as for
pleurisy.

The medicine Salome to be used against pain seems to be mentioned only
here. The name of the medicine suggests a Jewish connotation, being the
well-known personal name, of the Hasmonaean queen (Salome–Alexandra)
among others, and of Herod's sister, who had close connections with the
empress Livia (see above, Vol. I, p. 310). For other Jewish women called by
this name in the works of Josephus and in the New Testament, see Stähelin,
PW, Ser. 2, I, pp. 1995 ff. It may be that one of them gave her name to the
medicine, as Nicolaus of Damascus gave it to a famous species of dates; see
Plinius, *Naturalis Historia*, XIII, 45 (No. 214).

388

De Compositione Medicamentorum per Genera, II, 17, 22 — Kühn, XIII, pp. 536, 560

(17) Ἀσφάλτου Ἰουδαϊκῆς λίτρας ε΄ ... *(22)* ἀσφάλτου Ἰουδαϊκῆς μνᾶν α΄.

(17) 5 pounds of Judaean asphalt ... (22) 1 *mina* of Judaean asphalt.

389

Ad Pisonem de Theriaca, 12 — Kühn, XIV, p. 260

ἀσφάλτου Ἰουδαϊκῆς.

Judaean asphalt.

390

De Antidotis, I, 2 — Kühn, XIV, pp. 7 ff. = F87R

Κύπρον γοῦν ἱστορῆσαι βουληθεὶς ἐγὼ διὰ ταῦτα, φίλον τε ἔχων τὸν ἐν
αὐτῇ πολὺ δυνάμενον, ἑταῖρον ὄντα τοῦ προεστῶτος τῶν μετάλλων
ἐπιτρόπου Καίσαρος, καδμείαν τε πολλὴν ἐκεῖθεν ἐκόμισα καὶ διφρυγὲς
καὶ σπόδιον καὶ πομφόλυγα χαλκῖτίν τε καὶ μίσυ καὶ σῶρυ καὶ χάλκανθον,
5 ὥσπερ γε πάλιν ἐκ τῆς Παλαιστίνης Συρίας ὀποβάλσαμον ἀκριβές.
ἄσφαλτος μὲν γὰρ οὐδὲ δολωθῆναι δύναται πανούργως, ὥσπερ οὐδὲ ὁ τοῦ
ὀποβαλσάμου καρπὸς ἢ τὸ ξυλοβάλσαμον. ἔπλευσα δὲ καὶ ἐς Λῆμνον,
ἴσασι δὲ οἱ θεοί, δι' οὐδὲν ἄλλο ἢ διὰ τὴν Λημνίαν, εἴτε γῆν ἐθέλει τις
ὀνομάζειν, εἴτε σφραγῖδα, λέλεκται δὲ περὶ αὐτῆς αὐτάρκως ἐν τῷ περὶ τῆς
10 τῶν ἁπλῶν φαρμάκων δυνάμεως ἐνάτῳ. ταύτην οὖν εἴτε Λημνίαν γῆν, εἴτε
σφραγῖδα καλεῖν ἐθέλεις, παραποιοῦσιν, ὡς μηδένα δύνασθαι διαγνῶναι
τὴν ἀληθινὴν ἀπὸ τῆς παραπεποιημένης. καθάπερ γε τὸ καλούμενον
Ἰνδικὸν Λύκιον, ἕτερά τε πολλὰ δυσκολωτάτην ἔχοντα διάγνωσιν ἀπὸ τῶν
νενοθευμένων, ἃ χρὴ παρὰ τῶν εἰς τὰ χωρία πορευομένων, ἐπιτρόπων τε
15 καὶ συγκλητικῶν ἀρξάντων τῆς χώρας ἀθροίζειν, ἢ καὶ τῶν κατοικούντων
ἐν αὐτοῖς φίλων, ὥσπερ ἐμὲ ποιοῦντα τεθέασθε. κομίζεται γάρ μοι τὰ μὲν
ἐκ τῆς μεγάλης Συρίας, τὰ δ' ἐκ τῆς Παλαιστίνης, τὰ δὲ ἐξ Αἰγύπτου, τὰ δὲ
ἐκ Καππαδοκίας, ἐκ Πόντου δ' ἄλλα, καθάπερ γε καὶ Μακεδονίας τε καὶ
τῶν πρὸς τὴν δύσιν χωρίων, ἔνθα Κελτοὶ καὶ Ἴβηρες, οἵ τε κατὰ τὴν
20 ἀντικειμένην χώραν οἰκοῦντες Μαυρούσιοι.

Because of these things I wanted to see Cyprus, and as I had a friend
of much influence in the island who was a companion of the inspector
of the mines, the imperial procurator, I brought from there much
cadmia and pyrites from copper mines and spodion and zinc oxide
and copper ore and *misy* and *sory* [ferrous sulphate?] and copper
sulphate, as I also brought genuine opobalsamum from Palaestina
Syria. For the asphalt cannot be adulterated by trickery and the same
holds true of the fruit of the opobalsamum and xylobalsamum. I also
sailed to Lemnos, and, the gods know, for no other reason than to
procure the Lemnian earth, if one prefers to call it so, or the Lemnian

seal. I have sufficiently dealt with it in the ninth book of the work *De Simplicium Medicamentorum Temperamentis ac Facultatibus*. This Lemnian earth, or if you prefer to call it seal, is faked in such a way that no one can distinguish the authentic from the spurious, like the so-called Indian lycium and many other things that are very difficult to discern from the adulterated. To obtain the authentic products one has to collect them from the procurators who go to the place, or from the senatorial governors of the land, or from friends living there, as you have seen that I did. Some are brought to me from Great Syria, some from Palaestina, some from Egypt or Cappadocia, and others from Pontus and likewise from Macedon and the places in the west, where the Celts and the Iberians live, as well as the Mauri in the country opposite to them.

391

De Antidotis, I, 4 — Kühn, XIV, p. 25

ὡς οὖν ἐν Ῥώμῃ τῶν ἀρίστων φαρμάκων ἁπάντων εὐπορῆσαι μᾶλλόν ἐστιν, ἢ κατ᾽ ἄλλο χωρίον, οὕτως ἐν αὐτῇ τῇ Ῥώμῃ Καίσαρι σκευάζων τις, ἔτι μᾶλλον εὐπορεῖ πάντων τῶν εἰς ἄκρον ἀρετῆς ἡκόντων, οἴνου μὲν τοῦ Φαλερίνου καὶ μέλιτος Ὑμμητίου, ὀποβαλσάμου τε τοῦ Συριακοῦ
5 καλουμένου. διὰ δὲ τὸν τόπον ἐν ᾧ γεννᾶται πλεῖστόν τε καὶ κάλλιστον, ἕτερον ὄνομα δεύτερον ἔχον, τὸ Ἐγγαδηνὸν γὰρ ὀνομάζεται, κρεῖττον ὂν τῶν ἐν ἄλλοις χωρίοις τῆς Παλαιστίνης γινομένων·

Just as in Rome there is more abundance of all the best medicines than in any other place, so in Rome itself he who prepares them for the emperor has even more abundance of everything of supreme excellence, like the Falernian wine, the Hymmetian honey and the opobalsamum called the Syrian. This also has another name after the place where it grows in the largest quantity and is most beautiful, for it is named the Engadine, being superior to that which grows in other places of Palaestina.

τὸ Ἐγγαδηνὸν γὰρ ὀνομάζεται: Galen is the only pagan writer to connect expressly the balsam with Engedi. The fame of the place in this respect emerges from Josephus, *Ant.*, IX, 7: γεννᾶται δ᾽ ἐν αὐτῇ φοίνιξ ὁ κάλλιστος καὶ ὀποβάλσαμον. Cf. also Eusebius, *Onomasticon* (ed. Klostermann, p. 86): Ἐγγάδδι, παρακειμένη τῇ νεκρᾷ θαλάσσῃ, ὅθεν τὸ ὀποβάλσαμον; Hieronymus, *Commentarii in Hiezechielem*, XXVII:17 (*PL*, XXV, col. 256 = *CCSL*, LXXV, p. 371): "balsamum, quod nascitur in vineis Engaddi"; S. Lieberman, *Tarbiẓ*, XL (1970/1), pp. 24 ff.

Galen

For the medical qualities of the balsam, cf. Strabo, *Geographica*, XVI, 2:41, p. 763 (No. 115); Scribonius Largus (Nos. 155, 156); Quintus Serenus, *Liber Medicinalis*, ed. F. Vollmer, *Corpus Medicorum Latinorum*, II, fasc. 3, Leipzig–Berlin 1916, ll. 11 f.: "balsama si geminis instillans auribus addas, tum poteris alacrem capitis reparare vigorem"; see also, *ibid.*, ll. 26 ff. Balsam is mentioned also in other passages by Galen, though without specific connections with Judaea or Palestine; see *De Compositione Medicamentorum*, II, 1 (ed. Kühn, XII, p. 554); *De Simplicium Medicamentorum Temperamentis ac Facultatibus*, VI, 2:2 (ed. Kühn, XI, pp. 846 f.); *De Antidotis*, I, 13 (ed. Kühn, XIV, p. 62); *De Succedaneis* (ed. Kühn, XIX, pp. 726, 738).

392

De Antidotis, I, 12 — Kühn, XIV, pp. 60 f.

Πάντες γοῦν ἔγραψαν ἶριν μὲν ἀρίστην εἶναι τὴν ἐν Ἰλλυριοῖς
γεννωμένην, πετροσέλινον δὲ τὸ Μακεδονικόν, ἄσφαλτον δὲ τὴν
Ἰουδαϊκήν, ὥσπερ γε καὶ ὀποβάλσαμον, ἐπί τε τῶν ἄλλων ὁμοίως, ὑπὲρ ὧν
ἐφεξῆς κατὰ τὸν ἴδιον ἑκάστου λόγον οὐ παραλείψω τὴν ἀπὸ τῆς χώρας
5 ἀρετήν.

All indeed wrote that the best iris is that which grows in Illyria, the best parsley is the Macedonian, the best asphalt, as well as the opobalsamum, is the Judaean. The same holds true about other products concerning which I shall not omit to state the virtue of their lands sequentially at the proper place in the description of each of them.

393

De Antidotis, II, 10 — Kühn, XIV, p. 162

ἀσφάλτου Ἰουδαϊκῆς.

Judaean asphalt.

394

In Hippocratis Epidemiarum Libros Commentarius, I, 1 — Wenkebach, *Corpus Medicorum Graecorum*, V, 10, 1, p. 16 = Kühn, XVII, 1, p. 23

Τοῖς δὲ κατὰ Παλαιστίνην ἀριθμοῦσιν οἱ δώδεκα μῆνες ἀριθμὸν ἡμερῶν
γίνονται τριακοσίων πεντήκοντα τεσσάρων. ἐπειδὴ γὰρ ὁ ἀπὸ συνόδου

1 ἀριθμὸν Wenkebach ἀριθμὸς Ο 2 τριακοσίων πεντήκοντα
τεσσάρων Wenkebach τριακόσιαι πεντήκοντα τέσσαρες Q τῦδ MV

τῆς πρὸς ἥλιον σελήνης χρόνος ἄχρι πάσης ἄλλης συνόδου πρὸς τὰς ἐννέα
καὶ εἴκοσιν ἡμέρας ἔτι καὶ ἄλλης μέρος ἥμισυ προσλαμβάνει, διὰ τοῦτο
τοὺς δύο μῆνας ἡμερῶν γινομένους ἐννέα καὶ πεντήκοντα τέμνουσιν εἰς
ἄνισα μέρη, τὸν μὲν ἕτερον αὐτῶν τριάκοντα ἡμερῶν ἐργαζόμενοι, τὸν δ᾽
ἕτερον ἐννέα καὶ εἴκοσιν. ἀναγκάζονται τοιγαροῦν οἱ οὕτως ἄγοντες τοὺς
μῆνας ἐμβόλιμόν τινα ποιεῖν, ὅταν πρῶτον ἀθροίσθῃ τὸ τῶν ἔμπροσθεν
ἐνιαυτῶν ἔλλειμμα καὶ γένηται χρόνος ἑνὸς μηνός.

3 σελήνης Wenkebach   αὐτῆς Ο   4 ἄλλης Wenkebach
ἄλλο Ο   6 ἄνισα] ἔνια MQ / τριάκοντα Cornarius   τριάκοντα ἐννέα Ο

According to the counting of those in Palaestina the twelve months
amount to the number of 354 days. For, because the interval from the
meeting of the moon with the sun until the next full meeting takes up
in addition to the twenty-nine days also half of another day, they
therefore cut the two months, which together include fifty-nine days,
into two unequal parts, making one of the months consist of thirty
days, and the other of twenty-nine. Proceeding in this manner, they
were compelled to introduce an intercalated month as soon as the
arrears of the former years are put together and become a period of
one month.

For the Jewish system of intercalation, see S. Gandz, *JQR*, XXXIX (1948/9),
pp. 263 ff.; Schürer, ed. Vermes & Millar, I, pp. 587 ff.; M.D. Herr, apud:
S. Safrai & M. Stern (eds), *The Jewish People in the First Century*, II, Assen
1976, pp. 834 ff.

CXV. ARTEMIDORUS

Second half of the second century C.E.

The variegated picture of life presented by Artemidorus in his Onirocritica *includes two passages which have a direct bearing on Jews. In one (No. 395) the synagogue (προσευχή) is mentioned at the head of a list of apparitions that bode ill for those to whom they appear in dreams. The* προσευχή *is followed by several different expressions for beggars (μεταῖται, προῖκται, πτωχοί), after which are mentioned pitiable people in general.[1] All these apparitions foretell pain and anxiety.*

The second passage (No. 396) alludes to the Jewish revolt in Cyrenaica in the time of Trajan. It shows how great was the impression that the revolt made on both contemporaries and subsequent generations.[2]

---

1 For parallels between this passage and talmudic literature, see H. Lewy, *Rhein. Museum*, NS, XLVIII (1893), pp. 398 ff.; S. Lieberman, *Hellenism in Jewish Palestine*, New York 1950, p. 74.
2 Cf. also the commemoration of the victory over the Jews in the Oxyrhynchite nome in Middle Egypt, in *P. Oxy.*, No. 705 = *CPJ*, No. 450, dated 199/200 C.E.

395

Onirocritica, III, 53 — Pack

Προσευχὴ καὶ μεταῖται καὶ πάντες ἄνθρωποι προῖκται καὶ οἰκτροὶ καὶ
πτωχοὶ λύπην καὶ φροντίδα καὶ τηκεδόνα τῆς ψυχῆς καὶ ἀνδρὶ καὶ γυναικὶ
προαγορεύουσι· τοῦτο μὲν γὰρ οὐδεὶς ἄπεισιν εἰς προσευχὴν μὴ οὐχὶ
φροντίζων, τοῦτο δὲ καὶ οἱ μεταῖται πάνυ εἰδεχθεῖς ὄντες καὶ ἄποροι καὶ
5 μηδὲν ἔχοντες ὑγιὲς ἐμποδὼν ἵστανται πάσῃ προαιρέσει.

1 περὶ προσευχῆς LV 3 γάρ om. L / εὐχὴν L
4 φροντίζων σφόδρα V

A synagogue and beggars and all people who ask for gifts, and such as
arouse pity, and mendicants, foretell grief, anxiety and heartache to
both men and women. For on the one hand, no one departs for a
synagogue without a care, and, on the other, beggars who are very
odious-looking and without resources and have nothing wholesome
about them are an obstacle to every plan.

προσευχή: There can be no doubt that by προσευχή is meant the Jewish
house of prayer; cf. also Apion, quoted by Josephus, *Contra Apionem*, II, 10
(No. 164); Iuvenalis, *Saturae*, III, 296 (No. 297). The first known use of
προσευχή in this meaning occurs in an inscription from Schedia, dating from
the reign of Ptolemy III Euergetes (246–222 B.C.E.); cf. *OGIS*, No. 726 =
Frey, *CII*, No. 1440 = Gabba, No. 1 = Lifshitz, No. 92, p. 78. See M. Hengel,
in: *Festgabe für Karl Georg Kuhn*, Göttingen 1971, pp. 157 ff.
The use of the word in the sense of a house of prayer does not seem common
outside a Jewish environment or one not influenced by Jews. Yet at least one
exception seems to exist in an inscription from Epidaurus, dating from the
fourth century B.C.E.; cf. *IG*, Vol. IV, Part 1, *ed. minor*, p. 51, No. 106, l. 27:
τᾶς ποτευχᾶς [= τῆς προσευχῆς] καὶ τοῦ βωμο[ῦ].

396

Onirocritica, IV, 24 — Pack

Καὶ γάρ εἰσί τινες ⟨scil. ὄνειροι⟩ πρὸ ⟨τῆς⟩ ἀποβάσεως ἄκριτοι, οὓς κρίνων
μὲν ἐπιτυχὴς παρά γε ἐμοὶ εἶναι δόξεις, μὴ κρίνων δὲ οὐκ ἄτεχνος. οἷον
ἔδοξέ τις στρατοπεδάρχης ἐπὶ τῇ μαχαίρᾳ αὐτοῦ γεγράφθαι ικθ. ἐγένετο
πόλεμος ὁ Ἰουδαϊκὸς ἐν Κυρήνῃ, καὶ ἠρίστευσεν ἐν τῷ πολέμῳ ὁ ἰδὼν τὸν
5 ὄνειρον, καὶ τοῦτο ἦν ὃ εἴπομεν, ἀπὸ μὲν τοῦ ι Ἰουδαίοις, ἀπὸ δὲ τοῦ κ

1–2 ὁ μὲν κρίνων L 2 μὲν ἂν ἐπιτυχὴς V / ὁ δὲ μὴ κρίνων L
4 ὅ¹ om. V 5 ἦν ὃ εἴπομεν om. L / μὲν om. V

Artemidorus

Κυρηναίοις, ἀπὸ δὲ τοῦ ϑ̄ θάνατος. ἀλλὰ πρὸ μὲν ἀποβάσεως ἦν ἄκριτος, ἀποβάντων δὲ τῶν ἀποτελεσμάτων καὶ σφόδρα εὔκριτος.

There are some dreams that cannot be solved before the events come to pass. If you solve those dreams you will be lucky in my opinion, but if you fail you will not be reckoned unskilful. Of that kind was one in which a *praefectus castrorum* saw written upon his sword: ι κ ϑ. Then there came the Jewish war in Cyrene, and the fellow who had seen the dream distinguished himself in the war, and this was what the above-mentioned dream had signified: by the ι were meant the Jews, by the κ the C(K)yrenaeans, by the ϑ Thanatos (= Death). However, before it came to pass, this dream was unresolvable, but when the event happened, it was very manifest.

στρατοπεδάρχης: This usually translates the Latin *praefectus castrorum*. From what follows it appears that this officer took an actual part in the military operations against the Jews; see also W. Ensslin, PW, XXII, p. 1289. Similarly, command of the *vexillationes* of the two Egyptian legions at the siege of Jerusalem by Titus was put into the hands of Fronto Liternius, who was στρατοπεδάρχης τῶν ἀπὸ Ἀλεξανδρείας δύο ταγμάτων; cf. *BJ*, VI, 238; see H. J. Pflaum, *Les procurateurs équestres sous le Haut-Empire romain*, Paris 1950, p. 145; J. Lesquier, *L'armée romaine d'Égypte*, Cairo 1918, p. 130. Lesquier thinks that the official title of this commander during the operations in Judaea was more likely to be "praepositus vexillationibus legionum XXII Deioterianae et III Cyrenaicae", though formerly he held the position of *praefectus castrorum*. See also G. Lopuszański, *Mélanges d'archéologie et d'histoire*, LV (1938), pp. 151 ff. An inscription found in Pamphylian Attaleia refers to the task imposed on the *praefectus castrorum* of the Fifteenth Legion (the Apollinaris) by Trajan, and is connected with the resettlement of Cyrene; see *SEG*, XVII, No. 584.

πόλεμος ὁ Ἰουδαϊκὸς ἐν Κυρήνῃ: For the Jewish revolt in Cyrene, cf. Cassius Dio, LXVIII (No. 437), and the commentary *ad loc*. See S. Applebaum, *Zion*, XIX (1954), p. 38. For the use of πόλεμος for this revolt, cf. *SEG*, IX, No. 189: ἐκ πολέμοιο χαμαιριφῆ. The official description was "tumultus Iudaicus"; see *SEG*, IX, No. 252; cf. *SEG*, XVII, No. 804.

CXVI. DIOGENES LAERTIUS

Third century C.E.?

In the prologue to his Lives of the Philosophers *Diogenes Laertius*[1] *refers to views that philosophy had originated among the barbarians. The Jews and their sages are not ranked among the Persian Magi, the Chaldaeans, the Indian gymnosophists, and the Celtic Druids but appear only in connection with the view of Clearchus that the gymnosophists were descended from the Magi. Diogenes states that it was the opinion of certain people that the Jews likewise originated from the Magi.*

The second passage with a Jewish connection is from the "Life of Socrates". Justus of Tiberias, the Jewish historian, serves as the authority for an apocryphal statement concerning the intervention of Plato at the trial of his master. This is the only reference to Justus by a pagan writer. Diogenes does not mention that Justus was Jewish.

397

Vitae Philosophorum, I, 9 — Long = F98R = Bidez & Cumont, II, F D2, p. 68

Κλέαρχος δὲ ὁ Σολεὺς ἐν τῷ Περὶ παιδείας καὶ τοὺς γυμνοσοφιστὰς ἀπογόνους εἶναι τῶν Μάγων φησίν· ἔνιοι δὲ καὶ τοὺς Ἰουδαίους ἐκ τούτων εἶναι.

3 εἶναι+ἐπεὶ ἀβραὰμ ὁ τούτων πρόγονος χαλδαῖος ἦν. φ

Clearchus of Soli in his tract "On Education" further makes the Gymnosophists to be descended from the Magi; and some trace the Jews also to the same origin. (trans. R.D. Hicks, *LCL*)

1 The date of Diogenes Laertius is rather dubious. See A. Delatte, *La vie de Pythagore de Diogène Laërce*, Brussels 1922, pp. 6 f.; R. Hope, *The Book of Diogenes Laertius, Its Spirit and Its Method*, New York 1930, pp. 4 ff. For the suggestion to date Diogenes Laertius at the beginning of the second century C.E., see F. Kudlien, *Rhein. Museum*, CVI (1963), p. 254. This would make Diogenes a younger contemporary of Justus of Tiberias, who is quoted in the work. The solution depends largely on the dating of Sextus Empiricus, who also is mentioned by Diogenes Laertius (*Vitae Philosophorum*, IX, 87).

332

ἔνιοι δὲ καὶ τοὺς Ἰουδαίους ἐκ τούτων εἶναι: The early Hellenistic writers had pointed to the similarity between the Jews and the Indian sages; cf. Clearchus, apud: Josephus, *Contra Apionem*, I, 179 (No. 15); Megasthenes, apud: Clemens, *Stromata*, I, 15:72:5 (No. 14). Since the origin of the Indian gymnosophists had been traced to the Magi (see also F. Wehrli, *Die Schule des Aristoteles — Klearchos*², Basel–Stuttgart 1969, p. 50), it could be inferred that the Jews, who were akin to them, were likewise descended from the Magi. Various features of the religion and cult may also have suggested to some observers an affinity with Judaism; see T. Labhardt, *Quae de Iudaeorum Origine Iudicaverint Veteres*, Augsburg 1881, pp. 22 f. It is unlikely that the notion connecting the Jews and the Magi originated with Diogenes Laertius. On the use of his sources in the prologue of Diogenes Laertius, see W. Spoerri, *Späthellenistische Berichte über Welt, Kultur und Götter*, Basel 1959, pp. 53 ff. For the opinion that the view of the ἔνιοι should be attributed to Clearchus himself (cf. No. 15), see L. Robert, *CRAI*, 1968, p. 451.

398

Vitae Philosophorum, II, 41 — Long = *F. Gr. Hist.*, III, C734, F1

Κρινομένου δ᾽ αὐτοῦ φησιν Ἰοῦστος ὁ Τιβεριεὺς ἐν τῷ Στέμματι Πλάτωνα ἀναβῆναι ἐπὶ τὸ βῆμα καὶ εἰπεῖν, «νεώτατος ὤν, ὦ ἄνδρες Ἀθηναῖοι, τῶν ἐπὶ τὸ βῆμα ἀναβάντων»· τοὺς δὲ δικαστὰς ἐκβοῆσαι, «Κατάβα, κατάβα» — τουτέστι κατάβηθι.

3 Κατάβα, κατάβα Cobet post Menagium   καταβάντων codd.
4 τουτέστι κατάβηθι Scholium (fortasse ipsius Diogenis)   del. Cobet

Justus of Tiberias in his book entitled "The Wreath" says that in the course of the trial Plato mounted the platform and began: "Though I am the youngest, men of Athens, of all who ever rose to address you" — whereupon the judges shouted out: "Get down! Get down!"

(trans. R. D. Hicks, *LCL*)

Ἰοῦστος ὁ Τιβεριεὺς ἐν τῷ Στέμματι: Known as an opponent of the Jewish historian Josephus, Justus played an important role in the life of Tiberias during the Jewish war against Rome and also served as secretary to King Agrippa II. Some decades after the war he wrote a book on the Jewish revolt. Josephus was provoked by it to write his *Vita*, which is our main source of information about Justus.

Photius mentions a chronicle of Justus of the Jewish kings in *Bibliotheca*, 33, p. 6b (ed. Bekker = ed. Henry, I, p. 18) = *F. Gr. Hist.*, III, C734, T2: Ἰούστου Τιβεριέως Ἰουδαίων βασιλέων τῶν ἐν τοῖς στέμμασιν, which is said to have comprised the period from Moses to Agrippa II. A work of this kind was in the tradition of Jewish-Hellenistic literature, as exemplified by writers like Eupolemus and Demetrius.

A comparison between the expressions ἐν τῷ Στέμματι used by Diogenes Laertius and ἐν τοῖς στέμμασιν of Photius suggests that the same work is meant. On the other hand, it is hard to imagine any connection between the apocryphal Platonic episode related here and the history of Jewish kings. The best solution is to suppose that this history constituted only part of a comprehensive work by Justus, called Στέμματα, whatever its character, which included a section on Jewish kings; see Schürer, I, p. 62; F. Rühl, *Rhein. Museum*, LXXI (1916), pp. 294 f.; H. Luther, "Josephus und Justus von Tiberias", Ph. D. Thesis, Halle 1910, pp. 50 ff.; Otto, p. 16.

For a suggestion that the work referred to by Diogenes Laertius is to be identified with the *Commentarioli de Scripturis*, mentioned by Hieronymus, *De Viris Inlustribus*, 14 (ed. C. A. Bernoulli, Freiburg im Breisgau–Leipzig 1895, p. 16), see Luther, *op. cit.*, p. 54. However this identification has not much to commend it. On the other hand, the theory of Jacoby that the supposed work of Justus on the Jewish revolt was only the main part of a more comprehensive work is not very convincing either; see Jacoby, PW, X, pp. 1344 f.; A. M. Denis, *Introduction aux pseudépigraphes grecs d'Ancien Testament*, Leiden 1970, p. 267. Cf. also Momigliano, *CAH*, X, 1934, p. 886. Josephus, the literary rival of Justus, declares that the latter was acquainted with Greek culture (*Vita*, 40): καὶ γὰρ οὐδ᾽ ἄπειρος ἦν παιδείας τῆς παρ᾽ Ἕλλησιν; thus it is not surprising that he thought himself competent to deal with purely Greek subjects.

It has been maintained recently with much force that there is no real proof that Justus strayed beyond the boundaries of Jewish history, that the anecdote about Plato could well fit into a preamble or aside written in rhetorical style, and that the king-lists in general constituted a digression in the history of the Jewish war composed by Justus; see T. Rajak, *CQ*, NS, XXIII (1973), pp. 345 ff., especially pp. 362 ff. However it is more natural to assume that Diogenes Laertius used not a work by Justus bearing on an exclusively Jewish subject, i.e. the Jewish king-lists, excerpted from a history of the Jewish war, but one having more general purport.

Justus seems thus to have been one of the first Jewish writers to deal with non-Jewish subjects. One predecessor was the literary critic and historian, Caecilius of Caleacte in Sicily; see above, Vol. I, p. 566. For Justus, see now also B. Wacholder, *Eupolemus — a Study of Judaeo-Greek Literature*, Cincinnati 1974, pp. 298 ff.

CXVII. OPPIAN

c. 200 C.E.

The mention of the Palestinian myrrh in Oppian's Cynegetica *probably has some connection with the fame of the Judaean balsam; cf. also Statius,* Silvae, *V, 1:213 (No. 236): "Palaestini simul Hebraeique liquores".*[1]

399

Cynegetica, I, 338–341 — Mair

Ὡς δέ τις ἠϊθέων ὑπὸ νυμφοκόμοισι γυναιξὶν
εἵμασιν ἀργεννοῖσι καὶ ἄνθεσι πορφυρέοισι
στεψάμενος, πνείων τε Παλαιστίνοιο μύροιο,
ἐς θάλαμον βαίνησιν ὑμῆν ὑμέναιον ἀείδων.

Even as some youth, arrayed by the bridal women in white robes and purple flowers and breathing of the perfume of Palestine, steps into the bridal chamber singing the marriage song. (trans. A. W. Mair, *LCL*)

---

1 For a different explanation, see A. W. Mair in the Loeb edition of Oppian's *Cynegetica*, London 1928, p. 36, n. b.

CXVIII. ALEXANDER OF APHRODISIAS

Early third century C.E.

In his commentary on Aristotle's Meteorologica *Alexander repeats the information concerning the Dead Sea already given by Aristotle himself with some insignificant verbal changes.*[1]

400

In Aristotelis Meteorologicorum Libros Commentaria, II, p. 359a, apud: Commentaria in Aristotelem Graeca, III, 2, p. 88 — Hayduck

Μαρτυρίαν δὲ τοῦ κατὰ μῖξίν τινος γεώδους τόν τε χυμὸν ἁλμυρὸν γίνεσθαι καὶ παχύτερον ἅμα καὶ σωματωδέστερον τὸ ὕδωρ καὶ ἀπὸ ἱστοριῶν τινων παρατίθεται τήν τε ἐν Παλαιστίνοις λεγομένην λίμνην, ἣν ἅμα μὲν ἁλμυρὰν οὕτως εἶναι, ὡς μηδ' ἰχθύν τινα ἐν αὐτῇ γίνεσθαι, ἅμα δὲ
5 παχεῖαν οὕτως, ὡς μηδὲ εἰ συνδεθέν τι ζῷον τῶν βαρυτάτων εἰς αὐτὴν ἐμβληθῇ, καταφέρεσθαι αὐτὸ καὶ καταδύεσθαι, ἀλλὰ ἐπιπλεῖν· τὸ δ' αὐτὸ τοῦτο ὕδωρ ῥύπτειν τὰ ἱμάτια, ἂν διασείσῃ τις ἐν αὐτῷ αὐτὰ βρέξας.

| 3 παλαιστίνη AW | παλαιστίνειν a | 4 ὡς μὴ A |
| 5 συντεθὲν A / | τὸ βαρύτατον I | 6 ἐμβληθείη A Wa |

As evidence that the flavour becomes salty and water becomes thicker and more solid by the admixture of some earthy substance he [scil. Aristotle] adduces some stories and especially the lake said to be situated among the Palestinians. This lake is both salty to such a degree that no fish live in it, and so thick that not even a most heavy creature when bound and thrown into it is carried down and sinks, but floats over the water. The same water cleans clothes if one soaks them in it and shakes them.

---

1 On Alexander of Aphrodisias, see now G. Movia, *Alessandro di Afrodisia*, Padua 1970.

CXIX. ARISTOTELIAN *PROBLEMATA*

Second century C.E.?

Among the Pseudo-Aristotelian Problems there is one, first edited by Bussemaker in the Didot edition, which concerns the Dead Sea. It seems that the author of the following problem should be dated later than Alexander of Aphrodisias.[1]

401

Problemata Inedita, III, 49 — Bussemaker (Didot, IV), Paris, pp. 331 f.

Πόθεν δῆλον ὅτι ὅσον παχύτατόν ἐστι τὸ ὕδωρ, τοσοῦτόν ἐστι καὶ ἁλμυρώτατον; φασὶν ὡς ἡ ἐν Παλαιστίνῃ νεκρὰ θάλασσα παχυτάτη οὖσα, ἁλμυρωτάτη πάντων ἐστὶν ὑδάτων. καὶ πόθεν δῆλον ὅτι παχυτάτη ἐστίν; εἰ γάρ τις ἄνθρωπον, ἢ ζῷον ἕτερον, καταδήσας ἐμβάλῃ εἰς τὸ τῆς νεκρᾶς
5 θαλάσσης ὕδωρ, ἀνωθεῖται ὑπὸ τοῦ ὕδατος, καὶ οὐ γίνεται ὑποβρύχιον διὰ τὸ εἶναι παχὺ πάνυ καὶ βαστάζειν τὸ ἐμπεσόν. καὶ πόθεν δῆλον ὅτι ἁλμυρώτατόν ἐστιν; ἐπειδὴ ῥυπτικόν ἐστι παντὸς ῥύπου· σμήχει γὰρ τὸν ῥύπον, εἴπερ ἄλλο τι σμῆγμα, τὸ δὲ ῥύπτειν ἄκρας ἐστὶν ἁλμυρότητος· ἰδοὺ γάρ· ἅλες μὲν καὶ αὐτοὶ ῥύπτουσι, νίτρον δὲ πλέον, ὥσπερ
10 ἐπιτεταμένην ἔχον τὴν ἁλμυρότητα ἥπερ οἱ ἅλες.

Whence is it clear that the thicker the water, the more salty it is? It is said that the Dead Sea in Palestine, being the thickest, is the most salty of all waters. And whence is it clear that it is the thickest? If you bind a man or other living creature and throw it into the water of the

---

1 See Bussemaker, in: *Aristotelis Opera Omnia* (ed. Didot), IV, p. IX. For the *Problemata* attributed to Aristotle, but composed, it seems, by the later followers of the Peripatetic tradition, see C. Prantl, *Abhandlungen der philosoph.–philologischen Classe der königlich bayerischen Akademie der Wissenschaften*, VI (1852), pp. 339 ff.; E. S. Forster, *CQ*, XXII (1928), pp. 163 ff.; E. Richter, "De Aristotelis Problematis", Ph. D. Thesis, Bonn 1885.

Dead Sea they are pushed up by the water and do not sink because the water is very thick and lifts up that which is thrown into it. And whence is it clear that it is the most salty? Because it clears every dirt, for it wipes off the dirt like any other soap, and cleaning is a feature of extreme salinity. For let us see, salt itself cleans indeed, but sodium carbonate does it more so, since it has a more intense salinity than salt.

CXX. PHILOSTRATUS

Second half of the second century to forties of the third century C.E.

The sophist and versatile writer Philostratus refers to Jews in his Life of Apollonius of Tyana. *This work drew its inspiration from Julia Domna, the wife of Septimius Severus, and her circle* (Vita Apollonii, *I, 3), though it may have been published after the death of the empress in 217 C.E.[1] It reflects the admiration in which the sage Apollonius was held by the Severi, as attested by Cassius Dio, LXXVII, 18:4, and* Vita Alexandri Severi, *29:2 (No. 522).*

Philostratus shows no doubt about his attachment to Hellenic culture. His attitude to the various representatives of oriental wisdom, apart from the Indian sages, was by no means consistently enthusiastic, as shown by his depiction of the naked Egyptian sages and the attack he records by Apollonius of Tyana on the animal gods of Egypt.[2]

About the Jews, Philostratus records that they had long been in revolt, not only against the Romans, but against humanity, and that they "are separated from ourselves by a greater gulf than divides us from Susa or Bactra or the more distant Indies" (No. 403). However this view is put by Philostratus into the mouth of Euphrates, the opponent of Apollonius and one of the less attractive characters of the Life.[3]

The episode narrated by Philostratus concerning Apollonius' refusal to visit Judaea (No. 402) implies only the general Pythagorean abhorrence of shedding blood, while the assertion of Titus that he merely lent his arms to execute the wrath of God (No. 404a) reflects the Flavian propaganda also manifest in the account of Josephus.

---

1 See F. Solmsen, PW, XX, p. 139. On Philostratus, see also G. W. Bowersock, *Greek Sophists in the Roman Empire*, Oxford 1969, pp. 1 ff.

2 See Ed. Meyer, *Hermes*, LII (1917), p. 393 = *Kleine Schriften*, II, Halle 1924, p. 157.

3 Euphrates came from Tyre according to Philostratus, *Vitae Sophistarum*, I, pp. 488, 536; he is connected with the Syrian Epiphaneia by Stephanus Byzantius, s.v. Ἐπιφάνεια. He is referred to as an Egyptian by Eunapius, *Vitae Philosophorum et Sophistarum*, p. 454.

402

Vita Apollonii, V, 27 — Kayser

Οὐεσπασιανοῦ δὲ τὴν αὐτοκράτορα ἀρχὴν περινοοῦντος περὶ τὰ ὅμορα τῇ Αἰγύπτῳ ἔθνη, καὶ προχωροῦντος ἐπὶ τὴν Αἴγυπτον, Δίωνες μὲν καὶ Εὐφρᾶται, περὶ ὧν μικρὸν ὕστερον εἰρήσεται, χαίρειν παρεκελεύοντο ... ἐντεῦθεν ἀνέφυ λόγος, ὡς ἐνθύμιος μὲν αὐτῷ ⟨scil. Οὐεσπασιανῷ⟩ ἡ ἀρχὴ
5 γένοιτο πολιορκοῦντι τὰ Σόλυμα, μεταπέμποιτο δὲ τὸν Ἀπολλώνιον ὑπὲρ βουλῆς τούτων, ὁ δὲ παραιτοῖτο ἥκειν ἐς γῆν, ἣν ἐμίαναν οἱ ἐν αὐτῇ οἰκοῦντες οἷς τε ἔδρασαν οἷς τε ἔπαθον.

Vespasian was harbouring thoughts of seizing the absolute power, and was at this time in the countries bordering upon Egypt; and when he advanced as far as Egypt, people like Dion and Euphrates, of whom I shall have something to say lower down, urged that a welcome should be given to him ... This is how the story grew up, that it was during his conduct of the siege of Jerusalem that the idea of making himself emperor suggested itself to him [scil. Vespasian], and that he sent for Apollonius to ask his advice on the point; but that the latter declined to enter a country which its inhabitants polluted both by what they did and by what they suffered.

(trans. F.C. Conybeare, *LCL*)

For the visit of Vespasian to Egypt, cf. Josephus, *BJ*, IV, 656; *Vita*, 415; Tacitus, *Historiae*, III, 48. See also *CPJ*, No. 418a, and the discussion of Fuks in the commentary to the *Corpus*; A. Henrichs, *Zeitschrift für Papyrologie und Epigraphik*, III (1968), pp. 51 ff.; F. Grosso, *Acme*, VII (1954), pp. 391 ff.
πολιορκοῦντι τὰ Σόλυμα: Philostratus consistently uses the designation "Solyma" for Hierosolyma. The name Solyma is common in Latin poetry; cf. Valerius Flaccus, *Argonautica*, I, 13 (No. 226); Statius, *Silvae*, V, 2:138 (No. 237); Martialis, XI, 94:5 (No. 245); Iuvenalis, VI, 544 (No. 299). It is occasionally encountered in Greek prose from Manetho onwards; cf. apud: Josephus, *Contra Apionem*, I, 248 (No. 21); see also Pausanias, VIII, 16:5 (No. 358).

403

Vita Apollonii, V, 33–34 — Kayser = F96R

(33) Τὸ μὲν δὴ τῆς δυστυχίας ἐάσθω, τὸ δὲ τῆς δειλίας πῶς παραιτήσῃ, καὶ ταῦτα Νέρωνα δοκῶν δεῖσαι τὸν δειλότατόν τε καὶ ῥᾳθυμότατον; ἃ γὰρ ἐνεθυμήθη Βίνδιξ ἐπ' αὐτόν, σέ, νὴ τὸν Ἡρακλέα, ἐκάλει πρῶτον. καὶ γὰρ στρατιὰν εἶχες, καὶ ἡ δύναμις, ἣν ἐπὶ τοὺς Ἰουδαίους ἦγες, ἐπιτηδειοτέρα

5 ἦν τιμωρεῖσθαι Νέρωνα· ἐκεῖνοι μὲν γὰρ πάλαι ἀφεστᾶσιν οὐ μόνον
Ῥωμαίων, ἀλλὰ καὶ πάντων ἀνθρώπων· οἱ γὰρ βίον ἄμικτον εὑρόντες καὶ
οἷς μήτε κοινὴ πρὸς ἀνθρώπους τράπεζα μήτε σπονδαὶ μήτε εὐχαὶ μήτε
θυσίαι, πλέον ἀφεστᾶσιν ἡμῶν ἢ Σοῦσα καὶ Βάκτρα καὶ οἱ ὑπὲρ ταῦτα
Ἰνδοί· οὔκουν οὐδ᾽ εἰκὸς ἦν τιμωρεῖσθαι τούτους ἀφισταμένους, οὓς
10 βέλτιον ἦν μηδὲ κτᾶσθαι. Νέρωνα δὲ τίς οὐκ ἂν ηὔξατο τῇ ἑαυτοῦ χειρὶ
ἀποκτεῖναι, μονονοὺ πίνοντα τὸ τῶν ἀνθρώπων αἷμα καὶ ἐν μέσοις τοῖς
φόνοις ᾄδοντα; καίτοι ἐμοῦ τὰ ὦτα ὀρθὰ ἦν πρὸς τοὺς ὑπὲρ σοῦ λόγους, καὶ
ὁπότε τις ἐκεῖθεν ἀφίκοιτο τρισμυρίους Ἰουδαίων ἀπολωλέναι φάσκων
ὑπὸ σοῦ καὶ πεντακισμυρίους κατὰ τὴν ἐφεξῆς μάχην, ἀπολαμβάνων τὸν
15 ἥκοντα ξυμμέτρως ἠρώτων, τί δ᾽ ὁ ἀνήρ; μὴ μεῖζόν τι τούτων ... (34)
Τοσαῦτα τοῦ Εὐφράτου εἰπόντος ὁρῶν ὁ Ἀπολλώνιος τὸν Δίωνα
προστιθέμενον τῇ γνώμῃ, τουτὶ γὰρ καὶ τῷ νεύματι ἐπεδήλου καὶ οἷς
ἐπῄνει λέγοντα, «μή τι,» ἔφη, «Δίων, τοῖς εἰρημένοις προστίθης;» «νὴ
Δί᾽,» εἶπε, «πῇ μὲν ὅμοια, πῇ δὲ ἀνόμοια· τὸ μὲν γὰρ ὡς πολλῷ βελτίων ἂν
20 ἦν Νέρωνα καταλύων μᾶλλον ἢ τὰ τῶν Ἰουδαίων διορθούμενος, ἡγοῦμαι
κἀμοὶ πρός σε εἰρῆσθαι.»

10 οὐκ ἂν εὔξαιτο S

(33) As for the count of ill luck, I may dismiss it; but as for that of
cowardice, how can you avoid it? How escape the reproach of having
been afraid of Nero, the most cowardly and supine of rulers? Look at
the revolt against him planned by Vindex, you surely were the man of
the hour, its natural leader, and not he! For you had an army at your
back, and the forces you were leading against the Jews, would they
not have been more suitably employed in chastising Nero? For the
Jews have long been in revolt not only against the Romans but against
humanity; and a race that has made its own a life apart and
irreconcilable, that cannot share with the rest of mankind in the
pleasures of the table nor join in their libations or prayers or
sacrifices, are separated from ourselves by a greater gulf than divides
us from Susa or Bactra or the more distant Indies. What sense then or
reason was there in chastising them for revolting from us, whom we
had better have never annexed? As for Nero, who would not have
prayed with his own hand to slay a man well-nigh drunk with human
blood, singing as he sat amidst the hecatombs of his victims? I confess
that I ever pricked up my ears when any messenger from yonder
brought tidings of yourself, and told us how in one battle you had
slain thirty thousand Jews and in the next fifty thousand. In such cases
I would take the courier aside, and quietly ask him: "But what of the

great man? Will he not rise to higher things than this? ..." (34) Throughout Euphrates' long speech, Apollonius noticed that Dion shared his sentiments, for he manifested his approval both by gestures and the applause with which he hailed his words; so he asked him if he could not add some remarks of his own to what he had just heard. "By Heaven, I can," answered Dion, "and I should agree in part and in part disagree with his remarks; for I think I have myself told you that you would have been much better employed deposing Nero than setting Jewry to rights."

(trans. F. C. Conybeare, *LCL*)

33 ἃ γὰρ ἐνεθυμήθη Βίνδιξ: This accusation comes from the speech delivered before Vespasian by the opponent of Apollonius, the Stoic Euphrates; on him, see Grosso, *op. cit.* (supra, p. 340), pp. 418 ff.; P. Grimal, *Latomus*, XIV (1955), pp. 370 ff.; M. Pohlenz, *Die Stoa*, I², Göttingen 1959, p. 287; *ibid.*, II², 1955, p. 146. The remarks about Jewish exclusiveness express well-known views of the educated Graeco-Roman classes of that period, as attested by the great writers of the generation following Euphrates, such as Iuvenalis, XIV, 96–106 (No. 301); Tacitus, *Historiae*, V, 5 (No. 281); these sentiments can be traced from the writings of Hecataeus of Abdera onwards. For a discussion of the present passage, see also Weber, p. 112, n. 1.

οὓς βέλτιον ἦν μηδὲ κτᾶσθαι: For an expression of the same sentiment, cf. Rutilius Namatianus, *De Reditu Suo*, I, 395 f. (No. 542): "Atque utinam numquam Iudaea subacta fuisset Pompeii bellis imperioque Titi!"

404a

Vita Apollonii, VI, 29 — Kayser = F97R

Ἐπεὶ δὲ Τίτος ἡρήκει τὰ Σόλυμα καὶ νεκρῶν πλέα ἦν πάντα, τὰ ὅμορά τε ἔθνη ἐστεφάνουν αὐτόν, ὁ δὲ οὐκ ἠξίου ἑαυτὸν τούτου, μὴ γὰρ αὐτὸς ταῦτα εἰργάσθαι, θεῷ δὲ ὀργὴν φήναντι ἐπιδεδωκέναι τὰς ἑαυτοῦ χεῖρας, ἐπῄνει ὁ Ἀπολλώνιος ταῦτα, γνώμῃ τε γὰρ περὶ τὸν ἄνδρα
5 ἐφαίνετο καὶ ξύνεσις ἀνθρωπείων τε καὶ θείων, καὶ σωφροσύνης μεστὸν τὸ μὴ στεφανοῦσθαι ἐφ᾿ αἵματι. ξυντάττει δὴ πρὸς αὐτὸν ἐπιστολήν, ἧς διάκονον ποιεῖται τὸν Δάμιν, καὶ ἐπιστέλλει ὧδε·
«Ἀπολλώνιος Τίτῳ στρατηγῷ Ῥωμαίων χαίρειν.
Μὴ βουληθέντι σοι ἐπ᾿ αἰχμῇ κηρύττεσθαι, μηδ᾿ ἐπὶ δηίῳ αἵματι,
10 δίδωμι ἐγὼ τὸν σωφροσύνης στέφανον, ἐπειδὴ ἐφ᾿ οἷς δεῖ στεφανοῦσθαι, γιγνώσκεις. ἔρρωσο.
Ὑπερησθεὶς δὲ ὁ Τίτος τῇ ἐπιστολῇ, «καὶ ὑπὲρ ἐμαυτοῦ,» ἔφη, «χάριν οἶδά σοι καὶ ὑπὲρ τοῦ πατρός, καὶ μεμνήσομαι τούτων, ἐγὼ μὲν γὰρ Σόλυμα ἥρηκα, σὺ δὲ ἐμέ.»

342

After Titus had taken Jerusalem, and when the country all round was filled with corpses, the neighbouring races offered him a crown; but he disclaimed any such honour to himself, saying that it was not himself that had accomplished this exploit, but that he had merely lent his arms to God, who had so manifested his wrath; and Apollonius praised his action, for therein he displayed a great deal of judgement and understanding of things human and divine, and it showed great moderation on his part that he refused to be crowned because he had shed blood. Accordingly Apollonius indited to him a letter which he sent by the hand of Damis and of which the text was as follows:

"Apollonius sends greetings to Titus the Roman General.

Whereas you have refused to be proclaimed for success in war and for shedding the blood of your enemies, I myself assign to you the crown of temperance and moderation because you thoroughly understand what deeds really merit a crown. Farewell."

Now Titus was overjoyed with this epistle, and replied: "In my own behalf I thank you, no less than in behalf of my father, and I will not forget your kindness; for although I have captured Jerusalem, you have captured me." (trans. F. C. Conybeare, *LCL*)

τὰ ὅμορά τε ἔθνη ἐστεφάνουν αὐτόν: Cf. *BJ*, VII, 105: ἔνθα δὴ καὶ παρὰ τοῦ Πάρθων βασιλέως Βολογέσου πρὸς αὐτὸν ἧκον στέφανον χρυσοῦν ἐπὶ τῇ κατὰ τῶν Ἰουδαίων νίκῃ κομίζοντες.

θεῷ δὲ ὀργὴν φήναντι ἐπιδεδωκέναι τὰς ἑαυτοῦ χεῖρας: This conforms to the interpretation put on the events by Josephus; cf. *BJ*, V, 378: ἵνα γνῶτε μὴ μόνον Ῥωμαίοις πολεμοῦντες ἀλλὰ καὶ τῷ Θεῷ; *ibid.*, VI, 252 (one of the Roman soldiers, without receiving any order but moved by some supernatural impulse, started the conflagration of the Temple; see Bernays, II, p. 163).

404b

Vita Apollonii, VI, 34 — Kayser

Παρελθὼν δὲ ὁ Ἀπολλώνιος, «εἰ δὲ ἐνίους,» ἔφη, «τούτων ἐλέγξαιμι σοὶ μὲν καὶ πατρὶ τῷ σῷ πολεμίους, πεπρεσβευμένους δὲ ὑπὲρ νεωτέρων ἐς τὰ Σόλυμα, ξυμμάχους δ᾽ ἀφανεῖς τῶν σοι φανερωτάτων ἐχθρῶν, τί πείσονται,» «τί δὲ ἄλλο γε,» εἶπεν· «ἢ ἀπολοῦνται;»

Apollonius stepped forward and said: "Supposing I convicted some who are standing here of being your own and your father's enemies,

343

and of having sent legates to Jerusalem to excite a rebellion, and of being the secret allies of your most open enemies, what would happen to them?" "Why, what else," said the Emperor, "than instant death?" (trans. F. C. Conybeare, *LCL*)

εἰ δὲ ἐνίους ...: This passage occurs in Philostratus' account of the sojourn of Apollonius at Tarsus, where Titus was persuaded by Apollonius' arguments to confer favours on the people of that city; see Grosso, *op. cit.* (supra, p. 340), pp. 431 ff.

CXXI. ASINIUS QUADRATUS

First third of the third century C.E.

Asinius Quadratus is known to have written two historical works. The first was a history of the thousand years of the Roman state (χιλιετηρίς), from the foundation of Rome to the reign of Alexander Severus,[1] written in the Ionian dialect. The second was a Parthica, a work presumably similar to that of Asinius' predecessor Arrian.[2] Asinius seems to have acted as proconsul of Achaia, for whose official activities there is inscriptional evidence.[3] Stephanus Byzantius preserved some fragments of the Parthica, of which three belong to the ninth book. These are an allusion to Συρβανή, some island in the Euphrates; an explanation of the name Tigranocerta; and a reference to a city named Solyma. Solyma is said by Asinius to have been a city of Assyrians, so that he apparently located it in Assyria. He also states that it was founded after the capture of the Jerusalem Temple. Solyma, a quite common name for Jerusalem (Hierosolyma), occurs also in the work by Asinius' contemporary, Philostratus, Vita Apollonii, VI, 29 (No. 404a). There is no information about a city Solyma in Assyria. Asinius implies here that Jewish refugees from Jerusalem founded the city, a connection that certainly goes back to a Jewish tradition. The name "Assyrians" may be used here loosely and the township could have been in Babylonia. The Jewish tradition probably linked the foundation of that city with the destruction of the First Temple and the Babylonian exile. Asinius was undoubtedly referring to the foundation of the Assyrian Solyma retrospectively, within the narrative of one of the wars between Rome and Parthia. Possibly it was the war in the reign of Marcus Aurelius and Verus in the sixties of the second century C.E. In this war the

---

1 For an opinion that the χιλιετηρίς concluded with the millennial celebrations of 248 C.E., see Schwartz, PW, II, p. 1603; but that is not necessarily so.

2 Asinius is coupled with Arrian by Evagrius, *Historia Ecclesiastica*, V, 24.

3 See *Sylloge*, No. 887; E. Groag, *Die römischen Reichsbeamten von Achaia bis auf Diokletian*, Vienna–Leipzig 1939, pp. 90 f.; G. Barbieri, *L'albo senatorio da Settimio Severo a Carino*, Rome 1952, pp. 21 f.

Roman commander Avidius Cassius advanced towards the main centres of the Parthian empire and captured Seleucia and Ctesiphon.[4]

The use of the Jewish tradition by Asinius is paralleled by his reference to the Parthian language in the explanation proposed by him for the name of Tigranocerta: Τιγρανόκερτα· τὸ δ᾽ ἐστὶ τῇ Παρθυαίων φωνῇ Τιγρανούπολις.

405

Parthica, apud: Stephanus Byzantius, s.v. Σόλυμα — Meineke = *F. Gr. Hist.*, II, A97, F16 = H. Peter, *Historicorum Romanorum Reliquiae*, II, Leipzig 1906, p. 145, F22

Σόλυμα· πόλις ᾿Ασσυρίων, μετὰ τὴν ἅλωσιν τοῦ ναοῦ τοῦ ἐν ῾Ιεροσολύμοις κτισθεῖσα, ὡς Κουάδρατος ἐνάτῳ Παρθικῶν. τὸ ἐθνικὸν Σολυμηνός.

Solyma. A city of Assyrians. It was founded after the capture of the Jerusalem Temple, as Quadratus states in the ninth book of his *Parthica*. The ethnicon is Solymenos.

4 See N. C. Debevoise, *A Political History of Parthia*, Chicago 1938, pp. 247 ff.; F. Carrata Thomes, *Il regno di Marco Aurelio*, Turin 1953, pp. 76 ff.

CXXII. CASSIUS DIO

c. 160 C.E.–230 C.E.

The references made by Cassius Dio to Jews and Judaism in his Roman History are of no slight interest. His views reflect the social and cultural milieu of the Greek cities of Asia Minor at the end of the second century C.E., places with old-established contacts between Greeks and Jews. Dio also attained high positions in the Roman administration from the time of Septimius Severus to that of Alexander Severus, including the important military governorship of Pannonia Superior.[1] Some passages in his account constitute the most important literary source for crucial events of Jewish history in the Roman period, namely, the Jewish revolts under Trajan and Hadrian (Nos. 438, 440). They are also of value for supplementing the accounts of Josephus and the other sources for the history of the Jewish war against Rome (No. 430).

Whatever may have been his sources and the extent of his dependence on them in regard to the facts, Dio frequently colours his history by his own views and experience, especially when the subject is of interest to him, and, while relating the past, he does not lose sight of contemporary situations and implications.

The capture of Jerusalem by Pompey in 63 B.C.E. afforded Dio a suitable occasion for a description of the main features of the Jewish religion (No. 406). He states that the Jews are distinguished from the rest of mankind in practically every detail of life. Significantly, however, in contrast to earlier writers, he makes no attempt to explain Jewish separatism by misanthropy. Dio was acquainted with the monotheistic principle of the Jewish religion, and knew that the Jews had never set up a statue of their God, who is ineffable. This is also emphasized by Dio's presumed source for the history of the late Roman republic, i.e. the History of Livy[2] (No. 133). Two expressions of Jewish worship are especially mentioned by Dio, the large and beautiful

---

1 For the personality and social connections of Cassius Dio, see F. Millar, *A Study of Cassius Dio*, Oxford 1964, pp. 5 ff., 174 ff.; R. Syme, *Emperors and Biography*, Oxford 1971, pp. 143 ff.

2 See Schwartz, PW, III, pp. 1697 f. = *Griechische Geschichtschreiber*, Leipzig 1959, p. 414; A. Rosenberg, *Einleitung und Quellenkunde zur römischen Geschichte*, Berlin 1921, pp. 260 f.

Temple, and the dedication of the Day of Saturn to the Deity. Dio notes that the Jews keep many peculiar observances and engage in no serious occupations on that day. However, he neither considers the Sabbath a fast day nor confuses it with the Day of Atonement, unlike many of his pagan predecessors.

Although Dio emphasizes the military disadvantage suffered by the defenders of the Temple of Jerusalem as a result of the strict observance of the Sabbath, he refrains from making carping remarks about Jewish superstition. On one occasion he even speaks in a respectful tone of the devotion to their religion of the Jews serving in the forces of Antigonus (No. 414). As a contemporary of the Severi, he does not omit to mention that, though the Jews had often been repressed (in former times), they had won their right to freedom of religious observance (No. 406). On the other hand, he also states that the Jewish race is very bitter when aroused to anger, and his account of the Jewish revolt under Trajan includes a tale of atrocities perpetrated by Jews (No. 437). He records without comment that Vespasian and Titus did not assume the title of "Iudaicus" after their victory over the Jews (No. 430).

Dio was alert to the phenomenon of proselytism. He states that the name "Jews" applied also to aliens who followed Jewish customs (No. 406), and gives as a reason for the anti-Jewish measures introduced by Tiberius in 19 C.E. the success of Jewish religious propaganda (No. 419). He is the sole source to record that some Roman soldiers taking part in the siege of Jerusalem thought that the city was impregnable and deserted to the Jews (No. 430). In connection with the Jewish revolt under Hadrian Dio remarks that many foreign nations joined the Jewish rebels, though he adduces desire for gain and not sympathy with Judaism as their reason for doing so (No. 440).[3]

---

3 On Cassius Dio and the Jews, see also J. Schwartz, *L'antiquité classique*, XXXIX (1970), pp. 149 ff. See especially his interpretation of Cassius Dio, LXXVIII, 20:1–3.

(15:2) Ἐπ' οὖν τοῦτον ⟨scil. Ἀρέταν⟩ τούς τε πλησιοχώρους αὐτῷ ὁ
Πομπήιος ἐλάσας ἀκονιτί τε αὐτοὺς προσηγάγετο καὶ φρουρᾷ παρέδωκε.
κἀντεῦθεν ἐπὶ τὴν Συρίαν τὴν Παλαιστίνην, ὡς καὶ τὴν Φοινίκην
κακώσαντας, ὥρμησεν. ἦρχον δὲ αὐτῶν Ὑρκανός τε καὶ Ἀριστόβουλος
5 ἀδελφοί, καὶ ἐτύγχανον ὑπὲρ τῆς τοῦ σφετέρου θεοῦ, ὅστις ποτὲ οὗτός
ἐστιν, ἱερωσύνης (οὕτω γὰρ τὴν βασιλείαν σφῶν ὠνόμαζον) αὐτοί τε
διαφερόμενοι καὶ τὰς πόλεις στασιάζοντες· *(3)* ὁ οὖν Πομπήιος Ὑρκανὸν
μὲν οὐδεμίαν ἀξιόχρεων ἰσχὺν ἔχοντα ἀμαχεὶ εὐθὺς προσέθετο,
Ἀριστόβουλον δὲ ἐς χωρίον τι κατακλείσας ὁμολογῆσαί οἱ ἠνάγκασε, καὶ
10 ἐπειδὴ μήτε τὰ χρήματα μήτε τὸ φρούριον παρεδίδου, ἔδησεν αὐτόν. κἀκ
τούτου τοὺς μὲν ἄλλους ῥᾷον προσεποιήσατο, τὰ δὲ Ἱεροσόλυμα
πολιορκῶν πράγματα ἔσχε. *(16:1)* τὴν μὲν γὰρ ἄλλην πόλιν, ἐσδεξαμένων
αὐτὸν τῶν τὰ τοῦ Ὑρκανοῦ φρονούντων, ἀπραγμόνως ἔλαβεν, αὐτὸ δὲ τὸ
ἱερὸν προκατασχόντων τῶν ἑτέρων οὐκ ἀπόνως εἷλεν· *(2)* ἐπί τε γὰρ
15 μετεώρου ἦν καὶ περιβόλῳ ἰδίῳ ὠχύρωτο. καὶ εἴ γε ἐν πάσαις ταῖς ἡμέραις
ὁμοίως ἠμύνοντο, οὐκ ἄν αὐτὸ ἐχειρώσατο· νῦν δὲ τὰς τοῦ Κρόνου δὴ
ὠνομασμένας διαλείποντες, καὶ οὐδὲν τὸ παράπαν ἐν αὐταῖς δρῶντες,
παρέδωκαν τοῖς Ῥωμαίοις καιρὸν ἐν τῷ διακένῳ τούτῳ τὸ τεῖχος
διασεῖσαι. *(3)* μαθόντες γὰρ τὴν πτόησιν αὐτῶν ταύτην τὸν μὲν ἄλλον
20 χρόνον οὐδὲν σπουδῇ ἔπραττον, ταῖς δὲ δὴ ἡμέραις ἐκείναις, ὁπότε ἐκ τῆς
περιτροπῆς ἐπέλθοιεν, ἐντονώτατά οἱ προσέβαλλον. *(4)* καὶ οὕτως
ἑάλωσάν τε ἐν τῇ τοῦ Κρόνου ἡμέρᾳ μηδ' ἀμυνόμενοι, καὶ πάντα τὰ
χρήματα διηρπάσθη. ἥ τε βασιλεία τῷ Ὑρκανῷ ἐδόθη, καὶ ὁ
Ἀριστόβουλος ἀνηνέχθη. *(5)* ταῦτα μὲν τότε ἐν τῇ Παλαιστίνῃ ἐγένετο·
25 οὕτω γὰρ τὸ σύμπαν ἔθνος, ὅσον ἀπὸ τῆς Φοινίκης μέχρι τῆς Αἰγύπτου
παρὰ τὴν θάλασσαν τὴν ἔσω παρήκει, ἀπὸ παλαιοῦ κέκληται. ἔχουσι δὲ
καὶ ἕτερον ὄνομα ἐπίκτητον· ἥ τε γὰρ χώρα Ἰουδαία καὶ αὐτοὶ Ἰουδαῖοι
ὠνομάδαται· *(17:1)* ἡ δὲ ἐπίκλησις αὕτη ἐκείνοις μὲν οὐκ οἶδ' ὅθεν ἤρξατο
γενέσθαι, φέρει δὲ καὶ ἐπὶ τοὺς ἄλλους ἀνθρώπους ὅσοι τὰ νόμιμα αὐτῶν,
30 καίπερ ἀλλοεθνεῖς ὄντες, ζηλοῦσι. καὶ ἔστι καὶ παρὰ τοῖς Ῥωμαίοις τὸ
γένος τοῦτο, κολουσθὲν ⟨μὲν⟩ πολλάκις, αὐξηθὲν δὲ ἐπὶ πλεῖστον, ὥστε
καὶ ἐς παρρησίαν τῆς νομίσεως ἐκνικῆσαι. *(2)* κεχωρίδαται δὲ ἀπὸ τῶν
λοιπῶν ἀνθρώπων ἔς τε τἆλλα τὰ περὶ τὴν δίαιταν πάνθ' ὡς εἰπεῖν, καὶ
μάλισθ' ὅτι τῶν μὲν ἄλλων θεῶν οὐδένα τιμῶσιν, ἕνα δέ τινα ἰσχυρῶς
35 σέβουσιν. οὐδ' ἄγαλμα οὐδὲν ⟨οὐδ'⟩ ἐν αὐτοῖς ποτε τοῖς Ἱεροσολύμοις

8 ἀμαχεὶ Robertus Stephanus   ἀμαχὶ L   19 πτόησιν Boissevain
ἐμποίησιν L   31 ⟨μὲν⟩ Robertus Stephanus   35 οὐδὲν ⟨οὐδ'⟩ Herwerden

ἔσχον, ἄρρητον δὲ δὴ καὶ ἀειδῆ αὐτὸν νομίζοντες εἶναι περισσότατα
ἀνθρώπων θρησκεύουσι. (3) καὶ αὐτῷ νεών τε μέγιστον καὶ
περικαλλέστατον, πλὴν καθ᾽ ὅσον ἀχανής τε καὶ ἀνώροφος ἦν,
ἐξεποίησαν, καὶ τὴν ἡμέραν τὴν τοῦ Κρόνου καλουμένην ἀνέθεσαν, καὶ
40 ἄλλα τε ἐν αὐτῇ ἰδιαίτατα πολλὰ [ἃ] ποιοῦσι, καὶ ἔργου οὐδενὸς σπουδαίου
προσάπτονται.
(4) καὶ τὰ μὲν κατ᾽ ἐκεῖνον, τίς τε ἔστι καὶ ὅθεν οὕτως ἐτιμήθη, ὅπως τὲ
περὶ αὐτὸν ἐπτόηνται, πολλοῖς τε εἴρηται καὶ οὐδὲν τῇδε τῇ ἱστορίᾳ
προσήκει.

40 ἃ del. Reiske   πολλὰ ἃ secl. Dindorf

(15:2) Pompey accordingly marched against him [scil. Aretas] and his
neighbours, and, overcoming them without effort, left them in charge
of a garrison. Thence he proceeded against Syria Palaestina, because
its inhabitants had ravaged Phoenicia. Their rulers were two
brothers, Hyrcanus and Aristobulus, who were quarrelling themselves, as it chanced, and were creating factions in the cities on
account of the priesthood (for so they called their kingdom) of their
god, whoever he is. (3) Pompey immediately won over Hyrcanus
without a battle, since the latter had no force worthy of note; and by
shutting up Aristobulus in a certain place he compelled him to come
to terms, and when he would surrender neither the money nor the
garrison, he threw him into chains. After this he more easily
overcame the rest, but had trouble in besieging Jerusalem. (16:1)
Most of the city, to be sure, he took without any trouble, as he was
received by the party of Hyrcanus; but the temple itself, which the
other party had occupied, he captured only with difficulty. (2) For it
was on high ground and was fortified by a wall of its own, and if they
had continued defending it on all days alike, he could not have got
possession of it. As it was, they made an exception of what are called
the days of Saturn, and by doing no work at all on those days afforded
the Romans an opportunity in this interval to batter down the wall.
(3) The latter, on learning of this superstitious awe of theirs, made no
serious attempts the rest of the time, but on those days, when they
came round in succession, assaulted most vigorously. (4) Thus the
defenders were captured on the day of Saturn, without making any
defence, and all the wealth was plundered. The kingdom was given to
Hyrcanus and Aristobulus was carried away. (5) This was the course
of events at that time in Palestine; for this is the name that has been
given from old to the whole country extending from Phoenicia to

350

Egypt along the inner sea. They have also another name that they have acquired: the country has been named Judaea, and the people themselves Jews. (17:1) I do not know how this title came to be given them, but it applies also to all the rest of mankind, although of alien race, who affect their customs. This class exists even among the Romans, and though often repressed has increased to a very great extent and has won its way to the right of freedom in its observances. (2) They are distinguished from the rest of mankind in practically every detail of life, and especially by the fact that they do not honour any of the usual gods, but show extreme reverence for one particular divinity. They never had any statue of him even in Jerusalem itself, but believing him to be unnamable and invisible, they worship him in the most extravagant fashion on earth. (3) They built to him a temple that was extremely large and beautiful, except in so far as it was open and roofless, and likewise dedicated to him the day called the day of Saturn, on which, among many other most peculiar observances, they undertake no serious occupation.

(4) Now as for him, who he is and why he has been so honoured, and how they got their superstitious awe of him, accounts have been given by many, and moreover these matters have naught to do with this history. (trans. E. Cary, *LCL*)

15:2 Ἐπ' οὖν τοῦτον [scil. Ἀρέταν]: The account of Cassius Dio of the activities of Pompey against Aretas III, king of the Nabataeans, is not very accurate. Aretas helped Hyrcanus in his struggle against his brother Aristobulus, and the allies had started to besiege Jerusalem but were forced to raise the siege by the intervention of Scaurus (*Ant.*, XIV, 14 ff.; *BJ*, I, 124 ff.). After Pompey arrived in Syria he intended to invade Arabia (*Ant.*, XIV, 46), but in view of the situation in Judaea he determined to settle the affairs of that country first. The Romans launched an expedition against Petra in 62 B.C.E., only after the capture of Jerusalem and the transfer of the governorship of Syria to Scaurus that year. The success of this expedition was limited, though it was magnified by propaganda; cf. Orosius, VI, 6:1.

ἐπὶ τὴν Συρίαν τὴν Παλαιστινην: For the alternative use of the terms Syria Palaestina and Palaestina by Cassius Dio, cf. here below XXXVII, 16:5; XXXVIII, 38:4: Παλαιστίνους (No. 407); XXXIX, 56:6 (No. 408); XLI, 18:1 (No. 409); XLVIII, 26:2 (No. 412); XLVIII, 41:4 (No. 413); XLIX, 32:5 (No. 415); LV, 27:6: Ἡρώδης ὁ Παλαιστῖνος (No. 418); LX, 8:2: Ἀγρίππᾳ τῷ Παλαιστίνῳ (No. 423); LXVI, 9:2a (No. 431); LXVIII, 32:5 (No. 438). However, he still quite often uses the term Ἰουδαία; cf. XLVII, 28:3 (No. 410); LV, 23:4 (No. 417); LXV, 8:1, 3 (No. 427a); LXIX, 11:1 (No. 439); LXIX, 13:1; 14, 2 (No. 440); LXXV, 2:4 (No. 442). See also the general statement of Cassius Dio below, XXXVII, 16:5.

ὑπὲρ τῆς τοῦ σφετέρου θεοῦ, ὅστις ποτὲ οὗτός ἐστιν: The expression is common in Attic tragedy; cf. Aeschylus, *Agamemnon*, 160: Ζεύς, ὅστις ποτ᾽ ἐστίν; Euripides, *Troiades*, 885 f.: ὅστις ποτ᾽ εἶ σύ, ... Ζεύς. See E. Norden, *Agnostos Theos*, Leipzig–Berlin 1913, pp. 144 and 183, n. 1. Cassius Dio uses the expression in connection with the Jewish Deity since its name was unknown (*incertus*); cf. the commentary to Lucanus, *Pharsalia*, II, 593 (No. 191). Cf. also Iulianus, *Orationes*, VII, p. 231 A: ὦ Ζεῦ πάτερ, ἢ ὅ, τι σοι φίλον ὄνομα καὶ ὅπως ὀνομάζεσθαι.

ἱερωσύνης: Since the same person was usually both the high priest and the ruler in the Hasmonaean state, Cassius Dio identifies high priesthood with kingship; cf. Tacitus, *Historiae*, V, 8 (No. 281): "quia honor sacerdotii firmamentum potentiae adsumebatur" and in reference to Herod, cf. Strabo, *Geographica*, XVI, 2:46 (No. 115): παραδοὺς εἰς τὴν ἱερωσύνην.

αὐτοί τε διαφερόμενοι: For the appearance of Hyrcanus and Aristobulus before Pompey at Damascus, cf. *Ant.*, XIV, 41 ff.; Diodorus, XL, 2 (No. 64).

15:3 ἐς χωρίον τι κατακλείσας: I.e. the fortress of Alexandrion, where Aristobulus took refuge; cf. *Ant.*, XIV, 49; *BJ*, I, 134.

16:1 τὴν μὲν γὰρ ἄλλην πόλιν: Cf. *Ant.*, XIV, 59: οἱ δὲ ἕτεροι δεξάμενοι τὴν στρατιὰν ἐνεχείρισαν Πομπηΐῳ τήν τε πόλιν καὶ τὰ βασίλεια; *BJ*, I, 143.

αὐτὸ δὲ τὸ ἱερὸν ... οὐκ ἀπόνως εἷλεν: For the description of the siege, cf. *Ant.*, XIV, 58 ff.; Strabo, *Historica Hypomnemata*, apud: *Ant.*, XIV, 66–68 (No. 104).

16:2 καὶ εἴ γε ἐν πάσαις ταῖς ἡμέραις ὁμοίως ἠμύνοντο: Cf. *Ant.*, XIV, 64: ὃ δὴ καὶ Ῥωμαῖοι συνιδόντες κατ᾽ ἐκείνας τὰς ἡμέρας, ἃς δὴ σάββατα καλοῦμεν, οὔτ᾽ ἔβαλλον τοὺς Ἰουδαίους, οὔτε εἰς χεῖρας αὐτοῖς ὑπήντων, χοῦν δὲ καὶ πύργους ἀνίστασαν καὶ τὰ μηχανήματα προσῆγον, ὥστ᾽ αὐτοῖς εἰς τὴν ἐπιοῦσαν ἐνεργὰ ταῦτ᾽ εἶναι. Cf. also *BJ*, I, 146, and the commentary to Frontinus, *Strategemata*, II, 1:17 (No. 229).

νῦν δὲ τὰς τοῦ Κρόνου δὴ ὠνομασμένας διαλείποντες: Cassius Dio consistently calls the Sabbath by the name of the Day of Kronos, i.e. Saturn. Cf. the commentaries to Tibullus, I, 3:15–18 (No. 126), and Tacitus, *Historiae*, V, 4 (No. 281).

16:4 καὶ οὕτως ἑάλωσάν τε ἐν τῇ τοῦ Κρόνου ἡμέρᾳ: It is not certain that the Temple was actually captured on a Sabbath. Cassius Dio is mistaken about the Jewish attitude towards fighting on the Sabbath. After the time of Mattathias the Hasmonaean, the Jews used to defend themselves when faced with an assault by an enemy; cf. the commentary to Frontinus, *loc. cit.* Thus the previous statement of Cassius Dio (16:3) that the Romans ἐντονώτατά οἱ προσέβαλλον on the Sabbath can only be true if taken to mean the raising of earthworks rather than actual attack. What happened actually is described by Josephus, who asserts that if it were not for the Jewish national custom of resting on the Sabbath, the Romans would have been prevented by the defenders from finishing the raising of the earthworks; cf. *Ant.*, XIV, 63: ἄρχοντας μὲν γὰρ μάχης καὶ τύπτοντας ἀμύνασθαι δίδωσιν ὁ νόμος, ἄλλο δέ τι δρῶντας τοὺς πολεμίους οὐκ ἐᾷ. Cf. also Strabo, *Geographica*, XVI, 2:40, p. 763 (No. 115). Thus the capture of the Temple was made easier for the Romans by the accumulated result of continuous inaction by the Jews on the Sabbath — when the earthworks could be raised by the besiegers — rather than by the submission of the Jews to an actual Roman assault on the Sabbath day. The statement of Cassius Dio may therefore be due to a misunderstanding, but he is not guilty of Strabo's mistake in stating that the event occurred on the Day of Atonement; cf. the commentaries to Strabo, *Historica Hypomnemata, loc. cit.*, and *Geographica, loc. cit.*

πάντα τὰ χρήματα: Cassius Dio here somewhat contradicts the express statements of Cicero, *Pro Flacco*, 28, 67 (No. 68), and Josephus (*Ant.*, XIV, 72; *BJ*, I, 152 f.) that Pompey refrained from plundering the treasures of the Temple, though the other two writers differ in their explanations; see also Ed. Meyer, II, p. 312, n. 1. Perhaps Cassius Dio refers only to casual looting by the victorious soldiery.

ἥ τε βασιλεία τῷ Ὑρκανῷ ἐδόθη: This is inaccurate, since Hyrcanus was confirmed only in his office of high priest and ethnarch. That he was not king is proved by the fact that Josephus states only that he was reinstated as high priest (*Ant.*, XIV, 73; *BJ*, I, 153), and that in official documents from the time of Julius Caesar he is expressly designated as ethnarch (*Ant.*, XIV, 191, 194, 200, 209). It is unlikely that the official status of Hyrcanus deteriorated only under Julius Caesar. Probably after Pompey had considerably reduced the extent of Judaea he found it necessary to lower the status of its ruler. However, the title of king was still sometimes associated with Hyrcanus, as attested by *Ant.*, XIV, 157, 165, 172: ἄνδρες σύνεδροι καὶ βασιλεῦ; XV, 12, 15. Cf. also Florus, I, 40:30 (No. 321). For the right of Roman commanders to bestow the diadem on vassal rulers, see S. Weinstock, *Divus Julius*, Oxford 1971, pp. 337 f.

καὶ ὁ Ἀριστόβουλος ἀνηνέχθη: Aristobulus was brought to Rome and there adorned the triumph of Pompey; see the commentary to Appianus, *Liber Mithridaticus*, 117:571 ff. (No. 346).

16:5 Ἰουδαία: The name here denotes the whole of Palestine, the common usage among non-Jewish writers.

17:1 φέρει δὲ καὶ ἐπὶ τοὺς ἄλλους ἀνθρώπους: Cassius Dio emphasizes that to join the Jewish religion was tantamount to joining the Jewish nation. The statement may serve as evidence for the continuing power of proselytism in the time of the Severi; see Simon, pp. 315 ff.

ὥστε καὶ ἐς παρρησίαν τῆς νομίσεως ἐκνικῆσαι: In contrast to Christianity, Judaism as a religion enjoyed freedom of worship. Cassius Dio here refers both to former attempts to check the spread of Judaism and to the changed conditions under the Severi.

17:2 ἄρρητον δὲ δὴ καὶ ἀειδῆ αὐτὸν νομίζοντες: Cf. Livius, apud: Lydus, *De Mensibus*, IV, 53 (No. 134); *Scholia in Lucanum*, II, 593 (No. 133): "cuius deorum sit non nominant, neque ullum ibi simulacrum est."

17:3 ἀχανής τε καὶ ἀνώροφος ἦν: Cf. Strabo, *Geographica*, XIV, 1:5, p. 634 (concerning a temple at Milet).

407

Historia Romana, XXXVIII, 38:4 — Boissevain

Τί γὰρ δεῖ κἀνταῦθα καθ᾽ ἕκαστον ἐπεξιέναι τὴν Κρήτην, τὸν Πόντον, τὴν Κύπρον, τὴν Ἰβηρίαν, τὴν Ἀσιανήν, τὴν Ἀλβανίαν τὴν ἐκεῖ, Σύρους ἀμφοτέρους, Ἀρμενίους ἑκατέρους, Ἀραβίους, Παλαιστίνους;

2 Ἀσιανήν Bekker   ἀσίαν L

But here again why catalogue in detail Crete, Pontus, Cyprus, Asiatic Iberia, Farther Albania, both Syrias, the Arabs, and Palestine?

(trans. E. Cary, *LCL*)

Παλαιστίνους: The passage is taken from a speech by Julius Caesar before the battle with Ariovistus. Caesar enumerates the Roman conquests. Παλαιστίνους refers to the Jews; cf. the following passage and No. 418: Ἡρώδης ὁ Παλαιστῖνος.

408

Historia Romana, XXXIX, 56:5-6 — Boissevain = F100R

(5) Καταλιπὼν ⟨scil. Γαβίνιος⟩ οὖν ἐν τῇ Συρίᾳ Σισένναν τε τὸν υἱὸν κομιδῇ νέον ὄντα καὶ στρατιώτας μετ᾽ αὐτοῦ πάνυ ὀλίγους, τὴν μὲν ἀρχὴν ἐφ᾽ ἧς ἐτέτακτο τοῖς λῃσταῖς ἔτι καὶ μᾶλλον ἐξέδωκεν, (6) αὐτὸς δὲ ἐς τὴν Παλαιστίνην ἐλθὼν τόν τε Ἀριστόβουλον (διαδρὰς γὰρ ἐκ τῆς Ῥώμης
5   ὑπετάραττέ τι) συνέλαβε καὶ τῷ Πομπηίῳ ἔπεμψε, καὶ φόρον τοῖς Ἰουδαίοις ἐπέταξε, καὶ μετὰ τοῦτο καὶ ἐς τὴν Αἴγυπτον ἐνέβαλε·

(5) He [scil. Gabinius] left in Syria his son Sisenna, a mere boy, and a very few soldiers with him, thus exposing the province to which he had been assigned more than ever to the pirates. (6) He himself then reached Palestine, arrested Aristobulus, who had escaped from Rome and was causing some disturbance, sent him to Pompey, imposed tribute upon the Jews, and after this invaded Egypt.

(trans. E. Cary, *LCL*)

6 ἐς τὴν Παλαιστίνην ἐλθών: Gabinius acted as governor of Syria in the years 57–55 B.C.E. For his activities, cf. the commentary to Cicero, *De Provinciis Consularibus*, 5:10–12 (No. 70).
τόν τε Ἀριστόβουλον ... συνέλαβε: Aristobulus escaped from Rome in 56 B.C.E. with his son Antigonus; cf. *Ant.*, XIV, 92 ff.; *BJ*, I, 171 ff.; Plutarchus, *Vita Antonii*, 3:1 (No. 264). Returning to Judaea he attempted to restore the

Cassius Dio

fortifications of Alexandrion. Gabinius sent a Roman force under Sisenna, Antony and Servilius to capture him. Among those who joined Aristobulus was Peitholaus, the *hypostrategos* of Jerusalem. After he had suffered a defeat, Aristobulus retired to the fortress of Machairus, then surrendered to the Romans, and was sent back to Rome.

καὶ φόρον τοῖς Ἰουδαίοις ἐπέταξε: Pompey had already imposed taxes on Judaea (*Ant.*, XIV, 74; *BJ*, I, 154), but it seems that Gabinius introduced radical changes in the levying of taxes. He divided Judaea into five *synhedria* and abolished the part played by the Roman *publicani* in the collection of the taxes; see Momigliano, p. 202, and the commentary to Cicero, *loc. cit.*

409

Historia Romana, XLI, 18:1 — Boissevain = F101R

Ὁ δ' οὖν Καῖσαρ ταῦτά τε οὕτως ἐποίησε καὶ τὴν Σαρδὼ τήν τε Σικελίαν ἀμαχεὶ κατέσχεν, ἐκχωρησάντων τῶν τότε ἐν αὐταῖς ἀρχόντων. τόν τε Ἀριστόβουλον οἴκαδε ἐς τὴν Παλαιστίνην, ὅπως τῷ Πομπηίῳ τι ἀντιπράξῃ, ἔστειλε.

After taking these steps Caesar occupied Sardinia and Sicily without a contest, as the governors who were there at the time withdrew. Aristobulus he sent home to Palestine to accomplish something against Pompey. (trans. E. Cary, *LCL*)

τόν τε Ἀριστόβουλον οἴκαδε ... ἔστειλε: Cf. *Ant.*, XIV, 123 f.; *BJ*, I, 183 f. Cassius Dio seems not to have known about the death of Aristobulus at the hands of the partisans of Pompey, since in the subsequent narrative Aristobulus appears as still living (No. 412).

410

Historia Romana, XLVII, 28:3 — Boissevain = F102R

Παραλαβὼν ⟨scil. Κάσσιος⟩ οὖν τὴν Συρίαν ἐς τὴν Ἰουδαίαν ὥρμησε, πυθόμενος τοὺς στρατιώτας τοὺς ἐν τῇ Αἰγύπτῳ ὑπὸ τοῦ Καίσαρος καταλειφθέντας προσιέναι, καὶ ἐκείνους τε ἀκονιτὶ καὶ τοὺς Ἰουδαίους παρεστήσατο.

1 ⟨δ'⟩ οὖν? Bekker

So when Cassius had secured possession of Syria, he set out for Judaea on learning that the followers of Caesar who had been left

behind in Egypt were approaching; and without any difficulty he won
to his cause both them and the Jews.   (trans. E. Cary, *LCL*)

παραλαβὼν οὖν τὴν Συρίαν: The seizure of Syria by Cassius was one of the
chief steps in his preparations against an attack by the forces of Julius Caesar.
The military situation in Syria at that time was somewhat complicated. Sextus
Caesar, appointed governor of Syria by Julius Caesar, had been killed
(before the Ides of March) at the instigation of Caecilius Bassus, who took
over the command of his army. Bassus had to wage a war against the
Caesarian commanders and was in his turn besieged in Apamea by C.
Antistius Vetus. Antistius was aided by soldiers sent by Caesar and the
Caesarian party in the near neighbourhood, among them being the Jewish
statesman Antipater (*Ant.*, XIV, 268 f.; *BJ*, I, 217; cf. Cassius Dio, XLVII,
27:3). Later the command of the Caesarian forces was taken over by Q.
Marcius Crispus and L. Statius Murcus. When Cassius arrived in Syria he
won over both Caecilius Bassus and Murcus, thus becoming sole commander
of all the Roman forces in Syria; cf. Cicero, *Ad Familiares*, XII, 11 (No. 71).
ἐς τὴν Ἰουδαίαν ὥρμησε: Cassius was not unknown in Judaea. He had
already been active there in 53 B.C.E. after the defeat of Crassus by the
Parthians. Then he attacked the Galilaean township of Taricheae and,
according to Josephus, killed some thirty thousand Jews and formed
connections with Antipater (*Ant.*, XIV, 120; *BJ*, I, 180).
καὶ τοὺς Ἰουδαίους παρεστήσατο: Cf. *Ant.*, XIV, 272 ff.; *BJ*, I, 218 ff.
Cassius imposed a heavy tribute amounting to seven hundred talents of silver
on Judaea. Not all parts of the country paid the portions allotted to them, and
consequently the inhabitants of four Jewish townships (Gophna, Emmaus,
Lydda and Thamna) were reduced to slavery by Cassius. Herod exacted the
sum apportioned to Galilaea, and Hyrcanus even paid a hundred talents from
his own pocket. See Schürer, I, p. 350; Otto, pp. 21 f.; H. Buchheim, *Die
Orientpolitik des Triumvirn M. Antonius*, Heidelberg 1960, p. 63;
H. Volkmann, *Die Massenversklavungen der Einwohner eroberter Städte in
der hellenistisch-römischen Zeit*, Mainz–Wiesbaden 1961, pp. 181 (67) ff.

411

Historia Romana, XLVII, 30:1 — Boissevain

Ὁ δ᾽ οὖν Δολοβέλλας ἐγκρατὴς οὕτω τῆς Ἀσίας γενόμενος ἐς τὴν
Κιλικίαν ἦλθε, τοῦ Κασσίου ἐν τῇ Παλαιστίνῃ ὄντος, καὶ τοὺς Ταρσέας
ἑκουσίους προσλαβὼν φρουρούς τινας αὐτοῦ ἐν Αἰγέαις ὄντας ἐνίκησε, καὶ
ἐς τὴν Συρίαν ἐνέβαλε·

Dolabella, accordingly, after becoming in this way master of Asia,
came into Cilicia while Cassius was in Palestine, took over the people

of Tarsus with their consent, conquered a few of Cassius' guards who
were at Aegae, and invaded Syria. (trans. E. Cary, *LCL*)

τοῦ Κασσίου ἐν τῇ Παλαιστίνῃ ὄντος: Cassius Dio uses the names Ἰουδαία
and Παλαιστίνη alternately. Here Παλαιστίνη occurs in the passages
dealing with the invasion of Syria by Dolabella and his ultimate defeat by
Cassius; see T. Rice Holmes, *The Architect of the Roman Empire*, I, Oxford
1928, pp. 76 f.; see also J. Dobiáš, *Dějiny římské provincie syrské*, Prague
1924, pp. 179 ff.

412

Historia Romana, XLVIII, 26:2 — Boissevain = F103R

Οὗτοι μὲν ⟨scil. οἱ Τύριοι⟩ οὖν ἀνάλωτοι ἔμειναν· τὰ δ' ἄλλα ὁ Πάκορος
λαβὼν ἐς Παλαιστίνην ἐσέβαλε, καὶ τόν τε Ὑρκανόν, ὃς τότε τὰ
πράγματα αὐτῶν παρὰ τῶν Ῥωμαίων ἐπιτραπεὶς εἶχεν, ἔπαυσε, καὶ τὸν
Ἀριστόβουλον τὸν ἀδελφὸν αὐτοῦ ἄρχοντα κατὰ τὸ ἐκείνων ἔχθος
5 ἀντικατέστησεν.

2 ἐσέβαλλε L   4 ἔθος Robertus Stephanus

The Tyrians accordingly continued to be proof against capture but
Pacorus secured all the rest of Syria. He then invaded Palestine and
deposed Hyrcanus, who was at the moment in charge of affairs there,
having been appointed by the Romans, and in his stead set up his
brother Aristobulus as a ruler because of the enmity existing between
them. (trans. E. Cary, *LCL*)

τὰ δ' ἄλλα ὁ Πάκορος λαβών: I.e. the regions of Syria apart from Tyre. The
Parthian invasion of Syria was instigated by T. Labienus the Younger, who
had been sent by Cassius to ask for help against his Roman opponents from
Orodes II, the Parthian king. Labienus succeeded in persuading the
Parthians to start a war against Antony, and a strong Parthian force overran
Syria and large parts of Asia Minor at the end of 41 B.C.E. and the beginning
of 40 B.C.E.; for the chronology, see A. Bürcklein, "Quellen und
Chronologie der römisch-parthischen Feldzüge in den Jahren 713–718 d.
St.", Ph.D. Thesis, Leipzig 1879, pp. 49 ff.; Buchheim, *op. cit.* (supra, p. 356),
p. 118, n. 188. The Parthian army was under the leadership of Pacorus, the
king's son, and the satrap Barzaphranes. The main cities of Syria and
Phoenicia, namely Apamea, Antiochia, Sidon and Ptolemais, admitted the
Parthians, while only Tyre excluded them. Saxa, the Roman governor of
Syria, was killed. See N.C. Debevoise, *A Political History of Parthia*, Chicago
1938, pp. 108 ff.; D. Magie, *Roman Rule in Asia Minor*, I, Princeton 1950, pp.
430 ff.

καὶ τὸν ᾿Αριστόβουλον τὸν ἀδελφὸν αὐτοῦ: Here Dio is mistaken. The Parthian protégé was not Aristobulus, who was already dead, but his son Antigonus, the nephew of Hyrcanus. There is a contradiction below, where Dio expressly refers to the kingship of Antigonus; cf. Cassius Dio, XLVIII, 41:4 (No. 413); see Schürer, I, p. 354, n. 52. For Antigonus, see the commentary to Strabo, *Historica Hypomnemata*, apud: *Ant.*, XV, 8–10 (No. 108). Antigonus exploited the situation created by the Parthian invasion, and his partisans helped the Parthian advance in Judaea. For the events in Judaea, cf. *Ant.*, XIV, 330 ff.; *BJ*, I, 248 ff.; Syncellus (ed. Dindorf), I, p. 577; see Otto, pp. 25 ff.; A. Momigliano, *CAH*, X, 1934, pp. 319 ff.; A. Schalit, *König Herodes*, Berlin 1969, pp. 74 ff. Antigonus acted jointly with Lysanias of Chalcis throughout and made a pact with the Parthians to pay a large amount of money in return for the deposition of Hyrcanus and the destruction of Herod. The Jews living in the vicinity of Mount Carmel and in the Plain of Sharon joined Antigonus, and after some time Jerusalem was taken by the Parthians. Herod escaped from the city, and his brother Phasael and Hyrcanus fell into the hands of the Parthians, who made Antigonus king of Judaea.

413

Historia Romana, XLVIII, 41:4–5 — Boissevain = F103R

(4) ᾿Ανελπίστοις τε γὰρ ἅμα καὶ ἐλάττοσι τοῖς βαρβάροις σφῶν οὖσι προσπεσὼν ⟨scil. Οὐεντίδιος⟩ τόν τε Φραναπάτην καὶ ἄλλους πολλοὺς ἐφόνευσε, καὶ οὕτω τήν τε Συρίαν ἐκλειφθεῖσαν ὑπὸ τῶν Πάρθων ἀμαχεὶ πλὴν τῶν ᾿Αραδίων παρέλαβε, καὶ μετὰ τοῦτο τὴν Παλαιστίνην,
5 ᾿Αντίγονον τὸν βασιλεύοντα αὐτῆς ἐκφοβήσας, ἀπόνως κατέσχε. *(5)* καὶ ὁ μὲν ταῦτά τε διῆγε, καὶ χρήματα πολλὰ μὲν παρὰ τῶν ἄλλων ὡς ἑκάστων, πολλὰ δὲ καὶ παρὰ τοῦ ᾿Αντιγόνου τοῦ τε ᾿Αντιόχου καὶ Μάλχου τοῦ Ναβαταίου, ὅτι τῷ Πακόρῳ συνήραντο, ἐσέπραξε. καὶ αὐτὸς μὲν οὐδὲν ἐπ᾿ αὐτοῖς παρὰ τῆς βουλῆς, ἅτε οὐκ αὐτοκράτωρ ὢν ἀλλ᾿ ἑτέρῳ
10 ὑποστρατηγῶν, εὕρετο, ὁ δὲ ᾿Αντώνιος καὶ ἐπαίνους καὶ ἱερομηνίας ἔλαβεν.

(4) For Ventidius fell upon the barbarians when they were not expecting him and were at the same time in smaller force, and slew Phranapates and many others.
In this way he took over Syria without a battle, now that it was deserted by the Parthians, with the exception of the Aradii, and later occupied Palestine without trouble, after he had frightened the king, Antigonus, out of the country. (5) Besides accomplishing all this he exacted large sums of money from the rest individually, and large

358

sums also from Antigonus and Antiochus and Malchus the Nabataean, because they had given help to Pacorus. Ventidius himself received no reward for these achievements from the senate, since he was not acting with independent authority but as lieutenant to another; but Antony was honoured with eulogies and thanksgivings.   (trans. E. Cary, *LCL*)

4 ἀνελπίστοις ... παρέλαβε: For the victories of Publius Ventidius in 39 or 38 B.C.E. over the Parthians, cf. mainly Cassius Dio, XLVIII, 39:2 ff.; Iustinus, XLII, 4:10–16. In a series of engagements Ventidius completely broke the power of Parthia, Labienus lost his life, and the Romans regained Cilicia and Syria, destroying the Parthian force in the Battle of Gindarus; Pacorus himself fell on the battlefield; see T. Rice Holmes, *op. cit.* (supra, p. 357), pp. 121 f.; R. Syme, *The Roman Revolution*, Oxford 1939, pp. 223 f.; Buchheim, *op. cit.* (supra, p. 356), p. 76.
ʼΑντίγονον τὸν βασιλεύοντα αὐτῆς ἐκφοβήσας, ἀπόνως κατέσχε: Cf. *Ant.*, XIV, 392; *BJ*, I, 288.
5 πολλὰ δὲ καὶ παρὰ ʼΑντιγόνου ... ἐσέπραξε: Cf. *Ant.*, loc. cit.: τὸ δ' ὅλον ἦν αὐτῷ στρατήγημα χρήματα παρ' ʼΑντιγόνου λαβεῖν· ἔγγιστα γοῦν Ἱεροσολύμων στρατοπεδευσάμενος ἀποχρώντως ἠργυρίσατο τὸν ʼΑντίγονον; *BJ*, loc. cit. Malchus the Nabataean remained king after the complete Roman victory and throughout the ascendancy of Antony; see Schürer, I, p. 735; A. Kammerer, *Pétra et la Nabatène*, Paris 1929, pp. 184 ff.; Schürer, ed. Vermes & Millar, p. 580. However Antigonus was in a different category. He had come to the throne against the will of Rome, and his kingdom was bestowed by Rome upon Herod.

414
Historia Romana, XLIX, 22:3–23:1 — Boissevain = F104R

(22:3) Γάιος δὲ δὴ Σόσσιος τὴν ἀρχὴν τῆς τε Συρίας καὶ τῆς Κιλικίας παρ' αὐτοῦ λαβὼν τούς τε Ἀραδίους πολιορκηθέντας τε μέχρι τότε καὶ λιμῷ καὶ νόσῳ ταλαιπωρηθέντας ἐχειρώσατο, καὶ τὸν ʼΑντίγονον τοὺς φρουροὺς τοὺς παρ' ἑαυτῷ τῶν Ῥωμαίων ὄντας ἀποκτείναντα μάχῃ τε ἐνίκησε, καὶ
5 καταφυγόντα ἐς τὰ Ἱεροσόλυμα πολιορκίᾳ κατεστρέψατο. (4) πολλὰ μὲν δὴ καὶ δεινὰ καὶ οἱ Ἰουδαῖοι τοὺς Ῥωμαίους ἔδρασαν (τὸ γάρ τοι γένος αὐτῶν θυμωθὲν πικρότατόν ἐστι), πολλῷ δὲ δὴ πλείω αὐτοὶ ἔπαθον. ἑάλωσαν μὲν γὰρ πρότεροι μὲν οἱ ὑπὲρ τοῦ τεμένους τοῦ θεοῦ ἀμυνόμενοι, ἔπειτα δὲ καὶ οἱ ἄλλοι ἐν τῇ τοῦ Κρόνου καὶ τότε ἡμέρᾳ ὠνομασμένῃ. (5)
10 καὶ τοσοῦτόν γε τῆς θρησκείας αὐτοῖς περιῆν ὥστε τοὺς προτέρους τοὺς μετὰ τοῦ ἱεροῦ χειρωθέντας παραιτήσασθαί τε τὸν Σόσσιον, ἐπειδὴ

1 Σόσιος Dindorf

359

ἡμέρα αὖθις ἡ τοῦ Κρόνου ἐνέστη, καὶ ἀνελθόντας εἰς αὐτὸ πάντα μετὰ
τῶν λοιπῶν τὰ νομιζόμενα ποιῆσαι. (6) ἐκείνους μὲν οὖν Ἡρώδῃ τινὶ
ὁ Ἀντώνιος ἄρχειν ἐπέτρεψε, τὸν δ' Ἀντίγονον ἐμαστίγωσε σταυρῷ
προσδήσας, ὃ μηδεὶς βασιλεὺς ἄλλος ὑπὸ τῶν Ῥωμαίων ἐπεπόνθει, καὶ
μετὰ τοῦτο καὶ ἀπέσφαξεν. (23:1) ἐπὶ μὲν δὴ τοῦ τε Κλαυδίου τοῦ τε
Νωρβανοῦ τοῦθ' οὕτως ἐγένετο.

(22:3) And Gaius Sosius received from him the governorship of Syria
and Cilicia. This officer subdued the Aradii, who had been besieged
up to this time and had been reduced to hard straits by famine and
disease, and also conquered in battle Antigonus, who had put to
death the Roman guards that were with him, and reduced him by
siege when he took refuge in Jerusalem. (4) The Jews, indeed, had
done much injury to the Romans, for the race is very bitter when
aroused to anger, but they suffered far more themselves. The first of
them to be captured were those who were fighting for the precinct of
their god, and then the rest on the day even then called the day of
Saturn. (5) And so excessive were they in their devotion to religion
that the first set of prisoners, those who had been captured along with
the temple, obtained leave from Sosius, when the day of Saturn came
round again, and went up into the temple, and there performed all the
customary rites, together with the rest of the people. (6) These people
Antony entrusted to a certain Herod to govern; but Antigonus he
bound to a cross and flogged — a punishment no other king had
suffered at the hands of the Romans — and afterwards he slew him.
(23:1) This was the course of events in the consulship of Claudius and
Norbanus. (trans. E. Cary, *LCL*)

22:3 *Γάιος ... Σόσσιος*: For C. Sosius, see the commentary to Seneca the
Elder, *Suasoriae*, II, 21 (No. 149).
τὴν ἀρχὴν τῆς τε Συρίας καὶ τῆς Κιλικίας ... λαβών: For the history of the
administrative connections between Syria and Cilicia, see E.J. Bickerman,
AJP, LXVIII (1947), pp. 353 ff.
τούς τε Ἀραδίους ... ἐχειρώσατο: This city had already been besieged by
Ventidius in 39 B.C.E.; cf. Cassius Dio, XLVIII, 41:6; J.P. Rey-Coquais,
Arados et sa Pérée, Paris 1974, pp. 163 f.
φρουροὺς τοὺς παρ' ἑαυτῷ ... ἀποκτείναντα: Cf. *Ant.*, XIV, 448 f.; *BJ*, I, 323
f. This force was under the command of Joseph, Herod's brother, to whom
Machairas, a Roman officer, had sent Roman cohorts. Joseph hastened with
them to Jericho to avenge himself on his adversaries. His force was cut down
by Antigonus; Josephus states that the Roman cohorts were inexperienced in
war, since they consisted of new recruits, mostly from Syria (*Ant.*, XIV, 449).

μάχῃ τε ἐνίκησε: After the visit of Herod to the camp of Antony at Samosata, and the surrender of that town by Antiochus of Commagene, the Romans were free to help Herod in his struggle against Antigonus, and Antony gave Sosius instructions to that purpose. Sosius ordered two legions ahead to Judaea and then followed with his main army (Ant., XIV, 447; BJ, I, 327). Josephus mainly emphasizes the part played by Herod in the victory over Antigonus in the open country, stating that Sosius only reached Jerusalem. This may be literally true, but Herod's victories were made possible only by the help given him by the Romans, as is made clear by the narrative of Josephus himself (Ant., XIV, 451 ff.; BJ, I, 329 ff.). After Herod had learned the news of his brother's death he hastened to his kingdom, taking with him a Roman legion to Ptolemais, and so started the invasion of Galilee. He defeated his enemies and shut them up in a fortress, which surrendered before the battle fought in the vicinity of Jericho; the Roman commander Machairas took part in the fighting at Isana.

καὶ καταφυγόντα ... κατεστρέψατο: Cf. Ant., XIV, 468 ff.; BJ, I, 345 ff.

22:4 πολλὰ ... τοὺς Ῥωμαίους ἔδρασαν: Cf. Ant., XIV, 470 ff.

γένος ... πικρότατον: Cf. Ant., XIV, 475: ἀπονοίᾳ δὲ τὸ πλέον ἢ προμηθείᾳ χρώμενοι προσελιπάρουν τῷ πολέμῳ εἰς τοὔσχατον.

ἑάλωσαν μὲν γὰρ πρότεροι μὲν οἱ ὑπὲρ τοῦ τεμένους: The phases of the capture of Jerusalem are somewhat differently described by Josephus, Ant., XIV, 476 f. Josephus distinguishes between the capture of the outer precincts of the Temple and the Lower City on the one hand, and that of the inner precinct of the Temple and the Upper City on the other.

ἐν τῇ τοῦ Κρόνου καὶ τότε ἡμέρᾳ: Obviously Dio refers here to the Sabbath, on which day he also states that the capture of Jerusalem by Pompey took place (No. 406).

22:5 καὶ τοσοῦτόν γε τῆς θρησκείας αὐτοῖς περιῆν: Josephus relates another fact testifying to the consideration shown by Sosius for Jewish religious observances; the besieged Jews sent an embassy to the Roman general to request him to permit animals to be brought into Jerusalem for sacrifice. Sosius agreed to this in the belief that the Jews would surrender (Ant., XIV, 477).

22:6 τὸν δ' Ἀντίγονον ἐμαστίγωσε σταυρῷ προσδήσας: Cf. the commentary to Strabo, Historica Hypomnemata, apud: Ant., XV, 8–10 (No. 108); Plutarchus, Vita Antonii, 36:4 (No. 266).

23:1 ἐπὶ μὲν δὴ τοῦ τε Κλαυδίου τοῦ τε Νωρβανοῦ τοῦθ' οὕτως ἐγένετο: The consulate of Ap. Claudius and C. Norbanus is dated to 38 B.C.E.; see T. R. S. Broughton, The Magistrates of the Roman Republic, II, New York 1952, p. 390. Thus Dio contradicts Josephus, who states expressly that these events occurred during the consulship of Marcus Agrippa and Caninius Gallus (Ant., XIV, 487), that is in 37 B.C.E. We have to prefer the date of Josephus, which is supported here by the chronology of the sequence of events; see already J. A. van der Chijs, De Herode Magno, Leiden 1855, pp. 35 ff.; Bürcklein, op. cit. (supra, p. 357), pp. 61 ff.; Schürer, I, p. 358, n. 11. For the month of the capture of Jerusalem, see J. Kromayer, Hermes, XXIX (1894), pp. 563 ff.; Otto, p. 33, n. 2. It has recently been suggested that the event took place in 36 B.C.E.; see W.E. Filmer, *JTS* (1966), pp. 285 ff. This was also implied by J.v. Gumbach, *Über den altjüdischen Kalender*, Brussels 1848, pp. 268 ff. Against the latter view, see T.D. Barnes, *JTS*, XIX (1968), pp. 204 ff.; M. Stern, in: *The Jewish People in the First Century*, ed. S. Safrai & M. Stern, I, Assen 1974, pp. 64 ff.

415

Historia Romana, XLIX, 32:4–5 — Boissevain

(4) Ἐπὶ δὲ δὴ τῇ Κλεοπάτρᾳ μεγάλως διεβλήθη ⟨scil. *Ἀντώνιος*⟩, *ὅτι τε παῖδας ἐξ αὐτῆς, πρεσβυτέρους μὲν Ἀλέξανδρον καὶ Κλεοπάτραν (καὶ δίδυμοι γὰρ ἐτέχθησαν) νεώτερον δὲ Πτολεμαῖον τὸν καὶ Φιλάδελφον ἐπικληθέντα, ἀνείλετο, (5) καὶ ὅτι πολλὰ μὲν τῆς Ἀραβίας τῆς τε Μάλχου*
5 *καὶ τῆς τῶν Ἰτυραίων (τὸν γὰρ Λυσανίαν, ὃν αὐτὸς βασιλέα σφῶν ἐπεποιήκει, ἀπέκτεινεν ὡς τὰ τοῦ Πακόρου πράξαντα), πολλὰ δὲ καὶ τῆς Φοινίκης τῆς τε Παλαιστίνης, Κρήτης τέ τινα καὶ Κυρήνην τήν τε Κύπρον αὐτοῖς ἐχαρίσατο.*

(4) But in the matter of Cleopatra he [scil. Antonius] was greatly censured because he had acknowledged as his own some of her children — the elder ones being Alexandra and Cleopatra, twins at a birth, and the younger one Ptolemy, called also Philadelphus — (5) and because he had presented them with extensive portions of Arabia, in the districts both of Malchus and of the Ituraeans (for he executed Lysanias, whom he himself had made king over them, on the charge that he had favoured Pacorus), and also extensive portions of Phoenicia and Palestine, parts of Crete, and Cyrene and Cyprus as well. (trans. E. Cary, *LCL*)

5 *πολλὰ δὲ καὶ τῆς Φοινίκης τῆς τε Παλαιστίνης ... ἐχαρίσατο*: Cf. Plutarchus, *Vita Antonii*, 36 (No. 266).

416

Historia Romana, LIV, 9:3 — Boissevain = F105R

Τῷ τε Ἡρώδῃ Ζηνοδώρου τινὸς τετραρχίαν, καὶ Μιθριδάτῃ τινὶ τὴν Κομμαγηνήν, ἐπειδὴ τὸν πατέρα αὐτοῦ ὁ βασιλεὺς αὐτῆς ἀπεκτόνει, καίτοι παιδίσκῳ ἔτ' ὄντι ἐπέτρεψε ⟨scil. *Αὔγουστος*⟩.

To Herod he [scil. Augustus] entrusted the tetrarchy of a certain Zenodorus, and to one Mithridates, though still a mere boy, he gave Commagene; inasmuch as its king had put the boy's father to death.   (trans. E. Cary, *LCL*)

τῷ τε Ἡρώδῃ Ζηνοδώρου τινὸς τετραρχίαν: The bestowal of the tetrarchy of Zenodorus upon Herod is related by Cassius Dio among the various arrangements made by Augustus in 20 B.C.E. In 23 B.C.E. the kingdom of Herod was enlarged in the north-east; cf. *Ant.*, XV, 343; *BJ*, I, 398. The territory then ceded to Herod consisted of Trachonitis, Batanaea and Auranitis. It seems that these territories had also belonged wholly or in part to Zenodorus, whose policy caused Herod's territorial aggrandizement. According to Josephus, Zenodorus, who had leased the domain of Lysanias, increased his revenues by maintaining robber bands in Trachonitis. The main sufferers were the inhabitants of Damascus. When this became known to Augustus he ordered the annexation of Trachonitis to Herod's kingdom. Herod put down the brigandage in Trachonitis, though Zenodorus continued to cause trouble by stirring up the Arabs and instigating the citizens of Gadara to lodge accusations against Herod before Augustus. After the death of Zenodorus, Augustus bestowed the remainder of his territory upon Herod in 20 B.C.E. This territory lay between Trachonitis and Galilaea and contained Ulatha, Panias and the surrounding country; cf. Josephus, *Ant.*, XV, 360; *BJ*, I, 400. See Schürer, I, pp. 714 f.; Otto, p. 73; Schürer, ed. Vermes & Millar, I, pp. 565 f.; see also Kahrstedt, p. 89; Alt, II, p. 391.

417

Historia Romana, LV, 23:2–4 — Boissevain

(2) Τρία δὲ δὴ τότε καὶ εἴκοσι στρατόπεδα, ἢ ὥς γε ἕτεροι λέγουσι πέντε καὶ εἴκοσι, πολιτικὰ ἐτρέφετο. νῦν μὲν γὰρ ἐννεακαίδεκα ἐξ αὐτῶν μόνα διαμένει, τό τε δεύτερον τὸ Αὐγούστειον τὸ ἐν Βρεττανίᾳ τῇ ἄνω χειμάζον, καὶ τὰ τρία τὰ τρίτα, τό τε ἐν Φοινίκῃ τὸ Γαλατικόν,
5 καὶ τὸ ἐν Ἀραβίᾳ τὸ Κυρηναϊκόν, τό τε ἐν Νουμιδίᾳ τὸ Αὐγούστειον· (3) τέταρτον Σκυθικὸν ἐν Συρίᾳ, πέμπτον Μακεδονικὸν ἐν Δακίᾳ, ἕκτα δύο, ὧν τὸ μὲν ἐν Βρεττανίᾳ τῇ κάτω, τὸ τῶν νικητόρων, τὸ δὲ ἐν Ἰουδαίᾳ, τὸ σιδηροῦν, τέτακται· καὶ οἱ ἕβδομοι οἱ ἐν τῇ Μυσίᾳ τῇ ἄνω, οἵ καὶ τὰ μάλιστα Κλαυδίειοι ὠνομάδαται, οἵ τε ὄγδοοι Αὐγούστειοι,
10 ἐν τῇ Γερμανίᾳ τῇ ἄνω ὄντες· (4) καὶ οἱ δέκατοι ἑκάτεροι, οἵ τε ἐν Παννονίᾳ τῇ ἄνω οἱ δίδυμοι, καὶ οἱ ἐν Ἰουδαίᾳ ...

10 δέκατοι ἑκάτεροι Reimarus   δεκάτεροι M   δέκατοι Xiphilinus

(2) Twenty-three, or, as others say, twenty-five, legions of citizen

soldiers were being supported at this time. At present only nineteen of them still exist, as follows: the Second (Augusta), with its winter quarters in Upper Britain; the three Thirds — the Gallica in Phoenicia, the Cyrenaica in Arabia, and the Augusta in Numidia; (3) the Fourth (Scythica) in Syria; the Fifth (Macedonica) in Dacia; the two Sixths, of which the one (Victrix) is stationed in Lower Britain, the other (Ferrata) in Judaea; the Seventh (generally called Claudia) in Upper Moesia; the Eighth (Augusta) in Upper Germany; (4) the two Tenths in Upper Pannonia (Gemina) and in Judaea...

(trans. E. Cary, *LCL*)

3 τὸ δὲ ἐν 'Ιουδαίᾳ, τὸ σιδηροῦν: The Sixth Legion Ferrata constituted part of the garrison of Judaea from the time of Hadrian, though precisely when the transfer to Judaea occurred is a matter of dispute; cf. below, pp. 396 f. It was stationed at Kafar Cotni, south of Megiddo; cf. Ptolemaeus, *Geographia*, V, 15 : 3 (ed. Müller) (No. 337a); see *Mishna Gittin*, i : 5; E. Ritterling, *Rhein. Museum*, NS, LVIII (1903), pp. 633 ff.; idem, PW, XII, pp. 1587 ff.; R. K. McElderry, *CQ*, II (1908), pp. 110 ff. For inscriptions relating to this legion, see M. Avi-Yonah, PW, Suppl. XIII, pp. 400, 419 f.
4 οἱ δέκατοι ... οἱ ἐν 'Ιουδαίᾳ: The Tenth Legion Fretensis took part in the siege of Jerusalem by Titus, and after the capture of the city constituted the garrison of Judaea (*BJ*, VII, 5, 17). On this legion, see T. R. S. Broughton, in: Foakes Jackson & Kirsopp Lake (eds), *The Beginnings of Christianity*, V, London 1933, p. 434; Ritterling, PW, XII, pp. 1671 ff. At a later period the legion was transferred to Eilath; cf. Eusebius, *Onomasticon* (ed. Klostermann), p. 6, ll. 17 ff. Dio's statement refutes the view that the transfer had already taken place in the time of Septimius Severus. See also R. E. Brünnow & A. v. Domaszewski, *Die Provincia Arabia*, III, Strasbourg 1909, pp. 275 f. For a possible mention of the Tenth Legion in Judaea in 171 C.E., see P. Benoit, J. T. Milik & R. de Vaux, *Discoveries in the Judaean Desert*, II, Oxford 1961, No. 114.

418

Historia Romana, LV, 27 : 6 — Boissevain = F106R

"Ο τε 'Ηρώδης ὁ Παλαιστῖνος, αἰτίαν τινὰ ἀπὸ τῶν ἀδελφῶν λαβών, ὑπὲρ τὰς "Αλπεις ὑπερωρίσθη, καὶ τὸ μέρος τῆς ἀρχῆς αὐτοῦ ἐδημοσιώθη.

1 ἀπὸ] ὑπὸ Sturzius

Herod of Palestine, who was accused by his brothers of some wrongdoing or other, was banished beyond the Alps and his portion of the domain was confiscated to the state.   (trans. E. Cary, *LCL*)

Ἡρώδης ὁ Παλαιστῖνος ... ἐδημοσιώθη: Herod Archelaus, the son of Herod, is meant. Archelaus ruled over Judaea, Samaria and Idumaea from 4 B.C.E. to 6 C.E. Josephus never calls Archelaus by the name of Herod, but the coins confirm Dio's statement with the reading: Ἡρώδου ἐθνάρχου; see F. W. Madden, *Coins of the Jews*, London 1881, pp. 114 ff.; Schürer, I, p. 450, n. 4. On the banishment of Archelaus, cf. *Ant.*, XVII, pp. 342 ff.; *BJ*, II, 111. According to Josephus, Archelaus was accused by the Jews and Samaritans before Augustus and banished to Vienna in Gaul. Josephus does not refer to any accusation of Archelaus by his brothers in connection with the events of 6 C.E. The tension between Archelaus and his brother Herod Antipas, in company with other relations of Archelaus represented by his cousin Antipater, is related by Josephus in connection with the events of 4 B.C.E. Cf. also Nicolaus of Damascus, apud: Constantinus Porphyrogenitus, *Excerpta de Insidiis* (No. 97). Possibly strained relations continued in the family of Herod and these influenced the attitude of Augustus towards Archelaus.

For a suggested connection with the events related in Strabo, *Geographica*, XVI, 2:46, p. 765 (No. 115), see Otto, pp. 178 f. Otto thinks that Herod Antipas and Philip were called to Rome at the same time as Archelaus and that they thus had an opportunity to blame Archelaus; cf. the commentary to Strabo, *loc. cit.*

Dio dates the banishment of Archelaus to the consulate of Lepidus and Arruntius, that is to 6 C.E. This dating is in agreement with that of Josephus in *Ant.*, XVII, 342 (the tenth year of Archelaus' rule). Josephus dates it to the ninth year of Archelaus in *BJ*, II, 111.

419

Historia Romana, LVII, 18:5a — Boissevain

Τῶν τε Ἰουδαίων πολλῶν ἐς τὴν Ῥώμην συνελθόντων καὶ συχνοὺς τῶν ἐπιχωρίων ἐς τὰ σφέτερα ἔθη μεθιστάντων, τοὺς πλείονας ἐξήλασεν ⟨scil. Τιβέριος⟩.

As the Jews flocked to Rome in great numbers and were converting many of the natives to their ways, he [scil. Tiberius] banished most of them.

(trans. E. Cary, *LCL*)

τῶν τε Ἰουδαίων ... ἐξήλασεν: Cf. Tacitus, *Annales*, II, 85 (No. 284). Cassius Dio connects the expulsion of the Jews from Rome with their proselytizing activities. This is not referred to by Tacitus. The narrative of Josephus concerning the deception practised on the Roman lady Fulvia, who became a proselyte, agrees with Dio's account; cf. *Ant.*, XVIII, 81 ff.

420

Historia Romana, LIX, 8:2 — Boissevain

Ὁ γὰρ ⟨scil. Γάιος⟩ Ἀντιόχῳ τε τῷ Ἀντιόχου τὴν Κομμαγηνήν, ἣν ὁ πατὴρ αὐτοῦ ἔσχε, καὶ προσέτι καὶ τὰ παραθαλάσσια τῆς Κιλικίας δούς, καὶ Ἀγρίππαν τὸν τοῦ Ἡρώδου ἔγγονον λύσας τε (ὑπὸ γὰρ τοῦ Τιβερίου ἐδέδετο) καὶ τῇ τοῦ πάππου ἀρχῇ προστάξας, τὸν ἀδελφὸν ἢ καὶ τὸν υἱὸν 5 οὐχ ὅτι τῶν πατρῴων ἀπεστέρησεν, ἀλλὰ καὶ κατέσφαξε.

Thus it came about that the same ruler [scil. Gaius] who had given Antiochus, the son of Antiochus, the district of Commagene, which his father had held, and likewise the coast region of Cilicia, and had freed Agrippa, the grandson of Herod, who had been imprisoned by Tiberius, and had put him in charge of his grandfather's domain, not only deprived his own brother, or, in fact, his son, of his paternal inheritance, but actually caused him to be murdered.

(trans. E. Cary, *LCL*)

καὶ Ἀγρίππαν ... λύσας: Agrippa I was the grandson of Herod by his wife Mariamme the Hasmonaean, being the son of Aristobulus. For Agrippa's release from prison, cf. *Ant.,* XVIII, 236 f.; *BJ,* II, 181.

ὑπὸ γὰρ τοῦ Τιβερίου ἐδέδετο: On the imprisonment of Agrippa by Tiberius, cf. *Ant.,* XVIII, 168 ff.; *BJ,* II, 179 f. The reason for his imprisonment was a conversation between Caligula and Agrippa in which the latter expressed his wish for the death of Tiberius and the accession of Caligula. The conversation was overheard by a freedman of Agrippa who reported it to Tiberius.

καὶ τῇ τοῦ πάππου ἀρχῇ προστάξας: In fact in 37 C.E. Caligula made over to Agrippa the tetrarchy of his late uncle Philip; in 39 C.E. he added to it the tetrarchy of Herod Antipas, namely Galilee and Peraea. Agrippa's kingdom became approximately coextensive with that of his grandfather only after the death of Caligula in 41 C.E. For the life and reign of Agrippa I, see Schürer, I, pp. 549 ff.; Rosenberg, PW, X, pp. 143 ff.; E. Ciaceri, *Processi politici e relazioni internazionali,* Rome 1918, pp. 319 ff.; M.P. Charlesworth, *Five Men,* Cambridge (Mass.) 1936, pp. 1 ff.; Schürer, ed. Vermes & Millar, I, pp. 442 ff.; Stern, *op. cit.* (supra, p. 362), pp. 288 ff.

421

Historia Romana, LIX, 24:1 — Boissevain

Οὐ μέντοι ταῦθ' οὕτως αὐτοὺς ἐλύπει ὡς τὸ προσδοκᾶν ἐπὶ πλεῖον τήν τε ὠμότητα τὴν τοῦ Γαίου καὶ τὴν ἀσέλγειαν αὐξήσειν, καὶ μάλισθ' ὅτι ἐπυνθάνοντο τόν τε Ἀγρίππαν αὐτῷ καὶ τὸν Ἀντίοχον τοὺς βασιλέας ὥσπερ τινὰς τυραννοδιδασκάλους συνεῖναι.

All this, however, did not distress the people so much as did their expectation that Gaius' cruelty and licentiousness would go to still greater lengths. And they were particularly troubled on ascertaining that King Agrippa and King Antiochus were with him, like two tyrant-trainers. (trans. E. Cary, *LCL*)

Ἀγρίππαν αὐτῷ καὶ τὸν Ἀντίοχον: As known from Josephus, Agrippa had been a close friend of Caligula before the death of Tiberius and continued so during the reign of his friend. Something of the influence he had over Caligula may be learned from Agrippa's intervention on behalf of his compatriots over placing the statue of Caligula in the Temple of Jerusalem; cf. *Ant.*, XVIII, 289: προὔκοπτε φιλίᾳ τῇ πρὸς τὸν Γάιον μειζόνως. Antiochus king of Commagene also seems to have maintained good relations with Agrippa; cf. *Ant.*, XIX, 338, 355.

422

Historia Romana, LX, 6:6 — Boissevain = F107R

Τούς τε Ἰουδαίους πλεονάσαντας αὖθις, ὥστε χαλεπῶς ἂν ἄνευ ταραχῆς ὑπὸ τοῦ ὄχλου σφῶν τῆς πόλεως εἰρχθῆναι, οὐκ ἐξήλασε ⟨scil. Κλαύδιος⟩ μέν, τῷ δὲ δὴ πατρίῳ βίῳ χρωμένους ἐκέλευσε μὴ συναθροίζεσθαι.

As for the Jews, who had again increased so greatly that by reason of their multitude it would have been hard without raising a tumult to bar them from the city, he [scil. Claudius] did not drive them out, but ordered them, while continuing their traditional mode of life, not to hold meetings. (trans. E. Cary, *LCL*)

Τούς τε Ἰουδαίους πλεονάσαντας: Cf. the commentary to Suetonius, *Divus Claudius*, 25:4 (No. 307).

423

Historia Romana, LX, 8:2-3 — Boissevain = F107R

(2) Ἄλλῳ τέ τινι Μιθριδάτῃ, τὸ γένος ἀπ᾽ ἐκείνου τοῦ πάνυ ἔχοντι, τὸν Βόσπορον ἐχαρίσατο, καὶ τῷ Πολέμωνι χώραν τινὰ ἀντ᾽ αὐτοῦ Κιλικίας ἀντέδωκε. τῷ γὰρ Ἀγρίππᾳ τῷ Παλαιστίνῳ συμπράξαντί οἱ τὴν ἡγεμονίαν (ἔτυχε γὰρ ἐν τῇ Ῥώμῃ ὤν) τήν τε ἀρχὴν προσεπηύξησε καὶ τιμὰς ὑπατικὰς ἔνειμε. (3) τῷ τε ἀδελφῷ αὐτοῦ Ἡρώδῃ τό τε στρατηγικὸν

ἀξίωμα καὶ δυναστείαν τινὰ ἔδωκε, καὶ ἔς τε τὸ συνέδριον ἐσελθεῖν σφισι καὶ χάριν οἱ ἑλληνιστὶ γνῶναι ἐπέτρεψεν.

(2) To another Mithridates, a lineal descendant of Mithridates the Great, he granted Bosporus, giving to Polemon some land in Cilicia in place of it. He enlarged the domain of Agrippa of Palestine, who, happening to be in Rome, had helped him to become emperor, and bestowed on him the rank of consul; (3) and to his brother Herod he gave the rank of praetor and a principality. And he permitted them to enter the senate and to express their thanks to him in Greek.

(trans. E. Cary, *LCL*)

2 συμπράξαντί οἱ τὴν ἡγεμονίαν: Cf. *Ant.*, XIX, 236 ff.
τήν τε ἀρχὴν προσεπηύξησε: The enlargement of Agrippa's kingdom consisted mainly of the annexation of Samaria and Judaea proper; cf. *Ant.*, XIX, 274 f.; *BJ*, II, 215.
καὶ τιμὰς ὑπατικὰς ἔνειμε: Agrippa had already received *ornamenta praetoria* from Caligula; cf. Philo, *In Flaccum*, 40. Both Agrippa and his brother, who now also received the *ornamenta praetoria*, were Roman citizens, since Antipater, the father of Herod, had obtained Roman citizenship from Julius Caesar. See T. Mommsen, *Das römische Staatsrecht*, I³, Leipzig 1887, p. 464, n. 4.
3 τῷ τε ἀδελφῷ αὐτοῦ Ἡρώδῃ: The younger brother of Agrippa, known as Herod of Chalcis. He ruled over Chalcis until 48 C.E.; cf. *Ant.*, XIX, 277; *BJ*, II, 217.

424
Historia Romana, LXII, 20:2–3, 23:4 — Boissevain

(20:2) "Ὅτι ὁ Οὐλόγαισος ἀκούσας ὡς τὴν Ἀρμενίαν ὁ Νέρων ἄλλοις διένειμε καὶ τὴν Ἀδιαβηνὴν ὑπὸ τοῦ Τιγράνου πορθουμένην, αὐτὸς μὲν ὡς ἐς τὴν Συρίαν ἐπὶ τὸν Κορβούλωνα στρατεύσων ἡτοιμάζετο, τὸν δὲ τῶν Ἀδιαβηνῶν βασιλέα Μονόβαζον καὶ Μοναίσην Πάρθον ἐς τὴν Ἀρμενίαν
5 ἔπεμψεν. (3) οὗτοι δὲ τὸν Τιγράνην ἐς τὰ Τιγρανόκερτα καθεῖρξαν. καὶ ἐπεὶ ἐν τῇ προσεδρείᾳ οὐδὲν αὐτὸν ἐλύπουν, ἀλλὰ καὶ ὁσάκις προσμίξειάν οἱ ἀπεκρούοντο καὶ ὑπ᾽ ἐκείνου καὶ ὑπὸ τῶν Ῥωμαίων τῶν συνόντων αὐτῷ καὶ ὁ Κορβούλων ἀκριβῆ φρουρὰν τῆς Συρίας ἐποιήσατο, ἐγνωσιμάχησε καὶ τὴν παρασκευὴν ἀφῆκε ... (23:4) καὶ ὁ Μονόβαζος καὶ ὁ Οὐολόγαισος
10 πρὸς τὸν Κορβούλωνα ἦλθον καὶ ὁμήρους αὐτῷ ἔδωκαν·

(20:2) Vologaesus, on hearing that Nero had assigned Armenia to others and that Adiabene was being ravaged by Tigranes, made preparations to take the field himself against Corbulo in Syria, and sent into Armenia Monobazus, king of Adiabene, and Monaeses, a Parthian. (3) These two shut up Tigranes in Tigranocerta. But since they found that they could not harm him at all by their siege, but on the contrary, as often as they tried conclusions with him, were repulsed by both the native troops and the Romans that were in his army, and since Corbulo guarded Syria with extreme care, Vologaesus swallowed his pride and abandoned the expedition ... (23:4) Monobazus and Vologaesus also came to Corbulo and gave him hostages. (trans. E. Cary, *LCL*)

20:2 καὶ τὴν 'Αδιαβηνὴν ὑπὸ τοῦ Τιγράνου πορθουμένην: For the events, cf. Tacitus, *Annales*, XII, 13:1 (No. 286); on the Judaization of Adiabene, see the commentary *ad loc.*
23:4 καὶ ὁ Μονόβαζος καὶ ὁ Οὐολόγαισος πρὸς τὸν Κορβούλωνα ἦλθον: Like Tacitus, Dio does not refer to the Jewishness of the Adiabene dynasty.

425

Historia Romana, LXIII, 1:2, apud: Xiphilinus — Boissevain

Καὶ ὁ Τιριδάτης ἐς τὴν 'Ρώμην, οὐχ ὅτι τοὺς ἑαυτοῦ παῖδας, ἀλλὰ καὶ τοὺς τοῦ Οὐολογαίσου τοῦ τε Πακόρου καὶ τοῦ Μονοβάζου ἄγων, ἀνήχθη.

On the other hand, Tiridates presented himself in Rome, bringing with him not only his own sons but also those of Vologaesus, of Pacorus, and of Monobazus. (trans. E. Cary, *LCL*)

καὶ ὁ Τιριδάτης ἐς τὴν 'Ρώμην ... καὶ τοῦ Μονοβάζου ἄγων: This event belongs to 66 B.C.E.

426

Historia Romana, LXIII, 22:1a, apud: Zonaras — Boissevain

Ἔτι δ' ἐν τῇ Ἑλλάδι ὄντος τοῦ Νέρωνος 'Ιουδαῖοι εἰς πρoῦπτον ἀπέστησαν, καὶ ἐπ' αὐτοὺς τὸν Οὐεσπασιανὸν ἔπεμψε·

While Nero was still in Greece, the Jews revolted openly, and he sent Vespasian against them. (trans. E. Cary, *LCL*)

427a

Historia Romana, LXV, 8:1, 3, apud: Zonaras — Boissevain

(1) Ἐπὶ τούτοις ἠγγέλθη αὐτῷ ⟨scil. Οὐιτελλίῳ⟩ ἡ ἐν Ἰουδαίᾳ κατ' αὐτοῦ ἐπανάστασις. καὶ δεινῶς κατέδεισε δί αὐτὴν ... (3) Οὐεσπασιανὸς ἐν Ἰουδαίᾳ διατρίβων (ὡς γὰρ ἤδη ἱστόρηται, παρὰ Νέρωνος ἦν ἐκεῖσε σταλεὶς διὰ τὴν τῶν Ἰουδαίων ἀποστασίαν) τῷ μὲν Γάλβᾳ αὐταρχήσαντι
5 *τὸν υἱὸν ἔπεμψε Τίτον προσεροῦντα αὐτόν.*

(1) At this juncture the uprising against him in Judaea was reported to him [scil. to Vitellius]. And he was in great fear because of it ... (3) Vespasian, who was tarrying in Judaea (for as has already been related he had been sent thither on account of the revolt of the Jews), had sent his son to carry his greetings to Galba when the latter became emperor. (trans. E. Cary, *LCL*)

427b

Historia Romana, ibid., apud: Xiphilinus — Boissevain = F108R

Ἐπράχθη δὲ ταῦτα, καὶ ὁ Οὐεσπασιανὸς Ἰουδαίοις πολεμῶν, πυθόμενος τήν τε τοῦ Οὐιτελλίου καὶ τὴν τοῦ Ὄθωνος ἐπανάστασιν, ἐβουλεύετο ὅ τι χρὴ πρᾶξαι.

At the same time that this happened Vespasian, who was engaged in warfare with the Jews, learned of the rebellion of Vitellius and of Otho, and was deliberating what he should do. (trans. E. Cary, *LCL*)

428

Historia Romana, LXV, 9:2 — Boissevain = F108R

Τηνικαῦτα δὲ τὸν μὲν Μουκιανὸν ἐς τὴν Ἰταλίαν ἐπὶ τὸν Οὐιτέλλιον ἔπεμψεν ⟨scil. Οὐεσπασιανός⟩, αὐτὸς δὲ τά τε ἐν τῇ Συρίᾳ ἐπιδὼν καὶ τὸν πόλεμον τὸν πρὸς Ἰουδαίους ἄλλοις τισὶ προστάξας ἐς τὴν Αἴγυπτον ἐκομίσθη καὶ συνέλεγε χρήματα, ὧν που καὶ τὰ μάλιστα ἔχρῃζε, καὶ
5 *σῖτον, ἵν' ὅτι πλεῖστον ἐς τὴν Ῥώμην ἀποστείλῃ.*

For the time being he [scil. Vespasian] sent Mucianus to Italy against Vitellius, while he himself, after looking at affairs in Syria and entrusting to others the conduct of the war against the Jews, proceeded to Egypt, where he collected money, of which naturally he was greatly in need, and grain, which he desired to send in as large quantities as possible to Rome.　　　　　　(trans. E. Cary, *LCL*)

429

Historia Romana, LXVI, 1:1–4, apud: Xiphilinus — Boissevain = F108R

(1) Τήν τε ὕπατον ἀρχὴν ὁ Οὐεσπασιανὸς καὶ ὁ Τίτος ἔλαβον, ὁ μὲν ἐν τῇ Αἰγύπτῳ ὁ δὲ ἐν τῇ Παλαιστίνῃ ὤν. (2) Ἐγεγόνει μὲν οὖν καὶ σημεῖα καὶ ὀνείρατα τῷ Οὐεσπασιανῷ τὴν μοναρχίαν ἐκ πολλοῦ προδηλοῦντα ... (3) καὶ αὐτὸς ὁ Νέρων ἔδοξέ ποτε ἐν τοῖς ὕπνοις τὸν τοῦ Διὸς ὄχον ἐς τὴν τοῦ Οὐεσπασιανοῦ οἰκίαν ἐσαγαγεῖν. (4) ἀλλὰ ταῦτα μὲν ἑρμηνεύσεως ἔχρῃζεν, Ἰώσηπος δὲ ἀνὴρ Ἰουδαῖος ἀχθείς τε ὑπ' αὐτοῦ πρότερον καὶ δεθεὶς ἐγέλασε καὶ ἔφη· «νῦν μέν με δήσεις, μετ' ἐνιαυτὸν δὲ λύσεις αὐτοκράτωρ γενόμενος.»

(1) The consular office was assumed by Vespasian and Titus while the former was in Egypt and the latter in Palestine. (2) Now portents and dreams had come to Vespasian pointing to the sovereignty long beforehand ... (3) and Nero himself in his dreams once thought that he had brought the car of Jupiter to Vespasian's house. (4) These portents needed interpretation; but not so the saying of a Jew named Josephus; he, having earlier been captured by Vespasian and imprisoned, laughed and said: "You may imprison me now, but a year from now, when you have become emperor, you will release me."　　　　　　(trans. E. Cary, *LCL*)

4 *Ἰώσηπος δὲ ἀνὴρ Ἰουδαῖος*: Cf. Suetonius, *Divus Vespasianus*, 5:6 (No. 313). For the view that both Cassius Dio and Suetonius made use of the same source, see Weber, pp. 45 f.

430

Historia Romana, LXVI, 4–7 — Boissevain = F109R

(4:1) Ὁ δὲ Τίτος τῷ πρὸς Ἰουδαίους πολέμῳ ἐπιταχθεὶς ἐπεχείρησε μὲν αὐτοὺς λόγοις τισὶ καὶ ἐπαγγελίαις προσποιήσασθαι, μὴ πεισθεῖσι δὲ ἐπολέμει. καὶ μάχαις ⟨ταῖς⟩ μὲν πρώταις ἀγχώμαλα ἀγωνισάμενος, εἶτα

1 πρὸς Ἰουδαίους] τῶν Ἰουδαίων Uᵍ / προσταχθεὶς Uᵍ　　　3 ⟨ταῖς⟩ Reiske

κρατήσας ἐπολιόρκει τὰ Ἱεροσόλυμα. ἦν δὲ τρία αὐτοῖς σὺν τῷ τοῦ νεὼ
5 περιβόλῳ τείχη. (2) οἵ τε οὖν Ῥωμαῖοι χώματά τε πρὸς τὸ τεῖχος
ἐχώννυσαν καὶ μηχανήματα προσῆγον, τούς τε ἐπεκθέοντας ὁμόσε ἰόντες
ἀνέστελλον, καὶ τοὺς ἐπὶ τοῦ τείχους ἐπόντας σφενδόναις καὶ τοξεύμασιν
ἀνεῖργον· συχνοὺς γὰρ καὶ παρὰ βαρβάρων τινῶν βασιλέων πεμφθέντας
εἶχον· (3) καὶ οἱ Ἰουδαῖοι πολλοὶ μὲν αὐτόθεν πολλοὶ δὲ καὶ παρὰ τῶν
10 ὁμοήθων, οὐχ ὅτι ἐκ τῆς τῶν Ῥωμαίων ἀρχῆς ἀλλὰ καὶ ἐκ τῶν πέραν
Εὐφράτου, προσβεβοηθηκότες βέλη τε καὶ αὐτοὶ καὶ λίθους, τοὺς μὲν ἐκ
χειρὸς τοὺς δὲ καὶ μηχαναῖς, (4) σφοδρότερον ἅτε καὶ ἀφ' ὑψηλοῦ,
ἔπεμπον, καὶ ἐπεξιόντες, ᾗ καιρὸς ἦν, νυκτός τε καὶ ἡμέρας τὰς μηχανὰς
ἐνεπίμπρασαν, συχνοὺς ἀπεκτίννυσαν, τόν τε χοῦν ὑπορύσσοντες ὑπὸ
15 τὸ τεῖχος ὑφεῖλκον, καὶ τοὺς κριοὺς τοὺς μὲν βρόχοις ἀνέκλων τοὺς
δὲ ἁρπάγαις ἀνέσπων· ἑτέρων τὰς προσβολὰς σανίσι παχείαις
συμπεπηγμέναις τε καὶ σεσιδηρωμέναις, ἃς πρὸ τοῦ τείχους καθίεσαν,
ἀπέστρεφον. (5) τὸ δὲ δὴ πλεῖστον οἱ Ῥωμαῖοι τῇ ἀνυδρίᾳ ἐκακοπάθουν,
καὶ φαῦλον καὶ πόρρωθεν ὕδωρ ἐπαγόμενοι. οἱ δὲ Ἰουδαῖοι διὰ τῶν
20 ὑπονόμων ἴσχυον· ὀρωρυγμένους τε γὰρ αὐτοὺς ἔνδοθεν ὑπὸ τὰ τείχη
μέχρι πόρρω τῆς χώρας εἶχον, καὶ δι' αὐτῶν διεξιόντες τοῖς τε ὑδρευομένοις
ἐπετίθεντο καὶ τοὺς ἀποσκεδαννυμένους ἐλυμαίνοντο· οὕς ὁ Τίτος πάντας
ἀπέφραξε. (5:1) κἀν τοῖς ἔργοις τούτοις πολλοὶ ἐτιτρώσκοντο ἑκατέρων
καὶ ἔθνησκον, καὶ ὁ Τίτος αὐτὸς λίθῳ τὸν ἀριστερὸν ὦμον ἐπλήγη, καὶ ἀπ'
25 αὐτοῦ τὴν χεῖρα ἀσθενεστέραν εἶχεν· (2) χρόνῳ δ' οὖν ποτε τοῦ ἔξω
περιβόλου οἱ Ῥωμαῖοι ἐπέβησαν, ἐν μέσῳ δὲ τῶν δύο περιβόλων
στρατοπεδευσάμενοι πρὸς τὸ ἕτερον τεῖχος προσέβαλλον. οὐ μέντοι καὶ
ὁμοία ἡ πρόσμιξίς σφισιν ἐγίγνετο· ἀναχωρήσαντες γὰρ ἐς ἐκεῖνο πάντες
ῥᾷον, ἅτε καὶ ἐκ βραχυτέρας τῆς τοῦ κύκλου περιβολῆς, ἠμύνοντο. (3) ὁ οὖν
30 Τίτος κήρυγμα αὖθις, ἄδειαν αὐτοῖς διδούς, ἐποιήσατο. ἐκεῖνοί τε οὖν καὶ
ὣς ἐκαρτέρουν, καὶ οἱ ἁλισκόμενοι οἵ τε αὐτομολοῦντές σφων τὸ ὕδωρ τῶν
Ῥωμαίων λανθανόντως ἔφθειρον, καὶ τῶν ἀνθρώπων οὕς που μόνους
ἀπολάβοιεν ἔσφαζον. ὁ δὲ Τίτος οὐκέτ' οὐδένα αὐτῶν ἐδέχετο. (4) κἀν
τούτῳ καὶ τῶν Ῥωμαίων τινὲς ἀδημονήσαντες οἷα ἐν χρονίῳ πολιορκίᾳ,
35 καὶ προσυποτοπήσαντες ὅπερ ἐθρυλεῖτο, ἀπόρθητον ὄντως τὴν πόλιν
εἶναι, μετέστησαν· καὶ αὐτοὺς ἐκεῖνοι, καίπερ σπανίζοντες τῆς τροφῆς,
περιεῖπον ἐς ἐπίδειξιν τοῦ καὶ αὐτοὶ αὐτομόλους ἔχειν. (6:1) διακοπέντος
δὲ τοῦ τείχους μηχαναῖς κατὰ μὲν τοῦτο οὐδ' ὣς ἑάλωσαν, ἀλλὰ καὶ πάνυ
πολλοὺς ἐσβιαζομένους ἀπέκτειναν· ἐμπρήσαντες δέ τινα τῶν ἐγγὺς
40 οἰκοδομημάτων ὡς καὶ ἐκ τούτου τοὺς Ῥωμαίους περαιτέρω, κἂν τοῦ
κύκλου κρατήσωσι, προελθεῖν κωλύσοντες, τό τε τεῖχος ἐλυμήναντο καὶ
τὸν περίβολον τὸν περὶ τὸ τεμένισμα ἄκοντες συγκατέφλεξαν, καὶ

14 συχνούς τ' (?) Boissevain

ἀνεῴχθη ἡ ἔσοδος ἡ ἐπὶ τὸν νεὼν τοῖς Ῥωμαίοις. (2) οὐ μὴν καὶ
παραχρῆμα διὰ τὸ δεισιδαιμονῆσαι ἐσέδραμον, ἀλλ' ὀψέ ποτε, τοῦ Τίτου
σφᾶς καταναγκάσαντος, εἴσω προεχώρησαν. καὶ αὐτοὺς οἱ Ἰουδαῖοι πολὺ
προθυμότερον, ὥσπερ τι ἕρμαιον τὸ πρός τε τῷ ναῷ καὶ ὑπὲρ αὐτοῦ
μαχόμενοι πεσεῖν εὑρηκότες, ἠμύνοντο, ὁ μὲν δῆμος κάτω ἐν τῷ προνάῳ,
οἱ δὲ βουλευταὶ ἐν τοῖς ἀναβασμοῖς, οἵ θ' ἱερῆς ἐν αὐτῷ τῷ μεγάρῳ
τεταγμένοι. (3) καὶ οὐ πρότερόν γε ἐνικήθησαν, καίπερ ὀλίγοι πρὸς πολλῷ
πλείους μαχόμενοι, πρὶν ὑποπρησθῆναί τι τοῦ νεώ· τότε γὰρ ἐθελούσιοι οἱ
μὲν ξίφεσί σφας τοῖς τῶν Ῥωμαίων περιέπειρον, οἱ δὲ ἀλλήλους ἐφόνευον,
ἄλλοι ἑαυτοὺς κατεχρῶντο, οἱ δὲ ἐς τὸ πῦρ ἐσεπήδων. καὶ ἐδόκει πᾶσι μέν,
μάλιστα δὲ ἐκείνοις, οὐχ ὅτι ὄλεθρος, ἀλλὰ καὶ νίκη καὶ σωτηρία
εὐδαιμονία τε εἶναι, ὅτι τῷ ναῷ συναπώλλυντο. (7: 1) ἑάλωσαν δ' οὖν καὶ
ὣς ἄλλοι τε καὶ ὁ Βαργιορᾶς ὁ ἄρχων αὐτῶν· καὶ μόνος γε οὗτος ἐν τοῖς
ἐπινικίοις ἐκολάσθη. (2) οὕτω μὲν τὰ Ἱεροσόλυμα ἐν αὐτῇ τῇ τοῦ Κρόνου
ἡμέρᾳ, ἣν μάλιστα ἔτι καὶ νῦν Ἰουδαῖοι σέβουσιν, ἐξώλετο. καὶ ἀπ'
ἐκείνου δίδραχμον ἐτάχθη τοὺς τὰ πάτρια αὐτῶν ἔθη περιστέλλοντας τῷ
Καπιτωλίῳ Διί, κατ' ἔτος ἀποφέρειν. καὶ ἐπ' αὐτοῖς τὸ μὲν τοῦ
αὐτοκράτορος ὄνομα ἀμφότεροι ἔλαβον, τὸ δὲ δὴ τοῦ Ἰουδαϊκοῦ οὐδέτερος
ἔσχε· καίτοι τά τε ἄλλα αὐτοῖς, ὅσα ἐπὶ τηλικαύτῃ νίκῃ εἰκὸς ἦν, καὶ
ἀψῖδες τροπαιοφόροι ἐψηφίσθησαν.

48 ἱερῆς Boissevain   ἱερεῖς ABM   51 σφας om. BM   54 συναπώλοντο VC
55 Βαργιορᾶς Reimarus   καρπορᾶς V   βαρπορᾶς C   βασπόρης Uᵍ

(4:1) Titus, who had been assigned to the war against the Jews,
undertook to win them over by certain representations and promises;
but, as they would not yield, he now proceeded to wage war upon
them. The first battles he fought were indecisive; then he got the
upper hand and proceeded to besiege Jerusalem. This city had three
walls, including one that surrounded the Temple. (2) The Romans,
accordingly, heaped up mounds against the outer wall, brought up
their engines, joined battle with all who sailed forth to fight, and
repulsed them, and with their slings and arrows kept back all the
defenders of the wall; for they had many slingers and bowmen that
had been sent by some of the barbarian kings. (3) The Jews also were
assisted by many of their countrymen from the region about and by
many who professed the same religion, not only from the Roman
empire but also from beyond the Euphrates; and these, also, kept
hurling missiles and stones with (4) no little force on account of their
higher position, some being flung by the hand and some hurled by
means of engines. They also made sallies both night and day,

whenever occasion offered, set fire to the siege engines, slew many of their assailants, and undermined the Romans' mounds by removing the earth through tunnels driven under the wall. As for the battering rams, sometimes they threw ropes around them and broke them off, sometimes they pulled them up with hooks, and again they used thick planks fastened together and strengthened with iron, which they let down in front of the wall and thus fended off the blows of still others. (5) But the Romans suffered most hardship from the lack of water; for their supply was of poor quality and had to be brought from a distance. The Jews found in their underground passages a source of strength; for they had these tunnels dug from inside the city and extending out under the walls to distant points in the country, and going out through them, they would attack the Romans' water-carriers and harass any scattered detachments. But Titus stopped up all these passages. (5:1) In the course of these operations many on both sides were wounded and killed. Titus himself was struck on the left shoulder by a stone, and as a result of this accident that arm was always weaker. (2) In time, however, the Romans scaled the outside wall, and then, pitching their camp between this and the second circuit, proceeded to assault the latter. But here they found the conditions of fighting different; for now that all the besieged had retired behind the second wall, its defence proved an easier matter because its circuit was shorter. (3) Titus therefore once more made a proclamation offering them immunity. But even then they held out and those of them that were taken captive or deserted kept secretly destroying the Romans' water supply and slaying any troops that they could isolate and cut off from the rest; hence Titus would no longer receive any Jewish deserters. (4) Meanwhile some of the Romans, too, becoming disheartened, as often happens in a protracted siege, and suspecting, furthermore, that the city was really impregnable, as was commonly reported, went over to the other side. The Jews, even though they were short of food, treated these recruits kindly, in order to be able to show that there were deserters to their side also. (6:1) Though a breach was made in the wall by means of engines, nevertheless, the capture of the place did not immediately follow even then. On the contrary, the defenders killed great numbers that tried to crowd through the opening, and they also set fire to some of the buildings near by, hoping thus to check the further progress of the Romans, even though they should gain possession of the wall. In this way they not only damaged the wall but at the same time unintentionally burned down the barrier around the sacred precinct, so that the entrance to the temple was now laid open to the Romans. (2) Nevertheless, the soldiers because of their superstition did not immediately rush in; but at last, under compulsion from Titus, they made their way inside. Then the Jews defended themselves much more vigorously than before, as if they had discovered a piece of rare good fortune in being able to fight near the temple and fall in its defence. The populace was stationed below in the court, the councillors on the steps, and the priests in the sanctuary itself. (3) And though they were but a handful fighting against a far superior force, they were not conquered until a part of the temple was set on fire. Then they met death willingly, some throwing themselves on the swords of the Romans, some slaying one another, others taking their own lives, and still others leaping into the flames. And it seemed to everybody, and especially to them, that so far from being destruction, it was victory and salvation and happiness to them that they perished along with the temple. (7:1) Yet even under these conditions many captives were taken, among them Bargioras, their leader; and he was the only one to be executed in connection with the triumphal celebration. (2) Thus was Jerusalem destroyed on the very day of Saturn, the day which even now the Jews reverence most. From that time forth it was ordered that the Jews who continued to observe their ancestral customs should pay an annual tribute of two *denarii* to Jupiter Capitolinus. In consequence of this success both generals received the title of imperator, but neither got that of Judaicus, although all the other honours that were fitting on the occasion of so magnificent a victory, including triumphal arches, were voted to them.　　　　　　　　　　　　　　　　　　　(trans. E. Cary, *LCL*)

4:1 ὁ δὲ Τίτος ... ἐπιταχθείς: Cf. *BJ*, IV, 658: ... τὸν δὲ υἱὸν Τίτον μετὰ τῆς ἐκκρίτου δυνάμεως ἀπέστειλεν [scil. Οὐεσπασιανός] ἐξαιρήσοντα τὰ Ἱεροσόλυμα.

ἐπεχείρησε μὲν αὐτοὺς λόγοις ... : Josephus does not refer at this stage to any attempt by Titus to win over the besieged, relating such attempts later. In the more condensed narrative of Dio the various stages are somewhat confused.

μάχαις ... ἀγχώμαλα ἀγωνισάμενος: The danger in which Titus found himself as a result of a sudden attack by the Jews is described in *BJ*, V, 54 ff. For the Jewish assault on the Tenth Legion, cf. also, *ibid.*, 75 ff.

ἦν δὲ τρία αὐτοῖς ... τείχη: Cf. *BJ*, V, 136: τρισὶ δ'ὠχυρωμένη τείχεσιν ἡ πόλις. Cf. also the commentary to Tacitus, *Historiae*, V, 8 (No. 281).

4:2 συχνοὺς γὰρ καὶ παρὰ βαρβάρων τινῶν βασιλέων πεμφθέντας εἶχον: For the help sent to Titus by the allied vassal kings, cf. *BJ*, V, 47, 460 ff. (Antiochus of Commagene). See also *BJ*, V, 290.

4:3 καὶ ἐκ τῶν πέραν Εὐφράτου, προσβεβοηθηκότες: A Jewish warrior from Adiabene is referred to in *BJ*, V, 474. This man joined the forces of Simeon Bar Giora. We also read of some members of the royal house of Adiabene who were taken prisoner by Titus and afterwards released; cf. *BJ*, VI, 356 f.: κατὰ ταύτην τὴν ἡμέραν, οἵ τε Ἰζάτου βασιλέως υἱοὶ καὶ ἀδελφοὶ ... ἱκέτευσαν Καίσαρα δοῦναι δεξιὰν αὐτοῖς. These details, supplementing the express statement of Dio, testify to the part played by Jews from beyond the Euphrates in the defence of Jerusalem. On the other hand, cf. the speech put into the mouth of Agrippa II in *BJ*, II, 388 f. Here any hope of help being sent by compatriots in Adiabene is absolutely discounted.

4:4 τὰς μηχανὰς ἐνεπίμπρασαν: For Jewish attempts to burn the Roman engines and earthworks, cf. *BJ*, V, 287, 469 ff.

5:3 Τίτος κήρυγμα ... ἐποιήσατο: Cf. *BJ*, V, 361.

6:2 οἱ δὲ βουλευταί: The βουλευταί are the members of the *synhedrion* of Jerusalem, which fulfilled the functions of the highest religious authority for all Jews and also constituted the city council of Jerusalem. The question whether Jerusalem at that time may be thought to have been a *polis* is still debated. That this was so is maintained by, e.g., Schürer, II, p. 235; H. Dessau, *Geschichte der römischen Kaiserzeit*, Vol. II, Part 2, Berlin 1930, p. 795. This has been denied, however, by V. Tcherikover, *IEJ*, XIV (1964), pp. 61 ff. If by *polis* is understood all the cultural and political implications usually attached to the concept of the classical, and even the Hellenistic, *polis*, Jerusalem did not have this status. It had no *gymnasia* or regular political assemblies characteristic of Greek cities, and its instruments of government were of the traditional Jewish type. The *synhedrion* was the continuation of the old Jewish *gerousia*. At its head stood the high priest, not annually elected *archontes*. On the other hand, Jerusalem's jurisdiction extended to the surrounding territory, the terminology for its political and administrative organs became somewhat hellenized, and it acquired some characteristic features of the eastern Hellenistic cities. Such was the institution of the δέκα πρῶτοι; cf. *Ant.*, XX, 194. In general, see E. G. Turner, *JEA*, XXII (1936), pp. 7 ff.; L. Robert, *Documents de l'Asie mineure méridionale*, Geneva–Paris 1966, pp. 74 ff. Hence the Roman authorities addressed Jerusalem in official documents in a manner similar to that used in addressing the Greek *poleis*; cf. the letter of Claudius to Jerusalem in *Ant.*, XX, 11: Κλαύδιος Καῖσαρ ... Ἱεροσολυμιτῶν ἄρχουσι βουλῇ δήμῳ. Here also the *boulé* is identical with the *synhedrion*, and the same applies to the institution mentioned in *BJ*, II, 331, 336; V, 144, 532; VI, 354: τὸ βουλευτήριον. Its members are called βουλευταί by other writers besides Dio Cassius; cf. *BJ*, II, 405; Mark xv:43: Ἰωσὴφ ὁ ἀπὸ Ἀριμαθαίας εὐσχήμων βουλευτής; Luke xxiii:50. The designation βουλευταί even passed into the vernacular, and occurs in the talmudic and midrashic sources; cf., e.g., *TP Ta'anit*, iv, 69a: בולווטי ירושלים; *TP Yoma*, i, 38c: לשכת בולווטין.

6:3 οἱ δὲ ἐς τὸ πῦρ ἐσεπήδων: Cf. *BJ*, VI, 280: δύο γε μὴν τῶν ἐπισήμων, παρὸν σωθῆναι πρὸς Ῥωμαίους μεταστᾶσιν ἢ διακαρτερεῖν πρὸς τὴν

Cassius Dio

μετὰ τῶν ἄλλων τύχην, ἑαυτοὺς ἔρριψαν εἰς τὸ πῦρ καὶ τῷ ναῷ συγκατεφλέγησαν, Μηῖρός τε υἱὸς Βελγᾶ καὶ Ἰώσηπος Δαλαίου.

7:1 ἑάλωσαν δ' οὖν... καὶ ὁ Βαργιορᾶς: For the personality of Simeon Bar Giora, see the commentary to Tacitus, *Historiae*, V, 12 (No. 281). For his capture by the Romans after the fall of the Upper Town, see *BJ*, VII, 26 ff.

ὁ ἄρχων αὐτῶν: Simeon Bar Giora was not the sole commander of Jerusalem, but commander of the largest number of fighters (*BJ*, V, 248). He had at his disposal ten thousand fighters and also the cooperation of five thousand Idumaeans. His chief rival John of Gischala commanded only upwards of six thousand fighters, apart from the two thousand four hundred so-called Zealots.

μόνος ... ἐκολάσθη: Cf. *BJ*, VII, 154.

7:2 τὰ Ἱεροσόλυμα ἐν αὐτῇ τῇ τοῦ Κρόνου ἡμέρᾳ ... ἐξώλετο: I.e. on the day of Sabbath. A similar tradition occurs in *TB Ta'anit*, 29a, which states that the destruction of the Temple took place on Sabbath (מוצאי שבת); cf. Derenbourg, p. 291, n. 3. As already mentioned above, Dio does not distinguish between the different phases in the fall of Jerusalem. In general, for a comparison between Cassius Dio and Josephus, see I. M. J. Valeton, *Mnemosyne*, NS, XXVII (1899), pp. 90 f., 97 ff., 108 f., 133.

καὶ ἀπ' ἐκείνου δίδραχμον ἐτάχθη: Cf. the commentaries to Suetonius, *Domitianus*, 12:2 (No. 320); Cicero, *Pro Flacco*, 28:66–69 (No. 68); Tacitus, *Historiae*, V, 5 (No. 281). The Jewish tax contributed to the Temple of Jerusalem is also called δίδραχμον in other sources; cf. Philo, *Quis Rerum Divinarum Heres Sit*, 186; Josephus, *Ant.*, XVIII, 312; Matt. xvii:24.

τὸ δὲ δὴ τοῦ Ἰουδαϊκοῦ [scil. ὄνομα] οὐδέτερος ἔσχε: Cassius Dio seems surprised that the Flavians did not assume the title "Iudaicus", being accustomed to the practices of the Severi who assumed titles deriving from the names of the conquered nations as a matter of course after every successful campaign. However, this was much less common under the Flavians; cf. P. Kneissl, *Die Siegestitulatur der römischen Kaiser*, Göttingen 1969, p. 42. For other explanations, see Z. Yavetz, *Greek, Roman and Byzantine Studies*, XVI (1975), p. 432.

431

Historia Romana, LXVI, 9:2a, apud: Zonaras — Boissevain

Τὴν μὲν οὖν Αἴγυπτον δι' ὀλίγου κατεστήσατο ⟨scil. Οὐεσπασιανός⟩, καὶ σῖτον πολὺν εἰς τὴν Ῥώμην ἔπεμψεν ἀπ' αὐτῆς· τὸν δὲ υἱὸν αὐτοῦ Τίτον εἰς Ἱεροσόλυμα καταλελοιπὼς πορθῆσαι αὐτά, τὴν ἐκείνων ἀνέμεινεν ἅλωσιν, ἵνα μετὰ τοῦ υἱέος ἐπανέλθῃ πρὸς τὴν Ῥώμην.
5 τριβομένου δὲ χρόνου ἐν τῇ πολιορκίᾳ τὸν μὲν Τίτον ἐν τῇ Παλαιστίνῃ κατέλιπεν, αὐτὸς δὲ ὁλκάδος ἐπιβὰς εἰς Λυκίαν ἔπλευσε.

He [scil. Vespasian] soon restored order in Egypt and sent thence a large supply of grain to Rome. He had left his son Titus at Jerusalem to storm the place, and was waiting for its capture in order that he might return to Rome with him. But as time dragged on and the siege continued, he left Titus in Palestine and took passage himself on a merchantman; in this manner he sailed as far as Lycia.

(trans. E. Cary, *LCL*)

432

Historia Romana, LXVI, 12:1a, apud: Zonaras — Boissevain

Τῶν δ' Ἱεροσολύμων ἁλόντων ὁ Τίτος εἰς τὴν Ἰταλίαν ἐπανελθὼν τὰ ἐπινίκια αὐτός τε καὶ ὁ πατὴρ ἐφ' ἅρματος ἔπεμψαν· συνέπεμπε δέ σφισιν αὐτὰ καὶ ὁ Δομετιανὸς ὑπατεύων ἐπὶ κέλητος.

After Jerusalem had been captured Titus returned to Italy, and both he and his father celebrated a triumph, riding in a chariot. Domitian, who was consul, also took part in the celebration, mounted upon a charger.

(trans. E. Cary, *LCL*)

433

Historia Romana, LXVI, 15:3-5, apud: Xiphilinus — Boissevain

(3) Βερενίκη δὲ ἰσχυρῶς τε ἤνθει καὶ διὰ τοῦτο καὶ ἐς τὴν Ῥώμην μετὰ τοῦ ἀδελφοῦ τοῦ Ἀγρίππα ἦλθε· *(4)* καὶ ὁ μὲν στρατηγικῶν τιμῶν ἠξιώθη, ἡ δὲ ἐν τῷ παλατίῳ ᾤκησε καὶ τῷ Τίτῳ συνεγίγνετο· προσεδόκα δὲ γαμηθήσεσθαι αὐτῷ, καὶ πάντα ἤδη ὡς καὶ γυνὴ αὐτοῦ
5 οὖσα ἐποίει, ὥστ' ἐκεῖνον δυσχεραίνοντας τοὺς Ῥωμαίους ἐπὶ τούτοις αἰσθόμενον ἀποπέμψασθαι αὐτήν. *(5)* ἄλλως τε γὰρ πολλὰ ἐθρυλεῖτο, καί τινες καὶ τότε σοφισταὶ κύνειοι ἐς τὸ ἄστυ πως παραδύντες. Διογένης μὲν πρότερος ἐς τὸ θέατρον πλῆρες ἀνδρῶν ἐσῆλθε καὶ πολλὰ αὐτοὺς λοιδορήσας ἐμαστιγώθη, Ἡρᾶς δὲ μετ' αὐτόν, ὡς οὐδὲν
10 πλεῖον πεισόμενος, πολλὰ καὶ ἄτοπα κυνηδὸν ἐξέκραγε, καὶ διὰ τοῦτο καὶ τὴν κεφαλὴν ἀπετμήθη.

1 Βερενίκη Leunclavius   βερονίκη VC
4 προσεδοκᾶτο Robertus Stephanus   9 Ἡρᾶς Boissevain   ἠρὰς V   ἠρᾶς C

(3) Berenice was at the very height of her power and consequently came to Rome along with her brother Agrippa. *(4)* The latter was given the rank of praetor, while she dwelt in the palace, cohabiting with Titus. She expected to marry him and was already behaving in

378

every respect as if she were his wife; but when he perceived that the Romans were displeased with the situation, he sent her away. (5) For, in addition to all the other talk that there was, certain sophists of the Cynic school managed somehow to slip into the city at this time, too; and first Diogenes, entering the theatre when it was full, denounced the pair in a long, abusive speech; for which he was flogged; and after him Heras, expecting no harsher punishment, gave vent to many senseless yelpings in true Cynic fashion, and for this was beheaded.

(trans. E. Cary, *LCL*)

4 στρατηγικῶν τιμῶν ἠξιώθη: For the *ornamenta praetoria*, cf. Cassius Dio, LX, 8:3 (No. 423). See T. Frankfort, *Hommages à Albert Grenier*, Brussels–Berchem, II, 1962, p. 665.

ἀποπέμψασθαι αὐτήν: Cf. Quintilianus, *Institutio Oratoria*, IV, 1:19 (No. 231), and Suetonius, *Divus Titus*, 7:1–2 (No. 318). One suggestion for the chronology of events is that Berenice arrived at Rome only in 75 C.E. after the death of Mucianus and stayed there until 79 C.E. After putting Caecina and Eprius Marcellus to death, Titus gave in to public opinion and Berenice temporarily left Rome; see J.A. Crook, *AJP*, LXXII (1951), pp. 162 ff.

434

Historia Romana, LXVI, 18:1 — Boissevain

Ὁ δὲ δὴ Τίτος οὐδὲν οὔτε φονικὸν οὔτε ἐρωτικὸν μοναρχήσας ἔπραξεν, ἀλλὰ χρηστὸς καίπερ ἐπιβουλευθεὶς καὶ σώφρων καίτοι καὶ τῆς Βερενίκης ἐς Ῥώμην αὖθις ἐλθούσης ἐγένετο.

3 Βερενίκης Reimarus   βερονίκης VC

Titus after becoming ruler committed no act of murder or of amatory passion, but showed himself upright, though plotted against, and self-controlled; though Berenice came to Rome again.

(trans. E. Cary, *LCL*)

ἐς Ῥώμην αὖθις ἐλθούσης: This implies that Berenice returned to Rome after some absence.

435

Historia Romana, LXVII, 14:1–3, apud: Xiphilinus — Boissevain = F110R

(1) Κἀν τῷ αὐτῷ ἔτει ἄλλους τε πολλοὺς καὶ τὸν Φλάουιον ⟨τὸν⟩ Κλήμεντα

1 Φλάυιον Reimarus   φάβιον VC / ⟨τὸν⟩ Bekker

ὑπατεύοντα, καίπερ ἀνεψιὸν ὄντα καὶ γυναῖκα καὶ αὐτὴν συγγενῆ ἑαυτοῦ
Φλαουίαν Δομιτίλλαν ἔχοντα, κατέσφαξεν ὁ Δομιτιανός. (2) ἐπηνέχθη δὲ
ἀμφοῖν ἔγκλημα ἀθεότητος, ὑφ᾽ ἧς καὶ ἄλλοι ἐς τὰ τῶν Ἰουδαίων ἤθη
5 ἐξοκέλλοντες πολλοὶ κατεδικάσθησαν, καὶ οἱ μὲν ἀπέθανον, οἱ δὲ τῶν
γοῦν οὐσίων ἐστερήθησαν· ἡ δὲ Δομιτίλλα ὑπερωρίσθη μόνον ἐς
Πανδατερίαν. (3) τὸν δὲ δὴ Γλαβρίωνα τὸν μετὰ τοῦ Τραϊανοῦ ἄρξαντα,
κατηγορηθέντα τά τε ἄλλα καὶ οἷα οἱ πολλοὶ καὶ ὅτι καὶ θηρίοις ἐμάχετο,
ἀπέκτεινεν.

3 Φλαουίαν Bekker   φλαβίαν VC / Δομιτιανός Robertus Stephanus
                     δομίτιος VC

(1) And the same year Domitian slew, along with many others,
Flavius Clemens the consul, although he was a cousin and had to wife
Flavia Domitilla, who was also a relative of the emperor. (2) The
charge brought against them both was that of atheism, a charge on
which many others who drifted into Jewish ways were condemned.
Some of these were put to death, and the rest were at least deprived of
their property. Domitilla was merely banished to Pandateria. (3) But
Glabrio, who had been Trajan's colleague in the consulship, was put
to death, having been accused of the same crimes as most of the
others, and, in particular, of fighting as a gladiator with wild beasts.

(trans. E. Cary, *LCL*)

1 Φλάυιον ⟨τὸν⟩ Κλήμεντα ὑπατεύοντα: This occurred in 95 C.E.
καίπερ ἀνεψιὸν ὄντα: Usually this Flavius Clemens is regarded as having
been the nephew of Vespasian, i.e. the son of his brother Flavius Sabinus; see
Stein, PW, VI, pp. 2536 ff. However, for the cogently argued view that
Flavius Clemens was a grandson of the brother of Vespasian, see
G. Townend, *JRS*, LI (1961), pp. 54 ff.
κατέσφαξεν ὁ Δομιτιανός: Cf. Suetonius, *Domitianus*, 15:1: "Denique
Flavium Clementem patruelem suum contemptissimae inertiae, cuius filios
etiam tum parvulos successores palam destinaverat ... repente ex tenuissima
suspicione tantum non in ipso eius consulatu interemit." See also Eutropius,
VII, 23: "consobrinos suos interfecit"; Plinius, *Panegyricus*, 48:3;
Philostratus, *Vita Apollonii*, VIII, 25.
2 ἔγκλημα ἀθεότητος: This sort of accusation was raised against Jews at
different periods; cf. Apollonius Molon, apud: Josephus, *Contra Apionem*,
II, 148 (No. 49). For a connection between ἀθεότης and the refusal to take
part in the imperial cult in the time of Domitian, cf. M.P.Charlesworth,
HTR, XXVIII (1935), pp. 32 ff.
ὑφ᾽ ἧς καὶ ἄλλοι ἐς τὰ τῶν Ἰουδαίων ἤθη ἐξοκέλλοντες: Cassius Dio
expressly states that the accusation of ἀθεότης lodged against Clemens and
his wife implied an inclination towards Judaism. However many scholars

have thought that Christianity and not Judaism is meant here; see, e.g., J.B. Lightfoot, *The Apostolic Fathers*, I, London 1890, "S. Clement of Rome", I, p. 34 (cf. also a collection of passages bearing upon the persecution under Domitian and upon the family of Flavius Clemens, pp. 104 ff.); K.J. Neumann, *Der römische Staat und die allgemeine Kirche*, I, Leipzig 1890, p. 7; Linsenmayer, pp. 77 f.; Schürer, III, p. 64, n. 97; p. 168, n. 57; Harnack, II, p. 572; Stein, *op. cit.* (supra, p. 380), p. 2538; B.H. Streeter, *CAH*, XI (1936), p. 255; M. Sordi, *Il Cristianesimo e Roma*, Bologna 1965, p. 96; B. Grenzheuser, "Kaiser und Senat in der Zeit von Nero bis Nerva", Ph.D. Thesis, Münster 1964, pp. 123 f.; L.W. Barnard, *Studies in the Apostolic Fathers and Their Background*, Oxford 1966, pp. 13 f.; J. Vogt, *Gymnasium*, LXXXII (1975), p. 408.

On the other hand, a large number of scholars prefer to take the words of Cassius Dio at their face value, a view that seems more acceptable; see, e.g., H. Graetz, *Geschichte der Juden*, IV[4], Leipzig 1908, pp. 402 f.; Juster, I, p. 257, n. 1; E.T. Merrill, *Essays in Early Christian History*, London 1924, pp. 148 ff. (at least Flavius Clemens himself, if not his wife, was a Jew and not a Christian); Charlesworth, *op. cit.* (supra, p. 380), p. 33; E.M. Smallwood, *Classical Philology*, LI (1956), pp. 5 ff.; Leon, pp. 33 ff.; W.H.C. Frend, *Martyrdom and Persecution in the Early Church*, Oxford 1965, p. 113; W. Pöhlmann, "Die heidnische, jüdische und christliche Opposition gegen Domitian", Ph.D. Thesis, Erlangen 1966, pp. 33 ff.; T.D. Barnes, *JRS*, LVIII (1968), pp. 35 f.; W. Eck, *Chiron*, I (1971), pp. 392 f.; P. Keresztes, *Vigiliae Christianae*, XXVII (1973), pp. 7 ff.; Sevenster, p. 98. Also inclining to the view that Domitian aimed primarily at the Jews is Ed. Meyer, III, p. 555. There is no reason to assume that either Cassius Dio or his epitomator confused Christianity with Judaism, or that at the time of Domitian, many years after the persecution under Nero, the difference between the two creeds was still insufficiently clear to the Roman authorities. It is also noteworthy that no ancient Christian tradition has denoted Clemens a Christian. Eusebius does not associate him with Christianity although mentioning him as the uncle of Flavia Domitilla; see Eusebius, *Historia Ecclesiastica*, III, 18:4: ὡς καὶ τοὺς ἄποθεν τοῦ καθ᾽ ἡμᾶς λόγου συγγραφεῖς μὴ ἀποκνῆσαι ταῖς αὐτῶν ἱστορίαις τόν τε διωγμὸν καὶ τὰ ἐν αὐτῷ μαρτύρια παραδοῦναι, οἵ γε καὶ τὸν καιρὸν ἐπ᾽ ἀκριβὲς ἐπεσημήναντο, ἐν ἔτει πεντεκαιδεκάτῳ Δομετιανοῦ μετὰ πλείστων ἑτέρων καὶ Φλαυίαν Δομέτιλλαν ἱστορήσαντες, ἐξ ἀδελφῆς γεγονυῖαν Φλαυίου Κλήμεντος, ἑνὸς τῶν τηνικάδε ἐπὶ Ῥώμης ὑπάτων τῆς εἰς Χριστὸν μαρτυρίας ἕνεκεν εἰς νῆσον Ποντίαν κατὰ τιμωρίαν δεδόσθαι. See also Hieronymus, *Chronica* (ed. Helm[2]), p. 192: "Scribit Bruttius plurimos Christianorum sub Domitiano fecisse martyrium. Inter quos et Flaviam Domitillam, Flavii Clementis consulis ex sorore neptem, in insulam Pontiam relegatam."

The first to state that Clemens had been a Christian was the ninth-century Syncellus (ed. Dindorf, I, p. 650): πολλοὶ δὲ Χριστιανῶν ἐμαρτύρησαν κατὰ Δομιτιανόν, ὡς ὁ Βρέττιος ἱστορεῖ, ἐν οἷς καὶ Φλαυία Δομετίλλα ἐξαδελφὴ Κλήμεντος Φλαυίου ὑπατικοῦ, ὡς Χριστιανὴ εἰς νῆσον Ποντίαν φυγαδεύεται· αὐτός τε Κλήμης ὑπὲρ Χρίστου ἀναιρεῖται. Cf. *Eusebi Chronicorum Canonum Quae Supersunt*, ed. Schöne, II, Berlin 1866, p. 162. Syncellus, however, was unlikely to have had an ancient source referring to the Christianity of Clemens at his disposal. In the main he here follows Eusebius, who had only the episode of Domitilla in view. The short notice at the end of Syncellus' passage mentioning the martyrdom of Clemens reads as if it was an addition by a person who knew from his general reading that Clemens had been put to death on the orders of Domitian. If Clemens himself had indeed been accused of Christianity the more ancient Christian sources would not have kept silent. Nevertheless, the statement of Eusebius that Flavia Domitilla was a Christian seems to contradict that of Cassius Dio. It could be suggested that Flavia Domitilla, but not her husband, was converted to Christianity at some stage of her life, but it is more probable that the attribution of Christianity to Flavia Domitilla is also the product of a later age, though the specific reasons giving rise to this tradition may remain obscure; see Smallwood, *op. cit.* (supra, p. 381), pp. 8 f.

There is also no archaeological or epigraphical evidence to show that there was any connection between Roman aristocratic circles and Christianity before 200 C.E., and indeed it is not even possible to attribute with certainty any evidence of this kind to a Christian origin before this date. The famous Coemeterium Domitillae owes its name to the late *Index Coemeteriorum* (dated approximately to the seventh century), which, it seems, derived the name from a literary source, *Acta Nerei et Achillei*. On the oldest monuments of the Roman Church, see A.M. Schneider, *Festschrift zur Feier des zweihundertjährigen Bestehens der Akademie der Wissenschaften in Göttingen*, II, *Philologisch–historische Klasse*, 1951, pp. 166 ff. (for a detailed discussion of the Coemeterium Domitillae, see pp. 182 ff.); cf. Eck, *loc. cit.*; J. Vogt, *Reallexikon für Antike und Christentum*, II, Stuttgart 1954, p. 1169. Vogt is reserved towards Schneider's conclusions, yet does not state his reasons. For the interpretation of the passage of Cassius Dio, see also K.H. Waters, *Phoenix*, XVIII (1964), pp. 73 f. (whether Clemens was a convert to Christianity will probably never be ascertained); J.E.A. Crake, *Phoenix*, XIX (1965), pp. 65 ff.; J. Speigl, *Der römische Staat und die Christen*, Amsterdam 1970, pp. 28 ff.; *ibid.*, pp. 30 f.: "Das Christentum oder das Judentum des Clemens, das weder Christliche noch bzw. jüdische Tradition bestätigen, dürfte deswegen für die Verurteilung des Clemens nur ein Vorwand, oder überhaupt nur eine Kombination des Dio Cassius gewesen sein".

On the other hand there is some evidence that Judaism at that time won adherents and sympathizers from higher circles of Mediterranean and Roman society, not only from the lower classes. In the East, both the royal family of Adiabene and the rulers of Emesa and Cilicia became converts to Judaism; see *Ant.*, XX, 139, 145. The sympathy for Judaism of Julia Severa, a member of the local aristocracy of Acmonia in Phrygia, is well known; see *CII*, No. 766; her husband was L. Servenius Capito. Another of this family, L. Servenius Cornutus, became a Roman senator in the reign of Nero; see C.S. Walton, *JRS*, XIX (1929), pp. 44 f. In literary sources also there is a hint of the spread of Judaism among the higher classes of Roman society. However, a distinction must be made here between proselytes proper and sympathizers; see the commentary to Iuvenalis, XIV, 96–106 (No. 301). Proselytes were apparently to be found mostly among the lower classes; see Tacitus, *Annales*, II, 85 (No. 284). Sympathy for Judaism was sometimes shown even among persons of the senatorial order, who could not have become proselytes without seriously endangering their position. For women, the situation was somewhat different. Josephus states that Fulvia, the wife of Saturninus, a friend of the emperor Tiberius, became a proselyte; see *Ant.*, XVIII, 81 ff.: καὶ νομίμοις προσεληλυθυῖαν τοῖς Ἰουδαϊκοῖς. Another Roman lady who should be mentioned in this connection is Pomponia Graecina, the wife of Aulus Plautius, the conqueror of Britain under Claudius. Tacitus relates among the events of 57 C.E. that she became "superstitionis externae rea" and was judged by her husband; see Tacitus, *Annales*, XIII, 32 (No. 293). There is much to be said for the view that by "externa superstitio" Judaism is implied; see the commentary to Tacitus, *loc. cit.*

Another Plautia, the daughter of Aulus (scil. Plautius, presumably the *consul suffectus* of 1 B.C.E.), was the wife of Publius Petronius; see *CIL*, VI, No. 6866. Cf. also an inscription from Caunos; see G.E. Bean, *JHS*, LXXIV (1954), pp. 91 f. Petronius was *consul suffectus* of 19 C.E., and proconsul of Asia *c.* 29–35 C.E.; see D. Magie, *Roman Rule in Asia Minor*, II, Princeton 1950, p. 1363, n. 38. In the years 39–42 C.E. he was *legatus pro praetore* in Syria; for a biographical outline, see R. Hanslik, PW, XIX, pp. 1199 ff. As governor of Syria Petronius was bound to execute Caligula's policy and to desecrate the Jewish Temple by placing the emperor's statue in it. However Petronius was deterred by the Jewish opposition and did not put the imperial order into effect, thus jeopardizing his own life. Petronius' reactions may be accounted for both by political considerations and by reluctance to cause the bloodshed which he expected would ensue if he executed Caligula's orders. (Willrich takes Caligula's own explanation too seriously; see H. Willrich, *Klio*, III (1903), p. 417.) However, according to Philo, there was an additional factor conditioning Petronius' reaction to events. This was the attraction of Jewish philosophy and religion; cf. *Legatio ad Gaium*, 245: ἀλλὰ εἶχέ τινα καὶ αὐτός, ὡς ἔοικεν, ἐναύσματα τῆς Ἰουδαϊκῆς φιλοσοφίας ἅμα καὶ εὐσεβείας, εἴτε καὶ πάλαι προμαθὼν ἕνεκα τῆς περὶ παιδείαν σπουδῆς εἴτε καὶ ἀφ᾽ οὗ τῶν χώρων ἐπετρόπευσεν, ἐν οἷς Ἰουδαῖοι καθ᾽ ἑκάστην πόλιν εἰσὶ παμπληθεῖς, Ἀσίας τε καὶ Συρίας, εἴτε καὶ τὴν ψυχὴν οὕτω διατεθεὶς αὐτήκόῳ καὶ αὐτοκελεύστῳ καὶ αὐτομαθεῖ τινι πρὸς τὰ σπουδῆς ἄξια φύσει. Philo, stating that Petronius had some acquaintance with Jewish philosophy and religion, wonders whether he acquired this knowledge because of his general interest in culture, or only after he became the governor of provinces inhabited by large numbers of Jews, or alternatively perhaps because he had a natural inclination to seriousness.

Petronius' predecessor in the governorship of Syria was L. Vitellius, who also adopted a policy consistently favourable towards the Jews of Judaea. Vitellius not only deposed Pilate, upon the complaint of the Samaritans, but also alleviated the taxation in Jerusalem. He even changed the route of his troops in a campaign against the Nabataeans, to avoid their march passing through Judaea and offending the religious susceptibilities of the Jews by a display of the military standards (*Ant.*, XVIII, 120 ff.). Vitellius also went to Jerusalem to sacrifice in the Temple during the festival of Passover (*ibid.*, 90), a gesture which may be explained by considerations of political expediency. It seems worthwhile noting that there were some family connections between the Plautii, Petronii and Vitellii. See also A. Stein, *Der römische Ritterstand*, Munich 1927, p. 300, n. 3; Syme, I, p. 386.

A clearer example of a Roman from the higher classes who showed some sympathy for the beliefs of Jews and Christians is Sergius Paulus, governor of Cyprus, found in the company of the Jew Barjesus; cf. Acts xiii : 6 ff.; Groag, PW, Ser. 2, II, pp. 1715 ff.

The propagation of Judaism among senatorial circles after the destruction of the Temple is reflected in talmudic and midrashic literature; see Derenbourg, pp. 334 ff.; B.J. Bamberger, *Proselytism in the Talmudic Period*, Cincinnati 1939, pp. 235 ff.; G. Alon, *History of the Jews in Palestine in the Age of the Mishna and Talmud*, I, Tel Aviv 1958, pp. 74 ff. (in Hebrew). For the main relevant passages, see *TB 'Avoda Zara*, 10b; *Devarim Rabba*, ii : 24. The council of Trajan is said to be filled with impious Jews in *Acta Hermaisci*; see H. A. Musurillo, *The Acts of the Pagan Martyrs*, Oxford 1954, No. VIII (= *CPJ*, No. 157), Col. iii, ll. 42 f. In general, see M. Stern, *Zion*, XXIX (1964), pp. 155 ff.

ἐς Πανδατερίαν: Eusebius gives the locality as Pontia instead.

3 Γλαβρίωνα: On M' Acilius Glabrio, see v. Rohden, PW, I, p. 257; Groag, in: *PIR²*, I, pp. 9 f., No. 67. There is no reason whatever to assume that the Acilius Glabrio of the time of Domitian was a Christian (as is assumed, e.g., by S. Gsell, *Essai sur le règne de l'empereur Domitien*, Paris 1894, p. 293). Cf. Leon, p. 35, n. 2. There is no archaeological or epigraphical evidence to show that even the later Acilii were Christians and by no means can the supposed Christian inclinations of Acilius Glabrio himself be proved; see Eck, *op. cit.* (supra, p. 381), p. 392, n. 59. For a connection between Jews and Domitian's assassination, see S. Applebaum, *Scripta Classica Israelica*, I (1974), pp. 116 ff.

436

Historia Romana, LXVIII, 1:2, apud: Xiphilinus — Boissevain = F111R

Καὶ ὁ Νέρουας τούς τε κρινομένους ἐπ'ἀσεβείᾳ ἀφῆκε καὶ τοὺς φεύγοντας κατήγαγε, τούς τε δούλους καὶ τοὺς ἐξελευθέρους τοὺς τοῖς δεσπόταις σφῶν ἐπιβουλεύσαντας πάντας ἀπέκτεινε. καὶ τοῖς μὲν τοιούτοις οὐδ' ἄλλο τι ἔγκλημα ἐπιφέρειν ἐπὶ τοὺς δεσπότας ἐφῆκε, τοῖς δὲ ἄλλοις οὔτ'
5 ἀσεβείας οὔτ' Ἰουδαϊκοῦ βίου καταιτιᾶσθαί τινας συνεχώρησε.

3–4 οὐδ' ἄλλο] οὐδ' ὅλως Polak

Nerva also released all who were on trial for *maiestas* and restored the exiles; moreover, he put to death all the slaves and the freedmen who had conspired against their masters and allowed that class of persons to lodge no complaint whatever against their masters; and no persons were permitted to accuse anybody of *maiestas* or of adopting the Jewish mode of life. (trans. E. Cary, *LCL*)

ἀσεβείας: ἀσέβεια stands for *maiestas*, as is proved by many passages of Dio's History; cf., e.g., Cassius Dio, LVII, 9:2; LIX, 4:3, 6:2; LX, 4:2.
οὔτ᾽ Ἰουδαϊκοῦ βίου: For coins inscribed with the legend "Fisci Iudaici calumnia sublata", see A. Mattingly, *Coins of the Roman Empire in the British Museum*, III, London 1936, p. 15, No. 88; p. 17, No. 98.

437

Historia Romana, LXVIII, 32:1–3, apud: Xiphilinus — Boissevain = F112R

(1) Καὶ Τραϊανὸς μὲν ἐκεῖθεν οὕτως ἀπῆλθε, καὶ οὐ πολλῷ ὕστερον ἀρρωστεῖν ἤρχετο· καὶ ἐν τούτῳ οἱ κατὰ Κυρήνην Ἰουδαῖοι, Ἀνδρέαν τινὰ προστησάμενοί σφων, τούς τε Ῥωμαίους καὶ τοὺς Ἕλληνας ἔφθειρον, καὶ τάς τε σάρκας αὐτῶν ἐσιτοῦντο καὶ τὰ ἔντερα ἀνεδοῦντο τῷ τε αἵματι
5 *ἠλείφοντο καὶ τὰ ἀπολέμματα ἐνεδύοντο, πολλοὺς δὲ καὶ μέσους ἀπὸ κορυφῆς διέπριον· (2) θηρίοις ἑτέρους ἐδίδοσαν, καὶ μονομαχεῖν ἄλλους ἠνάγκαζον, ὥστε τὰς πάσας δύο καὶ εἴκοσι μυριάδας ἀπολέσθαι. ἔν τε Αἰγύπτῳ πολλὰ ἔδρασαν ὅμοια καὶ ἐν τῇ Κύπρῳ, ἡγουμένου τινός σφισιν Ἀρτεμίωνος· καὶ ἀπώλοντο καὶ ἐκεῖ μυριάδες τέσσαρες καὶ εἴκοσι. (3) καὶ*
10 *διὰ τοῦτ᾽ οὐδενὶ Ἰουδαίῳ ἐπιβῆναι αὐτῆς ἔξεστιν, ἀλλὰ κἂν ἀνέμῳ τις βιασθεὶς ἐς τὴν νῆσον ἐκπέσῃ θανατοῦται. ἀλλ᾽ Ἰουδαίους μὲν ἄλλοι τε καὶ Λούσιος ὑπὸ Τραϊανοῦ πεμφθεὶς κατεστρέψατο.*

2 Ἀνδρέαν Scaliger   ἀνδρίαν VC   Ἀνδρείαν Leunclavius
6 ἀλλήλους V   9 Ἀρτέμωνος? Boissevain   10 οὐδενὶ Sylburg
    οὐδὲν VC   11 ἐκπέσῃ Reiske   ἐμπέσῃ VC
    12 κατεστρέψατο Dindorf   κατεστρέψαντο VC

(1) Trajan therefore departed thence, and a little later began to fail in health. Meanwhile the Jews in the region of Cyrene had put a certain Andreas at their head, and were destroying both the Romans and the Greeks. They would eat the flesh of their victims, make belts for themselves of their entrails, anoint themselves with their blood and wear their skins for clothing; many they sawed in two, from the head downwards; (2) others they gave to wild beasts, and still others they forced to fight as gladiators. In all two hundred and twenty thousand

persons perished. In Egypt, too, they perpetrated many similar outrages and in Cyprus under the leadership of a certain Artemion. There, also, two hundred and forty thousand perished, (3) and for this reason no Jew may set foot on this island, but if one of them is driven upon its shores by a storm he is put to death. Among others who subdued the Jews was Lusius, who was sent by Trajan.

(trans. E. Cary, *LCL*)

1 ἐκεῖθεν οὕτως ἀπῆλθε: The retreat from the fortress of Hatra is meant. ἐν τούτῳ: For the chronological problems, cf. the commentary to Arrian (No. 332a).

κατὰ Κυρήνην Ἰουδαῖοι: On the events in Cyrenaica itself, see S. Applebaum, *Zion*, XIX (1954), pp. 23 ff. (for a detailed bibliography, see pp. 52 ff.); idem, *Journal of Jewish Studies*, II (1950/1), pp. 177 ff. and his survey, *ibid.*, XIII (1962), pp. 36 ff.; idem, *Greeks and Jews in Ancient Cyrene*, Jerusalem 1969, pp. 175 ff. (in Hebrew). On the diffusion of Jews in Cyrenaica and their history in the Hellenistic and early Roman period, see the commentary to Strabo, *Historica Hypomnemata*, apud: *Ant.*, XIV, 115 (No. 105). After the destruction of the Temple of Jerusalem, Cyrene became a centre of Jewish dissatisfaction. One of the extremists from Judaea, Jonathan the Weaver, took refuge there (*BJ*, VII, 437) and attempted to create disturbances. On the revolt in Cyrenaica, see also J.M. Reynolds, *Proceedings of the Cambridge Philological Society*, NS, V (1958–1959), pp. 24 ff.

Ἀνδρέαν τινά: Only Dio calls the leader of the revolt by this name. He is called Lukuas in Eusebius, *Historia Ecclesiastica*, IV, 2:3. See also U. Wilcken, *Hermes*, XXVII (1892), pp. 472, 479 f. Lukuas is not a Greek name, but probably a local Libyan one. The Jewish leader may have had two names (Ἀνδρέας ὁ καὶ Λουκούας). He is the only Jew mentioned by name in the sources that relate to the Jewish revolt in Egypt and Cyrenaica. It seems that he attracted Messianic hopes, being called king by Eusebius, *loc. cit.* Perhaps he is the person alluded to in the so-called *Acta Pauli et Antonini*; see H.A. Musurillo, *The Acts of the Pagan Martyrs*, Oxford 1954, No. IX = *CPJ*, II, No. 158a, Col. I, ll. 3 ff.: καὶ Θέω[ν] περὶ τούτ[ο]υ διάταγμα ἀνέγνω [τοῦ?] Λούπου, ὡς προάγειν αὐ[τ]οὺς [ἐ]κέλευε, χλευάζων τὸν ἀπὸ [σ] κηνῆς καὶ ἐκ μείμου βασιλέα. Wilcken maintains that the Jewish king was taken prisoner and surrendered to the Alexandrian mob; see U. Wilcken, *Zum alexandrinischen Antisemitismus (Abhandlungen der Königl. Sächsischen Gesellschaft der Wissenschaften, Philologisch-historische Klasse,* XXVII, 1909), p. 815 (35). However there is more probability in the view that it was only his image that was mocked by the Alexandrians; see A. v. Premerstein, *Hermes*, LVII (1922), p. 277. We do not have to accept that the man was a Greek converted to Judaism, as suggested by I. Heinemann, *Zion*, IV (1939), p. 278.

τούς τε Ῥωμαίους: The other principal sources for the history of the Jewish revolt in Cyrenaica are Artemidorus, *Onirocritica*, IV, 24 (No. 396); Eusebius, *Historia Ecclesiastica*, IV, 2:2–3; *Die Chronik des Eusebios aus dem armenischen*, translated by J. Karst, Leipzig 1911, p. 219; Hieronymus, *Chronica* (ed. Helm²), p. 196; Orosius, VII, 12:6; Syncellus (ed. Dindorf), I, p. 657; *The Chronicle of John, Bishop of Nikiu*, LXXII:14, translated by R.H. Charles, London 1916, p. 55. The fierceness of the fighting and the destruction that followed it emerge from both the literary and epigraphic sources; cf. Orosius, *loc. cit.*: "per totam Libyam adversus incolas atrocissima bella gesserunt; quae adeo tunc interfectis cultoribus desolata est, ut, nisi postea Hadrianus imperator collectas illuc aliunde colonias deduxisset, vacua penitus terra abraso habitatore mansisset." The picture is confirmed by the epigraphic material; cf., e.g., *SEG*, IX, Nos. 168, 189, 252 ("viam, quae tumultu Iudaico eversa et corrupta erat", etc.). For archaeological evidence, see also the articles of Applebaum, *op. cit.* (supra, p. 386).

καὶ τάς τε σάρκας...: For the view that the description of events found here does not derive from Cassius Dio but is to be accounted for by the anti-Semitic attitude of Xiphilinus, see M. Joël, *Blicke in die Religionsgeschichte zu Anfang des zweiten christlichen Jahrhunderts*, II, Breslau 1883, pp. 163 ff. His suggestion, though often repeated, seems hardly acceptable, and it is worthwhile recalling the strongly-coloured tale of atrocities committed by the British rebels under Boudicca against the Romans in Cassius Dio, LXII, 7; for the tale about the Egyptian rebels in the Delta in 171 C.E. who ate the body of a Roman centurion, see Cassius Dio, LXXI, 4:1; see also A. Henrichs, *Die Phoinikika des Lollianos*, Bonn 1972, pp. 33 f., 48 ff. Fear of the rebel Jews and their methods of fighting is reflected in a papyrus from Egypt; see *CPJ*, No. 437: οὐ μή σε ὀπτήσωσι. The war was waged fiercely on both sides; see Eusebius, *Historia Ecclesiastica*, IV, 2, 3: οἵ καὶ καταφυγόντες εἰς τὴν Ἀλεξάνδρειαν τοὺς ἐν τῇ πόλει Ἰουδαίους ἐζώγρησάν τε καὶ ἀπέκτειναν. Schwartz points out also the old Egyptian tradition about the cruelties perpetrated by the Persians on Egyptian soil; see J. Schwartz, *Chronique d'Égypte*, XXXVII (1962), pp. 350 f. For a suggestion that while Dio derives his material from a Greek anti-Jewish source, Eusebius draws on a source sympathetic to Jews, see U. Wilcken, *Hermes*, XXVII (1892), p. 479. Cf. also Appianus, *Bella Civilia*, II, 90:380 (No. 350), describing Trajan as ἐξολλύντα τὸ ἐν Αἰγύπτῳ Ἰουδαίων γένος.

2 ἔν τε Αἰγύπτῳ πολλὰ ἔδρασαν ὅμοια: Information on the revolt in Egypt has become much fuller following the papyrological discoveries; see the material collected by A. Fuks, in *CPJ*, Nos. 435–450; see also the commentary to *CPJ*, No. 452b; also A. Świderek, *The Journal of Juristic Papyrology*, XVI–XVII (1971), pp. 45 ff.; V. Tcherikover, *The Jews in Egypt in the Hellenistic–Roman Age in the Light of the Papyri²*, Jerusalem 1963, pp. 160 ff. (in Hebrew); A. Fuks, *Aegyptus*, XXXIII (1953), pp. 131 ff.; Tcherikover, in the Prolegomena to *CPJ*, I, pp. 86 ff.; Schwartz, *Chronique d'Égypte, op. cit.*, pp. 348 ff.; Smallwood, pp. 393 ff. In connection with the literary sources, apart from Eusebius and Orosius, cf. Appianus, *loc. cit.*; and also idem, *Liber Arabicus*, F19 (No. 348); *TP Sukka*, v, 55b, which refers to the great synagogue of Alexandria. The revolt in Egypt encompassed both

Alexandria and the χώρα. There are references to a battle in Alexandria, to Jewish activities in north-eastern Egypt (in the vicinity of Pelusium), in the Athribite *nomos*, in the vicinity of Memphis, in Faiyûm, in the Heracleopolite *nomos*, in the Oxyrhynchite, Cynopolite and Hermopolite *nomoi*, as well as in Upper Egypt (in Thebais, the Lycopolite and Apollinopolite *nomoi*).

It is not clear whether the revolt in Egypt or that in Cyrenaica came first. The sequence of events given by Dio seems to imply that the Egyptian revolt was subsequent to that in Cyrenaica. This sequence is supported by the fact that the one known leader (Andreas/Lukuas) came from Cyrene. Egypt is mentioned first by Eusebius, *Historia Ecclesiastica*, IV, 2:2: ἔν τε γὰρ Ἀλεξανδρείᾳ καὶ τῇ λοιπῇ Αἰγύπτῳ καὶ προσέτι κατὰ Κυρήνην, ὥσπερ ὑπὸ πνεύματος δεινοῦ τινος καὶ στασιώδους ἀναρριπισθέντες, ὥρμηντο πρὸς τοὺς συνοίκους Ἕλληνας στασιάζειν. For the losses sustained by the Roman forces during the revolt, see also J.F. Gilliam, *Bonner Historia Augusta Colloquium, Bonn 1964/1965* (1966), pp. 91 ff. (comments on *PSI*, No. 1063). See also, A. Kasher, *Zion*, XLI (1976), pp. 127 ff.

ἐν τῇ Κύπρῳ: The Jewish population of Cyprus in the Hellenistic and early Roman period seems also to have gained much importance, though the information on it is rather scanty; cf. Alon, *op. cit.* (supra, p. 384), I, p. 236. There were synagogues at Salamis; cf. Acts xiii:5. An inscription dating from the late Hellenistic age, a dedication in which the Jewish name Ὀνίας occurs, has been found in the acropolis of Kourion; see T.B. Mitford, *The Inscriptions of Kourion*, Philadelphia 1971, No. 70, p. 133 f.; see also idem, *AJA*, LXV (1961), pp. 118 f., No. 18, an inscription from Tremithus, dating from the reign of Domitian.

ἡγουμένου ... Ἀρτεμίωνος: This leader of the Jewish revolt in the island is mentioned only here.

καὶ ἀπώλοντο ... : The destruction of Salamis and the annihilation of the population there is emphasized by Eusebius, *Die Chronik aus dem armenischen, op. cit.* (supra, p. 387), p. 219. Cf. Hieronymus, *Chronica* (ed. Helm²), p. 196; Syncellus, I (ed. Dindorf), p. 657; Orosius, VII, 12:8. Inscriptions likewise show Roman military activities in the island at that time. On the Jewish revolt in Cyprus, see G. Hill, *A History of Cyprus*, I, Cambridge 1940, pp. 241 ff.; S. Applebaum, *Journal of Jewish Studies*, XIII (1962), pp. 41 f.; Smallwood, pp. 412 ff.

Among the inscriptions bearing upon the Jewish revolt in Cyprus is the important inscription found at Berytus, referring to Gaius Valerius Rufus, a tribune of the Legio VII Claudia, who was sent with a *vexillatio* to Cyprus by the emperor Trajan; see *ILS*, No. 9491 = Saxer, No. 45: "Cyprum in expeditionem". The only occasion which could necessitate this in the reign of Trajan was the Jewish revolt in the island. Another inscription found at Knodhara attests the presence in Cyprus of the Cohors VII Breucorum Civium Romanorum Equitata; see *CIL*, III, No. 215. It was usually stationed in Pannonia; see G.L. Cheesman, *The Auxilia of the Roman Imperial Army*, Oxford 1914, p. 154. Its transfer suggests a connection with the Jewish revolt at that time; see Hill, *op. cit.*, p. 242, n. 2; R. Paribeni, *Optimus Princeps*, II, Messina 1927, p. 199.

There is some reason to assume that the inscriptions from Salamis honouring Hadrian as εὐεργέτης καὶ σωτὴρ τοῦ κόσμου reflect the Roman victory; see *SEG*, XXIII, No. 609, dated 123 C.E. = T.B. Mitford & I.K. Nicolaou, *The Greek and Latin Inscriptions from Salamis*, Nicosia 1974, No. 92; *SEG*, XX, No. 123, dated 129–130 C.E. Another inscription to be considered in this connection is a soldier's epitaph found some nine miles north of Paphos; see T.B. Mitford, *Opuscula Archaeologica*, VI (1950), p. 54, No. 29.

3 καὶ διὰ τοῦτ᾽ οὐδενὶ Ἰουδαίῳ ἐπιβῆναι αὐτῆς ἔξεστιν: Inscriptions testifying to the renewal of Jewish settlements in Cyprus in the third and fourth centuries are an inscription from Lapethos dating from the third century; cf. *CII*, No. 736 = Lifshitz, No. 83; and an inscription from Golgoi dating from the fourth century; cf. *CII*, No. 735 = Lifshitz, No. 82. See also T. Reinach, *REJ*, XLVIII (1904), pp. 191 ff.; *ibid.*, LXI (1911), pp. 285 ff.; Mitford & Nicolaou, *op. cit.*, p. 118, n. 10; Hill, *op. cit.* (supra, p. 388), I, p. 243. For the inscription from Golgoi, see also O. Masson, *BCH*, XCV (1971), pp. 332 ff.

ἀλλ᾽ Ἰουδαίους μὲν ἄλλοι τε ...: Turbo was prominent among those who crushed the Jewish revolt in Egypt and Cyrenaica; cf. Eusebius, *Historia Ecclesiastica*, IV, 2:3 f.: ἐφ᾽ οὓς ὁ αὐτοκράτωρ ἔπεμψεν Μάρκιον Τούρβωνα σὺν δυνάμει πεζῇ τε καὶ ναυτικῇ, ἔτι δὲ καὶ ἱππικῇ. ὁ δὲ πολλαῖς μάχαις οὐκ ὀλίγῳ τε χρόνῳ τὸν πρὸς αὐτοὺς διαπονήσας πόλεμον, πολλὰς μυριάδας Ἰουδαίων, οὐ μόνον τῶν ἀπὸ Κυρήνης, ἀλλὰ καὶ τῶν ἀπ᾽ Αἰγύπτου συναιρομένων Λουκούᾳ τῷ βασιλεῖ αὐτῶν, ἀναιρεῖ. On the personality of Turbo, see H.G. Pflaum, *Les carrières procuratoriennes équestres sous le Haut-Empire romain*, I, Paris 1960, pp. 199 ff.; R. Syme, *JRS*, LII (1962), pp. 87 ff.; D. Rokeah, *Scripta Hierosolymitana*, XXIII (1972), pp. 79 ff.

Cyprus is mentioned in connection with the slaughter of the Jews in the time of Trajan in the talmudic literature also; cf. *TP Sukka*, v, 55b: ועירב דמן בדמן והלך הדם בים עד קיפרוס though here the blood shed by Trajan is not that of the Jews of Cyprus but presumably that of the Jews of Egypt (or Palestine) that flowed as far as Cyprus.

καὶ Λούσιος ὑπὸ Τραϊανοῦ πεμφθεὶς κατεστρέψατο: On Lusius Quietus and his origins, see Groag, PW, XIII, pp. 1874 ff.; W. den Boer, *Mnemosyne*, Ser. 4, I (1948), pp. 327 ff.; III (1950), pp. 263 ff., 339 ff.; Roos, *ibid.*, pp. 158 ff., 336 ff.; L. Petersen, *Das Altertum*, XIV (1968), pp. 211 ff. See also the commentary to Arrian (No. 332a).

438

Historia Romana, LXVIII, 32:5, apud: Excerpta Valesiana — Boissevain, III, p. 206

Τιμηθεὶς ⟨scil. Κυῆτος Λούσιος⟩ δὲ ἐπὶ τούτῳ πολὺ πλείω καὶ μείζω ἐν τῷ δευτέρῳ πολέμῳ ἐξειργάσατο, καὶ τέλος ἐς τοσοῦτον τῆς τε ἀνδραγαθίας ἅμα καὶ τῆς τύχης ἐν τῷδε τῷ πολέμῳ προεχώρησεν ὥστε ἐς τοὺς

ἐστρατηγηκότας ἐσγραφῆναι καὶ ὑπατεῦσαι τῆς τε Παλαιστίνης ἄρξαι· ἐξ
5 ὧν που καὶ τὰ μάλιστα ἐφθονήθη καὶ ἐμισήθη καὶ ἀπώλετο.

Being honoured for this he [scil. Lucius Quietus] performed far
greater and more numerous exploits in the second war, and finally
advanced so far in bravery and good fortune during this present war
that he was enrolled among the ex-praetors, became consul, and then
governor of Palestine. To this chiefly were due the jealousy and
hatred felt for him and his destruction.

(trans. E. Cary, *LCL*, Dio Cassius, VIII, p. 397)

439

Historia Romana, LXIX, 11:1, apud: Xiphilinus — Boissevain

Διὰ δὲ τῆς Ἰουδαίας μετὰ ταῦτα ἐς Αἴγυπτον παριὼν ⟨scil. Ἀδριανός⟩ καὶ
ἐνήγισε τῷ Πομπηΐῳ.

After this he [scil. Hadrian] passed through Judaea into Egypt and
offered sacrifice to Pompey.   (trans. E. Cary, *LCL*)

Διὰ δὲ τῆς Ἰουδαίας μετὰ ταῦτα ἐς Αἴγυπτον παριών: On Hadrian's
Egyptian visit, see W. Weber, *Untersuchungen zur Geschichte des Kaisers
Hadrianus*, Leipzig 1907, pp. 246 ff.; S. Follet, *Revue de Philologie*, XLII
(1968), pp. 54 ff. His visit is to be dated to 130 C.E.; see *ibid.*, p. 54, n. 4. Some
papyri attest to preparations already being made for this visit in 129.
Hadrian's first sojourn in Palestine, which preceded his Egyptian visit, is
illustrated by documents. Thus his presence at Gerasa in 129–130 C.E. is
evidenced by an inscription; see W. F. Stinespring, *JAOS*, LIX (1939), pp.
360 ff. Presumably Hadrian went to Jerusalem from Philadelphia, and then
went on to Gaza; cf. *CIL*, III, Suppl., No. 13596 (a milestone). The new
chronological system introduced in Gaza starting from 130 C.E. is
undoubtedly to be related to the visit of Hadrian and the benefits conferred
by him upon the city; see Weber, *op. cit.*, pp. 244 f.
Hadrian's visit to Judaea is attested also by the superscription "adventui
Aug(usti) Iudaeae" found on coins; see H. Mattingly, *Coins of the Roman
Empire in the British Museum*, III, London 1936, pp. 493 f., Nos. 1655–1661.
The main type of these coins depicts Judaea holding up a cup or a box; in
front of Judaea is seen a child holding a palm and behind her a second child.
Hadrian returned to Judaea on his way back from Egypt. There are
documents showing that Hadrian was still in Egypt at the very end of 130
C.E.; see A. & E. Bernand, *Les inscriptions grecques et latines du colosse de
Memnon*, Cairo 1960, Nos. 28–32, dated November 130; *P. Oslo*, III, No. 77, a

Cassius Dio

religious calendar from Tebtunis concerning the imperial cult (from l. 11 it ensues that Hadrian's ἐπίβασις was celebrated there on 1 December 130); *P. Oxy.*, XXXI, No. 2553, noting an entry by Hadrian into another town of Egypt, possibly Oxyrhynchus, to be dated to the first half of December 130. Hadrian must have therefore returned to Judaea and Syria at the beginning of 131.

440

Historia Romana, LXIX, 12:1–14:3; 15:1, apud: Xiphilinus — Boissevain = F113R

(12:1) Ἐς δὲ τὰ Ἱεροσόλυμα πόλιν αὐτοῦ ἀντὶ τῆς κατασκαφείσης οἰκίσαντος, ἣν καὶ Αἰλίαν Καπιτωλῖναν ὠνόμασε (scil. Ἀδριανός), καὶ ἐς τὸν τοῦ ναοῦ τοῦ θεοῦ τόπον ναὸν τῷ Διὶ ἕτερον ἀντεγείραντος πόλεμος οὔτε μικρὸς οὔτ' ὀλιγοχρόνιος ἐκινήθη. *(2)* Ἰουδαῖοι γὰρ
5 δεινόν τι ποιούμενοι τὸ ἀλλοφύλους τινὰς ἐς τὴν πόλιν σφῶν οἰκισθῆναι καὶ τὸ ἱερὰ ἀλλότρια ἐν αὐτῇ ἱδρυθῆναι, παρόντος μὲν ἔν τε τῇ Αἰγύπτῳ καὶ αὖθις ἐν τῇ Συρίᾳ τοῦ Ἀδριανοῦ ἡσύχαζον, πλὴν καθ' ὅσον τὰ ὅπλα τὰ ἐπιταχθέντα σφίσιν ἧττον ἐπιτήδεια ἐξεπίτηδες κατεσκεύασαν ὡς ἀποδοκιμασθεῖσιν αὐτοῖς ὑπ' ἐκείνων χρήσασθαι,
10 ἐπεὶ δὲ πόρρω ἐγένετο, φανερῶς ἀπέστησαν. *(3)* καὶ παρατάξει μὲν φανερᾷ οὐκ ἐτόλμων διακινδυνεῦσαι πρὸς τοὺς Ῥωμαίους, τὰ δὲ τῆς χώρας ἐπίκαιρα κατελάμβανον καὶ ὑπονόμοις καὶ τείχεσιν ἐκρατύνοντο, ὅπως ἀναφυγάς τε ὁπόταν βιασθῶσιν ἔχωσι καὶ παρ' ἀλλήλους ὑπὸ γῆν διαφοιτῶντες λανθάνωσι, διατιτράντες ἄνω τὰς
15 ὑπογείους ὁδοὺς ἵνα καὶ ἄνεμον καὶ φέγγος ἐσδέχοιντο. *(13:1)* καὶ τὸ μὲν πρῶτον ἐν οὐδενὶ αὐτοὺς λόγῳ οἱ Ῥωμαῖοι ἐποιοῦντο· ἐπεὶ δ' ἥ τε Ἰουδαία πᾶσα ἐκεκίνητο, καὶ οἱ ἁπανταχοῦ γῆς Ἰουδαῖοι συνεταράττοντο καὶ συνήεσαν, καὶ πολλὰ κακὰ ἐς τοὺς Ῥωμαίους τὰ μὲν λάθρα τὰ δὲ καὶ φανερῶς ἐνεδείκνυντο, *(2)* πολλοί τε ἄλλοι καὶ
20 τῶν ἀλλοφύλων ἐπιθυμίᾳ κέρδους σφίσι συνελαμβάνοντο, καὶ πάσης ὡς εἰπεῖν κινουμένης ἐπὶ τούτῳ τῆς οἰκουμένης, τότε δὴ τότε τοὺς κρατίστους τῶν στρατηγῶν ὁ Ἀδριανὸς ἐπ' αὐτοὺς ἔπεμψεν, ὧν πρῶτος Ἰούλιος Σεουῆρος ὑπῆρχεν, ἀπὸ Βρεττανίας ἧς ἦρχεν ἐπὶ τοὺς Ἰουδαίους σταλείς. *(3)* ὃς ἄντικρυς μὲν οὐδαμόθεν ἐτόλμησε τοῖς
25 ἐναντίοις συμβαλεῖν, τό τε πλῆθος καὶ τὴν ἀπόγνωσιν αὐτῶν ὁρῶν· ἀπολαμβάνων δ' ὡς ἑκάστους πλήθει τῶν στρατιωτῶν καὶ τῶν ὑπάρχων, καὶ τροφῆς ἀπείργων καὶ κατακλείων, ἠδυνήθη βραδύτερον μὲν ἀκινδυνότερον δὲ κατατρῖψαι καὶ ἐκτρυχῶσαι καὶ ἐκκόψαι αὐτούς.

9 ὡς] ὥστε Kuiper   15 ἄνεμον] ἀέρα? Bekker   17 ἐκεκίνητο Sturzius   κεκίνητο VC / πανταχοῦ V   20 καὶ del. Kuiper
26 λαμβάνων C

391

(14:1) ὀλίγοι γοῦν κομιδῇ περιεγένοντο. καὶ φρούρια μὲν αὐτῶν
30 *πεντήκοντα τά γε ἀξιολογώτατα, κῶμαι δὲ ἐνακόσιαι καὶ ὀγδοήκοντα*
καὶ πέντε ὀνομαστόταται κατεσκάφησαν, ἄνδρες δὲ ὀκτὼ καὶ
πεντήκοντα μυριάδες ἐσφάγησαν ἔν τε ταῖς καταδρομαῖς καὶ ταῖς
μάχαις (τῶν τε γὰρ λιμῷ καὶ νόσῳ καὶ πυρὶ φθαρέντων τὸ πλῆθος
ἀνεξερεύνητον ἦν), (2) ὥστε πᾶσαν ὀλίγου δεῖν τὴν Ἰουδαίαν
35 *ἐρημωθῆναι, καθάπερ που καὶ πρὸ τοῦ πολέμου αὐτοῖς προεδείχθη· τὸ*
γὰρ μνημεῖον τοῦ Σολομῶντος, ὃν ἐν τοῖς σεβασμίοις οὗτοι ἄγουσιν,
ἀπὸ ταὐτομάτου διελύθη τε καὶ συνέπεσε, καὶ λύκοι ὕαιναί τε πολλαὶ
ἐς τὰς πόλεις αὐτῶν ἐσέπιπτον ὠρυόμεναι. (3) πολλοὶ μέντοι ἐν τῷ
πολέμῳ τούτῳ καὶ τῶν Ῥωμαίων ἀπώλοντο· διὸ καὶ ὁ Ἀδριανὸς
40 *γράφων πρὸς τὴν βουλὴν οὐκ ἐχρήσατο τῷ προοιμίῳ τῷ συνήθει τοῖς*
αὐτοκράτορσιν, ὅτι· «εἰ αὐτοί τε καὶ οἱ παῖδες ὑμῶν ὑγιαίνετε, εὖ ἂν
ἔχοι· ἐγὼ καὶ τὰ στρατεύματα ὑγιαίνομεν» ... (15:1) ὁ μὲν οὖν τῶν
Ἰουδαίων πόλεμος ἐς τοῦτο ἐτελεύτησεν ...

29 γοῦν Bekker   δ' οὖν VC   31 κατεσκάφησαν Zonaras
       κατεστράφησαν VC   36 ὃν] ὁ Reiske

(12:1) At Jerusalem he [scil. Hadrian] founded a city in place of the one which had been razed to the ground, naming it Aelia Capitolina, and on the site of the temple of the god he raised a new temple to Jupiter. This brought on a war of no slight importance nor of brief duration, (2) for the Jews deemed it intolerable that foreign races should be settled in their city and foreign religious rites planted there. So long, indeed, as Hadrian was close by in Egypt and again in Syria, they remained quiet, save in so far as they purposely made of poor quality such weapons as they were called upon to furnish, in order that the Romans might reject them and that they themselves might thus have the use of them; but when he went farther away, they openly revolted. (3) To be sure, they did not dare try conclusions with the Romans in the open field, but they occupied the advantageous positions in the country and strengthened them with mines and walls, in order that they might have places of refuge whenever they should be hard pressed, and might meet together unobserved under ground; and they pierced these subterranean passages from above at intervals to let in air and light. (13:1) At first the Romans took no account of them. Soon, however, all Judaea had been stirred up, and the Jews everywhere were showing signs of disturbance, were gathering together, and giving evidence of great hostility to the Romans, partly by secret and partly by overt acts; (2) many outside nations, too, were joining them through eagerness for gain, and the whole earth, one might almost say, was being stirred up over the matter. Then, indeed, Hadrian sent against them his best generals. First of these was Julius Severus, who was dispatched from Britain, where he was governor, against the Jews. (3) Severus did not venture to attack his opponents in the open at any one point, in view of their numbers and their desperation, but by intercepting small groups, thanks to the number of his soldiers and his under-officers, and by depriving them of food and shutting them up, he was able, rather slowly, to be sure, but with comparatively little danger, to crush, exhaust and exterminate them. (14:1) Very few of them in fact survived. Fifty of their most important outposts and nine hundred and eighty-five of their most famous villages were razed to the ground. Five hundred and eighty thousand men were slain in the various raids and battles, and the number of those that perished by famine, disease and fire was past finding out. (2) Thus nearly the whole of Judaea was made desolate, a result of which the people had had forewarning before the war. For the tomb of Solomon, which[1] the Jews regard as an object of veneration, fell to pieces of itself and collapsed, and many wolves and hyenas rushed howling into their cities. (3) Many Romans, moreover, perished in this war. Therefore Hadrian in writing to the senate did not employ the opening phrase commonly affected by the emperors, "If you and your children are in health, it is well; I and the legions are in health ..." (15:1) This, then, was the end of the war with the Jews.

(trans. E. Cary, LCL)

These passages from Cassius Dio's History, even in the abridgement in which they have reached us through the epitome of Xiphilinus, constitute the main and most consistent survey of the Jewish revolt under Hadrian existing in ancient literature.

Dio's survey of the history of the revolt gives only the general outlines, describing cause, nature, tactics and results, but does not go into details. The only name mentioned is that of Julius Severus. Neither the governor of Judaea, Tineius Rufus, nor any of the κράτιστοι στρατηγοί sent to the province by Hadrian is called by name. Nor is it known from Dio's account which legions took part in the war.

Although Dio mentions the names of the leaders of the Jewish revolt in Cyrenaica (Andreas) and Cyprus (Artemion) in the time of Trajan, in the history of the revolt under Hadrian the name of Bar-Kokhba is missing. No localities are mentioned excepting Jerusalem and the tomb of Solomon, and

---

1 The translation according to the emendation of Reiske.

even the name of Beitar, the stronghold of the revolt whose fall signed the fate of the war, does not find place in Dio's account.

It seems likely that Dio used a literary source or sources for his narrative of the war, and only by such a supposition may we account for such details as the omens preceding the revolt. It is possible that both the wording of the letter of Hadrian quoted by Dio, and the numbers of the Jewish casualties and places captured, could derive directly or indirectly from Hadrian's reports to the senate; see Millar, *op. cit.* (supra, p. 347, n. 1), p. 62. However an additional literary source is required, which might already have included the quotation.

For the character and sources of the section on the reign of Hadrian in Dio's History, see also J. Plew, *Quellenuntersuchungen zur Geschichte des Kaisers Hadrian*, Strasbourg 1890, pp. 54 ff.; Millar, *op. cit.* (supra, p. 347, n. 1), pp. 60 ff.

The information supplied by other Greek and Latin writers concerning the Jewish revolt under Hadrian is comparatively meagre. Among them, cf. Appianus, *Syriacus Liber*, 50:252 (No. 343), seeming to imply the capture of Jerusalem by the Jews, and in any case its destruction by Hadrian at one stage of the revolt; Fronto, *De Bello Parthico*, 2 (No. 342), referring to the heavy losses sustained by the Roman forces in Judaea in the time of Hadrian; Apollodorus of Damascus (No. 322); Pausanias, *Graeciae Descriptio*, I, 5:5 (No. 353), stating the bare fact that Hadrian, though never waging any war willingly, had yet subdued the Hebrews. See also *Scriptores Historiae Augustae, Hadrianus*, 14 (No. 511), attributing the outbreak of the revolt to Hadrian's ban on circumcision; this information is wholly ignored by Dio.

A more important addition to Dio is found in Eusebius, *Historia Ecclesiastica*, IV, 6, where other points are emphasized than those in Dio's History or in the *Scriptores Historiae Augustae*. Eusebius gives no reason for the revolt, and refers only to the madness of the Jews, against which Tineius Rufus, the governor of Judaea, took action. Unlike the pagan writers, Eusebius refers to the leadership of Barchochebas (Bar-Kokhba), and the protracted siege of Beitar and its fall. He also stresses Hadrian's decrees preventing Jews from entering Jerusalem; here he refers to the lost work of Ariston of Pella. The transformation of Jerusalem into Aelia Capitolina is mentioned only after the crushing of the revolt. Eusebius also deals briefly with the Jewish revolt in his *Chronica* (ed. Karst, pp. 220 f.) and *Demonstratio Evangelica*; cf. the commentary to Appian (No. 343). The account of Eusebius set the later patristic and Byzantine tradition, though the latter did not remain wholly uninfluenced by that of Dio.

The talmudic and midrashic literature has much sporadic information on the revolt; it is collected in part by Derenbourg, pp. 412 ff.

Especially important for the subject are the new papyri discovered in the Desert of Judaea, published in part in *IEJ*, XI (1961), pp. 3 ff., 53 ff.; XII (1962), pp. 167 ff.; *Aegyptus*, XLII (1962), pp. 240 ff.; and in P. Benoit, J. T. Milik & R. de Vaux, *Discoveries in the Judaean Desert*, II — *Les grottes de Murabba'ât*, Oxford 1961.

For the Jewish numismatic material, see Y. Meshorer, *Jewish Coins of the*

Cassius Dio

Second Temple Period, Tel Aviv 1967, pp. 92 ff. For the Roman imperial coinage reflecting the Jewish revolt, see H. Mattingly, *Coins of the Roman Empire in the British Museum*, III, London 1936, p. CXLII. The main inscriptional material on the part played by the Roman military forces will be cited below. For a further study of the Jewish coins, see M. Philonenko, *CRAI* (1974), pp. 183 ff.

12:1 Ἐς δὲ τὰ Ἱεροσόλυμα πόλιν αὐτοῦ ἀντὶ τῆς κατασκαφείσης οἰκίσαντος, ἥν καὶ Αἰλίαν Καπιτωλῖναν ὠνόμασε: The decision to replace Jerusalem by a Roman city, and the laying of its foundations, seems to have taken place during Hadrian's visit to Jerusalem prior to his Egyptian journey of 130 C.E. We may discard both the date of 119, implied by *Chronicon Paschale*, I, p. 474 (ed. Dindorf), and that of Hadrian's visit in 117, to be inferred from Epiphanius, *De Mensuris et Ponderibus*, 14: μετὰ ἔτη μζ' τῆς τῶν Ἱεροσολύμων ἐρημώσεως; see Schürer, ed. Vermes & Millar, I, pp. 540 f.

The name Aelia derives from Aelius, the *gentilicium* of Hadrian; cf. Epiphanius, *loc. cit.*: ὡς γὰρ ἐκεῖνος ὠνόμαστο Αἴλιος Ἀδριανός, οὕτως καὶ τὴν πόλιν ὠνόμασεν Αἰλίαν. The epithet "Capitolina" comes from "Capitolinus", the designation of Jupiter. For the view that "Capitolinus" denotes Hadrian himself, see Weber, *op. cit.* (supra, p. 390), p. 241. Against this interpretation, see J. Beaujeu, *La religion romaine à l'apogée de l'empire*, I, Paris 1955, pp. 261 f.

The building operations of Hadrian in Palestine were not confined to Jerusalem. His visit was also connected with the raising of a temple in his honour at Tiberias; cf. Epiphanius, *Panarion*, XXX, 12: ναὸς δὲ μέγιστος ἐν τῇ πόλει προϋπῆρχε ... Ἀδριανεῖον τοῦτο ἐκάλουν. For the Hadrianeion in Caesarea, see *RB*, IV (1895), p. 76; *PEQ* (1896), p. 87. Cf. also F.M. Abel, *Histoire de la Palestine*, II, Paris 1952, pp. 79 ff.

Aelia Capitolina became a Roman colony. For the numismatic evidence, see G.F. Hill, *Catalogue of the Greek Coins of Palestine*, London 1914, pp. 82 ff.; L. Kadman, *The Coins of Aelia Capitolina*, Jerusalem 1956, p. 32. The fact is recorded in the *Digesta*, L, 15:1:6: "in Palaestina duae fuerunt coloniae, Caesariensis et Aelia Capitolina". See also G. Durand, *RB*, I (1892), pp. 369 ff.; H. Vincent & F.M. Abel, *Jérusalem*, II, Paris 1914, pp. 1 ff.; Abel, *Histoire de la Palestine*, *op. cit.*, pp. 97 ff.; A.H.M. Jones, *The Cities of the Eastern Roman Provinces*[2], Oxford 1971, p. 277.

ἐς τὸν τοῦ ναοῦ τοῦ θεοῦ τόπον ναὸν τῷ Διὶ ἕτερον ἀντεγείραντος: On the presence of Hadrian in Jerusalem, cf. Epiphanius, *De Mensuris et Ponderibus*, 14: καὶ ἄνεισιν ἐπὶ τὰ Ἱεροσόλυμα. The visit of Hadrian as described by Epiphanius is dated to 134 C.E. by Follet, *op. cit.* (supra, p. 390), pp. 68 ff. See also Hieronymus, *Commentarii in Esaiam*, i:2 (ed. M. Adriaen, *CCSL*, LXXIII, p. 33): "ubi quondam erat templum et religio Dei, ibi Adriani statua et Iovis idolum collocatum est"; idem, *Epistulae*, LVIII, 3:5 (ed. I. Hilberg, *CSEL*, LIV, pp. 531 f.): "ab Adriani temporibus usque ad imperium Constantini per annos circiter centum octoginta in loco resurrectionis simulacrum Iovis, in crucis rupe statua ex marmore Veneris a gentilibus posita." See also Iohannes Chrysostomus, *Adversus Iudaeos*, V, 11;

Cedrenus, I, pp. 437 f. (ed. Bekker); Nicephorus Callistus, III, 24 (*PG,* CXLV, pp. 944 f.).

πόλεμος ... ἐκινήθη: The statement of Dio that the outbreak of the revolt was caused by the foundation of Aelia Capitolina is seemingly contradicted by Eusebius, who refers to the change of the name of Jerusalem into Aelia Capitolina as an aftermath of the revolt; cf. *Historia Ecclesiastica,* IV, 6:4: οὕτω δὴ τῆς πόλεως ἐς ἐρημίαν τοῦ Ἰουδαίων ἔθνους παντελῆ τε φθορὰν τῶν πάλαι οἰκητόρων ἐλθούσης ἐξ ἀλλοφύλου τε γένους συνοικισθείσης, ἡ μετέπειτα συστᾶσα Ῥωμαϊκὴ πόλις τὴν ἐπωνυμίαν ἀμείψασα, εἰς τὴν τοῦ κρατοῦντος Αἰλίου Ἀδριανοῦ τιμὴν Αἰλία προσαγορεύεται. However, this apparent contradiction can be resolved. Once the revolt broke out conditions of war prevailed in Judaea, and Jerusalem seems to have fallen for some time into the hands of the Jews. Thus there could not have been enough time to carry out building operations on a large scale before what had been accomplished was destroyed by the rebels; see already F. Münter, *Der jüdische Krieg unter den Kaisern Trajan und Hadrian,* Altona–Leipzig 1821, p. 39.

πόλεμος οὔτε μικρός: That the war was heavy and strained the resources of the empire may be deduced from the large military forces employed by Hadrian and the losses sustained by the Romans, as implied by Hadrian's letter to the senate. It seems that the legionary garrison of Judaea had already consisted of two legions before the war, and that Bar-Kokhba had to withstand this force from the start of the revolt. One legion was undoubtedly the Legio X Fretensis, which constituted the garrison of Judaea from the year 70 C.E. A second legion was added at some time under the reign of Hadrian, but still before the outbreak of the war. This follows from the consideration that by then Judaea had already become a consular instead of a praetorian province, since it is known that at least Tineius Rufus, the governor of Judaea at the start of the war, was *consul suffectus* in 127 C.E., as attested by the *Fasti Ostienses*; cf. A. Degrassi (ed.), *Inscriptiones Italiae,* Vol. XIII, Part 1, Rome 1947, p. 205. Moreover, there is no cogent argument to make us assume that the elevation of Judaea from praetorian to consular rank took place only with the appointment of Tineius Rufus, and an earlier date is plausible; cf. L.J.F. Keppie, *Latomus,* XXXII (1973), pp. 859 ff. For dating the change to *c.* 129 C.E., if not a number of years earlier, see R. Syme, *Historia,* XIV (1965), p. 342.

New epigraphic evidence also points to the existence in the province of a second legion, whose camp is attested by a milestone, to be dated to 130 C.E., at Galilean Kafar Cotni. Since this is known to have been the place of encampment of the Legio VI Ferrata after the Roman victory (cf. above, p. 364), it was inferred that the inscription of 130 C.E. is to be connected with this legion; see B. Lifshitz, *Latomus,* XIX (1960), pp. 109 ff.; idem, *Hommages à Marcel Renard,* II, Brussels 1969, p. 461. The transfer of the legion to Judaea is even dated to 123 C.E., the time of Hadrian's first voyage to the east; cf. H.G. Pflaum, *IEJ,* XIX (1969), p. 232. For a suggestion that Legio II Traiana might have been the second legion garrisoning Judaea before the revolt, see Keppie, *op. cit.* This conjecture is based on the supposition that the Legio VI Ferrata then constituted the garrison of the province of Arabia; cf. also G. W. Bowersock, *Zeitschrift für Papyrologie und Epigraphik*, V (1970), pp. 40 ff. In any case Tineius Rufus evidently had two legions at his disposal at the initial stages of the war. See also M. Avi-Yonah, *IEJ*, XXIII (1973), pp. 209 ff., dating the transformation of Judaea into a consular province to 115/116 C.E. The correct solution seems to be that the Legio VI Ferrata at first constituted the garrison of Provincia Arabia, but was transferred to Judaea before 130 but after 117 C.E.; see G. W. Bowersock, *JRS*, LXV (1975), p. 184. On the Legio II Traiana and Judaea, see B. Isaac & I. Roll, *ZPE*, XXXIII (1979), pp. 149 ff.

There is no clear information concerning the strength of the legionary forces that took part in crushing the revolt under Hadrian, in contrast to the details supplied by Josephus for the Jewish war against Rome in the times of Vespasian and Titus. Apart from the information given by Cassius Dio, there is only the brief statement of Eusebius about military aid having been sent to Tineius Rufus by Hadrian; cf. Eusebius, *Historia Ecclesiastica*, IV, 6:1: στρατιωτικῆς αὐτῷ συμμαχίας ὑπὸ βασιλέως πεμφθείσης. We can base some inferences on the allusions to the strength and identity of the legionary garrisons of Judaea and the neighbouring provinces in the years preceding the revolt, and on inscriptions attesting to the presence of different military units and officers in Judaea during the war. Some of this evidence shows the part played in the fighting not only by the legions, but also by the *auxilia*, the fleet and the praetorian guard. The inscriptions often lend themselves to contradictory interpretations. However, it is clear that the war was a heavy strain on the resources of the imperial forces in Judaea, Syria and other parts of the empire, in both east and west.

The Legio X Fretensis was stationed in Judaea from the time of Titus, and epigraphical evidence confirms its presence there in the time of Hadrian; see A. Negev, *IEJ*, XIV (1964), p. 244; *ILS*, No. 2080; B. Lifshitz, *Latomus*, XXII (1963), p. 784; D. Barag, *IEJ*, XIV (1964), pp. 250 ff.; J. Olami & J. Ringel, *IEJ*, XXV (1975), pp. 148 ff. See also *PSI*, No. 1026 = S. Daris, *Documenti per la storia dell'esercito romano in Egitto*, Milan 1964, No. 98. It has already been shown that a second legion, perhaps the Legio VI Ferrata or Legio II Traiana, was also stationed in the province in the years immediately preceding the revolt.

Occasionally there is evidence of additional forces stationed in Judaea, either at the end of the reign of Trajan or during that of Hadrian. A dedication, dating presumably from the end of Trajan's reign, to "Iupiter optimus maximus" in honour of Trajan by a *vexillatio* of the Legio III Cyrenaica, known to have been stationed at that time in Egypt, has been found in Jerusalem; see *ILS*, No. 4393 = Saxer, No. 46. The presence of this *vexillatio* at Jerusalem may be accounted for by the fear of Jewish disturbances. From papyrological sources we have a receipt, to be dated to 128 C.E., issued to the weavers of Socnopaei Nesus, acknowledging the delivery of tunics and cloaks, of which five cloaks are destined for soldiers on service in "Iudaea"; see *P. Rylands*, II, No. 189. Cf. W. D. Gray, *The American Journal of Semitic Languages and Literatures*, XXXIX (1922–1923), pp. 254 f.

The two legions of the garrison of Judaea, the Legio X Fretensis and presumably the Legio VI Ferrata, were under the command of Tineius Rufus, the *legatus pro praetore* of Judaea, and these certainly bore the brunt of the first onslaught of the Jews. As could be expected, the first to come to the rescue of Tineius Rufus was Publicius Marcellus, the *legatus pro praetore* of Syria. In an inscription it is expressly mentioned that the man left in charge of the province, as a result of Publicius' departure from Syria for Judaea, continued to command the Legio IV Scythica; cf. *IGRR*, III, Nos. 174–175: ἡγεμόνα λεγιῶνος τετάρτης Σκυθικῆς καὶ διοικήσαντα τὰ ἐν Συρίᾳ πράγματα, ἡνίκα Πουβλίκιος Μάρκελλος διὰ τὴν κείνησιν τὴν 'Ιουδαϊκὴν μεταβεβήκει ἀπὸ Συρίας. This legion therefore did not accompany Publicius to Judaea, though he probably took the other Syrian legions with him. One of them seems to have been the Legio III Gallica, which usually belonged to the garrison of the province of Syria. It seems that one of its *emeriti* was honoured by Hadrian for his participation in the war; cf. *ILS*, No. 2313.

Whether the Legio II Traiana constituted part of the garrison of Judaea in the years preceding the war or not, the existence of a *vexillatio* of that legion in Judaea at the time of Hadrian is shown by an inscription from the aqueduct of Caesarea; cf. A. Negev, *IEJ*, XIV (1964), pp. 245 ff. It is difficult to say whether we can adduce additional evidence from *ILS*, No. 2083. This is an inscription commemorating a soldier, Gaius Nummius, decorated by Hadrian "ob bellum Iudaicum", who had served as *primus pilus* of the Legio II Traiana and also as *centurio* of the Legio III Cyrenaica and Legio VII Claudia. We cannot know in which capacity he fought in Judaea.

It may be surmised that the Legio VI Ferrata, which after the war constituted part of the garrison of the province, had also participated in the military operations. The whole legion may have been involved, or only some of its *vexillationes*, whether it had been stationed before the war in Judaea, Syria or Arabia.

It is usually assumed that also the Legio XXII Deioteriana took part in the imperial effort to crush the revolt. This legion was in Egypt in 119 C.E.; cf. *BGU*, I, No. 140 = Daris, *op. cit.* (supra, p. 397), No. 108. However its name is missing in *ILS*, No. 2288, a list of legions arranged according to the provinces and belonging fundamentally to the time of Antoninus Pius. It has been therefore suggested that this legion was wiped out at some stage of the war; see W. Pfitzner, *Geschichte der römischen Kaiserlegionen von Augustus bis Hadrianus*, Leipzig 1881, pp. 269 f.; Ritterling, PW, XII, pp. 1292, 1795; H. M. D. Parker, *The Roman Legions*, Oxford 1928, pp. 162 f.; J. F. Gilliam, *AJP*, LXXVII (1956), p. 362. Some doubts at this conjecture have been expressed by, e.g., P. Trommsdorff, "Quaestiones Duae ad Historiam Legionum Romanarum Spectantes", Ph. D. Thesis, Leipzig 1896, p. 93; Keppie, *op. cit.* (supra, p. 396), p. 863. However the view has not much to commend it (Trommsdorff's suggestion that the legion was lost in Trajan's Parthian war cannot be accepted since it was still in existence in 119 C.E.). If the legion was so destroyed, its defeat should have taken place before the full weight of the empire had been mobilized and thrown into the war.

For a suggestion that the Legio XII Fulminata, normally stationed in Cappadocia, took part in the war, cf. B. Lifshitz, *Latomus*, XXI (1962), p. 149. As happened in the first Jewish war against Rome, the army of the Danube also played its part in subduing the Jews. There is clear evidence for the presence in Palestine of *vexillationes* from two of the Lower Moesian legions, the Legio V Macedonica and the Legio XI Claudia, as well as from the Upper Pannonian Legio X Gemina. The evidence for the V Macedonica, which had taken part in the conquest of Galilee by Vespasian and of Jerusalem by Titus, and for the XI Claudia, comes from an inscription found near Beitar, the last stronghold of the revolt; cf. C. Clermont-Ganneau, *Archaeological Researches in Palestine*, I, London 1899, p. 465: "centur(iones) vexill(ationum) leg(ionis) V Mac(edonicae) et XI Cl(audiae)". Cf. also W. D. Carroll, *AASOR*, V (1925), pp. 84 f. (for 1923–1924). The view that the inscription is to be dated to the time of Trajan is not very likely, since its connection with Beitar renders a date during the Bar-Kokhba revolt almost certain; cf. B. Filow, *Die Legionen der Provinz Moesia von Augustus bis auf Diokletian*, Leipzig 1906, pp. 68 f. Nor is there more cogency in dating the inscription to post-Hadrianic times, as suggested by A. Schulten, *ZDPV*, LVI (1933), p. 184. The participation of the Legio XI Claudia is attested by an inscription relating to a soldier of that legion found at Beisan; cf. M. Avi-Yonah, *QDAP*, VIII (1939), pp. 57 ff.

The evidence for the Legio X Gemina consists of two inscriptions. One is *CIL*, VI, No. 3505 = Saxer No. 49. This states that Sextus Attius Senecio, a *praefectus alae* of I Flavia Gaetulorum and *tribunus* of the Legio X Gemina, was commissioned by Hadrian "in expeditione Iudaica ad vexilla[tiones deducendas in ...]". However, we cannot state the exact composition of the expeditionary force under the command of Senecio; see Saxer, *ad loc*. The other inscription attesting the presence of Q. Lollius Urbicus "in expeditione Iudaica", perhaps in the role of the commander of the Legio X Gemina, is *ILS*, No. 1065. Alongside of the legionary forces a number of auxiliary cohorts took part in the war. A prefect of the Cohors IV Lingonum was decorated by Hadrian "in expeditione Iudaica"; cf. *ILS*, No. 1092. This cohort is usually known as having been stationed in Britain, and is attested there in the years 103 and 146 C. E.; see G. L. Cheesman, *The Auxilia of the Roman Imperial Army*, Oxford 1914, p. 148. On the other hand Filow denies the presence of this cohort in Judaea, suggesting that the man acted there as a tribune of the Legio III Gallica, known in any case to have participated in the war; see the discussion by Filow, *op. cit.*, p. 69, n. 2. Three *alae* and twelve cohorts are referred to as being stationed in Syria Palaestina in *CIL*, XVI, No. 87, dated 139 C. E.

The activity of the praetorian cohorts, presumably accompanying the emperor, is to be inferred from *ILS*, No. 2081. The Classis Syriaca, probably created under the stress of the former Jewish war, again appears on the scene of operations; its prefect Sextus Cornelius Dexter was decorated by Hadrian for his service in "the Jewish war" (*ILS*, No. 1400). Another possible connection with the activities of the Classis Syriaca in the time of Hadrian is *CIL*, VI, No. 1565; see P. Thomsen, *ZDPV*, LXVIII (1946–1951), p. 80. For another view, see D. Kienast, *Untersuchungen zu den Kriegsflotten der römischen Kaiserzeit*, Bonn 1966, p. 96, n. 50.

The burden imposed by the war on the military resources of the empire may be illustrated by the special *dilectus* held at the time in Italy in order to restore the strength of the existing legionary forces; see J. C. Mann, *Hermes*, XCI (1963), p. 488; D. J. Blackman, *Akten des VI. Internationalen Kongresses für Griechische und Lateinische Epigraphik*, Munich 1972 (1973), p. 567.

The revolt is sometimes referred to in the Latin inscriptions of the period as "bellum Iudaicum" (*ILS*, No. 2083; *CIL*, VIII, No. 8934); sometimes it is denoted "expeditio Iudaica" (*CIL*, VI, No. 3505; *ILS*, Nos. 1071, 1092).

The strength of the Roman force employed in the war, the losses suffered in it, the duration of the conflict, and the remarks of Dio and Fronto (No. 342) seem fully to justify Mommsen's evaluation that this war "durch Intensität und Dauer in der Geschichte der römischen Kaiserzeit seines Gleichen nicht hat"; see T. Mommsen, *Römische Geschichte*, V[6], Berlin 1909, p. 545.

οὔτ᾽ ὀλιγοχρόνιος: The war seems to have lasted some three-and-a-half years; cf. Hieronymus, *Commentarii in Danielem*, ix, 24 = *CCSL*, LXXV A (ed. Glorie), p. 888 = PL, XXV, p. 553; *Seder 'Olam Rabba*, 30 (ed. Ratner, p. 146), where the manuscript evidence wavers between two-and-a-half and three-and-a-half years. This is the time given for the duration of the siege of Beitar in talmudic and midrashic sources; see *TP Ta'anit*, iv, 68d; *Midrash Ekha*, 2, 2. The *Chronica* of Eusebius dates the outbreak of the revolt to the year 2148 of Abraham's era (the sixteenth year of Hadrian) and the end of the revolt to the year 2151 (the nineteenth year of Hadrian), so that the duration of the revolt is dated by Eusebius between 132 and 135 C. E.; see *Die Chronik des Eusebius aus dem armenischen*, translated by J. Karst, Leipzig 1911, pp. 220 f.

According to Eusebius himself in the *Historia Ecclesiastica* (IV, 6: 3), the war reached its height in the eighteenth year of Hadrian, in the siege of Beitar: ἀκμάσαντος δὲ τοῦ πολέμου ἔτους ὀκτωδεκάτου τῆς ἡγεμονίας κατὰ Βηθθηρα. The official dating of Hadrian's reign commenced on 11 August 117 C. E., and the eighteenth year of Hadrian therefore ran from 11 August 134 to 10 August 135 C. E. About the siege and the fall of the fortress Eusebius states: τῆς τε ἔξωθεν πολιορκίας χρονίου γενομένης λιμῷ τε καὶ δίψει τῶν νεωτεροποιῶν εἰς ἔσχατον ὀλέθρου περιελαθέντων καὶ τοῦ τῆς ἀπονοίας αὐτοῖς αἰτίου τὴν ἀξίαν ἐκτίσαντος δίκην. The statements of Eusebius seem to imply that the decisive phase in the battle for Beitar fell in the eighteenth year of Hadrian. This is borne out by the epigraphic evidence. It is to be inferred from one source (*CIL*, XVI, No. 82) that by 14 April 135 Hadrian had not yet been acclaimed *imperator* for the second time. On the other hand, a Greek inscription from Syros (*IG*, XII, Suppl., No. 239) shows that this acclamation is to be dated in the nineteenth year of the *tribunicia potestas* of Hadrian, i.e. between 10 December 134 and 9 December 135, according to the most prevalent view concerning the counting of Hadrian's *tribunicia potestas*. If we take into consideration the first-mentioned inscription (*CIL*, XVI, No. 82), the acclamation must have taken place only after 14 April 135; see F. Heichelheim, *JQR*, XXXIV (1943/4), pp. 61 ff.;

idem, in: C. Seltman, *Hesperia*, XVII (1948), p. 85. For the problems connected with the years of the *tribunicia potestas* of Hadrian, see T. Mommsen, *Römisches Staatsrecht*, Vol. II, Part 2³, Leipzig 1887, pp. 799 f.; H. Mattingly, *JRS*, XX (1930), pp. 78 ff.; M. Hammond, *The Antonine Monarchy*, Rome 1959, pp. 72 f.; S. Follet, *Athènes au IIe et IIIe siècle*, Paris 1976, pp. 43 ff.

Hadrian had already been *imperator iterum* in 136 as known from the plentiful evidence attesting this for the twentieth year of his *tribunicia potestas*; cf. *CIL*, XIV, No. 4235; *ILS*, No. 317; *CIL*, VI, No. 975; *IGRR*, III, No. 896; *Année épigraphique*, 1928, No. 193; *P. Oslo*, III, No. 78.

Regarding the beginning of the revolt, it seems certain that Hadrian returned from Egypt to Judaea and Syria in 131. According to the succeeding passage of Dio, the Jews waited and did not revolt until Hadrian had left Syria. However, whether the war had already started in 131 or did not commence until 132 C.E. is still a matter of dispute. The exact date of Hadrian's departure from Syria cannot be stated, but his presence in Asia Minor in 131 seems to be certain, while dedications found in the Olympieion of Athens are dated in the sixteenth year of Hadrian's *tribunicia potestas* (10 December 131 to 9 December 132 C.E.); see P. Graindor, *Athènes sous Hadrien*, Cairo 1934, p. 40. The coins of Bar-Kokhba do not render much help concerning the dates of the beginning or end of the revolt or its duration. There are coins bearing the legend שנה אחת לגאלת ישראל "Year one of the Redemption of Israel", and שנה ב' לחרות ישראל "Year 2 of the Freedom of Israel". There are also coins attributed by the numismatists to the third year, but no express mention of a third year appears in the legends on the coins; see Y. Meshorer, *Jewish Coins of the Second Temple Period*, Tel Aviv 1967, pp. 94 f.

As we have seen, the date 132 C.E., i.e. the sixteenth year of Hadrian, is given for the start of the revolt by Eusebius, *Chronica*; see *Die Chronik des Eusebius aus dem armenischen, op. cit.* (supra, p. 400), p. 220. This date is now also defended on the basis of the document published by Benoit, Milik & de Vaux, *op. cit.* (supra, p. 394), No. 24; see M. R. Lehmann, *Revue de Qumran*, IV (1963), pp. 56 f. The dating of the editors implies the year 131 as the first of the redemption of Israel. The discussion turns mainly on the dating of the following sabbatical year mentioned in the document.

12:2 Ἰουδαῖοι γὰρ δεινόν τι ποιούμενοι τὸ ἀλλοφύλους τινὰς ἐς τὴν πόλιν σφῶν οἰκισθῆναι ... φανερῶς ἀπέστησαν: Dio's history is the only source to connect the outbreak of the revolt with the foundation of Aelia Capitolina. The cause of the war is explained as the prohibition imposed on circumcision in *Scriptores Historiae Augustae, Hadrianus*, 14:2 (No. 511). Some scholars give credence only to Dio; see F. Gregorovius, *Der Kaiser Hadrian*³, Stuttgart 1884, p. 189, n. 2; H. Strathmann, *Palästinajahrbuch*, XXIII (1927), pp. 101 ff. However, it seems reasonable to suppose that the legislation under Hadrian concerning circumcision played its part in stimulating the Jews to resort to force; see Schürer, I, pp. 674 ff.; M. P. Nilsson, *Imperial Rome*, London 1926, p. 52; S. Lieberman, *Annuaire de l'institut de philologie et d'histoire orientales et slaves*, VII (1939–1944), pp. 423 f.; B. d'Orgeval, *L'empereur Hadrien*, Paris 1950, p. 290; G. Alon, *History of the Jews in*

Palestine in the Age of the Mishnah and the Talmud, II, Tel Aviv 1955, pp. 10 ff. (in Hebrew); Simon, p. 126, n. 4; G. W. Bowersock, *JRS*, LXV (1975), p. 185. See also the commentary to No. 511.

For an attempt to dispose of Dio's account and his statement that the foundation of Aelia Capitolina was the cause of the revolt, cf. H. Mantel, *JQR*, LVIII (1967/8), pp. 224 ff., maintaining that this happened after the revolt and as a reaction to it. This opinion, however, is hardly defensible. Cf. now also Meshorer, *op. cit.* (supra, p. 401), pp. 92 f.

Clearly, in the years preceding the revolt, there existed a general atmosphere of tension and apprehension. The rebellious state of mind that characterized the Jews in most of the period of Roman rule in Judaea had apparently found an outlet at the end of Trajan's reign, and necessitated the strengthening of the legionary garrison of the province. The chief aim of Hadrian in founding Aelia Capitolina could have been his wish to weaken the Jewish element in Judaea and neutralize it by a strong settlement of foreigners in the centre of the country. Perhaps he could foresee some opposition to his plans, but he was probably surprised by the dimensions that it assumed.

ἀλλοφύλους ... οἰκισθῆναι: The colonization of Jerusalem by foreigners is also stressed in other sources; cf. Malalas, XI (ed. Dindorf), p. 279 = A. S. von Stauffenberg, *Die römische Kaisergeschichte bei Malalas*, Stuttgart 1931, p. 49: ὁ δὲ αὐτὸς Ἀδριανὸς ὀργισθεὶς κατὰ Ἰουδαίων ἐκέλευσεν εἰς τὴν Ἱερουσαλὴμ οἰκεῖν Ἕλληνας, μετονομάσας αὐτὴν πόλιν Αἰλίαν; cf. also Zonaras, *Annales* (II, ed. Pinder), XI, 23, p. 517: Ἰουδαῖοι δὲ μὴ φέροντες τῆς σφῶν παραπολαύοντας μητροπόλεως ἄλλους ὁρᾶν, Ἕλληνες γὰρ ἐν αὐτῇ κατῳκίσθησαν, μηδὲ ξενικοὺς τιμᾶσθαι θεοὺς ἐν αὐτῇ ἀνεχόμενοι. It has been maintained that Zonaras here comes nearer to the original of Dio than the epitome of Xiphilinus; see Weber, *op. cit.* (supra, p. 390), p. 241, n. 873.

πλὴν καθ' ὅσον τὰ ὅπλα τὰ ἐπιταχθέντα σφίσιν ἧττον ἐπιτήδεια ἐξεπίτηδες κατεσκεύασαν ὡς ἀποδοκιμασθεῖσιν αὐτοῖς ὑπ' ἐκείνων χρήσασθαι: This passage is explained against the background of tension and hostility between Rome and Parthia by F. Schehl, *Hermes*, LXV (1930), pp. 184 f.; cf. H. Kreissig, *Die sozialen Zusammenhänge des judäischen Krieges*, Berlin 1970, p. 57.

12:3 καὶ ὑπονόμοις ... ἐκρατύνοντο, ὅπως ἀναφυγὰς ... ἔχωσι: The subterranean places of refuge are well illustrated by the discoveries in the desert of Judaea.

13:1 ἐπεὶ δ' ἥ τε Ἰουδαία πᾶσα ἐκεκίνητο: It has been argued that Dio refers here only to Judaea proper and that the revolt was confined to this area; see A. Büchler, *JQR*, XVI (1904), pp. 144 ff. Judaea proper certainly constituted the main centre of the revolt, though at some stages of the war military operations presumably took place in other parts of the province as well; see S. Yeivin, *The War of Bar-Kokhba*, Jerusalem 1946, pp. 60 f. (in Hebrew); P. Prigent, *La fin de Jérusalem*, Neuchâtel 1969, p. 108. The high number of fortresses and villages captured by the Romans as given by Dio (fifty fortresses and nine hundred and eighty-five villages) also supports the view that the war was waged in other parts of Palestine as well. Some allusion to the devastation of Galilee in the time of Hadrian is found in the Talmud; see *TP Pe'a*, vii, 20a; as additional evidence implying offensive action on the part of the Jews outside Judaea, we may point to Sulpicius Severus, II, 31: "Syriam ac Palaestinam diripere conati". The same perhaps holds true of what Dio says about the Jews being joined by foreigners. It should also be added that although in Dio's time Judaea was no longer the official name for the whole Roman province, having been replaced by the term Syria Palaestina, Dio did not always conform to the official usage and continued to refer to the whole of the country as Judaea; see the commentary to Cassius Dio, XXXVII, 15:2 (No. 406). Among classical writers living after the incorporation of the whole of Palestine into the Judaean state as a result of the Hasmonaean conquests, usage of the term Judaea by pagan writers is restricted to the meaning of Judaea proper in one passage in the writings of Pliny (cf. No. 204) and perhaps in Mela (No. 152). Nevertheless the revolt only spread in a very limited way into other parts of the country, being centered mainly on Judaea proper.

The stronghold of the Jews where Bar-Kokhba made his last stand was Beitar in the vicinity of Jerusalem. It is to be identified with Khirbet el Yehoud near the village of Bettir, south-west of Jerusalem. The place is mentioned as Βηϑϑηρα by Eusebius, *Historia Ecclesiastica*, IV, 6:3; its memory looms large in the Talmud and Midrash; cf. *TP Ta'anit*, iv, 69a; *TB Giṭṭin*, 57a–b; 58a; *Ekha Rabbati*, ii:2. On the location of Beitar and its archaeological remains, see Carroll, *op. cit.* (supra, p.399), pp. 77 ff.; Schulten, *op. cit.* (supra, p. 399), pp.180 ff.; Strathmann, *op. cit.* (supra, p.401), pp.114 ff.; Abel, II, p. 271.

The places mentioned in connection with Bar-Kokhba in the documents from the desert of Judaea were also within Judaea proper. Thus for Herodium, see Benoit, Milik & de Vaux, *op. cit.* (supra, p. 394), No. 24; E. M. Laperrousaz, *Syria*, XLI (1964), pp. 347 ff.; for Engeddi, see *IEJ*, XI (1961), p. 47; *IEJ*, XII (1962), p. 250.

Dio also emphasizes the participation of world Jewry in the first Jewish war against Rome; cf. Cassius Dio, LXVI, 4:3 (No. 430): καὶ οἱ Ἰουδαῖοι πολλοὶ μὲν αὐτόθεν πολλοὶ δὲ καὶ παρὰ τῶν ὁμοήθων, οὐχ ὅτι ἐκ τῆς τῶν Ῥωμαίων ἀρχῆς ἀλλὰ καὶ ἐκ τῶν πέραν Εὐφράτου. Dio's account is the only source giving concrete information about Jews from other countries taking part in the war. In the chronicle of Syncellus the relevant passage is rather vague; cf. Syncellus, I (ed. Dindorf), p. 660.

Some nineteenth-century scholars suggest accounting for the journeys of R. Aqiva in the countries of the Diaspora as preparations for a revolt among the Diaspora Jews; cf. the reports in, e.g., *TB Rosh Hashana*, 26a; *TB Yevamot*, 115a; 121a; *TP 'Avoda Zara*, ii, 41b; see, e.g., Derenbourg, p. 418. However this view is now generally discounted; cf. Alon, *op. cit.* (supra, pp. 401 f.), II, p. 29. Possibly the Jews counted on some help from Parthia; see N. C. Debevoise, *A Political History of Parthia*, Chicago 1938, p. 242. If so, they were disappointed no less than in the times of the first Jewish war against Rome.

13:2 πολλοί τε ἄλλοι καὶ τῶν ἀλλοφύλων ἐπιθυμίᾳ κέρδους σφίσι συνελαμβάνοντο: In his history of the first Jewish war against Rome Dio also mentions the remarkable fact that foreigners joined the Jews engaged in fighting the Romans; cf. Cassius Dio, LXVI, 5:4 (No. 430). However the reasons given there, namely, the disheartening of some of the Roman soldiers and the belief that Jerusalem was impregnable, are indeed different; cf. the commentary *ad loc.*

Some confirmation of Dio's statement that foreigners took part in the war on the side of the Jews may have been found in the new documents discovered in the desert of Judaea. It is stated in *IEJ*, XI, p. 46: ותדברון ית תירסיס בר תינינוס ויתה עמכון. In his comments on the document (*ad loc.*) Y. Yadin thinks that the Thyrsis mentioned here could have been a non-Jew who joined the forces of Bar-Kokhba. The occurrence of non-Jewish names in the lists of the papyri, e.g., Γάϊος = Gaius, has also been explained by adherence to the Jewish cause of people drawn from the ranks of the proletariat of the Greek cities and runaway slaves; see B. Lifshitz, *IEJ*, XI, p. 61.

τότε τοὺς κρατίστους τῶν στρατηγῶν ὁ Ἀδριανὸς ἐπ᾽ αὐτοὺς ἔπεμψεν: At the time of the outbreak of the revolt Tineius Rufus acted as governor of Judaea; cf. Eusebius, *Historia Ecclesiastica*, IV, 6:1; Hieronymus, *Chronica* (ed. Helm²), p. 200; Syncellus, I (ed. Dindorf), p. 660. As emerges from the talmudic sources he acted in the same capacity after the quelling of the revolt, when he was instrumental in executing the anti-Jewish policy of Hadrian. He is the villain of the piece under the name טורנוס רופוס in the Jewish tradition; cf. *TB Ta'anit*, 29a.

Before Tineius Rufus arrived in Judaea he had already acted as *legatus pro praetore* in Thrace, presumably in 124–126 C.E.; in May 127 C.E. he became *consul suffectus*, a position he held until September of that year; cf. the *Fasti Ostienses* referred to above; see Degrassi, *op. cit.* (supra, p. 396). On Tineius Rufus, see Petrikovits, PW, Ser. 2, VI, pp. 1376 ff.; W. Eck, *Senatoren von Vespasian bis Hadrian*, Munich 1970, pp. 195, 204 f.; Keppie, *op. cit.* (supra, p. 396), p. 859. Publicius Marcellus, the *legatus pro praetore* of Syria, came to his aid, but without sufficient success; see above, on 12:1, supra, p. 398; on him, cf. H. Seyrig, *Antiquités syriennes*, III, Paris 1946, pp. 160 f.; Hanslik, PW, XXIII, pp. 1904 f. Inscriptional evidence attests his governorship of Syria *c.* 132 C.E.

ὧν πρῶτος Ἰούλιος Σεουῆρος ὑπῆρχεν: On the life and career of Julius Severus, see Groag, PW, XV, pp. 1813 ff.; E. Birley, *Roman Britain and the Roman Army*, Kendal 1961, pp. 28, 37 f.; A. R. Birley, *Epigraphische Studien*, IV (1967), pp. 70 f.; G. Alföldy, *Epigraphische Studien*, V (1968), pp. 116 ff.; M. G. Jarret & J. C. Mann, *Bonner Jahrbücher*, CLXX (1970), p. 187. Of utmost importance for the reconstruction of Julius Severus' career is *CIL*, III, No. 2830 = *ILS*, No. 1056. He was consul in 127 C.E., and then acted as governor of Dacia, Moesia and Britain. It was from Britain that he was called to Judaea.

ἀπὸ Βρεττανίας ... σταλείς: There is some difference of opinion concerning the date at which Julius Severus left Britain and arrived in Judaea, this being in either 133 or 134 C.E. For 134 C.E., see D. Atkinson, *JRS*, XII (1922), p. 66. However the chronology of the revolt dating its end to not later than 135, the decisive phase having been reached in 134, lends much support to the earlier of the two dates.

13:3 ἠδυνήθη ... ἐκκόψαι αὐτούς: According to the above-mentioned inscription (*ILS*, No. 1056) Julius Severus received in reward for his victory in Judaea the *ornamenta triumphalia*: "huic [senatus a]uctore [imp(eratore) Tra]ian(o) Hadrian[o Au]g(usto) ornamenta triu[mp]halia decrevit ob res in [Iu]dea prospere ge[st]as"; see Hammond, *op. cit.* (supra, p. 401), pp. 79, 111, n. 129, p. 299.

14:1 καὶ φρούρια μὲν αὐτῶν πεντήκοντα ... κατεσκάφησαν: Dio supplies no name for any of these fortresses. An attempt by Krauss to use the number of the fortresses given by Dio for undertaking a study of the Roman garrisons in the province has rather miscarried; cf. S. Krauss, *Magazin für die Wissenschaft des Judenthums*, XIX (1892), pp. 227 ff.

ἄνδρες δὲ ὀκτὼ καὶ πεντήκοντα μυριάδες ἐσφάγησαν ἔν τε ταῖς καταδρομαῖς καὶ ταῖς μάχαις: The enormous number of the Jewish casualties is stressed also by Eusebius, *Historia Ecclesiastica*, IV, 6:1: μυριάδας ἀθρόως ἀνδρῶν ὁμοῦ καὶ παίδων καὶ γυναικῶν διαφθείρων[scil. Tineius Rufus]. See also Hieronymus, *Commentarii in Danielem*, ix:24 (*CCSL*, LXXV A, ed. Glorie, p. 888 = *PL*, XXV, Col. 553): "sub Hadriano ... quando Hierusalem omnino subversa est et Iudaeorum gens catervatim caesa, ita ut Iudaeae quoque finibus pellerentur". The magnitude of the disaster is illustrated in the Talmud, especially by *TP Ta'anit*, iv, 69a–b, and the parallels. The number of Jews in Jerusalem during the siege in the time of Titus is assessed at six hundred thousand by Tacitus, *Historiae*, V, 13 (No. 281); cf. the commentary *ad loc*.

14:2 τὸ γὰρ μνημεῖον τοῦ Σολομῶντος ... ἀπὸ ταὐτομάτου διελύθη: Cf. *Itinerarium Burdigalense*, 598, in: Geyer, p. 25: "inde non longe est monumentum Ezechihel, Asaph, Iob et Jesse, Dauid, Salomon (at Bethleem)"; cf. also Cedrenus, I (ed. Bekker), p. 438: σημεῖον δὲ γέγονε τῆς ἁλώσεως αὐτοῦ ὡς τὸ τοῦ Σολομῶντος σημεῖον αὐτόματον διαλυθῆναι. However, Cedrenus derives his information from Dio.

14:3 πολλοὶ ... ἀπώλοντο· διὸ καὶ ὁ Ἀδριανὸς γράφων πρὸς τὴν βουλὴν οὐκ ἐχρήσατο τῷ προοιμίῳ τῷ συνήθει: The presence of Hadrian at the battlefields of Judaea is implied also by the letter of Apollodorus of Damascus (No. 322) and documentary evidence; see the introduction to Apollodorus.

There is proof that Hadrian was at Rome no later than 5 May 134; cf. *IGRR*, I, No. 149 = L. Moretti, *Inscriptiones Graecae Urbis Romae*, I, Rome 1968, No. 235. Presumably Hadrian returned to Rome after the fate of the war had already been decided, but before the fall of Beitar and the final subjugation of Judaea; see Schürer, ed. Vermes & Millar, I, p. 550. Yet some scholars think that Hadrian left Rome again for Judaea in the summer of 134; see W. Weber, *CAH*, XI (1936), p. 314; Follet, *op. cit.* (supra, p. 390), pp. 67 ff.

For a summary of the revolt, see now also Smallwood, pp. 428 ff.; M. Avi-Yonah, PW, Suppl. XIII (1973), pp. 400 ff.; cf. Y. Yadin, *Bar-Kokhba*, London–Jerusalem 1971; S. Applebaum, *Prolegomena to the Study of the Second Jewish Revolt (A.D. 132–135)*, Oxford 1976.

441

Historia Romana, LXXI, 25:1, apud: Xiphilinus — Boissevain

Ἐπεὶ δ᾽ οὐκ ἄν ποτε συγκαθεῖναι ἐς τοῦτο ὁ Κάσσιος ἐθελήσειε (πῶς γὰρ ἄν πιστεύσειέ μοι, ἄπιστος οὕτω περὶ ἐμὲ γεγενημένος), ὑμᾶς γε ὦ συστρατιῶται χρὴ θαρρεῖν. οὐ γάρ που κρείττους Κίλικες καὶ Σύροι καὶ Ἰουδαῖοι καὶ Αἰγύπτιοι ὑμῶν οὔτε ἐγένοντό ποτε οὔτε ἔσονται, οὐδ᾽ ἄν
5 μυριάκις πλείους ὑμῶν, ὅσῳ νῦν ἐλάττους εἰσίν, ἀθροισθῶσιν.

1 συγκαθεῖναι Robertus Stephanus   συγκαταθεῖναι VC

But since Cassius would never consent to adopt this course, — for how could he trust me after having shown himself so untrustworthy toward me? — you, at least, fellow-soldiers, ought to be of good cheer. For surely Cilicians, Syrians, Jews and Egyptians have never proved superior to you and never will, even if they should muster as many tens of thousands more than you as they now muster fewer.

(trans. E. Cary, *LCL*)

οὐ γάρ που κρείττους Κίλικες καὶ Σύροι καὶ Ἰουδαῖοι καὶ Αἰγύπτιοι ὑμῶν: The passage is taken from a speech by Marcus Aurelius before his soldiers in 175 C.E. He refers to the soldiers of the rebel Avidius Cassius, and to the Jews among them. This may perhaps suggest that Jews still occasionally served in the Roman armies; see, e.g., M. Brücklmeier, "Beiträge zur rechtlichen Stellung der Juden im römischen Reich", Ph.D. Thesis, Munich 1939, p. 62. For an explanation that the unsympathetic attitude of Marcus Aurelius to Jews reflected in the writings of Ammianus Marcellinus (cf. XXII, 5:5 = No. 506) was due to Jewish participation in the revolt of Avidius Cassius, see J. Schwartz, in: *Bonner Historia Augusta Colloquium*, Bonn 1963 (1964), pp. 148 f.

442

Historia Romana, LXXV, 2:4, apud: Xiphilinus — Boissevain

Μέγα δὲ καὶ ἐπὶ τούτῳ τῷ Σεουήρῳ φρονοῦντι, ὡς καὶ πάντας ἀνθρώπους καὶ συνέσει καὶ ἀνδρίᾳ ὑπερβεβηκότι, πρᾶγμα παραδοξότατον συνηνέχθη· Κλαύδιος γάρ τις λῃστὴς καὶ τὴν Ἰουδαίαν καὶ τὴν Συρίαν κατατρέχων καὶ πολλῇ διὰ τοῦτο σπουδῇ ζητούμενος, προσῆλθέ τε αὐτῷ
5 ποτε μεθ᾽ ἱππέων ὡς καὶ χιλίαρχός τις ὤν, καὶ ἠσπάσατο αὐτὸν καὶ ἐφίλησε, καὶ οὔτε εὐθὺς ἐφωράθη οὔθ᾽ ὕστερον συνελήφθη.

While Severus was pluming himself on this achievement, as if he surpassed all mankind in both understanding and bravery, a most incredible thing happened. A certain robber, named Claudius, who was overrunning Judaea and Syria and was being very vigorously pursued in consequence, came to him one day with some horsemen, like some military tribune, and saluted and kissed him; and he was neither discovered at the time nor caught later.   (trans. E. Cary, *LCL*)

Κλαύδιος γάρ τις λῃστής: For a connection between the activities of this Claudius and the "Jewish triumph" of Caracalla (cf. *Scriptores Historiae Augustae*, Caracallus 1, 6 = No. 517), see H. Graetz, *Geschichte der Juden*, IV⁴, Leipzig 1908, pp. 206 f.; cf. also J. Hasebroek, *Untersuchungen zur Geschichte des Kaisers Septimius Severus*, Heidelberg 1921, p. 71. However, it is not even certain whether Claudius was a Jew. The episode itself is to be compared with the account of the Italian brigand Bulla by Cassius Dio, LXXVI, 10.

CXXIII. AELIANUS

c. 170–235 C.E.

Two references of Jewish interest are found in the works of the Roman sophist Aelianus. One mentions the Jewish Sibyl (No. 444) and the other tells of the love of a serpent for a girl in the country of the Jews, or the Idumaeans, in the time of Herod (No. 443). It has not been possible to trace the origin of Aelianus' love story, which occurs only here, since his sources are not easy to identify.[1]
Elsewhere, Aelianus mentions the Syrian deer, which are born on the Carmel as well as on the Amanus and the Libanus; cf. De Natura Animalium, *V, 56:* Αἱ ἐν Σύροις ἔλαφοι γίνονται μὲν ἐν ὄρεσι μεγίστοις, Ἀμανῷ τε καὶ Λιβάνῳ καὶ Καρμήλῳ·

443

De Natura Animalium, VI, 17 — Hercher = F 114 R

Ἐν τῇ τῶν καλουμένων Ἰουδαίων γῇ ἢ Ἰδουμαίων ᾖδον οἱ ἐπιχώριοι καθ᾽ Ἡρώδην τὸν βασιλέα ἐρασθῆναι μείρακος ὡρικῆς δράκοντα μεγέθει μέγιστον, ὅσπερ οὖν ἐπιφοιτῶν εἶτα μέντοι τῇ προειρημένῃ συνεκάθευδε σφόδρα ἐρωτικῶς. οὐκοῦν ἡ μεῖραξ τὸν ἐραστὴν οὐκ ἐθάρρει, καίτοι
5 προσέρποντα ὡς ἐνῆν πρᾳότατά τε καὶ ἡμερώτατα. ὑπεξῆλθεν οὖν, καὶ διέτριψε μῆνα, οἷα δήπου λήθην τοῦ δράκοντος ἕξοντος κατὰ τὴν τῆς ἐρωμένης ἀποδημίαν. τῷ δὲ ἄρα ἡ ἐρημία ἐπέτεινε τὸ πάθος, καὶ ἐφοίτα μὲν ὁσημέραι καὶ νύκτωρ· οὐ μὴν ἐντυγχάνων ᾗ ἐβούλετο, ὡς ἐραστὴς ἀτυχῶν ἐν τῷ πόθῳ καὶ ἐκεῖνος ἤλγει. ἐπεὶ δὲ ἡ ἄνθρωπος ὑπέστρεψεν
10 αὖθις, ὁ δὲ ἀφικνεῖται, καὶ περιβαλὼν τῷ λοιπῷ σώματι, τῇ οὐρᾷ τὰς κνήμας τῆς ἐρωμένης πεφεισμένως ἔπαιεν, ὑπεροφθείς τε καὶ μηνίων δῆθεν.

In the country of those known as Iudaeans or Edomites the natives of the time of Herod the King used to tell of a serpent of enormous size being enamoured of a lovely girl: he used to visit her and later even

1 For a suggestion that Aelianus derived his material from the writer Pamphilus (first century C.E.), see M. Wellmann, *Hermes*, LI (1916), pp. 1 ff. Cf. K. Gerth, PW, Suppl. VIII (1956), pp. 732 ff.

slept with her like an ardent lover. Now the girl was terrified of her lover, although he slid up to her as softly and gently as he could. So she escaped from him and remained away for a month, supposing that the serpent in consequence of his darling's absence would forget her. But loneliness augmented his misery, and every day and night he used to haunt the place. Since he however did not find the object of his desire, he too felt all the pains of a disappointed lover. But when the girl came back once more, he arrived and, encircling her with the rest of his body, with his tail gently lashed her legs, presumably in anger at finding himself despised. (trans. A. F. Scholfield, *LCL*)

Ἐν τῇ ... Ἰουδαίων γῇ ἢ Ἰδουμαίων: For the interchange between Judaea and Idumaea in ancient literature, see the Introduction to Vergilius, *Georgica*, III, 12 (No. 125).

καθ' Ἡρώδην τὸν βασιλέα: This is another example of the fame attained by Herod in Graeco-Roman society; cf. Horatius, *Epistulae*, II, 2, 184 (No. 130), and Persius, *Saturae*, V, 180 (No. 190).

ἐρασθῆναι μείρακος ὡρικῆς δράκοντα: On the love of a dolphin for a boy, see the fragment from Duris of Samos, apud: Athenaeus, *Deipnosophistae*, XIII, 85, p. 606 C–D = *F. Gr. Hist.*, II, A 76, F 7. Cf. Plutarchus, *De Sollertia Animalium*, 18, p. 972 E–F. The story of a girl loved by an elephant is recorded in Plinius, *Naturalis Historia*, VIII, 14; and the love of a dolphin for a boy in the city of Iasos, in *ibid.*, IX, 27. On a dolphin and a boy in African Hippo, see Plinius, *Epistulae*, IX, 33.

444

Varia Historia, XII, 35 — Dilts = F115R

Σίβυλλαι τέτταρες, ἡ Ἐρυθραία ἡ Σαμία ἡ Αἰγυπτία ἡ Σαρδιανή. οἱ δὲ φασι καὶ ἑτέρας ἔξ, ὡς εἶναι τὰς πάσας δέκα, ὧν εἶναι καὶ τὴν Κυμαίαν καὶ τὴν Ἰουδαίαν.

1 ἢ³ om. X   2 ἑτέραι V

Four Sibyls, the Erythraean, the Samian, the Egyptian, the Sardian. There are some who count six more. Thus the total number comes to ten, among whom there are also the Cymaean and the Jewish.

καὶ τὴν Ἰουδαίαν: On the Jewish Sibyl, see the commentary to Pausanias, X, 12:9 (No. 360). See also Rzach, PW, Ser. 2, II, p. 2076. This Sibyl is commonly called the "Hebrew". She is so described by Pausanias himself (παρ' Ἑβραίοις); cf. also *Scholia Platonica ad Phaedrum*, 244 (No. 570); *Chronicon Paschale*, I (ed. Dindorf), p. 201; Suda (ed. Adler), IV, p. 354.

CXXIV. CORNELIUS LABEO

Third century C.E.

Through Macrobius we learn that the Roman antiquarian Cornelius Labeo,[1] in his work "De Oraculo Apollinis Clarii", discussed a Clarian oracle that called the "Highest God" by the name of Iao. The oracle identified him with Hades, Zeus, Helios and Dionysus.

---

1 On the date of Cornelius Labeo, see M.P. Nilsson, *Geschichte der griechischen Religion*², Munich 1961, p. 477, n. 8.

445

De Oraculo Apollinis Clarii, apud: Macrobius, Saturnalia, I, 18:18–21 — Willis

(18) Solem Liberum esse manifeste pronuntiat Orpheus hoc versu:

Ἥλιος ὃν Διόνυσον ἐπίκλησιν καλέουσιν.

Et is quidem versus absolutior, ille vero eiusdem vatis operosior:

Εἷς Ζεὺς εἷς ᾽Αίδης εἷς Ἥλιος εἷς Διόνυσος.

5 (19) Huius versus auctoritas fundatur oraculo Apollinis Clarii, in quo aliud quoque nomen soli adicitur, qui in isdem sacris versibus inter cetera vocatur ᾽Ιαώ. Nam consultus Apollo Clarius quis deorum habendus sit qui vocatur ᾽Ιαώ, ita effatus est:

(20) ὄργια μὲν δεδαῶτας ἐχρῆν νηπευθέα κεύθειν,

10 εἰ δ᾽ ἄρα τοι παύρη σύνεσις καὶ νοῦς ἀλαπαδνός,

φράζεο τὸν πάντων ὕπατον θεὸν ἔμμεν ᾽Ιαώ,

χείματι μέν τ᾽ ᾽Αίδην, Δία δ᾽ εἴαρος ἀρχομένοιο,

Ἥλιον δὲ θέρευς, μετοπώρου δ᾽ ἁβρὸν ᾽Ιαώ.

(21) Huius oraculi vim, numinis nominisque interpretationem, qua

15 Liber pater et sol ᾽Ιαώ significatur, exsecutus est Cornelius Labeo in libro cui titulus est De oraculo Apollinis Clarii.

---

2 Graeca om. TMA   3 is] his NB'V'R'   hic T   4 Graeca om. TMA
5 appollinis BZR / darii R   6 quoque om. R'   8 vocatus B'VZ /
affatus NDPT   9–13 Graeca om. TMA   13 ᾽Ιαώ] ῎Ιακχον Nilsson
15 sol ᾽Ιαώ edd.   solio NDP   sol T   sol AΩ MBVZ   sol YAΩ RFA /
significatus B   16 apollonis N

---

(18) That Liber is the sun, Orpheus clearly proclaims in the line:

The Sun that is called by name of Dionysus

And this verse certainly makes perfect sense, but another line by the same poet is rather more elaborate:

One Zeus, one Hades, one Sun, one Dionysus

(19) The authority of this last line is supported by an oracle of Apollo of Clarus, in which yet another name is attached to the sun, which is called in the same sacred verses, among other names, by the name of Iao. For when Apollo of Clarus was asked who among the gods should be identified with him that is called Iao he declared as follows:

(20) Those who have learned the *Orgia* should keep them in secrecy,

But if the understanding is little and the mind feeble,

Then ponder that Iao is the supreme god among all,

In winter he is Hades, at the beginning of the spring he is Zeus,

In summer he is Helios, while in autumn he is the graceful Iao.

(21) The meaning of this oracle, and the explanation of the deity and the name by which Iao is denoted Liber pater and the sun, are expounded by Cornelius Labeo in a book entitled "On the Oracle of Apollo of Claros".

19 *Nam consultus Apollo Clarius*: For the oracle of Apollo Clarius, see C. Picard, *Éphèse et Claros*, Paris 1922; idem, *Aegyptus*, XXXII (1952), pp. 3 ff.; H. Lewy, *Chaldaean Oracles and Theurgy*, Cairo 1956, pp. 63 f.

20 ὄργια μὲν δεδαῶτας ...: For this passage, see K. Buresch, *Klaros — Untersuchungen zum Orakelwesen des späteren Altertums*, Leipzig 1889, pp. 48 ff.; J. Muelleneisen, "De Cornelii Labeonis Fragmentis, Studiis, Adsectatoribus", Ph. D. Thesis, Marburg 1889, pp. 13 ff.; B. Boehm, "De Cornelii Labeonis Aetate", Ph. D. Thesis, Königsberg 1913, pp. 19 ff.; Ganschinietz, PW, IX, p. 708; W. Kroll, *Rhein. Museum*, LXXI (1916), pp. 314 ff.; Picard, *Éphèse et Claros, op. cit.*, p. 208, n. 5, p. 716; E. Peterson, Εἷς θεός, Göttingen 1926, pp. 243 f.; R. Reitzenstein, *Die hellenistischen Mysterienreligionen*³, Leipzig–Berlin 1927, pp. 148 f.; M. P. Nilsson, *Geschichte der griechischen Religion*², Munich 1961, pp. 477 f.; ὄργια here means simply "doctrine"; see A. D. Nock, *Gnomon*, XXIX (1957), p. 527 = Nock, II, p. 899.

τὸν πάντων ὕπατον θεὸν ἔμμεν Ἰαώ: For the diffusion of the name, see the commentary to Diodorus, I, 94 (No. 58). In view of the wide popularity enjoyed by Iao among non-Jews, as testified, e.g., by the magical papyri and kindred material, the appearance of Iao's name in an oracle of Claros is not entirely surprising. Also, as Nilsson stresses, there were many Jews then living in Asia Minor. The view expressed in the oracle that Hades, Zeus, Helios, and, it seems, also Dionysus, were the same divinity, identical with Iao, is well in accord with the theocrastic tendency of later antiquity. At Claros there was a systematic tendency towards the unification of creeds that could even include the God of Judaism; see A. D. Nock, *REA*, XXX (1928), p. 286.

μετοπώρου δ' ἁβρὸν Ἰαώ: Nilsson prefers to read here Ἴακχον, i.e., Dionysus. This suggestion seems to be supported by the statement of Macrobius: "qua Liber pater et sol Ἰαώ significatur". Cf. also the letter of P. Maas to Festugière, in: Le R.P. (A.J.) Festugière, *La révélation d'HermèsTrismégiste*, I², Paris 1950, p. 426: "der Dionysos dieser Zeit ist der typische ἁβρός und der typische Herbst".

21 *qua Liber pater et sol Ἰαώ significatur*: For the identification of "Liber pater" and the Jewish God, cf. Tacitus, *Historiae*, V, 5 (No. 281); Plutarchus, *Quaestiones Convivales*, IV, 5–6 (No. 258).

CXXV. MENANDER OF LAODICEA

End of the third century C.E.

It is interesting that the rhetor Menander[1] *gives a description of a Jewish* panegyris *which must have reflected a situation that had long since disappeared, i.e. the celebration of a festival in the period of the Second Temple at the time of its glory.*[2]

1 The dating of Menander to the end of the third century C.E. is accepted by Radermacher, PW, XV, p. 763. A date in the fourth century, and assuming that the reign of Diocletian constitutes the *terminus post quem* for the work, is put forward by C. Bursian, *Der Rhetor Menandros und seine Schriften (Abhandlungen der philosophisch-philologischen Classe der königlich bayerischen Akademie der Wissenschaften*, XVI, No. III, Munich 1882), pp. 16 f. Radermacher regards Menander as a Syrian, apparently assuming that he came from the Syrian city of Laodicea; see Radermacher, *op. cit.*, p. 764. However, it is more likely that Menander came from Laodicea ad Lycum; cf. Bursian, *op. cit.*, p. 15; Schmid & Stählin, II, p. 939. This supposition is based on the information of Suda (ed. Adler, III, p. 361): Μένανδρος, Λαοδικεὺς τῆς παρὰ τῷ Λύκῳ τῷ ποταμῷ, σοφιστής. ἔγραψεν ὑπόμνημα εἰς τὴν Ἑρμογένους τέχνην καὶ Μινουκιανοῦ προγυμνάσματα.

2 See already A.H.L. Heeren, *Menandri Rhetoris Commentarius de Encomiis*, Göttingen 1785, p. 112, n.q.

Epidictica, apud: C. Bursian, *Der Rhetor Menandros und seine Schriften* (*Abhandlungen der philosophisch–philologischen Classe der königlich bayerischen Akademie der Wissenschaften*, XVI, No. 3, Munich 1882), p. 68 = C. Walz, *Rhetores Graeci*, IX, pp. 210 f. = Spengel, *Rhetores Graeci*, III, p. 366

Συμβάλλεται γὰρ ἐπὶ δόξαν τῇ πανηγύρει καὶ τὸ ἐνδόξους εἶναι τοὺς
ἐπαγγέλλοντας τὴν σύνοδον· τῶν δὲ συνιόντων ὡς πλείστων ἢ ὡς
ἐνδοξοτάτων, ἐνδοξοτάτων μὲν ὡς οἱ Ὀλυμπίαζε· οἱ γὰρ γνωριμώτεροι
συνέρχονται· πλείστων δὲ ὡς τὸ περὶ τὴν πανήγυριν τῶν Ἑβραίων περὶ
5 τὴν Συρίαν τὴν Παλαιστίνην· ἐξ ἐθνῶν γὰρ ⟨πλείστων⟩ πλεῖστοι
συλλέγονται.

2 ἀπαγγέλλοντας PMv   3 ἐνδοξότατοι μὲν PvM / γνωρημότεροι PvM
    4 πλεῖστον δὲ PvM   4–5 ὡς ἐπὶ τὴν Συριαν τῶν Παλαιστίνων M
                            5 ⟨πλείστων⟩ Bursian

For the glory of the festival is enhanced when those who proclaim the
gathering are themselves of high repute, as well as when those who
assemble are either very great in number or of the highest repute. An
example of the last kind are those who go to Olympia, for the more
renowned meet there; while the largest multitudes are to be found at
the festival of the Hebrews living in Syria Palaestina, as they are
gathered in very large numbers from most nations.

περὶ τὴν πανήγυριν τῶν Ἑβραίων περὶ τὴν Συρίαν τὴν Παλαιστίνην: It is
difficult to imagine the existence in the time of Menander of a Jewish
πανήγυρις that would suit this description. Menander must have had the
period of the Second Temple in mind, when myriads of pilgrims from all the
countries of the Jewish Diaspora in the Roman empire and beyond its
borders went to Jerusalem to celebrate the three great festivals of the Jewish
year. Cf. the enthusiastic description of Philo, *De Specialibus Legibus*, I, 69:
καὶ τοῦδε σαφεστάτη πίστις τὰ γινόμενα· μυρίοι γὰρ ἀπὸ μυρίων ὅσων
πόλεων, οἱ μὲν διὰ γῆς, οἱ δὲ διὰ θαλάττης, ἐξ ἀνατολῆς καὶ δύσεως καὶ
ἄρκτου καὶ μεσημβρίας καθ᾽ ἑκάστην ἑορτὴν εἰς τὸ ἱερὸν καταίρουσιν.
For the huge numbers of the pilgrims, cf. Acts ii: 5 ff.; *BJ*, VI, 422 ff.; *TB
Pesaḥim*, 64b. See H. Graetz, *Geschichte der Juden*, Vol. III, Part 2[5], Leipzig
1906, pp. 815 ff.; Jeremias, pp. 89 ff. For the use of older sources by
Menander, see Radermacher, *op. cit.* (supra, p. 413, n. 1), p. 764.

CXXVI. CENSORINUS

Third century C.E.

The Jews find their place between Solon and the Etruscan books in Censorinus' display of erudition concerning the number seven, which forms the basis of the Jewish enumeration of the days.

447

De Die Natali, 11:6 — Hultsch = F195R

Alter autem ille partus, qui maior est, maiori numero continetur, septenario scilicet, quo tota vita humana finitur, ut et Solon scribit et Iudaei in dierum omnium numeris secuntur et Etruscorum libri rituales videntur indicare.

1 *maiore* V   3 *iudei* D   /   *sequuntur* V

However, the other pregnancy, which is longer, is counted by a greater number, namely, the number seven, which rules the whole of human life, as Solon writes, and this the Jews follow in their general division of days and so also the Etruscan books dealing with religious ceremonies seem to declare.

At the beginning of the chapter Censorinus defines two kinds of pregnancy, the shorter one of seven months and the longer one of ten months. Having stated that the shorter pregnancy is conditioned by the number six (*quorum prior ac minor senario maxime continetur numero*), he explains the origins of the longer pregnancy (*itaque ut alterius partus origo in sex est diebus, post quos semen in sanguinem vertitur, ita huius in septem*).

On the number seven in ancient literature, see F. Boll, *Neue Jahrbücher für das klassische Altertum*, XXXI (1913), pp. 112 ff.; W. H. Roscher, *Die Hebdomadenlehren der griechischen Philosophen und Ärzte*, Leipzig 1906.

ut et Solon scribit: See Solon, in: *Iambi et Elegi Graeci*, II, ed. M. L. West, Oxford 1972, No. 27; cf. Roscher, *op. cit.*, pp. 14 ff.

Etruscorum libri: See also Censorinus, *De Die Natali*, 14:6: "Etruscis quoque libris fatalibus aetatem hominis duodecim hebdomadibus discribi Varro commemorat."

CXXVII. SOLINUS

Third century C.E.?

C. Iulius Solinus incorporates material bearing on Judaea in his Collectanea,[1] *the main part of which derives from the* Naturalis Historia *of Pliny. However, Solinus gives some references and details that cannot be traced back to his principal source. Foremost among them is the reference to the destruction of Jericho by Artaxerxes.*[2]

1 For dating the *Collectanea*, cf. H. Walter, *Die "Collectanea Rerum Memorabilium" des C. Iulius Solinus*, Wiesbaden 1969, pp. 73 f. While the work has been dated to the third century (Mommsen), Walter does not exclude the possibility that it may have been written in the fourth century.
2 For the use of his sources by Solinus, see H. Walter, *Classica et Mediaevalia*, XXIV (1963), pp. 86 ff. For the passage of Solinus dealing with the Essenes in *Collectanea*, 35:9–12, see now C. Burchard, *RB*, LXXIV (1967), pp. 392 ff.

448

Collectanea Rerum Memorabilium, 1:56 — Mommsen = F196R

Bitumen in Iudaea quod Asphaltites gignit lacus adeo lentum mollitie glutinosa, ut a se nequeat separari, enimvero si abrumpere partem velis, universitas sequetur scindique non potest, quoniam in quantum ducatur extenditur. Sed ubi admota fuerint cruore illo polluta fila,
5 sponte dispergitur, et adplicita tabe diducitur paulo ante corpus unum, fitque de tenacitate conexa contagione partitio repentina.

1 *quod* om. P / *asfaltites vocatur* H / *adeo lentum*] *adcolentum* R
2 *nequeant* P 3 *velis*] *molieris* H / *sequeretur* S *sequitur* MP
4 *admonita* S

The bitumen found in Judaea, which the lake Asphaltites creates, is so viscous owing to its glutinous softness that it cannot be separated from itself. Indeed, if you want to sever a part, the whole follows and it cannot be torn away, for in proportion to its being drawn so it extends. But wherever you bring to it threads defiled by that blood, the bitumen scatters spontaneously, and what had shortly before been one body splits when that plague is applied, and through this contact its tenacious adhesion turns into a sudden division.

Sed ubi admota fuerint cruore illo polluta fila, sponte dispergitur: Cf. Plinius, *Naturalis Historia*, VII, 65 (No. 207); *ibid.*, XXVIII, 80 (No. 220).

449

Collectanea Rerum Memorabilium, 34–35 — Mommsen = F197R

(34:1) A Pelusio Cassius mons est et delubrum Iovis Cassii, atque ita Ostracine locus Pompeii Magni sepulchro inclitus. Idumaea inde incipit palmis opima. Deinde Ioppe oppidum antiquissimum orbe toto, utpote ante inundationem terrarum conditum. (2) Id oppidum
5 saxum ostentat, quod vinculorum Andromedae vestigia adhuc retinet. Quam expositam beluae non inritus rumor circumtulit: quippe ossa monstri illius M. Scaurus inter alia miracula in aedilitate sua Romae publicavit. (3) Annalibus nota res est: mensura quoque veracibus libris continetur, scilicet quod costarum longitudo

1 *est* om. N / *cassii* om. A 2 *idymea* NMP *idimea* LGS
3 *iope* NM 8 *mensurae* LMGSP 9 *continentur* LMGP

10 excesserit pedes quadraginta, excelsitas fuerit elephantis Indicis eminentior: porro verticuli spinae ipsius latitudine semipedem sint supergressi.

(35:1) Iudaea inlustris est aquis, sed natura non eadem aquarum omnium. Iordanis amnis eximiae suavitatis, Paneade fonte dimissus, 15 regiones praeterfluit amoenissimas; mox in Asphaltiten lacum mersus stagno corrumpitur. (2) Qui Asphaltites gignit bitumen, animal non habet, nihil in eo mergi potest: tauri etiam camelique inpune ibi fluitant. (3) Est et lacus Sara extentus passuum sedecim milibus, circumsaeptus urbibus plurimis et celebribus, ipse par 20 optimis. Sed lacus Tiberiadis omnibus anteponitur, salubris ingenuo aestu et ad sanitatem usu efficaci. (4) Iudaeae caput fuit Hierusolyma, sed excisa est. Successit Hierichus: et haec desivit, Artaxerxis bello subacta. Callirrhoe Hierusolymis proxima, fons calore medico probatissimus et ex ipso aquarum praeconio sic vocatus. (5) In hac 25 terra balsamum nascitur, quae silva intra terminos viginti iugerum usque ad victoriam nostram fuit: at cum Iudaea potiti sumus, ita luci illi propagati sunt, ut iam nobis latissimi colles sudent balsama. Similes vitibus stirpes habent: malleolis digeruntur, rastris nitescunt, aqua gaudent, amant amputari, tenacibus foliis sempiterno inum- 30 brantur. Lignum caudicis attrectatum ferro sine mora moritur: (6) ea propter aut vitro aut cultellulis osseis, sed in sola cortice artifici plaga vulneratur, e qua eximiae suavitatis gutta manat. Post lacrimam secundum in pretiis locum poma obtinent, cortex tertium, ultimus honos ligno. (7) Longo ab Hierusolymis recessu tristis sinus panditur, 35 quem de caelo tactum testatur humus nigra et in cinerem soluta. (8) Ibi duo oppida, Sodomum nominatum alterum, alterum Gomorrum, apud quae pomum quod gignitur, habeat licet speciem maturitatis, mandi tamen non potest: nam fuliginem intrinsecus favillaciam ambitio tantum eximiae cutis cohibet, quae vel levi pressa tactu

10 *excelsitas*] *sublimitas autem* SAP[1]   11 *latitudinem* NH   *latitudinis* SA
14 *iordanes* CNS / *paniade* M   16 *bitumen gignit* SAP   17 *eo*] *eum* P
18 *genesara* A[2] / *sedecim*] *xu* RC[1]   19 *ipse*] *in se* G   20 *tibiriadis* M /
omnibus] *his omnibus* LMG   21 *hierusolima* MS
hierosolyma vel *hierosolima* N   *iherosolima* [H]   22 *ierichus* G
iericus H   *hiericho* R   *iaericho* M   *macherus* P[2] ex Plino V, 72 /
haec] *haec caput esse* SAP[2]   om. R[a]   23 *proxuma* N
26 *at cum*] *ubi* SAP[2] / *sumus*] *eramus* SAP[2]   29 *aquis* SA   *aquas* P
31 *vitrio* N / *cultellis* [H] cum Plinio / *sola*] *ipso* SA   34 *hierosolima* SA /
recessus A   *regressu* M   36 *duo ibi* SAP / *gumorrum* N
gormorrum [H[a]]   37 *specimen* CLM[2]GSAP   38 *non* om. R[a] /
favillaciam] *vanam* P[2]

⁴⁰ fumum exhalat et fatiscit in vagum pulverem. (9) Interiora Iudaeae occidentem quae contuentur Esseni tenent, qui praediti memorabili disciplina recesserunt a ritu gentium universarum, maiestatis ut reor providentia ad hunc morem destinati. Nulla ibi femina: venere se penitus abdicaverunt. Pecuniam nesciunt. (10) Palmis victitant.
⁴⁵ Nemo ibi nascitur nec tamen deficit hominum multitudo. Locus ipse addictus pudicitiae est: ad quem plurimi licet undique gentium properent, nullus admittitur, nisi quem castitatis fides et innocentiae meritum prosequatur: (11) nam qui reus est vel levis culpae, quamvis summa ope adipisci ingressum velit, divinitus submovetur. Ita per
⁵⁰ inmensum spatium saeculorum, incredibile dictu, aeterna gens est cessantibus puerperiis. (12) Engada oppidum infra Essenos fuit, sed excisum est. Verum inclitis nemoribus adhuc durat decus lucisque palmarum eminentissimis nihil vel de aevo vel de bello derogatum. Iudaeae terminus Massada castellum.

41 *continentur* R   *continent* C   /   *hessenni* SAP   42 *ritu*] *more* SAP   /
   reor] *creditur* SAP²   43 *nullae ibi feminae* L¹G   /   *a venere* LMGP
   45 *ipse* om. SA   47 *fidei* H   51 *engaddi* A   *engeda* RN Leid
     engena C   *engela* [H]   /   *hessennos* AP   54 *missada* A

(34:1) After Pelusium comes Mons Cassius and the temple of Jupiter Cassius and then Ostracine, a place famous because of the tomb of Pompey the Great. Then Idumaea begins, rich in palms. Next comes Joppe, the most ancient city of all the world, inasmuch as it had been founded before the Flood. (2) This city points out a rock, which until now shows the marks of the chains of Andromeda, about whom a not unwarranted rumour circulated that she had been exposed to a monster. In fact Marcus Scaurus during his aedileship displayed to the public in Rome the bones of that monster among the rest of the marvels. (3) This event is known to the writers of the annals; the measure is also given in books of veracity, namely that the length of the ribs exceeded forty feet, while its height exceeded that of Indian elephants; moreover, the joints of its spine exceeded half a foot in breadth.

(35:1) Judaea is distinguished by its waters, but all waters do not partake of the same nature. The river Jordan is of extraordinary pleasantness. It derives from the spring Paneas, and flows past the most delightful regions. Soon afterwards it is merged into the Lake Asphaltites and is corrupted by its standing water. (2) This Lake Asphaltites produces bitumen, it harbours no animal, and nothing can sink in it; also bulls and camels float on it without damage. (3) There is also Lake Sara to the extent of sixteen miles, enclosed by many and famous towns; the lake itself can stand comparison with the most beautiful lakes. However, the Lake Tiberias excels all other lakes. It is healthful owing to its impetuous stream which is helpful to health. (4) The capital of Judaea was Jerusalem, but it has been demolished. Jericho succeeded it, but it also ceased to fill that place, since it was subdued in the War of Artaxerxes. Callirrhoe in the vicinity of Jerusalem is a source of approved goodness owing to its curative heat, and it derives its name from the fame of the water. (5) In this country the balsam grows. The forest of balsam was confined within the boundaries of twenty *jugera* until our victory. After we had become masters of Judaea, those extended so much, that now broad expanses of hills exude balsam for our benefit. They have stems similar to vines. They are diffused by mallet-shoots, raking makes them thrive, they rejoice in water and like to be pruned. Persistent leaves overshadow them perpetually. The wood of the stock when touched by iron dies immediately. (6) It is therefore nicked only by glass or by small knives made of bone, and this only in the bark through a skilful blow, when a juice extremely sweet in taste oozes out. After the tears, the second highest prices are fetched by the fruits, the third by the bark, and the last to be honoured is the wood. (7) At a great distance from Jerusalem a gloomy valley extends. That it was struck from heaven is testified by the black ground which is resolved into ashes. (8) Here there are two towns, one called Sodomum and the other Gomorrum, in whose vicinity, every fruit that is brought forth there, although it may look ripe, is inedible because the interior consists of ashy soot which is held together only by a very thin surrounding wrapping. Even when lightly touched, it exhales smoke and vanishes into vague dust. (9) The interior of Judaea which gazes at the west is occupied by the Essenes. These, provided with a memorable discipline, seceded from the customs of all other nations, having been destined for this way of life by divine providence. No woman is to be found among them and they have renounced sex completely. They ignore money (10) and live on palms. Nobody is born among them, yet their members do not decrease. The place is dedicated to chastity. There many people flock from every nation; however, nobody is admitted who has not a reputation for chastity and innocence. (11) For one who is responsible even for the smallest fault, although he may make the greatest effort

420

in order to obtain entrance, is kept away by divine command. Thus through innumerable ages (incredible to relate), a race in which no childbirths occur lives on for ever. (12) Lying below the Essenes was formerly the town of Engada, but it was razed. Certainly the famous wood still retains its glory and the outstanding groves of palms were not diminished either by age or by war. The boundary of Judaca is marked by the fortress of Massada.

34:1 *A Pelusio Cassius mons*: Most of the narrative that follows derives from the description in the Fifth Book of Pliny (No. 204), interspersed with information from other of his books. A noteworthy exception is the reference to the destruction of Jericho in the reign of Artaxerxes.

Idumaea inde incipit palmis opima: This designation of Idumaea does not emanate from Pliny, but is reminiscent of Lucanus, *Pharsalia*, III, 216 (No. 192): "et arbusto palmarum dives Idume."

34:2 *quippe ossa monstri illius M. Scaurus inter alia miracula in aedilitate sua Romae publicavit*: Cf. Plinius, IX, 11 (No. 209).

35:3 *lacus Sara*: This stands for Genesara (Plinius).

35:4 *Iudaeae caput fuit Hierusolyma, sed excisa est. Successit Hierichus: et haec desivit, Artaxerxis bello subacta*: This statement of Solinus is usually connected with what is related by Eusebius, *Chronica*, and writers drawing upon it, about the transportation of Jews from Judaea to Hyrcania in the vicinity of the Caspian Sea in the reign of Artaxerxes Ochus; cf. Eusebius, *Chronica* (ed. Schoene), II, p. 112; Hieronymus, *Chronica* (ed. Helm), p. 121; Orosius, III, 7:6: "Tunc etiam Ochus, qui et Artaxerxes, post transactum in Aegypto maximum diuturnumque bellum plurimos Iudaeorum in transmigrationem egit atque in Hyrcania ad Caspium mare habitare praecepit"; Syncellus (ed. Dindorf), I, p. 486: Ὦχος Ἀρταξέρξου παῖς εἰς Αἴγυπτον στρατεύων μερικὴν αἰχμαλωσίαν εἷλεν Ἰουδαίων, ὧν τοὺς μὲν ἐν Ὑρκανίᾳ κατῴκισε πρὸς τῇ Κασπίᾳ θαλάσσῃ, τοὺς δὲ ἐν Βαβυλῶνι, οἵ καὶ μέχρι νῦν εἰσιν αὐτόθι, ὡς πολλοὶ τῶν Ἑλλήνων ἱστοροῦσιν. Cf. G. Hölscher, *Palästina in der persischen und hellenistischen Zeit*, Berlin 1903, pp. 46 ff.; Schürer, III, p. 7, n. 11. That Jericho ceased to exist for some time after the middle of the fourth century B.C.E. has to some extent been corroborated by excavations there. The same seems to apply to some other sites in Persian Palestine that have been excavated (Hazor, Megiddo, Athlit, Lachish). For a connection with the general destruction resulting from the crushing of the rebellion headed by Tenes, king of Sidon, see D. Barag, *BASOR*, CLXXXIII (1966), pp. 6 ff. Cf. Diodorus, XVI, 40 ff.; R. Kittel, *Geschichte des Volkes Israel*, Vol. III, Part 2, Stuttgart 1929, p. 666. Engedi, so near to Jericho, also seems to have undergone a disaster at that time (c. 400 B.C.E.), remaining uninhabited for a long period; cf. B. Mazar & I. Dunayevsky, *IEJ*, XIV (1964), pp. 126 f.

That the Artaxerxes referred to by Solinus is to be identified with Ardashir, the founder of the Neo-Persian monarchy, is a suggestion put forward, following other scholars, by T. Reinach, *Semitic Studies in Memory of*

Alexander Kohut, Berlin 1897, pp. 457 ff.; but this has not much to recommend it. Against a similar interpretation by Dodwell, cf. already Mommsen in the introduction to his edition of Solinus, p. VII: "hoc scio neque a Solino usquam talia citari ipsius aetate gesta neque Artaxerxen illum attigisse Palaestinam". However, the way in which Solinus expresses himself is rather strange, since he gives the impression that chronologically Jericho succeeded Jerusalem as the chief city of Judaea.

35:5 *In hac terra balsamum nascitur*: Cf. Plinius, *Naturalis Historia*, XII, 111 (No. 213).

35:7–8 *Longo ab Hierusolymis ... et fatiscit in vagum pulverem*: From an unknown source.

Sodomum nominatum alterum, alterum Gomorrum: Sodoma is mentioned in Strabo, *Geographica*, XVI, 2:44, p. 764 (No. 115); Dio Chrysostomus (No. 251); Galenus, *De Simplicium Medicamentorum Temperamentis ac Facultatibus*, IV, 20 (No. 381); Gomorrum (Gomorra) is referred to here for the first time in pagan literature.

35:9 *Interiora Iudaeae occidentem quae contuentur Esseni tenent*: Cf. Plinius, *Naturalis Historia*, V, 73 (No. 204).

CXXVIII. PORPHYRY

232/233 to the beginning of the fourth century C.E.

Porphyry, a native of Tyre and pupil of Plotinus, and one of the most versatile scholars of late antiquity, showed great interest in Judaism. He viewed it both as one of the old religions of the East and as the creed that was the background of Christianity, which he opposed in his treatise Adversus Christianos. *This dual aspect of Judaism coloured Porphyry's attitude to it both positively and negatively in his various works.*[1]

The Jewish creed already receives much attention in what is probably the earliest of Porphyry's works, De Philosophia ex Oraculis Haurienda.[2] *In one of the texts the Jews are associated with the Phoenicians, Assyrians and Lydians as knowing the roads of happiness and truth (No. 450). A statement about the Father whom the Holy Hebrews honour concludes another of the oracles (No. 451). Even more interesting are certain comments made by Porphyry on the oracles. The Greeks, according to these comments, had been misled in seeking the way to the gods, and the discovery of the true road was vouchsafed to the Egyptians, Phoenicians, Chaldaeans (= Assyrians), Lydians and Hebrews (No. 450). Porphyry also expresses the view that Judaism is superior to Christianity and he justifies the execution of Jesus (No. 451). In another work Porphyry equates the demiurge of the world with the God worshipped by the Jews (No. 452). A sympathetic attitude to*

---

1 A Christian tradition, transmitted by the "Theosophy" of Aristocritus, states that Marcella, the wife of Porphyry, was a Jewess; for this passage, see K. Buresch, *Klaros*, Leipzig 1889, p. 124: φιλοχρήματος δὲ ὢν πλουσίαν ἔγημε γυναῖκα πέντε παίδων μητέρα, γεγηρακυῖαν ἤδη καὶ Ἑβραίαν. Cf. Porphyrios, Πρὸς Μαρκέλλαν, ed. Pötscher, Leiden 1969, pp. 60 f. The story that Porphyry had originally been a Christian and became a pagan as a result of a personal grievance seems to be pure invention; cf. Socrates, *Historia Ecclesiastica*, III, 23. The same story is recorded in Buresch, *loc. cit.*

2 An attempt to date the work later, after the Sicilian sojourn, has been made by J.J. O'Meara, *Porphyry's Philosophy from Oracles in Augustine*, Paris 1959, pp. 33 ff. This view seems to have been refuted by P. Hadot, *Revue des études augustiniennes*, VI (1960), pp. 205 ff.

Judaism may be traced also in Porphyry's De Abstinentia, *presumably written after the author's arrival in Sicily.*[3] *In the fourth book of* De Abstinentia *(No. 455), apart from using the long abstract by Theophrastus, Porphyry draws also upon the second book of Josephus,* Bellum Judaicum;[4] *actually he paraphrases the Jewish historian, with slight changes and omissions (cf. the commentary to No. 455). Above all, the introduction to the description of the tribulations and persecutions that the Jews suffered under both Antiochus and the Romans has a sympathetic ring; Porphyry also stresses the persistence of the Jews in abstaining from various animal foods:* διετέλουν πολλῶν μὲν ἀπεχόμενοι ζῴων, ἰδίως δὲ ἔτι καὶ νῦν χοιρίων.[5]

In two other of his works, the Vita Pythagorae *and* De Antro Nympharum, *Porphyry again makes favourable references to the Jewish people. In* Vita Pythagorae *he states that Pythagoras was a pupil of the Jews, who are given a place beside the Egyptians, Arabs and Chaldaeans (No. 456a). In* De Antro Nympharum *there is a quotation from Genesis, and Moses is called here simply the "Prophet" (No. 456b). However, in the first of these works Porphyry draws expressly upon Antonius Diogenes (No. 250), while in the second it is Numenius who speaks (No. 368).*

Porphyry also made some use of the Book of Genesis in Ad Gaurum *(No. 466), if indeed the work should be attributed to Porphyry, as is sometimes assumed.*[6] *There he cites "the theologian of the Hebrews" in connection with the view that, when the body of man had been formed,*

---

3 Cf. J. Bidez, *Vie de Porphyre*, Ghent 1913, pp. 98 ff.

4 Cf. J. Bernays, *Theophrastos' Schrift über Frömmigkeit*, Berlin 1866, pp. 22 f.

5 The similarity between *De Abstinentia*, IV, 18, and Josephus, *BJ*, VII, 352 ff., may not derive from the dependence of Porphyry on Josephus, but can be explained by the fairly common view taken of Indian philosophy, which may ultimately go back to Megasthenes; see W. Morel, *Rhein. Museum*, N.F., LXXV (1926), pp. 111 f. However, cf. the argumentation of G. C. Hansen, *Klio*, XLVIII (1967), pp. 199 f.

6 The arguments for attributing this work, transmitted under the name of Galen, to Porphyry have been stated by K. Kalbfleisch, "Die neuplatonische, fälschlich dem Galen zugeschriebene Schrift, Πρὸς Γαῦρον περὶ τοῦ πῶς ἐμψυχοῦται τὰ ἔμβρυα", *Abhandlungen der Königlichen Akademie der Wissenschaften zu Berlin*, 1895, pp. 15 ff. Their validity has been questioned by R. Beutler, PW, XXII, p. 290. However, Beutler does not deny that in any case we find in this work 'porphyrianisches Gedankengut'.

God breathed breath from himself into the body to act as a living soul. The great work of Porphyry, Adversus Christianos, *in fifteen books, is in a category apart. Here Porphyry displays much more knowledge of both the Old and the New Testaments than his predecessor Celsus. Fragments of the work, which has not been preserved, have been collected by modern scholars who have succeeded in restoring its main arguments.*[7] *The bulk of the fragments derives from a Christian polemic, the* Apocriticus *by Macarius Magnes.*[8]

7 The main collection of the fragments of Porphyry's Κατὰ Χριστιανῶν is to be found in A. v. Harnack, "Porphyrius, 'Gegen die Christen', 15 Bücher — Zeugnisse, Fragmente und Referate", *Abhandlungen der Königl. preussischen Akademie der Wissenschaften*, 1916, Philosophisch-historische Klasse, No. 1, Berlin. Some additional fragments have been dealt with by Harnack, "Neue Fragmente des Werks des Porphyrius gegen die Christen", *Sitzungsberichte der preussischen Akademie der Wissenschaften*, 1921, pp. 266 ff.; see also P. Nautin, *RB*, LVII (1950), pp. 409 ff.; F. Altheim & R. Stiehl, *Gedenkschrift für Georg Rohde*, Tübingen 1961, pp. 23 ff.; D. Hagedorn & R. Merkelbach, *Vigiliae Christianae*, XX (1966), pp. 86 ff.; G. Binder, *Zeitschrift für Papyrologie und Epigraphik*, III (1968), pp. 81 ff.; M. Gronewald, *ibid.*, p. 96; cf. T. D. Barnes, *JTS*, NS, XXIV (1973), pp. 424 ff.
For studies of the work, see Bidez, *op. cit.* (supra, p. 424, n. 3), pp. 65 ff.; A. B. Hulen, *Porphyry's Work Against the Christians — An Interpretation*, New Haven 1933; P. de Labriolle, *La Réaction païenne*, Paris 1934, pp. 223 ff.; J. Vogt, *Kaiser Julian und das Judentum*, Leipzig 1939, pp. 16 f.; P. Benoit, *RB*, LIV (1947), pp. 552 ff.; Beutler, *op. cit.* (supra, p. 424, n. 6), pp. 298 f.; H. O. Schröder, *Die Welt als Geschichte*, XVII (1957), pp. 196 ff.; W. H. C. Frend, *Martyrdom and Persecution in the Early Church*, Oxford 1965, pp. 483 ff.; W. den Boer, *Classical Philology*, LXIX (1974), pp. 198 ff.

8 The text of Macarius Magnes, the *Apocriticus*, was first published in 1876, after its discovery at Athens in 1867. See the first edition, by C. Blondel (& P. Foucart), Μακαρίου Μάγνητος ἀποκριτικὸς ἢ μονογενής, Paris 1876. There is certainly no agreement on how far the argumentation of the pagan critic of Christianity in the *Apocriticus* derives from the work of Porphyry. The main protagonists of the view that his statements reflect the work of Porphyry against the Christians are Wagenmann, *Jahrbücher für deutsche Theologie*, XXIII (1878), pp. 138 ff., 269 ff.; K. I. Neumann, *Iuliani Imperatoris Librorum Contra Christianos Quae Supersunt*, Leipzig 1880, pp. 14 ff.; G. Schalkhausser, *Zu den Schriften des Makarios von Magnesia (Texte und Untersuchungen zur Geschichte der altchristlichen Literatur*, XXXI, 4), Leipzig 1907; and, above all, A. Harnack in his *Kritik des Neuen Testaments von einem griechischen Philosophen des 3. Jahrhunderts, ibid.*, XXXVII, 4, Leipzig 1911, and in his introduction to

Much of the material also is found in the commentaries of Jerome.[9]
*In Harnack's collection the fragments have been arranged under the
following headings: Introduction; Criticism of the character and the
credibility of the evangelists; Criticism of the Old Testament; Criticism
of the works and sayings of Jesus; Dogma; The contemporary state of
the church. Porphyry obviously knew the arguments put forward by the*

the collection of fragments, "Gegen die Christen", *op. cit.* (supra, p. 425,
n. 7), in 1916. Here Harnack summarizes his view that Macarius had
composed his work against an anonymous excerptor of Porphyry; see
ibid., p. 21. Harnack admits that the excerptor may have introduced
stylistic changes in the text. It has been the view of most scholars that
Macarius' polemic was aimed at Porphyry; see, e.g., Bidez, Labriolle,
Beutler. However, from the beginning of the research into the text of
Macarius, another view is encountered, pointing to Hierocles, the author
of a polemical work in two books against the Christians: Φιλαηϑὴς πρὸς
Χριστιανούς. The derivation from Hierocles had already been upheld by
L. Duchesne, *De Macario Magnete et Scriptis Ejus*, Paris 1877. It was still
defended in 1914 by T. W. Crafer, *JTS*, XV (1914), pp. 360 ff., 481 ff.
According to Crafer, "in the *Apocriticus* we possess the words, not of
Porphyry, but of Hierocles, who copied his arguments but not his
language" (*ibid.*, p. 361). Geffcken also considers that although there is
much in the *Apocriticus* deriving from Porphyry, the anonymous
adversary of Christianity should not be identified absolutely with
Porphyry; see J. Geffcken, *Zwei griechische Apologeten*, Leipzig–Berlin
1907, pp. 301 ff. Among the more recent scholars, one view assumes that
Julian was the pagan opponent of Macarius; see P. Frassinetti, *Nuovo
Didaskaleion*, III (1949), pp. 41 ff. Cf. S. Pezzella, *Eos*, LII (1962), pp. 87
ff., concluding that, although the work of Macarius undoubtedly bears the
mark of Porphyry "poco o nulla alterata", there are also traces in it of a
polemical work written by Hierocles, and of other works difficult to
identify; this would make the work of Macarius a collection of
anti-Christian polemics in general. Cf. also Barnes, *op. cit.* (supra, p. 425,
n. 7), pp. 424 ff. Barnes thinks it more probable that Macarius quoted a
later polemic, which drew some of its material from Porphyry; thus
Macarius may be supposed to preserve something of the tenor and the
arguments of Porphyry's *Adversus Christianos*, but it should not be
assumed that Macarius preserves either his words or his precise
formulations.

9 For Jerome's commentary on Daniel, see J. Lataix, *Revue d'histoire et de
littérature religieuses*, II (1897), pp. 164 ff., 268 ff.; P. Frassinetti, *Istituto
Lombardo, Rendiconti (Classe di Lettere e Scienze Morali e Storiche)*,
LXXXVI (1953), pp. 194 ff.; cf. M. V. Anastos, in: *The Classical Tradition
— Literary and Historical Studies in Honor of Harry Caplan*, ed.
L. Wallach, Ithaca, N.Y., 1966, pp. 421 ff.; P. M. Casey, *JTS*, NS, XXVII
(1976), pp. 15 ff.

Jew in Celsus' work (No. 375) and was influenced by the arguments of current Jewish polemics.[10] *The attitude to Judaism emerging from his work is characteristic of the great pagan anti-Christian polemists from Celsus onwards. Porphyry attempts to undermine the specific sanctity accorded to the Old Testament in order to weaken the basis of the Christian religion, but in the crucial issue between Pauline teaching and Judaism his sympathy is with Jewish tradition. This attitude was to be expected from Porphyry, who considered that the divinity should be worshipped according to one's national tradition; cf. his* Ad Marcellam, 18: οὗτος γὰρ μέγιστος καρπὸς εὐσεβείας τιμᾶν τὸ θεῖον κατὰ τὰ πάτρια.*

In the introduction to his work (No. 458),[11] *Porphyry seems to have stressed that the Christians do not even follow the God worshipped by the Jews according to the usages of that people. The Christians prefer to choose a "new kind of track in a pathless desert", leading neither to the customs of the Greeks nor to those of the Jews. He refers to Paul as a hybrid personality, who, according to prevailing circumstances, assumes the character of a Jew, a Roman, or a Greek (No. 459d). Paul boasts of having received an excellent training in his ancestral law, and often refers to Moses, yet undermines Moses' authority. Owing to the nature of the work, Porphyry does not show here anything approaching the sympathy towards Jews that characterizes the passages of his* De Abstinentia *and* De Oraculis Hauriendis.

A prominent feature of Porphyry's criticism of the evangelists is his meticulous exposure of their inaccuracies in citing the Old Testament. Thus he points out that the evangelist (Matt. xiii:35) attributes to Isaiah what really belongs to the Psalms (No. 459b), while against Paul he cites passages from the law of Moses.

Porphyry also maintains that Moses nowhere alludes to the divinity of Jesus. Porphyry here states that the works of Moses were destroyed at the end of the period of the First Temple, when it was burned by the Babylonians. According to Porphyry, what passes under the name of the law of Moses was in fact compiled by Ezra

10 On the probability of a Jewish lead in discerning misquotations of the Old Testament in the New, see Hulen, *op. cit.* (supra, p. 425, n. 7), p. 38.
11 The view that Eusebius, *Praeparatio Evangelica*, I, 2:1 ff., derives from the introduction to Porphyry's work has been argued by U. v. Wilamowitz-Moellendorff, *ZNTW*, I (1900), pp. 101 ff., and accepted by Harnack.

(No. 465e), and even if it was composed by Moses Porphyry points out that there is no allusion in it to the divinity of Jesus or to his death by crucifixion. Porphyry also attacks the allegorical method applied by interpreters to Scripture.[12]

The whole twelfth book of Adversus Christianos *was devoted to criticism of the visions of Daniel. Much of the material and arguments it contained have been preserved in Jerome's Commentary to Daniel. The main contention of Porphyry was that the Book of Daniel had not been composed by the man under whose name it appears, but by a Jewish contemporary of Antiochus Epiphanes. It does not constitute, therefore, a prophecy, but a* vaticinium ex eventu *(cf. No. 464a: "non tam Danielem ventura dixisse, quam illum narrasse praeterita"). Porphyry consistently interpreted the text of Daniel in the light of actual events in the political history of the Hellenistic period, relying on a number of Greek historians for the historical facts.*[13]

One of the main elements in Porphyry's work is the scientific nature of the criticism he applies to the Old Testament, so that he becomes in this way a distant precursor of the modern biblical critics.

12 See Binder, *op. cit.* (supra, p. 425, n. 7).
13 For dating the Κατὰ Χριστιανῶν not before late in 270 C.E., and more likely in 271 or later still, see A. Cameron, *CQ*, NS, XVII (1967), pp. 382 ff. This date is also accepted by J.M. Demarolle, *Vigiliae Christianae*, XXVI (1972), p. 117. On the other hand, a date late in the third century or early in the fourth century C.E. is suggested by Barnes, *op. cit.* (supra, p. 425, n. 7), pp. 433 ff.

De Philosophia ex Oraculis Haurienda, apud: Eusebius, Praeparatio Evangelica, IX, 10:1–5 —
Mras = Porphyrii de Philosophia ex Oraculis Haurienda, ed. G. Wolff, Berlin 1856, pp. 139 ff.

(1) Ὁ δὲ Πορφύριος ἐν τῷ πρώτῳ τῆς Ἐκ λογίων φιλοσοφίας αὐτὸν εἰσάγει
τὸν ἑαυτοῦ θεὸν τῷ Ἑβραίων γένει μετὰ τῶν ἄλλων τῶν ἐπὶ συνέσει
βοωμέων ἐθνῶν σοφίαν ἐπιμαρτυροῦντα. *(2)* λέγει δὲ ὁ παρ' αὐτῷ
Ἀπόλλων δι' οὗ ἐκτίθεται χρησμοῦ τάδε· ἐκκειμένων δὲ ἔτι περὶ τῶν
5 θυσιῶν ἐπάγει οἷς προσέχειν δεῖ, ἅτε μεστοῖς οὖσι πάσης θεοσοφίας·
    αἰπεινὴ μὲν ὁδὸς μακάρων τρηχεῖά τε πολλόν,
    χαλκοδέτοις τὰ πρῶτα διοιγομένη πυλεῶσιν·
    ἀτραπιτοὶ δὲ ἔασιν ἀθέσφατοι ἐγγεγαυῖαι,
    ἃς πρῶτοι μερόπων ἐπ' ἀπείρονα πρῆξιν ἔφηναν
10 οἱ τὸ καλὸν πίνοντες ὕδωρ Νειλώτιδος αἴης·
    πολλὰς καὶ Φοίνικες ὁδοὺς μακάρων ἐδάησαν,
    Ἀσσύριοι Λυδοί τε καὶ Ἑβραίων γένος ἀνδρῶν·
καὶ τὰ τούτοις ἀκόλουθα. οἷς ὁ συγγραφεὺς ἐπιλέγει·
(3) Χαλκόδετος γὰρ ἡ πρὸς θεοὺς ὁδὸς αἰπεινή τε καὶ τραχεῖα, ἧς πολλὰς
15 ἀτραποὺς βάρβαροι μὲν ἐξεῦρον, Ἕλληνες δὲ ἐπλανήθησαν, οἱ δὲ
κρατοῦντες ἤδη καὶ διέφθειραν· τὴν δὲ εὕρησιν Αἰγυπτίοις ὁ θεὸς
ἐμαρτύρησε Φοίνιξί τε καὶ Χαλδαίοις (Ἀσσύριοι γὰρ οὗτοι) Λυδοῖς τε καὶ
Ἑβραίοις. *(4)* ἔτι πρὸς τούτοις καὶ ἐν ἑτέρῳ χρησμῷ φησιν ὁ Ἀπόλλων·
    μοῦνοι Χαλδαῖοι σοφίην λάχον ἤδ' ἄρ' Ἑβραῖοι,
20 αὐτογένεθλον ἄνακτα σεβαζόμενοι θεὸν ἁγνῶς.
(5) καὶ πάλιν ἐρωτηθείς, τίνι λόγῳ πολλοὺς λέγουσιν οὐρανούς, ἔχρησε
τάδε·
    εἷς ἐν παντὶ πέλει κόσμου κύκλος, ἀλλὰ σὺν ἑπτὰ
    ζώναισιν πεφόρηται ἐς ἀστερόεντα κέλευθα,
25 ἃς δὴ Χαλδαῖοι καὶ ἀριζήλωτοι Ἑβραῖοι
    οὐρανίας ὀνόμηναν, ἐς ἑβδόματον δρόμον ἕρπειν.

1 αὐτὸν om. B   3 παρ' αὐτῶν I   5 μεστοῖς οὖσι] μετὰ B
6 ἐπαινὴ I   7 διοιγομένοις I   8 δ' ἐπέασιν Wolff
8–9 ἐγγεγαυῖαι-ἔφηναν om. B   12 ἀνδρῶν] ἀνθρώπων N
13 καὶ...ἀκόλουθα om. B   15 ἀπεπλανήθησαν Theodoretus
17 Ἀσσύριοι γὰρ οὗτοι om. Theodoretus   18 Ἑβραίοις ὅμοιοι B
19 σοφίαν ION / ἤ δ' ἄρ I   ἤ δ' ἄρ N   20 αὐτογέννητον Iustinus
    21 ἔχρησεν οὕτως ON   24 ἐς Wolff   εἰς codd.
25 δὴ om. B / ἀριζήλωτοι Wolff   ἀριζήλοιτοι ON   ἀριζήλητοι BI
    26 ὠνόμηναν B / ἐς Wolff   εἰς codd. / ἔρπων Wolff

(1) But Porphyry, in the first book of his Philosophy from Oracles, introduces his own god as himself bearing witness to the wisdom of the Hebrew race as well as of other nations renowned for intelligence. (2) It is his Apollo who speaks as follows in an oracle which he is uttering; and while still explaining the subject of sacrifices, he adds words which are well worthy of attention, as being full of all divine knowledge:

> Steep is the road and rough that leads to heaven,
> Entered at first through portals bound with brass
> Within are found innumerable paths,
> Which for the endless good of all mankind
> They first revealed who Nile's sweet waters drink.
> From them the heavenward paths Phoenicia learned,
> Assyria, Lydia, and the Hebrew race.

And so forth, on which the author further remarks:
(3) "For the road to the gods is bound with brass, and both steep and rough; the barbarians discovered many paths thereof, but the Greeks went astray and those who already held it even perverted it. The discovery was ascribed by the god to Egyptians, Phoenicians, Chaldeans (for these are the Assyrians), Lydians and Hebrews."
(4) In addition to this Apollo also says in another oracle:

> Only Chaldees and Hebrews wisdom found
> In the pure worship of a self-born God.

(5) And being asked again, for what reason men speak to many heavens, he gave the following response:

> One circle girds the world on every side,
> In seven zones rising to the starlit paths:
> These, in their sevenfold orbits as they roll,
> Chaldees and far-famed Hebrews "heavens" surnamed.

(trans. E.H. Gifford, Oxford 1903)

451

De Philosophia ex Oraculis Haurienda, apud: Augustinus, *De Civitate Dei*, XIX, 23 —
Dombart & Kalb

Nam in libris quos ἐκ λογίων φιλοσοφίας appellat ⟨scil. Porphyrius⟩, in quibus exequitur atque conscribit rerum ad philosophiam pertinentium velut divina responsa, ut ipsa verba eius, quem ad modum ex Graeca lingua in Latinam interpretata sunt, ponam: "Interroganti,"

5 inquit, "quem deum placando revocare possit uxorem suam a
Christianismo, haec ait versibus Apollo." Deinde verba velut
Apollinis ista sunt: "Forte magis poteris in aqua inpressis litteris
scribere aut adinflans leves pinnas per aera avis volare, quam pollutae
revoces impiae uxoris sensum. Pergat quo modo vult inanibus
10 fallaciis ★ perseverans et lamentari fallaciis mortuum Deum cantans,
quem iudicibus recta sentientibus perditum pessima in speciosis ferro
vincta mors interfecit." Deinde post hos versus Apollinis, qui non
stante metro Latine interpretati sunt, subiunxit atque ait: "In his
quidem inremediabile sententiae eorum manifestavit dicens,
15 quoniam Iudaei suscipiunt Deum magis quam isti." Ecce, ubi
decolorans Christum Iudaeos praeposuit Christianis, confitens quod
Iudaei suscipiant Deum. Sic enim exposuit versus Apollinis, ubi
iudicibus recta sentientibus Christum dicit occisum, tamquam illis
iuste iudicantibus merito sit ille punitus. Viderint quid de Christo
20 vates mendax Apollinis dixerit atque iste crediderit aut fortasse
vatem, quod non dixit, dixisse iste ipse confinxerit. Quam sibi constet
vel ipsa oracula inter se faciat convenire, postea videbimus; hic tamen
Iudaeos, tamquam Dei susceptores, recte dicit iudicasse de Christo,
quod eum morte pessima excruciandum esse censuerint ... Sed ad
25 manifestiora veniamus et audiamus quam magnum Deum dicat esse
Iudaeorum. Item ad ea, quae interrogavit Apollinem, quid melius,
verbum sive ratio an lex: "Respondit," inquit, "versibus haec
dicens." Ac deinde subicit Apollinis versus, in quibus et isti sunt, ut
quantum satis est inde decerpam: "In Deum vero," inquit,
30 "generatorem et in regem ante omnia, quem tremit et caelum et terra
atque mare et infernorum abdita et ipsa numina perhorrescunt;
quorum lex est Pater, quem valde sancti honorant Hebraei." Tali
oraculo dei sui Apollinis Porphyrius tam magnum Deum dixit
Hebraeorum, ut eum ipsa numina perhorrescant.

5 *revocari* D¹   /   *posset* D²pe²   8 *inflans* AGrB¹a   /   *polluta* D¹ge
   9 *peragat* e   17 *suscipiunt* ep   32 *quem vel* p   /   *honorent* p¹
                           honorificant B

Cf. Lactantius, *De Ira Dei*, 23:12: "Apollo Milesius de Iudaeorum religione consultus
responso haec introducit: ἐς δὲ θεὸν βασιλῆα καὶ ἐς γενετῆρα πρὸ πάντων, ὃν
τρομέει καὶ γαῖα καὶ οὐρανὸς ἠδὲ θάλασσα. ταρτάρεοί τε μυχοί, καὶ δαίμονες
ἐρρίγασιν."

For in the book, entitled Oracular Philosophy, in which he [scil.
Porphyry] compiles and comments on responses, supposedly divine,

concerning matters pertaining to philosophy, he says (to quote his very words, translated from Greek into Latin): "To one who enquired what god's favour he should seek in order to recall his wife from Christianity, Apollo replied in the following verses." Then these words follow, as those of Apollo: "You may perchance more easily write in lasting letters on water, or spread light pinions and fly like a bird through the air, than recall to her senses an impious wife who has once polluted herself. Let her continue as she pleases, persisting in her empty delusions, and lamenting in song as a god one who died for delusions, who was condemned by judges whose verdict was just, and executed publicly by the worst iron-bound death." Then after these verses of Apollo (here rendered into Latin prose) Porphyry remarks: "In these verses Apollo made manifest the incurable weakness of the Christian belief, saying that it is the Jews who uphold God better than the Christians." Behold how he denigrates Christ, and prefers the Jews to the Christians when he expresses his belief that they are upholders of God. For this is his exposition of the verses of Apollo, in the course of which he says that Christ was slain by judges whose verdict was correct, as if he had been deservedly condemned to punishment by his judges. What the lying seer of Apollo said and Porphyry believed, or what Porphyry possibly invented as the seer's words, are their responsibility; I shall deal later with the consistency of Porphyry with himself, that is, how consistent he makes his very oracles with one another. In this passage, however, he says that the Jews, as God's champions, judged rightly in decreeing that Christ was to be tortured by the worst kind of death ... But let us come to plainer matters, and let us hear how great a god Porphyry says that the God of the Jews is. For example, Apollo, when asked which is the better, word (that is, reason) or law, replied, he says, in these verses, which he adds (and I select of them only the following, as sufficient): "In one truly God, the creator and the king prior to all things, before whom tremble heaven and earth and the sea and the hidden places beneath, and the very divinities shudder; their law is the Father whom the holy Hebrews greatly honour." In this oracle of his own god Apollo, Porphyry has cited the God of the Hebrews as being so great that the very divinities shudder before him.

(trans. W.C. Greene, LCL)

452

Commentarii in Oracula Chaldaica, apud: Lydus, De Mensibus, IV, 53, p. 110 — Wünsch

Ὁ μέντοι Πορφύριος ἐν τῷ ὑπομνήματι τῶν λογίων τὸν δὶς ἐπέκεινα τουτέστι τὸν τῶν ὅλων δημιουργὸν τὸν παρὰ Ἰουδαίων τιμώμενον εἶναι ἀξιοῖ, ὃν ὁ Χαλδαῖος δεύτερον ἀπὸ τοῦ ἅπαξ ἐπέκεινα, τουτέστι τοῦ ἀγαθοῦ, θεολογεῖ.

But Porphyry in his Commentary on the Oracles says that the god worshipped by the Jews is the second god, i.e. the creator of all things whom the Chaldaean in his discourse on the gods counts to be the second from the first god [the ἅπαξ ἐπέκεινα], i.e. the Good.

It is generally assumed that Lydus here draws upon Porphyry's *De Philosophia ex Oraculis Haurienda*; see the note of Wünsch to his edition of *De Mensibus*; H. Lewy, *Chaldaean Oracles and Theurgy*, Cairo 1956, p. 77, n. 43. However, it has been plausibly argued that Lydus has drawn in this passage on a commentary by Porphyry on the Chaldaean oracles written later than the *De Philosophia* and after Porphyry was influenced by Plotinus; see P. Hadot, in: "Porphyre", *Fondation Hardt pour l'étude de l'antiquité classique, Entretiens*, XII (1965), p. 133 (see also idem, *Revue des études augustiniennes*, VI (1960), pp. 214 f.). See also E. des Places, *Journal des Savants* (1973), p. 291, n. 4.

Porphyry here identifies the Jewish God with the demiurge, who, in accordance with the teaching of the Chaldaean Oracles, is identified as the Second God (ὁ δὶς ἐπέκεινα), that is to say the World-shaping intellect; see W. Kroll, *De Oraculis Chaldaicis*, Breslau 1894, pp. 16 f.; Lewy, *op. cit.*, p. 77, n. 43; pp. 114 ff., 318 f., 395. Kroll and Lewy quote the relevant texts bearing upon ἅπαξ ἐπέκεινα and δὶς ἐπέκεινα. Cf. also Numenius, *Fragments*, ed. E. des Places, Paris 1973, F16: ὁ γὰρ δεύτερος ⟨scil. θεός⟩ διττὸς ὢν αὐτοποιεῖ τήν τε ἰδέαν ἑαυτοῦ καὶ τὸν κόσμον, δημιουργὸς ὤν, ἔπειτα θεωρητικὸς ὅλως. Perhaps in his former work, *De Philosophia ex Oraculis Haurienda*, Porphyry had no difficulty in admitting that the God worshipped by the Hebrews was both the Creator God and the Highest God. However, the view expressed here, implying the identification of the Jewish God with the demiurge, influenced later Neoplatonism as evinced, e.g., by Julian. Cf. also P. Hadot, *Porphyre et Victorinus*, I, Paris 1968, p. 264.

453

De Abstinentia, I, 14 — Nauck = F116, §1R

Δικαίου δ' ὄντος τοῦ πρὸς τὰ θηρία πολέμου πολλῶν ἀπεχόμεθα τῶν συνανθρωπούντων. ὅθεν οἱ Ἕλληνες οὔτε κυνοφαγοῦσιν οὔθ' ἵππους

From Tacitus to Simplicius

ἐσθίουσιν οὔτ᾽ ὄνους· ⟨ὗς⟩ μέντοι ἐσθίουσιν ὡς ταὐτοῦ γένους τοῖς ἀγρίοις
τὸ ἥμερον· ὡσαύτως τε τοὺς ὄρνιθας· οὐδὲ γὰρ ἐστι χρήσιμον πρὸς ἄλλο
τι ὗς ἢ πρὸς βρῶσιν. Φοίνικες δὲ καὶ Ἰουδαῖοι ἀπέσχοντο, ὅτι οὐδ᾽ ὅλως
ἐν τοῖς τόποις ἐφύετο· ἐπεὶ οὐδὲ νῦν ἐν Αἰθιοπίᾳ φασὶν ὁρᾶσθαι τὸ
ζῷον τοῦτο.

3 ⟨ὗς⟩ Felicianus

Though we wage war against wild beasts on justified grounds, still we
abstain from many animals who live in association with men. This is
the reason why the Greeks do not eat dogs or horses or asses, but eat
pigs, the tame ones being of the same species as the wild, and this
holds true about the birds. For the pig is of no use but for food. But
the Phoenicians and Jews abstained from it, because in their places
pigs were not to be found at all. For it is said that even now this animal
is not to be seen in Aethiopia.

Φοίνικες δὲ καὶ Ἰουδαῖοι ἀπέσχοντο: The reason given by Porphyry for the
abstention from pork by the Phoenicians and Jews is that pigs were not to be
found in the countries of these peoples. This abstention contrasts with the
habits of the Greeks, who treat themselves to pork since that animal is of no
use but for food. Porphyry suggests also in the same passage that the absence
of pigs from Cyprus and Phoenicia is a reason for the fact that they are not
offered there as sacrifices, in the same way as no Greek sacrifices a camel or
an elephant to the gods. For the statement that the Phoenician law forbade
sacrifice of pigs, see also Herodianus, V, 6:9. Cf. also R. de Vaux, *ZAW*,
Suppl., LXXVII (1958), pp. 250 ff. (especially p. 258).
Porphyry returns to the question of the Jewish abstention from pork in a later
passage (No. 454), where it is coupled with the abstention of the Syrians from
fish, while the Phoenicians, like the Egyptians, are said not to partake of the
meat of cows, but pork is not mentioned in this connection.
For *De Abstinentia*, II, 26, cf. Theophrastus, above, Vol. I, No. 4.

454

De Abstinentia, II, 61 — Nauck = F116, §2R

Καὶ γὰρ δεινὸν ἂν εἴη, Σύρους μὲν τῶν ἰχθύων μὴ ἂν γεύσασθαι μηδὲ
τοὺς Ἑβραίους συῶν, Φοινίκων τε τοὺς πολλοὺς καὶ Αἰγυπτίων βοῶν
θηλειῶν, ἀλλὰ καὶ βασιλέων πολλῶν μεταβαλεῖν αὐτοὺς
σπουδασάντων θάνατον ὑπομεῖναι μᾶλλον ἢ τὴν τοῦ νόμου

1 μηδ᾽ ἂν Nauck   2 τε] δὲ ed. pr.   3 θηλειῶν Nauck   θηλείων codd.

5 παράβασιν, ἡμᾶς δὲ τοὺς τῆς φύσεως νόμους καὶ τὰς θείας
παραγγελίας φόβων ἕνεκα ἀνθρωπίνων ἤ τινος βλασφημίας τῆς ἀπὸ
τούτων αἱρεῖσθαι παραβαίνειν.

For it would be a terrible thing, that while the Syrians do not taste fish
and the Hebrews pigs and many of the Phoenicians and the Egyptians
cows, and even when many kings strove to change them they
preferred to suffer death rather than to transgress the law, we choose
to transgress the laws of nature and the divine orders because of fear
of men or some evil-speaking coming from them.

Σύρους μὲν τῶν ἰχθύων μὴ ἂν γεύσασθαι: The fish were sacred to
Atargatis. Devotees of the cult were absolutely forbidden to taste fish; cf.
G. Goossens, *Hiérapolis de Syrie*, Louvain 1943, p. 62.
βασιλέων πολλῶν μεταβαλεῖν αὐτοὺς σπουδασάντων θάνατον ὑπομεῖναι
μᾶλλον: So far as I know there is no evidence that Syrians were compelled by
foreign kings to eat fish, or Phoenicians to taste cows, though there was a
tradition of persecution of Egyptian cults and of the holy Apis by Persian
sovereigns. It seems likely that Porphyry is making a generalization here
from the history of the Hebrews, about whose fortitude in face of persecution
he has much to relate.

455

De Abstinentia, IV, 11-14 — Nauck = F116, §3R

(11) Τῶν δὲ γινωσκομένων ἡμῖν Ἰουδαῖοι, πρὶν ὑπ' Ἀντιόχου τὸ
πρότερον τὰ ἀνήκεστα παθεῖν εἰς τὰ νόμιμα τὰ ἑαυτῶν, ὑπό τε
Ῥωμαίων ὕστερον, ὅτε καὶ τὸ ἱερὸν τὸ ἐν Ἱεροσολύμοις ἑάλω καὶ πᾶσι
βατὸν γέγονεν οἷς ἄβατον ἦν, αὐτή τε ἡ πόλις διεφθάρη, διετέλουν
5 πολλῶν μὲν ἀπεχόμενοι ζῴων, ἰδίως δὲ ἔτι καὶ νῦν τῶν χοιρίων. τῶν δὲ
παρ' αὐτοῖς φιλοσοφιῶν τ ρ ι τ τ α ὶ ἰδέαι ἦσαν, καὶ τῆς μὲν προΐσταντο
Φαρισαῖοι, τῆς δὲ Σαδδουκαῖοι, τῆς δὲ τρίτης, ἣ καὶ ἐδόκει σεμνοτάτη
εἶναι, Ἐσσαῖοι. οἱ οὖν τρίτοι τοιοῦτον ἐποιοῦντο τὸ πολίτευμα, ὡς
πολλαχοῦ Ἰώσηπος τῶν πραγματειῶν ἀνέγραψεν. καὶ γὰρ ἐν τῷ
10 δευτέρῳ τῆς Ἰουδαϊκῆς ἱστορίας, ἣν δι' ἑπτὰ βιβλίων συνεπλήρωσεν,
καὶ ἐν τῷ ὀκτωκαιδεκάτῳ τῆς ἀρχαιολογίας, ἣν διὰ εἴκοσι βιβλίων
ἐπραγματεύσατο, καὶ ἐν τῷ δευτέρῳ τῶν πρὸς τοὺς Ἕλληνας, εἰσὶ δὲ
δύο τὰ βιβλία. εἰσὶ τοίνυν οἱ Ἐσσαῖοι Ἰουδαῖοι μὲν τὸ γένος,
φιλάλληλοι δὲ καὶ τῶν ἄλλων πλέον. οὗτοι τὰς μὲν ἡδονὰς ὡς κακίαν
15 ἀποστρέφονται, τὴν δὲ ἐγκράτειαν καὶ τὸ μὴ τοῖς πάθεσιν ὑποπίπτειν
ἀρετὴν ὑπολαμβάνουσι. καὶ γάμου μὲν παρ' αὐτοῖς ὑπεροψία, τοὺς δὲ

ἀλλοτρίους παῖδας ἐκλαμβάνοντες ἁπαλοὺς ἔτι πρὸς τὰ μαθήματα,
συγγενεῖς ἡγοῦνται καὶ τοῖς ἤθεσιν ἑαυτῶν ἐντυποῦσιν, τὸν μὲν γάμον
καὶ τὴν ἐξ αὐτοῦ διαδοχὴν οὐκ ἀναιροῦντες, τὰς δὲ τῶν γυναικῶν
20 ἀσελγείας φυλαττόμενοι· καταφρονηταὶ δὲ πλούτου, καὶ θαυμάσιον
παρ' αὐτοῖς τὸ κοινωνικόν, οὐδ' ἔστιν εὑρεῖν κτήσει τινὰ παρ' αὐτοῖς
ὑπερέχοντα. νόμος γὰρ τοὺς εἰς τὴν αἵρεσιν εἰσιόντας δημεύειν τῷ
τάγματι τὴν οὐσίαν, ὥστε ἐν ἅπασι μήτε πενίας ταπεινότητα
φαίνεσθαι μήθ' ὑπεροχὴν πλούτου, τῶν δ' ἑκάστου κτημάτων ἀνα-
25 μεμιγμένων μίαν ὥσπερ ἀδελφοῖς ἅπασιν οὐσίαν εἶναι. κηλῖδα δὲ
ὑπολαμβάνουσιν τοὔλαιον, κἂν ἀλειφθῇ τις ἄκων, σμήχεται τὸ σῶμα·
τὸ γὰρ αὐχμεῖν ἐν καλῷ τίθενται λευχειμονεῖν τε διὰ παντός.
χειροτονητοὶ δὲ οἱ τῶν κοινῶν ἐπιμεληταί, καὶ αἱρετοὶ πρὸς ἁπάντων
εἰς τὰς χρείας ἕκαστοι. μία δὲ οὐκ ἔστιν αὐτῶν πόλις, ἀλλ' ἐν ἑκάστῃ
30 κατοικοῦσι πολλοί. καὶ τοῖς ἑτέρωθεν ἥκουσιν αἱρετισταῖς ἀνα-
πέπταται τὰ παρ' αὐτοῖς, καὶ οἱ πρῶτον ἰδόντες εἰσίασιν ὥσπερ
συνήθεις. διὸ οὐδὲν ἐπικομιζόμενοι ἀποδημοῦσιν ἀναλωμάτων ἕνεκα.
οὔτε δὲ ἐσθῆτα οὔτε ὑποδήματα ἀμείβουσιν πρὶν διαρραγῆναι
πρότερον παντάπασιν ἢ δαπανηθῆναι τῷ χρόνῳ. οὐδ' ἀγοράζουσίν τι
35 οὐδὲ πωλοῦσιν, ἀλλὰ τῷ χρῄζοντι διδοὺς ἕκαστος τὰ παρ' ἑαυτοῦ τὸ
παρ' ἐκείνου χρήσιμον ἀντικομίζεται. καὶ χωρὶς δὲ τῆς ἀντιδόσεως
ἀκώλυτος ἡ μετάληψις αὐτοῖς παρ' ὧν ἂν ἐθέλωσιν.
(12) πρός γε μὴν τὸ θεῖον ἰδίως εὐσεβεῖς. πρὶν γὰρ ἀνασχεῖν τὸν ἥλιον
οὐδὲν φθέγγονται τῶν βεβήλων, πατρίους δέ τινας εἰς αὐτὸν εὐχάς,
40 ὥσπερ ἱκετεύοντες ἀνατεῖλαι. μετὰ ταῦτα πρὸς ἃς ἕκαστοι τέχνας
ἴσασιν ὑπὸ τῶν ἐπιμελητῶν ἀφίενται, καὶ μέχρι πέμπτης ὥρας
ἐργασάμενοι συντόνως ἔπειτα πάλιν εἰς ἓν ἀθροίζονται χωρίον,
ζωσάμενοί τε σκεπάσμασι λινοῖς οὕτως ἀπολούονται τὸ σῶμα ψυχροῖς
ὕδασι, καὶ μετὰ ταύτην τὴν ἁγνείαν εἰς ἴδιον οἴκημα συνίασιν, ἔνθα
45 μηδενὶ τῶν ἑτεροδόξων ἐπιτέτραπται παρελθεῖν· αὐτοί τε καθαροὶ
καθάπερ εἰς ἅγιόν τι τέμενος παραγίνονται τὸ δειπνητήριον.
καθισάντων δὲ μεθ' ἡσυχίας ὁ μὲν σιτοποιὸς ἐν τάξει παρατίθησιν
ἄρτους, ὁ δὲ μάγειρος ἓν ἀγγεῖον ἐξ ἑνὸς ἐδέσματος ἑκάστῳ.
προκατεύχεται δ' ὁ ἱερεὺς τῆς τροφῆς ἁγνῆς οὔσης καὶ καθαρᾶς, καὶ
50 γεύσασθαί τινα πρὶν τῆς εὐχῆς ἀθέμιτον· ἀριστοποιησάμενος δ'
ἐπεύχεται πάλιν, ἀρχόμενοί τε καὶ παυόμενοι γεραίρουσι τὸν θεόν.
ἔπειθ' ὡς ἱερὰς καταθέμενοι τὰς ἐσθῆτας πάλιν ἐπ' ἔργα μέχρι
δείλης τρέπονται. δειπνοῦσι δ' ὑποστρέψαντες ὁμοίως. συγ-
καθεζομένων τῶν ξένων, εἰ τύχοιεν αὐτοῖς παρόντες οὔτε δὲ
55 κραυγή ποτε τὸν οἶκον οὔτε θόρυβος μιαίνει. τὰς δὲ λαλιὰς ἐν τάξει
παραχωροῦσιν ἀλλήλοις, καὶ τοῖς ἔξωθεν ὡς μυστήριόν τι φρικτὸν ἡ

436

τῶν ἔνδον σιωπῇ καταφαίνεται. τούτου δ' αἴτιον ἡ διηνεκὴς νῆψις καὶ
τὸ μετρεῖσθαι παρ' αὐτοῖς τροφὴν καὶ ποτὸν μέχρι κόρου. τοῖς δὲ
ζηλοῦσι τὴν αἵρεσιν οὐκ εὐθὺς ἡ πάροδος, ἀλλ' ἐπ' ἐνιαυτὸν ἔξω
60 μένοντι τὴν αὐτὴν ὑποτίθενται δίαιταν, ἀξινάριόν τε καὶ περίζωμα
δόντες καὶ λευκὴν ἐσθῆτα. ἐπειδὰν δὲ τούτῳ τῷ χρόνῳ πεῖραν
ἐγκρατείας δῷ, πρόσεισι μὲν ἔγγιον τῇ διαίτῃ καὶ καθαρώτερον τῶν
πρὸς ἁγνείαν ὑδάτων μεταλαμβάνει, παραλαμβάνεται δὲ εἰς τὰς
συμβιώσεις οὐδέπω· μετὰ γὰρ τὴν τῆς καρτερίας ἐπίδειξιν δυσὶν
65 ἄλλοις ἔτεσιν τὸ ἦθος δοκιμάζεται, καὶ φανεὶς ἄξιος οὕτως εἰς τὸν
ὅμιλον ἐγκρίνεται.
(13) πρὶν δὲ τῆς κοινῆς ἅψασθαι τροφῆς, ὅρκους αὐτοῖς ὄμνυσι
φρικώδεις, πρῶτον μὲν εὐσεβήσειν τὸ θεῖον, ἔπειτα τὰ πρὸς
ἀνθρώπους δίκαια φυλάξειν καὶ μήτε κατὰ γνώμην βλάψειν τινὰ μήτ'
70 ἐξ ἐπιτάγματος, μισήσειν δὲ ἀεὶ τοὺς ἀδίκους καὶ συναγωνιεῖσθαι τοῖς
δικαίοις, τὸ πιστὸν πᾶσι μὲν παρέξειν, μάλιστα δὲ τοῖς κρατοῦσιν· οὐ
γὰρ δίχα θεοῦ περιγίνεσθαί τινι τὸ ἄρχειν. κἂν αὐτὸς ἄρχῃ,
μηδεπώποτε ἐξυβρίσαι εἰς τὴν ἐξουσίαν, μηδὲ ἐσθῆτι ἤ τινι πλείονι
κόσμῳ τοὺς ὑποτεταγμένους ὑπερλαμπρύνεσθαι, τὴν ἀλήθειαν
75 ἀγαπᾶν ἀεὶ καὶ τοὺς ψευδομένους προβάλλεσθαι· χεῖρας κλοπῆς καὶ
ψυχὴν ἀνοσίου κέρδους καθαρὰν φυλάξειν καὶ μήτε κρύψειν τι τοὺς
αἱρετιστὰς μήθ' ἑτέροις αὐτῶν τι μηνύσειν, κἂν μέχρι θανάτου τις
βιάζηται. πρὸς δὲ τούτοις ὄμνυσι μηδενὶ μὲν μεταδοῦναι τῶν δογμάτων
ἑτέρως ἢ ὡς αὐτὸς παρέλαβεν, ἀφέξεσθαι δὲ λῃστείας, καὶ
80 συντηρήσειν ὁμοίως τά τε τῆς αἱρέσεως αὐτῶν βιβλία καὶ τὰ τῶν
ἀγγέλων ὀνόματα. τοιοῦτοι μὲν οἱ ὅρκοι· οἱ δ' ἁλόντες καὶ
ἐκβληθέντες κακῷ μόρῳ φθείρονται. τοῖς γὰρ ὅρκοις καὶ τοῖς ἔθεσιν
ἐνδεδεμένοι οὐδὲ τῆς παρὰ τοῖς ἄλλοις τροφῆς δύνανται
μεταλαμβάνειν, ποηφαγοῦντες δὲ καὶ λιμῷ τὸ σῶμα διαφθειρόμενοι
85 ἀπόλλυνται. διὸ δὴ πολλοὺς ἐλεήσαντες ἐν ταῖς ἐσχάταις ἀνάγκαις
ἀνέλαβον, ἱκανὴν τιμωρίαν δεδωκέναι νομίζοντες ἐπὶ τοῖς ἁμαρτήμασι
τὴν μέχρι θανάτου βάσανον. τὴν δὲ σκαλίδα διδόασι τοῖς μέλλουσιν
αἱρετισταῖς, ἐπεὶ καὶ αὐτοὶ ἄλλως οὐ θακεύουσιν ἢ βόθρον ὀρύξαντες
εἰς βάθος ποδιαῖον, περικαλύψαντές τε θοἰματίῳ, ὡς μὴ ταῖς αὐγαῖς
90 ἐνυβρίζειν τοῦ θεοῦ. τοσαύτη δ' ἐστὶν αὐτῶν ἡ λιτότης ἡ περὶ τὴν
δίαιταν καὶ ὀλιγότης, ὡς τῇ ἑβδομάδι μὴ δεῖσθαι κενώσεως, ἣν τηρεῖν
εἰώθασιν εἰς ὕμνους τῷ θεῷ καὶ εἰς ἀνάπαυσιν. ἐκ δὲ τῆς ἀσκήσεως
ταύτης τοσαύτην πεποίηνται τὴν καρτερίαν, ὡς στρεβλούμενοι καὶ
λυγιζόμενοι καὶ καόμενοι καὶ διὰ πάντων ὁδεύοντες τῶν
95 βασανιστηρίων ὀργάνων, ἵν' ἢ βλασφημήσωσι τὸν νομοθέτην ἢ
φάγωσί τι τῶν ἀσυνήθων, οὐδέτερον ὑπομένειν. διέδειξαν δὲ τοῦτο ἐν

437

τῷ πρὸς Ῥωμαίους πολέμῳ, ἐπεὶ οὐδὲ κολακεῦσαι τοὺς αἰκιζομένους ἢ
δακρῦσαι ὑπομένουσι, μειδιῶντες δ' ἐν ταῖς ἀλγηδόσι καὶ κατ-
ειρωνευόμενοι τῶν τὰς βασάνους προσφερόντων εὔθυμοι τὰς ψυχὰς
100 ἠφίεσαν, ὡς πάλιν κομιούμενοι· καὶ γὰρ ἔρρωται παρ' αὐτοῖς ἥδε
ἡ δόξα, φθαρτὰ μὲν εἶναι τὰ σώματα καὶ τὴν ὕλην οὐ μόνιμον
αὐτῶν, τὰς δὲ ψυχὰς ἀθανάτους ἀεὶ διαμένειν, καὶ συμπλέκεσθαι μὲν
ἐκ τοῦ λεπτοτάτου φοιτώσας αἰθέρος ῥύμῃ φυσικῇ κατασπωμένας·
ἐπειδὰν δὲ ἀνεθῶσι τῶν κατὰ σάρκα δεσμῶν, οἷον δὴ μακρᾶς δουλείας
105 ἀπηλλαγμένας, τότε χαίρειν καὶ μετεώρους φέρεσθαι. ἀπὸ δὲ τῆς
τοιαύτης διαίτης καὶ τῆς πρὸς ἀλήθειαν καὶ τὴν εὐσέβειαν ἀσκήσεως
εἰκότως ἐν αὐτοῖς πολλοὶ οἳ καὶ τὰ μέλλοντα προγινώσκουσιν, ὡς ἂν
βίβλοις ἱεραῖς καὶ διαφόροις ἁγνείαις καὶ προφητῶν ἀποφθέγμασιν
ἐμπαιδοτριβούμενοι. σπάνιον δὲ εἴ ποτε ἐν ταῖς προαγορεύσεσιν
110 ἀστοχοῦσιν. τοιοῦτο μὲν τὸ τῶν Ἐσσαίων παρὰ τοῖς Ἰουδαίοις τάγμα.
(14) πᾶσί γε μὴν ἀπηγόρευτο ὑὸς ἐσθίειν ἢ ἰχθύων τῶν ἀφολιδώτων, ἃ
σελάχια καλοῦσιν Ἕλληνες, ἤ τι τῶν μωνύχων ζῴων. ἀπηγόρευτο δὲ
καὶ μηδὲ τὰ ἱκετεύοντα καὶ οἷον προσφεύγοντα ταῖς οἰκίαις ἀναιρεῖν,
οὐχ ὅτι μὴ ἐσθίειν. οὐδὲ νεοττοῖς ἐπέτρεψεν ὁ νομοθέτης τοὺς γονέας
115 συνεξαιρεῖν, φείδεσθαι δὲ [κελεύει] κἂν τῇ πολεμίᾳ τῶν
συνεργαζομένων ζῴων καὶ μὴ φονεύειν. καὶ οὐκ ἐφοβήθη μὴ
πληθῦναν τὸ γένος τῶν μὴ θυομένων ζῴων λιμὸν ἐργάσηται τοῖς
ἀνθρώποις· ᾔδει γὰρ πρῶτον μὲν ὅτι τὰ πολυτόκα ὀλιγοχρόνια, ἔπειτα
ὡς πολὺ τὸ ἀπολλύμενον, ὅταν μὴ τύχῃ τῆς ἐξ ἀνθρώπων ἐπιμελείας,
120 καὶ μὴν καὶ ὅτι ἔστιν ἄλλα ζῷα ἃ τῷ πληθύνοντι ἐπιτίθεται.

111 ἀπηγόρευτο Hercher   ἀπηγορεύετο codd.
115 κελεύει secl. Nauck   118 πολυτόκα Nauck   πολύτοκα καὶ codd.

(11) Among those known to us are the Jews, before they suffered
irremediably, first at the hands of Antiochus in the matter of their
laws and then later at the hands of the Romans, when also their
temple was captured and it became free of entry to all to whom it had
formerly been prohibited and the city itself was destroyed; [this
people] continued to abstain from many animals, and especially, even
now, from pigs. Among them philosophy took three forms; one was
represented by the Pharisees, another by the Sadducees, and the
third, which seemed to be the most august, by the Essaioi. The
last-mentioned created an association such as described by Josephus
in many places in his works, namely in the second book of his Jewish
History, which filled seven books, and in the eighteenth book of his
Antiquities, which he composed in twenty books, and in the second

book of his work "Against the Greeks", which consisted of two books. The Essaioi are thus of Jewish birth, but they show greater attachment to each other than the other sects. They shun pleasures as a vice and regard temperance and the control of the passions as a special virtue. Marriage they disdain, but adopt other men's children while yet pliable and docile, and regard them as their kin and mould them in accordance with their own principles. They do not, indeed, on principle condemn wedlock and the propagation thereby of the race, but they wish to protect themselves against women's wantonness. Riches they despise and their community of goods is truly admirable; you will not find one among them distinguished by greater opulence than another. They have a law that new members on admission to the sect shall hand over their property to the order, with the result, that you will nowhere see either abject poverty or inordinate wealth; the individual possessions join the common stock, and all, like brothers, enjoy a single patrimony. Oil they consider defiling, and anyone who accidentally comes in contact with it scours his person; for they make a point of keeping a dry skin and of always being dressed in white. They elect officers to attend to the interests of the community, the special services of each officer being determined by the whole body. They occupy no one city, but settle in large numbers in every town. On the arrival of any of the sect from elsewhere all the resources of the community are put at their disposal, just as if they were their own; and they enter the houses of men whom they have never seen before as though they were their friends. Consequently, they carry nothing whatever with them on their journeys for expense. They do not change their garments or shoes until they are torn to shreds or worn threadbare with age. They do not buy or sell, but each gives what he has to any in need and receives from him in exchange something useful to himself; they are, moreover, freely permitted to take anything from any of their associates without making any return.

(12) Their piety towards the Deity takes a peculiar form. Before the sun is up they utter no word on mundane matters, but offer to him certain prayers which have been handed down from their forefathers, as though entreating him to rise. They are then dismissed by their superiors to the various crafts in which they are severally proficient and are strenuously employed until the fifth hour, when they again assemble in one place and, after girding their loins with linen cloths, bathe their bodies in cold water. After this purification, they

assemble in a private apartment, which none of the uninitiated is permitted to enter; pure now themselves they repair to the refectory, as to some sacred shrine. When they have taken their seats in silence, the baker serves out the loaves to them in order, and the cook sets before each person one plate with a single course. The priest says grace before, the meal being holy and pure, and none may partake of it until after the prayer. When breakfast is ended, he pronounces a further grace; thus at the beginning and at the close they do homage to God. Then laying aside their garments, as holy vestments, they again betake themselves to their labours until the evening. On their return they sup in like manner, and any guests who may have arrived sit down with them. No clamour or disturbance ever pollutes their dwelling; they speak in turn, each making way for his neighbour. To persons outside the silence of those within appears like some awful mystery; it is in fact due to their invariable sobriety and the limitation of their allotted portions of food and drink to the demands of nature. A candidate anxious to join their sect is not immediately admitted. For one year, during which he remains outside the fraternity, they prescribe for him their own rule of life, presenting him with a small hatchet, a loin-cloth and white raiment. Having given proof of his temperance during this probationary period, he is brought into closer touch with the rule and is allowed to share the purer kind of holy water, but is not yet received into the meetings of the community. For after this exhibition of endurance, his character is tested for two years more, and only then, if found worthy, he is enrolled in the society. (13) But before he may touch the common food, he is made to swear tremendous oaths: first that he will practise piety towards the Deity, next that he will observe justice towards men; that he will wrong none whether of his own mind or under another's orders; that he will forever hate the unjust and fight the battle of the just; that he will forever keep faith with all men, especially with the powers that be, since no ruler attains his office save by the will of God; that should he himself bear rule, he will never abuse his authority nor, either in dress or by other outward marks of superiority, outshine his subjects; to be forever a lover of truth and to expose liars; to keep his hands from stealing and his soul pure from unholy gain; to conceal nothing from the members of the sect and to report none of their secrets to others, even though tortured to death. He swears, moreover, to transmit their rules exactly as he himself received them; to abstain from robbery; and in like manner carefully to preserve the books of the

440

sect and the names of the angels. Such are the oaths. The convicted and expelled come to a miserable end. For, being bound by their oath and usages, they are not at liberty to partake of other men's food, and so fall to eating grass, and wasting away, die. This led them in their compassion to receive many of them back in the last stage of suffering, deeming that torments which have brought them to the verge of death are a sufficient penalty for their misdoings. And they present a mattock to those intending to become members of the sect, since they themselves do not ease themselves otherwise than by digging a trench a foot deep and wrapping the mantle about them, that they may not offend the rays of the Deity. And such is the simplicity and scantiness of their food, that on the seventh day they have no need of easing themselves. They dedicate this day to hymns to the Deity and rest. Owing to this training they became capable of such perseverance that, on being racked and twisted and burnt and passing through every instrument of torture, in order to induce them to blaspheme their lawgiver or to eat some forbidden food, they refused to yield to either demand. They showed this in the war against the Romans, for they did not consent either to cringe to their persecutors or to shed a tear, but smiling in their agonies and mildly deriding their tormentors, they cheerfully resigned their souls, confident that they would receive them back. For it is a fixed belief of theirs that the body is corruptible and its constituent matter impermanent but that the soul is immortal and imperishable. The souls emanating from the finest ether become entangled being dragged down by natural force; but when once they are released from the bonds of the flesh, then, as though liberated from a long servitude, they rejoice and are borne aloft. As might be expected, owing to such a way of life and training aiming at truth and piety, there are many among them who foretell the future, being versed from their early years in holy books, various forms of purifications and apophthegms of prophets, and seldom, if ever, do they err in their predictions. Such is the order of the Essaioi among the Jews.

(14) To all Jews it was forbidden to eat pork or unscaled fish, which Greeks call cartilaginous, and also any of the uncloven animals. Moreover, it was forbidden to them to kill the animals which took refuge at their houses like suppliants, not to speak of eating them. Nor did the lawgiver allow to take away the parents together with the nestlings, and he enjoined that animals which are of help in work should be spared, even in enemy country, and not to slaughter them.

441

And he was not afraid lest the race of animals not liable to sacrifice would be multiplied and cause hunger to men; for first he knew that the prolific animals are short-lived, and then that many would die if they did not receive human attention and that there are other animals which attack the ones that multiply.

For a discussion, see Bernays, *op. cit.* (supra, p. 424, n. 4), pp. 22 ff.
11 τῶν δὲ παρ᾽ αὐτοῖς φιλοσοφιῶν τρίτται ἰδέαι ἦσαν: Cf. *BJ*, II, 119.
ἐν τῷ δευτέρῳ τῆς Ἰουδαϊκῆς ἱστορίας: I.e. the Jewish war against Rome. The description of the Essenes is found *ibid.*, II, 119–161.

ἐν τῷ ὀκτωκαιδεκάτῳ τῆς ἀρχαιολογίας... καὶ ἐν τῷ δευτέρῳ τῶν πρὸς τοὺς Ἕλληνας: Josephus describes the Essenes in *Ant.*, XVIII, 18 ff. The work against the Greeks mentioned by Porphyry is to be identified with *Contra Apionem*, the second book of which contains a survey of the Jewish religion but not specifically of that of the Essenes. Porphyry in any case uses in what follows only the *Bellum Judaicum*. Later, however, in dealing with the general observances of the Jews, he draws also on *Contra Apionem*.
Ἰουδαῖοι μέν: Porphyry here follows Josephus faithfully and does not use the designation Ἑβραῖοι, as is his general habit.
καὶ οἱ πρῶτον ἰδόντες εἰσίασιν ὥσπερ συνήθεις: Cf. *BJ*, II, 124: καὶ πρὸς οὓς οὐ πρότερον εἶδον.
ἀναλωμάτων ἕνεκα: Cf. *BJ*, II, 125: διὰ δὲ τοὺς λῃστὰς ἔνοπλοι. Porphyry may have deliberately introduced this change in order to omit any connection of the Essenes with arms; see Bernays, *op. cit.* (supra, p. 424, n. 4), pp. 26 f.
οὔτε δὲ ἐσθῆτα: Porphyry omits the passage of Josephus stating that in every city there was a member of the sect charged with attendance on guests and that in their dress and deportment they resembled children under strict discipline.
13 οἱ δ᾽ ἁλόντες καὶ ἐκβληθέντες κακῷ μόρῳ φθείρονται: Cf. *BJ*, II, 143: Τοὺς δ᾽ ἐπ᾽ ἀξιοχρέοις ἁμαρτήμασιν ἁλόντας ἐκβάλλουσι τοῦ τάγματος. ὁ δ᾽ ἐκκριθεὶς οἰκτίστῳ μόρῳ διαφθείρεται.
ἐν ταῖς ἐσχάταις ἀνάγκαις: Cf. *BJ*, II, 144: ἐν ταῖς ἐσχάταις ἀναπνοαῖς. Porphyry does not draw upon the passage, *BJ*, II, 145–147, which describes the judicial procedure of the Essenes, the reverence that they had for their lawgiver (Moses), the honour in which they held their elders, their respect for the wish of the majority, the care they took not to spit in the presence of other people, and their meticulous observance of the seventh day.
τὴν δὲ σκαλίδα διδόασι...: Some reworking is evident here; cf. *BJ*, II, 148: ταῖς δ᾽ ἄλλαις ἡμέραις βόθρον ὀρύσσοντες βάθος ποδιαῖον τῇ σκαλίδι, τοιοῦτον γάρ ἐστιν τὸ διδόμενον ὑπ᾽ αὐτῶν ἀξινίδιον τοῖς νεοσυστάτοις. The emphasis by Porphyry on the simplicity of the diet is absent from *BJ*. Josephus makes no allusion to its consequence for the seventh day but relates only that the Essenes do not go to stool on that day (*BJ*, II, 147). On the other hand, Porphyry omits some details found in *BJ*, as well as the general statement concerning the Essenes' ablutions after the discharge of

442

excrements, which, though a natural function, is treated by them as a defilement.

ἣν τηρεῖν εἰώθασιν εἰς ὕμνους τῷ θεῷ καὶ εἰς ἀνάπαυσιν: Josephus in this connection does not say that the Essenes dedicate the seventh day to reciting hymns to God and to rest.

ἐκ δὲ τῆς ἀσκήσεως ταύτης ...: An addition of Porphyry.

καόμενοι: After καόμενοι Porphyry omits κλώμενοι.

ῥύμῃ φυσικῇ κατασπωμένας: Cf. *BJ*, II, 154: ὥσπερ εἱρκταῖς τοῖς σώμασιν ἴυγγί τινι φυσικῇ κατασπωμένας. Cf. Bernays, *op. cit.* (supra, p. 424, n. 4), p. 26. Porphyry omits Josephus' observation (*BJ*, II, 155–157) about the similarity of the views of the Essenes and the Greeks concerning the abode of souls after death.

14 πᾶσί γε μὴν ἀπηγόρευτο ὑὸς ἐσθίειν ἢ ἰχθύων τῶν ἀφολιδώτων: Porphyry owes this statement to his own knowledge of the Bible; cf. Bernays, *op. cit.* (supra, p. 424, n. 4), p. 154.

ἀπηγόρευτο δὲ καὶ μηδὲ τὰ ἱκετεύοντα ...: Here Porphyry is dependent on *Contra Apionem*, II, 213.

456a

Vita Pythagorae, 11 — Nauck = F83 R; cf. Antonius Diogenes (No. 250)

Ἀφίκετο δὲ καὶ πρὸς Αἰγυπτίους, φησίν ⟨scil. ὁ Διογένης⟩, ὁ Πυθαγόρας καὶ πρὸς Ἄραβας καὶ Χαλδαίους καὶ Ἑβραίους, παρ' ὧν καὶ τὴν περὶ ὀνείρων γνῶσιν ἠκριβώσατο.

2 ἄρραβας V

He says [scil. Diogenes] that Pythagoras came also to the Egyptians, the Arabs, the Chaldaeans and the Hebrews, from whom he learnt the exact knowledge of dreams.

Porphyry's "Life of Pythagoras" constitutes a part of the first book of his Φιλόσοφος ἱστορία. His information about Pythagoras' visit to the Hebrews, as well as to the Arabs and Chaldaeans, derives from Antonius Diogenes, as he himself states. On Porphyry's *Vita Pythagorae*, see E. Rohde, *Kleine Schriften*, II, Tübingen–Leipzig 1901, pp. 125 ff.; H. Jäger, "Die Quellen des Porphyrios in seiner Pythagoras-Biographie", Ph. D. Thesis, Zurich 1919 (on the use of Antonius Diogenes by Porphyry, see pp. 34 ff.); Beutler, PW, XXII (1953), pp. 287 f.

The brief notice about the visit of Pythagoras to the Hebrews in Porphyry's works may be compared with the much more circumstantial account of Pythagoras' sojourn at Mount Carmel by Iamblichus, *De Vita Pythagorica*, 3:14 f.: διεπορθμεύθη ἀμελλητὶ ὑπό τινων Αἰγυπτίων πορθμέων καιριώτατα προσορμισάντων τοῖς ὑπὸ Κάρμηλον τὸ Φοινικικὸν ὄρος αἰγιαλοῖς, ἔνθα ἐμόναξε τὰ πολλὰ ὁ Πυθαγόρας κατὰ τὸ ἱερὸν ... ἀναμνησθέντες τε ὡς προσορμίσασιν εὐθὺς αὐτοῖς ὤφθη κατιὼν ἀπ' ἀκροῦ τοῦ Καρμήλου λόφου (ἱερώτατον δὲ τῶν ἄλλων ὁρῶν ἠπίσταντο αὐτὸ καὶ πολλοῖς ἄβατον).

456b

De Antro Nympharum, 10 — Nauck; cf. Numenius (No. 368)

Ἡγοῦντο γὰρ προσιζάνειν τῷ ὕδατι τὰς ψυχὰς θεοπνόῳ ὄντι, ὡς φησὶν ὁ Νουμήνιος, διὰ τοῦτο λέγων καὶ τὸν προφήτην εἰρηκέναι ἐμφέρεσθαι ἐπάνω τοῦ ὕδατος θεοῦ πνεῦμα.

1 συνιζάνειν M

They believed that the souls rest on the water, which is divinely animated, so Numenius asserts, saying that because of this the prophet said that the spirit of God is carried above the water.

457a

Chronica, apud: Eusebius, *Chronica*, I, p. 165 — Schöne = *Die Chronik aus dem armenischen*, ed. J. Karst, Leipzig 1911, pp. 76 f. = F. Gr. Hist., II, B 260, F 2 (9)

Postquam vero is ⟨scil. Ptolomaeus Alexander⟩ se fugae dedisset, ad maiorem fratrem Ptolomaeum Soterem nuntios mittentes Alexandrini, rursum ei regnum tradiderunt ex Cypro illuc naviganti. Cum vero anni insuper VII cum mensibus VI transissent; tot enim ⟨annos⟩
5 vixit, postquam illuc redux fuit; totum tempus post amborum patris mortem ad eum refertur, integro annorum XXXV numero, mensiumque sex conservato: distribuendo veraciter ⟨in⟩ Soterem Ptolomaeum diversis temporibus, annos XVII, et menses VI, et in secundum, qui et Alexander, intermedios ⟨annos⟩ in quibus maior
10 annos XVIII dominatus est; quos annos cum ex libro delere non possent ⟨Alexandrini⟩, etenim quantum ipsis licuit, expungebant, quia restitit ipsis per quaedam Iudaica subsidia, ideo haud ⟨ei⟩ tempora illa imputant, sed cunctos XXXVI annos fratri seniori adscribunt.

And after he [scil. Ptolemy Alexander] had fled, the Alexandrians sent envoys to the elder brother, Ptolemy Soter, and gave him the

444

kingship again when he sailed there from Cyprus. Since in addition seven years and six months passed — for he lived this long after his return there — the whole time from the death of the common father was attributed to him, thus retaining the full number of thirty-five years and six months.

According to the true distribution, however, seventeen years and six months fell to Ptolemy Soter at different periods, while there fell to the second [brother], Alexander, the eighteen intermediate years between those of his brother's rule. Since the Alexandrians could not expunge them from the book, they erased them as far as it lay in their power, because he had withstood them by means of some Jewish help. Thus they do not attribute those times to him, but count all the thirty-six years as those of his elder brother.

The above is the Latin translation by Schöne of the Armenian version of Eusebius' Chronicle. The following is the Greek text of the *Excerpta Eusebii*, as printed by J.A.Cramer, *Anecdota Graeca e Codd. Manuscriptis Bibliothecae Regiae Parisiensis*, II, Oxford 1839, p. 122 = Eusebius, *Chronica* (ed. Schöne), I, p. 166: Μετὰ δὲ τὴν τούτου φυγὴν πρὸς τὸν πρεσβύτερον Πτολεμαῖον τὸν Σωτῆρα οἱ Ἀλεξανδρεῖς πρεσβευσάμενοι παραδιδόασιν πάλιν τὴν βασιλείαν αὐτῷ ἐκ Κύπρου καταπλεύσαντι. διαγενομένων δὲ ἄλλων ἐτῶν ἑπτὰ πρὸς μησὶν ἕξ, τοσαῦτα γὰρ ἐπέζησε μετὰ τὴν κάθοδον, ὁ πᾶς χρόνος ὁ μετὰ τὸν τοῦ πατρὸς ἀμφοτέρων θάνατον εἰς τοῦτον ἀναφέρεται· τὸν μὲν ἀριθμὸν σῴζων λέ ἐνιαυτῶν πρὸς μησὶν ἕξ· διῳκηκὼς δὲ κατὰ τὴν ἀλήθειαν εἰς μὲν τὸν Σωτῆρα Πτολεμαῖον καὶ διαφόρους χρόνους δεκαεπτὰ ἔτη καὶ μῆνας ἕξ, εἰς δὲ τὸν δεύτερον τὸν καὶ Ἀλέξανδρον τοὺς μέσους, ὧν ἦρξεν ὁ πρεσβύτερος, ἐνιαυτοὺς δεκαοκτώ, οὓς καίτοι μὴ δυνηθέντες ἐκ τῆς ἀναγραφῆς ἀφανίσαι, τὸ ὅσον ἐφ᾽ ἑαυτοῖς ἀπαλείφουσι· προσέκρουσε γὰρ αὐτοῖς διά τινας Ἰουδαϊκὰς ἐπικουρίας· οὐ γὰρ ἀριθμοῦσι τούτους τοὺς χρόνους, τοὺς δὲ πάντας τὰ ἕξ καὶ τριάκοντα τῷ πρεσβυτέρῳ προσνέμουσιν·

The rivalry between the two brothers, Ptolemy Soter II, otherwise known as Ptolemy Lathyrus, and his younger brother, Ptolemy Alexander, was of long standing. Both were sons of Ptolemy Euergetes II (Ptolemy Physcon) and Cleopatra III. Cleopatra came to an open clash with Ptolemy Soter, and finally expelled him in 107 B.C.E. He took refuge at Cyprus, which became his main base, while his younger brother shared the rule with his mother. The Jews of Egypt, conspicuous among them the two Jewish generals Chelkias and Ananias, were staunch supporters of Cleopatra III and Ptolemy Alexander; see Strabo, *Historica Hypomnemata*, apud: Josephus, *Ant.*, XIII, 284–287 (No. 99), while Ptolemy Soter II (Lathyrus) displayed hostility towards the Hasmonaean state and aided its enemies. At the beginning of the reign of Alexander Jannaeus (103–76 B.C.E.) Ptolemy Soter II defeated the Jewish king's army. The Jews managed to remove Ptolemy Soter II from

Judaea only by the intervention of Cleopatra III, who sent an army commanded by the two above-mentioned Jewish generals; see above, Vol. I, pp. 269 f., 272.

After the death of the queen (101 B.C.E.) the Jews seem to have remained loyal to Ptolemy Alexander, who, presumably adhering to the policy of his mother, strengthened his rule by close connections with his numerous Jewish subjects. These events are borne out by the testimony of Porphyry, who considers that the Jewish support was a principal reason for the Alexandrians' dislike of Ptolemy Alexander, resulting in his expulsion and the recall of Ptolemy Soter II from Cyprus (88 B.C.E.).

Other sources referring to the expulsion of Ptolemy Alexander do not mention the part played by his Jewish connections; see Iustinus, XXXIX, 5:1; Pausanias, *Graeciae Descriptio*, I, 9:3; cf. Athenaeus, *Deipnosophistae*, XII, 73, p. 550. For the chronology of the year 88 B.C.E., see also the discussion by A. E. Samuel, *Chronique d'Égypte*, XL (1965), pp. 376 ff. (Some reservations are put forward by Fraser, II, pp. 220 f.)

However, one source with some bearing upon Alexandrian Jews in the time of Ptolemy Alexander is Iordanis, *Romana*, 81 (ed. T. Mommsen, Berlin 1882, p. 9): "Ptholomeus, qui et Alexander, ann. X. Quo regnante multa Iudaeorum populus tam ab Alexandrinis, quam etiam ab Anthiocensibus tolerabat." On this source, see H. Willrich, *Hermes*, XXXIX (1904), pp. 249 f.; B. Motzo, *Atti della reale Accademia delle Scienze di Torino*, L (1914–1915), pp. 216 f.; L. Fuchs, *Die Juden Aegyptens in ptolemäischer und römischer Zeit*, Vienna 1924, p. 16; H. I. Bell, *Juden und Griechen im römischen Alexandreia*, Leipzig 1926, p. 9; I. Lévy, *HUCA*, Vol. XXIII, Part 2 (1950–1951), pp. 127 ff.; V. A. Tcherikover, *CPJ*, p. 25, Prolegomena; H. Volkmann, PW, XXIII, p. 1746; O. Murray, *JTS*, NS, XVIII (1967), pp. 363 f. It is unnecessary to assume with Fuchs that Jordanis implies a change of attitude on the part of the Jews towards Ptolemy Alexander and a reconciliation with Ptolemy Soter (Lathyrus), so that in consequence Ptolemy Alexander launched a persecution against the Jews; against this interpretation, see already Bell, *op. cit.* It is equally not necessary to understand the passage of Jordanis as meaning that the sufferings of the Jews are to be dated to the time of the expulsion of Ptolemy Alexander; so, e.g., Volkmann, *op. cit.*; for another view, cf. Motzo, *op. cit.* p. 216, n. 2. It seems rather that the events occurred at some unknown occasion of tension between the Alexandrians and Ptolemy Alexander, as Jordanis states only that the Jews suffered during the reign of Ptolemy Alexander ("quo regnante"), without dating their suffering to any specific year.

This is one notice of Jordanis that he does not owe to Jerome; see Mommsen's introduction to his edition of Jordanis, *op. cit.*, pp. XXVII f. There is no reason for Lévy to doubt that Jordanis indeed refers to anti-Jewish disturbances in the reign of Ptolemy Alexander. What Porphyry writes about the Jewish support for Ptolemy Alexander, and the strength of the anti-Jewish feelings of the Alexandrians resulting from this, corroborates Jordanis' information about hardships endured by the Jews at the hands of the Alexandrians during the reign of Ptolemy Alexander.

Porphyry

457b

Chronica, apud: Eusebius, *Chronica*, I, p. 255 — Schöne = F117R = ed. Karst, *op. cit.*, p. 120 =
F. Gr. Hist., II, B260, F32 (18), p. 1217

Regnabat hic ⟨scil. Antiochus Sidetes⟩ quoque annis IX Iudaeosque
hic subegit, per obsidionem muros urbis evertebat, atque electissimos
ipsorum trucidabat anno tertio CLXII olympiadis.

And he [scil. Antiochus Sidetes] had also ruled for nine years, and he
subdued the Jews, and as a result of the siege he razed the walls of the
city [scil. Jerusalem], and the choicest of them he slaughtered, in the
third year of the 162nd Olympiad.

For these events, cf. Diodorus, XXXIV–XXXV, 1 (No. 63) and the
commentary *ad loc.* See also Plutarchus, *Regum et Imperatorum
Apophthegmata*, p. 184 E–F (No. 260).

458

Adversus Christianos, apud: Eusebius, *Praeparatio Evangelica*, I, 2:1–5 — Mras = Harnack, F1

(1) Πρῶτον μὲν γὰρ εἰκότως ἄν τις διαπορήσειεν, τίνες ὄντες ἐπὶ τὴν
γραφὴν παρεληλύθαμεν, πότερον Ἕλληνες ἢ βάρβαροι, ἢ τί ἂν γένοιτο
τούτων μέσον, καὶ τίνας ἑαυτοὺς εἶναί φαμεν, οὐ τὴν προσηγορίαν, ὅτι καὶ
τοῖς πᾶσιν ἔκδηλος αὕτη, ἀλλὰ τὸν τρόπον καὶ τὴν προαίρεσιν τοῦ βίου·
5 οὔτε γὰρ τὰ Ἑλλήνων φρονοῦντας ὁρᾶν οὔτε τὰ βαρβάρων ἐπιτηδεύοντας.
(2) τί οὖν ἂν γένοιτο τὸ καθ᾽ ἡμᾶς ξένον καὶ τίς ὁ νεωτερισμὸς τοῦ βίου; πῶς
δ᾽ οὐ πανταχόθεν δυσσεβεῖς ἂν εἶεν καὶ ἄθεοι οἱ τῶν πατρῴων θεῶν
ἀποστάντες, δι᾽ ὧν πᾶν ἔθνος καὶ πᾶσα πόλις συνέστηκεν; ἢ τί καλὸν
ἐλπίσαι εἰκὸς τοὺς τῶν σωτηρίων ἐχθροὺς καὶ πολεμίους καταστάντας καὶ
10 τοὺς εὐεργέτας παρωσαμένους καὶ τί γὰρ ἄλλο ἢ θεομαχοῦντας; *(3)* ποίας
δὲ καταξιωθήσεσθαι συγγνώμης τοὺς τοὺς ἐξ αἰῶνος μὲν παρὰ πᾶσιν
Ἕλλησι καὶ βαρβάροις κατά τε πόλεις καὶ ἀγροὺς παντοίοις ἱεροῖς καὶ
τελεταῖς καὶ μυστηρίοις πρὸς ἁπάντων ὁμοῦ βασιλέων τε καὶ νομοθετῶν
καὶ φιλοσόφων θεολογουμένους ἀποστραφέντας, ἑλομένους δὲ τὰ ἀσεβῆ
15 καὶ ἄθεα τῶν ἐν ἀνθρώποις; ποίαις δ᾽ οὐκ ἂν ἐνδίκως ὑποβληθεῖεν
τιμωρίαις οἱ τῶν μὲν πατρίων φυγάδες, τῶν δ᾽ ὀθνείων καὶ παρὰ πᾶσι

1 ἀπορήσειεν H   7 οἱ om. H   /   πατρίων ἐθῶν IGNV
9 εἰκὸς] ἀλλ᾽ εἰς H   10 γὰρ] δ᾽ G   11 δὲ] δὴ H   /
καὶ ἀξιωθήσεσθαι IGNV   /   τοὺς τοὺς] τοὺς HG   /   μὲν om. H
16 δ᾽ ὀθνείων] δὲ ξένων H

διαβεβλημένων Ἰουδαϊκῶν μυθολογημάτων γενόμενοι ζηλωταί; (4) πῶς
δ' οὐ μοχθηρίας εἶναι καὶ εὐχερείας ἐσχάτης τὸ μεταθέσθαι μὲν εὐκόλως
⟨τὰ⟩ τῶν οἰκείων, ἀλόγῳ δὲ καὶ ἀνεξετάστῳ πίστει τὰ τῶν δυσσεβῶν καὶ
20 πᾶσιν ἔθνεσι πολεμίων ἑλέσθαι, καὶ μηδ' αὐτῷ τῷ παρὰ Ἰουδαίοις
τιμωμένῳ θεῷ κατὰ τὰ παρ' αὐτοῖς προσανέχειν νόμιμα, καινὴν δέ τινα
καὶ ἐρήμην ἀνοδίαν ἑαυτοῖς συντεμεῖν, μήτε τὰ Ἑλλήνων μήτε τὰ
Ἰουδαίων φυλάττουσαν; (5) Ταῦτα μὲν οὖν εἰκότως ἄν τις Ἑλλήνων, μηδὲν
ἀληθὲς μήτε τῶν οἰκείων μήτε τῶν καθ' ἡμᾶς ἐπαΐων, πρὸς ἡμᾶς
25 ἀπορήσειεν. ἐπιμέμψαιντο δ' ἄν ἡμῖν καὶ Ἑβραίων παῖδες, εἰ δὴ
ἀλλόφυλοι ὄντες καὶ ἀλλογενεῖς ταῖς αὐτῶν βίβλοις ἀποχρώμεθα μηδὲν
ἡμῖν προσηκούσαις, ὅτι τε ἀναιδῶς, ὡς ἄν αὐτοὶ φαῖεν, καὶ ἀναισχύντως
ἑαυτοὺς μὲν εἰσωθοῦμεν, τοὺς δὲ οἰκείους καὶ ἐγγενεῖς τῶν αὐτοῖς πατρίων
ἐξωθεῖν παραβιαζόμεθα.

19 ⟨τὰ⟩ τῶν Stephanus   21 καινὴν] κενὴν H   25 ἀπορήσει G

(1) For in the first place any one might naturally want to know who we
are that have come forward to write, Are we Greeks or barbarians?
Or what can be intermediate to these? And what do we claim to be,
not in regard to the name, because this is manifest to all, but in the
manner and purpose of our life? For they would see that we agree
neither with the opinions of the Greeks, nor with the customs of the
barbarians. (2) What then may the strangeness in us be, and what the
new-fangled manner of our life? And how can men fail to be in every
way impious and atheistical, who have apostatized from those
ancestral gods by whom every nation and every state is sustained? Or
what good can they reasonably hope for, who have set themselves at
enmity and at war against their preservers and have thrust away their
benefactors? For what else are they doing than fighting against the
gods? (3) And what forgiveness shall they be thought to deserve, who
have turned away from those who from the earliest time, among all
Greeks and barbarians, both in cities and in the country, are
recognized as gods with all kinds of sacrifices and initiations, and
mysteries by all alike, kings, law-givers and philosophers, and have
chosen all that is impious and atheistical among the doctrines of men?
And to what kind of punishments would they not justly be subjected,
who deserting the customs of their forefathers have become zealots
for the foreign mythologies of the Jews, which are of evil report
among all men? (4) And must it not be a proof of extreme wickedness
and levity lightly to put aside the customs of their own kindred, and
choose with unreasoning and unquestioning faith the doctrines of the

impious enemies of all nations? Nay, not even to adhere to the God, who is honoured among the Jews according to their customary rites, but to cut out for themselves a new kind of track in a pathless desert, that keeps neither the ways of the Greeks nor those of the Jews? (5) These then are questions which any Greek might naturally put to us, having no true understanding either of his own religion or of ours. But sons of the Hebrews also would find fault with us, that being strangers and aliens, we misuse their books, which do not belong to us at all, and because in an impudent and shameless way, as they would say, we thrust ourselves in, and try violently to thrust out the true family and kindred from their own ancestral rights.

(trans. E. H. Gifford, Oxford 1903)

459a

Adversus Christianos, apud: Hieronymus, *Tractatus de Psalmo lxxxi* — *Anecdota Maredsolana*, III, 2, p. 80 = Harnack, F4 = *CCSL*, LXXVIII, p. 89

Totum orbem subegit Paulus ab Oceano usque ad Mare Rubrum. Dicat aliquis: "Hoc totum lucri causa fecerunt"; hoc enim dicit Porphyrius, "Homines rusticani et pauperes, quoniam nihil habebant, magicis artibus operati sunt quaedam signa. Non est autem grande
5 facere signa; nam fecerunt signa et in Aegypto magi contra Moysen, fecit et Apollonius, fecit et Apuleius, et infinita signa fecerunt."

The whole world from the Ocean to the Red Sea has been subjugated by Paul. Someone may say: "All this they [i.e. the Christians] did for love of gain." For this is what is said by Porphyry: "Rustic and poor people, since they owned nothing whatever, performed some miracles by magic arts; however, it is not much to perform miracles, for also the Magi in Egypt worked miracles against Moyses, and this same was done by Apollonius and Apuleius, who worked innumerable miracles."

459b

Adversus Christianos, apud: Hieronymus, *Tractatus de Psalmo lxxvii* — *Anecdota Maredsolana*, III, 2, p. 60 = Harnack, F10 = *CCSL*, LXXVIII, p. 66

Aperiam in parabola os meum, etc.: Hoc Esaias non loquitur, sed Asaph. Denique et inpius ille Porphyrius proponit adversum nos hoc

ipsum, et dicit: "Evangelista vester Matthaeus tam inperitus fuit, ut
diceret ⟨Matt. xiii:35⟩: 'Quod scriptum est in Esaia propheta:
5 Aperiam in parabolis os meum, etc.'"

I will open in a parable my mouth, etc.: This says not Esaia but Asaph.
Lastly also that impious Porphyry brings forth this very thing against
us and says: "Your evangelist Matthew was ignorant, so that he said
[Matt. xiii:35]: 'What was written in the prophet Esaia: I will open in
parables my mouth, etc.'"

459c

Adversus Christianos, apud: Hieronymus, *Commentarii in Danielem i* — Glorie, *CCSL*, LXXV, A,
p. 777 = *PL*, XXV, Col. 495 = Harnack, F 11

Et ob hanc causam secundum Matthaeum una videtur deesse
generatio ⟨Matt. i: 11–12⟩, quia secunda τεσσαραδέκας in Ioachim
desinit filio Iosiae, et tertia incipit a Joiachin filio Ioachim; quod
ignorans Porphyrius calumniam struit ecclesiae, suam ostendens
5 imperitiam, dum evangelistae Matthaei arguere nititur falsitatem.

1 *secundum* om. G / *deesse*] *de* sup. lin. M　　　2 τεσσαραδέκας μ Vallarsi
tessaresce decas A　　*tesseresce decadas* M　　*tesseriscedecac* F　　*tecceric* hE
DECΛΛΛ R τεσσαρακαιδέκας Pal.　　3 *ihoachim* A　　*Ioacim* μ Vallarsi
4 *instruit* MR et aliquot codd. Maurinorum　　5 *dum*] *cum* A

And it is for this reason that in the Gospel according to Matthew
[Matt. i: 11–12] there seems to be a generation missing, because the
second group of fourteen, extending to the time of Jehoiakim, ends
with a son of Josiah, and the third group begins with Jehoiachin, son
of Jehoiakim. Being ignorant of this factor, Porphyry formulated a
slander against the Church which only revealed his own ignorance, as
he tried to prove the evangelist Matthew guilty of error.

(trans. G.L. Archer Jr, Grand Rapids, Michigan 1958)

459d

Adversus Christianos, apud: Macarius Magnes, III, 30–33 — Blondel = Harnack, F 27–30

(30) Εἰ γὰρ τοῖς ἀνόμοις ἄνομος, ὡς αὐτὸς λέγει ⟨scil. ὁ Παῦλος⟩ ⟨I Cor.
ix:20–21⟩, «καὶ τοῖς Ἰουδαίοις Ἰουδαῖος» καὶ τοῖς πᾶσιν ὁμοίως
συνήρχετο, ὄντως πολυτρόπου κακίας ἀνδράποδον ... εἰ γὰρ ἀνόμοις

συζῇ καὶ τὸν Ἰουδαϊσμὸν ἐγγράφως ἀσμενίζει ἑκατέρου μετέχων,
5 ἑκατέρῳ συμπέφυρται συναναμιγνύμενος καὶ συναπογραφόμενος τῶν
οὐκ ἀστείων τὰ πταίσματα ...
(31) Ὁ δ' αὐτὸς οὗτος ἡμῖν, ὁ πολὺς ἐν τῷ λέγειν ὥσπερ τῶν οἰκείων
λόγων ἐπιλαθόμενός φησι τῷ χιλιάρχῳ οὐχὶ Ἰουδαῖον ἑαυτὸν ἀλλὰ
Ῥωμαῖον εἶναι, πρὸ τούτου φάς ⟨Acts xxii:3⟩· «Ἐγὼ ἀνὴρ Ἰουδαῖός
10 εἰμι, ἐν Ταρσῷ τῆς Κιλικίας γενόμενος, ἀνατεθραμμένος δὲ παρὰ τοὺς
πόδας Γαμαλιήλ, πεπαιδευμένος κατ' ἀκρίβειαν τοῦ πατρῴου νόμου.»
ὁ γοῦν εἰπών· «Ἐγώ εἰμι Ἰουδαῖος, καὶ Ἐγώ εἰμι Ῥωμαῖος», οὐδέτερόν
ἐστιν, ἑκατέρῳ προσκείμενος ... εἰ γοῦν Παῦλος ὑποκρινόμενος πῇ μὲν
Ἰουδαῖος, πῇ δὲ Ῥωμαῖός ἐστι, πῇ μὲν ἄνομος, πῇ δὲ Ἕλλην, ὅταν
15 ἐθέλῃ ἑκάστου πράγματος ὀθνεῖος καὶ πολέμιος, ἕκαστον ὑπεισελθὼν
ἕκαστον ἠχρείωκε, θωπείαις ἑκάστου κλέπτων τὴν προαίρεσιν ...
(32) Ὅτι δὲ κενοδοξίας ἕνεκεν τὸ εὐαγγέλιον καὶ πλεονεξίας τὸν νόμον
ὑποκρίνεται, δῆλος ἀφ' ὧν λέγει ⟨I Cor. ix:7⟩· «Τίς στρατεύεται ἰδίοις
ὀψωνίοις ποτέ; τίς ποιμαίνει ποίμνην καὶ ἐκ τοῦ γάλακτος τῆς ποίμνης
20 οὐκ ἐσθίει;» καὶ ταῦτα θέλων κρατῦναι τὸν νόμον τῆς πλεονεξίας
λαμβάνει συνήγορον, φάς· Ἦ καὶ ὁ νόμος ταῦτα οὐ λέγει; ἐν γὰρ τῷ
Μωσέως νόμῳ γέγραπται ⟨Deut. xxv:4⟩· «οὐ φιμώσεις βοῦν ἀλοῶντα.»
εἶτα ἐπισυνάπτει τὸν λόγον ἀσαφῆ καὶ μεστὸν φλυαρίας, τῶν ἀλόγων
τὴν θείαν ἀποτέμνων πρόνοιαν, φάσκων· μὴ τῶν βοῶν μέλει τῷ θεῷ;
25 ἢ δὶ ἡμᾶς λέγει; δὶ ἡμᾶς γὰρ ἐγράφη. δοκεῖ δέ μοι ταῦτα λέγων
ἱκανῶς ἐνυβρίζειν τῇ σοφίᾳ τοῦ κτίσαντος ὡς οὐ προνοουμένῃ τῶν
γενομένων [πάλαι]. εἰ γὰρ περὶ τῶν βοῶν οὐ μέλει τῷ θεῷ, τί καὶ
γέγραπται ⟨Ps. viii:7 ff.⟩· «Πάντα ὑπέταξας, πρόβατα καὶ βόας καὶ
κτήνη καὶ τοὺς ἰχθύας.» εἰ γὰρ ἰχθύων λόγον ποιεῖται, πολλῷ μᾶλλον
30 βοῶν ἀροτήρων καὶ καματηρῶν. ὅθεν ἄγαμαι τὸν οὕτω φένακα, τὸν
ἀπληστίας ἕνεκεν καὶ τοῦ λαβεῖν ἱκανὸν τῶν ὑπηκόων ἔρανον οὕτω τὸν
νόμον σεμνῶς περιέποντα.
(33) εἶθ' ὑποστρέψας αἰφνίδιον ὡς ὀνειροπλὴξ ἀφ' ὕπνου τινὸς
ἀναπηδήσας φάσκει ⟨Gal. v:3⟩· «μαρτύρομαι ἐγὼ Παῦλος ὅτι ἐάν τις
35 ἓν ποιήσῃ τοῦ νόμου, ὀφειλέτης ἐστὶν ὅλον τὸν νόμον ποιῆσαι» ἀντὶ
τοῦ· ὅλως οὐ χρὴ τοῖς λεγομένοις ὑπὸ τοῦ νόμου προσέχειν. ὁ
βέλτιστος οὗτος, ὁ φρενήρης, ὁ συνετός, ὁ κατὰ ἀκρίβειαν τοῦ πατρῴου
νόμου πεπαιδευμένος, ὁ τοσαυτάκις Μωσέως δεξιῶς μεμνημένος,
ὥσπερ ἐν οἴνῳ καὶ μέθῃ διαβραχείς, ἀναιρεῖ δογματίζων τοῦ νόμου τὸ
40 πρόσταγμα, λέγων Γαλάταις ⟨Gal. iii:1⟩· «Τίς ὑμᾶς ἐβάσκανεν τῇ
ἀληθείᾳ μὴ πείθεσθαι;» τουτέστι τῷ εὐαγγελίῳ· εἶτα δεινοποιῶν καὶ
φρικτὸν ἐργαζόμενός τινα τῷ νόμῳ πείθεσθαι λέγει ⟨Gal. iii:10⟩· «ὅσοι
γὰρ ἐξ ἔργων νόμου εἰσίν, ὑπὸ κατάραν εἰσίν.» ὁ γράφων Ῥωμαίοις, ὅτι ὁ

451

νόμος πνευματικός ἐστι ⟨Rom. vii:14⟩, καὶ αὖθις· ὁ νόμος
45 ἅγιος καὶ ἡ ἐντολὴ ἁγία καὶ δικαία ⟨Rom. vii:12⟩, τοὺς πειθομένους τῷ
ἁγίῳ ὑπὸ κατάραν τίθησιν.

(30) And if to those that are without law he [scil. Paul] joined as
without law, as he himself says [I Cor. ix:20–21], "and to the
Jews as a Jew", and likewise to all, being a slave of manifold
badness ... For if he lives with those without law and also
expressly in writing approves gladly of Judaism, sharing with each
each way of life, he is thus marred by having been associated with
each of them and having received the impression of the faults of
the uncivilized ...
(31) The very same man, who talks so much, as if he forgot his
own words, tells the tribune that he is not a Jew but a Roman,
though he said before [Acts xxii:3]: "I am a man which am a
Jew, born in Tarsus of Cilicia, yet brought up at the feet of
Gamaliel and taught according to the perfect manner of the law
of the fathers." For he who says: "I am a Jew, and I am a
Roman," is neither, though attaching himself to each ... If indeed
Paul pretends partly to be a Jew, and partly he is a Roman,
partly he is without law, partly a Greek, and when he so wishes,
being a stranger and an enemy to each, he damages each of them
by slipping in, while by flattery he steals the favour of each ...
(32) That he pretends to the Gospel because of vanity and to the
law because of greediness he makes clear by what he says [I Cor.
ix:7]: "Who goeth a warfare any time at his own charges? or who
feedeth a flock, and eateth not of the milk of the flock?" And in
order to strengthen his argument he takes the law as advocate for
greediness, saying: "Does not the law this? In the law of Moses
has been written [Deut. xxv:4]: 'Thou shalt not muzzle the ox
when he treadeth out the corn'." Then he joins to it the unclear
and nonsensical argument by which he excludes animals from
Divine Providence, saying: "Does God care for oxen? Or saith he
it altogether for our sakes? For our sakes, no doubt, this is
written." He seems to me by thus saying to so insult the wisdom
of the Creator as though it does not provide for animals that
came into being. For if God does not care for oxen, why has it
been written [Ps. viii:7 ff.]: "Thou hast put all things under his
feet; sheep and oxen, yea, and the beasts of the field and the
fish." If he pays attention to fish, the more so to oxen who

452

plough and toil. Therefore I wonder at such a great cheat, who, because of his insatiate greediness, and in order to obtain a large gift from his subjects, he thus solemnly handled the law.

(33) Then returning suddenly like one scared by a dream, jumping up from sleep, he says [Gal. v:3]: "I, Paul, testify that if one fulfils one item of the law, he is a debtor to the whole law", instead of saying: "One ought not to pay attention altogether to what is said by the law". The excellent fellow, the sound-minded, the intelligent, who was taught according to the perfect manner of the law of the fathers, who so often and so readily referred to the law of Moses, now, as if soaked in drunkenness, in stating his opinion abrogated the order of the law and says to the Galatians [Gal. iii:1]: "Who hath bewitched you, that ye should not obey the truth?", that is the Gospel. Then, having recourse to a terrifying language and thinking it awful that somebody obeys the law, he says [Gal. iii:10]: "For as many as are of the works of the law are under the curse." He who writes to the Romans that the law is spiritual [Rom. vii:14], and again that the law is holy, and the commandment holy and just [Rom. vii:12], put those who obey the holy under a curse.

460

Adversus Christianos, apud: Theodoretus, *Graecarum Affectionum Curatio*, VII, 36–37 — Raeder
= Harnack, F38

(36) Τούτοις ⟨scil. τοῖς προφήταις⟩ ἀκριβῶς ἐντυχὼν ὁ Πορφύριος (μάλα γὰρ αὐτοῖς ἐνδιέτριψε, τὴν καθ' ἡμῶν τυρεύων γραφήν), καὶ ἀλλότριον εὐσεβείας καὶ αὐτὸς ἀποφαίνει τὸ θύειν, παραπλήσιόν τι τοῖς πιθήκοις καὶ δρῶν καὶ πάσχων. (37) καθάπερ γὰρ ἐκεῖνοι μιμοῦνται μὲν τὰ τῶν
5 ἀνθρώπων ἐπιτηδεύματα, εἰς δέ γε τὴν τῶν ἀνθρώπων οὐ μεταβάλλονται φύσιν, ἀλλὰ μένουσι πίθηκοι, οὕτως οὗτος τὰ θεῖα λόγια κεκλοφὼς καὶ ἐνίων τὴν διάνοιαν τοῖς ξυγγράμμασιν ἐντεθεικὼς τοῖς οἰκείοις, μεταμαθεῖν οὐκ ἠθέλησε τὴν ἀλήθειαν, ἀλλὰ μεμένηκε πίθηκος ...

1 γὰρ om. BL	2 καὶ om. KMV	3 ἀποφαίνοι K
4 γὰρ om. K / μὲν om. C	7 τὴν ἐνίων M	τὴν om. KBL
8 καταμαθεῖν L		

(36) Porphyry, who read the prophets carefully, for he devoted much time to them when he concocted his writing against us, also expresses

his view that sacrifices are contrary to religion. Thus he acts and is affected like monkeys. (37) Because in the same way as these ape the habits of men, yet do not change their nature to human nature and remain monkeys, he, though he stole the divine sayings and inserted their thought into his own compositions, did not want to learn the truth, but remained a monkey.

461

Adversus Christianos, apud: Eusebius, *Chronica*, Praefatio, apud: Hieronymus, *Chronica*, pp. 7 f. — Helm² = Harnack, F40 = *F. Gr. Hist.*, II, B260, F33

Ex ethnicis vero impius ille Porphyrius in quarto operis sui libro, quod adversum nos casso labore contexuit, post Moysen Semiramin fuisse adfirmat, quae aput Assyrios CL ante Inachum regnavit annis. Itaque iuxta eum DCCC paene et L annis Troiano bello Moyses
5 senior invenitur.

Basing himself on pagan sources, that impious Porphyry asserts in the fourth book of the work which he contrived in vain toil against us that Semiramis, who reigned among the Assyrians one hundred and fifty years before Inachus, lived after Moyses. Thus, it follows according to him that Moyses preceded the Trojan war by almost eight hundred and fifty years.

The Chronicle of Porphyry seems to have started with the Trojan War; cf. *F. Gr. Hist.*, II, D, p. 878. Thus, it is not known in what connection he came to speak about the date of Moses. By implication the relative chronology suggested here would point to the great antiquity of Moses. See also J. Pepin, in: "Porphyre", *Fondation Hardt pour l'étude de l'antiquité classique, Entretiens*, XII (1965), pp. 231 ff.; R. Goulet, *Revue de l'histoire des religions*, CXCII (1977), pp. 137 ff.
ante Inachum: According to Ptolemy of Mendes, it was Inachus himself, the first of the Argive kings, who was a contemporary of Moses; cf. Ptolemaeus Mendesius, apud: Tatianus, *Oratio ad Graecos*, 38 (No. 157).

462

Adversus Christianos, apud: Eusebius, *Praeparatio Evangelica*, I, 9:20–21 — Mras = Harnack, F41 = *F. Gr. Hist.*, II, B260, F34

(20) Μέμνηται τούτων ὁ καθ᾽ ἡμᾶς τὴν καθ᾽ ἡμῶν πεποιημένος

Porphyry

συσκευὴν ἐν τετάρτῳ τῆς πρὸς ἡμᾶς ὑποθέσεως, ὧδε τῷ ἀνδρὶ
μαρτυρῶν πρὸς λέξιν ⟨No. 323⟩ *(21)·* «ἱστορεῖ δὲ τὰ περὶ Ἰουδαίων
ἀληθέστατα, ὅτι καὶ τὸ τοῖς τόποις καὶ τοῖς ὀνόμασιν αὐτῶν τὰ
5 συμφωνότατα, Σαγχουνιάθων ὁ Βηρύτιος …»

(20) The author in our day of the attack against us mentions these
things in the fourth book of his treatise "Against the Christians",
where he bears the following testimony to Sanchuniaton, word for
word [No. 323] (21): "Of the affairs of the Jews, the truest history,
because the most in accordance with their places and names, is that of
Sanchuniaton of Berytus…"   (trans. E. H. Gifford, Oxford 1903)

463

Adversus Christianos, apud: Severianus, Episcopus Gabalorum, *De Mundi Creatione*, Oratio
VI — *PG*, LVI, Col. 487 = Harnack, F42

Λέγουσι πολλοί, καὶ μάλιστα οἱ τῷ θεοστυγεῖ Πορφυρίῳ
ἀκολουθήσαντες τῷ κατὰ Χριστιανῶν συγγράψαντι καὶ τοῦ θείου
δόγματος πολλοὺς ἀποστήσαντι· λέγουσι τοίνυν· διὰ τί ὁ Θεὸς
ἀπηγόρευσε τὴν γνῶσιν τοῦ καλοῦ καὶ πονηροῦ; ἔστω, τὸ πονηρὸν
5 ἀπηγόρευσε· διὰ τί καὶ τὸ καλόν; εἰπὼν γάρ· «Ἀπὸ τοῦ ξύλου τοῦ
εἰδέναι καλὸν καὶ πονηρὸν μὴ φάγητε», κωλύει, φησίν, αὐτὸν τοῦ
εἰδέναι τὸ κακόν· διὰ τί καὶ τὸ ἀγαθόν;

Many say, and above all the followers of Porphyry, hated by God,
who wrote "Against the Christians" and caused many to revolt from
the divine creed. Well then, they say: Why did God forbid the
knowledge of Good and Evil? Well, he forbade the Evil, why also the
Good? For in saying: "Of the tree of the knowledge of good and evil,
thou shalt not eat of it", he states, he prevents him from knowing the
Evil, but why also from knowing the Good?

464a

Adversus Christianos, apud: Hieronymus, *Commentarii in Danielem*, Prologus — Glorie, *CCSL*,
LXXV, A, p. 771 = *PL*, XXV, Col. 491 = Harnack, F43A

Contra prophetam Danielem duodecimum librum scribit Porphyrius,

1 *scribit*] *scribens* corr. alt. m. F   *scripsit* Vallarsi

nolens eum ab ipso, cuius inscriptus est nomine esse compositum sed a quodam qui temporibus Antiochi, qui appellatus est Epiphanes, fuerit in Iudaea, et non tam Danielem ventura dixisse quam illum
5 narrasse praeterita, denique quidquid usque ad Antiochum dixerit, veram historiam continere, si quid autem ultra opinatus sit, quae futura nescierit esse mentitum.

6 *quae* F   *quia* cett.

Porphyry wrote his twelfth book against the prophecy of Daniel, denying that it was composed by the person to whom it is ascribed in its title, but rather by some individual living in Judaea at the time of that Antiochus who was surnamed Epiphanes. He furthermore alleged that "Daniel" did not foretell the future so much as he related the past, and lastly that whatever he spoke of up till the time of Antiochus contained authentic history, whereas anything he may have conjectured beyond that point was false, inasmuch as he would not have foreknown the future.   (trans. G. L. Archer)

464b

Adversus Christianos, apud: Hieronymus, *Commentarii in Danielem*, Prologus — Glorie, *CCSL*, LXXV, A, p. 773 = *PL*, XXV, Col. 492 = Harnack, F43B

Sed et hoc nosse debemus inter cetera Porphyrium in Danielis nobis libros obicere, idcirco illum apparere confictum nec haberi apud Hebreaeos, sed Graeci sermonis esse commentum, quia in Susannae fabula contineatur, dicente Daniele ad presbyteros ἀπὸ τοῦ σχίνου
5 σχίσαι καὶ ἀπὸ τοῦ πρίνου πρίσαι, quam etymologiam magis Graeco sermoni convenire quam Hebreaeo.

But among other things we should recognize that Porphyry makes this objection to us concerning the Book of Daniel, that it is clearly a forgery, not to be considered as belonging to the Hebrew Scriptures but an invention composed in Greek. This he deduces from the fact that in the story of Susanna, where Daniel is speaking to the elders, we find the expressions ἀπὸ τοῦ σχίνου σχίσαι ("to split from the mastic tree") and καὶ ἀπὸ τοῦ πρίνου πρίσαι ("to saw from the evergreen oak"), a word-play appropriate to Greek rather than to Hebrew.   (trans. G. L. Archer)

456

464c

Adversus Christianos, apud: Hieronymus, *Commentarii in Danielem*, Prologus — Glorie, *CCSL*, LXXV, A, p. 775 = *PL*, XXV, Col. 494 = Harnack, F43C = *F. Gr. Hist.*, II, B260, F36

Ad intellegendas autem extremas partes Danielis multiplex Graecorum historia necessaria est, Sutorii videlicet Callinici, Diodori, Hieronymi, Polybii, Posidonii, Claudii Theonis et Andronici cognomento Alipi, quos et Porphyrius esse secutum se dicit.

2 *Suctorii* Victorius

And yet to understand the final portions of Daniel a detailed investigation of Greek history is necessary, that is to say, such authorities as Sutorius Callinicus, Diodorus, Hieronymus, Polybius, Posidonius, Claudius Theon, and Andronicus surnamed Alipius, historians whom Porphyry claims to have followed.

(trans. G. L. Archer)

464d

Adversus Christianos, apud: Hieronymus, *Commentarii in Danielem ii:40* — Glorie, *CCSL*, LXXV, A, p. 795 = *PL*, XXV, Col. 504 = Harnack, F43D

Factus est mons magnus et implevit universam terram: Quod Iudaei et impius Porphyrius male ad populum referunt Israel, quem in fine saeculorum volunt esse fortissimum et omnia regna conterere et regnare in aeternum.

He became a great mountain and filled the whole earth: This last the Jews and the impious Porphyry wrongly apply to the people of Israel, who they insist will be the strongest power at the end of the ages, and will crush all realms and will rule forever. (trans. G. L. Archer)

464e

Adversus Christianos, apud: Hieronymus, *Commentarii in Danielem ii:46* — Glorie, *CCSL*, LXXV, A, p. 795 = *PL*, XXV, Col. 504 = Harnack, F43E

Hunc locum calumniatur Porphyrius, quod numquam superbissimus rex captivum adoraverit.

Porphyry falsely impugns this passage on the ground that a very proud king would never worship a mere captive. (trans. G. L. Archer)

464f

Adversus Christianos, apud: Hieronymus, *Commentarii in Danielem ii:48* — Glorie, *CCSL*, LXXV, A, p. 796 = *PL*, XXV, Col. 505 = Harnack, F43F

Et in hoc calumniator ecclesiae ⟨scil. Porphyrius⟩ prophetam reprehendere nititur, quare non recusarit munera et honorem Babylonium libenter susceperit.

2 *recusarit* FR μ Vall.   *recusaverit* GM   *recusaret ut* A

In this matter also the slanderous critic of the Church [scil. Porphyry] has ventured to castigate the prophet because he did not reject the gifts and because he willingly accepted honour of the Babylonians.

(trans. G. L. Archer)

464g

Adversus Christianos, apud: Hieronymus, *Commentarii in Danielem iii:98* — Glorie, *CCSL*, LXXV, A, p. 809 = *PL*, XXV, Col. 512 = Harnack, F43G

Epistola Nabuchodonosor in prophetae volumine ponitur, ut non fictus ab alio postea liber, sicut sycophanta ⟨scil. Porphyrius⟩ mentitur, sed ipsius Danielis esse credatur.

The epistle of Nabuchodonosor was inserted in the volume of the prophet, in order that the book might not afterwards be thought to have been manufactured by some other author, as the accuser [scil. Porphyry] falsely asserts, but the product of Daniel himself.

(trans. G. L. Archer)

464h

Adversus Christianos, apud: Hieronymus, *Commentarii in Danielem v:10* — Glorie, *CCSL*, LXXV, A, p. 824 = *PL*, XXV, Col. 520 = Harnack, F43J

Regina: Hanc Iosephus aviam Baldasaris, Origenes matrem scribunt, unde et novit praeterita, quae rex ignorabat. Evigilet ergo Porphyrius, qui eam Baldasaris somniavit uxorem et illudit plus scire quam maritum.

Queen: Josephus says that she was Belshazzar's grandmother, whereas Origen says that she was his mother. She therefore knew about previous events of which the king was ignorant. So much for Porphyry's far-fetched objection [literally: "Therefore let Porphyry stay awake nights"], who fancies that she was the king's wife, and makes fun of the fact that she knows more than her husband does.

(trans. G. L. Archer)

464i

Adversus Christianos, apud: Hieronymus, *Commentarii in Danielem vii: 7* — Glorie, *CCSL*, LXXV, A, p. 843 = *PL*, XXV, Col. 530 = Harnack, F43L

Porphyrius duas posteriores bestias, Macedonum et Romanorum, in uno Macedonum regno ponit et dividit, pardum volens intellegi ipsum Alexandrum, bestiam autem dissimilem ceteris bestiis quattuor Alexandri successores, et deinde usque ad Antiochum
5 cognomento Epiphanen decem reges enumerat, qui fuerint saevissimi, ipsosque reges non unius ponit regni, verbi gratia Macedoniae, Syriae, Asiae et Aegypti, sed de diversis regnis unum efficit regnorum ordinem, ut videlicet ea quae scripta sunt: "Os loquens ingentia" non de Antichristo, sed de Antiocho dicta credantur.

2 *unum* A	3 *autem* om. M	5 *fuerint* MFR *fueͬ* A
fuerunt μ Vallarsi	6 *regno* corr. F	7 *et* om. MR /
effecit corr. MF / *regnorum* F Glorie		*regni* MR
regum A μ Vallarsi	*regnum* PL	

Porphyry assigned the last two beasts, that of the Macedonians and that of the Romans, to the realm of the Macedonians and divided them up as follows. He claimed that the leopard was Alexander himself, and that the beast which was dissimilar to the others represented the four successors of Alexander, and then he enumerates ten kings up to the time of Antiochus, surnamed Epiphanes, and who were very cruel. And he did not assign the kings themselves to separate kingdoms, for example Macedon, Syria, Asia, or Egypt, but rather he made out of the various kingdoms a single realm consisting of a series. This he did of course in order that the words which were written: "a mouth uttering overweening boast" might be considered as spoken about Antiochus instead of about Antichrist.

(trans. G. L. Archer)

464j

Adversus Christianos, apud: Hieronymus, *Commentarii in Danielem vii : 8, 14* — Glorie, *CCSL*, LXXV, A, pp. 843, 848 = *PL*, XXV, Col. 531, 533 = Harnack, F43 M

(vii : 8) Frustra Porphyrius cornu parvulum, quod post decem cornua ortum est: Epiphanen Antiochum suspicatur, et de decem cornibus tria evulsa cornua: sextum Ptolomaeum cognomento Philometorem, et septimum Ptolomaeum Evergeten et Artarxiam regem Armeniae,
5   quorum priores multo antequam Antiochus nasceretur mortui sunt ... (vii : 14) Hoc cui potest hominum convenire, respondeat Porphyrius, aut quis iste tam potens sit, qui cornu parvum, quem Antiochum interpretatur, fregerit atque contriverit? Si responderit Antiochi principes a Juda Machabaeo fuisse superatos, docere debet,
10   quomodo cum nubibus caeli veniat quasi filius hominis.

4 *Armeniae*] *armoche* R   5 *mortuus est* A   7 *tam* om. MR   /
     parvulum μ Vallarsi   /   *quem*] *que* R   10 *veniat* FAμ Vallarsi
                             venit aut MR

(vii : 8) Porphyry vainly surmises that the little horn which rose after ten horns is Antiochus Epiphanes, and that the three uprooted horns out of the ten are Ptolemy VI surnamed Philometor, Ptolemy VII Euergetes, and Artarxias, king of Armenia. The first of these kings died long before Antiochus was born. ... (vii : 14) Let Porphyry answer the query of whom out of all mankind this language might apply to, or who this person might be who was so powerful as to break and smash to pieces the little horn, whom he interprets to be Antiochus? If he replies that the princes of Antiochus were defeated by Judas Maccabaeus, then he must explain how Judas could be said to come with the clouds of heaven like unto the Son of man.

(trans. G. L. Archer)

464k

Adversus Christianos, apud: Hieronymus, *Commentarii in Danielem ix : 1*—Glorie, *CCSL*, LXXV, A, p. 860 = *PL*, XXV, Col. 539 = Harnack, F43 N

Hic est Darius, qui cum Cyro Chaldaeos Babyloniosque superavit; ne putemus illum Darium, cuius secundo anno templum aedificatum est — quod Porphyrius suspicatur, ut annos Danielis extendat — vel eum qui ab Alexandro Macedonum rege superatus est.

2 *anno secundo* Vallarsi

This is the Darius who in cooperation with Cyrus conquered the Chaldaeans and Babylonians. We are not to think of that other Darius in the second year of whose reign the Temple was built (as Porphyry supposes in making out a late date for Daniel); nor are we to think of the Darius who was vanquished by Alexander, the king of the Macedonians.

(trans. G. L. Archer)

4641

Adversus Christianos, apud: Hieronymus, *Commentarii in Danielem xi: 13–19* — Glorie, *CCSL*, LXXV, A, pp. 909 ff. = *PL*, XXV, Cols. 563 f. = *F. Gr. Hist.*, II, B 260, F 45–47

Cumque Antiochus ⟨scil. Tertius⟩ teneret Iudaeam, missus Scopas Aetholus dux Ptolomaei partium adversus Antiochum fortiter dimicavit, cepitque Iudaeam et optimates Ptolomaei partium secum abducens in Aegyptum reversus est ... Antiochus enim Magnus
5 volens Iudaeam recuperare, et Syriae urbes plurimas, Scopam ducem Ptolomaei iuxta fontes Iordanis, ubi nunc Paneas condita est, inito certamine fugavit et cum decem milibus armatorum obsedit clausum Sidone. Ob quem liberandum misit Ptolomaeus duces inclytos Aeropum et Menoclea ⟨Meneclea⟩ et Damoxenum, sed obsidionem
10 solvere non potuit donec, fame superatus, Scopas manus dedit, et nudus cum sociis dimissus est. Quodque ait "comportabit aggerem" illud significat, quod praesidium Scopae in arce Hierosolymorum annitentibus Iudaeis multo tempore oppugnarit et ceperit et alias urbes, quae prius a Ptolomaei partibus tenebantur, Syriae et Ciliciae
15 et Lyciae ... De quibus universis et Graeca et Romana narrat historia ... Volens Antiochus non solum Syriam et Ciliciam et Lyciam et alias provincias, quae Ptolomaei fuerant partium, possidere, sed in Aegyptum quoque regnum suum extendere, filiam suam Cleopatram per Euclem Rhodium septimo anno regni adolescenti despondit
20 Ptolomaeo et tertio decimo anno tradidit, data ei dotis nomine omni Coelesyria et Iudaea.

> 2 *Aetholus* μ Vallarsi   *aetholi filius* codd.   /   *adversum* A
> 4 *abducens* Victorius   *adducens* codd.   /   *Magnus* A om. cett

And while Antiochus [scil. Antiochus III] held Judaea, a leader of the Ptolemaic party called Scopas the Aetolian was sent against Antiochus, and after a bold campaign he captured Judaea and took the aristocrats of Ptolemy's party back to Egypt with him on his return ... Purposing to retake Judaea and the many cities of Syria, Antiochus joined battle with Scopas, Ptolemy's general, near the sources of the Jordan where the city now called Paneas was founded, and he put him to flight and besieged him in Sidon together with ten thousand of his soldiers. In order to free him, Ptolemy dispatched the famous generals, Aeropus, Menocles [Menecles] and Damoxenus. Yet he was unable to lift the siege, and finally Scopas, overcome by famine, had to surrender and was sent away with his associates, despoiled of all he had. And as for the statement, "he shall cast up a mound", this indicates that Antiochus is going to besiege the garrison of Scopas in the citadel of Jerusalem for a long time, while the Jews add their exertions as well. And he is going to capture other cities which had formerly been held by the Ptolemaic faction in Syria, Cilicia and Lycia ... These things are related by both Greek and Roman historians ... Antiochus not only wished to take possession of Syria, Cilicia and Lycia, and the other provinces which had belonged to Ptolemy's party, but also to extend his empire to Egypt. He therefore used the good offices of Eucles of Rhodes to betroth his daughter, Cleopatra, to young Ptolemy in the seventh year of his reign; and in his thirteenth year she was given to him in marriage, professedly endowed with all of Coele-Syria and Judaea as her marriage-portion.   (trans. G. L. Archer)

Though Jerome does not state expressly that he derives his information on the Fifth Syrian War from Porphyry's work, it is almost certain that this is his source. On the events, cf. also the commentary to Polybius, apud: *Ant.*, XII, 135–136 (No. 32).

For the marriage between Cleopatra "the Syrian" and Ptolemy Epiphanes, cf. also *Ant.*, XII, 154; Appianus, *Liber Syriacus*, 5 : 18; Livius, XXXV, 13 : 4. Cf. M. Holleaux, *Études d'épigraphie et d'histoire grecques*, III, Paris 1942, p. 355, n. 2.

464m

Adversus Christianos, apud: Hieronymus, *Commentarii in Danielem xi: 20* — Glorie, *CCSL*, LXXV, A, p. 913 = *PL*, XXV, Col. 565 = Harnack, F43O = *F. Gr. Hist.*, II, B260, F48

Porphyrius hunc non vult esse Seleucum sed Ptolomaeum Epiphanen, qui Seleuco sit molitus insidias et adversum eum exercitum praepararit, et idcirco veneno sit interfectus a ducibus suis,

1 *non vult hunc* Victorius μ Vallarsi   2 *sit* om. M   3 *praepararet* MRA

quod cum unus quaereret ab illo: tantas res moliens ubi haberet
pecuniam respondit ei: amicos sibi esse divitias. Quod cum
divulgatum esset in populos, timuerunt duces, ne auferret eorum
substantias, et idcirco eum maleficis artibus occiderunt.

4 *ab illo quaereret* MRF   5 *sibi amicos* Victorius μ Vallarsi   6 *populo* MF
populis Victorius μ Vallarsi   7 *substantiam* Victorius μ Vallarsi

Porphyry, however, claims that it was not this Seleucus who is
referred to, but rather Ptolemy Epiphanes, who contrived a plot
against Seleucus and prepared an army to fight against him, with the
result that Seleucus was poisoned by his own generals. They did this
because when someone asked Seleucus where he was going to get the
financial resources for the great enterprises he was planning, he
answered that his financial resources consisted in his friends. When
this remark was publicly noised abroad, the generals became
apprehensive that he would deprive them of their property and for
that reason did him to death by nefarious means.   (trans. G. L. Archer)

464n

Adversus Christianos, apud: Hieronymus, *Commentarii in Danielem xi:21* f. — Glorie, *CCSL*,
LXXV, A, pp. 914 ff. = *PL*, XXV, Cols. 565 f. = Harnack, F43 P–Q = *F. Gr. Hist.*, B 260, F 49a

Hucusque historiae ordo sequitur et inter Porphyrium ac nostros
nulla contentio est. Cetera quae sequuntur usque ad finem voluminis,
ille interpretatur super persona Antiochi, qui cognominatus est
Epiphanes, fratre Seleuci, filio Antiochi Magni, qui post Seleucum
undecim annis regnavit in Syria obtinuitque Iudaeam ... "Stabit",
inquiunt, in loco Seleuci frater eius Antiochus Epiphanes, cui
primum ab his qui in Syria Ptolomaeo favebant, non dabatur honor
regius. Sed et postea simulatione clementiae obtinuit regnum Syriae
... et non solum, ait, Ptolomaeum vicit in fraudulentia, sed ducem
quoque foederis, hoc est Iudam Machabaeum superavit dolis, sive
quod dicit hoc est: cum ipse obtulisset pacem Ptolomaeo et fuisset
dux foederis, postea ei est molitus insidias; Ptolomaeum autem hic
non Epiphanen significat, qui quintus regnavit in Aegypto, sed

1 *ordo historiae* Victorius μ Vallarsi   4 *frater...filio* 1 m. A
frater...filius alt. m. A Victorius μ Vallarsi
8 *et* om. MRF Victorius μ Vallarsi

Ptolomaeum Philometora, filium Cleopatrae, sororis Antiochi, cuius
15 hic avunculus erat. Et cum post mortem Cleopatrae Eulaius
eunuchus nutritius Philometoris et Leneus Aegyptum regerent et
repeterent Syriam quam Antiochus fraude occupaverat, ortum est
inter avunculum et puerum Ptolomaeum proelium, cumque inter
Pelusium et montem Casium proelium commisissent, victi sunt duces
20 Ptolomaei. Porro Antiochus parcens puero et amicitias simulans
ascendit Memphim et ibi ex more Aegypti regnum accipiens
puerique rebus providere se dicens, cum modico populo omnem
Aegyptum subiugavit et abundantes atque uberrimas ingressus est
civitates, fecitque quae non fecerunt patres eius et patres patrum
25 illius; nullus enim regum Syriae ita vastavit Aegyptum, et omnes
eorum divitias dissipavit, et tam callidus fuit, ut prudentes
cogitationes eorum qui duces pueri erant, sua fraude subverteret. —
Haec Porphyrius sequens Suctorium sermone laciniosissimo pro-
secutus est, quae nos brevi compendio diximus.

14 *philometora* RF Glorie   *Philometorem* M Victorius μ Vallarsi
28 *Suctorium* Victorius μ   *Sutorium* MRA Vallarsi Glorie   *satorium* F

Up to this point the historical order has been followed, and there has
been no point of controversy between Porphyry and those of our side.
But the rest of the text from here on to the end of the book he
interprets as applying to the person of the Antiochus who was
surnamed Epiphanes, the brother of Seleucus and the son of
Antiochus the Great. He reigned in Syria for eleven years after
Seleucus, and he seized Judaea ... Our opponents say that the one
who was to "stand up in the place" of Seleucus was his brother,
Antiochus Epiphanes. The party in Syria who favoured Ptolemy
would not at first grant him the kingly honour, but he later secured
the rule of Syria by a pretence of clemency. ... And not only does the
text say that he conquered Ptolemy by fraud, but also the prince of
the covenant he overcame by treachery, that is, Judas Maccabaeus.
Or else this is what is referred to, that after he had secured peace with
Ptolemy and he had become the prince of the covenant, he afterwards
devised a plot against him. Now the Ptolemy meant here was not
Epiphanes, who was the fifth Ptolemy to reign in Egypt, but Ptolemy
Philometor, the son of Antiochus' sister Cleopatra; and so Antiochus
was his maternal uncle. And after Cleopatra's death Egypt was ruled
by Eulaeus, the eunuch who was Philometor's tutor, and by Leneus,

and they were attempting to regain Syria, which Antiochus had fraudulently seized, warfare broke out between the boy Ptolemy and his uncle. And when they joined battle between Pelusium and Mount Casius, Ptolemy's generals were defeated. But then Antiochus showed leniency towards the boy, and making a pretence of friendship, he went up to Memphis and there received the crown after the Egyptian manner. Declaring that he was looking out for the lad's interests, he subjected all Egypt to himself with only a small force of men, and he entered into rich and prosperous cities. And so he did things which his father had never done, nor his father's fathers. For none of the kings of Syria had ever laid Egypt waste after this fashion and scattered all their wealth. Moreover he was so shrewd that he even overcame by deceit the well-laid plans of those who were the boy-king's generals. This is the line of interpretation which Porphyry followed, pursuing the lead of Suctorius with much redundancy, discoursing of matters which we have summarized within a brief compass. (trans. G. L. Archer)

cui primum ab his qui in Syria Ptolomaeo favebant, non dabatur honor regius: On the conditions prevailing in Syria at the accession of Antiochus IV, see Holleaux, *op. cit.* (supra, p. 462), II, p. 130; P. van't Hof, *Bijdrage tot de kennis van Antiochus IV Epiphanes Koning van Syrië*, Amsterdam 1955, pp. 32 ff.; M. Zambelli, *Rivista di Filologia*, LXXXVIII (1960), pp. 363 ff.; O. Mørkholm, *Antiochus IV of Syria*, Copenhagen 1966, pp. 38 ff.; J. G. Bunge, *Historia*, XXIII (1974), pp. 57 ff.

464o

Adversus Christianos, apud: Hieronymus, *Commentarii in Danielem* xi:25 f. — Glorie, *CCSL*, LXXV, A, p. 918 = *PL*, XXV, Col. 567 = Harnack, F43R

Haec Porphyrius interpretatur de Antiocho, qui adversus Ptolomaeum sororis suae filium profectus est cum exercitu magno. Sed et rex austri, i.e. duces Ptolomaei, provocabuntur ad bellum multis auxiliis et fortibus nimis, et non poterunt resistere Antiochi
5 consiliis fraudulentis, qui simulabit pacem cum sororis filio et comedet cum eo panem et postea occupabit Aegyptum.

3 *provocabantur* M   *provocati sunt* μ Vallarsi
4 *potuerunt* R Victorius μ Vallarsi   5 *simulavit* MRF μ Vallarsi
6 *comedit* alt. m. M μ Vallarsi   /   *occupavit* MR μ Vallarsi

Porphyry interprets this as applying to Antiochus, who set forth with a great army on a campaign against his sister's son. But the king of the South, that is the generals of Ptolemy, will also be roused to war with many and very powerful auxiliary forces, but they will not be able to stand against the fraudulent schemes of Antiochus. For he will pretend to be at peace with his sister's son and will eat bread with him, and afterwards will take possession of Egypt.

(trans. G.L. Archer, with slight changes according to the readings of the MSS in Glorie's edition)

464p

Adversus Christianos, apud: Hieronymus, *Commentarii in Danielem* xi:27 f. — Glorie, *CCSL*, LXXV, A, pp. 918 f. = *PL*, XXV, Col. 567 = Harnack, F43S

Nulli dubium est, quin Antiochus pacem cum Ptolomaeo fecerit, et inierit cum eo convivium et dolos machinatus sit et nihil profecerit, quia regnum eius non potuit obtinere, sed a militibus Ptolomaei eiectus sit.

3 *obinere non potuit* MR   *non potuerit obtinere* F Victorius μ Vallarsi

There is no doubt but that Antiochus did conclude a peace with Ptolemy and ate at the same table with him and devised plots against him, and yet without attaining any success thereby, since he did not obtain his kingdom but was driven out by Ptolemy's soldiers.

(trans. G.L. Archer)

464q

Adversus Christianos, apud: Hieronymus, *Commentarii in Danielem* xi:29 ff. — Glorie, *CCSL*, LXXV, A, p. 919 = *PL*, XXV, pp. 567 f. = Harnack, F43 = *F.Gr.Hist.*, II, B260, F50

Et Graeca et Romana narrat historia postquam reversus est Antiochus, expulsus ab Aegyptiis, venisse eum in Iudaeam, hoc est adversus testamentum sanctum, et spoliasse templum et auri tulisse quam plurimum, positoque in arce praesidio Macedonum, reversum
5   in terram suam. Et post biennium rursum contra Ptolomaeum exercitum congregasse et venisse ad austrum.

1 *narrat*] *narrant* AF   3 *adversus* Victorius μ Vallarsi   *adversum* codd.

Both the Greek and the Roman historians relate that after Antiochus had been expelled from Egypt and had gone back once more, he

466

came to Judaea, that is, against the holy covenant, and that he despoiled the Temple and removed a huge amount of gold; and then, having stationed a Macedonian garrison in the citadel, he returned to his own land. And then two years later he gathered an army against Ptolemy and came to the south. (trans. G. L. Archer)

For the events, cf. I Macc. i : 20 ff.; II Macc. v : 11 ff.; *Ant.*, XII, 246 ff.; E. Bickermann, *Der Gott der Makkabäer*, Berlin 1937, pp. 70 ff.; Tcherikover, pp. 186 ff.

464r

Adversus Christianos, apud: Hieronymus, *Commentarii in Danielem* xi : 31 ff. — Glorie, *CCSL*, LXXV, A, pp. 921, 923, 925 f., 927 f. = *PL*, XXV, Cols. 569 ff. = Harnack, F 43 U = *F. Gr. Hist.*, II, B 260, F 51–55

(xi : 31 ff.) Brachia volunt autem eos significari qui ab Antiocho missi sunt, post biennium quam templum exspoliaverat, ut tributa exigerent a Iudaeis et auferrent cultum Dei, et in templo Hierusalem Iovis Olympii simulacrum et Antiochi statuas ponerent, quas nunc
5 "abominationem desolationis" vocat, quando ablatum est holocaustum et iuge sacrificium ... (xi : 34 f.) Parvulum auxilium Mathathiam significari arbitratur Porphyrius, de vico Modin, qui adversum duces Antiochi rebellavit et cultum veri dei servare conatus est; "parvum autem", inquit, auxilium vocat, quia occisus est in proelio
10 Mathathias, et postea Iudas, filius eius, qui vocabatur Machabaeus pugnans cecidit et ceteri fratres eius adversariorum fraude decepti sunt ... Porphyrius autem et ceteri qui sequuntur eum, de Antiocho Epiphane dici arbitrantur quod erectus sit contra cultum Dei et in tantam superbiam venerit, ut in templo Hierosolymis simulacrum
15 suum poni iusserit, quodque sequitur: "Et diriget, donec compleatur ira, quia in ipso erit consummatio", sic intellegunt, tam diu eum posse, donec irascatur ei Deus et ipsum interfici iubeat, si quidem Polybius et Diodorus qui bibliothecarum scribunt historias, narrant eum non solum contra Deum fecisse Iudaeae, sed avaritiae facibus
20 accensum, etiam templum Dianae in Elymaide, quod erat ditissimum, spoliare conatum, oppressumque a custodibus templi et vicinis circum gentibus et quibusdam phantasiis atque terroribus versum in amentiam ac postremum morbo interiisse, et hoc ei

6 *parvulum* Victorius μ Vallarsi   *parvum* codd.   20 *Aelymaide*? Glorie   *Elimaide* Victorius μ Vallarsi

accidisse commemorant, quia templum Dianae violare conatus sit ..
25 (xi:37 ff.) Deum Maozim ridicule Porphyrius interpretatus est, ut
diceret in vico Modin, unde fuit Mathathias et filii eius, Antiochi
duces Iovis posuisse statuam et compulisse Iudaeos, ut ei victimas
immolarent, i.e. deo Modin ... "Praesidia, etc.": quod Porphyrius ita
edisserit: "Faciet haec omnia, ut muniat arcem Hierusalem et in
30 ceteris urbibus ponat praesidia et Iudaeos doceat adorare deum
alienum, haud dubium quin Iovem significet. Quem cum illis
ostenderit et adorandum esse persuaserit, tunc dabit deceptis
honorem et gloriam plurimam et faciet ceteris, qui in Iudaea fuerint,
dominari, et pro praevaricatione possessiones dividet et dona
35 distribuet" ... (xi:40 f.) Et haec Porphyrius ad Antiochum refert,
quod undecimo anno regni sui rursus contra sororis filium
Ptolomaeum Philometorem dimicaverit. Qui audiens venire Antiochum congregavit multa populorum milia, sed Antiochus quasi
tempestas valida in curribus et in equitibus et in classe magna
40 ingressus sit terras plurimas et transeundo universa vastaverit
veneritque ad terram inclytam, id est Iudaeam ... et arcem munierit
de ruinis murorum civitatis et sic Aegyptum perrexerit ...
"Antiochus", aiunt, "festinans contra Ptolomaeum, regem austri
Idumaeos et Moabitas et Ammonitas, qui ex latere Iudaeae erant,
45 non tetigit, ne occupatus alio proelio Ptolomaeum redderet
fortiorem."

26 *Modaim* Glorie   42 *perrexerit Aegyptum* Victorius   *perrexerit in*
                          Aegyptum μ Vallarsi

(xi:31 ff.) But those of the other viewpoint claim that the persons
mentioned are those who were sent by Antiochus two years after he
had plundered the Temple in order to exact tribute from the Jews,
and also to eliminate the worship of God, setting up an image of
Jupiter Olympius in the Temple at Jerusalem, and also statues of
Antiochus himself. These are described as the "abomination of
desolation", having been set up when the burnt offering and
continual sacrifice were taken away ... (xi:34 f.) Porphyry thinks that
the "little help" was Mattathias of the village of Modin, for he
rebelled against the generals of Antiochus and attempted to preserve
the worship of the true God. He says he is called "a little help"
because Mattathias was slain in battle; and later on his son Judas, who
was called Maccabaeus, also fell in the struggle; and the rest of his
brothers were likewise taken in by the deceit of their adversaries ...

But Porphyry and the others who follow his lead suppose the reference to be to Antiochus Epiphanes, pointing out that he did raise himself up against the worship of God, and pushed his arrogance so far as to command his own statue to be set up in the Temple of Jerusalem. And as for the subsequent statement, "And he shall manage successfully until the wrath be accomplished, for the consummation shall be in him", they understand it to mean that his power will endure until such time as God becomes angry at him and orders him to be killed. For indeed Polybius and Diodorus, who composed the histories of the Bibliothecae, relate that Antiochus not only took measures against the God of Judaea, but also was impelled by an all-consuming avarice to attempt the plunder of the temple of Diana in Elymais, because it was so wealthy. But he was so beset by the temple guard and the neighbouring populace, and also by certain fearful apparitions that he became demented and finally died of illness. And the historians record that this befell him because he had attempted to plunder the temple of Diana ... (xi:37 ff.) As for the god Maozim, Porphyry has offered an absurd explanation, asserting that Antiochus' generals set up a statue of Jupiter in the village of Modin, from which came Mattathias and his sons; moreover they compelled the Jews to offer blood-sacrifices to it, that is, to the god of Modin ... "Garrisons, etc." ... Porphyry explained this as meaning that the man is going to fortify the citadel in Jerusalem and will station garrisons in the rest of the cities, and will instruct the Jews to worship a strange god, which doubtless means Jupiter. And displaying the idol to them, he will persuade them that they should worship it. Then he will bestow upon the deluded both honour and very great glory, and he shall make them rule over the rest in Judaea, and apportion estates unto them in return for their falsehood, and shall distribute gifts ... (xi:40 f.) This too is referred by Porphyry to Antiochus, on the ground that in the eleventh year of his reign he warred for a second time against his nephew, Ptolemy Philometor. For when the latter heard that Antiochus had come, he gathered many thousands of soldiery. But Antiochus invaded many lands like a mighty tempest, with his chariots and horsemen and large navy, and laid everything waste as he passed through. And he came to the glorious land, that is Judaea ... And Antiochus used the ruins of the wall of the city to fortify the citadel and thus he continued on his way to Egypt ... They say that in his haste to fight Ptolemy, the king of the south, Antiochus left untouched the Idumaeans, Moabites, and Ammonites, who dwelt to the side of Judaea, lest he should make Ptolemy the stronger by engaging in some other campaign. (trans. G. L. Archer)

xi:31 ff. Cf. Bickermann, *op. cit.* (supra, p. 467), pp. 90 ff.; J.C. Dancy, *A Commentary on I Maccabees*, Oxford 1954, pp. 78 ff. This is the only source to state expressly that Antiochus put statues of himself in the Temple, but Porphyry may have drawn on a good authority; see *ibid.*, p. 80; see also F.M. Abel & J. Starcky, *Les livres des Maccabées*, Paris 1961, p. 67.
xi:34 f. *quia occisus est in proelio Mathathias*: This is inaccurate, since, according to I Macc. ii, Mattathias died a natural death.
etiam templum Dianae ... violare conatus sit: On the death of Antiochus IV, see B. Motzo, *Saggi di Storia e Letteratura Giudeo-Ellenistica*, Florence 1924, pp. 128 ff.; Holleaux, *op. cit.* (supra, p. 465), III, pp. 255 ff.; C. Habicht, *2. Makkabäerbuch*, Gütersloh 1976, pp. 243 ff.

464s

Adversus Christianos, apud: Hieronymus, *Commentarii in Danielem* xi:44 f. — Glorie, *CCSL*, LXXV, A, pp. 931 ff. = *PL*, XXV, pp. 573 f. =. Harnack, F43 V = *F. Gr. Hist.*, II, B260, F56

Et in hoc loco Porphyrius tale nescio quid de Antiocho somniat. "Pugnans," inquit, "contra Aegyptios et Libyas Aethiopiasque pertransiens, audiet sibi ab aquilone et oriente proelia concitari; unde et regrediens capiet Aradios resistentes et omnem in littore
5 Phoenicis vastabit provinciam; confestimque perget ad Artaxiam regem Armeniae, qui de orientis partibus movebitur et interfectis plurimis de eius exercitu ponet tabernaculum suum in loco Apedno, qui inter duo latissima flumina est, Tigrin et Euphraten." Cumque hucusque processerit in quo monte inclyto sederit et sancto, dicere
10 non potest ... et stultum, sit, duo Mesopotamiae flumina duo maria interpretari. Montem autem inclytum idcirco praeteriit, quia secutus est Theodotionis interpretationem qui ait: "Inter media maria super montem Saba sanctum", cumque Saba nomen montis vel Armeniae vel Mesopotamiae putet, quare sit sanctus dicere non potest; etiam
15 hac licentia mentiendi, possumus nos addere quod ille conticuit, "sanctum", dici, "montem", quia iuxta errorem Armeniorum sit idolis consecratus. "Et veniet", inquit, "usque ad summitatem montis" in Elymaide provincia, quae est ultima Persarum ad orientem regio, ibique volens templum Dianae spoliare, quod
20 habebat infinita donaria, fugatus a barbaris est, qui mira veneratione fanum illud suscipiebant, et mortuus est maerore consumptus in

6 *movebitur* μ Vallarsi *movebatur* codd.

470

Tabes, oppido Persidis. Haec ille in suggillationem nostri artificiosissimo sermone composuit, quae etiamsi potuerit approbare, non de
Antichristo dicta, sed de Antiocho, quid ad nos, qui non ex omnibus
25 scripturarum locis Christi probamus adventum et Antichristi
mendacium? ... Haec quae manifesta sunt praeterit et de Iudaeis
asserit prophetari, quos usque hodie servire cognoscimus. Et dicit
eum, qui sub nomine Danielis scripsit librum, ad refocillandam spem
suorum fuisse mentitum — non quo omnem historiam futuram nosse
30 potuerit, sed quo iam facta memoraret; et in ultimae visionis
calumniis immoratur, flumina ponens pro mari et montem inclytum
et sanctum Apedno, quem ubi legerit, nullam potest proferre
historiam.

22–23 *artificiosissimo* Victorius μ Vallarsi   *artificam* A   *artifice* MR

Even for this passage, Porphyry has some nebulous application to
Antiochus, asserting that in his conflict with the Egyptians, Libyans,
and Ethiopians, passing through them he was to hear of wars that had
been stirred up against him in the north and the east. Thence he was
to turn back and overcome the resistance of the Aradians, and lay
waste the entire province along the coastline of Phoenicia. And then
he was to proceed without delay against Artaxias, the king of
Armenia, who was moving down from the regions of the East, and
having slain a large number of his troops, he would pitch his tent in
the place called Apedno, which is located between the two broadest
rivers, the Tigris and the Euphrates. But it is impossible to state upon
what famous and holy mountain he took his seat, after he had
proceeded to that point ... and it would be foolish to interpret the two
seas as being the two rivers of Mesopotamia. But Porphyry gets
around this famous mountain by following the rendering of
Theodotion, who said: "Upon the sacred Mount Saba between the
two seas". And even though he supposes that Saba was the name of a
mountain in Armenia or Mesopotamia, he cannot explain why it was
holy. To be sure, if we assume the right of making things up, we can
add the detail which Porphyry fails to mention, that the "mountain",
forsooth, was called "holy" because it was consecrated to idols in
conformity with the superstition of the Armenians. The account then
says: "And he shall come even unto the summit of that same
mountain" — supposedly in the province of Elymais which is the
easternmost Persian area. And there, when he purposed to plunder
the temple of Diana, which contained countless sums of money, he

471

was routed by the barbarians, for they honoured that shrine with a remarkable veneration. And Antiochus, being overcome by grief, died in Tabes, a town of Persia. By use of a most artificial line of argument Porphyry has concocted these details as an affront to us, but even though he were able to prove that these statements applied to Antiochus instead of the Antichrist, what does that matter to us? For do we not on the basis of all the passages of Scripture prove the coming of Christ and the falsehood of the Antichrist? ... Porphyry ignores these things, which are so very clear, and maintains that the prophecy refers to the Jews, although we are well aware that they are to this very day in a state of bondage. And he claims that the person who composed the book under the name of Daniel made it all up in order to revive the hopes of his countrymen — not that he was able to foreknow all of future history, but rather he records events that had already taken place. Thus Porphyry confines himself to false claims in regard to the final vision, substituting rivers for the sea, and positing a famous and holy mountain, Apedno, even though he is unable to furnish any historical source in which he has read about it.

(trans. G. L. Archer)

464t

Adversus Christianos, apud: Hieronymus, *Commentarii in Danielem xii : 1* ff. — Glorie, *CCSL*, LXXV, A, pp. 936 f. = *PL*, XXV, Cols. 575 f. = Harnack, F43W = *F. Gr. Hist.*, II, B 260, F57

Hactenus Porphyrius utcumque se tenuit et tam nostrorum imperitis quam suorum male eruditis imposuit. De hoc capitulo quid dicturus est, in quo mortuorum describitur resurrectio? ... Sed quid non faciat pertinacia? ... "Et hoc," inquit, "de Antiocho scriptum est, qui
5 vadens in Persidem Lysiae, qui Antiochiae et Phoeniciae praeerat, reliquit exercitum, ut adversus Iudaeos pugnaret urbemque eorum Hierusalem subverteret"; quae omnia narrat Iosephus historiae auctor Hebraeae, quod talis fuerit tribulatio, qualis numquam, et tempus advenerit quale non fuit ex quo gentes esse coeperunt usque
10 ad illud tempus. Reddita autem victoria et caesis Antiochi ducibus ipsoque Antiocho in Perside mortuo salvatus est populus Israel, omnes qui scripti erant in libro Dei, hoc est, qui legem fortissime defenderunt, et e contrario qui deleti sunt de libro, hoc est, qui praevaricatores existerunt legis et Antiochi fuerunt partium. "Tunc,"

3 *facit* Victorius μ Vallarsi   4 *qui* Victorius μ Vallarsi   *quia* codd.

472

15 ait, "hi qui quasi in terrae pulvere dormiebant et operti erant
malorum pondere et quasi in sepulcris miseriarum reconditi, ad
insperatam victoriam de terrae pulvere surrexerunt et de humo
elevaverunt caput, custodes legis resurgentes in vitam aeternam et
praevaricatores in opprobrium sempiternum. Magistri autem atque
20 doctores, qui legis habuere notitiam, fulgebunt quasi caelum, et qui
inferiores populos exhortati sunt ad custodiendas caeremonias Dei
ad instar astrorum splendebunt in perpetuas aeternitates." Ponit
quoque historiam de Machabeis, in qua dicitur, multos Iudaeorum
sub Mathathia et Iuda Machabaeo ad eremum confugisse et latuisse
25 in speluncis et in cavernis petrarum ac post victoriam procesisse, et
haec μεταφορικῶς quasi de resurrectione mortuorum esse praedicta.

19 *atque*] *atque et* R   *et* Victorius μ Vallarsi

Up to this point Porphyry somehow managed to maintain his position
and impose upon the credulity of the naïve among our adherents as
well as the poorly educated among his own. But what can he say of
this chapter, in which is described the resurrection of the dead? ...
But what will pigheadedness not resort to? ... This too, he declares,
was written with reference to Antiochus, for after he had invaded
Persia, he left his army with Lysias, who was in charge of Antioch and
Phoenicia, for the purpose of warring against the Jews and destroying
their city of Jerusalem. All these details are related by Josephus, the
author of the history of the Hebrews. Porphyry contends that the
tribulation was such as had never previously occurred, and that a time
came along as had never been, from the time that races began to exist
even to that time. But when victory was bestowed upon them, and the
generals of Antiochus had been slain, and Antiochus himself had
died in Persia, the people of Israel experienced salvation, even all
those who had been written down in the book of God, that is, those
who defended the law with great bravery. Contrasted with them were
those who proved to be transgressors of the law and sided with the
party of Antiochus. Then it was, he asserts, that these guardians of
the law, who had been, as it were, slumbering in the dust of the earth
and were cumbered with a load of afflictions, and hidden away, as it
were, in the tombs of wretchedness, rose up once more from the dust
of the earth to a victory unhoped for, and lifted up their heads, rising
up to everlasting life, even as the transgressors rose up to everlasting
disgrace. But those masters and teachers who possessed a knowledge
of the law shall shine like the heaven, and those who have exhorted

473

the more backward peoples to observe the rites of God shall blaze forth after the fashion of the stars for all eternity. He also adduces the historical account concerning the Maccabees, in which it is said that many Jews under the leadership of Mattathias and Judas Maccabaeus fled to the desert and hid in caves and holes in the rocks, and came forth again after the victory. These things, then, were foretold in metaphorical language as if it concerned a resurrection of the dead.

(trans. G. L. Archer)

464u

Adversus Christianos, apud: Hieronymus, *Commentarii in Danielem xii: 7, 11, 12*—Glorie, *CCSL*, LXXV, A, pp. 940 ff. = *PL*, XXV, Cols. 577 ff. = Harnack, F43W = *F. Gr. Hist.*, II, B260, F58

(xii:7) "Tempus et tempora et dimidium temporis" tres et semis annos interpretatur Porphyrius, quod et nos iuxta scripturarum sanctarum idioma non negamus ... Si itaque superiora, quae perspicue de Antichristo scripta sunt, refert Porphyrius ad
5 Antiochum et ad tres et semis annos quibus templum dicitur fuisse desertum, ergo et quod sequitur: "Regnum eius sempiternum, et omnes reges servient ei et obedient", debet probare super Antiocho vel, ut ipse putat, super populo Iudaeorum, quod nequaquam stare manifestum est ... "Quando populus dei dispersus fuerit" —
10 Antiocho persequente, ut vult Porphyrius ... "tunc haec omnia complebuntur"... (xii:11) Hos mille ducentos nonaginta dies Porphyrius in tempore vult Antiochi et in desolatione templi esse completos ... (xii:12) Porphyrius hunc locum ita edisserit, ut quadraginta quinque dies, qui super mille ducentos nonaginta sunt,
15 victoriae contra duces Antiochi tempus significent, quando Iudas Machabaeus fortiter dimicavit et emundavit templum idolumque contrivit et victimas obtulit in templo dei.

(xii:7) Porphyry interprets "a time and times and half a time" to mean three and a half years; and we for our part do not deny that this accords with the idiom of sacred Scripture ... If therefore the earlier references which were plainly written concerning the Antichrist are assigned by Porphyry to Antiochus and to the three and a half years during which he asserts the Temple was deserted, then he is under obligation to prove that the next statement, "His kingdom is eternal, and all kings shall serve and obey him", likewise pertains to Antiochus, or else (as he himself conjectures) to the people of the

474

Jews. But it is perfectly apparent that such an argument will never stand ... When it is stated that "the people of God shall have been scattered", "under the persecution of Antiochus", as Porphyry claims ... "at that time shall all these things be fulfilled" ... (xii:11) These thousand two hundred and ninety days Porphyry claims to have been fulfilled in the time of Antiochus and in the desolation of the Temple. (xii:12) Porphyry explains this passage in the following way, that the forty-five days beyond the one thousand two hundred and ninety signify the interval of victory over the generals of Antiochus, of the period when Judas Maccabaeus fought with bravery, and cleansed the Temple and broke the idol to pieces, offering blood-sacrifices in the Temple of God.   (trans. G. L. Archer)

xii:7   *tres et semis annos interpretatur Porphyrius*: See Bickermann, *op. cit.* (supra, p. 467), p. 143, n. 4.

464v

Adversus Christianos, apud: Hieronymus, *Commentarii in Esaiam xxx:1* ff. — Adriaen, *CCSL*, LXXIII, p. 383 = *PL*, XXIV, Col. 339 = Harnack, F43 X

Hoc annotavimus, ut quod in Danielis extrema legimus visione Deum Maozim ⟨מעוזים⟩, non ut Porphyrius somniat, deum viculi Modim, sed robustum Deum et fortem intellegamus.

That we noted in order that we should understand that what we read in the final vision of Daniel, namely the god Maozim [מעוזים], not the god of the village Modim, as Porphyry dreams, but a strong and brave god.

Deum Maozim, non ut Porphyrius somniat, deum viculi Modim: Cf. the commentary of Jerome to Daniel xi:37 ff., above (No. 464r).

464w

Adversus Christianos, apud: Hieronymus, *Commentarii in Osee i:2, 8* f. — Adriaen, *CCSL*, LXXVI, pp. 9, 14 = *PL*, XXV, Cols. 823, 827 = Harnack, F45

(i:2) Si quis autem contentiosus, et maxime gentilium, noluerit figuraliter dictum recipere, et irriserit prophetam fornicariae copulatum, opponamus ei ... (i:8 f.) Si quis autem contentiosus

interpres noluerit recipere ista, quae diximus, sed meretricem
nomine Gomer, filiam Debelaim, primum et tertium masculos,
secundam, quae media est, feminam intellexerit procreasse, hoc
volens scripturam sonare quod legitur, respondeat ...

5 *masculum* C   6 *procreare* C corr.

(i:2) However, if some contentious person, and above all one of the
gentiles, rejects the interpretation that it has been said figuratively
and laughs at the prophet as coupled with a prostitute, we shall
answer him ... (i:8 f.) However, if some contentious interpreter
rejects that which we have said, but has understood it to mean that a
harlot named Gomer, a daughter of Debelaim, gave birth to three
children, of which the first and the third were males and the second
that came between was a female, wishing the Scripture to have its
literal meaning, he should answer ...

465a

Adversus Christianos, apud: Augustinus, *Epistulae*, CII, 30 — Goldbacher, *CSEL*, XXXIV, 2
= *PL*, XXXIII, Col. 382 = Harnack, F46

Postrema quaestio proposita est de Iona nec ipsa quasi ex
Porphyrio sed tamquam ex irrisione paganorum; sic enim posita
est: "Deinde quid sentire," inquit, "debemus de Iona, qui dicitur
in ventre ceti triduo fuisse? quod satis ἀπίϑανον est et incredibile
transvoratum cum veste hominem fuisse in corde piscis; aut si
figura est, hanc dignaberis pandere. Deinde quid sibi etiam illud
vult supra evomitum Ionam cucurbitam natam? quid causae fuit,
ut haec nasceretur?"

1 *postremo* H   /   *posita* G   /   *ipse* HM (m. 2 *ipsa*)
6 *dignaueris* HACP (m. 2 *dignaberis*) G   /   *vult etiam illud* E

The last question has been raised concerning Jonas, not as if this
derives from Porphyry but rather from the mockery of the pagans in
general. It has been thus formulated: "Then what should we think,"
he says, "about Jonas who is said to have been in the belly of the
sea-monster for three days? This is sufficiently unlikely and
incredible that a man devoured with his dress should be in the heart of
a fish; and if this is said figuratively, you shall deem it worthy to
explain. Then what is the purpose of the gourd which sprang forth

476

above the disgorged Jonas? What was the reason for its appearance?"

465b

Adversus Christianos, apud: Eusebius, *Historia Ecclesiastica*, VI, 19:4–8 — Schwartz = Harnack, F39

(4) Ἄκουε δ' οὖν ἅ φησιν ⟨scil. Πορφύριος⟩ κατὰ λέξιν· «τῆς δὴ μοχθηρίας τῶν Ἰουδαϊκῶν γραφῶν οὐκ ἀπόστασιν, λύσιν δέ τινες εὑρεῖν προθυμηθέντες, ἐπ' ἐξηγήσεις ἐτράποντο ἀσυγκλώστους καὶ ἀναρμόστους τοῖς γεγραμμένοις, οὐκ ἀπολογίαν μᾶλλον ὑπὲρ τῶν
5 ὀθνείων, παραδοχὴν δὲ καὶ ἔπαινον τοῖς οἰκείοις φερούσας. αἰνίγματα γὰρ τὰ φανερῶς παρὰ Μωυσεῖ λεγόμενα εἶναι κομπάσαντες καὶ ἐπιθειάσαντες ὡς θεσπίσματα πλήρη κρυφίων μυστηρίων διά τε τοῦ τύφου τὸ κριτικὸν τῆς ψυχῆς καταγοητεύσαντες, ἐπάγουσιν ἐξηγήσεις.»
(5) Εἶτα μεθ' ἕτερά φησιν· «ὁ δὲ τρόπος τῆς ἀτοπίας ἐξ ἀνδρὸς ᾧ κἀγὼ
10 κομιδῇ νέος ὢν ἔτι ἐντετύχηκα, σφόδρα εὐδοκιμήσαντος καὶ ἔτι δι' ὧν καταλέλοιπεν συγγραμμάτων εὐδοκιμοῦντος, παρειλήφθω, Ὠριγένους, οὗ κλέος παρὰ τοῖς διδασκάλοις τούτων τῶν λόγων μέγα διαδέδοται. *(6)* ἀκροατὴς γὰρ οὗτος Ἀμμωνίου τοῦ πλείστην ἐν τοῖς καθ' ἡμᾶς χρόνοις ἐπίδοσιν ἐν φιλοσοφίᾳ ἐσχηκότος γεγονώς, εἰς μὲν τὴν τῶν λόγων
15 ἐμπειρίαν πολλὴν παρὰ τοῦ διδασκάλου τὴν ὠφέλειαν ἐκτήσατο, εἰς δὲ τὴν ὀρθὴν τοῦ βίου προαίρεσιν τὴν ἐναντίαν ἐκείνῳ πορείαν ἐποιήσατο.
(7) Ἀμμώνιος μὲν γὰρ Χριστιανὸς ἐν Χριστιανοῖς ἀνατραφεὶς τοῖς γονεῦσιν, ὅτε τοῦ φρονεῖν καὶ τῆς φιλοσοφίας ἥψατο, εὐθὺς πρὸς τὴν κατὰ νόμους πολιτείαν μετεβάλετο, Ὠριγένης δὲ Ἕλλην ἐν Ἕλλησιν
20 παιδευθεὶς λόγοις, πρὸς τὸ βάρβαρον ἐξώκειλεν τόλμημα· ᾧ δὴ φέρων αὐτόν τε καὶ τὴν ἐν τοῖς λόγοις ἕξιν ἐκαπήλευσεν, κατὰ μὲν τὸν βίον Χριστιανῶς ζῶν καὶ παρανόμως, κατὰ δὲ τὰς περὶ τῶν πραγμάτων καὶ τοῦ θείου δόξας ἑλληνίζων τε καὶ τὰ Ἑλλήνων τοῖς ὀθνείοις ὑποβαλλόμενος μύθοις. *(8)* συνῆν τε γὰρ ἀεὶ τῷ Πλάτωνι, τοῖς τε Νουμηνίου καὶ Κρονίου
25 Ἀπολλοφάνους τε καὶ Λογγίνου καὶ Μοδεράτου Νικομάχου τε καὶ τῶν ἐν Πυθαγορείοις ἐλλογίμων ἀνδρῶν ὡμίλει συγγράμμασιν, ἐχρῆτο δὲ καὶ Χαιρήμονος τοῦ Στωικοῦ Κορνούτου τε ταῖς βίβλοις, παρ' ὧν τὸν μεταληπτικὸν τῶν παρ' Ἕλλησιν μυστηρίων γνοὺς τρόπον ταῖς Ἰουδαϊκαῖς προσῆψεν γραφαῖς.»

5 φέρουσαν BD   10 τετύχηκα M   ξυντετύχηκα Suda
11 κατέλιπε M   12 μέγα om. M / δέδοται R   16 τοῦ βίου πορείαν B
17 ἐν Χριστιανοῖς om. M   25 τε[1] ABDM om. TER
27 κορνούτου TERM   κουρνούτου ABD / παρ' ὧν] παρὰ τῶν M

(4) But hear the very words that he [scil. Porphyry] uses: "Some, in their eagerness to find an explanation of the wickedness of the Jewish writings rather than give them up, had recourse to interpretations that are incompatible and do not harmonize with what has been written, offering not so much a defence of what was outlandish as commendation and praise of their own work. For they boast that the things said plainly by Moses are riddles, treating them as divine oracles full of hidden mysteries, and bewitching the mental judgement by their own pretentious obscurity; and so they put forward their interpretations."

(5) Then, after other remarks, he says: "But this kind of obscurity must be traced to a man whom I met when I was still quite young, who had a great reputation, and still holds it, because of the writings he has left behind him. I mean Origen, whose fame has been widespread among the teachers of this kind of learning. (6) For this man was a hearer of Ammonius, who had the greatest proficiency in philosophy in our day; and so far as a grasp of knowledge was concerned he owed much to his master, but as regards the right choice in life he took the opposite road to him. (7) For Ammonius was a Christian, brought up in Christian doctrine by his parents, yet, when he began to think and study philosophy, he immediately changed his way of life conformably to the laws; but Origen, a Greek educated in Greek learning, drove headlong towards barbarian recklessness; and making straight for this he hawked himself and his literary skill about; and while his manner of life was Christian and contrary to the law, in his opinions about material things and the deity he played the Greek, and introduced Greek ideas into foreign fables. (8) For he was always consorting with Plato, and was conversant with the writings of Numenius and Cronius, Apollophanes and Longinus and Moderatus, Nicomachus and the distinguished men among the Pythagoreans; and he used also the books of Chaeremon the Stoic and Cornutus, from whom he learnt the figurative interpretation, as employed in the Greek mysteries, and applied it to the Jewish writings."

(trans. J.E.L. Oulton, *LCL*)

465c

Adversus Christianos, apud: Macarius Magnes, III, 4 — Blondel = Harnack, F49

Φέρε γὰρ ὧδε τουτὶ σαφῶς ἐξετάσωμεν, πῶς ἐν Ἰουδαίᾳ γῇ τοσοῦτο πλῆθος τότε χοίρων ἐνέμετο τῶν μάλιστα ῥυπαρῶν καὶ μισουμένων τοῖς

478

Porphyry

Ἰουδαίοις βοσκημάτων ἄνωθεν, πῶς δὲ καὶ πάντες οἱ χοῖροι ἐκεῖνοι συνεπνίγησαν, λίμνης οὐ θαλάσσης βαθείας ὑπαρχούσης.

Come, let us clearly examine how in Judaea such a great number of swine was grazing, animals most sordid and from old hated by the Jews, and how those swine came to be drowned all of them, though it was a lake and not a deep sea.

465d

Adversus Christianos, apud: Macarius Magnes, IV, 9 — Blondel = Harnack, F52

Εἴ γε δεῖ κἀκείνην τὴν πεῦσιν μηρυκήσασθαι, ὡς Ἰησοῦς λέγει ⟨Matt. xi:25⟩· «Ἐξομολογοῦμαί σοι, πάτερ, κύριε τοῦ οὐρανοῦ καὶ τῆς γῆς, ὅτι ἀπέκρυψας ταῦτα ἀπὸ σοφῶν καὶ συνετῶν καὶ ἀπεκάλυψας αὐτὰ νηπίοις.» καὶ ἐν τῷ Δευτερονομίῳ ⟨xxix:28⟩ δὲ γέγραπται· «Τὰ κρυπτὰ
5   κυρίῳ τῷ θεῷ ἡμῶν καὶ τὰ φανερὰ ἡμῖν.» σαφέστερα οὖν δεῖ εἶναι καὶ οὐκ αἰνιγματώδη τὰ τοῖς νηπίοις καὶ ἀσυνέτοις γραφόμενα· εἰ γὰρ ἀπὸ τῶν σοφῶν κέκρυπται τὰ μυστήρια, νηπίοις δὲ καὶ θηλαζομένοις ἀλόγως ἐκκέχυται, βέλτιον τὴν ἀλογίαν ζηλοῦν καὶ τὴν ἀμαθίαν.

If there is a need to ruminate on the question, that Jesus says [Matt. xi:25]: "I thank thee, O Father, Lord of heaven and earth, because thou hast hid these things from the wise and prudent, and hast revealed them unto babes." And in Deuteronomy [xxix:28] it is written: "The secret things belong unto the Lord our God: but those things which are revealed belong unto us." Certainly those things for children and fools should be clearer and not in the way of riddles. For if the mysteries have been hidden from the wise and have been illogically poured upon children and sucklings, then it is better to pursue folly and boorishness.

465e

Adversus Christianos, apud: Macarius Magnes, III, 3 — Blondel = Harnack, F68

Ἔτι δὲ πολλῆς μοι γέμον τῆς ἀβελτηρίας φαίνεται τὸ λεχθέν· «Εἰ ἐπιστεύετε Μωσεῖ, ἐπιστεύετε ἂν ἐμοί· περὶ γὰρ ἐμοῦ ἐκεῖνος ἔγραψεν.» ὅμως δὲ Μωσέως οὐδὲν ἀποσῴζεται· συγγράμματα γὰρ

479

πάντα συνεμπεπρῆσθαι τῷ ναῷ λέγεται· ὅσα δ' ἐπὶ ὀνόματι Μωσέως
5 ἐγράφη μετὰ ταῦτα, μετὰ χίλια καὶ ἑκατὸν καὶ ὀγδοήκοντα ἔτη τῆς
Μωσέως τελευτῆς ὑπὸ Ἔσδρα καὶ τῶν ἀμφ' αὐτὸν ⟨οὐκ ἀκριβῶς⟩
συνεγράφη. εἰ δὲ καὶ Μωσέως δοίη τις εἶναι τὸ γράμμα, οὐ δυνατὸν
δειχθῆναι ὡς θεόν που λελέχθαι ἢ θεῖον λόγον τὸν Χριστὸν ἢ
δημιουργόν· ὅλως ⟨δὲ⟩ Χριστὸν σταυροῦσθαι τίς εἴρηκεν;

Also what is said seems to be full of silliness: "For had ye believed
Moses, ye would have believed me; for he wrote of me."
Nevertheless nothing has been preserved of Moses, as all his writings
are said to have been burnt together with the Temple. And all those
which were written under his name afterwards were composed
inaccurately one thousand one hundred and eighty years after Moses'
death by Ezra and his followers. And even if one concedes that the
work is by Moses, it is impossible to show that the Christus has been
said to be a god or a divine Logos or a demiurge. All in all, who had
ever spoken about the crucifixion of Christ?

465f

Adversus Christianos, apud: Macarius Magnes, IV, 21 — Blondel = Harnack, F76

Ἀνθρωποειδῆ δὲ τῶν ἀγαλμάτων εἰκότως εἶναι τὰ σχήματα, ἐπεὶ τὸ
κάλλιστον τῶν ζῴων ἄνθρωπος εἶναι νομίζεται καὶ εἰκὼν θεοῦ. ἔνι δ' ἐξ
ἑτέρου τοῦτο κρατῦναι τὸ δόγμα, διαβεβαιουμένου δακτύλους ἔχειν τὸ
θεόν, οἷς γράφει φάσκων ⟨Exod. xxxi: 18⟩· «Καὶ ἔδωκε τῷ Μωσῇ τὰς δύο
5 πλάκας τὰς γεγραμμένας τῷ δακτύλῳ τοῦ θεοῦ.» ἀλλὰ καὶ οἱ Χριστιανοὶ
μιμούμενοι τὰς κατασκευὰς τῶν ναῶν μεγίστους οἴκους οἰκοδομοῦσιν, εἰς
οὓς συνιόντες εὔχονται, καίτοι μηδενὸς κωλύοντος ἐν ταῖς οἰκίαις τοῦτο
πράττειν, τοῦ κυρίου δηλονότι πανταχόθεν ἀκούοντος.

The forms of the statues are likely to be in human shape, since man,
which is the finest of creatures, is also thought to be the image of God.
It is possible also to confirm this view by another passage, which
asserts by that which is written in it that God has fingers [Exod.
xxxi: 18]: "And he gave unto Moses, the two tables written with the
finger of God." But the Christians also imitate the constructions of
the temples by building very big houses in which they gather for
prayer, though nothing prevents them from doing this in their
dwelling-houses, since God clearly hearkens from everywhere.

465g

Adversus Christianos, apud: Macarius Magnes, IV, 23 — Blondel = Harnack, F78

Ἔχοιμι ἄν σοι καὶ ἀπὸ τοῦ νόμου δεῖξαι τὸ τῶν θεῶν πολύσεπτον
ὄνομα ἐν τῷ βοᾶν καὶ μετὰ πολλῆς αἰδοῦς νουθετεῖν τὸν ἀκούοντα
⟨Exod. xxii:28⟩· «Θεοὺς οὐ κακολογήσεις καὶ ἄρχοντα τοῦ λαοῦ σου οὐκ
ἐρεῖς κακῶς.» οὐ γὰρ ἄλλους παρὰ τοὺς ἡμῖν νομιζομένους ὧδε θεοὺς
5 λέγει, ἐξ ὧν ἴσμεν ἐν τῷ ⟨Jer. vii:6⟩· «Οὐ πορεύσῃ ὀπίσω θεῶν», καὶ
πάλιν ⟨Deut. xiii:3⟩· «Ἐὰν πορευθῆτε καὶ λατρεύσητε θεοῖς ἑτέροις».
ὅτι γὰρ οὐκ ἀνθρώπους, ἀλλὰ θεοὺς καὶ τοὺς ὑφ' ἡμῶν δοξαζομένους
λέγει οὐ μόνον Μωσῆς, ἀλλὰ καὶ Ἰησοῦς ...

It is possible for me to show you that the name of the gods is much
revered from the law itself, since it calls on and admonishes the
hearer with much reverence [Exod. xxii:28]: "Thou shalt not revile
the gods, nor curse the ruler of thy people." For he does not mean by
this any other gods than those considered so among us, as we learn
from such passages as [Jer. vii:6] "do not walk after gods", or again
[Deut. xiii:3] "If you go after and serve other gods". That not only
Moses but also Jesus speaks not about men but gods and moreover
about those who are held in honour by us ...

465h

Adversus Christianos, apud: Augustinus, *Epistulae,* CII, 8 — Goldbacher, *CSEL,* XXXIV, 2,
pp. 551 f. = *PL,* XXXIII, Col. 373 = Harnack, F81 = *F.Gr.Hist.,* II, B260, F60

"Sed ne dicant," inquit ⟨scil. Porphyrius⟩, "lege Iudaica vetere
hominum curatum genus, longo post tempore lex Iudaeorum
apparuit ac viguit angusta Syriae regione, postea vero prorepsit etiam
in fines Italos, sed post Caesarem Gaium aut certe ipso imperante."

3 *et viguit* G / *etiam* om. C

"But they should not say," he [scil. Porphyry] asserts, "that mankind
had been taken care of by the old Jewish law; the law of the Jews
made its appearance a long time afterwards and flourished only in a
small region of Syria; later, indeed, it was gradually extended to the
confines of Italy, yet this happened after Gaius Caesar, and certainly
not before his reign."

465i

Adversus Christianos, apud: Augustinus, *Epistulae*, CII, 16 — Goldbacher, *CSEL*, XXXIV, 2, p. 558 = *PL*, XXXIII, Col. 376 = Harnack, F79

"Accusant," inquit ⟨scil. Porphyrius⟩ "ritus sacrorum, hostias, tura et cetera, quae templorum cultus exercuit, cum idem cultus ab ipsis, inquit, vel a deo, quem colunt, exorsus est."

3 *inquit* om. E

"They," he [scil. Porphyry] says, "censure the rites of sacrifices, the victims, the incense and other things practised in the cult of the temples, while the same cult originated with themselves, or with the God whom they worship."

466

Ad Gaurum, 11 — Kalbfleisch, *Abhandlungen Berlin Akademie*, 1895, p. 48

Ἐμβαίνει δὲ ὁ κυβερνήτης εἰς φῶς προελθούσης τῆς φύσεως μετὰ τοῦ
ἔργου ⟨οὐκ⟩ ἀναγκαζόμενος. καθάπερ δ' ἐν τοῖς θεάτροις ἑώρακα, οἱ
τὸν Προμηθέα μιμούμενοι κειμένου τοῦ πλάσματος τὴν ψυχὴν ποιεῖν
ἀναγκάζονται εἰσδύνειν εἰς τὸ σῶμα, τῶν παλαιῶν ἴσως διὰ τοῦ μύθου
5 οὐκ ἀνάγκην παραστῆσαι βουλομένων τῆς εἰσκρίσεως, ὅτι δὲ μετὰ τὴν
κύησιν καὶ πλασθέντος τοῦ σώματος ἡ ἐμψύχωσις παριστάντων μόνον·
ὃ δὴ καὶ ὁ τῶν Ἑβραίων θεολόγος σημαίνειν ἔοικεν ὅταν
πεπλασμένου τοῦ ἀνθρωπίνου σώματος καὶ ἀπειληφότος πᾶσαν τὴν
σωματικὴν δημιουργίαν ἐμφυσῆσαι τὸν θεὸν αὐτῷ εἰς ψυχὴν ζῶσαν
10 λέγῃ τὸ πνεῦμα.

2 ⟨οὐκ⟩ Kalbfleisch   5 ἀνάγκην Kalbfleisch   ἀνάγκη P

The pilot enters uncompelled when the seed-power advances into light with its fruit. Certainly I saw that those who play Prometheus in the theatre are compelled to make the soul enter the body of the just-formed man lying on the ground. However, perhaps the ancients did not want to establish by the myth that the entry of the soul is compulsory but only to show that the animation takes place after the conception and formation of the body. The theologian of the Hebrews also seems to signify this when he says that when the human body was formed, and had received all of its bodily workmanship, God breathed the spirit into it to act as a living soul.

Porphyry

προελθούσης τῆς φύσεως μετὰ τοῦ ἔργου: The φύσις is identical with the δύναμις ἐν τῷ σπέρματι in the text of Kalbfleisch, *op. cit.* (supra, p. 424, n. 6), p. 46, ll. 25 f., or even with the vegetative soul of the embryo; cf. R.P. (A.J.) Festugière, *La révélation d'Hermès Trismégiste*, III, Paris 1953, p. 284, n. 1.

ὁ τῶν Ἑβραίων θεολόγος: Moses is labelled θεολόγος by Philo, *Vita Mosis*, II, 115; idem, *De Praemiis et Poenis*, 53.

ἐμφυσῆσαι τὸν θεὸν αὐτῷ εἰς ψυχὴν ζῶσαν λέγῃ τὸ πνεῦμα: Cf. Septuagint, Gen. ii : 7: καὶ ἐνεφύσησεν εἰς τὸ πρόσωπον αὐτοῦ πνοὴν ζωῆς, καὶ ἐγένετο ὁ ἄνθρωπος εἰς ψυχὴν ζῶσαν: See Tertullianus, *De Anima*, ed. with introduction and commentary by J.H. Waszink, Amsterdam 1947, pp. 193 ff.; J.G. Gager, *HUCA*, XLIV (1973), pp. 108 f.

CXXIX. IAMBLICHUS

Third century C.E.

In contrast to the extensive references to Judaism found in the works of Porphyry, their number in the works of his pupil Iamblichus is meagre indeed.[1] *The only certain reference seems to be the opinion of Iamblichus recorded by Lydus (No. 467), in which the God honoured by the Hebrews is equated with the demiurge, an equation that is already met in Porphyry,* Commentarii in Oracula Chaldaica, *apud:* Lydus, De Mensibus, *IV, 53 (No. 452).*

It is very doubtful that two passages of Iamblichus in De Mysteriis *show direct Jewish influence, or refer to the Jews, as is the opinion of some scholars.*[2] *It is stated in* De Mysteriis, *II, 3, pp. 80 f.*[3]: Ὡς δὲ καθ' ἕκαστον διορίσασθαι, μονοειδῆ μέν ἐστι φάσματα τὰ τῶν θεῶν, τὰ δὲ τῶν δαιμόνων ποικίλα, τὰ δὲ τῶν ἀγγέλων ἁπλούστερα μὲν ἢ κατὰ τοὺς δαίμονας, τῶν δὲ θείων ὑποδεέστερα, τὰ δὲ τῶν ἀρχαγγέλων μᾶλλόν τι τοῖς θείοις αἰτίοις συνεγγίζοντα ... καὶ τὰ μὲν τῶν θεῶν χρηστὰ τῇ ὄψει ἐλλάμπει, τὰ δὲ τῶν ἀρχαγγέλων βλοσυρὰ ἅμα καὶ ἥμερα, πραότερα δὲ τῶν ἀγγέλων, τὰ δὲ τῶν δαιμόνων φοβερὰ ... τὰ δὲ τῶν ἀρχαγγέλων, πλησιάζοντα τοῖς τῶν θεῶν, ἀπολείπεται αὐτῶν τῆς ταυτότητος· τὰ δὲ τῶν ἀγγέλων καὶ τούτων ἐστὶν ὑποδεέστερα, ἀμετάβλητα δὲ ... *However this passage can hardly be taken as a specific allusion to Judaism, from which the emergence of angels and archangels cannot be said to derive in view of the spread of their cult among other oriental religions also.*[4]

1 Plotinus, who would have been expected to include some observations on Judaism in his philosophical expositions, makes no direct reference to it, and there is no hint of any contact between him and the Jews in Porphyry's memoir of his mentor; cf. P. Merlan, *Journal of the History of Philosophy*, II (1964), p. 21. For the question of Plotinus' knowledge of Philo, see E. R. Dodds, *CQ*, XXII (1928), p. 140, n. 1; W. Theiler, in: *Porphyre (Fondation Hardt pour l'étude de l'antiquité classique, Entretiens*, XII, 1965), p. 102.

2 E.g., J. Vogt, *Kaiser Julian und das Judentum*, Leipzig 1939, p. 18, n. 2; T. Hopfner, *Die Judenfrage bei Griechen und Römern*, Prague 1943, p. 70. Cf. B. D. Larsen, *Jamblique de Chalcis — Exégète et philosophe*, Aarhus 1972, pp. 161 f. (on Philo and Iamblichus).

3 Iamblichus, *De Mysteriis*, ed. E. des Places, Paris 1966.

4 See F. Cumont, *RHR*, LXXII (1915), pp. 159 ff.

Iamblichus

The second passage is found in De Mysteriis, VII, 4 (ed. des Places):
τῶν ἱερῶν ἐθνῶν, ὥσπερ Ἀσσυρίων τε καὶ Αἰγυπτίων, οἱ θεοὶ τὴν
ὅλην διάλεκτον ἱεροπρεπῆ κατέδειξαν. Here again, it seems
unjustified on the part of modern scholars to identify the "holy nation of
the Assyrians", which takes precedence here even over the Egyptians,
with the Jews. We may assume that this is an allusion to the Aramaic
language and to the sacred wisdom of the Chaldaeans.[5]

467

apud: Lydus, De Mensibus, IV, 53 — Wünsch

Οἱ μέντοι περὶ Ἰάμβλιχον καὶ Συριανὸν καὶ Πρόκλον δημιουργὸν αὐτὸν
⟨scil. τὸν παρὰ Ἰουδαίων τιμώμενον θεόν⟩ νομίζουσιν εἶναι καλοῦντες
αὐτὸν τῆς τετραστοίχου θεόν.

But the schools of Iamblichus, Syrianus and Proclus consider him (i.e.
the god worshipped by the Jews) to be the demiurge, calling him the
god of the four elements.

5 Cf. (H.) J. Lewy, Zion, VI (1940/1), p. 13, n. 57 = Studies in Jewish
Hellenism, p. 233.

CXXX. ALEXANDER OF LYCOPOLIS

c. 300 C.E.

The work by the Neoplatonic thinker Alexander of Lycopolis opposing the Manichaeans[1] evidences the spread of the Manichaean religion in Egypt in the second half of the third century C.E.[2] Another example of the reaction against the impact of Manichaeism is to be found in a letter, probably written by the Alexandrian bishop Theonas, dating from the late third century C.E.[3] Alexander alludes twice to ἡ Ἰουδαίων ἱστορία, adducing two episodes from Genesis, the sacrifice of the son of Abraam and the sexual intercourse of the angels with the daughters of men.[4]

468

Contra Manichaei Opiniones Disputatio, 24 — Brinkmann

Τὸ μὲν γὰρ κατὰ τὸν ἐκκλησιαστικὸν λόγον εἰπεῖν εἰς λύσιν ἁμαρτιῶν
ἑαυτὸν ἐπιδεδωκέναι ἔχει πίστιν τινὰ πρὸς τοὺς πολλοὺς κἀκ τῶν ἱστοριῶν
τῶν καθ᾽ Ἕλληνας, ὅταν φῶσίν τινας ὑπὲρ σωτηρίας πόλεων ἑαυτοὺς
ἐπι⟨δε⟩δωκέναι, καὶ παράδειγμα τοῦ λόγου ἔχει καὶ Ἰουδαίων ἱστορία τὸν
5 τοῦ Ἀβραὰμ παῖδα εἰς θυσίαν τῷ θεῷ παρασκευάζουσα· τὸ δὲ εἰς

4 ἐπι⟨δε⟩δωκέναι Brinkmann   ἐπιδωκέναι M

---

1 See R. Reitzenstein, *Philologus*, LXXXVI (1931), p. 185.
2 See C. Schmidt & H.J. Polotsky, *Ein Mani-Fund in Ägypten (Sitz-ungsberichte der preussischen Akademie der Wissenschaften*, 1933), pp. 4 ff.; J. Schwartz, *Zeitschrift für Papyrologie und Epigraphik*, I (1967), p. 214.
3 See *P. Rylands*, III, No. 469, with Roberts' introduction = A. Adam, *Texte zum Manichäismus*, Berlin 1954, No. 35.
4 For the Manichaean γραφὴ τῶν γιγάντων, see Schmidt & Polotsky, *op. cit.* (supra, n. 2), p. 40. The Christian sympathies of Alexander of Lycopolis are stressed by C. Riggi, *Salesianum*, XXXI (1969), pp. 561 ff. For a balanced view, see P.W. van der Horst & J. Mansfeld, *An Alexandrian Platonist against Dualism — Alexander of Lycopolis' Treatise, 'Critique of the . Doctrines of Manichaeus'*, Leiden 1974, Introduction.

πράγματος ἐπίδειξιν τῷ παθήματι ὑπάγειν τὸν χριστὸν πολλῆς ἐστιν ἀμαθίας, εἰς διδασκαλίαν καὶ γνῶσιν τῶν ὄντων τοῦ λόγου ὄντος αὐτάρκους·

For to maintain, according to the Church doctrine, that he gave himself up for the remission of sins gains some belief in the eyes of many people in view of the stories told among the Greeks about some persons who gave themselves up for the safety of their cities; and also Jewish history furnishes an example of this doctrine, in preparing the son of Abraam for sacrifice to God. Still to make the Christ submit to the Passion in order to prove the thing is an expression of great folly, since for the teaching and knowledge of reality the doctrine itself is sufficient.

469

Contra Manichaei Opiniones Disputatio, 25 — Brinkmann

Ἃ δὲ λέγεται ὑπὸ τῶν ποιήσεων περὶ τῶν Γιγάντων, ἄντικρυς μῦθός ἐστιν. οἱ μὲν γὰρ περὶ τούτων διατάττοντες ἐν ἀλληγορίαις τὰ τοιαῦτα προφέρονται τὸ σεμνὸν τοῦ λόγου ἀποκρύπτοντες τῇ τοῦ μύθου ἰδέᾳ· οἷον ὅταν ἡ τῶν Ἰουδαίων ἱστορία φῇ τοὺς ἀγγέλους ταῖς θυγατράσι
5 τῶν ἀνθρώπων εἰς ἀφροδισίων συνεληλυθέναι μῖξιν, τὰς γὰρ θρεπτικὰς δυνάμεις τῆς ψυχῆς ἀπὸ τῶν ἄνω ἐπὶ τὰ τῇδε ⟨ ... ⟩ ἡ τοιαύτη προφορὰ τοῦ λόγου σημαίνει.

5 ἀφροδισίων Combefisius   ἀφροδίσιον M
6 ⟨ῥεπούσας⟩ vel ⟨νευούσας⟩ vel ⟨φερομένας⟩ Brinkmann

That which is said in the works of poetry about the giants constitutes an outright myth. Those who treat those matters proffer them in allegories, concealing the solemnity of the argument by the form of the myth. For example, when Jewish history states that the angels practised sexual intercourse with the daughters of men, such a manner of expression signifies the movement [descent] of the nourishing powers of the soul, from above to here below.

CXXXI. *ITINERARIUM ANTONINI AUGUSTI*

c. 300 C.E.

The Itinerary attributed to Antoninus Augustus, presumably the emperor Antoninus Caracalla, received its final revision not earlier than the time of Diocletian.[1] *The following extracts comprise the stations in the itinerary included in Judaea or having a specific Jewish connection.*

470a

Itineraria Romana, 149:5–150:4, ed. O. Cuntz, Leipzig 1929, p. 21

(149:5)	Sycamina	m.p. XXIIII
(150:1)	Caesarea	m.p. XX
(2)	Betaro	m.p. XVIII
(3)	Diospoli	m.p. XXII
(4)	Iamnia	m.p. XII

2 *cesarea* P   5 *iamia* P   *iammia* L   *iamnia* B

(149:5)	Sycamina	24 miles
(150:1)	Caesarea	20 miles
(2)	Betaro	18 miles
(3)	Diospolis	22 miles
(4)	Jamnia	12 miles

149:5 *Sycamina*: A township near Haifa. Its Jewish character under the late empire is attested by, e.g., Antoninus of Placentia, 3; see Geyer, p. 160.
150:2 *Betaro*: This station is mentioned also in the *Itinerarium Burdigalense*, apud: *Itineraria Romana*, 600 (ed. Cuntz, *op. cit.*, p. 98 = ed. Geyer, p. 25): "Item ab Hierusolyma, sic: Civitas Nicopoli mil. XXII; Civitas Lidda mil. X; mutatio Antipatrida mil. X; mutatio Betthar mil. X; Civitas Caesarea mil. XVI."
Betaro was probably situated in the territory of Antipatris and is sometimes

---

1 It has been suggested that the central part of the Itinerary (§§123–162) reflects an edict published at Rome which announced the plan of Caracalla's journey to the East, through the Balkans and Anatolia to Egypt, in 214 C.E.; see D. van Berchem, *Comptes rendus de l'Académie des Inscriptions* (1973), pp. 123 ff.

identified with the village et-Ṭire; cf. A. Alt, *Palästinajahrbuch*, XXI (1925), p. 46.

150:3 *Diospoli*: Diospolis, the ancient Jewish township of Lydda, obtained municipal status under Septimius Severus; see A.H.M.Jones, *The Cities of the Eastern Roman Provinces*, Oxford 1971, pp. 278 f. For its territory, see G. Beyer, *ZDPV*, LVI (1933), pp. 218 ff.; for the industrial importance of Lydda, see *Expositio Totius Mundi et Gentium*, 31 (No. 477).

470b

Itineraria Romana, 169:2–5 — Cuntz, *op. cit.*, p. 23

(169:2)	Babylona	m.p. XII
(3)	Heliu	m.p. XII
(4)	Scenas veteranorum	m.p. XVIII
(5)	Vico Iudaeorum	m.p. XII

1 *babilona* P *b*bylona* D *babylonia* L *babilonia* D
4 *iudeorum* PD

(169:2)	Babylon	12 miles
(3)	Heliu[polis]	12 miles
(4)	Scenae veteranorum	18 miles
(5)	The Village of the Jews	12 miles

169:5 *Vico Iudaeorum*: In view of the dense Jewish population in that part of Egypt in the Hellenistic and early Roman period it is not surprising that a village to the east of the Nile delta should be called "the Jewish Village"; cf. the Σύρων κώμη of *BGU*, VI, No. 1282; the τὸ καλούμενον Ἰουδαίων στρατόπεδον of *Ant.*, XIV, 133, and *BJ*, I, 191; and the "Castra Iudaeorum" of *Notitia Dignitatum*, Oriens, XXVIII, 42 (ed. Seeck, p. 60).

471a

Itineraria Romana, 199:1–4 — Cuntz, *op. cit.*, p. 27

(199:1)	Item a Caesarea Eleuteropoli	m.p. LXXVII
(2)	Betaro	m.p. XXXI
(3)	Diospoli	m.p. XXVIII
(4)	Eleuteropoli	m.p. XVIII

1 *cesarea* P *casarea* D 2 *eutoropoli* P *eletaepoli* D
euleuteropolim L 5 *eleutropoli* D *euleuteropolim* L

(199:1)	Likewise from Caesarea	
	to Eleutheropolis	77 miles
(2)	Betaro	31 miles
(3)	Diospolis	28 miles
(4)	Eleutheropolis	18 miles

199:1 *Eleuteropoli*: For Eleutheropolis and its importance, cf. the commentary to Ammianus Marcellinus, XIV, 8:11 (No. 505).

199:3 The author of the *Itinerarium* seems to have committed a mistake in reckoning the distance between Diospolis and Eleutheropolis at only eighteen miles. For a suggestion to emend the number XVIII to XXVIII, see Beyer, *op. cit.* (supra, p. 489), p. 224, n. 2.

471b

Itineraria Romana, 199:11–200:3 — Cuntz, *op. cit.*, p. 27

(199:11)	Item a Neapoli	
	Ascalona	m.p. LXXIIII
(200:1)	Elia	m.p. XXX
(2)	Eleuteropoli	m.p. XX
(3)	Ascalona	m.p. XXIIII

3 *alia* D   4 *eleteropoli* P

(199:11)	Likewise from Neapolis	
	to Ascalon	74 miles
(200:1)	Elia (Aelia)	30 miles
(2)	Eleutheropolis	20 miles
(3)	Ascalon	24 miles

CXXXII. HELLADIUS

First half of the fourth century C.E.

Helladius was a native of Egypt and author of a chrestomathy in iambic trimeters, of which Photius preserves a fragment in a prose paraphrase.[1] *Helladius relates that Moses was called "Alpha", because he was tainted with leprosy: ἀλφοῖς τὸ σῶμα κατάστικτος ἦν. This repeats the statements by the much earlier Nicarchus (No. 248), and Ptolemaeus Chennus (No. 331). However, Helladius does not refer to Nicarchus as his source, but to Philo, presumably Philo of Byblus (cf. No. 329).*

472

Chrestomathia, apud: Photius, Cod. 279, p. 529b — Bekker = F 117b R (pp. 362 f.)

῝Οτι φλυαρεῖ καὶ οὗτος τὸν Μωσῆν ἄλφα καλεῖσθαι, διότι ἀλφοῖς τὸ σῶμα κατάστικτος ἦν· καὶ καλεῖ τοῦ ψεύδους τὸν Φίλωνα μάρτυρα.

This man also talks nonsense in saying that Moses was called Alpha because his body was spotted with leprosy. For this lie he refers to the authority of Philo.

---

1 On Helladius, see Gudeman, PW, VIII, pp. 98 ff.; H. Heimannsfeld, *De Helladii Chrestomathia Quaestiones Selectae*, Bonn 1911.

CXXXIII. FIRMICUS MATERNUS

First half of the fourth century C.E.

In his astrological treatise, the Mathesis, *Firmicus Maternus mentions Abram four times as an astrological authority. In this respect he has a predecessor in Vettius Valens (Nos. 339 and 340).*[1]
In the first of the following passages (No. 473) Abram is given place beside the well-known astrological writers Petosiris, Nechepso and Critodemus. He is followed in the list by Orpheus.[2]

473

Mathesis, IV, Prooemium, 5 — Kroll & Skutsch

Omnia enim quae Aesculapio Mercurius ✶ einhnus vix tradiderunt, quae Petosiris explicavit et Nechepso et quae Abram, Orfeus et Critodemus ediderunt [et] ceterique omnes huius artis scii, perlecta pariter atque collecta et contrariis sententiarum diversitatibus
5 comparata illis perscripsimus libris divinam scientiam Romanis omnibus intimantes, ut hoc, quod quibusdam difficillimum videbatur propter Latini sermonis angustias, ostensa Romani sermonis licentia veris ac manifestis interpretationibus explicarem.

1 *emhnus* V   *et Hanubius* Teuffel
Hermemubius Serruys, *Revue de Philologie*, XXXII, pp. 147 f.
Chnubis Reitzenstein, Poimandres, 1904, pp. 125 f.   2 *abraam* M   /
orpheus MV   3 *et* del. ed. pr. / *scii* Sittl   *antisci*   (*antiscia* V) codd.
4 *pariter* om. M

1 On the personality of Firmicus Maternus, see C.H.Moore, "Julius Firmicus Maternus — Der Heide und der Christ", Ph.D.Thesis, Munich 1897. Firmicus Maternus may have been writing at the very end of Constantine's reign; see T.D.Barnes, *JRS*, LXV (1975), p. 40.
2 See J.Geffcken, *Hermes*, LV (1920), p. 282; W. & H.G.Gundel, *Astrologumena*, Wiesbaden 1966, pp. 227 ff.

All the things that Mercury and Chnubis [?][1] transmitted with difficulty to Aesculapius, and those that Petosiris and Nechepso disentangled, and those that Abram, Orfeus and Critodemus and all others who are experts in this profession related, we have read through in equal degree, and collected them, and after comparing the opposing diversities of their views we have written them down in books. Thus we have made known to all Romans the divine science, so that what seemed so difficult to some because of the limitations of the Roman language we set forth by means of a true and clear exposition, thereby displaying the possibilities of the Roman language.

Aesculapio Mercurius ... tradiderunt: Firmicus Maternus also records that Mercurius, i.e. Hermes, was the teacher of Aesculapius and passed down secrets to him; see Firmicus Maternus, *Mathesis*, III, 1.
Petosiris et Nechepso: These figure as a well-known pair in the astrological tradition; cf. also Firmicus Maternus, *Mathesis*, III, *Prooemium*, 4: "illi divini viri atque omni admiratione digni Petosiris ⟨et⟩ Nechepso"; IV, 22:2: "Nechepso, iustissimus Aegypti imperator et astrologus valde bonus". They were considered to be the joint authors of an astrological handbook as well as writers under their own names of other astrological works. On them, see W. Kroll, *Neue Jahrbücher für das klassische Altertum*, VII (1901), pp. 569 ff.; idem, PW, XVI, pp. 2160 ff.; XIX, p. 1165; F. H. Cramer, *Astrology in Roman Law and Politics*, Philadelphia 1954, pp. 17 ff.; Gundel & Gundel, *op. cit.* (supra, p. 492, n. 2), pp. 27 ff.; Fraser, I, p. 436; II, p. 630, n. 489.
Abram: On Abram as an astrological authority, see the introduction to Vettius Valens.
Orfeus: On the *Astrologumena* of Orpheus, see Ziegler, PW, XVIII, p. 1400.
Critodemus: Critodemus was one of the older astrological writers, presumably in the third century B.C.E.; see Cramer, *op. cit.*, pp. 14 f.; Gundel & Gundel, *op. cit.* (supra, p. 492, n. 2), pp. 106 f.; O. Neugebauer & H. B. van Hoesen, *Greek Horoscopes*, Philadelphia 1959, pp. 185 f.

474

Mathesis, IV, 17:2 — Kroll & Skutsch

Quae omnia tunc explicabimus, cum ad interpretationem venerimus sfaerae barbaricae; haec enim omnia divinus ille Abram et prudentissimus Achilles verissimis conati sunt rationibus invenire.

2 *abraam* M   3 *achiles* PR

1 According to the emendation of Reitzenstein.

All these things we shall set forth when we come to the exposition of the barbaric sphere. For that divine Abram and the very learned Achilles have attempted to find out all this by the truest calculations.

475

Mathesis, IV, 17:5 — Kroll & Skutsch

Ex hoc loco qualitatem vitae et patrimonii substantiam et felicitatis atque infelicitatis cursus ostendi datur. Amor etiam et adfectus virorum circa mulieres qualis sit, ex hoc loco discitur et nutrimentorum et desideriorum omnium effectus ex istius loci
5 substantia quaeritur. Hic locus patriam [vel huius loci quadrata latera] facili ratione demonstrat. Appellatur autem, sicut Abraham designat, Lunae locus.

5–6 *vel huius loci quadrata latera* secl. Sittl   6 *autem* om. M

From this position it is possible to disclose the quality of life, the richness of the patrimony and the progress of both happiness and unhappiness. Also from this position we learn about the nature of love and the fondness of men towards women, and from the essence of this position we inquire about the effects of all child-care and desires. By an easy calculation, this position [or the squared sides of this position] shows one's native country. It is called, as Abraham defines it, the Position of the Moon.

476

Mathesis, IV, 18:1 — Kroll & Skutsch

Locum daemonis ista ratione colligimus; quam ideo huic libro indidimus, quia Solis eum locum esse Abraham simili ratione monstravit et iniquum erat, ut a loco Lunae Solis separaretur locus.

3 *inicum* A[1]   *inimicum* cett.

The position of the daemon we deduce by this calculation; we inserted it into this book, because Abraham has shown by a similar calculation that this is the position of the Sun, and it seemed unfair for the position of the Sun to be separated from that of the Moon.

494

CXXXIV. *EXPOSITIO TOTIUS MUNDI ET GENTIUM*

c. 350 C. E.

The Expositio Totius Mundi ct Gentium (*No. 177*) *is a geographical survey which, from Chapter XXI onwards, concentrates on the various countries and cities of the Roman empire.*[1] *Interest in the economic sphere predominates in the* Expositio, *and the author dwells much on the products of the soil and industry, in particular textiles. The manner of his allusions to the old religion leaves hardly any doubt that the writer was an adherent of paganism.*[2] *The work displays more detailed knowledge of the countries of the East than of the West, and the author seems to be most closely associated with the cities of Syria, Phoenicia and Palestine. Thus we may safely assume that he came from the eastern part of the Roman world.*[3] *Among the cities of Palestine the author mentions Caesarea, defining it as a charming city abounding in everything and having a world-famous tetrapylon* (Expositio Totius Mundi et Gentium, *§26*). *It is also listed among the Syrian and Phoenician cities that participate in the circus games (§32), and, like Sarepta, Neapolis and Lydda, it exports* purpura alithina (*§31*). *Caesarea is also renowned for its pantomimes (§32).*

Other Palestinian cities given importance in the Expositio *are Neapolis, "ipsa civitas gloriosa et valde nobilis", Ptolemais, Eleutheropolis, Scythopolis, famous for its linen industry, Jericho, producing the palm known as "Nicolaean", Lydda, Gaza, which excels in reciters, and Ascalon, famous for its wrestlers.*

1 It is certain that the work was composed under Constantius, 337–361 C. E. On the various attempts to date the *Expositio* more exactly, cf. J. Rougé, *Expositio Totius Mundi et Gentium*, Paris 1966, pp. 9 ff. Rougé himself dates the *Expositio* to 359 C. E.

2 See *ibid.*, pp. 48 ff. Cf., e.g., §22: "Istae autem civitates semper stantes deorum et imperatoris sapientia"; §34: "Etenim ibi [scil. in Aegypto] deos habitasse aut et habitare scimus"; §35: "Et dii coluntur eminenter et templum Serapidis ibi est, unum et solum spectaculum novum in omni mundo". However, some glaring Christian interpolations are to be found in the *Expositio*; cf. passages in §§2–4.

3 See *ibid.*, pp. 27 ff. Rougé goes to the length of associating the author with Palestinian Neapolis (*ibid.*, p. 33): "notre auteur est originaire de Mésopotamie et, avant de venir s'installer à Tyr, sa famille a dû s'établir un temps à Naplouse".

Expositio Totius Mundi et Gentium, 30–31 — Rougé

(30) Neapolis et ipsa civitas gloriosa et valde nobilis. Tripolis et Scythopolis et Byblus et ipsae civitates in industria positae. Heliopolis quae propinquat Libano monti mulieres speciosas pascit, quae apud omnes nominantur Libanitides, ubi Venerem magnifice
5 colunt: dicunt enim eam ibi habitare et mulieribus gratiam formositatis dare. Sunt autem iterum civitates et ipsae Sidon, Sarepta, Ptolemais, Eleutheropolis optimae similiter et Damascus. (31) Quoniam ergo ex parte praedictas civitates descripsimus et diximus ⋆ necessarium mihi videtur ut etiam quidnam unaquaeque
10 civitas proprium habet exponamus, ut qui legit certam eorum scientiam habere possit ⋆. In linteamina sunt hae: Scythopolis, Laodicia, Byblus, Tyrus, Berytus quae linteamen omni orbi terrarum emittunt, et sunt eminentes in omni abundantia. Similiter autem et Sarepta et Caesarea et Neapolis, quomodo et Lydda, purpuram
15 alithinam. Omnes autem praedictae civitates gloriosae et fructiferae in frumento, vino et oleo ⋆ hi et omnibus bonis abundant ⋆ Nicolaum itaque palmulam in Palaestinae regione, loco qui sic vocatur Iericho, similiter et Damascenam et alteram palmulam minorem et psittacium et omne genus pomorum habent.

2 *Scytopolis* J Lu Si / *Bibilus* J Lu Si 4 *quae apud*] *que aput* J Lu / *Libanitides*] *Libanotides* Si *Libanotidas* J Go Riese Lu 6 *iterum*] *etiam* vel *item* Lu² / *ipsa* J Go Riese Lu Si 7 *Ptolemaes* J Lu Si / *obtima* J Riese Lu Si 9–11 lacunam cum D supplevit Rougé *necessarium est dicere quid singulae eorum habent* Si 11 *linteamina*] *litore enim* Si / *Scitopolis* J Lu *Scytopolis* Si 12 *Biblus* J Lu Si 13 *eminentes in omni* suprascriptum in J secundum Go 14 *Sarepta Sarafa* J Lu *Sarafta* Si *Saraphta* Go / *quomodo* om. Si 15 *alithinam*] *alitinam* Go Si *altinam* J Lu 16 *hi et* J Salmasius *his et* (?) Lu 17 *Nicolaam* Si *Nicholaum* J secundum Go Lu sed Salimasius testat *Nicolaum* / *Palaestinis* J Go Lu *Palaestines* Mu Riese Si / *regione*] *regio* J secundum Go Lu *regionis* Mu Si (*regione* Salmasius) 18 *Damascena* J Salmasius Lu om. Si 18–19 *altera palmula minore* J secundum Go Mu Lu 19 *psittacium*] *psittatium* J Go Riese Lu Si *pistacium* Salmasius *pistacio* Mu / *habent* testat Salmasius *habitantem* J secundum Go *habundanter* Go Si *habundantem* Lu Riese *abundantem* Mu

(30) Neapolis is also a famous and a very noble city. Tripolis and Scythopolis and Byblus are cities busy with industry. Heliopolis, which is situated in the vicinity of Mount Liban, nourishes beautiful

women, who are called by all Libanitides; here they worship Venus magnificently; it is said that she resides there and bestows upon the women the grace of beauty. In addition, also Sidon, Sarepta, Ptolemais, Eleutheropolis, and likewise Damascus are excellent cities. (31) Since we have described in part the above-mentioned cities and said ⋆ it seems necessary to me to set forth the specialities of each of them so that the reader may have an exact knowledge of them ⋆. The following are famous for linen clothes: Scythopolis, Laodicea, Byblus, Tyre, and Berytus, which export linen to the whole world and excel in the richness of all of those productions. Likewise Sarepta, Caesarea and Neapolis, as well as Lydda, export high-quality purple. All the above-mentioned cities are renowned for fertility in corn, vine and olive ⋆ they have a plenty of all goods ⋆ therefore they grow the Nicolaean palm in the land of Palestine, in a place called Jericho, and likewise that of Damascus and another palm, a smaller one, pistachio and all kinds of fruit.

30 *Neapolis et ipsa civitas gloriosa*: Neapolis was founded by Vespasian in 72 C.E. in the vicinity of ancient Shechem. It ranks among the "egregiae civitates" of Palaestina, alongside Caesarea, Eleutheropolis, Ascalon and Gaza, in the description by Ammianus Marcellinus, XIV, 8:11 (No. 505). Thus it does not owe its description as "gloriosa" and "nobilis" by the pagan writer of the *Expositio* to the part it played in biblical history or to its position as the Samaritan centre; nor do we have to explain this description by assuming that the author himself hailed from Neapolis, as does Rougé, *op. cit.* (supra, p. 495, n. 3). Other pagan sources also attest that in this period Neapolis was one of the most important cities of Palestine. An inscription from Aphrodisias in Caria, dating from the time of Marcus Aurelius, singles out Νέα πόλις τῆς Συρίας as a place where the athlete Aelius Aurelius Menander won his victories, the city being mentioned after Damascus, Berytus, Tyre, and Caesarea and before Scythopolis and Gaza; see L. Moretti, *Iscrizioni agonistiche greche*, Rome 1953, No. 72. For its importance in later times also, see Damascius, *Vita Isidori*, 141 (No. 548). *Tripolis et Scythopolis et Byblus*: The *Expositio* does not adhere to their geographical order in mentioning Scythopolis between Tripolis and Byblus, both of them cities of Phoenicia. For fourth-century Scythopolis, see also Ammianus Marcellinus, XIX, 12:8. On Jews in Scythopolis at the beginning of the fifth century, see N. Zori, *IEJ*, XVI (1966), pp. 123 ff.; idem, *Eretz-Israel*, XI (1973), pp. 229 f. Cf. also the inscription from late antiquity containing halakhic regulations bearing upon the sabbatical year found in the remains of an ancient synagogue 5 km south of Beth-Shean; see Y. Sussmann, *Tarbiz*, XLIII (1973/4), pp. 88 ff.
Eleutheropolis: On Eleutheropolis, see the commentary to Ammianus Marcellinus, XIV, 8:11 (No. 505).

31 *Scythopolis ... Berytus quae linteamen omni orbi terrarum emittunt*: The fame of the linen industry of Scythopolis is illustrated in both talmudic and midrashic literature; see *Bereshit Rabba*, 19 (ed. Theodor), p. 170; *ibid.*, 20, p. 196; *TP Ketubbot*, vii, 31c; *TP Qiddushin*, ii, 62c. It is also illustrated in the imperial legislation; cf. *Edictum Diocletiani*, in: S. Lauffer, *Diokletians Preisedikt*, 26–28, Berlin 1971, pp. 169 ff.; *Codex Theodosianus*, X, 20:8. On the textiles of Syria, see A. H. M. Jones, *The Later Roman Empire*, II, Oxford 1964, p. 837; L. C. West, *TAPA*, LV (1924), pp. 167 ff.

et Lydda: Lydda remained one of the main centres of Judaism in the age of the *amoraim*; cf. *Bereshit Rabba*, 94 (ed. Theodor–Albeck), p. 1184; *TP Pe'a*, viii, 21b; Hieronymus, *In Habacuc* ii:15 ff. (*CCSL*, ed. Adriaen, LXXVI, A, p. 610 = *PL*, XXV, p. 1301); idem, *Praefatio in Job* (*PL*, XXVIII, p. 1081), mentioning a Jewish teacher of Jerome at Lydda. Lydda suffered much as a result of the Jewish revolt in the time of Constantius in 351 C.E.; cf. Hieronymus, *Chronica* (ed. Helm²), p. 238; *Pesiqta Rabbati*, viii (ed. M. Friedman), p. 29b; see also the commentary to Aurelius Victor, *De Caesaribus*, 42:11 (No. 480); P. Thomsen, *Loca Sancta*, Halle 1907, p. 56; S. Lieberman, *Annuaire de l'institut de philologie et d'histoire orientales et slaves*, VII (1939–1944), pp. 411 f.

purpuram alithinam: See the comments of Rougé, *op. cit.* (supra, p. 495, n. 1). It seems that the designation *alithina* (ἀληθινή) signifies here high quality. *Nicolaum ... palmulam*: Cf. the commentary to Plinius, *Naturalis Historia*, XIII, 45 (No. 214).

loco qui sic vocatur Iericho: The area in the vicinity of Jericho continued to be inhabited by Jews in the early Byzantine period. On the synagogue near Tell es-Sultan and the Aramaic inscription on the front of the door, see D. C. Baramki & M. Avi-Yonah, *The Quarterly of the Department of Antiquities in Palestine*, VI (1938), pp. 73 ff.; see also Thomsen, *op. cit.*, pp. 71 f.

CXXXV. AURELIUS VICTOR

Fourth century C.E.

Aurelius Victor, a native of Africa, completed the Liber de Caesaribus *between 359 and 361 C.E.[1] The only information of any value about Jews to be derived from the work concerns the Jewish rebellion under Gallus (No. 480), Aurelius Victor being the only source to mention the name of the Jewish leader Patricius.*

1 See C.G. Starr, *American Historical Review*, LXI (1955–1956), p. 575; E. Hohl, *Historia*, IV (1955), p. 221. On Aurelius Victor, see also R. Syme, *Emperors and Biography*, Oxford 1971, pp. 228 ff.; H. W. Bird, *The Classical Journal*, LXX (1975), No. 4, pp. 49 ff.; W. den Boer, *Some Minor Roman Historians*, Leiden 1972, pp. 19 ff.; the introduction to the edition in the Budé series by P. Dufraigne, *Aurelius Victor — Livre des Césars*, Paris 1975. Dufraigne comes to the conclusion that the book should be dated between the end of 359 C.E. and September 360; see *ibid.*, p. XVI.

478

Liber de Caesaribus, 8:1 — Dufraigne

Ita ad Aulum Vitellium potestas delata, quae progressu funestior talibus initiis foret, si Vespasianus aliquamdiu Iudaeorum bello, quod Neronis iussu susceperat, impensius attineretur.

This power was conferred on Aulus Vitellius; an event that, with such beginnings, could in the course of time have had more fatal results if Vespasian had been excessively occupied in the war against the Jews, which he undertook at the behest of Nero, for a longer time.

479

Liber de Caesaribus, 9:10 — Dufraigne

At bello rex Parthorum Vologesus in pacem coactus, atque in provinciam Syria, cui Palaestinae nomen, Iudaeique, annitente filio Tito, quem, transgrediens in Italiam, reliquerat externae militiae moxque victorem praefectura praetorio extulerat.

1 *ac* P   2 *provinciam* Schott   *provincia* OP   /   *syriae* P

The king of the Parthians Vologesus was compelled to make peace, and Syria called Palaestina and the Jews were reduced into a province. That was achieved by the efforts of Vespasian's son Titus, whom he had left in charge of the foreign war when he himself crossed to Italy. Soon after he had gained the victory he promoted him to the rank of *praefectus praetorio*.

480

Liber de Caesaribus, 42:11 — Dufraigne

Et interea Iudaeorum seditio, qui Patricium nefarie in regni speciem sustulerant, oppressa.

1 *speciem* Dacier Pichlmayr   *specie* OP

And meanwhile the revolt of the Jews, who impiously raised Patricius to royalty, was crushed.

500

Iudaeorum seditio: The Jewish revolt in the time of Constantius in 351 C.E. was provoked by the policy of persecution adopted by the Christian emperors. Its outbreak was probably hastened by the war between Rome and Persia in that period. Aurelius Victor tells about the Jewish revolt after describing the war waged by Constantius against Magnentius and before mentioning the dismissal of Gallus. The Jewish revolt is referred to by various Christian writers; see Hieronymus, *Chronica* (ed. Helm²), p. 238, under the 282nd Olympiad; Socrates, *Historia Ecclesiastica*, II, 33; Sozomenus, *Historia Ecclesiastica*, IV, 7:5; Theophanes (ed. C. de Boor), I, Leipzig 1883, p. 40; Cedrenus (ed. Bekker), I, p. 524; Nicephorus Callistus, IX, 32 (*PG*, CXLVI, Col. 353); *Chronique de Michel le Syrien*, ed. J.B. Chabot, Paris 1899, I, p. 268; Agapius, in: *Patrologia Orientalis*, VII, pp. 571 f.

On the revolt, see H. Graetz, *Geschichte der Juden*, IV⁴, Leipzig 1908, pp. 312 ff., 455 f.; M. Avi-Yonah, *Geschichte der Juden im Zeitalter des Talmud*, Berlin 1962, pp. 181 ff. Aurelius Victor is the only writer to mention that there was a leader Patricius whom the Jews made king. On the other hand, Aurelius Victor is silent about the place of the revolt. According to the Christian sources the centre of the revolt was Diocaesarea (= Sepphoris), and Jerome adds Tiberias and Lydda. The events have echoes in the Midrash; cf. *Pesiqta Rabbati*, viii (ed. M. Friedman), p. 29b. See also *TP Yevamot*, xv, 15c; *TP Megilla*, iii, 74a; *TP Soṭa*, ix, 23c; *TP Berakhot*, v, 9a; *TP Shevi'it*, iv, 35a; *TP Beẓa*, i, 60c. These sources do not mention Gallus at all, but mention Ursicinus. To judge from the excavations there, Bet-Shearim was also destroyed during the revolt of the Jews; see Avi-Yonah, *op. cit.*, p. 184. Lieberman minimizes the importance of the revolt and reduces it to the level of a local incident connected with a Roman usurper (i.e. Patricius), supported by Diocaesarean Jews; see S. Lieberman, *JQR*, XXXVI (1945/6), pp. 340 f. However, both the language used here by Aurelius Victor ("Iudaeorum seditio" and "Patricium ... in regni speciem sustulerant"), as well as the implications of the other sources, suggest rather that Patricius was a Jew and that this Jewish revolt was of some importance. The revolt of Patricius and its suppression are not mentioned in the existing parts of the history of Ammianus Marcellinus. It has been recently suggested that he may have related these events in the lost book XIII of the history; see J. Geiger, *Liverpool Classical Monthly*, IV, No. 4 (1979), p. 77.

CXXXVI. JULIAN

331–363 C.E.

The most detailed exposition of Julian's views on Judaism is to be found in the "apostate" emperor's polemic against the Galilaeans, i.e. the Christians (No. 481a). The work was compiled by Julian during his sojourn at Antioch before he embarked on his Persian expedition.[1] As we find in Porphyry's similar work, the author's attitude to Judaism as displayed in Contra Galilaeos *is conditioned by his opposition to Christianity. Judaism and its scriptures are conceived of as the mainspring of Christianity, Judaism being an exclusive religion which on principle is hostile to other religions and despises their gods. In the terminology of both Julian and his predecessors, it is marked by* ἀθεότης. *However, Julian often praises the loyalty of the Jews to their ancestral worship and customs, to which he acknowledges that they have shown the utmost devotion. While he does not differ much from Porphyry in his general evaluation of Judaism, or of Christianity, in contrast to his predecessor, Julian allots a prominent place to Jewish sacrificial worship. In his estimation of sacrifices, as in other respects, he follows Iamblichus, for whom Julian had great admiration.*

Most of the extant passages from Julian's Contra Galilaeos *that refer to Judaism criticize the cosmogony depicted in Genesis and the "narrow" character of Jewish monotheism. Julian points to the meagre achievements of the Jews in the various spheres of civilization in comparison with other nations, an argument used by anti-Jewish polemists from Apollonius Molon onwards.*

Among the biblical stories singled out as specific targets for criticism is that of the planting of the Garden of Eden and the creation of Adam, the woman and the serpent. Julian stresses the fabulous character of the

---

1 It is expressly stated by Libanius that among the various occupations of Julian at Antioch was the composition of books in support of the gods; see Libanius, *Orationes*, XVII, 18. Julian's work "Against the Galilaeans" consisted of three books. The surviving passages from the polemical reply of Cyril of Alexandria to Julian's work refer to the first book. They have been edited by C. (K.) J. Neumann, *Iuliani Imperatoris Librorum Contra Christianos Quae Supersunt*, Leipzig 1880, and by W. C. Wright, in: *The Works of the Emperor Julian (LCL)*, III, pp. 318 ff.

story, remarking that as it was the serpent who enabled mankind to discern between good and evil he should be thought of as a benefactor of the human race (93 D).

On the other hand, God, who denies man the power of distinguishing between good and evil, must be characterized as envious. Julian places the Jewish myths on the same level as the incredible tales about the gods found in Greek mythology, such as the swallowing of his children by Kronos and the outrageous sexual behaviour of Zeus. In his view, the only course for justifying such stories would be to interpret them as having a hidden meaning (94 A). Julian adopts this method in discussing Greek mythology, but concerning the Jewish stories he only states that if one were to understand them literally they would seem highly blasphemous.

Julian also acknowledges that some of the opinions of the Jews are correct, but even these, as embodied in the story of Creation, fall below the truth of the Platonic cosmogony described in the Timaeus. Judaism ranks lower than Plato's theory not only in its general metaphysics, but also because of its narrow nationalist concept. Moses asserts that the demiurge of the universe elected the nation of the Hebrews and cares for them alone. But how the other nations are guided, and by which gods, Moses has not uttered a word. How could God have looked on inactively for myriads of years, or, according to the Christian and Jewish view, for thousands of years, while the whole of mankind was sunk in idolatry excepting only a little tribe that less than two thousand years previously had settled in one part of Palestine? It is therefore only natural to suppose that the God of the Hebrews is not the lord of the whole universe, but only one among the crowd of other gods (100 C). It is true that some Jews and Christians attained to the conception of a supreme God of the universe. Their God, however, is a jealous one, even avenging the sins of the fathers on the children. Preferable by far is the Greek view, i.e. the Neoplatonic doctrine, which maintains the existence of a demiurge who is indeed the common father and king of all, but at the same time assigns functions to national gods, and protectors to the various cities.

Differences among the national gods are reflected in national traits, and this explains the variety in national characters. The reason given for the dissimilarity of national languages by Moses in the story of the Tower of Babel is wholly fabulous. Even if we suppose that the god honoured among the Hebrews is indeed the demiurge of the universe, the Greek beliefs of him are nobler, for they do not imply that he is in any way the

503

rival of the national gods who are his subordinates. The famous Decalogue of Moses contains nothing very original, for eight of the commandments are common to the whole human race. As for the specific Jewish commandment forbidding the worship of other gods because of the jealousy of God, if a jealous man is considered blameworthy then jealousy can hardly be thought of as a divine quality (155D).

Another argument used by Julian is that God does not care for the Hebrews alone among the nations, for he has bestowed better gifts on other peoples. The Egyptians, Chaldaeans, Assyrians and Greeks can boast of more illustrious sons than the Hebrews. The Hebrews did not originate any of the sciences and philosophical studies and can show no one comparable with the great individuals produced by the Greeks. While the gods have granted Rome imperial power, they allowed the Jews to enjoy only a brief period of freedom. The Hebrews have had no general comparable to Alexander or Caesar, and even commanders inferior to these deserve more admiration than all the generals of the Jews put together (218C).

Julian opposes the Galilaeans as being worse than the Jews because they neither abide by the traditions of the Hebrews nor cleave to the law bestowed upon them by God. They have adopted the bad traits of both the Jews and the Gentiles. For the Hebrews have precise laws concerning religion, and countless observances that require a priestly life, and though their lawgiver forbade the worship of gods apart from the one "whose portion is Jacob, and Israel an allotment of his inheritance", he added also "Thou shalt not revile the gods". Only later generations added blasphemy to the neglect of worship, and this trait the Christians have in common with the Jews (238C). Julian states, moreover, that Moses himself calls the angels "gods". Moses also knew the various methods in which sacrifices are conducted and did not consider them impure. There is no ground for the view that the Jews do not conduct sacrifices. Even at present everything they eat is consecrated, but since they have been deprived of their Temple, they are precluded from sacrificing to God. The cause of division between the Jews and the Gentiles is the belief in only one God (306B): ἐκεῖνο γὰρ αὐτῶν μὲν ἴδιον, ἡμῶν δὲ ἀλλότριον. All the other appurtenances to sacrifices — temples, altars, and purifications — are common to both Jews and Gentiles.

One of the most significant passages in Contra Galilaeos *is that in which Julian declares that he has always revered the God of Abraham,*

Isaac and Jacob; these had been Chaldaeans, belonging to a sacred race and skilled in theurgy (354AB). They worshipped a God who has always been propitious to Julian himself, and to those who worship him after the way of Abraham. This God is indeed very great and powerful, but has nothing to do with the Christians, for these do not imitate Abraham by erecting altars to God as Abraham did, and worshipping him with sacrifices. Abraham himself used to sacrifice in the Hellenic way, applying divination to the shooting stars and augury to the flight of birds.

The references to Judaism and the Jews in the other works of Julian display the same attitude towards the Jewish religion. Julian shows a clear preference for Judaism over Christianity, expressing admiration for the God who is worshipped by the Greeks also, though under other names, and appreciation of the strict loyalty of the Jews to their national religion and customs. These views are again accompanied by disparagement of Jewish achievements in comparison with those of the Greeks, and by censure of the exclusiveness of monotheism.

Julian also shows a knowledge of Jewish society and its regulations. Thus in his letter to Arsacius (No. 482), specifying measures to be taken for the relief of the poor, he states that there are no beggars to be found among the Jews. In a letter to the Alexandrians (No. 485), he declares that it is disgraceful that a single Alexandrian should admit to being a Galilaean. For the ancestors of the genuine Hebrews were slaves of the Egyptians, while Alexander of Macedon, the founder of the city, was a god-fearing man. He resembled neither the Christians nor the Hebrews, though the latter have proved themselves highly superior to the Christians (μακρῷ γεγονότας αὐτῶν κρείττονας). However Ptolemy son of Lagus proved stronger than the Jews.

In the letter to Theodorus (No. 483) Julian states his attitude towards religion. He implies that he was not in favour of changes in matters concerning the gods, and advocates the observance of laws inherited from one's forefathers. He contrasts the indifference shown by the Greeks towards the gods with the zeal displayed by the Jews, who are even ready to sacrifice their lives for their religious observances. Julian finds them praiseworthy in worshipping a god who is most powerful and good, and governs the world of sense (ἐπιτροπεύει τὸν αἰσϑητὸν κόσμον). They err, however, in abstaining from the worship of other gods as well.

The specific importance of Julian's views on Judaism does not lie in their originality, since they derive mainly from the common stock of

Neoplatonic ideas, coloured above all by those of Porphyry and Iamblichus.[2] *They owe their interest to the position and personality of Julian, who also made an attempt to put his views into practice through the religious policy launched by him during his brief reign with the purpose of checking the advance of Christianity and restoring the old worship.*

The crux of his policy towards the Jews was his plan to restore the Temple at Jerusalem. This attempt is known to us both from the history of Ammianus Marcellinus, XXIII, 1:2–3 (No. 507), and from many patristic sources; it seems to be wholly ignored by talmudic literature. Julian's policy was inspired by his wish to deal a blow at the Christian doctrine, which implied that the desolation of the Temple at Jerusalem would be everlasting.[3] *This initiative was also consistent with his effort to restore the offering of sacrifices. The sources emphasize that the Jews are not allowed by their religion to sacrifice outside the Temple of Jerusalem. Thus if Julian wished to revive the Jewish sacrificial cult, he would have to restore the Temple.*[4] *Since the Jews constituted a by no*

2 On the influence of Celsus and Porphyry on Julian, see J. Geffcken, *Zwei griechische Apologeten*, Leipzig–Berlin 1907, pp. 305 f.; idem, *Neue Jahrbücher für das klassische Altertum*, XXI (1908), p. 170. For the views on sacrifices held by Iamblichus that influenced Julian, see Iamblichus, *De Mysteriis*, V, 9 (ed. des Places), pp. 163 f.; cf. the succinct justification of animal sacrifices by the Neoplatonist Sallustius, as given by him in *De Deis et Mundo*, 16: αἱ μὲν χωρὶς θυσιῶν εὐχαὶ λόγοι μόνον εἰσίν, αἱ δὲ μετὰ θυσιῶν ἔμψυχοι λόγοι ... ἐπεὶ τοίνυν ζωὴ μὲν πρώτη ἡ τῶν θεῶν ἐστι, ζωὴ δέ τις καὶ ἡ ἀνθρωπίνη, βούλεται δὲ αὕτη συναφθῆναι ἐκείνῃ, μεσότητος δεῖται ... ἡ δὲ μεσότης ὁμοία εἶναι τοῖς συναπτομένοις ὀφείλει· ζωῆς οὖν μεσότητα ζωὴν ἐχρῆν εἶναι, καὶ διὰ τοῦτο ζῷα θύουσιν ἄνθρωποι. Both Sallustius and Julian were influenced by the views of Iamblichus, who differed radically from Porphyry in his full acceptance of animal sacrifices. Julian's admiration for Iamblichus is also expressed in Iulianus, *Ad Helium Regem*, p. 146 A (Iamblichus is not inferior to Plato); pp. 157 C–158 A; idem, *Orationes*, IX (ed. Rochefort = ed. Hertlein, VI), p. 188 B; on Iamblichus as a forerunner of Julian, see, in general, R. E. Witt, in: *De Jamblique à Proclus (Fondation Hardt, Entretiens sur l'antiquité classique*, XXI, 1974 [1975]), pp. 35 ff.

3 See Iohannes Chrysostomus, *Adversus Iudaeos*, V, 11 (*PG*, XLVIII, Col. 900); idem, *De S. Babyla Contra Iulianum et Gentiles*, 22 (*PG*, L, Col. 568); Philostorgius, *Historia Ecclesiastica*, VII, 9; Theophanes, *Chronographia ad A. M. 5855*, I, p. 51 (ed. de Boor). Cf. Eusebius, *Demonstratio Evangelica*, VIII, 2:124–126.

4 See Iohannes Chrysostomus, *Adversus Iudaeos*, V, 11 (*PG*, XLVIII, Cols. 900 f.); idem, *De S. Babyla Contra Iulianum et Gentiles*, 22 (*PG*, L,

Julian

means negligible factor in the population of the empire, political
considerations may also have played some part in Julian's decision.[5]

Col. 568); Socrates, *Historia Ecclesiastica*, III, 20: φιλοθύτης γὰρ ὢν οὐ
μόνον αὐτὸς τῷ αἵματι ἔχαιρεν, ἀλλ᾽ εἰ μὴ καὶ ἄλλοι τοῦτο ποιῶσι,
ζημίαν ἐνόμιζεν; Theodoretus, *Historia Ecclesiastica*, III, 20:1;
Sozomenus, *Historia Ecclesiastica*, V, 22:3: ἴσως δὲ καὶ πρὸς
Ἑλληνισμὸν καὶ θυσίας ἑτοιμότερον αὐτοὺς ἐπάγεσθαι ᾤετο;
Rufinus, *Historia Ecclesiastica*, X, 38; Hieronymus, *Commentarius in
Danielem*, xi:35 (*PL*, XXV, Col. 570 = *CCSL*, LXXV A, pp. 923 f.).
On Julian's passion for sacrifices, cf. also Libanius, *Orationes*, XIV, 69;
XVII, 4: Τίνα μέντοι, τίνα θεῶν αἰτιατέον; ἢ πάντας ὁμοίως
ἐκλιπόντας φρουρὰν ἣν ὤφειλον τῇ γενναίᾳ κεφαλῇ ἀντὶ πολλῶν μὲν
ἱερείων, πολλῶν δὲ εὐχῶν, μυρίων δὲ ἀρωμάτων, πολλοῦ δὲ αἵματος
τοῦ μὲν νυκτός, τοῦ δ᾽ ἐν ἡμέρᾳ χυθέντος; οὐ γὰρ τοὺς μὲν εὐώχει, τοὺς
δὲ ὑπερέβαινεν ... ἀλλ᾽ ὅσους οἱ ποιηταὶ παρέδοσαν. πατέρας τε καὶ
παῖδας θεούς τε καὶ θεάς, ἄρχοντάς τε καὶ ἀρχομένους, ἅπασιν
ἔσπενδέ τε καὶ τοὺς ἁπάντων ἐνεπίμπλη βωμοὺς ἀρνῶν καὶ βοῶν;
ibid., XVIII, 126: Πρῶτον μὲν οὖν ὅπερ ἔφην, ὥσπερ φυγάδα τὴν
εὐσέβειαν κατήγαγε νεὼς τοὺς μὲν ποιῶν, τοὺς δὲ ἐπισκευάζων, εἰς δὲ
τοὺς εἰσάγων ἔδη; ibid., XXIV, 35: τίνα εἰκὸς εἰρῆσθαι περὶ τούτου τοῦ
τὰς ἁπάντων τῶν Ἑλλήνων ... παρελθόντος θυσίας; Ammianus
Marcellinus, XXII, 12:6: "Hostiarum tamen sanguine plurimo aras
crebritate nimia perfundebat, tauros aliquotiens immolando centenos et
innumeros varii pecoris greges, avesque candidas terra quaesitas et mari,
adeo ut in dies paene singulos milites carnis distentiore sagina, victitantes
incultius, potusque aviditate corrupti, umeris inpositi transeuntium, per
plateas ex publicis aedibus, ubi vindicandis potius quam cedendis
conviviis indulgebant, ad sua diversoria portarentur ..." Still one should
point out that Julian elsewhere asserts that all offerings brought to the
gods with piety have equal value, whereas sacrifices without piety have no
value whatever; see Iulianus, *Orationes*, VII, p. 213D.
On Julian's religious views, and attempts at reform in general, see
J. R. Asmus, *Zeitschrift für Kirchengeschichte*, XVI (1896), pp. 45 ff.;
G. Mau, *Die Religionsphilosophie Kaiser Julians*, Leipzig–Berlin 1907;
W. Koch, *Revue belge de philologie et d'histoire*, VI (1927), pp. 123 ff.;
R. Farney, *La religion de l'empereur Julien et le mysticisme de son temps*,
Paris 1934; P. de Labriolle, *La réaction païenne*, Paris 1934, pp. 369 ff.;
H. Raeder, *Classica et Mediaevalia*, VI (1944), pp. 179 ff.; J. Leipoldt,
*Der römische Kaiser Julian in der Religionsgeschichte (Sitzungsberichte
der sächsischen Akademie der Wissenschaften zu Leipzig, Philologisch-
historische Klasse*, CX, fasc. 1), Berlin 1964.
Important for the study of "Against the Galilaeans" in comparison with
other works of Julian is R. Asmus, *Julians Galiläerschrift im Zusam-
menhang mit seinen übrigen Werken (Beilage zum Jahresbericht des
Grossherzoglichen Gymnasiums zu Freiburg im Breisgau)*, Freiburg 1904.

5 This factor is underrated by J. Vogt, *Kaiser Julian und das Judentum*,

The imminent war with Persia lent importance to the attitude of the Jews in Mesopotamia and Babylonia. Though in the eyes of a doctrinaire like Julian politics might have been subordinated to religious considerations and principles, the results of the Persian war had great influence in determining the future creed of the Roman empire. According to Christian sources, the Jews eagerly responded to the call of Julian.[6] The work of restoration was put in the charge of Alypius.[7] What followed is well known. A natural disaster, presumably an earthquake, prevented the continuation of the work (see also the commentary to No. 507). Yet despite the view of some scholars (Bidez & Cumont, Vogt; see Bibliography) who agree with what is asserted by John Chrysostom,[8] it seems unlikely that Julian wholly renounced his original plan thereby admitting the validity of the Christian theological claim. It is more plausible to assume that the work was only temporarily discontinued because the emperor left for Persia.

The letter addressed by Julian to the community of the Jews (No. 486a) may represent the last stage of his policy, when he was still committed to the restoration of the Temple, before his departure for the Persian campaign.[9] The authenticity of this letter has been called in question by

Leipzig 1939, pp. 49 f., but much emphasized by M. Avi-Yonah, *Geschichte der Juden im Zeitalter des Talmud*, Berlin 1962, p. 192.

6 See Gregorius Nazianzenus, V, 4 (*PG*, XXXV, Col. 668); Theodoretus, *Historia Ecclesiastica*, III, 20:2; Socrates, *Historia Ecclesiastica*, III, 20; Rufinus, *Historia Ecclesiastica*, X, 38; Zonaras, XIII, 12 (ed. Büttner & Wobst, III, p. 62). For the summary of an unpublished Syriac source, a presumed letter of Cyril who was bishop of Jerusalem at that time, see S.P. Brock, *PEQ*, CVIII (1976), pp. 103 ff. Brock concludes that the letter is not authentic but was written *c.* 400 C.E. The letter gives a date for the attempted rebuilding of the Temple that coincides with the Jewish festival of Lag ba-'Omer, not otherwise attested in Antiquity.

7 See Ammianus Marcellinus, XXIII, 1:2 (No. 507), and the commentary *ad loc.*

8 See Iohannes Chrysostomus, *Adversus Iudaeos*, V, 11 (*PG*, XLVIII, p. 901).

9 For the chronology of Julian's sojourn in the East, see O. Seeck, *Regesten der Kaiser und Päpste*, Stuttgart 1919, pp. 209 ff. Julian arrived at Constantinople in December 361, and left for Persia at the beginning of March 363. Seeck dates the letter to the Jewish community to 1 March 363, at the end of the sojourn at Antioch; see *ibid.*, p. 212. For the relations between Julian and the Jews of Antioch, see Vogt, *op. cit.* (supra, n. 5), p. 50; cf. G. Downey, *A History of Antioch in Syria*, Princeton 1961, p. 382. Downey suggests that in establishing himself at Antioch Julian may have counted on the support of the important Jewish

generations of scholars. It has been declared spurious by Naber, Reinach, Lucas, Bidez, Vogt, and Speyer, among others, but its authenticity has been vigorously maintained by Hack and Lewy. Similar conclusions have been independently reached by W. den Boer. The letter is thought to be authentic also by scholars like Borries, Negri, Allard, Ensslin, Juster and Avi-Yonah. Wright defends the authenticity of the letter, though suggesting that it may have been rewritten or edited in a bureau.[10]

The contents of the letter do not imply anything to belie its attribution to Julian. The alleviation of the burden of the taxes, the blame put on the counsellors of Constantius, the view that people overcome by anxiety do not have much confidence when raising their hands in prayer, which does not seem of Jewish provenance, all accord well with what is known of the personality and views of Julian. Neither the allusion to offering prayers to the Great God, who has it in his power to direct Julian's reign, nor the emperor's hope of being able to glorify God in Jerusalem after gaining the victory, is out of place, if we take into consideration the syncretistic atmosphere of that age and the identification by Julian of the Jewish God with the ruler of the world of sense (No. 483). There is also his declaration that he has always revered the God of Abraham, Isaac and Jacob, a God worshipped by Greeks under other names (No. 481a).

The letter differs stylistically from other works of Julian; it is impregnated with the language of the Septuagint and shows a higher incidence of hiatus.[11] *Yet it would have been natural for Julian to use his wide knowledge of the Septuagint in a letter intended for Jews. Apparently the letter was already known to Sozomenus not later than the middle of the fifth century. Thus scholars who assume the letter to be spurious would have to suggest why a Jewish forger, living under*

community of that city; cf. R. Browning, *The Emperor Julian*, London 1975, p. 149.

10 See Wright's introduction in *LCL*, to *The Works of the Emperor Julian*, III, p. xxii.

11 It has been stated that Julian belonged to the category of writers who strove to omit the hiatus in their works, that in some of them he wholly omitted the hiatus, and that in the majority of them he used it less often than other writers; see C. Sintenis, *Hermes*, I (1866), pp. 69 ff. For the incidence of the hiatus in the writings of Julian, especially in those composed hastily, see F. K. Hertlein, *Hermes*, VIII (1874), p. 171. Cf. also M. Hack, *Yavneh*, II (1940), pp. 125 f. (in Hebrew), against Vogt, *op. cit.* (supra, n. 5), p. 65.

Christian rule in the decades following the death of Julian and presumably interested in obtaining the abolition of the tax levied by the Jewish Patriarch (see commentary ad loc.),[12] *should want to attribute his forgery to Julian the "apostate". The suggestion of Vogt that the letter was produced in order to influence the* praefectus orientis *Aurelianus, who was a pagan and an adherent of Neoplatonism, and thus one to whom the memory of Julian was dear, is ingenious but rather far-fetched.*[13]

There is no certainty that the letter mentioning Julian's plan to rebuild the Temple (No. 486b) actually preceded the letter discussed previously. Avi-Yonah has suggested that it should be regarded as part of a declaration issued by Julian to the Babylonian Jews on the eve of the Persian campaign.[14] *However, it could be another of the letters written by him to the Jews of the Roman empire, like the one he sent to the "Community of the Jews" at a somewhat earlier date. There is no doubt that the letter about the Temple also belongs to the last stages of Julian's activity, as Lydus expressly states that it was composed* ὅτε πρὸς Πέρσας ἐστρατεύετο. *We should not stress as significant the differences between the use here of the present tense in* ἀναγείρω *and of the future in the other letter for the purpose of their relative dating.*[15]

It is remarkable that the whole range of talmudic and midrashic literature maintains an almost complete silence both over Julian's attempt to restore the Temple at Jerusalem and over the Jewish response to the call of the new Cyrus. Nor does Ammianus Marcellinus, the only pagan writer to relate the events, refer to the Jewish reaction to the emperor's plan. It is only Christian writers like Gregory of Nazianzus and Jerome, and the ecclesiastical historians Theodoret, Sozomenus and Socrates, who show that the imperial policy concerning the Jews gained enthusiastic acceptance on their part and readiness to undertake heavy expenses for the rebuilding of the Temple.

---

12 For the view that the letter was composed by Jews who wanted to influence the patriarchs to give up the tax, at a date between 392 and 399 C.E., see L. Lucas, *Zur Geschichte der Juden im vierten Jahrhundert*, Berlin 1910, p. 53, n. 3.

13 See Vogt, *op. cit.* (supra, n. 5), p. 68.

14 See Avi-Yonah, *Geschichte der Juden im Zeitalter des Talmud, op. cit.* (supra, n. 5), p. 203.

15 There is an allusion to a letter that Julian addressed to the city of Tiberias; cf. Stephanus Byzantius, s. v. Τιβεριάς. However the occasion on which Julian wrote it is not known. See No. 486d and the commentary *ad loc.*

It stands to reason that the failure of Julian's plan made the Jews unwilling to dwell overmuch on any cooperation with him, and strengthened their misgivings as to the feasibility of the restoration of the Temple by a Gentile, although the Persian king might serve as a precedent. Apparently R. Aḥa, one of the contemporary amoraim, held in the time of Julian the opinion that the third temple would be restored before the advent of the Messiah of the Davidic house,[16] and thus approved the imperial initiative.[17] However, after the failure and ensuing disappointment, R. Aḥa himself seems to have repented of his former opinion and thought that what had happened was a disgrace. R. Aḥa's reversal of opinion is reflected in the Midrash, where we read in Qohelet Rabba, *ix : 10:* ברוך שהעביר חרפתו של לוליאנוס (*"blessed be He who removed the shame of Lulianus" as in the reading of the* editio princeps, *not "Lulianus and Pappus"). Lulianus seems to stand here for Julianus.*[18]

There is another allusion to Julian in the Jewish sources, in TP Nedarim, *iii, 37d:* 'והא לוליינוס מלכא כד נחת לתמן נחתון עימיה מאה כ ריבוון (*"When the Emperor Lulianus came down to Babylonia there came down with him one hundred and twenty myriads").*[19]

Bibliography

S. A. Naber, *Mnemosyne*, NS, XI (1883), pp. 387 ff.; G. (W.) Schwarz, *De Vita et Scriptis Iuliani Imperatoris*, Bonn 1888, p. 29; M. Adler, *JQR*, V (1893), pp. 591 ff.; Linsenmayer, pp. 266 f.; J. Geffcken, *Zwei griechische Apologeten*, Leipzig–Berlin 1907, pp. 304 ff.; H. Graetz, *Geschichte der Juden*, IV⁴, Leipzig 1908, pp. 457 ff.; L. Lucas, *Zur Geschichte der Juden im vierten Jahrhundert*, Berlin 1910, p. 53, n. 3; P. Allard, *Iulien l'Apostat*, III³, Paris 1910, pp. 130 ff.; J. Geffcken, *Kaiser Julianus*, Leipzig 1914, pp. 110 ff.; Juster, I, pp. 159 f.; E. v. Borries, PW, X, pp. 88 f.; W. Ensslin, *Klio*, XVIII (1923), p. 119, n. 9, pp. 189 f.; P. Regazzoni, *Didaskaleion*, VI (1928), fasc. III, pp. 1 ff.; J. Bidez, *La vie de l'empereur Julien*, Paris 1930, pp. 305 ff.; P. de Labriolle, *La réaction païenne*, Paris 1934, pp. 369 ff.; H. Zucker, *Studien zur jüdischen Selbstverwaltung im Altertum*, Berlin 1936, pp. 169 ff.; J. Vogt,

16 See *TP Ma'aser Sheni*, v, 56a.
17 See W. Bacher, *JQR*, X (1898), p. 169; idem, *Die Agada der palästinensischen Amoräer*, III, Strasbourg 1899, pp. 111 f.
18 See S. Lieberman, *Annuaire de l'institut de philologie et d'histoire orientales et slaves*, VII (1939–1944), pp. 412 ff.; idem, *JQR*, XXXVI (1945/6), pp. 243 ff.
19 See L. Zunz, *Die gottesdienstlichen Vorträge der Juden*², Frankfort on the Main 1892, p. 56; Lieberman, *Annuaire*, op. cit. (supra, n. 18), pp. 435 ff.

Kaiser Julian und das Judentum, Leipzig 1939, pp. 34 ff.; M. Hack, *Yavneh*, II (1940), pp. 118 ff. (in Hebrew); J. (H.) Lewy, *Zion*, VI (1940/1), pp. 1 ff. (in Hebrew) = *Studies in Jewish Hellenism*, Jerusalem 1960, pp. 221 ff.; F. M. Abel, *Histoire de la Palestine*, II, Paris 1952, pp. 282 ff.; G. Negri, *L'imperatore Giuliano l'Apostata⁵*, Milan–Varese 1954, pp. 182 ff.; E. E. Urbach, *Molad*, XIX (1961), pp. 372 ff. (in Hebrew); W. den Boer, *Vigiliae Christianae*, XVI (1962), pp. 186 ff.; M. Avi-Yonah, *Geschichte der Juden im Zeitalter des Talmud*, Berlin 1962, pp. 188 ff.; Simon, pp. 139 ff.; H. Mantel, *Studies in the History of the Sanhedrin*, Cambridge (Mass.) 1965, pp. 196, 239; Gager, pp. 101 ff.; W. Speyer, *Die literarische Fälschung im heidnischen und christlichen Altertum*, Munich 1971, p. 308, n. 2; R. Browning, *The Emperor Julian*, London 1975, pp. 149, 176; S. P. Brock, *PEQ*, CVIII (1976), pp. 103 ff.; G. W. Bowersock, in: P. Ducrey (ed.), *Gibbon et Rome à la lumière de l'historiographie moderne*, Geneva 1977, pp. 206 f.; idem, *Julian the Apostate*, London 1978, pp. 120 ff.

(42E) Μικρὸν δὲ ἀναλαβεῖν ἄξιον, ὅθεν ἡμῖν ἥκει καὶ ὅπως ἔννοια
θεοῦ τὸ πρῶτον, εἶτα παραθεῖναι τὰ παρὰ τοῖς Ἕλλησι καὶ παρὰ τοῖς
Ἑβραίοις ὑπὲρ *(43A)* τοῦ θείου λεγόμενα, καὶ μετὰ τοῦτο ἐπα-
νερέσθαι τοὺς οὔτε Ἕλληνας οὔτε Ἰουδαίους, ἀλλὰ τῆς Γαλιλαίων
5 ὄντας αἱρέσεως, ἀνθ' ὅτου πρὸ τῶν ἡμετέρων εἵλοντο τὰ παρ' ἐκείνοις,
καὶ ἐπὶ τούτῳ τί δή ποτε μηδ' ἐκείνοις ἐμμένουσιν, ἀλλὰ κἀκείνων
ἀποστάντες ἰδίαν ὁδὸν ἐτράποντο. ὁμολογήσαντες μὲν οὐδὲν τῶν
καλῶν οὐδὲ τῶν σπουδαίων οὔτε τῶν παρ' ἡμῖν τοῖς Ἕλλησιν οὔτε τῶν
παρὰ τοῖς ἀπὸ Μωυσέως Ἑβραίοις, ἀπ' ἀμφοῖν δὲ τὰς παραπεπηγυίας
10 ⟨τούτοις⟩ τοῖς ἔθνεσιν ὥσπερ τινὰς Κῆρας δρεπό*(43B)*μενοι, τὴν
ἀθεότητα μὲν ἐκ τῆς Ἰουδαϊκῆς ῥαδιουργίας, φαῦλον δὲ καὶ ἐπι-
σεσυρμένον βίον ἐκ τῆς παρ' ἡμῖν ῥᾳθυμίας καὶ χυδαιότητος, τοῦτο
τὴν ἀρίστην θεοσέβειαν ἠθέλησαν ὀνομάζεσθαι ... *(69B)* τί δεῖ μοι
καλεῖν Ἕλληνας καὶ Ἑβραίους ἐνταῦθα μάρτυρας; οὐδεὶς ἔστιν, ὃς
15 οὐκ ἀνατείνει μὲν εἰς οὐρανὸν τὰς χεῖρας εὐχόμενος, ὀμνύων ⟨δὲ⟩ θεὸν
ἤτοι θεούς, ἔννοιαν ὅλως τοῦ θείου λαμβάνων, ἐκεῖσε φέρεται ...
(44A) Οὐκοῦν Ἕλληνες μὲν τοὺς μύθους ἔπλασαν ὑπὲρ τῶν θεῶν
ἀπίστους καὶ τερατώδεις, καταπιεῖν γὰρ ἔφασαν τὸν Κρόνον τοὺς
παῖδας ⟨καὶ⟩ εἶτ' *(44B)* αὖθις ἐμέσαι. καὶ γάμους ἤδη παρανόμους·
20 μητρὶ γὰρ ὁ Ζεὺς ἐμίχθη. καὶ παιδοποιησάμενος ἐξ αὐτῆς ἔγημε μὲν
αὐτὸς τὴν αὐτοῦ θυγατέρα, μᾶλλον δὲ οὐδὲ ἔγημεν [αὐτὸς τὴν αὐτοῦ
θυγατέρα], ἀλλὰ μιχθεὶς ἁπλῶς ἄλλῳ παραδέδωκεν αὐτήν. εἶτα οἱ
Διονύσου σπαραγμοὶ καὶ μελῶν κολλήσεις. τοιαῦτα οἱ μῦθοι τῶν
Ἑλλήνων φασίν· *(75A)* τούτοις παράβαλλε τὴν Ἰουδαϊκὴν διδα-
25 σκαλίαν, καὶ τὸν φυτευόμενον ὑπὸ τοῦ θεοῦ παράδεισον καὶ τὸν
ὑπ' αὐτοῦ πλαττόμενον Ἀδάμ, εἶτα τὴν γινομένην αὐτῷ γυναῖκα.
λέγει γὰρ ὁ θεός ⟨Gen. ii:18⟩ «οὐ καλὸν εἶναι τὸν ἄνθρωπον μόνον·
ποιήσωμεν αὐτῷ βοηθὸν κατ' αὐτόν», πρὸς οὐδὲν μὲν αὐτῷ τῶν ὅλων
βοηθήσασαν, ἐξαπατήσασαν δὲ καὶ γενομένην παραίτιον αὐτῷ τε
30 ἐκείνῳ καὶ ἑαυτῇ τοῦ πεσεῖν ἔξω τῆς *(75B)* τοῦ παραδείσου τρυφῆς.
ταῦτα γάρ ἐστι μυθώδη παντελῶς. ἐπεὶ πῶς εὔλογον ἀγνοεῖν τὸν θεόν,

---

3–4 ἐπανέρχεσθαι M 　　 9 Μωυσέως Neumann 　　　 μωσέως MV Ψ
10 ⟨τούτοις⟩ Neumann 　 13 ἠθέλησαν ὀνομάζεσθαι Neumann 　 ὀνομάζεσθαι
ἠθέλησαν MΨ 　　 ὀνομαθέσθαι ἠθέλησαν V 　　　 15 ⟨δὲ⟩ Neumann
　 19 ⟨καὶ⟩ εἶτ' Neumann 　　 20–21 ἔγημε...μᾶλλον δὲ οὐδὲ om. VΨ
　　 21 αὐτοῦ Neumann 　　 αὐτοῦ M 　 / 　 21–22 αὐτὸς τὴν αὐτοῦ
θυγατέρα secl. Neumann 　　 23 τοιαῦτα] ταῦτα V 　　 26 γενομένην V
　　　　 29 παραιτίαν V

ὅτι τὸ γινόμενον ὑπ' αὐτοῦ πρὸς βοήθειαν οὐ πρὸς καλοῦ μᾶλλον, ἀλλὰ πρὸς κακοῦ τῷ λαβόντι γενήσεται; *(86A)* τὸν γὰρ ὄφιν τὸν διαλεγόμενον πρὸς τὴν Εὔαν ποδαπῇ τινι χρῆσθαι φήσομεν διαλέκτῳ;
35 ἆρα ἀνθρωπείᾳ; καὶ τί διαφέρει τῶν παρὰ τοῖς Ἕλλησι πεπλασμένων μύθων τὰ τοιαῦτα; *(89A)* τὸ δὲ καὶ τὸν θεὸν ἀπαγορεύειν τὴν διάγνωσιν καλοῦ τε καὶ φαύλου τοῖς ὑπ' αὐτοῦ πλασθεῖσιν ἀνθρώποις ἆρ' οὐχ ὑπερβολὴν ἀτοπίας ἔχει; τί γὰρ ἂν ἠλιθιώτερον γένοιτο τοῦ μὴ δυναμένου διαγινώσκειν καλὸν καὶ πονηρόν; δῆλον γάρ, ὅτι τὰ μὲν οὐ
40 φεύξεται, λέγω δὲ τὰ κακά, τὰ δὲ οὐ μεταδιώξει, λέγω δὲ τὰ καλά. κεφάλαιον δέ, φρονήσεως ἀπηγόρευσεν ὁ θεὸς ἀνθρώπῳ γεύσασθαι, ἧς οὐδὲν ἂν εἴη *(89B)* τιμιώτερον αὐτῷ· ὅτι γὰρ ἡ τοῦ καλοῦ καὶ τοῦ χείρονος διάγνωσις οἰκεῖόν ἐστιν ἔργον φρονήσεως, πρόδηλόν ἐστί που καὶ τοῖς ἀνοήτοις· *(93D)* ὥστε τὸν ὄφιν εὐεργέτην μᾶλλον, ἀλλ' οὐχὶ
45 λυμεῶνα τῆς ἀνθρωπίνης γενέσεως εἶναι. *(93E)* ἐπὶ τούτοις ὁ θεὸς δεῖ λέγεσθαι βάσκανος. ἐπειδὴ γὰρ εἶδε μετασχόντα τῆς φρονήσεως τὸν ἄνθρωπον, ἵνα μή, φησί, γεύσηται τοῦ ξύλου τῆς ζωῆς, ἐξέβαλεν αὐτὸν τοῦ παραδείσου διαρρήδην εἰπών ⟨Gen. iii:22⟩ «ἰδού, Ἀδὰμ γέγονεν ὡς εἷς ἐξ ἡμῶν τοῦ γινώσκειν καλὸν καὶ πονηρόν. καὶ νῦν μήποτε ἐκτείνῃ
50 τὴν χεῖρα καὶ λάβῃ ἀπὸ τοῦ ξύλου τῆς ζωῆς καὶ φάγῃ καὶ ζήσεται εἰς τὸν αἰῶνα.» τούτων τοίνυν ἕκαστον *(94A)* εἰ μὴ μῦθος ἔχων θεωρίαν ἀπόρρητον εἴη, ὅπερ ἐγὼ νενόμικα, πολλῆς γέμουσιν οἱ λόγοι περὶ τοῦ θεοῦ βλασφημίας. τὸ γὰρ ἀγνοῆσαι μέν, ὡς ἡ γινομένη βοηθὸς αἰτία τοῦ πτώματος ἔσται καὶ τὸ ἀπαγορεῦσαι καλοῦ καὶ πονηροῦ γνῶσιν, ὃ
55 μόνον ἔοικε συνέχειν τὸν νοῦν τὸν ἀνθρώπινον, καὶ προσέτι τὸ ζηλοτυπῆσαι, μὴ ⟨τοῦ ξύλου⟩ τῆς ζωῆς μεταλαβὼν ⟨ἄνθρωπος⟩ ἀθάνατος ἐκ θνητοῦ γένηται, φθονεροῦ καὶ βασκάνου λίαν ἐστίν.
(96C) Ὑπὲρ δὲ ὧν ἐκεῖνοί τε ἀληθῶς [ὑπὲρ θεοῦ] δοξάζουσιν ἡμῖν τε ἐξ ἀρχῆς οἱ πατέρες παρέδοσαν, ὁ μὲν ἡμέτερος ἔχει λόγος ὡδὶ τὸν
60 προσεχῆ τοῦ κόσμου τούτου δημιουργὸν ... ὑπὲρ γὰρ ⟨θεῶν⟩ τῶν ἀνωτέρω τούτου Μωσῆς μὲν εἴρηκεν οὐδὲν ὅλως, ὅς γε οὐδὲ ὑπὲρ τῆς τῶν ἀγγέλων ἐτόλμησέ τι φύ*(96D)*σεως. ἀλλ' ὅτι μὲν λειτουργοῦσι τῷ θεῷ πολλαχῶς καὶ πολλάκις εἶπεν, εἴτε δὲ γεγονότες, εἴτε ἀγένητοι, εἴτε ὑπ' ἄλλου μὲν γεγονότες, ἄλλῳ δὲ λειτουργεῖν τεταγμένοι, εἴτε
65 ἄλλως πως, οὐδαμόθεν διώρισται. περὶ δὲ οὐρανοῦ καὶ γῆς καὶ τῶν ἐν

42 αὐτῷ Neumann   ἀνθρώπῳ MV   45–46 δεῖ λέγεσθαι Neumann
λέγεται **MV**   49 ἐκτείνει V   51–52 μῦθος εἴη ἔχων θεωρίαν ἀπόρρητον M
        54 παραπτώματος V   55 συνέχειν ἔοικε V / τὸν νοῦν τὸν
        ἀνθρώπινον Neumann   τὸν ἀνθρώπινον βίον V   τὸν βίον τὸν
ἀνθρώπινον M   56 ⟨τοῦ ξύλου⟩ Neumann / ⟨ἄνθρωπος⟩ Neumann
58 ὑπὲρ θεοῦ secl. Neumann   59 ὡδὶ] οὐδὲ Neumann   61 ὅλως οὐδὲν V
        63 πολλαχῶς Neumann   πολλαχοῦ MV

514

αὐτῇ [καὶ] τίνα τρόπον διεκοσμήθη διέξεισι. καὶ τὰ μέν φησι κελεῦσαι
τὸν θεὸν γενέσθαι, ὥσπερ [ἡμέραν καὶ] φῶς καὶ στερέωμα, τὰ δὲ
ποιῆσαι, ὥσπερ οὐρανὸν καὶ γῆν, ἥλιόν τε καὶ σελήνην, τὰ δὲ ὄντα,
(96E) κρυπτόμενα δὲ τέως, διακρῖναι, καθάπερ ὕδωρ, οἶμαι, καὶ τὴν
70 ξηράν. πρὸς τούτοις δὲ οὐδὲ περὶ γενέσεως ἢ περὶ ποιήσεως τοῦ
πνεύματος εἰπεῖν ἐτόλμησεν, ἀλλὰ μόνον «καὶ πνεῦμα θεοῦ
ἐπεφέρετο ἐπάνω τοῦ ὕδατος»· πότερον δὲ ἀγένητόν ἐστιν ἢ γέγονεν,
οὐδὲν διασαφεῖ.

(49A) Ἐνταῦθα παραβάλωμεν, εἰ βούλεσθε, τὴν Πλάτωνος φωνήν. τί
75 τοίνυν οὗτος ὑπὲρ τοῦ δημιουργοῦ λέγει καὶ τίνας περιτίθησιν αὐτῷ
φωνὰς ἐν τῇ κοσμογενείᾳ σκόπησον, ἵνα τὴν Πλάτωνος καὶ Μωυσέως
κοσμογένειαν ἀντιπαραβάλωμεν ἀλλήλαις. οὕτω γὰρ ἂν φανείη, τίς ὁ
κρείττων καὶ τίς ἄξιος τοῦ θεοῦ μᾶλλον, ἆρ' ὁ τοῖς εἰδώλοις
λελατρευκὼς Πλάτων ἢ περὶ οὗ φησιν ἡ γραφή, ὅτι στόμα κατὰ *(49B)*
80 στόμα ὁ θεὸς ἐλάλησεν αὐτῷ ⟨Num. xii:8⟩· «Ἐν ἀρχῇ ἐποίησεν ὁ θεὸς
τὸν οὐρανὸν καὶ τὴν γῆν ...» ⟨Gen. i:1⟩. *(49D)* Ἐν δὴ τούτοις ⟨Μωυσῆς⟩
οὔτε τὴν ἄβυσσον πεποιῆσθαί φησιν ὑπὸ τοῦ θεοῦ οὔτε τὸ σκότος οὔτε
τὸ ὕδωρ· καίτοι χρῆν δήπουθεν εἰπόντα περὶ τοῦ φωτός, ὅτι
προστάξαντος θεοῦ γέγονεν, εἰπεῖν ἔτι καὶ περὶ τῆς νυκτὸς καὶ περὶ
85 τῆς ἀβύσσου καὶ περὶ τοῦ ὕδατος. ὁ δὲ οὐδὲν εἶπεν ὡς περὶ γεγονότων
ὅλως, καίτοι πολλάκις ἐπιμνησθεὶς αὐτῶν. πρὸς τούτοις οὔτε τῆς τῶν
ἀγγέλων μέμνηται γενέσεως ἢ ποιήσεως οὐδ' ὅντινα τρόπον
παρήχθησαν, *(49E)* ἀλλὰ τῶν περὶ τὸν οὐρανὸν μόνον καὶ περὶ τὴν
γῆν σκηνωμάτων, ὡς εἶναι τὸν θεὸν κατὰ τὸν Μωυσέα ἀσωμάτων μὲν
90 οὐδενὸς ποιητήν, ὕλης δὲ ὑποκειμένης κοσμήτορα. τὸ γὰρ ⟨Gen. i:2⟩
«ἡ δὲ γῆ ἦν ἀόρατος καὶ ἀκατασκεύαστος» οὐδὲν ἕτερόν ἐστιν ἢ τὴν
μὲν ὑγρὰν καὶ ξηρὰν οὐσίαν ὕλην ποιοῦντος, κοσμήτορα δὲ αὐτῆς τὸν
θεὸν εἰσάγοντος. Ὅ γε μὴν Πλάτων ἄκουε περὶ τοῦ κόσμου τί
φη*(57B)*σιν ⟨Timaeus 28B–C⟩ «Ὁ δὴ πᾶς οὐρανὸς ἢ κόσμος *(57C)* ἢ
95 καὶ ἄλλο, ὅ τί ποτε ὀνομαζόμενος μάλιστα ἂν δέχοιτο, τοῦτο ἡμῖν
ὠνομάσθω — πότερον ἦν ἀεί, γενέσεως ἀρχὴν ἔχων οὐδεμίαν, ἢ
γέγονεν, ἀπ' ἀρχῆς τινος ἀρξάμενος; γέγονεν· ὁρατὸς γὰρ ἁπτός τέ
ἐστι καὶ σῶμα ἔχων. πάντα δὲ τοιαῦτα αἰσθητά, ⟨τὰ δὲ αἰσθητά⟩, δόξῃ
περιληπτὰ μετὰ αἰσθήσεως, ⟨γιγνόμενα καὶ γεννητὰ ἐφάνη⟩ ... οὕτως
100 οὖν κατὰ τὸν λόγον τὸν εἰκότα δεῖ λέγειν τόνδε τὸν κόσμον ζῷον
ἔμψυχον ἔννουν τε τῇ ἀληθείᾳ διὰ τὴν τοῦ θεοῦ γενέσθαι *(57D)*
πρόνοιαν».

66 καὶ secl. Neumann   67 ἡμέραν καὶ secl. Neumann
81 ⟨Μωυσῆς⟩ Neumann   82 πεποιῆσθαί φησιν Neumann
φησι πεποιῆσθαι MVΨ

(57E) Ἔν δὲ ἑνὶ παραβάλωμεν μόνον· τίνα καὶ ποδαπὴν ποιεῖται δημηγορίαν ὁ θεὸς ὁ παρὰ Μωυσῇ καὶ ποδαπὴν ὁ παρὰ Πλάτωνι; (58A) ⟨Gen. i:26⟩ «Καὶ εἶπεν ὁ θεός· ποιήσωμεν ἄνθρωπον κατ᾽ εἰκόνα ἡμετέραν καὶ καθ᾽ ὁμοίωσιν» ...

(58B) Ἄκουε δὴ οὖν καὶ τῆς Πλατωνικῆς δημηγορίας, ἣν τῷ τῶν ὅλων περιτίθησι δημιουργῷ ⟨Timaeus 41A–C⟩ «θεοὶ θεῶν, ὧν ἐγὼ δημιουργὸς πατήρ τε ἔργων ἄλυτα ἔσται ἐμοῦ γε ἐθέλοντος» ... (99D) Οὐκοῦν ἐπειδήπερ οὐδὲ περὶ τοῦ προσεχοῦς τοῦ κόσμου τούτου δημιουργοῦ πάντα διειλεγμένος Μωυσῆς φαίνεται, τήν τε Ἑβραίων καὶ τὴν τῶν ἡμετέρων πατέρων δόξαν ὑπὲρ ἐθνῶν τούτων ἄν(99E)τιπαραθῶμεν ἀλλήλαις.

Ὁ Μωυσῆς φησι τὸν τοῦ κόσμου δημιουργὸν ἐκλέξασθαι τὸ τῶν Ἑβραίων ἔθνος καὶ προσέχειν ἐκείνῳ μόνῳ καὶ ἐκείνου φροντίσαι καὶ δίδωσιν αὐτῷ τὴν ἐπιμέλειαν αὐτοῦ μόνου. τῶν δὲ ἄλλων ἐθνῶν, ὅπως ἢ ὑφ᾽ οἷστισι διοικοῦνται θεοῖς, οὐδ᾽ ἡντινοῦν μνείαν πεποίηται· πλὴν εἰ μή τις ἐκεῖνα συγχωρήσειεν, ὅτι τὸν ἥλιον αὐτοῖς καὶ τὴν σελήνην ἀπένειμεν ⟨Deut. iv:19⟩. ἀλλ᾽ ὑπὲρ μὲν τούτων καὶ μικρὸν ὕστερον.

(100A) πλὴν ὅτι τοῦ Ἰσραὴλ αὐτὸν μόνου θεὸν καὶ τῆς Ἰουδαίας καὶ τούτους ἐκλεκτούς φησιν [εἶναι] αὐτός τε καὶ οἱ μετ᾽ ἐκεῖνον προφῆται καὶ Ἰησοῦς ὁ Ναζωραῖος ἐπιδείξω, ἀλλὰ καὶ τὸν πάντας πανταχοῦ τοὺς πώποτε γόητας καὶ ἀπατεῶνας ὑπερβαλλόμενον Παῦλον. ἀκούετε δὲ τῶν λέξεων αὐτῶν, ⟨καὶ⟩ πρῶτον μὲν τῶν Μωυσέως ⟨Exod. iv:22 f.⟩ «σὺ δὲ ἐρεῖς τῷ Φαραώ· υἱὸς πρωτότοκός μου Ἰσραήλ. εἶπον δέ· ἐξαπόστειλον τὸν λαόν μου, ἵνα μοι λατρεύσῃ. σὺ δὲ οὐκ ἐβούλου ἐξαποστεῖ(100B)λαι αὐτόν». καὶ μικρὸν ὕστερον ⟨Exod. v:3⟩ «καὶ λέγουσιν αὐτῷ· ὁ θεὸς τῶν Ἑβραίων προσκέκληται ἡμᾶς. πορευσόμεθα οὖν εἰς τὴν ἔρημον ὁδὸν ἡμερῶν τριῶν, ὅπως θύσωμεν κυρίῳ τῷ θεῷ ἡμῶν.» καὶ μετ᾽ ὀλίγα πάλιν ὁμοίως ⟨Exod. vii:16⟩ «κύριος ὁ θεὸς τῶν Ἑβραίων ἐξαπέσταλκέ με πρὸς σὲ λέγων ἐξαπόστειλον τὸν λαόν μου, ἵνα μοι λατρεύσωσιν ἐν τῇ ἐρήμῳ» ... Ἀλλ᾽ ὅτι μὲν Ἰουδαίων μόνων ἐμέ(106A)λησε τῷ θεῷ τὸ ἐξ ἀρχῆς καὶ κλῆρος αὐτοῦ γέγονεν οὗτος (106B) ἐξαίρετος, οὐ Μωυσῆς μόνον καὶ Ἰησοῦς, ἀλλὰ καὶ Παῦλος εἰρηκὼς φαίνεται· καίτοι τοῦτο ἄξιον θαυμάσαι περὶ τοῦ Παύλου. πρὸς γὰρ τύχας, ὥσπερ ⟨χρῶτα⟩ οἱ πολύποδες πρὸς τὰς πέτρας, ἀλλάττει τὰ περὶ θεοῦ δόγματα, ποτὲ μὲν Ἰουδαίους μόνον τὴν τοῦ θεοῦ κληρονομίαν εἶναι διατεινόμενος, πάλιν δὲ τοὺς Ἕλληνας ἀναπείθων αὐτῷ προστίθεσθαι, λέγων ⟨Rom. iii:29⟩

104 δημηγορίαν Neumann   δημιευργίαν ΜΥΨ   112 ἐθνῶν Neumann
    αὐτῶν MV   114 μωσῆς MV   120 αὐτὸν Neumann
      αὐτοῦ MV   121 εἶναι secl. Neumann

140 «μὴ Ἰουδαίων ὁ θεὸς μόνον, ἀλλὰ καὶ ἐθνῶν· ναὶ καὶ ἐθνῶν.» δίκαιον
οὖν ἐρέσθαι τὸν (106C) Παῦλον, εἰ μὴ τῶν Ἰουδαίων ἦν ὁ θεὸς μόνον,
ἀλλὰ καὶ τῶν ἐθνῶν, τοῦ χάριν πολὺ μὲν εἰς τοὺς Ἰουδαίους ἔπεμπε τὸ
προφητικὸν χάρισμα καὶ τὸν Μωυσέα καὶ τὸ χρῖσμα καὶ τοὺς
προφήτας καὶ τὸν νόμον καὶ τὰ παράδοξα καὶ τὰ τεράστια τῶν μύθων;
145 ἀκούεις γὰρ αὐτῶν βοώντων ⟨Ps. lxxvii:25⟩ «ἄρτον ἀγγέλων ἔφαγεν
ἄνθρωπος». ἐπὶ τέλους δὲ καὶ τὸν Ἰησοῦν ἔπεμψεν ἐκείνοις, ἡμῖν δὲ
οὐ προφήτην, οὐ χρῖσμα, οὐ διδάσκαλον, οὐ κήρυκα περὶ τῆς
μελλούσης ὀψέ ποτε γοῦν ἔσεσθαι καὶ εἰς ἡμᾶς ἀπ' αὐτοῦ
φιλανθρω(106D)πίας. ἀλλὰ καὶ περιεῖδεν ἐτῶν μυριάδας, εἰ δὲ ὑμεῖς
150 βούλεσθε, χιλιάδας ἐν ἀγνωσίᾳ τοιαύτῃ τοῖς εἰδώλοις, ὥς φατε,
λατρεύοντας τοὺς ἀπὸ ἀνίσχοντος ἡλίου μέχρι δυομένου καὶ τοὺς ἀπὸ
[μέσων] τῶν ἄρκτων ἄχρι μεσημβρίας ἔξω καὶ μικροῦ γένους οὐδὲ πρὸ
δισχιλίων ὅλων ἐτῶν ἑνὶ μέρει συνοικισθέντος τῆς Παλαιστίνης. εἰ γὰρ
πάντων ἡμῶν ἐστι θεὸς καὶ πάντων δημιουργὸς ὁμοίως, τί περιεῖδεν
155 ἡμᾶς; (100C) προσήκει ⟨τοίνυν⟩ τὸν τῶν Ἑβραίων θεὸν οὐχὶ δὴ παντὸς
κόσμου γενεσιουργὸν ὑπάρχειν οἴεσθαι καὶ κατεξουσιάζειν τῶν ὅλων,
συνεστάλθαι δέ, ὡς ἔφην, καὶ πεπερασμένην ἔχοντα τὴν ἀρχὴν
ἀναμὶξ τοῖς ἄλλοις νοεῖσθαι θεοῖς. (106D) ἔτι (106E) προσέξομεν
ὑμῖν, ὅτι τὸν τῶν ὅλων θεὸν ἄχρι ψιλῆς γοῦν ἐννοίας ὑμεῖς ἢ τῆς
160 ὑμετέρας τις ἐφαντάσθη ῥίζης; οὐ μερικὰ πάντα ταῦτά ἐστι; θεὸς
ζηλωτής· ζηλοῖ γὰρ διὰ τί καὶ [θεὸς] ἁμαρτίας ἐκδικῶν πατέρων ἐπὶ
τέκνα; ⟨Exod. xx:5⟩ ...
(134D) Ὁ μὲν γὰρ Μωυσῆς αἰτίαν ἀποδέδωκε κομιδῇ μυθώδη τῆς
περὶ τὰς διαλέκτους ἀνομοιότητος. ἔφη γὰρ τοὺς υἱοὺς τῶν ἀνθρώπων
165 συνελθόντας πόλιν ἐθέλειν οἰκοδομεῖν καὶ πύργον ἐν αὐτῇ
μέ(134E)γαν, φάναι δὲ τὸν θεόν, ὅτι χρὴ κατελθεῖν καὶ τὰς διαλέκτους
αὐτῶν συγχέαι. καὶ ὅπως μή τίς με νομίσῃ ταῦτα συκοφαντεῖν, καὶ ἐκ
τῶν Μωυσέως ἀναγνωσόμεθα τὰ ἐφεξῆς ⟨Gen. xi:4 ff.⟩ «καὶ εἶπον·
δεῦτε, οἰκοδομήσωμεν ἑαυτοῖς πόλιν καὶ πύργον» ... (135A) εἶτα
170 τούτοις ἀξιοῦτε πιστεύειν ἡμᾶς, ἀπιστεῖτε δὲ ὑμεῖς τοῖς ὑφ' Ὁμήρου
λεγομένοις ὑπὲρ τῶν Ἀλωαδῶν, ὡς ἄρα τρία ἐπ' ἀλλήλοις (135B) ὄρη
θεῖναι διενοοῦντο, «ἵν' οὐρανὸς ἀμβατὸς εἴη» ⟨Odyssea, XI, 316⟩. φημὶ
μὲν γὰρ ἐγὼ καὶ τοῦτο παραπλησίως ἐκείνῳ μυθῶδες εἶναι. ὑμεῖς δέ,
ἀποδεχόμενοι τὸ πρότερον, ἀνθ' ὅτου πρὸς θεῶν ἀποδοκιμάζετε τὸν

142 ἔπεμπε Neumann ex Theod. Mops.   ἔπεμψε MV   143 χάρισμα
Theod. Mops.   πνεῦμα MV   145 γὰρ Theod. Mops.   τε MV
146 τέλους Theod. Mops.   τέλει MV   152 μέσων secl. Neumann
154 τί περιεῖδεν Neumann   ἐστιν, οὐ περιεῖδεν M   εἰς τί περιεῖδεν V
155 τοίνυν add. Neumann   158 ὅλοις M   161 θεὸς secl. Neumann
171 ἀλωάδων MV

175 Ὁμήρου μῦθον; ἐκεῖνο γὰρ οἶμαι δεῖν σιωπᾶν πρὸς ἄνδρας ἀμαθεῖς,
ὅτι κἂν μιᾷ φωνῇ καὶ γλώσσῃ πάντες οἱ κατὰ πᾶσαν τὴν οἰκουμένην
ἄνθρωποι χρήσωνται, πύργον οἰκοδομεῖν οὐ δυνήσονται πρὸς τὸν
οὐρανὸν ἀφικνούμενον, κἂν ἐκπλινθεύσωσι τὴν γῆν πᾶσαν· ἀπείρων
γὰρ δεήσει (135C) πλίνθων ἰσομεγεθῶν τῇ γῇ ξυμπάσῃ τῶν
180 δυνησομένων ἄχρι τῶν σελήνης ἐφικέσθαι κύκλων. ὑποκείσθω γὰρ
πάντας μὲν ἀνθρώπους συνεληλυθέναι γλώσσῃ καὶ φωνῇ μίᾳ
κεχρημένους, πᾶσαν δὲ ἐκπλινθεῦσαι τὴν γῆν καὶ ἐκλατομῆσαι, πότε
ἂν μέχρις οὐρανοῦ φθάσειεν, εἰ καὶ λεπτότερον ἀρπεδόνος
ἐκμηρυομένων αὐτῶν ἐκταθείη; τοῦτον οὖν οὕτω φανερὸν ὄντα τὸν
185 μῦθον ἀληθῆ νενομικότες καὶ περὶ τοῦ θεοῦ δοξάζοντες, ὅτι
πεφόβηται τῶν ἀνθρώπων τὴν μιαιφονίαν τούτου τε (135D) χάριν
⟨καταπεφοίτηκεν⟩ αὐτῶν συγχέαι τὰς διαλέκτους, ἔτι τολμᾶτε θεοῦ
γνῶσιν αὐχεῖν;
(137E) Ἐπάνειμι δὲ αὖθις πρὸς ἐκεῖνο, τὰς μὲν γὰρ διαλέκτους ὅπως ὁ
190 θεὸς συνέχεεν. εἴρηκεν ὁ Μωυσῆς τὴν μὲν αἰτίαν, ὅτι φοβηθεὶς μή τι
κατ' αὐτοῦ πράξωσι προσβατὸν ἑαυτοῖς τὸν οὐρανὸν κατεργασάμενοι,
ὁμόγλωττοι ὄντες καὶ ὁμόφρο(138A)νες ἀλλήλοις· τὸ δὲ πρᾶγμα ὅπως
ἐποίησεν ⟨οὐδαμῶς, ἀλλὰ μόνον⟩, ὅτι κατελθὼν ἐξ οὐρανοῦ μὴ
δυνάμενος ἄνωθεν αὐτὸ ποιεῖν, ὡς ἔοικεν, εἰ μὴ κατῆλθεν ἐπὶ τῆς
195 γῆς. ὑπὲρ δὲ τῆς κατὰ τὰ ἤθη καὶ τὰ νόμιμα διαφορᾶς οὔτε Μωυσῆς
οὔτε ἄλλος ἀπεσάφησέ τις. καίτοι τῷ παντὶ μείζων ἐστὶν ἡ περὶ τὰ
νόμιμα καὶ τὰ πολιτικὰ τῶν ἐθνῶν ἐν τοῖς ἀνθρώποις τῆς περὶ τὰς
διαλέκτους διαφορᾶς ... (138C) εἰ τοίνυν τῶν ψυχικῶν ἡμῶν ἀγαθῶν
κατωλιγώρησεν, οὐδὲ τῆς φυσικῆς ἡμῶν κατασκευῆς προνοησάμενος,
200 οὔτε ἡμῖν (138D) ἔπεμψε διδασκάλους ἢ νομοθέτας ὥσπερ τοῖς
Ἑβραίοις κατὰ τὸν Μωυσέα καὶ τοὺς ἐπ' ἐκείνῳ προφήτας, ὑπὲρ τίνος
ἕξομεν αὐτῷ καλῶς εὐχαριστεῖν; (141C) Ἀλλ' ὁρᾶτε, μή ποτε καὶ ἡμῖν
ἔδωκεν ὁ θεὸς οὓς ὑμεῖς ἠγνοήκατε θεούς τε καὶ προστάτας ἀγαθούς,
οὐδὲν ἐλάττονας τοῦ παρὰ τοῖς Ἑβραίοις ἐξ ἀρχῆς τιμωμένου τῆς
205 Ἰουδαίας, ἧσπερ ἐκεῖνος προνοεῖν ἔλαχε μόνης, ὥσπερ ὁ Μωυσῆς ἔφη
καὶ οἱ μετ' ἐκεῖνον ἄχρις ἡμῶν. εἰ δὲ ὁ προσε(141D)χὴς εἴη τοῦ

177 χρήσονται V   178 ἐφικνούμενον Klimek   180 ἰσχύϊ ante ἄχρι M /
τῆς ante σελήνης V   182 χρωμένους V   183 ἄν] οὖν V /
φθάσαιεν M   185 τοῦ om. V   186 τὴν om. V / ὁμοφωνίαν V
187 καταπεφοίτηκεν add. Neumann   191 προσβατὸν ἑαυτοῖς Neumann
    προσβατὸν αὐτοῖς M   ἑαυτοῖς προσβατὸν V
193 ⟨οὐδαμῶς, ἀλλὰ μόνον⟩ Neumann   195 ἤθη Neumann   ἔθη MV
199 οὐδὲ Neumann   οὔτε MV   200 ἔπεμψε Neumann   πέμψας MV
    206 ἄχρις ὑμῶν V

518

κόσμου δημιουργὸς ὁ παρὰ τοῖς Ἑβραίοις τιμώμενος, ἔτι καὶ βέλτιον
ὑπὲρ αὐτοῦ διενοήθημεν ἡμεῖς ἀγαθά τε ἡμῖν ἔδωκεν ἐκείνων μείζονα
τά τε περὶ ψυχὴν καὶ τὰ ἐκτός, ὑπὲρ ὧν ἐροῦμεν ὀλίγου ὕστερον,
210 ἔστειλέ τε καὶ ἐφ᾽ ἡμᾶς νομοθέτας οὐδὲν Μωυσέως χείρονας, εἰ μὴ
τοὺς πολλοὺς μακρῷ κρείττονας ...
(146A) Ἔτι δὲ καὶ ὁ Μωυσῆς ἐπεκάλυπτε τὸ τοιοῦτον εἰδὼς οὐδὲ τὴν
τῶν διαλέκτων σύγχυσιν ἀνατέ(146B)θεικε τῷ θεῷ μόνῳ. φησὶ γὰρ
αὐτὸν οὐ μόνον κατελθεῖν οὐ μὴν οὐδὲ ἕνα συγκατελθεῖν αὐτῷ,
215 πλείονας δέ, καὶ τούτους οἵτινές εἰσιν οὐκ εἶπεν· εὔδηλον δέ, ὅτι
παραπλησίους αὐτῷ τοὺς συγκατιόντας ὑπελάμβανεν. εἰ τοίνυν πρὸς
τὴν σύγχυσιν τῶν διαλέκτων οὐχ ὁ κύριος μόνος, ἀλλὰ καὶ οἱ σὺν αὐτῷ
κατέρχονται, πρόδηλον, ὅτι καὶ πρὸς τὴν σύγχυσιν τῶν ἠθῶν οὐχ ὁ
κύριος μόνος, ἀλλὰ καὶ οἱ σὺν αὐτῷ τὰς διαλέκτους συγχέοντες,
220 εἰκότως ἂν ὑπολαμβάνοιντο ταύτης εἶναι τῆς διαστάσεως αἴτιοι.
(148B) Τί οὖν, ⟨οὐκ⟩ ἐν μακροῖς εἰπεῖν βουλόμενος, τοσαῦτα
ἐπεξῆλθον; ὥς, εἰ μὲν ὁ προσεχὴς εἴη τοῦ κόσμου δημιουργὸς ὁ ὑπὸ
τοῦ Μωυσέως κηρυττόμενος, ἡμεῖς ὑπὲρ αὐτοῦ βελτίους ἔχομεν δόξας
οἱ κοινὸν μὲν ἐκεῖνον ὑπολαμβάνοντες ἁπάντων δεσπότην, ἐθνάρχας
225 δὲ ἄλλους, οἳ τυγχάνουσι μὲν ὑπ᾽ ἐκεῖνον, εἰσὶ δὲ ὥσπερ ὕπαρχοι
βασιλέως, ἕκαστος τὴν ἑαυτοῦ διαφερόντως ἐ(148C)πανορθούμενος
φροντίδα· καὶ οὐ καθίσταμεν αὐτὸν οὐδὲ ἀντιμερίτην τῶν ὑπ᾽ αὐτὸν
θεῶν καθισταμένων. εἰ δὲ μερικόν τινα τιμήσας ἐκεῖνος ἀντιτίθησιν
αὐτῷ τὴν τοῦ παντὸς ἡγεμονίαν, ἄμεινον τὸν τῶν ὅλων θεὸν ἡμῖν
230 πειθομένους ἐπιγνῶναι μετὰ τοῦ μηδὲ ἐκεῖνον ἀγνοῆσαι, ἢ τὸν τοῦ
ἐλαχίστου μέρους εἰληχότα τὴν ἡγεμονίαν ἀντὶ τοῦ πάντων τιμᾶν
δημιουργοῦ.
(152B) Ὁ νόμος ἐστὶν ὁ τοῦ Μωυσέως θαυμαστός, ἡ δεκάλογος ἐκείνη
⟨Exod. xx:14 ff.⟩ «οὐ κλέψεις», «οὐ φονεύσεις», «οὐ ψευδο-
235 μαρτυρήσεις», γεγράφθω δὲ αὐτοῖς ῥήμασιν ἑκάστη τῶν ἐντολῶν, ἅς ὑπ᾽
αὐτοῦ φη(152C)σι γεγράφθαι τοῦ θεοῦ.
«Ἐγὼ εἰμι κύριος ὁ θεός σου ...»
(152D) Ποῖον ἔθνος ἐστί, πρὸς τῶν θεῶν, ἔξω τοῦ «οὐ προσκυνήσεις
θεοῖς ἑτέροις» καὶ τοῦ «μνήσθητι τῆς ἡμέρας τῶν σαββάτων», ὃ μὴ
240 τὰς ἄλλας οἴεται χρῆναι φυλάττειν ἐντολάς, ὡς καὶ τιμωρίας κεῖσθαι
τοῖς παραβαίνουσιν, ἐνιαχοῦ μὲν σφοδροτέρας, ἐνιαχοῦ δὲ
παραπλησίας ταῖς παρὰ Μωυσέως νομοθετείσαις, ἔστι δὲ ὅπου καὶ
φιλανθρωποτέρας;

207 τοῖς Ἑβραίοις Neumann   τῶν Ἑβραίων MV   212 ἔτι Neumann
    ὅτι MV   221 ⟨οὐκ⟩ Neumann   228 ἀντιτίθησιν Neumann
        ἀνατίθησιν MV   231 εἰληφότα V

519

(155C) Ἀλλὰ τὸ «οὐ προσκυνήσεις θεοῖς ἑτέροις» — ὃ δὴ μετὰ
245 μεγάλης περὶ τὸν θεόν φησι διαβολῆς. «θεὸς γὰρ ζηλωτής» ⟨Exod.
xx:5⟩ φησι· καὶ ἐν ἄλλοις πάλιν ⟨Deut. iv:24⟩ «ὁ θεὸς ἡμῶν (155D)
πῦρ καταναλίσκον«. εἶτα ἄνθρωπος ζηλωτὴς καὶ βάσκανος ἄξιος εἶναί
σοι φαίνεται μέμψεως, ἐκθειάζεις δέ, εἰ ζηλότυπος ὁ θεὸς λέγεται;
καίτοι πῶς εὔλογον οὕτω φανερὸν πρᾶγμα τοῦ θεοῦ καταψεύδεσθαι;
250 καὶ γὰρ εἰ ζηλότυπος, ἄκοντος αὐτοῦ πάντες οἱ θεοὶ προσκυνοῦνται καὶ
πάντα τὰ λοιπὰ τῶν ἐθνῶν τοὺς θεοὺς προσκυνεῖ. εἶτα πῶς οὐκ
ἀνέστειλεν αὐτὸς ζηλῶν οὕτω καὶ μὴ βουλόμενος προσκυνεῖσθαι τοὺς
ἄλλους, ἀλλὰ μόνον ἑαυτόν; ἆρ᾽ οὖν οὐχ οἷός τε ἦν ἢ οὐδὲ τὴν ἀρχὴν
ἢ(155E)βουλήθη κωλῦσαι μὴ προσκυνεῖσθαι καὶ τοὺς ἄλλους θεούς;
255 ἀλλὰ τὸ μὲν πρῶτον ἀσεβές, τὸ δὴ λέγειν ὡς οὐκ ἠδύνατο· τὸ δεύτερον
δὲ τοῖς ἡμετέροις ἔργοις ὁμολογεῖ. ἄφετε τοῦτον τὸν λῆρον καὶ μὴ
τηλικαύτην ἐφ᾽ ὑμᾶς αὐτοὺς ἕλκετε βλασφημίαν ... (160D) οὐδαμοῦ
χαλεπαίνων ὁ θεὸς φαίνεται οὐδὲ ἀγανακτῶν οὐδὲ ὀργιζόμενος οὐδὲ
ὀμνύων οὐδ᾽ ἐπ᾽ ἀμφότερα ταχέως ῥέπων ..., ὡς ὁ Μωυσῆς φησιν ἐπὶ
260 τοῦ Φινεές. εἴ τις ὑμῶν ἀνέγνω τοὺς ἀριθμούς, οἶδεν ὃ λέγω. ἐπειδὴ
γὰρ Φινεὲς τὸν τελεσθέντα τῷ Βεελφεγὼρ μετὰ τῆς ἀναπεισάσης
αὐτὸν γυναικὸς αὐτοχειρίᾳ λαβὼν ἀπέκτεινεν αἰσχρῷ καὶ ὀδυνηροτάτῳ
τραύματι, διὰ τῆς μήτρας, φησί, παίσας τὴν γυναῖκα, πεποίηται
λέ(160E)γων ὁ θεὸς ⟨Num. xxv:11⟩ «Φινεὲς υἱὸς Ἐλεάζαρ υἱοῦ Ἀαρὼν
265 τοῦ ἱερέως κατέπαυσε τὸν θυμόν μου ἀπὸ υἱῶν Ἰσραὴλ ἐν τῷ ζηλῶσαί
μου τὸν ζῆλον ἐν αὐτοῖς. καὶ οὐκ ἐξανήλωσα τοὺς υἱοὺς Ἰσραὴλ ἐν τῷ
ζήλῳ μου.» τί κουφότερον τῆς αἰτίας, δι᾽ ἣν θεὸς ὀργισθεὶς οὐκ ἀληθῶς
ὑπὸ τοῦ γράψαντος ταῦτα πεποίηται; (161A) τί δὲ ἀλογώτερον, εἰ δέκα
ἢ πεντεκαίδεκα, κείσθω δὲ καὶ ἑκατόν, οὐ γὰρ δὴ χιλίους ἐροῦσι —
270 θῶμεν δὲ ἡμεῖς καὶ τοσούτους τολμήσαντάς τι τῶν ὑπὸ τοῦ θεοῦ
τεταγμένων νόμων παραβῆναι· ἑξακοσίας ἐχρῆν διὰ τοὺς ἅπαξ χιλίους
ἀναλωθῆναι χιλιάδας; ὡς ἔμοιγε κρεῖττον εἶναι τῷ παντὶ φαίνεται
χιλίοις ἀνδράσι βελτίστοις ἕνα συνδιασῶσαι πονηρὸν ἢ συνδιαφθεῖραι
τοὺς χιλίους ἑνί ... (161B) εἰ γὰρ καὶ ἑνὸς ἡρώων καὶ οὐκ ἐπισήμου
275 δαίμονος δύσοιστος ἡ ὀργὴ χώραις τε καὶ πόλεσιν ὁλοκλήροις, τίς ἂν
ὑπέστη τοσούτου θεοῦ δαίμοσιν ἢ ἀγγέλοις ἢ καὶ ἀνθρώποις
ἐπιμηνίσαντος; (168B) ἄξιόν γέ ἐστι παραβαλεῖν αὐτὸν τῇ Λυκούργου
πραότητι καὶ τῇ Σόλωνος ἀνεξικακίᾳ ἢ (168C) τῇ Ῥωμαίων πρὸς τοὺς
ἠδικηκότας ἐπιεικείᾳ καὶ χρηστότητι. (171D) πόσῳ δὲ δὴ τὰ παρ᾽ ἡμῖν
280 τῶν παρ᾽ αὐτοῖς κρείττονα, καὶ ἐκ τῶνδε σκοπεῖτε. μιμεῖσθαι

244–245 μετά μεγάλης Neumann   μετὰ τῆς M   μέγα τῆς V
252 αὐτὸς Neumann   αὐτὸ MV   254 ἐβουλήθη V   255 ἐδύνατο V
261 Φινεὲς Neumann   φησι M   φησιν N   279 ἡμῖν] ἡμῶν V

κελεύουσιν ἡμᾶς οἱ φιλόσοφοι κατὰ δύναμιν τοὺς θεούς, εἶναι δὲ
ταύτην τὴν μίμησιν ἐν θεωρίᾳ τῶν ὄντων. ὅτι δὲ τοῦτο δίχα πάθους
ἐστὶ καὶ (171E) ἐν ἀπαθείᾳ κεῖται, πρόδηλόν ἐστί που, κἂν ἐγὼ μὴ
λέγω· καθ᾽ ὅσον ἄρα ἐν ἀπαθείᾳ γινόμ-θα, τεταγμένοι περὶ τῶν
285 ὄντων θεωρίαν, κατὰ τοσοῦτον ἐξομοιούμεθα τῷ θεῷ. τίς δὲ ἡ παρ᾽
Ἑβραίοις ὑμνουμένη τοῦ θεοῦ μίμησις; ὀργὴ καὶ θυμὸς καὶ ζῆλος
ἄγριος. «Φινεὲς» γάρ φησι ⟨Num. xxv: 11⟩ «κατέπαυσε τὸν θυμόν
μου ... ἐν αὐτοῖς.» εὑρὼν γὰρ ὁ θεὸς τὸν συναγανακτοῦντα καὶ
συναλγοῦντα ἀφεὶς τὴν ἀγανάκτησιν φαίνεται. (172A) ταῦτα καὶ τὰ
290 τοιαῦτα περὶ θεοῦ ἔτερα πεποίηται λέγων ὁ Μωυσῆς οὐκ ὀλιγαχοῦ τῆς
γραφῆς.

(176A) Ὅτι δὲ οὐχ Ἑβραίων μόνον ἐμέλησε τῷ (176B) θεῷ, πάντων
δὲ ἐθνῶν κηδόμενος ἔδωκεν ἐκείνοις μὲν οὐδὲν σπουδαῖον ἢ μέγα,
ἡμῖν δὲ μακρῷ κρείττονα καὶ διαφέροντα, σκοπεῖτε λοιπὸν τὸ
295 ἐντεῦθεν. ἔχουσι μὲν εἰπεῖν καὶ Αἰγύπτιοι, παρ᾽ ἑαυτοῖς
ἀπαριθμούμενοι σοφῶν οὐκ ὀλίγων ὀνόματα, πολλοὺς ἐσχηκέναι τοὺς
ἀπὸ τῆς Ἑρμοῦ διαδοχῆς, Ἑρμοῦ δέ φημι τοῦ τρίτου ἐπιφοιτήσαντος
τῇ Αἰγύπτῳ, Χαλδαῖοι δὲ καὶ Ἀσσύριοι τοὺς ἀπ᾽ Ὠάννου καὶ Βήλου,
μυρίους δὲ Ἕλληνες τοὺς ἀπὸ Χείρωνος. ἐκ τούτου γὰρ πάντες (176C)
300 ἐγένοντο τελεστικοὶ φύσει καὶ θεολογικοί, καθὸ δὴ δοκοῦσι μόνον
Ἑβραῖοι τὰ ἑαυτῶν ἀποσεμνύνειν ...

... (178A) Ἀλλ᾽ ἀρχὴν ἔδωκεν ὑμῖν ἐπιστήμης ἢ μάθημα φιλόσοφον;
καὶ ποῖον; ἡ μὲν γὰρ περὶ τὰ (178B) φαινόμενα θεωρία παρὰ τοῖς
Ἕλλησιν ἐτελειώθη, τῶν πρώτων τηρήσεων παρὰ τοῖς βαρβάροις ἐν
305 Βαβυλῶνι γενομένων· ἡ δὲ περὶ τὴν γεωμετρίαν ἀπὸ τῆς γεωδαισίας
τῆς ἐν Αἰγύπτῳ τὴν ἀρχὴν λαβοῦσα πρὸς τοσοῦτον μέγεθος ηὐξήθη·
τὸ δὲ περὶ τοὺς ἀριθμοὺς ἀπὸ τῶν Φοινίκων ἐμπόρων ἀρξάμενον τέως
★ εἰς ἐπιστήμης παρὰ τοῖς Ἕλλησι κατέστη πρόσχημα. τὰ δὴ τρία
μετὰ τῆς συναρίθμου μουσικῆς Ἕλληνες εἰς ἓν συνῆψαν, ἀστρονομίαν
310 γεωμετρίᾳ προσυφήναντες, ἀμ(178C)φοῖν δὲ προσαρμόσαντες τοὺς
ἀριθμοὺς καὶ τὸ ἐν τούτοις ἐναρμόνιον κατανοήσαντες. ἐντεῦθεν
ἔθεντο τῇ παρὰ σφίσι μουσικῇ τοὺς ὅρους, εὑρόντες τῶν ἁρμονικῶν
λόγων πρὸς τὴν αἴσθησιν τῆς ἀκοῆς ἄπταιστον ὁμολογίαν ἢ ὅτι τούτου
μάλιστα ἐγγύς.

315 (184B) Πότερον οὖν χρή με κατ᾽ ἄνδρα ὀνομάζειν ἢ κατ᾽
ἐπιτηδεύματα; ἢ τοὺς ἀνθρώπους, οἷον Πλάτωνα, Σωκράτην,
Ἀριστείδην, Κίμωνα, Θαλῆν, Λυκοῦργον, Ἀγησίλαον, Ἀρχίδαμον —

288 ἐν αὐτοῖς] ἐν υἱοῖς Ἰσραήλ V   302 Ἀλλ᾽ Neumann   ἀλλὰ MV
309 συναρίθμου] εὐρύθμου Neumann   313-314 τούτου ante μάλιστα pos.
Neumann   post μάλιστα pos. MV

ἢ μᾶλλον τὸ τῶν φιλοσόφων γένος, τὸ τῶν στρατηγῶν, τὸ τῶν δημιουργῶν, τὸ τῶν νομοθετῶν; εὑρεθήσονται γὰρ οἱ μοχθηρότατοι
320 καὶ βδελυρώτατοι τῶν στρατηγῶν ἐπιεικέστερον χρησάμενοι (184C) τοῖς ἠδικηκόσι τὰ μέγιστα ἢ Μωσῆς τοῖς οὐδὲν ἐξημαρτηκόσιν. (190C) τίνα οὖν ὑμῖν ἀπαγγείλω βασιλείαν; πότερα τὴν Περσέως ἢ τὴν Αἰακοῦ ἢ Μίνω τοῦ Κρητὸς ...
(194D) Ἆρα ἀξίως ἄν τις τοὺς συνετωτέρους ὑμῶν μισήσειεν ἢ τοὺς
325 ἀφρονεστέρους ἐλεήσειεν οἳ κατακολουθοῦντες ὑμῖν, εἰς τοσοῦτον ἦλθον ὀλέθρου, ὥστε τοὺς αἰωνίους ἀφέντες θεοὺς ἐπὶ τὸν Ἰουδαίων μεταβῆναι νεκρόν; ...
(198B) Τὸ γὰρ ἐκ θεῶν εἰς ἀνθρώπους ἀφικνούμενον (198C) πνεῦμα σπανιάκις μὲν καὶ ἐν ὀλίγοις γίνεται καὶ οὔτε πάντα ἄνδρα τούτου
330 μετασχεῖν ῥᾴδιον οὔτε ἐν παντὶ καιρῷ. ταύτῃ τοι καὶ τὸ παρ' Ἑβραίοις ⟨προφητικὸν πνεῦμα⟩ ἐπέλιπεν, οὐκοῦν οὐδὲ παρ' Αἰγυπτίοις εἰς τοῦτο σῴζεται ...
(201E) Τί δὲ τοιοῦτον ⟨ἑαυτοῖς⟩ Ἑβραῖοι καυχῶνται παρὰ τοῦ θεοῦ δεδόσθαι, πρὸς οὓς ὑμεῖς ἀφ' ἡμῶν αὐτομολήσαντες πείθεσθε; εἰ τοῖς
335 ἐκείνων γοῦν προσείχετε λόγοις, οὐκ ἂν παντάπασιν ἐπεπράγειτε δυστυχῶς, ἀλλὰ χεῖρον μὲν ἢ πρότερον, ὁπότε σὺν ἡμῖν ἦτε, οἰστὰ δὲ ὅμως ἐπεπόνθειτε ἂν καὶ φορητά. ἕνα γὰρ ἀντὶ πολλῶν θεῶν ἐσέβεσθε ἂν οὐκ ἄνθρωπον, μᾶλλον δὲ πολλοὺς ἀνθρώπους (202A) δυστυχεῖς. καὶ νόμῳ σκληρῷ μὲν καὶ τραχεῖ καὶ πολὺ τὸ ἄγριον ἔχοντι
340 καὶ βάρβαρον ἀντὶ τῶν παρ' ἡμῖν ἐπιεικῶν καὶ φιλανθρώπων χρώμενοι τὰ μὲν ἄλλα χείρονες ἂν ἦτε, ἁγνότεροι δὲ καὶ καθαρώτεροι τὰς ἁγιστείας. νῦν δὲ ὑμῖν συμβέβηκεν ὥσπερ ταῖς βδέλλαις τὸ χείριστον ἕλκειν αἷμα ἐκεῖθεν, ἀφεῖναι δὲ τὸ καθαρώτερον ...
(205E) Ἁγνείας μὲν οὐδὲ γὰρ εἰ πεποίηται μνήμην ἐπίστασθε·
345 ζηλοῦτε δὲ Ἰουδαίων τοὺς θυμοὺς καὶ τὴν πικρίαν, ἀνατρέποντες ἱερὰ καὶ βωμοὺς ... (209D) Ἀλλὰ τοῦτο μὲν οὐκ οἶδ' ὅθεν ὥσπερ ἐπιπνεόμενος ἐφθεγξάμην, ὅθεν δὲ ἐξέβην, ὅτι «πρὸς τοὺς Ἰουδαίους ηὐτομολήσατε, τί τοῖς ἡμετέροις ἀχαριστήσαντες θεοῖς;» ἆρ' ὅτι βασιλεύειν ἔδοσαν οἱ θεοὶ τῇ Ῥώμῃ, τοῖς Ἰουδαίοις ὀλίγον μὲν χρόνον
350 ἐλευθέρους εἶναι, δουλεῦσαι δὲ ἀεὶ καὶ παροικῆσαι; σκόπει τὸν Ἀβραάμ· οὐχὶ πάροικος ἦν ἐν [γῇ] ἀλλοτρίᾳ; τὸν Ἰακώβ· οὐ πρότερον

321 ἠδικηκόσι τὰ μέγιστα Neumann

τὰ μέγιστα ἠδικηκόσιν M 326 ὥστε ⟨καὶ⟩ Neumann 331 ⟨προφητικὸν
πνεῦμα⟩ Neumann 333 ⟨ἑαυτοῖς⟩ Neumann 335 οὐκ ἂν Neumann
καὶ οὐ M 337 ἐπεπόνθειτε Neumann πεπόνθειτε M
344 οὐδὲ γὰρ Neumann γὰρ οὐδὲ Aubert γὰρ οὐδὲ γὰρ M
345 Ἰουδαίων Neumann αὐτῶν M 351 γῇ secl. Neumann

μὲν *(209Ε)* Σύροις, ἑξῆς δὲ ἐπὶ τούτοις Παλαιστινοῖς, ἐν γήρᾳ δὲ
Αἰγυπτίοις ἐδούλευσεν· οὐκ ἐξ οἴκου δουλείας ἐξαγαγεῖν αὐτοὺς ὁ
Μωυσῆς ⟨φησιν⟩ ἐξ Αἰγύπτου ἐν βραχίονι ὑψηλῷ; κατοικήσαντες δὲ
355 τὴν Παλαιστίνην, οὐ πυκνότερον ἤμειψαν τὰς τύχας ἢ τὸ χρῶμά φασιν
οἱ τεθεαμένοι τὸν χαμαιλέοντα, νῦν μὲν ὑπακούοντες τοῖς κριταῖς, νῦν
δὲ τοῖς ἀλλοφύλοις δουλεύοντες· ἐπειδὴ δὲ ἐβασιλεύθησαν — ἀφείσθω
δὲ νῦν ὅπως· οὔτε γὰρ ὁ θεὸς ἑκὼν αὐτοῖς τὸ βασιλεύεσθαι
συνεχώρησεν, ὡς ἡ γραφή φησιν ⟨I Sam. viii:7⟩ *(210Α)*, ἀλλὰ βιασθεὶς
360 ὑπ’ αὐτῶν καὶ προδιαστειλάμενος, ὅτι ἄρα φαύλως βασιλευθήσονται.
πλὴν ἀλλ’ ᾤκησαν γοῦν τὴν ἑαυτῶν καὶ ἐγεώργησαν ὀλίγα πρὸς τοῖς
τριακοσίοις ἔτεσιν. ἐξ ἐκείνου πρῶτον Ἀσσυρίοις, εἶτα Μήδοις,
ὕστερον Πέρσαις ἐδούλευσαν, εἶτα νῦν ἡμῖν αὐτοῖς ... *(213Α)* ⟨καὶ⟩ ὁ
παρ’ ὑμῖν κηρυττόμενος Ἰησοῦς εἷς ἦν τῶν Καίσαρος ὑπηκόων ... ἀλλὰ
365 γενόμενος ⟨ἄνθρωπος⟩ τίνων *(213Β)* ἀγαθῶν αἴτιος κατέστη τοῖς
ἑαυτοῦ συγγενέσιν; οὐ γὰρ ἠθέλησαν, φασίν, ὑπακοῦσαι τῷ Ἰησοῦ. τί
δέ; ὁ σκληροκάρδιος καὶ λιθοτράχηλος ἐκεῖνος λαὸς πῶς ὑπήκουσε τοῦ
Μωυσέως; ...
(218Α) Νυνὶ δὲ ἀποκρίνεσθέ μοι πρὸς ἐκεῖνο. πότερον ἄμεινον τὸ
370 διηνεκῶς μὲν ἐλεύθερον εἶναι, ἐν δισχιλίοις ⟨δὲ⟩ ὅ*(218Β)*λοις ἐνιαυτοῖς
ἄρξαι τὸ πλεῖον γῆς καὶ θαλάσσης, ἢ τὸ δουλεύειν καὶ πρὸς ἐπίταγμα
ζῆν ἀλλότριον; οὐδεὶς οὕτως ἐστὶν ἀναίσχυντος, ὡς ἑλέσθαι μᾶλλον τὸ
δεύτερον. ἀλλὰ τὸ πολέμῳ κρατεῖν οἰήσεταί τις τοῦ κρατεῖσθαι χεῖρον;
οὕτω τίς ἐστιν ἀναίσθητος; εἰ δὲ ταῦτα ἀληθῆ φαμεν, ἕνα μοι κατὰ
375 Ἀλέξανδρον δείξατε στρατηγόν, ἕνα κατὰ Καίσαρα παρὰ τοῖς
Ἑβραίοις. οὐ γὰρ δὴ παρ’ ὑμῖν. καίτοι, μὰ τοὺς θεούς, εὖ οἶδ’ ὅτι
περιυβρίζω τοὺς ἄνδρας, ἐμνημόνευσα δὲ αὐτῶν ὡς γνωρίμων. *(218C)*
οἱ γὰρ δὴ τούτων ἐλάττους ὑπὸ τῶν πολλῶν ἀγνοοῦνται, ὧν ἕκαστος
πάντων ὁμοῦ τῶν παρ’ Ἑβραίοις γεγονότων ἐστὶ θαυμαστότερος.
380 *(221Ε)* Ἀλλ’ ὁ τῆς πολιτείας θεσμὸς καὶ τύπος τῶν δικαστηρίων, ἡ δὲ
περὶ τὰς πόλεις οἰκονομία καὶ τῶν νόμων τὸ κάλλος, ἡ δὲ ἐν τοῖς
μαθήμασιν ἐπίδοσις, ἡ δὲ ἐν ταῖς ἐλευθερίοις τέχναις ἄσκησις οὐχ
Ἑβραίων μὲν ἦν ἀθλία καὶ βαρβαρική; *(222Α)* καίτοι βούλεται ὁ
μοχθηρὸς Εὐσέβιος ⟨Praeparatio Evangelica, XI, 5:7⟩ εἶναί τινα καὶ
385 παρ’ αὐτοῖς ἐξάμετρα, καὶ φιλοτιμεῖται λογικὴν εἶναι πραγματείαν
παρὰ τοῖς Ἑβραίοις, ἧς τοὔνομα ἀκήκοε παρὰ τοῖς Ἕλλησι. ποῖον
ἰατρικῆς εἶδος ἀνεφάνη παρὰ τοῖς Ἑβραίοις, ὥσπερ ἐν Ἕλλησι τῆς

---

354 ⟨φησιν⟩ Neumann   355 πικνότερον Aubert   πικρότερον M
363 ⟨καὶ⟩ Neumann   365 ⟨ἄνθρωπος⟩ Neumann   366 φασίν Neumann
φησὶν M   370 ἐλεύθερον εἶναι Neumann
εἶναι ἐλεύθερον M / ⟨δὲ⟩ Neumann   387 τῆς Aubert   τὴν M

Ἱπποκράτους καί τινων ἄλλων μετ' ἐκεῖνον αἱρέσεων; (224C) ὁ
σοφώτατος Σολομῶν παρόμοιός ἐστι τῷ παρ' Ἕλλησι Φωκυλίδῃ ἢ
390 Θεόγνιδι ἢ Ἰσοκράτει; πόθεν; εἰ γοῦν παραβάλοις τὰς Ἰσοκράτους
παραινέσεις ταῖς ἐκείνου παροιμίαις, εὕροις ἄν, (224D) εὖ οἶδα, τὸν
τοῦ Θεοδώρου κρείττονα τοῦ σοφωτάτου βασιλέως. ἀλλ' ἐκεῖνος, φασί,
καὶ περὶ θεουργίαν ἤσκητο. τί οὖν; οὐχὶ καὶ ὁ Σολομῶν οὗτος τοῖς
ἡμετέροις ἐλάτρευσε θεοῖς, ὑπὸ τῆς γυναικός, ὡς λέγουσιν ⟨I Kings
395 xi:4⟩ ἐξαπατηθείς; ὦ μέγεθος ἀρετῆς. ὦ σοφίας πλοῦτος. οὐ
περιγέγονεν ἡδονῆς, καὶ γυναικὸς λόγοι τοῦτον ⟨παρήγαγον⟩. εἴπερ οὖν
ὑπὸ γυναικὸς ἠπατήθη [παρήγαγον], τοῦτον σοφὸν μὴ λέγετε. εἰ δὲ
πεπιστεύκατε [εἶναι] σοφόν, μή τοι παρὰ γυναικὸς αὐτὸν ἐξηπατῆσθαι
νομίζετε, κρίσει δὲ οἰ(224E)κείᾳ καὶ συνέσει καὶ τῇ παρὰ τοῦ
400 φανέντος αὐτῷ θεοῦ διδασκαλίᾳ πειθόμενον λελατρευκέναι καὶ τοῖς
ἄλλοις θεοῖς. φθόνος γὰρ καὶ ζῆλος οὐδὲ ἄχρι τῶν ἀρίστων ἀνθρώπων
ἀφικνεῖται, τοσοῦτον ἄπεστιν ἀγγέλων καὶ θεῶν. ὑμεῖς δὲ ἄρα περὶ τὰ
μέρη τῶν δυνάμεων στρέφεσθε, ἃ δὴ δαιμόνιά τις εἰπὼν οὐκ
ἐξαμαρτάνει. τὸ γὰρ φιλότιμον ἐνταῦθα καὶ κενόδοξον, ἐν δὲ τοῖς θεοῖς
405 οὐδὲν ὑπάρχει καὶ τοιοῦτον ... (238A) Ἀνθ' ὅτου ⟨δὲ⟩ μηδὲ τοῖς
Ἑβραϊκοῖς λόγοις ἐμμένετε μήτε ἀγαπᾶτε τὸν νόμον, ὃν δέδωκεν ὁ
θεὸς (238B) ἐκείνοις, ἀπολιπόντες δὲ τὰ πάτρια καὶ δόντες ἑαυτοὺς οἷς
ἐκήρυξαν οἱ προφῆται, πλέον ἐκείνων ἢ τῶν παρ' ἡμῖν ἀπέστητε; τὸ
γὰρ ἀληθὲς εἴ τις ὑπὲρ ὑμῶν ἐθέλοι σκοπεῖν, εὑρήσει τὴν ὑμετέραν
410 ἀσέβειαν ἔκ τε τῆς Ἰουδαϊκῆς τόλμης καὶ τῆς παρὰ τοῖς ἔθνεσιν
ἀδιαφορίας καὶ χυδαιότητος συγκειμένην. ἐξ ἀμφοῖν γὰρ οὔτι τὸ
κάλλιστον, ἀλλὰ τὸ χεῖρον ἑλκύσαντες παρυφὴν κακῶν εἰργάσασθε.
τοῖς μὲν γὰρ Ἑβραίοις ἀκριβῆ τὰ περὶ θρησκείαν ἐστὶ νόμιμα καὶ τὰ
σεβάσμα(238C)τα καὶ [τὰ] φυλάγματα μυρία καὶ δεόμενα βίου καὶ
415 προαιρέσεως ἱερατικῆς. ἀπαγορεύσαντος δὲ τοῦ νομοθέτου τὸ πᾶσι μὴ
δουλεύειν τοῖς θεοῖς, ἑνὶ δὲ μόνον, οὗ «μερίς ἐστιν Ἰακὼβ καὶ
σχοίνισμα κληρονομίας Ἰσραήλ» ⟨Deut. xxxii:9⟩, οὐ τοῦτο δὲ μόνον
εἰπόντος, ἀλλὰ γάρ, οἶμαι, καὶ προσθέντος «οὐ κακολογήσεις θεούς»,
ἡ τῶν ἐπιγινομένων βδελυρία τε καὶ τόλμα, βουλομένη πᾶσαν
420 εὐλάβειαν ἐξελεῖν τοῦ πλήθους, ἀκολουθεῖν ἐνόμισε τῷ μὴ
θεραπεύειν τὸ βλασφημεῖν, ὃ δὴ καὶ ὑμεῖς ἐντεῦθεν εἱλκύσατε (238D)
μόνον· ὡς τῶν γε ἄλλων οὐθὲν ὑμῖν τέ ἐστι κἀκείνοις παραπλήσιον.
ἀπὸ μὲν οὖν τῆς Ἑβραίων καινοτομίας τὸ βλασφημεῖν ⟨τοὺς παρ'

392 φασί Aubert   φησί M   396 ⟨παρήγαγον⟩ Aubert
397 παρήγαγον secl. Aubert   398 εἶναι secl. Neumann   400 πειθόμενον
Neumann   πειθόμενος M   405 ⟨δὲ⟩ Neumann   414 τὰ secl. Neumann
423–424 ⟨τοὺς παρ' ἡμῖν⟩ Neumann

524

ἡμῖν⟩ τιμωμένους θεοὺς ἡρπάσατε. ἀπὸ δὲ τῆς παρ' ἡμῖν θρησκείας τὸ
425 μὲν εὐσεβές τε ὁμοῦ πρὸς ἅπασαν τὴν κρείττονα φύσιν καὶ τῶν
πατρίων ἀγαπητικὸν ἀπολελοίπατε, μόνον δ' ἐκτήσασθε τὸ πάντα
ἐσθίειν ὡς λάχανα χόρτου ...
(253A) Ἐπειδὴ δὲ πρὸς μὲν τοὺς νυνὶ Ἰουδαίους δια*(253B)*φέρεσθαί
φασιν, εἶναι δὲ ἀκριβῶς Ἰσραηλῖται κατὰ τοὺς προφήτας αὐτῶν, καὶ τῷ
430 Μωυσῇ μάλιστα πείθεσθαι καὶ τοῖς ἀπ' ἐκείνου περὶ τὴν Ἰουδαίαν
ἐπιγενομένοις προφήταις, ἴδωμεν, κατὰ τί μάλιστα ὁμολογοῦσιν
αὐτοῖς. ἀρκτέον δὲ ἡμῖν ἀπὸ τῶν Μωυσέως, ὃν δὴ καὶ αὐτόν φασι
προκηρύξαι τὴν ἐσομένην Ἰησοῦ γέννησιν. ὁ τοίνυν Μωυσῆς οὐχ ἅπαξ
οὐδὲ δὶς οὐδὲ τρίς, ἀλλὰ πλειστάκις ἕνα θεὸν μόνον ἀξιοῖ τιμᾶν, ὃν δὴ
435 καὶ ἐπὶ πᾶσιν ὀνομάζει, θεὸν δὲ ἕτερον οὐδαμοῦ. *(253C)* ἀγγέλους δὲ
ὀνομάζει καὶ κυρίους καὶ μέντοι καὶ θεοὺς πλείονας, ἐξαίρετον δὲ τὸν
πρῶτον, ἄλλον δὲ οὐχ ὑπείληφε δεύτερον οὔτε ὅμοιον οὔτε ἀνόμοιον,
καθάπερ ὑμεῖς ἐπεξείργασθε ... *(253D)* καὶ τὸ «οὐκ ἐκλείψει ἄρχων ἐξ
Ἰούδα οὐδὲ ἡγούμενος ἐκ τῶν μηρῶν αὐτοῦ» ⟨Gen. xlix:10⟩ μάλιστα
440 μὲν οὐκ εἴρηται περὶ τούτου ⟨scil. Ἰησοῦ⟩, ἀλλὰ περὶ τῆς τοῦ Δαβὶδ
βασιλείας, ἣ δὴ κατέληξεν εἰς Σεδεκίαν τὸν βασιλέα. καὶ δὴ ἡ γραφὴ
διπλῶς πως ἔχει «ἕως ἔλθῃ τὰ ἀποκείμενα αὐτῷ», παραπεποιήκατε δὲ
ὑμεῖς «ἕως ἔλθῃ ᾧ ἀπόκειται».
(290B) Ὅτι δὲ Μωυσῆς ὀνομάζει θεοὺς τοὺς ἀγγέλους, ἐκ τῶν ἐκείνου
445 λόγων ἀκούσατε ⟨Gen. vi:2⟩ «ἰδόντες δὲ οἱ *(290C)* υἱοὶ τοῦ θεοῦ τὰς
θυγατέρας τῶν ἀνθρώπων ὅτι καλαί εἰσιν, ἔλαβον ἑαυτοῖς γυναῖκας
ἀπὸ πασῶν ὧν ἐξελέξαντο» καὶ μικρὸν ὑποβὰς «καὶ μετ' ἐκεῖνο ὡς ἂν
εἰσεπορεύοντο οἱ υἱοὶ τοῦ θεοῦ πρὸς τὰς θυγατέρας τῶν ἀνθρώπων, καὶ
ἐγεννῶσαν ἑαυτοῖς· ἐκεῖνοι ἦσαν οἱ γίγαντες οἱ ἀπ' αἰῶνος οἱ
450 ὀνομαστοί» ⟨Gen. vi:4⟩. ὅτι τοίνυν τοὺς ἀγγέλους φησίν, εὔδηλόν ἐστι
καὶ ἔξωθεν οὐ προσπαρακείμενον, ἀλλὰ καὶ δῆλον ἐκ τοῦ φάναι, οὐκ
ἀνθρώπους, ἀλλὰ γίγαντας γεγονέναι παρ' ἐκείνων. δῆλον γάρ, ὡς,
εἴπερ ἀνθρώπους ἐνόμιζεν αὐτῶν εἶναι *(290D)* τοὺς πατέρας, ἀλλὰ μὴ
κρείττονος καὶ ἰσχυροτέρας τινὸς φύσεως, οὐκ ἂν ἀπ' αὐτῶν εἶπε
455 γεννηθῆναι τοὺς γίγαντας· ἐκ γὰρ θνητοῦ καὶ ἀθανάτου μίξεως
ἀποφήνασθαί μοι δοκεῖ τὸ τῶν γιγάντων ὑποστῆναι γένος ... *(290E)*
ἕνα καὶ μόνον ἐδίδασκε ⟨scil. Μωυσῆς⟩ θεόν, υἱοὺς δὲ αὐτοῦ πολλοὺς
τοὺς κατανειμαμένους τὰ ἔθνη ...

429 Ἰσραηλῖται Neumann
Ἰσραηλίτας M   430 ἀπ' ἐκείνου Neumann   ἀπ' ἐκείνων M
431–432 ὁμολογοῦσιν αὐτοῖς Neumann   αὐτοῖς ὁμολογοῦσιν M
441 κατέληξεν Neumann   καταλῆξαι φαίνεται M / Σεδεκίαν Spanheim
ἐζεκίαν M

(299A) Ὑπὲρ δὲ ἀποτροπαίων ἐπάκουσον πάλιν ὅσα λέγει ⟨Lev. xvi:5⟩

460 «καὶ λήψεται δύο τράγους ἐξ αἰγῶν περὶ ἁμαρτίας» ... *(305B)* ὡς μὲν οὖν τοὺς τῶν θυσιῶν ἠπίστατο τρόπους Μωυσῆς, εὔδηλόν ἐστί που διὰ τῶν ῥηθέντων. ὅτι δὲ οὐχ ὡς ὑμεῖς ἀκάθαρτα ἐνόμισεν αὐτά, πάλιν ἐκ τῶν ἐκείνου ῥημάτων ἐπακούσατε «Ἡ δὲ ψυχή, ἥτις ἐὰν φάγῃ ἀπὸ τῶν κρεῶν τῆς θυσίας τοῦ σωτηρίου, ὅ ἐστι κυρίου, καὶ ἡ ἀκαθαρσία αὐτοῦ

465 ἐπ᾽ αὐτῷ, ἀπολεῖται ἡ ψυχὴ ἐκείνη ἐκ τοῦ λαοῦ αὐτῆς.» αὐτὸς οὕτως εὐλαβὴς ὁ Μωυσῆς περὶ τὴν τῶν ἱερῶν ἐδωδήν. *(305D)* προσήκει δὴ λοιπὸν ἀναμνησθῆναι τῶν *(305E)* ἔμπροσθεν, ὧν ἕνεκεν ἐρρήθη καὶ ταῦτα. διὰ τί γὰρ ἀποστάντες ἡμῶν οὐχὶ τὸν τῶν Ἰουδαίων ἀγαπᾶτε νόμον οὐδὲ ἐμμένετε τοῖς ὑπ᾽ ἐκείνου λεγομένοις; ἐρεῖ πάντως τις ὀξὺ

470 βλέπων· οὐδὲ γὰρ Ἰουδαῖοι θύουσιν. ἀλλ᾽ ἔγωγε ἀμβλυώττοντα δεινῶς αὐτὸν ἀπελέγξω, πρῶτον μέν, ὅτι μηδὲ τῶν ἄλλων τι τῶν παρὰ τοῖς Ἰουδαίοις νενομισμένων ἐστὶ καὶ ὑμῖν ἐν φυλακῇ· δεύτερον δέ, ὅτι θύουσι μὲν ἐν ἀδράκτοις Ἰουδαῖοι καὶ νῦν ἔτι πάντα ἐσθίου*(306A)*σιν ἱερὰ καὶ κατεύχονται πρὸ τοῦ θῦσαι καὶ τὸν δεξιὸν ὦμον διδόασιν

475 ἀπαρχὰς τοῖς ἱερεῦσιν, ἀπεστερημένοι δὲ τοῦ ναοῦ, ἤ, ὡς αὐτοῖς ἔθος λέγειν, τοῦ ἁγιάσματος, ἀπαρχὰς τῷ θεῷ τῶν ἱερείων εἴργονται προσφέρειν. ὑμεῖς δὲ οἱ τὴν καινὴν θυσίαν εὑρόντες, οὐδὲν δεόμενοι τῆς Ἱερουσαλήμ, ἀντὶ τίνος οὐ θύετε; καίτοι τοῦτο μὲν ἐγὼ πρὸς ὑμᾶς ἐκ περιουσίας εἶπον, ἐπεί μοι τὴν ἀρχὴν ἐρρέθη βουλομένῳ δεῖξαι

480 τοῖς ἔθνε*(306B)*σιν ὁμολογοῦντας Ἰουδαίους ἔξω τοῦ νομίζειν ἕνα θεὸν μόνον. ἐκεῖνο γὰρ αὐτῶν μὲν ἴδιον, ἡμῶν δὲ ἀλλότριον, ἐπεί τά γε ἄλλα κοινά πως ἡμῖν ἐστι, ναοί, τεμένη, θυσιαστήρια, ἁγνεῖαι, φυλάγματά τινα, περὶ ὧν ἢ τὸ παράπαν οὐδαμῶς ἢ μικρὰ διαφερόμεθα πρὸς ἀλλήλους ...

485 *(314C)* Ἀνθ᾽ ὅτου περὶ τὴν δίαιταν οὐχὶ τοῖς Ἰουδαίοις ὁμοίως ἐστὲ καθαροί, πάντα δὲ ἐσθίειν ὡς λάχανα χόρτου δεῖν φατε Πέτρῳ πιστεύσαντες ⟨Acts x:15⟩ ...

(319D) ἀλλὰ τί ταῦτα ἐγὼ μακρολογῶ λεγόμενα παρ᾽ αὐτῶν, ἐξὸν ἰδεῖν, εἴ τινα ἰσχὺν ἔχει; λέγουσι γὰρ τὸν θεὸν ἐπὶ τῷ προτέρῳ νόμῳ

490 θεῖναι τὸν δεύτερον. ἐκεῖνον μὲν γὰρ γενέσθαι πρὸς καιρὸν περιγεγραμμένον χρόνοις ὡρισμένοις, ὕστερον δὲ τοῦτον ἀναφανῆναι διὰ τὸ τὸν Μωσέως χρόνῳ τε καὶ τόπῳ περιγράφθαι. τοῦτο ὅτι ψευδῶς λέγουσιν, ἀποδείξω σαφῶς, ἐκ μὲν τῶν Μωυσέως οὐ δέκα μόνας, ἀλλὰ μυρίας παρεχόμενος μαρ*(319E)*τυρίας, ὅπου τὸν νόμον

495 αἰώνιόν φησιν ... *(340A)* σκοπεῖτε οὖν, ὅπως παλαιὸν ἦν τοῦτο τοῖς

473 ἐν ἀδράκτοις Aubert   ἀδράττοις M   488 παρ᾽ αὐτῶν Aubert
                          παρ᾽ αὐτὸν M

526

Ἰουδαίοις τῆς μαγγανείας τὸ ἔργον, ἐγκαθεύδειν τοῖς μνήμασιν
ἐνυπνίων χάριν ... (343C) ὑμεῖς δέ, ἃ μὲν ὁ θεὸς ἐξ ἀρχῆς ἐβδελύξατο
καὶ διὰ Μωυσέως καὶ τῶν προφητῶν, ἐπιτηδεύετε, προσάγειν δὲ ἱερεῖα
βωμῷ καὶ θύειν παρῃτήσασθε. πῦρ γάρ, φασίν, οὐ κάτεισιν, ὥσπερ
500 ἐπὶ Μωυσέως τὰς θυσίας ἀναλίσκον. ἅπαξ τοῦτο ἐπὶ (343D) Μωυσέως
ἐγένετο καὶ ἐπὶ Ἠλίου τοῦ Θεσβίτου πάλιν μετὰ πολλοὺς χρόνους.
ἐπεί, ὅτι γε πῦρ ἐπείσακτον αὐτὸς ὁ Μωυσῆς εἰσφέρειν οἴεται χρῆναι
καὶ Ἀβραὰμ ὁ πατριάρχης ἔτι πρὸ τούτου δηλώσω διὰ βραχέων ...
(346E) καὶ οὐ τοῦτο μόνον, ἀλλὰ καὶ τῶν υἱῶν Ἀδὰμ ἀπαρχὰς τῷ θεῷ
505 διδόντων, «ἐπεῖδεν ὁ θεὸς» φησὶν «ἐπὶ Ἄβελ καὶ ἐπὶ τοῖς δώροις
αὐτοῦ» ⟨Gen. iv:4⟩ ... (347C) «περὶ δὲ τὴν διαίρεσιν ὁ μὲν ἔτυχεν, ὁ δὲ
ἥμαρτε τοῦ σκοποῦ». πῶς καὶ τίνα τρόπον; ἐπειδὴ γὰρ τῶν ἐπὶ γῆς
ὄντων τὰ μέν ἐστιν ἔμψυχα, τὰ δὲ ἄψυχα, τιμιώτερα δὲ τῶν ἀψύχων
ἐστὶ τὰ ἔμψυχα τῷ ζῶντι καὶ ζωῆς αἰτίῳ θεῷ, καθὸ καὶ ζωῆς
510 μετείληφε καὶ ψυχῆς οἰκειοτέρας — διὰ τοῦτο τῷ τελείαν προσάγοντι
θυσίαν ὁ θεὸς ἐπηυφράνθη·
(354A) καίτοι, μὰ τοὺς θεούς, εἷς εἰμι τῶν (354B) ἐκτρεπομένων
συνεορτάζειν Ἰουδαίοις, ἀεὶ ⟨δὲ⟩ προσκυνῶν τὸν θεὸν Ἀβραὰμ καὶ
Ἰσαὰκ καὶ Ἰακώβ, οἳ ὄντες αὐτοὶ Χαλδαῖοι, γένους ἱεροῦ καὶ
515 θεουργικοῦ, τὴν μὲν περιτομὴν ἔμαθον Αἰγυπτίοις ἐπιξενωθέντες,
ἐσεβάσθησαν δὲ θεόν, ὃς ἐμοὶ καὶ τοῖς αὐτόν, ὥσπερ Ἀβραὰμ ἔσεβε,
σεβομένοις εὐμενὴς ἦν, μέγας τε ὢν πάνυ καὶ δυνατός, ὑμῖν δὲ οὐδὲν
προσήκων. οὐδὲ γὰρ τὸν Ἀβραὰμ μιμεῖσθε, βωμούς τε ἐγείροντες
αὐτῷ καὶ οἰκοδομοῦντες θυσιαστήρια καὶ θεραπεύοντες ὥς(354C)περ
520 ἐκεῖνος ταῖς ἱερουργίαις. (356C) ἔθυε μὲν γὰρ Ἀβραάμ, ὥσπερ καὶ
ἡμεῖς, ἀεὶ καὶ συνεχῶς· ἐχρῆτο δὲ μαντικῇ τῇ τῶν διαττόντων ἄστρων.
Ἑλληνικὸν ἴσως καὶ τοῦτο. οἰωνίζετο δὲ μειζόνως. ἀλλὰ καὶ τὸν
ἐπίτροπον τῆς οἰκίας εἶχε συμβολικόν. εἰ δὲ ἀπιστεῖ τις ὑμῶν, αὐτὰ
(356D) δείξω σαφῶς τὰ ὑπὲρ τούτων εἰρημένα Μωυσῇ ⟨Gen. xv:1⟩
525 «μετὰ δὲ τὰ ῥήματα ταῦτα ἐγενήθη κυρίου λόγος πρὸς Ἀβραὰμ λέγων
ἐν ὁράματι τῆς νυκτός· μὴ φοβοῦ, Ἀβραάμ, ἐγὼ ὑπερασπίζω σου. ὁ
μισθός σου πολὺς ἔσται σφόδρα ...» (356E) εἴπατέ ★ μοι ἐνταῦθα, τοῦ
χάριν ἐξήγαγεν αὐτὸν καὶ τοὺς ἀστέρας ἐδείκνυεν ὁ χρηματίζων
ἄγγελος ἢ θεός; οὐ γὰρ ἐγίνωσκεν ἔνδον ὤν, ὅσον τι τὸ πλῆθός ἐστι
530 τῶν νύκτωρ ἀεὶ φαινομένων καὶ μαρμαρυσσόντων ἀστέ(357A)ρων; ἀλλ'
οἶμαι, δεῖξαι τοὺς διᾴττοντας αὐτῷ βουλόμενος, ἵνα τῶν ῥημάτων

---

513 ⟨δὲ⟩ Neumann   514 οἳ Aubert   ὃν M / αὐτοὶ Neumann
οὗτοι M   519 οἰκοδομοῦντες Aubert   520 ἐκεῖνος Aubert   ἐκεῖνοι M
        οἰκοδομοῦν M

ἐναργῆ πίστιν παράσχηται τὴν πάντα κραίνουσαν καὶ ἐπικυροῦσαν
οὐρανοῦ ψῆφον. *(358C)* ὅπως δὲ μή τις ὑπολάβῃ βίαιον εἶναι τὴν
τοιαύτην ἐξήγησιν, ἐφεξῆς ὅσα πρόσκειται παραθεὶς αὐτῷ
535 πιστώσομαι. γέγραπται γὰρ ἑξῆς ⟨Gen. xv:7 ff.⟩ «εἶπε δὲ πρὸς αὐτόν·
ἐγώ εἰμι ὁ θεὸς ὁ ἐξαγαγών σε ἐκ χώρας Χαλδαίων ... *(358D)* κατέβη
δὲ ὄρνεα ἐπὶ τὰ διχοτομήματα καὶ συνεκάθισεν αὐτοῖς Ἀβραάμ». τὴν
τοῦ φανέντος ἀγγέλου πρόρρησιν ἤτοι θεοῦ διὰ τῆς οἰωνιστικῆς
ὁρᾶτε κρατυνομένην, οὐχ, ὥσπερ παρ' ὑμῖν, ἐκ παρέργου μετὰ θυσιῶν
540 δὲ τῆς μαντείας ἐπιτελουμένης; φησὶ δέ, ὅ*(358E)*τι τῇ τῶν οἰωνῶν
ἐπιπτήσει βεβαίαν ἔδειξε τὴν ἐπαγγελίαν. ἀποδέχεται δὲ τὴν πίστιν
[τοῦ] Ἀβραὰμ προσεπάγων, ὅτι ἀληθείας ἄνευ πίστις ἠλιθιότης ἔοικέ
τις εἶναι καὶ ἐμβροντησία. τὴν δὲ ἀλήθειαν οὐκ ἔνεστιν ⟨ἰδεῖν⟩ ἐκ
ψιλοῦ ῥήματος, ἀλλὰ χρή τι καὶ παρακολουθῆσαι τοῖς λόγοις ἐναργὲς
545 σημεῖον, ὃ πιστώσεται γενόμενον τὴν εἰς τὸ μέλλον πεποιημένην
προαγόρευσιν ...
(351D) πρόφασις ὑμῖν τῆς ἔν γε τούτῳ ῥᾳστώνης περιλέλειπται μία, τὸ
μὴ ἐξεῖναι θύειν ἔξω γεγονόσι τῶν Ἱεροσολύμων, *(324C)* καίτοι Ἡλίου
τεθυκότος ἐν τῷ Καρμηλίῳ ⟨I Kings xviii:19 ff.⟩ *(324D)* καὶ οὐκ ἔν γε
550 τῇ ἁγίᾳ πόλει.

542 ἀληθείας ἄνευ Neumann   ἄνευ ἀληθείας Μ
543 ⟨ἰδεῖν⟩ Neumann

(42 E) It is worthwhile to recall in a few words whence and how we
first arrived at a conception of God; next to compare what is said
about the divine among the Hellenes and Hebrews; (43 A) and finally
to enquire of those who are neither Hellenes nor Jews, but belong to
the sect of the Galilaeans, why they preferred the belief of the Jews to
ours; and what, further, can be the reason why they do not even
adhere to the Jewish beliefs but have abandoned them also and
followed a way of their own. For they have not accepted a single
admirable or important doctrine of those that are held either by us
Hellenes or by the Hebrews who derived them from Moses; but from
both religions they have gathered what has been engrafted like
powers of evil, as it were, on these nations — (43 B) atheism from the
Jewish levity, and a sordid and slovenly way of living from our
indolence and vulgarity; and they desire that this should be called the
noblest worship of the gods ...
(69 B) What need have I to summon Hellenes and Hebrews as

witnesses of this? There exists no man who does not stretch out his hands towards the heavens when he prays; and whether he swears by one god or several, if he has any notion at all of the divine, he turns heavenward ...

(44 A) Now it is true that the Hellenes invented their myths about the gods, incredible and monstrous stories. For they said that Kronos swallowed his children (44 B) and then vomited them forth; and they even told of lawless unions, how Zeus had intercourse with his mother, and after having a child by her, married his own daughter, or rather did not even marry her, but simply had intercourse with her and then handed her over to another. Then too there is the legend that Dionysus was rent asunder and his limbs joined together again. This is the sort of thing described in the myths of the Hellenes.

(75 A) Compare with them the Jewish doctrine, how the garden was planted by God and Adam was fashioned by Him, and next, for Adam, woman came to be. For God said [Gen. ii : 18], "It is not good that the man should be alone. Let us make him an help-mate like him." Yet so far was she from helping him at all that she deceived him, and was in part the cause of his and her own fall from their life of ease in the garden. (75 B) This is wholly fabulous. For is it probable that God did not know that the being he was creating as a help-mate would prove to be not so much a blessing as a misfortune to him who received her? (86 A) Again, what sort of language are we to say that the serpent used when he talked with Eve? Was it the language of human beings? And in what do such legends as these differ from the myths that were invented by the Hellenes?

(89 A) Moreover, is it not excessively strange that God should deny to the human beings whom he had fashioned the power to distinguish between good and evil? What could be more foolish than a being unable to distinguish good from bad? For it is evident that he would not avoid the latter, I mean things evil, nor would he strive after the former, I mean things good. And, in short, God refused to let man taste of wisdom, than which there could be nothing of more value for him. (89 B) For that the power to distinguish between good and less good is the property of wisdom is evident surely even to the witless; (93 D) so that the serpent was a benefactor rather than a destroyer of the human race. (93 E) Furthermore, their God must be called envious. For when he saw that man had attained to a share of wisdom, that he might not, God said, taste of the tree of life, he cast him out of

529

the garden, saying in so many words [Gen. iii:22], "Behold, Adam has become as one of us, because he knows good from bad; and now let him not put forth his hand and take also of the tree of life and eat and then live forever." (94 A) Accordingly, unless every one of these legends is a myth that involves some secret interpretation, as I indeed believe, they are filled with blasphemous sayings about God. For in the first place to be ignorant that she who was created as a help-mate would be the cause of the fall; secondly to refuse the knowledge of good and bad, which knowledge alone seems to give coherence to the mind of man; and lastly to be jealous lest man should take of the tree of life and from mortal become immortal, — this is to be grudging and envious overmuch.

(96 C) Next to consider the views that are correctly held by the Jews, and also those that our fathers handed down to us from the beginning. Our account has in it the immediate creator of this universe, as the following shows ... Moses indeed has said nothing whatsoever about the gods who are superior to this creator, nay, he has not even ventured to say anything about the nature of the angels. (96 D) But that they serve God he has asserted in many ways and often; but whether they were generated by one god and appointed to serve another, or in some other way, he has nowhere said definitely. But he describes fully in what manner the heavens and the earth and all that therein were set in order. In part, he says, God ordered them to be, such as light and the firmament, and in part, he says, God made them, such as the heavens and the earth, (96 E) the sun and moon, and that all things which already existed but were hidden away for the time being he separated, such as water, I mean, and dry land. But apart from these he did not venture to say a word about the generation or the making of the Spirit, but only this, "And the Spirit of God moved upon the face of the waters". But whether that spirit was ungenerated or had been generated he does not make at all clear.

(49 A) Now, if you please, we will compare the utterance of Plato. Observe then what he says about the creator, and what words he makes him speak at the time of the generation of the universe, in order that we may compare Plato's account of that generation with that of Moses. For in this way it will appear who was the nobler and who was more worthy of intercourse with God, Plato who paid homage to images, or he of whom the Scripture says that (49 B) God spake with him mouth to mouth [Num. xii:8]. "In the beginning, God

530

created the heaven and the earth …" [Gen. i: 1] (49 D) In all this, you observe, Moses does not say that the deep was created by God, or the darkness or the waters. And yet, after saying concerning light that God ordered it to be, and it was, surely he ought to have gone on to speak of night also, and the deep and the waters. But of them he says not a word to imply that they were existing at all, though he often mentions them. Furthermore, he does not mention the birth or creation of the angels or in what manner they were brought into being, (49 E) but deals only with the heavenly and earthly bodies. It follows that, according to Moses, God is the creator of nothing that is incorporeal, but is only the disposer of matter that already existed. For the words [Gen. i: 2], "And the earth was invisible and without form", can only mean that he regards the wet and dry substance as the original matter and that he introduces God as the disposer of this matter.

(57 B, C) Now on the other hand hear what Plato says about the universe [Timaeus, 28 B–C]: "Now the whole heaven or the universe — or whatever other name would be most acceptable to it, so let it be named by us — did it exist eternally, having no beginning of generation, or has it come into being starting from some beginning? It has come into being. For it can be seen and handled and has a body; and all such things are the objects of sensation, and such objects of sensation, being apprehensible by opinion with the aid of sensation are things that came into being, as we saw, and have been generated … It follows, therefore, according to the reasonable theory, that we ought to affirm that this universe came into being as a living creature possessing soul and intelligence in very truth, (57 D) both by the providence of God."

(57 E) Let us but compare them, point by point. What and what sort of speech does the god make in the account of Moses, and what the god in the account of Plato? (58 A) [Gen. i: 26] "And God said, Let us make man in our image and our likeness" …

(58 B) Now, I say, hear also the speech which Plato puts in the mouth of the Artificer of All [Timaeus, 41 A–C]: "Gods of Gods! Those works whose artificer and father I am will abide indissoluble, so long as it is my will" … (99 D) Accordingly, since Moses, as it seems, has failed also to give a complete account of the immediate creator of this universe (99 E) let us go on and set one against another the opinion of the Hebrews and that of our fathers about these nations.

Moses says that the creator of the universe chose out the Hebrew nation, that to that nation alone did he pay heed and cared for it, and he gives him charge of it alone. But how and by what sort of gods the other nations are governed he has said not a word — unless indeed one should concede that he did assign to them the sun and moon [Deut. iv:19]. However of this I shall speak a little later. (100 A) Now I will only point out that Moses himself and the prophets who came after him and Jesus the Nazarene, yes and Paul also, who surpassed all the magicians and charlatans of every place and every time, assert that he is the God of Israel alone and of Judaea, and that the Jews are his chosen people. Listen to their own words, and first to the words of Moses [Exod. iv:22 f.]: "And thou shalt say unto Pharaoh, Israel is my son, my firstborn. And I have said to thee, let my people go that they serve me. But thou didst refuse to let them go." (100 B) And a little later [Exod. v:3], "And they say unto him, the God of the Hebrews hath summoned us, we will go therefore three days' journey into the desert that we may sacrifice unto the Lord our God." And soon he speaks again in the same way [Exod. vii:16], "The Lord the God of the Hebrews hath sent me unto thee saying, Let my people go that they may serve me in the wilderness ..." (106 A) But that from the beginning God cared only for the Jews (106 B) and that He drove them out as his portion has been clearly asserted not only by Moses and Jesus but by Paul as well, though in Paul's case this is strange. For according to circumstances he keeps changing his views about God, as the polypus changes his colours to match the rocks, and now he insists that the Jews alone are God's portion, and then again, when he is trying to persuade the Hellenes to take sides with him, he says [Rom. iii:29], "Do not think that he is the God of Jews only, but also of Gentiles, yea of Gentiles also." Therefore it is fair to ask of Paul (106 C) why God, if he was not the God of the Jews only but also of the Gentiles, sent the blessed gift of prophecy to the Jews in abundance and gave them Moses and the oil of anointing and the prophets and the law and the incredible and monstrous elements in their myths? For you hear them cry aloud [Ps. lxxvii:25], "Man did eat angels' food." And finally God sent unto them Jesus also, but unto us no prophet, no oil of anointing, no teacher, no herald to announce his love for man which should one day, though late, reach unto us also. (106 D) Nay he even looked on for myriads, or if you prefer, for thousands of years, while men in extreme ignorance served idols, as

532

you call them, from where the sun rises to where it sets, yes and from North to South, save only that little tribe which less than two thousand years before had settled in one part of Palestine. For if he is the God of all of us alike, and the creator of all why did he neglect us? (100 C) Wherefore it is natural to think that the God of the Hebrews was not the begetter of the whole universe with lordship over the whole, but rather, as I said before, that he is confined within limits, and that since his empire has bounds we must conceive of him as only one of the crowd of other gods. (106 D–E) Then are we to pay further heed to you because you or one of your stock imagined the God of the universe, though in any case you attained only to a bare conception of Him? Is not all this partiality? God, you say, is a jealous God. But why is he so jealous, even avenging the sins of the fathers on the children? [Exod. xx : 5] ...

(134 D) Now of the dissimilarity of language Moses has given a wholly fabulous explanation. For he said that the sons of men came together intending to build a city, and a great tower therein, (134 E) but that God said that he must go down and confound their languages. And that no one may think I am falsely accusing him of this, I will read from the book of Moses what follows [Gen. xi : 4 ff.]: "And they said, Go to, let us build a city and a tower" ... (135 A) And then you demand that we should believe this account, while you yourselves disbelieve Homer's narrative of the Aloadae, (135 B) namely that they planned to set three mountains one on another, "that so the heavens might be scaled" [*Odyssea*, XI, 316]. For my part, I say that this tale is almost as fabulous as the other. But if you accept the former, why in the name of the gods do you discredit Homer's fable? For I suppose that to men so ignorant as you I must say nothing about the fact that even if all men throughout the inhabited world ever employ one speech and one language, they will not be able to build a tower that will reach to the heavens, even though they should turn the whole earth into bricks. For such a tower will need countless bricks, (135 C) each one as large as the whole earth, if they are to succeed in reaching to the orbit of the moon. For let us assume that all mankind met together, employing but one language and speech, and that they made the whole earth into bricks and hewed out stones, when would it reach as high as the heavens, even though they spun it out and stretched it until it was finer than a thread? Then do you, who believe that this so obvious fable is true, and moreover think that God was

afraid of the brutal violence of men, (135 D) and for this reason came down to earth to confound their languages, do you, I say, still venture to boast of your knowledge of God?

(137 E) But I will go back again to the question how God confounded their languages. The reason why he did so Moses has declared — namely, that God was afraid that if they should have one language and were of one mind, they would first construct for themselves a path to the heavens and then do some mischief against him. (138 A) But how he carried this out Moses does not say at all, but only that he first came down from heaven because he could not, as it seems, do it from on high, without coming down to earth! But with respect to the existing differences in characters and customs, neither Moses nor anyone else has enlightened us. And yet among mankind the difference between the customs and the political constitutions of the nations is in every way greater than the difference in their language ... (138 C) If, therefore, he paid no heed to our spiritual blessings, neither took thought for our physical conditions, and moreover, (138 D) did not send to us teachers or lawgivers as he did for the Hebrews, such as Moses and the prophets who followed him, for what shall we properly feel gratitude to him? (141 C) But consider whether God has not given to us also gods and kindly guardians of whom you have no knowledge, gods in no way inferior to him who from the beginning has been held in honour among the Hebrews of Judaea, the only land that he chose to take thought for, as Moses declared and those who came after him, down to our own time. (141 D) But even if he who is honoured among the Hebrews really was the immediate creator of the universe, our beliefs about him are higher than theirs, and he has bestowed on us greater blessings than on them, with respect both to the soul and to externals. Of these, however, I shall speak a little later. Moreover, he sent to us also lawgivers not inferior to Moses, if indeed many of them were not far superior.

(146 A) Furthermore Moses also consciously drew a veil over this sort of enquiry (146 B) and did not assign the confusion of dialects to God alone. For he says that God did not descend alone, but that there descended with him not one but several, and he did not say who these were. But it is evident that he assumed that the beings who descended with God resembled him. If, therefore, it was not the Lord alone but his associates with him who descended for the purpose of confounding the dialects, it is very evident that for the confusion of men's characters, also, not the Lord alone but also those who

534

together with him confounded the dialects would reasonably be considered responsible for this division.

(148 B) Now why have I discussed this matter at such length, though it was my intention to speak briefly? For this reason: If the immediate creator of the universe be he who is proclaimed by Moses, then we hold nobler beliefs concerning him, in as much as we consider him to be the master of all things in general, but that there are besides national gods who are subordinate to him and are like viceroys of a king, each administering separately his own province, (148 C) and moreover, we do not make him the sectional rival of the gods whose station is subordinate to his. But if Moses first pays honour to a sectional god, and then makes the lordship of the whole universe contrast with his power, then it is better to believe as we do, and to recognize the God of the All, though not without apprehending also the God of Moses; this is better, I say, than to honour one who has been assigned the lordship over a very small portion, instead of the creator of all things.

(152 B) That is a surprising law of Moses, I mean the famous decalogue [Exod. xx : 14 ff.]: "Thou shalt not steal." "Thou shalt not kill." "Thou shalt not bear false witness." (152 C) But let me write out word for word every one of the commandments which he says were written by God Himself.

"I am the Lord thy God ..."

(152 D) Now except for the command "Thou shalt not worship other gods", and "Remember the Sabbath day", what nation is there, I ask in the name of the gods, which does not think that it ought to keep the other commandments? So much so that penalties have been ordained against those who transgress them, sometimes more severe, and sometimes similar to, those enacted by Moses, though they are sometimes more humane.

(155 C) But as for the commandment "Thou shalt not worship other gods", to this surely he adds a terrible libel upon God. "For I am a jealous God" [Exod. xx : 5], he says, and in another place again, (155 D) [Deut. iv : 24] "Our God is a consuming fire". Then if a man is jealous and envious you think him blameworthy, whereas if God is called jealous you think it a divine quality? And yet how is it reasonable to speak falsely of God in a matter that is so evident? For if he is indeed jealous, then against his will are all other gods worshipped, and against his will do all the remaining nations worship their gods. Then how is it that he did not himself restrain them, if he is

535

so jealous and does not wish that the others should be worshipped, but only himself? Can it be that he was not able to do so, (155 E) or did he not wish even from the beginning to prevent the other gods also from being worshipped? However, the first explanation is impious, to say, I mean, that he was unable; and the second is in accordance with what we do ourselves. Lay aside this nonsense, and do not draw down on yourselves such terrible blasphemy ... (160 D) Nowhere is God shown as angry or resentful or wroth or taking an oath or inclining first to this side, then suddenly to that, ... as Moses tells us happened in the case of Phinehas. If any of you has read the Book of Numbers, he knows what I mean. For when Phinehas had seized with his own hand and slain the man who had dedicated himself to Baal-peor, and with him the woman who had persuaded him, striking her with a shameful and most painful wound through the belly, (160 E) as Moses tells us, then God is made to say [Num. xxv : 11]: "Phinehas, the son of Eleazar, the son of Aaron the priest, hath turned my wrath away from the children of Israel, in that he was jealous with my jealousy among them; and I consumed not the children of Israel in my jealousy." What could be more trivial than the reason for which God was falsely represented as angry by the writer of this passage? (161 A) What could be more irrational, even if ten or fifteen persons, or even, let us suppose, a hundred, for they certainly will not say that there were a thousand, — however, let us assume that even as many persons as that ventured to transgress some one of the laws laid down by God! Was it right that on account of this thousand, six hundred thousand should be utterly destroyed? For my part, I think it would be better in every way to preserve one bad man along with a thousand virtuous men than to destroy the thousand together with that one ... (161 B) For if the anger of even one hero or unimportant demon is hard to bear for whole countries and cities, who could have endured the wrath of so mighty a God, whether it were directed against demons or angels or mankind? (168 B) It is worth while to compare his behaviour with the mildness of Lycurgus and the forbearance of Solon, (168 C) or the kindness and benevolence of the Romans towards transgressors. (171 D) But observe also from what follows how far superior are our teachings to theirs. The philosophers bid us imitate the gods so far as we can, and they teach us that this imitation consists in the contemplation of realities. (171 E) And that this sort of study is remote from passion and indeed based on freedom from passion, is, I suppose, evident, even without my saying it. In proportion then as we, having been assigned to the contemplation of realities, attain to freedom from passion, in so far do we become like God. But what sort of imitation of God is praised among the Hebrews? Anger and wrath and fierce jealousy. For God says [Num. xxv : 11], "Phinehas hath turned away my wrath among them". For God, on finding one who shared his resentment and his grief, thereupon, as it appears, laid aside his resentment. (172 A) These words and others like them about God, Moses is frequently made to utter in the Scripture.

(176 A, B) Furthermore observe from what follows that God did not take thought for the Hebrews alone, but though he cared for all nations, he bestowed on the Hebrews nothing considerable or of great value, whereas on us he bestowed gifts far higher and surpassing theirs. For instance the Egyptians, as they reckon up the names of not a few wise men among themselves, can boast that they possess many successors of Hermes, I mean of Hermes who in his third manifestation visited Egypt, while the Chaldaeans and Assyrians can boast of Oannes and Belos, the Hellenes can boast of countless successors of Cheiron. (176 C) For thenceforth all Hellenes were born with an aptitude for the mysteries and theologians, in the very way, you observe, which the Hebrews claim as their own peculiar boast ...

(178 A) But has God granted to you to originate any science or any philosophical study? Why, what is it? (178 B) For the theory of the heavenly bodies was perfected among the Hellenes, after the first observations had been made among the barbarians in Babylon. And the study of geometry took its rise in the measurement of the land in Egypt, and from this grew to its present importance. Arithmetic began with the Phoenician merchants and among the Hellenes in course of time acquired the aspect of a regular science. These three the Hellenes combined with music into one science, for they connected astronomy with geometry and adapted arithmetic to both, (178 C) and perceived the principle of harmony in it. Hence they laid down the rules for their music, since they had discovered for the laws of harmony with reference to the sense of hearing an agreement that was infallible, or something very near to it.

(184 B) Need I tell over their names man by man or under their professions? I mean, either the individual men, as for instance Plato, Socrates, Aristides, Cimon, Thales, Lycurgus, Agesilaus, Archidamus, — or should I rather speak of the class of philosophers, of generals, of artificers, of lawgivers? For it will be found that even the

most wicked and most brutal of the generals behaved more mildly (184 C) to the greatest offenders than Moses did to those who had done no wrong. (190 C) And now of what monarchy shall I report to you? Shall it be that of Perseus, or Aeacus, of Minos of Crete ...
(194 D) Would not any man be justified in detesting the more intelligent among you, or pitying the more foolish, who, by following you, have sunk to such depths of ruin that they have abandoned the everliving gods and have gone over to the corpse of the Jew.
(198 B, C) For the spirit that comes to man from the gods is present but seldom and in few, and it is not easy for every man to share in it or at every time. Thus it is that the prophetic spirit has ceased among the Hebrews also, nor is it maintained among the Egyptians, neither down to the present ...
(201 E) But what great gift of this sort do the Hebrews boast of as bestowed on them by God, the Hebrews who have persuaded you to desert to them? If you had at any rate paid heed to their teachings, you would not have fared altogether ill, and though worse than you did before, when you were with us, still your condition would have been bearable and supportable. For you would be worshipping one god instead of many, not a man, or rather many wretched men. (202 A) And though you would be following a law that is harsh and stern and contains much that is savage and barbarous, instead of our mild and humane laws, and would in other respects be inferior to us, yet you would be more holy and purer than now in your forms of worship. But now it has come to pass that like leeches you have sucked the worst blood from that source and left the purer ...
(205 E) As for purity of life you do not know whether he so much as mentioned it; but you emulate the rages and the bitterness of the Jews, overturning temples and altars ... (209 D) But I know not whence I was as it were inspired to utter these remarks. However, to return to the point at which I digressed, when I asked, "Why were you so ungrateful to our gods as to desert them for the Jews?" Was it because the gods granted the sovereign power to Rome, permitting the Jews to be free for a short time only, and then forever to be enslaved and aliens? Look at Abraham: was he not an alien in a strange land? And Jacob: was he not (209 E) a slave, first in Syria, then after that in Palestine, and in his old age in Egypt? Does not Moses say that he led them from the house of bondage out of Egypt "with an out-stretched arm"? And after their sojourn in Palestine did they not change their fortunes more frequently than observers say the

chameleon changes its colour, now subject to the judges, now enslaved to foreign races? And when they began to be governed by kings, but let me for the present postpone asking how they were governed, for as the Scripture tells us [I Sam. viii : 7], God did not willingly allow them to have kings, (210 A) but only when constrained by them, and after protesting to them beforehand that they would thus be governed ill, still they did at any rate inhabit their own country and tilled it for a little over three hundred years. After that they were enslaved, first to the Assyrians, then to the Medes, later to the Persians, and now at last to ourselves ... (213 A) Even Jesus, who was proclaimed among you, was one of Caesar's subjects ... (213 B) But when he became man what benefits did he confer on his own kinsfolk? Nay, the Galilaeans answer, they refused to hearken unto Jesus. What? How was it then that this hard-hearted and stubborn-necked people hearkened unto Moses? ...

(218 A) But now answer me this: Is it better to be free continuously and (218 B) during two thousand whole years to rule over the greater part of the earth and the sea, or to be enslaved and to live in obedience to the will of others? No man is so lacking in self-respect as to choose the latter in preference. Again, will anyone think that victory in war is less desirable than defeat? Who is so stupid? But if this that I assert is the truth, point out to me among the Hebrews a single general like Alexander or Caesar! You have no such man. And indeed, by the gods, I am well aware that I am insulting these heroes by the question, but I mentioned them because they are well known. (218 C) For the generals who are inferior to them are unknown to the multitude, and yet every one of them deserves more admiration than all the generals put together whom the Jews have had. (221 E) Further, as regards the constitution of the state and the fashion of the law courts, the administration of cities and the excellence of the laws, progress in learning and the cultivation of the liberal arts, were not all these things in a miserable and barbarous state among the Hebrews? (222 A) And yet the wretched Eusebius [*Praeparatio Evangelica*, XI, 5 : 7] will have it that poems in hexameters are to be found even among them, and sets up a claim that the study of logic exists among the Hebrews, since he has heard among the Hellenes the word they use for logic. What kind of healing art has ever appeared among the Hebrews, like that of Hippocrates among the Hellenes, and of certain other schools that came after him? (224 C) Is their "wisest" man Solomon at all comparable with Phocylides or Theognis or Isocrates

among the Hellenes? Certainly not. At least, if one were to compare
the exhortations of Isocrates with Solomon's proverbs, you would,
(224D) I am sure, find that the son of Theodorus is superior to their
"wisest" king. "But," they answer, "Solomon was proficient in the
secret cult of God." What then? Did not this Solomon serve our gods
also, deluded by his wife, as they assert [I Kings xi:4]? What great
virtue! What wealth of wisdom! He could not rise superior to
pleasure, and the arguments of a woman led him astray! Then if he
was deluded by a woman, do not call this man wise. But if you are
convinced that he was wise, do not believe that he was deluded by a
woman, but that, trusting to his own judgement (224E) and
intelligence and the teaching that he received from the God who had
been revealed to him, he served the other gods also. For envy and
jealousy do not come even near the most virtuous men, much more
are they remote from angels and gods. But you concern yourselves
with incomplete and partial powers, which if anyone calls demonic he
does not err. For in them are pride and vanity, but in the gods there is
nothing of the sort. (238A) And why is it that you do not abide even
by the traditions of the Hebrews or accept the law which God has
given to them? (238B) Nay, you have forsaken their teaching even
more than ours, abandoning the religion of your forefathers and
giving yourselves over to the predictions of the prophets. For if any
man should wish to examine into the truth concerning you, he will
find that the impiety is compounded of the rashness of the Jews and
the indifference and vulgarity of the Gentiles. For from both sides
you have drawn what is by no means their best but their inferior
teaching, and so have made for yourselves a border of wickedness.
For the Hebrews have precise laws concerning religious worship
(238C) and countless sacred things and observances which demand
the priestly life and profession. But though their lawgiver forbade
them to serve all the gods save only that one, whose "portion is Jacob,
and Israel an allotment of his inheritance" [Deut. xxxii:9]; though he
did not say this only, but methinks added also, "Thou shalt not revile
gods"; yet the shamelessness and audacity of later generations,
desiring to root out all reverence from the mass of the people, has
thought that blasphemy accompanies the neglect of worship. (238D)
This, in fact, is the only thing that you have drawn from this source;
for in all other respects you and the Jews have nothing in common.
Nay, it is from the new-fangled teaching of the Hebrews that you have
seized upon this blasphemy of the gods who are honoured among us;

but the reverence for every higher nature, characteristic of our religious worship, combined with the love of the traditions of our forefathers, you have cast off, and have acquired only the habit of eating all things, "even as the green herb" ...

(253 A) Now since the Galilaeans say that, though they are different from the Jews, they are still, precisely speaking, Israelites in accordance with their prophets (253 B) and that they obey Moses above all and the prophets who in Judaea succeeded him, let us see in what respect they chiefly agree with those prophets. And let us begin with the teaching of Moses, who himself also, as they claim, foretold the birth of Jesus that was to be. Moses, then, not once or twice or thrice but very many times says that men ought to honour one God only, and in fact names him the Highest; but that they ought to honour any other god, he nowhere says! (253 C) He speaks of angels and lords and moreover of several gods, but from those he chooses out the first and does not assume any god as second, either like or unlike him, such as you have invented ... (253 D) And the words [Gen. xlix: 10], "The sceptre shall not depart from Judah, nor a leader from his loins" were most certainly not said of the son of Mary, but of the royal house of David, which you observe, came to an end with King Zedekiah. And certainly the Scripture can be interpreted in two ways when it says, "until there comes what is reserved for him", but you have wrongly interpreted it "until he comes for whom it is reserved" ...

(290 B) And that Moses calls the angels gods you may hear from his words [Gen. vi: 2], "The sons of God saw the daughters of men that they were fair, (290 C) and they took them wives of all which they chose." And a little further on: "And also after that, when the sons of God came in unto the daughters of men, and they bore children to them, the same became the giants which were of old, the men of renown" [Gen. vi: 4]. Now that he means the angels is evident, and this has not been foisted on him from without, but is clear also from his saying that not men but giants were born from them. For it is clear that if he had thought that men (290 D) and not beings of some higher and more powerful nature were their fathers, he would not have said · that the giants were their offspring. For it seems to me that he declared that the race of giants arose from the mixture of mortal and immortal ... (290 E) He taught [scil. Moses] that there was only one God, but that he had many sons who divided the nations among themselves ...

(299 A) And now observe again how much Moses says about the deities that are not evil [Lev. xvi : 5], "And he shall take two he-goats for a sin-offering" ... (305 B) Accordingly it is evident from what has been said, that Moses knew the various methods of sacrifice. And to show that he did not think them impure as you do, listen again to his own words, "But the soul that eateth of the flesh of the sacrifice of peace-offerings that pertain unto the Lord, having his uncleanness upon him, even that soul shall be cut off from his people." So cautious is Moses himself with regard to the eating of the flesh of sacrifice.

(305 D) But now I had better remind you of what I said earlier, (305 E) since on account of that I have said this also. Why is it, I repeat, that after deserting us you do not accept the laws of the Jews or abide by the sayings of Moses? No doubt some sharp-sighted person will answer, "The Jews too do not sacrifice." But I will convict him of being terribly dull-sighted, for in the first place I reply that neither do you also observe any one of the other customs observed by the Jews; and secondly, that the Jews do sacrifice in their own houses, and even to this day everything that they eat is consecrated (306 A); and they pray before sacrificing, and give the right shoulder to the priests as the first fruits; but since they have been deprived of their temple, or, as they are accustomed to call it, their holy place, they are prevented from offering the first fruits of the sacrifice to God. But why do you not sacrifice, since you have invented your new kind of sacrifice and do not need Jerusalem at all? And yet it was superfluous to ask you this question, since I said the same thing at the beginning, (306 B) when I wished to show that the Jews agree with the Gentiles, except that they believe in only one God. That is indeed peculiar to them and strange to us, since all the rest we have in a manner in common with them — temples, sanctuaries, altars, purifications, and certain precepts. For as to these we differ from one another either not at all or in trivial matters ...

(314 C) Why in your diet are you not as pure as the Jews, and why do you say that we ought to eat everything "even as the green herb", putting your faith in Peter [Acts x : 15] ...

(319 D) But why do I discuss at length these teachings of theirs [scil. of the Galilaeans], when we may easily see whether they have any force? For they assert that God, after the earlier law, appointed the second. For, say they, the former arose with a view to a certain occasion and was circumscribed by time and place. That they say this falsely I will clearly show by quoting from the body of Moses not

542

merely ten but ten thousand passages (319 E) as evidence, where he says that the law is for all time ...

(340 A) You observe, then, how ancient among the Jews was this work of witchcraft, namely sleeping among the tombs for the sake of dream visions ...

(343 C) But you, though you practise that which God from the first abhorred, as he showed through Moses and the prophets, have refused nevertheless to offer victims at the altar, and to sacrifice. "Yes," say the Galilaeans, "because fire will not descend to consume the sacrifices as in the case of Moses." Only once, I answer, did this happen (343 D) in the case of Moses, and again after many years in the case of Elijah the Tishbite. For I will prove in a few words that Moses himself thought that it was necessary to bring fire from outside for the sacrifice, and even before him, Abraham the patriarch as well ...

(346 E) And this is not the only instance, but when the sons of Adam also offered first fruits to God, the Scripture says [Gen. iv : 4], "And the Lord had respect unto Abel and to his offerings" ... (347 C) But in the matter of their division one of them hit the mark and the other fell short of it. How, and in what manner? Why, since of things on earth some have life and others are lifeless, and those that have life are more precious than those that are lifeless to the living God who is also the cause of life, inasmuch as they have also had a share of life and have a soul, more akin to his — for this reason God was more graciously inclined to him who offered a perfect sacrifice ...

(354 A, B) And yet, I call the gods to witness, I am one of those who avoid keeping their festivals with the Jews; but nevertheless, I revere always the God of Abraham, Isaac, and Jacob; who being themselves Chaldaeans of a sacred race, skilled in theurgy, had learned the practice of circumcision while they sojourned as strangers with the Egyptians. And they revered a God who was ever gracious to me and to those who worshipped him as Abraham did, for he is a very great and powerful God, but he has nothing to do with you. For you do not imitate Abraham by erecting altars to him or building altars of sacrifice or worshipping him (354 C) as Abraham did, with sacrificial offerings. (356 C) For Abraham used to sacrifice even as we do, always and continually. And he used the method of divination from shooting stars. Probably this also in an Hellenic custom. But for higher things he augured from the flight of birds. And he possessed also a steward of his house who set signs for himself. And if one of you doubts this, the very words which were uttered by Moses concerning

it (356D) will show him clearly [Gen. xv : 1]: "After these sayings the word of the Lord came unto Abraham in a vision of the night, saying, 'Fear not, Abraham! I am thy shield. Thy reward shall be exceedingly great.'" ... (356E) Tell me ＊ now why he who dealt with him, whether angel or God, brought him forth and showed him the stars? For while still within the house did he not know how great is the multitude of the stars that at night (357A) are always visible and shining? But I think it was because he wished to show him the shooting stars, so that as a visible pledge of his words he might offer to Abraham the decision of the heavens that fulfills and sanctions all things. (358C) And lest any man should think that such an interpretation is forced, I will convince him by adding what comes next to the above passage. For it is written next [Gen. xv : 7 ff.]: "And he said unto him, 'I am the Lord that brought thee out of the land of the Chaldees' ... (358D) And the fowls came down upon the divided carcasses, and Abraham sat down among them." You see how the announcement of the angel or god who had appeared was strengthened by means of the augury from birds, and how the prophecy was completed, not at haphazard as happens with you, but with the accompaniment of sacrifices? Moreover (358E) he says that by the flocking together of the birds he showed that the message was true. And Abraham accepted the pledge, and moreover declared that a pledge that lacked truth seemed to be mere folly and imbecility. But it is not possible to behold the truth from speech alone, but some clear sign that by its appearance shall guarantee the prophecy that has been made concerning the future ...

(351D) However, for your indolence in this matter there remains for you one single excuse, namely, that you are not permitted to sacrifice if you are outside Jerusalem, (324C) though for that matter Elijah sacrificed on Mount Carmel [I Kings xviii : 19 ff.], (324D) and not in the holy city.
                                              (trans. W. C. Wright, *LCL*)

42E Μικρὸν δὲ ἀναλαβεῖν ἄξιον, ὅθεν ἡμῖν ἥκει καὶ ὅπως ἔννοια θεοῦ τὸ πρῶτον: In what follows (52B) we read: ὅτι δὲ οὐ διδακτόν, ἀλλὰ φύσει τὸ εἰδέναι θεὸν τοῖς ἀνθρώποις ὑπάρχει. The view that the human race possesses the knowledge of God by nature is enshrined in a long tradition of Greek philosophy. It has formulation in Iamblichus, *De Mysteriis*, I, 3 (ed. des Places), pp. 41 f.: συννπάρχει γὰρ ἡμῶν αὐτῇ τῇ οὐσίᾳ ἡ περὶ θεῶν ἔμφυτος γνῶσις, κρίσεώς τε πάσης ἐστὶ κρείττων καὶ προαιρέσεως. It has been suggested that contrast to the Christian belief in revelation is implied; see Asmus, *Julians Galiläerschrift, op. cit.* (supra, p. 507, n. 4), pp. 6 f.

However the view was adopted by Christian writers, who gave it a monotheistic twist; see Arnobius, *Adversus Nationes*, I, 33: "Quisquamne est hominum, qui non cum istius principis notione diem primae nativitatis intraverit? Cui non sit ingenitum, non adfixum, immo ipsius paene in genitalibus matris non impressum, non insitum, esse regem ac dominum cunctorum quaecumque sunt moderatorem?" The views of Julian on this subject also find expression in his "Speech against the Cynic Heraclius", *Orationes*, VII, p. 209C.

43B τὴν ἀθεότητα μὲν ἐκ τῆς Ἰουδαϊκῆς ῥᾳδιουργίας: The Jews had already been accused of atheism by Apollonius Molon, apud: Josephus, *Contra Apionem*, II, 148 (No. 49). For the charge of atheism brought against Flavius Clemens and his wife, see Cassius Dio, LXVII, 14 (No. 435). The Christians became heirs to the same accusation, as we learn from various sources; see A. Harnack, *Der Vorwurf des Atheismus in den drei ersten Jahrhunderten* (*Texte und Untersuchungen*, NF, Vol. XIII, Part 4), Leipzig 1905; E. Fascher, *Festschrift für Otto Michel, Zum 60. Geburtstag*, Leiden–Cologne 1963, pp. 78 ff. There are not a few examples where Christians are labelled ἄθεοι: see, e.g., Iustinus, *Apologia*, I, 6; II, 3; *The Martyrdom of Polycarp*, 9, in: H. Musurillo, *The Acts of the Christian Martyrs*, Oxford 1972, No. 1, p. 8; Lucianus, *Alexander*, 25 (see H. D. Betz, *Lukian von Samosata und das Neue Testament*, Berlin 1961, p. 7); *Epistula ad Diognetum*, 2:6; Clemens Alexandrinus, *Stromata*, VII, 1:1; Arnobius, *Adversus Nationes*, I, 29; III, 28; VI, 27; Athenagoras, 3, 4, 10; Eusebius, *Historia Ecclesiastica*, IV, 13:3; 15:6; *CIL*, III, No. 12132, l. 22.

44A Οὐκοῦν Ἕλληνες μὲν τοὺς μύθους ἔπλασαν ὑπὲρ τῶν θεῶν ἀπίστους καὶ τερατώδεις: The Greek myths, as told for all time in the formative age of Greek poetry, had for long been an object of philosophical and moral criticism, and served as an easy target for the attacks of Jewish and Christian opponents of paganism. Julian is ready to admit with the former Greek philosophical critics that the Greek myths are absurd, but states that the biblical stories can have no claim to be better, more rational or more moral. See J. Pépin, *Mythe et allégorie — Les origines grecques et les contestations judéo–chrétiennes*, Paris 1958, pp. 466 ff. However, in contrast to Celsus, who similarly criticizes the biblical myths but does not admit the legitimacy of their having an allegorical interpretation, Julian displays a fair attitude. He is ready to admit that all the fables may have some secret meaning calling for an allegorical interpretation, for otherwise they are full of blasphemies concerning God. For Porphyry's disparagement of biblical myths, see Porphyrius, *Adversus Christianos*, apud: Eusebius, *Praeparatio Evangelica*, I, 2:3 (No. 458).

καταπιεῖν γὰρ ἔφασαν τὸν Κρόνον τοὺς παῖδας: The myth of Kronos always served as an easy target for the various critics of Greek mythology, and the answer to them was that it had an allegorical interpretation. Thus Pausanias (VIII, 8:3) suggests that the story about Kronos was a piece of Greek wisdom. A double allegorical interpretation of the myth of Kronos is offered by Sallustius in *De Deis et Mundo*, 4. He first interprets it as a theological myth, explaining the swallowing of the children by Kronos by the intellectuality of the god, and by the fact that all intellectuality is directed towards itself. He also interprets the story as a physical myth, which identifies Kronos with Χρόνος and calls the parts of Time the children of the whole, so that this is what is implied by the father swallowing his children.

ἔγημε μὲν αὐτὸς τὴν αὐτοῦ θυγατέρα: Cf. Tatianus, *Oratio ad Graecos*, 8: Ζεὺς τῇ θυγατρὶ συγγίνεται; Clemens Alexandrinus, *Protrepticus*, II, 16:1: μίγνυται δ᾽ αὖθις ὁ γεννήσας οὑτοσὶ Ζεὺς τῇ Φερεφάττῃ, τῇ ἰδίᾳ θυγατρί. Pépin remarks that Julian bases himself on an Orphic form of the legend of Persephone, according to which Dionysus and Zeus are merged into one; see Pépin, *op. cit.* (supra, p. 545), p. 467, n. 89.

93D ὥστε τὸν ὄφιν εὐεργέτην μᾶλλον, ἀλλ᾽ οὐχὶ λυμεῶνα τῆς ἀνθρωπίνης γενέσεως εἶναι: It has been suggested that in this glorification of the serpent Julian drew on Gnostic arguments; see N. Brox, *Jahrbuch für Antike und Christentum*, X (1967), pp. 181 ff. For the Gnostic interpretation of the serpent, see H.M. Schenke, *Der Gott «Mensch» in der Gnosis*, Göttingen 1962, p. 75.

94A εἰ μὴ μῦθος ἔχων θεωρίαν ἀπόρρητον εἴη, ὅπερ ἐγὼ νενόμικα: Julian expresses the necessity for an allegorical interpretation of myths elsewhere in his works. Especially important for the statement of his views concerning myths is his "Speech against the Cynic Heraclius", *Orationes*, VII, p. 222C–D. He states there that the more flagrant the incongruity of the myth, the more useful it is in stimulating people to give up the obvious meaning of the words and seek a way to comprehend the transcendental nature of the gods. The view is paralleled by Sallustius, *De Deis et Mundo*. The whole oration was composed by Julian as a reaction to the rendering of a myth in which the gods were treated with irreverence. Especially illuminating is the way in which Julian proceeds in his "Hymn to the Mother of Gods". According to Julian the Mother of Gods is the source of the intellectual and creative gods, and the myth of Attis is to be reinterpreted allegorically. Thus the castration of Attis is taken to signify the checking of the unlimited; see *Orationes*, VIII (ed. Rochefort = V, ed. Hertlein), p. 167C. Julian again stresses here the paradox and incongruity attached to myths, inducing men to search out the truth (*ibid.*, p. 170A).

The long history behind the Greek allegorical interpretation of myths may be traced back to thinkers like Theagenes of Rhegium or Metrodorus of Lampsacus. These attempted to give a profounder meaning to the Homeric poems and reinterpreted the Homeric heroes as powers of nature. Thus Achilles became the Sun, Helen the Earth, Agamemnon the Ether, and so on. Allegorical interpretation became a fashion among the Stoic philosophers Zeno, Cleanthes and Chrysippus, and was popularized by works like the "Homeric Allegories", ascribed to Heraclitus and presumably dating to the first century C.E.; see now the edition of Buffière, Paris 1962. See also W. Kroll, *Studien zum Verständnis der römischen Literatur*, Stuttgart 1924, pp. 81 ff.; Pépin, *op. cit.* (supra, p. 545), pp. 125 ff.; M. Pohlenz, *Die Stoa*², Göttingen 1959, pp. 97f.; R. Pfeiffer, *History of Classical Scholarship from the Beginnings to the End of the Hellenistic Age*, Oxford 1968, pp. 237f. This method was continued by the Neoplatonists. A conspicuous example of its use is by Porphyrius, *De Antro Nympharum*. Above all, Julian's views should be compared with those of his ideological associate Sallustius, expressed in his "Concerning the Gods and the Universe", which helps to clarify the relationship of Julian and his circle to the myths; see Sallustius, *De Deis et Mundo*, 3–4, with Nock's summary and comments in his edition, Cambridge 1926, pp. XLIII ff. Sallustius maintains that for the inspired poets, the foremost philosophers, and the founders of mysteries, the myths partake of a divine nature, while the god who spoke through oracles had recourse to myths. Since all things rejoice in likeness, it follows that what we have to say about gods ought to be like gods. The universe itself can be called a myth, whose outer shells conceal the inner realities. However Sallustius, like Julian, still has to account for the adulteries, thefts and other bizarre stories about the gods found in the myths. A possible reply is that these teach the human soul to think of the words as a veil, and of truth as a mystery. Sallustius also divides myths into various categories: theological, physical, material, and mixed. The story of Kronos is classified by Sallustius among the theological myths; the worst explanation given to such myths is the materialistic one fostered by the Egyptians. Sallustius also offers an example of a detailed allegorical explanation for the myth of Attis, and suggests that the rape of Kore signifies the descent of souls. For the influence on Julian of the exposition of the myth of Attis by Sallustius, see Nock's edition, *op. cit.*, pp. LI ff.

In his Orations Julian sometimes expressly shows his opposition to the crude myths. Thus he does not approve of what Hesiod says in his "Theogony" (l. 371) about the union and marriage of Hyperion and Thea, the parents of Helios; see the Julianic *Ad Helium Regem*, p. 136C: μὴ δὲ συνδυασμὸν μηδὲ γάμους ὑπολαμβάνωμεν, ἄπιστα καὶ παράδοξα ποιητικῆς μούσης ἀθύρματα. He also allows himself to differ from the traditional myth in respect of Athena Pronoia; cf. *ibid.*, p. 149B. Cf. also *Orationes*, VIII (ed. Rochefort = V, ed. Hertlein), p. 171 AB.

49D οὔτε τῆς τῶν ἀγγέλων μέμνηται γενέσεως: The angels played some part in Neoplatonic philosophy also, as may be seen from Iamblichus, *De Mysteriis*, and other writings; cf. the introduction to Iamblichus (supra, p. 484). For Celsus' view that the Jews worship angels, see Celsus, apud: Origenes, *Contra Celsum*, I, 26 (No. 375).

106E θεὸς ζηλωτής: Julian's attack on the anthropopathic nature of the Jewish God is anticipated by Celsus; see Origenes, *Contra Celsum*, IV, 72 (No. 375).

134D Ὁ μὲν γὰρ Μωυσῆς αἰτίαν ἀποδέδωκε κομιδῇ μυθώδη τῆς περὶ τὰς διαλέκτους ἀνομοιότητος: For the criticism of the biblical story of the confusion of languages, and the comparison between the building of the Tower of Babel and the Homeric story of the Aloadae, see already Celsus, apud: Origenes, *Contra Celsum*, IV, 21 (No. 375), and the commentary *ad loc.*

160D οὐδαμοῦ χαλεπαίνων ὁ θεὸς φαίνεται οὐδὲ ἀγανακτῶν ... ὡς ὁ Μωσῆς φησιν ἐπὶ τοῦ Φινεές: The personality of Phinehas and his action are generally praised in Jewish tradition. Phinehas became a prototype of the unflinching religious and national fighter; cf. I Macc. ii:26; Siracides xlv:23; IV Macc. xviii:12; *Midrash Tanḥuma, Pinḥas*, 3 (ed. Buber), p. 151; see M. Hengel, *Die Zeloten*², Leiden–Cologne 1976, pp. 160ff.; Ginzberg, III, pp. 386ff.; VI, pp. 137f. However one may hear some undertone of criticism of the zeal shown by Phinehas in *TP Sanhedrin*, xvi, 27b.

176A–178C: In his argumentation Julian combines the total pagan achievement throughout the ages and contrasts it with that of the Jews. By this procedure he forestalls Christian arguments that the wisdom of the barbarians was more ancient than that of the Greeks, and that the Greeks had obtained the rudiments of civilization from the older, eastern peoples; see the extreme formulation of this view in Clemens, *Stromata*, I, 16:74:1: οὐ μόνης δὲ φιλοσοφίας, ἀλλὰ καὶ πάσης σχεδὸν τέχνης εὑρεταὶ βάρβαροι.

201E μᾶλλον δὲ πολλοὺς ἀνθρώπους δυστυχεῖς: The cult of martyrs is implied.

209D–218B: For the argument based on the low political status of the Jews, see Celsus, apud: Origenes, *Contra Celsum*, V, 41; VIII, 69 (No. 375).

218B ἕνα μοι κατὰ Ἀλέξανδρον δείξατε στρατηγόν, ἕνα κατὰ Καίσαρα: Cf. Iulianus, *Ad Alexandrinos*, No. 111 (ed. Bidez & Cumont) (No. 485).

222A καίτοι βούλεται ὁ μοχθηρὸς Εὐσέβιος εἶναί τινα καὶ παρ' αὐτοῖς ἐξάμετρα: The attribution of hexameters to Hebrew poetry by Eusebius (cf. *Praeparatio Evangelica*, XI, 5:7) is in line with his whole concept of the seniority of Hebraic culture, on which, according to him, the Greeks drew so much.

224D–E: On Solomon, see *Midrash Tanḥuma, Wa-era*, 2 (ed. Buber), p. 18.

238D ὡς λάχανα χόρτου: See Iulianus, *Orationes*, IX (ed. Rochefort = VI, ed. Hertlein), p. 192D (No. 487).

253D ἕως ἔλθῃ ᾧ ἀπόκειται: Cf. Iulianus, apud: Gregorius Nazianzenus, *Orationes*, V, 3 (No. 486c).

340A παλαιὸν ἦν τοῦτο τοῖς Ἰουδαίοις ... ἐγκαθεύδειν τοῖς μνήμασιν ἐνυπνίων χάριν: Cf. Strabo, *Geographica*, XVI, 2:35, p. 761 (No. 115).

354B οἳ ὄντες αὐτοὶ Χαλδαῖοι, γένους ἱεροῦ καὶ θεουργικοῦ: The Chaldaic Oracles enjoyed immense prestige in the eyes of Julian and his contemporary Neoplatonists.

τὴν μὲν περιτομὴν ἔμαθον, Αἰγυπτίοις ἐπιξενωθέντες: Celsus also stressed the dependence of the Jews on the Egyptians in the matter of circumcision. The same argumentation by Celsus hints that the Jews were unoriginal even in this, the most typical institution of Judaism. Julian implies that the Jews have their share in the ancient civilization of mankind, and may be looked upon as one of its components.

356C Ἀβραάμ, ... ἐχρῆτο δὲ μαντικῇ τῇ τῶν διαττόντων ἄστρων: Cf. the introduction to Vettius Valens (supra, p. 173).

481b

Contra Galilaeos, F4 — Neumann

Μωυσῆς ἡμέρας τεσσαράκοντα νηστεύσας ἔλαβε τὸν νόμον, Ἡλίας δὲ τοσαύτας νηστεύσας θείων αὐτοψιῶν ἔτυχεν. Ἰησοῦς δὲ τί μετὰ τοσαύτην νηστείαν ἔλαβεν;

Moses after fasting forty days received the law, and Elijah, after fasting for the same period, was granted to see God face to face. But what did Jesus receive, after a fast of the same length?

(trans. W.C. Wright, *LCL*)

481c

Contra Galilaeos, Theologische Literaturzeitung, XXIV (1899), No. 10, p. 301

διὰ τί γὰρ οὐχὶ καὶ Μωυσῆς, ὃς ἀναιρέτης ἐλθὼν τῆς ἁμαρτίας πλειστη-ριάσας ταύτην κατείληπται;

Is not this true of Moses also, who came to take away sin, but has been detected increasing the number of sins? (trans. W.C. Wright, *LCL*)

481d

Contra Galilaeos, F15 — Neumann

Quod de Israel scriptum est, Matthaeus evangelista ad Christum transtulit, ut simplicitati eorum qui de gentibus crediderant illuderet.

The words that were written concerning Israel Matthew the Evangelist transferred to Christ, that he might mock the simplicity of those of the Gentiles who believed. (trans. W.C. Wright, *LCL*)

482

Ad Arsacium Archiereum Galatiae, No. 84a, p. 430 B–D — Bidez & Cumont, 1922 = Bidez (I, 2, Budé), p. 145 = Hertlein, No. 49 = Wright, No. 22

... Ξενοδοχεῖα καθ᾽ ἑκάστην πόλιν κατάστησον πυκνά, ἵν᾽ ἀπολαύσωσιν οἱ ξένοι τῆς παρ᾽ ἡμῶν φιλανθρωπίας, οὐ τῶν ἡμετέρων μόνον, ἀλλὰ καὶ

1 καθ᾽ ἑκάστην] κατὰ πᾶσαν V / πυκνά om. V et Cassiodorus

From Tacitus to Simplicius

τῶν ἄλλων ὅστις ἂν δεηθῇ. χρημάτων δ᾽ ὅθεν εὐπορήσεις, ἐπινενόηταί
μοι τέως· ἑκάστου γὰρ ἐνιαυτοῦ τρισμυρίους μοδίους κατὰ πᾶσαν τὴν
5 Γαλατίαν ἐκέλευσα δοθῆναι σίτου καὶ ἑξακισμυρίους οἴνου ξέστας· ὧν τὸ
πέμπτον μὲν εἰς τοὺς πένητας τοὺς τοῖς ἱερεῦσιν ἐξυπηρετουμένους
ἀναλίσκεσθαί φημι χρῆναι, τὰ δὲ ἄλλα τοῖς ξένοις καὶ τοῖς μεταιτοῦσιν
ἐπινέμεσθαι παρ᾽ ἡμῶν. αἰσχρὸν γάρ, εἰ τῶν μὲν Ἰουδαίων οὐδὲ εἷς
μεταιτεῖ, τρέφουσι δὲ οἱ δυσσεβεῖς Γαλιλαῖοι πρὸς τοῖς ἑαυτῶν καὶ τοὺς
10 ἡμετέρους, οἱ δὲ ἡμέτεροι τῆς παρ᾽ ἡμῶν ἐπικουρίας ἐνδεεῖς φαίνοιντο.

3 χρημάτων δ᾽ ὅθεν Nicephorus et Cobet
χρημάτων· ὅθεν δὲ (δ᾽ V) codd.   6 ὑπηρετουμένους b
8 an παρ᾽ ὑμῶν? Bidez & Cumont   /   οὐδεὶς b

In every city establish frequent hostels in order that strangers may
profit by our benevolence; I do not mean for our own people only, but
for others also who are in need. I have but now made a plan by which
you may be well provided for this with money;[1] for I have given
directions that 30,000 modii of corn shall be assigned every year for
the whole of Galatia, and 60,000 pints of wine. I order that one-fifth of
this be used for the poor who serve the priests, and the remainder
distributed by us to strangers and beggars. For it is disgraceful that,
when no Jew ever has to beg, and the impious Galilaeans support not
only their own poor but ours as well, all men see that our people lack
aid from us.   (trans. W. C. Wright, *LCL*)

1 The translation is according to the punctuation of Bidez & Cumont.

This letter has been preserved through the History of Sozomenus, V, 16:5ff.
It should probably be dated to July 362 C. E., at the time of Julian's arrival at
Antioch; cf. the introduction to the letter by Bidez & Cumont, p. 112. It is
somewhat earlier than the letter to Theodorus; see J. R. Asmus, *Zeitschrift
für Kirchengeschichte*, XVI (1896), p. 235. The addressee Arsacius, the high
priest of Galatia, is probably mentioned in Libanius, *Epistulae*, 386 (ed.
Foerster), X, p. 378; cf. *PLRE*, I, p. 110.
On the letter, written against the background of the pagan restoration of the
worship of the old gods, cf., in general, Asmus, *op. cit.*, pp. 227ff.; Negri, *op.
cit.* (supra, p. 512), pp. 247ff.; Leipoldt, *op. cit.* (supra, p. 507, n. 4), pp. 27ff.
εἰ τῶν μὲν Ἰουδαίων οὐδὲ εἷς μεταιτεῖ: This is the first statement of this kind
to be found in our collection. For the state of the Jews as depicted by older
writers, cf. Martialis, XII, 57:13 (No. 246); Iuvenalis, VI, 546 f. (No. 299);
Artemidorus, *Onirocritica*, III, 53 (No. 395). For the Jewish practice of
private and public charity, see Moore, II, pp. 162ff.; E. E. Urbach, *Zion*, Vol.
XVI, Parts 3–4 (1951), pp. 1ff. For charity practised by Christians as a factor
in advancing their mission, see Iulianus, *Misopogon*, p. 363 A; idem,

550

Julian

Fragmentum Epistulae, p. 305 B–C: ἐπειδὴ γάρ, οἶμαι, συνέβη τοὺς πένητας ἀμελεῖσθαι παρορωμένους ὑπὸ τῶν ἱερέων, οἱ δυσσεβεῖς Γαλιλαῖοι κατανοήσαντες ἐπέθεντο ταύτῃ τῇ φιλανθρωπίᾳ. See also Eusebius, *Historia Ecclesiastica*, IX, 8:14; H. Bolkestein, *Wohltätigkeit und Armenpflege in vorchristlichen Altertum*, Utrecht 1939, pp. 476 f.

483

Ad Theodorum, No. 89a, pp. 453 C–454 B — Bidez & Cumont, *op. cit.* = Bidez (I, 2, Budé), pp. 154 f.
= Hertlein, No. 63 = Wright, No. 20

Ὁρῶν οὖν πολλὴν μὲν ὀλιγωρίαν οὖσαν ἡμῖν πρὸς τοὺς θεούς, ἅπασαν δὲ εὐλάβειαν τὴν εἰς τοὺς κρείττονας ἀπεληλαμένην ὑπὸ τῆς ἀκαθάρτου καὶ χυδαίας τρυφῆς, ἀεὶ μὲν οὖν ὠδυράμην ἐγὼ κατ' ἐμαυτὸν τὰ τοιαῦτα, τοὺς μὲν ⟨Ἰουδαί⟩ων ⟨εὐσεβ⟩είας σχολῇ προσέχοντας οὕτω διαπύρους ὡς
5 αἱρεῖσθαι μὲν ὑπὲρ αὐτῆς θάνατον, ἀνέχεσθαι δὲ πᾶσαν ἔνδειαν καὶ λιμόν, ὑείων ὅπως μὴ γεύσαιντο, μηδὲ κρέως του μὴ παραχρῆμα ἀποθλιβέντος, ἡμᾶς δὲ οὕτω ῥᾳθύμως τὰ πρὸς τοὺς θεοὺς διακειμένους, ὥστε ἐπιλελῆσθαι μὲν τῶν πατρίων, ἀγνοεῖν δὲ λοιπὸν εἰ καὶ ἐτάχθη πώποτέ τι τοιοῦτον. ἀλλ' οὗτοι μὲν ἐν μέρει θεοσεβεῖς ὄντες, ἐπείπερ ὃν
10 τιμῶσι ... ἀλλ' ἀληθῶς ὄντα δυνατώτατον καὶ ἀγαθώτατον, ὃς ἐπιτροπεύει τὸν αἰσθητὸν κόσμον, ὅνπερ εὖ οἶδ' ὅτι καὶ ἡμεῖς ἄλλοις θεραπεύομεν ὀνόμασιν, εἰκότα μοι δοκοῦσι ποιεῖν τοὺς νόμους μὴ παραβαίνοντες, ἐκεῖνο ⟨δὲ⟩ μόνον ἁμαρτάνειν, ὅτι μὴ καὶ τοὺς ἄλλους θεούς, ἀρέσκοντες τούτῳ μάλιστα τῷ θεῷ, θεραπεύουσιν, ἀλλ' ἡμῖν
15 οἴονται τοῖς ἔθνεσιν ἀποκεκληρῶσθαι μόνοις αὐτούς, ἀλαζονείᾳ βαρβαρικῇ πρὸς ταυτηνὶ τὴν ἀπόνοιαν ἐπαρθέντες. οἱ δὲ ἐκ τῆς Γαλιλαίας δυσσεβεῖς ὥσπερ τι νόσημα τῷ βίῳ τὴν ἑαυτῶν ...

2–3 καὶ χυδαίας τρυφῆς Hertlein   ... (ας supra scripto) τρυφ.. V
καὶ...αίας τρυφῆς Vᵈ   ....τρυφ... U   3–4 τοὺς μὲν........εὐσεβείας U
τοὺς μὲν δυσσεβείας Spanheim   6–7 μηδὲ κρέως του μὴ παραχρῆμα ἀποθλιβέντος Bidez & Cumont   μὴ παρά.....ἀποθλιβέντος V   μηδὲ....
τοῦ μὴ παρά....ἀποθλιβέντος U   7 τὰ secl. Hercher   8 ἐπιλελῆσθαι
Spanheim   .....ῆσθαι V   ἐπιλε (clarum ex vestigiis) Vᵈ   ...λῆσθαι U
9 πώποτέ τι Spanheim   .. ποτέ τι VU ...   ἄλλῳ ποτέ τι Vd
9–10 ἐπείπερ θεὸν τιμῶσι τὸν ὡς ἀληθῶς ὄντα δυνατώτατον Cobet
11 ὅνπερ Spanheim   ... V   ο ... U   ὂν Hertlein   12 τοὺς
νόμους μὴ Spanheim   τοὺς (vel σοὺς) ... μὴ V   τοὺς (vel. σοὺς) μους μὴ Vᵈ
σοὺς......μὴ U   13 ἐκεῖνο ⟨δὲ⟩ Reiske   14 ἀρέσκοντες τούτῳ Cobet
ἀρέσκ(ον) ... τω (ut videtur) V   ἀρέσκοντες αυτῶ Vᵈ   ἀρέσκ.....τῷ U
15 ἀποκεκληρῶσθαι] ἀποκεκλη   ..σθαι V   ἀποκεκλη.....U
16 οἱ δὲ Dübner   ...ε V   ...U

Therefore, when I saw that there is among us great indifference about the gods and that all reverence for the heavenly powers has been driven out by impure and vulgar luxury, I always secretly lamented this state of things. For I saw that those whose minds were turned to the doctrines of the Jewish religion are so ardent in their belief that they would choose to die for it, and to endure utter want and starvation rather than taste pork or any animal that has not the life [i.e. the blood] squeezed out of it immediately;[1] whereas we are in such a state of apathy about religious matters that we have forgotten the customs of our forefathers, and therefore we actually do not know whether any such rule has ever been prescribed. But these Jews are in part god-fearing, seeing that they revere a god[2] who is truly most powerful and most good and governs this world of sense, and, as I well know, is worshipped by us also under other names. They act, as is right and seemly, in my opinion, if they do not transgress the laws; but in this one thing they err in that, while reserving their deepest devotion for their own god, they do not conciliate the other gods also; but the other gods they think have been allotted to us Gentiles only, to such a pitch of folly have they been brought by their barbaric conceit. But those who belong to the impious sect of the Galilaeans, as if some disease ...   (trans. W. C. Wright, *LCL*)

1 The translation is according to the text of Bidez & Cumont.
2 The translation is according to the emendation of Cobet.

Like the former epistle, this is one of the letters written by Julian in the East, after he had already experienced the indifference of the pagans towards the worship of the gods; for the date, see the introduction to the text by Bidez & Cumont, p. 123, against Geffcken, *Kaiser Julianus, op. cit.* (supra, p. 511), p. 153. Another letter addressed by Julian to Theodorus is *Epistula*, 30 (ed. Bidez & Cumont). Julian also in his "Hymn to the Mother of Gods" expresses himself rather disparagingly about the pig, banned as food during the sacred rites; see *Orationes*, VIII (ed. Rochefort = V, ed. Hertlein), p. 177 C.

484

Fragmentum Epistulae, No. 89b, pp. 289C–D, 291D–292C, 295B–296B, 300C–301B — Bidez & Cumont, *op. cit.* = Bidez (I, 2, Budé), pp. 156 f., 159 f., 163, 168 f. = F119R

(289C) Ὁρᾶτε ὅσα ἡμῖν δεδώκασιν ⟨scil. οἱ θεοί⟩ ἐκ τῆς γῆς ἀγαθά, τροφὰς παντοίας, καὶ ὁπόσας οὐδὲ ὁμοῦ πᾶσι τοῖς ζῴοις. ἐπεὶ δὲ ἐτέχθημεν γυμνοί, ταῖς τε τῶν ζῴων ἡμᾶς θριξὶν ἐσκέπασαν καὶ τοῖς

ἐκ τῆς γῆς φυομένοις καὶ τοῖς ἐκ δένδρων· καὶ οὐκ ἤρκεσεν ἁπλῶς
5 οὐδὲ αὐτοσχεδίως, (289D) καθάπερ ὁ Μωυσῆς ἔφη, τοὺς χιτῶνας
λαβεῖν δερματίνους, ἀλλ᾽ ὁρᾶτε ὅσα ἐγένετο τῆς ἐργάνης Ἀθηνᾶς τὰ
δῶρα ... (291D) ῎Ανθρωπος γὰρ ἀνθρώπῳ καὶ ἑκὼν καὶ ἄκων πᾶς ἐστι
συγγενής, εἴτε [γάρ], καθάπερ λέγεται παρά τινων, ἐξ ἑνός τε καὶ
μιᾶς γεγόναμεν πάντες, εἴθ᾽ ὁπωσοῦν ἄλλως, ἀθρόως ὑποστησάντων
10 ἡμᾶς τῶν θεῶν ἅμα τῷ κόσμῳ τῷ ἐξ ἀρχῆς, οὐχ ἕνα καὶ μίαν, ἀλλὰ
πολλοὺς ἅμα καὶ πολλάς. (292A) οἱ γὰρ ἕνα καὶ μίαν δυνηθέντες, οἷοί
τε ἦσαν ἅμα καὶ πολλοὺς καὶ πολλάς· καὶ γὰρ ὃν τρόπον τόν τε ἕνα
καὶ τὴν μίαν, τὸν αὐτὸν τρόπον τοὺς πολλούς τε καὶ τὰς πολλὰς ***
εἴς τε τὸ διάφορον ἀποβλέψαντα τῶν ἠθῶν καὶ τῶν νόμων, οὐ μὴν
15 ἀλλὰ καί, ὅπερ ἐστὶ μεῖζον καὶ τιμιώτερον καὶ κυριώτερον, εἰς τὴν τῶν
θεῶν φήμην, ἣ παραδέδοται διὰ τῶν ἀρχαίων ἡμῖν θεουργῶν, (292B)
ὡς, ὅτε Ζεὺς ἐκόσμει τὰ πάντα, σταγόνων αἵματος ἱεροῦ πεσουσῶν ἐξ
οὐρανοῦ τὸ τῶν ἀνθρώπων βλαστήσειε γένος· καὶ οὕτως οὖν συγγενεῖς
γινόμεθα πάντες, εἰ μὲν ἐξ ἑνὸς καὶ μιᾶς, ἐκ δυοῖν ἀνθρώποιν ὄντες οἱ
20 πολλοὶ καὶ πολλαί *** καθάπερ οἱ θεοί φασι, καὶ χρὴ πιστεύειν
ἐπιμαρτυρούντων τῶν ἔργων, ἐκ τῶν θεῶν πάντες γεγονότες. ὅτι δὲ
πολλοὺς ἅμα ἀνθρώπους γενέσθαι μαρτυρεῖ τὰ ἔργα, (292C)
ῥηθήσεται μὲν ἀλλαχοῦ δι᾽ ἀκριβείας· ἐνταῦθα δὲ ἀρκέσει τοσοῦτον
εἰπεῖν, ὡς ἐξ ἑνὸς μὲν καὶ μιᾶς οὖσιν οὔτε τοὺς νόμους εἰκὸς ἐπὶ
25 τοσοῦτον παραλλάξαι, οὔτε ἄλλως τὴν γῆν ὑφ᾽ ἑνὸς ἐμπλησθῆναι
πᾶσαν, οὐδὲ εἰ ἅμα πολλὰ καθάπερ αἱ σύες ἔτικτον αὐτοῖς αἱ
γυναῖκες· πανταχοῦ δὲ ἀθρόως νευσάντων θεῶν, ὅνπερ τρόπον ὁ εἷς,
οὕτω δὲ καὶ οἱ πλείους προῆλθον ἄνθρωποι, τοῖς γενεάρχαις θεοῖς
ἀποκληρωθέντες, οἳ καὶ προήγαγον αὐτούς, ἀπὸ τοῦ δημιουργοῦ τὰς
30 ψυχὰς παραλαμβάνοντες ἐξ αἰῶνος ... (295B) Μηδεὶς οὖν ἀπατάτω
λόγοις μηδὲ ταραττέτω περὶ τῆς προνοίας ἡμᾶς· (295C) οἱ γὰρ ἡμῖν
ὀνειδίζοντες τὰ τοιαῦτα, τῶν Ἰουδαίων οἱ προφῆται, τί περὶ τοῦ νεὼ
φήσουσι τοῦ παρ᾽ αὐτοῖς τρίτον ἀνατραπέντος, ἐγειρομένου δὲ οὐδὲ
νῦν; ἐγὼ δὲ εἶπον οὐκ ὀνειδίζων ἐκείνοις, ὅς γε τοσούτοις ὕστερον
35 χρόνοις ἀναστήσασθαι διενοήθην αὐτὸν εἰς τιμὴν τοῦ κληθέντος ἐπ᾽
αὐτῷ θεοῦ· νυνὶ δὲ ἐχρησάμην αὐτῷ, δεῖξαι βουλόμενος (295D) ὅτι τῶν
ἀνθρωπίνων οὐδὲν ἄφθαρτον εἶναι δύναται καὶ οἱ τοιαῦτα γράφοντες

8 γὰρ secl. Hertlein   11 δυνηθέντες ⟨ποιεῖν⟩? Bidez & Cumont
12 τόν τε Cobet / τότε codd.   13 lacunam indicaverunt Bidez & Cumont
πολλὰς ⟨χρὴ ὑπολαβεῖν γεγενῆσθαι⟩ Reiske   17–18 ἐξ οὐρανοῦ Bidez
& Cumont   ἐξ ὧν που codd.   19 εἰ...ὄντες secl. Petavius
20 lacunam indicaverunt Bidez & Cumont / ⟨εἰ δε⟩ καθάπερ Hertlein
27 νευσάντων codd.   ⟨φυτευσάντων τῶν⟩ θεῶν Hertlein
35–36 ἐπ᾽ αὐτῷ] Ὑψίστου? Bidez & Cumont

ἐλήρουν προφῆται, γραϊδίοις ψυχροῖς ὁμιλοῦντες. οὐθὲν δέ, οἶμαι,
κωλύει τὸν μὲν θεὸν εἶναι μέγαν, οὐ μὴν σπουδαίων προφητῶν οὐδὲ
40 ἐξηγητῶν τυχεῖν· αἴτιον δὲ ὅτι τὴν ἑαυτῶν ψυχὴν οὐ παρέσχον
ἀποκαθᾶραι τοῖς ἐγκυκλίοις μαθήμασιν, οὔτε ἀνοῖξαι μεμυκότα λίαν
τὰ ὄμματα οὐδὲ ἀνακαθᾶραι τὴν ἐπικειμένην αὐτοῖς ἀχλύν, (296A)
ἀλλ' οἷον φῶς μέγα δι' ὁμίχλης οἱ ἄνθρωποι βλέποντες οὐ καθαρῶς
οὐδὲ εἰλικρινῶς, αὐτὸ δὲ ἐκεῖνο νενομικότες οὐχὶ φῶς καθαρόν, ἀλλὰ
45 πῦρ, καὶ τῶν περὶ αὐτὸ πάντων ὄντες ἀθέατοι, βοῶσι μεγάλα·
«φρίττετε, φοβεῖσθε, πῦρ, φλόξ, θάνατος, μάχαιρα, ρομφαία», πολλοῖς
ὀνόμασι μίαν ἐξηγούμενοι τὴν βλαπτικὴν τοῦ πυρὸς δύναμιν, (296B)
ἀλλ' ὑπὲρ μὲν τούτων ἰδίᾳ βέλτιον παραστῆσαι πόσῳ φαυλότεροι τῶν
παρ' ἡμῖν οὗτοι γεγόνασι ποιητῶν οἱ τῶν ὑπὲρ τοῦ θεοῦ λόγων
50 διδάσκαλοι ... (300C) Ἁγνεύειν δὲ χρὴ τοὺς ἱερέας οὐκ ἔργων μόνον
ἀκαθάρτων οὐδὲ ἀσελγῶν πράξεων, ἀλλὰ καὶ ῥημάτων καὶ
ἀκροαμάτων τοιούτων. ἐξελατέα τοίνυν ἐστὶν ἡμῖν πάντα τὰ ἐπαχθῆ
σκώμματα, πᾶσα δὲ ἀσελγὴς ὁμιλία. καὶ ὅπως εἰδέναι ἔχῃς ὃ
βούλομαι φράζειν, ἱερωμένος τις (300D) μήτε Ἀρχίλοχον
55 ἀναγινωσκέτω μήτε Ἱππώνακτα μήτε ἄλλον τινὰ τῶν τὰ τοιαῦτα
γραφόντων. ἀποκλινέτω καὶ τῆς παλαιᾶς κωμῳδίας ὅσα τῆς τοιαύτης
ἰδέας· ἄμεινον μὲν γὰρ καὶ πάντα. πρέποι δ' ἂν ἡμῖν ἡ φιλοσοφία
μόνη *** καὶ τούτων οἱ θεοὺς ἡγεμόνας προστησάμενοι τῆς ἑαυτῶν
παιδείας, ὥσπερ Πυθαγόρας καὶ Πλάτων καὶ Ἀριστοτέλης οἵ τε ἀμφὶ
60 Χρύσιππον καὶ Ζήνωνα. προσεκτέον μὲν γὰρ οὔτε πᾶσιν οὔτε τοῖς
πάντων δόγμασιν, (301A) ἀλλὰ ἐκείνοις μόνον, καὶ ἐκείνων ὅσα
εὐσεβείας ἐστὶ ποιητικά, καὶ διδάσκει περὶ θεῶν πρῶτον μὲν ὡς εἰσίν,
εἶτα ὡς προνοοῦσι τῶν τῇδε, καὶ ὡς ἐργάζονται μὲν οὐδὲ ἕν κακὸν οὔτε
ἀνθρώπους οὔτε ἀλλήλους, φθονοῦντες καὶ βασκαίνοντες καὶ
65 πολεμοῦντες, ὁποῖα γράφοντες μὲν οἱ παρ' ἡμῖν ποιηταὶ
κατεφρονήθησαν, οἱ δὲ τῶν Ἰουδαίων προφῆται διατεταμένως
συγκατασκευάζοντες ὑπὸ (301B) τῶν ἀθλίων τούτων τῶν
προσνειμάντων ἑαυτοὺς τοῖς Γαλιλαίοις θαυμάζονται.

43 οἱ ἄνθρωποι] οἱ ἀνόητοι? Bidez & Cumont   55 μήτε[1] Hertlein
   μὴ δὲ codd.   58 lacunam indicaverunt Bidez & Cumont /
   οἱ ... προστησάμενοι Horkel   ἡ ... προστησαμένη codd.
59 ὥσπερ Hertlein   ὅπερ codd.   63–64 οὔτε...οὔτε Cobet
οὐδὲ...οὐδὲ codd.   64 ἀλλήλους Cobet   ἄλλους codd.
   66 διατεταμένως Reiske   διατεταγμένως codd.

(289C) You see all the blessings of the earth that they [scil. the gods]
have granted to us, food of all sorts, and in an abundance that they
have not granted to all other creatures put together. And since we

were born naked they covered us with the hair of animals, and with things that grow in the ground and on trees. Nor were they content to do this simply or off-hand, (289 D) as Moses tells us men took coats of skins, but you see how numerous are the gifts of Athene the Craftswoman ... (291 D) ... Because every man, whether he will or not, is a kin to every other man, whether it be true, as some say, that we are all descended from one man and one woman or whether it came about in some other way, and the gods created us all together at the first when the world began, not one man and one woman only, but many men and many women at once. (292 A) For they who had the power to create one man and one woman, were able to create many men and women at once; since the manner of creating one man and one woman is the same as that of creating many men and many women. ∗∗∗ And one must have regard to the differences in our habits and laws, or still more to that which is higher and more precious and more authoritative, I mean the sacred tradition of the gods which has been handed down to us by the theurgists of earlier days (292 B), namely that when Zeus was setting all things in order there fell from him drops of sacred blood, and from sky,[1] as they say, arose the race of men. It follows therefore that we are all kinsmen, whether, many men and women as we are, we come from two human beings, or whether, ∗∗∗ as the gods tell us, and as we ought to believe, since facts bear witness thereto, we are all descended from the gods. (292 C) And that facts bear witness that many men came into the world at once, I shall maintain elsewhere, and precisely, but for the moment it will be enough to say this much, that if we were descended from one man and one woman it is not likely that our laws would show such great divergence; nor in any case is it likely that the whole earth was filled with people by one man; nay not even if the women used to bear many children at a time to their husbands, like swine. But when gods all together had given birth to men,[2] just as one man came forth, so in like manner came forth many men who had been allotted by the gods who rule over births; and they brought them forth, receiving their souls from the Demiurge from eternity ... (295 B) Therefore let no man deceive us with his sayings or trouble our faith in a divine providence. (295 C) For as for those who make such a profanation a reproach against us, I mean the prophets of the

1 The translation is according to the text of Bidez & Cumont.
2 The translation is according to the text of Hertlein.

Jews, what have they to say about their own temple, which was overthrown three times and even now is not being raised up again? This I mention not as a reproach against them, for I myself, after so great a lapse of time, intended to restore it, in honour of the god whose name has been associated with it. But in the present case I have used this instance because I wish to prove (295 D) that nothing made by man can be indestructible, and that those prophets who wrote such statements were uttering nonsense, due to their gossiping with silly old women. In my opinion there is no reason why their god should not be a mighty god, even though he does not happen to have wise prophets or interpreters. But the real reason why they are not wise is that they have not submitted their souls to be cleansed by the regular course of study, nor have they allowed those studies to open their tightly closed eyes and to clear away the mist that hangs over them. (296 A) But since these men see as it were a great light through a fog, not plainly or clearly, and since they think that what they see is not a pure light, but a fire, and they fail to discern all that surrounds it, they cry with a loud voice; "Tremble, be afraid, fire, flame, death, a dagger, a broad-sword!" Thus describing under many names the harmful might of fire. (296 B) But on this subject it will be better to demonstrate how much inferior to our own poets are these teachers of tales about the gods ... (300 C) And the priests ought to keep themselves pure not only from impure or shameful acts, but also from uttering words and hearing speeches of that character. Accordingly we must banish all offensive jests and all licentious intercourse. And that you may understand what I mean by this, (300 D) let no one who had been consecrated a priest read either Archilochus or Hipponax or anyone else who writes such poems as theirs. And in Old Comedy let him avoid everything of that type — for it is better to avoid it entirely[3] — and philosophy alone will be appropriate for us ★★★ and of philosophers only those who choose the gods as guides of their mental discipline, like Pythagoras and Plato and Aristotle, and the school of Chrysippus and Zeno. For we ought not to give heed to them all nor to the doctrines of all (301 A) but only to those philosophers and those of their doctrines that make men god-fearing and teach concerning the gods, first that they exist, secondly that they concern themselves with the things of this world, and further that they do no injury at all either to mankind or to one another, out of

---

3 The translation is according to the text of Bidez & Cumont.

jealousy or envy or enmity. I mean the sort of thing our poets in the first place have brought themselves into disrepute by writing and in the second place such tales as the prophets of the Jews take pains to invent, (301 B) and are admired for so doing by those miserable men who have attached themselves to the Galilaeans.

(trans. W.C. Wright, *LCL*)

The addressee of this fragment remains unknown. Some scholars think that it constitutes a part of the previous letter, the end of which is missing; see Asmus, *Zeitschrift, op. cit.* (supra, p. 507, n. 4), followed by Bidez & Cumont, *op. cit.*, pp. 127 f., in the introduction to this text. For a different view, cf. Wright's introduction to the third volume of Julian's works in the Loeb edition, pp. LXII f. The passage already refers to Julian's design to restore the Temple of Jerusalem; it was therefore probably written during the emperor's sojourn at Antioch.

289 D καθάπερ ὁ Μωυσῆς ἔφη, τοὺς χιτῶνας λαβεῖν δερματίνους: Cf. Gen. iii:21.

291 D εἴτε ... ἐξ ἑνός τε καὶ μιᾶς γεγόναμεν πάντες: In what follows Julian criticizes this view, as it is unlikely that the whole earth is filled by people descended from one couple. Instead he expresses preference for the theory of creation as propounded in Plato's *Timaeus*.

295 C τί περὶ τοῦ νεὼ φήσουσι τοῦ παρ᾽ αὐτοῖς τρίτον ἀνατραπέντος: Two of the destructions of the Temple were carried out by Nebuchadnezzar and Titus respectively. In his reference to the third destruction, Julian seems to have had in mind the desecration of the Temple by Antiochus Epiphanes.

διενοήθην αὐτὸν εἰς τιμὴν τοῦ κληθέντος ἐπ᾽ αὐτῷ θεοῦ: In the opinion of Bidez & Cumont the use of the aorist in this sentence clinches the argument for the view that Julian finally gave up his intention to restore the Temple; see also Vogt, *op. cit.* (supra, pp. 507 f., n. 5), pp. 47, 53. However, that is not necessarily so.

485

Ad Alexandrinos, No. 111, pp. 433 A–C — Bidez & Cumont, *op. cit.* = Bidez (I, 2, Budé), pp. 188 f. = Hertlein, No. 51 = Wright, No. 47

Λίαν αἰσχύνομαι νὴ τοὺς θεούς, ἄνδρες Ἀλεξανδρεῖς, εἴ τις ὅλως Ἀλεξανδρέων ὁμολογεῖ Γαλιλαῖος εἶναι. τῶν ὡς ἀληθῶς Ἑβραίων οἱ πατέρες Αἰγυπτίοις ἐδούλευον πάλαι, νυνὶ δὲ ὑμεῖς, ἄνδρες Ἀλεξανδρεῖς, Αἰγυπτίων κρατήσαντες (ἐκράτησε γὰρ ὁ κτίστης ὑμῶν τῆς Αἰγύπτου) τοῖς
5   κατωλιγωρηκόσι τῶν πατρῴων δογμάτων δουλείαν ἐθελούσιον ἄντικρυς τῶν παλαιῶν θεσμῶν ὑφίστασθε. καὶ οὐκ εἰσέρχεται μνήμη τῆς παλαιᾶς ὑμᾶς ἐκείνης εὐδαιμονίας, ἡνίκα ἦν κοινωνία μὲν πρὸς θεοὺς Αἰγύπτῳ τῇ

557

πάσῃ, πολλῶν δὲ ἀπηλαύομεν ἀγαθῶν. ἀλλ᾽ οἱ νῦν εἰσαγαγόντες ὑμῖν τὸ
καινὸν τοῦτο κήρυγμα τίνος αἴτιοι γεγόνασιν ἀγαθοῦ τῇ πόλει, φράσατέ
10 μοι. κτίστης ὑμῖν ἦν ἀνὴρ θεοσεβὴς Ἀλέξανδρος ὁ Μακεδών, οὔτι μὰ Δία
κατά τινα τούτων ὤν, οὔτε κατὰ πάντας Ἑβραίους, μακρῷ γεγονότας
αὐτῶν κρείττονας. ἐκείνων μὲν οὖν καὶ ὁ τοῦ Λάγου Πτολεμαῖος ἦν
ἀμείνων. Ἀλέξανδρος δὲ καὶ Ῥωμαίοις ἐπὶ ἅμιλλαν ἰὼν ἀγωνίαν ⟨ἂν⟩
παρεῖχε.

13 καὶ] κἄν Hercher / ἐπὶ] εἰς Hertlein / ἀγωνίαν ⟨ἂν⟩ Bidez & Cumont ἀγῶνα v

I am overwhelmed with shame, I affirm it by the gods, O men of
Alexandria, to think that even a single Alexandrian can admit that he
is a Galilaean. The forefathers of the genuine Hebrews were the
slaves of the Egyptians long ago, but in these days, men of
Alexandria, you who conquered the Egyptians — for your founder
was the conqueror of Egypt — submit yourselves, despite your sacred
traditions, in willing slavery to men who set at naught the teachings of
their ancestors. You have then no recollection of these happy days of
old when all Egypt held communion with the gods and we enjoyed
many benefits therefrom. But those who have but yesterday
introduced among you this new doctrine, tell me of what benefit they
have been to the city? Your founder was a god-fearing man,
Alexander of Macedon, in no way, by Zeus, like any of these persons,
nor again did he resemble any Hebrews, though the latter have shown
themselves far superior to the Galilaeans. Nay, Ptolemy son of Lagus
proved stronger than the Jews, while Alexander, if he had had to
match himself with the Romans, would have made even them fight
hard for supremacy.   (trans. W.C. Wright, *LCL*)

This is one of the two letters addressed by Julian to the Alexandrians, both
being connected with the expulsion of Athanasius; see O. Seel, *Klio*, XXXII
(1939), pp. 175 ff. It was written in Antioch in November 362 C.E.
ἐκείνων ... καὶ ὁ τοῦ Λάγου Πτολεμαῖος ἦν ἀμείνων: Cf. Agatharchides of
Cnidus, apud: Josephus, *Contra Apionem*, I, 205–211 (No. 30a); Appianus,
Liber Syriacus, 50:251–252 (No. 343). Julian could have learned of this event
also from Plutarchus, *De Superstitione*, 8 (No. 256). For his knowledge of
Plutarch, cf. Iulianus, *Orationes*, II (ed. Bidez = III, ed. Hertlein), pp. 104A;
128C–D; IX (ed. Rochefort = VI, ed. Hertlein), p. 200B; VII, p. 227A;
Epistula ad Themistium, p. 265A; *Misopogon*, p. 359A; *Epistula ad
Alexandrinos*, p. 378D.
Ἀλέξανδρος ... Ῥωμαίοις ἐπὶ ἅμιλλαν ἰών: Cf. Livius, IX, 17; P. Treves, *Il
mito di Alessandro e la Roma d'Augusto*, Milan–Naples 1953. See also
Lucianus, *Dialogi Mortuorum*, 25.

Ad Communitatem Iudaeorum, No. 204, pp. 396D–398 — Bidez & Cumont, *op. cit.* = Hertlein, No.
25 = Wright, No. 51 = F118R

Ἰουλιανὸς Ἰουδαίων τῷ κοινῷ

Πάνυ ὑμῖν φορτικώτερον γεγένηται ἢ ἐπὶ τῶν παρῳχηκότων καιρῶν τὸ
ζυγὸν τῆς δουλείας τὸ δὴ διαγραφαῖς ἀκηρύκτοις ὑποτάττεσθαι ὑμᾶς καὶ
χρυσίου πλῆθος ἄφατον εἰσκομίζειν τοῖς τοῦ ταμείου λόγοις· ὧν πολλὰ
5 μὲν αὐτοψεὶ ἐθεώρουν, πλείονα δὲ τούτων ἔμαθον, εὑρὼν τὰ βρέβια τὰ
καθ᾽ ὑμῶν φυλαττόμενα. ἔτι δὲ καὶ μέλλουσαν πάλιν εἰσφορὰν καθ᾽ ὑμῶν
προστάττεσθαι εἶρξα, καὶ τὸ τῆς τοιαύτης δυσφημίας ἀσέβημα ἐνταῦθα
ἐβιασάμην στῆσαι, καὶ πυρὶ παρέδωκα τὰ βρέβια τὰ καθ᾽ ὑμῶν ἐν τοῖς
ἐμοῖς σκρινίοις ἀποκείμενα, ὡς μηκέτι δύνασθαι καθ᾽ ὑμῶν τινα τοιαύτην
10 ἀκοντίζειν ἀσεβείας φήμην. καὶ τούτων μὲν ὑμῖν οὐ τοσοῦτον αἴτιος
κατέστη ὁ τῆς μνήμης ἄξιος Κωνστάντιος ὁ ἀδελφός, ὅσον οἱ τὴν γνώμην
βάρβαροι καὶ τὴν ψυχὴν ἄθεοι, οἱ τὴν τούτου τράπεζαν ἐστιώμενοι· οὓς
ἐγὼ μὲν ἐν χερσὶν ἐμαῖς λαβόμενος εἰς βόθρον ὤσας ὤλεσα, ὡς μηδὲ
μνήμην ἔτι φέρεσθαι ἢ εἶναι παρ᾽ ἡμῖν τῆς αὐτῶν ἀπωλείας. ἐπὶ πλέον
15 δὲ ὑμᾶς εὐωχεῖσθαι βουλόμενος, τὸν ἀδελφὸν Ἴουλον, τὸν αἰδεσιμώτατον
πατριάρχην, παρῄνεσα καὶ τὴν λεγομένην [εἶναι] παρ᾽ ὑμῖν ἀποστολὴν
κωλυθῆναι, καὶ μηκέτι δύνασθαι τὰ πλήθη ὑμῶν τινὰ ἀδικεῖν τοιαύταις
φόρων εἰσπράξεσιν, ὡς πανταχόθεν ὑμῖν τὸ ἀμέριμνον ὑπάρχειν, τῆς
ἐμῆς βασιλείας ἵνα ἀπολαύοντες *** ἔτι μείζονας εὐχὰς ποιῆτε ⟨ὑπὲρ⟩
20 τῆς ἐμῆς βασιλείας τῷ πάντων κρείττονι καὶ δημιουργῷ θεῷ τῷ
καταξιώσαντι στέψαι με τῇ ἀχράντῳ αὐτοῦ δεξιᾷ. πέφυκε γὰρ τοὺς ἔν τινι
μερίμνῃ ἐξεταζομένους περισπᾶσθαι τὴν διάνοιαν καὶ μὴ τοσοῦτον εἰς
τὴν προσευχὴν τὰς χεῖρας ἀνατείνειν τολμᾶν, τοὺς δὲ πανταχόθεν

2 γεγένηται ἢ Bidez & Cumont   γεγέν ... V   γεγένηται Ald. /
παρῳχηκότων καιρῶν Ald.   παρ........ιρῶν V   παρω..........ρῶν U
2–3 τὸ ζυγὸν Bidez & Cumont   τῶν ζυγῶν codd.   3 δὴ e corr. V   δὲ U
om. Ald. / ἀκηρύκτοις ὑποτάττεσθαι Ald.   ἀκ......τοις υ..πλάττεσθαι
(τά supra πλά scripto) V   ἀκ..........πράττεσθαι U   4 λόγοις Ald.
...οις V ......U   7 προστάττεσθαι Klimek   προτάττεσθαι codd.
8 στῆναι Klimek   13 μηδὲ Hercher   μήτε codd.   14 ἢ εἶναι secl. Heyler
ἢ περιεῖναι Bidez & Cumont / παρ᾽ ἡμῖν Ald.   παρ᾽ ὑμῖν codd.
16 καὶ] ὡς Naber / λεγομένην Ald .... μένην VU /   εἶναι secl. Bidez &
Cumont   17 ὑμῶν τινὰ Ald.   .μῶν.... V   ὑμῶν τινὰς Vᵈ.......U
18 ἀμέριμνον Ald.   ἀμέ...νον V U / ⟨ἐπὶ⟩ τῆς Reiske   19 ἀπολαύοντες
⟨εἰρήνης⟩ Reiske / ⟨ὑπὲρ⟩ Reiske   21 ἀχράντῳ] ...χράντῳ V
22 περισπᾶσθαι Bidez & Cumont   περι...σθαι V U   περιδεῖσθαι Ald.
περιδινεῖσθαι Reiske

ἔχοντας τὸ ἀμέριμνον, ὁλοκλήρῳ ψυχῇ χαίροντας, ὑπὲρ τοῦ βασιλείου
25 ἱκετηρίους λατρείας ποιεῖσθαι τῷ μείζονι, τῷ δυναμένῳ κατευθῦναι τὴν
βασιλείαν ἡμῶν ἐπὶ τὰ κάλλιστα, καθάπερ προαιρούμεθα. ὅπερ χρὴ
ποιεῖν ὑμᾶς, ἵνα κἀγώ, τὸν τῶν Περσῶν πόλεμον διορθωσάμενος, τὴν ἐκ
πολλῶν ἐτῶν ἐπιθυμουμένην παρ' ὑμῶν ἰδεῖν οἰκουμένην πόλιν ἁγίαν
Ἱερουσαλὴμ ἐμοῖς καμάτοις ἀνοικοδομήσας οἰκίσω, καὶ ἐν αὐτῇ δόξαν δῶ
30 μεθ' ὑμῶν τῷ κρείττονι.

26 ἡμῶν Hertlein .. ὦν V .... U om. Ald. 28 παρ' ὑμῶν Reiske
παρ' ὑμῖν codd. 29 καὶ ἐν Ald. .....ἐν V U / δῶ Hertlein
δώσω codd.

To the Community of the Jews

By far the most burdensome thing in the yoke of your slavery, even
more than in times past, has been the fact that you were subjected to
unauthorized ordinances[1] and had to contribute an untold amount of
money to the accounts of the treasury. Of this I used to see many
instances with my own eyes, and I have learned of more, by finding
the records which are preserved against you. Moreover, when a tax
was about to be levied on you again I prevented it, and compelled the
impiety of such obloquy to cease here; and I threw into the fire the
records against you that were stored in my desks; so that it is no
longer possible for anyone to aim at you such a reproach of impiety.
My brother Constantius of honoured memory was not so much
responsible for these wrongs of yours as were the men who used to
frequent his table, barbarians in mind, godless in soul. These I seized
with my own hands and put them to death by thrusting them into the
pit, that not even any memory of their destruction might still linger
amongst us. And since I wish that you should prosper yet more, I have
admonished my brother Iulus your most venerable patriarch that the
levy which is said to exist among you should be prohibited, and that
no one is any longer to have the power to oppress the masses of your
people by such exactions; so that everywhere you may have security
of mind, and in the enjoyment of my reign ... may offer
more fervid prayers for my reign to the Most High God, the
Creator, who has deigned to crown me with his own immaculate right
hand. For it is natural that the spirit of men who are afflicted by any
anxiety should be distracted,[2] and they would not have so much
confidence in raising their hands to pray; but that those who are in all

1 The translation is according to the text of Bidez & Cumont.
2 The translation is according to the text of Bidez & Cumont.

560

respects free from care should rejoice with their whole hearts and offer their suppliant prayers on behalf of my imperial office to Mighty God, even to him who is able to direct my reign to the noblest ends, according to my purpose. This you ought to do, in order that, when I have successfully concluded the war with Persia, I may rebuild by my own efforts the sacred city of Jerusalem, which for so many years you have longed to see inhabited, and may bring settlers there, and, together with you, may glorify the Most High God therein.

(trans. W.C. Wright, *LCL*)

Ἰουδαίων τῷ κοινῷ: Cf. Iulianus, *Orationes*, III (ed. Bidez = II, ed. Hertlein), p. 72 B: τῷ κοινῷ δὲ τῶν Ἰταλῶν. The expression τὸ κοινόν is used for the community of Jerusalem by Josephus, *Vita*, 65, 72, 190, 254, 309, 341, 393.

τὸ ζυγὸν τῆς δουλείας: A common Greek expression; cf., e.g., Sophocles, *Aiax*, 944: δουλείας ζυγά.

τὸ δὴ διαγραφαῖς ἀκηρύκτοις ὑποτάττεσθαι: Julian's liberality towards his subjects and his reluctance to approve heavy taxation are well known. Thus he praises Constantius in his panegyric of him for not increasing taxation; cf. *Orationes*, I, 21 D: οὐκ αὔξων τοὺς φόρους οὐδὲ τὰς συντάξεις. For Julian's objection to raising taxation in Gaul under Constantius, see his letter to Oribasius, *Epistulae*, 14 (ed. Bidez & Cumont), p. 385 A–B; Ammianus Marcellinus, XVII, 3. After he had become emperor Julian remitted the arrears of the Thracians; see *Epistulae*, 73 (ed. Bidez & Cumont). We learn that he prohibited forceful exaction of the *aurum coronarium* from Codex Theodosianus, XII, 13:1: "Aurum coronarium munus est voluntatis, quod non solum senatoribus, sed ne aliis quidem debet indici. Licet quaedam indictionum necessitas postulaverit; sed nostro arbitrio reservari oportebit"; cf. H. Dessau, *Revue de Philologie*, XXV (1901), pp. 285 ff. See also Iulianus, *Misopogon*, p. 365 B; Libanius, *Orationes*, XVI, 19: ὁ τὴν ἀρχαίαν τοῦ χρυσοῦ φορὰν τοῖς δήμοις ἀνείς; XVIII, 193, 282; Ammianus Marcellinus, XXV, 4:15: "Liberalitatis eius testimonia plurima sunt et verissima, inter quae indicta sunt tributorum admodum levia, coronarium indultum, remissa debita multa ... vectigalia civitatibus restituta cum fundis"; cf. Ensslin, *op. cit.* (supra, p. 511), pp. 128 ff.

καὶ πυρὶ παρέδωκα: Cf. Cassius Dio, LXXI, 32:2; *Scriptores Historiae Augustae — Vita Hadriani*, 7:6: "ad colligendam autem gratiam nihil praetermittens infinitam pecuniam, quae fisco debebatur ... remisit syngrafis ... quo magis securitas omnibus roboraretur, incensis". It is worthwhile comparing the "infinita pecunia" of the *Vita Hadriani* with the χρυσίου πλῆθος ἄφατον of the present letter.

τὰ βρέβια τὰ καθ᾽ ὑμῶν ἐν τοῖς ἐμοῖς σκρινίοις ἀποκείμενα: This is not the only instance where Julian uses Latin words in his correspondence; cf., e.g., Iulianus, *Epistulae*, 84a (ed. Bidez & Cumont), p. 430 C (μοδίους ... ξέστας); *ibid.*, 115, p. 424 D (πριβάτοις). For the form βρέβιον, cf., e.g., *P. Lond.*, V, No. 1904 = *CPJ*, No. 504. A more common transcription seems to be

From Tacitus to Simplicius

βρέουιον; cf. S. Daris, *Aegyptus*, XL (1960), p. 195. For σκρίνιον, cf. *ibid.*, p. 284.

καὶ τούτων ... οὐ τοσοῦτον αἴτιος ... Κωνστάντιος ... ὅσον οἱ τὴν γνώμην βάρβαροι καὶ τὴν ψυχὴν ἄθεοι: Cf. Iulianus, *Orationes*, VII, pp. 232D–233A; *Epistulae*, 33 (ed. Bidez & Cumont), p. 389D; *ibid.*, 60, p. 379A–B; *Misopogon*, p. 357B: ἀλλὰ ὑμῖν μόνοις ἐκ πάντων Ῥωμαίων πολλῶν δοῖεν οἱ θεοὶ Κωνσταντίων πειραθῆναι, μᾶλλον δὲ τῶν ἐκείνου φίλων τῆς πλεονεξίας.

οὓς ἐγὼ ... ὤλεσα: For the punishment of Constantius' counsellors after the trials held at Chalcedon, cf. Libanius, *Orationes*, XVIII, 152; Ammianus Marcellinus, XXII, 3; see Allard, *op. cit.* (supra, p. 511), II, pp. 92 ff.; W. den Boer, *op. cit.* (supra, p. 512), pp. 191 f.

εἰς βόθρον ὤσας ὤλεσα: This has been sometimes felt to be non-Greek in expression; see L. H. Heyler, *Juliani Imperatoris Quae Feruntur Epistolae*, Mainz 1828, p. 276: "Pro verbis εἰς βόθρον Atticus scriptor εἰς βάραθρον dixisset"; one might see here a reminiscence from Psalms; see Septuagint Ps. xciii : 13: ἕως οὗ ὀρυγῇ τῷ ἁμαρτωλῷ βόθρος. Even so, this in itself would not constitute a proof that the letter is a Jewish forgery. If a pagan like Libanius seems to have known Psalms (cf. below, the introductory remarks to Libanius), it is all the more likely that a man like Julian, who was born and educated as a Christian and knew his Septuagint well, would have been able to use it at least in a letter to Jews. Cf. also Iulianus, *Orationes*, IX (ed. Rochefort = VI, ed. Hertlein), p. 192D (No. 487), where Julian uses a quotation from Genesis. Still, this has been viewed, not as an expression influenced by Psalms, but rather as a combination of the following three expressions: εἰς βάραθρον ὠθέω, known from Athens in connection with the execution of criminals; a Homeric phrase: τὸν δὲ Ζεὺς ὦσεν ὄπισθε (*Ilias*, XV, 694); and εἰς βόθρον θύειν, connected with sacrifices for the gods of the underworld; see Lewy, *op. cit.* (supra, p. 512), p. 27.

ὑμᾶς εὐωχεῖσθαι βουλόμενος: Perhaps this implies an allusion by contradiction to the counsellors of Constantius: οἱ τὴν τούτου τράπεζαν ἐστιώμενοι.

τὸν ἀδελφόν: Libanius is also designated ἀδελφός by Julian; cf. *Epistulae*, 96 (ed. Bidez & Cumont), p. 374D. The same applies to his reference to the High Priest Theodorus, *ibid.*, 30.

Ἰουλον: Ἰουλος is designated here as πατριάρχης. Only four names are repeatedly found in the history of the Hillelite dynasty of patriarchs: Hillel, Simeon, Gamaliel, and Judah. Thus there can be hardly any doubt that Ἰουλος stands for Hillel. The more usual transcription is Ἑλλήλ which may be read in Epiphanius, *Panarion Haeresium*, XXX, 4 : 3; *ibid.*, 7 : 1; cf. also the Latin transcription "Hellel" in Hieronymus, *Commentarius in Esaiam*, viii : 11 (*CCSL*, LXXIII, ed. Adriaen, p. 116 = *PL*, XXIV, Col. 119): "Sammai et Hellel". However a patriarch named Ἰουλλος occurs in Origenes, *Selecta in Psalmos* (*PG*, XII, Col. 1056); the same name is found also in a fourth-century inscription from Tiberias; see Lifshitz, No. 76, IV: Ἰουλλος προνούμενος πάντα ἐτέλεσε. We read also in a Jewish inscription from Rome (*CII*, No. 468), "Iulus Sabinus", but here Iulus may stand for

Julian

Iulius. For the inscription from Tiberias, see also *Journal for the Study of Judaism*, IV (1973), p. 52.

The Ἴουλος mentioned here should be Hillel II. Although not mentioned in the Talmud, he is well known in Jewish mediaeval tradition, which goes back to the Gaonim. This tradition lists Hillel II as the tenth of the Hillelite house, son of the Patriarch Judah III; see A. Zacut, *Sefer Juchassin*, ed. H. Filipowski, London–Edinburgh 1857, pp. 122, 129.

Jewish tradition attributes to the same Hillel the divulgation of the secrets of intercalation of the Jewish calendar, and dates this to the year 670 of the Seleucid era, i.e. to 358–359 C. E., as stated in the work of the Spanish–Jewish twelfth-century astronomer Abraham bar Ḥiyya; see Abraham bar Chiya, *Sefer Ha-ʿibbur*, ed. H. Filipowski, London 1851, p. 97. Abraham bar Ḥiyya states it on the authority of Rav Hai Gaon; cf. E. Mahler, *Handbuch der jüdischen Chronologie*, Frankfurt 1916, pp. 455 ff.

Some difficulty attaches to the fact that a contemporary patriarch named Ἴουλλος is mentioned by Origenes, *loc. cit.*: τὸ ὕστερον δὲ ἀνακινούμενος περί τινων λογίων θεοῦ Ἰούλλῳ τῷ πατριάρχῃ, καί τινι τῶν χρηματιζόντων παρὰ Ἰουδαίοις σοφῶν. See also Hieronymus, *Apologia Adversus Libros Rufini*, I, 13 (*PL*, XXIII, p. 408): "Origenes patriarchen Huillum, qui temporibus eius fuit, nominat." No patriarch proper named Hillel living in the time of Origen is known in Jewish tradition. However, there was a Hillel whose dates will suit those of Origen, and who, though he did not exercise the power of a patriarch, was a son of the patriarch Gamaliel III and a brother of the patriarch Judah II; cf. *Tosefta Moʿed Qaṭan*, ii: 15–16; *Tosefta Shabbat*, vii: 17; *TB Pesaḥim*, 51a; see H. Graetz, *MGWJ*, XXX (1881), pp. 433 ff.; C. Albeck, *Introduction to the Talmud, Babli and Yerushalmi*, Tel Aviv 1969, p. 167 (in Hebrew). It is quite likely that the designation "patriarch" is used by Origen in a rather loose way, which also allows other important members of the family to be called by that name; cf. M. Hengel, *ZNTW*, LVII (1966), p. 154, n. 27. For another interpretation, see now N. R. M. de Lange, *Origen and the Jews*, Cambridge 1976, pp. 23 f.

As mentioned before, Epiphanius refers to a patriarch named Ἑλλήλ. He is adduced in connection with the story of Joseph the Comes, a Jew of standing from the retinue of the patriarch who became a convert to Christianity and displayed much zeal in the propagation of his new faith; see M. Avi-Yonah, *Geschichte der Juden im Zeitalter des Talmud*, Berlin 1962, pp. 170 f.; A. H. M. Jones, *The Later Roman Empire*, II, Oxford 1964, p. 944. This Joseph, already an old man, met Epiphanius at Scythopolis, in the time of Constantius, but his connections with the Jewish patriarch Ἑλλήλ belonged to the reign of Constantine the Great. However, Epiphanius himself admits that he was not certain about the actual name of the patriarch; see Epiphanius, *Panarion Haeresium*, XXX, 4:3: ὁ δὲ πατριάρχης κατ' ἐκεῖνο καιροῦ Ἑλλήλ τοὔνομα ἦν (νομίζω γὰρ ὅτι οὕτως τὸ ὄνομα αὐτοῦ Ἰώσηπος ἔλεγεν, εἰ μὴ ἀπὸ τοῦ χρόνου σφάλλομαι).

τὸν αἰδεσιμώτατον: Cf. Iulianus, *Epistulae*, 85 (ed. Bidez & Cumont): Θεοδώρᾳ τῇ αἰδεσιμωτάτῃ. Julian himself is called βασιλεὺς αἰδέσιμος by Libanius, *Orationes*, XVI, 16. The *Codex Theodosianus* has a more official

563

designation for the patriarch; see *Codex Theodosianus*, XVI, 8:8: "virorum clarissimorum et inlustrium patriarcharum arbitrio — 392 C.E."; XVI, 8:11: "Si quis audeat inlustrium patriarcharum contumeliosam per publicum facere mentionem" — 396 C.E.; XVI, 8:15: "viris spectabilibus patriarchis" — 404 C.E.; XVI, 8:13: "qui inlustrium patriarcharum dicioni subiecti sunt" — 397 C.E.

πατριάρχην: In the fourth century C.E. πατριάρχης was undoubtedly the official title of the Jewish *nasi* (נשיא), the head of the Jewish community. The institution as such gained official recognition in the Roman empire not later than the second half of the second century C.E., though at first the official title may have wavered between ἐθνάρχης, the Greek title of the Jewish *nasi* from the time of Simeon the Hasmonaean (I Macc. xiv:47; xv:1–2), and πατριάρχης. In the famous passage of Origen, where he points to the immense power concentrated in the hands of the Jewish leader, he calls him ἐθνάρχης; see Origenes, *Ad Africanum de Historia Susannae*, 14 (*PG*, XI, Cols. 81 ff.): καὶ νῦν γοῦν Ῥωμαίων βασιλευόντων. καὶ Ἰουδαίων τὸ δίδραχμον αὐτοῖς τελούντων, ὅσα συγχωροῦντος Καίσαρος ὁ ἐθνάρχης παρ' αὐτοῖς δύναται. We meet again with ἐθνάρχης in Origenes, *De Principiis*, IV, 3 (*PG*, XI, Col. 348): φάσκοντας τὸν ἐθνάρχην ἀπὸ τοῦ Ἰούδα γένους τυγχάνοντα ἄρχειν τοῦ λαοῦ. On the other hand, in his *Selecta in Psalmos* (*PG*, XII, Col. 1056), Origen uses πατριάρχης. The term occurs in the meaning of a head of a family in the Greek translation of Chronicles; see I Chron. xxiv:31; xxvii:22; II Chron. xix:8; xxiii:20; xxvi:12. However in the plural it gradually became the designation for the great ancestors of the Jewish people, Abraham, Isaac and Jacob; see IV Macc. vii:19; xvi:25; Acts vii:8; Heb. vii:4 (in Acts ii:29, David is designated "patriarch").

Apparently the title πατριάρχης, enshrined in the biblical tradition and having more religious connotations, gradually supplanted ἐθνάρχης, a title of more secular nature (it appears in the Septuagint only in I Maccabees). The first documentary evidence for the title πατριάρχης is the famous inscription from Stobi; see *CII*, No. 694 = Lifshitz, No. 10: ὅς ἄν δὲ βουληθῇ τι καινοτομῆσαι παρὰ τὰ ὑπ' ἐμοῦ δοχθέντα, δώσει τῷ πατριάρχῃ δηναρίων (μ)υριάδας εἴκοσι πέντε. On the date, see Hengel, *op. cit.* (supra, p. 563), pp. 145 ff. Frey dates the inscription in his edition in *CII* to 165 C.E., and inclines to interpret πατριάρχης in the meaning of a local Jewish functionary. The existence of this type of Jewish dignitary is attested by *Codex Theodosianus*, XVI, 8:13, dated in 397 C.E. However, both Hengel and Lifshitz date the inscription to the second half of the third century; above all, the high sum of 250,000 denarii mentioned in the inscription points to that late date. Thus the evidence of the inscription would be somewhat later than that afforded by Origenes, *Selecta in Psalmos*.

Both the patriarch and the ethnarchs are mentioned in *CII*, No. 719 (cf. Lifshitz, pp. 64 f.): Αὐρήλιος Ἰωσῆς ἐνεύχομαι τὰς θείας καὶ μεγάλ[ας] δυνάμ(ει)ς τὰς τοῦ θεοῦ καὶ τὰ[ς] δυνάμ(ει)ς τοῦ Νόμου καὶ τὴν τιμὴν τῶν πατριαρχῶν καὶ τὴν τιμὴν τῶν ἐθν(ι)αρχῶν καὶ τὴν τιμὴν τῶν σοφῶν. The "patriarchs" here precede the "ethnarchs", who may have been local Jewish functionaries like the Jewish ethnarch of Alexandria; cf. Strabo, apud:

Julian

Josephus, *Ant.*, XIV, 117 (No. 105). On the other hand, the patriarchs here might mean the ancestors of the Jewish people, while the ethnarchs are the actual heads of the people, as suggested by Hengel, *op. cit.* (supra, p. 563), p. 156; the meaning occurs twice in the works of Origen. An inscription from Sicily, dated 383 C.E., registers an oath adjured by the honour of the patriarchs; cf. *CII*, No. 650: "Adiuro vos per honores patriarcarum".

From Palestine itself, there is inscriptional evidence from a synagogue in fourth-century Tiberias, the main seat of the Patriarchate. In the list of donors to the synagogue we read (cf. Lifshitz, No. 76, VII–VIII): Σενε[ρος] θρεπτὸς τῶν λαμπροτάτων πατριαρχῶν.

For the fourth century C.E. πατριάρχης is the common designation used in patristic literature; it is also used by Libanius (cf. Nos. 496–500, 503); in the *Scriptores Historiae Augustae* (No. 527); and in the *Codex Theodosianus*; cf. *Codex Theodosianus*, II, 1:10 (398 C.E.); XVI, 8:1 (315 C.E.); XVI, 8:2 (330 C.E.); XVI, 8:8 (392 C.E.); XVI, 8:11 (396 C.E.); XVI, 8:14 (399 C.E.); XVI, 8:15 (404 C.E.); XVI, 8:17 (404 C.E.).

On the history of the Patriarchate, see Juster, I, pp. 391 ff.; Zucker, *op. cit.* (supra, p. 511), pp. 148 ff.; S.W. Baron, *The Jewish Community*, I, Philadelphia 1942, pp. 140 ff.; Mantel, *op. cit.* (supra, p. 512), pp. 175 ff.; Jones, *op. cit.* (supra, p. 563), II, pp. 944 f.

τὴν λεγομένην παρ' ὑμῖν ἀποστολὴν κωλυθῆναι: In the meaning of a tax levied from the Jews on behalf of the patriarchs the term ἀποστολή occurs only here. In the *Codex Theodosianus* the tax is called "aurum coronarium"; see *Codex Theodosianus*, XVI, 8:29 (429 C.E.). The term ἀποστολή should be connected with the institution of the ἀπόστολοι. Their importance and the part played by them in the levy of taxes from the Jews of the Diaspora is attested in both the *Codex Theodosianus* and patristic literature; see *Codex Theodosianus*, XVI, 8:14 (399 C.E.): "Superstitionis indignae est, ut archisynagogi sive presbyteri Iudaeorum vel quos ipsi apostolos vocant, qui ad exigendum aurum atque argentum a patriarcha certo tempore diriguntur." This is paralleled by a passage of Epiphanius, *Panarion Haeresium*, XXX, 11:1 ff.: Συμβέβηκε γὰρ αὐτῷ τῷ Ἰωσήπῳ μετὰ τὸ ἀδρυνθῆναι Ἰούδαν τὸν πατριάρχην ... ἀμοιβῆς ἕνεκα γέρας τῷ Ἰωσήπῳ τῆς ἀποστολῆς δοῦναι τὴν ἐπικαρπίαν. καὶ μετ' ἐπιστολῶν οὗτος ἀποστέλλεται εἰς τὴν Κιλίκων γῆν· ὃς ἀνελθὼν ἐκεῖσε ἀπὸ ἑκάστης πόλεως τῆς Κιλικίας τὰ ἐπιδέκατα καὶ τὰς ἀπαρχὰς παρὰ τῶν ἐν τῇ ἐπαρχίᾳ Ἰουδαίων εἰσέπραττεν ... Cf. also, *ibid.*, 4:2.

On the ἀπόστολοι as emissaries of the Jewish leadership, though their specific function of fund-raising is not emphasized, cf. Eusebius, *In Isaiam* xviii:1 f. (*PG*, XXIV, Col. 213): Ἀποστόλους δὲ εἰσέτι καὶ νῦν ἔθος ἐστὶν Ἰουδαίοις ὀνομάζειν τοὺς ἐγκύκλια γράμματα παρὰ τῶν ἀρχόντων αὐτῶν ἐπικομιζομένους; Procopius Gazaeus, *Commentarii in Isaiam* (*PG*, LXXXVII, 2, Col. 2132). The meaning of ἀπόστολος is explained by Hieronymus, *Ad Galatas* i:1 (*PL*, XXVI, Col. 311): "Apostolus autem, hoc est, missus, Hebraeorum proprie vocabulum est, quod Silas (שליח) quoque sonat, cui a mittendo missi nomen impositum est." Theomnestus is probably an ἀπόστολος alluded to in Libanius, *Epistulae*, No. 1097 (No. 501).

Some of the sources are very unsympathetic to the patriarchs, and stress their greediness and accumulation of vast amounts of money at the expense of the Jewish people. The patriarch is labelled "depopulator Iudaeorum" in *Codex Theodosianus*, XVI, 8:14: "Noverint igitur populi Iudaeorum removisse nos depraedationis huiusmodi functionem. Quod si qui ab illo depopulatore Iudaeorum ad hoc officium exactionis fuerint directi, iudicibus offerantur, ita ut tamquam in legum nostrarum violatores sententia proferatur." The vast treasures acquired by the patriarch through the levy of taxes is attested by Iohannes Chrysostomus, *Contra Iudaeos et Gentiles*, 16 (*PG*, XLVIII, Col. 835): οὐ τοὺς ἁπάντων πανταχόθεν φόρους συνάγων ὁ πατριάρχης, ἀπείρους κέκτηται θησαυρούς; cf. also Palladius, *Dialogus de Vita S. Ioannis Chrysostomi*, 15 (*PG*, XLVII, Col. 51 = ed. P. R. Coleman-Norton, Cambridge 1928, p. 90): φασὶ δὲ τὸν λυμεῶνα καὶ ψευδώνυμον πατριάρχην τῶν Ἰουδαίων κατ᾽ ἔτος ἀμείβειν, ἢ καὶ παρ᾽ ἔτος, τοὺς ἀρχισυναγώγους ἐπὶ συλλογῇ τοῦ ἀργυρίου.

The remarks of the Christian writers accord with their unsympathetic attitude towards the institution of the Patriarchate as the last official expression of Jewish political power; cf., e.g., Hieronymus, *Commentarii in Esaiam iii:4* (*CCSL*, LXXIII, p. 49, ed. Adriaen = *PL*, XXIV, Col. 64): "Consideremus patriarchas Iudaeorum et iuvenes sive pueros effeminatos-que ac deliciis affluentes, et impletam prophetiam esse cernemus"; Cyrillus Hierosolymitanus, *Catechesis*, XII, 17 (*PG*, XXXIII, Col. 745).

Talmudic sources have less information about the patriarchs' emissaries to the Diaspora in their capacity of tax-collectors, and they appear rather as representatives of the rabbis or sages; see *TP Giṭṭin*, i, 43d; *Qiddushin*, iii, 64a (on missions to Babylonia); *Horayot*, iii, 48a; *Pesaḥim*, iv, 31b–c.

On the institution of the ἀπόστολοι, see H. Graetz, *Geschichte der Juden*, IV⁴, Leipzig 1908, pp. 441 ff.; H. Vogelstein, *MGWJ*, XLIX (1905), pp. 427 ff.; idem, *HUCA*, II (1925), pp. 99 ff.; S. Krauss, *JQR*, XVII (1905), pp. 370 ff.; Juster, I, pp. 388 ff.; Zucker, *op. cit.* (supra, p. 511), p. 160; Mantel, *op. cit.* (supra, p. 512), pp. 190 ff.; G. Alon, *History of the Jews in the Age of the Mishna and the Talmud*, I, Tel Aviv 1958, pp. 156 ff. (in Hebrew).

It is clear that nothing came of Julian's plan for the abolition or transformation of the ἀποστολή. In 399 C.E. the emperor of the West, Honorius, imposed a ban on sending out money to the patriarch (*Codex Theodosianus*, XVI, 8:14). Although Honorius asserts that he wants to prevent exploitation of the Jews by the patriarch, the real cause of his step is to be sought in the state of rivalry between the two parts of the Roman empire and the reluctance of Honorius and Stilicho to allow the export of gold to Palestine, then under the rule of their eastern antagonists. After the change in the political situation, the prohibition was abrogated in 404 C.E.; see *Codex Theodosianus*, XVI, 8:17: "Hadriano praefecto praetorio. Dudum iusseramus, ut ea, quae patriarchis a Iudaeis istarum partium a consuetudine praebebantur, minime praeberentur. Verum nunc amota prima iussione secundum veterum principum statuta privilegia cunctos scire volumus Iudaeis mittendi copiam a nostra clementia esse concessam." For Honorius' policy towards the Jews, see also E. Demougeot, *Hommages à*

Julian

Léon Herrmann, Brussels–Berchem 1960, pp. 277 ff. After the extinction of the Patriarchate in 429 C.E. it was ordered that the Jewish leaders ("Iudaeorum primates") should be prohibited from continuing to levy the tax, which was to become an imperial tax imposed on the Jews; cf. *Codex Theodosianus*, XVI, 8:29.

Julian's use of κωλυθῆναι has been interpreted as implying a change in the tax, rather than its absolute abolition; see Allard, *op. cit.* (supra, p. 511), III, p. 139. Following him, see also Juster, I, p. 387, n. 1; Hack, *op. cit.* (supra, p. 509, n. 11); Lewy, *op. cit.* (supra, p. 512). The latter authors think that Julian's purpose was only to introduce changes in the collection of the tax, which should continue to be levied for the benefit of the patriarch. The opinion of Zucker that Julian abolished the tax out of sheer ignorance does not seem probable; cf. Zucker, *op. cit.* (supra, p. 511), p. 171.

εὐχὰς ποιῆτε ... τῷ πάντων κρείττονι καὶ δημιουργῷ θεῷ: Later in this letter Julian refers to the Deity by the designations τῷ μείζονι and τῷ κρείττονι while the fragment of the letter preserved by Lydus has Ὕψιστος Θεός (No. 486b). In the present passage Julian identifies the Jewish God with the creator god (δημιουργὸς θεός). It is true that in opposing the Christians, when carried away by his polemic, Julian emphasizes the inadequacy of the Mosaic concept of the creator of the universe; cf. *Contra Galilaeos*, 99 E (No. 481a). Yet in his letter to Theodorus (No. 483), Julian states that the Jews revere a God who is most powerful and good, who governs the world of sense, and is worshipped by us also under other names. If this is what Julian has to say about the God of the Jews in a letter written to a non-Jew, it is even more understandable that he equates the Jewish God with the creator of the universe in a letter aimed at winning the sympathy of the Jewish people. Julian maintains that there is no reason why the Jewish God should not be a mighty god, even though he does not happen to have wise prophets or interpreters; see *Fragmentum Epistulae*, 295 D (No. 484).

Julian was not the first to equate the Jewish God with the demiurge. In this he followed his great Neoplatonic predecessors, Porphyry (cf. No. 452) and Iamblichus (cf. No. 467). According to the first, the Jewish God is ὁ τῶν ὅλων δημιουργός; according to the latter, he is δημιουργὸς τοῦ αἰσθητοῦ κόσμου. Cf. also Iulianus, *Orationes*, VIII (Rochefort = V, ed. Hertlein), p. 166D: οὕτω γὰρ ἔμελλεν ὁ μέγας Ἄττις καὶ κρείττων [κρείττων, Hertlein; κρεῖττον, codd.] εἶναι δημιουργός. The description κρείττων as belonging to the κοινὰ ὀνόματα suits the religious phraseology of the age. Thus τὸ κρεῖττον was a term favoured by Constantine; see Eusebius, *Vita Constantini*, II, 24, 25, 26, 28, 33, 67, 68, 71, 72. In general, the expression τὸ κρεῖττον (or ὁ κρείττων) was widely diffused among pagans as well as Christians; cf., e.g., Porphyrius, *De Abstinentia*, II, 50 (ed. Nauck, p. 177, ll. 6 f.); *Corpus Hermeticum*, X, 22; XIV, 3.

τῷ καταξιώσαντι στέψαι με τῇ ἀχράντῳ αὐτοῦ δεξιᾷ: An allusion to the acquisition of imperial power. In the same way, in his letter to the Athenians, Julian attributes his acceptance of the imperial crown from the hands of the soldiers in Gaul to the intervention of Zeus, who had given him a sign and bade him not to oppose the will of the army; cf. Iulianus, *Epistulae*, 48 =

Sozomenus, *Historia Ecclesiastica*, V, 17:3 (ed. Bidez), p. 284 C–D: Ἐν δὲ ταῖς δημοσίαις εἰκόσιν ἐπιμελὲς ἐποιεῖτο παραγράφειν αὐτῷ Δία μὲν οἷά γε ἐκ τοῦ οὐρανοῦ προφαινόμενον καὶ στέφανον καὶ ἀλουργίδα τὰ σύμβολα τῆς βασιλείας παρέχοντα. Cf. also Iulianus, *Ad Helium Regem*, p. 131 B. Here, in Julian's terminology, which adapts itself to his listeners, Zeus is synonymous with Sarapis and Helios; see Mau, *op. cit.* (supra, p. 507, n. 4), pp. 54 f.

For the use of ἄχραντος, cf., e.g., Iulianus, *Ad Helium Regem*, p. 134 B: νοῦ δὲ ἐνέργειαν ἄχραντον εἰς τὴν οἰκείαν ἕδραν ἐλλαμπομένην; ibid., p. 140 D; idem, *Orationes*, VIII (ed. Rochefort = V, ed. Hertlein), pp. 160 C, 166 D, 179 D. Cf. also Iamblichus, *De Mysteriis*, V, 9 (ed. des Places), p. 164: ἀχράντως; Proclus, *The Elements of Theology* (ed. Dodds), 154, 156 (p. 136, ll. 8, 27).

περισπᾶσθαι τὴν διάνοιαν: An expression current among Stoic writers; cf. Epictetus, I, 26:3; Marcus Antoninus, *Meditationes*, II, 7.

καὶ μὴ τοσοῦτον εἰς τὴν προσευχὴν τὰς χεῖρας ἀνατείνειν τολμᾶν: This expresses an idea that is less characteristic of Jewish religious tradition than of Neoplatonic philosophy, which postulated undisturbed concentration during prayer.

ὑπὲρ τοῦ βασιλείου ἱκετηρίους λατρείας ποιεῖσθαι τῷ μείζονι, τῷ δυναμένῳ κατευθῦναι τὴν βασιλείαν ἡμῶν ἐπὶ τὰ κάλλιστα: This may be compared not only with Jewish literature (cf. II Chron. xvii:5; Additamenta ad Esther viii:12 f.; III Macc. vii:2; Letter of Aristeas, 15), but also with the Christian prayer for the welfare of the emperors, as evidenced by the First Epistle of Clement lxi:2: σύ, κύριε, διεύθυνον τὴν βουλὴν αὐτῶν κατὰ τὸ καλὸν καὶ εὐάρεστον ἐνώπιόν σου.

There is much to be said for the view that this is an allusion to the official Jewish prayer delivered for the welfare of the emperor. The similar Christian prayer had its antecedents in the service of the synagogue; see Lewy, *op. cit.* (supra, p. 512), p. 28.

πόλιν ἁγίαν Ἰερουσαλήμ: Julian also uses the Hebrew biblical form Ἰερουσαλήμ, known to him from the Septuagint, in *Contra Galilaeos*, 306 A: οὐδὲν δεόμενοι τῆς Ἰερουσαλήμ. This weakens the argument that the use of Ἰερουσαλήμ instead of the Greek form Ἱεροσόλυμα proves that the author was a Jew (see the introductory remarks of Bidez & Cumont to their edition of Julian's letter). By denoting Jerusalem ἁγία Julian adopts the current Jewish terminology as it appears in the Septuagint and Jewish-Hellenistic literature; cf. Is. xlviii:2, lii:1; I Macc. ii:7; II Macc. i:7, ix:14, xv:14; III Macc. vi:5; Dan. iii:28.

486b

apud: Lydus, *De Mensibus*, IV, 53 — Wünsch = Bidez & Cumont, *op. cit.*, No. 134 = Bidez (I, 2, Budé), p. 197

Καὶ Ἰουλιανὸς δὲ ὁ βασιλεύς, ὅτε πρὸς Πέρσας ἐστρατεύετο, γράφων

Ἰουδαίοις οὕτω φησίν· «Ἀνεγείρω γὰρ μετὰ πάσης προθυμίας τὸν ναὸν τοῦ Ὑψίστου Θεοῦ.»

And King Julian, when he left for the campaign against the Persians, writing to the Jews, says as follows: "I raise with the utmost zeal the temple of the Highest God."

τὸν ναὸν τοῦ Ὑψίστου Θεοῦ: For the diffusion of the appellation *Hypsistos Theos* among Jews, Christians and pagans, cf. the commentaries to Celsus, apud: Origenes, *Contra Celsum*, I, 24 (No. 375); Damascius, *Vita Isidori*, 55–56 (No. 548). Its neutral character was well suited for use by Julian in a letter to Jews. *Hypsistos* is also used by Constantine; see Eusebius, *Vita Constantini*, II, 48, 51.

486c

apud: Gregorius Nazianzenus, *Oratio*, V, 3 = *P.G.*, XXXV, Col. 668 = Bidez & Cumont, *op. cit.*, No. 134

Τέλος ἐπαφῆκε ⟨scil. ὁ Ἰουλιανὸς⟩ καὶ τὸ Ἰουδαίων φῦλον ἡμῖν, τὴν παλαιάν τε αὐτῶν κουφότητα καὶ τὸ καθ' ἡμῶν ἄνωθεν ὑποσμυχόμενον ἐν αὐτοῖς μῖσος συνεργὸν λαβὼν τοῦ τεχνάσματος, ἐπιθειάζων τε δῆθεν ἐκ τῶν παρ' αὐτοῖς βίβλων καὶ ἀπορρήτων, ὡς
5 νῦν αὐτοῖς ἀποκείμενον εἴη κατελθεῖν εἰς τὴν ἑαυτῶν, καὶ τὸν νεὼν ἀναδείμασθαι, καὶ τῶν πατρίων τὸ κράτος ἀνανεώσασθαι, καὶ ἀποκρυπτόμενος εὐνοίας πλάσματι τὴν ἐπίνοιαν.

Finally he [scil. Julian] let loose upon us the Jewish nation, his artifice being assisted by the fickleness of the Jews and by hate of us smouldering of old in their hearts. Forsooth he referred to God, basing himself on their books and secret teachings, to show that it was destined for them to return to their country, to rebuild the temple and to restore their ancestral power, thus concealing his plan under the mask of goodwill.

νῦν αὐτοῖς ἀποκείμενον εἴη κατελθεῖν: Cf. Septuagint, Gen. xlix: 10: ἔλθη τὰ ἀποκείμενα αὐτῷ. Cf. also Iulianus, *Contra Galilaeos*, 253 D (No. 481a).
κατελθεῖν εἰς τὴν ἑαυτῶν: A common expression denoting return from exile.
καὶ τὸν νεὼν ἀναδείμασθαι: This may be a hint by Gregorius at the contents of the letter referred to by Lydus (No. 486b). However, an allusion to this source seems to be precluded by the difference between the contents of that

letter, which is fully preserved, and the statement of Gregorius. Thus there is no allusion to the ἀποκείμενον εἴη κατελθεῖν εἰς τὴν ἑαυτῶν. Of course nothing compels us to deny that Julian may have addressed a third letter to the Jews.

486d

Ad *Tiberiopolitas*, apud: Stephanus Byzantius, s.v. Τιβεριάς — Meineke = Bidez & Cumont, *op. cit.*, No. 154

Τιβεριάς, πόλις τῆς Ἰουδαίας πρὸς τῇ Γεννησαρίτιδι λίμνῃ. ἐκτίσθη δὲ
ὑπὸ Ἡρώδου. ἐκ ταύτης ἦν Ἰοῦστος ὁ τὸν Ἰουδαϊκὸν πόλεμον τὸν κατὰ
Οὐεσπασιανοῦ ἱστορήσας. ὁ πολίτης Τιβεριεύς. Ἰουλιανὸς δὲ ὁ βασιλεὺς
Τιβεριοπολίτας ἐπέγραψε, καὶ δῆλον ὡς τῆς πόλεως καλουμένης
5 Τιβεριουπόλεως

1 γεννησαρίτιδι H   γεννεσιρίτιδι X   κεννεσιρίτιδι AV   κενεσιριτίδι R

Tiberias, a city of Judaea near the lake of Gennesareth. It was founded by Herod. Justus, who wrote the history of the Jewish war against Vespasian, hailed from it. A citizen of it is designated "Tiberian". King Julian addressed them as "Tiberiopolitae", and it is obvious that the city was called Tiberiopolis.

Stephanus Byzantius expressly refers to a letter by Julian written to Tiberias, inferring from the fact that its people are addressed as "Tiberiopolitae" that the city was called Tiberiopolis. Founded by Herod Antipas and named after the Emperor Tiberius, Tiberias was given by its founder the typical organization of a Hellenistic *polis*, with a *boulē* and an archon to rule it and a board of δέκα πρῶτοι typical of the cities of the Roman empire at that time. The majority of the population was Jewish, and during the Jewish war against Rome a section of the people, headed by the Jewish archon of the city, threw in their lot with the rebels against Rome and severed connections with their direct sovereign, Agrippa II. It seems characteristic that the citizen assembly of Tiberias, the first Hellenistic *polis* having a Jewish majority, took place at least occasionally in the synagogue; see Josephus, *Vita*, 277. The Greeks seem to have belonged to the lower stratum of the population; see A. H. M. Jones, *The Cities of the Eastern Roman Provinces*[2], Oxford 1971, p. 276. On the government of Tiberias, see also H. W. Hoehner, *Herod Antipas*, Cambridge 1972, pp. 97 ff.
The situation changed somewhat after the time of Hadrian. There was a pagan temple at Tiberias, the Hadrianeum, and from then on the coinage of the city displays pagan types, among them the figures of Zeus, Poseidon and Sarapis. Nevertheless the importance of Tiberias as a Jewish center did not diminish in the later period but grew as the city gradually became the Jewish

religious and political capital. It became the seat of the Patriarchate and the Synhedrion, and many of the leading sages were connected with it. In the life of the city the Jewish influence became paramount, and the Jewish element could not be ignored by the Roman authorities. See also the remarks of M. Avi-Yonah, *Geschichte der Juden im Zeitalter des Talmud*, Berlin 1962, p. 46. Thus it is not preposterous to assume that the letter of Julian referred to by Stephanus was addressed to a city mainly Jewish and should be interpreted against the background of Julian's policy towards the Jews. It is not known where Stephanus obtained his knowledge of Julian's letter. The information he relates before quoting the letter, namely the location of Tiberias, its foundation and the reference to Justus' History of the Jewish War, could have been derived from Josephus. The name Tiberiopolis for Tiberias is hardly attested elsewhere. The coins of Tiberias show the official name of the city to have been Tiberias Claudiopolis: Τιβεριέων Κλαυδιοπολιτῶν; see G. F. Hill, *Catalogue of the Greek Coins of Palestine*, London 1914, p. XIV; A. Kindler, *Coins of Tiberias*, Tiberias 1961, p. 46. The name is also attested in inscriptions; see L. Moretti (ed.), *Inscriptiones Graecae Urbis Romae*, I, Rome 1968, p. 73, No. 82. The name Tiberiopolis is usually associated with the Tiberiopolis of Pacatian Phrygia; see Ruge, PW, Ser. 2, VI, pp. 790 ff.; D. Magie, *Roman Rule in Asia Minor*, II, Princeton 1950, p. 1359, n. 24; C. Habicht, *JRS*, LXV (1975), p. 72. There was another Tiberiopolis in Pisidia (Pappa-Tiberiopolis); see Magie, *op. cit.*, II, p. 1173, n. 25. The only inscriptional evidence that may seem to support Stephanus comes from Crete, dating to the first or second century C.E.; see M. Guarducci (ed.), *Inscriptiones Creticae*, I, Rome 1935, pp. 19 f., No. 25; cf. M. Schwabe, in: *Commentationes in Memoriam Iohannis Lewy*, ed. M. Schwabe & Y. Gutman, Jerusalem 1949, pp. 231 f. (in Hebrew). The Cretan inscription reads *T*]ιβεριοπολιτῶ[ν, and Guarducci suggests, without adducing Stephanus, that the Tiberiopolis implied here is the Palestinian Tiberias, and not the Phrygian Tiberiopolis. However, the arguments advanced by Guarducci are not strong, and one should rather identify the city in this inscription with the Phrygian or Pisidian Tiberiopolis; see also L. Robert, *REG*, LXXVIII (1965), pp. XXXVIII f.; J. & L. Robert, *REG*, XC (1977), pp. 382 ff.

ἐκτίσθη δὲ ὑπὸ Ἡρώδου: Herod Antipas is meant. On the foundation of Tiberias, see Hoehner, *op. cit.* (supra, p. 570), pp. 91 ff.

Ἰοῦστος: On Justus, see above, the commentary to No. 398.

487

Orationes, No. IX, p. 192 C–D — Rochefort = VI Hertlein

Οὕτως εἶ μνήμων; οὕτως εἶ σπουδαῖος, ὡς [ὁ] τοῦτο ὀνειδίζων τῷ κενοδόξῳ, κατὰ σὲ φάναι, Διογένει, κατ' ἐμὲ δὲ σπουδαιοτάτῳ θεράποντι καὶ

1 ὁ secl. Rochefort

ὑπηρέτῃ τοῦ Πυθίου, τὴν τοῦ πολύποδος ἐδωδήν, κατεδήδοκας μυρίους
ταρίχους, «Ἰχθῦς ὄρνιθάς τε φίλας θ᾽ ὅτι χεῖρας ἵκοιτο» Αἰγύπτιός γε ὤν,
οὐ τῶν ἱερέων, ἀλλὰ τῶν παμφάγων, οἷς πάντα ἐσθίειν νόμος ὡς λάχανα
χόρτου; γνωρίζεις, οἶμαι, τῶν Γαλιλαίων τὰ ῥήματα.

4 θ᾽ non habet Homer / γε Reiske   τε U

Is this the sort of memory you have? Is this your zeal for truth? For
though you criticized Diogenes the vain-glorious, as you call him —
though I call him the most zealous servant and vassal of the Pythian
god — for eating octopus, you yourself have devoured endless
pickled food, "fish and birds and whatever else might come to hand".
For you are an Egyptian, though not of the priestly caste, but of the
omnivorous type whose habit it is to eat "everything even as the
green herb". You recognize, I suppose, the words of the
Galilaeans. (trans. W. C. Wright, *LCL*)

οἷς πάντα ἐσθίειν νόμος ὡς λάχανα χόρτου: This allusion to Gen. ix: 3 (ὡς
λάχανα χόρτου δέδωκα ὑμῖν τὰ πάντα) is also made by Julian in *Contra
Galilaeos*, 238 D (No. 481); see the commentary, *ad loc.*

CXXXVII. SALLUSTIUS NEOPLATONICUS

Fourth century C.E.

The Neoplatonic philosopher and close associate of the emperor Julian refers to the Hebrews, among other nations, in order to explain his views on Providence.[1] Like earlier writers, Sallustius considers circumcision to be the most characteristic Jewish national custom; see, for example, Petronius, Satyricon, 102:14 (No. 194).

488

De Deis et Mundo, IX, 5 — Rochefort

Τὸ δὲ ἀδικίας τε καὶ ἀσελγείας ἐκ τῆς Εἱμαρμένης διδόναι, ἡμᾶς μὲν ἀγαθοὺς τοὺς δὲ θεοὺς ποιεῖν ἐστι κακούς· εἰ μὴ ἄρα ἐκεῖνο λέγειν ἐθέλοι τις ὡς ὅλῳ μὲν τῷ Κόσμῳ καὶ τοῖς κατὰ φύσιν ἔχουσιν ἐπ' ἀγαθῷ γίνεται πάντα, τὸ δὲ τραφῆναι κακῶς ἢ τὴν φύσιν ἀσθενεστέρως ἔχειν τὰ παρὰ τῆς Εἱμαρμένης ἀγαθὰ εἰς τὸ χεῖρον μεταβάλλει, ὥσπερ τὸν ἥλιον ἀγαθὸν ὄντα πᾶσι, τοῖς ὀφθαλμιῶσιν ἢ πυρέττουσι βλαβερὸν εἶναι συμβαίνει. διὰ τί γὰρ Μασσαγέται μὲν τοὺς πατέρας ἐσθίουσιν, Ἑβραῖοι δὲ περιτέμνονται, Πέρσαι δὲ τὴν εὐγένειαν σῴζουσι ⟨ἐκ μητέρων παιδοποιούμενοι⟩;

9 εὐτεκνίαν Rochefort / ⟨ἐκ μητέρων παιδοποιούμενοι⟩ Nock

On the other hand to suppose that acts of injustice and wantonness come from the Heimarmene is to make us good and the gods bad, unless what is meant thereby is that everything happens for the good of the universe as a whole and for all things in a natural condition, but that evil education or weakness of nature changes the blessings of Heimarmene to evil, as the sun, good as it is for all, is found to be harmful to those who suffer from inflammation of the eyes or from fever. Otherwise, why do the Massagetae eat their fathers and the

---

1 On the views of Sallustius, see A. D. Nock, *Sallustius — Concerning the Gods and the Universe,* Cambridge 1926, pp. XL ff.; G. Rochefort, *REG,* LXIX (1956), pp. 50 ff.

Jews circumcise themselves and the Persians preserve their nobility by begetting children on their mothers.

(trans. A. D. Nock, Cambridge 1926)

Τὸ δὲ ἀδικίας τε καὶ ἀσελγείας ἐκ τῆς Εἱμαρμένης ...: The passage occurs in Sallustius' discussion of Divine Providence. He considers that the fate ordained by the gods does not preclude human free will. It may only be admitted that the weakness of human nature and bad education transform the blessings of Fate into evil.

διὰ τί γὰρ Μασσαγέται ...: The idea is so briefly expressed as to be unintelligible; see Nock, *op. cit.* (supra, p. 573, n. 1), p. LXXII, Introduction. Nock interprets it as meaning "if Fate rules all, why do whole nations practise queer customs?" and expands the thought by adding: "their members cannot all have the same horoscopes".

Ἑβραῖοι δὲ περιτέμνονται: The Jews were not the only people to practise circumcision; cf. the commentary to Herodotus, II, 104 (No. 1). However, they were known as the circumcised *par excellence*.

Πέρσαι δὲ τὴν εὐγένειαν σώζουσιν: Cf. Philo, *De Specialibus Legibus*, III, 13: μητέρας γὰρ οἱ ἐν τέλει Περσῶν τὰς ἑαυτῶν ἄγονται καὶ τοὺς φύντας ἐκ τούτων εὐγενεστάτους νομίζουσι; Sextus Empiricus, *Hypotyposes*, III, 205; *Expositio Totius Mundi et Gentium*, 19 (ed. Rougé), pp. 152 ff.: "sicuti muta animalia, matribus et sororibus condormiunt." Cf. Bidez & Cumont, I, p. 79. εὐγένειαν should stand. Against Rochefort's emendation, cf. also L. G. Westerink, *Mnemosyne*, Ser. 4, XV (1962), pp. 74 f.

CXXXVIII. EUTROPIUS

Fourth century C.E.

Eutropius wrote his short history of Rome in the second half of the fourth century during the reign of Valens. While dealing with the history of the republic, he was dependent for his information on Livy.[1] For the history of the early empire Suetonius constituted his main source.

The dependence of Eutropius on these historians is well illustrated by his references to Jews. The narrative of the capture of Jerusalem by Pompey, notwithstanding its brevity, shows a striking similarity to that of Josephus, who himself had some direct or indirect knowledge of Livy; cf. Ant., XIV, 68 (No. 132). The reference to Titus' part in the siege of Jerusalem derives from Suetonius.

Eutropius is silent on the Jewish revolts under Trajan and Hadrian, as on all subsequent relations between Rome and the Jews.

489

Breviarium ab Urbe Condita, VI, 14:2, 16 — H. Droysen = F211R

(14:2) Inde ad Iudaeam transgressus ⟨scil. Pompeius⟩ Hierosolyma caput gentis tertio mense cepit, XII milibus Iudaeorum occisis, ceteris in fidem acceptis. His gestis in Asiam se recepit et finem antiquissimo bello dedit.

5 (16) Sescentesimo nonagesimo anno urbis conditae Decimo Iunio Silano et Lucio Murena consulibus Metellus de Creta triumphavit,

1 *transgressus est* GPD / *herosolimam* G¹ *hierosolimam* G² LP
hyerusolimam OD 2 *cepit*] *expugnavit* P 4 *dedit antiquissimo bello* G

1 Cf. A. Rosenberg, *Einleitung und Quellenkunde zur römischen Geschichte*, Berlin 1921, p. 152; W. den Boer, *Some Minor Roman Historians*, Leiden 1972, pp. 114 ff.

From Tacitus to Simplicius

Pompeius de bello piratico et Mithridatico. Nulla umquam pompa triumphi similis fuit. Ducti sunt ante eius currum filii Mithridatis, filius Tigranis et Aristobulus rex Iudaeorum, praelata est ingens pecunia, auri atque argenti infinitum.

10

9 *aristobulus* Lincolniensis, Paeanius   *aristobolus* cett.   /   *perlata* S
10 *et auri* PD   /   *infinitum pondus* LO

(14:2) Thence he [scil. Pompey] passed to Jerusalem, the capital of the nation, and captured it in the third month. Twelve thousand of the Jews were killed and the others surrendered. After this had been accomplished he returned to Asia and put an end to the very protracted war.
(16) In the six hundred and ninetieth year from the foundation of Rome, in the consulate of Decimus Iunius Silanus and Lucius Murena, Metellus celebrated his triumph over Crete and Pompey that over the pirates and Mithridates. There had never been a like triumphal procession. Before Pompey's chariot there were led the sons of Mithridates, the son of Tigranes and Aristobulus, the king of the Jews; also an enormous amount of money and countless quantities of gold and silver were carried before.

14:2 *Tertio mense cepit*: The capture of Jerusalem in the third month of the siege is confirmed by Josephus, *Ant.*, XIV, 66: ἀλούσης τῆς πόλεως περὶ τρίτον μῆνα. Josephus also means to indicate the third month of the siege here, and not the third month of the year; for this cf. *BJ*, I, 149; V, 397; see Schürer, I, p. 298, n. 23; above, vol. I, p. 276, the commentary to Strabo (No. 104).
XII milibus Iudaeorum occisis: The same number appears in *Ant.*, XIV, 71; *BJ*, I, 151.
16 *Nulla umquam pompa triumphi*: Cf. the commentary to Appianus, *Mithridaticus Liber*, 117:571 ff. (No. 346).

490

Breviarium ab Urbe Condita, VII, 10:3 — H. Droysen

Tanto autem ⟨scil. Augustus⟩ amore etiam apud barbaros fuit, ut reges populi Romani amici in honorem eius conderent civitates, quas Caesareas nominarent, sicut in Mauretania a rege Iuba et in Palaestina, quae nunc urbs est clarissima.

3–4 *sicut…clarissima* om. Paeanius

576

Eutropius

He [scil. Augustus] enjoyed so great love even among the barbarians that kings who were "friends of the Roman People" founded cities in his honour which they called Caesareas. Thus such a city was founded in Mauretania by King Juba, and in Palestine a city which is now most renowned.

quas Caesareas nominaret ... et in Palaestina: The foundation of Caesarea by Herod is meant here; cf. *Ant.*, XVI, 136; *BJ*, I, 408 ff. See B. Galsterer-Kröll, *Epigraphische Studien*, Bonn, IX (1972), pp. 46 ff.
quae nunc urbs est clarissima: In the time of Eutropius Caesarea was the capital of the province Palaestina Prima and an important cultural centre; see the commentary to Ammianus Marcellinus, XIV, 8:11 (No. 505).

491

Breviarium ab Urbe Condita, VII, 19:1, 3 (= F212R); 20:1; 21:2 — H. Droysen

(19:1) Vespasianus huic successit, factus apud Palaestinam imperator ... (19:3) Sub hoc Iudaea Romano accessit imperio et Hierusolyma, quae fuit urbs nobilissima Palaestinae ... (20:1) Hic cum filio Tito de Hierusolymis triumphavit ... (21:2) In oppugnatione Hierusolymorum sub patre militans duodecim propugnatores duodecim sagittarum confixit (scil. Titus) ictibus.

3 *hierusolima* GO   *iherosolimam* L   4 *hierosolimis* GL
5 *hierosolimarum* FGLO   6 *ictibus confixit* PD

(19:1) He [scil. Vitellius] was succeeded by Vespasian, who was made emperor in Palestine ... (19:3) In his reign Judaea was added to the empire, and Jerusalem which was the noblest city of Palestine ... (20:1) Vespasian celebrated with his son Titus a triumph over Jerusalem ... (21:2) In the storming of Jerusalem, while fighting [scil. Titus] under his father's command, he transfixed twelve of the defenders by twelve shots of arrows.

19:3 *urbs nobilissima Palaestinae*: For Eutropius Athens is just a "civitas Achaiae"; cf. Eutropius, V, 6; see W. den Boer, *op. cit.* (supra, p. 575, n. 1), p. 141.
21:2 *In oppugnatione Hierusolymorum*: The details derive directly from Suetonius, *Divus Titus*, 5:2 (No. 317).

CXXXIX. FESTUS

Fourth century C.E.

Rufius Festus, who served under Valens, presumably wrote his epitome of Roman history between 363 and 370 C.E.[1] His Breviarium *hardly adds anything substantial to the subject of Jews and Judaism. Judaea, or Jews, are mentioned three times, as having been conquered by the Romans; on the last occasion Pompey is expressly referred to as the conqueror. Festus draws on his usual sources, Florus and Eutropius, for this part of his work.*

492

Breviarium, 3 — Eadie

In Asia expulso Antiocho primum pedem posuere Romani, Mithridate victo Pontus regnum eius occupatum est, Armenia minor, quam idem tenuerat, armis obtenta est, in Mesopotamiam Romanus pervenit exercitus, cum Parthis foedus initum est, contra Carduenos
5 ac Saracenos et Arabas bellatum est, Iudaea omnis victa est, Cilicia, Syriae in potestatem populi Romani pervenerunt, Aegypti reges foederati erant.

2 *eius* om. Eα   4 *cardoenos* E   *cardoneos* WP¹W²   5 *ad arabes* E

The Romans first put their foot into Asia after the expulsion of Antiochus. After the victory over Mithridates of Pontus, his kingdom was occupied. Lesser Armenia, which belonged to the same king, was conquered by force, the Roman army reached Mesopotamia, an agreement was made with the Parthians, a war was waged against the Cardueni, Saracens and Arabs, the whole of Judaea was conquered,

1 See J.W. Eadie, *The Breviarium of Festus*, London 1967, p. 2 (critical edition with historical commentary). For the paganism of the compiler of the *Breviarium*, see *ibid.*, p. 9, n. 2; W. den Boer, *Some Minor Roman Historians*, Leiden 1972, pp. 178 ff. For a somewhat sceptical view, see A. Cameron, *The Classical Review*, NS, XIX (1969), p. 306. For Festus and his sources, see also Seeck, PW, VI, pp. 2257 f.; W. den Boer, *op. cit.*, pp. 173 ff.; B. Baldwin, *Historia*, XXVII (1978), pp. 197 ff.

Cilicia and the [various] parts of Syria came under the rule of the Roman people, the kings of Egypt were allies.

493

Breviarium, 14 — Eadie

Per confinia Armeniarum primum sub Lucio Lucullo Romana trans Taurum arma transmissa sunt. Phylarchi Saracenorum in Osrhoena cessere superati. In Mesopotamia ab eodem Lucullo Nisibis capta est. Postea per Pompeium eadem loca armis obtenta sunt. Syriae et Phoenice bello a Tigrane, Armeniorum rege, receptae sunt. Arabes et Iudaei in Palaestina victi sunt.

> 2 *fularchi* EWP¹P²   *fylarchi* BβW² / *oydroena* Eα   *osybenates* P
> 4 *postea*] *propterea* WP¹W²   6 *palestinam* E   *palestrina* W¹P³

The Roman forces crossed the Taurus for the first time through the Armenian boundaries under the command of Lucius Lucullus. The chiefs of the Saracens in Osrhoene surrendered after they had been overcome. The same Lucullus captured Nisibis in Mesopotamia. Afterwards the same places were overpowered by the arms of Pompey. The Syrias and Phoenicia were recovered in war from Tigranes, king of the Armenians. The Arabs and Jews in Palestine were defeated.

494

Breviarium, 16 — Eadie

Idem Pompeius Bosphorianis et Colchis Aristarchum regem inposuit, cum Albanis conflixit, Orhodi, Albanorum regi, ter victo pacem dedit, Hiberiam cum Artace rege in deditionem accepit, Saracenos et Arabas vicit. Iudaea capta Hierosolymam obtinuit, cum Persis foedus icit.

> 4 *arabes* BW   *arabos* P / *iherosolima* EW¹P³

The same Pompey imposed Aristarchus as king over Bosporus and Colchis. He came into conflict with the Albanians and granted terms to Orhodes, king of the Albanians, after defeating him thrice. He received the surrender of Hiberia with her king Artaces, and defeated the Saracens and Arabs. After conquering Judaea he took possession of Jerusalem. With the Persians he signed a treaty.

CXL. LIBANIUS

Fourth century C.E.

*Libanius of Antioch, the most famous rhetor of the fourth century C.E.,
had many opportunities to meet Jews on economic, social and cultural
levels. In his speech Περὶ προστασιῶν (No. 495a) Libanius refers to a
clash with his Jewish tenants, apparently caused by a proposed change
in their status. The incident was resolved in favour of the Jews through
the intervention of a military patron. In contrast, Libanius maintained
most friendly relations with the Jewish patriarch and the Jewish
community of Antioch, as well attested by his correspondence.[1]
The antagonism shown to the Jews in the above-mentioned speech was
over a financial matter, and thus may have given rise to Libanius'
ironical allusion to their character in the manner of the old
Graeco-Roman tradition of anti-Semitism; cf. the commentary to
Ἰουδαῖοι τῶν πάνυ (No. 495a). However, this is not the attitude that
Libanius reveals in his correspondence with the Jewish patriarch. Here
we feel a touch of sympathy for the Jews and their sufferings. Libanius
addresses the patriarch with words indicating deep respect, coupled
with a recognition of the virtues of both the patriarch and his people. His
sentiments may be accounted for by a fellow feeling in the common*

---

1 For possible biblical allusions in the speeches of Libanius, see
M. Schwabe, "Analecta Libaniana", Ph.D. Thesis, Berlin 1918, pp. 57 ff.
The following passages are quoted: (a) Libanius, *Orationes*, LIX, 169 (ed.
Foerster, IV, p. 294): δοκεῖ δή μοι καὶ τὸ βούλευμα τοῦ τὴν οἰκουμένην
συστησαμένου νῦν δὴ μάλιστα σῴζεσθαι. ἐπειδὴ γὰρ ἵδρυσε μὲν τὴν
γῆν, ἔχεε δὲ τὴν θάλατταν, ποταμοὺς δὲ προήγαγεν, ἔδειξε δὲ νήσων
περίρρυτον θέσιν, πάντα μὲν εἰς τὸ δημιουργηθὲν ἐγκατέθετο
σπέρματα καὶ βοσκήματα καὶ ὅλως ὁπόσων ἔμελλεν ἀνθρωπεία
φύσις. Cf., in general, Septuagint, Gen. Chap. i; Ps. lxxxviii: 12; ciii: 5;
Ezek. xxxi: 4; (b) Libanius, *Orationes*, LIX, 48 (ed. Foerster, IV, p. 232;
by inadvertence p. 231 is quoted): Ἀεὶ μὲν οὖν ἔγωγε τῆς παρούσης
βασιλείας τὸ πηδάλιον ἐν τῇ τοῦ κρείττονος ᾠήθην ἐγκεῖσθαι χειρί;
(c) Libanius, *Progymnasmata, Laudationes*, VI: 8 (ed. Foerster, VIII, p.
260): καί τις ἂν ὅλῃ πόλει τὰς αἰτίας ἀφείη τὸν δίκαιον αἰδεσθείς. Cf.
Septuagint Gen. xviii: 26: εἶπεν δὲ Κύριος Ἐὰν εὕρω ἐν Σοδόμοις
πεντήκοντα δικαίους ἐν τῇ πόλει, ἀφήσω πάντα τὸν τόπον δι᾽ αὐτούς.

plight in which both Jews and "Hellenes" found themselves under the yoke of Christian emperors.

The name of the patriarch is nowhere mentioned in the correspondence, nor is it expressly stated in any of the letters that a Jewish patriarch is implied. Nevertheless, it seems almost certain that the correspondence is with the Jewish head, and not a Christian patriarch, a conclusion which emerges from the following considerations:

a. It is clear that the majority of the letters addressed to the patriarch were dispatched to Palestine.[2] In the second half of the fourth century the official title of "patriarch" had not yet been attached to one of the heads of the Christian church in Palestine. The bishop of Jerusalem had that title conferred on him officially only at the Council of Chalcedon in 451 C.E., although the council might then have simply endorsed a title that had already been in common use some twenty years earlier.[3]

b. Some allusions in the correspondence preclude any possibility that the patriarch was a Christian; see, e.g., No. 496: τοιούτου γένους χρόνον οὕτω πολὺν κάμνοντος.

It should also be emphasized that there is no reason to consider that the patriarch of the correspondence was one of the secondary Jewish patriarchs, and not the Palestinian patriarch himself. Otherwise a general form of address would not have been adequate. Moreover, some of the letters imply that he wielded a power and influence that seems superior even to that of the civil governor of Palestine, to an extent that could lead to the latter's dismissal. Such a position would only fit the supposition that the correspondent of Libanius was none other than the representative of the illustrious house of Hillel.[4]

The patriarch appears to be a close friend of Libanius, and most of the correspondence comprises letters of recommendation in which the rhetor asks for some favour for his friends, who are sometimes also known to the patriarch. It is noteworthy that Libanius thinks of the patriarch as a man of accomplished Greek education, as seen by his allusions to the

---

2 Cf. the detailed proofs adduced by M. Schwabe, *Tarbiz*, Vol. I, No. 2 (1930), pp. 85 ff. (in Hebrew); see especially pp. 89 ff.

3 See R. Devreesse, in: *Mémorial Lagrange*, Paris 1940, p. 224; idem, *Le patriarcat d'Antioche*, Paris 1945, p. 46, n. 1.

4 See O. Seeck, *Die Briefe des Libanius zeitlich geordnet*, Leipzig 1906, p. 162; E. Richtsteig, *Index Libanianus*, s.v. Gamaliel; G. Downey, *A History of Antioch in Syria*, Princeton 1961, p. 382; M. Avi-Yonah, *Geschichte der Juden im Zeitalter des Talmud*, Berlin 1962, p. 228; R. Syme, *Ammianus and the Historia Augusta*, Oxford 1968, p. 63.

son of Lysimachus (= Aristides) and to the story of Telephus and Achilles (Nos. 500, 503). It remains doubtful, however, whether the information supplied by No. 502 has any bearing on the family of the patriarch (cf. the commentary ad loc.). If it had, this would have furnished a notable example of the way in which Greek education had penetrated the patriarch's house.

It is not easy to identify the patriarch with whom Libanius corresponded. The ἄρχων τῶν ἀρχόντων in No. 504, addressed to Priscianus and dated 364, must have been Hillel the son of Judah III. For the addressee of Libanius there are three candidates. His letters are dated 388, 390 and 393 C. E. According to Jewish tradition, after Hillel, the contemporary of Julian the Apostate, there were two Gamaliels who acted as patriarchs, and between them one Judah.[5] It is therefore to be inferred that the Gamaliel who was the last but one is reckoned the Fifth, while the last is considered the Sixth.[6]

Three Latin sources relating to the same age also refer to a Jewish patriarch called Gamaliel. They are as follows:

a. Hieronymus, Epistulae, 57 (PL, XXII, Col. 570): *"Dudum Hesychium virum consularem (contra quem Patriarcha Gamaliel gravissimas exercuit inimicitias) Theodosius princeps capite damnavit, quod sollicitato notario, chartas illius invasisset".*

b. Codex Theodosianus, XVI, 8:22 *(October 415): "Quoniam Gamalielus existimavit se posse inpune delinquere, quo magis est erectus fastigio dignitatum, inlustris auctoritas tua sciat nostram serenitatem ad virum inl(ustrem) mag(istrum) officiorum direxisse praecepta, ut ab eo codicilli demantur honorariae praefecturae, ita ut in eo sit honore, in quo ante praefecturam fuerat constitutus ..."*

c. Marcellus, De Medicamentis, XXIII, 77 *(at the time of Theodosius II): "Ad splenum remedium singulare, quod de experimentis probatis Gamalielus patriarchas proxime ostendit".[7] All these references are connected with the same person by Seeck.[8] However, it seems necessary*

---

5 According to Abraham Zacuto's *Sefer Hayuḥasin*; see *Liber Juchassin*, ed. H. Filipowski, London 1857, p. 122; A. Neubauer, *Mediaeval Jewish Chronicles*, Oxford 1895, II, p. 246.

6 See H. Graetz, *Geschichte der Juden*, IV⁴, Leipzig 1908, p. 449; W. Bacher, in: *Jewish Encyclopaedia*, s. v. Gamaliel; see also H. Mantel, *Studies in the History of the Sanhedrin*, Cambridge (Mass.) 1961, p. 2, n. 4.

7 See *Corpus Medicorum Latinorum*, V, ed. M. Niedermann, Leipzig–Berlin 1916, p. 185.

8 See Seeck, PW, VII, p. 690.

to distinguish between the letter of Jerome and the two other sources. It is clear that the Gamaliel of the Codex Theodosianus, *because of the date 415, should be identified with the last Gamaliel (VI), who died before 429 C.E. He must also be the same as the Patriarch Gamaliel about whom Marcellus, the contemporary of Theodosius II (408–450 C.E.), writes as one who has "recently"* (proxime) *invented the medicine. On the other hand, the letter of Jerome belonging to the nineties of the fourth century, would appear to refer to Gamaliel V.*[9] *This Gamaliel was presumably also the friend and correspondent of Libanius in the years 388–393 C.E. The case of Hesychius, a* vir consularis *who, according to Jerome's letter, was executed for misdeeds against Gamaliel, may be put on the same footing as the deposition of Hilarius, the governor of* Palaestina, *at the instigation of the same Gamaliel (No. 503).*[10]

9 See Graetz, *op. cit.* (supra, n. 6); Schwabe, *op. cit.* (supra, n. 2).
10 One should also consider the last Judah, who is wholly unknown apart from the reference to him in the mediaeval Jewish chronicle mentioned above.

495a

Oratio de Patrociniis, 13–17 — Foerster, Or. 47

(13) Ἰουδαῖοι τῶν πάνυ γῆν ἡμῖν πολὺν ἐργαζόμενοι χρόνον, γενεὰς
τέτταρας, ἐπεθύμησαν μὴ ὅπερ ἦσαν εἶναι καὶ τὸν παλαιὸν ἀπο-
σεισάμενοι ζυγὸν ἠξίουν ὁρισταὶ τοῦ πῶς ἡμῖν αὐτοῖς χρηστέον εἶναι.
ταῦτ᾽ οὐκ ἐνεγκόντες χρώμεθα δικαστηρίῳ. καὶ μαθὼν ὁ καθήμενος, τίνες
5 ὄντες εἰς τίνα παροινοῦσιν ἐν τίνι τὰς ἐλπίδας ἔχοντες, τοὺς μὲν ἔδησε
διπλῷ δεσμῷ, τῷ τε οἰκήματι καὶ σιδήρῳ, τοὺς δὲ τὰ ὄντα φράσοντας,
ἐκέλευσεν ἄγεσθαι. καὶ ταῦτα εἰπὼν καὶ χαλεπήνας πρὸς ἐμὲ μνησθέντα
λύσεως ᾤχετο ἀπιὼν ἑτέρωσε, οἱ δ᾽ ἐπὶ τὸ τῶν πολλῶν πάλαισμα, τὸν οἶκον
τοῦ στρατηγοῦ, καὶ τὴν ἐναντίαν τοῖς δικαίοις ἀσπίδα. καὶ κριθαὶ καὶ σῖτος
10 καὶ νῆτται καὶ χιλὸς ἵπποις. (14) καὶ ὁ μὲν προσέταξεν ἐᾶν τοὺς λιπόντας
τὴν τάξιν, ὁ δὲ ὑπήκουσέ τε καὶ ὑπέσχετο. καὶ ὁ δικάζων ὃ μὲν οὐκ ἦν, ἦν, ὃ
δ᾽ ἦν, οὐκ ἦν, ἀντὶ δικαστοῦ συνήγορος. τοιγαροῦν εἷλκεν ὑπὸ τὴν ψῆφον
ἡμᾶς καθ᾽ ἑκάστην ἡμέραν πέμπων ἄλλον ἐπ᾽ ἄλλῳ, τὸ ἤδη βουλόμενος,
τὸ μήπω μεμφόμενος, σπεύδων ἐπὶ τὴν ἐχθρὰν τοῖς θεοῖς χάριν. καὶ οὕτως
15 ἦν δῆλος τὸ δίκαιον προησόμενος τῇ χάριτι, ὥσθ᾽ οἱ νυκτὸς ἐξιόντες παρ᾽
αὐτοῦ τῶν ἡμῖν ἐπιτηδείων οἷς συντυγχάνοιεν ἔλεγον κεκρίσθαι μοι τὴν
δίκην καὶ τὸ κράτος ἔσεσθαι τῶν ἀντιδίκων. (15) καὶ ὡς τοῦθ᾽ οὕτως εἶχεν,
ἐδείχθη τῆς ἐπιούσης. οἱ μὲν γὰρ μεθ᾽ ἡμῶν ὄντες ῥήτορες ἤκουον, ὅτι δεῖ
σιωπᾶν ἐν ἀφθονίᾳ τῶν ἰσχυρῶν, τῶν δὲ σὺν ἐκείνοις οὐδὲν ἦν ἀσθενὲς ἐν
20 σκιαῖς τοῖς ἅπασι. τῆς ψήφου δὲ τεθείσης οἵαν τὸ κράνος καὶ ὁ θώραξ
ἤθελεν, αὐτὸν ἐδίωκεν ὁ ἐψηφισμένος, οὐ γὰρ εἴα τὸ συνειδὸς ἠρεμεῖν, καὶ
πρὸς τοὺς εἰσιόντας οὐδὲν αἰτιωμένους ὤμνυ πάντας ὅρκους ἦ μὴν ὀρθὴν
πεποιῆσθαι τὴν κρίσιν· ἧττον γὰρ ἡγεῖτο κακὸν τὴν εἰς τοὺς θεοὺς
ἀσέβειαν ἢ τὸ φθέγξασθαί τι τούτων ἃ σιγᾶσθαι βούλοιτ᾽ ἂν ὁ στρατηγός.
25 (16) ὃν ἠξίουν ἔγωγε μᾶλλον δεδιέναι τὸ λυμαίνεσθαι τοῖς δικαίοις ἢ τὸ
πυθέσθαι τινάς, ὡς αὐτὸς ταῦτα κελεύσειεν. ἃ εἰ μέν ἐστι δίκαια, τί ἂν
αἰσχύνοιτο; εἰ δὲ ἄδικα, τί τῶν τοιούτων ἐπιθυμεῖ; εἰ δ᾽ οὐδὲ ἐμοὶ τὸ
δίκαιον ἐσώθη τῷ πλεῖστα δὴ περὶ λόγους κάμνοντι καὶ γράμμασι δὴ
παρὰ σοῦ κεκοσμημένῳ καὶ τὴν τῶν πεφοιτηκότων ἔχοντι λύπην, τί χρὴ
30 περὶ τῶν ἄλλων οἷς οὐδὲν τούτων ἔστιν, ὑπολαμβάνειν; (17) Ταυτὶ μὲν οὖν
εἰς ἀπόδειξιν εἴρηταί μοι τοῦ ταῖς ἀποστροφαῖς ταυταισὶ ταῖς τῶν γεωργῶν
πολλοὺς οἴκους διασείεσθαι. καθ᾽ ἑκάστην γὰρ δὴ πόλιν τοιοῦτοι μὲν

6 ὄντα μὴ φράσοντας Gothofredus   φράσαντας? Reiske
10 προσέταξεν ἐᾶν Reiske   προσέταξε κἂν codd.
16 ἐντυγχάνοιεν Cobet   21 αὐτὸν Reiske   αὑτὸν codd. / ὁ om. I
25 ὃν] ὃ Reiske   31 ἀποστροφαῖς A (σ erasa)   ἀποτροφαῖς cett.
32 καθεκάστην I / δὴ om. B

γεωργοί, τοιαῦται δὲ θύραι, τοιοῦτοι δὲ μισθοί, τοιαῦται δὲ συνθῆκαι,
τοιαῦτα δὲ κέρδη, τοιαῦται δὲ ζημίαι, τοιαῦται δὲ εὐφροσύναι, τοιαῦται δὲ
35 κατήφειαι. καὶ γὰρ ἐκ τῶν ἄλλων ἀγρῶν οἷς ὁδὸς οὐκ ἔνι τὰ τοιαῦτα
ὑβρίζειν, γυναῖκας καταλιπόντες οὐκ ὀλίγοι καὶ τέκνα φέρονται πρὸς
τοὺς ἰσχύοντας ἐκείνους, τοὺς τοιούτους πύργους, ἀπολαύσοντες τῆς
παρανόμου δυνάμεως. κἂν ὁ κατηγορῶν γένηται τῶν τοῦ στρατηγοῦ τις,
αὐτῷ μέλειν εἰπὼν τοῦ κατηγορουμένου καταπαλαίσας τὸν αἰτιασάμενον
40 ἀπῆλθε.

33 θύραι] in θῆραι corr. M²   35 τὰ om. IBM   36 καὶ om. Gothofredus

(13) Some very typical Jews, who used to work on our land for a long
time, namely for four generations, have set their hearts on not being
as they had been before, and, throwing off the old yoke have claimed
to be arbiters of how we should employ them. I could not endure this
and had recourse to court. The judge, having learned who they were,
against whom they had displayed their drunken insolence, and in
what they placed their hopes, bound them by a double bond, by
prison and by iron. He also ordered the witnesses to be produced
before him to state the facts. Saying this, and being annoyed with me
for having mentioned their release, he left and went elsewhere, while
the others resorted to that trick of many, the residence of the military
commander and shield of injustice, and there was barley and wheat
and ducks and fodder for horses [brought as gifts to the military
commander]. (14) And the commander ordered that those who had
abandoned their post should be set free, and the judge obeyed and
gave his promise. Thus the judge became that what he was not, and
was not what he was, emerging as an advocate instead of a judge.
Therefore he dragged us every day to be judged, sending one [scil.
servant] after another, already wanting to accomplish the plan and
finding fault because it had not yet been accomplished. So he was in a
hurry to grant a favour abhorred by the gods. And it was clear so far,
that he was sacrificing justice to favour, so that people who went out
from him at night told those of my friends whom they happened to
meet that the verdict in my case had already been given and that my
opponents had obtained the upper hand. (15) That this was the case
was shown next day. The advocates on our side heard that they would
have to keep silence in spite of plenty of good arguments, while there
was nothing weak in the arguments of the other side, however feeble
they might have been. The vote was given according to the will of the
helmet and corslet, while the judge accused himself, since his

585

conscience did not let him keep quiet. To those who came in, though they did not charge him with anything, he used to swear all oaths that he had pronounced a just sentence. For he thought impiety towards gods a lesser evil than to utter something that the commander wanted to keep secret. (16) I would deem it more proper for him to fear to injure justice than that someone should hear that he ordered such things. If those were just, why should he be ashamed of them? If wrong, why does he desire such things? If justice has not been maintained even for one who has toiled so much in speech composition and was honoured by your diplomas, and who will receive expressions of sorrow from his pupils, what may one expect concerning others who have none of these advantages? (17) This has been said by me to show how many houses have been subverted by these defections of the peasants. For in every city there are such peasants, such doors to receive them, such rewards, such agreements, such gains, such losses, such rejoicings, such dejection. For also many peasants from other villages, to whom the road is not open to such acts of violence, leave their children, and wives, and hasten to put themselves under the protection of those powerful people, such strong towers, in order to enjoy illegal power. And even when the accuser is one of the entourage of the commander, the latter, asserting that he will deal with the accused, leaves the place only after overthrowing the accuser.

On this passage, see F. de Zulueta, in: *Oxford Studies in Social and Legal History*, Vol. I, Part 2, Oxford 1909, pp. 28 ff.; Juster, II, pp. 78 f., n. 2; G. MacLean Harper, *YCS*, I (1928), pp. 163 f.; F. Martroye, *Revue historique de droit français et étranger*, VII (1928), pp. 201 ff., 211 ff.; R. A. Pack, *Studies in Libanius and Antiochene Society under Theodosius*, Ph.D. Thesis, Michigan 1935, pp. 48 ff.; L. Harmand, *Libanius — Discours sur les patronages*, Paris 1955, pp. 67 ff., 78 ff., 109 f., 135 ff., 185 ff.; P. Petit, *Libanius et la vie municipale à Antioche au IVe siècle après J. C.*, Paris 1955, pp. 373 ff.; M. Rostovtzeff, *The Social and Economic History of the Roman Empire*[2], I, Oxford 1957, pp. 499 f.; J. H. W. G. Liebeschuetz, *Antioch — City and Imperial Administration in the Later Roman Empire*, Oxford 1972, pp. 44, 122, 203, 251, n. 3; G. Downey, *A History of Antioch in Syria*, Princeton 1961, p. 447; J. M. Carrié, *BCH*, C (1976), p. 162.

The speech περὶ προστασιῶν was, it seems, addressed to the emperor Theodosius I to inform him of the bad consequences of a situation in which villages and tenants were putting themselves under the patronage of military commanders, thus disturbing the existing social order. Libanius first mentions villages in which ownership of the land was divided among a number of farmers. These were buying the support of the military commanders and soldiers, and thus did much harm to their neighbours. One of the worst consequences of this practice, according to Libanius, was the distress caused to the Order of the Curiales, since it was no longer in their power to continue collecting the taxes. Libanius also dwells on another kind of patronage that has a bearing upon villages belonging to big landowners. In this case the tenants put themselves under military patronage without any regard to the landowners' lawful interests.

As an example of this state of affairs Libanius relates his own experience with his Jewish tenants, who had tilled the land owned by him for some generations, refused to continue doing so and tried to impose their conditions on him. Libanius brought the case before a court of justice, and the judge ordered the arrest of the tenants. The Jews, however, put themselves under the patronage of a local military commander, supplying him with food in return for his help (Liebeschuetz considers him to be the *magister militum per orientem*, in contrast to Harmand, who places the trial and the general in the village).

In his study of the speech Zulueta concludes that the example brought by Libanius from his own experience refers to an estate situated in Palestine. This interpretation is approved by Rostovtzeff. Zulueta suggests that the speech should be dated to the time preceding the *constitutio* that consolidated the institution of the colonate in Palestine (between 384 and 389 C.E.), by introducing there the *colonatus aeternitatis* similar to that existing in other countries; cf. *Codex Iustinianus*, XI, 51 (50): "Cum per alias provincias, quae subiacent nostrae serenitatis imperio, lex a maioribus constituta colonos quodam aeternitatis iure detineat, ita ut illis non liceat ex his locis quorum fructu relevantur abscedere neque ea deserere quae semel colenda susceperunt, neque id Palaestinae provinciae possessoribus suffragetur, sancimus, ut etiam per Palaestinas nullus omnino colonorum, suo iure velut vagus ac liber exsultet, sed exemplo aliarum provinciarum ita domino fundi teneatur, ut sine poena suscipientis non possit abscedere".

However, there is nothing in the speech itself to convince us that it reflects the conditions then prevailing in Palestine, and it is more probable that the Jewish tenants of Libanius were living on an estate belonging to him somewhere near Antioch; see the remarks of Juster, Pack, Harmand and Liebeschuetz. Enough is known about the large numbers of Jews then living in Syria, and especially in the near neighbourhood of Antioch, to justify this assumption.

Harmand has adduced good arguments for dating the speech between 386 and 392. The struggle between Libanius and the tenants seems to reflect an attempt made by that class to prevent the deterioration of its status within the process of the consolidation of the colonate. Military patronage would seem to them a means of attaining their object.

13 Ἰουδαῖοι τῶν πάνυ: Different views have been advanced as to the exact meaning of this expression. The best explanation seems to be that Libanius, with a touch of irony, alludes here to the national character of the Jews who were known to be a mutinous element; see Harmand, *op. cit.* (supra, p. 586), p. 73. For the expression itself, cf. Iulianus, *Orationes*, II (ed. Bidez = III, ed.

Hertlein), p. 110 B: Ἑλλήνων τῶν πάνυ; for traditional national prejudices in the works of Libanius, cf., e.g., *Orationes*, XIV, 55: κρείττων ἐγένετο τῆς Αἰγυπτίων φύσεως; cf. ibid., 56: καὶ ταῦτα Αἰγύπτιος.

γῆν ἡμῖν πολὺν ἐργαζόμενοι χρόνον: Libanius creates the impression here that the Jewish tenants had attempted to introduce a change in their position. But it is difficult not to suspect that it was Libanius who was the innovator, and that the tenants were only trying to preserve their former status of freedom.

τοὺς δὲ τὰ ὄντα φράσοντας: The judge ordered witnesses who knew the facts to be summoned.

μνησθέντα λύσεως: Libanius himself, generally a very humane person, wanted the tenants to be released.

τὸν οἶκον τοῦ στρατηγοῦ: There is no need to understand that the *strategos* here is the *dux provinciae*; he could be a local commander.

καὶ κριθαὶ ...: Since the tenants themselves were under arrest, all this was done by their friends.

495b

Orationes, XX, 30 — Foerster

Οἱ δὲ δὴ τὸν πατέρα τὸν Τίτου μηδέν σου ταύτῃ λείπεσθαι λέγοντες τὸν ἐν
μὲν ταῖς εἰκόσιν ὅμοια πεπονθότα, κτείναντα δὲ οὐδένα τῇ παρ᾽ ἑαυτοῦ
ψήφῳ, τά τε περὶ τὸν σῖτον οὐκ ἐθέλουσιν ὁρᾶν τά τε περὶ τοὺς ἐκ
Παλαιστίνης ἱκέτας, ὧν τὸ μὲν αὐτοῖς ἐποίει λιμόν, τὸ δὲ ἀσεβείας
5 ἀνάγκην.

1 τὸν τοῦ Τίτου Pa   1–2 μὲν ἐν I   2 ὅμοια οὐ πεπονθότα Reiske
     3 τὸν σῖτον... περὶ om. U   4 οἰκέτας B

Those who maintain that the father of Titus was not inferior to you in this respect, since he was affected by similar action with regard to his statues and yet sentenced no one to death, prefer to overlook his acts concerning the food supply and concerning the suppliants from Palestine. The first-mentioned caused famine among them, the second necessarily implied impiety.

The twentieth oration of Libanius reflects the aftermath of the riots which upset Antioch in the early part of 387 C.E. These riots constituted a direct offence to the emperor Theodosius, since they entailed the destruction of his statues; see R. Browning, *JRS*, XLII (1952), pp. 13 ff.; Downey, *op. cit.* (supra, p. 581, n. 4), pp. 426 ff.; A. Piganiol, *L'empire chrétien*, Paris 1972, pp. 274 f. In this oration Libanius praises Theodosius for the clemency he displayed towards the city of Antioch and puts him in this respect above the

Libanius

great examples of rulers in the remote, as well as in the recent, past, namely above Alexander, Philip, Constantine and Constantius. Libanius includes also Vespasian (i.e. the father of Titus), who also falls far short of Theodosius. In order to prove this last instance Libanius refers to two blameworthy acts connected with Vespasian. One was his plan to cause famine among the armed forces of his rival Vitellius in Italy and in the city of Rome by cutting off supplies of grain from Egypt and Africa; cf. Tacitus, *Historiae*, III, 48. The other such event in the political activity of Vespasian consisted of an impious act committed in regard to the suppliants of Palestine. The nature of this act may be explained by Josephus in his narrative concerning the treatment of the Jewish rebels at Taricheae; cf. *BJ*, III, 532 ff. According to the Jewish historian, Vespasian granted the rebels amnesty, and then, having been persuaded by his friends that against Jews nothing could be impious, he attacked them. A similar fourth-century episode about the Saxons who were slaughtered by the Romans is described by Ammianus Marcellinus, XXVIII, 5.

The *Jewish War* of Josephus was much used by Libanius' contemporaries, and above all by John Chrysostom, who quoted from Josephus more than from any other Greek prose writer, excepting Plato; see P. R. Coleman-Norton, *Classical Philology*, XXVI (1931), pp. 85 ff.; cf. H. Schreckenberg, *Die Flavius-Josephus-Tradition in Antike und Mittelalter*, Leiden 1972, pp. 90 f. The emphasis on Vespasian's impiety at Taricheae is consistent with Libanius' general attitude towards Jews.

The twentieth oration of Libanius was a written piece never delivered before Theodosius; see P. Petit, *Historia*, V (1956), p. 493.

496

Epistulae, 914, 1–3 — Foerster [W 832]

Τῷ πατριάρχῃ

(1) Τῶν εἰρημένων τούτων ἐν τοῖς γράμμασι τὰ μὲν ᾔδειν πάλαι, τὰ δὲ νῦν μεμάθηκα. καὶ πλείων ἡ λύπη μοι τῇ προσθήκῃ τῶν γραμμάτων γέγονε. τίς δ' οὐκ ἂν ἀχθεσθείη τοιούτου γένους χρόνον οὕτω πολὺν κάμνοντος; *(2)* 5 ὑπὲρ δὲ τῶν ἀδικούντων ὑμᾶς διελέχθη μὲν ἡμῖν οὐδεὶς ἐν ἐπιστολαῖς· εἰ δὲ καὶ πολλοὶ τοῦτ' ἐπεποιήκεσαν, οὐδὲν ἂν ἔπραττον οὐδ' ἂν ἐμαυτὸν ὑμᾶς ἀδικῶν ἠδίκουν. *(3)* ὃν δ' οἴει τῆς ἡμετέρας ἄρξειν καὶ εἶναί που πλησίον ἡμῖν, λόγος ὑμᾶς ὥσπερ ἡμᾶς οὐκ ἀληθὴς ἐξηπάτηκεν. ἀλλ' ἡμεῖς μὲν ἀπατώμενοι πεπαύμεθα, δεῖ δὲ καὶ ὑμᾶς νῦν, εἰ καὶ μὴ 10 πρότερον.

3 ἡ om. Ath.   5 ἡμῖν οὐδεὶς Va Ath   οὐδεὶς ἡμῖν V Vo
6 ἐπεποιήκεισαν Va Vo

589

From Tacitus to Simplicius

To the Patriarch

(1) That which was told to me in your letter, I knew in part before, and in part I have learned now. And my pain has been aggravated by the addition of the letter. Who will not be grieved that such a nation has suffered for so long a time? (2) Nobody spoke to me through letters on behalf of those who wronged you. Even if many had done this they would not have succeeded, for I would not wrong myself in wronging you. (3) Concerning the man who you think was to obtain the rule over our country and who is somehow near to us, a false rumour deceived you, as it did me. I have, however, become undeceived, as you should also, if it has not yet happened.

On this letter, see O. Seeck, *Die Briefe des Libanius zeitlich geordnet*, Leipzig 1906, p. 453; M. Schwabe, *Tarbiz*, Vol. I, No. 2 (1930), pp. 89, 93 ff., 107. Libanius writes in reply to a request by the patriarch, concerning some injustice done to Jews. The patriarch had received information that an attempt had been made by some people to influence Libanius to interfere on behalf of the wrongdoers. Libanius expresses his sorrow at what has happened, but denies in strong terms any attempt to influence him in favour of the malefactors. At the end of the letter there is an allusion to a change in the governorship of Syria. For the opinion that there was a connection between the wrong done to the Jews, mentioned in the letter, and the destruction of the synagogue at Callinicum, see Seeck, *op. cit.* Cf. Juster, I, pp. 75, 462, nn. 2 and 3; J. R. Palanque, *Saint Ambroise et l'empire romain*, Paris 1933, pp. 205 ff.; F. H. Dudden, *The Life and Times of St Ambrose*, Oxford 1935, II, pp. 371 ff.; A. H. M. Jones, *The Later Roman Empire*, I, Oxford 1964, pp. 166 f.; J. Matthews, *Western Aristocracies and Imperial Court, A. D. 364–425*, Oxford 1975, pp. 232 f.

1 τοιούτου γένους: By this is meant the Jewish nation, the nation of the patriarch. The mode of expression suits the style of Libanius, who prefers periphrasis to the use of a *nomen proprium*.

497

Epistulae, 917, 1–2 — Foerster [W835]

Τῷ πατριάρχῃ

(1) Ὑπὲρ Ἀμμωνίλλης δεύτερα ταῦτα ἔρχεται γράμματα τῶν προτέρων οὐδὲν δυνηθέντων διὰ τὸ δύνασθαι τοὺς κακῶς ποιοῦντας τὴν ἄνθρωπον. *(2)* τῇ τε οὖν προτέρᾳ συναχθόμενος ἐπιστολῇ καὶ τήνδε τιμῶν ποίησον 5 ἡμᾶς μὴ δεηθῆναι τρίτης.

1 ἀντιοχειας post πατριάρχῃ S

Libanius
To the Patriarch
(1) This is the second letter written on behalf of Amonilla, since the former was of no avail because of the power of those who do her harm. (2) Having been grieved by the former letter, honour also this and do your best so that I need not write a third one.

On this letter, see Seeck, *op. cit.* (supra, p. 590), p. 454; Schwabe, *op. cit.* (supra, p. 590), pp. 89 f., 95, 107. Libanius writes to the patriarch on behalf of a woman called Amonilla. He has already written a letter concerning her, but neither his efforts nor those of the patriarch were of much help.

498
Epistulae, 973, 1–3 — Foerster [W 892]

Τῷ πατριάρχῃ
(1) Μέγαν μὲν ἡμῖν Φιλιππιανὸν καὶ ἡ ζώνη ποιεῖ, μέγαν δὲ καὶ ὁ τρόπος ἀρετῆς ἐπιθυμῶν, μέγαν δὲ καὶ ὁ δώσων ἀγαθὰ ταῖς ὑμετέραις πόλεσι Φιλιππιανὸν φιλῶν. (2) γίγνεται δὲ καὶ τούτῳ μέγας, τῷ τῆς σῆς
5 ἐρασθῆναι φιλίας καὶ ταύτην αὐτῷ βουληθῆναι γενέσθαι δι' ἐμῆς ἐπιστολῆς. ἀπολαυσάτω τοίνυν τῶν παιδικῶν καὶ γεγράφθω φίλος καὶ οἷς ἐρεῖ περὶ τῶν ἐσομένων πρὸ τῶν ἔργων εὐφραινέτω. (3) δύναμαι δέ σε καὶ αὐτὸς εὐφραίνειν τοῖς εἰρημένοις περὶ σοῦ πρὸς ἐμὲ παρὰ τοῦ τὸν πατέρα καλῶς δεικνύντος Σιβουρίου. τοὺς γὰρ ἐπαίνους οἷς ἐχρώμην κατὰ σοῦ
10 πλείοσιν ἔστησε τοῖς παρ' ἑαυτοῦ.

1 Τῳ S   om. V Va Vo   3 ἡμετέραις S   5 αὐτῷ Foerster
    αὐτῷ V Va Vo   8 τοῦ τὸν] τοῦτον Vo S
9 Σιβουρίου. τοὺς γὰρ ἐπαίνους Reiske   σιβούριον. τοῖς γὰρ ἐπαίνοις codd.

To the Patriarch
(1) Philippianus is made great both by his girdle and by his character, which strives for virtue, and also by the fact that he who will bestow benefits upon your cities loves Philippianus. (2) However, he becomes great also by desiring your friendship and wishing to attain it through my letter. Let him, then, derive advantage from me being his darling, let him be inscribed as friend and let him make you rejoice by what he says about future things before he gives proof by doing them. (3) I myself have the power of making you rejoice by relating that which has been told me about you by Siburius, who represents his father well. For he confirmed the praises used by me with his own additional praises.

On this letter, see Seeck, *op. cit.* (supra, p. 590), p. 458; Schwabe, *op. cit.* (supra, p. 590), pp. 90, 95 f., 107 f. This is a letter of recommendation given to a man named Philippianus, who arrived in Palestine in the retinue of the governor, the *proconsul Palaestinae*, named Siburius (see *PLRE*, I, p. 839). At the end of the letter Libanius mentions the good opinion that Siburius has of the patriarch, an opinion expressed in a conversation with Libanius during the sojourn of Siburius in Antioch.

1 ἡ ζώνη ποιεῖ: The ζώνη is the symbol of officialdom; cf. Libanius, *Epistulae*, 1046.

2 παιδικῶν: This should be understood in the sense of friendship in general; see, e.g., Libanius, *Orationes*, XIV, 27: πρῶτον μὲν Ἕλλην ἐστίν, ὦ βασιλεῦ· τοῦτο δ' ἐστὶν ἕνα τῶν σῶν εἶναι παιδικῶν; see also A. J. Festugière, *Antioche païenne et chrétienne*, Paris 1959, p. 154, n. 4.

3 Σιβουρίου: He is the second of this name to be mentioned by Libanius, according to Seeck. He remained loyal to paganism, as emerges from Libanius, *Epistulae*, 975.

499

Epistulae, 974, 1–2 — Foerster [W 893]

Τῷ αὐτῷ

(1) Οὐχ ἵνα κτήσηταί σου τὴν φιλίαν ὁ χρηστὸς Εὐθύμιος, ἔδωκα τὴν ἐπιστολήν, ἔχει γάρ, ἀλλ' ἵνα γένηται μείζων ἐκείνη διὰ τὴν πρὸς ἐμὲ χάριν. οἶδα γὰρ ὡς ἐθελήσεις τούτῳ κοσμῆσαι τὴν ἐπιστολήν, ὥσπερ αὖ πολλὰς πρὸς τῇδε δι' ἴσων. *(2)* ὁ μὲν οὖν ἀνὴρ οἷός τε βοηθεῖν τοῖς χρῄζουσι συνδίκου καὶ λόγοις ἰσχύων καὶ νόμοις, κενὸν δὲ περιφέρων βαλάντιον βούλοιτ' ἂν αὐτὸ μὴ κενὸν περιφέρειν. τούτου δὲ μετὰ τὴν Τύχην σύ τε καὶ ὁ ἄρχων κύριοι, καὶ μᾶλλόν γε σὺ ἢ ὅτου γε τὸ ἄρχειν ἐστίν.

5

1 τῷ πατριάρχῃ S   5 πολλὰς Foerster e Vo   πολλαῖς V
(ἀς suprascr. m³)   πολλοῖς Va S   πολλοῖς πολλὰς Reiske   8 γε²] τε Wolf

To the same

(1) I gave the letter to Euthymius not in order that he should attain your friendship, for he has it already, but in order to strengthen it because of your fondness of me, as I know that by this you'll wish to adorn the letter, as well as many others in the same way. (2) For this fellow is able to help those who need an advocate, being strong both as a speaker and as a lawyer, yet he carries around an empty purse while he would like to carry it not empty. This after Tyche both you and the governor can bring to pass, and you more so than the governor.

Libanius

On this letter, see Seeck, *op. cit.* (supra, p. 590), p. 458; Schwabe, *op. cit.* (supra, p. 590), pp. 90, 96 f., 108. This letter of recommendation concerns a certain Euthymius. The contents of the letter show that the patriarch already knew the man.

500

Epistulae, 1084, 1–3 — Foerster [W 1004]

⟨τῷ⟩ πατριάρχῃ

(1) Ἔμελλες μέν, οἶμαι, καὶ μηδὲν ἐπιστείλαντός μου μεριμνήσειν ὑπὲρ τῶν Θεοφίλου πραγμάτων, ἀνδρὸς καὶ σοφωτάτου καὶ δικαιοτάτου καὶ ὃς ἐν μέσῳ βιβλίων καὶ ἐγρήγορε καὶ καθεύδει· τοιοῦτοι γὰρ ὑμεῖς οἱ τοῦ
5 γένους ἐκείνου· πᾶσι μὲν εἰώθατε βοηθεῖν, τοῖς δ' ἀρίστοις ⟨μάλιστα, μεριμνῶντες⟩ περὶ μὲν τοὺς ⟨ὡς⟩ ἀνθρώπους μόνον, περὶ δὲ τοὺς ὡς καὶ ἐν ἀρετῇ ζῶντας. *(2)* δείσας οὖν ἐγὼ μή με νομίσῃς ἢ οὐκ εἶναι φίλον αὐτῷ ἢ ἀργὸν εἶναι περὶ τοὺς φίλους ἔπεμψα τήνδε τὴν ἐπιστολήν, οὐχ ἵνα πείσω τὸν πεπεισμένον, ἀλλ' ἵνα αὐτὸς εὐδοκιμήσω παρὰ σοὶ τῷ τοιούτῳ
10 συμπράττων. *(3)* ἐκείνῳ μὲν οὖν ὀρθῶς εἴη τὰ πράγματα, ἐμοὶ δὲ ἔσται κέρδος τὰ σὰ γράμματα· μᾶλλον δέ, δύο κερδανῶ κέρδη, τά τε ἐσόμενά μοι γράμματα καὶ τὸ νενικῆσθαι τοὺς ἐπηρεάζοντας τῷ μιμουμένῳ τὸν Λυσιμάχου.

1 ⟨τῷ⟩ Foerster	3 ὃς Wolf ὡς codd.	4 ὑμεῖς Wolf
ἡμεῖς codd.	5–6 ⟨μάλιστα, μεριμνῶντες⟩ Foerster	6 ⟨ὡς⟩ Reiske
7 νομίσῃς Reiske νομίσῃ codd.	10 εἴη Foerster	εἰς codd.

[To the] Patriarch

(1) You would be worried about the affairs of Theophilus, a very wise and just man whose place is among books both when he is awake and sleeping, even if I did not write to you at all. For such people you are who belong to that nation. Since it is your habit to help everybody, but above all to help the best, taking care of all as human beings, but of the best as living a life of virtue. (2) Yet, fearing that you may think that I am not a friend of his or that I am lazy about my friends, I have sent you this letter, not in order to convince one that has already been convinced, but to gain myself a reputation in your eyes by helping such a man. (3) I wish him success in his business, while my gain will consist in your letter. I would rather have a double gain, the letter that I shall receive and the defeat of those who insult him who imitates the son of Lysimachus.

593

On this letter, see Seeck, *op. cit.* (supra, p. 590), pp. 464f.; Schwabe, *op. cit.* (supra, p. 590), pp. 90, 97 f., 108 f. This letter of recommendation concerns Theophilus, identical with No. V of the persons enumerated in the list of Seeck (so Schwabe correcting Seeck). On him, see Seeck, p. 312. This Theophilus, a pagan on friendly terms with Libanius, was born in Palestine. He now had a judicial case to plead in that country. Libanius requests both his own pupil Priscio and the patriarch to help Theophilus. In his letter to Priscio Libanius emphasizes the fact that the man is a "Hellene"; see Libanius, *Epistulae*, 1085: δεῖ τοίνυν καὶ ἐμὲ καὶ σὲ φανῆναι βοηθοῦντας ἀνδρὶ τῶν τε Ἑλλήνων ἀρίστῳ.

In the letter to the patriarch Libanius bestows high praise on the character of the Jews in general: τοιοῦτοι γὰρ ὑμεῖς οἱ τοῦ γένους ἐκείνου. He describes them as being used to give aid to all people, and especially the good ones, so that he feels that his request to the patriarch for help is rather superfluous, as the patriarch would in any case have given it.

3 τὸν Λυσιμάχου: Aristides, the son of Lysimachus, was famous for his honesty. Libanius refers to him not a few times; cf. the index of Richtsteig, *op. cit.* (supra, p. 581, n. 4). From the use by Libanius of this periphrastic expression without any explanation we may infer that he supposed the Greek erudition of the patriarch to be quite considerable.

501

Epistulae, 1097, 1–4 — Foerster [W 1017]

Τοῖς πατριάρχαις

(1) Οἶδα πολλὰ πραχθέντα Θεομνήστῳ τούτῳ βουληθέντος ἐμοῦ. ταύτας δὲ αὐτῷ τὰς χάριτας μέχρι τοῦ νῦν οὐκ ἀποδοὺς εὗρον ὅπως ἀποδοίην ἂν διὰ τῆσδε τῆς ἐπιστολῆς, ἣν ἐκεῖνος μὲν ᾔτησεν, ἐγὼ δὲ ἔδωκα νομίσας οὐ
5 παντάπασιν ἐμαυτὸν ἀμελεῖσθαι παρ' ὑμῖν. *(2)* καίτοι τινὲς ἦσαν οἱ τοῦτο καὶ λέγοντες καὶ πειρώμενοι δεικνύειν. ἀλλ' ἐμὲ τοῦτο πεισθῆναι τῶν ἀμηχάνων μεμνημένον τῶν ἔργων τῶν ὑμετέρων τῶν πολλῶν τε καὶ μεγάλων. *(3)* δότε δὴ χάριν καὶ μὴ κινεῖτε γῆρας κεῖσθαι μᾶλλον ἢ πορεύεσθαι βουλόμενον τὸ Θεομνήστου. δεῖ δὲ ὑμᾶς οὐ δεδιέναι μὴ
10 πολλὰς αἰτήσω χάριτας οὐ πολλὰς ἴσως ἡμέρας ἔτι βιωσόμενος. *(4)* εὔχομαι μὲν οὖν αὐτὸν τοῦ μείζονος τυχεῖν, τὸ δ' ἐστὶ μένειν· εἰ δὲ ἔστι τὸ διακωλύον, τό γε δεύτερον αἰτῶ, τάχιστα αὐτὸν αὖθις ἰδεῖν τὴν αὐτοῦ.

---

1 Τοῖς πατριάρχαις Foerster   πατριάρχαις V Vo   πατριάρχῃ Reiske
  8 κινεῖτε Foerster   κινῆτε codd.   11 ἐστὶ] ἔτι S
    12 αὐτοῦ Foerster   αὑτοῦ codd.

Libanius

To the Patriarchs

(1) I know that Theomnestus has done much according to my will. Since I have not so far repaid his favours, I found the opportunity to repay them through this letter, which he asked from me and I gave, thinking that I would not be utterly overlooked by you, (2) although there were some who have said that it may happen and who have even tried to prove it. However, for me it seems impossible to believe, when I remember your many and great deeds. (3) Do me the favour therefore and don't disturb the old age of Theomnestus, which requires rest rather than movement. You should not fear that I, who presumably have not many days more to live, may ask many favours. (4) I beseech you, therefore, that he may attain the best thing, namely to stay, but if this is precluded, I ask for the second best, that he may, as soon as possible, see his country again.

On this letter, see Seeck, *op. cit.* (supra, p. 590), p. 465; Schwabe, *op. cit.* (supra, p. 590), pp. 90, 99 ff., 109. Contrary to the former letters, which are addressed to the patriarch in the singular, this letter is addressed by Libanius to the "patriarchs". There is no reason to suppose that this is a textual corruption, since the plural occurs again at the end of the letter. The letter relates to a person called Theomnestus, who had performed various services for Libanius. Libanius now wants to repay his debt of gratitude. It emerges from the letter that Theomnestus was an old man, who longed for rest and wished to be released from some task imposed on him and that his "release" mainly depended on the "patriarchs". There is much to be said for Schwabe's supposition that Theomnestus was a Jew who acted as an *apostolos*. This interpretation also makes it easier to account for the change in the form of the addressee. It seems that Libanius officially addresses here the "patriarchs", i.e. the members of the Sanhedrin and not only the "patriarch" proper, because appointments of *apostoloi* were within the competence of the whole body only. On the *apostoloi*, see the commentary to No. 486a.

2 μεμνημένον τῶν ἔργων τῶν ὑμετέρων: Libanius had certainly been known not only to the patriarch, but also to the other Jewish leaders with whom he had sometimes cooperated; cf. above, *Epistulae*, 914 (No. 496).

502

Epistulae, 1098, 1–2 — Foerster [W 1018]

Τῷ αὐτῷ

(1) Ὁ παῖς σοι ἧκε δυνάμενος μανθάνειν, μετέσχε δὲ ἄρα μου, καὶ πρὶν ἰδεῖν, διὰ τῆς Ἀργείου περὶ λόγους ἰσχύος. ἐπὶ κάλλιον μὲν οὖν οὐδὲν

2 ἧκε Reiske   καὶ Vo (sed lacuna fere 14 litterarum praevia)

ἀφῖκται, κέρδος δὲ ἴσως αὐτῷ τὸ πολλὰς ἰδεῖν πόλεις, εἴπερ καὶ 'Οδυσσεῖ.
5 *(2) σὲ δὲ ἀξιῶ συγγνώμην ἔχειν αὐτῷ τοῦ δρασμοῦ καὶ μήτε χαλεπαίνειν
μήτε ἀπορεῖν ποιεῖν· ὃ λύπην δύναται φέρειν, ἢν καὶ τοῖς σφόδρα λόγων
ἐπιθυμοῦσιν ὁρῶμεν ἐμποδὼν γιγνομένην.*

4 πολλὰς Reiske   πολλάκις Vo

To the Same

(1) Your son has arrived, already knowing how to learn and having
participated in my teaching even before seeing me, thanks to
Argeius' power of speech. Thus nothing more beautiful awaited him.
Still perhaps some gain accrued to him, as to Odysseus, for he saw
many cities. (2) And I ask you to judge his running away kindly, and
not to be angry with him or cause him to be at loss, which may bring
him pain. For that, as we see, constitutes an obstacle also to those who
fervently long for the art of oratory.

On this letter, see Seeck, *op. cit.* (supra, p. 590), p. 84; Festugière, *op. cit.*
(supra, p. 592), pp. 138 f.; Schwabe, *op. cit.* (supra, p. 590), pp. 90, 102 ff., 109
f. I include this letter in the present collection with some hesitation. The
communication is addressed to "the same" (τῷ αὐτῷ), but some difficulty
attaches to this, since the preceding letter was addressed to the patriarchs in
the plural, while this is directed to a singular addressee. Most scholars still
think that by τῷ αὐτῷ the patriarch Gamaliel is implied; so, e.g., Richtsteig in
his index, *op. cit.* (supra, p. 581, n. 4); Schwabe, *loc. cit.*; Avi-Yonah, *op. cit.*
(supra, p. 581, n. 4), p. 228; P. Petit, *Les étudiants de Libanius,* Paris 1957, p.
59; R. Syme, *Emperors and Biography,* Oxford 1971, p. 23. Foerster in his
edition of Libanius also considers the possibility of a loss of one letter
between Nos. 1097 and 1098.
In the letter Libanius indicates that his pupil, the son of the addressee, has left
him and asks the father to forgive the boy. Since it is clear from the letter that
the addressee himself had received a good Greek education, and Greek
culture was traditional in the house of the patriarch, the above-mentioned
scholars saw no difficulty in identifying the boy of the letter with the son of the
patriarch. However, a certain Argeius is also mentioned as a former teacher
of the boy. This Argeius, the only person of this name referred to in the
correspondence of Libanius, was himself an old pupil of the latter. Argeius
was active in Pamphylia in the years 388–391 C.E. and it is hard to imagine
that the son of the patriarch went so far away for the purpose of study; see
Festugière, *loc. cit.* Schwabe suggests that at some time between 391 and 393
Argeius taught rhetoric in one of the cities nearer to the seat of the patriarch,
such as Berytus, and that the son of the patriarch had studied there under him
before he went for advanced studies under Libanius at Antioch. This is quite
possible, but in view of the uncertain identification of τῷ αὐτῷ, the
connection of the letter with Gamaliel still remains doubtful.

503

Epistulae, 1105 — Foerster [W 1025]

Τῷ πατριάρχῃ

Ὅσον χρόνον πράττει κακῶς Ἱλάριος, τοσοῦτον ἀμφότεροι λυπούμεθα,
καὶ ἐκεῖνος καὶ ἐγώ. ἔδει μὲν οὖν μηδὲν τούτων συμβεβηκέναι μηδὲ ἐν
ταῖς πόλεσι πολὺν εἶναι λόγον τῶν γεγενημένων· ἐπεὶ δὲ ἔδει τούτοις
5 αὐτὸν περιπεσεῖν πονηρᾷ τύχῃ, ἣ νοῦν ἔχοντα ἄνθρωπον ἁμαρτάνειν
ἠνάγκασεν — οὐ γὰρ ἂν μηδὲν ἔχων ἐγκαλεῖν τοιοῦτος ἐπεφήνεις περὶ
αὐτὸν ἀνὴρ φεύγων μὲν τό τινας κακῶς ποιεῖν, εἰωθὼς δὲ εὖ ποιεῖν —
γενοῦ τοίνυν Ἀχιλλεὺς Τηλέφῳ καὶ τὰ ἀπὸ τῆς ὀργῆς ἴασαι πραότητι καὶ
δὸς ἅπασι λέγειν ὡς οἰκίαν τὴν πρώτην τῶν παρ' ἡμῖν πολλῇ ζημίᾳ
10 κατενεχθεῖσαν ὤρθωσας·

6 ἐπεφήνεις Foerster e Vo   ἐπεφῆνω Wolf

To the Patriarch

Whenever Hilarius fares ill, then both of us are distressed, both he
and I. None of these things should have occurred, nor so much talk
taken place in the cities about the events. Since, however, he had to
be involved in these troubles, through bad luck which compelled a
sensible man to err — for you would not have assumed such an
attitude towards him with nothing to charge him with, you who shrink
from doing harm to anybody, but are in the habit of doing good.
Therefore become an Achilles to Telephus, heal the anger by
mildness, and cause everyone to say that you have raised up among us
the first house which tumbled down with much loss.

On this letter, see G. R. Sievers, *Das Leben des Libanius*, Berlin 1868, p. 185,
n. 92; Seeck, *op. cit.* (supra, p. 590), p. 465; Schwabe, *op. cit.* (supra, p. 590),
pp. 90 f., 98 f., 110.
Libanius implores the patriarch to help Hilarius, governor of Palaestina. It
seems that Hilarius was dismissed for improper behaviour and that the
patriarch was instrumental in his dismissal. Libanius does not attempt to
clear the official of the charge. However, knowing the character of the
patriarch, who hates hurting others and is more accustomed to the role of
benefactor, Libanius asks him to raise up the fallen house of Hilarius. The
letter testifies to the tremendous power of Gamaliel in Palestine.
Ἱλάριος: For Hilarius, governor of Palaestina, see Seeck, *op. cit.* (supra,
p. 590), pp. 178 f.; *PLRE*, I, p. 435.
Ἀχιλλεὺς Τηλέφῳ: Libanius again has recourse to a Greek mythological
allusion when writing to the patriarch.

504

Epistulae, 1251, 1–2 — Foerster [W 1342]

Τῷ αὐτῷ ⟨scil. Πρισκιανῷ⟩

(1) Θόρυβός τις ἐν τοῖς παρ᾽ ἡμῖν ἐγένετο Ἰουδαίοις ὡς ἥξοντος ἐπὶ τὴν
ἀρχὴν πονηροῦ τινος γέροντος, ὃν ἔχοντα αὐτὴν πρότερον ἐξέβαλον
τυραννίδα ποιήσαντα τὴν ἀρχήν. καὶ οἴονται τοῦτο ἐπιτάξειν τὸν τῶν
5 ἀρχόντων τῶν παρ᾽ αὐτοῖς ἄρχοντα σοῦ τοῦτο ἐθέλοντος. δέξασθαι γάρ σε
τοῦ γέροντος ἱκετείας ἀγνοοῦντα αὐτοῦ τὸν τρόπον, ὃν οὐδὲ τὸ γῆρας
ἐδυνήθη διορθώσασθαι. *(2)* ταῦτα οἴονται μὲν οὕτως ἔχειν οἱ
τεταραγμένοι, πεῖσαι δὲ οὐ δυνηθέντες τοῦτο ἐδυνήθησαν ἀναγκάσαι με
γράψαι. σὺ δὲ καὶ ἐμοὶ καὶ ἐκείνοις σύγγνωθι, ἐμοὶ μὲν ἡττηθέντι
10 τοσούτων, τοῖς δὲ παθοῦσιν, ὃ τῶν ὄχλων ἐστί, τὸ ῥᾳδίως ἐξαπατᾶσθαι.

2 Ἰουδαίοις Foerster   ιουδ V   ιοῦσι Wolf

To the Same [scil. to Priscianus]

(1) An uproar has arisen among our Jews because of the rumour that
some old rascal would come to obtain the archonship, which he had
held before and had been removed from by them because he had
turned it into a tyranny. And they believe that this has been ordered
by their "archon of archons" because you wish it. For you, not
knowing his character that even old age could not amend, have
accepted his supplication. (2) At least those people think so, who
being agitated think that this is the state of affairs, and though they
could not persuade me that this was so, they had power enough to
prevail over me to write. And you forgive both me and them, me for
conceding to so many, and them for being affected by what is typical
of crowds, namely to be easily deceived.

On this letter, see Seeck, *op. cit.* (supra, p. 590), p. 245; Schwabe, *Tarbiz*,
Vol. I, No. 3 (1930), pp. 107 ff.; H. Zucker, *Studien zur jüdischen
Selbstverwaltung im Altertum*, Berlin 1936, pp. 165 f.; S. W. Baron, *The
Jewish Community*, I, Philadelphia 1942, p. 142; G. Alon, *Studies in Jewish
History*, II, Tel Aviv 1958, pp. 315 f. (in Hebrew); F. M. Abel, *Histoire de la
Palestine*, II, Paris 1952, p. 283. The connection of this letter with the Jews
was revealed by the use of MS V in the edition of Foerster.

The letter is addressed by Libanius to Priscianus, who occupied various posts
in the administration and served at that time as *consularis Palaestinae*; on
him, see *PLRE*, I, p. 727. The letter refers to disturbances in the Jewish
community resulting from the spread of news that an elder who had formerly
been dismissed from the leadership of the community for tyrannical
behaviour is to return to his former position.

The situation that emerges from the letter seems to be as follows: The old man had previously served as archon of the Jewish community of Antioch; for the office of Jewish archon, see *BJ*, VII, 47; C.H. Kraeling, *JBL*, LI (1932), pp. 136 f. In order to regain this position he had appealed to Priscianus, who, as governor of Palaestina, had considerable influence on the attitude of the patriarch at Tiberias, i.e. the ἄρχων τῶν ἀρχόντων of the letter (the terminology again furnishes an instance of the style of Libanius, who prefers periphrastic designations to the ordinary title). This is the interpretation propounded by Schwabe. For the view that ἄρχων τῶν ἀρχόντων is to be understood in the sense of the leading archon of the Jewish community of Antioch, see Alon, *op. cit.* However, against this we should point out three considerations: (1) The use of the expression τὴν ἀρχήν proves that the old man was the archon *par excellence* of the local Jewish community. (2) The high-sounding ἄρχων τῶν ἀρχόντων suggests rather the illustrious personality of the Palestinian patriarch than the chairman of the archon committee of the Jews of Antioch. (3) The part played by Priscianus, the governor of Palaestina, in the whole affair is more in line with the identification of ἄρχων τῶν ἀρχόντων as the Palestinian patriarch.

CXLI. AMMIANUS MARCELLINUS

Fourth century C.E.

Ammianus Marcellinus, born in Antioch, and the last of the great pagan historians writing in Latin, refers four times to Jews in his History.[1] The first reference is included in a description of Palaestina (No. 505), following upon a brief survey of Syria and Phoenicia and preceding that of Arabia and Cyprus. Ammianus is impressed by the cultivation of the land in Palestine and the excellence of some of the cities, which do not yield to one another in comparison. Those mentioned here are Caesarea, the capital of the province, the Roman foundations of Eleutheropolis and Neapolis, and the ancient coastal cities of Ascalon and Gaza. Jerusalem is not listed among the splendid cities of the province.

It is interesting to find that in the work of Ammianus Marcellinus neither the Dead Sea nor the groves of balsam and the dates of Jericho, the almost permanent components of all ancient surveys of the country, are even mentioned. Instead we find an allusion to the warm springs, which are useful for medical purposes, coupled with a remark about the lack of more navigable rivers. This information is not conspicuous in works by earlier Greek and Latin authors, although Pliny alludes to Tiberias with its salubrious springs and to Callirrhoë as "calidus fons medicae salubritatis"; see his Naturalis Historia, V, 72 *(No. 204). Two historical events here barely mentioned by Ammianus are the foundation of Caesarea by Herod and the subjugation of the Jews and capture of Jerusalem by Pompey leading to the transformation of Judaea into a Roman province. The name of Herod is adduced without any explanation and is assumed to be well known to the readers;*

---

1 Among recent works on Ammianus Marcellinus, see S. Jannaccone, *Ammiano Marcellino*, Naples 1960; J. Vogt, *Ammianus Marcellinus als erzählender Geschichtsschreiber der Spätzeit (Akademie der Wissenschaften und der Literatur, Mainz, Abhandlungen der Geistes- und Sozialwissenschaftlichen Klasse*, 1963, fasc. 8), pp. 799 ff.; A. Momigliano, "The Lonely Historian Ammianus Marcellinus", *Annali della Scuola Normale Superiore di Pisa*, Ser. III, Vol. IV (1974), pp. 1393 ff.; R.C. Blockley, *Ammianus Marcellinus — a Study of His Historiography and Political Thought*, Brussels 1975.

contrast Macrobius, *Saturnalia, II, 4:11 (No. 543): "Herodes rex Iudaeorum". The capture of Jerusalem does not give rise to any remarks concerning the effect it had on Rome; cf. Rutilius Namatianus,* De Reditu Suo, *I, 395 ff. (No. 542). Ammianus Marcellinus felt no urge to imitate Tacitus in composing a digression on the Jews, though examples of such digressions, on a smaller scale, are afforded in other parts of his work, in the descriptions of the Saracens (Ammianus Marcellinus, XIV, 4), the Gauls (XV, 11–12), or the Persian kingdom (XXIII, 6).[2] The second reference to the Jews is in connection with an anecdote relating to Marcus Aurelius, an emperor held up for admiration by Ammianus Marcellinus (No. 506, and cf. the* commentary *ad loc.). The words attributed to Marcus Aurelius himself, in which the Jews are stated to be more unruly than the barbarian Marcomanni, Quadi and Sarmatians, have less significance than the manner in which they are introduced. We are told that the emperor became disgusted with the malodorous and rebellious Jews, and that this had caused his outburst. It is clear that Ammianus was unsympathetic to Jews, though the reading "fetentium" (= malodorous) has caused some uneasiness, and emendations have been proposed. Elsewhere Ammianus displays a critical attitude towards other nations also.[3]*

The most important reference of Jewish interest in the work of Ammianus concerns the attempt of the emperor Julian to restore the Temple of Jerusalem, for which Ammianus is our only non-Christian authority (No. 507). Although he narrates the event against the background of the preparations for Julian's Persian campaign, Ammianus does not suggest any connection between this campaign and Julian's Jewish policy, nor does he allude to the restoration of the Temple as part of a scheme aimed at refuting Christian theology. The well-known enthusiasm of the emperor for the ritual of sacrifices and

---

2 Ammianus mentions Antiochus Epiphanes, though not in the setting of his Jewish policy; he characterizes him as "rex iracundus et saevus" (Ammianus Marcellinus, XXII, 13:1). The description is in accord with a long line of historical tradition, going back to Polybius, which reveals a negative attitude to Antiochus. Tacitus, who in his existent works refers to Antiochus Epiphanes only in the Jewish excursus, describes him there as a champion against superstition and a propagator of Hellenism; cf. Tacitus, *Historiae,* V, 8:2 (No. 281).

3 Cf., e.g., the way Ammianus expresses himself in respect of the Egyptians (Ammianus Marcellinus, XXII, 6:1), or the Persians (XXII, 12:1).

renewal of traditional cults is also not adduced. The only explanation given is Julian's craving for glory, which seems to us rather superficial. Ammianus does not state his own view on the proposed restoration of the Temple, but confines himself to the story of the attempt and its failure. One should remember that Ammianus was both a pagan and a sincere admirer of Julian; see, above all, Ammianus Marcellinus, XVI, 1; cf. XVI, 5; XVI, 10:19; XXI, 12:20; XXII, 10:2. However, in his admiration for Julian Ammianus never went to the length of emulating the panegyric of his fellow-citizen Libanius. Ammianus sometimes also criticizes Julian. First, he censures this emperor's passion for sacrifices, a flaw which Julian shared, according to Ammianus, with the illustrious Marcus Aurelius; cf. Ammianus Marcellinus, XXV, 4:17: "Superstitiosus magis quam sacrorum legitimus observator innumeras sine parsimonia pecudes mactans ut aestimaretur (si revertisset de Parthis), boves iam defuturos, Marci illius similis Caesaris"; cf. also XXII, 12:6, 14:3.

Another point on which Ammianus criticizes Julian is his specifically anti-Christian policy, namely the law he promulgated which forbade Christian teachers of rhetoric and grammatica *to give instruction unless they agreed to worship pagan deities (Ammianus Marcellinus, XXII, 10:7; XXV, 4:20). Ammianus also disapproves of Julian's harsh procedure at the trial of Chalcedon (XXII, 3:10), and of the measures he adopted to lower prices of commodities at Antioch (XXII, 14:1; cf. the general summary of Julian's merits and defects, XXV, 4).*[4]

Ammianus takes care not to express himself in an offensive manner towards Christianity. In his characterization of Constantius, Ammianus even praises the original simplicity of the Christian faith, which had been disturbed by the emperor's superstition; see Ammianus Marcellinus, XXI, 16:18: "Christianam religionem absolutam et simplicem anili superstitione confundens". He ignores the struggle that occurred between the pagan senate and the imperial Christian government over the altar of Victoria.[5]

The religious views of Ammianus himself are mainly couched in expressions of belief in "supernum numen" (Ammianus Marcellinus,

---

4 See H. Gärtner, *Einige Überlegungen zur kaiserzeitlichen Panegyrik und zu Ammians Charakteristik des Kaisers Julian (Akademie der Wissenschaften und der Literatur)*, Mainz 1968; Blockley, *op. cit.* (supra, n. 1), pp. 73 ff.; G. A. Crump, *Ammianus Marcellinus as a Military Historian*, Wiesbaden 1975, pp. 17 ff.

5 See Momigliano, *op. cit.* (supra, n. 1), p. 1402.

*XIV, 11:24); "summum numen" (XV, 8:9); "numen sempiternum"
(XVII, 13:28; XXXI, 10:18); "caeleste numen" (XIX, 1:4; XXXI,
16:4); or "aeternum numen dei calestis" (XXV, 7:5).*[6]

*The historian's striving for religious toleration and the non-interference
of the state in matters of creed is voiced in the praise bestowed by him on
the emperor Valentinianus for his policy of religious toleration; see
ibid., XXX, 9:5: "Postremo hoc moderamine principatus inclaruit,
quod inter religionum diversitates, medius stetit, nec quemquam
inquietavit, neque ut hoc coleretur, imperavit aut illud, nec interdictis
minacibus subiectorum cervicem ad id, quod ipse coluit, inclinabat, sed
intemeratas reliquit has partes, ut repperit".*

*The last reference to Jews in the History of Ammianus concerns
Babylonian Jews who abandoned their city at the advance of the
Roman army (No. 508). This is related by Ammianus without
comment.*

---

6 On the religious views of Ammianus, see also A. Demandt, *Zeitkritik und
Geschichtsbild im Werk Ammians*, Bonn 1965, pp. 69 ff.; P. M. Camus,
*Ammien Marcellin — Témoin des courants culturels et religieux à la fin du
IVe siècle*, Paris 1967, pp. 133 ff., 247 ff. Cf. also S. D'Elia, *Studi Romani*,
X (1962), pp. 372 ff.; F. Paschoud, *Roma Aeterna*, Rome 1967, pp. 47 ff.

(11) Ultima Syriarum est Palaestina, per intervalla magna protenta, cultis abundans terris et nitidis, et civitates habens quasdam egregias, nullam nulli cedentem, sed sibi vicissim velut ad perpendiculum aemulas; Caesaream quam ad honorem Octaviani principis
5 exaedificavit Herodes, et Eleutheropolim et Neapolim, itidemque Ascalonem Gazam, aevo superiore exstructas. (12) In his tractibus navigerum nusquam visitur flumen, et in locis plurimis aquae suapte natura calentes emergunt, ad usus aptae multiplicium medellarum. Verum has quoque regiones pari sorte Pompeius, Iudaeis domitis et
10 Hierosolymis captis, in provinciae speciem delata iuris dictione formavit.

6 *Ascalona e⟨t⟩ Gazam* Heraeus   8 *emergunt* Wm2 BG   *emergent* V /
   aptae bG   *apti* V   10 *provinciae* Valesius   *in provincias reciem* V
   provinciarum speciem rectori BG

(11) The last region of the Syrias is Palestine, extending over a great extent of territory and abounding in cultivated and well-kept lands; it also has some splendid cities, none of which yields to any of the others, but they rival one another, as it were, by plumb-line. These are Caesarea, which Herodes built in honour of the emperor Octavianus, Eleutheropolis, and Neapolis, along with Ascalon and Gaza, built in a former age. (12) In these districts no navigable river is anywhere to be seen, but in numerous places natural warm springs gush forth, adapted to many medicinal uses. But these regions also met with a like fate, being formed into a province by Pompey, after he had defeated the Jews and taken Jerusalem, and left to the jurisdiction of a governor.   (trans. J.C. Rolfe, *LCL*)

11 *nullam nulli cedentem ... velut ad perpendiculum aemulas*: See P. de Jonge, *Sprachlicher und historischer Kommentar zu Ammianus Marcellinus, XIV*, II, Groningen 1939, pp. 75 f.
Caesaream quam ad honorem Octaviani principis exaedificavit Herodes: Cf. *Ant.*, XV, 331 ff.; Eutropius, VII, 10:3 (No. 490); Libanius, *Orationes*, XXXI, 42. See also A. Frova, in: *Scavi di Caesarea Maritima*, Rome 1966, p. 28; L. I. Levine, *Caesarea under Roman Rule*, Leiden 1975, pp. 11 ff.; H. Bietenhard, *Caesarea, Origenes und die Juden*, Stuttgart 1974, pp. 7 ff.
et Eleutheropolim: Eleutheropolis (Beit Gubrin) acquired its municipal rights in the time of Septimius Severus; see A. H. M. Jones, *JRS*, XXI (1931), p. 82; idem, *The Cities of the Eastern Roman Provinces*, Oxford 1971, pp. 278 f.;

G. Beyer, *ZDPV*, LIV (1931), pp. 209 ff.; Abel, II, p. 272; A. Spijkerman, *Studii Biblici Franciscani, Liber Annuus*, XXII (1972), pp. 369 ff.

et Neapolim: Flavia Neapolis was founded as a Roman colony in the vicinity of ancient Shechem after the crushing of the Jewish revolt against Rome (72 C.E.); see Abel, II, p. 396.

aevo superiore exstructas: I.e. they existed before the coming of the Romans.

12 *aquae suapte natura calentes*: The best known of the hot water springs of Palestine were those of Callirrhoë (Plinius, *Naturalis Historia*, V, 72 = No. 204), Gadara and Tiberias (*TB Sanhedrin*, 108a). See A. S. Herschberg, *Hatequfa*, VI (1920), pp. 215 ff. (in Hebrew).

in provinciae speciem ... formavit: The statement of Ammianus is not accurate. After the victory of Pompey, Judaea did not form a province by itself. This happened only after the deposition of Archelaus in 6 C.E. Pompey had left Judaea under the rule of the ethnarch and the high priest, Hyrcanus II, though it was at the same time subject to the supervision of the governor of Syria. Ammianus either did not know the details or did not trouble to be more precise, since in any case taxes were imposed by the Romans on Judaea, which lost its political independence; cf. *Ant.*, XIV, 74; *BJ*, I, 154; and cf. the commentary to Cicero, *De Provinciis Consularibus*, 5:10–12 (No. 70). Retrospectively, the details would appear of little importance for a general survey, and the incorporation of Judaea in the Roman republic emerged as the main act of Pompey relative to Judaea; see also Momigliano, p. 188. There is no reason to assume that Ammianus here is dependent on Festus, as in T. Mommsen, *Hermes*, XVI (1881), pp. 605 f.; see also W. den Boer, *Some Minor Roman Historians*, Leiden 1972, p. 192.

506

Res Gestae, XXII, 5:4–5 — Clark = F208R

(4) Quod agebat ideo obstinate, ut dissensiones augente licentia, non timeret unanimantem postea plebem, nullas infestas hominibus bestias, ut sibi feralibus plerisque Christianorum expertus. Saepeque dictitabat: "audite me quem Alamanni audierunt et Franci", imitari putans Marci principis veteris dictum. Sed parum advertit, hoc ab eo nimium discrepare. (5) Ille enim cum Palaestinam transiret, Aegyptum petens, Iudaeorum fetentium et tumultuantium saepe taedio percitus, dolenter dicitur exclamasse: "O Marcomanni o Quadi o Sarmatae, tandem alios vobis in⟨qui⟩etiores inveni."

3 *bestias ut sibi feralibus plerisque* Mommsen   *bestias sunt sibi feralibus plerique* V
         ut sunt G   *plerisque* G   6 *ille* Em2 BG   *illi* V
7 *fetentium Iudaeorum* tr. BG   *ferventium* Cornelissen   *petentium* Joël
         9 *inquietiores* G   *inetiores* V   *inertiores* WB   *ineptiores* E
                  deteriores A   *nequiores* Löfstedt

(4) On this he took a firm stand, to the end that, as this freedom increased their dissension, he might afterwards have no fear of a united populace, knowing as he did from experience that no wild beasts are such enemies to mankind as are most of the Christians in their deadly hatred of one another. And he often used to say: "Hear me, to whom the Alamanni and the Franks have given ear," thinking that in this he was imitating a saying of the earlier emperor Marcus. But he did not observe that the two cases were very different. (5) For Marcus, as he was passing through Palestine on his way to Egypt, being often disgusted with the malodorous and rebellious Jews, is reported to have cried with sorrow: "O Marcomanni, O Quadi, O Sarmatians, at last I have found a people more unruly than you."

(trans. J.C. Rolfe, *LCL*)

4 *Saepeque dictitabat*: These words of Julian are quoted in connection with the violent wrangles among the Christians.

Marci principis veteris dictum: For the admiration in which Marcus Aurelius was held by Ammianus, cf. especially Ammianus Marcellinus, XXX, 9:1, where this emperor serves, alongside Trajan, as an example of an excellent ruler. Cf. also XXI, 16:11; XXXI, 10:19. According to Ammianus, Julian strove to imitate him; cf. XVI, 1:4. Cf. Iulianus, *Caesares*, 328 B–D: ἔδοξε δὴ οὖν ὁ Μάρκος ... θαυμάσιός τις εἶναι καὶ σοφὸς διαφερόντως; see P. Allard, *Julien l'Apostat*, II³, Paris 1910, pp. 132 f.; W. Ensslin, *Klio*, XVIII (1923), p. 130; C. Lacombrade, *Pallas*, NS, XIV (1967), pp. 9 ff.

5 *cum Palaestinam transiret*: Cf. also the commentary to Cassius Dio, LXXI, 25:1 (No. 441).

fetentium: See S. Krauss, *Talmudische Archäologie*, I, Leipzig 1910, pp. 117, 494, n. 614. For the view that "faetere et tumultuare" should be understood in the sense of βδελύττεσθαι and θορυβεῖν, see J. Schwartz, *Chronique d'Égypte*, XXXVII (1962), p. 351. On the emendation *petentium* as giving some justification for censuring the Jews for their *ineptia*, see M. Joël, *Blicke in die Religionsgeschichte*, II, Breslau 1883, pp. 131 f.: "Denn die Thorheit (ineptia) der Juden kann doch nicht aus ihrem Athem, sondern nur aus ihren Forderungen (Petitionen) erkannt worden sein". This emendation, however, which makes *petere* intransitive, is not very likely.

dicitur exclamasse: The exclamation ascribed by Ammianus to Marcus Aurelius may prove that the philosophical emperor did not differ in his attitude to Jews from most of the educated Greeks and Romans of his time. For his religious policy in general and his attitude to Christianity, see J. Beaujeu, *La religion romaine à l'apogée de l'empire*, I, Paris 1955, pp. 331 ff.; A. S. L. Farquharson, *The Meditations of the Emperor Marcus Antoninus*, I, Oxford 1944, pp. 408 f.; A. Birley, *Marcus Aurelius*, London 1966, pp. 328 ff. The attribution of an exclamation of this kind to Marcus Aurelius may incidentally serve as some additional argument against those who identify Marcus Aurelius with the Antoninus who, according to Jewish tradition, was

606

the friend of Rabbi, i.e. Judah the Patriarch; cf. the commentary to *Scriptores Historiae Augustae, Caracallus*, 1:6 (No. 517).

inquietiores: This reading of Gelenius was received into the text by Clark and is approved also by, e.g., E.J. Bickerman, *RFIC*, XCVI (1968), p. 308, n. 3. Still it is rather hard to determine whether it is preferable to the *ineptiores* of E (*inetiores* V; cf. the critical apparatus). Some scholars follow WB in reading *inertiores*; see, e.g., H. Schenkl, *Rhein. Museum*, LXVI (1911), p. 398. However, though in pagan literature inertia because of the Sabbath rest may be acknowledged as characteristic of the Jews, the same cannot be said to characterize the Marcomanni, Quadi or Sarmatae. See also Birley, *op. cit.* (supra, p. 606), p. 263. The reading *inertiores*, interpreting *iners* here in the meaning of ἄτεχνος or even ἄμουσος, is also accepted by Schwartz, *loc. cit.*

507

Res Gestae, XXIII, 1:2-3 — Clark = F209R

(2) Et licet ⟨scil. Iulianus⟩ accidentium varietatem sollicita mente praecipiens, multiplicatos expeditionis apparatus flagranti studio perurgeret, diligentiam tamen ubique dividens, imperiique sui memoriam, magnitudine operum gestiens propagare, ambitiosum
5 quondam apud Hierosolyma templum, quod post multa et interneciva certamina, obsidente Vespasiano, posteaque Tito, aegre est expugnatum, instaurare sumptibus cogitabat inmodicis, negotiumque maturandum Alypio dederat Antiochensi, qui olim Brittanias curaverat pro praefectis. (3) Cum itaque rei idem fortiter
10 instaret Alypius, iuvaretque provinciae rector, metuendi globi flammarum prope fundamenta crebris adsultibus erumpentes, fecere locum exustis aliquotiens operantibus inaccessum, hocque modo elemento destinatius repellente, cessavit inceptum.

3 *dividens* Valesius	*diffidens* V	*diffundens* Bentley
5 *Hierosolyma* Bentley	*hierosolima* V	*Hierosolimam* PBG(-*ly* BG)
6 *posteaque* EAG	*post itaque* V	11 *assultibus* EBG *adsumptibus* V
	13 *inceptum* G	*incertum* V

(2) And although he [scil. Julian] weighed every possible variety of events with anxious thought, and pushed on with burning zeal the many preparations for his campaign, yet turning his activity to every part and eager to extend the memory of his reign by great works, he planned at vast cost to restore the once splendid temple at Jerusalem, which after many mortal combats during the siege by Vespasian and later by Titus, had barely been stormed. He had entrusted the speedy

performance of this work to Alypius of Antioch, who had once been vice-prefect of Britain. (3) But, though this Alypius pushed the work on with vigour, aided by the governor of the province, terrifying balls of flame kept bursting forth near the foundations of the temple, and made the place inaccessible to the workmen, some of whom were burned to death; and since in this way the element persistently repelled them, the enterprise halted. (trans. J. C. Rolfe, *LCL*)

2 *ambitiosum ... templum ... instaurare sumptibus cogitabat*: Ammianus' History is the only pagan source (apart from the testimony of Julian himself) to relate the attempt to restore the Temple of Jerusalem. The main Christian writers to record this event are Iohannes Chrysostomus, *Adversus Iudaeos*, V, 11; *Contra Iudaeos et Gentiles*, 16; *De S. Babyla contra Iulianum et Gentiles*, 22 (*PG*, L, p. 568); Gregorius Nazianzenus, V, 3–4; Rufinus, *Historia Ecclesiastica*, X, 38 ff.; Socrates, *Historia Ecclesiastica*, III, 20; Theodoretus, *Historia Ecclesiastica*, III, 20; Sozomenus, *Historia Ecclesiastica*, V, 22; Philostorgius, *Historia Ecclesiastica*, VII, 9 (cf. *Fragmente eines Arianischen Historiographen*, in: *Philostorgius*, ed. Bidez & Winkelmann, pp. 235 f.); *Theophanes ad A.M. 5855* (ed. de Boor), I, pp. 51 f.; Zonaras, XIII, 12:24–25 (ed. Büttner & Wobst); Michael Glycas IV (ed. Bekker), p. 470; cf. now also the summary of a presumed letter of Cyril, the contemporary bishop of Jerusalem, in: S. P. Brock, *PEQ*, CVIII (1976), pp. 103 ff.
Ammianus explains Julian's plan to restore the Temple as the emperor's wish to shed glory on his reign, and also accounts for Julian's Persian expedition by his burning desire for glory; cf. Ammianus Marcellinus, XXII, 12:2: "ornamentis inlustrium gloriarum inserere Parthici cognomentum ardebat". Certainly in regard to the Temple we cannot accept this reason as a sufficient explanation of the emperor's policy. The Christian writers emphasize that it was aimed at the Christian religion, it being the Apostate's wish to prove wrong Jesus' prophecy concerning the Temple of Jerusalem; cf. Matt. xxiv:2; Mark xiii:2; Luke xxi:6. Various Christian sources mention a conversation between the emperor and the Jews in which, in reply to Julian's question why they do not offer sacrifices in their religion, they say that they are only allowed to do so in their own Temple.
Ammianus himself did not share the emperor's enthusiasm for sacrifices; cf. Ammianus Marcellinus, XXII, 12:6, 14:3. See W. Ensslin, *Zur Geschichtschreibung und Weltanschauung des Ammianus Marcellinus*, Leipzig 1923, pp. 54 ff.
negotiumque maturandum Alypio dederat: Alypius, a near associate of the emperor, is referred to with hatred in Christian tradition; on him, cf. Libanius, *Epistulae*, 324; Philostorgius, *Historia Ecclesiastica*, VII, 9a (ed. Bidez & Winkelmann, p. 95); *Theophanes ad A.M. 5855* (ed. de Boor, p. 51); Seeck, *PW*, I, p. 1709; M. F. A. Brok, *De perzische expeditie van Keizer Julianus volgens Ammianus Marcellinus*, Groningen 1959, pp. 23 ff.; *PLRE*, I, pp. 46 f.
Some of the Christian writers (Rufinus, Theodoretus, Sozomenus) also

mention an earthquake, and there is evidence that at that time earthquakes occurred in other places in the eastern parts of the Roman empire, at Constantinople (Libanius, *Orationes*, XVIII, 177; Ammianus Marcellinus, XXIII, 1:7), at Nicomedia and Nicaea (*ibid.*, XXII, 13:5). This is also the explanation given by some modern scholars for what occurred in the Temple area; see M. Avi-Yonah, *Geschichte der Juden im Zeitalter des Talmud*, Berlin 1962, pp. 205 ff. Cf. also *Des Heiligen Ephraem des Syrers Hymnen de Paradiso und Contra Julianum*, translated by E. Beck, Louvain 1957, p. 84.

508

Res Gestae, XXIV, 4:1–2 — Clark = F210R

(1) In hoc tractu civitas ob muros humiles ab incolis Iudaeis deserta, iratorum manu militum conflagravit. Quibus actis pergebat ulterius imperator, placida ope numinis (ut arbitrabatur), erectior. (2) Cumque Maiozamalcha venisset, urbem magnam et validis circum-
5 datam moenibus, tentoriis fixis, providit sollicite ne castra repentino equitatus Persici turbarentur adcursu, cuius fortitudo in locis patentibus, inmane quantum gentibus est formidata.

4 *Maiozamalcha* Clark   *maozamalcha* V   *Maiozamalcham* G
      maiore malcha B

(1) In this tract a city which, because of its low walls, had been abandoned by its Jewish inhabitants, was burned by the hands of the angry soldiers. This done, the emperor went on farther, still more hopeful because of the gracious aid of the deity, as he interpreted it. (2) And when he had come to Maiozamalcha, a great city surrounded by strong walls, he pitched his tents and took anxious precautions that the camp might not be disturbed by a sudden onset of the Persian cavalry, whose valour in the open field was enormously feared by all peoples.   (trans. J. C. Rolfe, *LCL*)

The war between Julian and the Persians, which put an end to the emperor's life, lasted from the spring to the summer of 363 C.E. In January Julian had refused to negotiate with the Persian envoys, and on 5 March he left Antioch to begin the campaign. At Carrhae Julian divided his army. He himself accompanied the main force and advanced along the Euphrates in the direction of Babylonia and Ctesiphon, while another force under the command of the emperor's friend Procopius had to march on Nisibis, to cross the Tigris and conquer Adiabene. The same army then had to continue its advance along the Tigris and join Julian's main force somewhere near Ctesiphon. Julian acted according to plan, and reached the canal given by

Ammianus the name Naarmalcha ("The Royal Canal"), which in this case should be identified with Nahr Isa (known in Greek sources as Marses; the city of Pirisabora is situated on its east bank; cf. L. Dillemann, *Syria*, XXXVIII, 1961, pp. 153 ff.). Julian encamped with his army under the walls of Seleucia and defeated a Persian force under the command of the Surena in the vicinity of Ctesiphon. However, the Romans did not attempt to capture Ctesiphon but retreated northwards to meet the column of Procopius. In the battle that ensued Julian met his death (26 June 363).

Apart from the record of Ammianus Marcellinus, who himself took part in the campaign, there are historical monographs from other contemporaries, namely Julian's doctor Oribasius, Magnus of Carrhae, who influenced later tradition, Eutychianus the Cappadocian, and Callistion (cf. Socrates, *Historia Ecclesiastica*, III, 21). The accounts of Magnus and Eutychianus were used by Malalas; see the fragments surviving from the works of those historians in *F. Gr. Hist.*, II B, Nos. 221–226. Ammianus himself narrates the history of the campaign in Books XXIII, 2–XXV, 3, of his work. The main parallel narratives are to be found in Zosimus, *Historia Nova*, III, 12–29; Libanius, *Orationes*, XVIII, 204–273; Malalas (ed. Dindorf), pp. 328 ff. (dependent on Magnus); Festus, *Breviarium*, 28; Eutropius, X, 16; *Epitome de Caesaribus*, 43, 1–4; Socrates, *Historia Ecclesiastica*, III, 21; Philostorgius, *Historia Ecclesiastica*, VII, 15; Hieronymus, *Chronica* (ed. Helm²), p. 243. On the war between Julian and the Parthians, and the sources describing it, see A. Klotz, *Rhein. Museum*, LXXI (1916), pp. 461 ff.; O. Seeck, *Geschichte des Untergangs der antiken Welt*, IV², Stuttgart 1922, pp. 341 ff.; F. Cumont, *Études syriennes*, Paris 1917, pp. 1 ff.; J. Bidez, *La vie de l'empereur Julien*, Paris 1930, pp. 315 ff.; *F. Gr. Hist.*, II D, pp. 632 ff.; R. Andreotti, *Il regno dell' imperatore Giuliano*, Bologna 1936, pp. 157 ff. A. Piganiol, *L'empire chrétien*, Paris 1972, pp. 157 ff.; E. A. Thompson, *The Historical Work of Ammianus Marcellinus*, Cambridge 1947, pp. 134 ff.; W. R. Chalmers, *CQ*, NS, X (1960), pp. 152 ff.; L. Dillemann, *Syria*, XXXVIII (1961), pp. 115 ff.; idem, *Haute Mésopotamie orientale et pays adjacents*, Paris 1962, pp. 299 ff.; Brok, *op. cit.* (supra, p. 608); K. Rosen, "Studien zur Darstellungskunst und Glaubwürdigkeit des Ammianus Marcellinus", Ph. D. Thesis, Heidelberg 1968, pp. 149 ff.; N. J. E. Austin, *Athenaeum*, NS, L (1972), pp. 301 ff.; R. T. Ridley, *Historia*, XXII (1973), pp. 317 ff.; R. Browning, *The Emperor Julian*, London 1975, pp. 187 ff. See also, with reference to Julian's end according to a Christian legend, N. H. Baynes, *JRS*, XXVII (1937), pp. 22 ff.

For the effect of Julian's expedition on the Jewish settlements, see H. Graetz, *Geschichte der Juden*, IV⁴, Leipzig 1908, p. 345; S. Funk, *Die Juden in Babylonien 200–500*, II, Berlin 1908, pp. 78 ff.; G. Widengren, *Iranica Antiqua*, I (1961), p. 132; J. Neusner, *A History of the Jews in Babylonia*, IV, Leiden 1969, pp. 10 ff.

1 *civitas ... ab incolis Iudaeis deserta ... conflagravit*: The Roman army which invaded Babylonia certainly passed through a country densely populated by Jews. However the present source is the only reference to any Jewish reaction to the Roman advance. We learn that a township inhabited by Jews was deserted by them at the approach of the Romans. This supports

the view that Julian's policy of seeking popularity among the Jews and his plan for the restoration of the Temple did not affect the loyalty of the Babylonian Jews to their Persian sovereign and that they did not side with the Roman invaders.

Ammianus does not give the name of the place deserted by its Jewish inhabitants, but refers only to its destruction by the Roman army after the capture of Pirisabora, also a town with a large Jewish population; on Piruz-Sabur, see J. Obermeyer, *Die Landschaft Babylonien im Zeitalter des Talmuds und des Gaonats*, Frankfurt 1929, p. 57; J. Schmidt, PW, XX, pp. 1724 f.

Pirisabora is designated by Ammianus Marcellinus, XXIV, 2:9: "civitas ampla et populosa, ambitu insulari circumvallata". We are told that 2,500 prisoners were captured there by the Roman army, while the rest of the population had left the city in anticipation of the siege; the city was burned down by the Romans (XXIV, 2:22). The army continued to advance fourteen miles, came to some place where the fertility of the fields was ensured by the abundance of water (XXIV, 3:10), and then, after passing several islands, reached a place where the Euphrates is divided into many streams (XXIV, 3:14). It is in this connection that Ammianus relates that a city of the region had been abandoned by the Jews who inhabited it because of its low walls. It met the same fate as Pirisabora, being burned by the soldiers. The name of the next city to be mentioned is Maiozamalcha, which is stated to have been a great city surrounded by strong walls.

Zosimus mentions nothing about a Jewish township being captured and destroyed by the Roman army. However he does write about a canal identical with Ammianus' Naarmalcha, the arrival of Julian's forces at Bersabora (= Pirisabora) and its capture, the crossing of a river near a place called Phissenia, not mentioned by Ammianus and other sources, and the capture of a town called Bithra; see Zosimus, *Historia Nova*, III, 19:4: ἕως εἰς Βίθραν ἐληλύθει πόλιν, ἐν ᾗ βασίλεια ἦν καὶ οἰκήματα βασιλεῖ τε ὁμοῦ πρὸς ὑποδοχὴν ἀρκοῦντα καὶ στρατοπέδῳ. The designation Βίθρα stands for the place name Βίρθα; see Obermeyer, *op. cit.*, p. 73, n. 2; Dillemann, *Syria, op. cit.*, p. 146. Some scholars suggest that Birtha is the same township said to have been deserted by its Jewish inhabitants and burnt by the Romans. Thus Graetz, *op. cit.* (supra, p. 610); Juster, I, p. 201; J. Newman, *The Agricultural Life of the Jews in Babylonia*, London 1932, p. 14; Widengren, *op. cit.* (supra, p. 610). It is true that in his account Ammianus describes the destruction of the township situated between Pirisabora and Maiozamalcha, and that Zosimus refers to Βίρθα after the capture of Pirisabora and Maiozamalcha. However, Zosimus ignores both the Jewish character of the place and its burning by Roman soldiers. Libanius, who mentions Pirisabora and then Maiozamalcha, does not refer to other places in this phase of Julian's advance; see the useful table in Ridley, *op. cit.* (supra, p. 610), pp. 327 ff.

2 *Cumque Maiozamalcha*: Graetz's identification of Maogamalcha (= Maiozamalcha) with the well-known Jewish centre Maḥoza seems unwarranted; see Obermeyer, *op. cit.*, p. 178, n. 6.

CXLII. *SCRIPTORES HISTORIAE AUGUSTAE*

End of the Fourth Century C.E.

The nature, purpose and even the date of the biographies comprising the Historia Augusta *still present much of an enigma. The prevalent hypothesis now seems to be that, whoever might have been the author or authors of the work, it emanated from pagan circles and appeared towards the end of the fourth century.*[1] *Apparently the* Historia

1 The accepted dating of the publication of the *Historia Augusta* to the reigns of Diocletian and Constantine was first vigorously attacked by H. Dessau, *Hermes*, XXIV (1889), pp. 337 ff.; XXVII (1892), pp. 561 ff. Dessau saw the improbability of the apostrophes addressed to Diocletian, Constantius Chlorus and Constantine, and pointed out that the panegyric concerning the emperor Probus and the prophecy concerning his progeny (*Vita Probi*, 24) could only have had relevance after the rise of Sextus Petronius Probus, proconsul of Africa in 358 C.E., *consul ordinarius* in 371, and praetorian prefect of Italy, Africa and Illyricum in 383. Petronius Probus was connected by marriage with the noble house of the Anicii; cf. *ILS*, No. 1267: "Anicianae domus culmen". On him, see W. Seyfarth, *Klio*, LII (1970), pp. 411 ff.; P. R. L. Brown, *JRS*, LI (1961), p. 9; J. Matthews, *Western Aristocracies and Imperial Court, A.D. 364–425*, Oxford 1975, pp. 37 f., 195 ff.; M. T. W. Arnheim, *The Senatorial Aristocracy in the Later Roman Empire*, Oxford 1972, pp. 67, 196 f., 201. Dessau also attached importance to the year 395 C.E., for which two sons of Petronius Probus were appointed *consules ordinarii*, as well as the use by the *Historia Augusta* of the works of Aurelius Victor and Eutropius.

These arguments did not meet with universal acceptance, and Mommsen conceded only that the work had undergone a late revision; see T. Mommsen, *Hermes*, XXV (1890), pp. 228 ff. The earliest date was also defended by, e.g., H. Peter, *Die Scriptores Historiae Augustae*, Leipzig 1892; E. Klebs, *Rhein. Museum*, XLV (1890), pp. 436 ff. Even more recently the old dating has been thought possible; see A. H. M. Jones, *The Later Roman Empire*, III, Oxford 1964, p. 1, n. 1. However Dessau's view gradually became prevalent, and the majority of scholars treating the subject in recent years date the work to the nineties of the fourth century; see, e.g., W. Hartke, *Römische Kinderkaiser*, Berlin 1951, p. 242; A. Chastagnol, *Bonner Historia Augusta Colloquium*, Bonn 1963 (1964), pp. 43 ff.; L. Ruggini, *Atti del Colloquio Patavino sulla Historia Augusta*, Rome 1963, pp. 77 f. (the *terminus post quem* is 394 C.E.); R. Syme, *Ammianus and the Historia Augusta*, Oxford 1968, pp. 72 ff.; idem, *The*

Scriptores Historiae Augustae

Augusta reflects views and aspirations characteristic of Roman society at that time. However it is by no means certain that there is a definite political or religious programme common to all the biographies, and it may no more than indicate the atmosphere of the contemporary pagan aristocratic society of Rome.[2]

Historia Augusta — A Call of Clarity, Bonn 1971; idem, *JRS*, LXII (1972), pp. 123 ff.; cf. also the summary in idem, *Emperors and Biography — Studies in the Historia Augusta*, Oxford 1971, pp. 287 f.; J. Schwartz, *Bulletin de la Faculté des Lettres de Strasbourg*, XL (1961–1962), pp. 169 ff.; idem, *Historia*, XV (1966), pp. 454 ff.; W. Schmid, *Bonner Historia Augusta Colloquium*, Bonn 1964–1965 (1966), pp. 179 f.; K. P. Johne, *Kaiserbiographie und Senatsaristokratie*, Berlin 1976; R. Syme, *Latomus*, XXXVII (1978), pp. 173 ff.; T. D. Barnes, *The Sources of the Historia Augusta*, Brussels 1978, p. 18. Some scholars also go beyond the nineties of the fourth century and date the *Historia Augusta* to the first decade of the fifth century; see, e.g., O. Seeck, *Rhein. Museum*, XLIX (1894), pp. 208 ff. (407–411 C. E.); P. Horovitz, *Mélanges Piganiol*, III, Paris 1966, pp. 1743 ff. (between 406 and 408 C. E.). On the other hand, for a date in Julian's reign, see the notable book by N. Baynes, *The Historia Augusta — Its Date and Purpose*, Oxford 1926; while the years 352–354 C. E. are preferred by H. Stern, *Date et destinataire de l'Histoire Auguste*, Paris 1953. For the probability of a date near 350 C. E., see H. Mattingly, *HTR*, XXXIX (1946), pp. 213 ff. Dessau considered that the *Historia Augusta* was the work of a single author, and the same view is held by Syme in his various publications; see now P. White, *JRS*, LVII (1967), pp. 115 ff.; Syme, *Ammianus and the Historia Augusta, op. cit.*, pp. 176 ff.; J. N. Adams, *CQ*, NS, XXII (1972), pp. 186 ff. The problems of the study of the *Historia Augusta* and its trends have been subjected to a masterly review by A. Momigliano, *Journal of the Warburg and Courtauld Institutes*, XVII (1954), pp. 22 ff., with the conclusion that the problems surrounding the *Historia Augusta* have not yet been solved (*ibid.*, p. 43). More recently Momigliano has formulated his view in a way that does not exclude either a date of *c.* 395 C. E. or a single author for the whole work, and he also admits that some good arguments have lately been advanced to support its dating to the reign of Theodosius I. Yet, as he states, "I am, however, still waiting for an interpretation of the *H. A.* that tells me in simple words why a writer of about A. D. 395, if there was one, decided to split himself into six authors allegedly writing between *c.* 293 and 330"; see A. Momigliano, *The English Historical Review*, LXXXIV (1969), p. 569. For the view that the *Historia Augusta* was not all written at the same time, see A. Cameron, *Classical Review*, NS, XVIII (1968), p. 18.

2 The view that the *Historia Augusta* was written mainly to counter Christianity is expounded by J. Straub, *Heidnische Geschichtsapologetik*

The Jews loom quite large in the Historia Augusta, *being mentioned in some twenty passages.*[3] *First, some facts of political history connected with the Jews are related in the work. Thus we hear about the spirit of rebellion in Palestine at the beginning of Hadrian's reign* (Hadrianus, 5:2 = No. 509), *and about the suppression of a Jewish revolt by Turbo* (Hadrianus, 5:8 = No. 510). *The reason for the Jewish war against Rome under Hadrian is stated to be the ban imposed on circumcision: "quod vetabantur mutilare genitalia"* (Hadrianus, 14:2 = No. 511). *An interesting piece of information concerns the times of Antoninus Pius. The Jews are there allotted a place among the nations against whom the Roman empire waged war at that time, their revolt being crushed by the imperial legates* (Antoninus Pius, 5:4 = No. 512). *However, as usual with the* Historia Augusta, *it is doubtful how far the information may be taken at its face value when there is no confirmation from other sources.*

Most of the references of Jewish interest in the Historia Augusta *relate*

in der christlichen Spätantike, Bonn 1963, pp. 183 ff.; A. Alföldi, *Bonner Historia Augusta Colloquium*, Bonn 1963 (1964), pp. 1 ff. The opinion that the work of multiple authorship was written by convinced pagans hostile to Christianity, even though this is expressed overtly only in the case of Athanasius, is also held by H. Stern, *op. cit.* (supra, p. 613, n. 1), pp. 92 ff. Against this, Momigliano is convinced that Christianity was not the main concern of the author or authors of the *Historia Augusta* taken as a whole; see A. Momigliano, *Journal of the Warburg and Courtauld Institutes, op. cit.* (supra, p. 613, n. 1), p. 41. In the eyes of Syme, the author is "a classical scholar with the tastes of a *grammaticus* and a collector of oddities, perverse and whimsical"; see Syme, *Ammianus and the Historia Augusta, op. cit.* (supra, p. 612, n. 1), p. 52. Syme doubts whether this *scholasticus* had any political and social beliefs of a pronounced order; cf. *ibid.*, p. 191. Cf. also Syme, *Emperors and Biography, op. cit.* (supra, p. 613, n. 1), p. 201.

For an evaluation of the *Historia Augusta* as a historical source, see E. Hohl, *Über die Glaubwürdigkeit der Historia Augusta (Sitzungsberichte der Deutschen Akademie der Wissenschaften zu Berlin*, 1953, No. 2); on spurious documents, pp. 18 f.

3 For references to Jews in the *Historia Augusta*, see Syme, *The Historia Augusta — A Call of Clarity, op. cit.* (supra, pp. 612 f., n. 1), pp. 65 ff.; T. Liebmann-Frankfort, *Latomus*, XXXIII (1974), pp. 579 ff.; J. G. Gager, *HUCA*, XLIV (1973), pp. 96 f. However, it is perhaps going too far to agree that the author had a somewhat malicious interest in Jews, as suggested by J. F. Gilliam, *Bonner Historia Augusta Colloquium*, Bonn 1970 (1972), p. 133. On rabbinic parallels to the *Historia Augusta*, see also M. Hadas, *Classical Philology*, XXIV (1929), pp. 258 ff.

to the times of the Severi, and five references are found in the "Life of Alexander Severus" alone (Nos. 520–524). Septimius Severus is represented as revoking the punishment which had been imposed on the people of Palestine as a result of the war between Severus and Niger, though the Jews are not mentioned explicitly (Septimius Severus, 14:6 = No. 513). Septimius Severus is also said to have given his son (Caracalla) permission to celebrate a triumph over the Jews (Septimius Severus, 16:7 = No. 514); to have conferred numerous rights upon the people of Palestine during his visit there, and to have forbidden conversion to Judaism under heavy penalty (Septimius Severus, 17:1 = No. 515). Caracalla, the first emperor in the Historia Augusta shown to display sympathy towards Jews, does so when only a seven-year-old child (Antoninus Caracallus, 1:6 = No. 517).[4] Nevertheless this is the same emperor implied to have celebrated a triumph over the Jews, even if the authority for this information may be questioned. We are also asked to believe that Heliogabalus, perhaps the most abominable character depicted in the whole range of the Historia Augusta, intended to transfer the religions of the Jews and the Samaritans, together with the rites of the Christians, to the temple of the Syrian god Elagabalus on the Palatine hill (Heliogabalus, 3:5 = No. 518). The same emperor sometimes served ostriches at his banquets, saying that the Jews had been commanded to eat them (ibid., 28:4 = No. 519).

One of the most sympathetically depicted emperors in the whole collection of imperial biographies, Alexander Severus, emerges in the Historia Augusta as the tolerant emperor par excellence, and the respect shown by him for Judaism is paralleled by that he displayed towards the Christians. The "Life of Alexander Severus" contains the following items bearing upon Jews:

a. Alexander respected the privileges of the Jews and at the same time allowed the Christians to exist unmolested (Alexander Severus, 22:4 = No. 520).

b. The people of Antioch and Alexandria, wanting to annoy Alexander, called him a Syrian synagogue-chief (Alexander Severus, 28:7 = No. 521).

c. The biographer refers to a writer contemporary with Alexander Severus and states that in the sanctuary of his Lares the emperor kept

4 For the opinion that this incident does not signify any sympathy for Jews on the part of Caracalla, see Liebmann-Frankfort, op. cit. (supra, p. 614, n. 3), p. 590.

not only the images of the best among the deified emperors and of pagan celebrities like Apollonius, but also those of Christ and Abraham (Alexander Severus, *29:2 = No. 522*).

d. *It was the wish of Alexander Severus that every governor or procurator should be named publicly before his appointment, and the emperor used to refer to the custom of the Christians and Jews who always announced the names of those who were to be ordained priests* (Alexander Severus, *45:6–7 = No. 523*).

e. *Alexander Severus placed great importance on the golden rule of behaviour, which he is said to have learned from either a Jew or a Christian* (Alexander Severus, *51:7–8 = No. 524*).

In a multilingual royal inscription quoted in the biography of the three Gordiani, Jewish characters are listed with the Greek, Latin, Persian and Egyptian writing (Gordiani Tres, *34:2–3 = No. 525*).

The "Life of Claudius" contains a reference to Moses, the friend of God, "ut Iudaeorum libri locuntur", while God replying to Moses is labelled "an unknown god" ("incertum numen") (Divus Claudius, *2:4 = No. 526*).

There are also allusions to Jews in the letter written by Hadrian to Servianus listing the various components of the population of Egypt, and it is stated that no Jewish archisynagogus there is not an astrologer, a soothsayer or an anointer. The allusion to the "patriarch" in the letter must be to the Jewish patriarch of the house of Hillel (cf. Quadrigae Tyrannorum, *8:3–8 = No. 527*). *Mammon is the only god of all the inhabitants of Egypt: "Hunc Christiani, hunc Iudaei, hunc omnes venerantur et gentes". Subsequent to the biography of Septimius Severus none of the allusions to Jews have a bearing on their political history.[5]*

The Historia Augusta *does not contain any such expressions of hostility towards Jews or carping remarks concerning them as are found there in relation to, e.g., the Syrians, the Egyptians, or the Gauls.[6] In this respect*

---

5 The few references to Palestine in the later biographies do not add much to Jewish historiography; cf. *Aurelianus*, 33:4: "Praecesserunt [scil. in triumpho], elephanti viginti, ferae mansuetae Libycae, Palaestinae diversae ducentae"; *Quadrigae Tyrannorum*, 9:2: "Vir sapiens [scil. Saturninus] de Alexandrina civitate mox fugit atque ad Palaestinam rediit".

6 On the Syrians, see, e.g., *Scriptores Historiae Augustae, Aurelianus*, 31:1: "Rarum est ut Syri fidem servent". The ideal emperor Alexander Severus denies having Syrian ancestry; see *ibid., Alexander Severus*, 44:3; cf.

the Historia Augusta *differs considerably from the writing of another and presumably younger representative of western paganism of the age,* Rutilius Namatianus.

That the Jews figure quite conspicuously in the pages of the Historia Augusta *is mainly to be explained by the impact they still had on Roman society at the end of the fourth century. Such a conclusion is wholly in accord with what emerges from other sources of that time.[7] The references to the Samaritans (Nos. 518, 527) are also to be accounted for by the relative importance that this community assumed in the late Roman and Byzantine periods.*

ibid., 64:3; *ibid.*, *Tacitus*, 3:5: "tam leves esse mentes Syrorum". The Egyptians are defined as "furibundi, iactantes, iniuriosi atque adeo vani", in *Quadrigae Tyrannorum*, 7:4 (No. 527); cf. *ibid.*, 3:1: "Aegyptiorum incitatus furore"; *Marcus Antoninus*, 23:8: "vulgaritas Pelusiae" (or "Pelusiaca", according to the emendation of Novák). On the Gauls, see *Quadrigae Tyrannorum*, 7:1: "Saturninus oriundo fuit Gallus, ex gente hominum inquietissima et avida semper vel faciendi principis vel imperii"; cf. *ibid.*, 7:3; *Carus, Carinus et Numerianus*, 7:2.

7 On Jews in Italy in late Antiquity, see L. Ruggini, *Studia et Documenta Historiae et Iuris*, XXV (1959), pp. 186 ff.

509

Hadrianus, 5:2 — Hohl = F198a R

Nam deficientibus his nationibus, quas Traianus subegerat, Mauri lacessebant, Sarmat⟨a⟩e bellum inferebant, Brittanni teneri sub Romana dicione non poterant, Aegyptus seditionibus urgebatur, Libya denique ac Pal⟨a⟩estina rebelles animos efferebant.

4 *Libya* Casaubonus   *licya* P   *litia* Σ   /   *afferebant* PM

For the nations which Trajan had conquered began to revolt; the Moors, moreover, began to make attacks, and the Sarmatians to wage war, the Britons could not be kept under Roman sway, Egypt was thrown into disorder by riots, and finally Libya and Palestine showed the spirit of rebellion.   (trans. D. Magie, *LCL*)

For a comparison of this survey of Spartianus with Tacitus, *Historiae*, I, 2, see W. Weber, *Untersuchungen zur Geschichte des Kaisers Hadrianus*, Leipzig 1907, pp. 50 f.

Libya denique ac Palaestina rebelles animos efferebant: The correctness of the emendation "libya", for "licya" or "litia" of the MSS, is beyond doubt; see also Weber, *op. cit.*, p. 50, n. 171. Palaestina is joined to Libya by *ac*, which implies that the same kind of events is referred to in both countries, namely Jewish disturbances. For Libya as a centre of Jewish rebellion in the time of Hadrian's predecessor, cf. Cassius Dio, LXVIII, 32:1–2 (No. 437).

There is no clear evidence concerning the participation of Palestinian Jews in the great revolt by the Jews of the Diaspora in the last years of Trajan. However, the Roman government must have meant to take precautions against a revolt in Judaea by sending Lusius Quietus to govern there; cf. Cassius Dio, LXVIII, 32:4–5 (No. 438). Moreover, the talmudic sources, though not clear enough in this case, also give the impression that some clash between the Jews of Palestine and their Roman rulers occurred, and so lend support to the statement of the *Historia Augusta*. For a detailed analysis of the talmudic and oriental sources, see G. Alon, *A History of the Jews in Palestine in the Period of the Mishna and the Talmud*, I, Tel Aviv 1958, pp. 255 ff. (in Hebrew); for the conclusion that an actual rising indeed started in Palestine, but that the efficient measures taken by Quietus prevented a more serious revolt, see E. M. Smallwood, *Historia*, XI (1962), pp. 500 ff. See also the discussion of L. Motta, *Aegyptus*, XXXII (1952), pp. 486 ff.

510

Hadrianus, 5:8 — Hohl

Lusium Quietum sublatis gentibus Mauris, quos regebat, quia

1 *gentilibus* Mommsen   /   *quos*] *quas* Kellerbauer

suspectus imperio fuerat, exarmavit Marcio Turbone Iudaeis
conpressis ad deprimendum tumultum Mauretaniae destinato.

2 *iudei* P^a   *iudeis* P^b

He deprived Lusius Quietus of the command of the Moorish
tribesmen, who were serving under him, and then dismissed him from
the army, because he had fallen under the suspicion of having designs
on the throne; and he appointed Marcus Turbo, after his reduction of
Judaea, to quell the insurrection in Mauretania. (trans. D. Magie, *LCL*)

Lusium Quietum: For the personality of Lusius Quietus and the part he
played in the crushing of the Jewish revolt, see the commentaries to Arrian
(No. 332a), and Cassius Dio, LXVIII, 32:4 (No. 438).
Marcio Turbone Iudaeis conpressis: The *Historia Augusta* alludes here to the
activities of Turbo against the Jewish rebels in Cyrenaica and Egypt; see the
commentary to Cassius Dio, LXVIII, 32:1–2 (No. 437); see Liebmann-
Frankfort, *op. cit.* (supra, p. 614, n. 3), pp. 582 f.

511

Hadrianus, 14:1–2 — Hohl = F198bR

(1) Antiochenses inter haec ita odio habuit, ut Syriam a Phoenice
separare voluerit, ne tot civitatum metropolis Antiochia diceretur.
(2) Moverunt ea tempestate et Iudaei bellum, quod vetabantur
mutilare genitalia.

(1) In the course of these travels he conceived such a hatred for the
people of Antioch that he wished to separate Syria from Phoenicia, in
order that Antioch might not be called the chief city of so many
communities. (2) At this time also the Jews began war, because they
were forbidden to practise circumcision.   (trans. D. Magie, *LCL*)

2 *Moverunt ea tempestate et Iudaei bellum*: For this war, i.e. the revolt of
Bar-Kokhba, cf. Cassius Dio, LXIX, 12:1–14:3 (No. 440).
quod vetabantur mutilare genitalia: The *Historia Augusta* gives the ban on
circumcision as the reason for the revolt, while Cassius Dio attributes the
outbreak of the war to the foundation of Aelia Capitolina. Some scholars
give credence to Cassius Dio only and think that the *Historia Augusta*
confused the chronology of the events since the ban on circumcision was a
punitive measure adopted by the Roman government after putting down the
revolt; cf., recently, D. Rokeah, *Tarbiz*, XXXV (1966), pp. 127 ff. Still, it
seems that those historians who on the contrary maintain that the prohibition

preceded the revolt have a good case, and that this, coupled with the foundation of Aelia Capitolina, played some part in causing the outbreak; cf. the commentary to No. 440.

The ban on circumcision seems to have had a bearing on other sectors of the population in the Roman empire also, as proved by the following information: (1) After the conquest of Arabia the Romans imposed a ban on circumcision there according to a Syriac passage, which relates: "But as yesterday the Romans took Arabia, and abrogated all their ancient laws; and more especially that circumcision with which they circumcised"; see Bardesan, "The Book of the Laws of Countries", in: W. Cureton, *Spicilegium Syriacum*, London 1855, p. 30 = H. J. W. Drijvers, *The Book of the Laws of Countries*, Assen 1965, pp. 56 f. The most natural interpretation of the passage is that it alludes to the incorporation of the Nabataean kingdom into the Roman empire; see T. Nöldeke, *ZDMG*, XXXIX (1885), p. 343. It is hard to see the reasons why the passage should be connected not with the first conquest of Arabia in 106 C.E., but with the Arabian wars of Septimius Severus and Macrinus, the interpretation preferred by H. J. W. Drijvers, *Bardaisan of Edessa*, Assen 1966, p. 92, n. 3. (2) Egyptian priests had to obtain special permission for the performance of circumcision according to the papyrological evidence dating from the reigns of Antoninus Pius and Marcus Aurelius; see L. Mitteis & U. Wilcken, *Grundzüge und Chrestomathie der Papyruskunde*, Vol. I, Part 2, Leipzig–Berlin 1912, Nos. 76–77. See also J. Schwartz, *Annales du Service des Antiquités de l'Égypte*, XLIV (1944), pp. 235 ff. For the non-priestly population of Egypt circumcision was definitely forbidden, while on the other hand it seems that circumcision in the Hellenistic period was practised also by non-priests; see P. Wendland, *Archiv für Papyrusforschung*, II (1903), pp. 22 ff.; W. Otto, *Priester und Tempel im hellenistischen Ägypten*, I, Leipzig–Berlin 1905, p. 214, n. 4. (3) According to Modestinus (as quoted in the *Digesta*, XLVIII, 8:11), in the time of Antoninus Pius the Jews were allowed to perform circumcision only on their own sons, which seems to have been an exceptional concession. If the ban on circumcision was then of general validity, the Jews would have been prohibited from performing circumcision on non-Jews even if allowed to circumcise Jewish males. (4) After the ban had been removed with regard to Jews by Antoninus Pius the prohibition remained in force forbidding the Samaritans to circumcise their sons; cf. Origenes, *Contra Celsum*, II, 13. Origen states expressly that in his own time circumcision was permitted only to Jews.

There is no record of any Roman law imposing a ban on circumcision before the time of Hadrian. In the Julio-Claudian age there were even gentile rulers who underwent circumcision, e.g., Aziz of Emesa and Polemon of Cilicia; see Juster, I, p. 264, n. 2. Concerning the reign of Domitian, there is information only of a ban on castration; cf. Suetonius, *Domitianus*, 7; Martialis, VI, 2. This ban was confirmed by both Nerva and Hadrian; cf. Ulpianus, *Digesta*, XLVIII, 8:4:2: "Idem divus Hadrianus rescripsit: constitutum quidem est, ne spadones fierent, eos autem, qui hoc crimine arguerentur Corneliae legis poena teneri eorumque bona merito fisco meo vindicari debere"; see

620

T. Mommsen, *Römisches Strafrecht*, Leipzig 1899, pp. 637 ff.; B. d'Orgeval, *L'empereur Hadrien, oeuvre législative et administrative*, Paris 1950, pp. 324 f. It stands to reason that Hadrian's legislation dealing with circumcision was somehow a continuation of the civilizatory legislation concerning castration, and therefore not a specific measure aimed against Jews. For the character of Hadrian's legislation in general, but omitting the measures against castration or circumcision, see F. Pringsheim, *JRS*, XXIV (1934), pp. 141 ff. An example of Hadrian's civilizatory legislation were his measures against human sacrifices in Cyprus; cf. Lactantius, *Divinae Institutiones*, I, 21:1: "Aput Cyprios humanam hostiam Iovi Teucrus immolavit idque sacrificium posteris tradidit; quod est nuper Hadriano imperante sublatum". See also Z. Zmigryder-Konopka, *Eos*, XXXIII (1930–1931), pp. 334 ff.; E. M. Smallwood, *Latomus*, XVIII (1959), pp. 334 ff.; XX (1961), pp. 93 ff. For taking Juvenal's Fourteenth Satire (No. 301), dated 128 C. E., as the *terminus post quem* for the promulgation of the law against circumcision, see Smallwood, *Latomus*, XVIII, pp. 335 f. To state that a decree aimed against the institution of the Sabbath also preceded the revolt is wholly unwarranted; for this, see d'Orgeval, *op. cit.*, p. 32.

It may only be suggested that the general ban on circumcision, as ordained by Hadrian, left some room for special permission to be granted to Jews to circumcise their children, similar to the permission given to them later by Antoninus Pius and that given to the Egyptian priests. Thus, we may assume that the later Roman legislation relating to Jews was foreshadowed under Hadrian. Such an innovation, implying a limitation on proselytism, could well constitute one of the causes of the revolt.

As a result of the revolt the ban on circumcision became valid in Judaea and applicable to the Jews themselves, figuring among the other punitive measures taken at the time like the prohibitions against keeping the Sabbath and study of Jewish law. The talmudic and midrashic sources furnish no clear evidence to prove the existence of a prohibition imposed on circumcision in Judaea in the period preceding the revolt of Bar-Kokhba. The date of the passage adduced in *TB Bava Batra*, 60b, by Alon, *op. cit.* (supra, p. 618), II, pp. 11 f., and placed by him before the revolt, is rather disputable. The same holds true for *TB Shabbat*, 130a; *TB Yevamot*, 72a; for another view, see S. Lieberman, *Annuaire de l'institut de philologie et d'histoire orientales et slaves*, VII (1939–1944), p. 423. There are some allusions in the midrashic literature to the death penalty imposed on Jews who circumcised their sons; cf. *Mekhilta*, Tractate Baḥodesh, 6 (ed. Horovitz & Rabin), p. 227; *Wayyiqra Rabba*, 32. However, as circumcision is cited there only as the first among the Jewish religious observances to be banned, the plain inference is that the situation reflected here pertains to the aftermath of the revolt, when the Roman government was determined to extirpate Judaism from Judaea.

Recently it has been argued that Hadrian did not promulgate a general law against circumcision preceding the revolt and that the ban was imposed later as an act of retaliation; see J. Geiger, *Zion*, XLI (1976), pp. 139 ff. Against Geiger, See M. D. Herr, *ibid.*, XLIII (1978), pp. 1 ff. See also Smallwood, pp. 428 ff.

Antoninus Pius, 5:4 — Hohl = F 199 R

Nam et Brittannos per Lollium Urbicum vicit legatum alio muro
cespiticio summotis barbaris ducto et Mauros ad pacem postulandam
coegit et Germanos et Dacos et multas gentes atque Iud⟨a⟩eos
rebellantes contudit per praesides ac legatos.

For Lollius Urbicus, his legate, overcame the Britons and built a
second wall, one of turf, after driving back the barbarians. Through
other legates or governors, he forced the Moors to sue for peace, and
crushed the Germans and the Dacians and many other tribes, and
also the Jews, who were in revolt.   (trans. D. Magie, *LCL*)

Iudaeos rebellantes contudit: There is no certain information from other
sources about a Jewish revolt under Antoninus Pius. His reign put an end to
the anti-Jewish policy of Hadrian. Antoninus Pius gave the Jews permission
to practice circumcision among themselves; cf. Modestinus, apud: *Digesta*,
XLVIII, 8:11: "circumcidere Iudaeis filios suos tantum rescripto divi Pii
permittitur: in non eiusdem religionis qui hoc fecerit, castrantis poena
irrogatur". This permission, which implies the end of the persecution
initiated under Hadrian, is also referred to in *TB Rosh Hashana*, 19a, and
should probably be dated to the first years of Antoninus Pius' reign. Perhaps
the Jewish revolt referred to by the *Historia Augusta* should be dated to the
first half of the reign of Antoninus Pius and be seen as no more than the
aftermath of the struggle at the time of Hadrian. This date seems more
plausible than *c.* 156 C.E.; for this, cf. the proposal of Smallwood, *Latomus*,
XVIII (supra, p. 621), p. 341; for dating the revolt after 152 C.E., see also
W. Weber, *CAH*, XI, p. 337. One may argue on the other hand that after the
grant of the right of circumcision some other prohibitions were left that
continued to irritate the Jews and made them revolt. A connection between
the *Historia Augusta* and the talmudic traditions relating to the famous sage
Simeon bar Yohai's persecution by the Roman authorities is suggested by
H. Graetz, *Geschichte der Juden*, IV[4], Leipzig 1908, pp. 436 ff., n. 20; see also
E.E. Bryant, *The Reign of Antoninus Pius*, Cambridge 1895, p. 78; S. Krauss,
Antoninus and Rabbi, Frankfort on the Main 1910, pp. 108 ff.; Juster, II, p.
194, n. 3; W. Hüttl, *Antoninus Pius*, I, Prague 1936, pp. 315 ff.; F.M. Abel,
Histoire de la Palestine, II, Paris 1952, pp. 107 ff.; J. Beaujeu, *La religion
romaine à l'apogée de l'empire*, I, Paris 1955, pp. 327 f. We find a reference to a
veteran of Legio V Macedonica taking part in a military expedition in the
orient under Severus, consul of 155 C.E. and later governor of Palestine; cf.
ILS, No. 2311. However, there is no reason to connect this inscription with a
Jewish revolt, since Severus could have commanded a Roman force in the
East when filling another position than that of governor of Palestine; see
Groag, PW, X, pp. 821. For a suggestion that a revolt of Egyptian Jews is

implied, see Liebmann-Frankfort, *op. cit.* (supra, p. 614, n. 3), p. 585, n. 20 (referring to Garzetti). However, it can hardly be admitted that the Egyptian Jews at that time had enough power left them to attempt any revolt.

In general the information supplied by the *Vita Pii* is estimated highly by modern scholarship; see R. Syme, *Ammianus and the Historia Augusta*, Oxford 1968, p. 92, n. 7.

513

Septimius Severus, 14:6 — Hohl = F201bR

Pal⟨a⟩estinis poenam remisit, quam ob causam Nigri meruerant.

1 *nigro* P

He revoked the punishment which had been imposed upon the people of Palestine on Niger's account. (trans. D. Magie, *LCL*)

Palaestinis poenam remisit: If we accept the interpretation implying that the Jews had joined Septimius Severus right from the beginning — see Graetz, *op. cit.* (supra, p. 622), p. 206 — we should assume that the statement of Severus has a bearing only on the non-Jewish population of Palestine, e.g., the citizens of Flavia Neapolis; cf. *Septimius Severus*, 9:5: "Neapolitanis etiam Palaestinensibus ius civitatis tulit, quod pro Nigro diu in armis fuerunt". Indeed any connection between this statement and the Jews may be denied. However nothing is recorded about Jewish support for Septimius Severus (see Juster, II, p. 273, n. 3), and the evidence at our disposal shows only that the Sixth Legion joined Septimius Severus while the Tenth Legion, stationed at Jerusalem, did not; see Ritterling, PW, XII, pp. 1592 f.

514

Septimius Severus, 16:7 — Hohl = F201cR

Filio sane concessit, ut triumpharet; cui senatus Iudaicum triumphum decreverat, idcirco quod et in Syria res bene gestae fuerant a Severo.

Notwithstanding this, he gave permission that his son should celebrate a triumph; for the senate had decreed to him a triumph over Judaea because of the successes achieved by Severus in Syria.

(trans. D. Magie, *LCL*)

cui senatus Iudaicum triumphum decreverat: Many explanations have been suggested for the Jewish triumph granted to the son of Septimius Severus, i.e. to Caracalla. There is an allusion to a Jewish revolt in *P. Oxy.*, 705, Col. II, ll. 33 f. = *CPJ*, No. 450, dated 199–200. A connection with this passage is suggested by P. M. Meyer, *Klio*, VII (1907), pp. 131 ff. However, the document refers to a festival celebrated in Oxyrhynchus in commemoration of a victory won over the Jews at the time of their revolt under Trajan. More importance may attach to some information deriving from the literary sources. Thus, relative to the events of 197 C. E., Jerome writes in *Chronica²* (ed. Helm), p. 211: "Iudaicum et Samariticum bellum motum." This may be interpreted in two ways. It might refer to a joint revolt of Jews and Samaritans against Roman rule; cf. K. J. Neumann, *Der römische Staat und die allgemeine Kirche bis auf Diocletian*, I, Leipzig 1890, p. 156, connecting the "Iudaicus triumphus" with this revolt. Alternatively, it could imply a conflict between Jews and Samaritans. The first interpretation had already been adopted by Orosius, who refers to a revolt against the Romans (VII, 17:3): "Iudaeos et Samaritas rebellare conantes ferro coercuit". The Syriac chronographers followed the other view. There exists some remote possibility that against the background of the struggle between Septimius and Niger there occurred some collision between Jews and Samaritans, a conjecture disapproved of by G. Alon, *op. cit.* (supra, p. 618), II, pp. 100 ff. Taking the biography of Septimius Severus here at its face value, Juster supposes that the Jews had chosen the party of Niger and were consequently punished by Severus; see Juster, II, p. 195. In any case, in view of the other information available, it is hardly justifiable to take the "triumphus Iudaicus" of the *Historia Augusta* as proof of a revolt of the Jews in the time of Septimius Severus, whose reign and that of his son Caracalla have always been considered the heyday of cooperation between the Jews and the Roman empire. This is borne out by, e.g., Jerome's commentary to Dan. xi:34 (*PL*, XXV, Col. 570 = ed. Glorie, *CCSL*, LXXV, A, p. 924): "Hebraeorum quidam haec de Severo et Antonino principibus intellegunt, qui Iudaeos plurimum dilexerunt". At that time the Jews obtained the right to municipal honours; cf. *Digesta*, L, 2:3:3: "Eis, qui Iudaicam superstitionem sequuntur divi Severus et Antoninus honores adipisci permiserunt". In the reign of Septimius Severus there also began wide-scale building activities connected with the erection of new synagogues in Galilee; see, e.g., the dedicatory inscription dated 197 C. E. from Kasyoun in Upper Galilee; cf. *CII*, No. 972. Thus, if anything at all is to be inferred concerning the "Jewish triumph" of Caracalla, it is that some military achievements in Judaea are indeed implied here, but that these were not necessarily connected with the Jews, who no longer constituted at that time a majority of the population of Judaea proper. It has been suggested that the Jewish triumph of Caracalla should be explained by some success of the Roman army in Adiabene; see Avi-Yonah, *Geschichte der Juden im Zeitalter des Talmud*, Berlin 1962, p. 79, followed in this view by Liebmann-Frankfort, *op. cit.* (supra, p. 614, n. 3), pp. 588 f. This, however, is not very acceptable, since Adiabene seems no longer to have been ruled at that time by a Jewish dynasty. The reference has also been taken as an allusion to the activities of Claudius the Robber, referred to by Cassius Dio, LXXV, 2:4 (No. 442); see Graetz, *op. cit.* (supra, p. 622), pp. 206 f. However, it seems more probable that the statement about the Jewish triumph of Caracalla has no foundation in actual history but was invented under the influence of the accounts of the Jewish triumph of Titus, known to the author from Suetonius and Eutropius; see J. Hasebroek, *Untersuchungen zur Geschichte des Kaisers Septimius Severus*, Heidelberg 1921, p. 71; M. Platnauer, *The Life and Reign of the Emperor Lucius Septimius Severus*, Oxford 1918, pp. 121 f.

515

Septimius Severus, 17:1 — Hohl = F201dR

In itinere Pal⟨a⟩estinis plurima iura fundavit. Iudaeos fieri sub gravi poena vetuit. Idem etiam de C⟨h⟩ristianis sanxit.

1 *fundicuit* P¹

While on his way thither [scil. to Alexandria] he conferred numerous rights upon the communities of Palestine. He forbade conversion to Judaism under heavy penalties and enacted a similar law in regard to the Christians. (trans. D. Magie, *LCL*)

Iudaeos fieri ... vetuit. Idem etiam de Christianis sanxit: cf. Neumann, *op. cit.* (supra, p. 624), pp. 156 ff.; C. Lécrivain, *Études sur l'Histoire Auguste*, Paris 1904, p. 169; K.H. Schwarte, *Historia*, XII (1963), pp. 185 ff.; T.D. Barnes, *JRS*, LVIII (1968), pp. 40 f.; R. Freudenberger, *Wiener Studien*, NS, II (1968), pp. 206 ff. Septimius Severus did not start a new policy by his legislation relating to proselytizing activities but continued that decided upon in the time of Antoninus Pius; see the commentary to No. 512. This passage should be compared with Paulus, *Sententiae*, V, 22:3 f.: "Cives Romani, qui se Iudaico ritu vel servos suos circumcidi patiuntur, bonis ademptis in insulam perpetuo relegantur; medici capite puniuntur. Iudaei si alienae nationis comparatos servos circumciderint aut deportantur aut capite puniuntur". The need to take measures against proselytism in the time of Severus can certainly be accounted for by the continuation on the part of the Jews of proselytizing activity. For the expression "Iudaeos fieri", see Pseudo-Augustinus, *Questiones Veteris et Novi Testamenti* (ed. Souter), *CSEL*, L, 81, p. 137: "Non de proselitis dico, quos constat fieri Iudaeos".

516

Pescennius Niger, 7:9 — Hohl = F200R

Idem Pal⟨a⟩estinis rogantibus, ut eorum censitio levaretur, idcirco quod esset gravata, respondit: "vos terras vestras levari censitione vultis: ego vero etiam aerem vestrum censere vellem."

Likewise, when the people of Palestine besought him to lessen their tribute, saying that it bore heavily on them, he replied: "So you wish me to lighten the tax on your lands; verily, if I had my way, I would tax the air." (trans. D. Magie, *LCL*)

517

Antoninus Caracallus, 1:6 — Hohl = F202R

Septennis puer, cum conlusorem suum puerum ob Iudaicam religionem gravius verberatum audisset, neque patrem suum neque patrem pueri vel⟨ut⟩ auctores verberum diu respexit.

3 *velut* Casaubonus   *vel* codd.

Once, when a child of seven, hearing that a certain playmate of his had been severely scourged for adopting the religion of the Jews, he long refused to look at either his own father or the boy's father, because he regarded them as responsible for the scourging.

(trans. D. Magie, *LCL*)

On this passage, see A. v. Domaszewski, *Die Personennamen bei den Scriptores Historiae Augustae* (*Sitzungsberichte der Heidelberger Akademie der Wissenschaften, Philosophisch-historische Klasse*, 1918, No. 13), pp. 138 f.; W. Reusch, "Der historische Wert der Caracallavita in den Scriptores Historiae Augustae", *Klio*, Suppl., XXIV (1931), pp. 10 f. The story occurs in a context fairly favourable to Caracalla. Domaszewski seems to go too far in his interpretation here of the implication of the seventh year (the sabbatical year). See also K. Bihlmeyer, *Die "syrischen" Kaiser zu Rom (211–35) und das Christentum*, Rottenburg 1916, pp. 31 ff. The friendly attitude of Caracalla to the Jews is also illustrated by the commentary of Jerome to Daniel; see above, the commentary to No. 514. In view of this some scholars tend to identify Caracalla with the "Antoninus" who appears in talmudic and midrashic passages in connection with "Rabbi", i.e. the Patriarch Judah I; see, e.g., Alon, *op. cit.* (supra, p. 618), II, p. 94; Avi-Yonah, *op. cit.* (supra, p. 624), p. 39, n. 15. The relevant texts were collected by D. Hoffmann, *Magazin für die Wissenschaft des Judenthums*, XIX (1892), pp. 33 ff. Hoffmann himself, and before him Bodek, thought that the references were more likely to apply to Marcus Aurelius; see *ibid.*, pp. 245 ff.; A. Bodek, *Marcus Aurelius Antoninus als Zeitgenosse und Freund des Rabbi Jehuda ha-Nasi*, Leipzig 1868. For identifying the talmudic Antoninus with Avidius Cassius, see S. Krauss, *Antoninus und Rabbi*, Vienna 1910, pp. 88 ff., with a survey of former solutions at pp. 70 ff. For identification with Alexander Severus, see H. Graetz, *Geschichte der Juden*, IV⁴, Leipzig 1908, pp. 450 f.; for Antoninus Pius, see R. Leszynsky, *Die Lösung des Antoninusrätsels*,

Berlin 1910; S. Klein, *MGWJ*, LXXVIII (1934), p. 169. Another suggestion is that some Roman governor is implied by Antoninus, and not the emperor; see W. Bacher, *Agada der Tannaiten*, II, Strasbourg 1890, p. 458, n. 2. For a further theory according to which the older "Antoninus and Rabbi" traditions go back to an apocryphal colloquy between Marcus Aurelius Antoninus and the Patriarch Judah I, see L. Wallach, *JQR*, XXXI (1940/1), pp. 259 ff.; cf. also A. Birley, *Marcus Aurelius*, London 1966, p. 264.

While Caracalla emerges as displaying unequivocal sympathy for Jews in this biography, it is stated that the senate decreed a "Iudaicus triumphus" to the son of Septimius Severus, i.e. Caracalla, in *Septimius Severus*, 16:7 (No. 514, and the commentary *ad loc.*). Such a triumph, whatever its historicity, implies a clash between Caracalla and the Jews. See also H. Heinen, *Chiron*, I (1971), pp. 421 ff., especially p. 434.

It is worthwhile referring here to the biography of the Gordians, where the kindness of the second Gordian is illustrated by the fact that he could not restrain his tears whenever one of the schoolboys was being flogged; see *Gordiani Tres*, 18:1: "fuit ... bonitatis insignis, adeo ut semper in conlusu, si quis puerorum verberaretur, ille lacrimas non teneret".

518

Antoninus Heliogabalus, 3:4–5 — Hohl = F203aR

(4) Sed ubi primum ingressus est urbem, omissis, quae in provincia gerebantur, Heliogabalum in Palatino monte iuxta ⟨a⟩edes imperatorias consecravit eique templum fecit, studens et Matris typum et Vestae ignem et Palladium et ancilia et omnia Romanis veneranda in illud transferre templum et id agens, ne quis Romae deus nisi Heliogabalus coleretur. (5) Dicebat praeterea Iudaeorum et Samaritanorum religiones et Christianam devotionem illuc transferendam, ut omnium culturarum secretum Heliogabali sacerdotium teneret.

8 *secreta*? Peter

(4) As soon as he entered the city, however, neglecting all the affairs of the provinces, he established Elagabalus as a god on the Palatine Hill close to the imperial palace; and he built him a temple, to which he desired to transfer the emblem of the Great Mother, the fire of Vesta, the Palladium, the shields of the Salii, and all that the Romans held sacred, purposing that no god might be worshipped at Rome save only Elagabalus. (5) He declared, furthermore, that the religions of the Jews and the Samaritans and the rites of the Christians must

also be transferred to this place, in order that the priesthood of Elagabalus might include the mysteries of every form of worship.

(trans. D. Magie, *LCL*)

Iudaeorum et Samaritanorum religiones: This emphasis on the Samaritans is also found in *Quadrigae Tyrannorum*, 8:3 (No. 527).

ut omnium culturarum secretum Heliogabali sacerdotium teneret: For the transfer of the cult of Heliogabalus to Rome, see O.F. Butler, *Studies in the Life of Heliogabalus*, New York 1910, pp. 79 ff. Cf. also *Heliogabalus*, 7:4: "omnes sane deos sui dei ministros esse aiebat, cum alios eius cubicularios appellaret, alios servos, alios diversarum rerum ministros". See G. Wissowa, *Religion und Kultus der Römer*, Munich 1912, pp. 89 f. For the circumcision of Heliogabalus and his abstention from pork, see Cassius Dio, LXXIX, 11:1 f.; J.S. Hay, *The Amazing Emperor Heliogabalus*, London 1911, pp. 277 f. For justified doubts concerning the historicity of the passage, see T.D. Barnes, *JRS*, LVIII (1968), pp. 41 f.; see also T. Optendrenk, *Die Religionspolitik des Kaisers Elagabal im Spiegel der Historia Augusta*, Bonn 1968, pp. 45 ff.; T.D. Barnes, *Bonner Historia Augusta Colloquium 1970*, Bonn 1972, pp. 60 ff.

519

Antoninus Heliogabalus, 28:1–4 — Hohl = F203b R

(1) Canes quaternos ingentes iunxit ad currum et sic est vectatus intra domum regiam, idque privatus in agris suis fecit. (2) Processit in publicum et quattuor cervis iunctis ingentibus. Iunxit sibi et leones, Matrem magnam se appellans. Iunxit et tigres, Liberum sese vocans
5 eodemque habitu agens, quo dii pinguntur, quos imitabatur. (3) Aegyptios dracunculos Romae habuit, quos illi agathodaemonas vocant. Habuit et hippopotamos et crocodillum et rhinocerotem et omnia Aegyptia, quae per naturam sui exhiberi poterant. (4) Struthocamelos exhibuit in cenis aliquotiens, dicens praeceptum
10 Iudaeis, ut ederent.

2 *idemque* Peter

(1) He would harness four huge dogs to a chariot and drive about within the royal residence, and he did the same thing, before he was made emperor, on his country-estates. (2) He even appeared in public driving four stags of vast size. Once he harnessed lions to his chariot and called himself the Great Mother, and on another occasion, tigers, and called himself Dionysus; and he always appeared in the

particular garb in which the deity that he was representing was usually depicted. (3) He kept at Rome tiny Egyptian snakes, called by the natives "good genii", besides hippopotami, a crocodile, and a rhinoceros, and, in fact, everything Egyptian which was of such a kind that it could be supplied. (4) And sometimes at his banquets he served ostriches, saying that the Jews had been commanded to eat them.

(trans. D. Magie, *LCL*)

4 *Struthocamelos exhibuit in cenis aliquotiens, dicens praeceptum Iudaeis, ut ederent*: This constitutes a joke aiming at the well-known Jewish food tabus. The extraordinary interest in ostriches displayed by the *Historia Augusta* is pointed out by R. Syme, *Ammianus and the Historia Augusta*, Oxford 1968, p. 113. They are mentioned in the work on seven other occasions: *Heliogabalus*, 22:1; 30:2; 32:4; *Gordiani*, 3:7; *Probus*, 19:4; *Quadrigae Tyrannorum*, 4:2; 6:2. However, in the seven other cases the word used is *struthio* and not *struthocamelus*; see E. Alföldi-Rosenbaum, *Bonner Historia Augusta Colloquium 1970*, Bonn 1972, pp. 11 ff. Since ostriches were among the animals forbidden by Jewish law for food (see Lev. xi:16; Deut. xiv:15), it has been suggested that in the process of transmission of the *Historia Augusta* the negative has dropped out; see Gager, *op. cit.* (supra, p. 614, n. 3), p. 94.

520

Alexander Severus, 22:4 — Hohl = F204aR

Iudaeis privilegia reservavit. Christianos esse passus est.

He respected the privileges of the Jews and allowed the Christians to exist unmolested.   (trans. D. Magie, *LCL*)

Iudaeis privilegia reservavit: To respect the privileges of the Jews would be in line with the general policy of the Severi, but this does not suggest that Alexander Severus promulgated an edict confirming Jewish privileges; see Bihlmeyer, *op. cit.* (supra, p. 626), pp. 101 f.; Barnes, *op. cit.* (supra, p. 625), p. 42.

Christianos esse passus est: On his attitude to the Christians, see *Alexander Severus*, 43:6: "Christo templum facere voluit eumve inter deos recipere quod et Hadrianus cogitasse fertur". In addition to the passage in which Christians are coupled with the Jews, cf. also *ibid.*, 49:6. The wording of the *Historia Augusta* should not imply the declaration of Christianity as *religio licita*; see W. Schmid, *Mullus — Festschrift Theodor Klauser*, Münster 1964, p. 298.

Alexander Severus, 28:7 — Hohl

Volebat videri originem de Romanorum gente trahere, quia eum pudebat Syrum dici, maxime quod quodam tempore festo, ut solent Antiochenses, Aegyptii, Alexandrini lacessiverant conviciolis, et Syrum archisynagogum eum vocantes ⟨et⟩ archiereum.

2 *festo* Peter	*frusta* P	*frustra* Σ	3 *lacessiverant* Peter
lacessitus erat P		*lacessitus* Σ	4 ⟨*et*⟩ edd.

He wished it to be thought that he derived his descent from the race of the Romans, for he felt shame at being called a Syrian, especially because, on the occasion of a certain festival, the people of Antioch and of Egypt and Alexandria had annoyed him with jibes, as is their custom, calling him a Syrian synagogue-chief and a high priest.

(trans. D. Magie, *LCL*)

Syrum archisynagogum eum vocantes: For the *archisynagogus* in Jewish communities, see Schürer, II, pp. 509 ff.; Juster, I, pp. 450 ff.; Leon, pp. 171 f. In the Roman period the *archisynagogus* had the most important function in the Jewish communities. The supervision of the synagogue was concentrated in his hands and inscriptions testify to the existence of this office in the various countries of the Diaspora. Since this title was mainly connected with the Jewish cult, we may infer that the allusion here refers to the Jewish sympathies of the emperor. For a Jewish dedication to Alexander Severus, see an inscription from Intercisa (*CII*, No. 677): "Deo aeterno pro sal(ute) d(omini) n(ostri) Sev(eri) A(lexandri) p(ii) f(elicis) Aug(usti) ... Vot(um) red(dit) l(ibens) Cosmus pr(aepositus) sta(tionis) Spondilla synag(ogae)". Cf. also G. Alföldy, *Acta Antiqua Academiae Scientiarum Hungaricae*, VI (1958), pp. 177 ff. For a suggestion that Alexander Severus took upon himself the role of protector of synagogues and was designated honorary *archisynagogus* of one of them, see A. Momigliano, *Athenaeum*, NS, XII (1934), pp. 151 ff. The mediaeval commentary on the Bible by David Qimḥi on Gen. i:31, refers to a synagogue of Severus; see A. Epstein, *MGWJ*, XXXIV (1885), p. 341; D. Hoffmann, *Magazin für die Wissenschaft des Judenthums*, XIX (1892), pp. 53 ff.; A. Momigliano, *Gnomon*, XXXIV (1962), p. 180; S. Lieberman, *Hellenism in Jewish Palestine*, New York 1950, p. 23. A reference to the same synagogue is to be found also in *Midrash Bereshit Rabbati*, ed. Albeck, Jerusalem 1940, p. 209. This midrash was compiled by the mediaeval Rabbi Moshe Hadarshan.

Alexander Severus, 29:2 — Hohl = F204bR

Usus vivendi eidem hic fuit: primum ut, si facultas esset, id est si non cum uxore cubuisset, matutinis horis in lario suo, in quo et divos principes sed optimos electos et animas sanctiores, in quis Apollonium et, quantum scriptor suorum temporum dicit, Christum, Abraham et Orfeum et huiusmodi ceteros habebat ac maiorum effigies, rem divinam faciebat.

2 *larario* edd. *lario* codd. 5 *huiusmodi ceteros*] *huius ceteros* P Ch.

His manner of living was as follows: First of all, if it were permissible, that is to say, if he had not lain with his wife, in the early morning hours he would worship in the sanctuary of his Lares, in which he kept statues of the deified emperors — of whom, however, only the best had been selected — and also of certain holy souls, among them Apollonius, and, according to a contemporary writer, Christ, Abraham, Orpheus and others of the same character and, besides, the portraits of his ancestors. (trans. D. Magie, *LCL*)

Apollonium: Cf. Cassius Dio, LXXVII, 18:4; cf. also the passage in the "Life of Aurelian" where the author promises to put in writing the deeds of Apollonius (*Vita Aureliani*, 24:9): "Ipse autem, si vita suppetit atque ipsius viri favor viguerit, breviter saltem tanti viri facta in litteras mittam"; see P. Courcelle, *Latomus*, XI (1952), p. 116.

Abraham: The name of Abraham, though not in this accurate Hebrew form, already occurs in the older Greek literature; cf. Nicolaus of Damascus (No. 83); Charax of Pergamon (No. 335). Thus it is not surprising that the name was known by Alexander Severus in the third century C.E.; see Wissowa, *op. cit.* (supra, p. 628), p. 92. However, it is suspicious that the names of Abraham and Orpheus are coupled in the same way in Firmicus Maternus, *Mathesis*, IV, Prooemium, 5 (No. 474). For the view that the *Historia Augusta* may be dependent here on Firmicus Maternus, or that the passage derives from a Neoplatonic source, see J. Geffcken, *Hermes*, LV (1920), p. 282; see also Schmid, *Festschrift Klauser, op. cit.* (supra, p. 629), p. 300, n. 19; S. Settis, *Athenaeum*, L (1972), pp. 237 ff.

Orfeum: See W. Schmid, *Rhein. Museum*, XCVI (1953), p. 101, where it is pointed out that the Christians appropriated Orpheus to themselves. See also J. Straub, *op. cit.* (supra, pp. 613 f., n. 2), p. 169, n. 129. Straub emphasizes that in Christian gnostic sects adoration of Christ sometimes went hand in hand with that of pagan celebrities, namely Homer, Pythagoras, Plato, and Aristotle. For general remarks on the attitude of Alexander Severus to the Christians, see W. H. C. Frend, *Martyrdom and Persecution in the Early Church*, Oxford 1965, pp. 329 f.

Alexander Severus, 45:6–7 — Hohl = F204c R

(6) Et quia de publicandis dispositionibus mentio contigit: ubi aliquos voluisset vel rectores provinciis dare vel praepositos facere vel procuratores, id est rationales, ordinare, nomina eorum proponebat hortans populum, ut si quis quid haberet criminis, probaret
5 manifestis rebus, si non probasset, subiret poenam capitis; (7) dicebatque grave esse, cum id Christiani et Iudaei facerent in praedicandis sacerdotibus, qui ordinandi sunt, non fieri in provinciarum rectoribus, quibus et fortunae hominum committerentur et capita.

(6) Now since we happen to have made mention of his practice of announcing his plans publicly — whenever Alexander desired to name any man governor of a province, or make him an officer in the army or appoint him a procurator, that is to say, a revenue-officer, he always announced his name publicly and charged the people, in case anyone wished to bring an accusation against him, to prove it by irrefutable evidence, declaring that anyone who failed to prove his charge should suffer capital punishment. (7) For, he used to say, it was unjust that, when Christians and Jews observed this custom in announcing the names of those who were to be ordained priests, it should not be similarly observed in the case of governors of provinces, to whose keeping were committed the fortunes and lives of men.   (trans. D. Magie, *LCL*)

7 *cum id Christiani et Iudaei facerent in praedicandis sacerdotibus*: See Bihlmeyer, *op. cit.* (supra, p. 626), pp. 115 f.; on Christian ordination, see J. Straub, *Mullus — Festschrift Theodor Klauser*, Münster 1964, pp. 336 ff. A text referred to by Straub with special relevance here is Cyprianus, *Epistulae*, LXVII, 4: "ut sacerdos plebe praesente sub omnium oculis deligatur et dignus atque idoneus publico iudicio ac testimonio conprobetur, sicut in Numeris Dominus Moysi praecipit … coram omni synagoga iubet deus constitui sacerdotem, id est instruit et ostendit ordinationes sacerdotales non nisi sub populi adsistentis conscientia fieri oportere, ut plebe praesente vel detegantur malorum crimina vel bonorum merita praedicentur, et sit ordinatio iusta et legitima quae omnium suffragio et iudicio fuerit examinata".

Alexander Severus, 51:6–8 — Hohl = F204d R

(6) Si quis de via in alicuius possessionem deflexisset, pro qualitate
loci aut fustibus subiciebatur in conspectu eius aut virgis aut
condemnationi aut, si haec omnia transiret dignitas hominis,
gravissimis contumeliis, cum diceret: "visne hoc in agro tuo fieri quod
5 tu alteri facis?" (7) clamabatque saepius, quod a quibusdam sive
Iudaeis sive Christianis audierat et tenebat, idque per praeconem,
cum aliquem emendaret, dici iubebat: (8) "quod tibi fieri non vis,
alteri ne feceris." Quam sententiam usque adeo dilexit, ut et in
Palatio et in publicis operibus perscribi iuberet.

<blockquote>7 dic nubebat P¹   9 perscribi] praescribi Peter</blockquote>

(6) Moreover, if any man turned aside from the road into someone's
private property, he was punished in the Emperor's presence
according to the character of his rank, either by the club or by the rod
or by condemnation to death, or, if his rank placed him above all
these penalties, by the sternest sort of a rebuke, the Emperor saying,
"Do you desire this to be done to your land which you are doing to
another's?" (7) He used often to exclaim what he had heard from
someone, either a Jew or a Christian, and always remembered, and
he also had it announced by a herald whenever he was disciplining
anyone, (8) "What you do not wish that a man should do to you, do
not do to him". And so highly did he value this sentiment that he had
it written up in the Palace and in public buildings.

(trans. D. Magie, LCL)

7 *"quod tibi fieri non vis, alteri ne feceris"*: On this golden rule, see
W. H. P. Hatch, *HTR*, XIV (1921), pp. 193 ff.; A. Dihle, *Die goldene Regel;
Eine Einführung in die Geschichte der antiken und frühchristlichen
Vulgärethik*, Göttingen 1962; A. E. Harvey, *JTS*, NS, XV (1964), pp. 384 ff.
Knowledge of this maxim is well attested in Jewish literature; see Tobit
iv: 15: καὶ ὃ μισεῖς, μηδενὶ ποιήσῃς; Philo, apud: Eusebius, *Praeparatio
Evangelica*, VIII, 7: 6: ἅ τις παθεῖν ἐχθαίρει, μὴ ποιεῖν αὐτόν; see Bernays,
I, pp. 272 ff. Above all, this rule is known in its Aramaic form and ascribed to
Hillel; see *TB Shabbat*, 31a: דעלך סני לחברך לא תעביד; the same rule is
attributed to Rabbi Aqiva in *Aboth de-Rabbi Nathan* (ed. Schechter), Rec. B,
26, p. 53. See also the discussion in Geffcken, *op. cit.* (supra, p. 631), p. 285;
Straub, *Heidnische Geschichtsapologetik, op. cit.* (supra, pp. 613 f., n. 2), pp.
106 ff.; idem, *Atti del colloquio patavino sulla Historia Augusta*, Rome 1963,
pp. 21 ff. It is found in a pagan inscription from Salona: "Unusquisque quot

sibi fieri non vult facere non debet". The inscription, found in 1954, is dated to the reign of Alexander Severus by M. Sordi, *RFIC*, LXXXIX (1961), pp. 301 ff. For the text, see *ibid.*, p. 301; S. Panciera, *Latomus*, XIX (1960), p. 702. See now also B. Lifshitz, in: *CII²*, New York 1975, No. 680a, p. 62, Prolegomena; *Année épigraphique*, 1959, No. 251.

Evidently at that time the rule became a kind of *vulgare proverbium*, and is reflected in the speech of Maecenas in Cassius Dio, LII, 34:1: Πάνθ' ὅσα τοὺς ἀρχομένους καὶ φρονεῖν καὶ πράττειν βούλει, καὶ λέγε καὶ ποίει. However, the Syrian Alexander Severus might well have obtained his knowledge of the maxim directly from Jewish or Christian circles; see A. Cameron, *JRS*, LV (1965), p. 245. For bibliography on Alexander's relations with Jews and Christians, see also R. Soraci, *L'opera legislativa e amministrativa dell' imperatore Severo Alessandro*, Catania 1974, p. 222, n. 31.

525

Gordiani Tres, 34:2–3 — Hohl = F205R

(2) Gordiano sepulchrum milites apud Circesium castrum fecerunt in finibus Persidis, titulum huius modi addentes et Graecis et Latinis et Persicis et Iudaicis et Aegyptiacis litteris, (3) ut ab omnibus legeretur: "Divo Gordiano victori Persarum, victori Gothorum, victori Sarmatarum, depulsori Romanarum seditionum, victori Germanorum, sed non victori Philipporum."

    1 *Circesium* Casaubonus   *circeium* P   3 *legeretur*] *legetur* P

(2) The soldiers built Gordian a tomb near the camp at Circesium, which is in the territory of Persia, and added an inscription to the following effect in Greek, Latin, Persian, Hebrew, and Egyptian letters, (3) so that all might read: "To the deified Gordian, conqueror of the Persians, conqueror of the Goths, conqueror of the Sarmatians, queller of mutinies at Rome, conqueror of the Germans, but no conqueror of Philippi."   (trans. D. Magie, *LCL*)

2 *titulum huius modi*: The story of this inscription should not be thought authentic; see L. Homo, *Revue historique*, CLII (1926), p. 5. On the historical value of the *Gordiani* in general, see J. Burian, *Atti del colloquio patavino sulla Historia Augusta*, Rome 1963, pp. 41 ff.

addentes et Graecis et Latinis et Persicis et Iudaicis et Aegyptiacis litteris: The importance attached here to the Jewish letters, which are given equal status with the Greek, Latin, Persian and Egyptian ones, is noteworthy, but in accordance with the general tone of the *Historia Augusta*.

526

(4) Doctissimi mathematicorum centum viginti annos homini ad vivendum datos iudicant neque amplius cuiquam iactitant esse concessos, etiam illud addentes Mosen solum, dei, ut Iudaeorum libri locuntur, familiarem, centum viginti quinque annos vixisse; qui cum
5 quereretur quod iuvenis interiret, responsum ei ab incerto ferunt numine neminem plus esse victurum. (5) Quare etiamsi centum et viginti quinque annos Claudius vixisset, ne necessariam quidem mortem eius expectandam fuisse, ut Tullius de Scipione sic loquitur, stupenda et mirabilis docet vita.

5 *quod* ΣP corr   *quot* P   7 *ne necessariam* Salmasius   *necessariam* codd.

(4) Now the most learned of the astrologers hold that one hundred and twenty years have been allotted to man for living and assert that no one has ever been granted a longer span; they even tell us that Moses alone, the friend of God, as he is called in the books of the Jews, lived for one hundred and twenty five years, and that when he complained that he was dying in his prime, he received from an unknown god, so they say, the reply that no one should ever live longer. (5) But even if Claudius had lived for one hundred and twenty five years — as his life, so marvellous and admirable, shows us — we need not, as Tullius says of Scipio, have expected for him even a natural death.

(trans. D. Magie, LCL)

4 *centum viginti quinque annos vixisse*: see Geffcken, *Hermes, op. cit.* (supra, p. 631), pp. 293 f. According to Deut. xxxiv : 7, Moses reached the age of 120 years. The age of 120 years is fixed as the utmost limit of human life already in Gen. vi : 3; cf. *Ant.*, I, 152. Cf. Seneca, *De Brevitate Vitae*, 3 : 2: "Pervenisse te ad ultimum aetatis humanae videmus. Centesimus tibi vel supra premitur annus"; *Scriptores Historiae Augustae, Tacitus*, 15 : 2: "ipse victurus annis centum viginti". The figure of 125 years is nowhere given for the length of the life of Moses, but Benjamin died at the age of 125; cf. the Testaments of the Twelve Patriarchs, Testament of Benjamin, xii : 2; the same holds true of Asher; cf. Testament of Asher, i : 1. The age of 125 finds its place also among the examples of longevity listed by Plinius, *Naturalis Historia*, VII, 163 f. Thus the number given in the *Historia Augusta* is not so extraordinary as it may seem; see, e.g., Schmid, *Festschrift Klauser, op. cit.* (supra, p. 629), p. 305, n. 46: "Dies in Abweichung zu den apokryphen Texten, wo die Zahl 120 genannt ist. Ob ein Lapsus des Trebellius Pollio vorliegt oder bewusste Absicht, den Fall etwas über die von den Astrologen angegebene Grenze hinauszurücken, lässt sich nicht entscheiden".

qui cum quereretur quod iuvenis interiret: For the midrashic tradition on the death of Moses and his struggle against death, see Ginzberg, III, pp. 417 ff.

responsum ei ab incerto ferunt numine: The "incertum numen" (ἄγνωστος θεός) was the Jewish God; cf. Livius, apud: *Scholia in Lucanum*, II, 593 (No. 133); idem, apud: Lydus, *De Mensibus*, IV, 53 (No. 134); Lucanus, *Pharsalia*, II, 593 (No. 191). See Schmid, *Festschrift Klauser*, *op. cit.* (supra, p. 629), pp. 304 ff.

527

Quadrigae Tyrannorum, 7:4–8:10 — Hohl = *F. Gr. Hist.*, II, B257, F35 = *Bonner Historia Augusta Colloquium*, Bonn 1964–1965 (1966), pp. 160 f. — Schmid

(7:4) Sunt enim Aegyptii, ut satis nosti, ⟨in⟩ venti ventosi, furibundi, iactantes, iniuriosi atque adeo vani, liberi, novarum rerum usque ad cantilenas publicas cupientes, versificatores, epigrammatarii, mathematici, haruspices, medici. (5) Nam ⟨in⟩ eis C⟨h⟩ristiani, 5 Samaritae et quibus praesentia semper tempora cum enormi libertate displiceant. (6) Ac ne quis mihi Aegyptiorum irascatur et meum esse credat, quod in litteras rettuli, Hadriani epistolam ⟨p⟩romam ex libris Flegontis liberti eius proditam, ex qua penitus Aegyptiorum vita detegatur.

10 (8:1) "Hadrianus Augustus Serviano consuli salutem. Aegyptum, quam mihi laudabas, Serviane carissime, totam didici levem, pendulam et ad omnia famae momenta volitantem. (2) Illic qui Serapem colunt, C⟨h⟩ristiani sunt et devoti sunt Serapi, qui se C⟨h⟩risti episcopos dicunt, (3) nemo illic archisynagogus Iudaeorum, 15 nemo Samarites, nemo C⟨h⟩ristianorum presbyter non mathematicus, non haruspex, non aliptes. (4) Ipse ille patriarcha cum Aegyptum venerit, ab aliis Serapidem adorare, ab aliis cogitur Christum. (5) Genus hominum seditiosissimum, vanissimum, iniuriosissimum, civitas opulenta, dives, fecunda, in qua nemo vivat 20 otiosus. (6) Alii vitrum conflant, aliis charta conficitur, omnes certe linifiones ⟨aut⟩ cuiuscumque artis et ⟨professionis⟩ videntur; et habent podagrosi, quod agant, habent caesi quod agant, habent caeci, quod faciant, ne chiragrici quidem apud eos otiosi vivunt. Unus illis deus

1 ⟨in⟩ *venti* Hohl   *venti* P   *viri* Σ   2 *adeo vani* edd.   *adeo vasi* P
   avidi Σ   *adeo vafri* Baehrens   4 ⟨in⟩ *eis* Petschenig
7 *promam* Eyssenhardt   *roma* codd.   *ponam* Peter   9 *detegitur* Σ
12 *illic* Casaubonus   *illa* P   *illi* Σ   *illac* Petschenig   16 *aliptas* P
20 *cartha* P   21 ⟨aut⟩...⟨professionis⟩ Helm   22 *caesi*] *praecisi* Hohl
   laesi Schmid

nummus est. (7) Hunc Christiani, hunc Iudaei, hunc omnes
25 venerantur et gentes. Et utinam melius esset morata civitas, digna
profecto, quae pro sui fecunditate, quae pro sui magnitudine totius
Aegypti teneat principatum. (8) Huic ego cuncta concessi, vetera
privilegia reddidi, nova sic addidi, ut praesenti gratias agerent.
Denique ut primum inde discessi, et in filium meum Verum multa
30 dixerunt, et de Antinoo quae dixerint, comperisse te credo. (9) Nihil
illis opto, nisi ut suis pullis alantur, quos quem ad modum fecundant,
pudet dicere. (10) Calices tibi allassontes diversi coloris transmisi,
quos mihi sacerdos templi obtulit, tibi et sorori meae specialiter
dedicatos, quos tu velim festis diebus conviviis adhibeas. Caveas
35 tamen, ne his Africanus noster indulgenter utatur.''

24 *nummus* Vossius   *nullus* P om. Σ   26 *fecunditate*] *funditate* P
     28 *praesenti ⟨tamquam deo⟩*? Jacoby   30 *Antinoo* Casaubonus
antonino codd.   32 *diversi coloris*] *versicoloris* P   *id est versicolores* Salmasius

(7:4) For the Egyptians, as you know well enough, are puffed up,
madmen, boastful, doers of injury, and, in fact, liars and without
restraint, always craving something new, even in their popular songs,
writers of verse, makers of epigrams, astrologers, soothsayers,
quacksalvers. (5) Among them, indeed, are Christians and
Samaritans and those who are always ill-pleased with the present,
though enjoying unbounded liberty. (6) But, lest any Egyptian be
angry with me, thinking that what I have set forth in writing is solely
my own, I will cite one of Hadrian's letters, taken from the works of
his freedman Phlegon, which fully reveals the character of the
Egyptians.
(8:1) "From Hadrian Augustus to Servianus the consul, greeting.
The land of Egypt, the praises of which you have been recounting to
me, my dear Servianus, I have found to be wholly light-minded,
unstable and blown about by every breath of rumour. (2) There those
who worship Serapis are, in fact, Christians, and those who call
themselves bishops of Christ are, in fact, devotees of Serapis. (3)
There is no chief of the Jewish synagogue, no Samaritan, no Christian
presbyter, who is not an astrologer, a soothsayer, or an anointer. (4)
Even the Patriarch himself, when he comes to Egypt, is forced by
some to worship Serapis, by others to worship Christ. (5) They are a
folk most seditious, most deceitful, most given to injury; but their city
is prosperous, rich and fruitful, and in it no one is idle. (6) Some are
blowers of glass, others makers of paper, all are at least weavers of

637

linen or seem to belong to one craft or another; the lame have their occupations, the wounded have theirs, the blind have theirs, and not even those whose hands are crippled are idle. Their only god is money, (7) and this the Christians, the Jews and, in fact, all nations adore. And would that this city had a better character, for indeed it is worthy by reason of its richness and by reason of its size to hold the chief place in the whole of Egypt. (8) I granted it every favour, I restored to it all its ancient rights and bestowed on it new ones besides, so that the people gave thanks to me while I was present among them. Then, no sooner had I departed thence than they said many things against my son Verus, and what they said about Antinous I believe you have learned. (9) I can only wish for them that they may live on their own chickens, which they breed in a fashion I am ashamed to describe. (10) I am sending you over some cups, changing colour and variegated, presented to me by the priest of a temple and now dedicated particularly to you and my sister. I should like you to use them at banquets on feast-days. Take good care, however, that our dear Africanus does not use them too freely."

(trans. D. Magie, *LCL*)

8:1 *Serviano consuli salutem*: On Julius Servianus, the brother-in-law of Hadrian, see Groag, PW, X, pp. 882 ff.; idem, *PIR²*, III, p. 61, No. 186; Hohl, *op. cit.* (supra, p. 614, n. 2), p. 52, n. 63; H. G. Pflaum, *Bonner Historia Augusta Colloquium*, Bonn 1963 (1964), p. 97; A. N. Sherwin-White, *The Letters of Pliny — A Historical and Social Commentary*, Oxford 1966, p. 386. Servianus was consul three times. His third consulate is dated to 134 C.E.; cf. *ILS*, No. 2117: "missus ab imp. Hadriano Aug. Serviano III et Vibio Varo Cos". His second consulate went back to 102 C.E.; see Groag, *op. cit.*, p. 884. Thus the only consulate of Servianus which would fall in the reign of Hadrian is the third, and this is implied here.

8:3 *nemo illic archisynagogus Iudaeorum*: On the *archisynagogus*, see above, the commentary to *Alexander Severus*, 28: 7 (No. 521). See also *Codex Theodosianus*, XVI, 8: 14: "archisynagogi sive presbyteri Iudaeorum".

nemo Samarites: The Samaritans are conspicuous both here and in the biography of *Heliogabalus*, 3:5 (No. 518). On the Samaritans in the *Historia Augusta*, see H. Dessau, *Festschrift Lehmann-Haupt*, Leipzig–Vienna 1921, pp. 124 ff.; Baynes, *op. cit.* (supra, p. 613, n. 1), pp. 30 ff. The existence of a Samaritan community in Egypt itself may be followed from the very beginning of the Hellenistic age. Evidence is forthcoming from both the literary sources and the papyri. On the Samaritans at the time of Alexander, see *Ant.*, XI, 345; XII, 7; on a dispute between Jews and Samaritans before Ptolemy Philometor, see *ibid.*, XIII, 74 ff.; for Samaria as the name of a village in Ptolemaic Faiyûm, see *CPJ*, Nos. 22, 28, 128; *P. Rylands*, No. 71,

l. 22; M. Launey, *Recherches sur les armées hellénistiques*, II, Paris 1950, p. 1235; cf. also M. Nagel, *Chronique d'Égypte*, XLIX (1974), pp. 356 ff. (second century C. E.). The evidence continues for individual Samaritans living in Byzantine Egypt; cf. two papyri from Hermopolis, one a deed of divorce dated to 586 C. E. (*CPJ*, No. 513), and the other a receipt (*Papyri from Hermopolis*, ed. B. R. Rees, London 1964, No. 40); see also the passage from Eulogius, patriarch of Alexandria between 580 and 607 C. E., apud: Photius, Cod. 230 (ed. Bekker), p. 285a = ed. Henry, V, p. 60: τελευταῖον δὲ περιεῖχε τὸ βιβλίον λόγον ἐπιγραφὴν φέροντα· ὅρος ἐκφωνηθεὶς τοῖς Σαμαρείταις. Samaritans are already mentioned by older Latin historians; on the activities of the Samaritans in the times of Alexander the Great, cf. Curtius Rufus, IV, 8 : 34 : 9 (No. 197); cf. also, Tacitus, *Annales*, XII, 54 (No. 288), showing that the Roman historian was fully aware of the difference between Jews and Samaritans in the Julio-Claudian period and of their mutual antagonism. In both works the information bears upon Samaritans living in their homeland. Gradually, however, some references are made to Samaritans living outside Palestine and Egypt; e.g., for a Samaritan living in Rome in the time of Tiberius, see *Ant.*, XVIII, 167; on the doctor Rufus of Samaria, see above, the introduction to Galen. On Samaritan women in Attic inscriptions, see *IG*, II², Nos. 10219–10220; J. & L. Robert, *REG*, LXXXII (1969), pp. 476 ff. (though here we may surmise that the people implied are from the Hellenistic city of Samaria); on a Samaritan synagogue at Thessalonica, presumably of the fourth century C. E., see B. Lifshitz & J. Schiby, *RB*, LXXV (1968), pp. 368 ff.; cf. also E. Tov, *RB*, LXXXI (1974), pp. 394 ff. For Samaritans in Italy, see the inscription from Hipponion, published already in *Notizie degli Scavi*, 1921, p. 485, and then correctly read by L. Robert, *Hellenica*, III, Paris 1946, p. 97. On a synagogue of Samaritans at Rome, see Cassiodorus, *Variae*, III, 45 (*Monumenta Germaniae Historica, Auctores Antiquissimi*, XII, p. 101, ed. Mommsen).

The relative importance allotted in the *Historia Augusta* to Samaritans living in Egypt, and to the Samaritan cult in general, is well in accord with the advancement of the Samaritan element in the late Roman and Byzantine empire. This is excellently illustrated by *Codex Theodosianus*, XIII, 5 : 18: "Iudaeorum corpus ac Samaritanum" (390 C. E.); *ibid.*, XVI, 8 : 16 (404 C. E.); on the Samaritan mathematician and philosopher Marinus, see also Damascius, *Vita Isidori* (No. 548).

non aliptes: For the opinion that "aliptes" is reminiscent of Iuvenalis, *Saturae*, III, 76, see A. D. E. Cameron, *Hermes*, XCII (1964), p. 365.

8 : 4 *Ipse ille patriarcha cum Aegyptum venerit, ab aliis Serapidem adorare, ab aliis cogitur Christum*: It was common among scholars to assume that the Christian patriarch of Alexandria is implied here, and some even thought of an allusion to the great Athanasius; see, e.g., Baynes, *op. cit.* (supra, p. 613, n. 1), p. 66; H. Stern, *op. cit.* (supra, p. 613, n. 1), pp. 67 f. However, since the present letter states that when the patriarch comes to Egypt he is compelled to worship Christ, who in relation to the patriarch is put on the same level as Serapis, the obvious conclusion is that the person in question must be the Jewish-Palestinian patriarch of the house of Hillel; see, e.g., already E. Renan, *L'église chrétienne*³, Paris 1879, p. 189, n. 1; Harnack, I, p. 20, n. 2; more recently W. Schmid, *Bonner Historia Augusta Colloquium, op. cit.* (supra, p. 613, n. 1), pp. 153 ff.; Syme, *Ammianus and the Historia Augusta, op. cit.* (supra, p. 612, n. 1), pp. 62 ff.; idem, *Bonner Historia Augusta Colloquium*, Bonn 1966–1967 (1968), pp. 119 ff.; A. Momigliano, *The English Historical Review*, LXXXIV (1969), p. 569, n. 1.

At least from the third century C.E. onwards the literary sources testify that the Hillelite head of Palestinian Jewry was designated "patriarch"; cf. Origenes, *Selecta in Psalmos* (*PG*, XII, Col. 1056); see Juster, I, p. 394; cf. also the inscription from Stobi with the interpretation of M. Hengel, *ZNTW*, LVII (1966), pp. 152 ff.

8:6 *habent caesi quod agant*: The reading *cesi = caesi* in the meaning of "vulnerati", is defended by A. Önnerfors, in: Schmid, *op. cit.* (supra, p. 613, n. 1), pp. 183 f. Schmid himself prefers the emendation *lesi = laesi* (p. 184).

8:8 *in filium meum Verum multa dixerunt*: Hadrian did not adopt his son until the second half of 136 C.E., and it was the consul of that year, L. Ceionius Commodus, who was adopted; see Groag, PW, X, p. 888; A. Stein, *PIR*², II, pp. 138 ff. The account of Cassius Dio implies that as a result of this step Servianus and his grandson Fuscus were put to death by Hadrian on the ground that they were displeased at the adoption; see Cassius Dio, LXIX, 17:1: καὶ διὰ τοῦτο Κόμμοδον μὲν Λούκιον ... Καίσαρα Ῥωμαίοις ἀπέδειξε, Σερουιανὸν δὲ καὶ Φοῦσκον τὸν ἔγγονον αὐτοῦ ὡς καὶ ἀγανακτήσαντας ἐπὶ τούτῳ ἐφόνευσε, τὸν μὲν ἐνενηκοντούτην ὄντα τὸν δὲ ὀκτωκαιδεκέτην. There is also no kind of evidence that Ceionius Commodus was called Verus apart from the *Historia Augusta*.

8:9 *ut suis pullis alantur, quos quem ad modum fecundant, pudet dicere*: For an interpretation of the passage in the light of Aristoteles, *Historia Animalium*, VI, 2, p. 559b, l. 1, and Plinius, *Naturalis Historia*, X, 153 ("quaedam autem et citra incubitum sponte natura gignit ut in Aegypti fimetis"), see F. Dornseiff, *Aus der byzantinistischen Arbeit der deutschen demokratischen Republik*, I, ed. Johannes Irmscher, Berlin 1957, p. 45.

8:10 *ne his Africanus noster indulgenter utatur*: There was a consul Sextius Africanus of 112 C.E., but it is rather doubtful whether he may be identified with the Africanus of our letter; see Groag, PW, Ser. 2, II, p. 2044.

Most scholars deny the authenticity of this letter; see T. Mommsen, *Römische Geschichte*, V⁶, Berlin 1909, p. 576, n. 1; p. 585, n. 2; Lécrivain, *op. cit.* (supra, p. 625), p. 69; Groag, X, p. 887; E. Hohl, *Über die Glaubwürdigkeit der Historia Augusta, op. cit.* (supra, p. 614, n. 2), pp. 40 ff.; cf. *ibid.*, p. 48: "der Brief an Servian ist und bleibt eine von Anachronismen strotzende Fälschung"; B. W. Henderson, *The Life and Principate of the Emperor Hadrian*, London 1923, pp. 228 ff.; L. Homo, *Revue historique*, CLI (1926), pp. 179 f.; Jacoby, *F. Gr. Hist.*, II, D, p. 844 (there is no foundation for assuming a Greek original on the basis of the reading "allassontes versicolores"); Beaujeu, *op. cit.* (supra, p. 622), p. 274, n. 1 (stressing the use of "gentes" to designate the non-Christian and non-Jewish parts of the Alexandrian population and maintaining that this in itself furnishes sufficient ground for marking the letter as apocryphal); Schmid, *op. cit.*, pp. 153 ff. (the letter should be dated after the law promulgated in 399 C.E.; cf. *Codex Theodosianus*, XVI, 8:14; see especially Schmid, *op. cit.*, pp. 175 f.); Syme, *Ammianus and the Historia Augusta, op. cit.* (supra, p. 612, n. 1), pp. 60 ff.; idem, *Emperors and Biography, op. cit.* (supra, p. 613), pp. 19 f.; see also J. Schwartz, *Bonner Historia Augusta Colloquium*, Bonn 1972–1974 (1976), pp. 261 ff.

Still some maintain the authenticity of the letter; see H. Bardon, *Les empereurs et les lettres latines d'Auguste à Hadrien*, Paris 1940, pp. 398 ff.; B. d'Orgeval, *op. cit.* (supra, p. 621), pp. 312 f.; Dornseiff, *op. cit.* (supra, p. 640), pp. 39 ff. Others think that the original document was later reworked; see I. Dürr, *Die Reisen des Kaisers Hadrian*, Vienna 1881, pp. 88 ff.; J. Carcopino, *REA*, LI (1949), pp. 304 ff.

It seems, however, that the arguments adduced against the authenticity of the letter are irrefutable. Their main points are as follows:

a. The presumed date for the letter, if authentic, would be 130 C.E., the time of Hadrian's visit to Egypt. However Servianus was consul in 134, and it is rather problematic whether Hadrian paid a second visit to Egypt in 134 C.E., as upheld by S. Follet, *Revue de Philologie*, XLII (1968), pp. 54 ff.

b. The letter mentions a son of Hadrian, yet the emperor adopted Ceionius Commodus as late as 136 C.E. Moreover, the name of the son in the letter was Verus, a name not borne by Hadrian's adopted son.

c. Some minor points, such as calling the gentile population of Alexandria "gentes", the apparent allusion ("aliptes") to Juvenal in whom interest was revived in the latter part of the fourth century, and the importance attached to the Samaritans, all seem anachronistic.

d. After the revolt of Egyptian Jews was crushed at the very end of Trajan's reign, the sources testify to an almost total, though temporary, disappearance of the Jews from the Alexandrian scene. There is, for instance, no reference to Jews in the second-century *Gnomon of the Idios Logos*. Thus it is inconceivable that the Jews would have been so conspicuous in the life of Alexandria in the time of Hadrian. It is also unlikely that both the Samaritans and the Christians occupied such an important place as the letter seems to indicate in its description of Alexandria.

e. The content of the letter in the *Quadrigae Tyrannorum* is not free of inventions. Thus we read that Saturninus was a Gaul, and this gives the *Historia Augusta* an occasion to include some general remarks on the Gallic character. Yet it is stated that Saturninus hailed from Africa (γένει Μαυρούσιος) by Zosimus, *Nova Historia*, I, 66:1.

528

Quadrigae Tyrannorum, 12:3 — Hohl

Huic ⟨scil. Proculo⟩ uxor virago, quae illum in hanc praecipitavit dementiam, nomine Samso, quod ei postea inditum est, nam antea Vituriga nominata est.

His [scil. Proculus'] wife, who drove him to this act of madness, was a masculine woman called Samso — though this name was given her in her later years, for originally she was called Vituriga.

(trans. D. Magie, *LCL*)

nomine Samso: The name, Samso, which was adopted by the stout wife of Proculus (she formerly bore the name of Vituriga), is interpreted as an allusion to the biblical Samson by Syme, *Ammianus and the Historia Augusta, op. cit.* (supra, p. 612, n. 1), p. 57; cf. already A. v. Domaszewski, *Heidelberger Sitzungsberichte*, 1918, No. 13, p. 20.

CXLIII. THE ANONYMOUS AUTHOR OF *DE VIRIS ILLUSTRIBUS*

Fourth century C.E.

The anonymous author of De Viris Illustribus,[1] *whose accounts of famous men range from Proca, the ancient king of Alba, to Mark Antony, refers to Jews only in connection with the conquests of Pompey.*

529

De Viris Illustribus, 77 — Sherwin, Oklahoma 1973

Deinde mira felicitate rerum in septemtrionem Albanos, Colchos, Heniochos, Caspios, Iberos, nunc in Orientem Parthos, Arabas atque Iudaeos cum magno sui terrore penetravit ⟨scil. Pompeius⟩.

1 *facilitate et celeritate nunc in septemtrionem* op   *mira felicitate nunc in septemtrionem* Pichlmayr

Thereupon by wonderful good luck he [scil. Pompey] penetrated into the North, into the countries of the Albanians, Colchians, Heniochians, Caspians, and Iberians, and into the East, into the countries of the Parthians, the Arabs and the Jews, causing great fear.

1 See H. Peter, *Die geschichtliche Litteratur über die römische Kaiserzeit bis Theodosius I und ihre Quellen*, II, Leipzig 1897, pp. 367 ff.

CXLIV. THE ANONYMOUS AUTHOR OF *EPITOME DE CAESARIBUS*

Beginning of the fifth century C.E.

The Epitome de Caesaribus,[1] *dependent in its first eleven chapters on Suetonius, adds hardly anything to our knowledge of Jewish history. The only detail not found in other sources bears upon the relations between Caecina Alienus and Berenice.*

530

Epitome de Caesaribus, 4:6–7 — Pichlmayr & Gründel

(6) Ita liberti eius ⟨scil. Claudii⟩ potestatem summam adepti stupris exilio caede proscriptionibus omnia foedabant. (7) Ex quibus Felicem legionibus Iudaeae praefecit.

(6) In this way the freedmen of Claudius, after they attained to the highest power, polluted everything by debauchery, by sending people into exile, by murder and proscriptions. (7) One of this company, Felix, he appointed to the command of the legions of Judaea.

7 *Ex quibus Felicem legionibus Iudaeae praefecit*: For the procuratorship of Felix in Judaea, cf. Tacitus, *Historiae*, V, 9 (No. 281); Suetonius, *Divus Claudius*, 28 (No. 308). The language of the epitome echoes Suetonius: "Felicem, quem cohortibus et alis provinciaeque Iudaeae praeposuit"; see A. Cohn, *Quibus ex Fontibus S. Aurelii Victoris et Libri de Caesaribus et Epitomes Undecim Capita Priora Fluxerint*, Berlin 1884, pp. 10 ff.; Schlumberger (*infra*, n. 1), pp. 17 ff. However, the epitomator, through his ignorance of the former conditions and the true nature of the procuratorial provinces, made Felix a commander of legions instead of auxiliary troops.

1 On the *Epitome*, see J. Schlumberger, *Die Epitome de Caesaribus*, Munich 1974; T. D. Barnes, *Classical Philology*, LXXI (1976), pp. 258 ff.

531

Epitome de Caesaribus, 9:12–13 — Pichlmayr & Gründel

(12) Rex Parthorum Vologeses metu solo in pacem coactus est. (13) Syria, cui Palaestina nomen est, Ciliciaque ac Trachia et Commagene, quam hodie Augustophratensem nominamus, provinciis accessere. Iudaei quoque additi sunt.

1 *in pace* D

(12) Vologeses, king of the Parthians, was compelled to conclude peace only through fear. (13) Syria, called Palaestina, Cilicia, Thrace and Commagene, which in our times we call Augustophratensis, were included among the provinces. The Jews also were added to the empire.

532

Epitome de Caesaribus, 10:4–7 — Pichlmayr & Gründel

(4) Namque praefecturam praetorianam patre imperante adeptus ⟨scil. Titus⟩ suspectum quemque et oppositum sibi immissis, qui per theatra et castris invidiosa iactantes ad poenam poscerent, quasi criminis convictos oppressit. In quis Caecinam consularem adhibitum
5 coenae, vixdum triclinio egressum, ob suspicionem stupratae Berenicis uxoris suae iugulari iussit. (5) Iurgia autem sub patre venumdata rapinarum cupidum ⋆: unde Neronem cuncti opinantes vocantesque summam rerum nactum graviter acceperant. (6) Sed haec in melius conversa adeo ei immortalem gloriam contulere, ut
10 deliciae atque amor humani generis appellaretur. (7) Denique ut subiit pondus regium, Berenicen nuptias suas sperantem regredi domum et enervatorum greges abire praecepit.

1 *praetorialem* β

(4) For after Titus in his father's reign had attained to the post of prefect of the *praetoriani* he sent to the theatres and camps people who raised invidious charges against everybody who was suspected in his eyes and in opposition to him, and demanded their punishment. All these he executed as if already convicted of a crime. Among those executed was Caecina, an ex-consul, who was invited by him to dinner. He [scil. Titus] ordered him to be strangled as soon as he left

the dining-room, because he suspected him of committing adultery with his wife Berenice. (5) The judicial cases which had been put to sale by him during the life of his father [proved] him eager for plunder; hence all people who thought him and called him a Nero felt vexed when he obtained supreme power. (6) However, this expectation changed for the better to bring him immortal glory, so that he was called the darling and delight of the human race. (7) At last when he obtained royal power he enjoined Berenice, who hoped to be married to him, to return to her country. He also ordered the droves of effeminates to leave.

4 *In quis Caecinam*: I.e. Aulus Caecina Alienus, who helped the Flavian party a great deal in the struggle against Vitellius. He continued to maintain close ties of friendship with Titus, but at the end of the rule of Vespasian he was involved in a plot against the dynasty; cf. Suetonius, *Divus Titus*, 6:2; Cassius Dio, LXVI, 16:3; Zonaras, XI, 17. Caecina was executed at the command of Titus, but none of the sources apart from the *Epitome* connects his fall with Berenice; see M. Fortina, *L'imperatore Tito*, Turin 1955, p. 94, n. 51; J.A. Crook, *AJP*, LXXII (1951), p. 169, n. 31; Schlumberger, *op. cit.* (supra, p. 644, n. 1), p. 49.

5 *Iurgia autem sub patre venumdata rapinarum cupidum*: Cf. Suetonius, *Divus Titus*, 7:1: "suspecta rapacitas, quod constabat in cognitionibus patris nundinari praemiarique solitum; denique propalam alium Neronem et opinabantur et praedicabant".

6 *deliciae atque amor humani generis*: Cf. Suetonius, *Divus Titus*, 1: "amor ac deliciae generis humani".

7 *Berenicen nuptias suas sperantem regredi domum ... praecepit*: Cf. Suetonius, *Divus Titus*, 7:2 (No. 318): "statim ab urbe dimisit invitus invitam".

CXLV. *MULOMEDICINA CHIRONIS*

Second half of the fourth century C.E.

The Mulomedicina Chironis, *a compilation reflecting writings of different periods,*[1] *attests to the continued importance attached to the medical qualities of the Judaean bitumen.*

533

Mulomedicina Chironis, 193, 796 — Oder (cf. 870, 872, 874, 886, 888, 895, 902, 904, 908, 932, 935, 993)

(193) Ideoque praecipitur fumigare omnes ⟨scil. greges armentorum⟩ hac fumigatione: aspaltum Iudaicum, peucedanum, oppoponacum, castoreum, origanum … (796) Colliria ad omnia vitia oculorum … apobalsami Iudaicae …

(193) Therefore it is instructed to fumigate all the cattle by the following fumigation, which consists of Judaean bitumen, sulphur-wort, juice of *panax*, castor, marjoram … (796) Salves for all defects of the eyes … Judaean opobalsamum …

1 See Hoppe, PW, XVI, p. 506.

CXLVI. PELAGONIUS

Second half of the fourth century C.E.

The passage from Pelagonius' Ars Veterinaria,[1] *like the somewhat earlier preceding work* Mulomedicina Chironis, *reflects the popularity of the use of Judaean bitumen for medical purposes. Pelagonius also refers to the "Solomoniac stone".*

534a

Ars Veterinaria, 194, 338, 340, 491 — Ihm

(194) Ad recentia flemina ... bituminis Iudaici ... (338) Compositio emplastri. Nitri po. iiii, bituminis Iudaici po. iii ... (340) Compositio emplastri ... bituminis Iudaici selib., ... (491) ⟨Fragmentum ex Vegetio⟩ Pelagonius causticum ... hac ratione composuit ... asphalti
5 Iudaici pondera duo ...

(194) For fresh bloody swellings of the ankles ... Judaean bitumen ... (338) Composition of plaster: four pounds of nitrum, three pounds of Judaean bitumen ... (340) Composition of plaster ... a half-pound of Judaean bitumen...(491) [A fragment from Vegetius] Pelagonius made a burning medicament...in this way...two pounds of Judaean asphalt...

534b

Ars Veterinaria, 451 — Ihm

Remedium ad morbum sive ad umbras expulsandas de stabulo. Magnetis unc., lapidis Solomoniaci — II, opoponacis — I.

A medicine against illness or for thrusting out shadows from the stable. An ounce of magnet, of Solomoniac stone — two, juice of *panax* — one.

1 See K. Hoppe, *Die Commenta Artis Medicinae Veterinariae des Pelagonius* (*Abhandlungen aus der Geschichte der Veterinärmedizin*, fasc. 14), Leipzig 1927, p. 192; idem, PW, XVI, p. 510; Kroll, PW, XIX, p. 245.

CXLVII. *MEDICINA PLINII*

Fourth century C.E.

The Medicina Plinii *is a compilation by an unknown author who mainly used the* Naturalis Historia *of Pliny the Elder as his source, but occasionally resorted to other authors as well. It seems that he should be dated to the fourth century C.E.; certainly he was known at the beginning of the fifth century to the physician Marcellus, who used the work.*[1] *Its third book contains a reference to an amulet against tertian fever, on which Solomon's name appears as a threat to that illness. Solomon's fame in magic was of long standing, having its antecedents in ancient Judaism. His presumed power over demons is testified to by Josephus,* Ant., *VIII, 47; by the apocryphal work the Testament of Solomon,*[2] *and by magical papyri and amulets.*[3] *The exact wording of the* Medicina Plinii *"Solomon te sequitur [= persequitur = διώκει]" is found on Greek amulets.*[4]

1 See V. Rose, *Hermes*, VIII (1874), pp. 18 ff., on a date for the *Medicina Plinii* between 300 and 350 C.E.; Steier, PW, XV, pp. 81 ff.; cf. A. Önnerfors, *In Medicinam Plinii Studia Philologica*, Lund 1963, pp. 62 ff.

2 See C. C. McCown (ed.), *The Testament of Solomon*, Leipzig 1922, pp. 90 ff.

3 See K. Preisendanz, *Papyri Graecae Magicae*, I, Stuttgart 1973, No. IV, ll. 850 ff. (Σολομῶνος κατάπτωσις, a formula to be applied in order to throw a medium into trance); Ginzberg, IV, pp. 165 ff.; VI, 292, n. 56; C. Bonner, *Studies in Magical Amulets*, Ann Arbor 1950, pp. 208 ff.; cf. also D. C. Duling, *HTR*, LXVIII (1975), pp. 235 ff.

4 See Önnerfors, *op. cit.* (supra, n. 1), pp. 222 f.; R. Heim, *Incantamenta Magica*, Leipzig 1892 = *Jahrbücher für classische Philologie*, Suppl. XIX, p. 481, No. 61: Φεῦγέ με, μισουμένη, Σολομών σε διώκει, Σισίννιος Σισιννάριος.

535

Plinii Secundi Iunioris qui feruntur de Medicina Libri Tres, III, 15:7 — Önnerfors, *Corpus Medicorum Latinorum*, III, Berlin 1964

In charta virgine scribis quod in dextro brachio ligatum portet ille qui patitur: Recede ab illo Gaio Seio, tertiana, Solomon te sequitur.

2 *solo monte* VL   *solomonte* G   *SOLO. MODO: TE* C

You have to write on a virgin paper which the person suffering from the illness should bear on his right arm: "Depart from that Gaius Seius, tertian, Solomon pursues you."

CXLVIII. MARTIANUS CAPELLA

c. 400 C.E.

The description of Judaea in the compilation of Martianus Capella reflects his sources, Pliny and Solinus.[1]

536

De Nuptiis Philologiae et Mercurii, VI (*De Geometria*), 678–679 — Dick

(678) Verum Arabia tenditur usque odoriferam ac divitem terram. Sed iuxta est Syria multis distincta nominibus; nam et Palaestina est, qua contingit Arabiam, et Iudaea et Phoenicia et quantum interior habetur Damascene, in meridiem vergens Babylonia et eadem
5 Mesopotamia inter Euphraten et Tigrin, qua transit Taurum montem Sophene ... (679) Ostracine Arabia finitur, a Pelusio sexaginta sex milibus passuum. Apollonia Palaestinae per centum octoginta octo milia passuum procedens; supra Idumaeam et Samariam Iudaea longe lateque funditur. Pars eius Syriae iuncta Galilaea vocatur, a
10 ceteris eius partibus Iordane amne discreta, qui fluvius oritur de fonte Paneade ... secunda elatio Iudaeae ab Hierosolymis, in quo latere est fons Callirrhoe. Ab occidente Esseni, qui sine concubitu et cunctis cupiditatibus vivunt. Hinc aliquanto interius Masada castellum, in quo Iudaeae finis est; iungitur Decapolis dicta a numero civitatum.

2 *iuxta*] *iuncta* C   3 *qua* codex Grot. et Plin.   *quae* codd.   /
contingit] *contigit* M   *cingit* ΛLbCᵐ   *congit* B¹   9 *iuncta* βΛλM et Plin.
iniuncta (incuncta R¹) cett.   11 *hierosolimis* A¹ΛLBM   *ierusolimis* βaC

(678) Certainly Arabia extends to the perfume-producing and rich land. The next country is Syria, distinguished by many names. For it is

---

1 Martianus Capella was probably a pagan; see Wessner, PW, XIV, p. 2004. For a literary re-evaluation of Capella, see F. Le Moine, *Martianus Capella*, Munich 1972.

called Palaestina where it is adjacent to Arabia, and Judaea and Phoenicia, and the more inland part is known as Damascene; where it inclines to the south it is Babylonia and the same country is called Mesopotamia between the Euphrates and the Tigris, the district beyond Mount Taurus is Sophene ... (679) At Ostracine is the frontier of Arabia, 66 miles from Pelusium. Whence further away by 188 miles is situated Palestinian Apollonia. Beyond Idumaea and Samaria stretches the wide expanse of Judaea. The part of Judaea adjoining Syria is called Galilaea; it is separated from the other parts of Judaea by the river Jordan, which river rises from the spring Panias ... The second height [?] of Judaea next to Jerusalem, on which side is the spring Callirrhoë. On the west are the Essenes who live without sexual intercourse and all desires. From here somewhat in the interior is the fortress Masada, where is the limit of Judaea; to which is adjoined the Decapolis, so called from the number of its cities.

CXLIX. *SCHOLIA IN VERGILIUM*
(SERVIUS AND *BREVIS EXPOSITIO*)

First half ot the fifth century C.E.

Servius certainly had in mind the events of 139 B.C.E. when remarking on the expulsion from Rome of the Chaldaeans and the Jews in his commentary on Virgil (No. 537a).[1] The events are related by Valerius Maximus, I, 3:3 (No. 147) (see above, Vol. I, pp. 357 ff.). The passage from the Brevis Expositio *(No. 537c) alludes to the cold food that the Jews eat on the Sabbath.*

537a

Servius, *Commentarii in Vergilii Aeneida, VIII, 187* — Thilo

Veterumque ignara deorum: Duo dicit: non ideo Herculem colimus, aut quia omnem religionem veram putamus, aut quia deos ignoramus antiquos. Cautum enim fuerat et apud Athenienses et apud Romanos, ne quis novas introduceret
5 religiones: unde et Socrates damnatus est et Chaldaei vel Iudaei sunt urbe depulsi.

2 *veram*] *ream* H   5 *vel*] *et* Stephanus

Not having knowledge of the ancient gods: He [scil. Virgil] says two things, that we do not worship Hercules either because we think all religion true, or because we have no knowledge of ancient gods. For it had been provided by both the Athenians and the Romans that nobody should introduce new religious rites.

---

1 It has been the common view that Servius' commentary on Virgil was compiled between 395 and 410 C.E.; see H. Georgii, *Philologus*, LXXI (1912), pp. 518 ff. However, recently a somewhat later dating has been postulated (for the birth of Servius, 370–380 C.E.; for his commentary, 430–435); see N. Marinone, *Atti della Accademia delle Scienze di Torino (Classe di Scienze Morali, Storiche e Filologiche)*, CIV (1970), pp. 181 ff. For the view also that Servius' commentary could hardly have appeared much before 410, and possibly later, see A. Cameron, *JRS*, LVI (1966), p. 32.

Hence both Socrates was condemned and the Chaldaeans as well as the Jews were expelled from Rome.

537b

Servius, *Commentarii in Vergilii Georgica, III, 12* — Thilo

Quidam Idumaeas palmas ab Idyma, quae est urbs Lydiae palmarum ferax, dictas volunt. Plerique Idumam Syriae Iudaeae civitatem tradunt.

Some prefer the explanation that the Idumaean dates are so called after Idyma, a Lydian city fruitful in dates. However the majority asserts that Iduma is a city of Syria Judaea.

537c

Anonymos, *Brevis Expositio in Vergilii Georgica, I, 336* — Hagen

Frigida Saturni stella: Satis cognitum est, Saturni stellam frigidam esse et ideo apud Iudaeos Saturni die frigidos cibos esse.

The cold star of Saturn: It has been sufficiently known that the star of Saturn is cold and therefore the food among the Jews on the day of Saturn is cold.

On the *Brevis Expositio*, see Schanz & Hosius, II, p. 109.
apud Iudaeos Saturni die frigidos cibos esse: cf. Rutilius Namatianus, *De Reditu Suo*, I, 389 (No. 542): "cui frigida sabbata cordi".

CL. *SCHOLIA IN IUVENALEM*

c. 400 C.E.

This reference to the Jews and their journey to Aricia after being expelled from Rome (No. 538) is the only piece of information of any importance for Jewish history furnished by the scholia to Juvenal. Two expulsions of Jews from Rome during the period of the Roman empire are known. The first was under Tiberius in 19 C.E.; cf. Tacitus, Annales, II, 85 (No. 284). The other was under Claudius; cf. Suetonius, Claudius, 25 (No. 307). Some scholars connect the scholia to Juvenal with the second event,[1] while others prefer the first.[2] There still remains a possibility that the allusion of the scholiast implies another police measure, unknown from other sources.

538

Scholia in Iuvenalem Vetustiora — Wessner, p. 64

Dignus Aricinos qui mendicaret ad axes: Qui ad portam Aricinam sive ad clivum mendicaret inter Iudaeos, qui ad Ariciam transierant ex urbe missi.

2 *Ariciam* Pithou   *ariciem* PS

Well-fitted to beg at the wheels of Arician chariots: Who should go a-begging at the Arician gate or at the hill among the Jews, who passed over to Aricia after they had been expelled from Rome.

---

1 See, e.g., Schürer, III, p. 63; Juster, I, p. 180, n. 9.
2 See A. Momigliano, *Claudius the Emperor and His Achievement*, Oxford 1934, pp. 30, 96.

CLI. PSEUDACRO

Time unknown

The collection of scholia that goes under the name of Acro can hardly be connected with the second-century commentator on Horace known as Helenius Acro.[1] Pseudacro is the only ancient writer to call Moses a king. In the account of Pompeius Trogus, it was only Arruas, the supposed son of Moses, who became king of the Jews; see Pompeius Trogus, apud: Iustinus, XXXVI, 2:16 (No. 137). For circumcision as Iudaica nota, *cf.* Codex Theodosianus, *XVI, 8:22; cf. also Tacitus,* Historiae, *V, 5 (No. 281).*

539

Scholia in Horatium ad Sermones, I, 9:70 — Keller = F216R

Curtis Iudaeis: Ideo curtis, quia Moyses, rex Iudeorum, cuius legibus reguntur, neglegentia medici talis effectus et, ne solus esset notabilis, omnes circumcidi voluit.

2 *affectus* edd. ante Kellerum

The circumcised Jews: Therefore circumcised because Moyses the king of the Jews, by whose laws they are ruled, became so by the negligence of the physician, and in order not to be the only person conspicuous by this he wanted all to be circumcised.

1 See Schanz & Hosius, III, p. 166.

CLII. CLAUDIAN

c. 400 C.E.

Two allusions to Judaea or Jews are found in the In Eutropium *of Claudian.[1] In the first passage, Judaea takes its place, between the Cilicians and Sophene, among the provinces sold by the eunuch Eutropius (No. 540). The second and more interesting reference testifies to the celebrity achieved by the Jewish curtain-painters (No. 541).*

540

In Eutropium, I, 210–221 — Birt = F213R

Non pudet heu, superi, populos venire sub hasta?
Vendentis certe pudeat. Quod iure sepultum
mancipium, tot regna tenet, tot distrahit urbes?
Pollentem solio Croesum victoria Cyri
fregit ut eunucho flueret Pactolus et Hermus?
215 Attalus heredem voluit te, Roma, relinqui,
restitit Antiochus praescripto margine Tauri,
indomitos curru Servilius egit Isauros
et Pharos Augusto iacuit vel Creta Metello,
ne non Eutropio quaestus numerosior esset?
220 In mercem veniunt Cilices, Iudaea, Sophene
Romanusque labor Pompeianique triumphi.

> 212 *regna*] *iura* ς   *rura* Heinsius   217 *indomitus* P
> 220 *iudea* ΠP / *sofene* V¹PC   *soferne* V²   *sophoene* A   *sophone* ΛΠB

Ye gods, are ye not ashamed that whole peoples are sold beneath the hammer? At least let it shame you of the seller, when a slave, a chattel

---

1 Claudian's death is dated to 404 C. E. by A. Cameron, *Claudian — Poetry and Propaganda at the Court of Honorius*, Oxford 1970, p. XVI. For the religious outlook of Claudian, see *ibid.*, pp. 189 ff.; P. Fargues, *Claudien*, Paris 1933, pp. 153 ff.

the law counts dead, possesses so many kingdoms and retails so many cities. Did Cyrus' victory oust mighty Croesus from his throne that Pactolus and Hermus should roll their waves for a eunuch? Did Attalus make you, Rome, his heir, was Antiochus confined within the appointed bounds of Taurus, did Servilius enjoy a triumph over the hitherto unconquered Isaurians, did Egypt fall before Augustus, and Crete before Metellus, to ensure Eutropius a sufficient income? Cilicia, Judaea, Sophene, all Rome's labours and Pompey's triumphs, are there to sell.   (trans. M. Platnauer, *LCL*)

On the invective of Claudian against Eutropius the eunuch, who was all-powerful at the court of the emperor Arcadius, see Seeck, PW, VI, pp. 1520 f.; E. Stein, *Geschichte des spätrömischen Reiches*, I, Vienna 1928, pp. 357 ff.; A. H. M. Jones, *The Later Roman Empire*, I, Oxford 1964, pp. 177 f.; Cameron, *op. cit.* (supra, p. 657, n. 1), pp. 124 ff.
220 *Iudaea*: As a place name Judaea had hardly any political or administrative meaning at the time of Claudian. However, since the poet refers here to the time of Pompey, he finds it necessary to use the correct term applicable in the earlier period. In Claudian's day Palestine was under the rule of Arcadius and within the ambit of Eutropius.

541

In Eutropium, I, 346–357 — F214R

Fama prius falso similis vanoque videri
ficta ioco; levior volitare per oppida rumor
riderique nefas: veluti nigrantibus alis
audiretur olor, corvo certante ligustris.
350 Atque aliquis gravior morum: "si talibus, inquit,
creditur et nimiis turgent mendacia monstris,
iam testudo volat, profert iam cornua vultur;
prona petunt retro fluvii iuga; Gadibus ortum
Carmani texere diem; iam frugibus aptum
355 aequor et adsuetum silvis delphina videbo;
iam cochleis homines iunctos et quidquid inane
nutrit Iudaicis quae pingitur India velis."

346 *falsae* Heinsius   348 *veluti*] *sicut* BA   *ut si* Heinsius
353 *iuga*] *vada* ΠBV²   354 *Carmani* Heinsius   *Germani* Em
    Carmenii C   *Armeniis* V¹   *Armenii* V²φ / *traxere* B
        357 *quae*] *quod* Jeep

At first the rumour of Eutropius' consulship seemed false and invented as a jest. A vague story spread from city to city, the crime was laughed at as one would laugh to hear of a swan with black wings or a crow as white as privet. Thus spoke one of weighty character: "If such things are believed and swollen lies tell of unheard-of monsters, then the tortoise can fly, the vulture grow horns, rivers flow back and mount the hills whence they spring, the sun rise behind Gades and set amid the Carmanians of India; I shall soon see ocean fit nursery for plants and the dolphin a denizen of the woods; beings half-men, half-snails and all the vain imaginings of India depicted on Jewish curtains."   (trans. M. Platnauer, *LCL*)

The passage reflects the incredulous reaction of the poet to the rumour about the appointment of Eutropius to the consulate. It sounds improbable and is no less miraculous than a black-winged swan, or the picture that the curtains painted by Jews give of the wonders of India.

357 *Iudaicis quae pingitur India velis*: For a suggestion that curtain-painting was an occupation of Alexandrian Jews, see T. Birt, *Rhein. Museum*, XLV (1890), pp. 491 ff. See also Juster, II, p. 306, n. 8; *The Christian Topography of Cosmas Indicopleustes*, ed. E. O. Winstedt, Cambridge 1909, p. 121 = III, 70, ed. W. Wolska-Conus, I, Paris 1968, p. 511. For a possibility, on the other hand, that the tapestries are designated "Jewish" because their subject-matter derived from the Bible, and not because of their Jewish workmanship, see C. Roth, *Journal of the Warburg and Courtauld Institutes*, XVI (1953), p. 34, n. 3.

CLIII. RUTILIUS NAMATIANUS

Beginning of the fifth century C.E.

In an age in which Christianity was already dominant, the pagan aristocrat Rutilius Namatianus was probably the last non-Christian Latin writer to give vent to antipathy to Judaism. Born in southern Gaul, he attained high posts in the imperial service as magister officiorum *and* praefectus urbi. *At some time between 415 and 417 C.E. he left Rome to visit his property in his native Gaul, sailing northwards from Rome along the coast.[1] An unpleasant incident with a Jew in charge of fish-ponds near Faleria gave him the occasion for a rather disproportionate outburst against the Jews and their religion (No. 542). In general the poem expresses reverence for the majesty of Rome (see the exordium to the poem), and contains many allusions to classical Latin literature. These features are well reflected in the following passage. Its censure of Judaism echoes anti-Jewish motifs voiced by Seneca and other earlier Latin writers. There is also an argument used by anti-Christian sources, known to us from Celsus. Judaism is blamed not only for its intrinsic deficiencies but also as the "radix stultitiae", an epithet that seems to imply condemnation of the Jewish religion as the origin of Christianity. Indeed the dislike shown by Rutilius Namatianus for Judaism is more than equalled by his abhorrence of Christian monks.[2]*

---

1 For a discussion of the date of the journey, see I. Lana, *Rutilio Namaziano*, Turin 1961, pp. 11 ff. Lana himself argues in favour of 415 C.E. Good reasons for dating it to 417 C.E. are offered by A. Cameron, *JRS*, LVII (1967), pp. 31 ff. For 417 C.E., see also other scholars, e.g., J. Vessereau & P. Dimoff, *Revue de Philologie*, NS, XXX (1906), pp. 65 ff.; J. Carcopino, *Rencontres de l'histoire et de la littérature romaines*, Paris 1963, pp. 233 ff.; E. Doblhofer, *De Reditu Suo sive Iter Gallicum*, Heidelberg 1972, I, pp. 35 ff.; F. Paschoud, *Museum Helveticum*, XXXV (1978), pp. 319 ff.

2 For the paganism of Rutilius, see Doblhofer, *op. cit.*, pp. 27 ff.

Bibliography

A.W. Zumpt, *Observationes in Rutilii Claudii Namatiani Carmen, De Reditu Suo*, Berlin 1837, pp. 27 f.; C.H. Keene, *Rutilii Claudii Namatiani De Reditu Suo, Libri Duo*, London 1907, pp. 39 ff.; J.P. Postgate, *The Classical Review*, XXI (1907), pp. 24 f.; V. Ussani, *RFIC*, XXXVIII (1910), pp. 367 ff.; H. Schenkl, *Rhein. Museum*, LXVI (1911), pp. 394 ff.; W. Rettich, "Welt- und Lebensanschauung des spätrömischen Dichters Rutilius Claudius Namatianus", Ph.D. Thesis, Zurich 1918, pp. 9 f.; M. Schuster, *Philologische Wochenschrift*, XLV (1925), pp. 713 ff.; P. de Labriolle, *REL*, VI (1928), pp. 30 ff.; R. Helm, *Rutilius Claudius Namatianus, De Reditu Suo*, Heidelberg 1933, pp. 33 f.; M. Schuster, *Wiener Studien*, LVII (1939), pp. 156 ff.; N.W. Goldstein, *JR*, XIX (1939), pp. 357 f.; E. Merone, *Rutilio ellenizzante*, Naples [1954], p. 64; idem, *Rutilius Claudius Namatianus — De Reditu Suo*, Naples 1955, pp. 106 ff.; I. Lana, *Rutilio Namaziano*, Turin 1961, pp. 167 ff.; R.L. Wilken, *JR*, XLVII (1967), pp. 326 f.; F. Paschoud, *Roma Aeterna*, Rome 1967, pp. 159 f.

De Reditu Suo, I, 371–398 — Castorina = F215R

Lassatum cohibet vicina Faleria cursum,
quamquam vix medium Phoebus haberet iter.
Et tum forte hilares per compita rustica pagi
mulcebant sacris pectora fessa iocis:
375 Illo quippe die tandem revocatus Osiris
excitat in fruges germina laeta novas.
Egressi villam petimus lucoque vagamur:
stagna placent saepto deliciosa vado.
Ludere lascivos inter vivaria pisces
380 gurgitis inclusi laxior unda sinit.
Sed male pensavit requiem stationis amoenae
hospite conductor durior Antiphate:
Namque loci querulus curam Iudaeus agebat
humanis animal dissociale cibis.
385 Vexatos frutices, pulsatas imputat algas
damnaque libatae grandia clamat aquae.
Reddimus obscenae convicia debita genti
quae genitale caput propudiosa metit:
Radix stultitiae, cui frigida sabbata cordi,
390 sed cor frigidius religione sua.
Septima quaeque dies turpi damnata veterno,
tamquam lassati mollis imago dei.
Cetera mendacis deliramenta catastae
nec pueros omnes credere posse reor.
395 Atque utinam numquam Iudaea subacta fuisset
Pompeii bellis imperioque Titi!
Latius excisae pestis contagia serpunt
victoresque suos natio victa premit.

371 *lassantem* Baehrens   373 *et*] *nam* Kapp / *pagi* Castalio   *fagi* codd.
375 *revocatus*] *renovatus* BP   377 *lucoque*] *lutoque* RMP   *luthoque* B
ludoque Barth   382 *convictor* Heinsius / *durior*] *dirior* Drakenborch
crudior Mueller   *torvior* Baehrens   *acrior* Keene   390 *sua est* BP
391 *septima*] *optima* R   394 *pueros omnes*] *pueros parvos* (vel. *teneros*) Baehrens
pueros et anus Keene   *puerum in somnis* Duff   395 *subacta*] *capta* R
396 *imperioque*] *imperiisque* VR

The neighbouring Faleria checks our weary course, though Phoebus
scarce had reached his mid career. That day it happened merry

village-bands along the country cross-roads soothed their jaded
hearts with festal observances; it was in truth the day when, after long
time restored, Osiris wakes the happy seeds to yield fresh produce.
Landing, we seek lodging, and stroll within a wood; we like the ponds
which charm with their shallow enclosed basin. The spacious waters
of the imprisoned flood permit the playful fish to sport inside these
preserves. But we were made to pay dear for the repose of the
delightful halting-place, by a lessee who was harsher than Antiphates
as host! For a crabbed Jew was in charge of the spot — a creature that
quarrels with sound human food. He charges in our bill for damaging
his bushes and hitting the sea-weed, and bawls about his enormous
loss in water we had sipped. We pay the abuse due to the filthy race
that infamously practises circumcision; a root of silliness they are:
chill Sabbaths are after their own heart, yet their heart is chillier than
their creed. Each seventh day is condemned to ignoble sloth, as
'twere an effeminate picture of the god fatigued. The other wild
ravings from their lying bazaar methinks not even a child in his sleep
could believe. And would that Judaea had never been subdued by
Pompey's wars and Titus' military power! The infection of this
plague, though excised, still creeps abroad the more: and 'tis their
own conquerors that a conquered race keeps down.

(trans. J. Wight Duff & A. M. Duff, *LCL*)

---

371 *Faleria*: An Etrurian port south of Populonia facing Elba. Our
knowledge of Jews in ancient Etruria is rather meagre. For Jews in the
Etrurian town of Luna, see Gregorius, *Epistulae*, IV, 21; Juster, I, p. 181;
L. Ruggini, *Studia et Documenta Historiae et Iuris*, XXV (1959), p. 223, n. 88.
375 *revocatus Osiris*: Cf. Iuvenalis, *Saturae*, VIII, 29 f.: "populus quod
clamat Osiri invento". For the bearing of this on the date of the journey, see
R. Helm, *Philologische Wochenschrift*, LII (1932), pp. 972 f.; Lana, *op. cit.*
(supra, p. 660, n. 1), pp. 37 ff.; Cameron, *op. cit.* (supra, p. 660, n. 1), pp. 35 f.
377 *Egressi villam petimus*: A passage full of Vergilian reminiscences; see
the commentaries of Helm and Merone.
382 f. *conductor ... loci querulus curam Iudaeus agebat*: The Jew was
presumably in charge of the fish-ponds and their surroundings; see
M. Brücklmeier, "Beiträge zur rechtlichen Stellung der Juden im römischen
Reich", Ph.D. Thesis, Munich 1939, p. 43, n. 42. On Jews in Italian
agriculture, especially in later times, see, e.g., Gregorius, *Epistulae*, V, 8 (in
Sicily).
durior Antiphate: An allusion to the cruel king of the Laestrygonians, known
from *Odyssea*, X, 114, ff. Cf. also Ovidius, *Metamorphoses*, XIV, 234 ff.; *Ex
Ponto*, II, 9, 41.

384 *humanis animal dissociale cibis*: This sounds like an antithetical reminiscence of Seneca, *De Clementia*, I, 3:2: "qui hominem sociale animal communi bono genitum videri volumus". See also Tacitus, *Historiae*, V, 5 (No. 281): "separati epulis".

387 *Reddimus obscenae convicia debita genti*: Cf. Ovidius, *Metamorphoses*, XIV, 522: "addidit obscenis convicia rustica dictis". For the Jews as *obscena gens*, cf. Tacitus, *Historiae*, V, 4–5 (No. 281).

389 *Radix stultitiae*: Cf. Sulpicius Severus, II, 30 (No. 282): "radice sublata, stirpem facile perituram". This makes plausible the view held by most commentators on this passage that Christianity is implied.

cui frigida sabbata cordi: Cf. Meleager, in: *Anthologia Graeca*, V, 160 (No. 43). See also A. Garzya, *Studi Italiani di filologia classica*, XXXIII (1961), pp. 242 ff. In 412 C.E. legal provision was made for the undisturbed observance of the Sabbath; cf. *Codex Theodosianus*, XVI, 8:20. The policy of the then ruling emperor Honorius was in general tolerant towards the Jews, as rightly emphasized by Lana, *op. cit.* (supra, p. 660, n. 1), p. 168; cf. especially *Codex Theodosianus*, XVI, 8:21. Another passage in Latin literature where the frigidity of the Sabbath is stressed is the scholia to Vergilius, *Georgica, I, 336* (No. 537c): "apud Iudaeos Saturni die frigidos cibos esse".

391 *Septima quaeque dies turpi damnata veterno*: Cf. Seneca, *De Superstitione* (No. 186): "septimam fere partem aetatis suae perdant vacando". For the assumption that Rutilius had a knowledge of Seneca deriving from the *De Civitate Dei*, see Cameron, *op. cit.* (supra, p. 660, n. 1), p. 32. See also Iuvenalis, *Saturae*, XIV, 105 f. (No. 301): "cui septima quaeque fuit lux ignava"; Tacitus, *Historiae*, V, 4 (No. 281).

392 *tamquam lassati mollis imago dei*: The statement that God took a rest after the accomplishment of the work of creation (Gen. ii:2–3), had for long served as a target for attacks by the philosophical opponents of Christianity and Judaism, as attested by Celsus, apud: Origenes, *Contra Celsum*, VI, 61 (No. 375). For the uneasiness felt on the subject by Jewish and Christian thinkers, see Schenkl, *op. cit.* (supra, p. 661), pp. 399 ff.

394 *nec pueros omnes credere posse reor*: Cf. Iuvenalis, *Saturae*, II, 152: "nec pueri credunt, nisi qui nondum aere lavantur".

397 *Latius excisae pestis contagia serpunt*: Cf. Tacitus, *Annales*, XV, 44 (No. 294): "exitiabilis superstitio ... erumpebat".

398 *victoresque suos natio victa premit*: The passage is reminiscent of Horatius, *Epistulae*, II, 1:156: "Graecia capta ferum victorem cepit" (cf. Ovidius, *Fasti*, I, 523); above all, the words of Seneca concerning the Jews in his *De Superstitione* (No. 186): "victi victoribus leges dederunt"; cf. the commentary *ad loc.*

CLIV. MACROBIUS

First half of the fifth century C.E.

It quite accords with the antiquarian nature of the Saturnalia *of Macrobius[1] that the only reference in it with any bearing on Jewish history is connected with Herod, the contemporary of Augustus.*

543

Saturnalia, II, 4:11; cf. Cornelius Labeo (No. 445) — Willis = F214R

Cum audisset ⟨scil. Augustus⟩ inter pueros, quos in Syria Herodes rex Iudaeorum intra bimatum iussit interfici, filium quoque eius occisum, ait: "melius est Herodis porcum esse quam filium."

1 *siria* NDRA   3 *melius est*] *mallem* TBV / *porcus* TBV

When he [scil. Augustus] heard that among the boys under the age of two years whom in Syria Herodes the king of the Jews had ordered to be put to death was the king's own son, he exclaimed: "I'd rather be Herod's pig than Herod's son."

quos ... Herodes ... intra bimatum iussit interfici: Cf. Matt. ii:16: Τότε Ἡρῴδης ἰδὼν ὅτι ἐνεπαίχθη ὑπὸ τῶν μάγων ἐθυμώθη λίαν, καὶ ἀποστείλας ἀνεῖλεν πάντας τοὺς ἐν Βηθλέεμ καὶ ἐν πᾶσι τοῖς ὁρίοις αὐτῆς ἀπὸ διετοῦς καὶ κατωτέρω.
filium quoque eius occisum: Herod executed three of his sons. These were Alexander and Aristobulus, his sons by his Hasmonaean wife, in 7 B.C.E. (*Ant.*, XVI, 394; *BJ*, I, 551), and Antipater, just before his own death (*Ant.*, XVII, 187; *BJ*, I, 664; Nicolaus Damascenus = No. 97). None of them was a child when executed.

1 On the date and identity of Macrobius, see now A. Cameron, *JRS*, LVI (1966), pp. 25 ff.; see also the different view of S. Döpp, *Hermes*, CVI (1978), pp. 619 ff. Döpp thinks that the *Saturnalia* were published immediately after 402 C.E.

melius est Herodis porcum esse quam filium: This joke, based on the play of the Greek words υἱός and ὗς, loses its piquancy in the Latin translation. For the motif of the Jewish abstention from pork in pagan literature, see Petronius (No. 195); Sextus Empiricus, *Hypotyposes*, III, 223 (No. 334). See also Aelianus, *Varia Historia*, XII, 56: Διογένης ὁ Σινωπεὺς ἔλεγε πολλά, τὴν ἀμαθίαν καὶ τὴν ἀπαιδευσίαν τῶν Μεγαρέων διαβάλλων, καὶ ἐβούλετο Μεγαρέως ἀνδρὸς κριὸς εἶναι μᾶλλον ἢ υἱός. ἠνίττετο δὲ ὅτι τῶν θρεμμάτων ποιοῦνται πρόνοιαν οἱ Μεγαρεῖς, τῶν παίδων δὲ οὐχί.

It is generally agreed that Macrobius drew on ancient sources, and we may assume that the joke about Augustus and Herod also goes back substantially to an Augustan source; see G. Wissowa, *Hermes*, XVI (1881), p. 499; see also Norden, p. 429, n. 3. However, the original joke seems to have been contaminated by the Christian tradition as represented by Matthew; see Ed. Meyer, I, p. 58, n. 2. It is worthwhile recording in this connection what Seneca states about Augustus, when the latter was called upon to take part in the *consilium* of one Tarius, a man who detected his son plotting against his life; cf. Seneca, *De Clementia*, I, 15: "non culleum, non serpentes, non carcerem decrevit memor, non de quo censeret, sed cui in consilio esset; mollissimo genere poenae contentum esse debere patrem dixit in filio adulescentulo impulso in id scelus, in quo se, quod proximum erat ab innocentia, timide gessisset; debere illum ab urbe et a parentis oculis submoveri".

CLV. SYRIANUS

Fifth century C.E.

The Neoplatonic philosopher Syrianus is referred to by Lydus as holding the view that the Jewish God is the demiurge of the world of sense, being mentioned in this connection in conjunction with Iamblichus and Proclus. The concept may thus be thought traditional to the Neoplatonic school.

544

apud: Lydus, *De Mensibus*, IV, 53 — Wünsch, p. 110

Οἱ μέντοι περὶ Ἰάμβλιχον καὶ Συριανὸν καὶ Πρόκλον δημιουργὸν αὐτὸν τοῦ αἰσθητοῦ κόσμου νομίζουσιν εἶναι καλοῦντες αὐτὸν τῆς τετραστοίχου θεόν.

But the schools of Iamblichus, Syrianus and Proclus consider him [i.e. the God worshipped by the Jews] as the Demiurge of the world of sense, calling him the god of the four elements.

CLVI. PROCLUS

Second half of the fifth century C.E.

The extant works of the Neoplatonic philosopher Proclus make no allusion to Judaism. The sole reference bearing on the subject is by Lydus, who refers to Proclus as holding the common Neoplatonic view concerning the Jewish God whereby he is identified with the demiurge of the world of sense.

545

apud: Lydus, *De Mensibus*, IV, 53 — Wünsch, p. 110

Οἱ μέντοι περὶ Ἰάμβλιχον καὶ Συριανὸν καὶ Πρόκλον δημιουργὸν αὐτὸν τοῦ αἰσθητοῦ κόσμου νομίζουσιν εἶναι καλοῦντες αὐτὸν τῆς τετραστοίχου θεόν.

But the schools of Iamblichus, Syrianus and Proclus consider him [i.e. the God worshipped by the Jews] as the demiurge of the world of sense, calling him the god of the four elements.

CLVII. ZOSIMUS

c. 500 C.E.

The only mention of Jews in the New History of the pagan writer Zosimus[1] is in connection with the fate of the wife and daughter of the praetorian prefect Rufinus, both of whom took refuge at Jerusalem. Zosimus reminds his readers that Jerusalem had formerly been inhabited by Jews but from the time of Constantine was embellished with buildings by Christians. A pronounced pagan who hated the emperor Constantine, Zosimus counted the "apostate" emperor Julian among his heroes.[2] His work has even been defined as an antithesis to Orosius' Adversus Paganos.

1 For the date of Zosimus, see A. Cameron, *Philologus*, CXIII (1969), pp. 106 ff. Cameron dates at least the first part of the work between 498 and 502 C.E.; cf. the discussion on the date of Zosimus (between 425 and 518 C.E.) by F. Paschoud in the introduction to his edition of Zosimus (Budé), I, 1971, pp. XII ff. Zosimus is sometimes identified with the sophist Zosimus of Gaza; see Schmid & Stählin, Vol. II, Part 2, p. 1037. Against the identification, see L. Mendelssohn's introduction to the edition of Zosimus, Leipzig, 1887, pp. XI f. For the historical thought of Zosimus, see Z. Petre, *Studii Clasice*, VII (1965), pp. 263 ff.; R. T. Ridley, *Byzantinische Zeitschrift*, LXV (1972), pp. 277 ff.

2 Cf. Zosimus, II, 29; III, 2:4; Photius, *Bibliotheca*, Cod. 98, p. 84B (ed. Bekker = ed. Henry, II, p. 65): Ἔστι [scil. Ζώσιμος] τὴν θρησκείαν ἀσεβὴς καὶ πολλάκις ἐν πολλοῖς ὑλακτῶν κατὰ τῶν εὐσεβῶν.

546

Nova Historia, V, 8:2–3 — Mendelssohn

(2) Τῆς δὲ Ῥουφίνου γαμετῆς σὺν τῇ θυγατρὶ τῇ τῶν Χριστιανῶν ἐκκλησίᾳ προσδραμούσης δέει τοῦ μὴ συναπολέσθαι τῷ ἀνδρί, πίστιν δοὺς ὁ Εὐτρόπιος ἐφῆκεν αὐταῖς εἰς τὴν κατὰ Ἱεροσόλυμα πόλιν ἐκπλεῦσαι, πάλαι μὲν οἰκητήριον Ἰουδαίων οὖσαν, ἀπὸ δὲ τῆς Κωνσταντίνου
5 *βασιλείας ὑπὸ Χριστιανῶν τιμωμένην οἰκοδομήμασιν. (3) ἐκεῖναι μὲν οὖν αὐτόθι τὸν λειπόμενον τοῦ βίου διέτριψαν χρόνον.*

(2) The wife of Rufinus and his daughter took refuge in the Christian church from fear of perishing together with the man. Eutropius pledged his good faith and allowed them to sail away to Jerusalem, which in olden times had been inhabited by Jews but from the reign of Constantine onwards was honoured by Christian buildings. (3) There the two women passed the remainder of their lives.

δέει τοῦ μὴ συναπολέσθαι τῷ ἀνδρί: For the murder of Rufinus, which took place late in 395 C.E., see E. Stein, *Geschichte des spätrömischen Reiches*, I, Vienna 1928, p. 352; A. H. M. Jones, *The Later Roman Empire*, I, Oxford 1964, p. 177.
ἀπὸ δὲ τῆς Κωνσταντίνου βασιλείας ... τιμωμένην οἰκοδομήμασιν: See F. M. Abel, *Histoire de la Palestine*, II, Paris 1952, pp. 267 ff. See also J. Matthews, *Western Aristocracies and Imperial Court A. D. 364–425*, Oxford 1975, p. 136.

CLVIII. DAMASCIUS

First half of the sixth century C.E.

Damascius of Damascus, the Neoplatonic philosopher and follower of Proclus, belongs to the very last stage of the Graeco-Roman culture of Antiquity, being among the Hellenic scholars who left for Persia after the closure of the Academy at Athens by Justinian. His "Life of Isidorus" was compiled some time before 526 C.E.[1] Fragments of the work have mainly been preserved through Photius, while some passages have been regained by modern scholarship from biographical notices in Suda.[2] Both sets of fragments include some allusions to Judaism or to individual Jews. Thus there is an example of the part played by "the God of the Hebrews" in magical incantations (No. 547), and, as usual among writers of the period, the Jewish abhorrence of pork is assumed to be a matter of common knowledge (No. 549).

One of the most interesting aspects of the "Life of Isidorus" is that Damascius gives a glimpse into the cultural conditions of the age, above all among Neoplatonic circles. We learn that Jews and Samaritans actively participated in the contemporary scientific and intellectual life. There is mention of the Samaritan Marinus, who gained some distinction as a philosopher (No. 548), and of the Jewish doctor Domnus, who was overthrown by his pupil Gesius of Petra (No. 551). Zeno of Alexandria, another Jew, also belonged to the same circles (No. 550).

Both Marinus and Zeno defected from their ancestral religion. Marinus is said to have seceded to the Hellenic way of life from the Samaritan creed because it had changed much from the original "religion of Abramos". Zeno of Alexandria even became a militant apostate and purposely tried to offend the religious feelings of his former coreligionists. Damascius does not show much respect for Marinus, and even less for Zeno. Towards the first, Damascius' attitude is to be

---

1 On the date of the work, see Kroll, PW, IV, pp. 2039 ff.; in general, see also R. Strömberg, *Eranos*, XLIV (1946), pp. 175 ff. On the last days of the Academy at Athens, see also A. Cameron, *Proceedings of the Cambridge Philological Society*, XV (1969), pp. 7 ff.

2 See J. R. Asmus, *Byzantinische Zeitschrift*, XVIII (1909), pp. 436 ff.

671

accounted for by the views propounded by Marinus, and above all by the personal rivalry that existed between Marinus and Isidorus.
About Zeno too little is known for us to surmise the cause of his disparagement by Damascius. In any case, there is no reason for assuming that this has to be connected with anti-Jewish feelings on the part of the writer, especially as it is stated that Zeno did not remain a practising Jew. A passage that alludes to the hypothetical refusal by a Jew to taste pork even when it was prescribed for health reasons, and censures the Syrian Domninus for not adhering to his ancestral customs (No. 549), is well in accordance with the views held by Celsus, Porphyry and Julian, all of whom commended the virtue of loyal adherence to one's national traditions.[3]

3 I have not included in this collection of Damascius' references the passage alluding to the medical teacher Agapius; see Suda, s.v. Ἀγάπιος, I (ed. Adler), p. 20, deriving from *Vita Isidori* = *Vita Isidori*, F330 (ed. Zintzen), p. 261. He is taken to be a Jew by Wellmann, PW, I, p. 735. However the mere fact that although Agapius was an Alexandrian by origin he left Alexandria for Constantinople (ἀνελθὼν ἐς τὸ Βυζάντιον) does not warrant the assumption that he was among the Jews expelled from Alexandria at the instigation of Cyril in 414 or 415 C.E.; cf. Socrates, *Historia Ecclesiastica*, VII, 13; on this expulsion, see V.A. Tcherikover, *CPJ*, I, pp. 98 f., Prolegomena; R.L. Wilken, *Judaism and the Early Christian Mind — A Study of Cyril of Alexandria's Exegesis and Theology*, New Haven–London 1971, pp. 56 ff.
Perhaps more relevant for this collection are the fragments from Damascius' *Vita Isidori* relating to the famous physician Jacob. Damascius recounts that this Jacob, who was second to none in his time in the arts of diagnosis and healing, was an Alexandrian, though his father's family originated from Damascus. Jacob's father Hesychius was active in various places (Greece, Italy, Alexandria and Constantinople), and Jacob was born to him by a wife married in Greece. Jacob acted as a physician in the reign of the emperor Leo (457–474 C.E.). It emerges from this account that Jacob was not a Christian and that the Christians tried to put him into disrepute; see *Vita Isidori*, F194 (ed. Zintzen), p. 167: οἱ δὲ τῆς ἀλλοφύλου δόξης ἑταῖροι καὶ συστασιῶται διέβαλλον ... ὡς ὄντα οὐκ ἰατρόν, ἀλλὰ θεοφιλῆ τινα καὶ ἱερόν. The remark made by the Christian Photius about Hesychius and his son Jacob implies also that they were pagans; cf. *ibid.*, p. 168: ἄμφω δέ, καὶ ὁ παῖς καὶ ὁ φύσας, ἀσεβέε ἤστην. However, the name Jacob makes necessary the assumption that both he and his father were not born pagans, but only adopted paganism later. In view of the examples of Marinus and Zeno (Nos. 548, 550) one may suggest that Jacob and his father were born Jews, but the possibility exists that they were born Christians and later defected to paganism.

547

Vita Isidori, apud: Photius, Bibliotheca, Cod. 242, p. 339a,b = Zintzen, 55–56 = ed. Henry, Vol. VI, p. 18 = F120R

(55) Γυναῖκα παιδοποιὸν ἄγεται ⟨scil. Ἱεροκλῆς⟩. (56) ὡς δ' οὐκ ἐπείθετο τὸ δαιμόνιον τῆς γυναικὸς ἐξελθεῖν λόγοις ἡμερωτέροις, ὅρκῳ αὐτὸ ἐπηνάγκαζεν ὁ Θεοσέβιος, καίτοι οὔτε μαγεύειν εἰδὼς οὔτε θεουργίασμά τι μελετήσας. ὥρκιζε δὲ τὰς τοῦ ἡλίου προτείνων ἀκτῖνας καὶ τὸν Ἑβραίων θεόν. ὁ δὲ ἀπελήλατο ὁ δαίμων, ἀνακραγὼν εὐλαβεῖσθαι μὲν τοὺς θεούς, αἰσχύνεσθαι δὲ καὶ αὐτόν.

(55) Hierocles married a child-bearing woman. (56) As the evil could not be persuaded to leave the woman by gentle words, Theosebius compelled it to do so by an oath, although he was not versed in magic, nor practised any theurgy. He adjured it by invoking the rays of the sun and the God of the Hebrews. The bad spirit was expelled while crying out that he both reverenced the gods and felt shame before him.

55 Ἱεροκλῆς: On this Neoplatonic philosopher, see E. Zeller, *Die Philosophie der Griechen in ihrer geschichtlichen Entwicklung*[5], Leipzig 1923, Vol. III, Part 2, pp. 812 ff.; A. Elter, *Rhein. Museum*, NF, LXV (1910), pp. 175 ff.; Praechter, PW, VIII, pp. 1479 ff.
56 Θεοσέβιος: See Praechter, PW, Ser. 2, V, pp. 2245 ff.; for this passage, see p. 2246.
καὶ τὸν Ἑβραίων θεόν: The part played by "the God of the Hebrews" in the practice of ancient magic may well be illustrated by the reference in the great Paris magical papyrus, where this phrase is included in the formula of Pibeches; cf. *Papyri Graecae Magicae*, ed. K. Preisendanz, Vol. I, No. 4, ll. 3019 f.: ὁρκίζω σε κατὰ τοῦ θεοῦ τῶν Ἑβραίων Ἰησοῦ. The Jesus of the papyrus seems to be a late intruder, who replaced Iao; see S. Eitrem, *Symbolae Osloenses*, Fasc. Suppl. XX (1966), pp. 15 f. The marital life of Theosebius is again related by Photius.

548

Vita Isidori, apud: Photius, Bibliotheca, Cod. 242, p. 345b = Zintzen, 141–144 = ed. Henry, Vol. VI, p. 36 = F120R

(141) Ὅτι ὁ διάδοχος Πρόκλου, φησίν, ὁ Μαρῖνος, γένος ἦν ἀπὸ τῆς ἐν Παλαιστίνῃ Νέας πόλεως, πρὸς ὄρει κατῳκισμένης τῷ Ἀργαρίζῳ καλουμένῳ. εἶτα βλασφημῶν ὁ δυσσεβής φησιν ὁ συγγραφεύς· «ἐν ᾧ Διὸς

ὑψίστου ἁγιώτατον ἱερόν, ᾧ καθιέρωτο Ἄβραμος ὁ τῶν πάλαι Ἑβραίων
5 πρόγονος, ὡς αὐτὸς ἔλεγεν ὁ Μαρῖνος.» Σαμαρείτης οὖν τὸ ἀπ᾽ ἀρχῆς ὁ
Μαρῖνος γεγονὼς ἀπετάξατο μὲν πρὸς τὴν ἐκείνων δόξαν, ἅτε εἰς
καινοτομίαν ἀπὸ τῆς Ἀβράμου θρησκείας ἀπορρυεῖσαν, τὰ δὲ Ἑλλήνων
ἠγάπησεν. (142) ὅμως φιλοπονίᾳ τε καὶ ἀτρύτοις πόνοις ἐγκείμενος
εὐφυεστέρων ἤδη πολλῶν καὶ τῶν πρεσβυτέρων κατέχωσε δόξας τῷ
10 ἑαυτοῦ ὀνόματι ὁ Μαρῖνος. (143) οὐκ εἴα δὲ αὐτὸν ἐρωτᾶν ὁ Ἰσίδωρος
ἀσθενείᾳ σώματος ἐνοχλούμενον, εὐλαβείᾳ τοῦ ὀχλώδους. (144) πλὴν ὁ
Μαρῖνος ἐξ ὧν τε διελέγετο καὶ ἐξ ὧν ἔγραψεν (ὀλίγα δὲ ταῦτά ἐστι) δῆλος
ἦν οὐ βαθεῖαν αὔλακα τῶν νοημάτων καρπούμενος, ἐξ ὧν τὰ σοφὰ βλασ-
τάνει θεάματα τῆς τῶν ὄντων φύσεως.

7 θρησκείας] θυσίας M

(141) He says that the successor of Proclus, Marinus, came from
Neapolis in Palestine, a city situated near the mountain called
Argarizon. Then the impious writer uttered the blasphemy that on
this mountain there is a most holy sanctuary of Zeus the Highest, to
whom Abraham the father of the old Hebrews consecrated himself,
as Marinus himself maintains. Marinus, though originally a
Samaritan, gave up their creed, since it deviated from Abraham's
religion and introduced innovations in it, and fell in love with
paganism. (142) Nevertheless, by working hard, and untiring toil,
Marinus surpassed in renown the fame of many abler and elder men.
(143) Isidorus did not let Marinus be questioned as he had already
been troubled by weakness, and he took care not to annoy him. (144)
However, it is clear that Marinus, to judge from what he said and
what he wrote which did not amount to much, was not a profound
originator of the fruitful ideas that give rise to wise opinions about the
nature of things.

141 Μαρῖνος: See Suda, s.v. Μαρῖνος II: οὗτος τὴν Πρόκλου διατριβὴν
παραδεξάμενος καὶ Ἰσιδώρου τοῦ φιλοσόφου τῶν Ἀριστοτέλους λόγων
καθηγησάμενος. Marinus succeeded Proclus as head of the Platonic
Academy at Athens. In its loyalty to the old religion, the Athenian school of
Neoplatonism surpassed the Alexandrian; see, e.g., H.I. Marrou, in:
A. Momigliano (ed.), *The Conflict between Paganism and Christianity*,
Oxford 1963, pp. 136 f. Marinus represented the Aristotelian trend in the
Academy. Isidorus was critical of him, and according to his recorded words,
caused Marinus not to publish his commentary on Philebus; see *Vita Isidori*,
42 (ed. Zintzen), p. 66; Suda, III (ed. Adler), p. 324 = *Vita Isidori*, F 90 (ed.
Zintzen), p. 67. A criticism of Marinus' commentary to Parmenides is to be

Damascius

found in *Vita Isidori*, F244–245 (ed. Zintzen), pp. 199, 201. See also Damascius, *Dubitationes et Solutiones*, II, ed. C. A. Ruelle, Paris 1889, p. 294. Marinus is referred to also in Proclus' commentary on Plato's *Republic* (ed. Kroll, II, Leipzig 1901, p. 96, l. 2), and in Philoponus' commentary on Aristotle's *De Anima*, III, 5 (*Commentaria in Aristotelem Graeca*, XV, Berlin 1897, ed. Hayduck, p. 537, l. 12; p. 536, l. 6). Marinus compiled a biography of Proclus to be found now, edited by Boissonade, in the Appendix of the edition of Diogenes Laertius by Cobet (Didot); on the biography, see F. Leo, *Die griechisch-römische Biographie*, Leipzig 1901, pp. 263 ff.; on Marinus, in general, see also Schissel, PW, XIV, pp. 1759 ff. Marinus was well known as a mathematician, and we still have his introduction to Euclid's *Data* (ed. H. Menge, Leipzig 1896, pp. 234 ff.); see T. Heath, *A History of Greek Mathematics*, II, Oxford 1921, pp. 537 f.

Νέας πόλεως: On the Palestinian Neapolis, see Plinius, *Naturalis Historia*, V, 69 (No. 204).

πρὸς ὄρει ... τῷ Ἀργαρίζῳ καλουμένῳ ... ἐν ᾧ Διὸς ὑψίστου ἁγιώτατον ἱερόν: The old Samaritan temple on Mount Gerizim had been captured by John Hyrcanus (*Ant.*, XIII, 255 f.). In the second century C. E. the Romans built a temple there, presumably to Zeus Hypsistos. The cult of Zeus Hypsistos was practised throughout the Greek world; see A. B. Cook, *Zeus*, Vol. II, Part 2, Cambridge 1925, pp. 876 ff.; on the cult at Mount Gerizim, see *ibid.*, pp. 887 f.; C. Roberts, T. C. Skeat & A. D. Nock, *HTR*, XXIX (1936), pp. 39 ff. On the cult under the Roman empire as illustrated by the coins, see G. F. Hill, *British Museum Catalogue of the Greek Coins of Palestine*, London 1914, XXVIII ff.; E. Bickermann, *Der Gott der Makkabäer*, Berlin 1937, pp. 91 f.

Σαμαρείτης: The emergence of a Samaritan philosopher in the second half of the fifth century C. E. accords well with the general impression given by the sources of the strength of the Samaritan element both in Palestine and outside it in the Byzantine period. The Jewish origins of Marinus are emphasized without doing justice to his Samaritan antecedents by S. Krauss, *JQR*, IX (1897), pp. 518 f.

549

Vita Isidori, apud: Suda, s. v. Δομνῖνος et διαγκωνισάμενος = Zintzen, F227, 218

(227) Δομνῖνος, φιλόσοφος, Σύρος τὸ γένος ἀπό τε Λαοδικείας καὶ Λαρίσσης πόλεως Συρίας, μαθητὴς Συριανοῦ καὶ τοῦ Πρόκλου συμφοιτητής, ὥς φησι Δαμάσκιος. ἐν μὲν τοῖς μαθήμασιν ἱκανὸς ἀνήρ, ἐν δὲ τοῖς ἄλλοις φιλοσοφήμασιν ἐπιπολαιότερος. διὸ καὶ πολλὰ
5 τῶν Πλάτωνος οἰκείοις δοξάσμασιν διέστρεψε. καὶ διαλυμηνάμενος

4 ἐπιπολαιότερος Toup. Hemsterhuis   ἔτι παλαιότερος AM   ἔστι
παλαιότερος GI   5 τῶν] τοῦ V / διέτρεψε AG   διέτριψεν V
ἀνέτρεψε Μ

ἀποχρώσας ὅμως εὐθύνας τῷ Πρόκλῳ δέδωκε, γράψαντι πρὸς αὐτὸν
ὅλην πραγματείαν, καθαρτικὴν ὥς φησιν ἡ ἐπιγραφὴ τῶν δογμάτων
τοῦ Πλάτωνος. ἦν δὲ οὐδὲ τὴν ζωὴν ἄκρος οἷον ἀληθῶς φιλόσοφον
εἰπεῖν. (218) ὁ γὰρ Ἀθήνησιν Ἀσκληπιὸς τὴν αὐτὴν ἴασιν
10 ἐχρησμῴδει Πλουτάρχῳ τε τῷ Ἀθηναίῳ καὶ τῷ Σύρῳ Δομνίνῳ, τούτῳ
μὲν αἷμ᾽ ἀποπτύοντι πολλάκις καὶ τοῦτο φέροντι τῆς νόσου τὸ ὄνομα,
ἐκείνῳ δὲ οὐκ οἶδα ὅ τι νενοσηκότι. ἡ δὲ ἴασις ἦν ἐμπίπλασθαι
χοιρείων κρεῶν. ὁ μὲν δὴ Πλούταρχος οὐκ ἠνέσχετο τῆς τοιαύτης
ὑγιείας καίτοι οὐκ οὔσης αὐτῷ παρανόμου κατὰ τὰ πάτρια, ἀλλὰ
15 διαναστὰς ἀπὸ τοῦ ὕπνου καὶ διαγκωνισάμενος ἐπὶ τοῦ σκίμποδος
ἀποβλέπων εἰς τὸ ἄγαλμα τοῦ Ἀσκληπιοῦ (καὶ γὰρ ἐτύγχανεν
ἐγκαθεύδων τῷ προδόμῳ τοῦ ἱεροῦ), ὦ δέσποτα, ἔφη, τί δὲ ἂν
προσέταξας Ἰουδαίῳ νοσοῦντι ταύτην τὴν νόσον; οὐ γὰρ ἂν καὶ ἐκείνῳ
ἐμφορεῖσθαι χοιρείων κρεῶν ἐκέλευσας. ταῦτα εἶπεν, ὁ δὲ Ἀσκληπιὸς
20 ⟨ἱεὶς⟩ αὐτίκα ἀπὸ τοῦ ἀγάλματος ἐμμελέστατον δή τινα φθόγγον,
ἑτέραν ὑπεγράψατο θεραπείαν τῷ πάθει. Δομνῖνος δέ, οὐ [δὲ] κατὰ
θέμιν ⟨τὴν Σύροις πάτριον⟩, πεισθεὶς τῷ ὀνείρῳ [θέμιν τὴν Σύροις
πάτριον], οὐδὲ παραδείγματι τῷ Πλουτάρχῳ χρησάμενος ἔφαγέ τε τότε
καὶ ἤσθιεν ἀεὶ τῶν κρεῶν. λέγεταί που μίαν εἰ διέλειπεν ἡμέραν
25 ἄγευστος ἐπιτίθεσθαι τὸ πάθημα πάντως, ἕως ἐνεπλήσθη.

20 ⟨ἱεὶς⟩ Kassel

(227) Domninus, a philosopher, originally a Syrian coming from
Laodicea and Larissa, a city of Syria, a pupil of Syrianus and a
schoolmate of Proclus, as Damascius says. He was a man remarkable
in mathematics, yet in other fields of philosophy rather superficial.
He therefore also distorted much of Plato by his own opinions.
However, having thus mutilated the views of Plato, he was sufficiently
called to account for this by Proclus. Proclus wrote against him a
whole treatise, which, as it declares, was to purify the views of Plato
[scil. from the distortions of Domninus]. Nor was he so perfect in his
way of life that would really justify calling him a philosopher. (218)
Asclepius at Athens enjoined by means of incubation the same cure
to Plutarch the Athenian and the Syrian Domninus. Domninus
frequently used to spit out blood and bore this name of the disease
[scil. blood-spitter], while Plutarch had a disease the nature of which I
do not know: the remedy prescribed consisted of being filled with
pork. Plutarch, though it was not unlawful for him according to his
ancestral customs, could not bear such a cure, but stood up, and
leaning his elbow on his hammock and gazing at the statue of

Asclepius, for he happened to be sleeping in the *prodomos* of the sanctuary, exclaimed: "Lord, what would you have ordered a Jew if he had got this disease? Surely you would not have urged him to be filled with pork!" That is what he said, and Asclepius, immediately sending forth from the statue some harmonious sound, suggested another cure for the illness. On the other hand, Domninus, contrary to what had been traditionally allowed to the Syrians, was persuaded by the dream and did not take Plutarch for an example but partook of it then and always ate this meat. It is said that if he left an interval of even one day without taking this food, the malady would undoubtedly attack him until he was filled up with pork.

227 Δομνῖνος: Domninus was known as both a philosopher and a mathematician; see I. L. Heiberg, *Geschichte der Mathematik und Naturwissenschaften im Altertum*, Munich 1925, p. 45; Heath, *op. cit.* (supra, p. 675), II, p. 538; G. Sarton, *Introduction to the History of Science*, I, Baltimore 1927, p. 498; his short manual has been published in J. F. Boissonade, *Anecdota Graeca*, IV, Paris 1832, pp. 413 ff. It is commonly assumed that Domninus was a Jew by descent; see, e.g., Hultsch, PW, V, p. 1521; Schmid & Stählin, II, p. 1094; Schissel, *op. cit.* (supra, p. 675), p. 1759; S. W. Baron, *A Social and Religious History of the Jews*, VIII, New York 1958, pp. 57, 241. Yet the only support for this assertion seems to be the present passage from Suda. This, however, by no means supplies the proof but states merely that Domninus was a Syrian. The fact that it also states that the eating of pork was forbidden to Syrians does not warrant the supposition that Jews are implied here. Further aspects of this statement are discussed below. The evidence adduced, based mainly on the unproved identification of Domninus with the Jewish doctor Domnus (No. 551), is confused by S. Krauss, *JQR*, VII (1894/5), pp. 270 ff. Krauss mistakenly attributes the same identification to [L.] Zunz, "Namen der Juden", *Gesammelte Schriften*, II, Berlin 1876, p. 11. Zunz himself mentions only Domnus.

ἀπὸ τῆς Λαοδικείας καὶ Λαρίσσης: Perhaps there is a textual corruption here. Two separate cities of Syria are meant, both in the vicinity of Apamea. Evidently Domninus was a native of Larissa, and later lived in Laodicea; cf. Suda, s. v. μέτριοι (ed. A. Adler), III, p. 378; Honigmann, PW, XII, p. 716.

218 Πλουτάρχῳ ... τῷ Ἀθηναίῳ: On the philosopher Plutarch of Athens, see Zeller, *op. cit.* (supra, p. 673), Vol. III, Part, II, pp. 807 ff.

τί δὲ ἂν προσέταξας Ἰουδαίῳ νοσοῦντι ταύτην τὴν νόσον: The Jew is invoked hypothetically and the context by no means implies that the speaker is referring to Domninus.

οὐ[δὲ] κατὰ θέμιν... τὴν Σύροις πάτριον: The Jews were not the only nation to abhor pork. For the abstention of the Phoenicians, cf. Porphyrius, *De Abstinentia*, I, 14 (No. 453); similarly for the Egyptian priests, cf. Josephus in *Contra Apionem*, II, 141. At Hierapolis also pigs were neither eaten nor sacrificed, cf. Lucianus, *De Dea Syria*, 54; see G. Goossens, *Hiérapolis de*

Syrie, Louvain 1943, p. 46; J.G. Frazer, *Spirits of the Corn and of the Wild*, II (= *The Golden Bough*, VIII), London 1912, pp. 22 ff. If Domninus had indeed been a Jew, Damascius would no doubt have stated this more explicitly and not called him a Syrian. In contrast to the early Hellenistic age, during the period under consideration the Jews were not included among Syrians by pagan writers. Damascius refers specifically to the Jewish abstention from pork some sentences earlier.

550

Vita Isidori, apud: Suda, s.v. Ζήνων (VI) = Zintzen, F239

Ζήνων, Ἀλεξανδρεύς, ἀνὴρ Ἰουδαῖος μὲν γεγονώς, ἀπειπάμενος δὲ δημοσίᾳ πρὸς τὸ φῦλον τῶν Ἰουδαίων, ὡς παρὰ σφίσι νενόμισται, τὸν λευκὸν ὄνον ἐν τῇ ἀργούσῃ ἡμέρᾳ διὰ τῆς καλουμένης αὐτῶν συναγωγῆς ἐλασάμενος. οὗτος ὁ Ζήνων ἐπιεικὴς μὲν ἦν φύσει καὶ ἱερός, ἀλλὰ
5 νωθέστερος ἐν λόγοις καὶ μαθήμασιν, ἐφιέμενος μὲν ἀεί τι μανθάνειν καὶ ἐρωτῶν, ὅ τι ἂν ἀγνοοῖ, πάντα δὲ σχεδὸν ἀγνοῶν. καὶ γὰρ νοῆσαι βραδύτατος ἦν, καὶ τῶν νοηθέντων ὀψέ ποτε προδότης ὑπὸ λήθης ἑτοιμότατος.

Zeno, an Alexandrian born a Jew, renounced in public the nation of the Jews in the way usual among them, driving the white ass through their so-called synagogue on the day of rest. This Zeno was by nature a kindly person and a holy one, but was rather sluggish in dialectic and mathematics. However, he had always aimed at learning something and used to ask about what he did not know, yet he only knew next to nothing. For he was most slow to apprehend and very ready to throw away that what he learned with difficulty because of his forgetfulness.

ἐν τῇ ἀργούσῃ ἡμέρᾳ: I.e. on the day of Sabbath.
διὰ τῆς καλουμένης αὐτῶν συναγωγῆς ἐλασάμενος: Elisha ben Avuya, the famous apostate from Judaism in the second century C.E., rode near the synagogue of Tiberias on the Sabbath when his former pupil R. Meir was preaching there; see *TP Ḥagiga*, ii, 77b.

551

Vita Isidori, apud: Suda, s.v. Γέσιος = Zintzen, F335

Γέσιος· ἐπὶ Ζήνωνος ἦν λαμπρυνόμενος ἐπὶ τέχνῃ ἰατρικῇ, Πετραῖος τὸ

Damascius

γένος. καθελὼν δὲ τὸν ἑαυτοῦ διδάσκαλον Δόμνον τὸν Ἰουδαῖον καὶ τοὺς
ἑταίρους πρὸς ἑαυτὸν μεταστησάμενος ὀλίγου πάντας πανταχοῦ
ἐγνωρίζετο καὶ μέγα κλέος εἶχεν ...

Gesius. Under Zeno he distinguished himself in the art of medicine.
He hailed from Petra. He overthrew his teacher Domnus the Jew,
and, transferring almost all his companions to himself, became
known everywhere and attained great fame.

ἐπὶ Ζήνωνος: The reign of the emperor Zenon extended from 474 to 491
C.E.
Δόμνον τὸν Ἰουδαῖον: Domnus is also known as a commentator on
Hippocrates; see Wellmann, PW, V, p. 1526; Juster, II, pp. 255 f.
The part played by Jews in ancient medicine is already attested for the
Julio-Claudian period by Celsus, *De Medicina*, V, 19:11; V, 22:4 (Nos.
150–151); see the introduction to the texts, above, Vol. I, p. 368; see also the
introductions to Galen (supra, pp. 306 ff.), and Libanius (supra, p. 580).
Another Jewish medical celebrity at Alexandria was Adamantius, active
there at the beginning of the fifth century C.E.; see Socrates, *Historia
Ecclesiastica*, VII, 13; Wellmann, PW, I, p. 343. In this connection the
medical work of Asaf Iudaeus, the first known medical writer in Hebrew,
should be mentioned. He presumably wrote before the Arab conquest and
betrays the undoubted influence of Greek medicine; on him, see
L. Venetianer, *Asaf Judaeus, der aelteste medizinische Schriftsteller in
hebraeischer Sprache*, I–III, Budapest 1915–1917; S. Muntner, *Introduction to
the Book of Assaph the Physician* (in Hebrew), Jerusalem 1958; S. Pines,
"The Oath of Asaph the Physician and Yoḥanan ben Zabda", *Proceedings of
the Israel Academy of Sciences and Humanities*, V, Jerusalem 1975, No. 9, pp.
223 (1) ff.
"The Book of Mixtures and Potions" of S. Donnolo, the famous Jewish
physician and pharmacologist living under Byzantine rule in the tenth
century C.E., is wholly based on Greek medical tradition and does not show
any influence of Arab medicine; see H. J. Zimmels, "Science", *The Dark
Ages, The World History of the Jewish People*, Second Series, II, Tel Aviv
1966, pp. 298 f.; A. Sharf, *The Universe of Shabbetai Donnolo*, New York
1976, pp. 94 ff.

CLIX. OLYMPIODORUS

Sixth century C.E.

In his comments on Aristotle's Meteorologica, *Olympiodorus is more elaborate than his predecessor Alexander of Aphrodisias (No. 400).[1] He gives special attention to the way Aristotle expresses himself about the Dead Sea.[2]*

552

In Aristotelis Meteora Commentaria — Stüve, Commentaria in Aristotelem Graeca, Vol. XII, Part 2, Berlin 1900, pp. 163 f.; cf. Aristoteles, Meteorologica, II, p. 359a = above, Vol. I, No. 3

Ἰδοὺ γὰρ ἡ ἐν Παλαιστίνῃ Νεκρὰ μυθευομένη θάλασσα παχυτάτη οὖσα ἁλμυρωτάτη πάντων ἐστὶ τῶν ὑδάτων. καὶ ὅτι παχυτάτη ἐστί, δῆλον· εἰ γάρ τις ἄνθρωπον ἢ ἕτερόν τι ζῷον καταδήσας ἐμβάλοι εἰς τὸ τῆς Νεκρᾶς θαλάττης ὕδωρ, ἀνωθεῖται ὑπὸ τοῦ ὕδατος καὶ οὐ
5 γίνεται ὑποβρύχιον διὰ τὸ εἶναι παχὺ πάνυ καὶ βαστάζειν τὸ ἐμπεσόν.

5 βαστάζει a

1 There is no ground for the assumption that Olympiodorus was a Christian; see I. P. Sheldon-Williams, in: *The Cambridge History of Later Greek and Early Medieval Philosophy*, Cambridge 1967, p. 482.
2 The Dead Sea is also mentioned by Priscianus, one of the sixth-century Neoplatonic philosophers who left Athens for the court of Persia in the company of Damascius, in his *Solutiones Eorum de Quibus Dubitaverit Chosroës Persarum Rex*, preserved in a late Latin translation; see E. Zeller, *Die Philosophie der Griechen in ihrer geschichtlichen Entwicklung*, Vol. III, Part 2⁵, Leipzig 1923, p. 909, n. 1. See *Prisciani Lydi Quae Extant*, ed. I. Bywater (*Supplementum Aristotelicum*, Vol. I, Part 2, Berlin 1886, pp. 75 f., Chap. VI): "Declarat hoc et lacum talem narrando, in quem si quis immiserit ligans hominem seu iumentum, supernatare hoc, inquit, non tamen mergi aut etiam discindere aquam: esse autem amarum sic lacum et salsum, ut nullum nutriat piscem; vestimenta vero lavare si quis excusserit umectans. Manifestum itaque quia salsugo facit quoddam corpus crassum, et terreum est quod inest. Est autem lacus quidam alter in regione Palaestinorum qui dicitur Asphaltitis, quem etiam Mortuum vocant mare, quasi nihil vivificans in se: ab eo bitumen nascitur."

καὶ μή τις λεγέτω, ὅτι τῇ νηκτικῇ δυνάμει ἐπινήχεται τὸ ζῷον·
ὑπόκειται γὰρ δεδεμένον. οὕτω μὲν οὖν δήλη ἐστὶν ἡ τοῦ ὕδατος
παχύτης. ἀλλὰ μὴν καὶ ὅτι ἁλμυρώτατον ὕδωρ ἐστί, δῆλον· πρῶτον
μὲν, ἐπειδὴ ῥυπτικόν ἐστι παντὸς ῥύπου (σμήχει γὰρ τὸν ῥύπον τῶν
10 ἱματίων ἤπερ ἄλλο τι σμῆγμα), τὸ δὲ ῥύπτειν ἄκρας ἐστὶν
ἁλμυρότητος. ἰδοὺ γὰρ ἅλες μὲν καὶ αὐτοὶ ῥύπτουσι, νίτρον δὲ πλέον
ὡς ἐπιτεταμένην ἔχον τὴν ἁλμυρότητα ἤπερ οἱ ἅλες· ὅθεν καὶ διὰ τὴν
ἐπίτασιν ὑπόπικρόν ἐστι τὸ νίτρον. ἔπειτα καὶ τὸ εἶναι ἄγονον τὸ ὕδωρ
τοῦτο δῆλόν ἐστιν ὑπερβαλλούσης ἁλμυρότητος· οὐδὲ γὰρ ἰχθὺς ἢ
15 ἄλλο τι ἐγγίνεται ζῷον τῇ Νεκρᾷ θαλάσσῃ διὰ τὴν ἁλμυρότητα καὶ
πικρότητα. ἀλλ' ἄξιόν ἐστιν ἀπορίας, τί δήποτε ὁ φιλόσοφος
μυθεύεσθαι εἶπε τὴν Νεκρὰν θάλασσαν καίτοι ἐναργοῦς ὄντος τοῦ
τοιούτου ὕδατος· ἢ λέγομεν, ὅτι μυθεύεσθαι αὐτὴν εἶπε κατὰ τὸ
λέγεσθαι νεκράν· νεκρὰ γὰρ λέγεται μυθικῶς διὰ τὸ ἄγονον εἶναι
20 παντελῶς.

8 ὕδωρ om. V   10 ἤπερ a   εἴπερ V   ἤπερ Ideler
⟨μᾶλλον⟩ ἤπερ Stüve   14 ὑπερβαλούσης a

For, as you may see, the Dead Sea in Palestine, about which fabulous
stories are told, being the thickest of all waters is the most salty. That
it is the thickest is clear. For if one binds a man or other living creature
and throws it into the water of the Dead Sea, it is pushed above by the
water and does not go under because the water is very thick and lifts
up that which falls into it. And one should not say that the living
creature floats owing to its ability to swim, for it lies bound. Thus
certainly the thickness of the water is clear, but it is also clear that this
water is the most salty. First, it cleanses from every dirt, for it wipes
off the dirt of clothes more than any other detergent, and the
cleansing is a sign of the utmost saltiness. For, as you may see, salt in
itself cleanses, but nitrium cleanses more as it contains more intense
saltiness than salt. Hence because of this intensity the nitrium has a
flavour of bitterness. Secondly, it is clear that this water is sterile
because of the excess of saltiness, for no fish or other living creature
comes to existence in the Dead Sea as a result of the saltiness and
bitterness. However, one may be puzzled why the philosopher [i.e.
Aristotle] said that fabulous stories were told about the Dead Sea,
though the existence of such water is obvious. Or shall we say that he
said that fabulous stories were told about it as far as it was called
"Dead"? For the sea was called Dead mythically because of its
complete sterility.

681

CLX. LACTANTIUS PLACIDUS

Sixth century C.E.

The scholiast Lactantius Placidus[1] finds an occasion to discuss the nature of the Highest God when commenting upon Statius, Thebais, IV, 515 f., "Et triplicis mundi summum". A number of Platonizing elements of the Greek philosophical tradition are combined in the discussion which states that it is forbidden to know the name of the Highest God ("cuius scire non licet nomen"). Lactantius Placidus identifies the "summus deus" with the demiurge, a view which was out of accord with the prevalent conception in contemporary Neoplatonism; see Porphyrius, apud: Lydus, De Mensibus, *IV, 53 (No. 453); Iamblichus, apud: ibid. (No. 467). However it was consonant with both the Zoroastrian and the Jewish beliefs, according to which the Highest God is the Creator of the world.*

Lactantius attributes to the Persian Magi the view that, apart from the known gods who are worshipped in temples, there is a superior god who rules all the others and of whose kind there are only the sun and the moon ("Infiniti autem philosophorum Magorum Persae confirmarunt revera esse praeter hos deos cognitos, qui coluntur in templis, alium principem et maxime dominum, ceterorum numinum ordinatorem, de cuius genere sint soli sol atque luna").[2] For his assertion Lactantius calls upon the great authority of Pythagoras, Plato and Tages.[3] Lactantius protests against those who think that this God has anything

---

1 For the time of Lactantius Placidus, see Wessner, PW, XII, p. 358. Against the suggestion that Lactantius was a Christian, see A. Klotz, *Archiv für lateinische Lexikographie und Grammatik*, XV (1908), p. 514. The contrary view is held by F. Bretzigheimer, "Studien zu Lactantius Placidus und dem Verfasser der Narrationes Fabularum Ovidianarum", Ph. D. Thesis, Würzburg 1937, pp. 4 ff. The arguments that Lactantius was a pagan are stronger. For a detailed discussion of the relevant passages, see Bidez & Cumont, I, pp. 225 ff. For the problems of the text of the scholia of Lactantius in general, see R. D. Sweeney, *Prolegomena to an Edition of the Scholia to Statius*, Leiden 1969.

2 See W. Bousset, *Hauptprobleme der Gnosis*, Göttingen 1907, p. 86.

3 For the tradition on the Etruscan Tages, see Weinstock, PW, Ser. 2, IV, pp. 2009 ff.

to do with the practices of magic ("*sed dire sentiunt qui eum interesse nefandis artibus actibusque magicis arbitrantur*"), stating that although the Magi have "*sphragides*", supposed by them to contain the names of God, in fact the name of God can be known by none of mankind. Following upon this he expresses the philosophical tenet that the name of the Highest God cannot be known, and that it is only his virtues and powers diffused through the world that are worshipped and called upon by different names.⁴ Here Lactantius again invokes the authority of the Magi, and with them Orpheus,⁵ Moyses the priest of the Highest God,⁶ and Esaias, though what Lactantius exactly attributes to these authorities concerning the definition of God is rather obscure, its meaning apparently blurred by what may be a slovenly translation of some Greek philosophical original. Throughout the discussion Lactantius tends to confuse the concept of the "*Unknown Deity*" with that of the "*Ineffable Deity*", and perhaps his specific invocation of Moyses and Esaias has something to do with the awe felt in Jewish tradition for the ineffable name of God. This gains some probability from the tale that follows: "*Etrusci confirmant nympham, quae nondum nupta fuerit, praedicasse maximi Dei nomen exaudire hominem per naturae fragilitatem pollutionemque fas non esse: quod ut documentis assereret, in conspectu ceterorum ad aurem tauri Dei nomen nominasse, quem ilico ut dementia correptum et nimio turbine coactum exanimasse*".⁷

---

4 Thus Maximus of Madaura, apud: Augustinus, *Epistulae*, 16 (ed. Goldbacher, *CSEL*, XXXIV): "huius nos virtutes per mundanum opus diffusas multis vocabulis invocamus, quoniam nomen eius cuncti proprium videlicet ignoramus. Nam deus omnibus religionibus commune nomen est. Ita fit, ut, dum eius quasi quaedam membra carptim variis supplicationibus prosequimur, totum colere profecto videamur". This letter is referred to by Bidez & Cumont in their interpretation of the passage.

5 For the view that the coupling here of Moyses and Orpheus is not incidental, but that Orpheus owes his mention by Lactantius to the assimilation of Moyses to Musaeus, see Bidez & Cumont, I, p. 234. The assimilation is testified by, e.g., Numenius, apud: Eusebius, *Praeparatio Evangelica*, IX, 8:2 (No. 365).

6 "Deus summus" is here a translation of Ὕψιστος Θεός, a common designation of the Jewish God in the Greek world.

7 Cf. the reference by Bidez & Cumont, I, pp. 235 ff. (following K. O. Müller, *Die Etrusker*, II, ed. W. Deecke, Stuttgart 1877, pp. 38 f.), to a passage in Suda, s. v. Τυρρηνία: Ἱστορίαν δ' παρ' αὐτοῖς ἔμπειρος

From Tacitus to Simplicius

*In the foregoing passage Lactantius again confuses the issue at the end,
saying: "Sunt qui se — licet secreto — scire dicunt, sed falsum
sciunt, quoniam res ineffabilis comprehendi non potest".*[8] *However, in*

ἀνὴρ συνεγράψατο· ἔφη γὰρ τὸν δημιουργὸν τῶν πάντων θεὸν ιβ'
χιλιάδας ἐνιαυτῶν τοῖς πᾶσιν αὐτοῦ φιλοτιμήσασθαι κτίσμασι, καὶ
ταύτας διαθεῖναι τοῖς ιβ' λεγομένοις οἴκοις· καὶ τῇ μὲν α' χιλιάδι
ποιῆσαι τὸν οὐρανὸν καὶ τὴν γῆν· τῇ δὲ β' ποιῆσαι τὸ στερέωμα τοῦτο
τὸ φαινόμενον, καλέσας αὐτὸ οὐρανόν, τῇ γ' τὴν θάλασσαν καὶ τὰ
ὕδατα τὰ ἐν τῇ γῇ πάντα, τῇ δ' τοὺς φωστῆρας τοὺς μεγάλους, ἥλιον καὶ
σελήνην καὶ τοὺς ἀστέρας, τῇ ε' πᾶσαν ψυχὴν πετεινῶν καὶ ἑρπετῶν
καὶ τετράποδα, ἐν τῷ ἀέρι καὶ ἐν τῇ γῇ καὶ τοῖς ὕδασι, τῇ ς' τὸν
ἄνθρωπον. φαίνεται οὖν τὰς πρώτας ἓξ χιλιάδας πρὸ τῆς τοῦ ἀνθρώπου
διαπλάσεως παρεληλυθέναι· τὰς δὲ λοιπὰς ἓξ χιλιάδας διαμένειν τὸ
γένος τῶν ἀνθρώπων. ὡς εἶναι τὸν πάντα χρόνον μέχρι τῆς συντελείας
χιλιάδας ιβ'. The similarity between what is related in Suda and in the
Septuagint translation of Genesis has been pointed out. On the view that
there is a connection between this Etruscan cosmology and the story
related by Lactantius about the death of an ox after it had heard the
ineffable name of God, see Bidez & Cumont, *loc. cit.* Even the existence
of a Jewish apocryphon attributed to the old Etruscan Tages is suggested
by these scholars. For a further discussion of the episode of the ox in the
commentary of Lactantius, see E. Heikel, "Lactantii Placidi de Dei
Nomine Narratio", *Annales Academiae Scientiarum Fennicae*, Ser. B,
Vol. XII, No. 3 (1914), pp. 3 ff.

8 See the passage quoted from Maximus of Madaura (supra, p. 683, n. 4). It
is worthwhile also quoting the *locus classicus* of Pseudo-Aristoteles, *De
Mundo*, 7, p. 401a, l. 12 – 401b, l. 7: εἷς δὲ ὢν πολυώνυμός ἐστι,
κατονομαζόμενος τοῖς πάθεσι πᾶσιν ἅπερ αὐτὸς νεοχμοῖ, καλοῦμεν
δὲ αὐτὸν καὶ Ζῆνα καὶ Δία ... ἀστραπαῖός τε καὶ βρονταῖος καὶ αἴθριος
... καὶ μὴν ἐπικάρπιος μὲν ἀπὸ τῶν καρπῶν ... πάσης ἐπώνυμος ὢν
φύσεώς τε καὶ τύχης ἅτε πάντων αὐτὸς αἴτιος ὤν. Cf. Apuleius, *De
Mundo*, 27 : 350–351: "summum atque exsuperantissimus divum ... si ipse
in solio residat altissimo, eas autem potestates per omnes partes mundi
orbisque dispendat, quae sint penes solem ac lunam cunctumque
caelum"; 37 : 370: "Et cum sit unus, pluribus nominibus cietur ⟨propter⟩
specierum multitudinem". Cf. F. Regen, *Apuleius Philosophus
Platonicus*, Berlin 1971, pp. 74 f. The way in which Lactantius expresses
himself here baffles exact translation; see already C. G. Heyne, *Opuscula
Academica*, III, Göttingen 1788, p. 307, n. k. Heyne understood the
passage in the following way: "*Sed hoc dei vocabulum a nullo hominum
sciri potest*: magos tamen, cum virtutes dei per naturae potestates
designarent, pluribus nominibus deum appellasse, h. in plura numina dei
nomen distraxisse". That, however, would not square well with what
follows ("fecit et Moyses"), and Heyne added in relation to that
"Novissima an aliunde inserta sint, haud facile dixeris".

Commentaria in Aristotelis de Caelo — Heiberg, Commentaria in Aristotelem Graeca, VII,
Berlin 1894, p. 90

Εἰ γὰρ τοσοῦτον τὸ τοῦ οὐρανοῦ φῶς καὶ τὸ λαμπρὸν τῶν παρ' ἡμῖν
διαφέροντα μὴ τοῖς αὐτοῖς ὀνόμασιν ἐκεῖ τε καὶ παρ' ἡμῖν ἐκαλεῖτο,
οὐκ ἂν οὗτος ἐτόλμησεν εἰπεῖν τὸ τοῦ οὐρανοῦ φῶς καὶ ταῖς
πυγολαμπίσι καὶ ταῖς λεπίσι τῶν ἰχθύων ἐνυπάρχειν ... ὑπὸ δὲ
5 κενοδόξου φιλονεικίας ἔλαθεν ἑαυτὸν καὶ τῷ Δαυὶδ ἐκείνῳ, ὃν πάντως
τιμᾷ, τἀναντία διατατόμενος· ὅτι γὰρ οὐ τῆς αὐτῆς τοῖς ὑπὸ σελήνην
φύσεως ἐνόμισε τὰ οὐράνια, δηλοῖ τὸν οὐρανὸν διηγεῖσθαι τὴν δόξαν
τοῦ Θεοῦ λέγων καὶ τὴν ποίησιν τῶν χειρῶν αὐτοῦ τὸ στερέωμα
ἀναγγέλλειν, ἀλλ' οὐχὶ τὰς πυγολαμπίδας καὶ τῶν ἰχθύων λεπίδας.

1 τοσοῦτον om. E   2 μὴ] οὐ c / καὶ παρ' ἡμῖν] κἀνταῦθα E
3 ἐτόλμησεν οὗτος Eb / εἰπεῖν om. D   4 ὑπάρχειν D
5 δαβὶδ c   δᾱ῍δ ABDE   9 τῶν om. E

If the light of heaven and the brightness here, which differ so greatly
from one another, had not been called by the same names both there
and here, he [scil. Philoponus] would not dare to say that the light of
heaven is also to be found in the glow-worm and in the scales of fish.
And because of his vainglorious contentiousness it escaped him that
he put himself in a position which contradicted also that of David,
whom he certainly honours. For David made it clear that he did not
think that heavenly things partake of the same nature as the sublunar
ones by saying that the heavens declare the glory of God, and the
firmament shows his handywork, and not the glow-worm and the
scales of the fish.

οὗτος: Philoponus is often referred to as οὗτος by Simplicius; cf. Wellmann's
index to Heiberg's edition.
τὸν οὐρανὸν διηγεῖσθαι τὴν δόξαν τοῦ Θεοῦ: cf. Septuagint, Ps. xviii:2.

Commentaria in Aristotelis de Caelo — Heiberg, Commentaria in Aristotelem Graeca, VII,
Berlin 1894, pp. 141 f.

'Αλλὰ καὶ ὁ παρ' Ἰουδαίοις προφήτης Δαυὶδ περὶ τοῦ Θεοῦ λέγων «ἐν
τῷ ἡλίῳ» φησίν «ἔθετο τὸ σκήνωμα αὐτοῦ». καὶ ὅτι οὐχ ὡς πρὸς

1 δαβὶδ c   δᾱ῍δ ABDE   2 αὐτοῦ ADE

χρόνον τινὰ αὐτὸν εἰσοικισθῆναι νομίζει, δηλοῖ λέγων «ὁ θεμελιώσας
τὴν γῆν πρὸς τὸ μὴ κλιθῆναι εἰς τὸν αἰῶνα τῶν αἰώνων». δῆλον δέ,
5 ὅτι, κἂν «τῷ αἰῶνι» χρῆται πολλάκις ἀντὶ τοῦ πολλοῦ χρόνου, ἀλλὰ
«τὸν αἰῶνα τῶν αἰώνων» ὡς ἀνέκλειπτον παραλαμβάνει· εἰ δὲ ἡ γῆ
τοιαύτη, δῆλον, ὅτι καὶ ὁ οὐρανὸς καὶ ὁ ἥλιος.

3–4 νομίζει ... κλιθῆναι om. B / κλεισθῆναι A

Also the Jewish prophet David, when speaking about God, says that
he set his tabernacle in the sun. And that he [scil. David] considers it
to have been established not just temporarily he makes clear by
saying "having laid the foundation of the earth that it should not be
removed for ever and ever". It is clear that, even if he often uses "for
ever" instead of "for a long time", he takes "for ever and ever" in the
meaning of eternal. And if the earth is eternal, it is clear that the
heaven and sun are eternal as well.

ἐν τῷ ἡλίῳ ἔθετο τὸ σκήνωμα αὐτοῦ: Cf. Septuagint, Ps. xviii:5.
ὁ θεμελιώσας τὴν γῆν πρὸς τὸ μὴ κλιθῆναι: Cf. Septuagint, Ps. ciii:5. For
this argument, cf. also Simplicius' commentary to *De Caelo* (ed. Heiberg),
p. 117, ll. 24 ff.

688

ADDENDA AND CORRIGENDA TO VOLUME I

p. 9, notes, add: For a discussion of the relative chronology of Theophrastus and Hecataeus, see also M. Stern & O. Murray, *JEA*, LIX (1973), pp. 159 ff.

p. 25, Bibliography, add: J.C.H. Lebram, in: *Josephus-Studien — Otto Michel zum 70. Geburtstag gewidmet,* Göttingen 1974, pp. 244 ff.

p. 31, line 10, read: Panchaia

p. 41, line 4, add: On Ezekias, see also the interpretation of the coins from Tel Gamma as put forward by L.Y. Rahmani, *IEJ*, XXI (1971), pp. 158 ff.; cf. also N. Avigad, *Bullae and Seals from a Post-Exilic Judean Archive,* Jerusalem 1976, pp. 28 f.

p. 65, Bibliography, add: L. Troiani, *Studi classici e orientali,* XXIV (1975), pp. 97 ff.

p. 70, line 28, add: On the Hyksos invasion of Egypt, see also D.B. Redford, *Orientalia,* XXXIX (1970), pp. 1 ff.

p. 96, line 12, add: H. Jacobson, *REJ,* CXXXV (1976), pp. 145 ff.

p. 102, lines 10–11, for: under the leadership of Apis, read: in the reign of Apis

p. 126, notes, add: That Theophilus was a Jew is maintained by N. Walter, *Fragmente jüdisch-hellenistischer Historiker,* in: W.G. Kümmel (ed.), *Jüdische Schriften aus hellenistisch-römischer Zeit,* I, Gütersloh 1976, p. 109, n. 4.

p. 138, line 11, for: gravel, read: rubble

p. 140, line 22, add: See also H. Jacobson, *Mnemosyne,* XXX (1977), pp. 71 f.

p. 168, note 3, line 2, for: *Historiker,* read: *Geschichtschreiber*

p. 177, line 8 (35), read: ἐπιπηδῶσι

p. 187, line 5, following: *BJ,* add: I
line 12 from bottom, add: On Diodorus, XL, 2, see also T. Fischer, *ZDPV,* XCI (1975), pp. 46 ff.

p. 195, note 4, add: On Flaccus and the Jews of Asia, see also A.J. Marshall, *Phoenix,* XXIX (1975), pp. 139 ff.

p. 205, line 13, read: proconsul

p. 234, line 17 from bottom, read: Libya

p. 249, line 2 (11), read: Εὐρυσθεὺς

p. 250, lines 8–9, delete: and it was surpassed by Valerius Antias' work

p. 267, Bibliography, add: J.C.H. Lebram, in: *Josephus-Studien* — *Otto Michel zum 70. Geburtstag gewidmet,* Göttingen 1974, pp. 234 ff.; J.D. Gauger, *Historia,* XXVIII (1979), pp. 211 ff.

p. 285, lines 16, 19, for: Sosius' and Sosius, read: Antony's and Antony

p. 289, line 14, after: see, add: Polybius, V, 70:4: ἡ δὲ Φιλοτερία κεῖται παρ' αὐτὴν τὴν λίμνην εἰς ἣν ὁ καλούμενος Ἰορδάνης ποταμὸς εἰσβάλλων ἐξίησι πάλιν εἰς τὰ πεδία τὰ περὶ τὴν Σκυθῶν πόλιν προσαγορευομένην;

p. 321, line 13, for: a freedman, read: a freedman's son

p. 340, line 23, add: Concerning the description of Moses it is worthwhile referring also to Artapanus, apud: Eusebius, *Praeparatio Evangelica,* IX, 27, 37.

p. 358, line 10 from bottom, read: M. Popilius

p. 361, note 2, line 3, read: without

p. 362, note 7, line 1, read: Herrmann

p. 367, lines 16–17, for: ordering his enemy Antigonus to be beheaded, read: sending his enemy Antigonus to Antony who beheaded him

p. 391, on line 19, add: On Apion's nickname πλειστονίκης, see H. Jacobson, *AJP,* XCVIII (1977), pp. 413 ff.

p. 397, line 23, add: On the synchronization in Apion, see A. Momigliano, *Athenaeum,* NS, LV (1977), pp. 187 f.

p. 401, lines 5, 6, read: κάτοικοι
line 23, read: μέτοικοι

p. 412, line 5 from bottom, add: On the allegation of Jewish ritual murder raised by Apion, see also A. Henrichs, *Die Phoinikika des Lollianos,* Bonn 1972, pp. 33 f.

p. 430, note 4, line 3, read: Herrmann, *Musée belge*

p. 464, line 15, read: Ionian Sea

p. 478, line 7, add: On the toparchy of Herodium, see also P. Benoit, J.T. Milik & R. de Vaux, *Discoveries in the Judaean Desert,* II, Oxford 1961, No. 115, ll. 2, 21.

p. 559, line 6, read: *De Natura Animalium*
lines 2, 3 from bottom, following: IG², add: II–III

כתבי האקדמיה הלאומית הישראלית למדעים
החטיבה למדעי־הרוח

מקורות לתולדות עם ישראל

היהודים והיהדות בספרות היוונית והרומית

ההדיר וצירף מבואות וביאורים

מנחם שטרן

כרך שני
מטאקיטוס עד סימפליקיוס

ירושלים תש״ם